KARNATAKA
DEVELOPMENT REPORT

सत्यमेव जयते

PLANNING COMMISSION
GOVERNMENT OF INDIA

Karnataka
Development Report

सत्यमेव जयते

PLANNING COMMISSION
GOVERNMENT OF INDIA
NEW DELHI

Published by

ACADEMIC FOUNDATION
NEW DELHI

First Published in 2007 by
Academic Foundation
4772-73 / 23 Bharat Ram Road, (23 Ansari Road), Darya Ganj, New Delhi - 110 002 (India).
Phones : 23245001 / 02 / 03 / 04. Fax : +91-11-23245005. E-mail : academic@vsnl.com
www.academicfoundation.com

Published under arrangement with :
Planning Commission,
Government of India,
New Delhi.

Cover photographs, courtesy: Deccan Herald

Karnataka Development Report
ISBN 81-7188-579-9

Designed and typeset by Italics India, New Delhi
Printed and bound in India.

Contents

...CONTD. ...

...CONTD. ...

Core Group

Dr. Kirit S. Parikh *Member, Planning Commission*	**Chairman***
Dr. Renuka Viswanathan *Principal Adviser (SP-S)* *Planning Commission, New Delhi*	**Member**
Shri Gautam Basu *Principal Secretary (Planning),* *Government of Karnataka,* *Bangalore*	**Member**
Dr. Gopal K. Kadekodi *Director,* *Institute of Social and Economic Change,* *Bangalore*	**Member**

---

*Shri Kamaluddin Ahmed, Member, Planning Commission	from 27-09-2002 to 11-09-2003
*Dr. K. Venkata Subramaniam Member, Planning Commission	from 12-09-2003 to 02-08-2004

Contributors

Centre for Multi Disciplinary Development Research (CMDR), Dharwad

V. Annigeri

Nayana Tara Naik

Sailabala Devi

College of Fisheries, Mangalore

Ramachandra U. Bhatta

Institution of Agricultural Technology (IAT), Bangalore

A. Seetharam

B.R. Hegde

C. Vasudevappa

D.M. Hegde

K. Pandurangaiah

K.R. Kulkarni

K.V. Annayappa

M.A. Singlachar

M.G. Chandrakanth

M.M. Kailash

N. Ravi

N.L. Maurya

N.S. Adkoli

P. Parvathareddy

Ramachandra Bhat

S. Bisaliah

S. Lingappa

S.A. Patil

Satish Chandra CS

U.D Bongale

Indian Institute of Management (IIM), Bangalore

Chiranjib Sen*

D. Narasimha Rao

G. Ramesh*

Kalyani Sethuraman

M.S. Narasimhan*

Shainesh

T.V. Ramanayya

Institute of Social and Economic Change (ISEC), Bangalore

A.S. Seetharamu*

B.P. Vani

D. Rajasekhar

D.V. Gopalappa

G.K. Karanth*

G.S. Sastry

Gopal K. Kadekodi*

H.K. Amar Nath

Hemlata Rao*

K. Gayithri*

K.G. Gayathri Devi

K.N. Ninan*

K.V. Raju*

L. Venkatachalam

M. Devendra Babu

M. Jayakrishna

M. Mahadeva

M.D. Ushadevi

M.R. Narayana*

Maathai K. Mathiyazhagan*

Madhushree Sekhar

Manohar Yadav

Meenakshi Rajeev

P. Thippaiah

R.M. Vasanthakumari*

R.S. Deshpande*

S. Madheswaran

S.A. Pasha

S. Puttaswamaiah

S.N. Sangita*

T.V. Sekher

Mythic Society, Bangalore

Suryanath U. Kamath

NCAER, New Delhi

Shashanka Bhide

NIAS, Bangalore

B.K. Anitha

N. Shantha Mohan

N. Sudhamani

Romika

Sridhar

Srinath

Venugopal

---

* Chapter Coordinators

Preface

In the Golden Jubilee year of the formation of the Karnataka State this is considered to be most appropriate and privilege to bring out a Status Report on development in Karnataka. To begin with the Planning Commission and the Planning Department, Government of Karnataka approached the Institute for Social and Economic Change (ISEC) to act as a Nodal Agency to prepare the Karnataka Development Report. While accepting this task, ISEC involved four leading research institutions from Karnataka to shoulder this responsibility as partners. They are: Indian Institute of Management, Bangalore; Centre for Multi-Disciplinary Development Research, Dharwad; National Institute of Advanced Studies and Institution of Agricultural Technology, Bangalore.

The Report has three distinct features. Firstly, it is a Status Report, but with a rider. It is not a compendium of facts and figures on the trends and development outcomes over the different Plan periods. It was not the purpose here to make this an alternative to a State Plan document either. Rather, the Report tries to examine the process of development in the State, in terms of its dynamics of drivers, and the resultant impacts and changes. The drivers examined in the Report are technology, institutions, social and historical backdrops and synergies. Secondly, the Report is organised to cover almost all aspects of the development, from its historical and cultural roots to dynamic political framework, from sectoral to social development, from fiscal regimes of controls and commands to transparency and participatory governance, and from lessons to visions. Thirdly, the database and the bibliographical references provided in the Report are rich enough for anyone interested to operationalise the vision, be it a common person, policy maker, corporate planner, researcher or a teacher.

I, on behalf of all the five institutions would like to thank the Planning Commission and Government of Karnataka for having given us this opportunity to prepare the Report in the spirit of Public-Private Partnership.

I am extremely grateful to all the contributors, peer reviewers and supporter who have made the production of this document on time and with a value addition of highest order. Among the many, the untiring efforts and inputs put in by Mrs. R.M. Vasantha Kumari as Coordinator of the project and also tending to several editorial works are greatly appreciated.

Gopal K. Kadekodi
Institute for Social and Economic Change
Bangalore

" ಸುವರ್ಣ ಕರ್ನಾಟಕ – 2006 "

H.D. KUMARASWAMY
CHIEF MINISTER

VIDHANA SOUDHA, BANGALORE-560 001

MESSAGE

I am immensely pleased that a comprehensive "Karnataka Development Report" is being brought out at the instance of the Planning Commission.

The Institute for Social and Economic Change, Bangalore, with the support of other partner agencies, have documented with clarity and in detail the saga of development of the State since its formation, recognising its rich cultural heritage and progressive outlook. The Report also highlights the areas where greater pace and wider coverage of development are necessary.

The publication of the document has a special significance as this is being published in the Golden Jubilee celebration year of formation of the Karnataka State. I believe that this document—which is the outcome of sustained efforts by experts, scholars and institutions—will provide a wealth of essential information about the State's development for Researchers, Policy Makers and Administrators.

(H.D. KUMARASWAMY)
CHIEF MINISTER

सत्यमेव जयते

डॉ. किरीट एस. परीख
Dr. Kirit Parikh

सदस्य
योजना आयोग
योजना भवन
नई दिल्ली–110 001
MEMBER
PLANNING COMMISSION
YOJANA BHAWAN
NEW DELHI-110 001

MESSAGE

The Karnataka State Development Report has been prepared by the Planning Commission with the support of the State Government by a number of experts from various institutions led by the Institute for Social and Economic Change (ISEC).

The Planning Commission has initiated the preparation of State Development Reports (SDRs) by independent experts in coordination with the State Governments. Over the Tenth Plan period a majority of the States in the country have been covered. The main objective is to provide a quality reference document on the development profile of individual States and the policy alternatives and strategies available for accelerating development.

The present Report takes stock of the resources available in Karnataka and provides a road map for achieving a higher level of development. It is hoped that the report will stimulate debate and lead to better, widely acceptable development policy at the State level. The Report is expected to get integrated into the planning process of the State. For this purpose, the Planning Commission will like to disseminate the Report widely.

I hope the Report will be useful not only to the State Government, but also to non-governmental organisations, citizens' groups and others concerned with the formulation and implementation of the plans and policies oriented towards achieving a better quality of life for the people of the State.

I would like to place on record my deep appreciation of the significant contribution to this Report of Dr. Gopal K. Kadekodi, Director, Institute for Social and Economic Change, Bangalore; author, coordinator and leader of the team.

(Kirit Parikh)

दूरभाष :+91-11-23096568 टेलीफैक्स : +91-11-23096569
Telephone: +91-11-23096568 Telefax : +91-11-23096568, e-mail: kirit.parikh@nic.in

List of Tables, Figures, Boxes and Appendices

Tables

Figures

Boxes

Appendices

Executive Summary

Preamble

Karnataka has a long history of development over centuries. In the most recent past, it all began with Bharat Ratna Sir M. Visvesvaraya, who wanted to make Mysore (the erstwhile State of Kannada speaking people) a modern state with prosperity. As far back as 1902 when he initiated the construction of the first ever hydel dam and power generation plant at Shivanasamudram near Mysore, he had well thought out schemes of modernising the country by taking big leaps. He also had realised the weaknesses and strengths of the Karnataka people simultaneously. In his own words:

> The people themselves are, as a rule, passive and unaggressive. They are guided rather by the opinion of the caste or community than by a common national standard of life, thought and work, by century-old traditions and superstitions rather than by the collective experience of the modern world. .... Through leaning on others, large number of people have become reduced to social parasites. (1920: 8).

He went on to say:

> If, as suggested in this book, the utilisation of India's man power and material resources is placed in the forefront of national aims, if the people's general and technical knowledge is developed, if private initiative is stimulated, if all the latest inventions and discoveries are applied to increase production, if foreign experience is adapted to Indian conditions and fully utilised and useful foreign institutions readily adopted, if in short, all the improvements necessary and possible are introduced, the development of India, politically, economically and socially, will proceed at a pace which may be one of the outstanding futures of the coming generation (1920: 14).

Much prior to him, Karnataka also has a long history of development almost from the time of Rashtrakutas in the ninth century. There were instances of good governance in tank management, marketing, trade, and growth of artisanships based on the principle of cultural harmony, employment for all and social integration among all castes.

A document prepared in the year 2000, entitled *Karnataka: Future Vision and Current Action*, aimed at an overall growth rate of 8 per cent to 9 per cent with enhanced agricultural growth rate at 1.19-2.5 per cent, an average annual industrial growth at 12 per cent; fully tap the world markets in information technology, attaining information technology (IT) related exports of US$ 10 billion per year; and an average annual growth of employment at 3.15 per cent during 2000-2010. In addition, by 2005, the state aimed at, total literacy and primary health care for the entire population, reduction in population growth rate to 1.4 per cent, and attracting private investment in industrial sector to tune of Rs. 20,000 crores per annum, planting e-governance and total transparency at all levels.

Subsequently to that, Karnataka Government had set up a High Level Committee to examine the developmental status in the state with a focus on redressing regional imbalances. That report was also released in 2002. This report has extensively examined all aspects of social, economic and administrative status, imbalances in the state with remedial measures to be set out in a span of eight years.

ISEC as a nodal agency has prepared, jointly with several institutions and involving about 80 subject experts in various segments of development, a report: *Karnataka Development Report*, wherein some new foresights and visions have been knitted. The report is based on contributions from 80 subject specialists, coordinated by 20 experts from five major institutions, namely, Institute for Social and Economic Change; Indian Institute of Management, Bangalore; National Institute of Advanced Studies, Institution of Agricultural Technologists and Centre for Multi-Disciplinary Development Research.

The 18 chapters are:

- Chapter 1 : An Overview of Karnataka's Economy
- Chapter 2 : The Dynamics of Karnataka's Growth
- Chapter 3 : Natural Resources in Karnataka
- Chapter 4 : Human Resources of Karnataka
- Chapter 5 : Economic Infrastructure in Karnataka
- Chapter 6 : Social Infrastructure in Karnataka
- Chapter 7: Financial Infrastructure: Banking, Capital Markets and Cooperatives
- Chapter 8 : Political, Cultural and Social History of the State
- Chapter 9 : Social Sector Development
- Chapter 10 : Regional Dimensions of Development in Karnataka
- Chapter 11 : Politics, Governance and Service Delivery in Karnataka
- Chapter 12 : Karnataka State Finances
- Chapter 13 : Environment, Biodiversity, Climate Change and Urbanisation
- Chapter 14 : Agricultural and Allied Sectors: Need for Re-engineering
- Chapter 15 : Industrial Development in Karnataka
- Chapter 16 : Tourism, Entertainment and IT-enabled Services
- Chapter 17 : Vision of Development in Karnataka
- Chapter 18 : Policy Directions and Drivers for Future Development

Salient Features of Development in Karnataka

1) In terms of a number of indicators (be they income, human development, or governance), Karnataka has been above average the national level.
   - Per capita SDP (in 1993-94 prices) in 2002-03 was Rs. 14,083, far above the national average of 12,496.
   - Average annual growth rate of SDP (per cent) between 1994-95 and 2002-03 was 5.46 as against 4.03 at the all India level.
   - State's share in exports: 11.72 per cent of the country, 26.24 per cent of SDP.
   - Literacy rate: 67.04 in 2001 at the state level, as against 75.28 at the all India level.
   - Crude birth date: 22 per thousand in the state as against 26 at the all India level.
   - Infant mortality rate: 58 in 2001, as against 68 at the all India level.
   - Overall rank in HDI: 7 among the 15 states.
   - Per cent of people below poverty line: 20.04 in Karnataka, 26.1 at the all India level.
   - Governance: PRIs, growing public-private partnerships, large NGO sector, regular elections, *lokayukta*, several *adalats* and other regulatory institutions and e-governance.
2) Growth among the sectors and across the regions, however, have not been even or balanced.
   - Sectoral imbalance: Share of agriculture has declined from 34.29 per cent in 1994-95 to 22.36 in 2002-03, that of secondary sector remained steady at about 27 per cent, but that of tertiary sector increased from 38.27 per cent to 49.38.
   - Regional imbalance persists: Per capita income of districts such as Kodagu in 1997-98 was Rs. 24,623, but that of Bidar remained at Rs. 7861.
   - Social imbalance: Per cent of families below poverty line in 1993-94 were as high as 56.06 in Bidar, and as low as 8.91 in Dakshina Kannada.
   - Regional imbalance in sectoral development: Visible in irrigation, infrastructure, industrialisation, etc.
   - Rural-urban divide: High urban growth without matching infrastructure and social amenities such as schools, health care and security; yet at the same time, the rural urban divide seems to be converging.
3) Performance of decentralisation and deliveries of basic minimum needs seem to be working well.
   - *Gram panchayats*, which operate and maintain drinking water supply sources, have done well in improving access to drinking water and in the collection of water user charges. The performance of GPs in the provision of drinking water is likely to be improved if untied grants are linked to the performance of

GPs in the collection of water user charges and reduction of maintenance expenditure.

- The coverage of villages with community lighting is fairly good. However, GPs are not in a position to afford the provision of community lighting on account of non-fixation of meters to monitor the actual consumption of electricity and lack of policy to impose and collect light cess.
- With Stree-Shakthi programme expanding and large presence of NGOs, there are over 6,000 self-help groups in each of Karnataka's districts for women development and empowerment. For this vast social infrastructure to have meaningful impact on women development and empowerment, there is a need to reduce interest rates on bank finance to SHGs, form GP sub-committees with SHGs representatives as members to represent and secure women interests, and appoint women staff in each GP for resource convergence.

4) Karnataka has always shown its strength in technology development, role of private sectors and good governance.

Some details of the report are now presented in four parts.

PART ONE

Macro-perspectives and Sectoral Growths

There are at least four parameters to be kept track for a better understanding of the dynamics of growth and development in the state. They are: Rates of investments; shares of sectoral incomes; regional balance and employment.

Karnataka has all the potential for rapid growth, much higher than the national average rate of 8.1 per cent gross domestic product (GDP) growth (as targeted by the Tenth Five-Year Plan document of the Planning Commission). The per capita gross state domestic product of Rs. 14,083 (at 1993-94 prices) in 2002-03 is far above the national average (Rs. 12,496). The current rate of gross fixed capital formation (GFCF) has been about 47 per cent of the gross state domestic product (GSDP). GFCF has been increasing at an average annual rate of 22 per cent from 1993-94 to 2001-02. The infrastructural GFCF requirements for a stipulated 4 per cent growth rate in agriculture and around 10 per cent in all other sectors (same as stipulated at the all India level by the Planning Commission for the Tenth Plan period), are estimated to be around Rs. 13,250 crores on an average (at 1993-94 prices) per year for the coming years (as against the current rate of Rs. 11,000 crores).

Sources of investment in the state have been domestic savings (at around 20 per cent of SDP), inflow of private and foreign direct investments (FDIs) and borrowings. The capital formation in the infrastructure sector has recently registered a high average growth rate of about 12 per cent. In the recent past, more that 75 per cent of the overall investments have been coming from the private sector (of which about 10 per cent is in the form of FDIs), an indication of confidence in private governance and management. Since the private initiatives and investments have been rising in the state, it is indeed possible to peg the overall growth rate at 8 per cent of GSDP in the medium-term. This should be the overriding target for the state.

But there are many disturbing factors and adversaries to be reckoned with. If one examines the dynamics of growth in the state, the first disturbing factor is the annual fluctuations in the rates of capital formation and inflow of private investments: The annual growth rate of GFCF has been fluctuating from a low of (-)9.4 per cent to a high of 66.99 per cent; that of inflow of private investments varying from (-)25.98 per cent in 1993-94, 260.48 per cent in 1995-96, dropping to (-)22.02 per cent in 1997-98 and rising to 209.43 per cent in 2000-01. These fluctuation also made the capital formation/ output ratios fluctuate from a low of 26 per cent to a high of 48 per cent.

Growth of Gross Fixed Capital Formation by Industry in Karnataka: 1993-94 to 2001-02

	1993-94	*1994-95*	*1995-96*	*1996-97*	*1997-98*	*1998-99*	*1999-00*	*2000-01*	*2001-02*
Annual Growth of Total GFCF	-	32.33	18.78	21.35	13.68	29.10	-9.40	7.68	66.99
GFCF as a Per Cent of GSDP (at current prices)	26.94	30.56	30.95	32.39	32.85	35.27	29.56	28.93	47.77

Source: KDR, Chapter One (Appendix A-1.6).

Inflow of Private Investment in Karnataka: 1993-94 to 2001-02

Year	Total Investment (US$ million)	Annual Growth of Total Investment (per cent)
1993-94	1988.31	-25.98
1994-95	2626.50	32.10
1995-96	9468.09	260.48
1996-97	2386.52	-74.79
1997-98	1861.03	-22.02
1998-99	2214.02	18.97
1999-00	3031.85	36.94
2000-01	9381.35	209.43
2001-02	1673.34	-82.16

Source: KDR, Chapter One (Appendix A-1.8).

The challenge in this respect is to build confidence in investment channels. It requires building strong partnerships between public and private investments, such that in the years, when public investment is lacking, the private sector can move in. Otherwise, such wide fluctuations can make the investment climate very suspicious in the minds of potential investors.

The second macro-level concern is on the changing shares of sectoral incomes. The distribution of state income across primary, secondary and tertiary sectors shows a major shift towards the tertiary sector, and especially away from the primary sector. For instance, the share of tertiary sector in the state income increased from 38.3 per cent in 1993-94 to 50.0 per cent in 2002-03 and that of primary sector declined from 34 to 22 per cent. With new developments in the biotechnology sector enabling diversification in agriculture, completion of Upper Krishna River based irrigation and other schemes, and creating marketing facilities for horticulture and other agri-based industrial products, the share of agricultural contribution to the GSDP can be targeted higher. Based on the analysis of agricultural sector, the corresponding sectoral growth rate can be pegged at 4 per cent, higher than the observed average of 3.2 per cent since 1993-94, thereby also raising its share in GSDP.

The major steps required are:

- Arresting the declining trend in the average operational holdings.
- Taking advantage of IT and BT technologies.
- Better management of irrigation facilities, and deliveries (particularly to the tail enders).
- Reducing cropping violations.
- Switching to emerging alternative agricultural options: horticulture, sericulture, floriculture, poultry, etc.

If there is anything which is commonly talked about by all sections of the society, it is on employment. This is the third major challenge at the macro level. Planning Commission in its recent Vision 2020 document, brought out one fact for us to digest. That is about the scale of unemployment. At the national scale, there is a backlog of creating about 10 million jobs per year. (All together 300 million jobs in 30 years.) Even if one takes a reasonable minimum share of this for Karnataka, it will stand out to be about half a million per year. As against this, the current rate of workforce is of the order of 2.4 crores (of which, just about 19 lakhs are employed in the organised sector, and its growth rate is declining to –0.28 per cent in 1999-2000). The story from unorganised sector is still worse, highly fluctuating due to continued droughts, stagnancy in the development of infrastructural sector and so on. There is a very visible problem of

Growth of State Income in Karnataka State: 1994-95 to 2002-03

State Income Indicators [at factor cost and at constant (1993-94) prices]	Karnataka 1994-95	Karnataka 2002-03	India 1994-95	India 2002-03
1. Annual Growth of GSDP/GDP (per cent)	5.61	6.21	7.25	3.98
2. Per Capita GSDP/GDP (Rs.)	9027	14083	9229	12496
3. Annual Growth of Per Capita Income (per cent)	3.69	4.87	5.36	2.21
4. Distribution of GSDP/GDP by Sectors:				
4.1. Share of Primary Sector (per cent)	34.29	22.36	30.3	22.00
4.2. Share of Secondary Sector (per cent)	26.14	28.26	24.4	24.9
4.3. Share of Tertiary Sector (per cent)	38.27	49.38	45.3	53.1
4.4. Average Annual Growth (per cent) of GSDP/GDP during 1994-95 to 2002-03	-	7.00	-	5.99
4.5. Average Annual Growth (per cent) of Per Capita GSDP/GDP during 1994-95 to 2002-03	-	5.46	-	4.03

Source: KDR, Chapter One, (Appendix A-1.1).

employment in agriculture with the labour absorption declining from 30 per cent to 26 per cent. Any elementary economics will then tell us that this trend will lead to increasing income disparity and possibly adding to regional disparity also.

The remedy seems to be lying in reversing the trends in growths, away from service sector to agricultural sector, but taking all the advantages of the developments in the service sectors (such as communication, e-governance, IT, banking and so on).

Speaking about agriculture, a different package of agriculturally diversified productions with horticulture, agro-processing, fishery, poultry and such other activities taking a major lead over the traditional food and plantation crops is necessary.

Karnataka still has a high potential of sustaining the employment rate in the organised sector. This is possible because of high rate of technical and professional education in the state and the fast track service sectoral growth. However, several traditional un-organised sectors such as *beedi* making, silk industry, tile, fishery, horticulture and forest related activities share almost 75 per cent of total employment in the state. These sectors should be structured as semi-organised, with employment guarantee, wage fixation and other service regulations. Good training in processing, packaging, and delivery management in many of these export-oriented products can enhance the off-take as well as value added services. A related issue is in employment situation is reducing child labour. Properly designed social security system for the un-organised sectors can reduce this tendency. Opportunities such as transparency and involvement of civic societies be created to address this long standing human problem.

Resources for Development

Invariably, at the state level, one notices a mismatch between resources and development targets. The reasons are many. Resources are site specific, and not demand-specific. They are to be matched on a geographical scale as much as consistently over time.

Karnataka is emerging as a substitute for the Silicon Valley. But the current rate of investment in the IT sector of about Rs. 2000 crores has the potential of growing at a faster rate of over 15 per cent. Likewise, the BT sector, which currently growing at 28 per cent annually, can reach a satiety level soon. There is a every need to forewarn this and make the sector keep growing. This requires better tying up of this sector with pharmaceutical and drug sectors (most of which are out side of Karnataka), agriculture and seed sector, pesticide and fertiliser sectors and so on.

While Karnataka is shining as a Brain Bank of India in IT and BT and engineering technologies, it is equally necessary to cushion it from the bottom with a strong base at the literacy and primary education levels. Otherwise, the best of benefits from the investments on this brain sector will be at the national level, with minimum trickling down to the people of the state. Some of the challenges on this are:

- Bridging the literacy gap between female and male (currently at 22 per cent) and rural-urban gaps in literacy (currently 10 per cent): Apart from the usual public missions such as SSA on universalisation of literacy, methods of parent participation, corporate sectoral participation are to be built in.
- Enhancing regional capacities in human resources: Being a state with a vast artisanships, it will be loss for ever for the state to lose the 'forest for the wood'.
- Vocational training based on local level skills must be clubbed with private sectoral involvement in creating follow up employments.
- The natural resource base of the state should be fully understood and appreciated:
    - about 20 per cent of land is under forest cover;
    - about 10 per cent of geographical area is pasture and uncultivated lands;
    - about 117 lakh ha (62 per cent of geographical area) are under agriculture and cultivation;
    - about 7663 trillion metric cube (TMC) of water resources per year (of which about 50 per cent is dependable for use);
    - a maximum of 1,695 TMC (covering about 30 lakh ha of land under one form or other) under irrigation;
    - rich in mineral resources like iron ore (about 4000 million tonnes of reserves) and limestone and dolomite (about 20,000 million tonnes);
    - extraction of marine and inland fisheries of about 1.9 lakh tonnes of fish landings;
    - western Ghat region is one of the eight biospheres of India.

The new and needed emphasis are:

- The current forest cover of 20 per cent of geographical area should be enhanced to possible 30 per cent (though at the national level 33 per cent coverage is recommended).
- Irrigation potential can be increased to about 38 lakh hectares.
- Processing of mineral *in situ* before exporting.
- Enhancing fishery skills and landings.

Infrastructural Development

One of the most important infrastructure sector is power. There are two distinct aspects of this sector, namely the quality and quantity of supply. Some of these are resource linked, many others are linked to management and governance. Response to independent power producers (IPPs) received very poor responses so far. The major achievement has been only in un-buldling of generation, transmission and establishing four distribution companies. Further steps required are to restructure Karnataka Electricity Regulation Commission (KERC) itself, and bring the consumers much closer to the distribution system, with e-governance, subsidy reduction programme, loss reduction programme and physical upgradation programme. That requires a vision of good governance, public participation, transparency, disclosure mechanism and demand side management. For instance, the concept of power *adalat* should be universally used even at the *taluka* levels. Experiences all over the world show that with improved quality of power, people do not demand subsidy as much as in the situation of poor quality situations.

One of the hotly debated issue here is power subsidy to agriculture. Several studies have shown that while power sector in the state is targeting for the poor with subsidised power supply to the farmers, all the available statistics and field level studies reveal one fact: The small and marginal farmers, who are also the poor, are in dire need for subsidy, but are not at all the beneficiaries of the subsidy[1]. One can not find sufficient justification for power subsidy based on these factual information, unless we take the position that all farmers are poor.

The solution seems to be a mix of policies on restricting the use of groundwater as well as gradually raising power tariffs on a progressive basis. Alternative sources of energy such as solar and wind energies have ample scope in the state, which should receive some priorities.

PART TWO

Microeconomic and Social Issues

Development at the micro-level means to make it people oriented. Here, the issues of people viewed as class and caste, population, service delivery at the micro level, quality and dignity of life are all important. Quite often these are referred to as matters of human development distinct from economic development. The overall index of human development in Karnataka (ranked 7th at the national level in 1991) has marginally improved to 0.630 in 1998 from an earlier index of 0.47 in 1992.

The state's decadal growth rate of population has been declining, currently at 17.25 per cent in 2001, which is lower than at the national rate (21.34 per cent). Viewed from fast declining crude birth rate (22 per cent), death rate (7.8 per cent) and infant mortality rate (58 per 1000 live births), lower than the rates at national levels, Karnataka has shown trends of sustainable population dynamics. In the long run, it is visioned that the population growth in Karnataka can be stabilised at 1.3 per cent per year (an average of southern zone states in 2001). The regional variation in the fertility rates and population growths needs to be addressed in the coming years. This is a matter requiring considerable efforts to bring about harmonious changes.

Talking about human development, literacy (currently at 67 per cent) and education are two major milestones. The thrust of vision on the future should, however, be on raising rural and female literacy rates, bridging the gender and rural-urban gaps to nil by the year 2010. Other major challenges in this literacy mission are the quality of basic education, reduction of drop-out rates (particularly of girl child), and reduction in the long-standing gap of male-female literacy (of around 22 per cent). The next challenge is to implement the goal of Universal Elementary Education (also pending as a 2002 Bill before the Parliament).

In the light of regional disparity and sectoral imbalances referred to earlier, there is a need to switch the focus away from higher education (university degrees) to secondary and technical/vocational education (to raise vocational skills useful in industrial, maintenance and service sectors). Here some lessons

---

1. A recent study (Howes, 2003) based on NSS data shows that on average, land owners with pumpsets with less than one hectare of land receive just about Rs. 3.30 as subsidy per year, whereas land owners with more than four hectares of land get about Rs. 29.71.

from China are worth remembering: Both education and health care are linked to regional demands and necessities (with of course much restrictions on inter-regional migrations). In the activities such as floriculture, horticulture, herbiculture, maintenance, packaging and transport, sales and service of automobiles, electronics, and IT/BT sectors vocational and field training should be designed based on location-specific demands.

Next to literacy and education, the most important human needs are on health and quality of life. The vision on health care has to make a major turnaround now. It is not simply provisioning or public spending but making the system work. That requires several institutional changes in the health care delivery system. The buzzword today is the 'cooperative health care' system, in which even the poor 'pays' but also 'gets' the necessary health care. Programmes such as Yashaswini health plan need to be reexamined to make it on private and cooperative partnership basis. The *panchayats* should have their own choice of health care management system, be they with the involvement of corporate sector, or NGOs, other private provisioning, or cooperative and charity based health care systems.

All these in turn also make a case for building a strong institution of public-private partnership and education-health care-industry linkage. Resource mobilisation (estimated to the tune of about Rs. 4000 crores additionally and pegging a GSDP share of higher than the present four per cent for education) is feasible only under such partnerships in operationalising the process of linking education to job orientation.

Some of the micro level reforms needed are on drinking water supply, improved sanitation, urban and rural road systems, street lighting, micro-financing, etc. The challenges are many and very diversified on each of these questions. They are socially linked (e.g., culture, caste and habitation structures, gender), some of them are basic needs (e.g., drinking water), and some of them are having externalities (e.g., bad sanitation or quality of water, air and water pollution). As will be dealt later, these service delivery systems require decentralisation, involvement of civil society organisations and public-private partnerships.

All through the Five Year Plans, several schemes and special component programmes were introduced on matters of upliftment of socially deprived sections and castes. The social status and transformation among them are still at a slow ebb. What was considered to be the landmark in development in this direction, the 'land reforms' has not delivered the desired changes. With no more land available, and also given the fact that not many of the youths are willing to go back to land, it is better to switch to better training of youths, thrust on land management with agricultural diversification, ensuring literacy and education, better credit and easy access facilities for legal defence and social security, and their recognition in social and political arena. One remote possibility can also be on introducing land rights for women, a challenge at the national level as well (Agarwal, 2005).

An inter-phase between the macro and micro level issues is the issue of regional imbalances. What emerges from the Nanjundappa Committee report and the present report are summarised below:

First, the state should work out a revised formula on allocation of resources with a focus on regional disparities. This will amount to substantially augmenting the Gadgil formula, as much as the one recommended by the Second Finance Commission of the state. In any case, population size, geographical area and income per capita may not be sufficient to guide the allocations. Secondly, state alone can not drive the phase of development. There is every need for civil society groups at village, *taluka* and district levels that have to have a direct say on developmental matters, as much as the corporators, members of Legislative Assembly and other elected representatives. Thirdly, it is the prime opportunity to build a public-private partnership, on a number of socio-developmental issues such as literacy, drinking water supply, health care, etc. Finally, development should be viewed in the framework of decentralised development. After the major shift in the development strategy, devolution of decision power and economic instruments in respect of as many as 29 functions and activities have been transferred to *zilla*, *taluka* and *gram panchayats*. They have also been empowered to raise their own resources. Recently, the Karnataka Government has transferred as many as 180 state sector functions to the Panchayat Raj Institutions. Therefore, the challenge is now at the village, *taluka* and *zilla panchayat* levels. They are the first and best judges on identification of the gaps, deprivations and remedial solutions acceptable to the communities.

When it comes to decentalisation, there are several new emerging problems in the delivery system. First, an operational and implementable activity mapping has to be prepared on all the 29 functions identified for the Panchayat Raj Institutions in terms of their capabilities, capacities for their effective implementations and monitoring. For instance, the *zilla panchayats* can concentrate on both promoting public-private partnership and attracting industrial hubs. The *taluka panchayats* can take up implementing public-private partnerships with *taluka* level growth centres. The *gram panchayats* should concentrate on internalising the local talents in promoting employment and artisanships. They can easily involve the self-help groups (SHGs) and other NGOs in some of these functions. Second, a variant of this process of decentralisation is the vision of 'small village clusters'. Since many of the villages may not have all the complementary resources (land, water, forest, livestock, etc), it may be possible to encourage groups of villages to come together to take up common activities such as watershed development, establishing small rural industrial processing units, etc. This framework of promoting economic activity is meant to reverse the trend of rural people to migrate to urban areas, and take advantages of scale economies with emphasis on rural employment and promotion of artisanships. This new approach to decentralisation, however, requires some amendments to the existing devolution mechanisms.

PART THREE

Governance, Transparency and Accountability

On matters of governance, three major policy developments are in place in the state today. First, Karnataka enacted a Transparency Act in 2000. Transparency in administration and procurements, right to information, simplification of procedures and single windows for clearance has been introduced. Second, decentralisation in the development process at three-tier levels namely, *zilla, taluka* and *gram panchayats,* has been introduced since 1992. Third, the State introduced *lokayukta* as an anti-corruption institution at the state and districts levels, and several citizen charters and people's forums such as water and electricity *adalats.* With the Right to Information Act, 2005 coming in to play, the process of governance is expected to improve further.

But new sets of challenges crop up. As a process of political decentralisation, it is necessary to put into practice a strict process of 'inclusion' of all sections of the village and women representatives as per the reservations and requirements. But this be done based on the principle of participation and not simply as constitutional compliance or obligation. A system of accountability is yet to be developed as a database on each and every one of the publicly elected representatives. Secondly, political participation up to the level of district development committees and at all decision making levels in *gram panchayats* is to be ensured. Thirdly, administratively, it is absolutely necessary to transfer all the responsibilities of planning and implementation of development activities to local bodies and it is also necessary to make line departments fully accountable to the elected bodies such as PRIs. Fourthly, on fiscal and fund management a concept of devolution would mean the local bodies to have full powers in designing all aspects of budget including salaries, expenditures on developmental programmes etc., and also mobilising resources.

Then, there is a question of social transformation with good governance. It is hoped that the long pending 33 per cent representation for women in assemblies and much higher rates in all local bodies is realised soon. The state and the Centre need to carry forward the politics of positive discrimination. Given the fact that more than 35 per cent of our population live below the poverty line and the discrimination of and atrocities against Dalits and women never seem to stop, the state's intervention in this matter both to protect and empower them through legal measures and constitutional provisions become a priority. But this can be realised only with a revised approach of 'inclusion' process.

For all these to happen, there is a need for involving other institutions as well. The concept behind the evolution of such institutions is the principle of 'participation'. Viewed on these lines, the role of NGOs and government supported organisations such as self-help groups, *stree-shakti, swashakti* (under a promotive scheme of Department of Women and Child Welfare), water user associations, village protection committees of joint forest management (JFM) etc., and cooperative banks and certain segments of corporate bodies and hubs are important as civil society agents, regulators, monitors and implementers.

PART FOUR

Policy Drives

What Can Be the Overall Drivers?

Based on the analysis of past performance and the resource potentials, and the vision on sectoral and social dimensions, the overall GSDP growth rate at 8 per cent is feasible. This will have to be backed up by about 4 per cent growth rate in agriculture (all primary sectors), 10 per cent in the manufacturing and secondary sectors, and 12 per cent in the service sector.

Policies of Continuity and Change

Four major diversions and changes are worth considering in the coming years. They are about:

- Re-engineering with agricultural sector: The policy priority now should be to bring back agricultural sector on the rails of continuity in development.
- New phase of thrust on industry and infrastructural development: (1): The new policy thrust will have to be to decentralise more of the industrial units, in and around centres of engineering job shops. Such a policy will also neutralise the regional imbalances. (2) The main switch in policy required now is not just mobilising investable funds on infrastructural development, but to involving the private sector and making them also to manage them on a 'build-operate-transfer', 'build-own-operate', 'build-own-operate-transfer' or, 'build-operate-share-transfer' basis. This policy would not only reduce the pressure on the state for funds, but bring about more and more efficiency and accountability.
- Dismantling command and control regime: Change needed now is public-private partnership. A thrust on institutional change required now is regulation, in place of command. The sectors requiring some major shifts in this direction are power, irrigation, communication, road, tourism, urban water supply and so on.
- Promoting regional balance: The policy should be quickly switching to devolution of power to Panchayat Raj Institutions to raise the resources and use them for their own development. A fresh thinking on modifying the Second Finance Commission's Award is necessary to take cognizance of regional disparity in resource allocations.

New Strategic Considerations

Proactive planning

Consultative and participative approach

Public-private-hub-partnership

Small industrial and agricultural clusters approach

Newly emerging sectors: horticulture, aquaculture, packaging, etc.

From domestic to export-orientation

- A number of new Proactive strategies are to be introduced in the reforms period now. Among them, giving means and support for the IT, BT and service sectors for their global integration are a priority. Setting up of regionally spread IT and BT parks is another major step in this direction.
- Policy package is 'public-private-hub-partnership'. In sectors, which hitherto were exclusively under government control, such as roads and power, transport, tourism and so on, private sector participation is to be actively encouraged. Privatisation, restructuring and disinvestments are the directions in which the government has to move further.
- Switch from a purely domestic market-orientation to export-orientation is necessary. The role of the government should be more as 'supportive' and vigilant rather than purely providing incentives for markets to emerge.
- The new phase of industrialisation should consider the possibilities of 'small industrial clusters' in different districts to reduce the pressures on urban land and other resources.
- A strategy of consultative and participative approach: As a driving strategy, it is time to involve social groups at different levels in implementing such intermediary market based instruments. Participatory irrigation management to resolve the water management problems in the irrigation sector can be an example to cite. Bringing Karnataka Electricity Regulation Commission closer to people's groups is yet another strategy. *Panchayats* undertaking public distribution system, cooperative health care system, regulated price shops etc., are some of the other possibilities.

Addressing the Question of Poverty

- Whichever measure one uses, poverty estimates in the state show the concentration in the northern districts. As many as 48 *talukas* were found to be suffering from abject poverty (with more than 40 per cent families below poverty line) in the state, of which 30 were from north Karnataka. The estimate of people below poverty line is 33 per cent, higher than among the neighbouring states. On the basis of head-count rating, 6 districts of north Karnataka were worst in 1999-2000. More important for policy purposes is the fact that 60 per cent of the poor of the state lived in north Karnataka. Hence, it requires mixing up of policies on regional balance with sectoral strategies

- Instead of directly concentrating on attacking poverty reduction, incentive-based income approaches may be necessary.

Governance and Devolution Measures on PRIs

- On governance in general
  - making all public units and departments attuned to transparency and fiscal responsibility;
  - effective utilisation of information technology in all aspects of governance;
  - promotion of private Indian and foreign investment, and private-public partnership in owning, managing and financing of social and economic infrastructure sectors, and for promotion of tourism development, and
  - special promotional policies (including attracting foreign investment and increasing exports) on key sectors such as information and communication (including electronics), biotechnology, automobiles, handicrafts, readymade garments, general engineering, and agro-food processing industries.
- On improving governance and performance at the PRI levels several new initiatives are necessary. They are:
  - Political decentralisation to improve the inclusion process for marginalised and minority sections and women population in PRIs.
  - Administrative decentralisation in PRIs.
  - A fresh look at designing of activity mapping.
  - A separate cadre of officers for PRIs.
  - Fiscal decentralisation.

Sectoral Policies

1) Industrial Policies: Some New Thrusts

- Attraction of new private and FDI investments (to raise investments to the tune of Rs. 20,000 crores per year), effectively introducing single window agency, creation of industrial parks, special supports to small scale units are some of the new twists required now. With these, an employment target of at least 1.5 lakh per year can be targeted.
- Technology upgradation, infrastructure support, human resource development, deregulation of business environment, marketing assistance for the SSI Sector, classification of schemes for giving incentives into a system of economic zones (SEZ) as developed areas, developing areas, backward areas, export promotional industrial parks, and specialised industrial parks.
- Move from a Policy Orientation to a Project Orientation.

2) New Directions for Agriculture

The major issues to be tackled are: Stagnancy in agricultural technology, drought proneness of northern region, lack of crop diversification. Some of the major policy thrusts can be:

- Capital formation in the agricultural sector to grow at least at the rate of five per cent per annum. Inducing private capital formation is also important, particularly in seed development, storage, processing and transportation activities.
- The full potential of irrigation should be attained by the year 2010.
- Rainfed agriculture and livestock development should take advantage of new technologies such as biotechnology.
- Next phase of land reforms should provide flexibility as well as free operations in the land market without tampering with the Land Ceiling Act. The unabated conversion of agricultural land to non-agricultural uses has to be checked.
- Decongestion of farmlands is essential to enable dryland farming economically viable. This can happen through a deliberate plan to wean away a minimum number annually to alternate livelihood opportunities, as being initiated in China.
- Reforms in agricultural marketing are long due and particularly after the submission of Guru Committee and Patil Committee reports.
- Enhancement of investments in research and development and extension, both from public as well as private sources, to be targeted at Rs. 100 crores per year.

- Horticulture, floriculture, sericulture and fisheries are the emerging vanguards in the trade sectors. It will be necessary that the state undertake policies to make the producers and traders in these growth drivers to participate proactively in international trade along with post harvest processing. Specialised institutions like KAPPEC need to be strengthened to promote the participation and making the farming community reach international markets in these products.
- Establishment of biotechnology parks exclusively for marine resource development should be undertaken.

3) Re-orienting the Power Sector

- The first step in this direction is reforming Karnataka Electricity Regulation Commission itself. The E-Act relies heavily on KERC's decisionmaking authority to implement reforms—including open access rules and tariff rationalisation—as well as to guide future utility operation, including regulation of power purchase, utility performance, service quality, guiding on power purchase procurement, and ensuring competitive bidding and public participation.
- Secondly, eliminating cross-subsidies: Demand-side management, loss reduction and improved customer management (metering and billing) are necessary for reducing costs and future capacity needs. Distribution companies must be required to collect and disclose such information, and implement metering and IT system judiciously where most needed.
- The third policy thrust is on subsidy reduction. With tariff rationalisation, the current level of Rs. 1,800 crores should be reduced to below 1,000 crores. Subsidy if required should be based on the principle of performance, targeted to specific consumers. Financial incentives to support for physical system upgrade, including loss reduction, metering and IT deployment should be introduced.
- Finally, transparency and public scrutiny of utility operations through the avenues for public participation and consumer grievance provided by the regulatory process can improve SEB governance.

4) Policies on Water and Irrigation

- About 50 per cent of surface irrigation potential is yet to be tapped. The estimated cost is about Rs. 15,000 crores.
- Water Use Association Act is still to take its deep roots. Watershed development programmes should enable the User Association to come up.
- In the area of groundwater development, particularly, in the management of artificial recharging, treatment of aquifers etc., private agencies can be encouraged to come up, either on a cooperative basis or on a corporate sector basis. But, in the spirit of its ecological impacts, it should be fully priced. Groundwater regulations should be based on agro-climatic zones.

5) Policies on Delivery of Human Development

- Public-private partnerships: Linking PRIs, SHGs and other NGOs can lead to better deliveries.
- Clustering of villages around specified economic activities.
- Regional balance in primary education.
- Improving facilities and infrastructure in schools.
- Universalisation of Yashaswini Health Scheme.
- Enlarging social security to a larger section on the basis of economic status: housing, drinking water, lighting, health care, employment.
- Protecting cultural heritage of the regions.
- Empowerment of women with models of the type SEWA.
- E-governance at the GP level.

References

Agarwal, Bina (2005). "Landmark Step to Gender Equality", *The Hindu*, Magazine section, September 25.

Anonymous (2005). *Karnataka Development Report*, Draft report submitted to Planning Commission, Nodal Agency: Institute for Social and Economic Change.

Government of Karnataka (2000). *Karnataka: Future Vision and Current Action*, Karnataka State Industrial and Development Corporation Ltd., Bangalore.

———. (2002). *High Power Committee for Redressal of Regional Imbalances*, chaired by D.M. Nanjundappa.

Kadekodi, Gopal, B.P. Vani and H.K. Amarnath (2004). *An Enquiry in to the Nature of Regional Disparities: The Context of Human Development in Karnataka*, a draft report submitted to Karnataka Government, as part of *State Human Development Report*.

Howes, Stephen and Rinku Murgai (2003). "Karnataka: Incidence of Agricultural Power Subsidies", *Economic and Political Weekly*, April 19, pp. 1533-1535.

Visvesvaraya, M. (1920). *Reconstructing India*, Westminster, UK, P.S. King & Sons.

Chapter 1

An Overview of Karanataka's Economy

1.1 Introduction

Karnataka state was formed on 1st November 1956. For administrative purposes, the state is divided into 27 districts and 175 *taluka* (or subdistrict units). About 94 per cent of total villages (=29483) is inhabited. Total geographical area of Karnataka (192000 sq.km) is equal to 6.31 per cent of the nation's total.

1.1.1 Karnataka and Reforms

Three features characterise Karnataka's economic structure. First, Karnataka is a part of Indian federation. Second, Karnataka has a mixed economic system. Third, Karnataka is open to trade in goods and services and factor mobility with rest of India and the world. These features imply that the policies and programmes of the Union, state and local governments, role of private sector in product and factor markets, and international arrangements for trade and investment, have direct or indirect impact on socio-economic development of the state. In particular, since 1991, the national and state level economic reforms, and commitments to honouring the disciplines of the World Trade Organization (WTO) agreements in goods, services and intellectual property rights, have been speeding up the process of economic globalisation with attendant consequences on the economy, polity and society.

Over the years, Karnataka has accumulated a large infrastructure for human resources development. With more than 13 universities, 712 general education colleges, 97 medical colleges, 96 engineering colleges, 181 polytechnics, 300 industrial training centres, and several premier institutes/centres of research in pure and applied sciences, social sciences and humanities, management, information technology, biotechnology, fashion technology, legal education, manufacturing technology and foundry technology, the state is aptly called the "Brain Bank of India".

The state has earned a high reputation in initiating reforms for facilitating smooth, speedy and less costly transactions; liberalisation and simplifications of rules and regulations; transparency and accountability in public works and procurements; explicit role for participation of private sector, and public-private partnerships, in development of infrastructure; and in providing right to information for people. These reforms, among others, have been contributory to good governance measures of the state (Box 1.1).

Availability of skilled manpower, best corporate management and practices for global competitiveness, dynamism in the development and application of modern engineering technologies, and good governance measures have been the driving factors for enormous growth of high-tech industries and inflow of domestic and foreign investment in the state, especially in the information technology, electronics and communications, machine tools, engineering, automobiles, auto-components, food processing, agriculture, readymade garments, pharmaceuticals, and aerospace. Thus, Bangalore, the state's capital, is aptly called the "Silicon Valley of India", "IT Hub of Asia", and "IT Capital of India" with many global players, such as, Infosys and Wipro in the ICT sector.

In recognition of the importance of ICT for the common man, the state has been highly supportive and encouraging for use of ICT in education, revenue, employment, police, environment, transports and industry. These applications of ICT in the government sectors are popularly called e-governance. For instance, under Bhoomi, 20 million rural land records to 6.7 million farmers through 177 government owned kiosks

BOX 1.1

Good Governance Measures in Karnataka State

- Transparency, accountability, efficiency and fiscal responsibility by enacting special Acts.
- Effective utilisation of information technology in all aspects of governance.
- Decentralised governance and planning to ensure effective peoples' participation.
- Liberalisation of control and regulations through broader, faster and continuous economic reforms to create congenial economic environment.
- Promotion of private Indian and foreign investment, and private-public partnership, in owning, managing and financing of social and economic infrastructure sectors, and for promotion of tourism development.
- Further promotion of private sector in state-building activities, based on the historical experience of private sector's contributions to banking and finance, education, health, industry, agriculture, and service sectors.
- Formulation of development plans with growth-cum-equity objectives, instruments and strategies, especially to reduce transition costs of liberalisation and globalisation on vulnerable sections of population through poverty alleviation, employment generation, and human development programmes.
- Promotion for coexistence of small and large scale activities and enterprises for maximum utilisation of abundant human, natural, and man-made resources for attaining higher growth of income, employment, investment, and exports.
- Professionlisation of policymaking through setting up task forces, Administrative Reforms Commission, Tax Reforms Commission and High Power Committee for Redressal of Regional Disparities.
- Enhancement and strengthening of global competitiveness of economic activities under the WTO regime with special reference to small scale and size operations and activities through technology upgradation and market assistance programmes.
- Special promotional policies (including for attraction of foreign investment and for increasing exports) for key sectors, such as, information and communication (including electronics), biotechnology, automobiles, handicrafts, readymade garments, general engineering, and agro-food processing industries.

are delivered online. This has reduced, among others, red tape in the issue of land title records.

To ensure peoples' participation, and to utilise local information and resources in planning process, decentralised governance and planning has been practised in the state. Following the 73rd Amendment to the Indian Constitution, Karnataka Panchayat Raj Act, 1993 is enacted which provides three-tier system at the village, *taluka* and district levels. Up to March 2002, 5659 village *Panchayats* have been established, which, on an average, covers 5300 people. To review and guide the developmental tasks of village *Panchayats, Gram Sabhas* are constituted comprising persons on the electoral rolls in the village. To assist the district *Panchayats* in formulation of integrated development plans, District Planning Committees are constituted. To ensure participation of women and socially disadvantage groups of people, one-third of the membership is reserved for women, one-third for OBCs, and for SC/ST in proportion of their share in population of each village *Panchayat*. At the state level, one-third of the positions of Presidents as well as Vice-Presidents is reserved for SC/ST and OBCs. To review the finances and to make suitable recommendations for *Panchayats*, State Finance Commission is constituted once in every five years. For effective and informed participation of elected members, training for elected representatives in planning and governance is provided. A databank on finances of village level units is set up for financial planning purposes.

This Chapter presents an overview of Karnataka's economic growth (or state income), since 1991. In addition, major trends in (a) growth of employment, investment, and exports; and (b) income distribution (i.e. levels and inequality in consumption and extent of poverty) and human development indicators, are highlighted. Throughout, the state's economic performance is highlighted in comparison with national level and other southern states. These analyses are intended to draw implications on the nature and patterns of state's current growth competitiveness in the light of the past achievements and for the purpose of suggesting policy measures for future growth.

1.2 Economic Growth of Karnataka

Growth of GSDP (=gross state domestic product at factor cost and at constant (1993-94) prices) is an important indicator of economic growth of the state. Analysis of this indicator at aggregate and disaggregate levels leads to the following insights into the patterns and sources of growth.

1.2.1 Patterns of Aggregate Growth

Appendix A-1.1 presents select indicators of the economic growth of Karnataka from 1994-95 to 2003-04. In addition, these indicators are presented for the southern states and all India for purpose of comparative analysis.

Karnataka's annual growth of the GSDP has increased from 5.61 per cent in 1994-95 to 6.21 per cent in 2003-2004. At the same time, per capita GSDP has increased from Rs. 9027 to Rs. 14769 and annual growth of per capita GSDP from 3.69 per cent to 4.87 per cent.

State's annual growth of GSDP and per capita GSDP are lower than the annual growth of GDP and per capita GDP in 1994-95 as well as in 2003-04. In contrast, per capita GSDP was lower (or higher) than per capita GDP in 1994-95 (or 2003-04). Nevertheless, average growth of GSDP (= 7 per cent) and per capita GSDP (= 5.46 per cent) are higher than the average growth GDP and per capita GDP.

The distribution of GSDP across primary, secondary and tertiary sectors shows a major shift towards tertiary sector, and especially away from the primary sector. For instance, the share of tertiary (or primary) sector in the GSDP has increased (or declined) from 38.27 (or 34.29) per cent in 1994-95 to 51.55 (or 20.01) per cent in 2003-04. This shift from primary to secondary sectors is also evident at the national level as well as in other southern states. For instance, the share of tertiary (or primary) sector in the GDP has increased (or declined) from 45.3 (or 30.3) per cent in 1994-95 to 53.8 (or 21.7) per cent in 2003-04. In the same way, the share of tertiary (or primary) sector in the GSDP of Tamil Nadu has increased (or declined) from 41.52 (or 24.50) per cent in 1994-95 to 55.70 (or 11.37) per cent in 2003-04. Thus, the trends in relative share of primary, secondary and tertiary sectors in the state income are comparable with the relative share of the sectors in other southern states and at the national level.

As compared to other southern states, Karnataka has a higher economic growth by select indicators. First, average growth of GSDP and per capita GSDP of Karnataka is higher than that of Andhra Pradesh, Kerala, and Tamil Nadu. Second, per capita GSDP of Karnataka is higher than that of Andhra Pradesh Kerala in 2003-04. Third, share of primary sector in GSDP of Karnataka is higher than that of Andhra Pradesh; and share of secondary sector in GSDP of Karnataka is higher than that of Andhra Pradesh and Kerala, in 2003-04. Further, between 1994-95 and 2003-04, share of tertiary sector in Karnataka's GSDP has changed by 13.28 percentage points. This change is higher than for Andhra Pradesh (5.92 percentage points) and at all India level (8.5 percentage points).

In what follows, a disaggregate analysis of Karnataka's economic growth is undertaken to identify the sectoral, industrial, and spatial sources for Karnataka's economic growth during 1994-95 to 2003-04.

1.2.2 Disaggregation of Economic Growth by Sectors and Industry

Appendix A-1.2 presents the sources and extent of variability in annual growth by sectoral and industry compositions from 1994-95 to 2003-04. The trends in the compositions imply the following:

In absolute terms, the GSDP has increased over the years; from Rs. 4,33,869 million in 1994-95 to Rs. 6,06,196 million in 1998-99 and to Rs. 8,05,501 million in 2003-04. At the same time, annual growth rate of GSDP has fluctuated from 3.69 per cent in 1994-95 to 11.21 per cent in 1998-99, and to 4.87 per cent in 2003-04. During 1994-95 to 2003-04, the lowest annual growth (= 2.50 per cent) is evident for 2001-02 and is attributable for negative growth of primary sector [= (-) 14.24 per cent]. In fact, since 2001-02, annual growth of GSDP is lowered by the negative growth rate of primary sector.

Most importantly, in 2003-04, the negative growth rate of primary sector [= (-) 6.48 per cent] is continued, but that of secondary sector (= 6.90 per cent) and tertiary sector (= 10.88 per cent) has improved, which have enabled the aggregate state's or all sectors' growth rate to rise to 4.87 per cent. The effect of severe drought in the successive years, though affected the aggregate growth in 2001-02, the other sectors pulled it out of what would otherwise have been a severe economic crisis in the state.

Per capita GSDP of the state has increased from Rs. 9,027 in 1994-95 to Rs. 11,851 in 1998-99 and to Rs. 14,769 in 2003-04. The annual growth of per capita GSDP varies from 3.69 per cent in 1994-95 to 11.21 per cent in 1998-99, and 4.87 per cent in 2003-04. The lowest growth of per capita GSDP (=1.01 per cent) in 2001-02 is attributable to the (a) above sources of negative growth of GSDP, and (b) continued growth of total population in the state.

Trends in annual growth of GSDP and per capita GSDP show two features. First, annual growth of GSDP has remained higher than the annual growth of per capita GSDP. This is shown in Figure 1.1 and implies that annual population growth has remained less than the annual growth of GSDP. Second, average growth of GSDP and per capita GSDP has been positive in the state. For instance, average growth of GSDP is equal to 7 per cent and per capita income is equal to 5.46 per cent during 1994-95 to 2003-04. This suggests that the state should target for a higher annual growth of state income and/or lower growth of population in order to attain a higher average growth of per capita GSDP in future.

FIGURE 1.1

Trends in Annual Growth of GSDP and Per Capita GSDP: 1994-95 to 2003-04

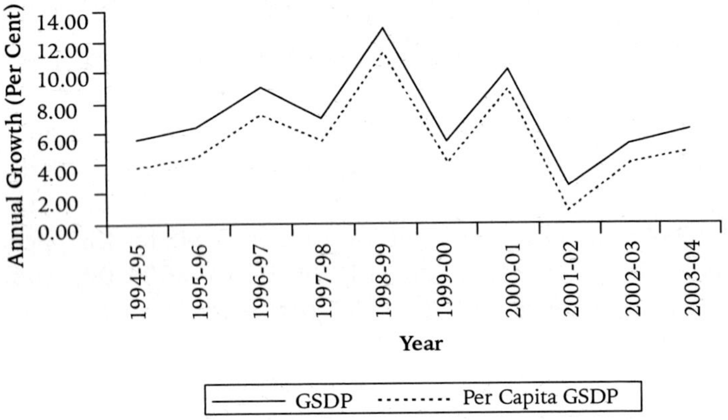

Share of primary (or tertiary) sector in state's GSDP has declined (or increased) from 36.32 (or 38.27) per cent in 1993-94 to 28.51 (or 41.97) per cent in 1998-99 and to

FIGURE 1.2

Trends in Sectoral Share in GSDP: 1993-94 to 2003-04

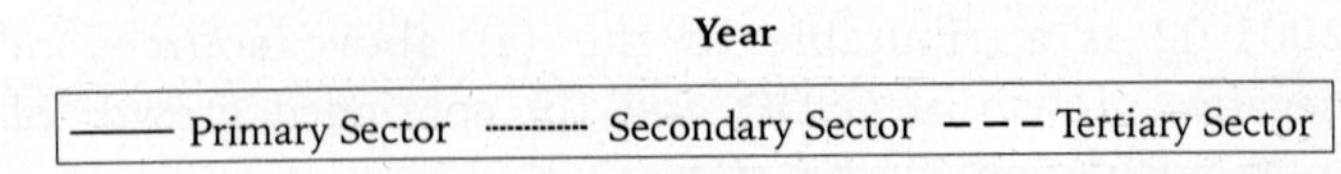

20.01 (or 51.55) per cent in 2003-04. This is shown in Figure 1.2. At the same time, the share of secondary sector has increased from 25.40 per cent in 1993-94 to 29.52 per cent in 1998-99 and has declined to 28.44 per cent in 2003-04. The average growth of tertiary sector is equal to 10.21 per cent as compared to 8.34 per cent of secondary sector and 1.09 per cent of primary sector. Thus, the tertiary sector has emerged as the most important contributor to the state's GSDP since 1993-94.

Within each sector, the most dominant activity/industry is evident in terms of its largest share in the state income. That is, agriculture in primary sector, manufacturing in secondary sector, and trade, hotels and restaurants in tertiary sector. The share of these activities/industries in GSDP is equal to 17.48 per cent, 19.43 per cent and 14.06 per cent respectively in 2003-2004 (Appendix A-1.3). Thus, special policy support for manufacturing sectors, and industry-oriented service sectors by the state government is evident in the diversified industrial policies since 1995 (Box 1.2).[1]

BOX 1.2

Policies for Promotion and Development of Industries in Karnataka State

The Government of Karnataka has the general industrial policy, complementary policies for the general industrial policy and sector-specific industrial policies for promotion and development of industries in the state. These policies include:

General Policies

- New Industrial Policy, 2001-06.

Complementary Policies

- Export Promotion Policy, 2002-07.
- Tourism Policy, 2002-07.
- Industries (Facilitation) Bill, 2002.
- Infrastructure Policy, 1997.
- Power Sector Policy, 1997.

Sector-specific Industrial Policies

- Agro-food Processing, Policy 2003.
- The Millennium BPO Policy, 2002.
- The Millennium IT Policy, 2000.
- Industrial Promotion Policy for the Automobile Industry, 2000.
- The Millennium Biotech Policy, 2000.

1. Details of select policies are available on: *http://www.kumbangalore.com/kar_policy/policy.htm.*

Further, the key industries, which contribute to sectoral growth, are identifiable by average growth rates. Thus, mining and quarrying (9 per cent) and fishing (6.44 per cent) are key contributing activities in the primary sector. Construction (10.66 per cent), and electricity, gas, and water supply (5.48 per cent) in the secondary sector. Within the tertiary sector, the key contributing service industries include communication (23.09 per cent), railways (12.90 per cent), transport by other means (8.55 per cent), and banking and insurance (11.48 per cent).

Variability of the GSDP by each industry in each year and over the years is captured in terms of coefficient of variation. First, inter-industry (for 13 industries, however) variations in the GSDP which was about 100 per cent up to 2001-02 declined subsequently. Second, of the sectors, variability of GSDP is highest in tertiary sector (29 per cent) as compared to 23 per cent in secondary sector and 11 per cent in primary sector. Within the sectors, variability of income is highest in mining and quarrying (25 per cent) in primary sector, construction (32 per cent) in secondary sector, and communication (64 per cent) in tertiary sector. However, these industries are not dominant in terms of their share in state income.

A comparison between the average growth and coefficient of variation for each industry during 1994-95 to 2002-03 shows that higher growth is associated with higher variability. This is clearly evident for mining and quarrying in primary sector, construction in secondary sector, and communication in tertiary sector.[2]

1.2.3 Disaggregation of Growth by Districts

Disaggregating economic growth by districts in the state identifies spatial sources of variations in annual growth of state and per capita income. With the formation of seven new districts (*viz.*, Bagalkote from Bijapur, Chamrajnagar from Mysore, Udupi from Dakshina Kannada, Davangere from Chitradurga, Gadag and Haveri from Dharwad, and Koppal from Raichur) from the 20 districts in 1997-98, district level income data are available for all 27 districts only from 1998-99. Appendices A-1.3 and A-1.4 present the trends and patterns of annual growth and sectoral shares in gross district income—at constant (1993-94) prices—by primary, secondary and tertiary sectors as well as by levels of per capita district income.

Sectoral variations are evident in the annual growth of primary, secondary and tertiary sectors in all districts. Most importantly, several districts experienced negative annual growth in different years, mainly in primary and secondary sectors. For instance, the number of districts, which have experienced negative annual growth is equal to 6 (or 1) in primary (or secondary) sector in 1999-00 and 22 (or 3) in 2002-03. Nevertheless, only 12 districts in primary sector and 2 districts in secondary sector have experienced a negative average growth rate during 1999-00 to 2002-03. The decline in annual growth in secondary sector is evident for 12 districts, *viz.*, Bagalkote, Bangalore Rural, Bidar, Bijapur, Chamrajnagar, Gadag, Gulbarga, Hassan, Haveri, Kodagu, Koppal, and Uttara Kannada.

All the districts have experienced a positive annual growth of tertiary sector, except Bijapur and Hassan districts in 2002-03. Most importantly, no district in tertiary sector has experienced a negative average growth during 1999-00 to 2002-03. In view of this, the average growth of aggregate gross district income is positive in all districts. This implies that the growth of tertiary sector has been a major source of positive growth of gross district income in the state.

Annual growth of primary sector is negative in 22 districts in 2002-03. This offers evidence for the spatial source of the state's negative annual growth of GSDP from the primary sector in 2002-03 (= -6.36).

Interdistrict variations in sectoral incomes and per capita income are evident in the coefficient of variation. Of the sectors, interdistrict variations in gross district income are highest in secondary sector and lowest in primary sector. For instance, coefficient of variations is equal to 177 (or 47) per cent for secondary (or primary) sector in 1999-00 and 174 (or 42) per cent in 2002-03, with that of tertiary sector in between. On the other hand, a decline in interdistrict variations in per capita district income is evident in the reduction of value of coefficient from 41 per cent 1999-00 to 34 per cent in 2002-03.

In addition, interdistrict disparity in sectoral district incomes and per capita district income is evident in the number of districts above the state's average growth rate: 16 districts in primary sector, 19 districts in secondary sector, 10 districts in tertiary sector, 20 districts in aggregate income and 11 districts in per capita income.

Districts with low share of primary sector in gross district income (e.g. Bangalore Urban, Dakshina Kannada, Dharwad, Uttara Kannada and Udupi) have a

2. Correlation coefficient between average growth and coefficient of variation by industry is equal to 0.81 in primary sector, 0.94 in secondary sector and 0.98 in tertiary sector.

higher share of tertiary sector than secondary sector. These districts have experienced a higher annual growth of district income due to higher growth of tertiary sector in their district incomes. A notable exception, for instance, is Mysore, which has a higher composition of tertiary sector income (44.70 per cent) with 28.62 per cent of district income from the primary sector.

Most importantly, the contribution of primary sector to the gross district income in all the northern districts (i.e. Bagalkote, Bellary, Bidar, Bijapur, Gadag, Gulbarga, Koppal and Raichur) has been above the state's average since 1999-00. At the same time, the contribution of secondary and tertiary sectors in the gross district income has been below the state's average. This suggests that the northern districts have smaller secondary and tertiary bases for their economic growth.

1.3 Growth of Investment, Employment and Exports

At the state level, the growth of employment, investment and exports are contributory to economic growth. Thus, the growth of these variables is emphasised below.

1.3.1 Growth of Investment

Investment (or creation of capital) is one of the key determinants of economic growth. As a mixed and open economy, Karnataka is open for private domestic and foreign investment, as well as for public investment, in all state-building activities. Thus, growth and composition of investment is analysed by capital formation in public and private sectors, and by inflow of private investments.

Capital Formation

An important indicator for investment is capital formation. Within the sectoral framework of the state income estimations, gross fixed capital formation (GFCF) is estimated by industry and by public and private sectors.[3]

Appendix A-1.6 presents the trends in the annual growth of GFCF by industry from 1993-94 to 2001-02. Total GFCF for all industries has increased from Rs. 11,067 crore in 1993-94 to Rs. 23,996 crore in 1997-98 and to Rs. 50,476 crore in 2001-02. Annual growth of GFCF fluctuated from 32.33 per cent in 1994-95 to 13.68 per cent in 1997-98 and 66.99 per cent in 2001-02. The average annual growth rate during 1993-94 to 2001-02 was positive and equal to 22.57 per cent. The share of GFCF in the state income varies from 26.94 per cent in 1993-94 to 32.85 per cent in 97-98 and to 46.30 per cent in 2001-02. Further, the average growth by industry is highest for Storage (49.20 per cent) and is followed by Agriculture (47.27 per cent), Registered Manufacturing (35.60 per cent), and Transport by other means (35.17 per cent). This analysis excludes two special cases. First, Mining and Quarrying (62.17 per cent due to a rise in GFCF from Rs. 37 crore in 1999-00 to Rs. 210 crore in 2000-01) and Forestry and Logging (93.05 per cent due to a rise in GFCF from Rs. 269 crore in 2000-01 to Rs. 1,990 crore in 2001-02).

In terms of industrial composition of GFCF, higher capital formation is evident in Agriculture, Registered Manufacturing and Other Services. The share of these three industrial groups in the total GFCF is equal to 45.69 per cent in 1993-94, 58.77 per cent in 1997-98, 70.40 per cent in 1999-00 and 70.86 per cent in 2001-02. The Supra Regional Sectors, comprising Railways, Communication, Banking and Insurance, and Central Government administration accounted for 13.83 per cent in 1993-94, 6.65 per cent in 1997-98 and 3.51 per cent in 2001-02.

Appendix A-1.7 presents the share of private sector in the GFCF by industry from 1993-94 to 2001-02. The contribution of private sector is 100 per cent in (a) fishing, (b) unregistered manufacturing, and (c) real estate, ownership of dwellings and business services. Further, the contribution of private sectors is over 75 per cent in (i) registered manufacturing, (ii) construction, (iii) trade, hotels and restaurants, and (iv) other services. In the same way, private sector's share is higher in transport by other means and storage.

Most importantly, the annual share shows variations in the total (or for all sectors) GFCF between years: 63.29 per cent in 1993-94, 71.19 per cent in 1995-96, 82.09 per cent in 1998-99 and 44.77 per cent in 2001-02. The recent decline in the private sector's share in 2001-02 is evident for all industries except unregistered manufacturing, real estate, ownership of dwellings and business services, and other services.

Inflow of Private Investment

Since 1991, national reforms for attraction of foreign investment and complementary reforms at the state

3. The Directorate of Economics and Statistics (DES), Government of Karnataka (Bangalore) estimates the GFCF and all estimates are provisional. Thus, the correlation coefficient between the growth of state income and GFCF is not computed. The methodology for estimation is detailed in the processed document of the DES: *Methodology Used for Preparing the Estimates of GFCF at State Level.*

level (i.e. as a part of various industrial policies, listed in Box 1.2) have impacted on larger inflow of private investment into the state. Major advantages of private (especially, private foreign) investment include non-debt financing of economic development, access to state-of-art technology and access to national and global markets. In this section, the size and composition of private investment inflows into Karnataka are highlighted. At the state level, Karnataka Udoyg Mitra (KUM), under the Department of Industries and Commerce, is a facilitating and promotional body for promotion and approval of investment proposals.

Under the existing policy framework, private industrial investments are cleared and approved by (a) foreign direct investment by the Foreign Investment Promotion Board of the Government of India and, subsequently, by the Karnataka Udyog Mitra; (b) small size domestic investment proposals (i.e. investment of less than Rs. 3 crore) by District Level Single Window Clearance Committee; (c) large size investment proposals (i.e. investment of Rs. 3 crore or more but less than Rs. 50 crore) by the State Level Single Window Clearance Committee; and mega investment proposals (i.e. investment of Rs. 50 crore or more) by the High Level Clearance Committee.[4]

Opportunities for investment in Karnataka are available in different sectors, such as, informatics, computer software, IT-enabled services, telecom, auto and auto components, precision engineering, machine tools, mineral based industries, food processing, floriculture and biotechnology. The utilisation of these opportunities is evident, among others, in the growth of investment in IT and BT sectors. For instance, in 2002-03, total number of IT companies is equal to 116 (comprising 79 foreign equity companies) with a total investment of Rs. 1,708 crore (comprising Rs. 1025 crore of FDI). The number of electronic and hardware (or BPO) companies is equal to 31 (or 41) with a total investment of Rs. 448 (Rs. 512) crore. On the other hand, the number of BT companies is equal to 22 (comprising 14 foreign equity companies) with a total investment of Rs. 758 crore (comprising Rs. 425 crore of FDI).[5]

Appendix A-1.8 presents the trends in size and types of private investment inflows (at current prices) into Karnataka from 1993-94 to 2003-04. The main insights from this analysis are as follows:

Total investment (excluding investment of less than Rs. 3 crore) has fluctuated between years: from Rs. 6622.64 crore in 1993-94, Rs. 9937.61 crore in 1998-99, and to Rs. 8233.88 crore in 2003-04. The annual growth of total investment has varied from (-) 20.16 per cent in 1993-94, (-) 28.16 per cent in 1998-99 and to 56.32 per cent in 2003-04. However, the average annual growth of total investment is equal to 38.68 per cent. The annual growth of total investment is positively correlated with annual growth of total state income (=0.17) during 1994-95 to 2003-04.

Per cent of foreign direct investment approvals in the total investment approvals have fluctuated from 4.92 per cent in 1993-94, 49.99 per cent in 1997-98, and 5.43 per cent in 2003-04. These investments have come from countries, such as, USA (31.67 per cent), Mauritius (7.43 per cent), UK (7.39 per cent), Japan (6.09 per cent), Germany (8.69 per cent), and Singapore (4.63 per cent). In addition, about 0.29 per cent is contributed by Euro Issues, 6.70 per cent by NRIs, and 17.95 per cent by others.

Investment per foreign direct investment project has varied from Rs. 5.25 crore in 1993-94, Rs. 60.13 crore in 1997-98, and Rs. 1.57 crore in 2003-04. In the same way, investment per large project varied from Rs. 8.55 crore in 1993-94, Rs. 23.87 crore in 1998-99, and to Rs. 23.74 crore in 2003-04; and investment per mega project varied from Rs. 486.96 crore in 1993-94, Rs. 677.47 crore in 1998-99, and to Rs. 56.43 crore in 2003-04.

Share of total private investment in state's GSDP has varied from 16.12 per cent in 1993-94, 11.31 per cent in 1998-99, 45.73 per cent in 2000-01, and to 6.21 per cent in 2003-04.[6]

Karnataka's performance in attracting FDI is highlighted in the national context by the state's share in total approved FDI in India. The share exhibits wide variations between years: 4.32 per cent in 1993-94, 17.25 per cent in 1997-98, and 19.62 per cent in

4. Foreign direct investment refers to inflows under the following routes: Government (SIA/FIPB), RBI, NRI, acquisition of shares, equity capital of unincorporated bodies, reinvested earnings, and other capital.

5. These data are compiled from Government of Karnataka's website: *www.karnataka.com/industry*.

6. It might be added here that data on project investments (from the CapEx Survey) are published by the CMIE (2003). This data is useful, among others, for interstate comparison of investment inflows. For instance, for the quarter ending October 2003, total investment (includes private and public investment in manufacturing and service sectors) under implementation in Karnataka is equal to Rs. 44283 crore. As a per cent of total investment in the nation, Karnataka's investment comprised 6.40 per cent. This share is lower than for Andhra Pradesh (7.87 per cent), but higher than for Tamil Nadu (6.29 per cent) and Kerala (2.59 per cent). For lack of comparability between the CMIE and KUM investment data, only KUM (or official) investment data is analysed above.

2000-01. Except in 1993-94 and 1998-99, Karnataka's share remained higher than 5 per cent in the nation's total.

1.3.2 Growth of Employment

Availability of low cost and high quality labour is an important determinant of productivity and competitiveness of economic activities and, hence, higher economic growth. At the same time, higher economic growth is essential for generation and expansion of productive employment opportunities. Thus, growth of employment is both a determinant and consequence of economic growth. Further, full employment of labour complements to the realisation of potential economic growth. This has implications for reduction in income or consumption inequality and poverty in the state. Appendix A-1.9 presents select indicators of growth of employment in Karnataka in comparison with the national level and between 1993-94 and 1999-00. These indicators imply the following:

Number of persons in the labour force, or labour force participation rate (LFPR), has declined in total, and in both urban and rural areas in the state, between 1993-94 and 1999-00.[7] For instance, LFPR has declined in rural (or urban) areas from 75.7 (or 58) per cent in 1993-94 to 72.2 (or 52.7) per cent in 1999-00. However, all indicators of LFPR in the state are higher than the national level in both 1993-94 and 1999-00.

Annual growth of employment during 1993-94 to 1999-00 is higher for urban employment (= 2.8 per cent) than for rural employment (= 1.2 per cent) in the state.[8] Annual growth of employment in the state is equal to the national level in total employment, higher than rural employment and lower than urban employment.

Incidence of unemployment in total (1.4 per cent) and in rural areas (0.7 per cent) has remained constant, and has declined in urban areas from 3.7 per cent in 1993-94 to 3.4 per cent in 1999-00.[9] This also implies that the incidence of urban unemployment has remained higher than in rural areas. The incidence of total, rural and urban unemployment in the state has remained lower than at the national level.

Growth of employment in the organised sector of Karnataka has declined from 3.12 per cent in 1993-94 to 0.44 per cent in 1999-00. This decline is evident at the national level. However, the annual growth of employment in Karnataka has remained higher than at the national level. The average annual growth of organised employment in Karnataka (= 2.74 per cent) is about 3.7 times higher than at the nation level (= 0.74 per cent).

An important reason for higher growth of organised employment in Karnataka is attributable to higher share of state government employment within the public sector employment. This is evident, for instance, by the share of state government in employment generation within the public sector in 1991 as well as in 2000 is higher in Karnataka (43.46 per cent and 49.96 per cent) than in Andhra Pradesh (26.1 per cent and 27.58 per cent), Kerala (44.22 per cent and 45.09 per cent), Tamil Nadu (38.61 per cent and 39.59 per cent) and at the all-India level (37.32 per cent and 38.62 per cent).

Karnataka shares about 6.8 per cent of total unorganised units (i.e. enterprises and establishments) in the nation's total (= 25 million units) in 1993-94. This share has marginally declined to 6.3 per cent in 1999-00. Growth of total unorganised units during 1993-94 to 1999-00 is lower in the state (1.6 per cent) than at the national level (= 2.7 per cent). Further, growth of unorganised units is lower in Karnataka than in other southern states. For instance, the growth of unorganised units is equal to 2.1 per cent in Andhra Pradesh, 4.4 per cent in Kerala and 2.4 per cent in Kerala.

Most importantly, along with the decline in the number of unorganised units, employment per unit has declined in Karnataka from 3 persons to 2.75 persons. This decline is evident at the national level as well as in other southern states. Nevertheless, employment per unit in Karnataka has remained higher than at the national level. As compared to other southern states, employment per unit in Karantaka is higher than in Andhra Pradesh (2.59 persons) and Kerala (2.46 persons), but lower than in Tamil Nadu (2.86 persons) in 1998. However, between 1990 and 1998, growth of per unit employment in the state is equal to Kerala [(-)1 per cent] and lower than in Tamil Nadu [(-)0.4 per cent] and Andhra Pradesh [(-) 0.6 per cent].

The share of unorganised employment in the total (organised and unorganised) employment indicates the

---

7. LFPR "is the proportion of persons in the age group 15 years and above who were either working (i.e. employed) on the usual principal and subsidiary status or seeking or available for work (i.e. presently unemployed)", Planning Commission, *National Human Development Report* 2001, Government of India 2002: p.155,

8. Annual growth of employment is estimated in Government of India (2002) "as compound annual growth in the persons employed in the age group 15 years and above on the usual principal and subsidiary status" (p.159).

9. Incidence of unemployment is equal to "the percentage of persons unemployed in the age group 15 years and above on the usual principal and subsidiary status to the total number of persons in the labour force", Planning Commission, *National Human Development Report 2001*, Government of India, 2002: p.163.

relative size of employment between the organised and unorganised sectors. This share is equal to 77.84 per cent in 1993-94, but has declined to 73.98 per cent in 1999-00, in Karnataka state. This implies an increase in organised employment in total employment of the state. This is in contrast at the national level where the relative size of unorganised employment has increased from 79.07 per cent in 1993-04 to 81.07 per cent in 1999-00.

Employment elasticity (i.e. ratio of growth of employment to growth of output) during 1993-94 to 1999-00 is higher in the state (= 0.188) than at the national level (0.160). Further, available evidence for other southern states suggests that employment elasticity is higher in Karnataka than in Andhra Pradesh (0.067 per cent), Kerala (0.013 per cent), Tamil Nadu (0.052 per cent) and at the all India level (0.160 per cent). This implies that the responsiveness of employment to output growth, or productive employment, is higher in the state as compared to other southern states and at the national level.

1.3.3 Growth of Exports

Exports are the major sources of external demand and precious foreign exchange. Karnataka is a pioneer in establishing a database on exports from 1993-94. The export data is compiled and processed by Visveswaraya Industrial and Trade Centre, Department of Industries and Commerce. In total, exports are grouped under 19 commodities. Appendices A-1.10 and A-1.11 present the commodity composition and annual growth of exports by commodities from 1993-94 to 2003-04.

Total value of exports (at current prices) has grown from Rs. 3025 crore in 1993-94 to Rs. 10039.48 crore in 1998-99 to Rs. 41670.24 crore in 2003-04. This has increased the state's contribution to national exports from 3.51 per cent in 1993-94 to 5.14 per cent in 1998-99 to 10.22 per cent in 2003-04. Further, exports as a percentage of state's GSDP (at factor cost and current prices) has increased from 7.36 per cent in 1993-94 to 11.43 per cent in 1998-99 and to 31.45 per cent in 2003-04. In fact, share of exports in the GSDP has been higher than the share of exports in GDP (at factor cost and at market prices) since 1999-00.

Of the 19 commodities, seven traditional exports (*viz.*, readymade garments, coffee products, iron ore and minerals, engineering, silk products, chemicals and allied products, and leather products) have declined from 88.80 per cent in 1993-94 to 88.53 per cent in 1998-99 and to 83.91 per cent in 2003-04. On the other hand, the composition of electronics and computer software has increased from 7.77 per cent in 1993-94 to 42.76 per cent in 1998-99 and to 49.25 per cent in 2003-04.

Annual growth of exports varies between years: from 32.08 per cent in 1994-95 to 19.06 per cent in 1998-99 and to 39.37 per cent in 2003-04. However, the average growth of total exports from 1994-95 to 2003-04 is positive and equals to 30.22 per cent. Most importantly, the annual growth of total exports of Karnataka has remained higher than the annual total exports of India. This is shown in Figure 1.3.

FIGURE 1.3

Trends in Growth of Exports from Karnataka and India: 1994-95 to 2003-04

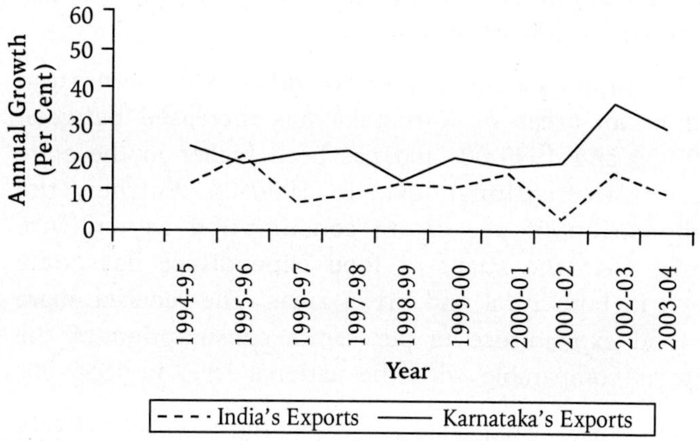

Annual growth of exports by commodities shows wide variations. For instance, the average growth (during 1994-95 to 2003-04) is higher for tobacco/*beedi* (151.76 per cent), wool and woolen products (118.46 per cent), agriculture and processed food products (113.11 per cent), electronics and computer software (59.59 per cent), and cashew and cashew kernals (55.53 per cent). About 11 commodities have recorded a higher average annual growth than at the state level (30.22 per cent).

Variability of exports of each commodity is evident in the value of coefficient of variation. Higher variability is evident for wool and woollen products (211 per cent), agriculture and processed food products (194 per cent), tobacco/*beedi* (112 per cent), electronics and computer software (103 per cent), cashew and cashew kernels (89 per cent). Thus, commodities, which have a record of higher average annual growth, have a higher variability of their annual exports over time.

1.4 Trends and Patterns of Consumption and Extent of Poverty

Differential levels and inequality of household consumption, and extent of poverty are the most important indicators of income distribution. Differential level of household consumption is measurable by per capita expenditure by food and non-food, and by rural and urban, distinctions. Gini ratio for household consumption is a measure of inequality in consumption. Per cent of population by rural and urban areas measures the extent of rural and urban poverty. Appendix A-1.12 presents these indicators for 1993-94 and 1999-00 for Karnataka state and at all India level, using the per capita (household) consumption expenditure data from 50th and 55th Rounds of the National Sample Survey of Household Consumer Expenditure, and estimation of poverty line and per cent of population below the poverty line by the Planning Commission.

Per capita consumption expenditure in both rural and urban areas of Karnataka has increased between 1993-94 and 1999-00, and has been higher in the state than at the national level in 1999-00. Further, the composition of per capita consumption expenditure shows that the share of food expenditure has come down in both rural and urban areas. The reduced share of food expenditure in per capita consumption of the state is comparable with the national level in 1999-00.

Gini ratio for per capita consumption expenditure has declined (or increased) in rural Karnataka from 1993-94 to 1999-00. Qualitatively, this pattern is similar at the national level. This implies a decline (or an increase) in rural (or urban) consumption inequality in Karnataka.

Extent of poverty has declined in the state in terms of the number of persons below the poverty line. This is evident not only for the entire population, but also for rural as well as for urban areas. Most importantly, rural poverty is lower than urban poverty in the state, and all poverty indicators in the state are lower than at the national level except for urban poverty.

A comparison of income distribution indicators between Karnataka and other southern states (i.e. Andhra Pradesh, Tamil Nadu and Kerala) imply the following:[10]

- Per capita consumption expenditure in rural and urban Karnataka is lower than in rural and urban Tamil Nadu and Kerala.
- Gini ratio for per capita consumption in rural Karnataka was higher than in rural Andhra Pradesh and Kerala in 1993-94 as well as in 1999-00. However, Gini ratio for per capita consumption in urban Karnataka was lowest as compared to all other southern states in both 1993-94 and 1999-00.
- Composition of food consumption in rural Karnataka was higher than in rural Andhra Pradesh and Kerala in 1993-94 and higher than in rural Tamil Nadu and Kerala in 1999-00.
- Composition of food consumption in urban Karnataka was highest (or lowest) among the southern states (or except Andhra Pradesh) during 1993-94 (or 1999-00).
- Extent of poverty (or per cent of population below poverty line) was higher in rural Karnataka than in rural Andhra Pradesh and Kerala, and highest in urban Karnataka, in 1993-94.
- Extent of poverty (or per cent of population below poverty line) is higher in rural Karnataka than in rural Andhra Pradesh and Kerala in 1993-94 as well as in 1999-00; and extent of poverty in urban Karnataka is the highest in 1993-94, but higher than in Kerala and Tamil Nadu in 1999-00.

Thus, as compared to other southern states, Karnataka has much scope to improving the indicators of income distribution.

1.5 Human Development Indicators

In recent years, analysis of economic growth has an added dimension in terms of human development. Human development captures distribution of gains from economic development in a multidimensional way. A Human Development Index (HDI) is constructed as a composite of attainments in education, health and economic growth. Changes in HDI measures the relative variations in the levels and growth of human development. This helps in identifying the source/s of low and high performance in human development. Accordingly, the HDI guides the policy makers for design and implementation of policies for attaining a higher and balanced human development in the state. The first Report of Human Development in Karnataka was prepared in 1999, and the second report is under preparation, by the Government of Karnataka.

10. The following analysis is based on the state-wise consumption indicators in *National Human Development Report 2001*, Planning Commission, Government of India (2002).

Select human development indicators of the state are summarised in Appendix A-1.13 For comparison purposes, the value of all indicators is given for two points in time (i.e. 1991 and 2001) for the state as well as for India.

Karnataka shares 5.31 per cent of nation's total population (846.30 million) in 1991 and 5.17 per cent of nation's total population (1027.02 million) in 2001. The share of rural population in the state [69.08 (or 66.02) per cent in 1991 (or 2001)], and the state's decadal growth rate of total population [21.12 (or 17.25) per cent in 1991 (or 2001)] is lower than at the national level. In fact, the share of rural population in the state has declined from about 69 per cent in 1991 to about 66 per cent in 2001. Alternatively, the share of urban population in state's total has increased from 31 per cent in 1991 to 34 per cent in 2001.

In terms of crude birth rate, death rate and infant mortality rate, Karnataka state has a remarkable achievement as compared to national level. For instance, the infant mortality rate in the state (or nation) is equal to 77 (or 80) in 1991 and 58 (or 68) in 2000.

Literacy in the state has improved from 1991 to 2001 and is higher than the national level by indicators, such as, total literacy rate by male and female, and by literacy rate in rural and urban areas. For instance, literacy rate for total population has increased from 56.04 per cent to 67.04 per cent, as compared to the national level increase from 52.21 per cent to 65.28 per cent.

Female literacy is lower than male literacy in Karnataka. Both female and male literacy in the state is higher than at the national level. For instance, literacy rate in the state (or nation) in 2001 is equal to 76.29 (or 75.29) per cent for males and 57.45 (51.2) per cent for females.

Urban literacy is higher than rural literacy in the state, and state's rural and urban literacy are higher than at the national level. For instance, rural (or urban) literacy in the state was equal to 47.69 (or 74.20) per cent in 1991; 59.68 (or 81.05) per cent in 2001. At the national level, rural (or urban) literacy was equal to 44.69 (or 73.08) per cent in 1991 and 59.21 (or 80.06) per cent in 2001.

Nevertheless, the rank of the state in the Human Development Index (among 15 major states, however) has remained at 7 in 1991 and 2001. This suggests that further efforts are essential to improving the state's competitive performance of human development at the national level.

The Report on Human Development in Karnataka in 1999 [Government of Karnataka (1999)] showed that the education index (=0.596) contributed to 42.27 per cent of the state's total human development in 1991. This contribution is slightly smaller than the contribution of health index (43.83 per cent), but far higher than the contribution of income index (13.90 per cent). However, interdistrict variations do exist in the attainment of human development within the state. For instance, the northern districts ranked at the bottom in the Human Development Index (HDI) (i.e. of the 20 districts): 20th rank by Raichur, 19th rank by Gulbarga, 18th rank by Bidar, 17th rank by Bellary and 14th rank by Bijapur. Further, 12 had lower value of HDI than at the state level.

In addition, the Government of Karnataka's Final Report of the High Power Committee for Redressal of Regional Imbalances in 2002 has constructed the HDI for 20 districts and for reference year 1998. The value of HDI in 1998 (=0.63) is higher than in 1991 (=0.47). This indicates an improvement in the overall level of human development in the state. Nevertheless, inter-district disparities in the levels of human development persisted. For instance, 12 districts had lower value of HDI than at the state level as in 1991. In the same way, the relative ranking of northern districts has remained the same as in 1991, such as, Raichur (20th rank), Gulbarga (19th rank), Bidar (18th rank), Bellary (17th rank), and that of Bijapur worsened (16th rank).

Thus, corrections for spatial disparities in the attainment of human development are one of the major policy challenges for the state.

1.6 Price Variations

Unlike at the national level, no Index of wholesale price change is constructed to measure the rate of inflation at the state level. Rather, consumer price indices are constructed for different groups of workers/labourers, such as, industrial workers and agricultural labourers. The consumer price index for industrial workers is a measure of retail price inflation for the state. Analysis of the trends in annual growth of these indices shows the nature and magnitude of price changes in the process of regional economic growth.

Variations in prices in Karnataka are captured in terms of changes in three consumer price indices: (a) Consumer Price Index for Industrial Workers (CPI-IW);[11] (b) Consumer Price Index for Urban Non-Manual

11. Constructed by the Directorate of Economics and Statistics (Bangalore) for 12 series and by the Labour Bureau (Shimla) for 4 series. The average of the 16 series with the base year 1960 is used for the analysis.

Workers (CPI-UNMW);[12] and (c) general Consumer Price Index for Agricultural Labourers (CPI-AL-G).[13]

Trends in the growth of prices by annual per cent changes in these indices are presented from 1994-95 through 2003-04 in Appendix A-1.14. For comparison purposes, annual growth of the indices are presented at the all India level.

Annual price changes show considerable variations by all the three indices in Karnataka during 1994-95 to 2003-04. For instance, the annual growth of CPI-IW is equal to 10.44 per cent in 1994-95, 8.30 per cent in 1998-99 and 4.39 per cent in 2003-04. In the same way, the annual growth of CPI-UNMW (or CPI-AL) is equal to 10.19 (or 11.89) per cent in 1994-95, 0.00 (or 11.04) per cent in 1998-99 and 4.87 (or 14.89) per cent in 2003-04. However, it is apparent that, as compared to the annual 1994-95, annual growth of price change by all indices has declined in 2003-04.

In terms of average growth rate, CPI-UNMW shows the highest variation (7.20 per cent) as compared CPI-IW (7.04 per cent) and CPI-AL (6.45 per cent). In terms of coefficient of variation of annual growth, the highest variation is evident for CPI-AL (91.81 per cent) and is followed by CPI-UNMW (48.03 per cent) and CPI-IW (46.64 per cent).

The annual growth of price changes by all indices in Karnataka is different from that of all-India level. Thus, average growth and coefficient of variation of annual growth of all indices of price change differ between Karnataka and all-India level. In particular, the average growth of CPI-IW and CPI-UNMW (or CPI-AL) is higher (or lower) in Karnataka than at the all-India level. The coefficient of variation for CPI-UNMW and CPI-AL (or CPI-IW) in Karnataka is higher (or lower) than at the all-India level.

The CPI-IW is popularly called "retail price inflation" in India. The trends in the annual growth of CPI-IW shows that Karnataka's retail price inflation has remained lower than at the all-India level, except in 1994-95, 1997-98, and 1999-00. Thus, the average growth and coefficient of variation of CPI-IW in Karnataka is smaller than at the all-India level.

12. Constructed by the Central Statistical Organisation (New Delhi) for four centres for the base year 1984-85. The average of four centres indices is used for the analysis.

13. Constructed by the Labour Bureau (Shimla) for the base year 1960-61.

1.7 Concluding Remarks

This chapter has highlighted the salient features and competitive performance of Karnataka's economic growth since 1991. Competitive performance is measured by higher performance of Karnataka over other southern states as well as at the national level. In addition, contribution of Karnataka to the national economic development is measured by the state's share in national exports, employment and investments.

The main lessons of Karnataka's development experiences since 1991 are as follows:

- Karnataka has been responsive to changing local, regional, national and global economic scenario by making timely and sequential policy initiative (including measures for good governance). The combined impact of these policies has resulted in strengthening of economic and social infrastructure, and creation of congenial business and investment climate in the state. Thus, Karnataka has emerged, among others, as the Brain Bank of India and Bangalore has been called Silicon Valley of India.
- Economic growth shows high fluctuations in terms of annual growth and by sectoral and industry compositions. Thus, lack of consistency is experienced in the process of state's economic growth since 1991. Slow and negative growth of secondary and primary sectors, especially since 1999-00, is attributable for the high variations in the state's growth. Consequently, growth of per capita income has experienced high fluctuations along with the growth of state income, as the population growth has remained positive.
- Tertiary sector has emerged as a major contributor of state income. Growth of transport and communication, and banking and finance are contributory for tertiary sector's growth. Available evidence suggests that contribution of recent and fast growing activities, such as, IT (including IT-enabling services), private social infrastructure sectors (e.g. private educational institutions in higher education), and export performance are yet to be adequately accounted for growth of state income. In the event of accounting for full contribution of these in secondary and tertiary sectors, both the growth and composition of state income might undergo major positive changes.
- As a consequence of promotional measures in industrial and non-industrial policies, Karnataka

has successfully attracted considerable amount both private foreign direct investment and domestic investment. The share of total private investment in the state's gross state domestic product was highest (60.36 per cent) in 1995-96; and the share of state's FDI in the nation's total approved FDI inflows was highest (28.81 per cent) in 2002-03. In 2003-04, these shares stood at 6.21 per cent and 7.16 per cent respectively.

- Poverty and inequality in consumption persists in the state. A rise in inequality in consumption in urban Karnataka is a matter of serious policy concern, especially in the presence of transitional costs of economic reforms and process of globalisation on socially vulnerable groups and spatially backward areas. In addition, social and spatial disparities are evident in the attainment of human development in the state. Thus, further neglect of distributional implications may lead to human defacing of future reforms and globalisation in Karnataka.
- The *Report of the Special Group on Targeting Ten Million Employment Opportunities per year over the Tenth Plan Period* (Planning Commission, Government of India, 2002: Chairman: S.P.Gupta) has targeted an increase in employment opportunities of 50 million (10 million per annum on average) during the 10th Five Year Plan period (2002-03 to 2006-07). Contribution of manufacturing sector is estimated at 23.71 per cent; agriculture and allied activities at 19.63 per cent; and service activities at 56.96 per cent. Further, contribution of small and medium enterprises (SMEs) and self-employed (mainly in the informal sector) is estimated to be about 90 per cent in the projected total employment generation. From this viewpoint, policies for promotion of employment generation in SMEs in organised and unorganised (or informal) sectors will have a critical impact on accomplishing the employment targets. In particular, Karnataka has experienced a decline in the growth of unorganised enterprises and employment per unit in the 1990s. This process needs to be reversed through special policy focus on employment generation in SMEs in both organised and unorganised sectors. Otherwise, prospects for a larger and wider employment generation in the state seem to be bleak with attendant consequences on income distribution.
- Government of Karnataka's *Karnataka: Future Vision and Current Action* (2000), aims, among others, at an overall growth rate of 8 per cent to 9 per cent; average annual industrial growth at 12 per cent; fully tap world markets in information technology; and average annual growth of employment at 3.15 per cent, during 2000-2010. In addition, by 2005, the state aims, among others, at total literacy of population; reduction in population growth rate to 1.4 per cent; and attracts private investment in industrial sector to the tune of Rs. 20000 crore per annum. The lessons from the development experience of Karnataka since 1991, as elaborated in this Report, should be the basis for appropriate redesign and implementation of policies to accomplish the above long-and medium-term targets of the state.

APPENDIX A-1.1

Economic Growth of Karnataka: 1994-95 to 2003-04: A Comparison with Southern States and All-India

Growth Indicators	*Karnataka*		*Andhra Pradesh*		*Kerala*		*Tamil Nadu*		*India*	
	1994-95	*2003-04*	*1994-95*	*2003-04*	*1994-95*	*2003-04*	*1994-95*	*2003-04*	*1994-95*	*2003-04*
1. Annual Growth of GSDP/GDP (%)	5.61	6.21	5.61	7.64	4.52	6.31	12.57	3.55	7.25	8.51
2. Per Capita GSDP/GDP (Rs.)	9027	14769	8636	13261	9368	13208	11105	16035	9229	13332
3. Annual Growth of Per Capita Income (%)	3.69	4.87	3.95	6.31	3.22	5.34	11.28	2.50	5.36	6.69
4. Distribution of GSDP/GDP by Sectors										
4.1. Share of Primary Sector (%)	34.29	20.01	33.39	27.84	30.95	16.74	24.50	11.37	30.3	21.7
4.2. Share of Secondary Sector (%)	26.14	28.44	23.57	23.20	21.06	20.51	34.63	31.03	24.4	24.5
4.3. Share of Tertiary Sector (%)	38.27	51.55	43.04	48.96	48.80	62.75	41.52	55.70	45.3	53.8
4.4. Average Growth (%) of GSDP/GDP during 1994-95 to 2003-04	-	7.00	-	5.67	-	5.13	-	5.20	-	6.24
4.5. Average Growth (%) of Per Capita GSDP/GDP during 1994-95 to 2003-04	-	5.46	-	4.47	-	4.21	-	4.15		4.30

Notes: (1) GSDP (or GDP) refers to Gross State Domestic Product (or Gross Domestic Product) at factor cost and constant (1993-94) prices.

Sources: (1) *Economic Survey 2004-05*, Planning Department, Government of Karnataka, Bangalore, 2005. (2) *National Accounts Statistics 2001 and 2005*, Central Statistical Organisation, and Government of India, 2001 and 2005. (3) Processed State Income Data by the Planning Commission 2005, Government of India (New Delhi).

APPENDIX A-1.2

Annual Growth of Gross State Domestic Product of Karnataka State: 1994-95 to 2003-04

(in per cent)

Industry	*1994-95*	*1995-96*	*1996-97*	*1997-98*	*1998-99*	*1999-00*	*2000-01*	*2001-02*	*2002-03*	*2003-04*	*Average Growth %*	*Coefficient of Variation*
Agriculture	-1.30	2.24	4.11	-2.73	13.17	9.83	12.81	-16.05	-7.50	-6.48	0.81	0.12
Forestry and Logging	10.14	-2.51	13.44	-7.07	1.53	-3.10	0.39	6.42	-4.98	4.92	1.92	0.04
Fishing	12.17	29.92	3.66	1.98	-10.74	10.98	5.35	-14.30	33.06	-7.67	6.44	0.13
Mining and Quarrying	5.86	1.37	11.78	26.92	-24.60	15.58	7.94	17.53	9.51	18.14	9.00	0.25
Primary	-0.31	2.24	4.87	-2.27	10.87	9.18	11.93	-14.24	-6.36	-4.98	1.09	0.11
Manufacturing	11.90	3.99	9.15	12.78	17.96	-10.19	2.90	11.89	13.40	7.63	8.14	0.21
Registered	15.28	3.85	9.68	16.37	23.26	-17.50	-1.41	17.23	18.09	8.32	9.32	0.23
Unregistered	6.48	4.24	8.22	6.50	7.84	5.81	10.25	3.76	5.30	6.30	6.47	0.19
Construction	-4.47	21.25	14.17	22.48	19.49	12.20	3.15	6.90	5.72	5.75	10.66	0.32
Electricity, Gas and Water supply	12.73	1.00	1.10	4.65	19.38	-3.01	14.45	10.13	-9.70	4.11	5.48	0.17
Secondary	8.70	6.73	9.39	14.09	18.42	-4.55	3.92	10.42	9.35	6.90	8.34	0.23
Transport, Storage and Communication	9.88	15.71	20.28	9.96	12.51	18.08	23.17	13.55	17.80	19.74	16.07	0.46
Railways	7.21	13.40	62.85	-39.43	13.24	16.82	19.91	22.94	5.69	6.40	12.90	0.32
Transport by Other Means	5.52	9.28	15.77	9.81	14.65	5.09	5.93	4.88	7.77	6.75	8.55	0.24
Storage	10.17	18.34	6.04	14.09	9.36	10.55	7.14	19.42	7.28	-2.96	9.94	0.29
Communication	16.64	24.43	19.32	19.99	10.29	32.00	38.08	18.36	24.60	27.20	23.09	0.64
Trade, Hotels and Restaurants	15.16	9.91	17.73	3.69	17.12	-0.64	14.78	8.89	7.11	4.78	9.85	0.26

Contd. ...

Contd. ...

Industry	*1994-95*	*1995-96*	*1996-97*	*1997-98*	*1998-99*	*1999-00*	*2000-01*	*2001-02*	*2002-03*	*2003-04*	*Average Growth %*	*Coefficient of Variation*
Banking and Insurance	16.94	12.67	9.04	18.86	-0.08	16.39	11.87	10.11	11.47	7.50	11.48	0.31
Real Estate, Ownership of Dwellings and Business Services	4.39	5.40	5.14	6.61	7.72	10.24	10.89	7.90	8.02	14.58	8.09	0.25
Public Administration	-0.68	9.92	2.48	8.99	3.85	12.16	-1.45	3.71	-0.63	4.76	4.31	0.14
Other Services	4.87	7.55	10.41	14.84	10.98	15.02	9.57	9.01	6.86	13.86	10.30	0.31
Teritary	**9.20**	**9.81**	**11.97**	**9.34**	**10.24**	**9.66**	**12.63**	**9.28**	**9.05**	**10.88**	**10.21**	**0.29**
Total GSDP	**5.62**	**6.41**	**8.96**	**6.91**	**12.72**	**5.33**	**10.09**	**2.50**	**5.26**	**6.21**	**7.00**	-
Total GSDP (Rs. in Million)	433869.3	461668.1	503022	537778.2	606196.4	638511	702952.2	720535.6	758413.8	805500.6	-	0.21
Per Capita GSDP	3.69	4.45	7.21	5.41	11.21	3.97	8.84	1.01	3.96	4.87	5.46	-
Per Capita GSDP (Rs.)	9027	9429	10109	10656	11851	12322	13411	13546	14083	14769	-	0.28
Coefficient of Variation	1.11	1.07	1.03	0.98	1.01	0.98	0.99	0.88	0.85	0.82	-	-

Source: Computed by using the basic data from the State Income Division, Directorate of Economics and Statistics, Government of Karnataka (Bangalore).

APPENDIX A-1.3

Share of Gross State Domestic Product of Karnataka State by Sectors: 1993-94 to 2003-04

(in per cent)

Industry	*1993-94*	*1994-95*	*1995-96*	*1996-97*	*1997-98*	*1998-99*	*1999-00*	*2000-01*	*2001-02*	*2002-03*	*2003-04*
Agriculture	32.95	30.79	29.58	28.27	25.72	25.82	26.92	27.59	22.59	19.86	17.48
Forestry and Logging	2.22	2.32	2.13	2.21	1.92	1.73	1.59	1.45	1.51	1.36	1.35
Fishing	0.40	0.42	0.52	0.49	0.47	0.37	0.39	0.37	0.31	0.39	0.34
Mining and Quarrying	0.75	0.75	0.72	0.74	0.87	0.58	0.64	0.63	0.72	0.75	0.83
Primary	36.32	34.29	32.94	31.71	28.98	28.51	29.55	30.04	25.14	22.36	20.01
Manufacturing	17.86	18.93	18.50	18.53	19.55	20.45	17.44	16.30	17.80	19.17	19.43
Registered	11.00	12.00	11.71	11.79	12.84	14.04	10.99	9.84	11.26	12.63	12.88
Unregistered	6.87	6.92	6.78	6.74	6.71	6.42	6.45	6.46	6.54	6.54	6.54
Construction	5.09	4.60	5.25	5.50	6.30	6.68	7.11	6.66	6.95	6.98	6.95
Electricity, Gas and Water supply	2.45	2.61	2.48	2.30	2.25	2.39	2.20	2.29	2.46	2.11	2.06
Secondary	25.40	26.14	26.22	26.33	28.10	29.52	26.75	25.25	27.20	28.26	28.44
Transport, Storage and Communication	4.57	4.75	5.17	5.71	5.87	5.86	6.57	7.35	8.14	9.11	10.27
Railways	0.31	0.31	0.33	0.49	0.28	0.28	0.31	0.34	0.41	0.41	0.41
Transport by Other Means	2.51	2.50	2.57	2.73	2.81	2.86	2.85	2.74	2.81	2.87	2.89
Storage	0.02	0.02	0.02	0.02	0.02	0.02	0.02	0.02	0.02	0.02	0.02
Communication	1.74	1.92	2.25	2.46	2.76	2.70	3.39	4.25	4.90	5.81	6.95
Trade, Hotels and Restaurants	10.93	11.92	12.31	13.31	12.90	13.41	12.65	13.19	14.01	14.25	14.06
Banking and Insurance	4.81	5.33	5.64	5.64	6.27	5.56	6.14	6.24	6.71	7.10	7.19
Real Estate, Ownership of Dwellings and Business services	6.90	6.82	6.76	6.52	6.50	6.22	6.51	6.55	6.90	7.08	7.64
Public Administration	4.40	4.14	4.27	4.02	4.10	3.77	4.02	3.60	3.64	3.44	3.39
Other Services	6.66	6.61	6.68	6.77	7.27	7.16	7.82	7.78	8.27	8.40	9.00
Teritary	38.27	39.57	40.83	41.97	42.92	41.97	43.70	44.71	47.67	49.38	51.55
Total GSDP	**100.00**	**100.00**	**100.00**	**100.00**	**100.00**	**100.00**	**100.00**	**100.00**	**100.00**	**100.00**	**100.00**

Source: Same as in Appendix A-1.2.

APPENDIX A-1.4

Annual Growth of Gross District Income by Sectoral Composition in Karnataka State: 1999-00 to 2002-03

(in per cent)

District	*Annual Growth-1999-00*					*Annual Growth-2002-03*					*Average Growth-1999-00 to 2002-03*				
	Primary	*Secondary*	*Tertiary*	*Total*	*Per Capita*	*Primary*	*Secondary*	*Tertiary*	*Total*	*Per Capita*	*Primary*	*Secondary*	*Tertiary*	*Total*	*Per Capita*
Bagalkote	11.02	9.74	6.43	9.25	6.71	-12.26	3.61	1.40	-3.78	-4.76	-1.28	9.63	5.58	3.38	1.77
Bangalore Urban	72.04	1.79	13.30	10.04	-5.51	-18.65	34.26	0.64	13.11	11.96	0.29	11.56	10.14	9.96	5.01
Bangalore Rural	-0.89	4.46	33.41	12.61	16.16	-10.84	-42.94	2.26	-15.45	-16.31	8.08	24.82	19.86	14.56	14.35
Belgaum	10.31	5.69	9.57	8.99	7.48	-7.33	9.80	0.39	0.07	-0.95	-3.08	6.49	5.72	2.25	0.92
Bellary	1.85	3.26	8.87	4.91	-0.77	-5.06	51.93	8.81	12.84	11.70	1.13	8.34	7.63	4.90	2.49
Bidar	13.79	10.10	3.70	8.71	5.15	8.31	3.00	0.14	3.47	2.42	2.76	8.25	5.45	4.75	2.86
Bijapur	45.81	9.08	13.60	24.58	22.26	5.77	6.14	-0.28	3.01	1.97	8.01	6.74	5.41	6.23	4.69
Cham-rajnagar	-64.84	8.42	8.88	-31.23	8.04	-0.21	3.77	0.05	0.53	-0.49	42.12	7.14	5.77	9.82	3.82
Chickmagalur	23.42	6.93	12.84	17.46	21.31	-2.42	53.74	3.22	6.08	5.00	5.46	21.10	7.98	8.09	8.05
Chitradurga	-0.61	8.75	9.96	4.89	5.57	-2.62	9.18	0.31	0.71	-0.31	2.32	10.44	8.47	5.93	5.08
Dakshina Kannada	5.10	-1.07	26.65	10.00	9.61	13.39	42.37	2.87	13.85	12.69	7.49	-4.91	10.05	1.09	0.05
Davangere	19.66	8.14	12.09	14.95	16.02	-12.02	13.25	-3.27	-3.57	-4.55	-1.13	11.00	5.87	3.55	2.87
Dharwad	5.33	6.21	5.60	5.67	4.96	13.57	47.00	1.69	17.01	15.82	3.00	22.07	4.11	7.36	6.17
Gadag	-8.31	9.13	19.84	7.24	9.71	-17.83	6.17	1.09	-3.59	-4.57	7.13	8.29	15.09	9.79	9.36
Gulbarga	17.35	8.98	7.04	11.01	6.14	6.56	0.51	1.80	3.04	1.99	3.52	5.95	4.82	4.09	1.91
Hassan	24.45	11.99	9.46	16.52	22.99	-8.91	4.60	-1.67	-3.72	-4.70	1.92	8.92	6.26	4.67	5.32
Haveri	18.06	8.05	22.03	17.58	20.05	-12.77	-17.84	0.21	-8.72	-9.65	-4.52	20.43	9.43	4.06	3.75
Kodagu	8.96	15.81	8.49	9.32	13.76	-5.99	6.13	2.13	-1.62	-2.62	0.74	10.83	6.90	3.96	4.09
Kolar	18.67	2.55	7.65	12.10	14.01	-12.11	-14.42	1.16	-7.14	-8.08	-2.18	6.84	6.62	2.49	2.01
Koppal	33.75	4.93	16.93	19.98	10.64	-25.48	54.42	0.15	7.85	6.75	-0.63	29.36	9.94	11.28	8.10
Mandya	24.19	1.42	10.16	15.12	24.51	-20.82	30.21	2.55	-2.87	-3.85	-3.98	10.30	4.88	1.43	2.85
Mysore	18.51	3.29	11.35	10.96	11.57	-18.26	36.01	0.58	5.91	4.83	-4.28	14.31	4.91	4.35	3.36
Raichur	25.57	13.19	8.43	16.98	10.84	-6.94	25.26	5.05	2.79	1.75	1.56	12.17	7.16	5.10	2.61
Shimoga	9.91	6.82	8.20	8.57	11.34	-9.34	11.86	7.38	2.19	1.15	-1.96	0.88	6.23	1.99	1.73
Tumkur	-9.56	8.56	6.13	-0.03	3.50	-9.15	20.27	0.14	1.09	0.06	-2.73	5.23	5.56	1.64	1.56
Udupi	-1.39	6.19	19.29	10.25	22.08	-0.72	18.13	0.41	3.64	2.59	6.03	14.25	9.55	9.24	11.16
Uttara Kannada	4.98	9.29	12.92	9.63	14.28	-0.09	-33.73	0.35	-9.45	-10.37	-0.24	-3.53	5.92	1.51	1.71
State	**11.54**	**3.88**	**12.75**	**9.92**	**9.00**	**-6.71**	**20.40**	**1.37**	**4.13**	**3.08**	**-0.28**	**7.02**	**7.88**	**5.19**	**3.85**
CV of GDI (%)	0.47	1.77	1.33	1.06	0.41	0.42	1.74	1.44	1.13	0.34	0.42	1.95	1.43	1.23	0.38

Notes: CV refers to coefficient of variation, and GDI refers to gross district income at constant (1993-94) prices.

Source: Same as in Appendix A-1.2.

APPENDIX A-1.5

Share of Sectoral Composition in Gross District Income in Karnataka State: 1999-00 to 2002-03

(in per cent)

District	*Sectoral Share-1999-00*			*Sectoral Share-2000-01*			*Sectoral Share-2001-02*			*Sectoral Share-2002-03*		
	Primary	*Secondary*	*Tertiary*	*Primary*	*Secondary*	*Tertiary*	*Primary*	*Secondary*	*Tertiary*	*Primary*	*Secondary*	*Tertiary*
Bagalkote	47.44	20.62	31.93	47.18	20.78	32.04	41.83	24.18	33.99	38.15	26.03	35.82
Bangalore Urban	4.64	40.15	55.21	1.97	41.43	56.60	1.76	38.08	60.16	1.26	45.21	53.53
Bangalore Rural	32.82	25.67	41.51	23.69	40.90	35.42	31.58	30.03	38.39	33.30	20.27	46.43
Belgaum	42.03	22.12	35.85	43.61	20.59	35.80	34.28	24.71	41.01	31.75	27.12	41.14
Bellary	33.85	26.58	39.57	38.18	22.00	39.82	35.29	20.70	44.01	29.69	27.87	42.44
Bidar	41.04	16.65	42.30	36.20	17.48	46.33	34.12	18.81	47.07	35.72	18.72	45.56
Bijapur	42.79	15.41	41.81	37.43	16.42	46.15	35.61	17.73	46.66	36.57	18.26	45.17
Chamrajnagar	27.78	22.58	49.65	54.22	13.59	32.18	48.38	16.48	35.14	48.02	17.01	34.97
Chickmagalur	52.15	9.72	38.13	49.46	11.49	39.05	48.21	11.05	40.74	44.35	16.01	39.64
Chitradurga	43.64	16.79	39.57	46.46	15.91	37.63	40.17	17.85	41.98	38.84	19.35	41.81
Dakshina Kannada	11.91	45.31	42.78	20.01	26.01	53.98	16.96	23.29	59.75	16.89	29.12	53.98
Davangere	48.84	16.47	34.69	49.05	16.97	33.98	41.09	19.91	39.00	37.49	23.39	39.12
Dharwad	25.58	23.01	51.41	31.95	20.05	48.00	17.88	29.12	53.00	17.35	36.59	46.06
Gadag	30.95	22.89	46.16	40.30	17.37	42.33	30.19	20.42	49.39	25.73	22.49	51.79
Gulbarga	36.22	22.10	41.68	33.04	28.43	38.53	32.11	22.65	45.24	33.20	22.10	44.70
Hassan	47.77	13.48	38.74	45.01	14.25	40.74	41.60	15.27	43.14	39.36	16.59	44.06
Haveri	48.97	16.55	34.48	39.54	28.40	32.06	37.08	22.81	40.11	35.44	20.53	44.03
Kodagu	55.10	8.28	36.63	54.05	8.69	37.26	50.79	9.37	39.84	48.53	10.10	41.36
Kolar	50.11	13.79	36.10	46.06	14.66	39.29	40.70	18.60	40.70	38.52	17.14	44.34
Koppal	38.89	20.53	40.58	37.66	20.62	41.73	29.34	28.04	42.62	20.27	40.15	39.58
Mandya	49.44	14.82	35.74	42.01	20.00	37.98	42.69	16.49	40.83	34.80	22.10	43.10
Mysore	28.62	26.68	44.70	22.40	35.92	41.68	23.88	27.73	48.39	18.43	35.62	45.96
Raichur	49.69	12.45	37.87	50.51	12.04	37.45	42.12	13.82	44.05	38.13	16.85	45.02
Shimoga	38.62	20.28	41.11	41.13	17.73	41.14	35.78	17.83	46.39	31.74	19.51	48.74
Tumkur	38.62	23.98	37.41	44.64	19.98	35.39	36.28	21.45	42.27	32.61	25.52	41.87
Udupi	28.01	18.89	53.10	29.12	21.18	49.69	28.63	20.09	51.28	27.42	22.90	49.68
Uttara Kannada	27.59	27.49	44.92	26.96	26.22	46.81	24.59	28.43	46.98	27.13	20.81	52.07
State	**30.05**	**26.37**	**43.58**	**30.55**	**26.09**	**43.36**	**26.18**	**25.63**	**48.19**	**23.45**	**29.63**	**46.92**

Source: Same as in Appendix A-1.2

APPENDIX A-1.6

Growth of Gross Fixed Capital Formation by Industry in Karnataka: 1993-94 to 2001-02

Industry	*Annual Growth of Gross Fixed Capital Formation (%)*									*Average Growth (%)*
	1993-94	*1994-95*	*1995-96*	*1996-97*	*1997-98*	*1998-99*	*1999-00*	*2000-01*	*2001-02*	
Agriculture	21.33	17.58	15.59	13.07	13.09	9.71	14.62	14.03	34.66	47.27
Forestry and Logging	0.99	0.79	0.75	0.69	0.68	0.82	0.83	0.89	3.94	93.05
Fishing	0.23	0.34	0.35	0.45	0.37	0.31	0.39	0.36	0.21	22.63
Mining and Quarrying	1.69	2.81	2.21	1.36	1.23	0.26	0.13	0.69	0.69	62.17
Manufacturing (Registered)	13.67	14.34	20.83	32.31	33.69	48.85	37.40	33.24	22.78	35.60
Manufacturing (Unregistered)	8.42	7.41	7.24	6.63	6.38	5.62	7.37	6.96	4.30	11.31
Construction	0.95	1.25	1.64	0.90	1.77	1.18	1.29	1.35	0.92	29.04
Electricity, Gas and Water Supply	9.42	8.67	7.42	6.85	8.78	5.33	3.67	5.30	5.14	17.41
Transport by other Means	3.98	5.27	5.48	4.96	3.55	1.85	3.48	3.48	5.12	35.17

Contd. ...

Contd. ...

Industry	Annual Growth of Gross Fixed Capital Formation (%)									Average Growth (%)
	1993-94	1994-95	1995-96	1996-97	1997-98	1998-99	1999-00	2000-01	2001-02	
Storage	0.04	0.03	0.04	0.04	0.03	0.02	0.04	0.04	0.07	49.20
Trade, Hotels and Restaurants	3.59	4.40	5.34	3.12	2.70	2.60	2.36	2.59	1.66	13.44
Real Estate, Ownership of Dwellings and Business Services	8.76	7.33	7.51	7.05	6.97	0.80	1.10	1.29	0.86	4.34
Public Administration	2.40	2.26	3.04	2.57	2.13	3.32	3.95	4.08	2.73	26.63
Other Services	10.69	10.98	11.05	10.21	11.99	14.84	18.38	19.73	13.43	25.29
Supra Regional Sectors*	13.83	16.53	11.50	9.80	6.65	4.49	4.97	5.96	3.51	4.52
Total	**100.00**	**100.00**	**100.00**	**100.00**	**100.00**	**100.00**	**100.00**	**100.00**	**100.00**	
Total GFCF (Rs. in Crore)	(11067)	(14644)	(17397)	(21111)	(23996)	(30979)	(28106)	(30228)	(50476)	
Annual Growth of Total GFCF	-	32.33	18.78	21.35	13.68	29.10	-9.40	7.68	66.99	22.57
GFCF as a per cent of GSDP	26.94	30.56	30.95	32.39	32.85	35.27	29.59	28.91	46.30	

Notes: 1. *Supra Regional Sectors include Railways, Communication, Banking & Insurance and Central Government Administration.

2. GSDP refers to Gross State Domestic Product at factor cost and current prices.

Source: Same as in Appendix A-1.2.

APPENDIX A-1.7

Share of Private Sector in Gross Fixed Capital Formation in Karnataka: 1993-94 to 2001-02

(in per cent)

Industry	Share of Private Sector in Gross Fixed Capital Formation (%)								
	1993-94	1994-95	1995-96	1996-97	1997-98	1998-99	1999-00	2000-01	2001-02
Agriculture	39.73	41.86	47.71	47.63	49.22	29.06	22.00	22.83	4.77
Forestry and Logging	2.73	2.59	2.29	2.76	3.07	3.14	3.42	2.23	0.25
Fishing	100.00	100.00	100.00	100.00	100.00	100.00	100.00	100.00	98.10
Mining and Quarrying	4.28	6.33	3.12	12.50	13.51	32.91	51.35	8.57	7.78
Manufacturing (Registered)	81.89	86.48	86.83	93.30	93.26	98.35	97.56	95.16	79.21
Manufacturing (Unregistered)	100.00	100.00	100.00	100.00	100.00	100.00	100.00	100.00	100.00
Construction	86.67	91.80	92.66	89.95	94.34	91.83	91.74	81.86	75.38
Electricity, Gas and Water Supply	3.07	12.60	11.00	17.15	11.20	17.57	32.01	21.04	13.10
Transport by Other Means	67.27	77.98	78.49	79.66	70.04	110.82	83.96	91.15	41.31
Storage	50.00	75.00	42.86	66.67	50.00	60.00	25.00	33.33	11.11
Trade, Hotels and Restaurants	97.48	95.81	98.82	98.18	96.91	97.89	99.25	98.34	96.78
Real Estate,Ownership of Dwellings and Business Services	100.00	100.00	100.00	100.00	100.00	100.00	100.00	100.00	100.00
Public Administration	0.00	0.00	0.00	0.00	0.00	0.00	0.00	0.00	0.00
Other Services	94.00	95.90	93.76	93.46	92.04	94.82	95.30	95.81	96.71
Total GFCF	**63.29**	**67.28**	**71.19**	**76.77**	**75.59**	**82.09**	**77.68**	**74.85**	**44.77**

Source: Same as in Appendix A-1.2.

APPENDIX A-1.8

Inflow of Private Foreign and Domestic Investment into Karnataka: 1993-94 to 2003-04

Year	*Total Investment (Rs. in Crore)*	*Annual Growth of Total Investment (Per Cent)*	*Per cent of Foreign Direct Investment (FDI) in Total Investment*	*Per cent of Mega Investment in Total Investment*	*Investment Per FDI Project (Rs. in Crore)*	*Investment Per Large Project (Rs. in Crore)*	*Investment Per Mega Project (Rs. in Crore)*	*Total Investment as a per cent of Gross State Domestic Product*	*Share of Karnataka's FDI in Nation's Total Approved FDI*
1993-94	6622.64	-20.16	4.92	80.88	5.25	8.55	486.96	16.12	4.32
1994-95	9171.41	38.49	10.08	77.99	8.25	10.23	447.06	19.14	9.26
1995-96	33933.89	270.00	6.67	88.96	19.51	10.02	1118.08	60.36	6.10
1996-97	11609.67	-65.79	27.03	59.17	19.25	11.45	343.48	17.81	7.80
1997-98	13832.56	19.15	49.99	43.76	60.13	8.24	378.28	18.94	17.25
1998-99	9937.61	-28.16	6.27	74.99	7.89	23.87	677.47	11.31	2.06
1999-00	14367.32	44.58	8.56	76.94	11.39	22.89	736.91	15.13	6.84
2000-01	47808.64	232.76	10.36	80.20	22.32	15.45	435.71	45.73	19.62
2001-02	8785.59	-81.62	9.17	67.69	2.52	19.74	283.19	8.06	5.55
2002-03	5267.47	-40.04	43.36	22.38	7.88	19.00	168.40	4.39	28.81
2003-04	8233.88	56.32	5.43	47.29	1.57	23.74	56.43	6.21	7.16

Notes: 1) All investment figures are in current prices.

2) GSDP refers to Gross State Domestic Product at factor cost and current prices.

3) Number of large projects and investment on large projects in 2003-04 covers from March 2003 to August 2004.

Source: Computed by using the basic data in the (a) records and website of Karnataka Udyog Mitra: *http://www.kumbangalore.com/kar_projects/projects.htm;* (b) State Income Division, Directorate of Economics and Statistics; (c) Reserve Bank of India's website: *http://www.rbidocs.rbi.org.in/rdocs/bulletin/docs/66793.xls;* (d) Government of India's *Economic Survey 2001-02*; and (e) *Monthly Review of the Indian Economy* (January 1998 and December 2005), Centre for Monitoring of the Indian Economy (Mumbai).

APPENDIX A-1.9

Employment in Karnataka State: 1993-94 to 1999-00

Indicators of Employment	*Karnataka*		*India*	
	1993-94	*1999-00*	*1993-94*	*1999-00*
Labour Force Participation Rate				
Persons in Labour Force in Total (%)	68.6	65.6	64.50	61.80
Per cent of Labour Force in Rural Areas	75.7	72.2	68.80	66.20
Per cent of Labour Force in Urban Areas	58	52.7	53.0	51.10
Estimated Annual Growth of Employment During 1993-94 to1999-00 (%)				
Total Employment	NA	1.6	NA	1.6
Rural Employment	NA	1.2	NA	1.3
Urban Employment	NA	2.8	NA	2.4
Incidence of Unemployment	NA		NA	
Total Unemployment	1.4	1.4	2.0	2.3
Rural Unemployment	0.7	0.7	1.2	1.5
Urban Unemployment	3.7	3.4	4.6	4.8
Employment in Organised Sector				
Annual Growth (%)	3.12	0.44	0.84	-0.28
Average Annual Growth during 1991-92 to 2000-01 (%)	NA	2.74	NA	0.74
Employment in Unorganised Sector: 1990 and 1998				
Share of Unorganised Units (%)	6.8	6.3	25.00 million	30.35 million
Growth of Unorganised Units (%)		1.6		2.7
Employment Per Unit (Persons)	3	2.75	2.88	2.74
Ratio of Unorganised Employment in Total (Organised+Unorganised) Employment	77.84	73.98	79.07	81.07
Employment Elasticity				
Employment Elasticity during 1993-94 to 1999-00 (%)	NA	0.188	NA	0.160

Notes: (1) NA refers to not applicable.

Sources: (1) *National Human Development Report 2001*, Planning Commission, Government of India (New Delhi): 2002; *Selected Socio-Economic Statistics*, India 2001, Central Statistical Organisation, Government of India; (3) *Economic Survey 2002-03*, Government of India; and (4) *Economic Survey 2002-03*, Government of Karnataka.

APPENDIX A-1.10

Commodity Composition of Exports from Karnataka State: 1993-94 to 2003-04

(in per cent)

Commodities	*1993-94*	*1994-95*	*1995-96*	*1996-97*	*1997-98*	*1998-99*	*1999-00*	*2000-01*	*2001-02*	*2002-03*	*2003-04*
Electronics and Computer Software	7.77	10.25	15.17	19.52	37.12	42.76	50.38	55.07	57.25	53.18	49.25
Readymade Garments	21.91	22.72	20.48	18.60	15.19	15.22	11.73	13.95	14.00	13.38	9.69
Coffee Products	13.22	13.77	12.99	11.62	9.86	10.40	9.21	5.97	NA	6.41	10.73
Iron Ore and Minerals	12.13	8.75	8.74	6.69	6.18	6.50	6.06	4.23	5.20	5.52	4.56
Engineering	9.21	7.93	7.72	7.52	7.03	6.47	5.21	4.20	3.43	5.10	5.02
Silk Products	9.80	4.65	5.00	3.65	3.04	3.56	4.06	4.82	3.34	2.50	2.32
Cashew and Cashew Kernals	1.79	1.75	1.68	3.41	2.80	2.37	1.96	1.17	4.38	2.44	1.82
Chemical and Allied Products	7.28	5.62	4.06	2.92	2.38	2.03	1.74	1.15	1.59	1.38	1.56
Gem and Jewellery	1.38	1.94	2.68	2.15	2.18	1.86	1.57	1.37	1.73	1.23	0.87
Agriculture and Processed Food Products	1.01	1.12	0.99	2.43	1.90	1.65	1.52	1.48	1.40	0.99	6.31
Basic Chemicals, Pharmaceuticals and Cosmetics	1.85	1.55	1.40	1.18	0.87	2.01	1.51	1.83	0.81	0.94	0.64
Leather Products	7.47	6.53	6.20	4.68	3.43	1.58	1.14	1.49	0.24	0.87	0.78
Marine Products	NA	2.83	1.97	1.54	1.39	0.80	0.68	0.59	1.18	0.74	0.66
Plastic Goods	0.48	0.39	0.56	0.47	0.45	0.36	0.58	0.42	1.00	0.72	0.81
Spices	NA	NA	NA	NA	NA	0.60	0.47	0.46	0.43	0.32	0.20
Wool and Woollen Products	NA	0.21	0.28	0.26	0.22	0.18	0.34	0.19	0.41	0.32	1.80
Handicrafts	NA	NA	NA	NA	0.15	0.15	0.16	0.20	0.34	0.31	0.24
Tobacco/*Beedi*	0.37	0.33	0.36	0.06	0.13	0.08	0.13	0.02	0.22	0.26	0.21
Miscellaneous and Others	4.31	9.65	9.73	13.32	5.69	1.41	1.55	1.37	3.05	3.40	2.53
Total	**100.00**	**100.00**	**100.00**	**100.00**	**100.00**	**100.00**	**100.00**	**100.00**	**100.00**	**100.00**	**100.00**
Total Exports (Rs. in Crore)	(3025.00)	(3995.55)	(5002.54)	(6453.33)	(8432.21)	(10039.48)	(12854.25)	(16027.46)	(20145.58)	(29897.99)	(41670.24)
Share of Karnataka's Exports in Nation's Total	3.51	3.93	3.83	4.46	5.10	5.14	5.65	5.76	6.93	8.41	10.22
Per Cent of Total State's Exports in GSDP	7.36	8.34	8.90	9.90	11.54	11.43	13.53	15.33	18.48	24.90	31.45
Per Cent of Total National Exports in GDP	11.03	11.08	12.18	11.65	11.88	12.22	12.92	14.62	13.97	15.77	16.18

Notes: 1. NA refers to not available. 2. GSDP (or GDP) refers to gross state domestic product (or gross domestic product) at factor cost and current prices.

Source: Computed by using the basic data on export performance of Karnataka State, Visveswaraya Industrial and Trade Centre (VITC), Government of Karnataka, Bangalore, 2003: Processed.

APPENDIX A-1.11

Annual Growth of Exports by Commodities in Karnataka State: 1994-95 to 2003-04

(in per cent)

Commodities	*1994-95*	*1995-96*	*1996-97*	*1997-98*	*1998-99*	*1999-00*	*2000-01*	*2001-02*	*2002-03*	*2003-04*	*Average Growth*	*Coefficient of Variation*
Electronics and Computer Software	74.32	85.23	66.00	148.47	37.16	50.88	36.27	30.67	37.86	29.07	59.59	1.03
Readymade Garments	36.96	12.84	17.14	6.75	19.28	-1.29	48.25	26.12	41.84	0.95	20.88	0.62
Coffee Products	37.50	18.18	15.38	10.80	25.60	13.43	-19.12	NA	NA	133.53	29.41	0.94
Iron Ore and Minerals	-4.65	25.00	-1.28	20.76	25.30	19.37	-12.93	54.41	57.44	15.11	19.85	0.66
Engineering	13.74	21.77	25.65	22.27	9.61	3.08	0.46	2.75	120.39	37.36	25.71	0.73
Silk Products	-37.38	34.60	-5.85	8.77	39.79	45.64	48.18	-12.97	10.99	29.74	16.15	0.57
Cashew and Cashew Kernals	29.44	20.04	161.81	7.27	0.85	5.69	-25.27	368.89	-17.11	3.68	55.53	0.89
Chemical and Allied Products	1.99	-9.64	-7.07	6.32	1.57	9.60	-17.25	73.28	29.07	57.07	14.49	0.51
Gem and Jewellery	85.48	72.55	3.43	32.43	2.02	7.70	8.54	59.70	5.00	-1.56	27.53	0.54
Agriculture and Processed Food Products	45.60	10.72	216.67	2.30	3.11	18.16	21.80	18.13	5.27	789.30	113.11	1.94
Basic Chemicals, Pharmaceuticals and Cosmetics	10.54	13.09	8.84	-3.86	175.85	-4.18	51.65	-44.30	71.11	-5.04	27.37	0.60
Leather Products	15.41	18.86	-2.58	-4.30	-45.00	-8.00	63.01	-79.62	436.28	24.45	41.85	0.36
Marine Products	NA	-12.71	0.53	18.18	-31.64	8.94	7.89	152.14	-6.76	24.79	17.93	0.51
Plastic Goods	7.70	80.09	7.30	26.39	-5.46	107.55	-9.58	196.35	7.03	57.23	47.46	1.11
Spices	NA	NA	NA	NA	NA	1.67	20.89	16.30	13.00	-15.82	7.21	0.19
Wool and Woollen Products	NA	68.88	18.07	12.89	-3.16	141.89	-28.57	166.08	16.58	673.51	118.46	2.11
Handicrafts	NA	NA	NA	NA	21.74	29.72	57.50	118.11	32.60	8.65	44.72	0.77
Tobacco/*Beedi*	19.53	36.16	-77.78	175.00	-29.18	108.60	-80.12	1276.47	72.74	16.21	151.76	1.12
Miscellaneous and Others	195.48	26.23	76.63	-44.20	-70.54	41.20	10.37	179.28	65.28	3.61	48.33	0.67
Total Exports from Karnataka State	32.08	25.20	29.00	30.66	19.06	28.04	24.69	25.69	48.41	39.37	30.22	0.85
Total Exports from India	**17.95**	**28.67**	**10.80**	**14.05**	**18.21**	**16.60**	**22.15**	**4.54**	**22.29**	**14.69**	**16.99**	**0.49**

Note: NA refers to not available or applicable.

Source: Computed by using the basic data on export performance of Karnataka State, Visveswaraya Industrial and Trade Centre (VITC), Government of Karnataka, Bangalore, 2003: Processed.

APPENDIX A-1.12

Income Distribution in Karnataka State: 1993-94 to 1999-00

Indicators	*Karnataka*		*India*	
	1993-94	*1999-00*	*1993-94*	*1999-00*
Household Consumption Levels				
Per Capita Total Consumption Expenditure in Rs. Per Month	318.5	638.8	328.2	591.0
Per Capita Consumption Expenditure in Rural Areas (Rs. Per Month)	269.4	499.8	281.4	486.1
Per Capita Consumption Expenditure in Urban Areas (Rs. Per Month)	423.1	911.0	458.0	855.0
Composition of Food Expenditure in Per Capita Consumption Expenditure in Rural Areas (%)	61.95	59.1	618	59.4
Composition of Food Expenditure in Per Capita Consumption Expenditure in Urban Areas (%)	55.7	46.3	54.7	48.1
Consumption Inequality				
Gini Ratio for Per Capita Consumption Expenditure in Rural Areas	0.269	0.241	0.282	0.258
Gini Ratio for Per Capita Consumption Expenditure in Urban Areas	0.315	0.321	0.340	0.341
Extent of Poverty				
Poverty Line (Rs.)	186.63	302.89	205.84	281.35
Percentage of Population Below the Poverty Line: Total	31.6	20.04	36.0	26.1
Percentage of Population Below the Poverty Line: Rural	29.88	17.38	37.3	27.1
Percentage of Population Below the Poverty Line: Urban	40.14	25.25	32.4	23.6

Source: Planning Commission (2002). *National Human Development Report 2001*, Government of India, New Delhi.

APPENDIX A-1.13

Human Development Indicators of Karnataka State: 1991 and 2001

Indicators	*Karnataka*		*India*	
	1991	*2001*	*1991*	*2001*
Population Growth				
Per cent Share in Nation Population	5.31	5.17	846.30 million	1027.02 million
Share of Rural Population in Total Population	69.08	66.02	74.27	72.20
Annual Average Growth of Total Population: 1981-91 and 1991-2001	21.12	17.25	286	21.34
Crude Birth Rate: 1991 and 2000	26.8	22	29.5	25.8
Crude Death Rate	9	7.8	8.5	8.5
Infant Mortality Rate:	77	58	80	68
Ranking among 15 Major States in Human Development Index	7	7	-	-
Literacy				
Literacy Rate for Total Population (%)	56.04	67.04	52.21	65.28
Literacy Rate for Total Male Population (%)	67.26	76.29	64.1	75.9
Literacy Rate for Total Female Population (%)	44.34	57.45	39.2	51.2
Literacy in Rural Areas (%)	47.69	59.68	44.69	59.21
Literacy in Urban Areas (%)	74.20	81.05	73.08	80.06

Sources: (1) *Economic Survey 2002-03*, Government of India, New Delhi. (2) *Economic Survey 2002-03*, Planning Department, Government of Karnataka, Bangalore: 2003. (3) *National Human Development Report 2001*, Planning Commission, Government of India (New Delhi): 2002. (4) *Selected Educational Statistics 1998-99*, Ministry of Human Resource Development, Department of Secondary Education and Higher Education, (New Delhi): 2000.

APPENDIX A-1.14

Trends in Growth of Prices in Karnataka State: 1994-95 to 2003-04

(in per cent)

Year	*Annual Growth Karnataka State*			*Annual Growth All India*		
	CPI-IW	*CPI-UNMW*	*CPI-AL-G*	*CPI-IW*	*CPI-UNMW*	*CPI-AL-G*
1994-95	10.44	10.19	11.89	8.14	9.72	11.94
1995-96	10.87	10.50	17.74	12.19	9.28	10.75
1996-97	8.90	11.41	6.18	9.27	9.27	9.05
1997-98	7.04	8.87	3.07	7.02	6.71	3.39
1998-99	8.30	0.00	11.04	13.11	11.59	10.98
1999-00	4.09	9.09	4.17	3.38	4.45	4.46
2000-01	3.28	6.61	-2.36	3.74	5.40	-0.33
2001-02	3.51	5.93	-0.22	4.28	5.12	1.11
2002-03	3.68	4.58	4.73	4.10	3.85	3.13
2003-04	4.39	4.87	14.19	3.73	3.70	3.89
Average Growth (%)	6.45	7.20	7.04	6.90	6.91	5.84
Coefficient of Variation (%)	46.64	48.53	91.81	53.13	41.00	76.10

Source: Computed from the basic data in the *Economic Survey 2004-05*, Government of Karnataka, 2005.

Chapter 2

The Dynamics of Karnataka's Growth

2.1 Introduction—the Economic Reform Context

The growth path of the Karnataka economy has been strongly influenced by the recent change in policy climate brought about by the economic reforms introduced in 1991. The growth rate of SDP (at current prices) observed during the 1990s in Karnataka was 8.2 per cent per year, which was the highest among all the major states in India.[1] The corresponding figure for the 1980s was 5.4 per cent. Clearly, in aggregative terms, Karnataka has responded well to the new policy environment. Karnataka's relative economic status, compared with the other states, has steadily improved over time. From being a 'middle-ranking' Indian state, whose per capita income was below the national average in the early years of planning (Rao *et al.* 1975), it is now recognised as a 'fast growing' state.[2] In per capita terms, the ratio of Karnataka state's per capita NSDP to the national average for all states has moved from 0.98 in 1981-83 to 1.03 in 1990-93, and further to 1.23 in 1998-2001. This confirms the impression of the state's superior relative performance, particularly during the 1990s.[3]

A key element of this new policy environment of the 1990s is globalisation. Our objective in this chapter is to understand the broad dynamics of Karnataka under globalisation and attendant policies of domestic market liberalisation, and to note the patterns of continuity and change in the evolution of the state's economy. Since the time that economic reforms were launched by the national government headed by Sri P.V. Narasimha Rao, India has remained firmly committed to globalisation of its economy. Though the approach to globalisation has been cautious and gradual, progress along the globalisation path has been steady—import tariffs and non-tariff barriers have been substantially lowered, import licensing nearly abolished, export controls have been reduced. The exchange rate has been increasingly market determined, and current account convertibility has been established. Ownership caps on foreign direct investment have been eased, making it possible to have 100 per cent foreign ownership in much of manufacturing and infrastructure. India is an active participant in the WTO negotiations. The results of these policies can be seen in the key parameters of the external sector. These include doubling of India's trade-GDP ratios, rising foreign investment flows, and the growing number of international firms operating in India. India's longstanding global linkages have been deepened further through the presence of substantial communities of overseas Indians throughout the world. As many commentators have noted with some surprise, successive governments after 1991, despite changes in the political and ideological composition of the ruling coalition, have continued this policy. This process seems poised to continue.

Karnataka is at the centre-stage of this process of global (and national) economic integration, and has been so throughout the decade of the 1990s. With the

1. Planning Commission, Tenth Five Year Plan, Chapter 3 (Development Trends), Table 3.2. The all-India growth rate was 6.8 per cent, while Assam grew the slowest at 2.7 per cent. Other states which showed improved growth rates during the 1990s were Gujarat, Tamil Nadu, Maharashtra, Rajasthan and West Bengal. Though current price figures have obvious limitations, the broad patterns of relative state-wise performance may be reasonably inferred from them.

2. Bhattacharya, B.B. N.R. Bhanumurthy, Sabyasachi Kar and S. Saktivel, (2004). "Forecasting State Domestic Product and Inflation: Macroeconomic Model for AP, Karnataka and UP", *Economic and Political Weekly*, July 31, The estimated annual growth rate for Karnataka GSDP during 1981-2000 is 6.7 per cent, compared with the all-India figure of 5.7 per cent. The authors report finding a positive 'structural shift' in the growth rate in the mid-90s.

3. These data are from the publication *Domestic Product of States of India, 1960-61 to 2000-01*, EPW Research Foundation May 2003, Table 8.4. The NSDP figures are 3-year averages. The all-India figures refer to the averages for all the states for the sake of comparability, (and not to the CSO all-India NDP estimates).

economic reforms and decontrol, the importance of state-level policies has increased, as each state seeks to attract national and international investment. In the case of Karnataka, these efforts at revamping the policy framework have been bolstered with multilateral assistance. Karnataka responded rapidly, and during this decade of the 1990s, emerged as one of the 'reform leaders'. Among the most significant and discussed national economic phenomena of the decade is the dramatic success of the services sector, especially the information technology and software services in the global market. Bangalore, in particular, plays a very special role as the leading IT hub, recognised for its supportive environment for high-tech industry, cosmopolitan urban culture, and as a key destination for FDI. International integration *via* FDI now goes both ways. Dynamic firms operating out of Bangalore, such as Infosys Technologies and Wipro Limited, have acquired firms and located design and production activities in other countries. Not only have international firms found Bangalore attractive, the economic boom has also drawn many skilled migrants and young students and professionals, as well as poorer workers from different parts of the country.

The state, as the data cited earlier indicate, has clearly benefited from the economic reforms process. Along with the potential benefits that have been derived by the state during this period, some serious challenges have also come about. These need to be addressed in order to ensure the long-term sustainability of the development process. The proper response to these challenges requires farsightedness and cooperation between the government, the business and the civil society in a new and creative way. As we shall note below, cooperation between government and industry has been a long tradition in Karnataka's industrial history. Visionary government leadership laid the foundation for modern industry in Karnataka, and the relationship between the government and the private sector has been generally proactive. We can hope that this will be the case in the future as well.

While the new economic environment has made possible high economic growth rates, the ability to realise the even higher potential benefits depends on how swiftly and smoothly the region is able to undergo the required 'structural transformation'. This involves being able to shift resources into activities that can stand the test of competition. The task of development policy under these conditions involves creating enabling conditions for economic units to upgrade their competitive capabilities. These enabling conditions include physical and social infrastructure that permit firms to be flexible; access to technology and to capital and credit facilities; labour markets which can meet the specific needs of skills and competence, and so on. Successful policy for sustaining the growth process also implies the ability to phase out those activities that are not able to meet the minimum conditions of competitiveness. This process is, however, fraught with political and economic risks.

A deep problem is rooted in the unequal preparedness of different sectors and segments of society to respond to the opportunities provided by liberalisation and globalisation. Certain so-called 'new economy' services such as information technology and communications have prospered, whereas the 'old economy' sectors such as agriculture, infrastructure and some manufacturing areas have been economically constrained. The agriculture sector in Karnataka has, for example, remained relatively stagnant for several decades. The policy response has been inadequate. During the 1990s, the relative position of agriculture has worsened. Large tracts of land rely on rainfall, and are drought-prone. Output has shown instability during the decade, with four episodes of deceleration.[4] Total factor productivity in Karnataka agriculture has decelerated, and the SDP per worker in the agriculture sector has declined in real terms. There are regions that have experienced environmental degradation due to the excessive use of HYV seed-fertiliser technology. Under such conditions, and the fact that the secondary and tertiary sectors are growing rapidly, the relative per capita income of the rural population is declining rapidly. The implications of this imbalance for the overall development of the state's economy can be gauged from the fact that 60 per cent of the population derives its income from agricultural activities.[5] The contrast with the dynamic sectors of the economy is quite stark. Development policy needs to address both the extreme segments of the economic spectrum.

2.2 Key Features of Karnataka's Growth

2.2.1 Origins of Industrial Development and Trends

Karnataka enjoyed an early start in modern economic development, particularly in the erstwhile Mysore state. As early as 1903, the first ever hydel power plant in Asia was established in Sivasamudram. Thanks to the efforts of Sir M. Visvesvaraya, then *Dewan* of the

4. For a detailed analysis of the agriculture and allied sectors, see Chapter 14. These decelerations in agricultural output growth occurred in 1993-94, 1996-97, 1998-99 and 2000-01.

5. Chapter 14, Section 14.1.2.

Princely State, a number of state enterprises were started in the early decades of the 20th century. The industrialisation of the region was further bolstered through the early presence of such leading scientific and technological academic institutions as the Indian Institute of Science, and large central public sector undertakings.[6]

Most of these public sector units were established during the 1950s and 60s, though some had earlier origins. Many of them were in high technology and engineering-based industries. There is little doubt that the presence of these industries, alongside leading research institutions such as the laboratories of the Defence Research & Development Organisation (DRDO) and the Indian Space Research Organisation (ISRO) contributed to the creation of a rich scientific and technical human resource pool in Bangalore. This made it possible for the city to carve out a unique niche as high-tech industrial and service sector base in later decades.

The Hindustan Aeronautics Limited (HAL) actually began as Hindustan Aircraft Limited in 1940. It was an early example of public-private partnership—a collaborative venture between the princely state of Mysore and the industrialist Walchand Hirachand to initiate the Indian aircraft industry. It later merged with two other companies to form HAL in 1964. Similarly, ITI Limited began as Indian Telephone Industries in 1948, as a departmental undertaking of the Central Ministry of Post and Telegraph. Another important electronics enterprise—Bharat Electronics Limited (BEL) was established in 1954, with its headquarters in Bangalore. The company is engaged in design development and manufacture of advanced electronics equipments and components. Apart from these high-tech advanced industries, Karnataka took lead in establishing several consumer oriented local resource based industries such as Mysore sandal soaps and detergents, Mysore silks board, etc. Thus, it is important to note that through an intensive public policy the state has played a catalytic role in development. At the same time, the government's approach towards the private sector has been supportive.[7]

Over the last two decades, there has been a significant transformation of the state's economy in terms of the composition of the major productive sectors (Figure 2.1). The relative weight of the tertiary sector has increased to make it the dominant sector in the economy accounting for 55.4 per cent of net state domestic product (in current prices). Correspondingly, the proportion contributed by the primary sector has come down sharply from 43 per cent in 1980-81 to 24.4 per cent in 2002-03. The secondary sector's relative weight in NSDP (in current prices) has also decreased during the same period, from 23 to 20.3 percent. These numbers sum up in a succinct manner the essential elements of Karnataka's recent economic evolution—the dynamism of services, the relative stagnancy of agriculture and allied activities, and modest performance of the secondary sector (manufacturing, construction and infrastructure).

FIGURE 2.1

Sectoral Composition of State Income

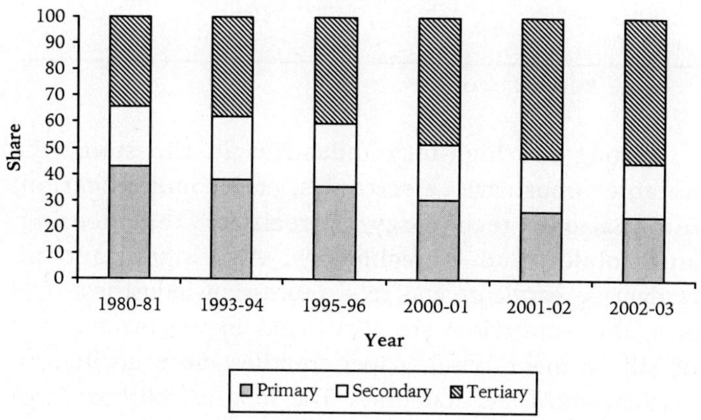

Source: Directorate of Economics and Statistics, Government of Karnataka, Bangalore.

As a result of the higher than national average growth, Karnataka has attained a better degree of labour utilisation than the all-India average. Despite the modest performance of the rural economy, in 1999-00, the current daily status rural unemployment rate in Karnataka for persons was 43 per thousand, as compared with 71 for all-India. The corresponding figures for urban unemployment were 54 and 77, respectively.[8] The official unemployment rate for 1999-00 was 4.61 per cent (GoK, 2004).

While the industrial sector of the state's economy has not expanded significantly in relative terms, it is one of India's top five industrialised states. There are

6. The Indian Institute of Science (IISc) was an early example of public-private partnership. It was established in 1909 through a tripartite collaboration involving J.N. Tata, the Government of the *Maharaja* Krishnaraja Wodeyar, and the colonial Government of India. The Mysore Government provided land free of cost.

7. For a more detailed account, see Chapter 15.

8. *Report of the Special Group on Targeting Ten Million Employment Opportunities per Year*, Government of India, Planning Commission, May 2002, Table 17. For some more details on employment in the state see Chapter 4.

some notable enterprises operating in Karnataka. These dominant industrial units are technologically advanced. Because of this fact, the state projects an image of being highly modern and industrialised—a base for 'high-tech' activities. Building on a long history of industrialisation, Karnataka's industrial base is diversified. It combines large public sector enterprises, private-sector large and medium enterprises and a much larger number of small enterprises (Table 2.1). An examination of the modern segment of Karnataka's industrial and IT sectors reveals the imprint of an impressive pattern of integration into the world economy, (Appendices A-2.1 and A-2.2).

TABLE 2.1

Size Distribution of Industries in Karnataka (2001-02)

Type of Industries	*No. of Units*	*Investment (in US$ Million)*	*Employment*
Large and Medium Industries	1068	6813	4,46,809
Small Scale Industries	252671	1102	1,505,800

Source: Karnataka Udyog Mitra.

Among the high-tech industries in the state, the notable ones are electronics, telecommunication, information technology, precision engineering, automobiles, and biotechnology. Also significant are readymade garments and food processing industries. 'Old economy' enterprises are also found in the manufacture of silk, cement, steel, paper, textiles, auto ancillaries, machine tools and foundries. The long established, large public sector undertakings in the state include Indian Telephone Industries (ITI), Hindustan Aeronautics Limited (HAL), Hindustan Machine Tools (HMT), Bharat Earth Movers Limited (BEML) and Bharat Electronics Limited (BEL). In addition, Bharat Petroleum Corporation Ltd., Hindustan Petroleum Corporation Ltd., Steel Authority of India Ltd., Bharat Heavy Electricals Ltd., and Videsh Sanchar Nigam Ltd., are other major PSUs operating in the state. The auto industry has an annual turnover of over Rs. 2000 crores. In the auto sector, companies such as Volvo and TELCO (heavy vehicles), TVS (two wheelers), and Toyota Kirloskar (utility vehicles) are among the majors with units in the state. Auto component manufacturers in the state include many reputed firms as Mico-Bosch, Delphi, Denso, Amco-Yuasa, TG-Kirloskar, which have foreign collaborations.

The industrialisation process in Karnataka in the last three decades has witnessed some broad trends, which has left a mark on the composition of the industrial sector as a whole.[9] Initially aiming to take advantage of the favourable electric power availability, many large enterprises were energy-intensive, and not particularly employment-intensive. By the mid-1970s, the power constraint became severe, and industrial policy sought to diversify the industrial base. Earlier efforts to promote light industries, and to encourage the small and medium enterprises had been made, with only modest success. The small industries sector contains a wide range of enterprises, differentiated by size, technological sophistication and organisation. During the late 1980s and the 1990s, a modern segment within the small industrial sector has emerged. Some of them are technologically sophisticated and serve the market for ancillary activities to the larger enterprises, and exports. But these dynamic small enterprises constitute a minority. There are, on the other hand, a large number of unregistered enterprises, which account for over half the value of manufacturing output of the state. These are mainly traditional household enterprises producing a range of handicraft and sericulture products. More than 60 per cent of these operate in the rural sector. The economic condition of the unregistered enterprises is unstable, even as they account for a large proportion of non-agricultural employment. Even the registered SSI units (numbering 1.10 lakh, according to the *All-India Census of Small Scale Industries,* 2001-02) are bedeviled by economic difficulties. More than 15 per cent of these are 'sick' units.

2.2.2 Salient Features of Information Technology and High-tech Enterprises

In the field of information technology, the dominant Indian firms Infosys Technologies, Wipro and TCS are based in the state. In biotechnology, the firm Biocon is a leader in the field, and is based in Bangalore. An increasing number of international high-tech firms have begun operations in the state, particularly, Bangalore. These include Hewlett Packard, Motorola, TI, Oracle, Dell Computers, Intel and IBM. In all, according to official figures, there are 150 units affiliated with multinational companies in the state. Karnataka contributes around 35 per cent of India's software exports, and 20 per cent of the country's electronics hardware production.[10]

9. See Chapter 15 for a detailed account.

10. *Welcome to Karnataka—the New Economy Hub* (Promotional material prepared by the Government of Karnataka, on the basis of data available with government departments.)

TABLE 2.2

IT Growth in Karnataka

Year	1999-00	2000-01	2001-02	2002-03	Up to Jan. 2004
No. of Companies	782	928	1038	1154	1285
Investment (Rs. in Crores)	-	825	1383	1708	2029
Exports (Rs. in Crores)	4400	7475	9903	12350	10200
Turnover (Rs. in Crores)	2692	5949	3578	10281	-

Source: Visvesvaraya Industrial Trade Centre (VITC), Bangalore.

TABLE 2.3

India and Karnataka's Software Exports

Year	India		Karnataka		Share of IT in India (in per cent)
	Rs. Crores	In USD	Rs. Crores	In USD	
1997-98	6530	1759	2246	478	4.90
1998-99	10940	2600	3915	833	7.60
1999-00	17150	3962	4400	957	10.60
2000-01	28150	6217	7475	1600	13.80
2001-02	36500	7647	9903	2063	17.00
2002-03	47500	9693	12350	2572	20.40

Source: Visveswaraya Industrial Trade Centre (VITC), Bangalore.

Likewise, Karnataka has shown a lead in the development of biotechnology (BT) sector. More than 40 Biotechnology companies were established in the state between 2000-2003, taking the cumulative total to about 92. This accounts for nearly half of all biotech companies in India. Karnataka has a large number of biotech companies, ranging from start-ups to well established concerns such as AstraZeneca India, Biocon India, Cadilla, SmithKline Beecham and Wockhardt. The industry has attracted more than Rs. 1000 crores of investment, of which Rs. 140 crores is venture capital.[11] The rate of growth (28 per cent on average) has exceeded that of any other state in the country. Almost 90 per cent of BT units are in Bangalore. Apart from the number of establishments, the export performance from this sector has also been rising very fast, with the current rate at about 62 per cent.

The approach of the state government to the biotech sector has been extremely proactive. It was quick to put in place a 'Millennium Biotech Policy' in 2000-2001, and announced plans to support the industry in several ways—including fiscal concessions, designated infrastructure (biotech parks, biotech corridor, etc.), and an institutional framework (besides the Department of IT and BT, including several bodies with outside participation such as the Vision Group on Biotechnology, the Karnataka Biodiversity Committee, State Biotechnology Coordination Committee, the Single Window Agency, etc.).[12]

2.2.3 *Karnataka's Export Performance*

Karnataka has, with reasonable success, been able to derive a growth stimulus from exports. Precise data on state level exports are not available. However, on the basis of data compiled by the Vișvesvaraya Industrial Trade Centre (VITC), one can make some tentative inferences. Karnataka is one of the more open sub-regions in the nation, in terms of participation in international trade and investment. The share of Karnataka in all-India exports is around 12 per cent, which implies that the state has a significantly higher export to SDP ratio than the average (Table 2.4). A fairly diverse export mix exists, which may be grouped under the following broad categories, reflecting the comparative advantage of the state. These are skilled labour-intensive services, labour-intensive products, natural resource-intensive products, and agro-based products.

TABLE 2.4

Karnataka: Exports

	2001-02	2002-03	2003-04
Karnataka's Share in All-India's Exports (in per cent)	8.21	9.99	11.92

Source: Information Brochure on Karnataka, 2003.

Electronics and Software Exports

The export performance, not surprisingly, is dominated by electronics and computer software.[13] This item accounts for 55 per cent of the state exports during 2001-2003. There were 1038 software development centres in the state in 2003. The software exporters belong to different categories of firms: small and medium enterprises, foreign equity companies and major Indian companies. The relative shares of each of

11. See *http://www.karnataka.com/industry/biotech/*.

12. See *http://www.bangaloreit.com/index.asp* which has links to the Biotechnology Policy of the state.

13. Based on data from STPI, Bangalore.

these categories in software exports were 13.7 per cent, 45.1 per cent and 41.2 per cent, respectively. The linkage with the USA is particularly strong in this sector. That country is the main importer of software from the state, accounting for 69 per cent of the exports, followed by Europe at 21 per cent (Figure 2.2, Tables 2.5, 2.6 and 2.7).

FIGURE 2.2

Destination of Software Exports

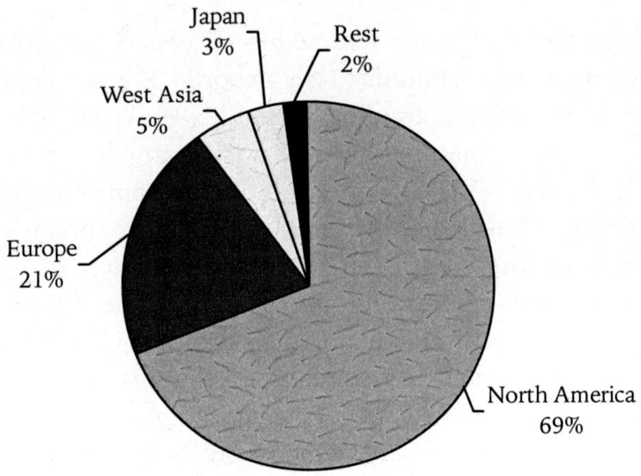

Source: Visveswaraya Industrial and Trade Centre, Government of Karnataka, Bangalore.

TABLE 2.5

Company-wise Share of Software Exports

Companies	*Exports (in Million $)*
Small and Medium Enterprises	283
Foreign Equity Companies	930
Major Indian Companies	850

Source: Visvesvaraya Industrial and Trade Centre (VITC), Bangalore.

TABLE 2.6

Segment-wise Software Exports.

Software Exports (Segment-wise)	Percentages
Application Development	37
Telecom	18
System Software	17
Embedded	7
Chip Design	6
ITES	5
Others	10

Source: Visvesvaraya Industrial and Trade Centre, Bangalore.

TABLE 2.7

Software Exports 2001-02 (Secondary Cities)

Software Export 2001-02 (Secondary Cities)	*US$ in Millions*
Mangalore	50.52
Mysore	8.12

Source: Visvesvaraya Industrial Trade Centre, Bangalore.

Other Exports

The next most important export item is readymade garments (14 per cent of state's total exports). Other export products/services include petroleum and petro-products, engineering, coffee products, silk products, iron ore and minerals, basic chemicals, pharmaceuticals and cosmetics, gems and jewellery, agriculture and processed food products, handicrafts, leather products, chemical and allied products, plastic goods, spices and wool and woollen products.

2.2.4 Inflows of Foreign Direct Investment

Karnataka has also welcomed FDI. The trends in FDI into Karnataka since 1991 and the country wise sources of FDI are shown in Appendices A-2.3 and A-2.4. The cumulative FDI flows approved for Karnataka from 1991 through 2003 has been just over 5.5 billion US dollars. These pertain to 1407 projects, reflecting plans of investors, mainly from an assortment of OECD countries. Of this, $ 2.95 billion of FDI (in 713 projects) has actually been implemented, as per the latest information available. The country composition of the FDI approvals again shows the importance of the USA, which has the highest number of projects (451). However, in relation to the quantum of investment flow, the EU is dominant, with Belgium, Germany and the United Kingdom as the major contributors. Japan is the most important investor from the Asian region.

2.3 Karnataka's Growth Dynamics—Some Issues of Concern

Despite the overall positive growth performance of the state, and the impressive progress of the modern and technologically advanced sectors as noted above, there are certain aspects of the growth process, which require policy attention. These are discussed below.

2.3.1 *Regional Imbalance in Growth*

Right from the very start of Karnataka as a state, the issue of regional balance and equity has been an important issue in policy and planning. Today, in the era of economic reforms, it continues to be an issue that is both economically and politically important.

The regional inequality in development within the state has historical origins. The state was created in 1956 by joining together Kannada-speaking regions, which had distinct administrative histories. Some areas were already well developed, whereas others were relatively neglected peripheral areas of their erstwhile administrative units. The erstwhile Mysore State (then composed of Mysore, Mandya, Bangalore, Kolar, Tumkur, Chitradurga, Chickmagalur, Davangere, Shimoga and Hassan), which was the portion under princely rule by the Wodeyars, had received a head start in modernisation, because of enlightened developmental policies. Legendary figures, such as Sir M. Visvesvaraya, Seshadri Iyer and Mirsa Ismail, as *dewans*, pursued far-sighted developmental policies in the late 19th and early 20th centuries. But the Northern districts that came under the jurisdiction of the Bombay and Madras presidencies, or the Nizam of Hyderabad's rule, were developmentally neglected.

This concern with intrastate inequality has persisted into the era of market reforms. The natural flow of investment is towards areas that offer location advantages. Regions better endowed with infrastructure, serve as a magnet for investment flows.[14] Others tend to be left behind. In Karnataka, an expert committee appointed to examine regional disparities within the state, observed that interdistrict disparities in per capita income have widened during the 1990s, whereas during the 'pre-globalisation' period, the trend had been in the opposite direction.[15] As we shall see below, the new industrial policy of the state, announced in 2001, attempts to address the issue once again.

The Appendix A-2.5 presents data, relating to the 1990s, on the regional dimensions of Karnataka's economy.[16] It can be noticed that the range of variation in the per capita income is quite significant across the districts. It varies from Rs. 25,740 in Bangalore Urban to Rs. 7,861 in Bidar—implying a 325 per cent ratio between the richest and the poorest district. The broad divergence between the north and the south districts is also apparent. The richest district in north Karnataka, (Belgaum), ranks only 7th in per capita income. It is also worth noting that there is no clearly noticeable association between the relative importance of the primary sector in the composition of district income, and the level of per capita income. Normally, one might expect to observe that the 'more industrialised' districts would be more prosperous. However, the top 3 ranked districts (by per capita income) reveal a sharp contrast in respect of the share of the primary sector in district income. These are Bangalore (Urban), Kodagu and Dakshina Kannada districts, in which the share of the primary sector is 3 per cent, 57 per cent and 29 per cent. Even leaving aside the special case of Bangalore (Urban), this suggests that there are key differences in sectoral productivity levels across the districts. This points to the distinct growth histories and regional comparative advantage within the state, which has shaped the regional specialisation of economic activity of the economically successful districts. Some regions have emerged as industrial hubs, while others specialise in commercial agricultural activities. However, the bottom ranked 3 districts with respect to per capita income reveal a uniformity of specialisation. All of them have primary sector shares in excess of 40 per cent in other words, all poor districts are primary sector-dependent, but not all rich districts have diversified away from the primary sector. The Nanjundappa Committee has cautioned against assuming homogeneity of conditions in regions, and observed that there are significant variations in development indicators, even within districts. It has urged a focus on the *talukas* while designing regional development strategies.

The Committee also carried out an analysis of trends in regional inequality over time. They compared the district indicators for several parameters in 1957-58 with 1998-99.[17] The findings relating to development of irrigation and industry present an interesting contrast. During this period, with respect to irrigation, there has been a policy of irrigation development in north Karnataka, which had lagged behind earlier. This has led to a remarkable reversal in the regional inequality in irrigation status between south and north Karnataka. The north Karnataka districts have increased their share in the net irrigated area from 29 per cent in 1957-58 to 58.3 per cent in 2000-01. The shares of the two regions in the incremental shares of the 17.9 lakh hectares of irrigated area that have been added during this period

14. Factors other than physical infrastructure can also play a role in this respect.Other factors, particularly the availability of a pool of appropriately skilled labour is also important, as Karnataka's own experience shows.

15. *High Power Committee for Redressal of Regional Imbalances*, chaired by D.M. Nanjundappa, submitted its final report in June 2002.

16. The Nanjundappa Committee has presented a detailed picture of inter-district variations, covering all dimensions. We confine ourselves here to making a few general observations.

17. *ibid.*, Chapter 4.

varies widely. As much as 71 per cent of the incremental irrigation capacity created has been in north Karnataka, and 29 per cent in south Karnataka. At present, the irrigation status of the area under cultivation in the two regions, as measured by the per cent of net irrigated to net sown area is roughly equal. It is 25.6 per cent in south Karnataka, as compared with 24.3 per cent in the northern Karnataka (Appendix A-2.6).

With regard to industry, however, the situation remains biased in favour of south Karnataka. The data, compiled by the Nanjundappa Committee on the regional distribution of the number of factories, indicate that the share of south Karnataka has increased from 63.5 per cent to 72.6 per cent between 1957 and 1998-99. The contribution of Bangalore alone to this phenomenon is considerable. This district accounts for as much as 46 per cent of the number of factories in Karnataka in 1998-99, having increased its share from 30 per cent in 1957. The relative status of several other erstwhile important industrial locations—in both north and south Karnataka has declined. This includes Dakshina Kannada and Mysore in the south, and Belgaum, Dharwad and Bellary in the north. Thus, the trend towards increasing regional concentration of industry in south Karnataka, and in particular around Bangalore, has been a key feature of the state's growth dynamics. This has emerged as an issue for policy attention, both from considerations of political economy, as well as that of long-term sustainability (Appendix A-2.7).

2.3.2 *Uneven Urbanisation Pattern*

The regional imbalance in growth discussed above is closely associated with the observed pattern of urbanisation in Karnataka.[18] The state, with 31 per cent of its population in urban areas, was ranked fourth in the nation in terms of urbanisation, according to the 1991 Census. Within the urban settlements, there is a high degree of concentration of the urban population. The 21 Class I cities (with population of 100000 and above), accounting for 8.27 per cent of the number of urban settlements in the state, had amongst them 64.7 per cent of the urban population. Bangalore alone accounted for 30 per cent of the state's urban population. Bangalore thus dominates the state's urban scene. The next largest cities—Mysore and Hubli-Dharwad, each have populations that are only 16 per cent that of Bangalore.

The urbanisation trend in the state is different from the all-India pattern in respect of the components of the increase in urban population. A very large proportion of the urban population growth is based on migration, and this has been significantly higher than the all-India level. This pattern may be inferred from the fact that the measured spread of urbanisation arises from two sources. The first relates to the creeping growth of urban population, which leads to the official reclassification of peripheral urban or semi-urban areas as urban, and the second source is the intensification of the population size within existing urban areas. In Karnataka, nearly 90 per cent of the growth of urban population was based on migration and natural increase.[19] A mere 10 per cent is due to reclassification of settlements as urban. The picture that emerges from this pattern, in broad terms, is that the relatively large urban centres formed the focus of urban growth by attracting and retaining population, whereas by and large, the smaller towns grew much slower. The urban population of the state resides predominantly in the southern districts (52 per cent), followed by the northern districts (33 per cent), with the balance shared equally between the Coastal and the Malnad regions.

There is, in addition, a rather notable spatial pattern to the spread of urbanisation in Karnataka, which is rooted in the transportation linkage routes between major economic agglomerations. These are referred to as "urban corridors". The trends reflect the underlying market-determined growth process, and related flows of commerce and people, and this pattern of urbanisation has implications that are elaborated below (Table 2.8).

18. See *The Future of Urbanisation—Spread and Shape in Selected States*, Centre for Policy Research, New Delhi June 2001, which is the main source for this subsection. The discussion here is based on data up to 1991 Census.

19. The data here pertain to the 1971-81 decade, during which migration accounted for 55 per cent, natural increase 35 per cent and reclassification of urban areas for 10 per cent of the increase in urban population. The corresponding figure for migration at the all-India level was 40 per cent.

TABLE 2.8

Urbanisation by Region

Urban Corridors	*1991*	
	Urban Population	*% of Total Urban Population*
Bangalore-Belgaum	6688598	40.08
Mysore–Bangalore–Kolar (Excluding Bangalore)	1516417	10.90
Coastal Corridor (Mangalore–Udupi–Karwar)	815740	5.86
Total	**9020755**	**64.85**

Source: Centre for Policy Research, 2001.

The rapid growth of Bangalore has clearly boosted the state's economic growth performance. However, there are emerging problems and constraints, which have implications for sustainability of the present growth patterns. There are severe pressures on infrastructure—power, roads and public transportation, water, sewerage, sanitation and air pollution. Of these, water is perhaps the most serious emerging constraint.[20] The other major urban centres of Karnataka, such as Hubli-Dharwad, face similar or worse infrastructural constraints. A closely connected issue is that of land utilisation. Urban policy and urban governance therefore would need to form a crucial part of future development strategy of Karnataka.

The spatial trends of the growth process in the state appear to be generating a particular pattern of urbanisation. The spread of urbanisation is developing through the formation of urban settlements along certain 'corridors' enabled by national highways. These corridors include the Bangalore-Belgaum corridor, the Mysore-Bangalore-Kolar corridor, and the coastal Managalore-Udupi-Karwar corridor. Nearly 65 per cent of the urban population of Karnataka resides within these corridors, and the projections indicate that by 2021, this figure will rise to 76 per cent. Unplanned spread of urbanisation will lead to the clogging of urban spaces, which in the longer run will choke off the potential growth. Bangalore city is already experiencing a chaotic expansion at its fringes. Residential developments with poor basic services are encroaching upon agricultural lands and the green belt. Such phenomena are likely to occur elsewhere and intensify over time (Centre for Policy Research, 2001: 181). A conscious policy of urban development, which recognises the economic forces underlying the emergence of these corridors, is needed for planning the creation of adequate regional infrastructure. Such a strategy would enable a comprehensive development plan in which the functional relations between the core and fringe urban areas can develop harmoniously.

2.3.3 Stagnation and Underperformance in the Agricultural Sector

The decline in the relative share of agriculture in the composition of the state's domestic output has been noted earlier, in connection with the relative decline of the primary sector. To some extent, the relative underperformance can be explained by the dynamism of the services sector and the modest performance of the industry sector. However, the weak performance of the agricultural sector itself is an important direct cause. In fact, the slow growth of the sector, on which two-thirds of the population relies for its livelihood, has been a longstanding source of concern to policy makers. The problem has been evident for some time. The growth performance has been oscillating over time. During the 1980s, the average growth rate of agriculture was dismal (Hanumappa, 2000). Foodgrain production was stagnant during the first half of the 1980s, and during the remainder of the decade it grew at 1.94 per cent. The trend in the crop yield for major crops, (such as paddy, *jowar, ragi,* maize, *tur,* gram and oilseeds), had been negative for the period of nearly a decade and half ending in 1990 (Hanumappa, 2000:2). During the 1990s, the performance did improve somewhat. However, the early years of the decade of 2000 have again exposed the weakness of the agricultural economy. A key factor has been the vulnerability to the fluctuations in the monsoon. Production has fallen short of targets (GoK, *Economic Survey* 2003-2004, Ch. 1 & 2). Farmers' distress has been reported and the recent spate of suicides by some farmers has once again focused public scrutiny on the economics of the agricultural sector.

The main structural features of the sector having a bearing on the long-term dynamics of the state's agriculture are the following:[21]

20. An assessment of the inadequacies in each of the above dimensions of infrastructure and infrastructure services may be found in *The Future of Urbanisation—Spread and Shape in Selected States, op.cit.* A sobering assessment of the overall water resource situation in Karnataka may be found in the *State Water Policy 2002,* Government of Karnataka, Water Resources Department. The Policy preamble states, "The State is endowed with limited water resources that are stressed and depleting...Unless water resources are properly developed and managed, the State will face acute crisis within the next two decades."

21. Hanumappa, *op.cit.,* which in turn has drawn on the findings of the *Report of the Committee on Stagnation of Agricultural Productivity in Karnataka* (Chairman: T.R. Satishchandran), Government of Karnataka, 1993.

1. There has been a fall over time in the average size of operational holdings in the state. Underlying this trend is a significant rise in the proportion of households cultivating less than two hectares, and the share of total cultivated area under such marginal farms. Several factors have contributed to this trend, of which demographic pressure and the impact of land reforms are the most important. This trend is more marked in the southern and coastal regions.

2. Technological factors underlie the weak performance of agricultural production. This includes the inability to adopt the new high yielding variety (HYV) technology effectively, and to adapt it appropriately to the local agro-climatic conditions. This has resulted in the suboptimal utilisation of modern inputs such as fertiliser and pesticides. The same is true for soil and water conservation practices. Extension services appear to have been inadequate.

3. Even though the irrigation infrastructure has expanded substantially, the management of irrigation has not been satisfactory. Water has been wastefully utilised and poorly distributed. Water-intensive cultivation of paddy and sugarcane by upstream farmers has been accompanied by scarcity of water supply for the tail-end farmers. The inefficiency in water use has been encouraged by the perverse nature of pricing of this resource, as well as that of power. Both of these crucial inputs have been subsidised through extreme degree of underpricing. Apart from implicit subsidy, the utilisation of irrigation has been below potential due to the underdevelopment of supporting irrigation infrastructure in the form of delivery systems canal distributaries and field channels, and land development. This state of affairs has contributed to land degradation in large tracts.

4. The economics of cultivation has been adverse—the price has been low in relation to costs at existing levels of productivity. On the other hand, there is a significant gap in actual yields obtained by farmers, as compared with what is demonstrated to be possible in the laboratories. The yields obtained vary widely but the gaps are quite stark, generally farmers obtain about 55 to 65 per cent of the demonstration yields. However, much larger gaps have been observed (Hanumappa, 2000:13).

5. During the economic reforms' period, beginning 1991, the policy environment has changed considerably. With liberalisation, the flow of credit to the rural economy through the banking channels reduced. There is greater reliance on market forces, and some efforts at increasing exports. However, a significant positive impact on Karnataka's agriculture is yet to be observed. On the contrary, there have been claims in the media about agrarian distress (Deshpande, 2002). Some of the market reform elements such as the power sector reforms, which sought to rationalise the power tariff structure proved politically costly for the Krishna government, particularly in the context of droughts. During the 1990s, there has been an intensification of the incentive structure towards commercialisation of agriculture. There have been changes in the cropping pattern towards commercial and horticultural crops, and also towards more technologically sophisticated, and higher risk activities such as food processing and horticultural exports. Investment needs for agricultural activities have increased, and along with this, so have cash needs. Marginal lands are being brought into cultivation, and monoculture seems to have increased. These trends have contributed to the increase in the stress on the soil, and indirectly to higher risk in agricultural activities. This is particularly the case in the un-irrigated tracts, where the climatic risk is compounded by the lack of adequate technical, marketing and credit support for the new activities.

6. Thus, the condition of the agrarian economy remains a crucial constraint on the future growth prospects of the sector, and thus of the economy of the state as a whole. An appropriate agrarian strategy is needed to set the stage for the next phase of Karnataka's growth. The elements of a policy response have been elaborated in Chapter 14. These include shifting the policy focus from irrigation expansion to rainfed agriculture, with special attention to utilisation of water and land, through an integrated approach of watershed development. The second element of a desirable strategy concerns the strengthening of the economic viability of the small and marginal farmers through appropriate reorientation of the policy framework (including institutional, technological and financial components). Attention to sustainability of the natural resource base for

agriculture is essential through revamping organic agriculture. The third element is improving the marketing infrastructure, and the credit delivery system.

2.4 Karnataka's Economic Growth Policy Priorities—Continuity and Change

Development strategy has played a key role in shaping the pattern of growth dynamics noted above. It is instructive to examine the main elements of policy thinking, as they have evolved over time. For this purpose, a comparison of the policy thinking that was reflected in the discussions that took place in the early 1970s, with the policy approaches that are being contemplated today may be useful.[22] It can be noted that some ideas that are being proposed today were present in embryonic form several decades ago.

During the early period of planning, the main focus of development strategy was clearly on the agricultural sector. Between Plan I and Plan IV, the proportion of outlays on agriculture more than doubled, from 11 per cent to 23 per cent. If the outlays on cooperation, community development and irrigation are included, the total outlay on sectors related to agricultural development was between 40-50 per cent (Rao *et al.*, 1975, ch. 1). The areas receiving attention in the strategy were irrigation, application of scientific knowledge, provision of finance, seeds and fertilisers, as well as land redistribution. In subsequent years, the relative importance of agriculture in plan outlays has declined significantly. By the Ninth Five-Year Plan (1997-2002), the share of the agricultural sector had declined to 31 per cent.

It is interesting to note that industry had been a relatively neglected sector in the early plans, accounting for 5 per cent to 8 per cent of outlays in the First and Second Plans respectively.[23] However, the private sector was perceived to be fairly active in the state. Tentative estimates at the time put the quantum of private investment at double that of public investment.

The development strategies and associated policy priorities that were contemplated at the time are briefly summarised below:

The weakness of the agrarian economy was already causing concern. The problems of the small and marginal farmers were noted, and their disadvantages (both economic and social) in participating in the opportunities available for development were identified as a crucial constraint for agricultural growth. The low level of labour absorption in agriculture was beginning to show up as unemployment. By 1965-66 (years of agricultural crisis), the unemployment was 7.45 per cent. Policy attention focused on 'employment generation' through a vigorous expansion of agriculture and ancillary activities (Mazumdar and Seshaiah, 1975). The perceived failure of macro-level plans to make an impact on grassroots development led to the endorsement of the idea of district-level planning. Decentralised governance arrangements for development programmes, with devolution of funds to local government, thus came to be advocated quite early (Nanjundappa, 1975).

With respect to industry, the early approach of the state government[24] was to build on the progressive policies of the past towards stimulating the growth of private enterprise. The main instruments were: (a) the setting up of a supportive network of institutions, and (b) the creation of infrastructure. The policy approach did not favour an aggressive public sector-driven industrialisation through the establishment of many new industrial enterprises under the auspices of the state government. However, the state's industrial development did benefit enormously from the presence of a number of major central government enterprises, such as ITI and HAL, which helped lay the foundations for the science-based industrial development that occurred in Bangalore.

The institutional support structure that was developed to support industrial development followed the national model. Financial institutions to provide long-term loan finance and venture capital, and to provide land and sheds were established. These included the State Financial Corporation, the State Investment and Development Corporation, the Small Industries Corporation and the Industrial Area Development Board. Infrastructure spending was also stepped up, and the state government allocated between 30 per cent to 40 per cent of total plan expenditure during the early plans to power, transport, communication and technical education. Apart from this, the government provided a

22. Our main source for the early discussions is V.K.R.V Rao, H.K. Mazumdar and Amal Ray (eds.), *Planning for Change: Issues in Mysore's Development*, Vikas Publications, 1975. This publication is of some historical interest, being the proceedings of the first major seminar organised by the Institute for Social and Economic Change. It brought together many leading academics and policy practitioners to deliberate on the development strategy for the state.

23. These figures refer to the direct outlays on industry, and do not include the expenditure on infrastructure.

24. T.R. Satishchandran, "Industrial Development in Mysore", in V.K.R.V. Rao *et al. op. cit.* Most of the data cited in the following paragraphs relating to industrial development have been drawn from this source.

number of promotional subsidies and tax exemptions to industry.[25]

The impact of these policies on industrial development was modest in the modern sector, though small-scale industrial enterprise appears to have responded strongly to the policy environment. There were very few large and medium industrial enterprises—numbering 167 out of more than 9600 that were estimated in 1970. The vast majority of enterprises belonged to the small-scale industry category. Their numbers expanded rapidly, multiplying three-fold during the 1960s. These enterprises were mainly engaged in producing textiles, general engineering goods, and food, beverages and tobacco products.

Regional imbalance in industrial development was already a major issue. The continuity of this policy issue over three decades can be seen in the recent deliberations and recommendations of the High Power Committee for Redressal of Regional Imbalances in 2002. The overwhelming dominance of Bangalore was already causing policy concern at the time. It accounted for 40 per cent of all industrial units and 33 per cent of invested capital. Eleven out of the 19 districts of the time were deemed to be industrially backward.[26]

The idea of regionally dispersing industrial centres was already under consideration in the 1970s, and 11 such locations ('second line of cities') had been selected for industrial development. Creation of adequate infrastructure was seen to be the most effective means for achieving this objective. The continuity of policy concern in this area is thus interesting and noteworthy. At the time, the main constraining factor was deemed to be shortage of plan funds, because a comprehensive approach was required to create sufficiently attractive locations for large industry. Not only was a good infrastructure required (roads, railways and power), but social amenities such as good education and medical institutions, as well as adequate housing for industrial workers were also needed. All this required substantial funds, which were not available to the government. The inadequacies in this regard had resulted in an industrial growth pattern that was biased in favour of small enterprises.

25. These related to such items as preparation of feasibility studies, sales tax refund, exemption from electricity tax, waiver of fines for conversion of agricultural land to industrial use, etc.

26. Though some of these erstwhile backward districts have shown signs of industrial development, such as Dharwad, Belgaum and Mysore, the basic problem remains.

Despite a clear identification of the major constraints and desirable direction of policy intervention in the policy discourse of the 1970s, clarity of purpose with respect to development policy was lost in the next decade or two. The 1980s and 1990s may be characterised as a period of policy drift in the state, during which the above mentioned policy concerns have become more acute. The resource constraints on growth-promoting investments worsened. The slow growth rate in the major production sectors, particularly agriculture, led to the adoption of defensive economic policies, rather than on well-coordinated, proactive development strategies. This trend was compounded by the political economy of competitive electoral politics. However, a part of the reason for this blurring of policy focus, particularly in the 1990s, is due to the sharp change in the policy environment introduced by the national level economic reform itself. The early years of the reform sought to correct the national balance of payments imbalance and to free the private sector from control *raj*. However, it had no clear message for state-level planning or state-level policy reform. In Karnataka, large and widespread subsidies were resorted to and persisted with, which weakened the government's resource position without creating a sustainable framework for growth (Rao, 2003). These were mainly in the form of implicit subsidies, that is, they were given in the form of low prices for government-supplied goods and services. The sectors covered by subsidies included power, irrigation, food and agriculture, housing, education and industry.

Turning specifically to the impact of these subsidies on the key production sectors, the emerging picture is as follows. In agriculture, studies found that in practice the subsidies had a perverse incidence (Deshpande *et al.*, 2003). Most of the subsidies on inputs were captured by the better-off regions and by the farmers with large operational holdings. The effect on the growth process was also suboptimal. While no clear association has been found across regions between input subsidy received and the rate of agricultural growth, there is evidence that these subsidies distorted the choice of crops by farmers, and also led to the inefficient use of precious inputs such as water and fertiliser. Moreover, the abysmally low levels of cost recovery in irrigation water use has led to the significant weakening of maintenance and operation of the existing irrigation assets. At the same time, emphasis has been placed on starting new irrigation projects. Given the implied reallocation of funds to new projects, without completion of ongoing projects, has led to significant cost and time overruns on the latter (Raju and Amar Nath, 2003).

In the case of industry (Gayathri, 2003), throughout the 1970s and 80s the government had provided incentives aimed at regionally dispersing industry *via* tax concessions. During the 1990s, the subsidies were intensified. The capital investment subsidy was an important instrument used. Once again, the actual regional incidence of the subsidy was biased in favour of the districts already well endowed with industry, in apparent contradiction to the objective of regional dispersal. Bangalore alone accounted for nearly 18 per cent, and the 5 most industrially advanced districts together accounted for 56 per cent of the total capital subsidy disbursed. Despite the availability of these and other subsidies and concessions to entrepreneurs in all the districts, the designated growth centres in underdeveloped regions such as Raichur and Hassan have not developed industrially. In short, as a policy instrument for industrial development, the subsidies have not been effective.

To sum up, an examination of the broad outlines of the evolution of development thinking and experience in Karnataka indicate that certain issues and structural problems have persisted over several decades. The core problems relate to the long-term weakness of the agricultural sector, and the regionally concentrated growth of the industry and services sector. Backward regions and economically vulnerable sections of the population have remained so, despite the reasonably satisfactory overall growth performance in the state. Though the problems have been clearly discerned, the proposed solutions could not be implemented satisfactorily. In spite of rising development expenditures, the development stimuli has not made a sustained positive impact, and in many cases has actually created unintended effects that defeat the original purpose of the policy intervention, such as in the efforts to disperse industry or distribute growth. At the same time, the spontaneous forces of the market unleashed by liberalisation and supported by an investor-friendly policy posture have helped propel Bangalore into a major global IT centre with very strong export linkages. There was perhaps, during the 1990s, a diminution of the focus on the rural economy and economic development goals more generally. Policy makers were focused on reforming the investment climate, attracting FDI, and rationalising the user charges on power, and so on.

2.5 The Emerging Policy Scenario and Strategic Considerations

The policy challenges now confronting the government now consist of finding a means of achieving two goals simultaneously. First, it must continue to strengthen the competitiveness of the IT, BT and service sectors and its global integration, which is the principal source of the private sector growth that is buoying the Karnataka economy. In spite of the over-dominance of Bangalore in the state's economy, the goal of policy must be to sustain its IT-based, horticulture linked BT and other high-tech industry. Second, the strategy must contain an effective policy package to stimulate growth in the backward districts and in the rural economy more generally. Detailed discussions of the current situation and related policy issues for each of the major production sectors, and the supporting physical and social infrastructure sectors are available in the following chapters of the report. In this section, some observations and suggestions on the general directions of the emerging policy are made.

The policy approach in evidence since 2000 has certain discernible elements. These reflect the national and international policy environment, as well as the state's own economic conjuncture. A fundamental consideration in the design of the current development strategy is the understanding on the part of policy makers about the appropriate role of the state. The post-reform approach of the state has broadly followed a liberal model, which has welcomed the increased role of the private sector. In the modern industrial and services sector, the government has sought to stimulate private investment. In areas where private enterprise has generally operated, policy stimuli have taken the form of providing a variety of incentives, and simplifying of governmental procedures. In sectors, which hitherto were exclusively under government control, such as roads and power, private sector participation is being actively encouraged. Many different forms are being tried out—from outsourcing to joint investment and co-production. The state public enterprises have been under scrutiny from a Commission appointed for the purpose. Privatisation, restructuring and disinvestments are the directions in which the government has signalled that it wants to go.[27]

All this is of course not unique to Karnataka. However, it is among the more agile states in embracing the new ethos of liberalisation. In this new environment, the nature and scope of 'planning' is greatly transformed. Much greater reliance must be placed on the compliance of non-governmental actors with the actions and responses desired by the government. Given the earlier observations about the

27. See Parvathi Menon, "Karnataka's Agenda", *Frontline*, January 18-31, 2003 (Vol 20, Issue 01), for a report on the Disinvestment programme of the state government.

inadequate correspondence between policy objectives and economic outcomes, a major issue that arises in the present context is how to bring about such a correspondence. If the task was difficult earlier, it is even more difficult now with less instruments of control at the disposal of the government. The present situation does not call for a major macro level reorientation, as was called for in 1991, when the reforms began. The direction of structural readjustment has clearly set in. As noted earlier in the chapter, the switch from a purely domestic market orientation to export-orientation has occurred, not only in the IT and BT sectors but also in sectors like textiles and garments. Foreign direct investment is taking place.

What then needs to be done? A set of basic approaches that need to be incorporated in the design of Karnataka's development strategy can be mentioned. The first need is to have a proactive approach towards the market. One may call this 'proactive planning'. This would involve the alignment of the structure of incentives such that the market forces can be harnessed in support of development goals. Rather than trying to impose a structure of incentives on the economy, it might make more sense to first analyse the economic, demographic and other structural trends, and examine how one can take advantage of it. For example, consider the goal of regional dispersal of industry. As noted earlier, this has been a longstanding goal that has been difficult to achieve. Various incentives offered for industrial dispersal have not worked. Industrial location is the result of economic calculation by investors and entrepreneurs. The study of spatial trends, as noted earlier, suggests that economic forces seem to be pointing towards the formation of 'urban corridors', along certain arterial transport routes. The industrial dispersal strategy might seek to take advantage of this trend, and work proactively to set up industrial centres and supporting systems along these corridors. This, if properly done, might actually decongest Bangalore effectively, and allow a smoother transition than the chaotic low quality semi-urban sprawl that typically occurs in unplanned settings. The advantage here would be that the market forces would be on the side of policy. True, this would not result in a uniform distribution of industry across districts. But, this may lead to a more rational attainment of regional comparative advantage, and also generate more resources for redistributive policies with regard to social amenities and infrastructure. In view of the serious nature of regional inequality as discussed above, such policy aimed at securing balance in amenities and infrastructure needs to be continued in parallel. The economic strategy should follow its own logic based on regional comparative advantage, while the social development strategy should be based on the logic of assuring equity. The two strategies should be allowed to strengthen each other and not to work at cross-purposes.

Similar considerations can guide industrial and export policies in the state. Awareness of emerging market trends can lead to the government helping the private sector to seize market opportunities in world markets. Here the government has shown agility by moving quickly to announce its Millennium BPO Policy and Millennium Biotech Policy to take advantage of the opportunities afforded by the IT and BT enabled services market. The policy calls for providing such services as a state-level mechanism for certification and accreditation of HR Training Agencies so that good quality human resources can be accessed quickly, and in creating a framework that ensures data security and customer secrecy. The step is truly commendable. However, it is important to appreciate that this type of 'proactive planning' has been possible because of close cooperation between the IT department of government of Karnataka, Karnataka Biotechnology Development Council and industrial bodies such as the CII. In short, this cooperation has enabled the policy makers to access market knowledge and business trends, and thus improve the quality of planning, and provide the necessary 'public goods'.[28]

At the same time, it is important to ensure that the private sector does its share in helping solve the 'problems of the commons'. Increasingly, urban congestion and environmental stress are becoming acute. It is necessary therefore to rationalise the pattern of utilisation of peripheral urban and semi-urban land. The present chaotic situation needs to be corrected. It may require the transfer of some portion of privately held land to the government for the creation of roads, hospitals, parks and other public facilities.[29] In short, rules and institutions are needed to

---

28. The cooperative relationship between the government and the IT industry has a fairly long tradition and developed at the national level, even before the economic reforms of 1991. It took an intense form during the 1990s when N. Vittal headed the Department of Electronics(DoE). Innovations such as the Software Technology Parks (STPs), and liberal policies were introduced. Bangalore was fortunate in being among the earliest locations of an STP. At the national level, the close interaction between the NASSCOM and the government helped evolve sound policies that allowed the industry to attain international competitiveness. See Balaji Parthasrathy, "Globalizing Information Technology: The Domestic Policy Context for India's Software Production and Exports", *Iterations*, May 2004.

29. It is interesting to note that in Gujarat (an industry leader among states), the Town Planning Act was amended in 1999. Now the law requires buyers of barren and undeveloped land under urban development authorities "to keep or surrender 50 per cent of the land for various infrastructure developments like roads, hospitals, parks, green land, and so on." Earlier the ration was 35 per cent. The private party may retain ownership of the land and develop the infrastructure, while charging users of the facilities. Alternatively, the land may be sold to the urban development authorities, which would develop the infrastructure. See Ravindra H. Dholakia, "The Role of the State Government in Promoting Private Sector Growth", in Stephen Howes, Ashok Lahiri and Nicholas Stern (eds.), *State Level Reforms in India*, Macmillan India Ltd., 2003.

promote a two-way collaboration in the production and creation of public goods. There are indications that industry in Karnataka, particularly in Bangalore, is willing to cooperate with government in the creation of infrastructure. In recent years, the private sector, catalysed by the BATF, has contributed to improving urban amenities such as parks and bus shelters in Bangalore city. According to latest media reports, leading high-tech sector companies have pledged to financially support the government in major urban infrastructure investments, such as the construction of new elevated roads for enabling fast access to the 'Electronic City'—where a cluster of these firms are located.

A second key consideration in strategy is to recognise that in the present phase what is needed is institutional reform. Though resource constraints for the government pose a serious problem, the need for appropriate institutional mechanisms to regulate and guide the economy is equally strong. In relation to the industrial policy approaches discussed above, the institutionalisation of consultative and participative policymaking is an important ingredient of success. Institutional reform needs to encompass the policymaking process itself. Karnataka has innovated in the area of participatory policymaking through such mechanisms as the participatory task forces that were set up in 2000. These may be helpful, not only through the induction of better knowledge into the policy process, but also in managing the politics of implementation of the policies through easing the formation of consensus. Among the task forces, some such as the Bangalore Agenda Task Force came to be better known. The design of such institutional mechanisms needs to be experimented with and refined, such that they are able to improve the content of policy, without being viewed as being overly influenced by any particular powerful interest group.

Another area for institutional change is regulation. In many areas where the government used to enjoy monopoly power, notably the power sector, the entry of private participation has made it necessary to institute appropriate regulatory institutions. Though the issues here are complex, and the country does not have a wealth of historical experience to draw from, the establishment of regulatory frameworks is vital. Given the large volumes of investments that are needed in these sectors, and the fact that infrastructure constraints are at the root of industrial stagnation, action in this dimension is urgent. Though the government has set up a regulatory authority in the power sector, the degree of independence that it enjoys, and the analytical skills at its disposal are matters of concern.

What ought to be done about those sectors of the Karnataka economy that are outside the orbit of market dynamism—such as the backward and deprived regions, and the economically marginal groups? Here the experience of Karnataka that we have reviewed above, suggests that this condition persists despite the step up of development expenditure. An example is that of irrigation. The efforts to introduce institutional innovations for management of irrigation systems do not seem to have worked. This clearly constitutes the most difficult set of problems. Market mechanisms typically have little to offer to such groups and areas. Gradualist and incremental incentives offered by the government seem to be either ignored or misused. In these circumstances, some kind of social 'big bang' approach may be desirable to shift the social and economic equilibrium. Concerted public campaigns—'people's campaigns' need to be organised, involving the government and non-governmental actors, around activities that would have strong developmental effects, and hold the promise of improving the well-being of the people. In some states, such as Kerala, movements and campaigns organised around literacy, poverty alleviation through self-help groups engaged simultaneously in microcredit, and micro-enterprises seem to have had a very positive effect. Such innovative initiatives may help break the current economic confinement. These subeconomies need to be diversified, their internal savings to be mobilised and deployed, and networks for collective and cooperative activities created and strengthened.

In this context, it is interesting to note that the State Water Policy, 2002 of the Government of Karnataka contains elements of such a collective approach to resolve the water management problems in the irrigation sector. It declares the government's intention to adopt a participatory approach to the management of water resources, and the willingness to introduce the necessary legal and institutional changes to enable its 'ultimate goal' which is to "transfer operation, maintenance, management and collection of water charges to user groups". The Policy also proposes to undertake campaigns aimed at creating awareness among citizens regarding user participation and decision making (GoK, 2002). We may hope that adequate emphasis will be given to this dimension of institutional strategy in the actual implementation of the policy.

Another numerically important constituent of the Karnataka economy is the small-scale industrial sector. It remains, however, relatively weak in terms of productivity and economic performance, particularly in comparison to the IT services sector. The New Industrial Policy, 2001 states its intention to promote entrepreneurship and human resources to help develop this sector. Again, it is worth noting the state government's approach, which envisions establishing a partnership with the private sector in capacity building. For example, the policy proposes the involvement of the private sector in Rural development and self-employment institutes, to be set up in all districts. Similarly, it proposes to involve industry associations in establishing specialised training institutes for such industrial fields as steel technology and automotive technology.

While such initiatives are in the correct direction, there is the need for a comprehensive and effective strategy for the small-scale industrial sector. Post-independence experience with promotion of small industries has not been particularly successful in India, and may be described as one of the main failures of the planning era. The small-scale sector typically suffers from both internal and external weaknesses. Internal weakness stems from low productivity arising from scale of production, backward technology, inadequacies of organisation, management skills and finance. External weakness arises from inability to access market information, to market products widely and to bargain effectively. There are examples, however, of countries where the small-scale sector has managed to overcome these disadvantages. Among these, the Italian example is notable, and this has led to the emergence of new thinking about the development of the small-scale sector.[30] The basic lessons may have some relevance for Karnataka's emerging strategy in this sector. The task at hand is to facilitate the transformation of a small-scale industrial sector based on traditional artisan-based organisation to one that can compete effectively without a host of subsidies. Small firms can achieve competitiveness by organising into networks to reap collective economies. This permits the formation of closely interconnected clusters of firms, which can work collectively to develop new products and processes. The firms can flexibly share segments of production processes among themselves by assigning work among themselves. In this type of set-up, the role of the industry associations becomes very important, for it is these organisations that enable the firms to share joint expenditures, which otherwise would render the individual firm uncompetitive. The associations can provide cooperative services related to administrative work, book-keeping, acquiring raw materials, coordinating credit, etc. For more sophisticated services such as marketing, advertising and financial services, these could be provided through public-private partnerships.

To summarise, in relation to the emerging economic strategy of the state, we have proposed two innovative approaches. The first is 'proactive planning', which seeks to leverage the energies of the market system by strengthening areas where the economy has a demonstrable comparative advantage. Policy should seek to anticipate areas of potential weakness, particularly in areas requiring collective action—such as urban congestion. At the same time, it should strengthen its redistribution strategy by separating the economic growth strategy from the regional redistribution strategy. Second, we have suggested an emphasis on institutional innovation for better policy planning and implementation. In the case of IT and modern industry, we have suggested participative policymaking and partnership. In the case of the weaker sectors, such as agriculture and small industry where individualised subsidies do not seem to have worked, we have proposed variants of a strategy aimed at fostering cooperation and collective action to break the current deadlock.

30. For a survey of the literature on small industry development and the key features of the Italian experience, see Sumangala Damodaran, *Export Orientation and Industrial Clustering—Organisational Structure, Growth and Performance of the Leather and Leather Products Industry in India*, Ph. D dissertation, Jawaharlal Nehru University, 2003 (unpublished).

References

Centre for Policy Research (2001). *The Future of Urbanisation—Spread and Shape in Selected States*, New Delhi, June.

Deshpande, R. S. (2002). "Suicides by Farmers in Karnataka—Agrarian Distress and Possible Alleviatory Steps", *Economic and Political Weekly*, June 29.

Deshpande, R.S., M.J. Bhende and T. Raveendra Naik (2003). "Volume and Composition of Subsidies in Food and Agriculture", in M. Govinda Rao, (ed.), *Volume and Composition of Budgetary Subsidies in Karnataka*, Institute for Social and Economic Change, Bangalore.

Gayathri, K. (2003). "Industrial Incentives in Karnataka", in M. Govinda Rao, (ed.), *Volume and Composition of Budgetary Subsidies in Karnataka*, Institute for Social and Economic Change, Bangalore.

Government of Karnataka, *State Water Policy 2002*, Item 6.7, 6.8 and 6.9.

———. *Economic Survey 2000-04*.

Hanumappa, H. G. (2000). "State Policy Initiatives and Agricultural Development: A Case Study of Karnataka", *Working Paper 57*, Institute for Social and Economic Change, Bangalore.

Mazumdar, H. K. and S. Seshaiah (1975). "A Brief Survey of Problem of Development in Mysore State—Some Background Notes", in V.K.R.V. Rao *et al.*, *Planning for Change: Issues in Mysore's Development*, Vikas Publications.

Nanjundappa (1975). "Planning from Below and Development Finance", in V.K.R.V. Rao *et al. Planning for Change: Issues in Mysore's Development*, Vikas Publications.

Raju, K.V. and H. K. Amar Nath (2003). "Irrigation Subsidies in Karnataka", in M. Govinda Rao, *Volume and Composition of Budgetary Subsidies in Karnataka*, Institute for Social and Economic Change, Bangalore.

Rao, M. Govinda (ed.) (2003). *Volume and Composition of Budgetary Subsidies in Karnataka*, Institute for Social and Economic Change, Bangalore.

Rao, V.K.R.V., H.K. Mazumdar and Amal Ray (eds.) (1975). *Planning for Change: Issues in Mysore's Development*, Vikas Publications, Ch.1.

APPENDIX A-2.1

Size Distribution of Small Industrial Enterprises in Karnataka

Type of Establishment	*Establishments*	*Employment*	*Employment Per Establishment*
Rural			
All Establishments	310227	11884243	4
	100.00	100.00	
Private Establishments	206564	815854	4
	66.58	68.89	
Cooperative Establishments	13750	52625	4
	4.43	4.44	
Government	89913	315764	4
	28.98	26.66	
Urban			
All Establishments	330991	1805544	5
	100.00	100.00	
Private Establishments	300228	1352578	5
Cooperative Establishments	6065	55863	9
	1.83	3.09	
Government	24698	397103	16
	7.46	21.99	
Rural and Urban			
All Establishments	641218	2989787	5
	100.00	100.00	
Private Establishments	506792	2168432	4
	79.04	72.53	
Cooperative Establishments	19815	108488	5
	3.09	3.63	
Government	114611	712867	6
	17.87	23.84	

Source: Fourth Economic Census of Karnataka, 1998.

APPENDIX A-2.2

Size Distribution of Industrial Enterprises in Karnataka—Distribution of Non-agricultural Enterprises by Types of Major Activity Groups

Major Activity Group	*OAE*	*%*	*Establishments*	*%*	*All*	*%*
Mining and Quarrying	2359	0.23	2316	0.36	4675	0.28
Manufacturing and Repair Services	259670	25.68	128665	20.07	388335	23.50
Electricity, Gas and Water	251	0.02	476	0.07	727	0.04
Construction	10034	0.99	6059	0.94	16093	0.97
Wholesale Trade	21279	2.10	16319	2.55	37598	2.28
Retail Trade	438738	43.39	156323	24.38	595061	36.01
Hotels and Restaurants	61063	6.04	34765	5.42	95828	5.80
Transport	14096	1.39	10681	1.67	24777	1.50
Storage and Warehousing	1216	0.12	1321	0.21	2537	0.15
Communications	5943	0.59	9166	1.43	15109	0.91
Finance, Insurance, etc.	27705	2.74	30265	4.72	57970	3.51
Community, Social and Other Services	164184	16.24	244829	38.18	409013	24.75
Others (unspecified)Activities	4697	0.46	33	0.01	4730	0.29
All Activities	1011235	100.00	641218	100.00	1652453	100.00

Source: Fourth Economic Census of Karnataka, 1998.

APPENDIX A-2.3

Foreign Direct Investment in Karnataka: Country-wise Details of Foreign Direct Investment Approved by Government of India for Karnataka

Country	*No. of Projects*	*Investment (US$ Million)*
USA	451	721.12
Mauritius	126	365.14
UK	96	241.70
Japan	65	418.10
Germany	124	490.40
France	26	60.38
Netherlands	51	66.95
Singapore	66	89.56
Belgium	14	889.49
Canada	11	50.78
Sweden	13	49.96
Euro Issues	5	1615.63
NRIs	126	262.88
Others	233	241.85
Total	**1407**	**5563.94**

Source: FIPB/Karnataka Udyog Mitra.

APPENDIX A-2.4

Foreign Direct Investment in Karnataka: Year-wise Details of Foreign Direct Investment Approved by Government of India for Karnataka

Year	*No. of Projects*	*Investment (US$ Million)*
1991-92	22	4.28
1992-93	30	19.89
1993-94	62	102.83
1994-95	112	294.33
1995-96	116	676.57
1996-97	163	883.81
1997-98	115	1860.40
1998-99	79	148.14
1999-00	108	283.94
2000-01	222	1084.64
2001-02	319	168.89
2002-03	59	36.22
Total	**1407**	**5563.94**

Source: FIPB/Karnataka Udyog Mitra.

APPENDIX A-2.5

Aspects of Regional Development of the Karnataka Economy

District	*Share of Primary Sector (1996-97) (%)*	*Per Capita Income (1997-98) (Rs.)*	*Per Capita Income 1997-98 (Rank)*	*Percentage of Families Below Poverty Line 1993-94*	*Percentage of Families Below Poverty Line 1993-94 (Rank)*
South Karnataka	30				
Bangalore Urban	3	25740	1	31.42	9
Bangalore Rural	38	12215	9	38.17	8
Chickmagalur	55	17609	4	15.61	18
Chitradurga	44	10989	13	39.00	7
Dakshina Kannada	29	20167	3	8.91	20
Hassan	49	12346	8	14.44	19
Kodagu	57	24623	2	20.73	17
Kolar	44	10013	16	48.45	3
Mandya	43	11081	12	30.16	10
Mysore	35	14576	5	28.94	13
Shimoga	44	13970	6	25.56	14
Tumkur	46	9011	18	40.64	6
North Karnataka	41				
Belgaum	44	13377	7	29.86	11
Bellary	46	12200	10	44.5	5
Bidar	40	7861	20	56.06	1
Bijapur	49	10049	15	28.98	12
Dharwad	34	10397	14	49.75	2
Gulbarga	35	9516	17	45.54	4
Raichur	47	8688	19	25.11	15
U.Kannada	31	12019	11	24.97	16

Source: High Power Committee for Redressal of Regional Imbalances, chaired by D.M Nanjundappa, June 2002.

APPENDIX A-2.6

Trends in Regional Irrigation Status

Districts	*Share in the State Total of Net Area Irrigated (Per cent)*		*Percentage of Net Area Irrigated to Net Area Sown*	
	1957-58	*2000-01*	*1957-58*	*2000-01*
Bangalore	5.0	2.9	10.9	19.4
Chitradurga	5.1	7.7	7.3	24.6
Kolar	5.9	2.5	17.0	18.8
Shimoga	14.0	5.3	41.5	61.4
Tumkur	6.2	4.5	9.6	19.2
Chickmagalur	8.1	1.0	3.3	8.7
Dakshina Kannada	6.2	4.1	24.7	44.5
Hassan	5.3	3.1	15.7	21.7
Kodagu	0.8	0.1	6.8	2.1
Mandya	7.7	4.2	26.0	43.8
Mysore	6.7	6.3	11.7	29.5
Bellary	2.8	6.3	3.5	32.9
Bidar	1.3	1.5	2.7	10.2
Gulbarga	2.3	6.2	1.4	13.7
Raichur	1.6	9.9	1.2	29.5
Belgaum	7.3	13.5	5.9	40.7
Bijapur	3.5	12.7	1.8	26.4
Dharwad	7.2	7.2	5.0	17.3
Uttara Kannada	3.0	1.0	20.5	22.1
South Karnataka (Net Area Irrigated Hectares)	71.0 (5,38,943)	41.7 (10,62,188)	16.5	25.6
North Karnataka (Net Area Irrigated Hectares)	29.0 (2,20,409)	58.3 (14,85,481)	3.2	24.3
State Total (Net Area Irrigated Hectares)	100 (7,59,352)	100 (25,47,669)	7.5	24.8

Source: High Power Committee for Redressal of Regional Imbalances, chaired by D.M Nanjundappa, June 2002.

APPENDIX A-2.7

Regional Trends in Industrial Location

District	*Industry*			
	District Share in the State Total of Factories			
	1957	*Rank*	*1998-99*	*Rank*
Bangalore	30.18	1	45.9	1
Chickmagalur	1.02	14	2.5	10
Chitradurga	3.71	8	4.1	7
Dakshina Kannada	9.70	4	6.9	2
Hassan	0.96	15	0.5	19
Kodagu	0.90	16	1.7	13
Kolar	2.57	10	1.6	14
Mandya	0.84	18	0.7	18
Mysore	8.56	5	4.8	5
Shimoga	2.81	9	2.1	11
Tumkur	2.22	11	1.7	12
South Karnataka	63.47		72.6	
Belgaum	9.88	3	5.8	4
Bijapur	6.05	6	4.7	6
Dharwad	10.42	2	6.8	3
Uttara Kannada	0.90	17	0.9	17
Bellary	5.69	7	3.0	9
Bidar	0.18	19	1.0	16
Gulbarga	1.36	13	1.4	15
Raichur	2.04	12	3.8	8
North Karnataka	36.53		27.40	
Karnataka	**100.00**		**100.00**	

Source: High Power Committee for Redressal of Regional Imbalances, chaired by D.M Nanjundappa, June 2002.

Chapter 3

Natural Resources in Karnataka

3.0 Introduction

Sustainable development and reduction in regional imbalances in any state depends on level of natural resources of the region including land, forests, water and minerals. The resources may often get regionally fixed like land, forests and minerals. Water resources, as in the case of river, may be taken as mobile insofar as its course cuts across geographical boundaries of various regions, districts or state. They are not evenly distributed. Consequently, the High Power Committee for Redressal of Regional Imbalances (GoK, 2002a) has recognised that regional imbalances can manifest as barrier to develop and manage these natural resources. Fair and equitable development of natural resources across the Karnataka state requires a well thought out development efforts both by government, planning and policy and by private investment.

Efficient and scientific utilisation of land ensures ecological balance of an ecosystem. Land could be utilised for different purposes but their sustainability depends on their appropriate use and management. As population increases, the demand for land (for crop cultivation, housing, industries, etc.) also increases. But since the land area is fixed, it cannot be expanded along with the rise in population and its demand for land. Further, not all the available land could be brought under crop cultivation. Certain amount of it needs to be preserved as natural forests and as uncultivated lands (barren, pastures non-agricultural land, cultivable waste, and other common lands like grazing) so that the complementarities and supplementarities between crop cultivation, livestock rearing and other rural livelihood systems are maintained.

The contribution of uncultivated lands including forests to local economy is outside the market framework, which are both its strength as well as weakness. Strength in the sense of social justice, that it supports rural families. Weakness lies in unsustainable exploitation of these lands, which would result in the tragedy of these resources'. It is argued that weakness or tragedy could be averted through 'cooperative game' of all stakeholders, contributing to both local economy and individual welfare of all participants (Nadkarni and Pasha, 1991). Further, uncultivated lands and forest are being an economically important part of the overall land use system and hence, proper use and treatment of these resources can lead to full realisation of their potential. There also exists symbiotic relationship between cultivated and uncultivated lands with different institutional situations.

3.1 Land Use

About 83 per cent of the land area in Karnataka is suitable for agriculture, and the remaining 17 per cent is not well suited for farming, which could be appropriately utilised for forestry, pasture, silvipasture, and wildlife conservation. Table 3.1 shows that at the state level the proportion of net sown area including current fallow was as high as 61.7 per cent of the total geographical area of the state during 1999-00, though it has increased marginally during the period 1991-92 and 1999-00. This has happened at the cost of uncultivated lands i.e., permanent pastures and other grazing lands, barren and uncultivable and cultivable waste lands. The share of uncultivated lands, in total geographical area was 18.4 per cent during 1991-92, which has remained more or less same during 1999-00. The low proportion of these lands has affected the farming and livelihood systems in many parts of the state. The meagre proportion (around 19 per cent) of available uncultivated lands during 1999-00 could hardly meet the biomass needs of the people in rural areas. Even this proportion as per the official landuse statistics may not be actually available when we look into their status at the micro-level (Nadkarni and Pasha, 1991). If the actual status is assessed the proportion of net sown area would further increase, leaving very little as pastures and other uncultivated lands (CPRs).

Area under forests has marginally decreased at the state level from 30.75 lakh hectares during 1991-92 to 30.63 lakh hectares during 1999-00 (Table 3.1). Its proportion to total geographical area has remained same (16 per cent) during the same period, and it is far below the recommended proportion of 33 per cent. Even the existing forest area of 30.63 lakh hectares during 1999-00 may not be under proper forest cover.

TABLE 3.1

Land Utilisation ('000 ha)

	1991-92	*1999-00*
Total Geographical Area	19179	19050
Forests	3075 (16.0)	3063 (16.1)
Barren and Non-agricultural Land	1993 (10.4)	2085 (10.9)
Cultivable Waste	445 (2.3)	439 (2.3)
Permanent Pastures and Other Grazing Lands	1097 (5.7)	1005 (5.3)
Land under Miscellaneous Trees and Groves	316 (1.6)	313 (1.6)
Other Fallow	431 (2.3)	399 (2.1)
Net Sown Area (including Current Fallow)	11693 (61.0)	11747 (61.7)

Note: Figures in the parentheses are percentages to total geographical area.

Source: (1) *Karnataka at a Glance 2001-02*, Directorate of Economics and Statistics, Government of Karnataka, Bangalore.

(2) *Indian Agricultural Statistics 1991-92*, Vol I and II, All India, State-wise and District-wise, Ministry of Agriculture, Government of India.

Across districts there are variations both in area of forest and uncultivated lands. In the forest rich district of Uttara Kannada in the Western Ghats, the proportion of forest to total geographical area has declined from 80.6 per cent during 1991-92 to 79.5 per cent in 1999-00. The proportion of uncultivated lands has increased from 7.5 per cent to 8.8 per cent in this period. In other districts of the Western Ghats the proportion of forest area to total geographical area has remained more or less same during the same period. The proportion of forest area to total geographical area of the districts in the northern Maidan area of the state has remained more or less same during the period 1991-92 to 1999-00, ranging from 4.0 per cent to 12.0 per cent across districts of the region.(Appendix A-3.1)

3.1.1 Soil Type and Degradation

Soils in the state have been classified into 6 major types. Red soil constitutes around 37 per cent followed by black cotton soil, 27.8 per cent of total area. The other major types are alluvial soils, 15.7 per cent followed by lateritic soil, 11.6 per cent. Soils in the state have been degraded due to activities like intensive agriculture, over grazing, deforestation, enhanced industrial growth, soil compaction, salinisation, loss of nutrients and toxicity problems. It is reported that in Karnataka around 7.7 million hectares, constituting 40.3 per cent of the total geographical area (TGA) has been affected due to various soil degradation problems. Water erosion is the major problem causing loss of topsoil and terrain deformation in 5.9 M ha (30.9 per cent of TGA). Karnataka has 80 per cent of the land under rainfed cultivation and around 20 per cent covered under irrigation next only to Rajasthan. As much as 70 per cent of the total geographical area of the state falls under arid climatic zone where the rainfall is scanty and the mean temperature high. The rainfed crop production is in this region. As the state's major area falls in the arid and semi-arid zone, moisture is the major limiting factor in crop production. Out of 120.85 lakh ha of cultivated area, 68 lakh ha (57 per cent of total geographical area) needs soil and moisture conservation treatment.

3.1.2 Land Degradation

As said earlier soils have been degraded by human activities like intensive irrigated agriculture, over grazing, deforestation, enhanced industrial growth, and contamination which has led to water and wind erosion, soil compaction, salinisation, loss of nutrients and toxicity problems. Such degradation processes in turn limit the productive capacity of lands making it more difficult and expensive for the farmers to increase production of food, fibre and fodder. It is reported that about 7.7 million ha representing 40.3 per cent of the total geographical area of the state is affected by various soil degradation problems in the three landforms of South Deccan Plateau, Western and Eastern Ghats and Coastal Plains. Water erosion is the major problem causing loss of topsoil and terrain deformation.

Poor soil and water conservation measures and lack of watershed approaches have resulted in land degradation in many ways. It is estimated that nearly 250 tonnes of soil per ha is washed away annually. So far 32 lakh ha has been brought under watershed projects and still more than 50 per cent area is left uncovered. The salinity has become very acute in the command areas of Tungabhadra, Kabini, Ghataprabha, Malaprabha,and Upper Krishna, etc. It is reported that nearly 1.27 lakh ha of land is affected by waterlogging, salinity and alkalinity accounting for 10 per cent of the total land under irrigation in the state (Kushalapa, 2003).

3.1.3 Issues

Following are the broad issues related to land degradation (GoK, 2004):

- Soil and water erosion due to unsustainable practices leading to loss of fertility of farm lands.
- Excessive irrigation and faulty water regimes causing land degradation.
- Lands of vegetation and increasing pressure on the land capacity.
- Use of chemicals in agriculture which leads to soil and water contamination.
- Mining and quarrying leading to land degradation.
- Developmental activities fragmenting the landscape and habitants.

3.2 Forest Sector

The state is endowed with fairly good forest cover constituting five forest types: 1. Tropical Wet Evergreen, 2. Tropical Semi Evergreen, 3. Tropical Moist Deciduous, 4. Tropical Dry Deciduous, and 5. Tropical Thorn Forests. The forests of Karnataka are valuable due to their several economically important species such as sandalwood, rosewood, teak, white cedar forests, etc. The state is also rich in biological diversity with its Western Ghats as one of the world's biodiversity hot spots. It has 20 wildlife sanctuaries covering an area of about 3,931 sq. km, and 5 national parks with an area of 2,472 sq.km., inhabited with rich wildlife and indigenous tribal population. At the same time the state's forests are subjected to heavy biotic pressures, and the sustainable management of forests has become a challenging task. In fact, from 1978 onwards nearly 96,744 ha of forest area have been encroached upon by more than 116,822 families indicating nearly 2 per cent of the total households in the state. An area of 10,492 ha has been encroached between 1998 and 2002 by 15,791 families. And the area released for various developmental activities accounts for 34,138 ha (0.9 per cent of forest area) from 1980 to 2002 (Kushalapa, 2003).

3.2.1 Extent of Forests as per Forest Assessment Report (FAR)

It can be seen from Table 3.2 that as per legal classification (recorded forests) the total forest area remains same between 1990-91 and 1999. But there is a slight

TABLE 3.2

Extent of Forests in Karnataka as per FAR (Million ha)

	1990-91	*1999*
Cultivated Area (Net Sown Area and Current Fallow)	11.73 (61.6)	11.75 (61.3)
Land under Tree Crops and Groves	0.32 (1.7)	0.32 (1.7)
Forest Area as per Legal Classification:		
(i) Reserved Forests	2.86 (14.9)	2.86 (14.9)
(ii) Protected Forests	0.39 (2.2)	0.39 (2.2)
(iii) Others	0.61 (3.2)	0.61 (3.2)
Total (i) + (ii) + (iii)	3.86 (20.1)	3.86 (20.1)
	1991 Assessment	1999 Assessment
Forest Area as per Assessment by Forest Survey of India based on Satellite Imagery		
(i) Dense Forests (Crown Density 40 per cent and above)	2.49 (13.1)	2.48 (12.9)
(ii) Open Forests (Crown Density from 10 to less than 40 per cent)	0.73 (3.8)	0.76 (4.0)
(iii) Mangrove Forests	Nil	Nil
Total Forest Area (i)+(ii)+(iii)	3.22 (16.9)	3.24 (16.9)
Scrub Area (Less than 10 per cent Crown Density)	0.46 (2.4)	0.45 (2.3)
Other Uncultivated Lands (excluding Barren Lands and Lands under Non-agricultural Use)		
(i) Permanent Pastures and Other Grazing Lands	1.10 (5.8)	1.02 (5.3)
(ii) Cultivable Waste	0.45 (2.4)	0.44 (2.3)
(iii) Fallow Other than Current Fallow	0.40 (2.1)	0.40 (2.1)
Total (i)+(ii)+(iii)	1.95 (10.3)	1.86 (9.7)

Note: Figures in parentheses are percentages to total geographical area.

Source: Forest Assessment Reports, Ministry of Environment and Forests, Government of India, Dehradun.

change in forest cover during the same period as per the Forest Assessment Reports. The interesting point is that area under dense forests has declined, whereas area under open forests slightly increased during the same period. This may give a picture of forest degradation taking place during this period (Table 3.2). The protection, regeneration and afforestation of the available 1.86 million hectares (around 10 per cent of total geographical area) of uncultivated lands has good potential, and needs attention.

3.2.2 Contribution to Economy

Forests in Karnataka occupy an important place in the State's economy, and play an important role in the farming and livelihood systems of rural households. Forests are also important for the state to maintain the ecological balance and biodiversity conservation. Forestry and logging sector's contribution to gross state domestic product (GSDP) at current prices, was Rs. 914 crores (2.2 per cent of total GSDP) during 1993-94, which increased to Rs. 1942 crores (1.5 per cent of total GSDP) during 2003-04 (Table 3.3). In absolute terms though it has increased, its share in GSDP is declining. The state's total annual consumption of fuel wood is estimated at 4.2 million tonnes during 2001, and the projected estimate for 2006 is around 4.6 million tonnes. The average annual per capita consumption of fuel wood in forest areas has been estimated at 406 kilogrammes, and availability of fuel wood has been estimated at 16.7 lakh cubic metre per annum.

TABLE 3.3

Contribution of Forestry and Logging to Gross State Domestic Product at Factor Costs

(Rs. in Crores)

Year	*At Current Prices*	*At Constant (1993-94) Prices*
1993-94	914 (2.2)	914 (2.2)
2003-04 QE	1942 (1.5)	1084 (1.3)

Note: Figures in parentheses are percentages to Total (Gross) State Domestic Product.
QE: Quick Estimates.

Source: State Domestic Product- Karnataka 1993-94 to 2000-2001, Directorate of Economics and Statistics, Government of Karnataka, Bangalore.

3.2.3 Forestry in Karnataka

Acknowledging the role of forest as biodiversity reserves, required for ecological balance, efforts are being made to reduce the biotic pressure on forests. At the same time, the livelihoods of many families depending on forests needs to be safeguarded. And thus it is inevitable to have a comprehensive policy that can act as a balancing force. In this direction, Karnataka has adopted, a policy and following the guidelines of the National Forest Policy 1998, the Government of Karnataka issued an order during 1993 in this regard, and forestry programmes are since being implemented under the new institutional framework of Joint Forest Planning and Management (JFPM).

For many years, the state or its functionary, the Forest Department exercised its powers and controlled the use and management of forests. Other common property resources (CPRs) both under the control of Revenue Department and Forest Department are largely found in the form of open access resources. Of late, realising the gravity of the problem of degradation and decline of these resources, the Forest Department is working towards establishing appropriate institutions and institutional arrangements at the grassroots level through participatory processes, for management and use of these resources jointly by the state (Forest Department) and local communities. In this direction, social forestry programme was initiated in the early 1980s, and Joint Forest Planning and Management (JFPM) is being implemented since the 1990s. It is aimed at promoting grassroots level decision making bodies for sustainable use and management of forests. New institutions and institutional arrangements at the grassroots level in the form of village forest committees (VFCs) are being formed.

3.2.4 Development Programmes and People Participation

The Forest Department of Karnataka implemented several projects to conserve, develop, regenerate and for the sustainable use and management of Karnataka's forests since 1980s. The major projects implemented in this direction are the Karnataka Social Forestry Project (KSFP) supported by the World Bank and Overseas Development Administration (ODA) of the United Kingdom and the Karnataka Western Ghats Forestry and Environmental Project (KWGFEP) funded by the ODA. After the successful implementation of these two major projects, the Forest Department of Karnataka has launched one more ambitious afforestation project for the Eastern Plains of Karnataka covering the period, 1996-97 to 2001-02, with the total project cost of Rs. 598.28 crores. The Eastern Karnataka Afforestation Project (EKAP) is funded by the Japan Bank for International Cooperation (JBIC). The Forest Department is implementing EKAP in 23 districts of the state. Under this project the target was to conserve, regenerate and develop around 4.975 lakh hectares, 3 lakh hectares in private lands, and the remaining uncultivated lands, which include reserve forests, common lands, tank beds, foreshores and other public lands. All these are to be achieved with the help of people's participation and involvement in project activities through JFPM. This will be done also by meeting the biomass requirements of the local communities. So far, more than 3000 village forest committees (VFCs) have been formed. The Eastern Plains are in semi-arid areas and face the risk of degradation unless protected by carefully planned afforestation and land use. The crucial aspect of EKAP's implementation is to see that the local people are involved more effectively in afforestation programmes, thereby their livelihoods could be improved and the forests are maintained in sustainable ways.

a) **State Sector Plan Scheme:** Beneficiary oriented programmes under the special component and tribal subplan with components like creation of social security plantations, supply of bamboo and canes, creation of bamboo plantations.

b) **Vanavikasa Yojana:** Objective of the scheme is to distribute five crore seedlings over a period of three years starting from 2001-02.

c) **Central Plan Schemes:** Under Area Oriented Fund and Fodder Project, 7024 ha of plantation is being maintained. Under the schemes like Area Oriented Fuelwood and Fodder Project (AOFF) and conservation and Management of Mangroves on usufruct sharing basis, 2139.5 hectares of plantations have been raised.

d) **Eco-development Project:** The India Eco-development Project is being implemented with assistance from International Development Agency (IDA) and Global Environmental Facility (GEF), with total project cost of Rs. 39.493 crores, from 1997-98 to 2001-02. During 2002-03, Rs. 500 lakhs have been earmarked for Improved Protected Area Management, Village Eco-development Programme, Impact Monitoring Research and Information Technology.

Key Constraints: Some of the key constraints are related to a) problems related to conservation and scientific working, b) biotic pressure—fuel wood, fodder, grazing, c) encroachments and diversion of forest lands, d) forest fires, e) wide range of conflicts, and f) ecological balance-fragile to be resilient—adverse impacts (environmental, economic, and social). It is required to arrest forest decline and degradation, restore the forest quality and to stabilise the management and use by,

- Limiting consumption level—sustainable level. Resource consumption should be less than resource regeneration.
- Protecting and enhancing forest area.
- Extend forest cover—both on public and private lands.
- Alternative sources to bridge the gap between demand and supply of forest products.

Some of the major problems faced by the State Forest Department are:

- **Financial resource crunch**: By and large sufficient fund is not available for silviculture, afforestation and for protection, other than the funds for externally aided specific projects.
- **Staff**: Most of the field staff have become old and weak, and there is no provision to recruit new and young field staff. The staffing pattern at present is 'V' shaped, i.e. more staff at the top and very few at the bottom. It is suggested that the staffing pattern should be like a pyramid, wherein top is narrow and sharp, and the bottom is wide.

3.2.5 Some Issues and Opportunities

a) **Efficiency:** The village forest committee (VFC) members expect the Forest Department to replant the harvested forest areas and hand them over to them after maturity. There is no plan or thinking among VFC members to invest a part of the village development fund (VDF) on afforestation. The only tangible benefit from the plantation to the locals was some fuel wood. A few members including chairmen prefer fruit yielding trees like tamarind to be planted for tangible benefits. In many villages, there is no common and collective understanding among the villagers. There is no clear awareness and understanding among many villagers about the role and functions of VFCs. In many cases, the village *Panchayat* (VP) members are manipulating the VFC fund, and VDF is being used for VP work, i.e. fund diversion from VFC to VP. Since VFC is at the village level and VP for a group of villages, there is no coordination between the two. There is confusion among people as to which organisation they belong to. Also, some of the villagers are members of both VFC and VP, and they come across with two different perceptions. It is said that the same person has to sit in one meeting (of VP), which is political with different approach and attitude, and also he has to attend another meeting (of VFC) with a different approach and attitude. Even though it is stated that both are for the development of the village, one can find clash of interests between the two.

The problem is also with the perspectives among people about VFC and VP. VFC is being equated with VP in terms of its organisation, structure, power and finance. There is hardly any effective existence of *Gram Sabhas* in many villages, VP and VFC work on their own and hardly discuss their plans, programmes and actions at the village level.

b) **Equity:** Forests and other uncultivated lands (UCLs) such as pastures, C and D lands and other barren public lands, as common property resources (CPRs), are important to maintain and ensure livelihood and farming systems of rural communities, as also to maintain the ecological balance. In fact, empirical research shows that due to bad management of these resources, ecology and environment as well as the livelihoods of many people is being affected to a considerable extent. In particular, the poor are the worst affected lot through the processes of wrong decision making and bad management options (Pasha, 1992). Further, as in the past, most of the villages in Karnataka hardly have forests or CPRs of their own, and depend for their biomass requirements on government forests and other open access resources. As far as JFPM plantations are concerned, by and large the common man is getting very little except some fuel wood from these resources. There is no voice of the common man in decision making. For example, the chairman of VFC, in many cases an elite, uses his people and power in decision making, which is in his own interest. He himself operates the beneficiaries' share of money kept in a bank. JFPM plantation and VFC have become private property of a few, instead of being a CPR.

c) **Sustainability:** Broadly, sustainability is in terms of sustainable forests management, and optimising benefits. In many villages, there is no coordination and benefit sharing among all the members. Though some villagers are members of both VP and VFC, they hardly take a collective and holistic approach for the village. It is perceived that the VP is for the village and VFC is for and of the Forest Department. It is also observed that most of the VFC members would like to utilise the VDF of VFC for VP activities. It is perceived and argued that the developmental activities of the village through VP are more important than the forestry programmes. The funds available for VP are inadequate, and hence the funds of VDF of VFC should also be utilised for VP activities, which may include items like *choultry* (wedding hall) for the village, and a common building for the people to rest!

d) **Institutional:** i) *Gram Sabhas* (GS), Village *Panchayat*, VFCs and self-help groups (SHGs) which work in different directions, without coordination need to become effective and efficient, ii) lack of appropriate and clear property rights, and iii) lack of effective benefit sharing mechanisms.

e) **Non-timber Forest Produce (NTFP)**

- NTFP: Efficiency in collection and equity in distribution of NTFP are important for sustainable management of forests. In addition to rural livelihoods, efficiency in NTFP collection is also compatible with conservation of biodiversity, carbon sequestration and other environmental functions.
- Good research (data) on NTFP is required.
- NTFPs are facing extinction due to neglect, or threatened with extinction due to over and unscientific exploitation.
- In many cases NTFPs are collected as CPRs. So regulations in their collection are required. And the locals should have a stake i.e. clear property rights and tenure. There is no clarity on property rights or ownership of NTFPs.
- NTFPs should be operated through VFCs.

f) **Governance/Organisation**: Forestry in Karnataka is passing through a tough path. It is not just silviculture and conservation which are important. Equally important are the sustainability of forest use and management depend on favourable social, economic, ecological, political and institutional conditions. It is not that forests should be managed for revenue, not only for rural livelihoods (that forests as a source of poverty reduction), not also for purely ecological reasons without the social element in it, and not only for biodiversity. Forests have to be managed taking into account all of their multiple functions. Multiple functions relate to forestry economics, economics of forests, conservation of biodiversity, ecological functions and for livelihood security.

Some Issues

- GS should be powerful, and should work with VFC. All the members of the village hamlet should be members of GS, whereby they will become general body members of VFC enabling both to work together.
- Many villages/hamlets have no forests, and some do not even have CPRs. Therefore, only those villages/hamlets, which are close to forests or CPRs, need to be involved. Other villages without CPRs/forests should be involved in roadside plantations, tank foreshores, institutional plantations (schools, etc.), and benefit could be shared. Even with this it may not be possible to bring all the villages/hamlets into forestry programmes. But there is hope. Under the new programme, Forest Development Agencies (FDAs) are formed at the division level, and FDA can plan activities in such a way that most of the locals are involved.
- Registration of VFC under Societies Act is difficult owing to legal problems.
- Auditing of VFC or FDA will be a problem—VFC not to register under the Society's Act due to auditing.
- Inconsistency between guidelines under NFAP and the work order—a serious problem. For example, in Tamil Nadu as per the work order, VFC fund should be operated single handedly by the forester/RFO, whereas in Andhra Pradesh it is to be jointly operated by the forest official (forester/RFO) and the VFC (VSS) chairman. And the guidelines are common that it should be operated jointly. Forest officials of Karnataka Government in general suggest that account and power to draw money should lie with the forester/RFO, and not to be operated jointly.
- Preparation of micro plans—top down. Everything is fixed by top i.e. guidelines. For example plantation models, number of seedlings to be planted, etc.

In order to ensure efficient and effective protection, management and use of forests and forest resources within the broad framework of decentralised institutions, the following points could be useful:

- To have accurate village wise data on forests and other common property resources (CPRs).
- JFPM plantations and other CPRs should be with *Gram Sabha* and village forest committees (VFCs).
- Reserved and protected forests, which are important for biodiversity and ecological importance, could be with the Forest Department, but VFC/GS members should also be involved in the management through employment and benefit sharing.
- Clarity of tenure on trees, minor forest products, CPRs and forests; and GS and VFC members should be well versed with it.
- Information centres at the village level.
- VFC and GS should be unit of local organisation with effective people's participation.
- Creating awareness about forest and forestry programmes.

It is also important that role, responsibilities, and duties of GS along with VFC, i.e., in planning, decision making, and implementation of forestry programmes and schemes should be mentioned clearly. Meetings should be conducted at least four times a year, and issues related to forest protection, and use and management of minor forest products, etc. should be discussed.

3.3 Water Resources in Karnataka

3.3.1 The Issues

Water has become an extremely 'scarce commodity' in Karnataka state. The scarcity phenomenon is reflected in terms of 'depletion' and 'degradation' of water resources that the state is endowed with. The seriousness of the scarcity issue and the urgent need for addressing this issue at the state level have also been emphasised in the Karnataka Water Policy, 2002. It should be noted that despite several measures to deal with this issue at the state level, it poses serious threat to both present and future development of the state. This is because, present scarcity phenomenon is caused mainly by 'pull' and 'push factors'. The major 'pull factor' is, rapidly increasing competition among agriculture, domestic and industry sectors for the limited amount of 'utilisable' water resources available in the state. The nature of the competition for the 'quantity' of water is highly intensified when the negative externality caused by deterioration in the 'quality of water' is brought into the picture. The quality related issue makes the problem more acute in the sense that even if there is adequate amount of water available for different uses, a slight deterioration in the quality will make the entire quantity unfit for particular use. The deterioration in the water quality is caused by point (such as, industrial effluents) and non-point source pollution (such as agricultural run-off, urban sewage, etc.). On the other hand, the 'push factors' are also contributing to the severity of the water scarcity problem in the state. The push factors are: failure of rainfall, catchment degradation, and deterioration of the traditional sources like tanks, growth of invasive species that evapotranspire large quantity of water, etc. These factors made the water as a 'critical success factor' in the state, whose availability/non-availability has its own impact on the economic, social and political variables in the state.

One of the emerging issues in the state is the 'increased economic cost' in terms of 'damage cost' and 'environmental expenditures' (also, called 'defensive expenditures') that rapidly and negatively affect the sustainable development of the state. For example, groundwater depletion leads to additional expenditures on pumping cost, rainwater harvesting measures, measures to augment alternative sources of water supply, etc. In the case of water pollution, costs such as health cost, damage to land quality, and the resulting reduction in agricultural productivity, damage to valuable biodiversity, etc., increase enormously the volume of the total damage cost in the state. All these environmental related costs are embedded somewhere in the system and so far no serious attempt has been made to estimate the actual volume of the environmental damage cost in the state—thanks to non-availability of information and the existing weak institutions. At the political level, the scarcity issue leads to severe conflicts among different kinds of water users, sometimes even leading to suicide by particular type of stakeholders, like farmers. Therefore, enhancing the sustainable development of the state and resolving the social conflicts arising out of water related issues be mainly on how effectively the depletion and degradation issues are dealt with appropriately in the state.

Understanding the above issues, which are critical for water resource planning and management in the state in coming years, has larger implications on the policy initiatives to be carried out in order to achieve efficient water management. For example, the institutional arrangements for popularising the usage of water saving technologies in the agricultural sector such as sprinkler and drip irrigation systems depend how scarcity of water plays a major role in mediating this linkage between water and regional economic development. In high water scarce areas, regulations with appropriate incentives and disincentives should be in place so that over exploitation of groundwater and the associated quality related issues could be managed within the economically feasible limits. With the given level of information on water resources and the related issues on sectoral developments, we are constrained to formulate appropriate policies with incentives and disincentives to address the economic consequences of water resource management at regional level.

3.3.2 Status of Water Resources in Karnataka

In the following section, we would discuss the issues in the water sector in relation to both quantity and quality.

Issues Related to Quantity: The average annual rainfall received by the state is 1138 mm which suggests that the availability of water through precipitation is adequate. However, the level of average rainfall differs among different regions leading to unequal distribution of water availability. For example, in the eastern part of the state, the average annual rainfall is only 569 mm while that of the western part is 4092 mm. In other words, the west-flowing rivers of the state receive relatively higher amount of rainfall while the east flowing rivers receiving relatively lower amount. Therefore, there exists a distributional discrepancy in relation to water availability in different regions of the state. Even within the 'water abundant' regions, non-availability of water for economic use poses serious problem. For example, it is estimated that around 80 per cent of the water resources in the west-flowing rivers is not utilisable for any economic use because of difficulties in constructing storage reservoirs.

The estimates on total availability of water resources in all the seven river basins in the state, is 7663 TMC and the net water resources at 3418 TMC per year (at 50 per cent dependability). Approximately 58 per cent of the water resources is found in the west-flowing rivers where, a larger percentage of water could not be harnessed for any effective use. Altogether, it is estimated that in the state, only 1695 TMC of surface water could be 'economically utilisable' for irrigation purpose. In the case of groundwater, it has been estimated that 485 TMC of groundwater is available in the state. However, the distribution of groundwater and its exploitation are not uniform throughout the state. A substantial amount of groundwater is found in the coastal areas, which cannot be effectively utilised. The situation with the status of groundwater use is also not satisfactory. For example, the Department of Mining and Geology has identified 56 watersheds (out of 380 in the state) in the state as 'overexploited' watersheds where the rate of exploitation of groundwater is found to be greater than the rate of recharge. One more important aspect is that the estimates of surface and groundwater resources were based on the crude methodology and were unreliable since information about various parameters to be included in the methodology such as evapotranspiration, evaporation, deep percolation, etc. is not readily available. However, sources at Water Resources Department of the state reveal that the Hydrology Project Stage–1 has taken care of these methodological issues and therefore, these kinds of information should be utilised for making water resource planning in the state in coming years. All these suggest that the problem of water scarcity in the state is much more severe than what is being projected at present.

Sectoral Utilisation: It may be noted that data on sectoral utilisation of water in actual terms for the state as a whole is not readily available. However, projections made by the Water and Land Management Institute, Dharwad in 1998 reveal that the percentage of water utilised in the agriculture sector decreases (but in absolute terms, increases) during the next 20 years while that of the 'other uses' would increase (Table 3.4). However, how to augment the additional amount of water required (i.e. around 520 TMC) in 2025 is a major issue challenging the organisations dealing with the water sector in the state.

A State Environment Report prepared recently by Centre for Multi-disciplinary Research, Dharwad which has reported sectoral water utilisation pattern in some of the major river basins of the state such as Krishna, Cauvery and west-flowing rivers, reveals unequal utilisation of water in different sectors. For example, in rivers like Krishna and Cauvery, around 94 per cent of the water available is utilised for irrigation purpose, whereas in the case of west-flowing rivers irrigation use constitutes only around 10 per cent. In the case of household water use, the percentage of water utilised for this purpose ranges from 0.86 (in west-flowing rivers) to 4.24 per cent (in Cauvery basin). Even in the case of sectoral utilisation, there exists a discrepancy across different river basins in the state. This reason for this discrepancy can not be answered easily because it requires further information such as the proportion of demand from various sectors and the technical difficulties in developing water resources for different uses. But some of the initiatives of the state government such as the study of the topography of the areas in the western region of the state, developing infrastructure profile for industrial locations, etc. should provide further strength to address the discrepancy.

TABLE 3.4

Projections for Sectoral Water Demand in Karnataka (in TMC)

Sectors	*Years*	
	2000	*2025*
Household Sector (or Drinking Purpose)	58.15 (4.4)	91.62 (4.95)
Agriculture Sector	1110.06 (84.0)	1356.00 (73.33)
Industrial Sector	47.57 (3.6)	125.10 (6.76)
Hydro/Thermal Power	52.86 (4.00)	65.19 (3.52)
Others	52.86 (4.00)	211.44 (11.43)
Total	**1321.44 (100.00)**	**1850.10 (100.00)**

Note: Figures in parentheses are proportion to total.
Source: Water and Land Management Institute (1998), Dharwad.

As per the government's priority for water allocation is concerned, the State Water Policy, 2002 has identified various priority areas, in line with the National Water Policy, 2002. State Water Policy 2002 gives topmost priority to drinking water, followed by irrigation, hydropower, aquaculture, and so on, in terms of allocation of water. It may be noted that even though the priorities have been identified broadly at the macro level, there exists a need for addressing the allocation issues at the micro level too between agriculture and other sectors. As we have already discussed, in some of the river basins more than 90 per cent of the water available is utilised in the agricultural sector, which is in fact considered as 'economically inefficient'. This has been supported by some studies elsewhere in the past which found that efficiency in the agriculture sector could be improved greatly whereby a substantial amount of water used in the agricultural sector could be diverted to other high value uses without affecting the agricultural productivity. Therefore, the allocation decisions should not be based merely on arbitrary rankings but more on the efficiency and economic values.

Issues Related to Quality: The assessment of water resources in the state at present ignores the interrelationship between the quantity and quality aspects of water resources. More precisely, separate assessments are made for these two aspects, by separate agencies in the state. The quality related issue has emerged as a serious problem in the state. For example, a comprehensive sample survey conducted by the Rural Development Engineering Department (RDED) during 1999 and 2001 all over the state reveals that out of all the 2 lakh sample rural habitations, 20,929 habitations experienced water quality problems caused by excess fluoride, excess iron, excess nitrate and brackishness (GoK, 2002a). Since all these contaminated sources of water supply are still being used by households due to non-availability of alternative sources, the hidden economic cost in terms of health hazards would be enormous in the state.

The quality related issues are caused by many different factors, which warrant for identification and appropriate action for control. One of the major problems is urban sewage resulting from inefficient utilisation of water in urban areas. Studies in the past have found out that around 85 per cent of the water used in the household sector can turnout as wastewater that ultimately joins the streams and rivers, which are sources for water supply in the downstream areas. The existing wastewater related problems are due to two major factors: (a) the urban sewage falls under 'non-point source pollution' category and therefore, collection and treatment of sewage may not be technically feasible; and (b) at present, the sewage treatment is viewed as a 'costly' affair. The fallacy here is that the planners always look at the direct costs of treating sewage rather than looking holistically at the 'social cost' imposed by the untreated sewage on the society. Even though the exact volume of wastewater generated in all the urban and semi-urban areas of Karnataka is not known, sewage is a major issue in almost all these areas in the state (Table 3.5).

TABLE 3.5

Quantum of Wastewater Generated by Some of the Towns and Cities in Karnataka

(in Terms of M^3 Litres Per Day)

Town/City	*Wastewater Generated*
Gokak	2500
Bagalkot	3100
Soundatti	2400
Khanapur	425
Rabakavi	2325
Yadgir	855
Afzalpur	855
Jewargi	410
Shahabab	2992
Hospet	4800
Siraguppa	240
Kampli	544
Gangavati	3648
Shringeri	472
T. Narasipur	316
Kanakapur	1744
Sakaleshpur	1008
Kushalanagar	450
Dandeli	80000
Bantwala	1200
Payaswini	1440

Source: CMDR (2003), Dharwad.

The problem caused by urban sewage is aggravated if we take into account the run-off from rural areas caused especially by open-air defecation. For the state as a whole, the percentage of households having toilet facilities amounts to only 6.85 per cent as per 1991 estimates. The implication is that around 93 per cent of the households in rural areas adopt open-air defecation, which has larger implications on the environmental costs.

It is being held that the high ratio of wastewater to the total water used could be attributed to the inefficient use of water in general. But a close look at the issue reveals that the inefficient use is the major outcome of the disparity between what the households actually want from the water supply authorities and what the authorities actually want to deliver. In other words, some loopholes in the policy formulation related to water supply leads to inefficient use of water in the household sector. For instance, inappropriate pricing of water, excess quantity of water supplied to households (because of improper assessment of current level of per capita availability of water at the household level), lack of information about households' preferences regarding additional amount of water, willingness to pay for water, and so on can be attributed to the present level of inefficiency in water use.

Another non-point source pollution whose negative impact on land quality and public health is very severe but whose impact has not been fully understood and estimated in economic terms is the agricultural run-off. Even though the amount of fertiliser and pesticides used may not be excess (compared to total cultivable areas), the way in which the fertiliser and pesticides is used may be the cause for the present problem. Apart from urban sewage and agricultural run-off, pollution from small industries also affects the water quality drastically. In addition, the state experiences water quality problem related to alkalinity, salinity, water-logging, etc. which pose major threat to the agricultural sustainability in the state. Therefore, the water quality related issues in the state assume paramount importance in the overall sustainable development of the state.

Institutional Set-up: For development and conservation of water resources, recently the state has revamped the institutional structure. Box 3.1 describes organisational structure of institutions dealing with issues related to water sector in the state.

It should be noted that even though there exists a strong organisational structure to deal with the issues related to water resources, the problems seem to continue and even would intensify due to various reasons that are discussed later.

Policy and Conservation Measures: The state government has initiated several measures to develop and manage the water resources. In the case of irrigation sector, a substantial amount of investment has been made on the irrigation projects with a view to achieve the goal of 'crop per drop'. However, the recent State Water Policy, 2002 recognised that additional amount of investment is required in distribution canals so that the water lost during distribution is adequately dealt with. Since there is no proper pricing policy on irrigation sector, the revenue from the water charges is not adequate to meet the expenses on additional investment. The State Water Policy has also identified many different policy measures in the area of development and conservation of water resources. For example, improving the tanks, developing the groundwater sources for drinking purposes, preventing degradation from agro-chemicals, industrial and domestic pollution, waterlogging and salinisation, etc. are some of the measures mentioned in the State Water Policy, 2002. Moreover, the state government is implementing watershed programmes in dry areas of the state with the view to improve the soil quality and water use. It may be noted that a total amount of Rs. 566.48 crore has been spent on development of watersheds in the state between 1984 and 2000. During this period, 22,06,208 hectares of land had been treated with improved soil and water conservation measures. Despite all these measures, the problems related to quantity and quality of water resources in the state have assumed serious proportion which will affect the sustainable development of the state in a big way.

BOX 3.1

Organisational Structure of State, District and Village Level

Name of the Organisation	*Important Tasks*
State Level Organisations	
Water Resources Development Organisation (WRDO)	Development of major and medium irrigation, collection of information related to hydrology, command area development and research and developmental activities.
Command Area Development Authority	Identification of and protection of command areas at river basins.
Department of Minor Irrigation	Identification of areas for taking up new tanks, trapping the silt and rejuvenation of tanks.
Department of Mines and Geology (Groundwater Wing)	Hydrological Survey and identification of watersheds.
Soil Survey Division	Assessing soil quality; suggestions for cropping pattern for command areas.
Watershed Department (Department of Agriculture)	Identifying watershed areas and identifying the agencies for watershed programmes.
Drought Monitoring Cell	Review of drought situation and information sharing with other line departments.
Regional Remote Sensing Centre	Generating information about the water resources, planning and modelling.
Karnataka Engineering Research Station	Developing training modules, conducting training to engineers.
Directorate of Economics and Statistics	Collection of information and dissemination.
Department of Environment, Ecology and Forests	Formulation of rules and regulations for preventing environmental pollution.
Karnataka State Pollution Control Board	Monitoring pollution from industries and other sources and ensuring implementation of pollution control.
District Level	
Zilla Panchayat	District level programmes on watershed, etc.
Urban Local Bodies	Water supply and sanitation programmes.
Village Level	
Gram Panchayats	Implementation of programmes at the local level.

Source: CMDR (2003), Dharwad.

Therefore, in the following section we would discuss some concrete policy measures that have been suggested for improving the situation, at least in future.

3.3.3 Development of Irrigation Infrastructure Sources of Irrigation

Covering a vast Malnad region with parts of Western Ghat belt, and with normal rainfall of over 1000 mm per year in the Deccan region, Karnataka state is endowed with enormous water resources. The state consists of five major river basins, namely, Krishna, Cauvery, Godavary, several west flowing rivers, and North and South Pennar. Of the total estimated catchment yield of 98,406 m.cum of rainfall water, about 48,000 m.cum of water is economically utilisable within the state. However, irrigation development in Karnataka as compared to many other states and the country as a whole is quite low. This is because, some of the perennial rivers are west-flowing and the topography is not conducive for utilising substantial amount of water available in these rivers.

Important sources of irrigation in Karnataka are canals, wells, tanks, lift irrigation, pickup and anecuts. Recent data on source-wise gross irrigated area (30.22 lakh ha) shows that 40 per cent of the irrigated area is under canal irrigation, followed by 33 per cent under groundwater (includes 21 per cent under dugwells) and 12 per cent by tanks, lift irrigation schemes and other sources together irrigate 14 per cent of the total area. Area irrigated more than once is canal irrigation (3.3 lakh ha) followed by dugwell irrigation (1.11 lakh ha) and borewell irrigation (0.99 lakh ha).

Karnataka has about 36,672 minor tanks (command area less than 2000 ha) with a total command area of around 6.9 lakh ha distributed in 27 districts, amounting to an average 19 ha of land irrigated by one tank. Ninety per cent of these tanks have a command area of less than 40 ha. The actual irrigated area is estimated to be not more than 2.4 lakh ha (35 per cent of the potential). Over the years, there has been a decrease in the net irrigated area through tanks in comparison with other sources of irrigation (Table 3.6). Around 27 per cent increase in the land under borewell/tube well irrigation explains the reduction in the tank-irrigated area in the state.

TABLE 3.6

Sources of Irrigation

Sources of Irrigation	*(Area in Thousand Ha)* 1961	1981	1994	1997
Channels (Major and Medium Irrigation)	236	547	934	918
Open Wells	133	364	487	466
Bore/Tube wells	-	-	290	367
Tanks	344	304	273	240

Source: Raju *et al.*, 2003.

Groundwater Irrigation

Currently about 30.22 lakh ha of irrigated area is under one or other forms of groundwater exploitation in the state. In most parts of the state, particularly in eastern and southern plains, groundwater depletion is taking place (up to 800 feet depth) faster than the earlier projections made by the Department of Mines and Geology. Out of the remaining potential, another 0.45 million ha metres can still be exploited at the state level. However, as many as 56 *talukas* fall in the category of 'over developed in watershed'; of these 56 *talukas*, nearly 98 per cent fall in southern Karnataka. There are two different major problems with groundwater development in Karnataka. First, according to the Department of Mines and Geology, overexploitation of groundwater has taken place in 43 *talukas* under the 'above 65 per cent' category (defined as Grey and Dark blocks). Second, there is a problem of increasing alkalinity, nitrates, fluorides and other hardness factors. Because of these factors, a large number of *talukas* falling in the category of 'White' are unfit for any groundwater exploitation.

In Karnataka state, gross groundwater recharge is estimated at around 16.18 lakh ha mts (net 13.76 lakh ha mts; it is 85 per cent of the gross recharge estimated, leaving 15 per cent for domestic, industrial, and other uses, except irrigation. Total number of wells are about 5.77 lakhs, of which borewells constitutes about 38 per cent, followed by 9 per cent dug cum borewells, 52 per cent by dug cum borewells, dugwells by 37 per cent and negligible portion by others. So, in total, a net quantity of 4.96 lakh ha mts. (36 per cent of net recharge) being utilised against the net recharge of 13.76 lakh ha mts. The remaining amount of water is available either in hard-rock areas or in areas where exploitation is difficult.

Till 1993-94, created potential under groundwater is 7.27 lakh ha as against the revised ultimate groundwater potential of 25.72 lakh ha. At national level, groundwater development is around 65 per cent, while in Karnataka it is only 29 per cent. Around 34 per cent of the area under borewells and 22 per cent under well irrigation has been irrigating more than once, contributing to the gross area of 3.90 and 5.98 lakh ha respectively (in 1993-94). The ultimate irrigation potential, from all sources has been estimated at 55 lakhs ha. Due to overexploitation of groundwater resources in many parts of the state, more then 3 lakh dugwells have dried. Shallow borewells have failed and yield in deep borewells are declining. Area irrigated by groundwater extraction structures is decreasing. Consequently, more than Rs. 2,000 crores of investment made by the individual farmers on the construction of wells, pumping equipments, pipelines, development, etc. have become non-performing assets.

Subregional Analysis

Subregions in Karnataka

Twenty-seven districts of Karnataka fall in two agro-climatic zones of the country; namely Zone-X and Zone-XII. Fourteen districts of Zone-X are clustered into three subregions, and the remaining five districts of Zone-XII are clustered into fourth subregion based on agro-climatic features such as soil type, rainfall pattern and crop pattern. Thus, Karnataka state has been divided into four subregions (SR) as shown in Table 3.7.

TABLE 3.7

Districts of Karnataka State Falling under Different Subregions

Subregions	*Districts*
SR-1	Belguam, Bellary, Bijapur, Bidar, Dharwad. Gulburga, and Raichur.
SR-2	Bangalore, Chitradurga, Kolar, and Tumkur
SR-3	Mandya, Mysore, and Hassan.
SR-4	Chickmagalur, Kodagu, Shimoga, Dakshina Kannada, and Uttara Kannada.

Soure: High Power Committee, GoK, 2002.

TABLE 3.8

Subregion-wise Net Irrigated Area (NIA) to Net Sown Area (1956-59, 1985-88 and 2000-01) in Percentages

Sub-regions	*1956-59*		*1985-88*		*2000-01*	
	NIA ('000 ha)	*Per Cent of NIA to NSA*	*NIA ('000 ha)*	*Per Cent of NIA to NSA*	*NIA ('000 ha)*	*Per Cent of NIA to NSA*
SR-1	193	3	904	14	1024	20.43
SR-2	172	10	340	16	202	19.19
SR-3	152	17	256	23	301	27.04
SR-4	242	29	280	26	391	36.33
Total	**759**	**8**	**1780**	**17**	**1918**	**24.80**

Source: High Power Committee, GoK, June 2002

It can be seen from Table 3.8 that, net area irrigated had increased from about 7.59 ha to 19.18 lakh ha over the last four decades. The table also shows that SR-1, which had only 3 per cent of its net area sown under irrigation during the first period had gone up to 20 per cent by year 2001. While SR-2 is almost doubled, net irrigated area in SR-3 has gone up from 17 per cent to 27 per cent of the total net sown area.

Source-wise Irrigation

SR-1, has recorded positive growth and topped in all cases (except in tank irrigation) compared to other subregions of the state. In case of canal irrigation, SR-1 has recorded an increase of 114 per cent, while the state has achieved 71 per cent. Except Bidar, all other districts of SR-1 have increased tremendously (27 times), owing to introduction of Upper Krishna Project, Ghataprabha and Malaprabha irrigation projects. SR-3 stood second (36 per cent) because of Hassan district followed by SR-2 (22 per cent), and Kodagu district in SR-4 recorded two and a half times increase due to Harangi and Bhadra irrigation projects.

Area under tube well irrigation has shown positive change in all SRs. SR-3 is on top (increased by 10 times) though actual area increased is not very high (11,727 ha). In SR-1 tube well area has increased in all districts (13,045 ha). In case of area under well irrigation, SR-2 has shown negative growth, while SR-3 and SR-1 have indicated an increase of 52 per cent and 64 per cent respectively. SR-4 with 78 per cent increase topped the list. But in terms of actual area increase, SR-1 is on top with 27,123 ha increase against 20,321 ha of SR-4. In other sources of irrigation, SR-1 leads with an increase of 156 per cent, whereas SR-2 and SR-3 have recorded negative (-70 per cent and -32 per cent respectively). The state has achieved 67 per cent.

Tank irrigated area has been declining in all SRs. Decline is less in SR-1 (-6 per cent), followed by SR-3 (-7 per cent). But this area has been reportedly increased in districts like Bijapur (244 per cent), Raichur (77 per cent), and Gulburga (26 per cent) of SR-1 and Kolar (30 per cent) of SR-2. In case of SR-1, net irrigated area (NIA) and gross irrigated area (GIA) have respectively recorded an increase of 123 per cent and 128 per cent against the state average of 71 per cent and 77 per cent respectively. Other SRs area in the range of 18-42 per cent (NIA) and 17-58 per cent (GIA). The districts of SR-1 have recorded higher increase for both NIA (32 to 36 per cent) and GIA (78 to 51 per cent), when compared to remaining districts of other SRs.

District Level Irrigation

In canal irrigated area, 13 districts (of the earlier 19) have recorded positive growth and 6 of them are in SR-1; these 6 districts are in the range of 0-50 per cent; 3 of the 13 districts have reported between 101 to 300 per cent positive change. In tank irrigated area, only 6 out of the 19 districts have recorded increase and some 11 districts have recorded negative between 0-50 per cent. In case of tube well irrigation, all districts (except Kodagu) have reported positive change. Out of the 19 districts, 13 have recorded positive and 6 of them with 51-100 per cent, followed by 3 districts with 26-50 per cent. However, 3 districts are on negative side, in the range of 0-25 per cent. Both NIA and GIA have increased in all districts (except in Chickmagalur with 12 per cent NIA). Across the districts 0-50 per cent increase has been shown in their NIA (10 districts) and GIA (9 districts) respectively.

Overall, a large number of districts have registered increase in irrigated area: canal (13 districts), tank (6), tube well (all except Kodagu), well (13), other sources (9), NIA (18), and GIA (19). Decrease in area is also seen in some districts: canal (6 districts), tank (13), well (6), others (9), NIA (1), and on tube wells data is not available.

3.3.4 Growth of NIA and GIA across Subregions

The future of irrigation development in Karnataka belongs to SR-1. Majority of the investments in irrigation is being made in SR-1. The investments though deferred and escalated over time (till 1998, Rs. 5,000 crores) has started to yield returns. Phenomenal growth in NIA has taken place in SR-1. The percentage change is substantially high owing to the Upper Krishna Project in Gulburga (362 per cent) and Bijapur (205 per cent) districts. On the other hand, Tungabhadra project has boosted up NIA in Raichur (154 per cent) and Bellary (74 per cent), while Ghataprabha and Malaprabha projects jacked up NIA in Belgaum district by 73 per cent. For the total NIA development, in terms of area, though canal irrigation has improved by 3.10 lakh ha, tube well irrigated area has shown a massive improvement of 25430 per cent (up by 1.29 lakh ha from mere 511 ha) and wells irrigated area contributed 64 per cent change.

Three major projects, located in northern Karnataka covering SR-1, are being developed in recent years. Major irrigation investments of the state are also being made in this subregion. Thereby, high growth in irrigated area has taken place in the districts of SR-1. While the state as a whole has gained by 71 per cent change in NIA area (1980-81 to 93-94), SR-1 has led by 123 per cent. Large investments in major irrigation projects have boosted up canal area by 114 per cent.

SR-2, a dry land zone, with entrepreneurial farmers and better rural infrastructure facilities has moved ahead with 42 per cent change in NIA and 58 per cent (highest across SRs) in GIA. Kolar district with 91 per cent change in GIA has proved that by utilising groundwater efficiently, farmers can jack up their GIA. Easy access to urban markets and better rural infrastructure facilities also influence these developments.

The SR-3 is getting stagnated or moving up slowly; its canal irrigation potential has already expanded (Hassan achieved 162 per cent, and Mysore 60 per cent) and pressure is mounting up on groundwater usage; in Mysore district, though actual number of tube wells are not many, in terms of tube well irrigated area change is significant by 31,300 per cent and well area by 92 per cent in Mysore district. SR-3 is a moderate subregion with NIA change of 29 per cent and GIA of 35 per cent.

Indeed, the poor performer is SR-4. In spite of being bestowed with natural bounties, and good rainfall, the SR could not built up structures and adequately maintain the existing structures to harvest rainwater. As a result, the SR-4 has lost in tank area by 17 per cent, gained only 9 per cent through canals. However, wells have shown promise by increasing about 78 per cent. Overall, its NIA has increased by only 18 per cent, lowest among the SRs.

In summary, together all SRs in Karnataka state have registered 71 per cent increase in NIA and 77 per cent in GIA. In this process of development, SR-1 has the highest share (change by 123 per cent and 128 per cent), followed by SR-2 (with 42 per cent and 58 per cent). Most of the districts have joined the group with a positive change; NIA in 18 and GIA in 19 districts have showed upward movement. Table 3.9 presents subregion-wise, percentage changes in NIA and GIA.

TABLE 3.9

Changes (during 1998-1999) in NIA and GIA across the Subregions in Karnataka

(in per cent)

Subregions	*NIA*	*GIA*
1	123	128
2	42	58
3	29	35
4	18	17
State	**71**	**77**

Source: Department of Water Resources, Govt. of Karnataka, 2002.

3.3.5 Financing Irrigation Development

Investment Profile

Development of irrigation has absorbed massive investments over the years. The total investment up to March 2001 on irrigation in the state was Rs. 14,267 crores comprising, Rs. 13,399 crores on major and medium irrigation and Rs. 868 crores on minor irrigation (using surface water). In terms of irrigated area, minor irrigation covered 3.88 lakh ha in the pre-plan period (i.e., before 1951), which increased to 5.12 lakh ha by 1991-92. Area under major and medium irrigation has increased from 5.99 lakh ha in the pre-plan period to 16.81 lakh ha by 1991-92; another 2.63 lakh ha was developed from 1992-93 to 1996-97.

From 1951-56 (First Five-Year Plan) to 1991-92 (Annual Plan), Rs. 431 crores have been spent in developing irrigated area under minor irrigation (surface) and between 1992-93 and 1996-97, Rs. 291 crores have been spent. For the surface water projects, until now (1951-56 to 1996-97) Rs. 7,372 crores have been spent. Out of that, major portion is for major and medium irrigation. From 1951-52 to 1991-92, the amount spent was Rs. 3,110 crores (42 per cent of the total) and the remaining 58 per cent was spent during 1992-93 to 1996-97.

During 2000-2001 an outlay of Rs. 2,754.58 crores has been allocated for major and medium irrigation projects. It is programmed to create an additional outlet potential of 76,722 ha. This includes an outlay of Rs. 1902.93 crores to be spent on UKP through Krishna Bhagya Jala Nigam Limited and Rs. 665 crores through Karnataka Neeravari Nigama Limited for Karnataka Neeravari Nigam Limited projects (Table 3.10).

TABLE 3.10

Financial and Physical Achievements on Major and Medium Irrigation

Sl.No	*Sector*	*Allocation (Rs. in Crores)*	*2000-2001 Programme* Physical Programme (in ha)	*Investment per ha (in Rs.)*
	Capital Outlay			
I	Major & Medium			
	a) Plan projects	2754.58	177969	15477
	b) Projects pending approval	300.00	35223	8517
	Total	3054.58	213192	14328
II	Survey & Investigation etc.	7.80		
	Total (I &II)	**3062.38**	**213,192**	

Source: Department of Water Resources, Government of Karnataka, 2002.

The loss of annual returns from irrigation investment has increased from Rs. 0.61 crores in 1956-57 to Rs. 94.56 crores in 1986-87. In case of investment in major and medium irrigation, the annual loss has increased from Rs. 0.31 crores to Rs. 69.46 crores, whereas the annual loss in the case of minor irrigation has risen from Rs. 0.30 crores to Rs. 25.10 crores, for the same period. Further, for major, medium and minor irrigation between 1956-57 and 1986-87, it was observed that a cumulative loss of Rs 511.38 crores from major and medium irrigation projects, Rs. 257.29 crores from minor irrigation (surface) projects has occurred, which is equivalent to almost 90 per cent of total cost invested on the irrigation projects. At the disaggregated level, this was around 87 per cent of major and medium irrigation and around 96 per cent in case of minor surface irrigation.

It may be noted (Appendix A-3.3) that the actual expenditure incurred, which is estimated in terms of per hectare value (i.e. column 9), stands at 1.5 lakhs per hectare in the Cauvery Basin followed by Krishna Basin, with 1.3 lakhs. In the case of Godavari and other north flowing river basins, the figure for actual per hectare investment provides a sordid picture. Future investment requirements for developing the irrigated areas in each basin have been calculated in terms of the actual per hectare investment made in the past. Around Rs. 14,118 crores is required for developing an area of 11.12 lakh ha of land in all the river basins. However, this figure is only a conservative estimate and the actual cost due to escalations, etc. may go many times greater than this. A realistic estimate based on the detailed assessment is required for allocating financial resources for irrigation developments in the state in future.

Water Rates

Water rates, were raised by about 2.5 per cent over that of the 1985 rates (Table 3.11). Despite the revision, there is an estimated shortfall in operation and maintenance requirement varying from Rs. 500 to 600 per ha to achieve full cost recovery. Collection of water charges is as low as 30 per cent (though reported at 60 per cent). In the case of minor irrigation tanks, the water rates are only a fraction of those levied for major projects (one-half for the first one-third length of the main canal and one-fourth for the remaining two-thirds). Low cost recovery contributes to the poor maintenance and operation of the irrigation systems, which, in turn, makes it even more difficult to collect the water charges currently levied.

TABLE 3.11

Water Fee on Crop-Area Basis

Crops	*Earlier Rates (Revised in July 1985)*		*Revised Rates (Effective from July 2001)*	
	Rs./ha	*Rs./Acre*	*Rs./ha*	*Rs./Acre*
Sugarcane	555.75	225*	988.45	400
Paddy	86.45	35**	247.10	100
Cotton	98.80	40	148.25	60
Horticultural Crops	98.80	40	148.25	60
Wheat	54.34	22	148.25	60
Groundnut	59.28	24	148.25	60
Sunflower	-	-	148.25	60
Jowar, Maize, *Bajra*, *Ragi* and Semi-dry Crops	49.40	20	86.50	35
Pulses	37.05	15	86.50	35
Tobacco	61.75	25	86.50	35
Fodder Crops	19.76	8	37.05	15
Others	-	-	86.50	35

Note: * For 12-18 months crop. For less than 12 months crop, Rs. 150.

** For the 1st crop. For the 2nd crop onwards Rs. 40.

Source: Department of Minor Irrigation, Bangalore, 2001.

Irrigation Department prescribes the norms which are revised once in five years for land holdings under the tanks and pickups with no assured supply of water. On the other side, normal water rates are levied for the head reaches of the tank command comprising two-thirds of the total land and reduced water rates are applied for the rest of the area in lower reaches. The agricultural lands coming under the command area of the pickup and percolation tanks shall be treated as dry lands. For unauthorised use of water and violation of cropping pattern, the rates are 15 and 10 times more.

3.3.6 Monitoring and Implementation Issues

Some of the major problems in the irrigation sector in the state are:

1. Delay in executing irrigation projects; in turn, raising project costs, postponing in realising the benefits.
2. Poor quality structures; particularly canal distribution network structures; in some places, both in old and new projects, major canals breaches; this has led to additional expenses, and crop loss; local newspapers regularly feature the short comings and problems in the irrigation project areas.
3. Inadequate maintenance and repairs; thereby, the whole system and its users, continuously face water shortages, both in time and quantity.
4. The Irrigation Department is dominated by single discipline; skill upgradation and training is not given adequate importance; improved management of irrigation systems necessitates multi-disciplinary personnel.
5. Owing to persisting inadequacies in the irrigation sector, as the National Water Policy, 1987, has suggested and many research and action research studies have recommended, management transfer through participatory irrigation management at different levels of the system. This will enhance, as the studies found, water efficiency, improved revenue collections to the state, reduced expenditure on operation and maintenance, and improved management of the irrigation systems. So, there is a strong need to bring in users role in planning, execution, system rehabilitation, operation, and maintenance, water distribution, fee collection, and conflict resolution.
6. To facilitate the above process, the state needs to suitably modify its irrigation acts and administrative rules. There is a need to rethink in the existing conditions, what kind of legal framework is required.
7. The state has to seriously think and act to bring out suitable guidelines and followed by administrative rules to take care of the emerging conflicting demands by the three different sectors—domestic, industrial, and agricultural. Currently, the conflicting demands are met mostly though *ad hoc* measures. In the process, the agricultural sector is getting deprived.
8. Currently the concerned department is known as the irrigation department (It has been renamed as Water Resources Development Organisation). It has to broaden its purview, both in its personnel skill and coverage, to restructure its focus to whole water resources, rather than mere irrigation. The Department has to reorganise and downsize some wings and create new wings, to meet the emerging demands of the sector for the next 20 years. Probably, it can follow '2020 Vision' as envisaged by the International Food Policy Research Institute and supported by the World Bank. Alternatively, the state can formulate its own long-term vision.
9. Water Resources Department should focus more on resource consolidation, effective harvesting of

its various sources of water, its sustainable development and efficient usage, design rule making and rule enforcement mechanisms, guidelines for effective implementation of its plans and programmes, wholeheartedly support users' participation in its activities, open up the sector for private participation, bring in and maintain the transparency and accountability in the Department's activities.

10. The current allocation levels for operation and maintenance are inadequate: Up to 60 per cent is spent on establishment and related costs, thereby, actual work component gets lower than required; this has severely affected maintenance and repairs of distribution structures. As a result, canals carrying capacity has reduced, in some cases up to 50 per cent.

11. In the present context, the field offices are not in a position to guarantee the supply quantity and timeliness. This is true both at main system and outlet level. Owing to this, users are not keen to participate in the system management and on the other hand, field officials are not in a position to collect water fees.

12. To execute all of the above, the state has to set a time bound action plan.

3.3.7 *Critical Issues*

a) Owing to expansion of irrigation with its emphasis on new construction, the performance of irrigation and the sector's broader management needs have been neglected. The development impact of irrigation is much less than its potential and deficiencies in implementation have accumulated over time. The sector is now in crisis. Four issues are of particular concern: productivity, sustainability, investment focus and financial discipline, and sector management.

b) The productivity of irrigation is low and well below potential. On the majority of surface irrigation schemes, suboptimal distribution of water (timing, reliability, and spatial distribution) result in low yields and cropping intensity and reduced opportunities for diversifying agriculture. Deficiencies in agricultural extension, limited research on irrigation technology, and insufficient piloting of innovations compound the situation. Poor design and project preparation of many surface irrigation schemes and deteriorating infrastructure are also having significant deleterious effect.

c) The sustainability of Karnataka's irrigation investment is in serious question, mainly due to a marked decline in maintenance of infrastructure and a similar decline in the quality of construction over the past three decades. On the other hand, over exploitation of groundwater in some parts has been a major phenomenon. Rehabilitation requirements are already large and threaten to dominate expenditure unless maintenance and construction are improved. Additionally, environmental problems are mounting, requiring substantial attention to them, drainage, and resettlement of displaced communities. Even new projects are facing growing salinity problem (e.g., UKP 14,000 ha). A void in water resource planning and coordination of usage urgently needs to be filled.

d) The investment focus and financial discipline of irrigation require rethinking and reform. Substantial reallocation of government expenditures is required to support investment for improving productivity, adequate maintenance, and completion of ongoing projects, drainage, and micro-network and groundwater investment by farmers. Sharp financial deterioration of the sector poses a serious threat. Recurrent expenditures have ballooned in the past decade, with most of the increase going to unproductive staff growth and wastage due to lax control of expenditures and works. Cost recovery has dwindled and irrigation-related subsidies, including power subsidies to pumpsets, now loom large in state government budgets. These impacts are crowding out worthwhile investment.

e) Ineffective sector management underlies most of these deficiencies. Sector institutions, notably State Irrigation Department, have undergone little change over many decades, while sectoral priorities have changed and execution has become more complex. The Department's structure, functions and approach are predominantly construction engineering; this orientation is inadequate in face of the need for a broader management culture and sharper diagnosis and response to the sector's weaknesses and opportunities. The roles of other state institutions involved with irrigation need better definition and coordination among them. The vitality and capital of non-government sources are not being captured, and significant opportunity for greater involvement of farmers and the private sector has been virtually ignored.

f) If these issues are not resolved, productivity will remain low; infrastructure will progressively deteriorate, leading to declining irrigated area or insupportable rehabilitation needs; financial imbalances will continue to widen; and most seriously, there will be little scope for maintaining the agricultural growth rate.

3.3.8 Institutional and Financial Reforms

Understanding the situation of irrigation in India requires looking from the macro to the micro level. Many policies regarding irrigation, including much of the investment in systems, originate at the national level. However, because irrigation is a state subject, it is implemented by the states, through specific irrigation projects, with the outcomes being ultimately determined at the local level.

Water control is essential for agricultural progress. Many states have ongoing investments in major canal irrigation systems, as well as the need to maintain older systems. Some states which face greater pressures to develop its water resources (like in Krishna basin), have implemented an innovative corporate structure to finance the capital cost of irrigation development. Many states have also adopted policies of 'Participatory Irrigation Management' to improve ongoing operation and maintenance.

Despite the vast amount of money that has gone into irrigation system development and operation, there has been relatively little attention to financing issues, especially of capital costs (except in few states). Official statistics underrepresent the magnitude of irrigation expenditure, by neglecting the effect of inflation, gestation lags, and pure time preference. The empirical studies suggest that it is not only physical drought, but also financial drought, that irrigation systems need to worry about.

It is also necessary to look at the question of whether the irrigated farmers are extracting large rents at the expense of the rest of society, by looking at the full picture of direct and indirect financing. This has changed over time, from direct cost recovery in the colonial period, to more indirect charges on irrigated farmers after Independence. In the context of ongoing economic liberalisation, there is a case for shifting back from indirect to direct cost recovery to improve the efficiency of irrigation system management. We need to examine a number of types of irrigation fees, including volumetric pricing, wholesaling to water users' associations, and crop-area base charges in terms of their practical feasibility, as well as the incentives they create for water conservation.

Recent institutional reforms focused to set up financially autonomous irrigation agency, like the Krishna Bhagya Jal Nigam Limited in Karnataka. Such financially autonomous agencies have also been suggested as a powerful means of restructuring agency staff incentives, to make them more client-oriented toward farmers, when the agency becomes dependent on the irrigation service charges collected. The Study (Raju, Ashok Gulati, and Ruth Meinzen-Dick, 1999) finds that the Nigam structure has allowed the state to mobilise large amounts of money from private sources, to complete the irrigation project in an accelerated manner. However, it has not had a major influence on the motivation of agency staff to work with farmers.

If farmers cannot be persuaded to pay more for the government staff to do proper operation and maintenance of the irrigation systems, participatory irrigation management reforms attempt to get farmers to take on more of the operation and maintenance tasks directly. It should be noted that trend in the capital cost of irrigation per hectare, trend in the cost of supply per hectare and its components, annual loss in the revenue and the cost of debt service on irrigation investment are some of the serious issues that need attention in coming years in the state. Across the states, various approaches have been adopted in terms of level of organisation of the users and changes in irrigation charges, and then reviews the types of legislative reforms required for participatory irrigation management policy statements to succeed in changing the management of irrigation systems. Water charges for different crops in the state *vis-à-vis* in other neighbouring states need to be carefully reviewed and appropriate reforms need to be initiated. Policy reforms in this regard cannot be carried out by the government alone—they require farmers to play an active role.

3.3.9 Economic Reforms

In Karnataka, revenue generation from the irrigation sector is not very encouraging. Out of Rs. 230 crores outstanding, actual collection was only Rs. 30 crores. Penal water fees of around Rs. 215 crores were waived during the Parliamentary Elections held in March 1996. To add to this, current water fee levels in Karnataka are quite low, ranging from Rs. 37 to Rs. 370 per ha, depending on the crop. A High Level Committee set up in 1993 to consider enhancing the water fee levels, had not come out with clear suggestions even by mid-1998. The committee headed by the current Finance Minister is also equally concerned about the political implications of any enhancement in the fee level. However, the Committee in its July 1998 meeting suggested (not yet officially announced) doubling the current water fee level, and gradually raising it by four times. These recommendations are nowhere close to the suggestions made by the Water Pricing Committee of the Planning Commission in 1992 (popularly known as Vaidyanathan Committee). The senior official in the Irrigation Department said, "If we follow the Pricing Committee's recommendations, then we have to raise the water fee levels by 20 to 30 times, which is very unlikely for any state government."

- Taking into the potentials at the major, medium and minor irrigation, and also groundwater exploitation, it has already been mentioned that about Rs. 15,000 crore will have to be earmarked for the development of irrigation sector in the state during the coming eight years. This will have to be phased out by emphasising on the minor irrigation first, development of recharging structures for groundwater potentials and completion of ongoing major and medium irrigation projects and to undertake new projects.
- Secondly, it is extremely important to recognise that it costs to supply water. With the approval of the government about formation of Water Users' Association with effect from June 2000, the water users in major, medium and minor irrigation areas are to be encouraged to form such cooperative associations charged with the responsibilities of recovering the irrigation charges collectively. This will make the use of water more and more purposeful and productive. Such associations should be encouraged to work out the cropping patterns on the basis of water availability and individual farmer's ability to pay for it. Furthermore, they can also work out a part of the user charges for investment towards groundwater recharging, construction of augmentation of borewells and canals, etc.
- Thirdly, in the area of groundwater development, particularly, in the management of artificial recharging, treatment of aquifers, etc. private agencies can be encouraged to come up, either on a cooperative basis or on a corporate sector basis. This way of approaching the problems can reduce the regional imbalances in a faster way.
- Finally, like in many programmes and schemes, one runs into some bad experience at the level of implementation, etc. It is necessary to make the necessary corrections immediately on such schemes, or abandon them without wasting any more resources and time. The lift irrigation schemes introduced in selected districts of north Karnataka are glaring examples. Almost 40 per cent of the lift irrigation schemes implemented in districts of Raichur, Gubarga, Bidar, Bellary, and Bijapur are just not working; even those that are working are providing just about 36 per cent of potential water. A sum of Rs. 17.59 crore has been invested to get irrigation benefits to just about 9,203 hectares. High Power Committee is of the opinion that whether it is irrigation, or industry; the efficiency of the delivery system should be the guideline for rating the projects, and not just figures of implementation.

Strategic Choices

a) Facing with inefficiencies in performance of the irrigation sector necessitates answers to four simple questions:

   i) What is possible and how should this be planned?

   ii) What are the priorities for public expenditure?

   iii) How can technical implementation be improved?

   iv) Who should manage and execute in order to get the best results?

Answers to these simple questions will comprise the sector's strategic framework for the future decades. In concert, the answers will guide policy makers and implementers on actions to improve productivity, ensure sustainability, refocus investment, and strengthen sectoral management. Four major actions are required:

b) **Forge a Coherent Water Resources Policy**. Complete data on the availability and distribution of water are needed as first step in planning investment for effective usage of limited resources. The natural hydrological unit, the river basin, is the essential planning unit. Ground rules and mechanism for sharing water and coordinating usage across boundaries and among competing users—municipalities, agriculture, and industry—need to be hammered out. Holistic planning and management are needed as demands for water sharing increase. With this approach, firmer grounds are established for investment choice that is responsive to users, sectors, regions and technology. Environmental and resettlement policies also need improvement.

c) **Prioritise Expenditure and Tighten Financial Management**: Public fund for investment in irrigation is limited by budgetary constraints and further is being squeezed by recurrent expenditure and power subsidies. More transparent budgeting and accounting procedures would point to shrinkage in investment *per se*. The widening discrepancy between expenditure and revenue is rooted in extremes of both sides of the ledger—rapidly rising staff costs and declining revenue from user charges. Both must be brought under control. Investment must be prioritised to achieve maximum impact. These context envelopes decisions on whether to upgrade existing infrastructure or build new capacity and on what balance to strike among groundwater, surface irrigation, and drainage investment, to cite a few.

d) **Improve Technical Performance**: Improving sector performance hinges on more than narrow technical choices. Broadly, it encompasses strategy, agro-climate, project design, construction, operation, maintenance, management, and responsiveness to community needs. The overall scope for improvement on all these fronts is considerable. In particular, technical implementation requires improvement in water management, maintenance, design and construction. e.g., installation of solar pumps, improving performance efficiency of diesel and electric pumpsets, reducing conveyance losses of groundwater, and importantly increase surface water use efficiency.

e) **Reorder Government/Private Roles and Build Capacity**: Investment in irrigation does not necessitate exclusive public management and investment. Government cannot afford to undertake and manage all irrigation investment. Nor should it. Critical analysis is needed on what government should be doing and where privatisation would be beneficial. Autonomous commands, farmer operated and maintained commands, joint management, and NGO and university and research institutes involvement in data collection, analysis, project planning and design are only a few of the possibilities. Where government does plan and execute, its capacity to do so must be enhanced and its units restructured to accommodate more specialist expertise across more disciplines. The construction engineering approach should give way to a broader-spectrum management culture. Also essential is, revising the State Irrigation Act and administrative guidelines to facilitate, a) irrigation management transfer to users and b) for better accountability of staff.

3.3.10 Policy and Legal Framework

Major and medium irrigation systems in Karnataka have been wholly state managed with little users participation. At the state level, the government has been attempting to revise the existing and formulate new policies and design programmes to provide long-term physical and financial support for the implementation of participatory irrigation management. The Command Area Development Programme identified farmer involvement in system management as part of the programme when it was started in 1974. However, no significant efforts were made in this area until the mid-1980s. The Sixth Five-Year Plan emphasised the need for participation of farmers in the scientific management of water resources. The Seventh Five-Year Plan reiterated the need for participation of farmers in the management of irrigation. Since, 1985, the CAD programme has issued a series of guidelines, exhortations, and offers to the states to take up aspects of irrigation management transfer. The National Water Policy (both 1987, and 1999) has also stressed the involvement of farmers in various aspects of the management of the irrigation system, particularly in water distribution and collection of water rates. In recent years, initiatives to implement participatory irrigation management included setting up of High Power Committee, revising the State Irrigation Act, holding frequent workshops and seminars, and training programmes for field officials and farmers.

Owing to inadequate policy and legal framework to support participatory irrigation management in the Irrigation Act, water users' associations have remained weak. In recent years, as per the High Power Committee's suggestions, the Irrigation Act was revised, to include legislative backing for participatory irrigation management practices in the state. However, the state is yet to formulate a comprehensive and integrated water resources policy.

3.3.11 Some Suggestions

To address the depletion and degradation issues related to water resources, which assumes paramount importance in the context of sustainable development of the state, following aspects have been recommended. It may be noted that these recommendations are not new and have been articulated by many in the past. However, we present a consolidation of all the recommendations and also added certain new things together so that the approach towards water policy in the state could be a 'comprehensive approach':

1. Even though the 'river basin' has been recognised as a planning unit, a concrete system to account for dynamics of water resources and issues related to it has not yet been developed. In this direction, it is suggested that a complete 'water accounting system' for the water sector in each river basin has to be developed. This water accounting system should be holistic in nature in the sense that it is based on inputs from disciplines such as hydrology, economics, engineering, remote sensing, and sociology. Initially, this system can start with 'hydro-economic modelling' for water resources in the basin. While the hydrology part deals with the dynamism that is taking place within the water sector, the economics part can deal with how much water is being used in each sector (including the 'ecology' sector) and how efficiently water is used in these sectors, etc. This type of exercise would guide on both intra-sectoral and inter-sectoral allocation of 'scarce water' in the basin. Future projections about water allocation in relation to level of scarcity could be made with this type of accounting system suggested. Moreover, the economics part of the exercise will deal with the economic costs of environmental damage in each sector so that appropriate pollution control can be achieved. This exercise needs expertise in the area of hydrology, economics, remote sensing, and so on.
2. It should be recognised that the quantity and quality aspects are highly inter-related to each other and the reinforcing effect between these two aspects is realised everywhere. Integrating the quantity and quality aspects together to assess the water potential in different parts of the state is highly warranted for. Therefore, implementing the holistic accounting approach suggested above would be an effective way in which both quantity and quality aspects could be dealt with simultaneously.
3. Developing Basin Boards for 'scarce' river basins is warranted for in the state. The State Water Policy, 2002 argues for establishing a 'State Water Resources Board for 'multi-sectoral water planning, inter sectoral water allocation, planning of water development programmes, management decisions, and resolution of water resources issues'. Though this is a welcoming idea, a 'centralised' board may not be effective in dealing with the water related issues at the river basin level. Therefore, Basin Boards, consisting of all the stakeholders in the basin can be formed and these boards can be empowered to make important decisions regarding water resources. The 'water accounting system' suggested above could help the board in the decision making process.
4. Groundwater Regulation Act should be implemented in the state in due course. However, rules and regulations should be framed according to the regional agro-climatic factors influencing the groundwater exploitation.
5. It is suggested that an effective and efficient pricing policy is warranted for in the water sector so that the scarcity of water could be managed through a regulated market mechanism. Recognition of opportunity costs of water use in each sector is the prerequisite for formulating an appropriate pricing policy and recognition of other economic values (namely, ecological values) of water use should be an important component in the pricing mechanism. However, 'pricing of water' is a political issue but economics plays a major role in this. Pricing of water in non-agricultural sectors is being met with lot of resistance and this may be due to peoples' uncertainty regarding assured water supply. Many empirical studies all over the world had demonstrated that people will not be willing to pay increased tariff for the 'existing' water supply that is unreliable. If they are convinced that they are going to get improved and assured water supply through improved water supply

schemes, then their willingness to pay is found to be more. In the agricultural sector, an efficient pricing policy that tries to address the scarcity issue has to be based mainly on the farmers' willingness to pay, apart from other factors such as the regional productivity differences, cost of production, etc. In this direction, more number of micro level studies should be conducted to understand people's willingness to pay for improved water supply and this kind of information should be used for formulating water supply policies in general and pricing or tariff policy in particular.

6. Creating a Water Pricing Regulatory Committee at the state level, in line with the Electricity Regulatory Committee, would be a good initiative in the area of pricing of water. In countries like Australia and France, regulated markets in the water sector plays a major role in addressing the water scarcity problem especially at the river basin level. Even the farmers are allowed to 'trade' their own share of water with others who need it and this kind of mechanism lead to optimise the water used at sectoral level. The proposed Regulatory Committee can be a starting point so that the state could gradually move towards fully integrating water sector with the market economy. The Committee can have constant interaction with line departments and basin boards of various river basins in the state so as to address the issues if 'spillover effects' and inter-river basin disputes over water pricing among the river basins.

7. Removing subsidies that are indirectly influencing the overexploitation of groundwater in a phased manner is desirable. In the case of electricity subsidy-water extraction linkages, critical areas need to be identified and subsidies could be provided only in these areas. In the case of electricity charge to be fixed for the agricultural motors, the price should reflect the opportunity cots of water extraction. For example, cost of irrigation through diesel pumpsets may be considered as the basis for fixing electricity charge. However, before taking any appropriate decision some relevant research studies on a pilot basis need to be initiated in these areas.

8. At present, suggestions on institutional arrangements for managing and allocating water revolves only around the political institutions such as water user associations (WUAs). However, there are strong evidences to show as to how these 'static and externally imposed' institutions have failed to achieve the desired goals. This being the case, there exists a need for introducing innovative approaches such as introduction of water trading among the stakeholders and introduction of tradable permits for controlling pollution at the industry level. The state may look for strengthening the participatory irrigation management (PIM) system with appropriately designing incentives and disincentives. The financial resources of PIM should be strengthened by way of designing the appropriate water rates and increasing the share of water rates.

9. Recycling and reuse of water in different sectors depends mainly on the 'incentive' structure embedded in the pricing mechanism. Therefore, the pricing policy should be formulated in such a way that it has some desirable impact on recycling and reuse of water in each sector.

10. Exploring the role of private sector in water supply and wastewater treatment and involving the private sector in some of these activities will result in increased benefits. However, if the existing public policies on water supply are improved with more inputs from 'demand side' factors, the government itself can provide the water supply services more efficiently.

11. Coordination among different line departments is important and there exists a lot of replication of activities between different departments dealing with the water sector. Even though certain measures have been taken in this regard by the state, lot more needs to be done in terms of brining all the activities under one umbrella.

12. Quality related issues need to be addressed very seriously. Pollution control should be made more effective in the state. Apart from the existing command-and-control method, the market-based instruments based on 'polluter-pays-principal' will have to be introduced in the area of pollution control. Initially, the tradable permits system could be introduced among the clustered polluting industries on an experimental basis. Stringent measures and institutional arrangements to control non-point

source pollution are required. Complete review of state pollution control policies based on the local conditions is warranted for.

13. Environmental Cells with the experts in various fields should be created in key departments like Department of Water Resources. Regional Environmental Cells must also be created. All the water quality related activities need to be coordinated by these Cells.

3.4 Marine Resource Exploitation and Management in Karnataka

India is the fourth largest fish producer in the world, second in Asia next only to China (MPEDA, 2003). As a result of concerted efforts by the Central and the State Governments, fish production has been increasing in the country, reaching a record level of 5.96 million tonnes during 2000-01. The country has recorded strident progress in fish production, which was just 0.75 million tonnes in 1950-51. The marine fisheries sector in India has grown from its subsistence level during the early 1950s to a major industry level with a gross capital investment of around Rs. 41,170 million at 1995 price level (Pillai *et al.*, 2001). The marine fish landings of 1.7 million tonnes during 2000 earned a gross income of Rs. 102,000 million at the landing centre price level. The annual production from marine resources is fluctuating around 2.5 million tonnes, showing signs of stagnation. The contribution of fisheries to Indian GDP and NDP at constant prices of 1980-81 has been meagre 0.79 per cent and 0.74 per cent respectively in 1993-94. But these figures are moving upwards and contribution of fisheries is increasing. Thus, though the percentage contribution of total agriculture sector as a whole including livestock and forestry to the total GDP is decreasing, the contribution of fisheries has not declined but maintained its position. It shows that fisheries and aquaculture in absolute terms has increased its stake in the national income of the economy. As per 1996 estimates, around 6 million of population is directly dependent upon fisheries which is about 0.7 per cent of the total production. More than 4 million people are believed to have been engaged in fish processing and marketing.

The marine fisheries modernisation programme was started as early in 1953, under the Indo-Norwegian Project in Kerala, which attempted to introduce motors for the artisanal fishing crafts, especially in gill nets. The increase in the international demand for shrimps led to the designing and development of fishing technology, with the introduction of 32 coastal trawlers as a demonstration vessel. Although efforts were made by the governments to see that the traditional fishermen adopt the new trawl technology, due to institutional factors a number of outside investors and middlemen secured the benefit of the scheme and reaped the profits (SIFFS, 1991). The coastal trawlers, which were relatively small, targeted the prawn resources of 0-50 metre depth range. Due to their ability to tap demersal resources, their impact was positive on total production. Over the years during 60s and 70s the number of trawlers increased significantly and the catch per unit of fishing effort started declining, which necessitated them to diversify and expand their fishing operation into deeper waters. However with the improvement in the landings from mechanised fishing, the artisanal sector suffered a decline in the landings. Table 3.12 presents the landings from different mechanised and non-mechanised sectors in India.

TABLE 3.12

Marine Fish Production in India

Year	*Total Catch in Tonnes*	*Share in %*		
		Mechanised	*Motorised*	*Traditional*
1982	1415219	62.9*	—	37.1
1985	1565893	74.9*	—	25.1
1990	2142713	45.3	34.2	20.6
1995	2258832	51.0	35.3	13.8
2000	2700263	66.0	26.0	8.0

Note: * Includes the contribution from Motorised sector also. In those years the catch was classified as from mechanised and Non-mechanised.

Source: Compiled from CMFRI Annual Reports.

The marine fishing in Karnataka is patterned on Kerala model, although there are some differences with respect to the artisanal and motorised sectors. In Kerala attempts for the replacement of artisanal crafts with motorised and mechanised boats have met with partial success and many outside capitalistic investors have entered into the fishery. On the other hand, in Karnataka, due to the efforts of the state government, the traditional fishing communities, who were traditional fishermen, acquired most of the mechanised crafts. Although there were conflicts between the fisher-groups against the introduction of purse seiners they were sorted out by the community organisations.

Table 13.3 presents the group-wise growth in fish production of Karnataka for select years from 1969-2001. Total fish production increased from 75,793 tonnes in 1969 to 1,93,680 tonnes in 2001. The annual average landings in this period worked out to 1,39,787 tonnes. Incidentally, it may be mentioned that fish production touched a peak of 2,51,012 tonnes in 1989 and thereafter it stared declining from that level.

TABLE 3.13

Marine Fish Landings in Karnataka during 1969-2001

Year	Total Landings (in Tonnes)	Percentage Share of Individual Groups to the Total Landing				
		Pelagic	Demersal	Molluscs	Crustaceans	Miscellaneous
1969	75793	72.86	12.04	0.08	5.29	9.75
1975	87494	79.49	11.44	0.20	6.43	2.43
1980	115322	72.69	17.95	0.11	5.29	3.96
1985	118654	72.65	13.30	0.20	12.33	1.51
1990	178334	70.66	11.98	1.28	15.29	0.79
1995	116579	52.20	21.83	7.75	17.92	0.29
1998	139676	55.96	26.58	5.21	11.60	0.66
1999	165098	58.20	23.56	4.90	13.34	-
2000	181600	54.28	30.32	4.89	10.52	-
2001	193680	51.70	34.25	2.88	11.17	-
Annual Average Landings (1969-2001)	139787	63.17	18.03	2.16	12.92	4.09

Source: Marine Fisheries Information Service T& E Ser. No. 41, 52, 67, 136. Annual Reports of Central Marine Fisheries Research Institute, Cochin.

The contribution of annual pelagic fish production varied between 80 per cent in 1975 to 51 per cent in 2001. Considering the fact that the pelagic fishes constitute the basic fisheries and provide food security to the local communities a decline in the share of pelagic fishes shows the vulnerability of the local fishing communities to poverty. The percentage of demersal fishes varied between 9 per cent in 1971 to 34 per cent in 2001. Crustaceans which, accounted for 15 per cent in 1991 declined to 13 per cent in 2001.

3.4.1 Growth in Fishing Effort

The growth in the number of fishing vessels, which represents the intensity of fishing, is presented in Tables 3.14 and 3.15. In contrast to the growth in fishery production, the total number of mechanised fishing boats doubled during the last two decades. During the corresponding period, the number of non-mechanised boats also increased. Almost all these non-mechanised boats are motorised and fitted with outboard engines. The increase in the number of boats is also coupled with the enhancement of fishing capacity in terms of size (OAL), engine horsepower, electronic equipments, etc. that is not properly reflected and quantified. Thus, one of the most important reasons for non-increasing landings could be over harvesting.

TABLE 3.14

Growth of Mechanised Fishing Units in Karnataka

(No. of Vessels)

Year	*Trawlers*	*Purse Seiners*	*Gill-netters*	*Long Liners*	*Others*	*Total Mechanised*
1985-86	1984	396	722	22	7	3131
1991-92	1938	369	884	56	599	3846
1995-96	2471	327	1639	-	983	5420
1998-99	2506	360	3385	-	67	6318
2002-03	3215	646	4108	68	55	7678

Source: Department of Fisheries, Government of Karnataka, Bangalore.

TABLE 3.15

Growth of Non-mechanised Fishing Units in Karnataka

(No. of Vessels)

Year	*Rampanies*	*Dugout Canoes*	*Plank Built Boats*	*Pattabale Units*	*Others*	*Total Non-mechanised*
1985-86	74	5534	2202	1201	8143	17154
1990-91	72	4526	2274	1160	3828	11860
1995-96	148	4070	1874	838	4603	11533
1998-99	283	1570	1553	6677	9209	19292
2002-03	308	6852	1859	1350	8817	19186

Source: Department of Fisheries, Government of Karnataka, Bangalore.

As per the latest estimates of the Directorate of Fisheries, Government of Karnataka (2000) there are more than 25,610 fishing units operating in the three coastal districts; out of which 25 per cent are mechanised and remaining are motorised with outboard engines. During the last 15 years the fishing and fish processing sectors have experienced large-scale mechanisation. This mechanisation process was facilitated by the state and central governments directly and through financial and cooperative organisations. It should be noted that traditional gears in rivers and estuaries also harvest a small proportion of high valued fish, although these traditional systems are increasingly replaced by modern methods. The observations show that the traditional *rampani* fishing, which once accounted for 60-70 per cent of the annual catch in the state, has almost disappeared.

TABLE 3.16

Changing Structure of Marine Fishing Technologies

Particulars	*1991*	*1995*	*2001*
Total Landings	156654	148941	193680
Share of (in per cent)			
Mechanised	91.5	86.2	86.5
Motorised	2.8	11.2	8.8
Non-motorised	5.7	2.6	4.7
Total No. of Boats	15706	16953	26864
Share of (in per cent)			
Mechanised	24	32	29
Motorised	51	41	39
Non-motorised	24	27	33

Source: Department of Fisheries, Government of Karnataka, Bangalore.

Table 3.16 shows that the mechanised fishing vessels contribute 90 per cent of the total production with only 25-30 per cent of the total fishing vessels. The motorisation of traditional crafts supported by the state policies has gained momentum and its share in the total production has increased from 2.8 per cent in 1990 to 8.8 per cent in 2001. On the other hand the share of motorised boats has declined from 50 per cent to 39 per cent indicating the increased fishing capacity of these intermediate fishing technologies. The traditional fishers contribute 25-30 per cent of the total fishing capacity but share only 4-5 per cent of the total landings indicating the inequity in the distribution of the benefits.

The total number of mechanised boats increased by three times during the 20-year period and non-mechanised boats by two times. During the period from 1980-81 to 2003 the number of trawlers has increased from 1833 to 3215 and the gill-netters have increased from 104 to 4108 (Government of Karnataka, 2003). The discussions with the officials of the Department of Fisheries reveal that most of the non-mechanised boats are motorised and fitted with outboard engines capable of fishing up to 50–100 metre depth. This increase in number is also accompanied by increase in harvesting capacity (fishing power) in terms of size, horsepower, electronic equipment, etc. Since 1996, multi-day fishing fleets were introduced in Karnataka capable of fishing in deeper waters (150-200 metre depth) for 10-15 days. Currently, more than 60 per cent of the day trawlers are converted into multi-day fishing vessels.

Comparative analysis of cost and returns of mechanised vessels during last decade presented in Table 3.17 shows that while the net profitability of trawlers has increased by five times from 60,000 in 1992 to 3,27,000 in 2003 the purse seiners are just sustaining with marginal increase. The erosion of profitability of purse seining was mainly due to the development of more efficient small scale gears on the one hand and decline in the pelagic resources on the other. Further major part of the deep sea pelagic resources are also being harvested by multiday fishing vessels leading to conflicts in resource harvesting. The development of ring seiners and mini purse seiners operating in near shore waters compete with purse seiners.

TABLE 3.17

Comparison of Fishing Operations in Karnataka

Particulars	*1992*		*2003*	
	Trawler	*Purse Seiner*	*Trawler*	*Purse Seiner*
Length of the Boat	30-36	38-50	44-58	42-58
Average Hp of the Engine	37-98	98-108	98-120	90-110
No. of Fishing Days	167	183	238	241
No. of Days/Trip	1	1	7-10	1
Capital Investment	288345	1630460	1899536	2056201
Annual Fixed Cost	38414	182831	548059	593506
Annual Variable Cost	254168	775388	1906591	1710577
Annual Total Cost	292582	958219	2454650	2304083
Fuel Cost	75588	143720	812469	615280
Labour Payment	92302	347363	648103	712617
Catch (in Kgs)	69219	459160	79051	173557
Gross Revenue	352193	1217708	2781712	2610003
Net Revenue	59610	259489	327062	305920

Source: Aithal (1992), updated with primary data, 2003.

Annual Costs and Returns of Fishing Units: The operating costs account for a high proportion of (92.17 per cent) of the total cost in traditional fishing units followed by ring seine (89.36 per cent), gill net (84.73 per cent), trawler (77.67per cent) and purse seine unit (74.24 per cent) (Table 3.18). The high operating cost of most of the fishing unit is due to the higher cost on fuel as well as the crew share. It can be also seen that the gross revenue as well as net revenue go hand in hand across different fishing units. The net revenue of trawler and purse seiner was more than Rs. 3,00,000, Rs. 2,40,000 in ring seine, whereas the same was Rs. 59,000 for gill net and Rs. 22,0000 for traditional fishing units.

TABLE 3.18

Annual Cost and Returns of Fishing Units (in Rupees)

Particulars	Mechanised		Motorised		
	Trawler	Purse Seiner	Ring Seine	Gill Net	Traditional
1. Fixed Cost	548059 (22.33)	593506 (22.76)	209340 (10.64)	65360 (15.27)	5712 (7.83)
2. Operating Cost	1906591 (77.67)	1710577 (74.24)	1758640 (89.36)	362538 (84.73)	67192 (92.17)
3. Total Cost	2454650 (100.00)	2304083 (100.00)	1967980 (100.00)	427898 (100.00)	72904 (100.00)
4. Catch (in Kg)	79051	173557	127695	10362	2805
5. Gross Revenue	2781712	2610003	2204624	486891	94604
6. Net Operating Profit (5-2)	875121	899426	445984	124353	27412
7. Net Profit (5-3)	327062	305920	236644	58993	21700

Note. Figures in the parentheses indicate the percentages to their respective totals.

Source: Primary Data, 2003.

Sharing of Risks and Returns in Marine Fishing: The payment of a part of the share in the total output is universal in marine fisheries in view of the risk factors and incentives based on technical skill and expertise. The sharing system although common for all fishing technologies there are differences between fishing methods based on capital intensity, type of fish harvested, social structure and ownership pattern. The system of sharing of risk and income is presented in Table 3.19

TABLE 3.19

Sharing Pattern in Karnataka (in Percentages)

Particulars	Mechanised		Motorised		Traditional	
	Owner	Crew	Owner	Crew	Owner	Crew
Commission Charge	50	50	50	50	50	50
Fuel Charge	100	0	50	50	-	-
Food Charge	50	50	50	50	-	-
Net Profit	70	30	40	60	34	66

Source: Primary Data, 2003.

Thus the crew income depends on the sharing system and total income generated in fishing. It is important to note that in traditional fishing system, there are shares for the community and social organisations, which is absent in the mechanised fishing. Therefore, to some extent an informal social security system seems to prevail under the traditional system, which is absent in, mechanised fishing, as there is no homogeneity among the investors and crewmen. The government has introduced many schemes to provide support for vulnerable sections of the fishing community. For example under the 'Yashaswini' insurance scheme fishermen below the poverty line are provided with free life insurance support.

3.4.2 *Subsidy for Marine Fishing*

The technological advancement in the mechanised sector and consequent decline in the catches of traditional sector led to two developments:

- Institutions and organisations for the protection of traditional fishermen.
- Motorisation of the traditional crafts.

The development of organisations, unions of traditional fishermen for pressuring government to secure more subsidies, and exercising their rights over the resource is an important development during the period. The 1980s and early 1990s were a time of ambitious industrialisation programme in many of the states. The emphasis of the policy has been to increase fish production for domestic consumption and export. This has been sought through various devices such as motorisation, port development, and providing new boats and fishing gears.

The fishing subsidy consists of both capital and operational subsidy. The capital subsidy was introduced with the intention to increase the fish production through advanced fishing technologies. Whereas, the operational subsidy was introduced to boost the fishing activity in order to improve the profitability of the fishing operations. The capital subsidy availability is more for motorised compared to the mechanised fishing units. Under mechanised fishing units the operational subsidy was Rs. 1, 28,284 and Rs. 97,149 in trawler and purse seiner respectively, and it was Rs. 11,700 and Rs. 4,875 respectively in gillnet under motorised fishing units (Table 3.20). It accounted more than 5 per cent of the annual cost in mechanised and about one per cent of the annual cost in motorised fishing units. The total subsidy available for trawlers was about Rs. 1,40,184 (5.40 per cent of the total annual cost), followed by Rs. 98,483 (4.10 per cent) for purse seiner, Rs. 20,470 (1.03 per cent) for ring seine and Rs. 9,585 (2.19 per cent) for the gill net fishing unit. On an average the subsidy on total cost was higher for mechanised fishing units than the motorised.

TABLE 3.20

Annual Subsidies for Fishing Units

(Rs./Unit)

Subsidy on	*Mechanised*				*Motorised*			
	Trawler		*Purse Seiner*		*Ring Seine*		*Gill Net*	
	Amount	*%**	*Amount*	*%**	*Amount*	*%**	*Amount*	*%**
Capital Investment	34000	1.76	3812	0.19	31950	4.04	16490	7.17
Fixed Cost	11900	2.13	1334	0.22	8770	4.02	4710	6.72
Operating Cost	128284	6.30	97149	5.37	11700	**0.66**	4875	1.33
Total Cost	**140184**	**5.40**	**98483**	**4.10**	**20470**	**1.03**	**9585**	**2.19**

Note: * indicates the percentage subsidy available to the capital investment, annual fixed, operational and total cost.

Source: Directorate of Fisheries, Government of Karnataka, Bangalore.

The contribution of the subsidy to the mechanised fishing units is more than the motorised units. So if the subsidy is removed, the mechanised fishing units will be affected much by reduction in the net returns because of increase in the cost of fish harvest, than the motorised units. The motorised fishing unit also faces the same situation, but the intensity is relatively less. The increase in the cost of harvesting the fish for mechanised fishing units is nearly three times more than the increase in the cost of harvesting of motorised fishing units. The interesting fact is that subsidy does not have direct impact on the earnings of the active fishers (crews) in the mechanised sector as indicated by the returns to labour. But there may be indirect influence on their employment as there is a possibility to refrain from fishing by the owners of fishing vessels. The returns to labour decreases by Rs. 2.31 for ring seine and Rs. 3.47 for gill net. This is mainly because of the sharing pattern prevailed in the respective sectors. The decrease in returns to capital can be seen in all the fishing units with variations. It is pointed out that the subsidy has no direct impact on the socio-economic status of mechanised active fishers and the benefits of the subsidy is enjoyed by the owners themselves.

3.4.3 Variability of Supply

The marine fish production is highly seasonal in their availability. It was observed that September to February was the season of bulk landings. The quantity of fish landed, during different months are also undergoing changes during the last 30 years (Table 3.21).

TABLE 3.21

Changes in the Quarterly Marine Fish Landings in Karnataka

(Quantity in Metric tonnes)

Quarterly Marine Fish Landings	*1968*		*1998*		*2002–03*	
	Quantity	*Percentage to Total*	*Quantity*	*Percentage to Total*	*Quantity*	*Percentage to Total*
January-March	7125	8.11	56929	29.99	36336	20.17
April-June	8978	10.22	26323	13.87	36829	20.44
July-September	5857	6.67	29632	15.61	57686	32.02
October-December	65857	74.99	76929	40.53	49310	27.37
Total	**87817**	**100**	**189813**	**100**	**180161**	**100.00**

Source: Reports of the Directorate of Fisheries, Government of Karnataka, Bangalore.

An analysis of the species-wise landings shows that the production of some species such as sharks, soles, mackerel and oil sardines which were hitherto used for drying, curing, etc. apart from fresh fish, has been fluctuating over the years. There has been some shift in the catch composition from high valued prawns, seer fishes and pomfrets to low valued varieties such as squilla, lizard fish, pink perch, croakers, etc. which are now contributing significantly to the total production. In 1970, the proportion of mackerel, oil sardine and prawns together constituted 85 per cent of the total landings of Karnataka (87708 metric tonnes). In 2003 the proportion of these species have declined to 23 per cent (44210 metric tonnes) (Government of Karnataka, 2003). Thus there has been a decline of these species by 50 per cent leading to non-availability of fish for drying and curing by the fisher women. There has been a continuous demand from the fisher groups that they should be given special support due to declining fish production resulting in loss of income. The district administration of the Dakshina Kannada and Udupi districts accepted several representations of the fisher groups and requested the state government to meet some of their demands. During the year 1997 the state government waived-off the payment of Rs. 11.00 lakh due from the fishermen cooperatives and rescheduled some of the short-term loans. The state government has not formulated any guidelines to consider a famine situation.

The pelagic fishes, such as mackerel, and anchovies are showing a declining trend while the oil sardine is increasing during the last three years. The ribbonfish production is increasing with increased share of multi-day fishing vessels in the total catch. The trend in the production of carangids is also declining. Among the demersal fishes the declining landings of elasmobranches could be due to the recent ban on fishing by the Government of India under the Wildlife Protection Act of 1972. Catfishes are among those affected due to purse seining, with their catch declining to 27 tonnes in 2000 from a maximum catch of 10,000 tonnes in 1980. The croakers are showing a declining trend during the last one-decade. The production of perches has significantly increased with the introduction of multi-day fishing vessels. The landings of soles reached their peak during 1991-92, but thereafter they have been declining with some minor peaks. One of the disturbing factors is that the landings of stomatopods are declining and it was difficult to identify the actual reasons. Similarly, the production of prawns and cephalopods is showing stagnation and a gradual decline in spite of significant increase in the trawl effort and total trawl landings. The effort and catch rate of trawlers are showing a continuous increase in respect of some of the species such as perches. However, the catch rate of prawns, cephalopods and ribbonfish is showing a declining trend. The total purse seine landings and also the catch rate are showing a declining trend, on account of the introduction of other efficient gears.

3.4.4 Fish Famine, Fishing Ban and Livelihood Issues

There has been a continuous demand from the fisher groups that they should be given special support due to declining fish production resulting in loss of income. The district administration of the Dakshina Kannada and Udupi districts have accepted several representations of the fisher groups and requested the state government to meet some of their demands. During the year 1997 the state government waived of the payment of Rs. 11.00 lakh due from the fishermen cooperatives and rescheduled some of the short-term loans. Personal discussions with the officials of the State Fisheries Department in Mangalore revealed that the landings statistics clearly present a decline in fish production to the extent of 20 per cent during 2001-02, although there was some improvement at the end of the fishing season. On the other hand the Central Marine Fisheries Research Institute (CMFRI), Mangalore maintained that although there is fluctuation in the landings of individual species there are no indications of total decline and there are no specific reasons to believe that there is fish famine. In a seminar organised by the Fishery Survey of India (December 2001) it was concluded that there is vast scope for exploiting resources of the deep sea. Thus, clearly there has been a difference of opinion between the state fisheries department on the one hand and CMFRI scientists on the other. Another problem is with the exact definition of the fish famine. The state government has not formulated any guidelines to consider a famine situation. The fish famine is a situation, which leads to severe shortage of food due to decline in the production and lack of accessibility and entitlements.

For a proper conservation of fish on a sustainable basis, there has to be uniform dates with regard to fishing ban in all the states on the Western Coast. The Central Government is actively considering imposing a uniform ban on fishing throughout the West Coast during the southwest monsoon. Hence, in the larger interest of justice, to conserve the fish on a sustainable basis, the High Court of Goa has directed the Central Government to impose such a uniform ban on fishing, fixing uniform dates for all the coastal states on the Western coast during the southwest monsoon, before the onset of the next monsoon in May 2003. During the aforesaid ban period, state governments should strictly implement the above fishing ban against all kinds of mechanised vessels, including country crafts and boats/canoes fitted with inboard or outboard motor and other mechanised boats using nets for the purpose of fishing within the territorial waters of the state Goa, i.e. 22 kms from the seacoast. It is made clear that the traditional fishing by boats, without any mechanised motors, etc. are permissible and this order will not come in the way of the 'ramponkars', earning their day-to-day livelihood by traditional fishing. However, today most of the traditional boats are fitted with mechanised engines of varying capacity. Those fishing units, which are currently earning their livelihood by fishing during the monsoon period, will be deprived of their livelihood since they cannot compete with larger mechanised boats during the fishing season. Hence, simultaneous efforts should be made to provide opportunities for the small-scale fishermen to get a share in the fish production through allocating certain fishing areas for their exclusive fishing. Some of the important suggestions for the conservation of marine resources are presented below:

a. **The conservation of fish breeding grounds**: The Department of Fisheries can undertake the task, with the help of experts and local people, to identify fish breeding areas. Till such time all wetlands and backwater areas could be declared as fish breeding centres. A notice to the *Panchayats* could be issued indicating the reason for declaring areas as such and soliciting their cooperation in protecting the place. Perhaps the Department of Fisheries could spell out what activities will/will not be allowed. Important fish breeding grounds could be declared as sanctuaries under the provisions of the Wildlife Protection Act.

b. **Recognise the preferential access rights of coastal fishing communities:** The preferential rights of coastal fishing communities to responsibly and sustainably use and access coastal and marine resources, should be recognised by putting in place systems that promote legal security of tenure. This would also be in keeping with Article 6.18 of the FAO Code of Conduct for Responsible Fisheries that encourages states to "...appropriately protect the rights of fishers and fish workers, particularly those engaged in subsistence, small-scale and artisanal fisheries, to a secure and just livelihood, as well as preferential access, where appropriate, to traditional fishing grounds and resources in the waters under their national jurisdiction."

c. **Recognise the use of sustainable traditional fishing gear and practices:** Traditionally, coastal fishing communities have used a range of selective fishing gear and practices to target fisheries resources, including highly migratory fish stocks. The use of such gear and practices has been consistent with the principles of sustainable use of biodiversity. The rights of artisanal and small-scale fish workers to pursue their livelihoods using such forms of selective gear, under effective management systems, including in all categories of protected areas, should be recognised, as a means of attaining the objectives of the Convention on Biological Diversity. This would be consistent with Article 10 (c) of the Convention that highlights the need to "protect and encourage customary use of biological resources in accordance with traditional cultural practices that are compatible with conservation or sustainable use requirements." Further, positive incentives should be provided to promote the use of selective gear and practices, as through social labelling and eco-labelling. Alternative livelihood opportunities, including community-based tourism, should be promoted with a view to phasing out destructive fishing practices and gear.

d. **Prioritise the livelihood interests of natural-resources-dependent communities:** The importance of stakeholder participation is well recognised. It is, however, imperative to recognise and prioritise, in all management initiatives and decisionmaking processes, including the establishment and management of protected areas, and within the framework of sustainable resource use, the interests and participation of traditional and local communities who depend on the natural resource base for a livelihood.

e. **Economic liberalisation and fishery sector:** Under various Export-Import Policies of GoI in the period 1991-2002, 21 items of fish can be imported without any licence. Another 62 items can be imported against special import licence (SIL). Many of these items are available in the Indian waters. This has a direct and negative impact on local prices and markets, which ultimately would end up by further marginalising the community.

f. **Develop suitable deep-sea fisheries policies** The deep-sea vessels fishing in Indian EEZ are required to obtain licence from the Government of India. The Indian fishing companies registered under the Marine Products Export Development Authority Act, with the Ministry of Commerce. However, they sometimes do not follow the state regulations. For example, although shark fishing was prohibited recently under the Karnataka Marine Fisheries Regulation Act by the Karnataka state, the neighbouring state deep-sea fishers were not willing to follow the order as they were licenced under a different regulation. Thus, the conservation measures affected local fishers.

3.5 Minerals and Mineral Development

3.5.1 Background

Karnataka forms one of the leading states of the Indian Union in the field of minerals and is known for the wide variety of minerals it contains. At present income originating from mining and quarrying is Rs. 73,638 lakh in 2002-03 at current prices. The state ranks fifth among the mineral producing states in India. The sale value of minerals exploited in Karnataka in 2002-03 was over Rs. 2500 crore. The state has also been one of the pioneer states in India in the investigation and exploration of mineral deposits and in the starting of mineral-based industries. It is no doubt endowed with a large number of minerals of economic importance spread over 40,000 sq. kms and had the unique distinction of being a primary gold producing state in the country. There are over a hundred old workings of gold in the state. Now Gujarat, Jharkhand and Andhra Pradesh states are also producing gold. It has large reserves of high grade iron ore of exportable quality, besides other ferrous minerals like manganese and chromite. Again, Karnataka is the only other state besides Orissa to possess sizeable resources of chromite essential to the production of alloy and tool steel. Of the other non-metallic minerals, the state has large resources of clay, limestone and dolomite. Other minerals having industrial importance are corundum, gamet, emery, asbestos, bauxite, kaolin, fuller's earth, ochre, quartz, feldspar, silica, and vermiculite. It has limited resources of non-ferrous metals like copper, lead and zinc. Diamond occurrences have been reported from parts of Karnataka.

3.5.2 *Mineral Reserves, Production and Value*

As said earlier Karnataka is one of the mineral rich states of the country. At present about 20 varieties of major minerals and five varieties of minor minerals are being exploited in the state (Table 3.22). Up to March 31, 2003, 528 mining leases of major minerals, 6196 quarry leases of minor minerals, 30 reconnaissance permits (RPs) and 5 prospecting licences (PL) have been sanctioned.

TABLE 3.22

Mining Resources

Minerals	*Reserves*
Gold and Silver and Other Precious Metals	The state is having more than 40,000 sq. kms of green stone belts in which precious metals are known to occur. Exploration is taking place in Kolur, Hatti, Ajjanahalli, Hirebudini, etc..
Diamond and Other Precious Stones	Bellary, Gulbarga, Dharwad, districts have been reported to contain Diamondifferous Kimberlite pipes.
Corundum and Garnet	Available in Tumkur, Mysore, Coorg, Dakshina Kannada and Kolar District. No systematic exploration is done.
Iron Ore	Total iron ore deposits both hematite and magnetite are available. Total iron ore deposits are about 4000 million tonnes. It is being exploited for exports to a small extent in the captive steel plants like M/S Jindal Vijayanagar Steel Ltd, M/S VISL and M/S Bellary Steel and Alloys Ltd. Huge reserves of low-grade iron ore are also available.
Limestone and Dolomite	There are vast reserves of limestone and dolomite and the total reserves is 20,000 million tonnes which is available primarily in Gulbarga, Bijapur, Bagalkot, Belgaum and Tumkur districts.
Granite	Total estimated reserves is more than 220 million cubic metres. The famous varieties of granite are Ilkal Pink, Multicolour granite, Black granite, Grey granite, Juparano, Hassan green, Cats-eye, Pink Porphyry, etc.
Other minerals	Appreciable reserves of important industrial minerals are available such as, asbestos, bauxite, china clay chromite, copper ore nanganese, quartz silica and vanadium, talc, clay, kyanite and mangnesite,

contd. ...

...contd. ...

TABLE 3.23

Deposits of Ornamental Granite

Ornamental Variety	*Reserves (Inferred) (in million cubic Metres)*
Pink Multicoloured Granite	132.55
Pink Granite	6.96
Grey Granite	64.84
Block Granite	3.95
Prophery	12.80
Total	**221.10**

Source: Department of Mines and Geology, Government of Karnataka.

Note: The details regarding recoverable mineral reserves in Karnataka as on April 1, 1995 are presented in Table 3.24.

TABLE 3.24

Karnataka's Mineral Resources

Name of Mineral/Ore	*Recoverable Reserves Unit: '000 Tonnes*			
	Proved	*Probable*	*Possible*	*Total*
Asbestos		122764	167832	290596
Bauxite	1801	5860	19671	27332
China Clay	225	2818	9814	12857
Chromite	502	756	194	1452
Copper-ore	963	3820	886	5669
Corundum	768	667	13859	15294
Dolomite	7404	11831	326917	346152
Feldspar	28000	99640	60000	187640
Fire Clay	1394	1951	5425	8770
Fullers Earth		405	901	1360
Gold-ore*	3270984	8910250	682200	12863434
Granite (0.0 Cum)		124186	78800	202986
Graphite	75000	187500	—	262500
Iron Ore Hemetite (m.t)**	665	219	188	1072
Iron Ore Magnetite (m.t)**	1427	371	986	2784
Kyanite	233	395	705	1323
Limestone	839490	7169842	9430184	17439516
Magnesite	300	89	840	1229
Manganese Ore	6474	10408	24172	41054
Quartz/Silica Sand	10275	7981	19787	38043
Silver-ore*	2283376	2811613	282735	5377624
Talc/Steatite/Soap Stone	318	471	771	1622
Titaniferrous Magnetite	—	100	8069	8169
Vermiculite	—	1093	40746	41839

Note: * There are large no. of small gold deposits in the state. To asses the exact resources detailed explorations are required.
** Many mines have gone beyond proved depths. Further explorations are required to assess lumpy and fine ore.

Source: Department of Mines and Geology, Government of Karnataka.

In respect of minor minerals, Karnataka is endowed with rich varieties of granite resources. Approximately there are 100 varieties of rocks available in the state. Granites with pleasing textures and colour, apart from the attractive gneisses, migmatetes and sober dyke rocks are abundantly available. The past two decades have seen an upward trend in the granite industry with increase in consumption of decorative granite. Karnataka is the leading producer of dimension stones. The government of Karnataka has made an assessment of the reserves of different ornamental granite deposits.

3.5.3 Mineral Production and Value

During 2000-01, out of 3012 reporting mines in India 194 were from Karnataka. The state has large number of metallic minerals mines next only to Orissa—53 iron ore mines, 16 manganese ore mines and out of 6 gold mines in the country, 4 are in Karnataka. The total value of all minerals mined in Karnataka was Rs. 142.84 crore in 2002-03 comprising of Rs. 1005.94 crore worth of major minerals and 136.90 crore worth of minor minerals. The details of quantity and value of various minerals produced are summarised in Tables 3.25 and 3.26 (Appendix A-3.2).

TABLE 3.25

Output of Important Minerals in Karnataka

(Value Rs. in '000s)

Minerals	*1960-61*	*1970-71*	*1980-81*	*1990-91*	*2000-01*	*2002-03*
Bauxite	38	1077	1851	5496	5481	3425
Gold	56756	77974	258930	544003	1004425	1232303
Iron Ore	7424	18948	96057	1742142	6308458	7641457
Manganese Ore	11339	13671	52037	208999	173537	164462
Silver	71	122	407	744	1654	2145
Dolomite	68	17	414	882	12431	22593
Kaolin	155	505	914	864	6603	10655
Limestone	4771	16527	30631	257183	723435	868858
Magnetise	287	288	3068	20898	27370	17747
Quartz and Silica Sand	256	501	2295	10039	7049	7070
Total Major Minerals	81372	131023	459556	2860677	8380319	10059404
Total Minor Minerals	502	4290	79517	127211	929762	1369002
Total Minerals	**81874**	**135313**	**539073**	**2987888**	**9310081**	**11428406**

Source: Department of Mines and Geology, Government of Karnataka.

TABLE 3.26

Quantity and Value of Gold Produced

Year	*Quantity (in Kgs.)*	*Value (Rs. '000s)*
1956-57	5574	51377
1960-61	4995	56756
1970-71	3511	77974
1980-81	2355	258930
1990-91	1521	544003
2000-01	2140	1004425
2001-02	2475	1133448
2002-03	2705	1232303

Source: Department of Mines and Geology, Government of Karnataka.

The output of gold is on the decline because of depleting reserves in the existing mines. Hutti Gold Mines Ltd. (HGML) which is a 100 per cent state owned company, remains the sole gold producer in the country since the closure of the Central Government—owned Bharath Gold Mines Ltd. (BGML) at Kolar Gold Field. HGML is embarking on modernisation and expansion of its milling plant. Global tenders are being floated for installing a new plant with a milling capacity of 1,600 tonnes per day. After the new plant is commissioned its annual gold output is expected to increase to 4,000 kg from 2,500 kg anticipated during 2002. The mine deposits will also be developed from 760 m to 1,000 m over next five years. The output of manganese ore which was as high as 5598.38 lakh tonnes in 19754-75 is slowly declining and touched a level of less than half of this at 2229.00 lakh tonnes in 2002-03. On the other hand, the output of iron ore and limestone is increasing steadily. Further, many new minerals have come into limelight such as shale, fire clay, limeshell, ochre and kaolin, etc. In the overall value of all minerals produced in India in 2000-01 of Rs. 56807.09 crore, Karnataka's share is very small at Rs. 99351.16 lakh mainly because this value also includes the high value fuel items like natural gas, coal and crude petroleum which are absent in Karnataka. But in term of metallic minerals Karnataka takes the second place next to Orissa. Karnataka in all-India occupies the first place in respect of gold, felsite, lumeshell, and magnesite, second place in kyanite, third position in chromite, iron ore, manganese, and shale, fourth position in silver, limestone and red ochre and fifth position in respect of, corrundum (Government of Karnataka, 2000).

TABLE 3.27

Important Minor Minerals Produced in Karnataka

Mineral	*Quantity Mined*
Building Stone (Tonnes)	1847698
Ordinary Sand (Tonnes)	127053
Shabad Stones (Sq. Feet)	3810177
Brick Earth	3769218
Granite (Million Cubic Metres)	127053

Source: Department of Mines and Geology, Government of Karnataka.

3.5.4 Mineral Policy, Regulation and Administration

Considering the valuable importance of minerals for industrial use and also as commodities for earning foreign exchange, Karnataka was one of the earliest states to establish in 1894, an exclusive Department of Mines and Geology for exploration and exploitation of ores and minerals. Since then the Department has been undertaking systematic geological and mineral surveys including drilling with a view to deciphering the geology of the state. Further the Department is also vested with compilation of geological map delineation, potential economic mineral bearing zones, locate, assess and develop economic mineral deposits. In addition, the Department also carries out systematic exploration to develop the groundwater resource utilisation particular to boost agriculture production in the state.

Mineral Regulation

As regards the Government's policy in respect of mines and minerals, while the mineral wealth rests with respective state governments, the subject of regulation of mines and minerals development is governed by entry 54 of the Union List under Seventh Schedule of the Constitution of India. Therefore, Parliament has the exclusive power to make laws with respect to mines and mineral development. Basically all mining activities are governed by the Mines and Minerals (Development and Regulation) Act, 1957 under which Mineral Rules, 1960 and the Mineral Conservation and Development Rules, 1988 have been framed. Both the rules are applicable to all minerals except coal, atomic minerals and minor minerals.

The Department of Mines and Geology, Government of Karnataka has major regulatory functions like controlling the commercial exploitation of minerals (major and minor) and enforcing of laws and rules framed by the Central and state government and to issue mining and quarrying leases under the above principle legal framework. The Department is the sole authority to collect royalty on both major and minor minerals. The Department also endeavours to achieve its goals through: a) auditing the mining and quarrying account each year to raise demand, b) recommending several idle leases for determination to facilitate private sector to take up mining and quarrying, c) notify areas available for leasing for grant to public, d) facilitate the exploitation of economically important minerals, survey and prospecting by adopting latest techniques and finally carry out systematic appraisal of ground water resources of the state through detailed survey drilling operation; geophysical surveys and laboratory test to analyse ores, minerals and water samples. With the diversified functions and increasing role, the Department has turned out to be one of the revenue earning departments. The revenue realisation of the Department, which was just Rs. 12 crores 10 years ago, has increased to Rs. 175 crore at present.

3.5.5 Policy Liberalisation

All the states have been delegated with rule making powers in respect of minor mines under the provisions of Act 1957 Section 15 of the Mines and Minerals Development & Regulation (MMDR). The MMDR Act, 1957 stipulates that prior approval of government of India is necessary before grant of mineral concession for minerals specified in Schedule I of the Act. Of the 22 minerals included in this schedule, 11 are atomic minerals, fuel (coal and light) and the remaining 10 are metallic ores and industrial minerals.

The Karnataka government has been giving permission with the approval of Government of India, for prospecting of leasing of mine. Following economic liberalisation 1991, the government of India has been embarking on a large-scale deregulation drive.The state governments too followed in line in their respective jurisdiction. In the National Minerals Policy 1993, the government of India has brought about radical changes in the licensing and leasing policy by liberalising all minerals except atomic minerals and hydrocarbon energy minerals. A major change which has facilitated increased role for private sector in mining sector is the deletion of 13 minerals from the reserved list such as iron ore, manganese, chrome, sulphur, gold, diamond, copper, lead, zinc, molybdenum tungsten, nickel, and platinum group of minerals. Second, in encouraging foreign investment and technology the ceiling on foreign equity has been removed. Thirdly, limestone has been deleted from the list of scheduled minerals thus dispensing with the prior approval of Government of

India. Karnataka stands to gain immensely in view of its large-scale reserves of iron ore, manganese, gold, and limestone.The opening up of the Indian mining sector generated considerable global interest attracting many multinational companies for investment in mineral exploration and mining. Therefore, the government of Karnataka also effected necessary changes in order to realise the potential by optimum exploitation of the natural resources without disturbing the ecological balance. First the Karnataka Minor Minerals Concession Rules, 1994 were promulgated with effect from 28th May 1994. Later the state announced its first ever Mineral Policy—'The Karnataka Mineral Policy 2000'.

In fact, much earlier itself, Karnataka has been relaxing controls and bringing about gradual privatisation in respect of leasing out granite to private people. The year 1990-91, saw furthermore deregulation. During 1990-91, the state government relaxed the earlier ban imposed on leasing out coloured granites to private people by promulgating amendments *vide* 22nd May 1990 and 4th January 1991, which was contested in the Karnataka High court. There are several problems and constraints faced by the state government in this regard. People resorting to movement of minor mineral without paying royalty was a major problem. The system of inspection of quarry areas before issue of permit and checking of unauthorised granite quarrying and movement of granite were not at all at the desired level because of lack of facilities such as manpower and inadequate regulatory provisions in the Rules. The state government made concerted efforts to prevent leakages of royalty and export of unauthorisedly moved granite blocks at the ports, by making appeal to government of India, (Port and Customs) to cooperate with state government, etc. Further, the Department of Mines and Geology has to handle over 1000 court orders of various types in respect of granite quarry operators, which increased the quantum of workload to the legal section by way of para-wise comments and contesting the clauses.The liberalised action, of the Karnataka government, of relaxation and partial privatisation became a matter of litigation and the High court has set aside the Government Order of 18th June 1991 and all leases declared null and void. However, following the recommendation of the Interim Report of the Joint Legislatures House Committee and its implementation the situation improved and the government could address some of these problems without much difficulty. An important outcome of this was that a new Comprehensive Karnataka Minor Mineral Concession Rules was notified and brought into effect from May 28, 1994. These rules are more progressive and aim at benefiting public at large and also encourage systematic and scientific developments of quarrying. The Rules were made more stringent so as to virtually stop unauthorised and illegal transportation of minerals and granite. But at the same time an element of flexibility was induced in the Rules. Royalty rates were aligned with the market rates as also with the rates prevailing in the neighbouring states. This brought significant improvement in the mineral administration and led to higher revenue realisation.

During 1994-95, the Department of Mines and Geology was empowered to cause tender-cum-auction. In the following year 11 new checkposts were set up and two years later 6 more checkposts and these checkposts made it possible to effectively monitor and check the unauthorised and illegal mining activities in the state. After consolidation of all steps, the state government organised the Karnataka Mineral Conference on September 13 and 14, 2000 at Bangalore and it was at this time the Karnataka Mineral Policy 2000 was released by the Hon'ble Chief Minister of Karnataka to attract more foreign and private investments in the mining sector.

3.5.6 The Karnataka Mineral Policy 2000

The Karnataka Mineral Policy, 2000 is the first evercomprehensive policy framed by the state government with the basic objective of supporting private participation in mining activities by encouraging the principle of first come first served. The main objectives *inter alia* include, value addition through promotion of processing units and mineral based industries; encourage export of minerals having export potential; increase employment opportunities in the mining sector and exploit mineral deposits by promoting adoption of mechanised and scientific mining with due regard to optimum exploitation, mine safety and minimising the adverse effects of mineral development on the forests, environment and ecology. The state government would facilitate exploratory activities in the field of mineral exploration, support mineral based industries, strengthen the machinery to check unauthorised mining and leakage of revenues, and specify and notify adequately the Minor Mineral Concession Rules to ensure better mineral administration. The state would seek further delegation of powers to the state government from the Government of India. The Mineral Policy through mineral surveys and prospecting endeavours to search new deposits in more difficult terrains, issue reconnaissance permits and prospecting licences to competent and capable national and multinational companies on first come first served basis. Detailed investigations which were hitherto confined to major minerals now would be extended to minor minerals also. The mineral administration include facilitating mineral exploration by overseas investors and provide help to domestic, foreign investors in putting up mineral/mining based industries having a capital outlay of more than Rs. 5 crore. A State Level Facilitation Group to provide single window clearance is set up. Further a Mining Special Assistance Cell has been established to provide escort services. In addition, several Central Government agencies are also engaged in mineral exploration. The state government would ensure proper coordination amongst all these agencies for optimum use of resources.

Export promotion of minerals such as iron, ore, granite, semi-precious stones, would be achieved by organising fairs, exhibitions, visits to national, international trade fairs, exhibitions, seminars, participation of lessees, etc. The Policy also addresses the many problems in minerals development due to various forest laws operating in the mining areas which are conflicting to each other. The critical issues of rehabilitation of mining areas is very important and the Policy contemplates to earmark funds for this purpose. The government also emphasises the welfare of mineral workers and their wards and finally ensure mine safety.

3.5.7 Exports of Minerals

Karnataka has good potential for export of iron ore, granite and semi-precious stones. At present the quantity of exports of these minerals are relatively small. In the recent years, exports of iron ore and minerals have been valued in the range of Rs. 678 crore and Rs. 780 crore. There is a great demand in the international markets for coloured and ornamental granite from Karnataka. The state's share in exports of granite is estimated at 65 per cent to 75 per cent. However, due to various reasons the state's share has declined drastically to 15 per cent. Karnataka granite (particularly from North Karnataka with appealing colours and uniform textures) is catching the world market. As at the end of March 2003, the state has accorded 580 ornamental stone leases. The state has taken new initiatives to promote granite industry such as, implementation of Granite Conservation and Development Rules, 1999 for quick disposal of leases application, reducing delays through self assessment of granite, etc.

There are some constraints in increasing the exports of minerals from the state. Both the policies namely Karnataka Mineral Policy, 2000 and the Karnataka Export Promotion Policy, 2002-2007 have addressed these issues at length and have recommended various strategies to promote exports such as, improving their quality acceptable to foreign markets and also providing adequate incentives, adoption of standard equipments and latest technologies and development of infrastructure such as ports, etc. Priority is being given in the grant of mining leases to those who put up export-oriented units in the state. The state however endeavours to increase export of minerals and value-added mineral based products so as to achieve Rs. 1000 crore mark per annum in a three-year period.

3.5.8 Other Issues

There are several issues and concerns with regard to mineral development in Karnataka like in any other states. They are: a) systematic mining, b) mining and environment, c) rehabilitation of mining areas, and d) welfare of mine workers, etc.

Systematic mining includes measures such as review of prescribed minimum size of lease area, amalgamation of adjoining minor mineral leases of small size into a single lease net exceeding five hectares, identify non-working mines, following appropriate productivity norms, induction of foreign technology, and strict compliance of stipulation prescribed, etc.

Environment and mining are conflicting to each other. The key environmental problems on account of mining activities are, degradation of land, forest and loss of biodiversity, surface and groundwater pollution by siltation and mine drainage, air pollution by emission of suspended and respirable dust particles and environment degradation due to abandoned or closed mines. The state has taken cognizance of these concerns and contemplates to strike a balance between environment and mineral development by creating greater environment awareness, orientation of lease holders for preservation of ecological balances, and their participation in aforestation in degraded areas, sponsoring studies on reduction and utilisation of mining waste, efforts to convert old disused mining sites into forests, allowing the waste arising out of dimensional granite for any use on payment of royalty, etc.

Rehabilitation of mining areas presupposes that the mining areas are properly prospected and mineral deposits proved. To prevent the adverse impact of mining on environment, mining areas need to be rehabilitated. Necessary financial resources have to be mopped up to provide health facilities to the people living in the mining region and to combat mining related health hazards, growing trees and plants in the mining areas, stabilisation of the slopes and the dumps are all, the essential components of the rehabilitation programmes.

Employees working in mines face greater risks and dangers to life. At present the welfare amenities available to mine workers are inadequate and far from satisfactory. The Karnataka state government has decided to share 50 per cent of the cost of the construction of amenities like schools, hospitals, dispensaries, housing and drinking water facilities under various developmental schemes. The balance 50 per cent would be borne by the mining lease. The state has also proposed to provide special welfare amenities for children of mine workers and steps would be taken to eliminate forced labour in mines and quarries.

References

Aithal, P.V. (1992). "Economics of Marine Fishing in South Kanara District of Karnataka", *M.Sc Thesis*, University of Agricultural Sciences, Bangalore.

CMDR (Centre for Multi-disciplinary Development Research), (2003). *State of Environment Report–Karnataka*, CMDR, Dharwad.

CMFRI (Central Marine Fisheries Research Institute) 1980-2002, *Annual Reports*, Central Marine Fisheries Research Institute, Cochin.

Government of India (1988). *National Forest Policy*, Ministry of Environment and Forests, New Delhi.

———. *Indian Agricultural Statistics 1991-92*, Vol. I and II, All India, State-wise and District-wise, Ministry of Agriculture.

———. *Indian Minerals Year Book 1998-1999*, Indian Bureau of Mines, Department of Mines and Minerals.

———. Reports of Indian Bureau of Mines, Ministry of Mines.

Government of Karnataka. *Economic Development of Mysore, 1956-69*, Bureau of Economics and Statistics.

———(1986). Proceedings of the Government, *Government Order No.FFD 75 FAP 83*, Bangalore July 23.

———(1996). *Human Development in Karnataka 1999*, Planning Department, Bangalore. *Mineral Policy 2000*, Department of Mines and Geology.

———. *Karnataka at a Glance 2001-02*, Directorate of Economics and Statistics.

———. (2002a). *High Power Committee for Redressal of Regional Imbalances*, Final Report.

———. (2002b). *State Water Policy, 2002*.

———. (2003). *Statistical Bulletin of Fisheries*. Directorate of Fisheries, Bangalore.

———. 2004. *State of the Environment Report and Action Plan-2003*. Department of Forest, Ecology and Environment, Bangalore.

———. *Karnataka Export Promotion Policy 2002-2007*, Department of Industries and Commerce.

———. Various Annual Reports of the Department of Mines and Geology.

———. *Statistical Abstracts of Karnataka*, and *Karnataka at a Glance*, various issues, Directorate of Economics and Statistics.

———. *Ornamental Stones of Karnataka*, Department of Mines and Geology.

———. *Ornamental Granite Tracks of Karnataka (At a Glance)*, Department of Mines and Geology.

———. *Economic Survey* of various years, Planning and Statistics Department.

———. *Unearthing Karnataka's Hidden, Treasure*, Department of Mines and Geology.

Kushalapa, K.A. (2003). "Land and Forest Degradation Sector", Draft Final Report, *State of Environment Report and Action Plan 2002-2003*, Government of Karnataka.

Marine Fisheries Information Service. Central Marine Fisheries Research Institute, Cochin.

MPEDA (2003). *Marine Products Export Review*, Marine Products Export Development Authority, Cochin.

Nadkarni, M. V. and Syed Ajmal Pasha (1991). "Developing Uncultivated Lands: Some Issues from Karnataka's Experience in Social Forestry", *Indian Journal of Agricultural Economics*, 46 (4), October-December.

Pillai, N.G.K., Mohan Joseph Modayil and U. Ganga (2001). "Marine Fishing Practices and Aquaculture Technologies in India", Paper presented at the Inception Workshop on *Supply and Demand for Fish*, p.42, ICLARAM, Penang, Malaysia.

Pasha, Syed Ajmal (1992). "CPRs and Rural Poor: A Micro-Level Analysis", *Economic and Political Weekly*, 27(46), November.

Raju, K.V., G.K. Karanth and M.J. Bhende (2003). *Rejuvenating Tanks: A Socio-Ecological Approach*, Books for Change, Bangalore.

Raju, Ashok Gulati and Ruth (1999). *Financial Reforms in Irrigation Sector: A Case Study of Krishna Bhagya Jal Nigam Limited*, a India paper presented in the First International Water Management Conference held at Islamabad, Pakistan, July 18-19, 2000.

South Indian Federation of Fishermen Society (SIFFS) (1991). *A Census of the Artisanal Marine Fishing Fleet of Kerala*.

APPENDIX A-3.1

District-wise Land Use Pattern in Karnataka (Area in '00 Hectares)

District	*1999-2000*					*1991-92*				
	TGA	*Forest*	*UCLs*	*UCLs+Forest*	*NSA*	*TGA*	*Forest*	*UCLs*	*UCLs+Forest*	*NSA*
Bangalore (Urban)	2174	33.0(1.5)	1083.4(49.8)	1116.4(51.4)	1057.7(48.7)	8005	845.7 (10.6)	2449 (30.6)	3294.7 (41.2)	4733.7 (59.1)
Bangalore (Rural)	5854.3	812.7(13.9)	1697.3(29.0)	2510.0(42.9)	3344.3(57.1)	—	—	—	—	—
Chitradurga	7707.0	737.2(9.6)	2212.0 (28.7)	2949.2(38.3)	4757.8(61.7)	10852	908.3(8.4)	2882.7 (26.6)	3791.0 (34.9)	6364.1 (58.6)
Davanagere	5976.0	899.2(15.1)	1032.5(17.3)	1931.7(32.3)	4044.3(67.7)		—			
Kolar	7794.7	703.2(9.0)	2845.2(36.5)	3548.4(45.5)	4246.2(54.5)	8223	703.2 (8.6)	2928 (35.6)	3631.2 (44.2)	4163.5 (50.6)
Shimoga	8477.8	2768.6(32.7)	3435.9(40.5)	6204.5(73.2)	2273.4(26.8)	10553	3274.3(31.0)	3842.3 (36.4)	7116.6 (67.4)	3458.9 (32.8)
Tumkur	10647.5	449.8(4.2)	3654.8(34.3)	4104.7(38.6)	6542.9(61.5)	10598	449.8(4.2)	3744.7 (35.3)	4194.5 (39.6)	6453.1 (60.9)
Belgaum	13443.8	1904.2(14.2)	1613.6(12.0)	3517.8(26.2)	9926.0(73.8)	13415	1904.2(14.2)	1593.6 (11.9)	3497.8 (26.1)	9946.0 (74.1)
Bijapur	10534.7	19.8 (0.2)	824.1(7.8)	843.9(8.0)	9690.8(92.0)	17069	831.0(4.9)	1484.8 (8.7)	2315.8 (13.6)	14808.0 (86.7)
Bagalkot	6588.8	811.3(12.3)	687.2(10.4)	1498.5(22.7)	5090.3(77.3)	—	—	—	—	—
Dharwad	4273.3	352.4(8.3)	426.7(10.0)	779.1(18.2)	3494.2(81.8)	13738	1153.0(8.4)	1229.3 (8.9)	2382.3 (17.3)	11400.0 (83.0)
Gadag	4657.1	326.1(7.0)	335.2(7.2)	661.4(14.2)	3995.8(85.8)	—	—	—	—	—
Haveri	4851.6	474.5(9.8)	589.1(12.1)	1063.7(21.9)	3787.9(78.1)	—	—	—	—	—
Uttar Kannada	10246.8	8150.4(79.5)	907.2(8.8)	9057.6(88.4)	1189.2(11.6)	10291	8296.1(80.6)	772.9 (7.5)	9069.0 (88.1)	1177.8 (11.4)
Bellary	8132.0	970.2(11.9)	1638.4(20.1)	2608.5(32.1)	5523.4(67.9)	9885	1192.5(12.1)	1853.3 (18.7)	3045.8 (30.8)	6516.4 (65.9)
Bidar	5417.6	250.9(4.6)	1167.5(21.5)	1418.4(26.2)	3999.2(73.8)	5448	250.9(4.6)	1240.1 (22.8)	1491.0 (27.4)	3926.7 (72.1)
Gulbarga	16102.1	687.6(4.3)	1990.2(12.4)	2677.8(16.6)	13424.3(83.4)	16224	681.7(4.2)	2204.6 (13.6)	2886.3 (17.8)	13216.0 (81.5)
Raichur	8358.4	181.7(2.2)	1312.8(15.7)	1494.5(17.9)	6863.9(82.1)	14017	476.2(3.4)	2200.4 (15.7)	2676.6 (19.1)	11207.0 (79.9)
Koppal	5524.9	294.5(5.3)	976.9(17.7)	1271.4(23.0)	4253.5(77.0)	—	—	—	—	—
Chickmagalur	7220.7	2004.9(27.8)	2189.8(30.3)	4194.6(58.1)	3026.1(41.9)	7201	2004.9(27.8)	2292.2 (31.8)	4297.0 (59.7)	2923.7 (40.6)
Dakshina Kannada	4771.5	1284.8(26.9)	2082.7(43.6)	3367.5(70.6)	1404.0(29.4)	8441	2267.5(26.9)	3716.8 (44.0)	5984.3 (70.9)	2351.7 (27.9)
Udupi	3564.5	994.4(27.9)	1500.5(42.1)	2494.9(70.0)	1069.6(30.0)	—	—	—	—	
Hassan	6626.0	540.4(8.2)	1945.1(29.4)	2485.6(37.5)	4140.5(62.5)	6814	540.3(7.9)	2137.1 (31.4)	2677.4 (39.3)	3948.6 (57.9)
Kodagu	4107.7	1346.0(32.8)	1231.1(30.0)	2577.1(62.7)	1530.7(37.3)	4102	1346.0(32.8)	1241.3 (31.3)	2587.3 (63.1)	1520.5 (37.1)
Mandya	4982.4	247.7(5.0)	1868.5(37.5)	2116.2(42.5)	2866.3(57.5)	4961	237.7(4.8)	1800.2 (36.3)	2037.9 (41.1)	2944.6 (59.3)
Mysore	6763.8	628.5(9.3)	2069.4(30.6)	2697.9(39.9)	4066.0(60.1)	11954	3384.6(28.3)	3202.8 (26.8)	6587.4 (55.1)	5875.4 (49.1)
Chamrajnagar	5699.0	2756.1(48.4)	1078.7(18.9)	3834.8(67.3)	1864.2(32.7)	—	—	—	—	—
Total	**190498.4**	**30630.0(16.1)**	**42396.0(22.3)**	**73025.9(38.3)**	**117472.5(61.7)**	**191791**	**30748.0(16.0)**	**42816 (22.3)**	**73564.0 (38.4)**	**116934.0 (61.0)**

Note: TGA=Total geographical area, UCLs= Total land not available for cultivation + Total uncultivable land + Other fallow land, UCLs+Forest= Total land not available for cultivation + Total other uncultivable land+ Other fallow land + Forest, NSA= Net Sown Area including Current Fallow.

The figures in parentheses stand for proportion to the total geographical area (TGA).

Source: (1) *Karnataka at a Glance 2001-02*, Directorate of Economics and Statistics, Government of Karnataka, Bangalore.

(2) *Indian Agricultural Statistics 1991-92*, Vol I and II, All India, State-wise and District-wise, Ministry of Agriculture, Government of India.

APPENDIX A-3.2

Quantity and Value of Mineral Production in Karnataka 1960-61 to 2002-03

Minerals	Unit	1960-61		1970-71		1980-81		1990-91		1991-92		1992-93	
		Quantity	Value	Quantity	Value	Quantity	Value	Quantity	Value	Quantity	Value	Quantity	Value
I Metallic Minerals													
Bauxite	Tonnes	2248	38	73046	1077	68447	1851	57944	5496	18884	1574	13178	1373
Chromite	Tonnes	594	49	4870	292	54349	4876	46478	25058	38420	31027	37173	32051
Copper Ore	Tonnes			135	10	41771	6335	100925	31280	106591	34439	93864	30242
Gold	Kgs	4995	56756	3511	77974	2335	258930	1521	544003	1477	544621	1245	472170
Iron Ore	'000 Tonnes	1872	7424	3168	18948	4189	96057	12338	1742142	12360	2380988	11043	1703296
Manganese Ore	Tonnes	302216	11339	429825	13671	465680	52037	345241	208999	350945	257637	398783	367443
Tungsten Conc.	Kgs												
Silver	Kgs	360	71	264	122	172	407	140	744	135	719	127	667
Total I	**Tonnes**		**75677**		**112094**		**420493**		**2557722**		**3251005**		**2607242**
II Non-metallic Minerals													
Asbestos	Tonnes	288	20	184	92	291	48	59	3	59	3	41	2
Clay(others)	Tonnes			23902	29	17818	97						
Corundum	Tonnes	24	2	186	112	62	51	16900	13	10000	8	3250	2
Dolomite	Tonnes	5159	68	1556	17	17594	414	5765	882	5965	257	400	23
Felsite	Tonnes		19	0	0	1129	217			1004	633	999	593
Felspar	Tonnes		14	0	0	4435	263					2352	248
Fire Clay	Tonnes	9216	15	24397	216	5841	80	5411	1173	4872	703	4047	943
Kaolin	Tonnes	22462	155	26086	505	13247	914	6263	864	7192	1069	9598	2381
Kyanite	Tonnes	51	2	243	17	790	84	555	56	540	54	700	158
Limestone	'000 Tonnes	1033	4771	2393	16527	2030	30631	5234	257183	6842	360986	7012	367866
Lime Shell	Tonnes			0	0	843	43	49371	4717	59492	6344	34169	3995
Magnesite	Tonnes	4445	287	7336	288	8700	3068	36045	20898	39827	25335	38919	28977
Ochre	Tonnes	4490	83	15788	287	10259	279	19130	1305	21584	1440	12407	713
Quartz & Silica Sand	Tonnes	19227	256	33432	342	52784	2261	57766	5701	41840	5892	65905	8296
Fuchsite Quartzite	Tonnes			13	33	8	4	3	3				
Silica Sand	Tonnes			8781	159	1047	34	123930	4338	125809	5912	77790	3694
Moulding Sand	Tonnes			28955	160	27381	228						
Sillimanite	Tonnes			0	0								
Steatite	Tonnes	208	3	329	74	9738	327	1527	87	1020	63	492	38
Vermiculite	Tonnes			800	24	190	15						
Staruolite	Tonnes			82	40	6	5						
Dunite				0	0								
Shale	Tonnes			0	0			244638	5732	120870	2790	124220	2867
Calcite	Tonnes			462	5								
Garnet (Abrasive)				12	2								
Total II			**5695**		**18929**		**39063**		**302955**		**411489**		**420796**
III Major Minerals I to II			**81372**		**131023**		**459556**		**2860677**		**3662494**		**3028038**
IV Minor Minerals			502		4290		79517		127211		257975		305274
V Total III & IV			**81874**		**135313**		**539073**		**2987888**		**3920469**		**3333312**

Contd. ...

Contd. ...

Minerals	Unit	1993-94		1994-95		1995-96		1996-97		1997-98		1998-99	
		Quantity	Value	Quantity	Value	Quantity	Value	Quantity	Value	Quantity	Value	Quantity	Value
Metallic Minerals													
Bauxite	Tonnes	18860	1919	19563	2224	31772	3495	24956	2920	7969	877	21806	2399
Chromite	Tonnes	33921	49802	24072	49265	62513	87217	43277	59179	35990	45906	15200	34162
Copper Ore	Tonnes	92446	42414	60870	24567	38662	16638						
Gold	Kgs	1311	630784	1642	705309	1424	792557	1842	959728	1969	897114	1953	1190922
Iron Ore	'000 Tonnes	12042	2826329	12431	3120387	12846	3620989	12905	4265103	16123	5449389	15024	5451072
Manganese Ore	Tonnes	372451	288535	383576	274629	405441	295501	390994	305023	323988	256582	272959	232483
Tungsten Conc.	Kgs												
Silver	Kgs	130	611	149	698	128	848	172	1224	204	1250	212	1633
Total I	**Tonnes**		**3840394**		**4177079**		**4817245**		**5593177**		**6651118**		**6912671**
Non-metallic Minerals													
Asbestos	Tonnes	59	3		2								
Clay (others)	Tonnes												
Corundum	Tonnes	500		15									
Dolomite	Tonnes	23724	2773	27409	4819	46932	8749	54588	9071	58988	9629	52180	7702
Felsite	Tonnes	964	694	1021	527	1183	677	1209	1068	1481	1105	657	670
Felspar	Tonnes	5814	1395	7107	1950	7715	2592	4543	1526	2766	737	2089	574
Fire Clay	Tonnes	5610	840	6238	1316	5414	1061	9129	1980	11453	2698	6727	1801
Kaolin	Tonnes	16678	4185	12242	5023	15184	6031	15805	6121	18334	9465	12676	7674
Kyanite	Tonnes	4378	1083	575	96	854	138	1837	648	613	182	657	230
Non-metallic Minerals													
Limestone	'000 Tonnes	7514	400671	8012	448795	8398	525024	8796	547103	9803	650524	8775	640304
Lime Shell	Tonnes	23848	3978	21873	3640	41507	6210	35313	7902	34402	9755	46334	16092
Magnesite	Tonnes	38036	30241	27805	23293	26167	21533	31085	17332	35388	19240	35107	23835
Ochre	Tonnes	11468	706	16304	1032	23811	1771	22824	1501	25880	1757	21254	1946
Quartz & Silica Sand	Tonnes	34511	7515	41604	8112	16836	2610	33888	5521	27219	4378	25295	2201
Fuchsite Quartzite	Tonnes	154	77	17	9	29	15	1	1			195	39
Silica Sand	Tonnes	95518	5344	94315	7334	102729	7241	122181	10305	116565	8600	120531	919
Moulding Sand	Tonnes												
Sillimanite	Tonnes												
Steatite	Tonnes	358	30	253	21	483	43	624	56	235	74	250	28
Vermiculite	Tonnes											1220	800
Staruolite	Tonnes												
Dunite		7597	2667	57334	23736	135717	54287	146860	51401	184819	64687	219288	76312
Shale	Tonnes	148824	3078	158005	6597	140130	5850	198090	12149	130575	8694	168885	10766
Calcite	Tonnes												
Garnet (Abrasive)													
Total II		**465280**		**536302**		**643832**		**673685**		**791525**		**800167**	
III Major Minerals I to II		**4305674**		**4713381**		**5461077**		**6266862**		**7442643**		**7712838**	
IV Minor Minerals		**415095**		**582713**		**602538**		**1640584**		**2519115**		**989924**	
V Total III & IV		**4720769**		**5296094**		**6063615**		**7907446**		**9961758**		**8702762**	

Contd. ...

...Contd. ...

Minerals	Unit	1999-2000		2000-01		2001-02		2002-03	
		Quantity	Value	Quantity	Value	Quantity	Value	Quantity	Value
Metallic Minerals									
Bauxite	Tonnes	30177	3319	49830	5481	52345	6072	29529	3425
Chromite	Tonnes	12918	32365	14820	23858	17937	30880	19139	30825
Copper Ore	Tonnes								
Gold	Kgs	1969	1113845	2140	1004425	2475	1133448	2705	1232303
Iron Ore	'000 Tonnes	17213	6094903	18902	6308458	22595	7740503	24044	7641457
Manganese Ore	Tonnes	274052	206437	218882	173537	213346	174104	222899	164462
Tungsten Conc.	Kgs								
Silver	Kgs	281	2188	219	1645	275	2126	270	2145
Total I	**Tonnes**		**7453057**		**7517404**		**9087133**		**9074617**
Non-Metallic Minerals									
Asbestos	Tonnes								
Clay (others)	Tonnes					2500	250		
Corundum	Tonnes								
Dolomite	Tonnes	43582	6139	92780	12431	123025	19589	166967	22593
Felsite	Tonnes	656	581	928	695	1121	787	1094	723
Felspar	Tonnes	11082	4001	6270	2273	4925	1830	6288	1967
Fire Clay	Tonnes	3325	665	3346	669	15360	3620	11296	2427
Kaolin	Tonnes	14616	7794	13377	6603	15781	10599	14978	10655
Kyanite	Tonnes	162	89	355	195	230	110	297	163
Limestone	'000 Tonnes	9725	710437	9903	723435	10481	761380	12181	868858
Lime Shell	Tonnes	54767	17492	56720	25696	89224	45252	87712	37824
Magnesite	Tonnes	35950	21771	25534	27370	21214	23954	17179	17747
Ochre	Tonnes	22299	2131	25776	2221	25047	3636	34349	4793
Quartz & Silica Sand	Tonnes	19816	1590	10260	1675	6849	1174	2973	465
Fuchsite Quartzite	Tonnes					149	19		
Silica Sand	Tonnes	131115	8965	92574	5374	81993	5872	91213	6595
Moulding Sand	Tonnes								
Sillimanite	Tonnes								
Steatite	Tonnes							1892	123
Vermiculite	Tonnes								
Staruolite	Tonnes								
Dunite		217503	76126	155081	54278	42102	12558	11515	691
Shale	Tonnes					224298	4050	488810	9163
Calcite	Tonnes								
Garnet (Abrasive)									
Total II			**857781**		**862915**		**894680**		**984787**
III Major Minerals I to II			**8310838**		**8380319**		**9981813**		**10059404**
IV Minor Minerals			1004815		929762		1452389		1369002
V Total III & IV			**9315653**		**9310081**		**11434202**		**11428406**

Source: Department of Mines and Geology, Government of Karnataka.

APPENDIX A-3.3

Irrigation Potential Created, Investment Made and Potential to be Utilised

Projects (Major and Medium)	*Potential (in Ha)*			*Financial Outlay (in Lakhs)*			*Investment Required**		
	Planned	*Created up to 3/2001*	*Balance*	*Admn. Approved Cost*	*Present Cost*	*Expenditure up to 3/2001*	*Balance*	*Investment @ Present (Rs. in Lakhs per Ha) Created*	*Investment Required for Remaining Area to be (Rs. Crores)*
1	2	3	4	5	6	7	8	9	10
Krishna	2072291	1286546	785745	588535	1786362.30	937801.79	848560.51	1.3	10214.68
Cauvery	727692	503116	224576	96604	686403	331006.53	355396.47	1.5	3368.64
Godavari	43113	21127	21986	30979	47821	34788.35	13032.65	0.60	131.91
Others	80604	0	80604	1353	71090	2963.53	68126.47	0.50**	403.02
Total	**2923700**	**1810789**	**1112911**	**717471**	**2591676**	**1306560.20**	**1285116.10**	**1.38**	**14118.25**

Notes: *Column 9 is derived by multiplying figures in column 4 with column 8; Column 10 is derived by multiplying column 4 with column 9.

**Since actual expenditure incurred is not available, we make an assumption of Rs. 50,000 per hectare as the actual expenditure incurred.

Source: Department of Water Resources, Government of Karnataka and HPC 2002.

Chapter 4

Human Resources of Karnataka

4.1 Perspective

The spread and quality of human resources in a region is a parametrical determinant of the spread, efficiency and levels of economic, social, political, civic and cultural development of that region. This proposition holds good even for Karnataka state. Development is engineered by a variety of factors such as infrastructure facilities, institutional structures, legal framework and resources. In case of resources, there are two types—natural and human. Vision-led, goal-oriented, efficient and effective use of natural resources and infrastructure facilities within given institutional structures and legal frameworks lead to desired development. The extent and quality of this utilisation depends upon the quality of the population, the human resources of the region.

4.1.1 Linkages

Quality of the population of a region is an extensive and comprehensive concept. It includes therein the health, nutritional status, spread of literacy and educational levels attained by the people, employment status and quality of employment. Employment is a proxy for income and income gets reflected in current consumption and savings for the future. The health, fitness and educational levels of the people facilitate their choice of employment within given market conditions. They also contribute to the productivity of the people wherever they work. In this way, quality of life of the people and quality of people contribute to the overall growth process. Human Capital theory (T. W. Schultz, Gary Becker, Dale Jorgenson, Mc Clelland, Robert Solow, Abramovitz, Harbison and Myers, Mary Jean Bowman and Charles Anderson, Psacharopoulos among others) has clearly and unequivocally unravelled the values of the quality of people to economic growth and social development. The spread of health, fitness, education and employment across discrete population groups such as sex, age-groups, region and units of development administration reflect the distributional status of the quality of people. It addresses the concerns of justice and equality in realisation of the quality of life of the people and the possibility of all round contribution to the growth process.

4.1.2 Objectives

This chapter addresses the issues and concerns of human resources in Karnataka state. Specifically it has three-fold objectives. They are:

(a) to review the performance of Karnataka state in regard to production and promotion of human resources,

(b) to examine the potential for growth and development as indicated through the current levels and quality of human resources, and

(c) to foresee the prospects for development of human resources in the state.

4.1.3 Scope

Performance of Karnataka in regard to development of human resources would keep in view the development since the last four decades. However, the interest would be specifically confined to the reform period, that is from 1991 onwards. Analysis of performance and review of prospects would include regional, sex and interdistrict differentials. Prospects for the future would discuss the needed policy shifts as well as strategic interventions for the future. This would also be within a framework of an overall vision of growth and development in the state. The chapter unfolds itself with the foregoing perspective.

4.2 Demographic Profile

This section includes trends and levels in population growth in the state, concerns of sex ratios, mortality, nuptiality, family planning, fertility, urbanisation and migration.

4.2.1 Trends and Levels in Population Growth

The population of Karnataka, which stood at 13 million in 1901 increased to 19 million by 1951 and to 52 million by 2001. Thus, the population in the state increased by four times in the last century. Out of the total increase in population in the state, between 1901-2001, about 84 per cent of the increase occurred in the last 50 years (Appendix A-4.1).

Karnataka, with an area of 1,91,791 sq. kms and a total population of 5,27,33,958 accounts for 5.83 per cent of the total geographical area and 5.13 per cent of the total population of the country. Karnataka occupies eighth rank among 15 major states both in respect of area and population as per the 2001 Census. Out of the total geographical area of the state, south Karnataka, comprising of Bangalore and Mysore revenue divisions accounts for 48.58 per cent, whereas north Karnataka comprising of Belgaum and Gulbarga revenue divisions accounts for 51.42 per cent. In terms of geographical area, Bangalore (urban) district is the smallest district sharing 1.14 per cent of state's area followed by Kodagu (2.14 per cent). Gulbarga district is the biggest district sharing 8.46 per cent of the total area of the state, followed by Belgaum (6.99 per cent).

Out of the total population of the state, south Karnataka and north Karnataka account for 57.28 per cent and 42.72 per cent respectively. Bangalore (urban) district, which is the smallest in area, is the biggest district in population size, sharing 12.37 per cent of the total population of the state followed by Belgaum (7.98 per cent). Kodagu is the smallest district sharing 1.03 per cent of state's population preceded by Chamrajnagar (1.83 per cent).

The population growth in the state has not been uniform in the last century, with variations from decade to decade. There was a slight fall in the population during the period 1911 to 1921 mainly due to famines and epidemics after the First World War. Historically, the population growth in Karnataka has been close to the national average. However, there was a sharp decline in the growth rate in the last two decades (Figure 4.1).

The decadal growth rate of population reached the highest level of 26.43 per cent during 1971-81 since the beginning of the last century, slowed down to 21.12 per cent during 1981-91 and further declined to 17.25 per cent during the last decade (Appendix A-4.2). The north Karnataka region registered higher population growth (21.39 per cent) in comparison to south Karnataka region (16.45 per cent) during 1991-2001.

FIGURE 4.1

Population Growth in Karnataka and India: 1911 to 2001

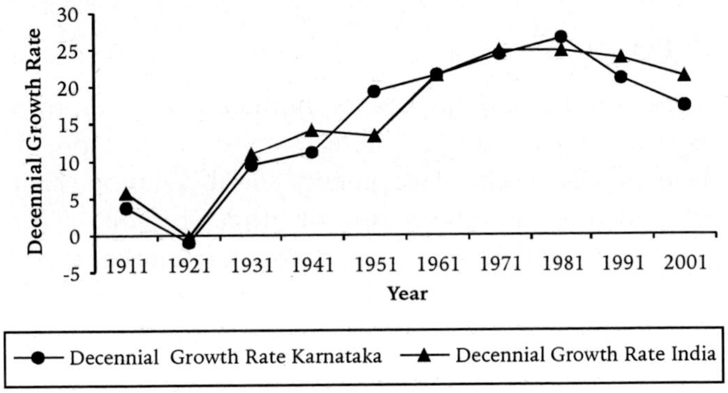

Source: Population Census of respective years.

The growth rates vary widely across the districts. It is observed that until 1940, districts like Kodagu and Chickmagalur experienced decline in their respective population due to the scourge of malaria. The fastest growing region in the state was southern Maidan comprising districts belonging to old Mysore state, followed by northern Maidan, coastal and Malnad areas. But, the northern districts (coming under Gulbarga division) experienced higher growth during the last two decades. Good irrigation facilities also encouraged large-scale migration into Bellary and Raichur districts in the eighties, which led to higher growth rate of population in this region. Of the remaining districts, except Bangalore (the capital city of Karnataka), all other districts had annual growth rates less than 2 per cent. Bangalore district recorded the highest decadal growth rate (34.8 per cent) while Udupi registered the lowest growth rate (6.9 per cent) in the state during 1991-2001. The northern Maidan districts registered a decadal growth rate of 18.76 during the period 1991 to 2001 whereas the growth rate in coastal and Malnad districts was only 11.47 per cent (Appendix A-4.3). The decadal growth rate in southern Maidan region is 14.35 per cent.

According to the population projections of the Registrar General of India, Karnataka's population will be 59 million by 2011 and 63 million by 2016. The aged population (60 years above) would increase from 43 lakh in 2006 to 61 lakh by 2016 (Appendix A-4.4). However, it is noted that the growth rate of schoolgoing child population will decline over the years.

The density of population (number of persons per square kilometre) increased from 68 persons in 1901 to 101 by 1951 and to 275 by 2001. The highest population density was observed in Bangalore division, followed by Mysore division. Bangalore district was the most densely populated district in the state in 2001, mainly due to the high density of Bangalore urban agglomeration, which comprised 85 per cent of the population of the district, followed by Dakshina Kannada and Mysore. The less densely populated districts were Uttara Kannada and Kodagu. Population density was considerably lower in Karnataka compared to the national average (324 per sq. km).

Scheduled Caste and Scheduled Tribe Population

More than one-fifth of the total population in the state belonged to scheduled caste (16.2 per cent) and scheduled tribe (6.6 per cent) category. Over the years, their share in the total population has increased. There were large variations in their concentration by districts. While Kolar, Chamarajnagara and Gulbarga districts had a larger share of scheduled castes, Raichur, Bellary and Chitradurga had bigger share of scheduled tribes (Appendix A-4.5). There were five districts in the state which had SC population of more than 20 per cent. In 8 districts of Karnataka, the ST population comprised of 10 to 20 per cent.

4.2.2 Sex Ratio

Karnataka's sex ratio (number of females per 1,000 males) of 964 in 2001 was higher than the all-India figure of 933. The sex ratio of the state was adverse to women and it continued to be adverse during the last century. In 1891 AD, there were 991 females per 1,000 males and a century later, the sex ratio had declined to 960. Most of the districts in the state (except Udupi, Dakshina Kannada and Hassan) had adult sex ratios unfavourable to women.

If we look at the recent trends in sex ratio, particularly the decadal changes in child sex ratio (population below the age of seven years), Karnataka has shown an increasing deficit of females. Though there was a marginal increase in adult sex ratio during 1991-2001, the child sex ratio declined from 960 to 949 in the state. The lowest child sex ratio was recorded in Belgaum district (924). Even in a district like Dakshina Kannada, which had an adult sex ratio favourable to women (1,023), the child sex ratio was only 952 (Appendix A-4.6). Same is the case with Udupi district (adult sex ratio is 1,127 whereas child sex ratio was only 955 in 2001). What is more alarming was the lowest child sex ratios registered in some *talukas* of the state (879 in Chikkodi of Belgaum district and 896 in Siddapur of Uttara Kannada district).

The widening gap in the ratio of girls to boys has been clearly brought to light in 2001 Census, confirming a trend that has been in place for many decades. The imbalance in sex ratio was most pronounced in the youngest age group (0-6 years), thus indicating the scale of injustice as well as the long-term social and economic consequences implied. The Census lists 'sex-selective female abortions', 'female infanticide', and 'female neglect'—as important reasons for this shocking anomaly (Hatti *et al.*, 2004). Such choices could be possible with the progress of medical technology.

4.2.3 Population Composition

The young population below the age of 14 years and the old (60 years and above) form the dependent groups. The young population was 36.0 per cent and old population was 7 per cent in 1991. As per 2001 Census, proportion of young population, has come down to 32 per cent whereas the proportion of elderly (60+ years) has increased to 8 per cent (Appendix A-4.7). The average household size for the state was 5.7 persons in 1991 has come down to 5.0 in 2001. The northern districts of Bidar and Bijapur had the high percentage of large households (6 and more persons), whereas Kodagu showed a different picture. The household size in rural Karnataka was 5.8 persons and in urban Karnataka 5.4. Hindus constituted 84 per cent of the state's population, Muslims 12 per cent and Christians 2 per cent as per the 2001 Census. (Appendix A-4.8).

4.2.4 Mortality

During 1951-1991, the death rate in the state came down sharply, mainly due to the control of epidemics. According to the sample registration system (SRS), the crude death rate of Karnataka was 7.6 (8.2 in rural and 6.4 in urban areas) in 2001. The respective figures for India were 8.4, 9.0 and 6.3. SRS also estimated that the infant mortality rate (IMR), widely recognised as a sensitive indicator of both the socio-economic development and the access to health services, was 53 per thousand live births in the state, compared to 66 at the national level (2001). But considerable variations can be observed between rural and urban areas of the state (69 and 27 respectively). From 95 in 1971, IMR declined considerably to 53 in 2001. But the rural-urban differential was more pronounced in the state than at the national level. According to the National Family Health Survey (1998-99), the infant mortality rate for the state was 51.5 and under-five mortality rate was 69.8. According to NFHS-2 estimates, the IMR in Karnataka (52) was much lower than the national IMR of 68. Moreover, in recent years the IMR in Karnataka has been declining twice as fast as in India as a whole. Despite the substantial decline in infant and child mortality rates in Karnataka, however, one in every 19 children born during the five years (1994-1998) died within the first year of life, and one in every 14 children died before reaching age five. Rural mortality rates were considerately higher than urban mortality rates. The IMR was 41 per cent higher in rural areas than in urban areas. Variations across districts in the state were also significant. In 1991, infant and child mortality rates were 79 and 119 in Bellary district, whereas it was only 29 and 46 respectively in Dakshina Kannada district.

In 1951, the expectation of life at birth for both the men and women was 42 years. It increased to 62.07 years in 1991(60.6 years for men and 63.61 for women). According to the projections, the life expectancy in Karnataka will be 63 for male and 67 for female by 2011 (Appendix A-4.9). Across districts, Dakshina Kannada had the highest (68.52 years) and Bellary (60.32 years) the lowest life expectancy in 1991 (Government of Karnataka, 1999).

4.2.5 Nuptiality

As per the 1991 Census data, the average age at marriage for females in the state was 20.15 years whereas for males it was 26.22 years. Historically, age at marriage has been lower in the districts of northern Karnataka and higher in the coastal and Malnad areas of the state. The singulate mean age at marriage was 26 years for males and 19 years for females in 1991. The differences between rural and urban areas were on expected lines—25 years in rural and 27 years in urban areas for males and 18 years and 20 years respectively for females. The difference between the lowest and the highest age at marriage in the districts of Karnataka was about 5 years for both sexes, both in urban and rural areas. While the difference between male and female age at marriage was usually about 7 years, the difference between the urban and rural areas was only about 2 years. According to NFHS-2, urban women married about two years later than the rural women did and males married about 7 years later than females in Karnataka. Despite the evidence of a rising age at marriage of women in Karnataka, nearly half of them still marry before reaching the legal minimum age at marriage of 18 years, as set by the Child Marriage Restraint Act of 1978 (IIPS and ORC Macro, 2001). It is interesting to note that marriage between relatives (consanguineous marriage) was quite common in the state, particularly among the lower castes. As per the NFHS (1995), more than one-fourth of women married a first cousin and about nine per cent married a second cousin, uncle or other blood relative.

However, variation across districts was quite remarkable. In Dakshina Kannada, 94 per cent of the females in the age group 15-19 years were unmarried in 1991. But, in Raichur and Bijapur districts, the proportion was only about 52 per cent. Age at marriage of females was highest in Dakshina Kannada (23.4 years) followed by Kodagu (22 years). In six districts of Karnataka, the average age at marraige for women was between 18 and 19 years. But, in rural areas of Raichur and Bijapur, the age at marriage for women was less than 18 years in 1991 (2001 data not yet available).

4.2.6 Family Planning

Karnataka had an early start in family planning. Two government sponsored family planning clinics were opened, one in Bangalore and one in Mysore as early as 1930 (Rayappa and Sekher, 1998). These were the first official family planning clinics in the world. According to NFHS, the knowledge of family planning was universal in Karnataka, with 99 per cent of ever-married women reporting knowledge of at least one modern method of birth control. Even though knowledge of family planning was almost universal, the actual use of contraception was relatively lower in the state. According to NFHS (1998-99), current contraceptive use was 58.3 per cent. About 57 per cent were using a modern method (52.2 per cent sterilisation, mostly female sterilisation and only 5 per cent spacing methods). The ideal family size preferred by the women was on an average 2.2 children. NFHS (1998-99) also indicated that 11.5 per cent of the currently married women had an unmet need for family planning. If all the women with an unmet need for family planning were to adopt it, the current contraceptive use rate would increase to 70 per cent.

4.2.7 Fertility Levels and Differentials

The crude birth rate (CBR) has been declining in Karnataka since early 1970s. CBR, which remained relatively stable at a higher level of about 40 or more in the 1950s and 1960s, reached a level of about 28 by 1990. According to SRS, the CBR was 22.2 in 2001 (23.6 in rural and 19 in urban areas). At the national level, the figures were 25.4, 27.1 and 20.2 for total, rural and urban areas respectively. The total fertility rate (TFR) was 4.4 in 1971, which declined to 2.5 in 1997. In urban Karnataka, it was 2 per cent according to NFHS-2 (1998-99). Karnataka will attain the replacement level fertility by 2010, or even before.

There were considerable fertility variations across the state. There existed disparities with regard to health and demographic indicators between the regions of the state. Fertility decline has been faster in southern and coastal regions, and at a tardy pace in backward northern districts characterised by low literacy, low female age at marriage, poor health infrastructure and low status of women (Sekher *et al.*, 2004).

Using 2001 Census data, it was estimated that the crude birth rate (CBR) of Karnataka was 20.9 and total fertility rate (TFR) was 2.9. Among the districts, Koppal, Gulbarga and Raichur were having high CBR while the lowest birth rates were in Udupi and Mandya (Appendix A-4.10). With regard to TFR, 10 districts were below 2.1. However, there were 7 districts where the TFR was 3 and above (Gulbarga, Koppal, Bidar, Raichur, Bellary, Bagalkot and Bijapur).

High fertility in the state is essentially a problem of a few districts in northern Karnataka. Based on a regional analysis using NFHS data, Bhat and Zavier (1999) observe that for almost all socio-demographic variables, the Northeastern Plateau in the state (districts of Bidar, Bijapur, Gulbarga and Raichur) showed very poor performance. The region had the lowest percentage of literate females (22 per cent) and the highest concentration of certain religious groups (12 per cent) in the state. The mean age at first marriage of females was less than 18 years and the couple protection rate was below 40. The backwardness and poor health infrastructure of the region was evident from the fact that it had the lowest percentage of institutional deliveries (17) whereas the state average was 38 per cent, and the lowest per cent of fully immunised children (30). The districts of northern Maidan and the region as a whole showed lower level of achievement compared to other parts of the state with regard to human development and health indices as well as in the availability of public health care facilities. The socio-economic backwardness of the region characterised by limited exposure to mass media and low status of women in a way explain the tardy decline of fertility in the northern districts. If the state can make substantial efforts for improvement in the quality of life in the northern backward districts, fertility transition may be achieved sooner than expected (Sekher *et al.*, 2001). The poor heath infrastructure existing here makes it extremely difficult to effectively implement the family planning programme. No programme can make a significant dent in fertility reduction without certain levels of infrastructural support, conducive social atmosphere and economic development.

4.2.8 Urbanisation

The proportion of urban population in Karnataka was always higher than it was for the country as a whole. In 1901, only 12.6 per cent of the state's population was considered as urban. By 2001, every third person in the state was living in an urban area (34 per cent). Karnataka was the fourth most urbanised among the major states of India. The city of Bangalore exercised tremendous influence on the urban growth of the state by attracting large number of migrants, particularly from the neighbouring states. The state accounted for 6.28 per cent of the country's urban population. Bangalore grew to become the fifth largest urban centre in India and accounted for 24 per cent of the urban population in Karnataka in 2001. The least urbanised district was Kodagu with 86 per cent of its population residing in rural areas.

The urban population of Karnataka, which was about 1.6 million in 1901, had increased to 17.9 million in 2001. Out of the total increase in urban population in 100 years i.e., between 1901 and 2001, about 83 per cent increase was in the last 50 years. There were 237 towns in the state as per the 2001 Census. Most of the urban population in the state was concentrated in class I towns (population of more than 100,000) (Appendix A-4.11 and 4.12).

Among districts, the proportion of urban population in Bangalore district was the highest (88 per cent). The district accounted for over 32 per cent of the urban population of the state. The next higher proportion of urban population was observed in Dharwad district (55 per cent).

4.2.9 Migration

Migration data from 1991 Census indicate that about 87 per cent of the total migrants recorded were interdistrict or intradistrict migrants within the state. Among the migrants, only 12.5 per cent were from other states of India as per the 1991 data. Among the districts, as expected, Bangalore urban district had the highest share of interstate migrants. Border districts like Bellary, Kodagu, Bidar and Kolar also had high proportion migrants from other states.

4.2.10 Insights on Demographic Profile

It has been a convention to view Karnataka state to comprise of southern and northern regions. While districts of Bangalore and Mysore revenue divisions comprise the southern region, districts of Belgaum and Gulbarga revenue divisions comprise the northern region. It is observed that the southern region occupies lesser geographical space (48.58 per cent) than the northern region while it carries a higher population size (57.28 per cent) of the state. Much of this differential is accounted by Bangalore urban district which accounts for 12.37 per cent population of the state with only 1.14 per cent of the state's area, Bangalore city being the capital of the state (over one-eighth share of population in the state in 1 out of 27 districts).

The decadal growth rate of population in the state reveals a declining trend. However, the districts of the most backward region of the state, the Gulbarga division, recorded high growth rates. It is a matter of serious concern that the 7 districts of Gulbarga division carry a population which is 24.56 per cent as a proportion to the total state population while the sum of gross domestic income of these 7 districts of Gulbarga division is only 18.31 per cent. Even when Bangalore urban district's gross income is removed from the total income of the state and the income of Gulbarga division is calculated as a proportion of state's total income, this figure falls short of its share of population.

The high growth rates are also a cause for concern because of several other reasons. This region recorded high poverty ratios as per 1993-94 estimates by the DES/GoK using NSS samples (pp.92-94, 1999, GoK). The SC and ST population proportions in this region were 19.11 and 11.75 per cent while similar figures for the state were 16.2 and 6.6 per cent. It is common knowledge that low incomes and high poverty ratios are prominent among these social groups. It also needs to be noted that the high growth rates of population in this region are with unfavourable sex-ratios in 0-6 population in Bagalkot (939), Gulbarga (937), Koppal (938) and Bellary districts (949), the state average in 2001 being 957. The 2001 Census has also revealed that while the total fertility rate was 2.4 per cent at the state level, all the 7 districts of this region and only this region in the state has recorded a TFR of more than 3.0 per cent.

It is evident from the foregoing set of insights that if Karnataka has to achieve the replacement level fertility by 2010 as visualised by the State Health Policy of 2004, then it has to concentrate its efforts on the overall development of the districts of the Gulbarga division.

4.3 Literacy in the State

Special attention to education in Karnataka state is focused in Chapter 6 of this report. Hence, this section will confine itself to literacy in the state.

4.3.1 Literacy at the State Level

Literacy rates have moved up from 29.80 per cent in 1961 to 67.04 per cent by 2001 in the state. The increase in rates during the four decadal periods were 7.03, 9.38, 9.83 and 11.00 per cent respectively (Table 4.1). It is to be noted that population growth also slowed down during 1991 to 2001. The crude annual average literacy gain during 1961 to 2001 has been 0.931 per cent per year. The gap in literacy in 2001 from 100 per cent coverage is 32.96 per cent. At this pace of 0.931 per cent per year, full literacy (cent per cent) may be achieved in the state, as per crude estimates, by only 2036 AD. But it may not be the case because of the following reasons: (a) Literacy promotes literacy. The gains from school education and efforts in promotion of adult literacy would boost the demand for schooling and literacy attainments. There are several districts (8) whose literacy rates were more than 70 per cent by 2001. Concentration of efforts in future can be

TABLE 4.1

Literacy Rates in Karnataka

(in per cent)

Gender	*1961*	*1971*	*1981*	*1991*	*1996*	*2001*
Male	42.29	48.51	58.73	67.26	73.75	76.29
Female	16.70	24.56	33.17	44.34	52.65	57.45
Total	**29.80**	**36.83**	**46.21**	**56.04**	**63.42**	**67.04**

Source: Human Development in Karnataka, 1999; GoK, 1999 and *Census of India,* 2001.

on those districts which are lagging far behind. (b) Population growth rate is going down and a large volume of illiterates from older age-groups may disappear. (c) The state has set a target of universalisation of primary education by 2007 AD and higher primary education by 2010 AD. With increasing investments of time, efforts and resources on elementary education in the state, the time-ceiling for realisation of 100 per cent literacy may get reduced. It is envisioned that Karnataka may achieve full literacy by 2020. Most of the districts may hit this target. A few districts may lag behind and require some more time. Districts which need additional attention for full literacy are discussed at a later section.

FIGURE 4.2

Progress of Literacy in Karnataka

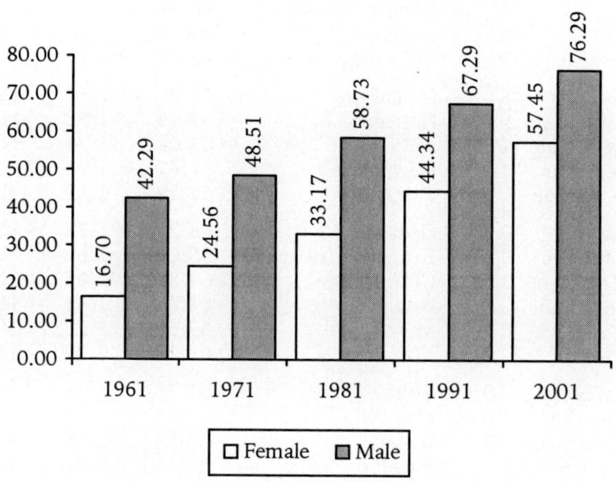

Source: *Population Census* of respective years.

The progress of literacy in the state has been steadily increasing over the years. The average literacy rates between 1961 and 2001 has increased by 40 per cent from 25 per cent to 65 per cent. The figures also show that the female literacy rates when compared to the male literacy rates in 1961 were less than half (Figure 4.2). Over the years the gap, between the male and female literacy rates is reducing but the pace suggests that overall the gap in the literacy rates even in 2001 is a cause for concern. This is despite the fact that the state government had adopted several schemes to target the girl children in their drive for universal elementary education. This trend is seen even when one compares the data of the literacy rates at the national level.

According to 2001 Census, the literacy rate of Karnataka was slightly higher than the national average by about a little less than 2 percentage points. The literacy rate in Karnataka was 67.04 per cent with a decadal growth rate of 10 per cent in Karnataka, which is marginally higher than the national growth rate of 9.6 per cent. According to the 2001 Census, literacy rates of women and men in Karnataka were 57.45 per cent and 76.29 per cent as against 44.3 per cent and 67.3 per cent respectively in 1991. In actual numbers 1,29,57,306 women out of a total of 2,58,77,615 (in 2001) in the state were illiterate. Though the literacy rate of women has increased from 29.8 per cent in 1961 to 57.4 per cent in 2001, as a result of several state initiated literacy programmes, it is observed that the gap in female and male literacy rates is still wide.

4.3.2 Comparison of Division-wise Literacy Rate 1991-2001

A division-wise comparison of literacy rates is more interesting particularly to trace its growth over the decade (Figure 4.3). This analysis gains immensely from the fact that while breakdown of numbers at divisional level has something more to tell than drawing conclusions only from the comparison of the state figures of 1991 and 2001.

FIGURE 4.3

Division-wise Literacy Rates: 1991-2001

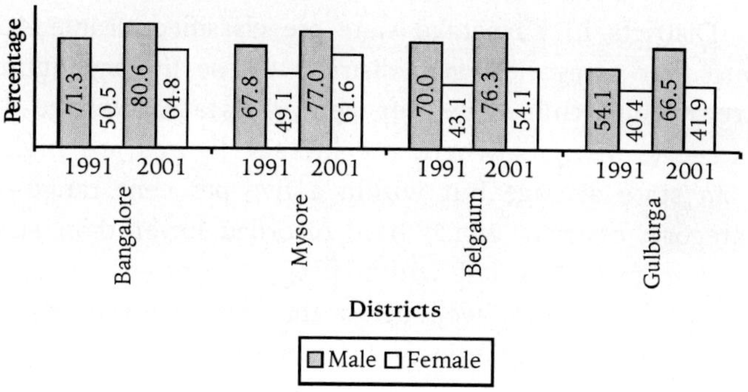

Source: *Population Census* of respective years.

In addition, the gender breakup of the literacy rates of the different divisions also throws light on the contribution of specific divisions within the state to the slow pace of the state in closing the gender gap. The literacy rates at the divisional level for the males clearly show that the increase in the rates for the past decade spans from close to 6 per cent points to about 12 per cent. The lowest was in the Belgaum division and the highest in the Gulbarga division. The decadal increase of the female literacy rates across the divisions was from around 11 per cent to over 15 per cent, which is an encouraging trend. In this case too, Belgaum registers the lowest increase while Gulbarga recorded the maximum increase. While examining the gender gap in the literacy rates for the years 1991 and 2001, there is a tendency of the gap reducing by 3 to 5 per cent. It must be noted that only the Bangalore division has closed the gap by 5 per cent. The other two divisions namely Mysore and Gulbarga have reduced the gender gap in 2001 when compared to 1991 by around 3 per cent. Belgaum division has reduced the gender gap by 4.66 per cent close to the Bangalore division, although it has the second lowest female literacy rates next only to Gulbarga in 2001. Hence, the government needs to increase its efforts on increasing the female literacy in both the Mysore and Belgaum divisions (Appendix A-4.13).

4.3.3 Comparison of District Literacy Rates

Literacy in the Districts

It is common knowledge that there are regional imbalances in literacy attainments in the state. A simple analysis based on 2001 Census data on literacy in districts of Karnataka state and the average annual exponential growth rates that they have achieved during 1991-2001, in the light of state average performance, would indicate whether total (85 per cent) and full (100 per cent) literacy will be achieved by 2020.

Districts in Karnataka state are classified (Table 4.2) into four categories, *viz.*, districts whose literacy figures are higher than five per cent of state average—A category; districts where the literacy figures are higher than state average but within a five per cent range—B category; districts which have recorded lower than state average rates but fall within five per cent—C category; districts which are well below the state average beyond a five per cent difference—D category.

While reviewing the performance of districts, their average annual exponential growth rate between 1991-2001 is also considered. This will give an indication of their future potential.

Analysis reveals that all A category districts have recorded lower than state average (LSA). Low growth rate among A category may be because they find it difficult to reach illiterate population, that is, those who are on the margin. These districts need to concentrate more on the marginal illiterate population, non-enrolled/drop-out children, child labourers, street children and difficult to reach tribal/remote rural population in future.

Dharwad district in B category. It needs to intensify its efforts as its growth rate is lower than state average. Similarly LSA growth rate districts in A Category viz., Shimoga and Chickmagalur also need to step up their efforts for higher growth rate.

Gadag district is in C category, but is still recording LSA growth rate.

TABLE 4.2

2001 Literacy Rates across Districts in Karnataka State Average: 67.04 per cent (Persons) State Average Annual Exponential Growth: 1.81 per cent

Category	*Sl.No.*	*District Rate*	*Literacy Annual Growth Rate*	*Average*	*G.R. HSA/ LSA*
A Category > 5 per cent of State Average	1	Bangalore (Urban)	83.91	0.96	LSA
	2	Dakshina Kannada	83.47	0.84	LSA
	3	Udupi	79.87	0.70	LSA
	4	Kodagu	78.17	1.35	LSA
	5	Uttara Kannada	76.59	1.39	LSA
	6	Shimoga	74.86	1.60	LSA
	7	Chickmagalur	72.63	1.75	LSA
B Category 0.1 and up to 5 per cent Lower than State Average	8	Dharwad	71.87	1.37	LSA
	9	Hassan	68.75	1.92	HSA
	10	Haveri	68.09	1.96	HSA
	11	Davangere	67.67	1.92	HSA
	12	Tumkur	67.19	2.12	HSA
C Category 0.1 and up to 5 per cent Lower than State Average	13	Gadag	66.27	1.72	LSA
	14	Bangalore (Rural)	65.00	2.62	HSA
	15	Chitradurga	64.88	2.18	HSA
	16	Belgaum	64.42	1.91	HSA
	17	Mysore	63.69	2.27	HSA
	18	Kolar	63.14	2.27	HSA
D Category Lower than State Average beyond 5 per cent Difference	19	Bidar	61.98	3.23	HSA
	20	Mandya	61.21	2.43	HSA
	21	Bellary	58.04	2.38	HSA
	22	Bagalkot	57.81	0.76	LSA
	23	Bijapur	57.46	0.16	LSA
	24	Koppal	55.02	3.71	HSA
	25	Chamrajnagar	51.26	2.99	HSA
	26	Gulbarga	50.65	2.77	HSA
	27	Raichur	49.54	3.73	HSA

Note: LSA Lower than state average figure.
HSA Higher than state average figure.

Source: Census of Population, 2001.

Serious cases among D Category districts are Bagalkot and Bijapur whose growth rate are LSA. All the 9 districts under D Category and especially Raichur, Gulbarga, Chamarajnagar need intensive care.

Having examined the trends in the literacy rates over the past decade across divisions, this section examines the variation of literacy rates in the year 2001 across districts with urban and rural breakups (Appendix A-4.14).

The state figure for female literacy rate in rural Karnataka was 48.50 as against 70.63 per cent for the males. A further breakup of female literacy rates at the district level reveal that, 14 of the districts were below the state figure. Among the 14 districts, Raichur and Gulbarga were the most backward at 26.38 and 26.97 per cent respectively.

Drawing attention to the wide gender gap in the literacy rates in some districts, the High Power Committee for the Redressal of Regional Imbalances has recommended, that as far as redressal measures are concerned, 5 districts (Koppal, Raichur, Gulbarga, Bagalkot and Gadag) figure in the more deprived category and hence attract remedial action in the first phase.

While it is important to break up data of the state to districts to highlight deprivation among the districts, it may also be required to further breakdown the data at the *taluka* level and locate variations even within the district. The Task Force on Women's Empowerment has done this exercise and pointed out to the fact that with respect to rural female literacy, one needs to take note of the *talukas* of Yadagiri (18.67 per cent), Shahpur (23.21 per cent), Raichur (24.76 per cent) and Devadurga (25.22 per cent), which rank the lowest in women literacy rates. As expected, these *talukas* are located in the two most backward districts namely Raichur and Gulbarga. In urban areas, Siraguppa (40.74 per cent) in Bellary district. Deodurg (43.85 per cent) and Manvi (46.75 per cent) both in Raichur district and Basavana Bagewadi (50.22) in Bijapur district are the most backward *talukas*. These *talukas* within the districts must be prioritised for intervention by the state.

TABLE 4.3

Distribution of Districts and *Talukas* in Karnataka based on the Female Literacy Rate in Karnataka

Women Literacy Rate	*Districts*	*Talukas*
More than 57.45	11	64
Less than 57.45	16	111
Total	**27**	**175**

Source: Census of Population, 2001.

As regards concentration of female illiteracy in the state, the Task Force on Women's Empowerment has reported that of the 175 *talukas* in the state, the literacy rate of women was less than the state's figure of 57.45 per cent in as much as 111 *talukas* (Figure 4.4).

FIGURE 4.4

Distribution of Women Literacy

(a) District Level

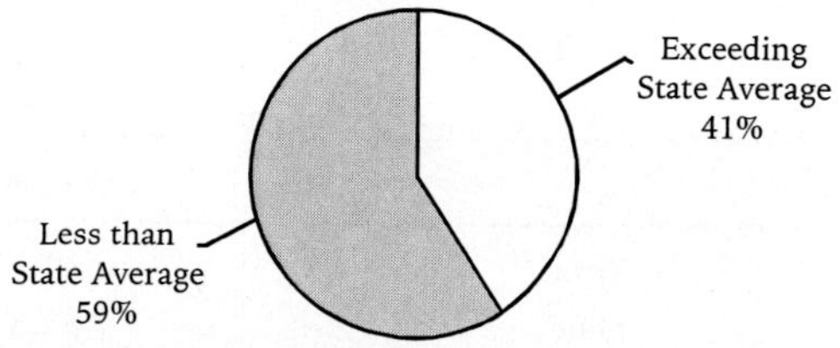

(b) *Taluka* Level

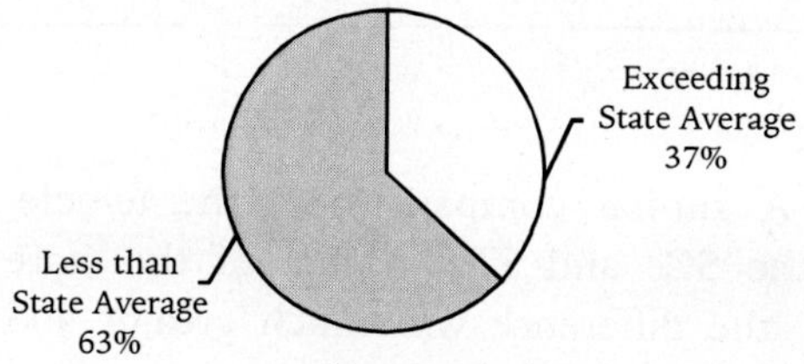

Source: Task Force on Women Empowerment, *Ensure Women Welfare Schemes Reach Target Audience*, Government of Karnataka.

Only four districts in the state have a women literacy rate of more than 70 per cent, which are Bangalore Urban (77.68 per cent), Dakshina Kannada (77.36 per cent), Udupi (74.02 per cent), and Kodagu (72.53 per cent). Sixteen districts namely, Bangalore Rural, Belgaum, Bagalkot, Bellary, Bijapur, Bidar, Gulbarga, Gadag, Chamrajnagar, Koppal, Chitradurga, Kolar, Mandya, Tumkur, Mysore and Raichur have women literacy rate of less than 57.45 per cent. Surprisingly, the agriculturally developed districts like Mandya (51.62 per cent) and Mysore (55.81 per cent) too, have not shown any improvement in the growth of literacy rates for women. It is a matter of concern that the women literacy rates in the districts of Gulbarga (38.40 per cent) and Raichur (36.84 per cent) are so low and stands apart from the rest of the districts in the state.

4.3.4 Progress of Literacy among the Scheduled Castes and Scheduled Tribes

The Scheduled Castes and Scheduled Tribes have always been a disadvantaged group and hence their progress in literacy, and for that matter in education as a whole, lags behind those attained by the general population. The literacy rates for these special groups as per the 2001 Census, show that for Karnataka the figures for SC male was 63.8 per cent almost 12 per cent less than the state figure, i.e., 76.29 per cent for males in the year 2001 (Table 4.4). The corresponding figures for the ST males was 59.7 per cent, which was 16.6 per cent less than the literacy rates for males in the state. A similar comparison of the female literacy rates for the SCs and STs to that of the state figures reveal that the difference was much greater and was in fact 15.75 per cent and 20.85 per cent respectively. The gap between the literacy rates of these disadvantaged groups and the overall literacy rates need to be bridged so that they too can be a part of the mainstream.

TABLE 4.4

Literacy Rates among SC & ST in 2001

(in per cent)

SC	**Total**	**52.9**
	Male	63.8
	Female	41.7
ST	**Total**	**48.3**
	Male	59.7
	Female	36.6

Source: Census, 2001.

4.3.5 Public-Private Enterprise in Achieving Total Literacy

In recent years the role of private enterprise to tackle illiteracy and achieve the fundamental right to education has increased considerably. Several NGOs in the state have made concerted efforts to increase literacy rates among the underprivileged in rural areas and urban slums in the state. Some of the note-worthy efforts are by organisations like MAYA, Mahila Samakhya, Pratham, Suvidhya, Samuha. Several NGOs who have been in the field of development and have worked for women's empowerment have also focused their energies both physical and financial to promote literacy among women. Additionally, they have directed efforts to increase the participation of students particularly girls in elementary school education.

The last few years have also seen the active role of the state both the Centre and state in promoting the education of girls and particularly focusing on retaining children in school through the Sarva Shiskshan Abhyan. This programme adopts many of the successful approaches of the earlier government programmes. It focuses on providing girls access to education through local specific initiatives.

The Mahila Samakhya Programme launched in the state in 1989 is stated to be a women's empowerment project which does not aim at services delivery but seeks to bring about a change in women's perception about themselves and of society, in regard to women's traditional roles. It endeavours to create an environment for women to seek knowledge and information in order informed choices and create circumstances in which women can learn at their own pace.

The efforts of the NGOs and the government and more importantly the private sectors like the Azeem Premji Foundation(WIPRO), INFOSYS and the Tata Trusts have all in some way or the other contributed to promoting elementary education which will have a long range impact in reducing the illiteracy in the state.

4.3.6 Urban Literacy in Karnataka

Literacy rates on the whole are improving in India and in Karnataka too. The urban literacy rate for Karnataka which was a mere 35 per cent in 1951 improved gradually and the increase was more pronounced in 1991 when it touched 74 per cent. As per 2001 Census the urban literacy rate was 81.05 per cent which means less than 20 per cent of Karnataka's urban population remains illiterate. The urban-rural the gap in literacy which widened for three consecutive decades in 1961, 1971 and 1981, narrowed to 26 per cent in 1991 and furthermore to 21 per cent in 2001 (Figure 4.5)

FIGURE 4.5

Karnataka: Urban and Rural Literacy Rates and Gap 1951-2001

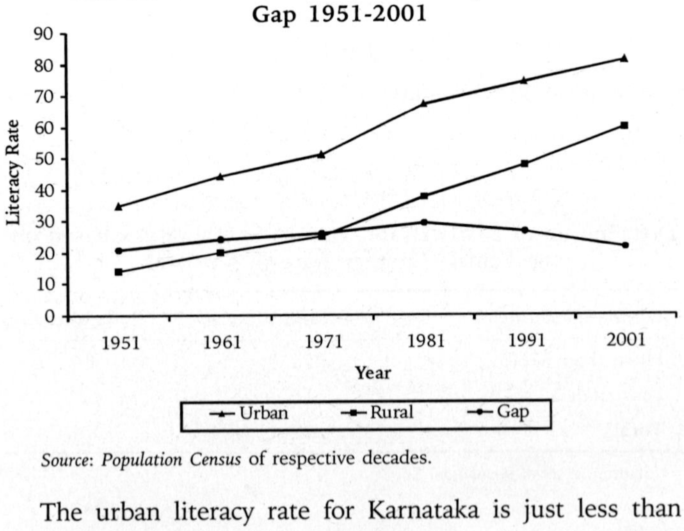

Source: Population Census of respective decades.

The urban literacy rate for Karnataka is just less than 1 per cent higher than the all-India rate of 80.06 in 2001 but it is lower than the neighbouring states like Kerala, Tamil Nadu and Maharashatra. Only Andhra Pradesh recorded lower urban literacy rate than Karnataka. The difference in urban literacy rates between 1991 and 2001 was highest for Andhra Pradesh at 10.04 per cent followed by Karnataka at 6.85 per cent. The urban-rural gap for 2001 was lowest for Kerala at 3.33 per cent (Tables 4.5 and 4.6 and Figure 4.6).

TABLE 4.5

Rural-Urban Gap in Literacy Rates for Select States

(in per Cent)

States	*1981*	*1991*	*2001*
Karnataka	29.28	26.51	21.37
Andhra Pradesh	33.15	30.61	21.06
Kerala	6.60	3.33	3.33
Tamil Nadu	28.25	23.40	15.41
Maharashtra	28.64	23.68	14.92
All-India	-	**28.41**	**20.85**

Source: Population Census and *National Human Development Report*, 2001.

TABLE 4.6

Difference in Urban Literacy Rates 1991-2001 in Selected States

(in per Cent)

States	*1991*	*2001*	*Difference*
Karnataka	74.21	81.05	6.85
Andhra Pradesh	66.35	75.39	10.04
Kerala	92.25	93.38	1.13
Tamil Nadu	77.99	82.07	4.08
Maharashtra	79.2	85.76	6.56
All-India	**73.08**	**80.06**	**6.98**

Source: Population Census and *National Human Development Report* 2001.

FIGURE 4.6

Difference in Urban Literacy Rates 1991-2001 in Select States

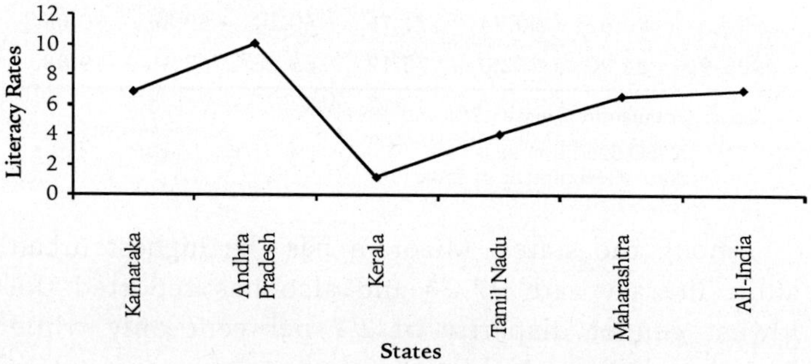

Source: Population Census and *National Human Development Report* 2001.

4.3.7 Gender-wise Urban Literacy

The female literacy rates have been always lower than those of the males and urban literacy is not an exception. Nevertheless one noticeable development in female literacy in Karnataka is, that it has been growing at a faster rate than male literacy with a result the gender divide is narrowing. This phenomenon is seen in almost all the states (Tables 4.7 and 4.8).

TABLE 4.7

Urban Literacy: Males and Females in Karnataka

(in Per Cent)

Years	*Males*	*Females*	*Gap between Males and Females*	*Difference in Growth Rates*	
				Males	*Females*
1951	47.00	23.00	24.00	-	-
1961	-	-	-	-	-
1971	60.00	42.00	18.00	13.00	19.00
1981	76.54	56.41	20.13	16.54	14.41
1991	82.04	65.74	16.30	5.50	9.33
2001	86.85	74.87	11.98	4.82	9.13

Source: Population Census of respective decades.

TABLE 4.8

Urban Literacy: Males and Females in Select States

(in per cent)

States	*1981*		*1991*		*2001*	
	Males	*Females*	*Males*	*Females*	*Males*	*Females*
Karnataka	76.54	56.41	82.04	65.74	86.85	74.87
Andhra Pradesh	72.58	48.70	75.87	56.41	83.21	69.34
Kerala	92.00	81.99	95.58	89.06	96.07	90.87
Tamil Nadu	83.76	62.23	86.06	69.61	88.40	75.64
Maharashtra	82.90	63.94	86.41	70.87	91.42	79.25
All-India	-	-	-	-	**86.42**	**72.99**

Source: Population Census and *National Human Development Report, 2001*.

4.3.8 Urban Literacy-Regional Distribution

The highest literacy rate was attained by Kodagu district in 2001 i.e., 89.7 per cent overtaking Dakshina Kannada district which had the highest literacy of 84.51 per cent in 1991. The lowest literacy was in Raichur district at 66.9 per cent in 2001 which was the same as in 1991 also at 56.38 per cent. The difference between the highest rate and lowest rate which was 28.13 per cent in 1991 narrowed to 22.8 per cent which is a good sign.

It may be seen from the Table 4.9 that no district (urban) had attained a literacy rate of above 85 per cent in 1991 whereas in 2001 four districts had attained, namely, Coorg 89.7 per cent, Udupi 89.5 per cent, Dakshina Kannada 89.1 per cent and Uttara Kannada 86.3 per cent. While in 1991 maximum number of districts (six) were in the relatively low literacy range below 70 and above 60 per cent where as in 2001 only two districts were in this range. Furthermore in 2001 maximum number districts i.e., 10 were in higher literacy range of below 85 and above 80 per cent (Appendix A-4.15 and A-4.16)

TABLE 4.9

Number of Districts in Different Literacy Ranges: Urban Karnataka

Range of Literacy (in per cent)	*No. of Districts*	
	1991	*2001*
85 and above	-	4
Below 85 and above 80	3	10
Below 80 and above 75	5	4
Below 75 and above 70	5	7
Below 70 and above 60	6	2
Below 60	1	-
Total	20	27

Source: Population Census 2001.

The following table presents a clear picture of the gender divide among the districts both for 1991 and 2001.

TABLE 4.10

Urban Literacy: Males and Females in Districts for Karnataka

Range of Literacy (in Per Cent)	*No. of Districts*			
	1991		*2001**	
	Males	*Females*	*Males*	*Females*
90 and above	1	-	4	-
Below 90 and above 85	3	-	10	2
Below 85 and above 80	8	-	8	2
Below 80 and above 75	5	2	5	6
Below 75 and above 70	2	5	-	6
Below 70 and above 60	1	6	-	9
Below 60	-	5	-	2
Below 50	-	2	-	-
Total	20	20	27	27

Note: *Seven districts were newly formed subsequent to 1991 Census.

Source: Population Census 1991 and 2001.

The gender gap though narrowed in 2001 as compared with 1991, it is large in some districts like Bagalkot, Raichur, Koppal, Gadag and Bellary which is above 20 per cent. Even districts such as Bijapur, Gulbarga and Bellary, are in fact very close to this gap. The highest gap is 21.5 per cent for Bagalkot and the lowest is 7.1 per cent in Kodagu. The difference between the highest and lowest gap is skewed considering the fact that for the state as a whole, the gap is 2.0 per cent only in 2001. The details of district-wise urban literacy rates are given in Appendix A-4.15.

4.3.9 Adult Urban Literacy

A scenario with total literacy without addressing adult illiteracy is incomplete. The adult literacy rate in India is defined as the proportion of literate population in age group of 15 years and above. Adult literacy is a prevalent measure of education that reflects average social effort, in a society over the period.

Adult literacy rates are also increasing over a period of time. However nearly one-fourth of the urban adult population in Karnataka remain illiterate. Further urban adult literacy for the state, which was lower than the all-India rate in 1981 improved marginally in 1991 but again slipped below the all-India rate in 1995-96. The adult literacy rate for males was 84.20 per cent and that of females was 65.20 per cent in 1995-66 and the gap was19 per cent. This gap was much larger than the total literacy rates of 2001 and 1991 of 11.98 per cent and 16.30 per cent respectively (Table 4.11).

TABLE 4.11

Adult Urban Literacy Rates

(in per cent)

Years	*Karnataka*			*All-India*		
	Male	*Female*	*Persons*	*Male*	*Female*	*Persons*
1981	75.96	51.67	64.46	76.29	51.9	65.11
1991	80.62	60.74	71.15	80.14	59.86	70.68
1995-96	84.20	65.20	75.12	65.68	67.35	79.68

Source: Population Census 1981 and 1991.
NSSO 52nd Round as reported in *National Human Development Report 2001*, Government of India.

Among the states, Mizoram has the highest urban adult literacy rate 97.07 and also has reported the lowest gender disparity of 2.7 per cent only while Rajasthan has the highest disparity of 29.1 per cent. In the five-year period between 1991 and 1995-96, Karnataka could reduce the disparity only fractionally by less than 1 per cent whereas the other comparable states had done much better (Table 4.12).

TABLE 4.12

Gender Gap in Adult Literacy: Urban Karnataka and Select States

States	*1981*	*1991*	*1995-96*
Karnataka	24.29	19.88	19.00
Andhra Pradesh	28.24	18.70	20.10
Kerala	12.53	7.81	5.10
Tamil Nadu	26.01	19.86	18.30
Maharashtra	23.28	19.46	17.40
All-India	24.39	20.28	18.33

Source: *Population Census* 1981 and 1991.
NSSO 52nd Round as reported in *National Human Development Report 2001*, Government of India.

4.3.10 Urban Literacy as Revealed by NSSO 55th Round 1999-2000

As per the 55th Round of NSS 1999-2000 in a sample of 1000 persons, literates were 821 and the 'not literates' were 179. The breakup of males and females reveals that male literates are more than the female literates i.e., 880 for males and 757 for females. The level of education of literates is given below separately for males and females (Table 4.13).

TABLE 4.13

Level of Urban Literacy out of a Sample of 1000 Persons

Details	*Males*	*Females*	*Persons*
Total Literates	**880**	**757**	**821**
Literates below Primary	123	121	122
Primary	137	129	133
Middle	185	181	183
Secondary	189	172	181
Higher Secondary	103	77	91
Graduates and Above	143	76	111

Source: NSSO 55th Round 1989-90.

The level of literacy is seem to be somewhat distributed among all levels of education. Persons with middle and secondary levels account for less than 50 per cent at 44.3. The lowest percentage was recorded in the higher secondary level implying that people who have studied up to higher secondary have peursued their studies to graduates and above which accounts for 13.5 per cent of the literates. Similar is the picture both for males and females. Among females, the level of literacy was highest in the middle level whereas for males it was at the secondary level. Below primary level the difference is negligible between females than males. However people in the 'not literates' category in the urban areas is still high at 17.9 per cent. The 100 per cent literacy level is still a long way to achieve.

The monthly per capita expenditure (MPCE) is an important determining factor of literacy and is directly related with it. This can be seen from the following data (Table 4.14).

TABLE 4.14

Urban Literacy as per MPCE out of a Sample of 1000 Persons

MPCE	*Males*		*Female*		*Total*	
(in Rupees)	*Literates*	*Non-literates*	*Literates*	*Non-literates*	*Literates*	*Non-literates*
0-300	550	450	383	617	467	533
300-500	652	348	442	558	550	450
350-425	800	200	608	392	704	296
425-500	770	230	629	371	701	299
500-575	804	196	696	304	749	251
575-665	834	166	711	289	774	226
665-775	906	94	749	251	829	171
775-915	948	52	775	225	864	136
915-1120	967	33	867	133	919	81
1120-1500	953	47	893	107	925	75
1500-1925	980	20	964	36	973	27
Above 1925	985	15	946	54	968	32
All	**880**	**120**	**757**	**243**	**821**	**179**

Source: NSSO 55th Round 1989-90.

Lower the income higher is the proportion of non-literate persons and *vice versa.* This phenomenon is seen in both males and females. Likewise among the literates, higher the income, higher is the level of education. Out of 821 literates, 'graduates and above' were 395 in MPCE of Rs.1925 and above. Similarly more literates 467 with lowest level of education i.e., below primary are found in the lowest MPCE of Rs.300 and The number of literates with lower level education i.e., below primary is found to be in the higher at 467 MPCE of Rs.300 whereas only 3 are found in the highest education level of graduates and above.

Literacy and illiteracy as per household type for persons above age 7 has been captured by NSSO 55th Round 1999-2000. As for the household activity, illiteracy was high among the casual labour, 39.4 per cent for total persons, 32.0 per cent for males and 47.0 per cent for females.

Variations among the social groups as revealed by the same Round for urban Karnataka, Scheduled Tribe households account for highest illiteracy of 46.1 per cent followed by Scheduled Caste 34.4 per cent while for other backward classes it was 20.4 per cent and for others it was 11.1 per cent. For males and females similar trend has been observed.

Variations across religions among the illiterates reveal that, Islam accounts for 22.9 per cent, followed by Hinduism 17.1 per cent and Jainism 14.0 per cent. The trend is similar to both for for both males and females.

4.3.11 *Intensity of Formal Education*

The National Human Development Report, 2001 has observed that enrolment rate as indicator to capture the spread of education is not accurate with this magnitude of dropouts. Therefore, the Report has constructed the mean year of schooling or intensity of formal education. Intensity of formal education is based on stage-wise enrolment completion rates and it attempts to capture current progress in spread of education among school going children the entire population. This indicator according to the report not only values education in early years of an individual's life but it also lays importance on a structured formal system of education and more importantly weighs progressively the capacity of the education system to successfully retain enrolled students over successive stages from class I to XII. The intensity of formal education has been constructed at two different point of time 1978 and 1993 separately for rural and urban and for males and females. For Karnataka these indicators are given below (Table 4.15).

TABLE 4.15

Intensity of Formal Education in Urban Karnataka (in Years)

	Boys		*Girls*		*Children*	
	1978	*1993*	*1978*	*1993*	*1978*	*1993*
Rural	3.60	4.31	2.99	3.88	3.36	4.12
Urban	5.18	5.34	4.67	5.09	4.96	5.22
Total	**4.16**	**4.68**	**3.65**	**4.34**	**3.95**	**4.53**

Source: National Human Development Report, 2001.

For the whole state of Karnataka, the intensity of formal education was 3.95 years in 1978 which was lower than 4.03 years for all-India. This increased 15 years later in 1993 to 4.53 years for Karnataka and 4.63 years for all-India. The increase was seen in all both rural and urban and for boys and girls. In urban areas, the gender disparity which was wider in 1978 narrowed sizeably in 1993.

4.3.12 *Adjusted Intensity of Formal Education*

The NHDR, 2001 also observes that this indicator of intensity of formal education ignores the children who are not enrolled and therefore it is necessary to adjust it for gross enrolment ratio and estimate the adjusted intensity of formal education. While doing so importance is placed on school enrolments and at the same time, the capacity of the system to retain those who are enrolled over successive classes. The adjusted figures for 1978, and 1993 are presented below (Table 4.16).

TABLE 4.16

Adjusted Intensity of Formal Education in Karnataka (in Years)

	Boys		*Girls*		*Children*	
	1978	*1993*	*1978*	*1993*	*1978*	*1993*
Rural	1.98	2.92	1.14	2.15	1.57	2.54
Urban	4.63	4.25	3.16	3.67	3.89	3.97
Total	**2.65**	**3.35**	**1.68**	**2.64**	**2.17**	**3.00**

Source: National Human Development Report 2001.

The adjusted intensity of formal education from the above suggests that for urban areas the adjustment was minimum as compared to rural areas. Here again the gap between girls and boys is not significant in urban areas compared to rural areas. Among the states as usual the adjusted and unadjusted ratios for 1993 are higher in Kerala (3.94), followed by Tamil Nadu (3.86), Maharashtra (3.41) and Andhra Pradesh was lower at 2.28 years. In overall, union territory of Pondicherry registered the highest at 4.81 years.

4.3.13 *Policy and Intervention Programmes to Reduce Urban Literacy in Karnataka*

According to the house-to-house children Census for the age group 6-14 years conducted every year by the Government of Karnatka since 2001, the number of out of school children was 10.53 lakh, 6.66 lakh and 4.06 lakh in February 2001, 2002 and 2003 respectively.

In fact this was very high in 1996-97 at 26.05 lakh (estimated). The Government of Karnataka had taken up many varieties of schemes to improve accessibility of children in schoolgoing age group, to schools and increasing enrolments which have brought about positive impact in improving student retention rates. Between 2001 and 2003 about 6.47 lakh children were admitted to schools and mainstreamed. Another 2.08 lakh children were brought back to the mainstream through various programmes. This is reflected in the sharp fall in out of school children from 10.53 lakh in 2000-01 to 2.81 lakh in 2003-04 and furthermore to 1 lakh in 2004-05.

To achieve the goal of Universalitation of Elementary Education, both the Karnataka and the Central Governments have formulated various programmes under 'Sarva Shiksha Abhiyan' (SSA). SSA was launched very recently by the Government of India which has been planned to be initiated in low female literacy districts spread over 15 states. SSA which has replaced the DPEP, is a variant of DPEP and envisages to develop district-specific elementary education with a focus on *Panchayati Raj* Institutions. To begin with, it would develop educational plans with the involvement of local people in a participatory planning mode. SSA is a holistic programme which envisages community involvement in a big way and community ownership is central to the SSA Programme. Another feature of SSA is that all the existing centrally sponsored schemes have been brought under one umbrella i.e., SSA. SSA is being implemented in 27 revenue districts of Karnataka from the year 2001-02. The funding which was shared among the Centre and states in varying ratios is now being funded fully by the International Development Association (IDA) under its credit agreement with effect from 2004-05.

Some of the measures introduced in Karnataka to encourage enrolment and retention are, free education to girls studying in Std. I-XII in government institutions and also free textbooks and uniforms for girls students in Std. VII-X in government institutions, massive mid-day meal programme, free school bags, and free six notebooks to SC and ST girls in classes V to VII in government primary schools.

The details of the schemes targeting the out of school children (6-14) in urban areas in Karnataka are given below. It may be mentioned that a good number of schemes mentioned below are common to both urban and rural areas. Most of the urban oriented programmes are concentrated in Bangalore city and Bangalore urban where the adverse fall out of urbanisation is reflected in increasing number of slums, working children and the street children.

i. Chinnara Angala

The Chinnara Angala Summer Course Programme is aimed at bringing back out of school children into schools. The out-of school children fall into two categories: a) those who were never enrolled in school, and b) those who have dropped out of school at either the lower primary level or the upper primary level. The Chinnara Angala is aimed at enabling these children in the age group of 6-14 years to enrol themselves into regular schools. Earlier a para-teacher appointed from amongst the village youths taught the children and now regular teacher is looking after the Chinnara Angala Centre with the assistance of the volunteer who is the local youth. An intensive, condensed form of the curriculum is taught, at the end of which the children are enrolled in the appropriate regular classes. The duration of the intervention was initially proposed to be of 60 days. Later it was decided that it would continue till all the children were enrolled into formal school.

When first started in 10 programme blocks, 3,100 children were enrolled in the course, and as many as 2,600 children from amongst them were enabled to join the mainstream formal schools. It shows acceptance of the intervention by the community. This also indicates growing awareness among people about the need for education. In the beginning the programme personnel spent considerable time convincing people about the benefits of the interventions, which was crucial for the success of this intervention.

The Akshara Foundation, an NGO has been very active in running this programme in Bangalore. All the existing 194 Chinnara Angala learning centres reaching out to 4,600 children in the city have been coordinated by the Foundation with the help of other NGOs like MAYA, Mobility India, APSA, REDS and Rashtrothana Parishat.

Akshara, in collaboration with Madhyam, another NGO, has launched a 100 per cent enrolment campaign in 30 slums in the city. Along with the field publicity office of the Ministry of Information, they conducted awareness programmes on Chinnara Angala in another 35 slums in the city.

ii. Coolieyinda Shalege Programme: (Labour to School)

Commonly children in the age group of 6-14 are found employed in places such as factories, shops, households, hotels, garages, etc. mainly to supplement income of their parents for their livelihood. Coolieyinda Shalege Programme has been launched to bring these children to the school fold from their work places. In this programme parents and employers of the children are warned citing the provision of the prevention of Child Labour Act. Awareness has been created among them regarding importance of education. This has helped to bring the children into the school fold. This programme is being implemented with the coordination of the other departments like Police, Women and Child Development, Social Welfare and Labour Department. This campaign is to liberate such working children from the bondage of labour. Handouts and posters have been made with the appeal of Hon'ble Chief Minister of Karnataka to bring these children to the school fold. Advertisement and T.V. jingles and street plays are made to create the awareness among the parents and society in coordination with NGOs.

iii. Flexi Schools

Eight flexi schools have been started in Bangalore (urban and city). These schools were started with the working children in view who cannot attend the formal school due to their time frame in the workplace, and are running from 8.00 a.m. to 8.00 p.m., so that the working children can attend classes and learn their lessons at hours convenient to them. Hence the name 'flexi schools'. These schools which are not permanent formal schools, aim at infusing confidence and strengthening their knowledge and thus helping these children to bridge with the formal school children. After this children can join the formal school without any difficulty. Till date, 280 children are admitted to these schools. Several NGOs are also cooperating to run these schools including the Akshara Foundation and the Center for Working Children who have joined in the effort on their own initiative. In order to attract working children to these schools, departments such as, the Labour, the Social Welfare and the Department of Minority in addition to several voluntary organisations are cooperating with the Education Department of the State Government.

iv. Mobile Schools

These schools were started to give education to slum dwelling children and children of construction workers, especially in the city areas. At present eight mobile schools are working in Bangalore city. These mobile schools collect children from the slums in and around the city and take them in a bus to a good environment where their teachers will teach them. The inside of the bus is modified into a classroom. Learning levels will be improved and interest will be created in these schools. After achieving the minimum level, these children are admitted to formal schools. The Karnataka State Road Transport Corporation has donated eight buses for this purpose. State government is providing free uniform, free textbooks and mid-day meals to these children.

v. Beediyinda Shalege (From Street to School)

For the children who are in the street in the age of group of 6-14 and not getting education, the Education Department is preparing some innovative programmes to bring them into the school fold with NGO's coordination. As per the survey of street children conducted by the 'the Bangalore City Forum for Street and Working Children', there are 12,284 street children who are out of schools. To address these children a provision has been made in the Annual Work Plan 2004-05 to bring them to school.

vi. Baa Baale Shalege (Bringing the Girl Child to School)

Baa Baale Shalege is yet another special initiative to bridge the gender gap. The main strategies adopted under this campaign are:

- To make women officials of the Education Department motivate themselves to adopt an educational block each and evince special interest in the education of girls in that block.
- To make the women officials adopting a block to meet women teachers in the particular block and motivate them to achieve the aims of this programme voluntarily.
- To make all voluntary organisations such as stree-shakti/self-help groups, *mahila/yuvathi mandals* and women representatives to evince interest and take responsibility for the tasks.
- To ensure that girls participate effectively in the 20-point programme under the Learning Achievement Year.
- To persuade NGOs to take active part in the campaign.

vii. Kishori Kendra

This programme is launched with the coordination of Mahila Samkhya, an NGO. This is exclusively for girls who are deprived of school education. Two residential

Bridge Courses, one in Bellary and another in Koppal are being conducted and 135 girls were enrolled in 2003-04.

viii. Enrolment Drive

Every year in the beginning of the academic year the Department of Education undertakes enrolment drive for active participation of people for 100 per cent enrolment in the age group of 6-14 years. This is one kind of an effort to bring back dropout children to schools and all efforts are made to see that they continue their studies.

ix. Samudayadatta Shale (School with Community Initiative)

The Samudayadatta Shale programme is move towards the community and helps to bring back the dropout children and non-enrolled children. This is an effort to increase awareness among the community about their children education and the role of parents in the particular village/habitation, people of their children and the school.

The details regarding the children mainstreamed through various programmes under the Sarva Shiksha Abhiyan Samithi for Karnataka for up to 2003-04 are summarised in Table 4.17 below:

TABLE 4.17

Number of Children Mainstreamed through Sarva Shiksha Abhiyan Samithi

Schemes	*No. of Children Mainstreamed*
Chinnara Angala	1,07,085
Maa Marali Shalege	21,878
Kooliyinda Shalege	3,261
Beediyinda Shalege	1,117
Baa Bale Shalege	10,645
Special Enrolment Drive	57,632
Through EGS	5,441
Flexi School	427
Mobile School	454
Grand Total	**2,07,940**

Source: Commissioner for Public Instruction, Government of Karnataka.

Chinnara Angala Scheme appears to be the driving force for mainstreaming the out of school children. Special enrolment drive, Baa Marali Shalege and the Baa Bale Shalege are also effective schemes. Among the districts, the literacy backward districts of Raichur, Gulbarga, Yadgir, Koppal and Bidar in the Gulbarga division account for more than 50 per cent. The number of children mainstreamed through Chinnara Angala in different phases are given below (Table 4.18).

TABLE 4.18

Number of Children Mainstreamed through Chinnara Angala

Stages/Schemes	*Year*	*Target*	*Actuals*
I Phase	2000	-	2500
II Phase	2001	101101	82708
Special Chinnara Angala Scheme	2001	22244	15468
III Phase	2002	125000	92382
Special Chinnara Angala (only for Bangalore Urban District)	2002	-	5126
IV Phase	-	-	-
No. of Children Covered by District Deputy Directors	2003	125573	107426
Baa Marali Shalege	2002	-	225852
Cooliyinda Shalege	-	-	3270

Source: Commissioner for Public Instruction, Government of Karnataka.

As per the above information the achievements are far below their respective targets.

x. Literacy Campaign

A nationwide effort was set in motion in 1988 with the establishment of National Literacy Mission which has sought to impart functional literacy to 100 million illiterates in the 15-35 age group by the end of the Eighth Five-Year Plan. Karnataka was one of the first states to take up comprehensive programmes for total literacy. Beginning with the district of Dakshina Kananada in 1990, now the literacy campaign is covering all the districts in the state. There is a separate department *viz.*, the Directorate of Mass Education which is the nodal agency for implementation of the literacy programmes in Karnataka. The implementation of total literacy campaign, post literacy campaign and Kannada Nadu Sakshkara Nadu have all been completed in all the districts and, except Gulbarga, have passed through the Post Literacy phase between 1990-91 and 1999-2000. The outcome of the programme is that among the identified 77.16 lakh non-literates in the 9-35 age group, 43.08 lakh non-literates were made literate (Directorate of Mass Education, Government of Karnataka).

Progress of the Total Literacy Campaign is given in Appendix A-4.17.

xi. Gender Equity

In order reduce the boy-girl divide to less than five in the project blocks, special measures were initiated by the Government of Karnataka. i) removal of gender bias in textbooks, ii) gender sensitisation, iii) representation of women in committees, iv) upgradation of schools, v) provision of toilets, vi) appointment of women teachers, vii) appointment of women village teacher motivators, and viii) incentives to girls.

xii. Child Labour and Education

Child labour is a serious problem particularly in urban areas and cities. International organisations are bringing pressure to eradicate child labour but it is not an easy task to completely eradicate child labour in a country like India with such high illiteracy and large section of people below poverty line. However Karnataka Government has taken serious and sincere efforts to address this issue. Karnataka became the first state to undertake a survey of working children in prohibited dangerous and non-dangerous establishments in 2002. The survey revealed that 7,112 children were working in dangerous and hazardous work and another 23,118 children in non-hazardous establishments. Considering the magnitude, the state government put in place an action plan to end child labour by the year 2007. The State Labour Department launched Child Rights Cells in Bangalore and 202 educational blocks which would receive public complaints and attend to their redressal in three days. The aim is to admit such children to schools. It is a matter of pride that Karnataka is also the first state to ban child labour in non-hazardous jobs within the existing legal framework through the Shops and Commercial Establishments Act, 1961. According to the Government of Karnataka Economic Survey 2003-2004, the state rescued 88,000 such child workers and sent them to 180 special schools under the National Child Labour Project. A pilot project was launched with Norwegian aid whereby 21 special schools were started for such rescued child workers and nearly 560 children have been enrolled. The Education Department of Government of Karnataka brought back 30,000 working children to schools under the scheme, 'Cooliyinda Shalege' and about two lakh school dropouts, also were are back in the school through 'Baa Marali Shalege'. Akshara Dashoha scheme launched recently for children in Government primary schools, stand to benefit 46 lakh children besides indirect benefits of providing employment to 80,000 women cooks.

4.3.14 Assessment

Eradication of illiteracy has been a major concern for the government since independence. The governments both at the national and the sub-national levels have initiated series of new programmes and projects in the past 10 years to meet the goal of Education. for All (EFA). The National Policy on Education of 1986 and the revised one of 1992 and the World Declaration on Education for All 1990 adopted in Jomtien have all provided greater momentum to the national commitment for reaching basic education for all children. The Jomtien Declaration to which India is a signatory along with several novel schemes adopted particularly in the 1990s have brought to the central stage the need for reviewing basic education as a fundamental right of every citizen in the country.

Basic education policies and programmes in the recent years have gone beyond the mere emphasis on numbers to focus on quality concerns in basic education, on the education of girls and disadvantaged section of the society, the need for people's involvement in basic education programmes and decentralisation of education management. In addition to the schemes which focus on rural, urban slums and tribal areas, there exists a number of private, fee charging nursery schools, the licensing or recognition of which is not mandatory, to cater to the needs of the parents living in urban and semi-urban areas.

Between 1991 Census and 2001 Census, urban literacy rate increased significantly from 56.0 per cent to 81.05 per cent. That means illiteracy in urban areas was brought down from 44 per cent in 1991 to 18.95 per cent in 2001. The urban illiterate population account for less than 20 per cent as opposed to 40.32 per cent in the rural segment. Male literacy rate in urban Karnataka increased from 67.3 per cent in 1991 to 86.85 per cent in 2001 leaving behind 13.15 per cent of urban males illiterate. But it is noteworthy that the increase in female literacy accelerated in this period from a mere 44.3 per cent in 1991 to 74.87 per cent in 2001, leaving behind about 25 per cent of the urban females as illiterates. The difference in increase in literacy rates between 1991 and 2001 was 25.05 per cent for males and 30.57 per cent for females.

Although illiteracy levels are coming down over the period, nearly one-third of Karnataka's population which is illiterate poses a bigger challenge for the state in order to attain 100 per cent literacy. The foregoing analysis tells us vividly how much Karnataka has done to reduce illiteracy. Despite literacy improvement, it is a matter of concern that the state which had the 12th position in urban literacy among the states in India in 1981, slipped to the 14th place in 1991 and further more down to 16th place in 2001. In

1991 the two states which overtook Karnataka were Madhya Pradesh and Sikkim, and in 2001 two more states which overtook Karnataka were Manipur and Orissa. Even the newly formed states of Uttaranchal and Chhattisgarh have recorded higher urban literacy rates than Karnataka.

Tackling urban illiteracy is not vastly different from that of rural illiteracy. Both formal and informal education strategies were adopted. All projects adopted under Education for All (EFA) take care of literacy programmes of urban areas also. Each project or programme has set specific targets and also incorporated various monitoring and evaluation mechanisms. Despite the significant achievement and positive goal orientation it is a worrisome matter that there are serious problems of gender, regional, sectional and social disparities at the primary education level. A significant portion of students more of girls continue to drop out due to various socio-economic and cultural factor as also lack of adequate infrastructure (toilets), shortage of teachers and unsatisfactory quality of education provided. While enrolment of children in primary level is the first step, containing dropout rates and the retention and improving completion in the subsequent stages are the major challenges.

One need not be complacent about 80 plus literacy rate in the urban Karnataka. In fact there is still more than a quarter of female population who are illiterates. Moreover there is large and incessant influx of population in to the urban areas for various reasons. Between 1951 and 2001 while the rural population increased by 2.48 times, the urban population increased by 4.57 times. The number of rural males and rural females each increased each by 2.48 times, the corresponding increases for urban areas were 4.86 times for males and 4.45 times for females. The failure of monsoon which is more often and recurring droughts in Karnataka are the major compulsions for migration from rural to urban. In addition, the lack of proper marketing facilities and unremunarative prices are pushing the farmers in to distress sales and the lower wages for agricultural labourers *vis-á-vis* labourers in construction activities are also responsible for increase in urban population. Since this is going to be a recurring feature in years to come, coping up with the already inadequate infrastructure more so of education poses major problem. Further, although the state government has been implementing very good schemes for tackling urban illiteracy of children and adults there is need to bring about increasing awareness of these facilities by vigorous and whole hearted efforts both by the public and private sector. Private sector should come forward in a big way to help the government to attain total literacy. The Azim Premji Foudation and efforts of FICCI are some of such initiatives. But they are far inadequate. Private schools should also endeavour to help reducing the gender gap by extending the incentives given by the government schools to promote girls' education.

4.3.15 Recent Initiatives

In order to fulfil the goal of universal elementary education, Constitutional (86th Amendment) Act 2002 has been passed by the Parliament. A Central Bill containing the detailed mechanism to implement the Amendment has been circulated to states and Members of Parliament for their comments. The Bill once enacted, the Legislation would be a milestone in the country's march towards Universal Elementary Education. The country has not yet achieved the goal of expenditure on education at 6 per cent of GDP as contemplated in the National Policy on Education. The total expenditure on education by both Central and state government was only 3 per cent of GDP in 2002-03 (revised estimates). The Tenth Five-Year Plan (2002-07) has accorded high priority to this sector. The Common Minimum Programme of the newly formed government at the Centre pledges to raise public spending in education to 6 per cent of GDP with at least half this amount being spent on primary and secondary sectors. The latest Union Budget 2004-05 of July 2004 has already imposed the 2 per cent education cess on all central taxes to finance the commitment to universalise access to quality basic education. Further, the Central Government proposes to set up a National Commission on Education to monitor allocate resources and to monitor programmes.

The Karnataka Government's expenditure on education has been hovering around 3.20 per cent of its GDP. Its per capita expenditure on education is less than that in Hariyana, Tamil Nadu, and Maharashtra. [World Bank Report: *Challenges, as Reported Encyclopedia of Indian Education*, NCERT , Vol.1 (A-K)]. In The Medium-Term Fiscal Plan 2000-2001 to 2004-2005 adopted by the Karnataka Government provides substantial funding to the school education sector to realise the target of UEE up to eight years of school education by 2007. It is expected that these measures would enable the Karnataka Government to achieve total literacy much earlier than expected. According to the same report, mentioned in this para, that the state may universalise primary education well before 2010 and it will achieve full literacy i.e., 80 per cent and above in another 10 years.

4.3.16 Insights on Literacy in the State

1. Male–Female gap in literacy

1961	1971	1981	1991	2001
21.96	20.62	21.10	22.92	21.91

   It is clearly evident that just as the growth in total literacy rate in the state is quite tardy, the efforts in bridging the male-female differentials also follow the same pace.

2. Decadal gains are marginal in Bangalore Rural (4.83), Bagalkot (4.23) and Bijapur (00.91) while the gain at the state level is 11 per cent. There is a negative growth of literacy rate among males in Bijapur district.

   Districts which are far below the state average in growth rate of literacy are, in increasing order of gap, Bellary, Bagalkot, Bijapur, Bagalkot, Koppal, Chamarajanagar, Gulbarga and Raichur. Five of these seven districts belong to Hyderabad Karnataka region, Gulbarga Division.

   Just as all districts need to improve their performance in regard to literacy attainments, the following districts need intensive care: Raichur, Gulbarga and Chamarajnagar.

3. A *taluka* level analysis has shown that status of women's literacy is quite pathetic in Yadgir, Shahpur, Raichur and Devadurg *talukas.* and 111 out of a total of 175 *talukas* composing 27 districts have literacy rates lower than that of state average of female literacy which is 57.5 per cent in 2001.

4. The rural-urban gap in literacy rates is quite high in Karnataka state as compared to other South Indian states except Andhra Pradesh. Gains in urban literacy in Karnataka during 1991-2001 in is close to similar gains at the all-India level.

5. Gender-gap in urban literacy is narrowing over the period 1981-2001 in the state. Difference in literacy rates between highest literacy district (Kodagu) and lowest literacy district (Raichur) narrowed from 28.13 per cent in 1991 to 22.8 per cent in 2001. This may mean that interdistrict imbalances in literacy performance has narrowed, though prominent.

6. Capacity to spend a minimum of nearly Rs. 665 per month per person averaging an annual family expenditure (4 persons) of Rs. 32,000 is essential for achieving full literacy (80 per cent and above) in any region of the state. (Based on NSSO 55th Round 1989-90.) However, it is to be noted that the average per capita consumption in rural Karnataka is around Rs. 500 per month for all groups and lower still for SCs and and STs, and nearing the average for OBCs. Even in Urban Karnataka the MPCE for SCs & and STs is well below the desired figure of Rs. 665 (NSSO 1999-2000; GoK, Feb. 2004, p.321). The first source of data of Rs. 665 per month was of 1989-90 while the second source was of 1999-2000. Hence, the figure of Rs. 665 would be an underestimate by 1999-2000.

   It is also true that the income levels of the marginalised populations would get accelerated through their educational attainments. This is a vicious circle beginning with: low or no educational attainments—access only to unskilled occupations as agricultural labour or low level construction labour or coolie in a market yard and the like—low income levels—poverty—inadequate capacity to send children to schools or employment of children in labour—child labourers without schooling becoming unskilled adult illiterate labourers repeating their parents' life cycle. Hence, this vicious circle needs to be broken by ensuring minimum wages for unskilled labour as per the Labour Act, attracting children to schools with adequate monetary and non-monetary incentives.

   The inference is that realisation of targets of full literacy in the state is also strongly associated with income levels of population. Income levels are quite low among marginalised groups in the state. Hence, literacy promotion would be a challenging proposition in these groups. It is possible that as their income levels rise, they would turn their mind-set away from contingencies of existence to acquisition of literacy.

7. Proportion of out-of-school children in Karnataka state has been going down sharply.

This augurs well for literacy situation in the state. Additions to the existing stock may get reduced.

8. A variety of intervention programmes are being operated by the Government of Karnataka to realise EFA targets. They are: EGS, Chinnara Angala, Coolieyinda Shalege, Flexi Schools, Mobile Schools, Beedhiyinda Shalege, Baa Baale Shalege, Kishori Kendra, Dhakhalathi Andolana, Samudayadatta Shale, School Adoption Programme, Tent School, Bridge Course, Home-based Education, Management of School by Stakeholders (SDMC), training at Block (BRC) and Cluster of Villages (CRC) levels, training through teleconferencing, action research and documentation, etc. These programmes are backed up by post literacy and continuing education programmes as well as village library movement. These interventions particularly in the primary education subsequent to 2001 have made a dent in the number of out of school children whereby over 9 lakh children were brought into the mainstream in a period of five years. Hence, it may possibly be expected that the state would achieve full literacy and EFA by expected target dates: UPE by 2007, UEE by 2010, full literacy—80 per cent by 2015 and 100 per cent by 2020. The period 2015 to 2020 may be earmarked for strong and sustained efforts to close gaps in literacy and school education for gender, region and, social groups.

4.4 Human Capital in Karnataka State

Human capital in generic framework represents endowments such as skills, knowledge and health, which enable an individual either to be productive or provide the ability to command labour. However, in economic sense, human capital is considered, as an investment for which there is a definite return. Therefore, as more and more people invest their time, effort and money to acquire the relevant capabilities and skills through formal education and training, the country prospers in terms of its human capital assets correspondingly. Therefore it would be worthwhile to examine the nature and amount of human capital formed at different points of time. It is against this backdrop, the growth of human capital in the state of Karnataka is examined.

The growth of human capital in this analysis is captured in terms of both quantity and nature (type) over a period of time from pre-economic reform (1991) to the present reform period (2001). While the quantity is being assessed in terms of demographic changes in the number of educated population at certain levels, the nature of human capital is assessed in terms of the kind of education acquired at different levels. The analysis is being confined to Karnataka state and to the secondary, post-secondary and higher education only.

Presently, Karnataka is being recognised as the new growth centre in a reforming Indian economy powered by knowledge-based industries such as software, electronics, biotechnology, pharmaceuticals and back offices for many overseas companies. The state, which started a software revolution has been aggressively wooing job-seekers not only from across the country but also from overseas. Karnataka in recent times seems to be surging ahead powered by its booming higher education sector to produce manpower for diverse jobs in a booming economy. Therefore it is in this context the assessment of human capital in terms of quantity and nature would not only indicate the direction in which the state is moving so far as secondary and higher education is considered but also the spread of education across the state.

4.4.1 Focus of the Analysis

1. To examine the human capital accumulation during pre-and the present-reform period.
2. To study regional and gender disparities in human capital accumulation.
3. To capture trends and patterns in quantity and nature of human capital formation across regions and between sex.

4.4.2 Stock of Human Capital

Looking at the availability of the human capital in the state during the pre-reform period, it may be seen from Appendix A-4.18 that there was an overall total stock of 6.8 per cent with secondary education, 2.3 per cent with higher secondary, 0.3 per cent each with technical and non-technical diploma/certificate and 2.5 per cent with degree and beyond attainment. The ratio of secondary/higher secondary to post-secondary diploma and higher (university degree) in the demographic composition in the state works out to 9.1:0.6:2.5. This evidently points to the state's low priority to post secondary technical education (diploma) as against university degree education. It is to be noted that the post secondary technical education (diploma) offers the advantage of obtaining specialised technical/professional/vocational skills for large majority of maintenance and repair jobs in the service sector as well as for junior level supervisory and mechanical operators in the industrial production and manufacturing sectors. As against this, the university general degree provides for very limited options in the job market. Besides, higher secondary education has become the basic eligibility for clerical and lower level managerial jobs both in public and private sectors. It is also the basic minimum qualification for admission to almost all professional courses including teacher training (elementary) nursing, pharmacy, etc.

Thus considering the cumulative stock of human capital at secondary level and beyond above the state revealed 12.2 per cent in its demographic composition. In terms of urban-rural composition with this level of educational attainment, it is noticed that the cumulative figure for rural was 6.8 per cent and that of urban areas was 24.5 per cent thus revealing a huge disparity of 17.7 percentage points. Considering the cumulative educational attainment at this level for males and females, it is noticed that the male composition in the state is 16.3 per cent and that of female is 8.0 per cent thus revealing a disparity of over 8.0 per cent.

4.4.3 Educational Attainment of Human Capital

Considering the male-female differences in educational attainment at this level in urban and rural areas separately it is noticed that the educational attainment is highest among the urban males (30.1 per cent) and lowest among rural females (3.3 per cent). The disparity is much wider between males and females in urban than in rural areas (11.7 per cent as against 6.8 per cent).

However, what is more interesting is that the educational attainment among urban females (18.4 per cent), which is not only above the overall state average, but is also above that of the male's attainment in the state as a whole. Urban women are placed second best in the social stratification in terms of their educational attainment at secondary and beyond level. The rural females seem to be the most discriminated in terms of their educational attainment at all levels considered in this analysis. Their conspicuous absence at the technical diploma levels points to the rural areas being deprived of female technicians for certain routine maintenance and repair jobs as well as for emerging IT related jobs in the e-governance sectors.

As for the secondary education attainment separately, it may be noticed from A-4.18 that while urban composition is 12.4 per cent, the same for rural is 4.3 per cent thus revealing a disparity to the extent of 8.1 per cent in terms of educational attainment at this level. Similarly while the male composition is 8.7 per cent, the female composition is 4.8 per cent revealing a disparity of 3.9 per cent. At the male female disparity between rural and urban areas is very marginal. The bottom line, it is the urban male who seem to have gained the most (14.4 per cent) in terms of secondary education attainment followed by urban females (10.3 per cent).

Similarly looking at the higher secondary education attainment, it varies from 0.5 per cent (among rural females) to 5.6 per cent (among the urban males). Once again the urban segment including the urban females is relatively better placed over their rural counterparts, although the disparity between male-female is highest in the urban region (4.1 per cent).

In regard to the post secondary diploma education, it may be seen that the percentage of population is less than 1 per cent or about 1 per cent (excepting urban males) across different population segments. This is true of either technical or non-technical. Quite interestingly, although the percentage of this population is quite negligible, yet the urban females seem to have an edge over the other population segments in terms of non-technical diploma educational attainment.

Considering the degree and above educational attainment, the proportion of this population is higher than that of technical and non-technical diploma put together (2.5 per cent as against 0.6 per cent). Clearly, this is an indication of the state's lopsided priority in favour of university education rather than post-secondary technical. Evidently, the university education has been a monopoly of urban males (8.1 per cent) and urban females (3.8 per cent).

4.4.4 Spread of Human Capital across the Regions in the State

The accumulation of human capital in terms of educational attainment for secondary and beyond across four geographical regions is examined during 1991 (Figures 4.7, 4.8 and 4.9). As could be seen from the Figure 4.7 Bangalore division reveals highest average cumulative accumulation (13.4) followed by Mysore, Belgaum and Gulbarga. Thus in terms of average percentage, the regional variation is not too wide.

However, the disparity in human capital accumulation becomes glaring uniformly across all the four regions when rural-urban and male-female differentials are examined. While, male population reveal two times more accumulation than their female counterparts in almost all the regions (Figure 4.8), the the urban population reveal three times more accumulation than their female counterparts (Figure 4.9). Clearly the trends point to biases against the females and the rural population segments.

FIGURE 4.7

Cumulative Percentage of Population with Secondary and Higher Education-1991 (Total)

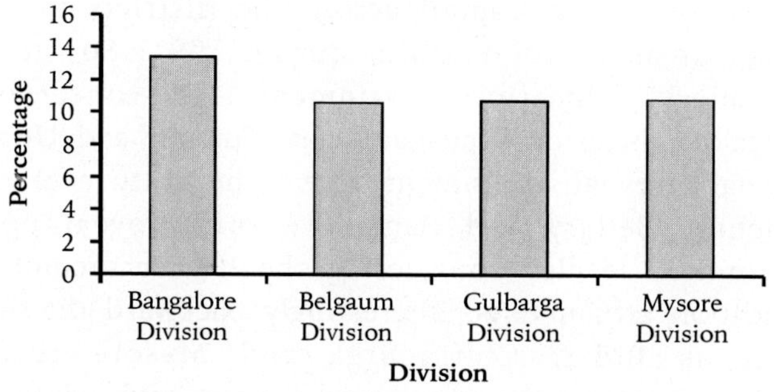

Source: Computations based on Population Census Data, 1991.

FIGURE 4.8

Cumulative Percentage of Population with Secondary and Higher Education-1991 (Male-Female)

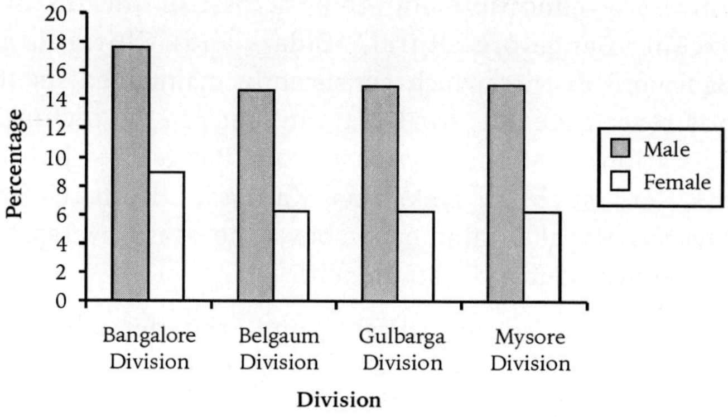

Source: Computations based on Population Census Data, 1991.

FIGURE 4.9

Cumulative Percentage of Population with Secondary and Higher Education-1991 (Rural-Urban)

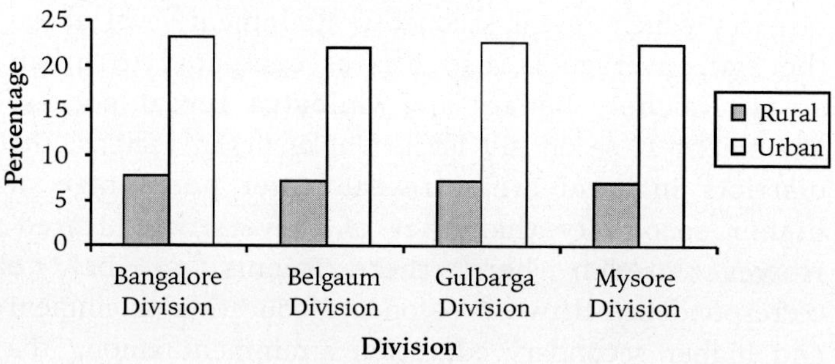

Source: Computations based on Population Census Data, 1991.

4.4.5 Spread of Human Capital across the Districts in the State

How do the districts in the state fare themselves in terms of cumulative accumulation of educational attainment at secondary and beyond? The Appendix A-4.19 gives the position of the districts with respect to the same. As could be observed it is the Bangalore city urban district, which consistently reveals top position for all population segments. Similarly Raichur is seen consistent with respect to lowest position for all population segments. There are only four districts which reveal percentages above the state average. They are Bangalore, Uttara Kannada, Dakshina Kannada, and Kodagu. Similarly, for males, only Bangalore and Dakshina Kannada reveal percentage above state average for the same. So far as female educational attainment is considered, Bangalore, Shimoga, Chickmagalur, Uttara Kannada, Kodagu reveal percentage above state average for the same. With regard to rural areas 11 districts reveal figures above state average. For urban areas, Bangalore, Mysore, Tumkur, Kodagu and Dakshina Kannada reveal percentage above state average for the same. Surprisingly, Tumkur which maintained below state average status for all segments has emerged as the second best district in the urban area.

4.4.6 Spread and Nature of Human Capital

The nature of human capital available in an economy clearly indicates the state's planning priorities for sustained economic growth. As the productive sectors in the economy are expanded and diversified for achieving the intended growth and development, it becomes very crucial to produce skilled manpower for such an economy. In recent times, with shifting emphasis to market economy, the emergence of service sector has fuelled demand for service and maintenance oriented jobs. In addition, the growth of knowledge industry has generated unprecedented demand for knowledge-intensive specialised skills and competencies, which university level education is expected to fulfil. The middle level maintenance and service skills and competencies for the knowledge industry are expected to be provided by the post-secondary level technical and non-technical education. It is in the light of this, it would be worthwhile to examine the kind of human capital that is being accumulated in the state over the years. To benchmark this, the state's position and the district-wise scenario that prevailed in the pre-reform period is being analysed. It is already seen from the earlier analysis (Appendix A-4.19) that the state revealed an aggregate pool of 12.2 per cent of its human resource with secondary and beyond education, out of which the rural reserve was 6.8 per cent and that of urban 24.5 per cent. In the forthcoming section, the spread of human capital in the state, across the districts and its type are being discussed.

Considering the spread of human capital in the state with respect to secondary, post-secondary and beyond education attainment, it is seen from Appendix A-4.18 that during 1991, the matriculates constituted highest composition in the demography. They were 6.8 per cent in the state, 9.3 per cent in urban and 4.3 per cent in rural regions. Among the male population the figures showed 8.7 per cent and 4.8 per cent among female population. Thus both urban region and male population revealed percentage higher than that of the state average in terms of acquiring secondary education.

The higher secondary stage which is a forerunner for higher education revealed a state average of 2.3 per cent with 1.3 for rural and 1.9 for urban regions. The male composition in the state with this level of education was 3.1, which was higher than that of the state average. The female constituted 1.4 per cent with this level of education.

In comparison, the post-secondary technical/non-technical educational attainment was seen to be less than 1 per cent at the state level. While it was 0.3 per cent in rural areas, the same in urban areas was 0.4 per cent. The male population with this educational attainment constituted 1.0 per cent which was slightly higher than the state average. The female population was only 0.4 with this educational attainment. However, the University level educational attainment in the state during the period stood at 2.5 per cent, with 0.9 per cent rural and 1.6 urban. The males constituted 3.5 per cent in the state, which was more than the state average. The females' attainment with respect to university education was 1.4 per cent. Interestingly the university educated population in the state (2.5 per cent) as well as among the male population (3.5 per cent) revealed higher percentage than the higher secondary educated for the corresponding segments (2.3 per cent and 3.1 per cent) in the state during the period. The female composition with university level education was much the same as that of higher secondary female educated in the state (1.4 per cent).

It is clearly evident from Appendix A-4.21 that the spread of human capital across the districts in the urban areas is not uniform during 1991. So far as secondary education attainments is concerned, Bangalore, Belgaum, Kodagu, Kolar, Tumkur and Uttara Kannada reveal attainment above the state average. Raichur, Bellary and Bangalore rural reveal poor attainment levels. Considering the higher secondary education attainments, interestingly backward districts such as Bidar, Chitradurga and Mysore reveal attainment above the state average along with advanced districts like Bangalore, Dakshina Kannada, Hassan, Kodagu and Tumkur. However, there seems to be no correspondence between secondary and higher secondary education attainment among the districts. Attainments in higher secondary education is lower than that of university education uniformly across all the districts except Bangalore Rural, Bidar and Chitradurga. Bangalore district which consistently maintained its top position acceded to Kolar in terms of technical education attainment. Apart from Bangalore district, districts such as Dakshina Kannada, Kodagu, and Mysore reveal attainments above the state average in university education attainment.

Contrary to the urban trend, the percentage of population with secondary education attainment in almost all the districts in rural regions is just half of the same in urban areas (Appendix A-4.22). This is primarily due to lack of access to higher secondary and university education in rural areas as compared to urban areas. Excluding Bangalore district it is the Kodagu and Uttara Kannada which reveal highest secondary education attainment. Besides, the number of districts which reveal secondary attainment level above the state average is also less as compared to urban areas. Raichur, Bellary and Gulbarga reveal poorest attainment at secondary level. Unlike urban regions, the districts in rural areas, reveal lower percentage of higher secondary than that of university educated. However, even here there seems to be no correspondence between secondary education attainment and higher secondary education attainment among the districts. Technical education attainment in all the districts is low. Kodagu consistently reveals top position with respect to education attainment at all levels excepting secondary education.

4.4.7 Human Capital Accumulation among Men and Women

The spread of human capital in terms of educational attainment at secondary and beyond level between male and female population across the districts reveals certain interesting patterns. Excluding the Bangalore district, which has consistently maintained the top position, only three districts (Belgaum, Uttara Kannada and Kodagu) reveal percentage above the state average of 8.7 in terms of secondary education achievement among males. However, the same level attainment among females reveals that there are five districts (Dakshina Kannada, Kodagu, Shimoga, Uttara Kannada, Chickmagalur) above the state average of 4.8 for female with secondary education attainment. Similarly, for higher secondary attainment, while for male population there are four districts (Bidar, Chitradurga, Dakshina Kannada, Dharwad) above the state average of 3.1, for female population, there are five districts (Dakshina Kannada, Kodagu, Shimoga, Uttara Kannada, Chickmagalur) above the state average of 1.4. The backward districts revealing better positions for higher secondary education is noteworthy. However, these districts slip back to lower positions at the post-secondary and university level education. Technical education appears to be a low priority for both males and females as they reveal negligible percentage all through the districts. However, districts such as Kolar and Shimoga reveal percentage above the state average of 1.0 for males. Similarly, districts such as Uttara Kannada Kodagu and Dakshina Kannada reveal percentage above state average of 0.4 for females. At the university level education, while Dakshina Kannada, Kodagu and Uttara Kannada reveal percentage above state average for both male and female population, Tumkur district also reveals above state average for females. In terms of male-female disparities in educational attainment at different levels, it is seen that female population have accumulated just half of what males have achieved thereby pointing to gender bias. This picture emerges across all the districts excepting Dakshina Kannada, Kodagu, Uttara Kannada and Shimoga. Thus the analysis clearly points to the uneven spread of human capital accumulation across the districts, between urban and rural and among male and female population.

4.4.8 Human Capital Accumulation—The Reform Years

Having seen the status of human capital formation in the state during 1990s, an attempt has been made to trace the growth in the 2000s. As 2001 Census figures are not available as yet, some suggestive indicators such as enrolment, enrolment per lakh population, instutional facilities, etc, are considered for this period. It is clearly seen from Appendix A-4.24 that there has been an appreciation both in number of institutions and enrolment at secondary and beyond level in the state between the pre-reform period (1990s) and the post-reform period (2000 onwards). However, the increase in enrolment has been quite marginal in case of polytechnics, primary TTI and B.Ed., colleges, others except higher secondry reveal considerable rise. The professional engineering colleges in the state has been growing at an alarming rate mostly in the private sector to meet the rising demands of the IT sector (both domestic and international). As of now (2004) there are close to 150 engineering colleges in the state. With waning demand for mechanical skills and slump in the industrial productions, and simultaneous demand for electronic and soft skills in the knowledge intensive economy both polytechnics and ITI seem to have been marginalised as they have not been able to adequately respond to the demands of the job market. Most courses offered in ITI and polytechnics are not only traditional types, but also in terms of their entry requirements still admit matriculation pass. However, in Teacher Training (elementary), Library Science, Pharmacy, Nursing, etc. even at the diploma level, the entry level requirement has been enhanced from matriculation pass to higher secondary pass.

Alternatively, there has been a proliferation of the self-accredited proprietary training colleges offering a variety of job skills and placement support for the non-traditional and glamorous occupations in the emerging job market for the secondary and higher secondary graduates (computer training colleges, NIIT, NTTF, Fashion Design, Cosmetology, Company Secretary, Business executives, personality grooming, etc.). This demand is also being driven by the global markets for outsourcing professionals in the service sector. However, the growth of these institutions is not uniform across the state rather is mostly restricted to urban and semi-urban regions).

4.4.9 Institutional Facilities and Enrolment across Regions

It may be seen that the distribution of institutional facilities is not uniform across the regions in the state. While Bangalore region continues its dominance in terms of having highest educational facilities at all levels, Gulbarga region continues to receive a raw deal at all levels. The unequal distribution in educational facilities is quite evident across districts in the state (Appendix A-4.25). Even considering the enrolment across regions, the regional imbalances are clearly evident thus indicating the direct correspondence between the facilities and the participation (Appendix A-4.26).

Considering yet another indicator of number of students per lakh population, at the general degree level, it is seen from Appendix A-4.27, that the state average for number of college students enrolled per lakh population was 669 in 2000. Bangalore, Dakshina Kannada., Dharwad and Uttara Kannada districts were placed above the state average. Of the districts Dakshina Kannada revealed highest ratio of 1,164 followed by Uttara Kannada (1097) and Bangalore (1,078). It is to be noted that Bangalore which consistently revealed first position in terms of educational attainment in 1991 at all levels has slipped to third position so far as college education is considered. Anyway it is to be noted that these figures are partial representation of higher education as they are limited to only colleges coming under collegiate department. Professional, technical and university enrolments are excluded from this. As such it is quite likely that districts like Dakshina Kannada and Uttara Kannada have surpassed Bangalore.

In order to track the human capital accumulation in the pre and the post-reform period across the districts in the state, an attempt has been made to assign ranks to the districts on the basis of educational attainment at different levels at two points of time-1990s and 2000 (Appendix A-4.28). It is observed that at the secondary, higher secondary and degree levels, more than half of the districts in the state reveal positive improvements, while for technical levels, a reverse trend is observed.

Another indicator of availability of human capital is the Employment Exchange Registration. (Note: There are reservations in the use of this data source.) It is seen that percentage increase between 1991 and and 2001 was highest among the ITI certificate holders followed by diploma holders. Although degree holders are larger than the diploma holders, the percentage increase during the decade was only 46 (Appendix A-4.29). A similar analysis of the district-wise status for the registration in 2001 reveals that Bangalore urban district had the highest number (2,51,566) followed by Bangalore rural (1,10,227) and Gulbarga with 1,02,339. Kodagu being the smallest district reveals the lowest number of 15,257 on the live register. Considering these figures across different types of education, it is seen that graduates seem to be more in number in all the districts as compared to diploma holders. However, the ITI/ATS certificate holders are seen in greater number than diploma holders in all districts excepting Udupi. Thus the above trends clearly suggest that the state's priority to university education as compared to post-secondary technical. It is seen that there were 5732, 237 and 617 institutions at the secondary, technical and degree levels respectively in the state. Their distribution across the districts reveals that Bangalore urban had highest proportion of them while Kodagu had least proportion at the secondary level. Similarly, considering technical institutions, Bangalore district reveals highest and both Bangalore rural and Kodagu reveal the lowest. At the degree level, once again it is Bangalore, which reveals highest number and Kodagu the lowest. However considering the educational attainment at different levels, it has already been noted earlier that Kodagu was placed in an advantageous position with second highest at secondary level, and third highest at higher secondary level. Similarly, Bangalore revealed highest attainment at higher secondary, technical and university level education. While, Raichur revealed lowest attainment at higher secondary and technical, at university level, both Raichur and Bangalore rural revealed lowest attainment.

As the number of institutions in a district is determined by the population, an attempt has also been made to look at the distribution of institutions across districts. However, it is to be noted that these institutions do not necessarily serve the local population, but also from other districts and other states as well. Particularly, when higher education institutions offer residential facilities, then it is likely that non-locals will also like to receive the benefit. Thus based on the density of the institutions per lakh population, it is noticed that the positions of districts varies. Even the districts with low educational attainments seem to reveal comparatively better density with that of the advanced districts. Thus, the density of institutions across the districts for various levels of education does not seem to be related to their corresponding educational attainment.

4.4.10 Insights on Human Capital in the State

1. Structure of human capital in the state is quite imbalanced as viewed from the perspectives of the needs of the economy and the new economic policies adopted by the Indian state since 1991, and hence one would expect an intense supply of technical skills among the educated population. The availability of technical skills is hardly 0.3 per cent of the total secondary/post-secondary educated persons, which has to be noted with the stock of graduates (2.5 per cent is higher than the stock of higher secondary educated persons (2.3 per cent). This imbalance is more pronounced among males and among urban population.
2. Non-technical diploma appears to be most popular among urban females though the overall proportion in the state is quite low.
3. It is sad to note that hardly 3.3 per cent of women in rural areas of the state possess secondary and post-secondary qualifications.
4. As can be expected Bangalore urban agglomeration has the highest stock of human capital in the state. Differentials across divisions are observed in decreasing order from Mysore through Belgaum, Bangalore (net of Bangalore city) and Gulbarga divisions. These differentials which are marginal are contributed by gross imbalances in stocks of urban/rural and male/female differentials within and across the divisions.
5. A notable feature of growth of institutions in the state is that Engineering Colleges, Industrial Training Institutions and management colleges have grown at a fast rate during 1991-2001. There is also a proliferation of unregistered/unrecognised institutions for vocational training in computer services. A proposal for regulating these institutions under Private Educational Institutions Regulation provision of the Karnataka Education Act, 1993 is under consideration. A crude estimate reports nearly 400 computer-training centres across the 100 wards of Bangalore city alone. There is no estimate on figures for the whole state.
6. A mismatch is regularly being observed between need and availability of human capital in the state. Market surveys on manpower needs and manpower demand for the whole economy and the sectors and sub-sectors therein are limited in number, not readily accessible and left unused. 'Trial and error' market logic is still ruling the dynamics of human capital formation and utilisation in Karnataka state.

4.5 Labour and Employment in Karnataka State

The need to ensure adequate growth in employment opportunities for providing productive employment for the continually growing labour force is widely regarded as one of the most important problems facing the country. The expansion of productive employment is also crucial for sustained poverty reduction, as labour is the main asset for a majority of the poor. Karnataka is basically an agrarian economy where a majority of the population depends on the primary sector. Employment is largely unorganised, rural and non-industrial in nature. For an overall development of the state, the Tenth Five-Year Plan of Karnataka stressed employment generation as the priority sector (Planning, Statistics and Science and Technology Department, 2002). It identified the growing problem of unemployment needs to reverse the observed phenomenon of secondary and tertiary sectors which were not proportionately absorbing as much of the disguised unemployment in the primary sector as their growth would warrant. In addition, it aimed at providing direct and indirect employment through antipoverty, rural development and construction programmes. Unemployment rate among educated was higher than the unemployment rate of the illiterates. These considerations have led to the demand for greater attention to the employment objective. In this section, we present an assessment of the employment problem in Karnataka based on recent trends in employment and unemployment. This section also offers some policy suggestions for employment promotion in the state. The section is organised as follows: Section 4.5.1 examines the employment situation by presenting the growth in employment in recent years. Unemployment trends are discussed in Section 4.5.2. Section 4.5.3 describes the quality of employment in Karnataka. The last Section deals with some policy suggestions for employment generation in the state.

4.5.1 Employment Situation and Trends

Any vision of the future has to be rooted in the current reality and policies, and the processes have to be identified to bridge the gap between current reality and future vision. It is, therefore, essential to have an understanding of the broad employment and unemployment scenario as it exists today, which would also indicate directions for improvement in future. In view of this, we examine employment situation and trends in employment based on Population Census and National Sample Survey (NSS) data.

Workforce

The data on labour force from NSS have been presented for two-points in Appendix A-4.30, for Karnataka and India, separately for males and females in rural and urban locations. The following observations are based on these data. First, the rural labour force growth (1.2 per cent) is lower than the urban (2.8 per cent) across sex, which is usually the case because of differences in educational opportunity in urban areas. However, the higher labour force in the case of rural females as compared to urban females is noteworthy. Second, the most peculiar feature of the data is that there has occurred a significant decline in labour force for females and males in both rural and urban locations between 1993-94 and 1999-2000. On the whole, it implies that there have been squeezes in labour force during the second half of 1990s.

Distribution of Workers

Distribution of workers in Karnataka during 1991 and 2001 has been presented in Appendix A-4.31. From 1991 to 2001, the workforce in the state increased from 189 lakh to 235 lakh, a growth of 2.5 per cent per annum. Number of agricultural labourers has grown from 56.53 lakh in 1991 to 62.09 lakh in 2001. The growth rate in agricultural labourers was 0.98 per cent per annum. The proportion of agricultural labourers to total labourers has decreased from 29.9 per cent in 1991 to 26.4 per cent in 2001. The composition of cultivators declined from 35.4 per cent in 1991 to 29 per cent in 2001. Workers in household industry increased from 3.53 lakh to 9.36 lakh a growth of 16.5 per cent per annum. Its share increased from 1.9 per cent in 1991 to 4 per cent in 2001. The other workers in household industry rose from 61.88 lakh to 94.41 lakh with an annual average rate of growth of 5.3 per cent. As compared to the total growth per annum, cultivators and agricultural labourers have registered lower growth rates whereas other categories recorded higher growth rates. On the whole, the traditional occupations are having negligible growth compared to other sectors in Karnataka state.

As per 2001 Census, proportion of agricultural labourers was almost double in north Karnataka (36.2 per cent) as compared to south Karnataka (19.4 per cent) Among divisions, the highest proportion of agricultural labourers was in Gulbarga division (40.6 per cent) followed by Belgaum division (33 per cent), Mysore division(18.7 per cent) and Bangalore division (19.8 per cent). The proportion of agricultural labourers varies significantly among districts. It is as high as 45 per cent in Raichur district followed by Haveri district 43.6 per cent and Chamrajnagar district with 42.9 per cent. The proportion of agricultural labourers was less than 5 per cent in Bangalore (2.5 per cent), Dakshina Kannada (4.4 per cent) and Kodagu (4.2 per cent). This proportion was higher than that of the state in 16 districts namely Chitradurga, Davanegere, Kolar and Shimoga in Bangalore division, Chamrajnagar in Mysore division, Bagalkote, Belgaum, Bijapur,Gadag, Dharwad and Haveri in Belgaum division and Bidar, Bellary, Gulbarga, Raichur and Koppal in Gulbarga division.

Worker Participation Rate

Appendix A-4.32 provides work participation rates (WPR) in Karnataka and all-India by area for the period 1993-94 to 1999-2000. The participation rates in rural Karnataka and India declined significantly between 1993-94 and 1999-2000. The WPRs for rural Karnataka were much higher than all-India. Urban Karnataka also showed the participation rates higher than that for all-India. However, it declined in both Karnataka and all-India for both males and females except in urban Karnataka where it remained constant.

Age specific WPR in rural and urban Karnataka during 1993-94 and 1999-00 is presented in Appendix A-4.33 and A-4.34. Three points need to be noted in connection with the decline in the worker-population ratio from these tables. First, the declines in WPR are not offset by any significant rise in the ratio of unemployed in the population on usual status categorisation. Second, age-specific WPRs have declined between 1993-94 and 1999-00 in each and every age group. So the observed decline in crude worker-population ratios is not merely due to shifts in the age structure of the population. Third, the reduction in worker-population ratios reflects a beneficial rise in the student-population ratios. Not only in the 5-9 and 10-14 age groups covering the primary and middle school system, but also in the 15-19 and 20-24 age-groups indicating a rising participation in secondary and higher level education. These gains have been particularly impressive for rural girls below 20 years of age.

Main and Marginal Workers

The workers comprise main workers and marginal workers in the proportion of 82.3 per cent and 17.7 per cent respectively in the state in 2001. The proportion of main workers to the population is 36.7 per cent, whereas the proportion of marginal workers is 7.9 per cent. Out of 27 districts in the state, 13 districts have proportion of main workers higher than that of the state. Those districts are Bangalore (Rural), Chitradurga, Kolar and Tumkur in Bangalore division; Chickmagalur, Dakshina Kannada, Hassan, Kodagu Mandya and Udupi in Mysore division; Gadag and Haveri in Belgaum division; and Bellary in Gulbarga division.

Contrary to main workers there has been a spectacular increase in marginal workers in 2001. The proportion of marginal workers which stood at 3.5 per cent in 1991 has reached the level 7.9 per cent in 2001, showing more than two-fold increase. It is worth noting that proportion of marginal workers among females (11 per cent) is more than double that of males (5 per cent). Among female marginal workers the proportion is more than 5 times in rural (15.2 per cent), as compared to that in urban areas (2.6 per cent). There is a wide variation in the proportion of marginal workers in the districts. This proportion was the highest in Chamrajanagar district (11.6 per cent) and the lowest in Bangalore district (2.8 per cent). Among districts only two districts namely Kodagu and Bangalore have registered less than 5 per cent of the marginal workers to total population of the respective districts. Out of 27 districts, 10 districts namely Shimoga, Chickmagalur, Gadag, Mysore, Udupi Dharwad, Bellary, Dakshina Kannada, Kodagu and Bangalore have the proportion of marginal workers less than that of state.

The proportion of marginal workers is significantly higher in rural areas (10.5 per cent) as compared to that in urban areas (2.8 per cent). In rural areas, the proportion of female marginal workers is higher than that of male marginal workers, while in urban areas the proportion of female marginal workers is slightly lower than that of male marginal workers.

The above analysis reveals that there is an increase in tendency among females to enter the workforce as main workers as well as marginal workers in rural and urban areas despite the fact that men dominate in main workforce. The proportion of men and women in main workforce is higher in rural areas as compared to urban areas, whereas the proportion of men is higher than that of women in both areas. The female work participation rate though increased, is considerably lower than the corresponding rate for males. More women are found as marginal workers especially in rural areas where the workers are seasonal in nature and also low paid. This phenomenon is not particular to north or south Karnataka but it is throughout the state. As against the common belief that urban areas provide more employment opportunities, the work participation is generally higher in rural areas than in urban areas.

Incidence of Child Labour

Child labour is a complex phenomenon basically rooted in poverty; there is unwavering commitment by the government and the people of Karnataka to combat it. Children constituted about 34 per cent of the total labour force by 2001 in Karnataka. Of these children, 9 out of every 10 worked in their own rural family settings. Nearly 85 per cent were engaged in traditional agricultural activities. Less than 9 per cent worked in manufacturing, services and repairs and the remaining worked in factories. Overall, the percentage of child workers to the child population was around 5.6 per cent in 2001. Appendix A-4.35 and A-4.36 shows that percentage of child labour among children in Karnataka and India across areas and sex in 1993-94 and 1999-00. Child labour was clearly on the decline in Karnataka and all-India between 1993-94 and 1999-00. Likewise, the percentage of working children between the ages of 5 and 14 had come down. There seems to be some correlation between the women's work participation rate and the child labour. Currently, a sectoral approach of targeting certain identified sectors employing child labour has by passed large segments of child labour. Hence, there is a need to shift emphasis by having geographical area approach. Often, the manufacturing sector is targeted, in a tokenised manner, while the greatest numbers of child labourers are in agriculture (much in bondage), in the urban and semi-urban informal sector and in family labour. The sectoral approach has been driving children from the targeted sector to other non-targeted sectors. It needs to be considered whether it would be better to focus on those districts where incidence of child labour is more and parallelly encourage district administration with less number of child labour to strive towards a child labour free district.

Besides, the NSS report also shows that the supply of child labour generally tended to come from households of rural areas who were landless, had low monthly per capita expenditure, were average in size and were belonging to socially backward classes, were headed by male and employed as labourers or self-employed. Though the role of the market might be important in the changed scenario in the globalisation and competition, the state had to remain the main provider particularly at the primary level and especially for the poor.

The Action Plan on Child Labour has remained a broad policy document and a 'Statement of intent' (Lukose, 2004). But it has not been broken into defined action points identifiable in terms of definite physical and financial targets. Responsibility for the same was not fixed on a specific officer or authority. It does not say who does what, when, where, how and how much. A new legislation on the lines of the one proposed by Second Law Commission *viz.*, Inductive Child Labour Law which prohibits child labour and makes compulsory primary education mandatory in tune with the 86th Constitutional Amendment (21A), is necessary as the elimination of child labour and the universalisation of elementary education are inseparable processes.

The policy measures aimed at poverty reduction, physical and social infrastructure department might also reduce child labour. Intervention like micro-credit for households, food for work and enforcement of labour laws might also work towards achieving this goal. Increased community participation and government expenditure on education and poverty reduction is necessary for solving the solution for the problem of child labour (Ravallion, 2000; Dev, 2003).

Employment Growth

The important question is have economic reforms reduced employment growth? Appendix A-4.37 depicts that employment growth declined drastically in the 1990s as compared to the decade of 1983 to 1993-94. In rural Karnataka, it declined from 2.3 per cent per annum during 1983 to 1993-94 to 1.2 per cent during 1993-94 to 1999-00. The corresponding numbers for urban areas were 2.2 per cent and 2.8 respectively. Similar decline also could be noticed for all India. According to the Special Group on Employment (Planning Commission, 2002b), rural employment growth in all-India declined from 1.8 per cent during the period 1983-1994 to 1.3 per cent during the period 1994-2000. During the same period, urban employment growth as per all-India level declined from 2.9 per cent to 2.4 per cent. In the case of Karnataka, the employment growth (both rural and urban) declined from 2.3 per cent during 1983 to 1993-94 to 1.6 per cent during 1993-94 to 1999-2000. What are the reasons for the decline in employment growth in the 1990s? One of the reasons could be the decline in participation rates of younger age group. However, it may be noted that the participation rates declined for all age groups although the decline was sharper for younger age groups. Another explanation could be that the economic opportunities had not increased in the reform period in spite of higher growth.

Proliferation of Marginal and Small Farmers

Operational holding is defined as the land wholly or partly used for agricultural production and operated as one technical unit by one person, alone or with others, without regard to title, legal form, size or location. The percentage of landholdings in the marginal groups increased while semimedium to large size group holdings decreased indicating more fragmentation due to mounting demographic pressure. The growing population and the inability of the non-agriculture sector to absorb additional workforce led to unabated sub-division of operational holdings. Appendix A-4.38 shows district-wise per capita land holdings in Karnataka between 1990-91 and 1995-96. The number of operational holdings had grown and an average area per holder was nearly 1.95 hectare in 1995-96. There was a significant decline in the share of per capita area operated in large holdings from 2.13 hectare in 1990-91 to 1.95 hectare in 1995-96 in Karnataka. This has its own implications on land utilisation, agricultural productivity and land degradation. At the district level, the per capita land holding was highest in Bijapur followed by Gulbarga whereas Mandya stood at the bottom. There seems to be some correlation between the unfertile and low irrigated districts and per capita landholdings in Karnataka. Bijapur remained on top across per capita operational holdings except large farmers in both 1990-91 and 1995-96. A majority of the marginal families were underemployed in the state. The size of landholding of these farmers was uneconomical and a majority of them also worked as agricultural labourers to sustain their livelihood. The highest per capita landholdings was in Chitradurga district in 1990-91 and Chikmagalur district in 1995-96 among large farmers. The reason attributed to the fact being the existence of rigid joint-family system in the farming families in these districts. On the whole, in the 1990s, the share of agricultural labourers was on the increase while the numbers of cultivators were declining. The cultivators, seems to have become agricultural labourers over time in Karnataka.

Changes in the Sectoral Distribution of Workers and Rural Non-farm Employment

Appendix A-4.39 indicates that there was a considerable fall in the share of employment in the primary sector, which largely comprised agriculture. The share of total workforce in the primary sector in Karnataka was higher than that of India, which was 66.8 per cent in 1987-88, fell to 58.4 per cent in 1999-00 as against India's 58.82 per cent and 52.43 per cent respectively. In particular, the dependence on agriculture remained high and there was no steady decline in the percentage of workers engaged in agriculture. The percentage of workers in secondary sector in Karnataka was 12 per cent in 1987-88 and marginally declined to 11.5 per cent in 1999-00; while in India as a whole it remained at 10.8 per cent during the same period. In 1987-88, the tertiary sector's share in Karnataka was 21.2 per cent, which was lower than that for India. By 1999-00, the share of tertiary sector in Karnataka was 30 per cent whereas it was higher at 36.7 per cent for India. On the whole, in the 1990s, it appears that people in Karnataka had diverted towards tertiary sector from both agricultural and industry.

Appendix A-4.40 shows that the percentage of rural non-form employment in Karnataka tended to be stagnant. This is true for both males and females. In other words, jobs in the rural non-agricultural sector were created slowly. Since the rural labour absorption in the non-form sector is crucial for poverty reduction, the Karnataka experience in the 1990s with regard to non-form employment creation was quite disturbing.

Employment in the Organised Sector: Public and Private Sectors

Most of the social security laws are applicable only to organised workers, who constitute about 10 per cent of the total workforce. The distinction between the organised and unorganised sector workforce has important implications for the quality of employment. Although, employment situation is deteriorating and that this is adding to the process of marginalisation, its situation during the last decade has not been encouraging. The annual growth rate of Karnataka state's employment in the organised sector (1 per cent) was much higher than India's growth rate of 0.1 per cent. In fact, other south Indian states were trailing behind the employment generation in the organised sector, which means that Karnataka was much ahead in implementation of reform measures in the state. Growth rate of women employment in organised sector was higher than the national average and across southern states in both private and public sectors. Employment in the unorganised sector mainly comes from the agricultural and service sectors, whereas in the organised sector it was generated by industries and government sponsored schemes.

The organised sector is dominated by the public sector, which contributes mainly to the total employment in this sector in Karnataka. Organised sector employment is mainly in the area of wholesale and retail trade, transport, storage and communication, finance, insurance, real estate and community and social services. Appendix A-4.41 shows the distribution of employment by sectors across gender in Karnataka during 1990-91 to 2001-02. Women employees' representation in Karnataka has been growing over the years from 17.4 per cent in 1990-91 to 31 per cent in 2001-02. Further, women employees grew at an annual growth of 5.4 per cent in public sector and 22.5 per cent in private sector during 1990-91 and 2001-02. Likewise, male employees accounted an annual growth of-0.2 per cent in public sector and 0.6 per cent in private sector. On the whole, employment in the public sector showed signs of deceleration from 70.3 per cent in 1990-91 to 58.7 per cent in 2001-02 due to government's policy of downsizing (often called as right-sizing) public sector labour force through voluntary retirement scheme.

Distribution of Workforce by Industry

The main source of employment generation in the unorganised sector of the economy including self-employment and small business wherein the present contribution is as high as 90 per cent of the total employed labour force. The main employment generating activities are manufacturing, wholesale and retail trade, hotels and restaurants and social and personal services. Employment and its growth in various industries in Karnataka during 1993-94 to 2002-03 have been given in Appendix A-4.42. The manufacturing sector, which provides substantial employment next to agriculture, is growing significantly. Plantation and forestry, mining and quarrying, electricity, gas and water; and construction have shown negative growth. All other industries have shown positive growth. Wholesale and retail trade, hotels and restaurants; finance, insurance, real estate and business services and social and personal services have shown considerable growth. Although other industries are important, manufacturing industries should still be considered as a major concern for employment. Social and personal services need a major change in composition in favour of health, education, etc. and only then they can substantially contribute to the growth. Given the Tenth Plan target on education, literacy and health standards (Planning Commission, 2002c), the scope of its growth and potential employment generation is very high. On the whole, reforms have not been able to alter the employment pattern in any of the industry including the manufacturing sector where no abnormal change has been noticed.

Employment in the Informal Sector

The informal sector is either in rural and urban areas where most of the employment is going to be created. This sector has been so far completely neglected by planners, which is why it is characterised by low productivity. It has both self-employed and wage workers but most of them work under deplorable working conditions with low earnings. Accordingly, a well-planned support system should be provided for the growth of this sector in the form of marketing, credit, training and upgradation of technology, etc. Occupational safety and health have been largely neglected in this sector and they should receive utmost priority. For enhancing the capabilities of the workers in the informal sector the proper blend of education and training in a flexible manner is extremely desirable. The workers in this sector although extremely vulnerable are practically devoid of any safety-net mechanism, except a statutory minimum wages, which are generally set below poverty line income and mostly not implemented.

Subsequent to the Structural Adjustment Programme the process of causualisation and absorption of labour in the informal sector in India are on the rise. Within the rural areas, the growth of non-farm sector, which is predominated by informal sector activities, is governed by two major forces. First, it expands in response to those who are thrown out of the agricultural sector and second, with industrial dispersal, increasing commercialisation and rising public works programmes the demand induced component of this sector has undergone marked increase particularly during the 1980s. It may nonetheless be argued that urban informal sector is highly demand responsive. This is mainly because of its weak linkages with the formal sectors, particularly the organised industry and its limited access to the external market. The relationship between informal sector, employment and industrialisation, which has already been a matter of interest for long, has drawn further attention in the context of structural adjustment.

Elasticity of Employment

Appendix A-4.43 presents estimates of elasticities of employment with respect to growth rate for the major sectors of the Karnataka economy. The estimated elasticities are less than unity in almost all the cases. The results show elasticity of employment is declining in agricultural, mining and quarrying, manufacturing and electricity, gas and water supply. In construction, transport, storage and communication and finance and insurance services, the elasticity of employment has increased. This obviously reflects accelerations in the growth of productivity per person employed, which is a desirable outcome, especially if it is taking place in the sectors where productivity per person employed is very low. We also note that employment elasticity may be very low in sectors where there is a great deal of underemployment, which means there is considerable room for output to expand without an expansion in measured employment.

Creation of new job opportunities is important to provide work to those already unemployed and new entrants in the labour force. But for reduction in poverty, which is a much larger problem than unemployment, it is necessary to reduce underemployment and raise productivity and earnings of working poor. It is important to keep growth in the centre of employment and poverty reduction strategy. While the need for selective and well-targeted programmes for direct attack on poverty in the short run is important, the emphasis on growth based on employment and poverty reduction strategy is necessary to evolve a long-term and sustainable solutions to these problems. The integration of growth and employment objectives in development strategy is not an easy task: often, employment elasticities of output growth are low and declining or more people get engaged or employed without any significant increase in productivity so that, employment expansion is not accompanied by commensurate growth of output. It is possible to achieve both the objectives by promoting faster growth of sectors with relatively higher employment elasticities, so that output growth is contributed both by expansion of employment and increase in productivity, rather than ending up with jobless growth or growth less expansion of employment (GoK, 2002).

4.5.2 Unemployment Situation and Trends

Incidence of Unemployment

The incidence of unemployment is defined as the percentage of persons not having work or unemployed in the age group of above 14 years on the usual principal and subsidiary status to total number of persons in the labour force. Appendix A-4.44 shows the incidence of unemployment by gender and rural-urban residence, for 1993-94 and 1999-00. Given the increase in the labour force, a decline in the growth of employment in the 1990s had increased the incidence of unemployment. There was decrease in the incidence of unemployment both for males and females on the whole and in particular, for urban areas in Karnataka and all-India except for males between 1993-94 and 1999-00. In case of rural areas, however, there was a sharp increase between 1993-94 and 1999-00 from 1.2 per cent to 1.5 per cent in all-India whereas Karnataka remained at 0.7 per cent. The data confirm much higher rates of unemployment, particularly in urban areas. Although the rates seem to have remained at 1.4 per cent in Karnataka as against an increase from 2 per cent to 2.3 per cent for India during the last inter-survey periods among rural as well as urban areas.

Unemployment Rate

The unemployment rate for the population as a whole masks important variations for different categories of the labour force. It is traditionally higher in urban areas than in rural areas because the greater dominance of the organised sector in urban areas forces people to be either employed or unemployed. This pattern is evident from Appendix A-4.45 It is interesting to note, however, that the difference in unemployment rates between rural and urban areas *vis-à-vis* females and males narrowed considerably in Karnataka and India during the 1990s. The reason for the observed increase in unemployment rates in rural areas can be shift from self-employment to casual labour, and the number of women entering the labour force is likely to increase. However, unemployment rate in Karnataka is decelerating as against all-India, which was growing between 1993-94 and 1999-00.

Underemployment

Underemployment refers to a situation in which a person is employed for a certain length of time but seeking or is available for additional work. It is quite high in various segments of the labour force. In spite of the fact that the incidence of underemployment was reduced substantially in the 1990s, the unemployed person days for rural females in Karnataka increased from 2.5 per cent in 1993-94 to 2.9 per cent in 1999-00 (Appendix A-4.46). Likewise, it increased for India. For the females, the percentage of employed increased significantly while that of not in the labour force declined in Karnataka and all-India during the period 1993-94 and 1999-00. It may be noted that the extent of underemployment was higher for rural and urban male workers compared to female workers in Karnataka and all-India. As regards the trend in the rate of open unemployment, there was apparently a clear-cut pattern that the labour force grew faster than employment opportunities in the economy in the 1990s.

4.5.3 Quality of Employment

So far we have discussed employment and unemployment problems, which have failed to capture the quality of employment. Income or wages may be one of the variables reflecting quality. Many people get employment but they get low wages and income. In this part, we examine the changes in variables representing the quality of employment such as casualisation of labour, labour productivity, real wages and poverty.

Causalisation of Labour

Changes in the composition of employment between self-employment, regular salaried employment and casual employment have been shown in Appendix A-4.47. The share of self-employment has been declining over time. This has occurred primarily in rural areas reflecting the decline in the proportion of farmers cultivating their own land owing to the fragmentation of holdings. The proportion of self-employment to total employment in the urban areas has been more or less constant. There has been a marginal increase in regular salaried employment. However, there has been a marginal increase in the share of casual employment in rural areas over time. This reflects the displacement of marginal cultivators and their conversion into agricultural labour. As a result, casual labour increased from 39.3 per cent of rural employment in 1993-94 to 44.5 per cent in 1999-00. The share of casual labour in urban employment was constant over time in Karnataka whereas it fluctuated over the past two decades in India. The increase in the share of casual labour in total employment is sometimes regarded as an indication of deteriorating employment quality since this type of employment is not associated with job security or other employment benefits.

The quality of a great deal of wage employment is very low in Karnataka and this is a major problem. A law to regulate and improve employment conditions for nearly one crore workers in various segments of the unorganised sector in Karnataka is soon to be enacted. With the growing casualisation and contractualisation of labour and the steep fall in numbers of the organised labour force, which is an outcome of the economic liberalisation of the 1990s, a comprehensive law for unorganised labour has been a major demand in the state. More flexible labour laws would encourage greater dependence upon regular employment with an improvement in the quality of employment for labour as a whole.

Employment and Education

It is not easy to quantify the level of skills in the labour force because data on skill levels are not readily available. What is available is information on the educational attainment of the labour force and the relevant data for 1983/1999-00 have been summarised in Appendix A-4.48. It is evident that education levels in the labour force are very low. First, the proportion of the illiterate workers has declined. Second, in each of the three major sectors, our attention is drawn to the increase in the proportion of educated workers. However, the proportion of educated workers has been increasing the least in the primary, and the most in the tertiary sector. Consequently, the intersector variations in the quality of labour force have been widening. Third, the pattern of improvement in the quality of labour force has been different between 1983/1993-94 and 1993-94/1999-00. The improvement during 1983/1993-94 reflected itself in terms of the declining proportion of illiterate workers and increasing proportion of primary-pass workers, while during 1993-1994/1999-00, the ascendancy stood more in favour middle-pass workers. The net result was to shift the Indian labour force from low level (illiterates) to middle level (primary and/or middle level of schooling) of human capital in a big way, and to high levels, in a modest way. Fourth, in spite of the steady improvement in the quality of labour force, especially the proportion of educated workers, the scenario seems fairly depressing even at the dawn of new century. The situation is most depressing for the primary sector, the proportion of educated workers engaged in agriculture being less than 10 per cent. We are persuaded to emphasise that a weak human capital base continues to be the real Achilles heel of Indian agriculture.

Our analysis clearly shows that the situation on the front of human capital is anything but pleasing. Our economy stands clearly divided into three segments: primary sector overwhelmingly thronged by the illiterate or semi-educated persons, mostly self-employed, operating at low level of productivity; secondary sector, highly dominated by the semi-educated persons, mostly wage-employed, operating at productivity levels substantially higher than those in the primary sector; and the territory sector, with a fairly high presence of educated workers, both self-and wage-employed, operating at productivity levels superior to those in the secondary, and much more so in the primary sector. In other words, a preponderant majority of the educated job seekers seem to be ' accommodated' in the territory sector; the secondary sector, and to a much larger extent, the primary sector, become the job-hunting ground for the illiterate and/or semi-educated job aspirants. The peacock is right here. Its feathers are in the teritary and, to a lesser extent, secondary sectors while its feet are firmly rooted in the primary sector. In terms of its sheer weight, the clumsy part poses serious concerns (Chadha, 2004).

The Indian policy makers have, thus, to think seriously for the future cadres of employment seekers. In our view, three types of policy interventions are called for. The first must aim at improving the quality of would be workers. The second needs to focus on training/retraining of the existing workforce. The third intervention needs to take note of the existing stock of human capital, and the one likely to emerge in the next five years or so, and launch sector-specific priorities of development that would match the supply of human capital; a case for enhanced focus on manufacturing comes up well.

The system is also highly oriented towards general education. The preference of general education was mainly driven by the perception that an academic degree was necessary to obtain a government job or status in society. The net result was that the education system neglected the need to provide vocational and technical skills to generate demand among students for acquiring marketable skills. In the long term, a strategy to impart vocational and technical skill will facilitate increase in the income from labour. A massive expansion of training facilities is needed.

Labour Productivity

Productivity is a measure of efficiency with which resources, both human and material, are converted into goods and services. Faster economic growth can be ensured through accelerated production and higher proclivity in all branches of economic activity. Human resources, being an important input, their productivity plays a significant role in determining the overall economic growth. Sector-wise labour productivity since 1987-88 is provided in Appendix A-4.49.

Labour productivity in agriculture has increased constantly during 1987-88 to 1999-00 in Karnataka. As against this, labour productivity in construction declined. However, the transport sector increased between 1987-88 and 1993-94 before declining significantly in 1999-00. On the other hand, labour productivity in manufacturing sector recorded significant increase during 1987-88 and 1999-00. A comparison with all-India in 1993-94, the levels of labour productivity in Karnataka, in the sub-sectors of agriculture, transport and trade were higher than that of all-India levels. But, sub-sectors like Construction, Services and Manufacturing were lower than that of all-India. On the whole, 1990s witnessed a significant growth in major sectors of Karnataka's economy. Inter-sector comparison reveals that the labour productivity was highest in Manufacturing. In general, the late 1990s witnessed a significant growth in major sectors of Karnataka economy. Although it is comforting to note that Indian productivity has kept up a rising trend, it has not been sufficiently high to make Indian products compete successfully in the international market.

Real Wage Rates, Poverty and Wage Employment

Agricultural labourers in Karnataka constitute the bulk of rural poor. Any policy concerned with improvement in their living standards has to take into consideration their income-earning opportunities and wage-rates, the return on their main endowment—labour.

Increases in real wages over time are, therefore, likely to be good proxies for fall in poverty incidence, and have the advantage of being relatively easy to monitor. If we look at Appendix A-4.50, male non-agricultural wage rates are invariably higher than female wage rates. Growth rates for casual labour wage rates in both sectors were highest between 1983 and 1987-88. These growth rates collapsed between 1987-88 and 1993-94, but recovered to varying degrees, during the second part of the 1990s.

In agriculture, however, growth rates in real wage rates from 1993-94 to 1999-00 remained well below the levels recorded in the period 1983 to 1987-88, for both males and females (Appendix A-4.50). The collapse of demand for farm labour undoubtedly accounts for much of this deceleration in the growth rates of real agricultural wages. In non-agriculture, on the other hand, the rate of growth of casual labour wage rates for males and females was higher towards the end of the 1990s than at any time previously. Female casual non-farm wage growth rates also recovered nicely from the trough of the late 1980s and early 1990s, but did not quite reach the high rates of growth of the earlier 1980s.

Implementation of minimum wages alone will not benefit wage workers. The effective enforcement of statutory entitlement along with provision of equal wages for both sexes is also vital in the state.

The next important aspect is employment stability, which has a direct impact on the macro economic growth distribution. This can be explained by wage employment stability. The National Council for Applied Economic Research (NCAER) survey provides the evidence of the average days worked per adult wage earners and then effective wage rate, which has been reported in Appendix A-4.51. The effective wage rate explains the employment stability.

If we consider the number of working days, Karnataka, in both agriculture and non-agriculture and all wage-working activities, stood above the all-India average for both male and female employees. When it came to effective wages rate, Karnataka fell below the all-India average. Particularly, in the case of agriculture male workers and female workers the variation was more in Karnataka. In the case of non-agriculture also the disparity remained high. From the above table, one can also observe that though the number of man-days were more, the wage level was low, which resulted in less income generation to the adult employees. Another interesting observation is that the non-agricultural effective wage rates were higher than those for agriculture. It implies that diversification to non-agriculture might be due to both pull and push factor. Public policy should aim at improving entitlement through creation of larger number of employment days and then improve wage payments. Implementation of minimum wages alone will not benefit wage workers. The effective enforcement of statutory entitlement is more vital in the state.

Poverty, in a broad sense, does not only refer to deprivation with reference to a minimum basket of goods and services that are essential for existence. It also includes socially perceived deprivation with respect to individual basic needs like shortfalls in health and education, inadequacy of shelter and deprivation associated with rigidities in social stratification (Planning Department, 1999). Appendix A-4.52 presents the per cent of population below poverty line in Karnataka and India in 1987-88 and 1999-00. Poverty reduction seems to be more pronounced in rural areas despite the fact that income per worker in the primary sector was the lowest in Karnataka and India. This might be due to increase in the wage rate of workers, which has shown significant increase during the period. Between 1987-88 and 1999-00, the proportion of population below poverty line declined from 37.5 per cent to 20 per cent in Karnataka against a decline from 38.9 per cent to 26 per cent at the national level. Such a substantial number even after five decades of independence is a matter of concern. On the whole, incidence of poverty was higher in urban areas while declining drastically during the 1990s in Karnataka and India as a whole.

In view of the poverty reduction, government is creating additional employment through many welfare schemes. They provide employment for the rural poor in the process of creating productive assets. Appendix A-4.53 gives the distribution of wage employment among various schemes in Karnataka during 1995-96 to 2002-03. The state has nine categories of programmes, which created about 1,108 lakh man-days during 2002-03. This is slightly lower than what was achieved during the earlier years. Wage-employment generation through government-sponsored programmes has been drastically declining over the recent past. Employees Assurance Scheme (EAS) provided 84.6 lakh man-days of work during 2002-03. This was usually towards the creation of productive assets in the rural areas such as roads, watershed management, minor irrigation, and other such works. In addition, there were a few other programmes, which also generated employment to the tune of about 70 lakh man-days per year in rural areas besides food security and creation of durable community, social and economic and infrastructure development in rural areas. Essentially, these jobs were provided to the agricultural labourers and marginal farmers but they were seasonal in nature. Growth rate of wage employment generation was high for CADA and Watershed Development programmes as against JRY/JGSY, EAS and buildings, which had the negative growth. On the whole, the prospects of employment in the state are not very bright. The incremental employment over a decade has been in the range of about one lakh man-days per year. Given the supply of labour, extent of poverty and deprivation, this achievement is little. Inadequate investments on infrastructure development, specifically the rural infrastructure is a significant cause of shortfall of full employment norm. This cause is also to be viewed from the perspective of competitive investment environment, perceived priorities of the state and very importantly the limited potentials for investment. It is also to be noted that no target date has been fixed even at the national level for full employment and poverty alleviation.

4.5.4 Some Policy Suggestions

Strategic Options

Unemployment has been a cause of worry in India for a very long time. However, unemployment is a derivative from the variables labour force and Employment. The Planning Commission has had the objective of removing unemployment and severe underemployment right from 1977-78, spread over a period of 10 years. This has not happened so far though the National Development Council in September 1992 meeting approved the strategy for removal of unemployment and severe under-employment over the next 10 years. In this context, there is a need to have strategies for improving the livelihoods. The first strategy should aim at rural and urban masses who are illiterate/semi-literate, unskilled, semi-literate/skilled. The second strategy has to address the educated unemployed. The policy goal should be to improve economic growth in rural areas with emphasis on employment for the poor, and shift workers from agriculture to non-agriculture activities, particularly services in rural areas. Thus, the task of generating employment is an urgent one and needs a range of concerted actions from the government, donors, banks and the private sector and from civil society institutions. Third, the better infrastructure also promotes the shift from low productivity casual labour to more productive casual work in the non-farm sector. Infrastructure is the key to higher real wages, and one of the keys to improvements in literacy and school attendance. Thus, the poverty reduction pay-off to investment in rural infrastructure in backward areas through employment generation programmes is likely to be greater than the returns to expenditure on assorted anti-poverty programmes. Programmes targeting individual poor households will still be needed especially to take care of special groups, such as poor female headed households, destitute old people, the disabled, the drought stricken and the totally unemployed. But the right track in the direction of raising the labour productivity of the people, who can and do work as casual labourers, is increasing productive employment opportunities for them, particularly in the non-farm sector. In short, 'infrastructure is everything' may be the appropriate slogan for the attack on chronic poverty in rural India.

Fourth, one might question the sustainability of high economic growth driven by the isolated growth of the service sector in the long run. This is because of various demand constraints (no demand from the other two sectors) and supply constraints (input supply to the other sectors). President Abdul Kalam and Y. S. Rajan (1998) highlight the complementarity of the three sectors in the following words:

"A country like India cannot hope to build its future on the services sector alone though it can be and will be a major component of the economy. India cannot afford not to build its strengths in agriculture for reasons for food and nutritional security. Nor can it afford to ignore manufacturing strengths for reasons of economic and national security. Based on the strength of these two sectors, it can build a major economic infrastructure for the services sector and use it to generate great wealth and employment for her people" (p. 158).

They add that if the services sector is properly developed along with the other two important and basic sectors, it can become instrumental in employment generation and individual prosperity, as it covers the multiple sectors of technology and manufacture.

Kalam and Rajan (1998) expect that the existing strong complementarity amongst the three sectors will increase in the near future, with the introduction of newer technologies necessitating skill upgradation in all three sectors, which would further accelerate the growth of the services sector. For example, the agriculture sector might witness more intense use of it than what it is doing now, be it in the use of remote sensing though satellite for regular monitoring of crops, soil conditions, water resources, for weather forecasts through satellites and ground borne systems, or in the use of modern communications to be in contact with markets. Similarly, in the industrial sector, the reorientation of skills from a lower to a higher level will become almost a necessity with the use of sensors, modern electronics and IT. According to them, "installation of IT systems for all these sectors, training, persons at all levels and maintaining and improving their skills would be a major service industry" (p. 159). Consequently, the growth of skilled and professional services would alleviate the acute problem of the educated unemployed.

In the context of poverty alleviation and employment generation, particularly for low-skill labour, the interdependent growth of all the three sectors should be emphasised so that the country can achieve a sustained 8 per cent rate of growth in real GDP, as has been envisaged in the Tenth Five Year Plan (Planning Commission, 2001). Once this happens, there will be a trickle-down effect making growth an instrument of poverty alleviation and employment generation. This would happen, particularly in the services sector, through inter-sectoral linkages. For instance, when the IT, telecom, retail trade and automobile sectors, etc. grow and expand, they directly create demand for skilled labour. But, for instance, the latter would employ more drivers, car cleaners, domestic help, security personnel, and a host of other low-skill workers. Such employment generation, which helps in poverty alleviation, will in fact follow the growth of sectors employing high-skill workers.

The same may also be expected to happen in the rural sector where the growth of high value crop production, particularly the commercial farm sector (horticulture, floriculture, herbiculture, agro-processing and so on) would create demand for the low-skill labour in poor families. Incidentally, the demand for such high value crops would have been generated by the aforementioned newly spawned urban production activities like the IT sector and so on. Our argument here visualises the interdependence of activities in all the three sectors, whose vigorous growth would help in poverty removal and employment generation. However, poverty removal would require vigo rous growth of the social sector (primarily education and health, etc.) and poverty alleviation focused intervention by the government.

Employment Generation Policy

Economic policy needs to be formulated and implemented in such a way as to deploy the national and local resources for creating large-scale employment opportunities in the growth process. The employment expansion that does not flow from the growth process is likely to be, at best, a mere palliative. There are three elements to the strategy to expand employment: (a) redistribution of income in favour of the low-income groups, (b) creation of public investment; and (c) provision of incentives to private investment. The growth strategy that can generate decent full employment cannot be based solely or even mainly on private investment. The *sine qua non* of such a growth strategy is investment by the state. Investment in agriculture and necessary infrastructure in terms of roads and electrification would play a crucial role in employment and income generation and poverty reduction in India. Land reform, as the experiences of various states including Karnataka have shown, plays a crucial role in mitigating the exclusion of poorer groups from growth and development in rural areas.

Agriculture will continue to play a dominant role in the creation of employment. As the average income of a worker in the agricultural sector is extremely low, the emphasis should be on creating productive employment and not treating it as a residual sector for the surplus labour. Development of agriculture in backward regions has very high potentiality for creating employment and reducing poverty. In agriculture, the potential for indirect employment in the form of agro-industries like food processing seems to be higher than that of direct employment. Allied activities like the dairy sector also have a high potential for employment. All these have a large export potential as well as the possibility of expanding domestic market, which can create significant employment. But in order to effectively tap this potential, a concerted policy and action plans are needed to develop them by adequate investment, suitable technological upgradation and proper marketing arrangements.

Along with agriculture, the non-farm sector has the potential for employment generation in rural areas. The relatively faster growth of employment in this sector in recent times has been widely discussed. There is clearly a need in favour of focusing on dynamic sub-sectors with comparative advantage and potentially wider markets and providing them with adequate credit, technology and other support.

It is not appropriate to project GSDP growth and employment elasticities over a long period of 25 years. The scenario of employment in 2020 will be based on certain underlying trends in regard to factors, which prevail in the longer term. Though the growth of labour force will slow down, but the elasticity of employment will also fall, which means that pressure on labour market will not ease. As agricultural work opportunities continue to shrink, the informal sector will grow rapidly. To cope up with such expected trends, strategies are needed to promote labour intensive and capital saving technologies. Employment creation in small establishments will have to be promoted by incentives linked with jobs created rather than capital invested.

4.5.5 *Insights on Labour and Employment in Karnataka State*

- While population in Karnataka grew from a total of 4.49 crores in 1991 to 5.27 crores in 2001, the workforce increased from 1.9 crores to 2.4 crores. Still, a decline is observed in labour force and workforce participation in the state over the years. This decline is apparent rather than real as population growth rates are declining faster than the growth rate of workforce. There is no cause for worry on the declining rates of labour force and work force though the gap between the two may be considered with concern.
- Agricultural labour has been growing at 0.98 per cent per annum during 1991 to 2001. But its proportion in the labour force has decreased from 29.9 to 26.4 per cent. The cause for concern is that the proportion is still 40.6 per cent in Gulbarga division, 43.8 per cent among females and specifically SC/ST women. There is a world of difference between proportion of agricultural labour in north Karnataka (36.2 per cent) and south Karnataka (19.4 per cent). It is well known that agricultural labour is highly associated with poverty, illiteracy, and other correlates of the world of the poor.
- Only 7 districts recorded workforce participation rates above state average both during 1991 and 2001. They are Bellary, Chikmagalur, Kodagu, Mandya, Raichur, Tumkur and Hassan. This trend was consistent even across sexes and regions (rural/urban) in only Kodagu and Tumkur.
- A serious cause for concern is the increase of marginal workers from 3.5 per cent in 1991 to 7.9 per cent in 2001.
- Child labour has been declining as expected. But it is still high in some of the north Karnataka districts.
- Employment growth in the state during 1990-1991 to 2001-02 was 2.6 per cent. The growth has been quite fast in the private sector since 1995-96, especially in favour of females. In fact, public sector male growth rate has been negative.
- A casual observer may notice an inconsistency between the two facts presented here. A question may be placed as to how can there be rising unemployment in the state when the state has recorded a 2.6 per cent average annual growth rate in employment between 1990-91 to 2001-02. This will not appear as a contradiction to a professional critic. Growth rate in

employment is always calculated for a given base. 2.6 growth rate means, for the 1990-91 base and for successive years taken as bases for calculation there is addition of 2.6 per cent to the workforce. Unemployment is a net figure of the difference between labour force and workforce. Labour force may be increasing at a rate faster than 2.6 per cent. In that case unemployment may increase in spite of rising growth rates in employment. One may also wonder as to why labour force increases are faster than workforce growth rates. It may be because of loss of land by agriculturists with marginal lands, migration of marginal and small farmers to urban areas and similar causes of casualisation of labour.

- Unemployment is on the rise in the state. The worst affected category are scheduled caste women, especially in rural areas. They are in labour force as per their usual principal status (UPS). But their proportion is quite low on current daily status (CDS) in relation to the usual principal status (UPS) status. On any day 4.45 per cent of SC women failed to get employment, during 1993-94 to 1999-2000. Statistics, sometimes suppress realities as they are expressed in percentages.
- Employment grew from 2.52 million to 5.76 million for women and from 11.95 to 12.79 million for men in the state from 1990-1991 to 2001-02 at a rate of 0.6 per cent for men (because of a high base) and 2.6 per cent for women. This is a welcome trend.
- One-third of employment growth between 1993-94 to 2001-02 has been contributed by the manufacturing sectors, may be specifically the ready-made garments. The manufacturing sector also has the highest growth rate of 4.7 per cent in the state.

In terms of volume the service sector contributed 40 per cent of employment. Together these two sectors contributed 73 per cent of employment in the state. The IT, BT, electronics, automobiles sectors are growing at a fast pace creating vast service sector employment opportunities.

- Casual labour is on the rise in rural Karnataka. Own account employment has come down.
- Labour productivity is quite high and rising in all the three sectors *viz*; agriculture, industry and the services in only two districts of the state *viz*; Shimoga and Mandya. Overall, labour productivity is higher than state average (0.25) in only 6 of the 20 districts of the state.
- Real wages increased by 40 per cent for men and 25 per cent for women between 1993-94 and 1999-00. In contrast, cost of living in the state increased by 68 per cent between 1993-94 to 2000-01 (GoK, 2002-03).
- Analysis of wage employment created by the Government under Employment Assurance Scheme (EAS) during 95-96 to 2002-03 falls short of full employment norm.
- The service sector throws new opportunities for creation of employment. Growth in automobiles, electronics, computers, telecommunications, information technology and biotechnology generates the needs for maintenance and repairs, sales and service and marketing which are service sector jobs. In this way service sector has enormous potential for absorption of skilled labour. Likewise, in agriculture emerging areas of hope are horticulture, floriculture, herbiculture and BT agri-business. With adequate and organised market support for finance and goods handicrafts and other village industries also throw up promise.
- Employment is the only social security for the poverty-gripped people. Imaginative (type of work), target (time, full employment norms) oriented, satisfactory quality (wage rates) employment for both men and women in rural and urban areas across all districts and all social groups can guarantee equity and justice in the state. If this employment is generated in all sectors with emphasis on emerging areas in agriculture, the service and the industry sectors, it heralds alround growth in the state. Heavy investments on 'infrastructure development and maintenance' in all sectors would be a panacea for large scale generation of employment and consequently poverty alleviation. Growth with justice is the objective of all policies of the state including the Employment Policy. 'Right to work' will become a reality only in such a scenario.

4.6 Summative Observations

Human beings are ends in themselves. They are the ultimate goal of all development efforts of a state. They should not be looked upon as mere resources. They have resources. They are not resources. Their resources should be used to develop themselves and incidentally also promote the community/national goals. This should be the perspective of all development efforts.

The quality of human resources is quite poor and wanting in Karnataka state. Literacy status—general and differentiated across social groups, gender and regions, health status and family welfare mindset among people, work status and quality of employment, quality of human capital, would all indicate towards such an inference.

There are several efforts by the state to improve the quality of people in the areas of health care, literacy and employment and human capital formation. Going by results as well as examination of status it may be inferred that what is being done is grossly inadequate. Vigorous, renewed and additional efforts are needed by the state to develop human beings *per se* and also develop in them capacities of value for social and economic growth and development in the state.

Backward districts of the state, identified in this study, need special attention. There is a need for district-specific time/goal targeting for all districts whether it is literacy, gender-parity, employment or human capital formation. Though such targeting is meaningful for the whole state, it is practicable to engage in district-specific targeting. Inter-*taluka* differentials get better addressed in district-specific planning and reviews.

Technical/vocational education needs special, intensive, area-planning. Emerging concerns in employment in the areas of floriculture, horticulture, herbiculture; maintenance, sales and service of automobiles, electronics, IT/BT sectors should be linked with technical/vocational courses.

A holistic perspective is the need in human development. It is rather difficult to address concerns of literacy leaving squarely the concerns of poverty and food security. The concerns of poverty need to be met within a framework of meaningful employment. As such the intricate and complex web of relationships between and across literacy, health, and fitness, employment, social security/food security, gender and regional parity, social groups upliftment and a fair deal for agricultural labour needs to be recognised within development plans and reviews. Employment is the key to poverty alleviation. Investments in 'development and maintenance of infrastructure' in all sectors of economy is essential for employment. Generation of appropriate skills in primary, secondary and tertiary sectors for emerging areas which will match the generated employment, would match the efforts in investment in infrastructure development.

The objective of growth should be all round, that is across all sectors and sub-sectors of development in a region keeping in view its natural resource potential and human resources base. As of now it is observed that across districts, growth is not taking place across all sectors/sub-sectors. Natural resources may set limits. But service sector growth depends on proper planning, finance, marketing support and supply of technical/vocational skills. This kind of integrated planning is not visible in the state.

Proportion of marginal workers is increasing substantially. Women from marginalised social groups are the worst affected in this scenario. Further, it is observed that the rise in real wage rates has not been able to keep pace with the rate at which cost of living is rising. Such facts as these need to form the information base for planning and implementation of 'full employment' programmes in the state.

What is ultimately desired is that there is a need for a renewed faith in the quality of people in the state and a recognition that such quality acts as a lever for economic growth and social development. Development performance in the state does not reflect such a faith in a prominent way.

References

Department of Technical Education. *Annual Administration Reports, 2000-2001; 1994-95; 1993-94,* Bangalore.

Karnataka Regional Engineering College (2001). *Annual Technical Manpower Review, Karnataka State-1997-2001*, Surathkal.

Bhalla, S. (2000). "Behind Poverty: The Qualitative Deterioration of Employment Prospects for Rural Indians", *Working Paper No.7*, IHD.

———.(2001). "Assessing Quality of Employment Growth Using National Sample Survey Data", paper presented at NSSO Golden Jubilee Seminar, Pune, April 6-7.

Bhat, P.N.M. and Francis Zavier (1999). "Findings of National Family Health Survey: Regional Analysis", *Economic and Political Weekly*, XXXIV (42-3): 3008-32.

Census of India (1991). *Karnataka State District Profile 1991*, pp. 50-75, Registrar General and Census Commissioner, New Delhi.

———.(2001). "Provisional Population Totals: Distribution of Workers and Non-workers", *Series 30*, Census Operations, Bangalore.

———.(1991). *General Economic Tables*, Series II-Karnataka Part-II B Series.

Chadha (2004). "Human Capital Base of Indian Labour Market: Identifying Worry Spots", *The Indian Journal of Labour Economics*, Vol. 47, No.1.

Dev, S. Mahendra. and Vijay Mahajan, (2003). "Employment and Unemployment", *Economic and Political Weekly*, 38 (12 and 13): 1252-1261.

Government of India (2001). *District-wise Social Economic Demographic Indicators*, National Commission on Population, New Delhi.

———. *Common Minimum Programme of the United Progressive Alliance*.

———. *Economic Survey* of various years.

———. *Encyclopaedia of Indian Education*, NCERT, Vol.1 (A-K)

———. *National Human Development Report 2001*.

———. NSSO 47th, 50th, 52nd, 54th and 55th Rounds.

———. *Population Census* of various years.

———. (2002). *Select Education Statistics*, MHRD.

———. (2004). *Union Budget 2004-05*, July.

Government of Karnataka (1999). *Human Development in Karnataka, 1999*, Planning Department, Bangalore.

———. *Karnataka at a Glance* Directorate of Economics and Statistics, (2000 and 2001), Bangalore.

———. (2001). *Functional Review Reports*, Karnataka Administrative Reforms Commission, December.

———. (2001). *Annual Report–2001*, Department of Employment & Training.

———. (2002). *High Power Committee for Redressal of Regional Imbalances*, Final Report, June.

———. (2004). *Karnataka State Integrated Health Policy*, Department of Health and Family Welfare, Bangalore.

———. (2001). *Karnataka towards Equity, Quality and Integrity in Health*, Final Report of the Taskforce on Health and Family Welfare, Bangalore.

———. (2002). *High Power Committee for Redresssal of Regional Imbalances*, pp. 227-250, Education for All, Directorate of Mass Education.

———. (2004). *Budget 2004-05: Speech of the CM* , pp. 1-36, Finance Department Bangalore.

———. *Karnataka Economic Survey* of various years.

———. (1999). *Karnataka Human Development Report 1999*.

———. *Statistical Abstract 1998-99*, Commission of Government of Karnataka.

———. (1999). *Annual Plan 1999-2000*, Vol.1: 3 Planning, Institutional Finance and Statistics and Science and Technology Department, Bangalore.

———. Planning, Statistics and Science and Technology Department, (2002) *Draft Tenth Plan 2002-2007 and Annual Plan 2002-2003*, Vol.1, Bangalore.

———. *Seventh All-India School Education Survey: September 2002*, Report on Provisional Statistics.

———. (2003). *Shaikshanika Anki Amshagala* Pakshinota 2002-03, Office of the Commissioner of Public Instruction, New Public Offices, Bangalore.

Government of Karnataka and Sekher T.V. (2001). *Functional Review of Department of Health and Family Welfare in Karnataka*, Functional Review Reports, KARC, Bangalore.

Guilmoto, C.Z. and S. Irudaya Rajan (2002). "District Level Estimates of Fertility from India's 2001 Census", *Economic and Political Weekly*, XXX VII, (7): 665-72.

Hatti, Neelambar, T.V. Sekher and Mattias Larsen (2004). "Lives at Risk: Declining Child Sex Ratios in India", *Lund Papers in Economic History*, No. 93, Lund University, Lund (Sweden).

IIPS and ORC Macro (2001). *National Family Health Survey (NFHS-2)—India 1998-99, Karnataka*, International Institute for Population Sciences, Mumbai.

Kalam, Abdul and Y.S. Rajan (1998). *India 2020 – A Vision for the New Millennium*, Viking Penguin, India.

Lukose, Vallutharai (2004). "Child Labour", paper presented at the *Workshop on Karnataka Human Development Report-II*, Bangalore, August 2004.

NCAER (1999). Survey on Human Development, New Delhi.

NSS (1996). *Sarvekshana*, 20(1), "Survey results of Fifth Quinquennial Survey on Employment and Unemployment (1993-94)", July-September: 20-150.

———. (1997). *"Employment and Unemployment Situation among Social Groups in India: 1993-94", Fifth Quinquennial Survey, 50th Round, Report No.425*, pp. 36-93, Department of Statistics, Delhi.

———. (1998). *"Employment and Unemployment Situation among Religious Groups in India: 1993-94", Fifth Quinquennial Survey, 50th Round, Report No.438*, pp. 34-59, Department of Statistics.

———. (2000). *"Employment and Unemployment in India: 1999-00", Sixth Quinquennial Survey, 55th Round, Department of Statistics*, New Delhi: 5-14.

———. (2001a). *"Employment and Unemployment Situation among Religious Groups in India: 1999-2000", Sixth Quinquennial Survey, 55th Round, Report No.468*, pp. 43-64, Ministry of Statistics and Programme Implementation, Delhi.

———. (2001b). *"Employment and Unemployment Situation among Social Groups in India: 1999-2000", Sixth Quinquennial Survey, 55th Round, Report No.469*, pp. 37-102, Ministry of Statistics and Programme Implementation, Delhi.

Planning Commission (1992). *Eighth Five-Year Plan: 1992-1997*, Vol.1, New Delhi: 117.

———.(2001). *Approach to Tenth Five Year Plan.*

———.(2002a). *Report on Labour and Employment*, pp. 21-65, Academic Foundation, New Delhi.

———.(2002b). *Special Group on Targeting Ten Million Employment Opportunities per Year*, New Delhi.

———. (2002c). *Tenth Five-Year Plan: 2002-2007*, Vol.1: 141-176, New Delhi.

Ravallion, M. (2000). "What is Needed for a More Pro-poor Growth Process in India?" *Economic and Political Weekly*, 35 (13): 1089-1093.

Rayappa, P.H. and T.V. Sekher (1998). "Administration of Health Services in Karnataka", in S. Ramanathan (ed.), *Landmarks in Karnataka Administration*, IIPA and Uppal Publishers. New Delhi.

Registrar General, India (1996). *Population Projections for India and States 1996 – 2016*.

Sekher, T.V, K.N.M. Raju and M.N. Sivakumar (2001). "Fertlity Transition in Karnataka: Levels, Trends and Implications", *Economic and Political Weekly*, XXXVI (51): 4742-52.

Sekher,T.V. and K.N.M.Raju (2004). "Fertility Transition in Karnataka", *Monograph* No: 5, Bangalore, Institute for Social and Economic Change.

Sundaram, K. (2001). "Employment and Unemployment Situation in the Nineties: Some Results from NSS 55th Round Survey", *Economic and Political Weekly*, 36(11): 931-940.

Visaria, Pravin (1997). "Women in the Indian Working Force: Trends and Differentials", *Artha Vijnana*, 39(1): 1-136.

APPENDIX A-4.1

Basic Demographic Data of Districts of Karnataka: 2001

State/District	Population			Decadal Growth Rate	Sex Ratio	Density	Literacy Rate (7+ age)		
	Total	Males	Females	(1991-2001)			Persons	Males	Females
India	**1027015247**	**531277078**	**495738169**	**21.34**	**933**	**324**	**65.38**	**75.85**	**54.16**
Karnataka	**52850562**	**26898918**	**25951644**	**17.25**	**964**	**275**	**66.6**	**76.1**	**56.9**
Belgaum	4214505	2150090	2064415	17.40	960	314	64.21	75.70	52.32
Bagalkot	1651892	834247	817645	18.84	980	251	57.30	70.88	43.56
Bijapur	1806918	926424	880494	17.63	950	172	57.01	69.94	43.47
Gulbarga	3130922	1592789	1538133	21.02	966	193	50.01	61.77	37.90
Bidar	1502373	771022	731351	19.56	949	276	60.94	72.46	48.81
Raichur	1669762	841840	827922	21.93	983	241	48.81	61.52	35.93
Koppal	1196089	603312	592777	24.57	983	166	54.10	68.42	39.61
Gadag	971835	493533	478302	13.14	969	209	66.11	79.32	52.52
Dharwad	1604253	823204	781049	16.65	949	376	71.61	80.82	61.92
Uttara Kannada	1353644	686876	666768	10.90	971	132	76.60	84.53	68.47
Haveri	1439116	740469	698647	13.29	944	298	67.79	77.61	57.37
Bellary	2027140	1029714	997426	22.30	969	240	57.40	69.20	45.28
Chitradurga	1517896	776221	741675	15.05	955	179	64.45	74.66	53.78
Davangere	1790952	917705	873247	14.78	952	302	67.43	76.37	58.04
Shimoga	1642545	830559	811986	12.90	978	193	74.52	82.01	66.88
Udupi	1112243	522231	590012	6.88	1130	286	81.25	88.23	75.19
Chickmagalur	1140905	574911	565994	11.98	984	158	72.20	80.29	64.01
Tumkur	2584711	1313801	1270910	11.87	967	243	67.01	76.78	56.94
Kolar	2536069	1286193	1249876	13.83	972	307	62.84	73.17	52.23
Bangalore	6537124	3426599	3110525	34.80	908	2979	82.96	87.92	77.48
Bangalore Rural	1881514	962183	919331	12.21	955	323	64.70	73.99	54.99
Mandya	1763705	888034	875671	7.14	986	355	61.05	70.50	51.53
Hassan	1721669	859086	862583	9.66	1004	253	68.63	78.37	59.00
Dakshina Kannada	1897730	938434	959296	14.51	1022	416	83.35	89.70	77.21
Kodagu	548561	274831	273730	11.64	996	133	77.99	83.70	72.26
Mysore	2641027	1344670	1296357	15.04	964	383	63.48	70.88	55.81
Chamrajnagar	965462	489940	475522	9.16	971	189	50.87	59.03	42.48

Source: *Census of India*, Karnataka, 2001.

APPENDIX A-4.2

Population Growth in Karnataka: 1901-2001

Year	Persons	Population		Decennial Growth Rate	
		Males	Females	Karnataka	India
1901	13054754	6582195	6472559	-	-
1911	13525251	6827801	6697450	3.6	5.75
1921	13377599	6793718	6583881	-1.09	-0.31
1931	14632992	7445458	7187534	9.38	11
1941	16255368	8294043	7961325	11.1	14.2
1951	19401956	9866923	9535033	19.4	13.3
1961	23586772	12040923	11545849	21.6	21.5
1971	29299014	14971900	14327114	24.2	24.8
1981	37043451	18869494	18173957	26.4	24.8
1991	44977201	22951917	22025284	21.1	23.9
2001	52733958	26856343	25877615	17.3	21.3

Source: Registrar General, India, various years.

APPENDIX A-4.3

Decadal Variation in Population Growth by Regions in Karnataka: 1901-2001

State/Regions	*1901-11*	*1911-21*	*1921-31*	*1931-41*	*1941-51*	*1951-61*	*1961-71*	*1971-81*	*1981-91*	*1991-2001*
Karnataka	+ 3.60	-1.09	+9.38	+11.09	+19.36	+21.57	+24.22	+26.43	+21.12	+17.25
	(+3.55)	(-1.10)	(+9.01)	(+10.57)	(+17.85)	(+19.72)	(+21.92)	(+23.73)	(+19.16)	(+15.91)
Coastal and Malnad	- 0.51	-1.11	+5.71	+7.81	+17.24	+32.67	+24.19	+24.33	+13.13	+11.47
Northern-Maidan	+ 3.15	- 4.98	+9.96	+11.05	+15.60	+19.27	+22.53	+23.60	+23.00	+18.76
Southern-Maidan	+ 6.44	+3.35	+10.42	+12.81	+24.25	+19.55	+25.90	+30.15	+22.62	+14.35
All India	**+ 5.75**	**- 0.31**	**+11.00**	**+14.22**	**+13.31**	**+21.51**	**+24.80**	**+24.66**	**+23.51**	**+21.34**
	(+ 5.60)	**(-0.31)**	**(+10.49)**	**(+13.39)**	**(+12.58)**	**(+19.78)**	**(+22.40)**	**(+22.36)**	**(+21.12)**	**(+20.27)**

Note: Coastal and Malnad region comprises six districts, namely, Dakshina Kannada, Udupi and Uttara Kannada (Coastal), Chickmagalur, Shimoga and Kodagu (Malnad).

Southern Maidan comprises Bangalore urban, Bangalore rural, Chamarajnagara, Chitradurga, Davangere, Hassan, Mandya, Mysore, Kolar and Tumkur districts.

Northern Maidan includes the districts of Bagalkot, Belgaum, Bellary, Bidar, Bijapur, Dharwad, Gadag, Gulbarga, Haveri, Koppal and Raichur.

Figures in the parentheses are decadal exponential growth rates.

Source: *Census of India*, (various years).

APPENDIX A-4.4

Population Projections for Karnataka: 2006-2016 (in '000)

	2006			*2011*			*2016*		
Age Group	*Male*	*Female*	*Total*	*Male*	*Female*	*Total*	*Male*	*Female*	*Total*
Under 15	7970	7673	15642	7736	7427	15163	7866	7562	15428
15-49	16122	15776	31897	17250	16968	34217	17891	17512	35403
50-59	2373	2114	4486	2732	2542	5274	3007	3050	6057
60+	2188	2210	4398	2579	2585	5163	3056	3062	6118
Total	**28652**	**27772**	**56424**	**30295**	**29520**	**59815**	**31821**	**31186**	**63007**

Source: Registrar General, India, 1996.

APPENDIX A-4.5

Total, Scheduled Castes and Scheduled Tribes Population in the Districts of Karnataka: 2001

	Population				
State/District	*Total*	*Scheduled Castes*	*% of SC Population*	*Scheduled Tribes*	*% of ST Population*
Karnataka	52850562	8563930	16.2	3463986	6.6
Belgaum	4214505	462020	11.0	243451	5.8
Bagalkot	1651892	250604	15.2	80181	4.9
Bijapur	1806918	334254	18.5	30051	1.7
Gulbarga	3130922	717595	22.9	154195	4.9
Bidar	1502373	298812	19.9	182219	12.1
Raichur	1669762	317276	19.0	303042	18.1
Koppal	1196089	185209	15.5	138588	11.6
Gadag	971835	137414	14.1	54410	5.6
Dharwad	1604253	131969	8.2	70442	4.4
Uttara Kannada	1353644	101896	7.5	23781	1.8
Haveri	1439116	175360	12.2	127163	8.8

Contd. ...

...*Contd.* ...

State/District	*Population*				
	Total	*Scheduled Castes*	*% of SC Population*	*Scheduled Tribes*	*% of ST Population*
Bellary	2027140	374218	18.5	364638	18.0
Chitradurga	1517896	336487	22.2	266235	17.5
Davangere	1790952	333227	18.6	209701	11.7
Shimoga	1642545	269519	16.4	55997	3.4
Udupi	1112243	67689	6.1	41613	3.7
Chickmagalur	1140905	233134	20.4	41019	3.6
Tumkur	2584711	474044	18.3	193819	7.5
Kolar	2536069	671692	26.5	205711	8.1
Bangalore	6537124	851047	13.0	86018	1.3
Bangalore (Rural)	1881514	377679	20.1	61555	3.3
Mandya	1763705	247213	14.0	17193	1.0
Hassan	1721669	311726	18.1	26451	1.5
Dakshina Kannada	1897730	131160	6.9	62936	3.3
Kodagu	548561	67422	12.3	46115	8.4
Mysore	2641027	467640	17.7	271351	10.3
Chamrajnagar	965462	237624	24.6	106111	11.0

Source: Final population totals, *Census of India, 2001*.

APPENDIX A-4.6

Sex Ratio and Child Sex Ratio of Karnataka by Districts: 1991 and 2001

State/Region	*2001*		*1991*	
	Sex Ratio of Total Population	*Sex Ratio of 0-6 Population*	*Sex Ratio of Total Population*	*Sex Ratio of 0-6 Population*
Karnataka	964	949	960	960
Belgaum	959	924	954	955
Bagalkot	977	939	-	960
Bijapur	948	971	962	956
Gulbarga	964	937	962	959
Bidar	948	967	952	962
Raichur	980	962	979	973
Koppal	982	938	-	958
Gadag	968	951	-	955
Dharwad	948	944	944	953
Uttara Kannada	970	946	966	949
Haveri	942	961	-	953
Bellary	969	949	965	959
Chitradurga	955	946	944	965
Davangere	951	949	-	954
Shimoga	977	959	960	965
Udupi	1127	955	-	970
Chickmagalur	984	964	977	978
Tumkur	966	952	959	970
Kolar	970	976	965	971
Bangalore Urban	906	940	903	950

Contd. ...

...Contd. ...

State/Region	*2001* Sex Ratio of Total Population	*2001* Sex Ratio of 0-6 Population	*1991* Sex Ratio of Total Population	*1991* Sex Ratio of 0-6 Population
Bangalore (Rural)	953	941	945	957
Mandya	985	937	963	959
Hassan	1,005	964	999	967
Dakshina Kannada	1,023	952	1,063	952
Kodagu	996	977	979	957
Mysore	965	970	953	969
Chamrajnagar	968	957	-	959

Note: Seven districts were created in 1997.
Source: *Census of India*, 1991, 2001—Karnataka

APPENDIX A-4.7

Population Data by Religion: Karnataka—2001

Religion	*Total Population*	*Proportion to Total Population*	*Sex Ratio*	*Sex Ratio (0-6)*	*Proportion of Child Population (0-6 yrs)*	*Literacy Rate*	*Female Literacy Rate*	*Work Participation Rate*
Hindus	44,321,279	83.9	966	945	13.3	65.6	55.3	45.9
Muslims	6,463,127	12.2	957	950	16.1	70.1	63.0	36.4
Christians	1,009,164	1.9	1030	961	11.1	87.4	84.0	39.5
Sikhs	15,326	0.0	739	882	11.9	83.7	77.3	38.4
Buddhists	393,300	0.7	907	953	15.3	54.8	42.0	41.7
Jains	412,659	0.8	926	892	12.0	84.3	77.2	39.3
Other Religions	115,460	0.2	966	949	13.8	68.2	57.2	43.9

Source: The First Report on Religion: *Census of India* 2001 (released in September, 2004).

APPENDIX A-4.8

Population in Five-Year Age Groups by Residence and Sex-2001: Karnataka

Age Group	*Total*			*Rural*			*Urban*		
	Persons	*Males*	*Females*	*Persons*	*Males*	*Females*	*Persons*	*Males*	*Females*
All Ages	**52850562**	**26898918**	**25951644**	**34889033**	**17648958**	**17240075**	**17961529**	**9249960**	**8711569**
0-4	4942594	2537476	2405118	3397862	1742354	1655508	1544732	795122	749610
5-9	5681431	2893477	2787954	3904587	1984925	1919662	1776844	908552	868292
10-14	6221576	3189233	3032343	4251140	2177833	2073307	1970436	1011400	959036
15-19	5381672	2840330	2541342	3484228	1852678	1631550	1897444	987652	909792
20-24	4886225	2541933	2344292	2985560	1546091	1439469	1900665	995842	904823
25-29	4578219	2216303	2361916	2848720	1359926	1488794	1729499	856377	873122
30-34	3821205	1917602	1903603	2430733	1198795	1231938	1390472	718807	671665
35-39	3918079	1926776	1991303	2530832	1228241	1302591	1387247	698535	688712
40-44	3058456	1636842	1421614	1997708	1058414	939294	1060748	578428	482320
45-49	2713842	1434271	1279571	1774819	928804	846015	939023	505467	433556
50-54	2109655	1117489	992166	1399820	733108	666712	709835	384381	325454
55-59	1423742	694759	728983	959486	458153	501333	464256	236606	227650
60-64	1498909	728997	769912	1059747	510997	548750	439162	218000	221162
65-69	953187	441373	511814	669806	307599	362207	283381	133774	149607
70-74	799497	382616	416881	579970	276687	303283	219527	105929	113598
75-79	353230	168279	184951	247996	117686	130310	105234	50593	54641
80+	457199	202465	254734	332075	147877	184198	125124	54588	70536
Age not Stated	51844	28697	23147	33944	18790	15154	17900	9907	7993

Source: *Census of India*, 2001 (*www.censusindia.net*).

APPENDIX A-4.9

Estimates of Birth Rate and Total Fertility Rate for Districts of Karnataka from 2001 Census

State/District	*Crude Birth Rate*	*Total Fertility Rate*
Karnataka	**20.9**	**2.4**
Bagalkot	25.1	3.1
Bangalore	18.7	1.9
Bangalore (Rural)	17.9	2.2
Belgaum	22.8	2.7
Bellary	25.1	3.1
Bidar	25.1	3.4
Bijapur	24.4	3.0
Chamrajnagar	17.9	2.0
Chickmagalur	18.3	1.9
Chitradurga	20.4	2.3
Dakshina Kannada	17.6	1.7
Davangere	20.7	2.4
Dharwad	21.1	2.5
Gadag	22.0	2.6
Gulbarga	26.7	3.5
Hassan	17.6	1.9
Haveri	21.8	2.6
Kodagu	19.2	2.0
Kolar	20.5	2.5
Koppal	27.4	3.4
Mandya	16.9	1.9
Mysore	18.9	2.1
Raichur	26.5	3.3
Shimoga	19.5	2.0
Tumkur	18.3	2.2
Udupi	15.0	1.5
Uttara Kannada	19.7	2.2

Source: Guilmoto and Rajan, 2002.

APPENDIX A-4.10

Projected Levels of the Expectation of Life at Birth in Karnataka and India: 1996-2016

Year	*Karnataka*		*India*	
	Male	*Female*	*Male*	*Female*
1996-2001	61.7	65.4	62.4	63.4
2001-2006	62.4	66.4	64.1	65.4
2006-2011	63.1	67.4	65.6	67.2
2011-2016	63.7	68.4	66.9	68.8

Source: Report of the Technical Group on Population Projections, 1996, Registrar General, India.

APPENDIX A-4.11

Urban Population by Classification of Towns in Karnataka, 2001 and the Projections for 2011

Population Range	Class of Town	2001 Census		Projection for 2011	
		Urban Population	% Share of Urban Population	Urban Population	% Share of Urban Population
1 Lakh or More	Class I	12043036	67	15792075	70
50000-99999	Class II	1726134	10	3002218	13
20000-49999	Class III Cities/Towns	3096525	17	3042434	13
10000-19999	Class IV Towns	839021	5	624630	3
5000-9999	Class V Towns	192477	1	195437	1
Less than 5000	Class VI Towns	22665	0	17598	0
Karnataka Urban	All Towns	17919858	100	22674392	100

Source: Government Karnataka, *State of the Environment Report and Action Plan, 2003, Census of India, 2001.*

APPENDIX A-4.12

Percentage of Urban Population: Karnataka—2001

State/District	Percentage of Urban Population
Karnataka	**33.98**
Belgaum	24.06
Bagalkot	29.00
Bijapur	21.87
Gulbarga	27.13
Bidar	22.94
Raichur	25.42
Koppal	16.61
Gadag	35.18
Dharwad	54.98
Uttara Kannada	28.67
Haveri	20.79
Bellary	34.86
Chitradurga	18.15
Davangere	30.30
Shimoga	34.79
Udupi	18.60
Chickmagalur	19.52
Tumkur	19.64
Kolar	24.75
Bangalore	88.08
Bangalore (Rural)	21.67
Mandya	16.02
Hassan	17.70
Dakshina Kannada	38.41
Kodagu	13.79
Mysore	36.90
Chamrajnagar	15.37

Source: *Census of India*, 2001, Karnataka

APPENDIX A-4.13

Male/Female Differentials in Literacy in Karnataka 1991 and 2001

	Gains			Decadal Gains	2001-1991
Districts	2001	1991	Decade	Male	Female
Karnataka	**67.04**	**56.04**	**11.00**	**9.03**	**13.11**
Bangalore	83.91	76.27	7.64	5.42	10.17
Banaglore (Rural)	65.00	50.17	4.83	12.92	16.97
Chitradurga	64.88	52.28	12.60	10.19	15.24
Davanagere	67.67	55.96	8.31	9.62	14.04
Kolar	63.14	50.45	12.69	10.45	15.06
Tumkur	67.19	54.48	12.71	10.39	15.25
Belgaum	64.42	53.00	11.42	9.24	13.84
Bagalkot	57.81	53.58	4.23	2.53	5.91
Gadag	66.27	55.88	10.39	7.92	12.90
Dharwad	71.87	62.73	9.14	6.82	11.79
Haveri	68.09	56.10	11.99	9.89	14.32
Uttara Kannada	76.59	66.73	9.86	8.09	11.71
Gulbarga	50.65	38.54	12.11	10.44	13.91
Bijapur	57.46	56.55	00.91	-2.40	4.38
Bidar	61.98	45.11	16.87	14.32	19.48
Raichur	49.54	34.34	15.20	15.27	15.14
Koppal	55.02	38.23	16.79	15.68	17.98
Bellary	58.04	45.89	12.75	10.48	13.92
Mysore	63.69	50.88	12.81	11.59	14.21
Hassan	68.75	56.85	11.90	9.42	14.42
Mandya	61.21	48.15	13.06	11.53	14.92
Chamrajnagar	51.26	38.19	13.07	11.94	14.42
Chickmagalur	72.63	61.05	11.58	10.12	13.16
Kodagu	78.17	68.35	9.82	8.45	11.31
Udipi	79.87	74.47	05.40	3.01	07.98
Shimoga	74.86	63.90	10.96	9.20	12.91
Dakshina Kannada	82.47	76.74	6.73	4.86	8.55

Source: *Population Census*, 2001.

APPENDIX A-4.14

District-wise Rural-Urban Literacy Rates by Sex in Karnataka: 2001 (in per cent)

Districts	Rural		Urban		Total	
	Male	Female	Male	Female	Male	Female
Bagalkot	66.01	36.33	82.40	60.87	70.88	53.56
Bangalore	78.82	60.78	89.13	79.70	87.92	77.48
Bangalore (Rural)	71.88	50.95	-	-	73.99	54.99
Belgaum	71.53	45.80	88.43	72.53	75.70	52.32
Bellary	63.49	36.82	79.41	60.69	69.20	45.28
Bidar	69.22	43.64	83.14	66.47	72.46	48.81
Bijapur	65.95	37.32	83.86	64.89	69.94	43.47
Chamrajnagar	55.64	38.59	77.69	63.86	59.03	42.48
Chickmagalur	78.42	60.70	87.77	77.78	80.29	64.01
Chitradurga	71.84	49.12	87.21	74.74	74.66	53.78
Dakshina Kannada	87.07	72.69	93.78	84.47	89.70	77.21
Davanagere	73.04	52.02	83.90	71.89	76.37	58.04
Dharwad	73.13	47.70	87.00	73.28	80.82	61.92
Gadag	76.40	46.28	84.60	63.88	79.32	52.52
Gulbarga	54.93	29.43	79.16	60.49	61.77	37.90
Hassan	75.94	54.72	89.34	79.35	78.37	59.00
Haveri	76.61	54.52	81.44	68.17	77.61	57.37
Kodagu	82.14	70.10	93.19	86.11	83.70	72.26
Kolar	68.87	44.99	86.18	74.27	73.17	52.23
Koppal	66.10	35.81	79.67	58.34	68.43	39.61
Mandya	67.82	47.65	84.31	72.26	70.50	51.53
Mysore	61.01	42.31	87.33	78.12	70.88	55.81
Raichur	56.09	28.86	76.76	56.54	61.52	35.93
Shimoga	78.45	60.66	88.53	78.50	82.01	66.88
Tumkur	74.25	52.29	86.91	76.35	76.78	56.94
Udupi	86.85	72.97	93.83	85.31	80.23	75.19
Uttara Kannada	81.58	63.52	91.79	80.59	84.53	68.47

Source: *Population Census of India*, 2001.

APPENDIX A-4.15

District-wise Ranking of Urban Literacy Rate by Sex in Karnataka: 1991

District	Male	District	Female	District	Total
Dakshina Kannada	90.87	Dakshina Kannada	78.21	Dakshina Kannada	84.51
Coorg	88.43	Coorg	77.76	Coorg	83.27
Uttara Kannada	88.12	Uttara Kannada	73.79	Uttara Kannada	81.10
Bangalore	85.24	Bangalore	72.68	Bangalore	79.53
Chickmagalur	84.73	Chikmagalur	72.03	Chikmagalur	78.59
Shimoga	84.23	Shimoga	71.35	Shimoga	78.01
Hassan	84.02	Hassan	71.08	Hassan	77.76
Belgaum	83.54	Tumkur	67.79	Tumkur	75.61
Tumkur	82.61	Mysore	66.91	Kolar	74.09
Kolar	81.63	Kolar	66.15	Belgaum	73.59

Contd. ...

...Contd. ...

District	*Male*	*District*	*Female*	*District*	*Total*
Chitradurga	81.20	Chitradurga	65.05	Chitradurga	73.52
Bijapur	80.88	Belguam	62.99	Mysore	73.50
Dharwad	79.82	Mandya	60.66	Dharwad	70.20
Bidar	78.76	Dharwad	59.93	Mandya	68.46
Mysore	76.69	Bangalore (Rural)	59.68	Bijapur	68.42
Gulbarga	75.86	Bidar	55.91	Bidar	68.03
Mandya	75.75	Bijapur	55.27	Bangalore (Rural)	67.39
Bangalore (Rural)	74.56	Gulbarga	51.87	Gulbarga	64.36
Bellary	71.93	Bellary	49.32	Bellary	60.93
Raichur	68.53	Raichur	43.59	Raichur	56.38
Karnataka	82.40		65.74		74.20

Source: *Population Census*, 1991.

APPENDIX A-4.16

District-wise Ranking of Urban Literacy Rate by Sex in Karnataka: 2001

Rank	*District*	*Total %*	*District*	*Male %*	*District*	*Female %*	*District*	*Male-Female Gap %*
1	Kodagu*	89.74	Udupi*	93.78	Kodagu	86.11	Bagalkot*	21.53
2	Udupi	89.47	Dakshina Kannada	93.19	Udupi*	85.31	Koppal*	21.33
3	Dakshina Kannada	89.10	Kodagu	93.13	Dakshina Kannada	84.47	Gadag*	20.72
4	Uttara Kannada	86.27	Uttara Kannada	91.79	Uttara Kannada	80.59	Raichur	20.22
5	Bangalore	84.65	Hassan	89.34	Bangalore	79.70	Bijapur	18.97
6	Hassan	84.43	Bangalore	89.13	Hassan	79.35	Bellary	18.72
7	Shimoga	83.60	Shimoga	88.53	Shimoga	78.50	Gubarga	18.67
8	Chickmagalur	82.87	Belguam	89.43	Mysore	78.12	Bidar	16.67
9	Mysore	82.80	Chickmagalur	87.77	Chickmagalur	77.78	Belgum	15.90
10	Tumkur	81.80	Mysore	87.33	Tumkur	76.35	Chamarajnagar*	13.83
11	Chitradurga	21.14	Chitradurga	87.21	Chitradurga	74.74	Dharwad	13.72
12	Belgaum	80.66	Dharwad	87.00	Kolar	74.27	Haveri*	13.27
13	Kolar	80.31	Tumkur	86.91	Dharwad	73.28	Chitradurga	12.47
14	Dharwad	80.31	Kolar	86.18	Belgaum	72.53	Mandya	12.05
15	Mandya	78.39	Gadag*	84.60	Mandya	72.26	Davanagere*	12.01
16	Davangere*	78.08	Mandya	84.31	Davangere*	71.89	Kolar	11.91
17	Bangalore (Rural)	75.97	Davangere*	83.90	Bangalore (Rural)	69.97	Bangalore (Rural)	11.64
18	Bidar	75.14	Bijapur	83.86	Haveri*	68.17	Uttara Kannada	11.20
19	Haveri*	74.98	Bidar	83.14	Bidar	66.47	Tumkur	10.5
20	Bijapur	74.59	Bagalkot*	82.40	Bijapur	64.89	Shimoga	10.03
21	Gadag*	74.40	Bangalore (Rural)	81.61	Gadag*	63.88	Chickmagalur	9.99
22	Bagalkot*	71.75	Haveri*	81.44	Chamarajnagar*	63.86	Hasan	9.99
23	Chamrajnagar*	70.88	Koppal*	79.67	Bagalkot*	60.87	Bangalore	9.43
24	Bellary	70.24	Bellary	79.41	Bellary	60.69	Mysore	9.21
25	Gulbarga	70.12	Gulbarga	71.16	Gulbarga	60.49	Udupi*	8.77
26	Koppal*	69.14	Chamarajnagar*	77.69	Koppal*	58.34	Dakshina Kannada	8.72
27	Raichur	66.86	Raichur	76.76	Raichur	56.54	Kodagu	7.02
	Karnataka	**74.90**		**81.10**		**86.90**		**5.80**

Note: *Newly Formed Districts.

Source: *Population Census*, 2001.

APPENDIX A-4.17

Total Literacy Campaign Progress Report

Name of the Project	Target (in Lakhs)			Achievment (in Lakhs)		
	Male	Female	Total	Male	Female	Total
Dakshina Kannada	0.70	1.74	2.44	0.58	1.48	2.06
Bijapur	2.74	2.72	5.46	0.96	0.96	1.92
Mandya	1.74	2.36	4.10	1.49	2.03	3.52
Shimoga	1.33	1.80	3.31	1.22	1.38	2.60
Tumkur	1.28	1.99	3.27	1.18	1.58	2.76
Raichur	2.64	3.74	6.38	0.87	1.02	1.89
Bidar	0.92	1.16	2.53	0.73	1.28	2.01
Dharwad I Phase	1.53	2.19	3.72	1.13	1.61	2.74
Dharwad II Phase	0.95	1.53	2.48	0.69	0.83	1.52
Mysore I Phase	1.24	1.64	2.88	0.60	0.57	1.17
Mysore II Phase	1.49	1.74	3.23	0.59	0.70	1.29
Uttara Kannada	0.54	1.01	1.55	0.37	0.72	1.09
Bangalore (Rural)	1.31	1.86	3.17	0.24	0.24	0.48
Chickmagalur	0.59	0.92	1.51	0.45	0.76	1.21
Kodagu	0.27	0.36	0.66	0.08	0.19	0.27
Gulbarga	2.62	3.36	5.98	0.77	1.13	1.90
Belgaum	2.06	3.48	5.51	1.28	2.79	1.07
Kolar	1.39	2.28	3.67	0.46	0.59	1.05
Chitradurga	1.70	2.44	4.14	1.03	1.45	2.48
Bellary	1.72	2.39	4.11	0.92	1.09	2.01
Hassan	1.07	1.76	2.83	0.74	0.86	1.60
Bangalore (Urban)	0.54	0.73	1.27	0.49	0.63	1.12
Bangalore City	1.41	1.70	3.11	0.83	1.49	2.32
Total	**31.78**	**45.38**	**77.16**	**17.70**	**25.38**	**43.08**

Source: Directorate of Mass Education, Commissioner of Public Instruction, Government of Karnataka.

APPENDIX A-4.19

Cumulative Percentage of Population with Secondary and beyond Secondary Educational Attainment across District

District	Total	Male	Female	Rural	Urban
Bangalore	28.1	33.4	22.1	10.9	30.9
Bangalore (Rural)	8.7	12.4	4.7	7.0	16.0
Belgaum	11.2	16.1	6.2	7.5	23.7
Bellary	8.2	11.7	4.5	4.4	17.1
Bidar	9.1	13.2	4.0	6.4	20.0
Bijapur	9.4	14.2	4.4	6.3	19.7
Chickmagalur	11.3	14.5	8.0	8.8	23.7
Chitradurga	11.1	15.4	6.7	7.2	22.0
Dakshina Kannada	13.9	16.9	11.1	9.7	24.6
Dharwad	11.5	15.8	7.0	6.6	20.8
Gulbarga	8.2	12.5	3.8	4.7	19.7
Hassan	9.6	13.1	6.1	6.6	23.8
Kodagu	13.9	15.6	12.2	12.4	26.4
Kolar	9.8	13.5	5.8	6.1	22.1
Mandya	9.7	13.9	5.3	7.6	20.6
Mysore	10.8	13.9	7.2	4.5	25.8
Raichur	6.2	9.5	2.9	3.7	15.9
Shimoga	12.2	16.0	8.3	8.1	23.6
Tumkur	10.7	14.8	6.1	7.7	25.1
Uttara Kannada	12.8	15.6	9.9	9.3	23.9
State	**12.2**	**16.3**	**8.0**	**6.8**	**24.5**

Source: Original Source: *Census of India 1991*, Series II-Karnataka, General Economic Tables, Part-III-B Series. Computations by the author.

APPENDIX A-4.18

Percentage of Population with Educational Attainment of Secondary and Above (Rural-Urban & Male-Female) in Karnataka

Education	Total			Rural			Urban		
	T	M	F	T	M	F	T	M	F
Matriculation/Secondary	6.8	8.7	4.8	4.3	6.2	2.4	12.4	14.4	10.3
Higher Secondary/Equivalent	2.3	3.1	1.4	1.3	1.9	0.5	4.6	5.6	3.5
Diploma/Certificate (Non-technical)	0.3	0.4	0.3	0.2	0.4	0.1	0.5	0.5	0.6
Diploma/Certificate (Technical)	0.3	0.6	0.1	0.09	0.2	0.0	0.9	1.5	0.2
Graduates & above	2.5	3.5	1.4	0.9	1.4	0.3	6.1	8.1	3.8
Total	**12.2**	**16.3**	**8.0**	**6.8**	**10.1**	**3.3**	**24.5**	**30.1**	**18.4**

Source: Original Source: *Census of India* 1991, Series II-Karnataka, General Economic Tables, Part-III-B Series. Computations by the author.

APPENDIX A-4.20

Breakup of Educational Attainment in the Demographic Composition (Overall Total)

(in per cent)

District	*Matric*	*Hr. Sec.*	*Tech/Non-Tech Diploma*	*University*	*Disparity between D & E*
A	*B*	*C*	*D*	*E*	*F*
Bangalore	14.1	4.8	1.7	7.5	5.8
Bangalore (Rural)	5.5	1.6	0.3	1.1	0.8
Belgaum	7.0	1.9	0.5	1.8	1.3
Bellary	4.5	1.6	0.5	1.6	1.1
Bidar	5.3	2.0	0.4	1.4	1.0
Bijapur	5.3	2.0	0.5	1.6	1.1
Chickmagalur	6.2	2.4	0.6	2.1	1.5
Chitradurga	6.3	2.3	0.6	1.9	1.3
Dakshina Kannada	7.2	3.1	0.7	2.9	2.2
Dharwad	6.4	2.2	0.7	2.2	1.5
Gulbarga	4.8	1.7	0.4	1.4	1.0
Hassan	5.6	1.8	0.5	1.7	1.2
Kodagu	7.9	2.8	0.3	2.9	2.6
Kolar	6.1	1.5	0.8	1.4	0.6
Mandya	5.8	1.9	0.5	1.5	1.0
Mysore	5.6	2.0	0.6	2.6	2.0
Raichur	3.6	1.3	0.2	1.1	0.9
Shimoga	7.0	2.3	0.7	2.2	1.5
Tumkur	6.5	1.9	0.6.	1.7	1.1
Uttara Kannada	7.8	1.9	0.6	2.5	1.9
State	**6.8**	**2.3**	**0.6**	**2.5**	**1.9**

Source: Original Source: *Census of India 1991*, Series II-Karnataka, General Economic Tables, Part-III-B Series. Computations by the author.

APPENDIX A-4.21

Breakup of Educational Attainment in the Demographic Composition: Urban Areas

District	*Matric*	*Hr. Sec.*	*Tech/Non-. Tech Diploma*	*University*	*Disparity between D & E*
A	*B*	*C*	*D*	*E*	*F*
Bangalore	15.2	5.3	1.9	8.5	6.6
Bangalore (Rural)	9.5	3.0	0.7	2.9	2.2
Belgaum	13.1	4.4	1.1	5.1	4.0
Bellary	8.9	3.3	1.0	3.9	2.9
Bidar	10.2	4.7	1.0	4.1	3.1
Bijapur	10.4	4.0	0.9	4.3	3.4
Chickmagalur	11.9	4.4	1.6	5.8	4.2
Chitradurga	11.1	4.9	1.2	4.8	3.6
Dakshina Kannada	11.6	5.6	1.1	6.2	5.2
Dharwad	10.8	4.0	1.2	4.8	3.6
Gulbarga	10.4	4.0	1.0	4.2	3.2
Hassan	11.8	4.8	1.3	6.0	4.8
Kodagu	13.1	5.6	0.9	6.9	5.0
Kolar	12.4	3.7	2.2	3.8	1.6
Mandya	10.9	4.1	1.2	4.4	3.2
Mysore	12.0	4.9	1.6	7.3	5.7
Raichur	8.5	3.2	0.8	3.4	2.6
Shimoga	12.2	4.5	1.7	5.3	3.6
Tumkur	12.9	4.7	1.6	5.9	4.3
Uttara Kannada	13.2	3.8	1.2	5.7	4.5
State	**12.4**	**4.6**	**1.4**	**6.1**	**4.7**

Source: Original Source: *Census of India 1991*, Series II-Karnataka, General Economic Tables, Part-III-B Series. Computations by the author.

APPENDIX A-4.22

Breakup of Educational Attainment in the Demographic Composition (Rural Areas)

(in per cent)

District	*Matric*	*Hr. Sec.*	*Tech/Non-. Tech Diploma*	*University*	*Disparity between D & E*
A	*B*	*C*	*D*	*E*	*F*
Bangalore	7.4	1.7	0.8	1.3	0.8
Bangalore (Rural)	4.7	1.2	0.3	0.8	0.5
Belgaum	5.1	1.2	0.4	0.8	0.4
Bellary	2.7	0.9	0.3	0.6	0.3
Bidar	4.1	1.4	0.2	0.7	0.5
Bijapur	3.7	1.4	0.4	0.8	0.4
Chickmagalur	5.0	2.0	0.4	1.4	1.0
Chitradurga	4.5	1.4	0.4	0.9	0.5
Dakshina Kannada	5.5	2.1	0.5	1.6	1.1
Dharwad	4.1	1.3	0.4'	0.8	0.4
Gulbarga	3.0	0.9	0.2	0.5	0.3
Hassan	4.3	1.2	0.3	0.8	0.5
Kodagu	6.9	2.3	1.0	2.2	1.2
Kolar	4.2	0.9	0.4	0.6	0.3
Mandya	4.9	1.5	0.3	0.9	0.6
Mysore	2.9	0.8	0.2	0.6	0.4
Raichur	2.3	0.7	0.2	0.5	0.3
Shimoga	5.1	1.5	0.4	1.1	0.7
Tumkur	5.2	1.3	0.4	0.8	0.4
Uttara Kannada	6.1	1.4	0.4	1.4	1.0
State	**4.3**	**1.3**	**0.3**	**0.9**	**0.6**

Source: Original Source: *Census of India 1991*, Series II-Karnataka, General Economic Tables, Part-III-B Series. Computations by the author.

APPENDIX A-4.23

Breakup of Educational Attainment in the Demographic Composition: Male-Female

(in per cent)

District	Sec		Hr.Sec		Tech		Univ	
	M	F	M	F	M	F	M	F
Bangalore	16.0	11.9	5.6	3.9	2.4	0.9	9.4	5.4
Bangalore (Rural)	7.6	3.3	2.7	0.9	0.2	0.02	1.9	0.4
Belgaum	9.5	4.3	2.9	0.9	0.8	0.2	2.9	0.7
Bellary	6.2	2.8	2.2	0.9	0.9	0.1	2.5	0.7
Bidar	2.0	2.7	3.2	0.8	0.6	0.1	2.4	0.4
Bijapur	7.6	2.9	3.1	0.8	0.8	0.2	2.7	0.5
Chickmagalur	7.5	4.9	3.1	1.7	0.9	0.2	3.0	1.2
Chitradurga	8.3	4.2	3.3	1.3	0.9	0.4	2.9	0.8
Dakshina Kannada	8.4	6.2	3.7	2.5	0.9	0.5	3.9	1.9
Dharwad	8.3	4.4	3.2	1.3	1.0	0.3	3.3	1.0
Gulbarga	7.1	2.4	2.5	0.8	0.6	0.2	2.3	0.5
Hassan	7.3	3.9	2.5	1.1	0.7	0.2	2.6	0.9
Kodagu	8.8	6.9	2.9	2.7	0.3	0.3	3.6	2.3
Kolar	8.1	3.9	2.1	0.9	1.2	0.4	2.1	0.6
Mandya	7.9	3.7	2.9	0.9	0.7	0.2	2.4	0.5
Mysore								
Raichur	5.4	1.8	1.9	0.6	0.4	0.1	1.8	0.4
Shimoga	8.6	5.3	3.0	1.6	1.2	0.3	3.2	1.1
Tumkur	8.5	4.3	2.8	0.9	0.9	0.2	2.6	1.7
Uttara Kannada	8.9	6.6	2.5	1.4	0.7	0.5	3.5	1.4
State	**8.7**	**4.8**	**3.1**	**1.4**	**1.0**	**0.4**	**3.5**	**1.4**

Source: Original Source: Census of India 1991, Series II-Karnataka, General Economic Tables, Part-III-B Series.

APPENDIX A-4.24

Institutions and Enrolment

	1990-91		2000-01/01-02	
	Institutions	Enrolment	Institutions	Enrolment
Secondary	5020	1334000	8612	1951313
Higher Secondary	1322	465000	2184	322893
General Degree Colleges	419	225300	916	3523000
Polytechnics	165	46339	196	47103
Engg. Colleges	51	57834	112	90841
ITI	35	7896	331**	18089
TTIs (P.pry+Pry)	(48+127)175	(1172+11249) 12421	135*	15173*
B.Ed.	64	6618	73	7300

Note: * Figures relate to 1998-99 and includes only Pry.TTI.

Statistical Abstract of Karnataka 1998-99, p.310.

Statistical Abstract of Karnataka 1993-94, p.324.

** Includes both government and private (Source: *Karnataka–A Manpower Profile 2000-01*, GoK).

Source: *All India Educational Survey (AIES)*, 2003 except for ITI data *Manpower Profile 2000-01*, MP & E Division, GoK, 9.84.

APPENDIX A-4.25

Institutional Facilities across Districts: 2001-02

District	Sec 1999-00	Hr. Sec	Polytechnics 1998-99	Degree Colleges 2000-01	Engg. Colleges
A	B	C	D	E	F
Bangalore	1018	230	52	200	51
Bangalore (Rural)	298	59	6	19	6
Belgaum	575	122	11	63	4
Bellary	211	50	6	19	3
Bidar	309	64	5	28	3
Bijapur	510	126	7	55	3
Chickmagalur	221	48	3	15	1
Chitradurga	570	168	8	63	7
Dakshina Kannada	463	156	9	75	6
Dharwad	597	155	14	83	5
Gulbarga	415	100	8	49	2
Hassan	372	78	4	22	2
Kodagu	99	32	2	7	1
Kolar	338	73	10	21	2
Mandya	313	76	3	22	1
Mysore	510	121	11	53	6
Raichur	280	63	6	24	1
Shimoga	302	68	8	35	1
Tumkur	541	144	5	39	6
Uttara Kannada	240	59	6	24	1
State	**8182**	**1992**	**184**	**916**	**112**

Source: Shaikshanika Anki Anshagala Pakshinota 2002-03. Office of the Commissioner for Public Instruction, New Public Offices, Bangalore, 2003.

Karnataka at a Glance 2000-01, Directorate of Economics and Statistics, Bangalore, 2001.

APPENDIX A-4.26

Number of Secondary, Higher Secondary, Technical and Degree Colleges: 1993-94

Districts	Sec	%	No. of Sec. Schs. per Lakh Pop.	Polytechnic and Engg. College	No.of tech. Colleges per Lakh Pop.	Degree College	No.of Degree Colleges per Lakh Pop.
Bangalore	65	(11.4)	13.5	63	1.3	88	1.8
Bangalore (Rural)	183	(3.2)	10.9	2	0.1	12	0.7
Belgaum	423	(7.4)	11.8	13	0.4	46	1.3
Bellary	170	(2.9)	8.9	7	0.4	17	0.9
Bidar	169	(2.9)	13.5	9	0.7	19	1.5
Bijapur	382	(6.7)	13.0	13	0.4	38	1.3
Chickmagalur	173	(3.0)	17.0	4	0.4	13	1.3
Chitradurga	432	(7.5)	19.8	13	0.6	43	1.9

Contd. ...

...*Contd.* ...

Districts	Sec	%	No. of Sec. Schs. per Lakh Pop.	Polytechnic and Engg. College	No.of tech. Colleges per Lakh Pop.	Degree College	No.of Degree Colleges per Lakh Pop.
Dakshina Kannada	279	(4.9)	10.4	12	0.4	64	2.4
Dharwad	391	(6.8)	11.2	19	0.5	60	1.7
Gulbarga	290	(5.1)	11.2	10	0.4	39	1.5
Hassan	328	(5.7)	20.9	9	0.6	18	1.1
Kodagu	71	(1.2)	14.5	2	0.4	5	1.0
Kolar	212	(3.7)	9.6	13	0.6	15	0.7
Mandya	166	(2.9)	10.1	4	0.2	16	0.9
Mysore	364	(6.4)	11.5	16	0.5	33	1.0
Raichur	135	(2.4)	5.8	6	0.3	16	0.7
Shimoga	300	(5.2)	15.7	8	0.4	33	1.7
Tumkur	408	(7.1)	17.7	10	0.4	23	1.0
Uttara Kannada	201	(3.5)	16.5	7	0.6	19	1.6
State	**5732**		**12.7**	**237**	**0.5**	**617**	**1.4**

Note: Figures in parentheses indicate percentage for each district.

Source: *Statistical Abstract Karnataka 1997-98*. Bureau of Economics and Statistics, Government of Karnataka.

Government of Karnataka, High Power Committee for Redressal of Regional Imbalances, *Final Report*, June 2002.

APPENDIX A-4.27

Number of Degree College (Government and Aided) Students Enrolled per Lakh Population in 2001

District	*No. of Students*
Bangalore	1078
Bangalore (Rural)	371
Belgaum	607
Bellary	668
Bidar	551
Bijapur	641
Chickmagalur	458
Chitradurga	371
Dakshina Kannada	1164
Dharwad	712
Gulbarga	355
Hassan	616
Kodagu	587
Kolar	620
Mandya	576
Mysore	508
Raichur	213
Shimoga	659
Tumkur	564
Uttara Kannada	1097
State	**669**

Source: High Power Committee for Redressal of Regional Imbalances, Final Report Part VII, Appendix, June 2002.

APPENDIX A-4.28

Rank Positions of Districts in Terms of Educational Attainment in 1991 and 2000 for Secondary and beyond Stage

District	*Secondary*		*Hr. Secondary/PUC*		*Technical*		*Degree*		*No. of College Students per Lakh Population 2000*
	90s	*2000*	*90s*	*2000*	*90s*	*2000*	*90s*	*2000*	
Bangalore	1	1	1	1	1	1	1	1	3
Bangalore (Rural)	15	10	17.5	16	18.5	17	19.5	18	17
Belgaum	5.5	2	12.5	7	13	3	10	4	10
Bellary	19	17	17.5	14	13	6	13.5	12	5
Bidar	16.5	16	9	17	16.5	16	17	17	13
Bijapur	16.5	6	9	4	13	10	13.5	6	7
Chickmagalur	11	19	4	19	8	20	8	19	16
Chitradurga	10	17	5.5	5	8	9	9	8	17.5
Dakshina Kannada	4	4	2	3	4	2	2.5	2	1
Dharwad	9	3	7	2	4	4	6.5	3	4
Gulbarga	18	11	16	10	16.5	8	17	13	19
Hassan	14	13	15	13	13	15	11.5	15	9
Kodagu	2	20	3	20	18.5	19	2.5	20	14
Kolar	12	9	19	9	2	7	17	9	8
Mandya	13	12	12.5	11	13	18	15	16	11
Mysore	13.5	5	9	6	8	5	4	5	15
Raichur	20	15	20	15	20	14	19	7	20
Shimoga	5.5	14	5.5	12	4	13	6.5	14	6
Tumkur	8	8	12.5	8	8	11	11.5	11	12
Uttara Kannada	3	18	12.5	18	8	12	5	10	2

Source: *Population Census*, Government of India, 1991 and High Power Committee for Redressal of Regional Imbalances, Government of Karnataka, 2002.

APPENDIX A-4.29

Registrants on the Live Registers of Employment Exchange in Karnataka, Qualification-wise and District-wise: 2000-01

District	*P.G*	*Graduates*	*Dip. Holders*	*ITI/ATS/Certificate Holders*	*Matriculates & below Stenographers*	*Matriculation*	*Total*
Bangalore (Urban)	7366.5	24968.5	8955	12658	154730	42888	251566
Bangalore (Rural)	7366.5	24968.5	8955	12658	154730	42888	251566
Chitradurga	-	3662	397	1540	43190	7068	55857
Davanagere	-	2970	982	2092	52673	8021	66738
Kolar	-	4567	1622	6886	69334	13048	95457
Shimoga	-	4570	1699	1576	36465	12228	56538
Tumkur	-	6240	1368	2134	72694	10315	92751
Bagalkote	-	2653	583	1897	31759	8142	54034
Belgaum	-	8542	1925	2105	83864	13791	110227
Bijapur	-	2905	556	1679	33709	9239	48088
Dharwad	-	4334	1031	2026	32422	16130	55943
Gadag	-	2105	353	1354	25857	5029	34698
Haveri	-	3173	429	1698	29548	4009	38857
Uttara Kannada	-	4302	2071	2127	34395	11380	54175
Chamrajnagar	-	2306	287	713	23077	3525	29908
Chickmagalur	-	3685	487	990	24896	8384	38442
Dakshina Kannada	-	6656	1551	2855	24819	10517	46398
Hassan	-	11140	687	1913	33787	27760	75287
Kodagu	-	1352	195	418	10297	2995	15257
Mandya	-	4558	933	1648	43434	12776	63349
Mysore	-	5615	1308	2851	57469	18702	85945
Udupi	-	3169	1135	753	15790	4333	25180
Bellary	-	7756	1414	4863	42702	14926	71661
Bidar	-	3762	743	1208	49999	3824	59536
Gulbarga	-	8099	1607	4237	71832	16564	102339
Koppal	-	2432	302	1410	18712	3141	25997
Raichur	-	3721	1092	2646	39168	8999	55626
State	**14833**	**164211**	**42767**	**79034.97**	**1311452**	**340721**	**1953019**

Source: *Annual Report*-2001, Department of Employment and Training, GoK, 2001.

APPENDIX A-4.30

Persons in the Labour Force in Karnataka: 1993-94 and 1999-00

(per cent)

Area	*Gender*	*1993-94*		*1999-00*		*Annual Growth*	
		Karnataka	*India*	*Karnataka*	*India*	*Karnataka*	*India*
Rural	Female	61.5	48.8	55.5	45.6	0.3	0.8
	Male	89.4	87.6	88.5	85.4	1.8	1.6
	Persons	75.7	68.8	72.2	66.2	1.2	1.3
Urban	Female	24.7	23.4	25.2	20.9	3.9	1.5
	Male	80.6	79.9	78.3	78.6	2.5	2.6
	Persons	53.8	53.3	52.7	51.1	2.8	2.4
Total	Female	49.8	42.0	45.4	38.5	0.8	0.9
	Male	86.5	85.4	85.0	83.5	2.0	1.9
	Persons	68.6	64.5	65.6	61.8	1.6	1.6

Note: Figures relate to usual principal and subsidiary status of individuals.

Source: NSS, 1997 and 2001.

APPENDIX A-4.31

Distribution of Workers in Karnataka: 1991 and 2001

Category	*1991 (Lakhs)*	*Per Cent to Total*	*2001 (Lakhs)*	*Per Cent to Total*	*Annual Growth Rate*
Cultivators	66.92	35.4	69.36	29.5	0.4
Agriculture Labourers	56.53	29.9	62.09	26.4	1.0
Workers in Household Industry	3.53	1.9	9.36	4.0	16.5
Others	61.88	32.8	94.41	40.0	5.3
Total	**188.87**	**100**	**235.22**	**100**	**2.5**

Source: *Economic Survey of Karnataka*, 2004.

APPENDIX A-4.32

Work Participation Rates in Karnataka and India: 1993-94 and 1999-00

(per cent)

		Karnataka		*India*	
Area	*Gender*	*1993-94*	*1999-00*	*1993-94*	*1999-00*
Rural	Female	43.0	38.0	32.8	29.8
	Male	60.4	59.5	55.3	53.1
	Persons	51.7	48.7	44.4	41.7
Urban	Female	18.1	17.8	15.4	13.9
	Male	54.2	54.5	52.0	51.8
	Persons	36.6	36.6	34.7	33.7

Notes and Source: Same as in A-4.30.

APPENDIX A-4.33

Age-specific Work Participation Rates in Rural Karnataka: 1993-94 and 1999-00

(per cent)

Age (in Years)	*Females*		*Males*		*Persons*	
	1993-94	*1999-00*	*1993-94*	*1999-00*	*1993-94*	*1999-00*
5-9	3.8	1.3	3.3	0.9	3.6	1.1
10-14	25.1	15.3	25.0	15.1	25.1	15.2
15-19	50.3	42.1	67.2	64.4	59.4	54.2
20-24	62.0	48.1	88.4	88.4	75.3	68.7
25-29	64.1	63.5	98.4	97.4	79.3	79.5
30-34	76.2	71.4	98.1	98.2	87.5	84.3
35-39	74.6	71.0	98.7	99.1	86.9	85.4
40-44	73.7	66.5	99.7	97.8	87.7	82.8
45-49	75.8	61.8	98.1	97.9	86.7	81.4
50-54	68.7	56.3	96.0	94.4	82.2	75.2
55-59	50.6	49.9	95.8	88.1	70.8	67.1
60 & above	26.2	26.1	65.2	65.0	47.8	44.8
All	**43.0**	**38.0**	**60.4**	**59.5**	**51.7**	**48.7**

Notes and Source: Same as in A-4.30.

APPENDIX A-4.34

Age-specific Work Participation Rates in Urban Karnataka: 1993-94 and 1999-00

(per cent)

Age (in Years)	*Females*		*Males*		*Persons*	
	1993-94	*1999-00*	*1993-94*	*1999-00*	*1993-94*	*1999-00*
5-9	0.1	0.2	1.5	0	0.8	0.1
10-14	4.5	4.2	10.9	7.3	8.0	5.9
15-19	15.8	13.9	41.0	33.7	29.0	24.1
20-24	24.6	22.7	68.7	62.7	48.3	42.2
25-29	29.7	22.0	90.3	90.7	57.8	55.4
30-34	29.5	36.6	97.4	97.0	65.2	67.9
35-39	38.2	33.6	98.5	99.2	69.3	65.2
40-44	34.6	34.1	98.3	98.6	69.6	70.3
45-49	32.8	27.0	98.7	97.8	68.7	62.4
50-54	27.6	27.8	92.5	93.1	62.3	65.5
55-59	22.9	17.8	79.1	87.3	50.9	51.0
60 and above	12.6	9.9	43.7	31.4	26.5	20.1
All	**13.0**	**17.8**	**54.2**	**54.5**	**36.6**	**36.6**

Notes and Source: Same as in A-4.30.

APPENDIX A-4.35

Child Labour in Karnataka and India: 1993-94 and 1999-00

(per cent)

Area	*Gender*	*Age Group (in years)*	*Karnataka*		*India*	
			1993-94	*1999-00*	*1993-94*	*1999-00*
Rural	Females	5-9	3.8	1.3	1.4	0.7
		10-14	25.1	15.3	14.1	9.6
	Males	5-9	3.3	0.9	1.1	0.6
		10-14	25.0	15.1	13.8	9.1
	Persons	5-9	3.6	1.1	1.3	0.7
		10-14	25.1	15.2	14.0	9.3
Urban	Females	5-9	0.1	0.2	0.5	0.2
		10-14	4.5	4.2	4.5	3.6
	Males	5-9	1.5	0.0	0.5	0.3
		10-14	10.9	7.3	6.6	4.9
	Persons	5-9	0.8	0.1	0.5	0.3
		10-14	8.0	5.9	5.6	4.3

Source: Same as in A-4.30.

APPENDIX A-4.36

Child Workforce Participation Rate (5-14 years): District Level: 1991

District	*Total*		*Rural*		*Urban*	
	Male	*Female*	*Male*	*Female*	*Male*	*Female*
Karnataka	8.23	6.50	9.80	8.30	4.47	2.19
Bangalore*	4.68	2.30	6.71	4.07	4.32	1.80
Belgaum	7.72	5.40	9.01	6.55	3.26	1.45
Bellary	13.87	14.68	16.40	18.19	7.26	5.63
Bidar	7.25	4.91	8.25	5.90	3.12	0.65
Bijapur	8.76	7.47	10.09	9.23	4.30	1.48
Chickmagalur	6.37	7.92	7.03	5.54	3.24	1.91
Chitradurga	8.84	7.61	10.09	9.57	5.36	2.15
Dakshina Kannada	2.67	5.55	2.73	6.21	2.47	3.61
Dharwad	9.69	8.22	11.97	16.94	5.22	2.75
Gulbarga	11.40	8.63	13.85	11.00	3.40	1.03
Hassan	6.99	4.69	7.69	5.30	3.81	1.69
Kodagu	5.16	5.14	5.53	5.58	3.23	2.99
Kolar	8.85	8.91	10.19	10.86	4.39	2.34
Mandya	8.90	4.34	9.65	4.80	5.06	1.99
Mysore	9.05	3.66	11.24	4.56	4.30	1.33
Raichur	13.14	12.36	15.05	14.63	5.76	3.23
Shimoga	6.75	4.83	7.65	6.05	4.20	1.27
Tumkur	7.18	5.68	7.61	6.30	4.97	2.41
Uttara Kannada	4.45	3.11	5.17	3.55	2.17	1.70

Note: Male and female child workforce participation rates have been calculated as a percentage of male and female child population (5-14 years) respectively.

* Bangalore district was bifurcated in the 1991 Census. For purposes of comparison with the other Census data, Bangalore Rural and Bangalore Urban have been combined.

Source: Calculated from Census data, 1991.

APPENDIX A-4.37

Employment Growth in Karnataka and All- India: 1983 to 1999-00

(per cent per annum)

Year	*Gender*	*Rural*		*Urban*	
		Karnataka	*All-India*	*Karnataka*	*All-India*
1983 to 1993-94	Females	2.7	1.5	0.6	3.2
	Male	2.0	2.0	2.7	2.8
	Persons	2.3	1.8	2.2	2.9
1993-94 to 1999-00	Females	0.3	0.8	3.9	1.5
	Male	1.8	1.6	2.5	2.6
	Persons	1.2	1.3	2.8	2.4

Notes: Figures relate to usual principal and subsidiary status of individuals.

Source: Computations based on NSS Data of Respective Years.

APPENDIX A-4.38

District-wise Distribution of Per Capita Landholding in Karnataka: 1990-91 and 1995-96

(Hectares)

Districts	*Marginal*		*Small*		*Semi-medium*		*Medium*		*Large*		*Total*	
	1990-91	*1995-96*	*1990-91*	*1995-96*	*1990-91*	*1995-96*	*1990-91*	*1995-96*	*1990-91*	*1995-96*	*1990-91*	*1995-96*
Bangalore (Rural)	0.48	0.47	1.43	1.42	2.68	2.71	5.77	5.62	12.00	14.81	1.35	1.28
Bangalore (Urban)	0.48	0.47	1.45	1.43	2.91	2.74	5.60	5.73	12.00	16.38	1.51	1.39
Belgaum	0.49	0.49	1.48	1.46	2.79	2.74	5.93	5.88	14.82	15.37	2.38	2.16
Bellary	0.64	0.54	1.47	1.46	2.73	2.77	6.04	5.87	14.60	14.81	2.80	2.48
Bidar	0.52	0.62	1.45	1.47	2.78	2.72	5.92	6.03	15.13	14.04	2.70	2.35
Bijapur	0.58	0.62	1.54	1.53	2.79	2.78	6.15	6.07	14.20	14.18	3.75	3.32
Chickmagalur	0.56	0.52	1.45	1.43	2.72	2.70	5.80	5.83	15.56	23.66	2.56	1.78
Chitradurga	0.53	0.56	1.44	1.45	2.59	2.70	5.83	5.84	21.33	15.06	1.97	2.32
Dakshina Kannada	0.37	0.37	1.41	1.41	2.78	2.73	5.75	5.70	17.50	20.39	1.17	1.06
Dharwad	0.56	0.60	1.50	1.49	2.80	2.78	6.09	5.94	14.62	13.98	3.28	2.76
Gulbarga	0.58	0.60	1.51	1.49	2.76	2.77	5.97	5.96	14.25	14.91	2.90	2.90
Hassan	0.46	0.45	1.40	1.39	2.70	2.69	5.93	5.61	18.50	19.88	1.32	1.22
Kodagu	0.50	0.53	1.41	1.42	2.70	2.78	5.61	5.88	18.00	18.57	1.46	2.47
Kolar	0.50	0.48	1.38	1.41	2.91	2.71	6.13	5.64	20.33	14.72	3.09	1.37
Mandya	0.37	0.38	1.38	1.39	2.67	2.67	5.57	5.43	12.00	18.76	0.83	0.77
Mysore	0.62	0.48	1.49	1.42	2.79	2.63	5.91	5.48	14.71	15.31	2.97	1.22
Raichur	0.49	0.62	1.41	1.47	2.65	2.75	5.43	5.88	18.00	14.29	1.39	2.64
Shimoga	0.57	0.56	1.42	1.41	2.73	2.72	5.94	5.71	18.00	14.71	1.76	1.63
Tumkur	0.33	0.48	1.37	1.44	2.80	2.74	5.17	5.76	10.00	15.11	1.04	1.69
Uttara Kannada	0.47	0.34	1.43	1.42	2.71	2.73	5.77	5.59	16.40	13.39	1.65	0.98
Karnataka	**0.47**	**0.48**	**1.46**	**1.45**	**2.75**	**2.74**	**5.93**	**5.87**	**15.28**	**15.02**	**2.13**	1.95

Note: Marignal refers to below 1 hectare, Small to 1-2 hectares, Semi-medium to 2-4 hectares, Medium to 4-10 hectares and Large to above 10 hectares.
Source: Directorate of Economics and Statistics, 2000-01, Government of Karnataka.

APPENDIX A-4.39

Sectoral Distribution of Employment in Karnataka and India: 1987-88 to 1999-00

(per cent)

Year	*Primary*		*Secondary*		*Tertiary*	
	Karnataka	*India*	*Karnataka*	*India*	*Karnataka*	*India*
1987-88	66.80	58.82	12.00	10.85	21.20	30.33
1993-94	66.37	58.41	10.64	10.10	22.99	31.49
1999-00	58.40	52.43	11.52	10.87	30.08	36.71

Notes: Same as in A-4.31.
Source: Computation based on NSS Data of respective years.

APPENDIX A-4.40

Non-farm Employment in Rural Karnataka and Rural All-India

(per cent)

Year	*Females*		*Males*	
	Karnataka	*India*	*Karnataka*	*India*
1993-94	17.0	13.9	21.2	26.6
1999-00	12.2	14.6	21.5	28.7

Source: Same as in A-4.18.

APPENDIX A-4.41

Distribution of Employment by Sectors in Karnataka: 1990-91 to 2001-02

(in Thousands)

Year	Public Sector		Private Sector		Total		Grand Total
	Females	Males	Females	Males	Females	Males	
1990-91	160.0	857.3	92.1	337.9	252.1	1195.2	1447.3
	(11.1)	(59.2)	(6.4)	(23.3)	(17.4)	(82.6)	(100.0)
1991-92	167.0	861.0	98.2	353.3	265.2	1214.3	1479.5
	(11.3)	(58.2)	(6.6)	(23.9)	(17.9)	(82.1)	(100.0)
1992-93	170.7	855.3	110.7	364.3	281.4	1219.6	1501.0
	(11.4)	(57.0)	(7.4)	(24.3)	(18.7)	(81.3)	(100.0)
1993-94	178.6	854.2	127.8	369.8	306.4	1224.0	1530.4
	(11.7)	(55.8)	(8.4)	(24.2)	(20.0)	(80.0)	(100.0)
1994-95	190.5	860.1	138.5	389.1	329.0	1249.2	1578.2
	(12.1)	(54.5)	(8.8)	(24.7)	(20.8)	(79.2)	(100.0)
1995-96	199.0	859.4	273.8	427.1	472.8	1286.5	1759.3
	(11.3)	(48.8)	(15.6)	(24.3)	(26.9)	(73.1)	(100.0)
1996-97	216.9	866.8	289.4	442.5	506.3	1309.3	1815.6
	(11.9)	(47.7)	(15.9)	(24.4)	(27.9)	(72.1)	(100.0)
1997-98	223.0	863.0	308.6	448.4	531.6	1311.4	1843.0
	(12.1)	(46.8)	(16.7)	(24.3)	(28.8)	(71.2)	(100.0)
1998-99	234.6	857.4	310.5	446.5	545.1	1303.9	1849.0
	(12.7)	(46.4)	(16.8)	(24.1)	(29.5)	(70.5)	(100.0)
1999-00	251.8	862.2	310.0	440.0	561.8	1302.2	1864.0
	(13.5)	(46.3)	(16.6)	(23.6)	(30.1)	(69.9)	(100.0)
2000-01	254.5	858.1	314.2	452.9	568.7	1311.0	1879.7
	(13.5)	(45.7)	(16.7)	(24.1)	(30.3)	(69.7)	(100.0)
2001-02	255.5	834.5	320.5	445.4	576.0	1279.9	1855.9
	(13.8)	(45.0)	(17.3)	(24.0)	(31.0)	(69.0)	(100.0)
Growth Rate	**5.4**	**-0.2**	**22.5**	**2.9**	**11.7**	**0.6**	**2.6**

Notes: Figures in the parentheses are per cent to total.

Source: Various issues of *Economic Survey of Karnataka*.

APPENDIX A-4.42

Industry-wise Employment in Karnataka: 1993-94 to 2001-02

(in Lakhs)

Industry	1993-94	1994-95	1995-96	1996-97	1997-98	1998-99	1999-00	2000-01	2001-02	Growth Rate
Plantation and Forestry	0.56	0.58	0.57	0.56	0.56	0.56	0.53	0.53	0.52	-0.9
	(3.7)	(3.7)	(3.2)	(3.1)	(3.0)	(3.0)	(2.8)	(2.8)	(2.8)	
	[NA]	[3.6]	[-1.7]	[-1.8]	[0.0]	[0.0]	[-5.4]	[0.0]	[-1.9]	
Mining and Quarrying	0.27	0.27	0.27	0.25	0.21	0.21	0.22	0.2	0.19	-3.7
	(1.8)	(1.7)	(1.5)	(1.4)	(1.1)	(1.1)	(1.2)	(1.1)	(1.0)	
	[NA]	[0.0]	[0.0]	[-7.4]	[-16.0]	[0.0]	[4.8]	[-9.1]	[-5.0]	
Manufacturing	4.38	4.49	6.08	6.25	6.36	6.29	6.18	6.18	6.01	4.7
	(28.6)	(28.4)	(34.6)	(34.4)	(34.5)	(34.0)	(33.2)	(32.9)	(32.4)	
	[NA]	[2.5]	[35.4]	[2.8]	[1.8]	[-1.1]	[-1.7]	[0.0]	[-2.8]	

Contd. ...

...*Contd.* ...

Industry	*1993-94*	*1994-95*	*1995-96*	*1996-97*	*1997-98*	*1998-99*	*1999-00*	*2000-01*	*2001-02*	*Growth Rate*
Electricity, Gas and Water	0.5	0.49	0.47	0.45	0.46	0.46	0.45	0.44	0.41	-2.3
	(3.3)	(3.1)	(2.7)	(2.5)	(2.5)	(2.5)	(2.4)	(2.3)	(2.2)	
	[NA]	[-2.0]	[-4.1]	[-4.3]	[2.2]	[0.0]	[-2.2]	[-2.2]	[-6.8]	
Construction	0.6	0.62	0.59	0.58	0.55	0.53	0.52	0.5	0.48	-2.5
	(3.9)	(3.9)	(3.4)	(3.2)	(3.0)	(2.9)	(2.8)	(2.7)	(2.6)	
	[NA]	[3.3]	[-4.8]	[-1.7]	[-5.2]	[-3.6]	[-1.9]	[-3.8]	[-4.0]	
Wholesale and Retail Trade, Hotels and Restaurants	0.32	0.34	0.36	0.37	0.37	0.37	0.38	0.38	0.38	2.3
	(2.1)	(2.2)	(2.0)	(2.0)	(2.0)	(2.0)	(2.0)	(2.0)	(2.0)	
	[NA]	[6.3]	[5.9]	[2.8]	[0.0]	[0.0]	[2.7]	[0.0]	[0.0]	
Transport, Storage and Communications	1.55	1.55	1.6	1.6	1.63	1.62	1.64	1.67	1.66	0.9
	(10.1)	(9.8)	(9.1)	(8.8)	(8.8)	(8.8)	(8.8)	(8.9)	(8.9)	
	[NA]	[0.0]	[3.2]	[0.0]	[1.9]	[-0.6]	[1.2]	[1.8]	[-0.6]	
Finance, Insurance, Real Estate and Business Services	1.12	1.16	1.19	1.25	1.33	1.34	1.35	1.38	1.37	2.8
	(7.3)	(7.3)	(6.8)	(6.9)	(7.2)	(7.2)	(7.2)	(7.3)	(7.4)	
	[NA]	[3.6]	[2.6]	[5.0]	[6.4]	[0.8]	[0.7]	[2.2]	[-0.7]	
Social and Personal Services	6.02	6.3	6.46	6.84	6.96	7.11	7.37	7.52	7.54	3.2
	(39.3)	(39.9)	(36.7)	(37.7)	(37.8)	(38.5)	(39.5)	(40.0)	(40.6)	
	[NA]	[4.7]	[2.5]	[5.9]	[1.8]	[2.2]	[3.7]	[2.0]	[0.3]	
Total	15.32	15.8	17.59	18.15	18.43	18.49	18.64	18.8	18.56	2.6
	(100.0)	(100.0)	(100.0)	(100.0)	(100.0)	(100.0)	(100.0)	(100.0)	(100.0)	
	[NA]	[3.1]	[11.3]	[3.2]	[1.5]	[0.3]	[0.8]	[0.9]	[-1.3]	

Note: 1. Figures in the parentheses are percentage to total. 2. Figures in the square parentheses are growth rates. 3. NA refers to not applicable.
Source: Various issues of *Economic Survey of Karnataka.*

APPENDIX A-4.43

Employment Elasticity by Sector: 1993-94 to 1999-00

Sector	*Elasticity*
Agriculture	-0.05
Mining and Quarrying	-2.02
Manufacturing	-0.05
Electricity, Gas and Water Supply	-1.10
Construction	0.80
Transportation, Storage and Communication	0.45
Financial and Insurance Services	0.20

Note: Figures relate to usual principal status of individuals.
Source: Calculated based on NSS Data 1997 and 2001.

APPENDIX A-4.44

Incidence of Unemployment in Karnataka and India: 1999-00

(Per Cent)

Area	*Gender*	*Karnataka*		*India*	
		1993-94	*1999-00*	*1993-94*	*1999-00*
Rural	Female	0.3	0.4	0.8	1.1
	Male	0.9	0.9	1.5	1.7
	Persons	0.7	0.7	1.2	1.5
Urban	Female	6.5	4.8	6.6	5.9
	Male	3.0	2.9	4.1	4.5
	Persons	3.7	3.4	4.6	4.8
Total	Female	1.3	1.2	1.7	1.8
	Male	1.4	1.5	2.1	2.5
	Persons	1.4	1.4	2.0	2.3

Source: Same as in A-4.18.

APPENDIX A-4.45

Unemployment Rate in Karnataka and India: 1993-94 and 1999-00

Area	Gender	Karnataka		India	
		1993-94	1999-00	1993-94	1999-00
Rural	Female	3.9	4.0	5.6	7.0
	Male	4.7	4.4	5.6	7.2
	Persons	4.4	4.3	5.6	7.1
Urban	Female	8.9	5.9	10.5	9.4
	Male	5.6	5.3	6.7	7.3
	Persons	6.3	5.4	7.4	7.7

Note: Figures relate to current daily status of individuals.

Source: Same as in A-4.18.

APPENDIX A-4.47

Distribution of Workers by Category of Employment in Karnataka and All-India: 1993-94 and 1999-00

(Per Cent)

Area	Category	Karnataka		India	
		1993-94	1999-00	1993-94	1999-00
Rural	Self-employed	55.9	50.2	58.1	56..0
	Regular Employed	4.8	5.3	6.4	6.7
	Casual Labour	39.3	44.5	35.6	37.3
Urban	Self-employed	41.3	38.8	42.4	42.2
	Regular Employed	36.9	39.6	39.5	40.0
	Casual Labour	21.8	21.6	18.3	17.8

Note: Figures relate to usual principal and subsidiary status of individuals.

Source: Same as in A-4.18.

APPENDIX A-4.46

Underemployment in Karnataka and India: 1993-94 and 1999-00

(Per Cent)

Area	State/Country	Employed		Unemployed		Not in Labour Force	
		1993-94	1999-00	1993-94	1999-00	1993-94	1999-00
				Female			
Rural	Karnataka	69.6	76.4	2.5	2.9	27.9	20.7
	India	66.3	67.6	3.0	4.1	30.6	28.3
Urban	Karnataka	77.7	87.4	1.7	0.8	20.6	11.9
	India	76.6	79.1	2.4	2.2	21.0	18.7
				Male			
Rural	Karnataka	90.9	91.0	3.6	3.1	5.5	5.9
	India	90.9	89.7	4.0	5.3	5.1	5.1
Urban	Karnataka	94.0	94.8	2.6	2.2	3.4	3.1
	India	94.9	94.2	2.7	2.7	2.5	3.1

Note and Source: Same as in A-4.18.

APPENDIX A-4.48

Distribution of Principal Status Workers by their Level of Education: 1983/1999-2000

Levels of Education	1983			1993-94			1999-00		
	Primary Sector	Secondary Sector	Tertiary Sector	Primary Sector	Secondary Sector	Tertiary Sector	Primary Sector	Secondary Sector	Tertiary Sector
Illiterate	69.0	41.8	25.1	64.0	38.1	21.4	61.8	29.3	19.2
Primary	20.8	33.4	24.0	21.3	28.9	21.6	18.8	23.5	15.9
Middle	6.9	11.5	16.8	8.6	12.4	16.4	10.4	19.5	17.8
Secondary and above	3.3	13.3	34.2	6.2	20.5	40.6	9.0	27.7	47.0

Source: Household data on CD-ROM supplied by NSSO, New Delhi.

APPENDIX A-4.49

Labour Productivity in Different Sectors in Karnataka and All India

Years	Agriculture	Construction	Services	Manufacturing	Transport	Trade
Karnataka GSDP per Person						
1987-88	2684.86	8678.42	13696.35	6805.60	10510.42	8684.12
1993-94	3045.33	8479.20	11180.35	9740.18	15669.17	11865.45
1999-00	3965.00	8057.00	N.A.	22371.00	12035.00	N.A.
Average of 16 States GSDP per Person						
1987-88	2532.92	6160.88	10714.26	8453.60	10005.86	8359.71
1993-94	2870.87	9139.12	12326.58	10800.23	11468.26	9678.27

Note: Figures are in 1980-81 constant prices in rupees.
GSDP per UPSS workers is the labour productivity.

Source: Bhalla, 2000; Bhalla, 2001.

APPENDIX A-4.50

Real Wage Rate in Agriculture and Non-agriculture by Sex: 1999-2000 in Constant Prices

Gender	*1983*	*1987-88*	*1993-94*	*1999-2000*
Real Wage Rate in Agriculture Males	21.15 (5.68)	27.12 (3.06)	32.5 (3.59)	40.15 (4.17)
Real Wage Rate in Non-agriculture Males	32.56 (1.73)	35.18 (4.76)	46.5 (3.93)	58.59 (3.45)
Real Wage Rate in Agriculture Females	15.06 (3.08)	17.26 (4.97)	23.09 (2.79)	27.23 (4.15)
Real Wage Rate in Non-agriculture Females	15.38 (9.07)	22.73 (3.32)	27.64 (4.17)	35.33 (5.74)

Note: Figures in parentheses indicates growth rates.

Source: Bhalla *et al.* (2004)

APPENDIX A-4.51

Average Days Worked per Adult Wage Earners and Effective Wage Rate for Agriculture and Non–agricultural Wage Work

Category	*State/Country*	*Agriculture*			*Non-agriculture*			*All Wage Workers*		
		Male	*Female*	*Total*	*Male*	*Female*	*Total*	*Male*	*Female*	*Total*
Avg. Days of Work	Karnataka	155	135	146	174	175	174	165	145	156
	All-India	145	124	137	157	133	152	172	137	160
Effective Wage Rate (Rs. per Day)	Karnataka	19.3	14	17.3	27.9	14	23.3	21.9	14	18.7
	All-India	23.4	16.4	20.9	30.5	18.7	28.4	26.4	16.9	23.6

Source: *NCAER Survey*, 1999.

APPENDIX A-4.52

Population Below Poverty Line in Karnataka and India: 1987-88 to 1999-00

(Per Cent)

Year	*Rural*		*Urban*		*Total*	
	Karnataka	*India*	*Karnataka*	*India*	*Karnataka*	*India*
1987-88	32.82	39.09	48.42	38.20	37.53	38.86
1993-94	29.88	37.27	40.14	32.36	33.16	35.97
1999-00	17.38	27.09	25.25	23.62	20.04	26.10

Source: Computation based on NSS Data of respective years.

APPENDIX A-4.53

Wage Employment Generation in Karnataka: 1995-96 to 2002-03 in Lakh Man-Days

Programmes	*1995-96*	*1996-97*	*1997-98*	*1998-99*	*1999-2000*	*2000-01*	*2001-02*	*2002-03*	*Growth Rate*
1. Jawahar Rojgar Yojana, Jawahar	524.86	250.94	265.9	222.05	176.48	128.94	140.81	73.57	-12.3
Grameena Swaraj Yojana Sampoorna	31.9	16.1	18.5	14.4	13.1	7.8	9.5	6.6	
Grameena Swaraj Yojana	NA	-52.2	6.0	-16.5	-20.5	-26.9	9.2	-47.8	
2. Employees Assurance Schemes	352.76	238.56	352.76	177.06	165.59	103.56	124.4	84.57	-10.9
	21.4	15.3	24.5	11.5	12.2	6.3	8.4	7.6	
	NA	-32.4	47.9	-49.8	-6.5	-37.5	20.1	-32.0	
3. Major and Medium	300.4	705.63	522.15	652.12	602.4	939.89	734.24	414.21	5.4
Irrigation and Flood Control	18.3	45.3	36.3	42.2	44.6	57.0	49.5	37.4	
	NA	134.9	-26.0	24.9	-7.6	56.0	-21.9	-43.6	
4. Minor Irrigation	79.61	69.92	39.28	60.58	63.34	48.22	43.56	43.98	-6.4
	4.8	4.5	2.7	3.9	4.7	2.9	2.9	4.0	
	NA	-12.2	-43.8	54.2	4.6	-23.9	-9.7	1.0	
5. Command Area Development	11.65	27.4	30.67	21.67	6.68	15.77	38.8	39.75	34.5
Authority Activities CADA	0.7	1.8	2.1	1.4	0.5	1.0	2.6	3.6	
	NA	135.2	11.9	-29.3	-69.2	136.1	146.0	2.4	
6. Roads and Bridges	257.86	185.24	148.05	291.25	258.21	331.62	298.62	357.61	5.5
	15.7	11.9	10.3	18.9	19.1	20.1	20.2	32.3	
	NA	-28.2	-20.1	96.7	-11.3	28.4	-10.0	19.8	
7. Buildings	100.45	53.9	59.96	96.8	70.88	51.38	62.67	57.47	-6.1
	6.1	3.5	4.2	6.3	5.2	3.1	4.2	5.2	
	NA	-46.3	11.2	61.4	-26.8	-27.5	22.0	-8.3	
8. Watershed Development	18.16	24.72	19.46	22.25	8.51	29.27	38.8	36.89	14.7
	1.1	1.6	1.4	1.4	0.6	1.8	2.6	3.3	
	NA	36.1	-21.3	14.3	-61.8	243.9	32.6	-4.9	
Total	**1645.75**	**1556.31**	**1438.23**	**1543.78**	**1352.09**	**1648.65**	**1481.9**	**1108.05**	**-4.7**
	100.0	**100.0**	**100.0**	**100.0**	**100.0**	**100.0**	**100.0**	**100.0**	
	NA	**-5.4**	**-7.6**	**7.3**	**-12.4**	**21.9**	**-10.1**	**-25.2**	

Notes and Source: Economic Survey of Government of Karnataka, various issues.

Chapter 5

Economic Infrastructure in Karnataka

5.1 Introduction

Development of physical infrastructure is essential for all economic activities to enable production and distribution of goods and services for human welfare. Infrastructural development includes a variety of heterogeneous components such as transportation infrastructure (e.g., roads, bridges, railways, ports or airports), power, communication, irrigation and many more. This development requires relatively large financial outlays and returns from them are over the long-term with some gestation lags, depending upon the technology. Often, it is the state initiative that leads to the creation of such infrastructure assets, particularly in the early stages of economic development. It also entails numerous positive externalities that the private provider of services finds difficult to internalise in its costs without appropriate regulatory mechanisms. Historically therefore, the development of infrastructure was initially left to the governments. In India also, much of the physical infrastructure has been built by the Central and state governments under various Five Year Plans, while the role of private sector has begun as a complementary provider in the more recent period, more so in the last decade.

The drivers of infrastructural development have been changing over the years. As an instance, the development of irrigation has been generally the responsibility of state governments, marginally also of farmers themselves. But, in the case of telecommunications, the Central Government had the exclusive rights to develop the sector until the 1990s when the private sector was allowed to participate as a service provider. In the cases of railway transport, airports and shipping till recently, the services are provided exclusively by the Central Government. Involvement of private sectors has been emerging in the construction and management of many infrastructural developments. In the case of power and roads, till recently, both the states and Centre provide the investment funds for development and maintenance, when private sector has been able to develop some segments of the roads, power plants and airports on build-operate-transfer mode of contract.

In Karnataka, recognition of the need to pursue a coherent approach to the development of infrastructure is reflected in its 1997 Infrastructure Development Policy. Karnataka Government has a separate Department of Infrastructure Development. Subsequently several measures, institutions and policies have also been instituted to promote public and private climate for infrastructure development.

This chapter is addressed to these developments in the state, with a view on the vision and policy directions for the future. Firstly, while presenting some macro-picture of the status of economic infrastructure, several indicators of performance and efficiency are analysed. Subsequently, five major infrastructural developments are addressed in some detail. The specific sub-sectors are communication, irrigation, power, roads and railways (also marginally touching on development of ports and airports).

5.2 Some Aggregate Perspectives on Infrastructure

5.2.1 Karnataka in Comparison to the Other States

Any comparison of infrastructure status across the states is not easy. The infrastructure needs of different states may differ substantially. However, with a view to draw some broad comparative picture between the states, only 15 states for few selected sectors are analysed here with only one indicator per sector. The indicators selected for different states are: road length per square km of geographical area (measured in km), railway length per square km of area (measured in km), number of post offices per capita, number of telephone exchanges per capita, number of registered motor vehicles per capita and installed power capacity per capita (in MW). Position of each state with respect to different indicators (*Statistical Abstracts*, Government of India) mentioned above is depicted in Figures 5.1-5.7 below. It may be noted that barring irrigation, railways and roads, Karnataka figures among the upper 7 states of the 15 states considered here in all other sectors.

FIGURE 5.1

Ratio of Area Covered by Railways to Total Geographical Area of the States*

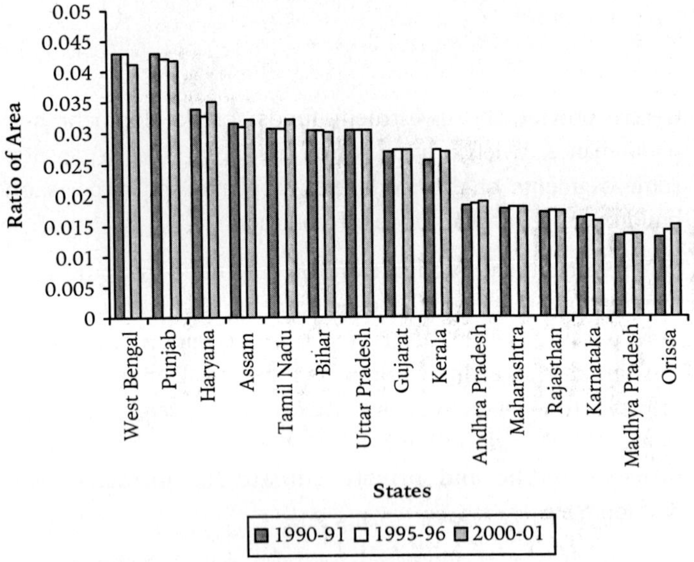

Note: *Railway length and geographical area are in sq. kms.

Source: *Statistical Abstracts*, various issues.

FIGURE 5.2

Ratio of Area Covered by Roads to Total Geographical Area of the States*

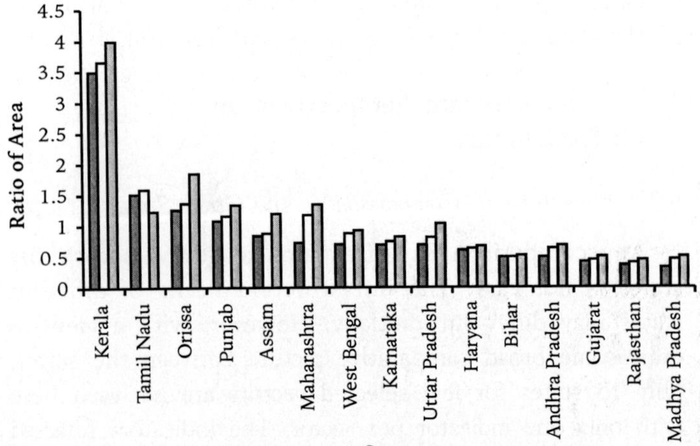

Note: *Both areas are in sq. kms.

Source: *Statistical Abstracts*, various issues.

FIGURE 5.3

Telephone Exchange Per Capita

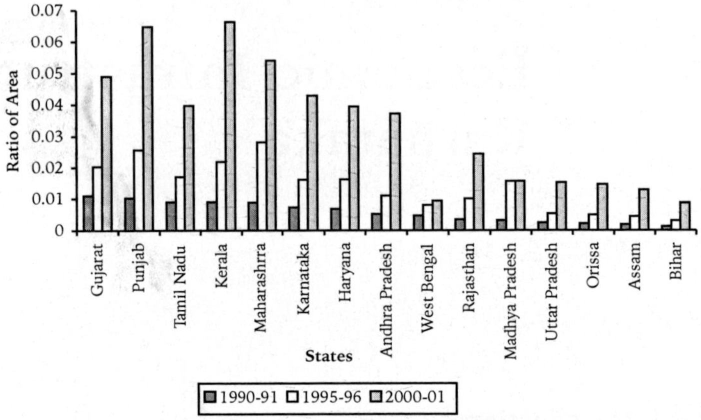

Source: *Statistical Abstracts*, various issues.

FIGURE 5.4

Registered Motor Vehicles Per Capita

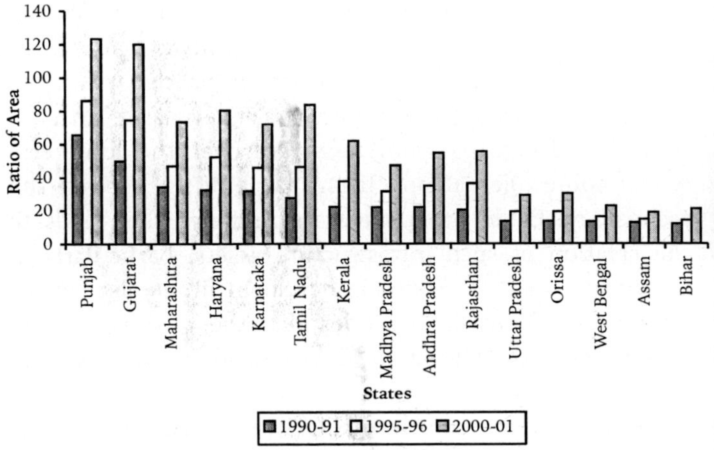

Source: *Statistical Abstract*, various issues.

FIGURE 5.5

Number of Post Offices Per Capita

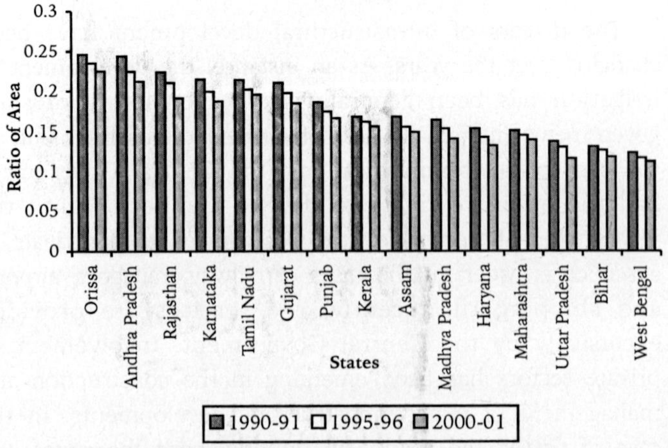

Source: *Statistical Abstracts*, various issues.

FIGURE 5.6

Installed Capacity (in kWh Per Capita)

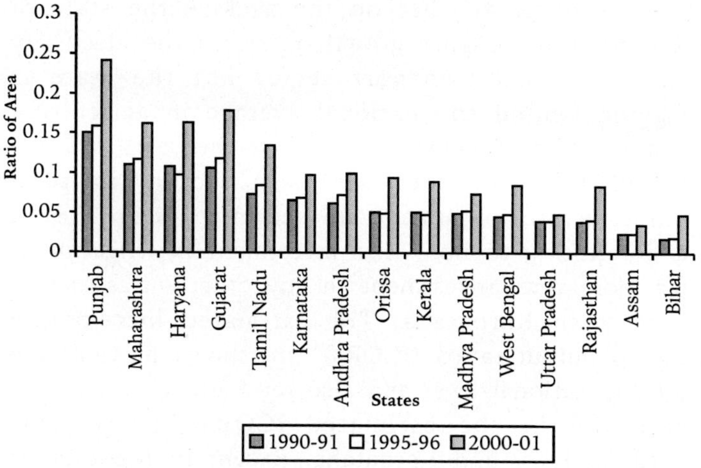

Source: *Statistical Abstracts,* various issues.

TABLE 5.1

Ranking of the States Using Infrastructure Indices

State	*1990-91*	*1995-96*	*2000-01*
Punjab	0.60	0.65	0.83
Haryana	0.42	0.46	0.59
Tamil Nadu	0.41	0.46	0.58
Gujarat	0.38	0.44	0.59
Kerala	0.37	0.42	0.58
Andhra Pradesh	0.31	0.34	0.44
Uttar Pradesh	0.31	0.33	0.37
West Bengal	0.30	0.33	0.35
Karnataka	**0.29**	**0.32**	**0.42**
Maharashtra	0.28	0.35	0.47
Orissa	0.28	0.29	0.37
Assam	0.26	0.26	0.30
Bihar	0.25	0.26	0.30
Rajasthan	0.25	0.29	0.36
Madhya Pradesh	0.20	0.25	0.27

Source: *Statistical Abstracts,* Government of India.

FIGURE 5.7

Share of Irrigated Area to Gross Cropped Area

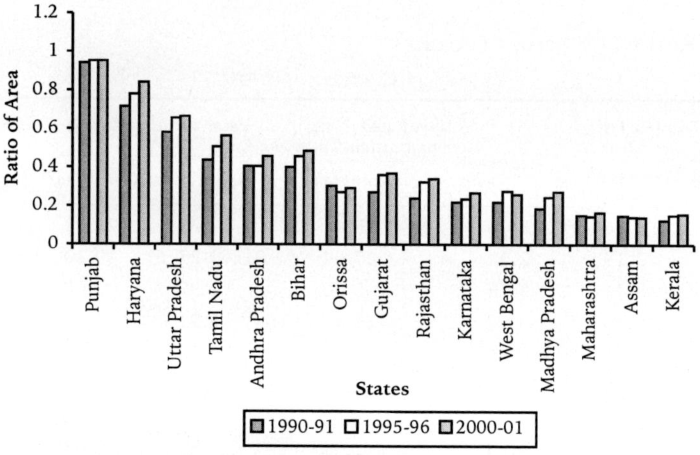

Source: *Statistical Abstracts,* various issues.

FIGURE 5.8

Infrastructure Indices

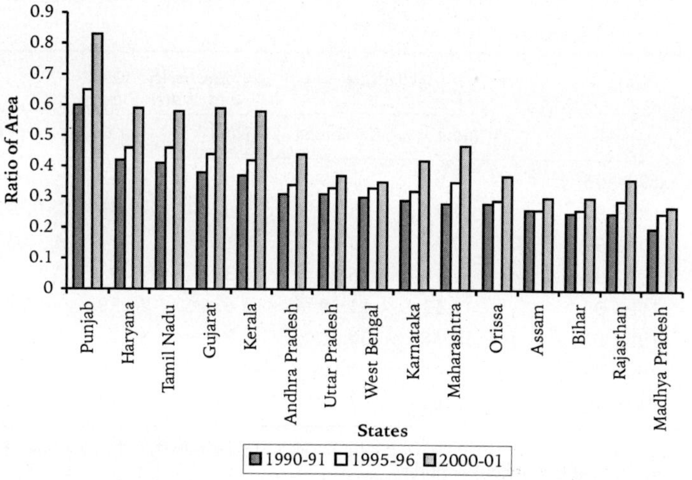

5.2.2 An Integrated View on the Status of Infrastructure Development

In order to get an integrated view, different indicators of infrastructure are combined by first developing an index for each infrastructure, subsequently aggregating them by assigning equal weights to each of the indices. The combined infrastructure index for different states for three different years is presented in Table 5.1 and Figure 5.8. Once again the position of Karnataka is in the middle, with Punjab and Haryana being consistently at the top since 1990-91.

Infrastructure development can be a driver for economic growth. As can be seen from the correlation coefficients between per capita state domestic product and Indices of infrastructure (Table 5.2) one can certainly assert about its direct relevance in economic development of the states. Furthermore, it can be noted that there is an increasing trend of this link as viewed from the correlation coefficients over the years. Two points emerge from this analysis. First, there is a further need for infrastructure improvement in Karnataka, to take more strides in economic development. Second, this calls for substantial investments to make the vision of sustained income growth in the state.

TABLE 5.2

Correlation between SDP and Infrastructure Indices

Year	*Correlation Coefficient between SDP Values and Infrastructure Indices*	*Spearman's Rank Correlation Coefficient***
1990-91	0.668*	0.726
1995-96	0.806*	0.752
2000-01	0.833*	0.815

Source: *Statistical Abstracts*, Government of India.

Note: * Significant at 1 per cent level; ** Ranking of the states are done with respect to SDP values and infrastructure indices.

5.2.3 Assessing Investment Needs for Infrastructure Development

There is no consistent statistical information on investment in infrastructure, except for estimates of gross fixed capital formation (GFCF) by the Central Statistical Organisation and the Directorate of Economics and Statistics in Karnataka. Treating GFCF data to be a close proxy for such investments some analysis on the future needs for the development of this sector can be made. Several assumptions and proxies had to be used in this analysis. As a proxy for investment in irrigation, data on capital formation in the agriculture sector is used. In the case of roads, capital formation in the construction sector has been used as a proxy, for power sector capital formation in the electricity and gas sector is used. Capital formation in railway and communication sectors corresponds to these respective infrastructure sectors. The Table 5.3 shows the growth rates of capital formation in these sectors at the national as well at the state levels from 1993 -2001.

It is observed that on the average the state of Karnataka has higher growth rates for the electricity and gas, road transport sector but the state is lagging behind the national average in agriculture and railways. Average shares (over the years 1993-94 to 2001-02) of each of these sectors in total infrastructure investment are shown in Figure 5.9. It is interesting to note that investment in irrigation is far more than investment in any other infrastructure sectors in Karnataka. The estimated incremental capital output ratios (ICORs)[1] are shown in Table 5.4 for the national level and also for Karnataka. There is variation in the estimated ICORs between the national level and Karnataka. Except in the case of transportation other than railways, ICORs in Karnataka are higher than the national ICORs. Based on these ICORs and the projected rate of growth of state's GSDP, some indications of investment needs have been projected for Karnataka, as shown in Table 5.5. For example for the agricultural sector the existing trend growth rate is 2.8 per cent (over the years 1993-94 to 2001-02). To maintain this growth rate the capital requirement for the agricultural sector for the year 2003-04 would be Agri $GFCF_{2003\text{-}04}$ = Agri ICOR * .028 * Agri $GDP_{2002\text{-}03}$, where Agri GDP is the sectoral GDP estimate for the

TABLE 5.3

Annual Rates of Growth of Real GFCF across Sectors

(in per cent)

Year	*Agriculture*		*Electricity, Gas and Water Supply*		*Transport by Other Means*		*Railway and Communication*		*Total Infrastructure*	
	India	*Karnataka*	*India*	*Karnataka*	*India*	*Karnataka*	*India*	*Karnataka*	*India*	*Karnataka*
1994-95	8.64	-1.68	-8.62	11.43	35.20	53.36	5.06	45.41	9.23	22.01
1995-96	4.86	-5.10	-5.67	-7.45	4.92	23.19	2.92	-27.04	1.27	-9.20
1996-97	0.24	-8.29	9.12	4.14	-0.39	3.05	-3.76	-5.60	1.99	-2.68
1997-98	-1.18	6.75	0.33	38.93	-22.32	-17.53	-3.87	-29.47	-8.91	-1.91
1998-99	-5.11	-11.39	13.85	-24.99	11.25	5.54	-0.24	-11.25	7.30	-12.38
1999-00	10.38	30.38	-1.23	-39.75	16.86	32.42	14.57	0.49	8.95	6.68
2000-01	0.44	1.82	-3.58	46.78	11.68	6.43	26.94	13.42	7.48	11.84
Average	**2.61**	**1.79**	**0.60**	**4.16**	**8.17**	**15.21**	**5.95**	**-2.01**	**3.90**	**2.05**

Source: Computed from GFCF data provided by Directorate of Economics and Statistics, Government of Karnataka and Central Statistical Organisation (CSO), Government of India.

1. GFCF in a particular year gives, by how much amount total investment/capital has increased in that year. Thus ICOR at period t is defined as GFCFt/(GDPt-GDPt-1).

agricultural sector. Using the above procedure three alternative scenarios are considered to provide estimates of investment needs for Karnataka for the year 2003-04.

Scenario I: Agriculture is assumed to grow at 4 per cent and the rest of the sector at 10 per cent (column 1 in Table 5.5).

Scenario II: Agriculture is assumed to grow at 5 per cent and the rest of the sectors at the existing trend growth rates (column 2 in Table 5.5)

Scenario III: All the sectors are assumed to grow at the existing trend growth rate (column 3 in Table 5.5). Existing trend growth rate over the period 1993-94 to 2001-02 are as follows:

Agriculture sector: 2.8 per cent, electricity, gas and water: 6.9 per cent, transport: 9.46 per cent, storage: 10.75 per cent, railways and communication: 20.56 per cent.

FIGURE 5.9

Average Shares (Over the Years 1993-94 to 2001-02) of GFCF of Different Sectors to Total GFCF

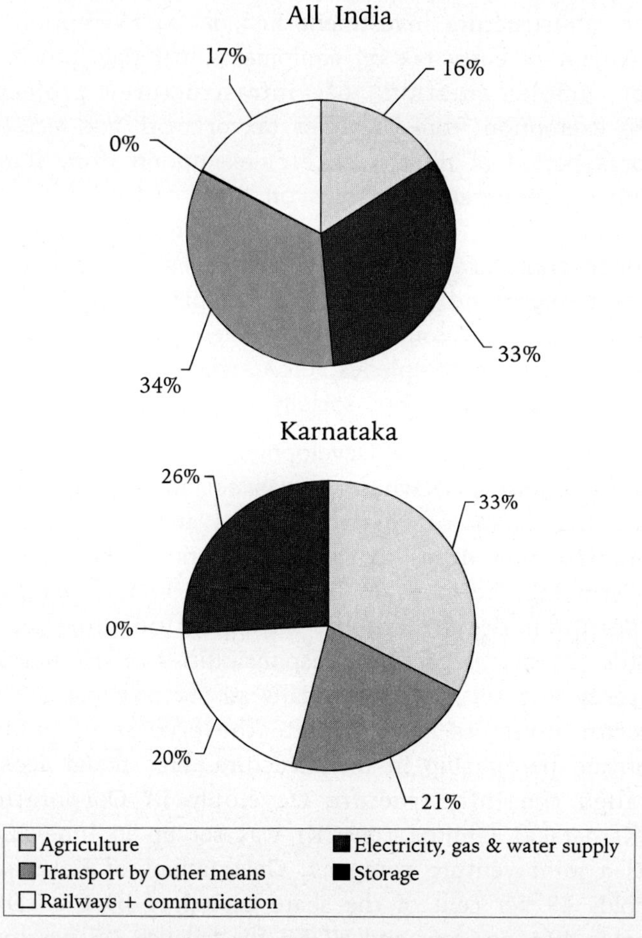

Source: Computed from GFCF data provided by Directorate of Economics and Statistics, Government of Karnataka and Central Statistical Organisation (CSO).

TABLE 5.4

Incremental Capital-Output Ratios

Sectors	*All India*	*Karnataka*
Agriculture	2.16	4.44
Electricity, Gas, Water	14.98	20.86
Transport	8.65	7.40
Storage	2.08	5.40
Supra (Railways, Telecommunication)	3.40	4.99

Source: Computed from GFCF data provided by Directorate of Economics and Statistics, Government of Karnataka and Central Statistical Organisation (CSO), Government of India

TABLE 5.5

Projected Gross Fixed Capital Formation (Rs. Lakhs)* based on Stipulated Growth Rates of SDP

Sectors	*Projected GFCF Requirements** (2003-04)*	*Projected GFCF Requirements++ (2003-04)*	*Projected GFCF Requirements to Maintain Existing Growth Rates (2003-04)*
Agriculture	281371	351714	196960
Electricity, Gas, Water	324765	227011	227011
Transport	496478	469668	469668
Storage	843	907	907
Supra Sectors (Railways, Telecommunication)	222035	456504	456504

Note: *In Rs. lakhs at 1993-94 prices.

**4 per cent growth rate for agriculture and 10 per cent for the other sectors

++5 per cent growth rate for agriculture and rest of the sector maintaining the existing trend growth rate.

Source: Computed from GFCF data provided by Directorate of Economics and Statistics, Government of Karnataka and Central Statistical Organisation (CSO), Government of India

The estimated financial requirements as per scenario I, II and III in 2003-04 are Rs. 13,255, Rs. 15,058 and Rs. 13,510 crores respectively (in 1993-94 prices) for the development of the infrastructure sector to achieve the desired rates of economic growth. Given the stringent fiscal situation it is often difficult for the state government to raise such substantial amount of resources for investment purposes. It is in this respect that seeking private investment is important for the government. Karnataka government has taken a positive step in this direction. Notable cases are on airport, metro railways, bridges, IT and BT, communications, and several more.

TABLE 5.6

Share of Public Sector in Infrastructure GFCF

(in per cent)

Year	*Agriculture*		*Electricity, Gas and Water Supply*		*Transport by Other Means*		*Railway and Communication*		*Total*	
	India	Karnataka	India	Karnataka	India	Karnataka	India	Karnataka	India	Karnataka
1993-94	34.85	60.28	76.63	96.93	41.13	32.79	100	100	37.66	32.09
1994-95	35.08	58.14	87.25	87.40	20.97	21.97	100	100	37.50	27.88
1995-96	32.69	52.29	87.89	89.00	16.14	21.53	100	100	28.88	26.19
1996-97	30.02	52.38	81.25	82.85	15.05	20.33	100	100	27.56	21.59
1997-98	31.79	50.78	85.93	88.80	18.23	29.98	100	100	28.25	23.37
1998-99	24.24	70.95	80.06	82.43	18.24	-10.73*	100	100	31.02	17.21
1999-00	27.61	78.01	79.95	67.98	15.81	16.01	100	100	32.30	21.01
2000-01	25.53	77.18	81.66	78.97	15.11	8.88	99.99	100	32.44	24.03
Average	**30.23**	**62.50**	**82.58**	**84.30**	**20.08**	**17.59**	**100**	**100**	**31.95**	**24.17**

Note: * GFCF is negative for this year.

Source: Computed from GFCF data provided by Directorate of Economics and Statistics, Government of Karnataka and Central Statistical Organisation (CSO), Government of India.

5.2.4 Encouraging Private Investment in Infrastructure

Preamble to the Infrastructure Policy of 1997 accepts the fact that the infrastructure facilities in the state are inadequate and available resources for infrastructure development have progressively diminished in the face of increasing demands from other sectors. In fact, government is finding it difficult to maintain the existing infrastructure facilities. Given the importance of this sector government therefore, has unambiguously declared to the potential investors its commitment to encouraging private investment in infrastructure in the state.

The present shares of public sector investment in total investment (measured in terms of GFCF) in both Karnataka and at all-India level are provided in Table 5.6 above.

It is observed that there is scope for enhancing private investment in the power sector. The state of Karnataka has involved the private sector for infrastructure development, in particular, in the power sector (e.g. Tannir Bhavi). Several other sectors including roads and bridges/flyovers, air and sea ports, transport system have also been identified for private participation. Generally infrastructure projects will be offered to the private sector through open competitive bidding. In this respect several types of arrangements are feasible e.g. build-operate-transfer (BOT), build-own-operate (BOO), build-own-operate-transfer (BOOT), build-operate-share-transfer (BOST) and so on. Government also recognised the fact that private participation in infrastructure projects requires the projects to be commercially viable. Various incentives for infrastructure investment include: a) exemption of payment of entry tax on equipments/materials procured for implementation of infrastructure projects, (b) exemption from the sales tax or work contract tax for a period of three years, (c) exemption from stamp duty or registration charges on sales of land for such projects, (d) provision of Government land at concessional rate, (e) allowing investors to charge users' fees, and (f) allowing the private sectors to engage in other commercial activities (such as building of commercial complexes, etc.), when they undertake financially unviable but socially relevant projects.

The Infrastructure Development Department of the Government of Karnataka was set up during 1996. Among its major responsibilities are to determine infrastructure needs in various sectors of the state by identifying the areas to be developed and to act as a consultant department for infrastructure projects. In order to discharge these responsibilities, a nodal state agency was set up. Its mandate was to promote private sector investors and facilitate the process of public-private partnership in infrastructure. This nodal agency called the Infrastructure Development Corporation (Karnataka) Limited (IDeCK) was set up in June 2000 as a joint venture company. Government of Karnataka holds 49 per cent of the share capital of IDeCK, IDFC holds 49.5 per cent and HDFC the balance 1.5 per cent. Besides, share capital, GoK provides funds to IDeCK for development of projects. Its aim is to help government establish state level priorities in infrastructure development and act as a platform to catalyse and harness both public and private investments and to ensure that projects actually happen. Two of the major projects IDeCK has been handling in the recent years are Bangalore-Maddur State Highway project and the Landfill Project for Bangalore Mahanagara Palika. Both the projects have been allocated to private investors through open competitive international bidding system under build-operate-maintain-transfer-basis. It may be necessary to establish a separate Viability Gap Fund to leverage with private initiation in infrastructure investments.

In order to invite more private investment in the power distribution, this function has been unbundled from KPTCL. Four independent government owned electricity supply companies (ESCOMS) were formed on regional basis with their headquarters located at Bangalore, Mangalore, Hubli and Gulbarga. Government of Karnataka has in fact decided to invite private sector participation in distribution of electricity and intends to attempt privatisation of all four companies (GoK, 2003-04). In addition to the development of roads through private investments, private participation is also encouraged for the developments of ports in the state. In this regard, development of new sites, and support to infrastructure and maritime related industries are being provided by the Government. Karnataka Industrial Investment and Development Corporation has been appointed as he nodal agency for implementation of such policies. At present Government has decided to allow private participation in three ports *viz.*, Belekere, Tadri and Old Mangalore. Detailed bids are awaited. However, for Tadri port selection process of the developer has been completed (GoK, 2003-04). Similarly, K-RIDE was set up with the objective of developing and implementing rail infrastructure projects in Karnataka and leverage private participation. Four projects are initially identified for development through K-RIDE. In particular, gauge conversion of Hassan-Mangalore rail line was found to be commercially viable and apart from the state investment, investment from the strategic investors will be sought (Economic Survey, GoK, 2003-04). For the construction of a state-of-art international airport 4,300 acres of land has been acquired 30 kms away from main Bangalore city in a location named Devanahalli. Private investment is forthcoming for the development of the airport.

5.3. Development of Communication Sector

5.3.1 Introduction

When it comes to sending, receiving and transmitting all forms of information (i.e. text, voice and imaged based) communication is the medium. The modes of communication include telecommunication (e.g. telephones) and information technology (e.g. Internet), post and telegraph, and mass media. Mass media includes print media (e.g. newspapers and magazines), audio (e.g. radio) and audio-visual (e.g. television) media. Communication is essential for all information-based economic activities, such as, production, consumption, allocation, exchange and distribution. Communication sector comprises production of hardware, establishment of network and provision of services. Thus, communication is contributory to economic development through its contribution to state income in both secondary and tertiary sector activities, directly and indirectly.

The network of post offices and telephone exchanges has been a vehicle to provide communication infrastructure for postal and telecommunication services in the state. In the nineties, telecommunication infrastructure has taken a leap forward with the advent of cellular telephones. The entry of private sector in this segment has made rapid progress possible. Several benefits to the private investors are given to attract private investment in this sector.

As a segment of infrastructure development, the analysis of communication services is restricted to telecommunication and postal services for their growth in terms of institutional network and provision of services.[2] In addition, network, quality, usage and access of services are examined. Both telecom and postal services are in the Central list of the Indian Constitution. The policies for planning, development, regulation and pricing of these services are being formulated and implemented for the nation as a whole. Since 1991, provisioning of telecom and postal services in Karnataka and in all other states have been

2. Thus, it excludes the role of electronics, information technology, and mass media. However, there exists complementarity between electronics and telecommunication on the hardware part, and information technology and telecommunication on the service part. Given the focus on communication services, electronics hardware is not focused. Information technology is not focused, as it is separately discussed elsewhere. Moreover, as per the existing definition and composition of communication sector in state's income, only telecom and postal services are relevant. Nevertheless, the impact of communication services on economic development goes beyond its contribution to state's tertiary sectoral income (e.g. communication as an input in the production process). These impacts are not captured for lack of data on input-output relationships between industries or sectors in the state.

undergoing remarkable improvements due to major policy reforms in the communication sector including privatisation.

5.3.2 *Role of Communication Sector in State's Economic Development*

Contribution of communication sector to state's gross and net domestic product, measured at factor costs and constant (1993-94) prices, from 1994-95 through 2002-03 is presented in Appendix A-5.1. Three indicators highlight the contribution: (a) annual growth of income from the communication sector, (b) share of communication sector in state's total income and (c) share of communication sector in state's total income from the tertiary sector. It may be noted that:

- The annual growth rate of state income from the communication sector is higher than that for gross and net state income in all the years (as given in Chapter 1, however) except in 1998-99. For instance, the average annual growth over 1994-95 to 2002-03 of income from the communication sector in the NSDP is equal to 23.39 per cent, which is much higher than the annual average growth of NSDP and tertiary sector.
- The share of communication sector as well as the tertiary sector has been increasing in the state income over the years. For instance, the average annual share of communication sector in NSDP is equal to 3.40 per cent.
- The share of communication sector in the tertiary sector has also been increasing over the years.

5.3.3 *Telecom Services*

Growth of Public Telecom Sector in Karnataka State: An Overview

The major insights from the trends in indicators of growth of public telephone, telegraph, telegram and telex infrastructure and service from 1991-92 through 2002-03 are as follows (Appendix A-5.2):

- Equipped capacity [i.e. number of Direct Exchange Line (or DEL)] that a telephone exchange is equipped to provide per exchange has increased by 1.82 times during 1991-92 to 1995-96, 2.39 times during 1995-96 to 2000-01 and by 1.13 times during 2001-02 to 2002-03.
- Equipped capacity per exchange has remained higher than the number of DEL per exchange, indicating for extent of capacity utilisation (83 per cent).
- Over the years, both access and usage demand for telecom services have increased (as viewed from tele-density from 0.83 in 1991-92 to 5.18 in 2002-03, and number of metered calls per DEL from 5,120 in 1991-92 to 5580 in 2002-03).
- The number of public telephones has increased 2.8 times during 1991-92 to 1995-96 as well as during 1995-96 to 2000-01, and 1.7 times between 2000-01 to 2002-03. At the same time, public telephones as a percentage of total DEL has increased from 2.52 per cent in 1991-92 to 3.43 per cent in 1995-96, 3.62 per cent in 2000-2001 and 4.72 per cent in 2002-03.
- There exists unmet demand in terms of waitlisted telephones. This is evident by the share of DEL in total registered/expressed demand, 73.97 per cent in 1991-92, 83.85 per cent in 1995-96, 92.92 per cent in 2000-01 and 95.60 per cent in 2002-2003. This implies that: (a) the unmet demand has declined over the years, and (b) lack of demand may not be attributable for lack of capacity utilisation, and lack of capacity may not be attributable to unmet demand. Consequently, supply side bottlenecks (e.g. timely laying of cables) could be a reason for lack of capacity utilisation and for existence of unmet demand.
- Overall quality of telephone services has improved, as is evident by the decline in the per cent of billing complaint from 0.99 per cent in 1991-92 to 0.28 per cent in 1995-96, 0.10 per cent in 2000-01 and in subsequent years.
- Growth of other components of telecom sector, such as, telex, trunk calls and telegram, do not show positive trends during 1991-92 to 2002-03, rather stagnant or declining.

Interdistrict Variations in Telecom Development

At the outset, it should be emphasised that, over the years, interdistrict disparities have declined in regard to the distribution of: (a) number of telephone exchanges, (b) DEL, (c) loading, and (d) number of waitlisted telephones. However, the provisioning of telecom services shows considerable variations between 20 telecom districts in Karnataka state. Coefficient of variation for the distribution of number of telephone exchanges (or DEL) across the telecom districts have remained fairly constant. But variation on distribution of loading (or waitlisted telephones) has declined from 163.16 (or 133.05) per cent in 1996-97 to 3.83 (or 89.37) per cent in 1999-00, and to 4.56 (or 97.07) per cent in

2002-03. Some major observations on such regional variation in 2002-03 from Appendix A-5.3 are:

- The highest share of telephone exchanges is in Dakshina Kannada (9.12 per cent) and lowest in Mandya (2.41) per cent. In terms of total population per telephone exchange, the highest is evident for Bangalore Urban (about 60,960) and lowest is evident for Kodagu (7,180). In addition, about 12 districts have less population served by one exchange than at the state's average (19,560 persons).
- Of the total 2,753,499 DEL in the state, the combined share of Bangalore Urban (32.24 per cent) Dakshina Kannada (10.23 per cent), Belgaum (5.35 per cent) and Hubli (5.63 per cent) is 53.45 per cent, taking away the major share. In the same way, teledensity in about 14 districts taken together is less than at the state level (5.22 per cent).
- Capacity utilisation in terms of loading varies between districts: highest in Bangalore Urban (87.13 per cent) and lowest in Bidar (63.24 per cent). About 16 districts have less loading than the state level (81.78 per cent).
- The district-wise distribution of waitlisted telephones shows that the unmet demand is relatively higher in Dakshina Kannada (23.78 per cent), Belgaum (7.98 per cent), Shimoga (6.67 per cent), Bijapur (5.48 per cent), Kolar (5.07 per cent), Bangalore Urban (4.78 per cent) and Mysore (3.41 per cent). About 12 districts have their unmet demand above the state average level (3.66 per cent).

Contrasting Provisioning of Telecom Services across the States

Five different indicators are relevant for contrasting Karnataka's performance with select neighbouring states. They are: (a) rate of public provisioning, (b) access to basic and cellular mobiles phones, (c) private-public provisioning of basic and cellular mobile phones, (d) rural and urban divide in provisioning and access, and (e) efficiency of service delivery system.

Appendix A-5.4 presents the growth of public provisioning of telecom network in Karnataka from 1991-92 through 2003-04 in contrast to those in southern states and at all-India level. Annual growth of DEL in the southern states has been positive throughout except in 2003-04, but with fluctuations over the years. However, the 13 year average number of DEL per exchange in Karnataka is less than for other southern states (1.05 times higher in Andhra Pradesh, 2.37 times in Kerala and 1.4 times in Tamil Nadu) and at the all-India (1.31 times). Also the 13-year average growth of DEL is lower in Karnataka than for other southern states. Thus, the network growth in Karnataka seems to be lagging behind the neighbouring states.

In contrast to public telecom provisioning, state's access to fixed and total (i.e. fixed and cellular mobile) by both public and private telecom operators can be viewed from (Appendix A-5.5 and Figures 5.10 and 5.11). Comparison across the southern states reveals that:

- Teledensity (i.e. number of telephones per 100 population) of fixed phones in Karnataka has been increasing from 0.83 in 1991-92 to 1.62 in 1995-96 and from to 4.91 in 2001-02 to 6.28 in 2003-04. Moreover, the tele-density of fixed phones in Karnataka has remained higher than in Andhra Pradesh, Tamil Nadu and the all-India level, but lower than in Kerala. This is evident, for instance, in the higher average annual tele-density of Karnataka (=2.86) as compared to Andhra Pradesh (=2.30), Tamil Nadu (=2.49) and at all-India (=2.20).
- Total (fixed and mobile) teledensity has a marked increase since 2000-01 in Karnataka and other states due to growth of cellular mobile phones. For instance, total teledensity of Karnataka has increased 4.75 in 2000-01 to 9.46 in 2003-04. As in the case of tele-density of fixed phones, tele-density of total phones in Karnataka has remained higher than other southern states (except Kerala) and all-India. Implicitly, this increase accounts for a shift from fixed line connectivity to mobile connections in recent years.

FIGURE 5.10

Growth of Teledensity without Cellular/Mobile Phones: 1991-92 to 2003-04

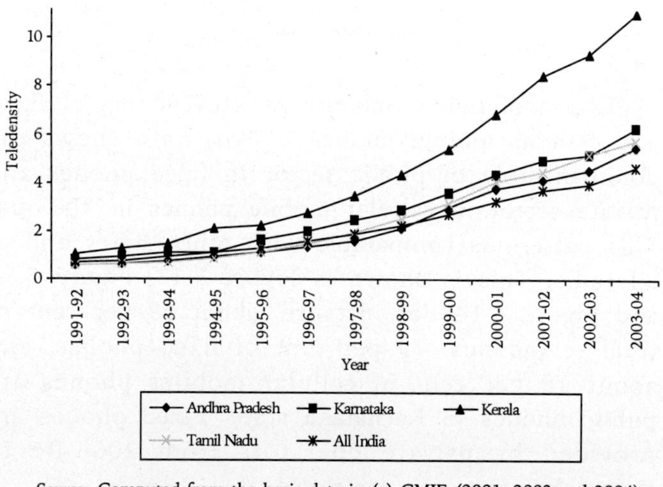

Source: Computed from the basic data in (a) CMIE (2001, 2003 and 2004), and (b) *Annual Report* 2003-04, Department of Telecommunication, Government of India (New Delhi).

FIGURE 5.11

Growth of Teledensity with Cellular/Mobile Phones: 1991-92 to 2003-04

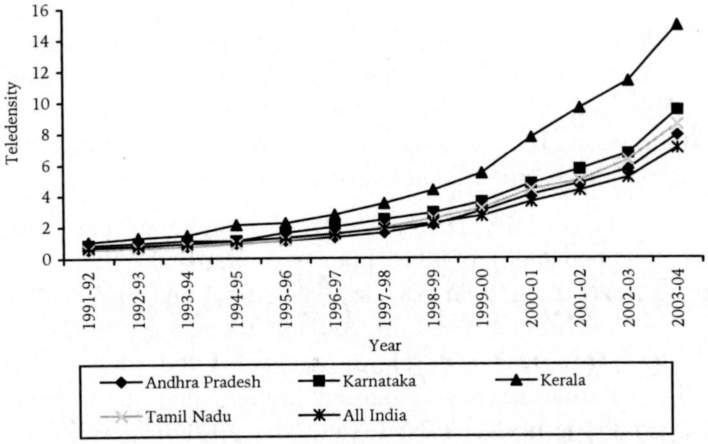

Source: Computed from the basic data in (a) CMIE (2001, 2003 and 2004), and (b) *Annual Report* 2003-04, Department of Telecommunication, Government of India (New Delhi).

FIGURE 5.12

Share of Public and Private Operators in Total Phones: 2003-04

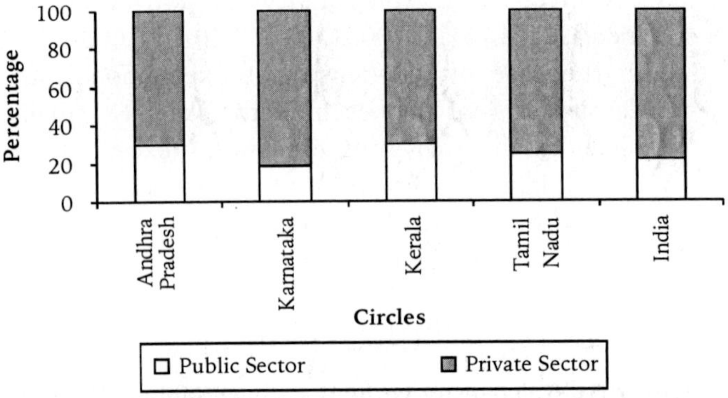

Source: Computed from the basic data in (a) CMIE (2001, 2003 and 2004), and (b) *Annual Report* 2003-04, Department of Telecommunication, Government of India (New Delhi).

Pattern of public and private provisioning of fixed and cellular mobile phones in Karnataka shows the dominant role of public sector in fixed phones and private sector in cellular mobile phones in 2003-04. This pattern is comparable with other states and at all India. This is shown is Figure 5.12, Figure 5.13 and Figure 5.14 For instance, about 59 per cent of total telephones, 79 per cent of fixed phones, and about 19 per cent of cellular mobiles phones are public phones in Karnataka state. Fixed phones are provided by private operators from 2003-04 in Karnataka state.

FIGURE 5.13

Share of Public Sector and Private Operators in Fixed Telephone: 2003-04

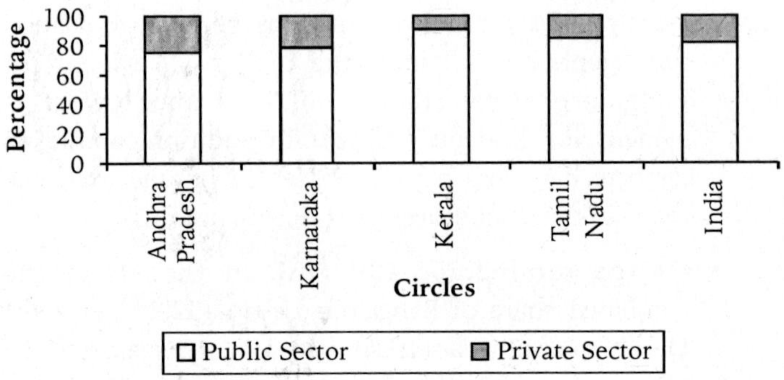

Source: Computed from the basic data in (a) CMIE (2001, 2003 and 2004), and (b) *Annual Report* 2003-04, Department of Telecommunication, Government of India (New Delhi).

FIGURE 5.14

Share of Public and Private Operators in Cellular/Mobile Telephone: 2003-04

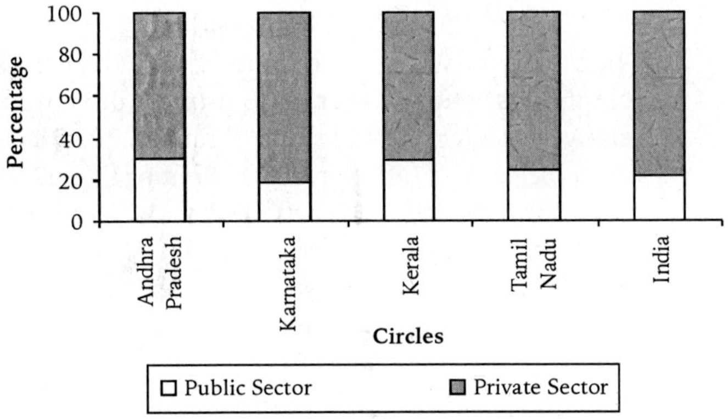

Source: Computed from the basic data in (a) CMIE (2001, 2003 and 2004), and (b) *Annual Report* 2003-04, Department of Telecommunication, Government of India (New Delhi).

Contrast between rural and urban divide in the provisioning and access to overall (i.e. fixed and cellular mobiles services by both public and private operators) telecom services is evident in Karnataka and other states (Appendix A-5.6).[3] The evidence suggests the following.

- Levels and growth of access to telecom services differ between rural and urban areas. For instance, increase in rural and urban tele-density

3. It should be emphasised that provisioning of telecom services by private sector include Internet and broadband services over the telephone networks. For lack of data at the state and district levels, these services are not explicitly analysed.

between 2000-01 to 2003-04 is equal to 0.62 in rural areas and 12.25 in urban areas in Karnataka. This increase in rural tele-density is lowest as compared to other states and all India, but increase in urban tele-density is higher than in all other states (except Kerala) and at all India level.

- Access to telecom services in rural areas, as viewed from the share of rural DEL in the overall telephones, has declined from 27.7 per cent in 2000-01 to 16.1 per cent in 2003-04. This decline is evident in all other states and at all India level. However, decline in Karnataka (11.1 percentage points) is highest except the decline in Kerala (12.3 percentage points).
- The difference in unmet demand indicates the differential access to telecom services. Karnataka's share on this is around 6 per cent during 1993-94 to 2000-01 (and comparable with Andhra Pradesh and Tamil Nadu; but it is still quite high in Kerala (26.54 per cent).

Quality of telecom services is of critical importance for the final delivery of services. Based on the indicators and benchmarks set up by TRAI (2003), Appendix A-5.7 summarises the efficiency and competitiveness in the delivery of select telecom services. Here, the BSNL is identified with public sector provider. The average value of performance indicators of private providers in each state is considered for total private sector performance.

The results for basic services show that the public sector is more efficient than the private sector in Karnataka state. This is in contrast with private sector being more efficient than the public sector in Tamil Nadu and Andhra Pradesh, or equally efficient as in the case of Kerala. On the other hand, the relative efficiency of the states is indicated by the number of performance indicators, which meet with national level benchmarks, for the combined or total value of the indicators. In this regard, in basic services Karnataka is least performing (=1) and Tamil Nadu is best performing (=5), as compared to Andhra Pradesh (=4) and Kerala (=3). Poor performance of the private sector in Karnataka is reflected here. Thus, improvement of quality of telecom services in the private sector is of vital importance for enhancing both efficiency and competitiveness of basic telecom services in Karnataka.

Unlike in basic services, the public and private sector are equally efficient in the delivery of cellular services in Karnataka. This is in contrast with all other states where the private sector offers more efficient quality of services than the public sector. Most importantly, Karnataka's efficiency in the delivery of services by all providers (=4) is equal with Kerala and better than Tamil Nadu (=3) and Kerala (=3). These results, however, must be considered initial and indicative, as they are based on a select quarterly data.

5.3.4 Postal Services

Postal services have been the most important mode of communication in the state, especially before the recent widespread development and utilisation of telecom services and still remain essential for many reasons, particularly in places and for people where telecom services are unavailable, inaccessible, and unaffordable. In general, the services include booking and delivery of registered and unregistered articles and letters, newspapers and money orders, and savings bank. More recent services include speed post, and use of information technology for postal banking and speed post, and delivery of telephone services in rural areas through village postmen.

Growth of Postal Institutional Network

The growth of postal network can be viewed in terms of changes in total number of post offices, rural-urban location of total post offices, population served per post office, total letter boxes and rural and urban location, summarily put in Appendix A-5.8. The number of post offices have increased from 9,762 in 2002-03 to 9,911 in 2003-04, recording an annual growth rate of less than one per cent. Further, the share of rural post offices in the total number of post offices has remained about 86 per cent throughout.[4] Post offices with full range of services (i.e. money order, savings bank and delivery services) are equal to 89.64 per cent. Post offices with one delivery are equal to 89.49 per cent and two deliveries are equal to 2.17 per cent. Total population served per post office has increased marginally from 4,706 in 1992-93 to 5004 in 1995-96 and to 5321 in 2003-04. In contrast, at the all-India level, total population per post office was equal to

4. Three criteria contribute for establishment of a new rural post office; (a) Population size e.g. 3000 population in a group of villages in plain areas, and 500 population in individual villages or 1000 population in a group of villages in hilly, tribal, desert and inaccessible areas. (b) Distance (e.g. minimum 3 kms away from the existing post office). (c) Anticipated income (e.g. minimum 1/3rd of the cost). In urban areas, the criteria include the following: (i) The minimum distance is 1.5 km in cities with 20 lakh population and above, and 2 km in other urban areas. (ii) Minimum 5 percent profit (or cost recovery) for further retention. (iii) No extra-departmental post offices to be opened. Thus, lack of fulfilment of these criteria may contribute to slow growth of number of rural and urban post offices.

6,115 in 1995-96 and 6,629 in 2000-01, indicating marginally higher performance in Karnataka. Total number of letterboxes (= sum of letterboxes in and away from post offices) has increased from 27,391 in 1991-92 to 29,174 in 1995-96 and to 34,715 in 2003-2004. The share of rural letterboxes has also increased from about 66 per cent in 1991-92 to about 77 per cent in 1995-96 and to 78.38 per cent in 2003-04.

Performance of Postal Services

Three aspects of postal services are important, namely, composition, distance and modes. The composition of total postal traffic includes unregistered mail, registered articles and parcel, insured letters and parcels, and value paid (VP) letters and parcels. Distance over which the total traffic is carried is given by route length in kilometre by modes. Modes include railway, water transport, and motor services, runners and other modes (e.g. cycles). The growth of postal traffic in Karnataka from 1992-93 through 2002-03 presented in Appendix A-5.9 is summarised below:

- The average annual growth in postal traffic during 1992-93 to 2002-03 is positive and equals to 3.04 per cent, but with fluctuations (1.32 per cent in 1992-93, 0.26 per cent in 1996-97 and -8.65 per cent in 2002-03).
- The share of registered mails dominate over other components in the total postal traffic. For instance, the share of registered (or unregistered) mails is equal to 91.98 (or 1.96) per cent in 1992-93, 90.52 (or 2.77) per cent in 1996-97 and 88.07 (or 1) per cent in 2002-03.
- The distance over which the traffic is carried has increased over the years, from about 1.25 lakh km in 1992-93 to 1.48 lakh km in 1996-97 and to 1.51 lakh km in 2002-03. Of the modes of total traffic, the share of railways and motor services dominate over other modes: 60.75 per cent in 1992-93, 70.35 per cent in 1997-98 and 72.16 per cent in 2002-03. However, the share shows marked decline in 1995-96 and 1996-97, mainly due to the decline in the share of motor services from 1.14 lakh km in 1994-95 to 0.51 lakh km in 1995-96 and 0.54 lakh km in 1996-97.
- The value of money orders (MOs) booked per money order has increased from about Rs.131 in 1992-93 to Rs. 220 in 1996-97 and to Rs.399 in 2002-03. In the same way, the value of MOs paid per MO paid has increased from about 176 in 1992-93 to Rs. 260 in 1996-97 and to Rs. 377 in 2002-03. Thus, overall transactions in MOs show an increase between these years.

Interdistrict Variations in Postal Services

The performance of this sector at the district levels is viewed through two indicators, namely, the share of total number of post offices in the state and total population per post office. Appendix A-5.10 presents these indicators for 1997-98 and 2001-02.

Except for four districts (*viz.*, Belgaum, Gulbarga, Tumkur and Uttara Kannada), all the remaining districts have less than 5 per cent share in the total number of post offices in the State. The combined share of these four districts is equal to 21.43 per cent in 2001-02.

A comparison between the per cent distribution of state's total post offices and total population by districts show two interesting patterns. First, except for the Bangalore Urban district, the per cent share of state's total post offices by districts is in consonance with the per cent share of state's total population by district (with a simple correlation coefficient of 0.8). But inter-district variations are evident in the total population served by one post office in each district. For instance, the highest (or lowest) population per post office is in Bangalore Urban in 2001-02 being 18,479, whereas it is as low as 2,479 in Kodagu. In addition, as compared to the state average level, 18 districts in 1997-98 and 17 in 2001-02 have less population per post office.

5.3.5 Policy Directions and Vision for the Communication Sector

Undisputedly, communication sector is contributory to economic development in Karnataka in terms of its share in the state income. The nature and coverage of services differ between the telecom and postal services, complementing each other. Furthermore, the objectives of service access and affordability of overall communication services for all economic activities are being kept in mind. The growth of private sector is remarkable in the provisioning of cellular mobile services and in increasing the tele-density in both rural and urban areas. Further, private operators have begun to provide fixed phone services in Karnataka from 2003-04. Thus, public sector is faced with competition from the private sector in both fixed and cellular mobile phones.

Lack of capacity utilisation and existence of unmet demand pose contradictions in the planning and development of the public fixed telecom services in the state. This suggests the supply side bottlenecks are to be eliminated to attain higher capacity utilisation and meeting with full demand for telecom services. In this regard, improving the expressed demand for fixed telecom services (i.e. basic, value added and broadband services by fixed and mobile services) deserve special consideration for implementation (Narayana, 2003).

Efficient and competitive delivery of communication services is important for attraction and sustainability of economic development in the state. Initial evidence suggests that, as compared to other southern states, Karnataka state lags behind in both efficiency and competitiveness in delivery of telecom services. This implies that need for a focus on improving service delivery, as per the TRAI's national level benchmarks, particularly in private sector.

Information-technology (IT) sector and communication sector are mutually complementary. For instance, growth of telecom is essential for the growth of Internet and *vice versa*. Many of the recent postal services use information technology for speedy and efficient delivery of services. It is gratifying to note that, way back in 1997, Karnataka was the first state in India to announce a separate policy for promotion and development of information technology in the state (i.e.Information Technology Policy, 1997) with objectives to increase domestic and export earnings. Subsequently, the state has announced the Millennium IT Policy in 2000 (called Mahithi). The objectives of the policy included important social and cultural aspects, such as, use of IT technology in the overall goal of the Government of Karnataka in eradicating poverty and empowering women and to promote the usage of Kannada in IT. Thus, over the years, Karnataka has emerged as a 'Silicon Valley of India' Most of the 20 top IT companies in the country are located in the state. Bangalore has shown tremendous progress in attracting national and MNCs in IT sector, it is called IT Capital of India.

In recognition of the above important roles of the IT sector, the Tenth Five-Year Plan of India has set specific objectives and targets, which include emphasis on e-commerce, e-governance, e-education and IT-enabled services (e.g. Call Centres/Customer Interaction Services, BPO, Insurance Claim Processing, Medical Transcription, Legal Database, Online Education, Payroll/HR Services and Web Services). In fact, Karnataka has a major role in accomplishing the above objectives and targets. Consequently, Karnataka's thrust areas in the IT-sector in the Tenth Plan should include: (a) software development and exports and IT-enabled services; and (b) priority for e-governance, development of software in Indian languages. IT for masses, distance education, and e-commerce. Thus, policy coordination between communication sector and information technology is essential for the overall growth of the ICT sector for state's current and future economic development.

5.4 Power Sector Development

5.4.1 An Overview

Growth of both industrial and agricultural sectors heavily depend upon power as an essential infrastructure input. It is essential for modern life styles as well.

Karnataka has had to invest heavily in new capacity to keep up with rapid economic growth. With hydel generation ranging from 30-50 per cent of total generation, the state is still dependent on the monsoons for supply adequacy. Yet, over the years, the thermal share of generation has been increasing, with most new generation coming from diesel/naphtha and coal.

The increasing transmission and distribution losses have caused serious shortfalls in revenue realisation and increasing cost of electricity supply. The average revenue realisation rate was at Rs 2.57 per unit during 2002-03 as against average cost of generation of Rs 3.49. Regional variations in supply provision between urban and rural areas persist, with urban areas having substantially better loss levels, revenue recovery, collection efficiency and power quality. The increasing burden of subsidy is becoming beyond the capacities of ESCOMs to absorb them.

Reforms in the nineties and in the Electricity Act have focused on encouraging private investment. So far, Karnataka has failed to attract substantial domestic or foreign private investments. The public sector still generates over 90 per cent of the 30,788 million units (MU) in 2003-04. The basic reason for poor private investment inflow into the sector is that of uncertainty over minimum returns and a politicised decisionmaking process. It has been felt in this regard that reforms should start with privatisation of distribution sector (GoK, 2003-04).

5.4.2 Karnataka's Demand Profile

Karnataka's per capita electricity consumption has fluctuated around 350 units (kwh) in the nineties, as against the national average growing from 275 to over 350 Figure 5.15. Its consumer profile is heterogeneous, with a mix of agriculture, commercial and industrial load, as can seen from Figure 5.16. Industrial consumption comprises 30 per cent of load, while agricultural load is estimated to be around 40 per cent. Residential load and domestic lighting follow with shares of around 10-12 per cent.

FIGURE 5.15

Per Capita Electricity Consumption-India *versus* Karnataka

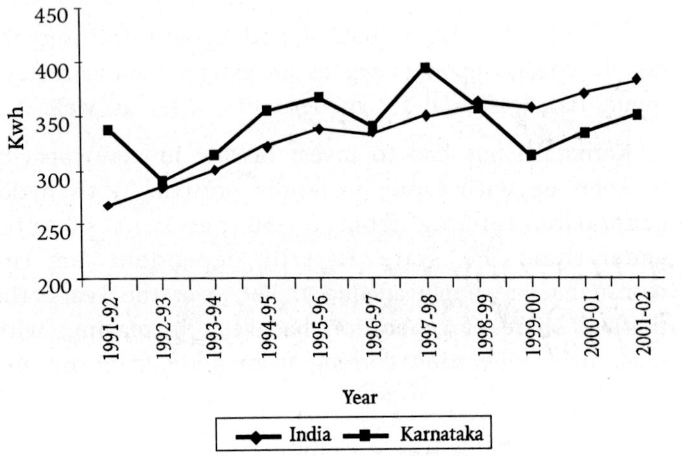

Note: All India 2001-01 and 2000-02 projected based on historical growth rate.

Source: Annual Report on Working of SEBs 2001-2002; Planning Commission, KPTCL Annual Administration Report 2001-2002.

FIGURE 5.16

Consumption Breakdown

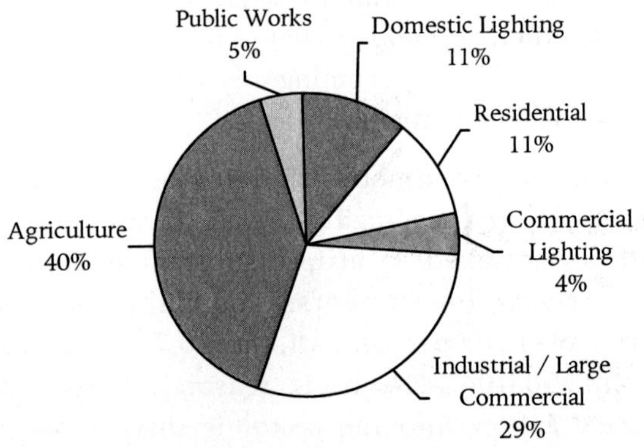

Historical Demand Growth

The load growth over the last 10 years is fluctuating between 6 and 8 per cent in the early nineties, and between 4.8 and 5.6 per cent in the late nineties (Figure 5.17). GDP, on the other hand, grew at an average rate of 7.3 per cent in the early nineties, and 8.3 per cent in the late nineties. All these indicate that the power sector has not kept up with economic growth in Karnataka. From an energy perspective, the sale of irrigation pump sets and residential (all electric home) loads have been the largest drivers of demand, followed by industrial demand (which includes service industries). While industrial and agricultural load growth predictably fluctuate with overall load growth, residential demand has grown steadily.

FIGURE 5.17

Demand Growth by Consumer Class (Connected Load)

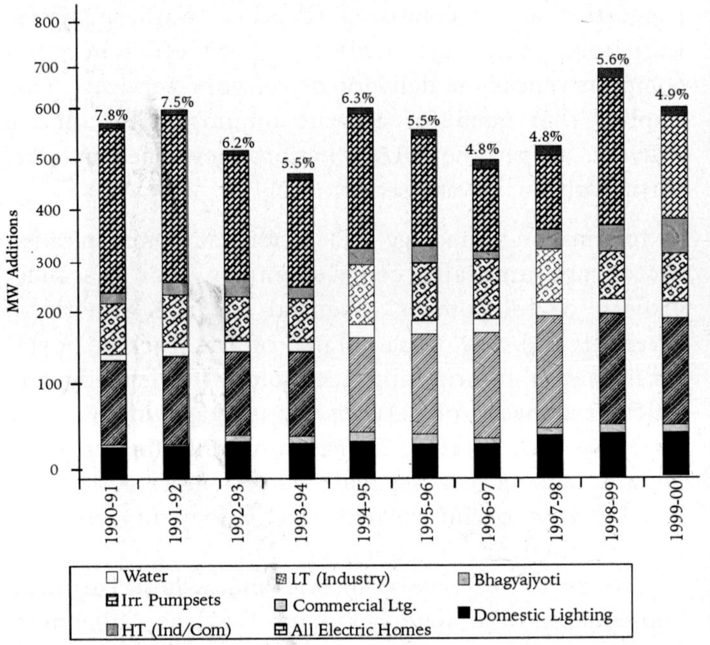

Source: KPTCL, 2004.

Industrial and residential growth has centered around Bangalore, with the rise in immigration and the development of service industries in the last decade. Coastal areas (MESCOM) have been the focus of development in the last few years, and are likely to see substantial industrial demand growth. Load growth in from an energy perspective, the sale of irrigation pump sets and residential (all electric home) loads have been the largest drivers of demand, followed by industrial demand (which includes service industries). While industrial and agricultural load growth predictably fluctuate with overall load growth, residential demand has grown steadily. Gulbarga and Hubli, however, will most likely remain predominantly agricultural. This regional breakdown is evident in Table 5.7. Bangalore zone has over 50 per cent of the residential, commercial and industrial load in the State, but the lowest agricultural load. On the other extreme, Gulbarga and Hubli zones have about 35 per cent each of agricultural load, and less than 10 per cent of the other categories. By the end of 2002-2003, 97 per cent of Karnataka's 27,585 villages (2001, Census) and about 40 per cent of its 27,000 odd hamlets have been electrified. However, Karnataka continues to ration power to rural areas. They receive three-phase power for only 8 hours at night for agricultural purposes, with another 8-hour block available for domestic lighting only (single-phase).

TABLE 5.7

Energy Consumption (MU)—Breakdown by ESCOM (Zone) 2002-2003

	Bangalore	*Mangalore*	*Hubli*	*Gulbarga*
Residential	2,021	858	492	309
Commercial	784	257	124	87
Industrial	2,128	1,042	501	474
Agriculture	4	10	18	17

Source: ESCOM filings to KERC.

Such divergent growth along zonal lines explains the divergence in ESCOM finances as well, since industrial growth creates financial surpluses, while agricultural growth drains them.

Future Demand

Future growth projections are as uncertain as predictions of GDP growth. But, strong growth can be expected. So far, there is little indication that immigration of people and businesses into Bangalore will slow down. Mangalore has also developed into a major port and attracted many infrastructure projects and businesses. Rural demand, which is part suppressed, will grow faster as supply adequacy improves. The relative composition of growth will depend on state industrial and agricultural/irrigation policy.

Because of the supply rationing, the true nature of demand for electricity will not be known until supply constraints are released. No doubt, the future demand growth would be higher than currently observed six per cent.

5.4.3 State Utility Performance—Physical

According to state power sector ratings by independent consultants (CRISIL/ICRA), Karnataka rates high for its generation performance, which is driven largely by the performance of its 1260 MW thermal unit at Raichur, whose average PLF increased from 81 per cent in 1993-94 to 88 per cent in 2001-2002 (Planning Commission 01-02). Aside from Raichur, KPTCL meets its base load requirements through its allocations from Central stations, and bilateral contracts. These have been requisitioned whenever available—the only failure in their delivery is due to lack of availability, which reflects on the performance of the respective central generating stations and not on KPTCL. Its other thermal units are two diesel-fired peaking units. Their plant load factor is not an accurate measure of performance, because they are not meant to run continuously. The main uncertainty in their performance is that they are underutilised to save money. Informally, it is well known that utilities use load shedding freely to balance demand and supply and reduce costs.[5]

The utilisation of hydro units is more difficult to assess. The key observation is that the dispatch is conducted in an opaque and *ad hoc* manner, with insufficient transparency and use of analytical tools. Karnataka typically faces water deficiency in summer months, but often carries a surplus in the rest of the year. Generally operations are maximised on hydro use for meeting summer peaking requirements, aside from minimising outflow requirements. With the peak summer period coming right before the monsoon, the utility has to find a balance between exhausting resources before the summer comes, and maintaining a surplus to carry to the next year, subject to any operational constraints.

To what extent hydro dispatch is optimised, merits further investigation. According to KERC at the end of each monsoon, based on water levels, the utility sets an average daily dispatch rate for the rest of the year to reach depletion by summer end. A more dynamic approach that is responsive to system conditions, particularly weather, could improve hydro utilisation. As followed in several other countries, a hydro-based optimisation tools can be deployed to determine year-round dispatch based on load projections, a step that KPTCL can consider urgently.

The efficiency of IPP dispatch has been poor mainly due to contract limitations and high fuel cost. The Tannir Bhavi unit, a naphtha-based combined-cycle unit contracted for 85 per cent PLF, has been dispatching only 40-50 per cent of the time in the last two years, and most often during peak load hours. Even if it were dispatching in all peak hours but had been idle in off-peak periods, its dispatch would be less than 70 per cent. It is perhaps an imprudent investment choice;

5. Under the Electricity Grid Code, utilities with insufficient supply of their own would end up procuring energy on the inter-regional balancing market (the Unscheduled Interchange, or UI, market) to meet load. Thus, they have an incentive to curtail load to avoid these charges.

peaking units should have been built instead, which cost 30 per cent less than base load units.

Thus, to improve resource utilisation, two important changes are required. First, the KERC must enforce transparency in utility operations, so that KPTCL is held accountable to its dispatch method and decisions. Second, KPTCL must be encouraged to deploy analytical tools to optimise dispatch, particularly since a high hydro presence increases the complexity of dispatch.

Transmission and Distribution Losses

T&D (technical and commercial) losses over the last decade has deteriorated from 20 per cent to 36 per cent in 2001-02. Official loss estimates currently stand at around 30 per cent. These are better performance indicators than only three other SEBs (Uttar Pradesh, Jammu and Kashmir, and Delhi), but much higher than the national average of 27 per cent in 2001-2002 (Planning Commission, 2001-02). In financial year 2001-02, KPTCL was not able to meet KERC's loss reduction targets. However, it appears to have reversed this in 2002-2003, as shown in Table 5.8.

TABLE 5.8

Historical T&D Losses (Technical and Commercial)

(Per Cent)

Year	*1990-1991*	*1997-1998*	*2001-2002*	*2002-2003*
T&D Losses	20.1	18.4	36	30.7

Source: Planning Commission, Annual Report on the Working of SEBs, 2001-2002, and KERC for 2002-2003.

Of the 30 per cent T&D losses, transmission losses are 6 per cent, while the rest comprise some combination of technical losses and collection losses. International standards for technical distribution losses are below 10 per cent. Since supply to agricultural uses (accounting for about 40 per cent of distribution) is not metered, actual losses can be still higher than this. Improving distribution losses by 5 percentage points would save about Rs 100 crores in energy costs annually, and free up a third of estimated unmet energy requirements in 2002-03.[6] Moreover, peak demand would be reduced by 600 MW, which could defer investment requirements of over Rs. 2,000 crores for 2-3 years, and probably cost far less to implement.

6. Five per cent on 30,000 MU, assuming Rs. 2000 crores to be the costs of energy losses. This latter figure has been calcuated from plant incremental costs provided by SRLDC.

This emphasises the need to focus on loss reduction as a prime objective of forthcoming state policy. For this, two policy trends must continue: that KERC must continue to set tariffs based on stringent loss reductions; and the state government does not deviate from pre-allocated subsidies. In fact, as promised in the 2003-04 Karnataka Budget, the state should go further and link future subsidy allocations to past performance.

State Utility Performance—Supply Adequacy

Karnataka had an annual met peak and energy demand of 5,445 MW and 30,788 million units (MU) respectively in 2003-2004 (including losses), as against the KPTCL's true demand estimates of 6,440 MW and 37,000 MU of capacity, respectively. The installed generation capacity in 2003-04 was however 5197 MW only. Most power systems worldwide plan for a reserve margin above peak demand, usually 15 per cent, to allow for plant outages and adverse weather conditions. Thus, for an estimated peak load of 6,440 MW, Karnataka would ideally have to have 7,360 MW. But, as in most states, Karnataka has struggled to keep pace even with the peak demand.

The acute dependence on the monsoons is a genuine problem. Of the total capacity, about half (3,085 MW) of Karnataka's capacity is hydro based, which means its annual energy availability depends on the monsoon, and its maximum availability during peak demand depends on the pattern of its usage over the year. Thus, it is difficult to *a priori* state whether Karnataka has sufficient capacity for its current needs. In addition to hydro (including about 150 MW of mini-hydel), Karnataka has about 100 MW of wind projects, 450 MW of naphtha and diesel plants, and about 1,500 MW from coal plants. Karnataka also has about 1,100 MW of capacity allocated to it from central generating stations (CGS), which include 150 MW from nuclear plants, and the rest from coal. Karnataka also may import up to 150 MW from the eastern region. As shown in Figure 5.18, the energy contribution from hydro to meeting demand shows variations up to 30 per cent, but depending on rainfall patterns it can contribute over 50 per cent of energy consumed. With KPCL having plans for building over 800 MW of hydro capacity, dependence on hydro power will go up further.

Figure 5.19 shows the breakdown of demand and supply, which provides many insights. Over 40 per cent of perceived demand is just the losses incurred to support the actual end use demand. Losses at peak are higher than average losses, because they are

FIGURE 5.18

Historical Hydro Level and Demand Growth

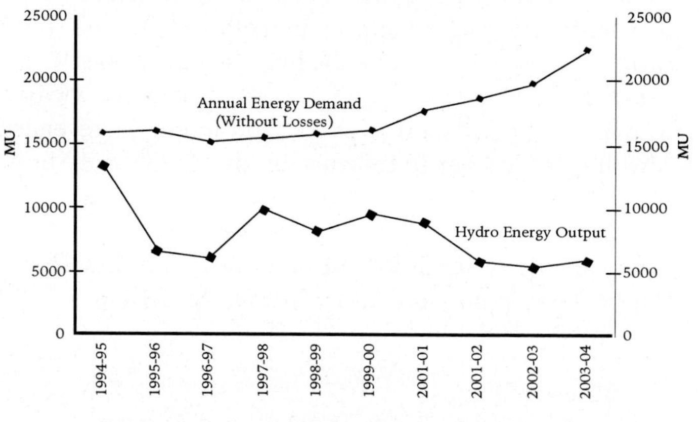

Source: KPTCL Systems Planning Group, 2004.

FIGURE 5.19

Supply Adequacy Illustration

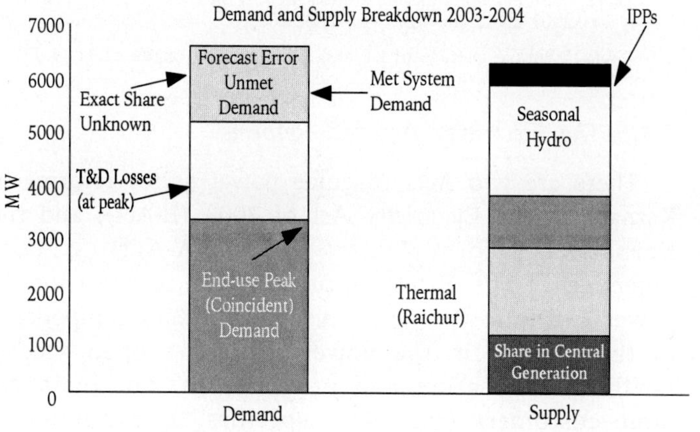

Source: Calculations based on the data provided by KPTCL Systems Planning Group, 2004.

proportional to the square of flowing energy. Thus, T&D losses impose a sizeable burden on peak capacity requirements, and not just on energy. Second, true peak demand is poorly understood due to inadequate metering and data infrastructure. On the one hand, demand forecasts tend to be consistently aggressive. However, the practice of load shedding also suppresses demand. As shown in Figure 5.19, met demand, including losses was 5,445 MW, while estimated actual demand is 6,440 MW. The difference includes some combination of unmet, but connected load, and forecast error, compounded by the proliferation of illegal connections.

Conventional presentations of supply inadequacy rely on tenuous demand estimates, and place undue emphasis on the need for generation additions, at the expense of load management and loss reduction. Institutional and operational failures, both in supply utilisation and in the delivery system, obscure the distinction between true supply deficits and poor resources utilisation. Past resource planning has failed in ensuring cost efficiency. In future, this combination of inadequate demand assessment, supply-side focus and cost inefficiency must be broken of to avoid continued wasteful expenditure and develop a viable power sector.

Future Capacity Needs

The KPTCL projects about 4 per cent demand growth over the next 5 years. This creates new supply requirements of about 1,400 MW, or investment requirements of Rs. 5,000-6,000 crores in that period. A large number of projects are already in development, totalling more than 4,900 MW (Table 5.9). Not all of these necessarily would sell power to Karnataka utilities.

If these projects materialise, Karnataka would have excess supply as early as in 2008. However, none of these projects have begun construction, while some have not even achieved financial closure. No projects are due to come online in the next 2-3 years. Thus, near-term demand growth would have to be met from purchases outside the state (open access) or, as discussed above, from demand reduction.

The key lesson is that budgetary allocations ought not to revolve any more around generation capacity additions. Instead, the focus must shift to transmission and distribution upgrades, to support growth, imports into Karnataka (to facilitate open access and trade), and most of all to reduce losses and improve demand management. In the new regionalised market regime, as long as import capability exists, Karnataka will be able to rely on other regions to a greater extent than before. Planning no longer needs to be based on local, physical generation addition to meet demand growth.

5.4.4 Utility Financial Performance

Overview

Both average costs and subsidy requirements have steadily increased over the nineties, despite an increase in industrial tariffs and connections, but due mainly to deterioration in delivery, increased power purchase costs and drop in agricultural tariffs. KPTCL's subsidy burden in the last few years has gradually increased to Rs. 1,800-2,200 crores, which corresponds to an average realisation shortfall of about Rs. 0.75 to Rs 1 per unit. The average cost of energy, after accounting for losses,

TABLE 5.9

Capacity Expansion in Development

Project	*Type*	*Capacity (MW)*	*Cost (Crore)*
KPCL	Hydro	1,290*	675**
KPCL-Bellary	Coal	500	2100
KPCL-Bidadi	Nat. Gas	1,400	4100
KPCL-Raichur	Coal	210	
Jindal	Coal/Gas	500	
Nagarjuna	Coal	1000	
Total		**4,900**	

Note: *Several projects lumped together, ** Excluding Almatti Dam Power Plant.

Source: KPCL Brochure, 2004, KPCL personnel.

TABLE 5.10

Historical Revenue Shortfall—Nominal Terms

Rs./Unit	*1990-1991*	*1997-1998*	*2002-2003*
Average Cost	0.83	1.79	3.49
Average Tariff	0.81	1.64	2.57
Revenue Shortfall	0.02	0.25	0.92

Source: Planning Commission, Annual Report on the Working of SEBs, 2001-2002, and KERC for 2002-2003.

TABLE 5.11

Financial Performance by ESCOM: 2002-2003

Rs./Unit	*Bangalore*	*Mangalore*	*Hubli*	*Gulbarga*
Average Revenue	3.08	3.09	2.27	2.34
Average Dist. Cost	0.48	0.74	0.68	0.65
Average Subsidy	0.41	0.48	1.58	1.67

Source: ESCOM filings with KERC.

is around Rs. 3.50 per unit. As can be seen from Table 5.10 both average costs and revenue shortfall over the nineties have increased. In fiscal year 2003-04, the subsidy burden is projected to decrease to about Rs. 1,400 crores. This is based in part on the improvement in loss reduction achieved in fiscal year 2002-03. Table 5.11 shows the regional differences in financial performance, which are clear fallouts of the companies consumer profiles. BESCOM and MESCOM have the larger shares of industrial and commercial customers, and therefore have the highest average revenue and lowest subsidy burden.

History of Tariff Changes

Table 5.12 shows the tariff changes over the last decade. Industrial rates have gone up, while agricultural tariffs have dropped from 0.87 to 0.70 Rs./unit in the last five years. These tariff changes indicate that cross subsidies from commercial and industrial customers to others, including agricultural, have likely increased. With the implementation of E-Act provisions, this trend of tariff-setting will have to be revisited. With loss reduction (particularly in collection), and tariff rationalisation, the subsidy burden could easily fall below Rs. 1,000 crores. Just a 5 per cent point increase in collections can yield over Rs. 200 crores in revenues. The impending tariff reforms in the E-Act will bring about more transparency in cost of supply and cross subsidies. This will allow regulators to better parse out utility inefficiencies from subsidies. This process should inform state policy on future subsidy provision.

TABLE 5.12

Historical Tariffs—Nominal and Average

Rs./Unit	*1997-1998*	*2002-2003*
Commercial	5.00	5.96
Industrial	3.03	4.45*
Agricultural	0.87	0.70

Source: Planning Commission, Annual Report on the Working of SEBs, 2001-2002, and KERC for 2002-2003.

Note: * Simple average of LT and HT industrial tariffs (4.41, 4.52), 2002-2003, from KPTCL's website.

5.4.5 The Electricity Act and Reforms

There are two Acts to guide power sector reforms in Karnataka: The Electricity Act of 2003 (E-Act), and the Karnataka Reform Act of 1999 (KA-Act). A core objective of the E-Act is to generate competition in power supply at the retail level. Three main components of the reforms in the power sector are open access, tariff rationalisation and privatisation. For instance, large customers (the E-Act specifies, at a minimum, customers with 1 MW load) can purchase power from other IPPs, captive power units, or utilities, while they still take delivery of some power from the SEB. This requires the creation of a set of rules to permit such transactions, and compensate SEBs for various delivery costs incurred. This is known as open access.

With a view to privatisation, the erstwhile Karnataka SEB has been unbundled into separate generation, transmission and distribution companies (ESCOMs) in four zones (Bangalore, Mangalore, Gulbarga and Hubli). The state government developed a privatisation strategy, which culminated in Draft Amendments to the 1999 Act to accommodate private distribution. BESCOM has a relatively good collection rate, low losses and lucrative customer profile, and it is expected to have a good success. However, other zones are in greater need of operational improvements. On their own they may not attract investors. privatisation, thus, may start and stop with BESCOM.

Karnataka has a poor record of IPP investments since 1991. Four IPP projects totalling 429 MW have materialised since 1991, including one coal, two diesel and one naphtha project. Two IPP projects have faced controversy over dubious project approval processes. Cogentrix's 1,000 MW project in Mangalore is a well-known failure, wherein the sponsors abandoned the project after several years of delay caused by public interest litigation concerning their spurious environmental clearances.

If Karnataka is to invest efficiently, in addition to improved adequacy analysis and planning, it must adhere strictly to a competitive, transparent process of project selection and abandon the MoU route. Already, KPCL is planning, in various stages of development, 3,500 MW of projects, all effectively on an MoU basis (Table 5.9). At the same time, several private IPPs are in development as well. Once these projects get underway, KERC may face tremendous pressure to approve these, even if they do not meet its needs assessment guidelines.

In order to permit SEBs to remain revenue-neutral, the E-Act calls for bringing customer tariffs close to their cost of supply, so as to gradually obviate the need for cross subsidies. Second, the E-Act allows to impose surcharges on migrating customers to compensate for the cross subsidies and stranded costs. In many ways the E-Act enables state regulators develop a road map for open access, calculate tariff based on cost of supply (eliminating cross subsidies), and calculate surcharges.

Under the E-Act there is much scope to develop a more sophisticated information infrastructure to understand customer load patterns—through metering, energy management systems, and better billing systems. Only with these could Karnataka develop a sound techno-economic basis for SEB and tariff restructuring.

Karnataka promulgated an Anti-Theft Law in 2002-2003, which has been implemented mostly by BESCOM. This has been one of the reasons why it has been able to reduce distribution losses in Bangalore, which contributed to the unprecedented loss reduction achieved in Fiscal Year 2002-03 discussed earlier. Finally, Karnataka has requisitioned funds from the Central Government as part of the Accelerated Power Reforms Development Program (APDRP) to invest in physical system upgrades. In 2003-04, 687 crores were obtained, and in 2004-05 the projected outlay is 1544 crores. Unfortunately, most of these funds (986 crores in 04-05) have been earmarked for Bangalore, which reflects an urban-centric approach. This represents a lost opportunity to have invested heavily in rural areas, which have the lowest quality and the highest consequent financial burden on the state.

5.4.6 Institutional Evolution in the State Power Sector

Karnataka has undertaken two important institutional and structural changes in the last one decade. The erstwhile KSEB was unbundled into generation, transmission and four distribution companies; and the Karnataka Electricity Regulatory Commission (KERC) was formed pursuant to the Electricity Regulatory Commission Act of 1998. Both these changes were critical for further reforms. The impending structural change is that of privatisation, which is much more controversial and uncertain.

As said earlier KSEB has been unbundled into six companies, pursuant to the KA Reforms Act 1999. KPCL is operating its thermal and hydro generating units as per the directions of KPTCL, which is the State Load Dispatch Centre (SLDC). KPTCL manages the SLDC and is the owner of the transmission network lines of 66 KV and above in Karnataka. The four zonal ESCOMs were corporatised and unbundled in June 2002, and have filed independent annual reports and accounts with the KERC. This has improved transparency and information access to utility operations.

Pursuant to the Electricity Act, KPTCL no longer bears the risks and responsibility of power purchase PPAs for generation with KPCL have been allocated to the ESCOMs at a single bulk supply tariff set by the KERC on the basis of projected costs and T&D losses. Thus, the KPTCL now operates as a 'wires' companies, while ESCOMs handles power purchase decisions.

The benefits of such a shift in purchase responsibilities are many. First, resource planning would cater more closely to load requirements. Second, the separation of transmission from bulk supply would reduce conflict of interest between the KPTCL as a transmission operator and market participant. Further, the allocation of PPAs to ESCOMs will provide an opportunity for the state to align supply costs with consumer tariffs, based on individual ESCOM's consumer profiles of cost-to-serve and affordability.

The evolution of the Three-Member Karnataka Electricity Regulatory Commission (KERC) is one of the noteworthy achievements of the sector. The KERC has already promulgated several regulations pursuant to the E-Act on open access, trading, guidelines for demand forecasting and power purchase, among others. They set tariffs for Fiscal year 2001-02 and Fiscal Year 2002-03 on the basis of a 5.5 and 5 per cent reduction in T&D losses respectively to force KPTCL to invest in loss reduction. They took a strong position against the controversial Tannir Bhavi Project by disallowing pass through of disputed fixed costs to consumers (KERC, 2003).

Unfortunately, the KERC's progressive orders and positions have been able to protect the consumer, but not the taxpayer. This is because the ultimate financial accountability of state-owned SEBs rests with the government. In the case of Tannir Bhavi, the project company was able to recover its dues from an escrow mechanism set up pursuant to the PPA. KPTCL did not achieve their loss reduction targets set by the KERC in Fiscal Year 2001-02, but the government agreed to cover the resulting increase in subsidies.

The KERC has been at the forefront of encouraging public participation and servicing consumer grievances. The KERC, through its Office of Consumer Advocacy, has supported workshops across the state, and publishes a bilingual, monthly newsletter, Consumer Power. The KERC funded the formation of ECON (Electricity Consumers' Network), which is a network of consumer organisations across the state.

Consumer organisations have benefited from the KERC's open process, and intervened on several occasions. KERC received over 9,000 objections to its tariff revision. It held public hearings to address most of these, but also held 243 personal hearings. ECON also conducted a survey of billing for consumers across the state. It has made other interventions related to IPP projects. Within the framework of E-Act, 2003, KERC can bring many such reforms in governance and accountability towards higher efficiency in the delivery system.

5.4.7 *Vision for the Future*

Power sector reforms in the nineties have achieved moderate success at best. The thrust of reforms was to attract independent power producers (IPPs) to boost generation investments. But the response on this has been very poor with only four projects, totalling 430 MW. The state has been attempting privatisation of distribution for a few years now, but without concrete results. Meanwhile, by 2001-02 the transmission and distribution (T&D) losses increased to 36 per cent (which improved marginally in 2003), and the annual subsidy burden increased to Rs. 1,800 crores.

The main success of the sector has come from institutional reforms. The erstwhile Karnataka State Electricity Board (KSEB) unbundled into separate generation, transmission and four distribution companies (ESCOMs). This has brought about some transparency in finances. The Karnataka Electricity Regulatory Commission (KERC) has made strides in forcing loss reduction and accountability. It has also provided a forum for an active consumer voice in Karnataka.

Looking forward, the Electricity Act 2003 (E-Act) has heralded a paradigm shift by allowing competition in all sectors, and offering the benefits to both wholesale and retail consumers (through open access). With generation delicensed, IPPs can exploit open access to sell power directly to consumers and across regions. The E-Act also calls for eliminating cross subsidies, which implies that tariffs have to be revised toward cost of supply. These provisions provide many opportunities to relieve industry and improve SEB's financial health, but they also pose considerable risks to residential and rural consumers. In the short term, the SEB could face stranded costs, and further revenue shortfalls.

But these outcomes will require proactive intervention by the state government, both in policy and rule-making. The vision for Karnataka's power sector therefore must be defined in terms of the building blocks needed to implement effectively and sustain these reforms at all level, of generation, transmission and distribution.

The first of these building blocks is the KERC. The E-Act relies heavily on the KERC's decisionmaking authority to implement reforms—including open access rules and tariff rationalisation—as well as to guide future utility operation, including regulation of power purchase, utility performance, and service quality. KERC needs to grow its internal capabilities and needs state's support to recognise and enforce its authority under the E-Act. For example, the KERC's authority to guide power purchase procurement must be adhered to ensure cost-efficient resource planning. Instead of negotiated and MOU-based contracts between project sponsors and government, competitive bidding processes must be adhered to. Public sector projects must also be subject to planning prudence and oversight. Second, a transparent decision making process under the aegis of the KERC that involves public participation, and forces scrutiny and accountability of individual decisions must be developed.

A second critical building block is that of an infrastructure for information assimilation, disclosure and verification about the customer. The E-Act's objective of eliminating cross subsidies requires understanding customers' cost of supply, which relies heavily on customer load profiles. Further, demand-side management, loss reduction and improved customer management (metering and billing) are necessary for reducing costs and future capacity needs. Distribution companies must be required to collect and disclose such information, and implement metering and IT system judiciously where most needed.

State financial support will be required in two forms: first, the process of subsidy reduction must be continued. The current level of Rs 1,500 crores should be reduced to below Rs 1,000 crores as tariffs are rationalised and T&D losses are reduced. Subsidy administration needs to change. The state must provide performance-based subsidies, targeted to specific consumers, and avoid truing up excess shortfalls. Second, the state must continue to provide financial support for physical system upgrade, including loss reduction, metering, billing and collection procedures with IT deployment, as it has in the Accelerated Power Reforms Development program (APDRP). However, the focus of APDRP has been excessively in the Bangalore ESCOM, and with questionable project selection. Instead, funding must be channelled to Gulbarga and Hubli, where investments are most needed and neglected.

Finally, policy makers must recognise that the E-Act, despite its far-reaching nature, has one major lacuna: that of improving SEB governance. Only transparency and public scrutiny of utility operations through the avenues for public participation and consumer grievance provided by the regulatory process can fill this void.

In summary, the vision of the power sector must be one that is built on transparent operations, efficient delivery, and competitive resource allocation and utilisation. The financial burden will only reduce if state utilities are forced to operate as corporate entities, face competition, and with full disclosure to the public. The state's role to facilitate this is to limit its involvement to provide clear, targeted subsidies upfront, provide financial support for physical system expansion, but allow the regulator to assume the reigns of decision making, and guide the sector toward financial viability under the auspices of the E-Act.

5.5 Road Development

5.5.1 Introduction

Roads are always recognised as an infrastructure and arteries of the nation. Roads play a decisive role in initiating and accelerating the process of development. Road network of Karnataka is 1,34,062 km in length and spreads over a geographical area of 1,91,791 sq. km of the state (as of March 2002), amounting to an average road length of 70 km per 100 sq. km. Started initially with a substantial responsibility of the state, in the recent periods participation of the private sector has been initiated in financing and developing road and bridges infrastructure. Karnataka Road Development Corporation has been set up in 1999 with the expectation that the corporation would raise resources from market and financial institution, and take up economically viable and strategically important roads for development and earn returns. In addition under various different central/state schemes financial assistance has been provided for investment in roads and bridges. For instance, the Karnataka State Highways Project with World Bank assistance is under formulation for the improvement of 900 kms of state highways. An amount of Rs 520 crores is provided in the Annual Plan 2003-04 for the project to be carried out from July 2001 to December 2006. As far as rural roads are concerned, Rs 106.40 crores have been provided during the Annual Plan of 2003-04 under Prime Minister Gramodaya Sadak Yojana (PMGSY). For the construction of rural roads through NABARD assistance and Rs 120 crores is provided during the Annual Plan of 2003-04.

Studies indicate that there exists a very high correlation between road development and indicators of economic developments such as gross domestic product, industrial and agricultural production. The investment in road sector generates greater employment than many sectors for the same investment. Investment in roads and employment generation as can be viewed in Table 5.13 and Figure 5.20.

TABLE 5.13

Recent Investment and Employment Linkages with Road Development

Year	*Investment (Rs. Cr.)*	*Employment (Lakh Persons)*
1981-86	4000	12
1986-91	11500	35
1991-96	21000	63
1996-01	27752	83

Source: Report of Task Force, *Road Improvement in Karnataka*, Sept. 2000.

5.5.2 Current Status in Karnataka

Total road length in Karnataka comprises of national highways, state highways, important district roads, other district roads, ZP roads, and village roads. The total length of road at present is of the order of 154 thousand kilometres in 2003-04, of which 62.70 per cent is surfaced road. On an average, about 80 kilometres of road exists per every 100 sq. km of geographical area. However, the distribution of the roads between the districts, and within the districts is not at all balanced. The national standard envisages a road network of about 100 kms per 100 sq. km of area. Thus, the state as a whole is lagging behind the suggested norms. The breakups of these by districts are shown in Appendix A-5.11 The road development by types of roads in Karnataka are shown in the subsequent tables.

TABLE 5.14

Details of Growth in Road Lengths in Karnataka State

Category of Roads	*Road Length—Km.*			
	1991-92	*1995-96*	*2000-01*	*2003-04*
National Highways	1997	1997	3728	3967
State Highways	11288	11395	9829	9590
Major District Roads	18063	28311	28247	38247
Other District Roads	3179	2090	-	-
Municipal Roads	8056	8366	8366	8366
Other Roads	91494	85361	104034	94034
All Roads	**133987**	**137520**	**145204**	**154164**

Note: Reduction in road length under some categories is due to upgradation of roads to higher categories.

From 2000-01 onwards, the category 'other roads' include ODR and village roads.

Source: Economic Survey, 2004-05 Government of Karnataka, March 2002.

In the rural segment there has been substantial improvement in the accessibility of villages by roads. There are as of 2003-04 only 27 villages which remain unconnected by roads in the state. In 1991-92, they were 199. The number of villages connected by all-weather roads is also progressing from 12649 in 1991-92 to 18,295 in 2003-04. And likewise, there has been a reduction in the number of villages connected by *kutcha* and non-motorable roads from 7433 to 3501 in this period.

In order to develop roads and bridges in rural areas the state has utilised the Rural Infrastructure Development Fund (RIDF) under its different tranches. The road length improved up to March 2003 was 1693 kilometres under RIDF-II, 2985 kilometres under RIDF-III, 2319 kilometres under RIDF-IV, 2535 kilometres under RIDF-V, 2201 kilometres under RIDF-VI, 518 kilometers under RIDF-VII and 44 kilometers under RIDF-VIII. Out of 1,535 number of road project works taken up under all these tranches, 1,336 projects have been completed. In respect of bridges, the number of

FIGURE 5.20

Recent Investment and Employment Linkages with Road Development (Investment in Crores)

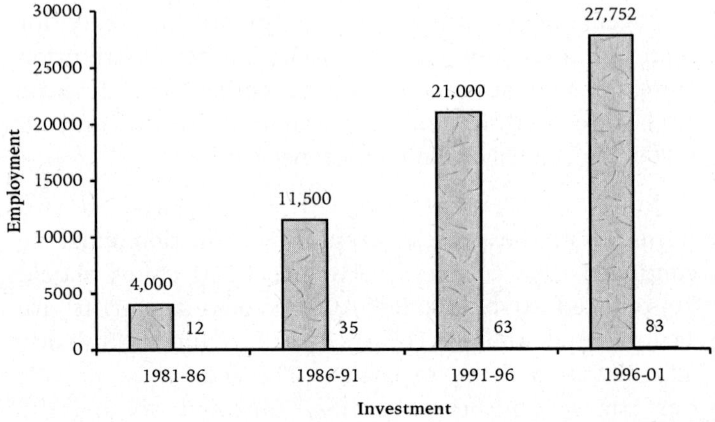

projects taken up was 391 in this period of which 339 were completed. Under the Pradhan Mantri Gram Sadak Yojana launched in 2000 in Karnataka, all unconnected rural inhabitations with a population of more than 1,000 persons is expected to be covered in the next 3 years. Funds for this programme are being provided by the Centre as additional central assistance and a sum some of Rs. 416.66 crore have been spent up to December 2004 and a road length of 1,336 kilometres has been asphalted.

A number of departments are associated in the development of road network. Agency-wise break up of road length in Karnataka is shown in Figure 5.21. It should be noted that *Zilla Panchayats* under the decentralised development have a larger share of responsibility in the development of rural roads in Karnataka (as can be seen from Figure 5.21 also). The quality of the roads viewed by the types of roads are shown in Table 5.15.

With respect to the lane width, out of the total 10,021 kms of state highways, single lane roads account for 59 per cent, intermediate lane roads 31 per cent, and less than 10 per cent are double lane roads. In case of major district roads, 93 per cent are single lane roads, 6 per cent intermediate lane roads and less than 1 per cent are double lane roads.

5.5.3 Organisational Structure on Road Development

Public Works Department (PWD)

PWD is one of the very old departments of the state. For a long time this is the only engineering department looking after all engineering related activities. Subsequently the original department was bifurcated into PWD (Roads and Buildings) and Irrigation Departments.

Associated organisations with PWD are:

- Karnataka Road Development Corporation Limited (KRDCL).
- Karnataka State Highway Improvement Project (KSHIP).
- The Chief Architect, Karnataka, Bangalore (CA).
- Port and Inland Water Transport (PIWT).
- Karnataka Land Army Corporation (KLAC).
- Karnataka State Construction Corporation (KSCC).
- Karnataka State Police Housing Corporation (KSPHC).
- Karnataka Engineering Research Station (KERS).

The major activities of the Department are:

- Collection of field data on existing road network (NH, SH and MDR) and bridges for upgradation, improvement and maintenance.
- Traffic survey and preparation of database.
- Investigation, survey, planning, design, preparation of estimates, tendering, implementation of new road projects, upkeep and routine annual maintenance of existing roads including quality assurance/checking.
- Preparation of estimates, including structural designs, for the buildings of Government departments, construction including quality checking/assurance.

With increasing deterioration of roads, it is necessary to concentrate more and more on maintenance. It is always felt that PWD should concentrate on maintenance activity of roads alone and leave the construction activity to other bodies/cells such as KRDCL and KSHIP. For instance, Karnataka state Highway Improvement Project (KSHIP) is a special project implementation unit (PIU) in the mainline PWD. The main functions of KSHIP are upgrading 991.38 km of state highways and major maintenance of 2,268.50 km of state highways, costing Rs. 2,030 crores (mainly funded by World Bank). KSHIP functions like a corporate entity with adequate financial freedom.

FIGURE 5.21

Agency-wise Breakup of Road Length

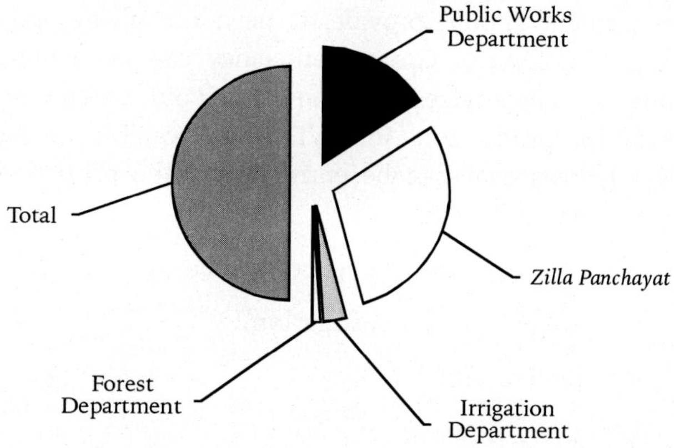

Source: Report of Task Force, *Road Improvement in Karnataka*, Sept. 2000.

The Task Force for Road Works set up by Government of Karnataka in September 2000 felt that there is no synergy between the road maintenance activity and building maintenance activity, without building construction. Therefore, it is recommended that the buildings related activity be separated from PWD.

TABLE 5.15

Surface Type-wise Breakup of Different Categories of Roads

Surface Type	*Length of Road Category—Km*								
	NH	*SH*	*MDR*	*ODR*	*Village Road*	*Taluka Devl. Road*	*Irrigation Dept.*	*Forest*	*Total*
Cement Concrete	90	108	24	--	6	--	3	--	231
Bituminous	3407	9899	22626	1116	10712	368	646	15	48789
Water Bound Macadam	--	8	5338	509	24445	6092	4791	490	41673
Others	--	6	259	9	9846	24686	3977	2077	40860
Total	**3497**	**10021**	**28247**	**1634**	**45009**	**31146**	**9417**	**2582**	**131553**

Source: Report of Task Force, 2000.

As an efficiency augmenting measure, there is a need to make a distinction between public provision and public production. In case of PWD, while Government should provide, it need not always produce the entire service. Greater efficiency can be achieved if some of the services are contracted out to the private sector for production. In PWD, it is possible to explore several areas that can be entrusted to the private sector for greater efficiency.

The ares of outsourcing could be:

- surveys and investigation,
- quality control,
- guest houses,
- vehicles of the department, and
- gangmen for maintenance.

Karnataka Road Development Corporation Limited (KRDCL)

KRDCL, which is the wholly owned enterprise of the state government, was created in July 1999 for the development of road infrastructure in Karnataka. It is governed by a Board, which is the final decision making authority. Main functions of KRDCL include:

- building roads and bridges,
- facilitate BOT entrepreneurship and collection of tolls,
- to take up priority works, and
- to borrow funds for the above.

The Corporation has taken up mini works and the important ones are:

i) Construction of 147 bridges on the various state highways and major district roads of the state.

ii) Maintenance of 7,038 kilometres of state highways,

iii) Strengthening and four-laning of existing Bangalore Mysore State Highway in different phases, etc.

Most of the road construction activity is undertaken by KRDCL and KSHIP, leaving behind only the maintenance of the road network (state highways and MDR) to PWD staff. The improvements and maintenance of national highway is taken up by PWD staff under National Highway Zone with funds from Government of India.

Vehicular traffic in Karnataka irrespective of inadequate infrastructure facilities has increased phenomenally in the recent year. In 1990-91, the number of motor vehicles were 14,33,000 and this increased more than four-fold to 48,76,000 in 2003-04. Motor vehicles per lakh of population has touched 6,879 in 2001-02 much above the all-India number of 5,723 but below that of Kerala, Tamil Nadu and Maharashtra.

5.5.4 Resource Allocation on Road Development

Inefficiency in resource utilisation stems from the processes followed in the Government towards decisionmaking and disbursement of funds. While funds do flow through the government, in case of the corporations/PIU, the funds are in the nature of a dedicated account and there is no uncertainly in terms of flow of funds. In the case of department, processes are too cumbersome, flow of funds is erratic, and disbursement of funds is influenced by several other considerations as can be seen from Table 5.16. It can be noted that in case of state funded works, only 40 per cent of the letter of credits (LoCs) sought are released whereas in the case of NABARD, almost the entire amount was released.

TABLE 5.16

Disbursement of Funds under Different Schemes (2000-01)

Month	*LoCs Sought (Rs. in lakhs)*		*LoCs Released (Rs. in lakhs)*	
	State	*NABARD*	*State*	*NABARD*
April 2000	273.1	700.0	0.0	0.0
May	258.0	900.0	25.5	1600
June	253.0	500.0	0.0	0.0
July	278.5	700.0	45.5	1200.0
August	490.5	500.0	236.6	500.0
September	475.0	600.0	147.0	600.0
October	446.0	525.0	112.0	516.0
November	529.0	350.0	63.0	350.0
December	521.0	600.0	205.0	587.0
January 2001	821.0	900.0	2.5	900.0
February	856.5	500.0	306.0	0.0
March	1985.0	500.0	1746.9	1000.0
Total	**7182.6**	**7275**	**2884**	**7253**

Source: Functional Review of PWD, October 2001.

The increase in growth in the traffic volume, the ever increasing loads and overloading cause greater distress on the road pavement, calling for higher outlays for the maintenance and development of the road network. Proper maintenance is essential to provide desired quality of riding and performance. The budgetary allocations both at national and state level always fall short of the requirements.

The existing sources of financing are as under:

- government budget including sovereign borrowings,
- central road fund,
- fee/toll on bridges,
- market committee fee, and
- other levies/surcharge.

The plan outlays and expenditure on roads and bridges showed a quantum jump from Rs. 953 crore during Ninth Five Year Plan period (1997-2002) to Rs. 3949.46 crore in the Tenth Five Year Plan period (2002-2007). In the annual plans of the Tenth Five Year Plan which was lower in the First Annual Plan 2002-03 at Rs. 602.39 crores was raised to Rs. 1,074.94 crore in 2003-04 and little less than this in 2004-05 at Rs. 1,057.89 crores. Similarly, in respect of outlays were enhanced progressively. But, as observed earlier, these are far inadequate to meet the ever increasing traffic volume in the state. This is revealed also in the budgetary allocation of the state. In Karnataka, budgetary allocations are not adequate to meet the growing demands. Budgetary allocations of the state in the last five years is shown in Table 5.17.

TABLE 5.17

Budgetary Allocations—PWD: Government of Karnataka (State Highways and Main District Roads)

(Rs. in Lakhs)

		1995-96	*1996-97*	*1997-98*	*1998-99*	*1999-00*
Plan	Allocation	5437.11	5180.00	4449.00	2203.00	1830.00
	Expenditure	4605.10	7752.82	4376.48	1865.06	1272.46
Non-plan	Allocation	6149.66	6606.41	9500.00	11800.00	14782.62
	Expenditure	6620.33	7741.33	7466.04	9838.71	10092.70

Source: Report of Task Force, *Road Improvement in Karnataka*, Sept. 2000.

Clearly, there is a need to enhance budgetary allocations on road developments. It is estimated that the funds needed to maintain the existing network in Karnataka are about Rs. 9,100 crores at 2000-01 price level. Thus, the budgetary allocation are quite insufficient to meet this demand.

In order to meet the ever-increasing demand for maintenance and to expand the road network, there is a need to tap all possible sources of finance—public, private and foreign. It is, therefore, recommended to create a separate road fund for the state. The funds raised from every source may be credited into this fund.

- Levy of cess on transport related items-petrol, diesel, various engine oils, CNG used as fuel by automobiles, tyres and tubes, motor vehicle spares, etc.
- Toll on roads and bridges—developed out of dedicated fund.
- Special cess on the use of the roadway by agencies like electricity, telephone, water supply, sewerage, Internet service providers, cable operators, etc.
- Betterment levy on land and property where there is value addition due to formation of new roads.
- Commercial exploitation of land adjoining highways—motels and resorts, service facilities, workshops, truck terminals, etc.
- Private participation and development of roads-construction of bypasses, bridges, improvements of road on BOT, BOOT, BOST, BT, BOO, BOLT, etc.
- External aid—World Bank, ADB, OECF, borrowing from domestic financial institutions.
- Fines and penalties levied on vehicles carrying overload.
- Certain contribution/levies by industries such as cement manufacturers, vehicle manufacturers, etc.
- A cess on activities such as ore carrying, movement of granite blocks, etc. that cause higher distress to the road pavement.
- Open market borrowings by bonds, debentures.
- Road cess on first time registration in the state.
- Highway Infrastructure Savings scheme similar to NSCs, KVPs, etc.

It is advisable to give top priority for improvement in road maintenance standards in the state by making the required investment. A part of this expenditure may be recovered from the beneficiaries or the road users, by charging special levy or cess on petroleum products, tyres and automobile parts. This is in tune with the present day concept of user or beneficiaries to pay for the services.

The National Highway Act 1956 and Karnataka Highway Act 1964 have been amended to permit private entrepreneur to undertake National Highway and state road projects on build own and transfer (BOT) basis and recover the investments through tolls. Policies have been framed both by the Central and the state governments extending financial support to investors. New road links such as bypass roads and major bridges may be opened for private sector under BOT system.

5.5.5 Towards Better Governance

New thinking on several counts are necessary if major shifts in road development and maintenance are to be scaled up. Capacity building and human resource development on a continual level is a must for any development organisation. Side by side, one has to improve the capability for efficient delivery of programmes and this would need attention on several fronts, first being the PWD and KRDCL departments, directly concerned with roads.

Secondly, some alternative strategy is also worth experimenting. For sustained improvement in implementation of projects, development of contracting industry in the highways sector on healthy lines is imperative. A major push in the direction of improving the contracting industry in India came in 1985 when for the first time, the Government of India, while seeking loan assistance for roads from the World Bank (WB) accepted to adopt international competitive bidding (ICB) procedures for the highway projects forming part of the loan package. In order to encourage modernisation and mechanisation (both these words were considered synonymous), size of the project was kept at Rs. 100 to Rs. 150 million at that time. State PWDs and NHAI have huge road upgradation programmes in their hands. The volume of works envisaged is 5 to 6 times the current capacity of contractors in the highway sector. It will, thus, be necessary to create conditions of growth for domestic contractors and support from foreign contractors.

Thirdly, some changes in construction technology are also necessary. India's road construction technology was essentially labour-oriented till the 1980s. The strategy then suited the needs to absorb the unemployed in road construction and maintenance, working with small size of contract packages, and loaded with a policy of import-substitution, which prevented the state-of-art equipment to be imported into the country. The economic reforms introduced in 1991 has enabled a major impetus to import world-class road making equipments. The tightening of the specifications facilitated the use of modern equipment. The use of vibratory rollers for compaction has become common. Electronic sensor controlled asphalt pavers have replaced the old technology mechanical pavers.

Fourthly, there is a need for consistency in the quality of road construction and incorporation of quality aspects in the organisations and agencies entrusted with the task of road construction has assumed paramount importance. Adoption of ISO 9000 systems has a good impact on quality, productivity and cost reduction. Both the government departments and the private sector contractors and consultants are progressing in acquiring such certifications as a demonstration of their determination and resolve in supplying quality product and/or service.

The Indian Roads Congress have evolved guidelines on quality systems for roads and bridges to facilitate preparation of appropriate quality system for individual road and bridge projects. Application of these guidelines by all those involved in road building activity would lead to achievement of high quality in highway projects. The major components of quality assurance consists of:

- supplier's quality policy,
- purchaser's quality policy,
- internal quality systems,
- inspection and audit,
- documentation, and
- work culture.

5.5.6 Policy and Vision for the Future

Karnataka is one of the well developed states of India. However, the growth of road network in the state of Karnataka has not kept pace with the requirements. It is a recognised fact that modernisation of infrastructure, specially transportation plays a vital role in enhancing the growth rate any region. It is important to recognise the fact that road connectivity to rural areas is a must for improving the socio-economic conditions of rural people. The major objectives of the road sector development should aim at creating adequate capacity to match the demand, all-weather roads for all villages, modernisation of construction activities and appropriate strategies to maintain the road networks.

The state is borrowing money from external agencies, specially from World Bank to the tune of Rs. 2,300 crores for maintenance and upgradation of state highways. Government of Karnataka has created a Special Cell, known as Karnataka State Highway Improvement

Project (KSHIP) as a project implementation unit in the main line Public Works Department to utilise these funds. Karnataka Road Development Corporation was set up in 1999 to undertake maintenance of 75,000 kilometres of road network and construction of 150 bridges and to borrow money from external agencies. Along with these privatised ventures, the PWD also requires a face life. It should be made responsible only for road works, delinking from building maintenance activities.

A perusal of Public Works Department expenditure reveals that the meagre amounts allocated to training and development of staff, is not utilised. In this era of specialisation it is essential to upgrade skill and competence of the staff of the department through refresher courses, long-term training and research. There is no human resource policy followed in rewarding the performers in the department. There is an urgent need to upgrade capacity building and human resource development in the organisation associated with road development.

There is also a need to change the current practices in the contracting industry and construction technology. Quality systems for different components of the road sector need to be reviewed and upgraded. It is felt that quality assurance activity may be outsourced for better quality control. The state does not maintain a well-developed database covering the road network, traffic data, accident records and maintenance information. Development of such a database helps in preparing long-term maintenance management plans. Being an IT hub in the country, the state can develop such a database very easily.

In order to derive optimal benefits from scarce resources it is essential to develop master plans for roads in each district, based on the guidelines developed by Indian Roads Congress. Combining all the district master plans could develop a perspective plan covering a time period of 20 years. It helps in prioritising the road construction activities in different districts based on the resource availability.

There is a necessity to augment the resources for highway projects by allowing private sector participation in highway projects. It is estimated that to maintain the existing road network in Karnataka, about Rs. 9,000 crores are required at 2001 price level. Furthermore, a number of additional levies on transport related activities such as additional cess on petrol/diesel, motor vehicle spares, etc. could be considered. It is felt that a Karnataka Road Fund may be created and all the revenues generated for the road development may be transferred to this fund. In order to encourage professionalism in road sector this fund may be managed by a group of experts drawn from different stakeholders.

The vision for the state should be to raise the road coverage to around one km per one sq. km area. Such a vision should be targeted in the next 10 years, ahead of other developments. After all 'it is not the wealth that builds the road but it is the roads that build the wealth'.

5.6 Rail Infrastructure

5.6.1 An Overview

One of the critical sectors which determines the pace of economic development of a state is the basic transport infrastructure, of which rail network is very important, perhaps next only to roads. Karnataka as a state has a unique geographic position as it is flanked by major metro cities *viz.* Chennai in the extreme east, Hyderabad in north, and Bombay on western side; besides, Karnataka has a coastal belt with an average width of 50 to 80 kms and covers a distance of about 267 kms from north to south with Mangalore as a major commercial port and nine other minor/ intermediate ports. Bangalore, one of the fastest growing cities in the world, is the preferred investment destination for many multinational and global business houses. Karnataka has emerged as an educational hub in the country, attracting students and teachers from all over the country. It has also recently, become a hub of employment opportunities for various backward areas of the country. For a city that is so networked, transport connectivity is essential. The northern parts of the state are rich in mineral resources, especially iron ore it is against this backdrop that the development of rail infrastructure for Karnataka state assumes increasing significance.

5.6.2 Recent Policy Development and Impacts

The three major factors that have influenced the growth and development of railways, which in turn had a major impact on the economy of the state and will continue to do so in the future, are the following:

- active participation of the state government in major railway projects;
- the uni-gauge policy of Indian Railways, and
- formation of South Western Railway.

In September 2000, Government of Karnataka entered into an Memorandum of Understanding with the Ministry of Railways to form the Karnataka Rail Infrastructure Development Company Ltd., (K-RIDE) with the specific objective of developing and financing rail infrastructure projects in the state. K-RIDE has since been incorporated and a business plan prepared. Among the projects taken up by K-RIDE, that would play an important role, in development in the years to come are the following:

- Hassan-Mangalore gauge conversion project (185 kms. at the cost of Rs. 312 crores). This line provides critical linkage to the New Mangalore port for movement of iron ore, general cargo (about 4.66 million tonnes per year), and POL.
- Sholapur-Gadag gauge conversion: Connectivity to heritage and tourists centres like Bijapur, Hampi, Aihole, Badami, Pattadakal and Koodalsangama. GoK and MoR are jointly implementing this 134 crores project that is expected to be completed by 2005 to handle a cargo traffic of 2.33 million tonnes per year.
- Conversion of part of the line between Sholapur and Bijapur (94 kms.) was completed in 1998 and balance 190 kms. stretch from Bijapur to Gadag remains to be converted.
- New line between Kottur and Harihar: (65 km, Rs. 124 crores): The cost sharing is between GoK (2/3) and MoR (1/3). The project when completed will provide a direct line for moving iron ore from Bellary and Hospet to Mangalore port.
- Doubling of Bangalore-Kengeri-Ramanagaram line (45 kms., Rs. 91 crores): One-third cost being borne by Railways and two-thirds by Government of Karnataka.
- Hospet-Guntakal doubling (115 kms. Rs. 154 crores): This is expected to handle iron ore traffic of about 12.67 million tonnes per year.
- New line between Hubli and Ankola: (167 kms., Rs. 998 crore) The projected traffic for this line after commissioning is expected to be about 11.72 million tonnes per year.

Besides these K-Ride projects, as many as 43 rail overbridges and rail underbridges have been sanctioned on cost sharing basis with Government of Karnataka. In addition, there are as many as at least 5 new projects under consideration.

South Western Railway was created as a new railway zone consisting of 3 divisions at Hubli, Mysore and Bangalore and with headquarters at Hubli. It has provided a major impetus in the development of the Railway over the state, covering 2,559 BG and 492 MG kilometres touching 5 states *viz.* Karnataka, Andhra Pradesh, Tamil Nadu, Maharashtra and Goa. With its head quarters at Hubli, it is expected that this will also enable to reduce the regional disparity within Karnataka. A large number of gauge conversion projects have already been initiated after the creation of this new division. About 25 gauge conversion projects have been either completed or in progress, whereas 25 projects have been identified with a total of 2,645 kilometre lengths to be taken up in due course.

5.6.3 Impact of Gauge Conversion on Rail Traffic

The impact of gauge conversion, in terms of traffic handled, over the three divisions in Karnataka has not been uniform. Being a passenger traffic oriented division, having no major freight loading station in this jurisdiction no major freight change has been observed in Bangalore Division, attributable to gauge conversion.

Mysore Division which is a small division in terms of traffic handled, recorded significant impact in respect of operating indices. A comparison of 1985-86 and 2002-03 situation (Tables 5.18 and 5.19) indicates that:

- The wagon balance has dropped by 32 per cent, because of 95 per cent improvement in wagon turnaround.
- The wagon kms have also improved by 9.62 per cent.

TABLE 5.18

Performance Prior to Gauge Conversion (Mysore Division)

Category	*1985-86*	*1986-87*	*1987-88*	*1988-89*	*1989-90*
Wagon Balance	2273	2206	2197	2195	1948
Wagon Turnaround	4.3	4.2	4.3	3.9	3.7
Throughput	1595	1531	1596	1584	1349
NTKMs	756	754	804	847	746
Wkms	63.8	68.2	74.6	74.7	62.5
Loading	92	90	109	92	76
EKMs (Steam)	105	122	119	132	145
EKMs (Diesel)	453	452	433	447	451

Source: RITES Report-1.

TABLE 5.19

Performance Post Gauge Conversion (Mysore Division)

Category	*1995-96*	*1996-97*	*1997-98*	*1998-99*	*1999-00*	*2000-01*	*2001-02*	*2002-03*	*2003-004*
Wagon Balance	688	885	1050	1227	1114	1192	1581	1548	1523
Wagon turnaround	2.6	2.8	2.9	2.9	2.5	2.4	3.0	2.6	2.2
Throughput	736	962	1015	1350	1694	1695	1357	2218	2348
NTKMs	1061	172	994	1050	1312	1585	1232	1653	-
WKMs	88.7	85.3	82.0	85.0	104	120	102	116	120
Loading	44.1	59.0	97	122	105	136	167	197	246
EKMs	476	510	525	420	555	557	588	556	545

Source: RITES Report-1.

- The locomotive utilisation (EKM) has shown an improvement of 30 per cent.
- The total quantum of traffic handled has also improved substantially and increase of 125 per cent. This is despite the fact that BG wagons carry one-third more freight.
- The number of wagon releases has increased by 49 per cent. The number of wagons moved (i.e. throughput) over the divisions has also increased by 47 per cent.
- As far as loading is concerned, the best loading done during MG was 5.83 1.1 tonnes in 1987-88 as against 1.67 tonnes in 2002-2003—an increase of 130 per cent.

The Hubli Division showed maximum change as the division's growth was drastically handicapped by its meter gauge infrastructure as can be see from Tables 5.20, 5.21 and 5.22. Till the broad gauge conversions were pending, the Hubli division was very seriously affected in its traffic handling. The gauge conversion, therefore, resulted in a phenomenal growth in traffic on the Hubli division, as can been from the indicators such as:

- Loading went up from 2.7 metric tonne to 8.5 metric tonne an increase of 214 per cent.
- Passenger service improved steadily after gauge conversion and went up from 9,197 to in 1994-95 to 28,087 in 2002-2003—an increase of 205 per cent.
- The total earnings went up from Rs 11,073 to 42,473 lakhs—an increase of 280 per cent.

As far as passenger traffic is concerned, the number of passengers carried by the South Western Railways went up from 14.3 million in 1994-95 to 26.9 million in 2001-02-an increase of 88 per cent.

TABLE 5.20

Freight Loading (Hubli Division)

Year	*Loading in MT*	*Year*	*Loading in MT*
1994-95	2.749	2000-01	6.615
1995-96	2.444	2001-02	7.788
1996-97	3.225	2002-03	8.524

Source: RITES Report-1.

TABLE 5.21

Passenger Services (Hubli Division)

Year	*Total Passenger*		*Year*	*Total Passenger*	
	Mail/Exp.	*Pass*		*Mail/Exp.*	*Pass*
1994-95	3620	5577	2000-01	8700	18716
1995-96	5934	9710	2001-02	8964	18689
1996-97	7623	10984	2003-03	9222	18865

Source: RITES Report-1.

TABLE 5.22

Earnings (Hubli Division)

(Rs. lakhs)

Year	*Earnings*
1991-92	11073
1992-93	12057
1993-94	14747
2000-01	36551
2001-02	41712
2002-03	42473

Source: RITES Report-1.

5.6.4 Future Directions

While surveys for gauge conversions and new line construction have been conducted and many projects are underway, it would be essential to ensure that execution is completed in the shortest possible time. The Indian Railways are facing a resource crunch with dwindling budgetary support and reducing freight earnings. While state sharing of financial resources has helped mitigate this problem to some extent it may be judicious to consider the possibilities of private participation in some of these projects. Already Konkan Railway Corporation is operating in about 200 kms along the coastal line of Karnataka. As mentioned earlier, many of these projects would benefit export and movement of goods from interior areas. Hence, possible partners for these sections would be iron ore exporters, coffee growers and other commodity exporters.

As far as the problem of Bangalore city is concerned, immediate action to introduce metrorail system is necessary. The growth of population in Bangalore urban area, from just about 16.64 lakh in 1971, having gone up to 56.87 lakh in 2001 is indicative enough to make a case for a rapid rail network inside the city. A good suburban rail network (either underground or elevated like in Chennai) could help considerably traffic congestion without disrupting the road network. The Government of Karnataka has commissioned a study for evaluating the feasibility of commuter rail services for Bangalore. In terms of the study, the estimated cost of development works for operationalisation of commuter rail services is estimated at Rs.1025 crore, which includes cost of the land also, and to be implemented in the phased manner. The dialogue on the proposal for cost sharing is going on with the Ministry of Railways and Union Ministry of Urban Development.

The Government of Karnataka is funding the implementation of ROB/RUB projects in the state on a 50:50 cost sharing basis with the Ministry of Railways. The Ministry of Railways has sanctioned 38 projects in the state such projects. The Infrastructure Development Corporation (iDeCK) (Karnataka) Ltd. has been providing advisory assistance to Hassan-Mangalore Rail Development Corporation (HMRDC) for implementation of the Hassan-Mangalore gauge conversion project including technical assistance to HMRDC coordination with Government of Karnataka, banks and equity investors for mobilising the necessary funds for the project and management of the company's finances. The project which is in advance stage is nearing completion. iDeCK has also prepared a business plan for implementation of the development of rail link to Devanahalli Airport. The business plan which has been reviewed has been accepted by the technical committee and is awaiting the approval of the State Cabinet whereupon it would be posed the Ministry of Railways.

5.6.5 Ports and Airports

In Karnataka state, the coastal belt with an average width of 50 to 80 km covers a distance of about 267 km from north to south encompassing 3 districts *viz.*, Uttara Kannada, Dakshin Kannada and Udupi. It has a total of 10 ports. The ports in Karnataka need further development and a New Port Policy has been formulated to meet this objective. The New Port Policy emphasises the strategic location of the Karnataka coast, halfway between Gujarat and Kerala on the Western Coast line. It also stresses the need to develop export-oriented and maritime industries like ship building. Integration of the growth of fisheries with port development is also emphasised in port policy. The Government has decided to seek private investment for the development of ports. Annual Plan allocation for the development of port and inland water transport has however seen a decline. Port-wise traffic handled also shows a declining trend (Table 5.23). Expenditure under Annual Plan 2002-03 was Rs 7 crore whereas annual outlay for 2003-04 is Rs 6 crore. Both Mangalore port and Karwar port get an allocation of Rs. 2.5 crore in the current Annual Plan. Port-wise traffic handled by the major ports are shown in Table 5.23. A sum of Rs. 60 lakhs has been provided in the Annual Plan 2003-04 for the development of railway over- and under-bridges on state highways and major district roads.

TABLE 5.23

Port-wise Traffic Handled: 2001-2004

(Thousand Tonnes)

Port	*2001-02*	*2002-03*	*2003-04 (anticipated)*
Karwar	556	545	550
Malpe	9	10	10
Mangalore (Old)	182	120	122
Other Ports	1	1	1
Total	**748**	**676**	**683**

Source: Annual Plan 2003-04 and Director of Ports and Inland Water Transport.

Bangalore International Airport Project has achieved some important milestones during 2004-05. The Bangalore International Airport Limited (BIAL) successfully concluded the Concession Agreement with Government of India in July 2004 after protracted negotiations and discussions with Government of India for over two years. this is considered to be a major breakthrough for this project as this is the first such agreement for public-private partnership venture in the aviation sector of the country. The other achievemnents include: (i) handing over of forest land of 1,394 acres 20 *guntas* for forest department to KSIIDC, (ii) KIADB successfully acquired an extent of 2,649 acres of private land and handed over the same to KSIIDC in August 2004 and Revenue Department has also transferred an extent of 403 acres to KSSIDC through mutation. Thus, a total of 4,266 acres of land has been assembled for this project, (iii) executing the land lease agreement between KSIIDC and BIAL for agreeing to these an extent of 3,884 acres, 25 *guntas* to BIAL in January 2005, (iv) state support agreement providing for state financial support of Rs. 350 crores for the project apart from other concessions was executed in January 2005, (v) all other major project agreements such as EPC agreement, OMS agreement, CNS/ATM agreement and financing agreement have been concluded, (vi) amendment in the shareholders' agreement has been finalised, (vii) ICICI bank has sanctioned a rupee term loan of Rs.743 crores to BIAL for financing the project, (vii) National Highway Authority of India have finally agreed to provide Trumpet Inter-change from National Highway-7 to meet an access road to the airport site, (viii) with an achievement of financial close the project is expected to take-off immediately and the airport is expected to be ready in a period of 33 months from then.

As regards the development of minor airport and regional air services the Bajpe Airport at Mangalore is on the improvement and upgradation path with a new runway under construction. At the Hubli Airport, Airport Authority of India (AAI) is providing night landing facilities in order to commence night air services between Hubli and Mumbai. Proposal for setting up the airport at Gulbarga is under the consideration of Government of India. The Mysore Airport also will be re-operationalised and upgraded.

References

Chowdary, T.H. (2003). "Challenges for Indian Telecommunications: the 1990's and beyond", in Gary Madden (ed.), *World Telecommunications Markets, The International Handbook of Telecommunications Economics*, Vol.III, pp.400-412, Edward Elgar, Cheltenham.

CMIE (2001). *Infrastructure: January 2001*, Economic Intelligence Service, Centre for Monitoring Indian Economy Pvt. Ltd., Mumbai.

———. (2003). *Infrastructure: February 2003*, Economic Intelligence Service, Centre for Monitoring Indian Economy Pvt. Ltd., Mumbai.

———. (2004). *Infrastructure: March 2004*, Economic Intelligence Service, Centre for Monitoring Indian Economy Pvt. Ltd., Mumbai.

Dossani, Rafiq (2003). *Telecommunication Reform in India*, Viva Books Pvt. Ltd., New Delhi.

Government of Karnataka (1995). *Brochure on Irrigation Statistics in Karnataka, 1980-81 to 1993-94*, Department of Economics and Statistics, Bangalore.

———. (1995). *Groundwater Resource Status of Karnataka as on 31st December 1994*, Department of Mines and Geology Bangalore.

Government of India. (2003). *Annual Administrative Report for the Year 2002-03*, Karnataka Postal Circle, Bangalore.

———. *Annual Report 2002-03*, Department of Telecommunications, New Delhi.

———. (2004). *Annual Report 2002-03*, Department of Telecommunications, New Delhi.

———. *Annual Plan-2002-03*, Vol. I, Department of Planning, Statistics & Science and Technology.

———. (2002). *High Power Committee for Redressal of Regional Imbalances*, Final Report June.

———. *Irrigation in Karnataka-2002-03*, Irrigation Department, *http://www.waterresourecs.kar.nic.in,.*

———. *Irrigation in Karnataka-2002*, Water Resource Department, *http://www.kar.nic.in.*

———. *Karnataka Budget Document 2003-04*, Detailed Estimates of Expenditure. Vol. II.

———. (1993). *Stagnation of Agricultural Productivity in Karnataka during 1980s*, Report of the Expert Committee, Bangalore.

———. (1994). *Economic Survey 1993-94*, Planning Department, Bangalore.

———. (1995). *Minor Irrigation Statistics at a Glance 1994-95*, Minor Irrigation Department. Bangalore.

———. (1997). *Irrigation in Karnataka*. Irrigation Department, Bangalore.

———. (1997). *Report on Studies on Conjunctive Use of Surface and Groundwater Resources in Ghataprabha Irrigation Projects*, Directorate of Southwest Region, CGWB Bangalore.

———. (1993). *Public Investments in Irrigation in Karnataka: Issues in Financial Management*. Special Studies Division of the Planning Department, Bangalore.

———. (2000). *Vision 2020 Document.*

———. (2003-04). *Economic Survey of Karnataka 2003-04.*

Indian Roads Congress (1984). *Road Development Plan for India.*

Karnataka Electricity Regulatory Commission, (2003). *KA Tariff Order 2003*, Karnataka Electricity Regulatory Commission.

———. *Monthly Data Furnished to KERC*, 2003-2004, *www.kerc.org* (Power Data / Distribution).

KPTCL website (2004). *www.kptcl.com.*

Narayana, M.R. (2003). *Consumer Demand for Telecom Services in Karnataka and Goa*, Department of Telecommunications, Government of India, New Delhi.

Prayas Energy Group (2002). *A Good Beginning, but Challenges Galore*, Survey of Electricity Regulatory Commission in India.

Planning Commission of India. *Annual Report on the Working of SEBs*, 2001-2002.

PWD, 1999 and 2000. Budget Book.

Raju K.V, Ashok Gulati, and Ruth Meinzen-Dick (1999). "Krishna Bhagya Jal Nigam Limited: Pointer Towards Institutional Reforms in Irrigation Financing ?", Paper presented in the National Workshop on *Participatory Irrigation Management*, held on January 19-24, Hyderabad, Andhra Pradesh, organised by the Ministry of Water Resources, Government of India.

Ramanayya T.V, Shyamal Roy, V. Nagadevara (2001). *Functional Review of Public Works Department*, October.

Report of Task Force, *Road Improvement in Karnataka*, September 2000.

TRAI (Telecom Regulatory Authority of India) (2003). *The Indian Telecom Services Performance Indicators : April-June'03*, TRAI House, New Delhi.

World Bank (1991). *India Irrigation Sector Review* (in two volumes), Washington D.C.

———. (1995). *Economic Developments in India: Achievements and Challenges*, A World Bank Country Study, Washington D.C.

APPENDIX A-5.1

Contribution of Communication Sector to State Income: 1994-95 to 2002-03

Indicators of State Income and Communication	*1994-95*	*1995-96*	*1996-97*	*1997-98*	*1998-99*	*1999-00*	*2000-01*	*2001-02*	*2002-03*
***Sector* Gross State Domestic Income (GSDP) at constant (1993-94) prices**									
Annual Growth of Communication Sector (%)	16.64	24.43	19.32	19.99	10.29	32.00	38.08	14.40	22.50
Share of Communication Sector (%)	1.92	2.25	2.46	2.76	2.70	3.39	4.26	4.92	5.80
Share of Communication Sector in Tertiary Sector (%)	4.38	4.62	4.81	4.99	4.77	4.90	5.12	5.23	5.95
Net State Domestic Income at constant (1993-94) prices									
Annual Growth of Communication Sector (%)	16.98	26.59	20.88	21.63	10.10	35.20	40.58	14.89	23.70
Share of Communication Sector (%)	1.79	2.16	2.39	2.74	2.65	3.42	4.36	5.09	6.00
Share of Communication Sector in Tertiary Sector (%)	4.56	5.24	5.62	6.23	6.18	7.60	9.43	10.16	11.61

Source: Computed by using the basic data from the files (GSDP_NSDP2004&DIS 01_02.xls SDP2003 (2) page 1 through 4) in the State Income Division, Directorate of Economics and Statistics, Government of Karnataka (Bangalore).

APPENDIX A-5.2

Select Indicators of Growth of Public Telecom Services in Karnataka State: 1991-92 to 2002-03

Indicators	*1991-92*	*1992-93*	*1993-94*	*1994-95*	*1995-96*	*1996-97*	*1997-98*	*1998-99*	*1999-00*	*2000-01*	*2001-02*	*2002-03*
Equipped Capacity per Exchange	250	280	328	413	462	546	658	766	950	1105	1229	1251
DEL per Exchange	220	241	272	334	388	462	565	654	777	903	985	1013
Loading (Per cent)	88.04	86.20	82.98	80.95	83.96	84.61	85.92	85.39	81.79	81.78	80.18	81.01
Teledensity	0.83	0.95	1.08	1.34	1.60	1.97	2.45	2.89	3.56	4.33	4.91	5.18
Number of Metered Telephone Calls per DEL ('000)	5.12	5.61	4.89	5.48	7.45	7.53	7.79	7.52	6.28	6.37	4.56	5.58
Total Number of Public Telephones	9469	11458	14020	21462	26883	34152	45330	53061	61911	75656	89550	128853
Per cent of Local Public Telephones	66.77	59.34	54.35	23.72	22.42	19.46	18.41	16.55	15.01	15.20	19.25	40.12
Per cent of STD Public Telephones	21.47	26.57	28.58	28.83	27.88	29.49	35.65	39.45	43.31	49.04	50.53	38.88
Per cent of Village Public Telephones	11.76	14.09	17.07	47.45	49.70	51.05	45.94	44.00	41.67	35.76	30.22	21.01
Total Public Telephones as a Per cent Of Total DEL	2.52	2.64	2.76	3.33	3.43	3.51	3.69	3.62	3.38	3.35	3.46	4.72
DEL as a Percentage of Registered Demand	73.97	71.30	75.38	83.85	83.61	85.48	91.64	94.00	84.63	92.92	96.10	95.60
Per cent of Billing Complaint	0.99	1.01	0.75	0.49	0.28	0.23	0.2	0.15	0.13	0.1	0.1	0.1
Number of Telex Lines	2956	2982	2940	2907	2753	2221	1698	1245	954	582	582	582
Telex Lines as a Percentage of Registered Telex Demand	82.85	78.74	85.61	95.44	99.64	99.91	99.94	100.00	100.00	100.00	100.00	100.00
Number of Metered Telex Call Units per Telex Line ('000)	15.05	14.27	8.57	8.39	7.70	4.57	4.15	3.53	5.00	4.39	2.92	2.63
Number of Trunk Calls Booked ('000)	219.96	189.21	140.69	112.52	93.52	169.8	62.62	53.9	41.21	35.56	35.56	35.56
Effective Trunk Calls as a Percentage of Trunk Calls Booked	80.25	78.80	78.75	78.42	77.02	78.50	84.11	80.15	80.64	81.24	83.75	83.65
Total Number of Inland Telegram Booked ('000)	**3798**	**4342**	**4300**	**4456**	**4052**	**4154**	**4050**	**3695**	**3122**	**2228**	**2228**	**2228**

Note: DEL refer to Direct Exchange Lines. This is a measure of number of fixed telephones or landline connections.

Source: Computed by using basic data in various issues of annual reports of the Karnataka Telecom Circle (Bangalore).

APPENDIX A-5.3

Interdistrict Variations in the Provision of Telecom Services: 2002-03

Telecom	*Percentage of Telephone Exchange in State's Total*	*Population (in '000 Served by One Telephone Exchange*	*Per Cent of DEL in State's Total*	*Teledensity*	*Loading Per Cent*	*Per Cent of Waitlisted Telephones*	*DEL as a Per Cent of Registered Demand*
Bangalore (Rural)	3.71	18.77	3.11	4.56	81.1	7.36	91.75
Bangalore (Urban)	3.97	60.96	32.24	13.61	87.13	4.78	99.44
Belgaum	6.97	22.38	5.35	3.50	83.98	7.98	94.64
Bellary	4.27	17.61	2.26	3.07	73.83	0.24	99.60
Bidar	2.89	19.25	1.36	2.49	63.24	1.34	96.38
Bijapur	7.20	17.84	3.48	2.77	74.68	5.48	94.36
Chickmagalur	5.53	7.64	2.43	5.88	79.92	2.26	96.60
Dakshina Kannada	9.12	12.22	10.23	9.37	81.21	23.78	91.89
Chitradurga	4.90	25.00	3.05	2.55	79.33	2.85	96.57
Gulbarga	5.97	19.41	2.69	2.37	75.64	2.97	95.97
Hassan	3.78	16.88	3.01	4.81	80.24	3.67	95.58
Hubli	6.19	24.03	5.63	3.86	82.73	5.07	96.70
Kodagu	2.82	7.18	1.74	8.79	75.89	3.17	93.54
Kolar	5.38	17.40	3.48	3.79	81.58	5.25	94.58
Mandya	2.41	27.10	1.86	2.90	75.22	4.85	90.98
Mysore	5.16	25.82	5.69	4.36	85.58	3.41	97.78
Raichur	4.53	23.29	2.36	2.29	75.91	3.35	94.89
Shimoga	5.19	11.71	3.77	6.33	80.98	6.67	93.71
Tumkur	4.19	22.83	3.07	3.28	75.08	4.22	95.05
Uttara Kannada	5.82	8.62	3.20	6.51	76.84	1.29	98.50
Total	**100.00**	**19.56**	**100.00**	**5.22**	**81.78**	**100.00**	**96.34**
	(2696)		**(2753499)**		**(80.99)**	**(104506)**	

Note: Population deflator in computing (a) population per exchange and (b) teledensity refers to 2001 Census.

Source: Computed by the author using basic data from the *Annual Report 2003-04*, Karnataka Telecom Circle (Bangalore).

APPENDIX A-5.4

Comparative Growth of Public Telecom Network in Karnataka State: 1991-92 to 2003-04

Year	*Andhra Pradesh*		*Karnataka*		*Kerala*		*Tamil Nadu*		*All India*	
	Annual Growth of DEL	*DEL per Exchange*	*Annual Growth of DEL*	*DEL per Exchange*	*Annual Growth of DEL*	*DEL per Exchange*	*Annual Growth of DEL*	*DEL per Exchange*	*Annual Growth of DEL*	*DEL per Exchange*
1991-92	11.65	189	12.87	220	17.57	453	9.2	250	14.49	361
1992-93	16.67	221	15.85	241	23.47	549	13.06	281	16.98	389
1993-94	14.86	251	16.93	272	14.89	607	18	328	18.08	423
1994-95	27.17	317	26.77	334	21.42	725	25.56	399	22.05	486
1995-96	23.18	387	21.73	388	29.22	890	28.06	496	22.29	566
1996-97	19.27	459	24.19	462	25.36	1077	31.28	631	21.41	655
1997-98	22.77	558	26.14	566	26.93	1325	32.26	813	22.41	761
1998-99	34.69	724	19.3	654	25.01	1594	30.67	1000	21.3	868
1999-00	41.66	927	24.9	777	25.83	1845	26.49	1194	22.77	976
2000-01	27.43	1029	23.35	904	26.77	2188	28.56	1381	22.35	1015
2001-02	10.33	1043	14.63	984	24.47	2473	12.2	1407	16.22	1076
2002-03	8.29	NC	6.42	NC	12.26	NC	3.96	NC	7.76	NC
2003-04	-1.14	NC	-0.04	NC	7.85	NC	-0.80	NC	0.60	NC
Average Annual Growth and DEL Per Exchange	**19.76**	**555**	**17.93**	**527**	**21.63**	**1248**	**19.88**	**743**	**17.59**	**689**

Note: NC refers to not computable due to non-availability of data on number of telephone exchanges in 2002-03 and 2003-04.

Source: Computed from the basic data in (a) CMIE (2001, 2003 and 2004), and (b) *Annual Report 2003-04*, Department of Telecommunication, Government of India (New Delhi).

APPENDIX A-5.5

Comparative Growth of Teledensity in Karnataka State: 1991-92 to 2003-04

Year	*Andhra Pradesh*	*Karnataka*	*Kerala*	*Tamil Nadu*	*All-India*
1991-92	0.57	0.83	1.05	0.56	0.69
1992-93	0.65	0.95	1.28	0.63	0.79
1993-94	0.74	1.09	1.45	0.73	0.91
1994-95	0.93	1.11	2.13	0.90	1.09
1995-96	1.12	1.62	2.23	1.14	1.31
1996-97	1.32	1.97	2.76	1.48	1.56
1997-98	1.60	2.45	3.48	1.94	1.87
1998-99	2.13	2.89	4.33	2.51	2.22
1999-00	2.99	3.56	5.41	3.15	2.68
2000-01					
(A) Without Cellular Phones	3.76	4.33	6.83	4.01	3.22
(B) With Cellular Phones 2001-02	4.04	4.75	7.73	4.37	3.57
(A) Without Cellular Phones	4.11	4.89	8.45	4.45	3.67
(B) With Cellular Phones	4.76	5.65	9.61	4.93	4.30
2002-03					
(A) Without Cellular Phones	4.52	5.18	9.30	5.16	3.92
(B) With Cellular Phones	5.66	6.67	11.33	6.22	5.11
2003-04					
(A) Without Cellular Phones	5.44	6.28	11.01	5.75	4.62
(B) With Cellular Phones	7.85	9.46	14.87	8.54	7.02
Average Annual Teledensity					
(A) Without Cellular Phones	1.81	2.33	3.58	1.96	1.82
(B) With Cellular Phones	1.89	2.44	3.77	2.03	1.91

Notes: Teledensity without (or with) cellular mobile phone represents teledensity of fixed (or fixed and cellular mobile phones) provided by both public and private operators.

Source: Computed from the basic data in CMIE (2001, 2003 and 2004) and *Annual Report 2003-04*, Department of Telecommunication, Government of India (New Delhi).

APPENDIX A-5.6

Access to Telecom Services in Rural and Urban Karnataka: 2000-01 to 2003-04

Indicators of Telecom Services	*Andhra Pradesh*	*Karnataka*	*Kerala*	*Tamil Nadu*	*All India*
Teledensity in Rural Areas					
2000-01	1.47	1.79	5.05	0.49	0.9
2001-02	1.83	2.13	6.59	0.46	1.21
2002-03	2.03	2.37	7.85	2.12	1.49
2003-04	2.33	2.41	8.60	2.35	1.57
Teledensity in Urban Areas					
2000-01	11.16	10.33	15.14	12.82	10.37
2001-02	13.24	12.29	17.58	11.65	12.03
2002-03	15.42	14.78	21.28	12.28	14.32
2003-04	22.70	22.58	32.82	17.21	20.74
Per cent of Rural DEL to Overall DEL					
2000-01	28.6	27.7	55.2	6.9	20.6
2001-02	33.0	29.0	59.0	6.0	24.0
2002-03	26.15	23.2	51.3	20.3	20.9
2003-04	21.58	16.6	42.9	16.1	16.1
Per cent of Waitlisted Telephones in Nation's Total					
1993-94	6.22	6.64	12.59	12.46	100 (=2496850)
1995-96	5.93	6.75	18.24	15.01	100 (=2277021)
1997-98	7.78	4.14	25.10	9.08	100 (=2705741)
2000-01	4.49	5.89	26.54	5.13	100 (=2916718)

Source: Computed from the basic data in CMIE (2001, 2003 and 2004) and *Annual Report 2003-04*, Department of Telecommunication, Government of India (New Delhi).

APPENDIX A-5.7

Efficiency and Competitiveness in Delivery of Quality Telecom Services in Karnataka State: 2003

Benchmark for Indicators of Quality of Telecom Services	*Average Value of the Performance Indicator*											
	Andhra Pradesh			*Tamil Nadu*			*Karnataka*			*Kerala*		
	Public	*Private*	*Total*	*Public*	*Private*	*Total*	*Public*	*Private*	*Total*	*Public*	*Private*	*Total*
Basic Services												
1. Fault Repairs												
1.1. Less than 3 Fault Incidence per 100 Subscribers per Month	7.88	0.85	4.37	6.04	3.15	4.60	6.34	0.44	3.39	8.23	0.00	4.12
1.2. More than 90 per cent of Fault Repair by Next Working Day:												
October	86.70	98.31	92.50	96.55	99.29	97.92	95.17	66.21	80.69	91.38	100.00	95.69
November	94.77	98.88	96.83	96.38	99.47	97.92	96.43	56.35	76.39	91.28	100.00	95.64
December	94.86	98.56	96.71	96.36	99.87	98.12	96.38	66.37	81.38	91.31	100.00	95.66
1.3. Mean Time to Repair is Less than 8 Hours	5.00	4.65	4.83	8.00	3.60	5.80	3.00	2.47	2.74	14.00	2.70	8.35
1.4. Percentage of Repeat Faults is Less than 0.1 per cent:												
October	4.65	43.99	24.32	1.18	32.62	16.90	6.62	6.21	6.41	5.14	0.00	2.57
November	5.53	4.10	4.82	1.39	32.80	17.10	6.03	6.10	6.07	5.39	0.00	2.70
December	8.48	3.25	5.87	1.36	33.20	17.28	5.50	5.31	5.41	6.10	0.00	3.05
2. Call Completion, Call Assistance and Metering/Billing												
2.1. More than 65 per cent of Call Completion Rate in Local Network	45.80	72.69	59.25	55.70	61.12	58.41	49.50	62.26	55.88	58.50	67.96	63.23
2.2. Metering and Billing Credibility is Less than 0.1 per cent of Bills Disputed	0.78	0.10	0.44	0.06	0.10	0.08	0.04	0.34	0.19	0.04	0.16	0.10
Total Number of Indicators which Meets with the Benchmarks for Basic Services	3	6	4	4	4	5	5	2	1	4	8	3
Cellural Services												
(a) Call Success Rate (within licencees own network)—More than 99 per cent	98.00	98.08	98.04	94.50	99.34	96.92	98.10	98.53	98.32	89.09	99.49	94.29
(b) Service Access Delay—Between 9 to 20 Seconds	6.00	8.64	7.32	11.85	13.72	12.79	8.83	6.35	7.59	3.73	9.63	6.68
(c) Call Drop Rate (per cent)—Less than 3 per cent	1.83	1.47	1.65	1.61	1.37	1.49	1.34	1.16	1.25	1.63	1.16	1.39
(d) Per cent of Connection with Good Voice Quality—More than 95 per cent	98.00	96.18	97.09	95.89	96.72	96.31	97.00	96.97	96.99	95.00	99.05	97.03
(e) Number of faults per 100 Subscribers per Month—Less than One per cent	1.78	0.05	0.91	1.85	0.10	0.98	2.80	0.21	1.50	1.81	0.19	1.00
(f) Faults Cleared within 24 Hours—100 per cent	99.00	99.33	99.17	99.00	86.63	92.82	100.00	100.00	100.00	99.99	99.50	99.75
Total Number of Indicators which Meets with the Benchmarks for Cellular Services	**2**	**3**	**3**	**2**	**4**	**3**	**3**	**3**	**4**	**3**	**5**	**4**

Source: Computed by using the basic data in Annex 1.2 'A' and Annex 2.3 in TRAI (2003).

APPENDIX A-5.8

Growth of Postal Network in Karnataka: 1992-93 to 2003-04

Year	*Total Number of Post Offices*	*Annual Growth of Total Post Offices*	*Per Cent of Rural Post Offices*	*Population per Post Office*	*Total of Letter Boxes*	*Per Cent of Rural Letter Boxes*
1992-93	9762	NA	86.05	4706	27391	66.22
1993-94	9781	0.19	86.09	4797	27899	77.50
1994-95	9785	0.04	86.24	4899	28079	77.73
1995-96	9787	0.02	86.25	5004	29174	77.49
1996-97	9805	0.18	86.44	5033	29351	77.45
1997-98	9837	0.33	86.46	5089	29138	77.41
1998-99	9852	0.15	86.57	5152	28807	78.72
1999-00	9873	0.21	86.58	5210	29654	77.37
2000-01	9895	0.22	86.59	5264	30367	73.31
2001-02	9901	0.06	85.51	5326	33376	74.56
2002-03	9908	0.07	86.50	5322	34292	79.31
2003-04	9911	0.03	86.80	5321	34715	78.38

Source: Computed from basic data from the Office of the Chief Post Master General, Karnataka Postal Circle (Bangalore).

APPENDIX A-5.9

Growth of Postal Traffic in Karnataka: 1992-93 to 2002-03

Year	*Total Traffic (Number of Articles and Newspapers (in Lakh)*	*Annual Growth of Total Postal Traffic*	*Share of Unregistered Articles in Total Postal Traffic*	*Share of Registered Articles in Total Postal Traffic*	*Total Distance Over which the Total Traffic Carried (in Kms)*	*Total Distance Over which the Total Traffic Carried by Rail and Road*	*Value of MOs per MO Booked (Rs.)*	*Value of MOs per MO Paid (Rs.)*
1992-93	8100	-1.32	91.98	1.96	124554	68.75	130.59	175.67
1993-94	6577	-18.80	87.71	5.67	121788	79.39	175.96	189.32
1994-95	6500	-1.16	87.69	5.69	149320	80.88	169.21	203.01
1995-96	6501	0.01	87.68	5.72	144027	42.07	219.84	279.98
1996-97	6518	0.26	90.52	2.77	147904	43.31	220.41	259.87
1997-98	6811	4.50	91.03	2.45	151032	70.35	252.49	285.16
1998-99	7390	8.50	84.91	1.86	159344	69.72	318.07	386.96
1999-00	9196	24.44	86.99	1.34	156430	71.53	123.59	336.88
2000-01	10195	10.85	87.30	1.12	159080	65.24	407.71	361.36
2001-02	11705	14.82	87.91	2.01	162785	70.20	388.63	454.42
2002-03	10693	-8.65	88.07	1.00	150756	72.16	399.09	377.38

Note: MO refers to money order.

Source: Computed by using basic data from the Office of the Chief Post Master General, Karnataka Postal Circle (Bangalore).

APPENDIX A-5.10

Inter-Distribution Variations in the Postal Network and Access to Postal Services: 1997-98 and 2001-02

Districts	*Per Cent of Post Offices in State's Total*		*Total Population per Post Office*	
	1997-98	*2001-02*	*1997-98*	*2001-02*
Bagalkote	3.36	3.35	4791	4977
Bangalore (Urban)	3.57	3.57	15681	18479
Bangalore (Rural)	3.35	3.33	5766	5689
Belgaum	7.25	7.35	5718	5779
Bellary	4.62	4.61	4137	4441
Bidar	3.09	3.07	4695	4939
Bijapur	4.26	4.23	4163	4317
C R Nagar	2.03	2.05	5013	4750
Chickmagalur	3.08	3.12	3815	3686
Chitradurga	3.20	3.35	4742	4549
D. Kannada	4.85	4.93	3893	3886
Davanagere	2.80	2.61	6455	6937
Dharwad	2.40	2.20	6632	7357
Gadag	2.06	1.76	4813	5586
Gulbarga	6.32	6.29	4720	5016
Hassan	4.25	4.26	4271	4079
Haveri	2.11	2.61	6935	5573
Kodagu	2.24	2.22	2535	2479
Kolar	4.29	4.26	5976	5980
Koppal	2.32	2.32	4778	5189
Mandya	3.70	3.69	5143	4827
Mysore	4.21	4.21	6264	6295
Raichur	2.85	2.82	5481	5908
Shimoga	3.65	3.67	4602	4517
Tumkur	5.79	5.77	4604	4518
Udupi	3.31	3.33	3703	3362
U.Kannada	5.03	5.02	2800	2723
State	**100.00**	**100.00**	**5199**	**5326**
	(9837)	**(9901)**		

Note: Projected population in 1998-99 for 27 districts is used to arrive at total population per post office in 1997-98.

Source: Computed by using the basic data from the Office of the Chief Post-Master General, Karnataka Postal Circle (Bangalore).

Chapter 6

Social Infrastructure in Karnataka

6.0 Introduction

Social infrastructure is a comprehensive structure of public goods and services that must be available to all people in the nation. It ranges from education, training, health care, water supply and sanitation, and housing to integrated child development services. Evidences show that regions and countries that fail to invest in basic social infrastructure can expect substandard economic growth. Indeed, it is a fundamental task for all the states in India. However, there is no general consensus that social infrastructure such as education, health, housing and social network is responsible for the economic growth of any region. Some believe that high rates of human capital development have been a major factor responsible for the success of some countries in Asian region (World Bank, 1993; Thant, 1999). Some refute this argument that heavy investments in education led the balanced economic growth in fast growing economies of Southeast Asia. The governments of these countries have been especially judicious at planning educational development in order to meet the demands of the fast-changing labour market. This is because in several cases it is clear that educational and skill bottlenecks have forced governments into relying on expatriate labour, and in some cases retarded the economic growth (Booth, 1999). In fact, the direct interventions by the state for provisions of various social services such as education, health, housing, and social network measures are required to ensure a balanced economic development that encompasses a sustained rate of economic growth and an equitable distribution of income.

In recent years, UNDP reports strongly argue that neither social nor economic development can take place in isolation and both should be viewed as an integral part of a single phenomenon of development. In fact, the contemporary research on the interrelationship between economic and social developments has proceeded in two different directions. One side argues that the social indicator approach uses both monetary and non-monetary indicators reflecting the various aspects of economic and social lives to study the relationship. The chosen indicators are usually the output indicators measuring the progress in economic or social areas (or both), which are the result of a number of composite indices of socio-economic development. Another side argues that the social expenditure approach uses certain input indicators reflecting the costs of providing various social services and then seeks to determine the impact of such costs on economic growth measured by changes in per capita GDP. This Chapter is designed for the combination of both input and output indicators of social sector, which includes education, health, nutrition, housing, water supply and sanitation, integrated child development services, and social security through self-help groups.

6.1 Educational Infrastructure

Recognising the importance of education for realising its goal of improved growth with equity, the government of Karnataka has initiated many studies/ schemes and initiatives for the overall development of education in the state along with promotion of private of private sector in the development of education. Currently, the state (0.45) is slightly above the national average (0.42) in respect of its Human Development Index. Of course, a progress in respect of human development can be achieved through the provision of high quality education and health services with the given infrastructures. In this context, it may be useful to examine the initiatives taken so far by the government of Karnataka in the field of educational infrastructures and suggest policy measures for sustainable development in the education.

6.1.1 Development of Education in Karnataka

Educational progress can be assessed in terms of outcomes, such as literacy rates, educational attainments and enrolment and also of input indicators into the educational system, such as the number of institutions, teachers and school infrastructure. The education system in Karnataka consists of lower primary from classes I-IV, upper primary from classes V-VII, and secondary covering the classes IX and X. Only recently, the government of Karnataka has lengthened the duration of primary education from 4 years to 5 years, middle to 3 years and secondary constitutes 2 years as earlier (5+3+2). At present all the schools have not adopted this system but nearly two-thirds of the schools have adopted the new form (Seetharamu, 2002).

In the year 1956, the number of schools was 22,250 and it increased to 57,905 by the turn of the century showing a compound growth rate of 2 per cent per annum. The enrolment increased by 3.9 per cent and the number of teachers by 3.8 per cent during the same period. It is significant to note that in case of primary and secondary education, the growth of enrolment is less than the growth of institutions while in case of higher education the pattern is reversed (Appendix A-6.1). The enrolment in professional education falls short of the growth in institutions. It leads a situation that there is no need to open any new schools both at the primary and secondary level. It is due to the low growth of children in this particular age group in the state. In the case of propositional education, there is a negative growth of enrolment in the state.

Karnataka is a medium developed state insofar as the educational development is concerned as it occupies the 7th position among the 16 major states in the country. The relative development status of education of the districts reveals that all the districts of north Karnataka (NK) have occupied lower rank while the districts of South Karnataka (SK) except a few are much better. In fact, the rank of North Karnataka districts in respect of educational development has either remained unchanged or their rank has become lower in 2002 than in 1991. Therefore, the development of education in the north Karnataka districts over the period of time has become stagnant, which is a matter of great concern.

6.1.2 Growth of Educational Institutions

Primary Schools

The distribution of primary schools by management indicates that the growth of private managed schools (4.81 per cent) is about four times that for the government schools (1.4 per cent) during the period 1990-91 to 2002-03 (Figure 6.1). The unaided schools grew at a compound growth of 7 per cent per annum, as against this, the private aided schools grew at 2 per cent. The state government adopted a policy of providing a primary school for a population of 200 persons as against the government of India's norm of 300 persons. The government of Karnataka is able to fulfil this norm as on

FIGURE 6.1

Number of Primary Schools by Management in Karnataka

(a) 1990-91

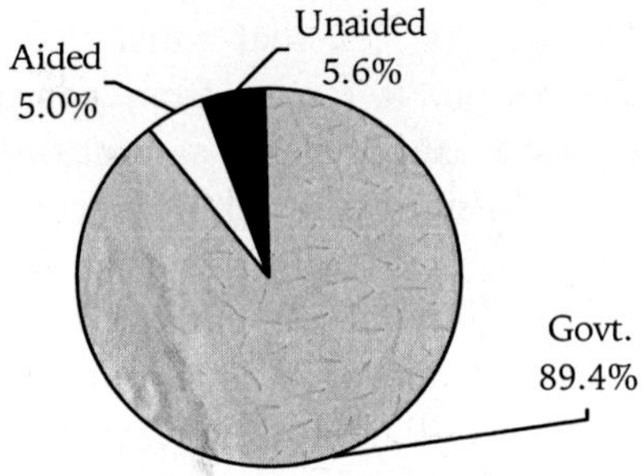

(b) 2002-03

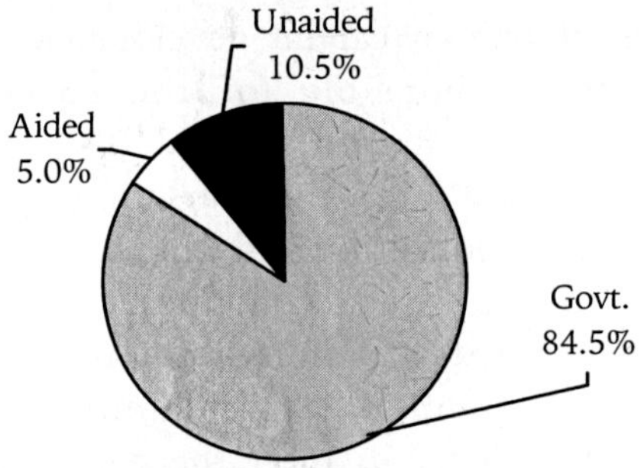

Source: Commissioner of Public Instruction, Education Department, Government of Karnataka, Bangalore.

FIGURE 6.2

Number of High Schools by Management in Karnataka

(a) 1990-91

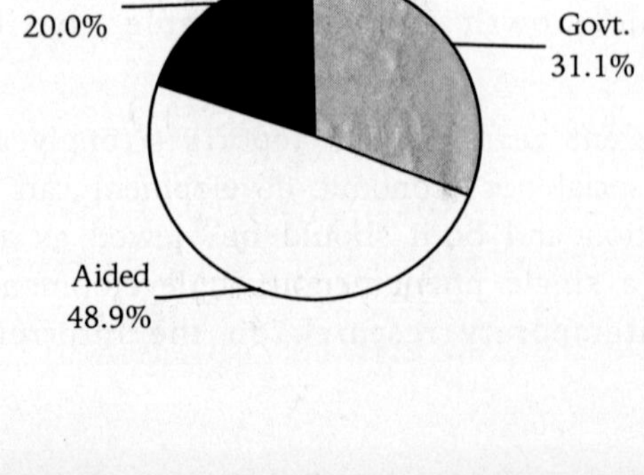

(b) 2002-03

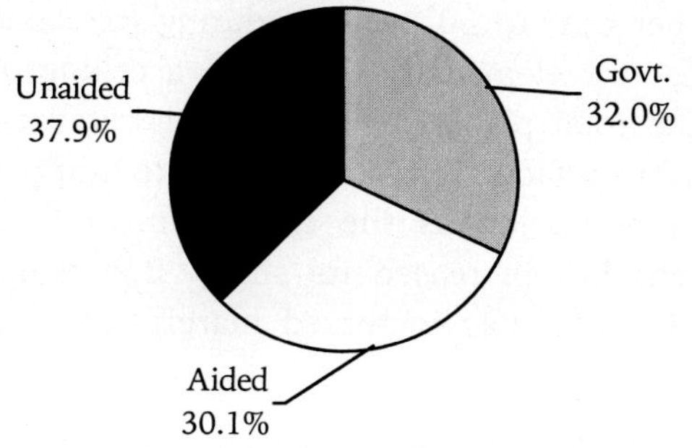

Source: Commissioner of Public Instruction, Education Department, Government of Karnataka, Bangalore.

an average there is more than one school (1.14) for a population of 200 in the age group of 6-14 years children in the year 2002-03. Of the 27 districts, 15 districts (12 South Karnataka and 3 Uttar Karnataka) have one or more than one school for 200 persons while 12 districts (8 North Karnataka and 4 South Karnataka) do not fulfil the norm of providing a primary school for a population of 200 persons. Over the years there is a steady increase of the unaided primary schools. However, the government managed schools at the primary level are found to be the highest.

High Schools

The high schools by management show that the unaided schools grow at a faster rate than other schools. During 1990-91 the number of aided schools was the highest and during 2002-03 there was a shift towards the growth of unaided schools and the picture was reversed. The Figure 6.2 provides the high schools by management.

Higher Educational Institutions

During the last decade (1990-91 to 2000-2001) there was a significant increase in the number of institutions of higher learning as the growth of higher, general and professional institutions were 7.08 and 7.20 per cent respectively. The growth of primary schools during the same period was the lowest (1.89 per cent). Even the universities and other institutes grew at a higher rate (4.91 per cent) than the primary schools (Figure 6.3) The faster growth of professional and higher educational institutions in the state may be due to the mushroom growth of private sector educational institutions in the state.

6.1.3 Public Expenditure on Education

Education in the state is financed by the public and the private sectors. In the public sector both the state and the Central Governments spend for education,

FIGURE 6.3

Growth of Educational Institutions in Karnataka

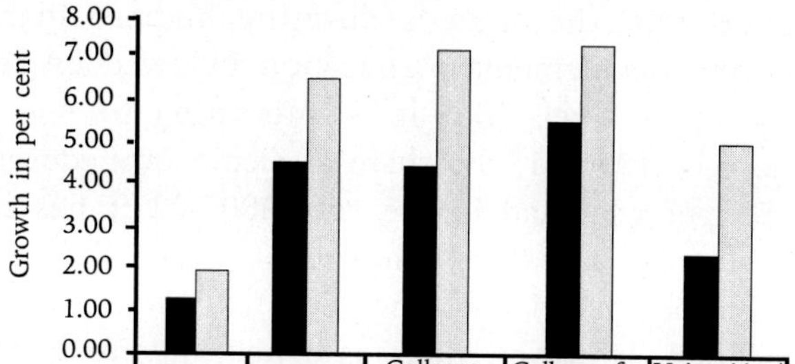

	Primary Schools	High Schools	Colleges for General Education	Colleges for Professional Education	Universities/ Deemed Universities
□CGR for 1980-81 to 1990-91	1.24	4.45	4.36	5.40	2.31
■CGR for 1990-91 to 2001-02	1.89	6.38	7.08	7.20	4.91

while in the private sector it is the households and other private organisations and corporate bodies spend on education. In the case of aided schools, the contribution of the government also needs to be reckoned. The state governments have the major responsibility for secondary education and direct responsibility for elementary education. The education sector has multiple sources of finance. These include the states' own revenue (both tax and non-tax revenues), transfers from the Central Government, the block assistance for the state plan and the centrally sponsored plans of the Central Ministry of Human Resources. The state government finances its own institutions and the privately aided institutions.

Share of Education in SDP

In spite of fairly high rate of growth of income (12 per cent GSDP growth) in the state during the nineties, the proportion of income devoted to education is only slightly higher (4 per cent) as compared to the all India average (3.7 per cent) and also in relation to that found in many other states (Figure 6.4).

FIGURE 6.4

Share of Total Educational Expenditure in SDP in Karnataka

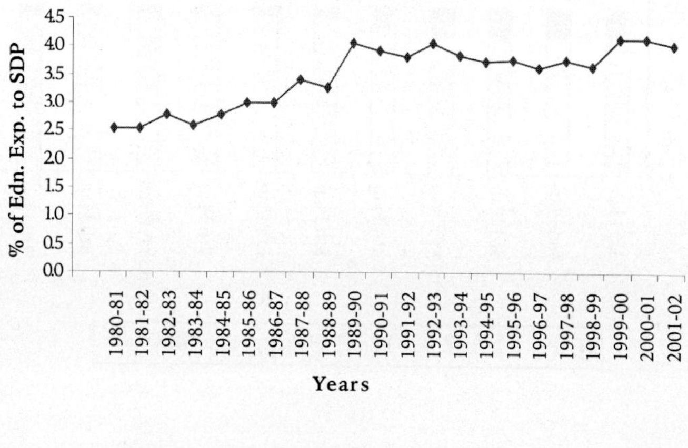

As regards the share of total expenditure in SDP it is more realistic to examine the share of expenditure of each level of education in SDP (Appendix A-6.2). It is found that the state is devoting highest share of its income on elementary education followed by secondary and other levels. But it is interesting to note that in the year 1990-91, the share of elementary education was 1.63 per cent and in the year 2001-02 it has remained unaltered. On the other the share of higher and technical education during these two points of time has declined. However, there is a necessity to enhance the share of elementary education in the state income but it should not be at the cost of higher education and technical education.

Intrasectoral Budgetary Allocations in Education

The budgetary allocation to different levels and types of education indicated that more than 50 per cent of the total allocation goes in favour of elementary education, while the rest of the fund are allocated to other levels of education (Appendix A-6.3). For the development of other levels of education particularly secondary level, this allocation seems to be inadequate to meet the challenges in the present day context. There is a very marginal increase in the allocation of resources for secondary education while the share of higher education over the period of time is scaling down particularly in the year 2001.

Plan–Wise Allocation of Resources to Education

The plan-wise allocation of resources to different levels of education shows that elementary education gets the highest share (Figure 6.5). During the First Plan, it was about 44 per cent of the total expenditure and it increased to 51 per cent in the Ninth Plan, while the share of secondary education has increased from 18 per cent to 30 per cent during the same period. Under SSA for elementary education a ceiling of 33 per cent of the total plan size has been allocated to provide infrastructure facilities. Realising the importance of secondary education as the crucial turning point, the government has increased its share. But, the share of higher education has increased marginally over all the plans.

FIGURE 6.5

Plan-wise Expenditure on Different Sectors of Education in Karnataka

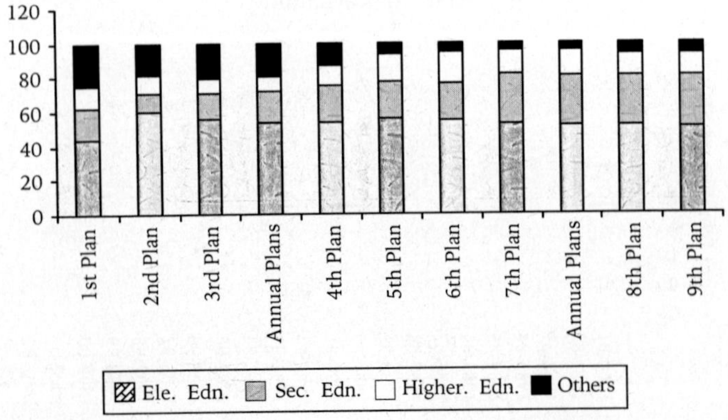

Per Student Cost of Education

The unit cost reflects the quality of education to some extent. It is found that the per student expenditure on elementary education increased by more than 10 times at current prices while the same has increased slightly higher than 2 times at constant prices (Appendix A-6.4). Further, it is observed that the real expenditure on higher education declined substantially from 1995-96 to 1999-00 and it has picked up in the year 2000-01, which affects the quality of higher education to a great extent.

Object-wise Classification of Expenditure on Education

The item-wise expenditure on education in Appendix A-6.5 may provide some idea about the quality of education. It is found that the expenditure on teacher training, scholarships, examinations and textbooks not only is very negligible but has constantly declined over the period of time. The quality of education depends largely on these items. The share of these items in the total expenditure on school education was 5.19 per cent in 1991-92 and it declined to 1.80 per cent in the year 2001-02. Major proportion of the expenditure goes in terms of grant and the same has increased over the years, which is spent mainly to meet the salaries of the staffs. In this background it may be observed that the quality of education at the school level is likely to be affected in negative way.

Centrally Sponsored Schemes

The financing under centrally sponsored schemes (CSS) are made by the Central Government in order to promote regional equity by providing incentives for education to backward regions and backward class children. The schemes like Operation Black Board (OBB), Non-formal Education (NFE), and Teacher Education (TE) are some of the centrally and District Primary Education Programme (DPEP) is an externally funded scheme. All the centrally sponsored schemes aim at providing financial support to elementary education, while DPEP finances are meant for primary education only. DPEP allows financing of all the components that are also funded by the other CSS, including classroom construction, appointment of new teachers, teaching learning equipment and NFE centres. One of the important objectives of all the CSS schemes is to reduce regional disparities in education and to achieve horizontal equality across states. The distribution of fund under various schemes indicates that there is no uniformity in the distribution of grants keeping in view the backwardness of the state. For example, under OB schemes many educationally backward states (West Bengal, Bihar, Uttar Pradesh Assam) received smaller grants than the advanced states like Maharastra and Karnataka. Similar is also the case with the distribution of funds in case of teacher education. However, the fund distribution for NFE is found to be somewhat skewed. The DPEP funds seem to be distributed more uniformly and the outcome of DPEP is also found to be satisfactory in the state (Box 6.1). The fund flow from various centrally sponsored schemes needs to be effectively managed by the states for the best result of elementary education.

BOX 6.1

DPEP: A Success story

In Karnataka, total 11 districts (Phase I, 4 districts and 7 districts in phase II) were covered under DPEP. The DPEP in Karnataka, though, has been able to reduce dropout rates, lags behind its set target of bringing dropout rates below 10 per cent. The 12th Joint Review Mission (JRM), 2000 notes with satisfaction the dropout of girls in 1-4 years is lower than that of boys (14 per cent for boys and 12 per cent for girls). However, several qualitative changes have been brought by DPEP interventions. Repetition rates for both boys and girls have declined to 3.45 per cent for boys and 4.16 per cent for girls during 1999-00. For SC boys and girls it is 6 per cent and 7 per cent during the same period. Achievements in learning also are lower among SC/ST children particularly for language testing for standard IV. Girl's achievement is generally equivalent to or better than that for boys.

R. Kanbargi (2002). *Equity in Education in Karnataka*, Education Dept. Government of Karnataka.

6.1.4 Educational Indicators in the State

Literacy Scenario

Educational indicators are the outcomes of the input indicators such as infrastructures for given financing provisions of the state. Literacy is considered as one of the most important outcome indicators of educational status of the population. Karnataka has made steady progress in not only the literacy rate but also the gender disparity in literacy,[1] which has declined from 0.47 in 1961 to 0.18 in 2001 (Appendix A-6.6).

Interdistrict Variation in Literacy

The inter-district variations in literacy rates are estimated in terms of mean, standard deviation and coefficient of variation. The average literacy rate of the state has increased sharply from 55.23 per cent in 1991 and 66.05 per cent in 2001 (Appendix A-6.7). The mean literacy rate of all population is higher than scheduled caste population and there is not much difference between Scheduled Caste and Scheduled Tribe mean literacy rate. It is further revealed that the coefficient of variation of literacy among females declines more significantly than that for the male. Across regions the variation in rural literacy is higher than urban literacy. In spite of the steady progress in literacy rate there are disparities in literacy rate by gender and by region. The variation in literacy over the years is narrowing down for all caste groups. The variation in female literacy is found to be almost double of the male literacy and this pattern is observed amongst all groups of population (Appendix A-6.7).

The mean literacy rate between different districts of the state also shows wide variation particularly between north and south Karnataka (Figure 6.6). The mean

FIGURE 6.6

Coefficient of Variation in Literacy

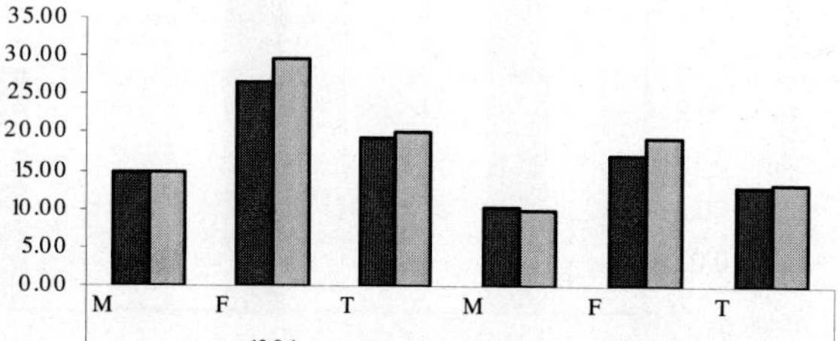

	1991 M	1991 F	1991 T	2001 M	2001 F	2001 T
South Karnataka	14.97	26.65	19.37	10.18	17.09	13.00
North Karnataka	14.86	29.66	20.02	9.75	19.36	13.47

1. Disparity Index = $\text{Log}(X_1/X_2) + \text{Log}\,[(Q-X_1)/(Q-X_2)]$, where $X_2 \geq X_1$ and $Q \geq 200$. Sopher, D.K. (1974). "Measurement of Disparity", *The Professional Geographer*, 26/2, (Nov.), pp. 380-92.

literacy rate of the districts of north Karnataka[2] (61.48 per cent) is less than those of south Karnataka[3] (69.71 per cent). The gender gap in literacy in north Karnataka districts is also higher than that of south Karnataka districts implying a low female literacy rate in north Karnataka. There is a sharp decline in the variation in literacy rate during the decade among districts both of south and north Karnataka. The literacy status of the districts in the state of Karnataka indicates clearly that only a group of districts in south Karnataka are taken care, while the districts in north Karnataka seems to be neglected. The Figure 6.6 gives a clear idea about the literacy achievements in the north and south Karnataka.

Intradistrict Disparity (Gender Disparity)

There is also an intra-district disparity in literacy rates between male and female. As per the Sopher's (1974) disparity index, the gender disparity in all the 12 districts of north Karnataka (except Uttar Kannada and Dharwad) is higher than the state average implying higher gender disparity (lower female literacy). As against this, out of the 15 districts of south Karnataka, 9 districts have very low gender disparity (below state average) and 6 districts have the disparity above state average but the difference is very marginal.

The gender disparity among the scheduled caste population is higher than the general population but the disparity among the scheduled tribe is higher than the scheduled caste population (Figure 6.7). The disparity in rural areas is higher than that in urban areas. This is due to the fact that rural female literacy is much lower.

FIGURE 6.7

Gender Disparities in Literacy: 1991

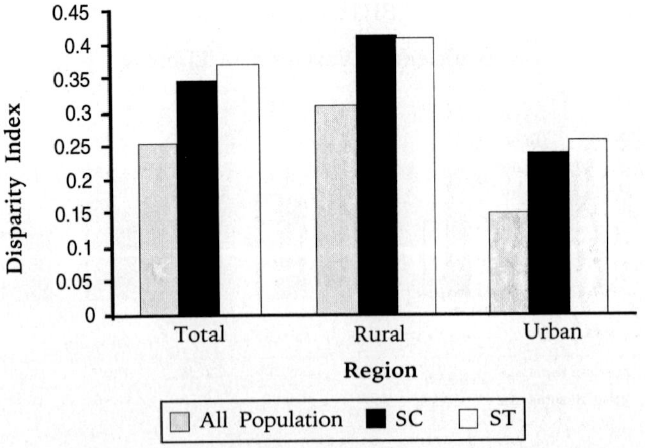

6.1.5 *Education Levels of the Population*

Though literacy is the most commonly used indicator of educational development of a region, it does not provide an idea about the different educational levels of population. As per the estimations from the NFHS in 1998-99, the educational levels of the population of Karnataka are less than 20 per cent (19.6 per cent) for male population, who have completed primary education and slightly higher than 13 per cent had above higher secondary education. The proportion of female population in each level of education is found to be less than their male counterparts.

The computation of median years of education of the population from the NFHS–I and NFHS–II indicates that considerable progress is made in the median years of schooling in the state of Karnataka particularly for females over the period 1992-93 to 1998-99. The median years of schooling for females was zero in 1992-93 and it rose to 3.2 years in 1998-99. The median years of schooling for the total population also has improved by 2 years, whereas the years of schooling for males have not shown much improvement. Despite the sharp improvement in years of schooling (particularly females), the females are behind their male counterparts.

The education status of the state can be explained in terms of enrolment, enrolment ratios, and girls/boys ratio, which provide the current status of education in the state. There is a sharp increase in the enrolment of children at the primary level over the years as it has increased from 49.86 lakhs in 1980-81 to 83 lakhs in 2003-04. The growth rate of enrolment in primary education during 1980-81 to 1990-91 was 3.06 per cent and it declined to 0.8 per cent during 1990-91 to 2002-2003. It may be due to the population transition in Karnataka during the last decade. Even the enrolment in secondary schools show a declining trend as it grew at 4.86 per cent during 1980-81 to 1990-91 and it declined to 2.99 per cent during 1990-91 to 2002-03.

There is a marked improvement in the enrolment of girls as seen from the gender parity index. In 1980-81, the parity index was 75.74 and it rose to 93.38 in the year 2002-03 at the primary level and if this increasing rate continues the hope of achieving the goal of 'universalisation of elementary education' (UEE) and of removing gender disparity would not be a very distant

2. North Karnataka includes: Belgaum, Bijapur, Bagolkot, Dharwad, Gadag, Haveri, Uttar Kannada, Bellary, Bidar, Gulbarga, Raichur, and Koppal.

3. South Karnataka includes: Bangalore Urban, Bangalore Rural, Chitradurga, Davangere, Kolar, Shimoga, Tumkur, Chickmagalur, Dakshina Kannada, Udupi, Hassan, Kodagu, Mandya, Mysore, and Chamrajnagar.

goal for the state. The gender parity index at secondary level has also shown more improvement (56.88 to 85.49) than in the case of primary level during the same period (Appendix A-6.8).

The enrolment of children and their growth are certainly important but the absolute numbers do not tell much about the proportion of children to the relevant age group of population enrolled in a particular level of education in the school. In order to assess the extent of achievement in the context of UEE, gross enrolment rate (GER) is a better measure. GER is the ratio of the number of children enrolled in a particular stage of education to the total number of children in the age group corresponding to that stage. The numerator is likely to include children outside the relevant age group due to late entry or slow progress through the school. Hence, gross enrolment exceeds 100 per cent. The GER has increased considerably during the last decade as it was 91.67 in 1996-97 and it increased to 104.37 in 2002-2003 (Appendix A-6.9). As against this the net enrolment ratio is considered to be a more correct measure of enrolment, as it does not include the over and underaged children in a particular level of education as in case of GER. The net enrolment rate (NER) was 72.28 in 1996-97 and it increased to 82.27 in the year 2002-03 (Appendix A-6.9). As such the net enrolment ratio is much below 100. Despite the steady increase in enrolment, the net enrolment ratio for girls is lower than that of boys over the years and it seems to be a more distant goal to have 100 per cent NER. Across social groups, it is found that the GER has increased for general children and Scheduled Tribe (ST) children, while the same has declined for Scheduled Caste (SC) children during the last decade. The GER for boys is always found to be higher than girls despite the increase in GER during the decade (Appendix A-6.10).

There is also a substantial improvement in girls' enrolment in professional higher education during the same period, the growth rate being one per cent and six per cent respectively for boys and girls. Despite the rapid increase in enrolment of girls in professional education, the gender parity index is lower than that of general higher education. The gender parity index of enrolment in higher education in the state shows that girls/females are increasingly well/over represented in general higher education (even better than primary and secondary education) while they are under represented in case of professional higher education, which is a cause of concern (Figure 6.8). This adds to the gender imbalances in enrolment in education as a whole. The main reason for their over representation in general

FIGURE 6.8

Gender Parity Index in Enrolment by Level/Type of Education in Karnataka

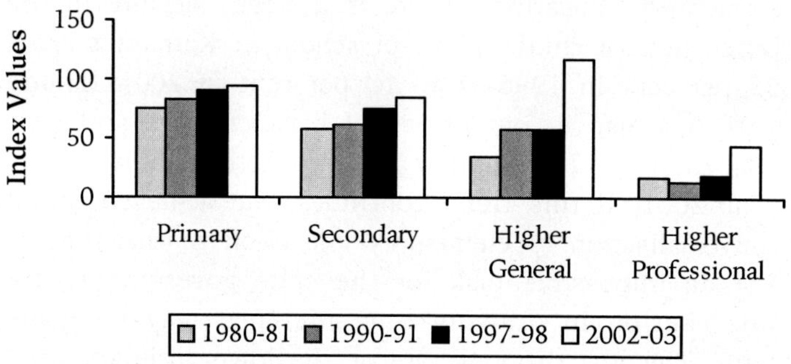

higher education may: (i) the subjects of general higher education are blindly considered as 'female subjects'; and (ii) since the investment is very high in the case of professional education, parents prefer to invest on their male child for this type of education mainly due to socio-cultural reasons.

6.1.6 Major Challenges

Dropout Rate

Student dropout in primary school is the major concern in the state. Though there is a sharp decline in the dropout rate over the decade for both boys and girls particularly at the lower primary level, there is not much difference between boys and girl's dropout at the lower primary level (Appendix A-6.11). In fact, the gap has widened at the higher primary level implying more dropouts of girls at the higher primary level. With the increase in the level of education the drop out rate increases, 52 per cent of children enroled in class one do not complete elementary education and 59 per cent drop out before completing class X (not shown in the Appendix). It indicates that the retention rate of children declines as they move towards higher levels of education but the retention rate of girls at the upper primary level is found to be lower than for their male counterparts. The gender gap in dropout increases with the rise in the level of education. In the year 2000-01, the gender gap was one at the lower primary level and it increased to 14 at the higher primary level. The gender gap in dropout rate in the year 1992-93 was 4 at the lower primary level and it declined to 1 by the year 2000-01. At the upper primary level it was 10 in 1992-1993 and it increased to 14 in the year 2000-01 which is a matter of serious concern.

Out of School Children

In addition to the dropout rate, the children not attending school also is one of the major constraints of the achievement of the goal of 'universalisation of elementary education'. There is a steady decline in the proportion of children out of school in Karnataka from 28 per cent in 1996-97 to 10 per cent in 2001 (Figure 6.9). The gap in out of school between boys and girls was more in 1996 and it reduced considerably in the year 2001. If this trend continues, the achievement of universalisation of elementary education in the state is not an impossible task for the state government. But one caution in drawing this inference may be made here. The low dropout rate at the lower primary level may be due to the state government's policy of 'no detention till class V', if the students attend the school for a minimum number of days irrespective of their learning achievements.

FIGURE 6.9

Percentage of Out of School Children for 6-14 Years

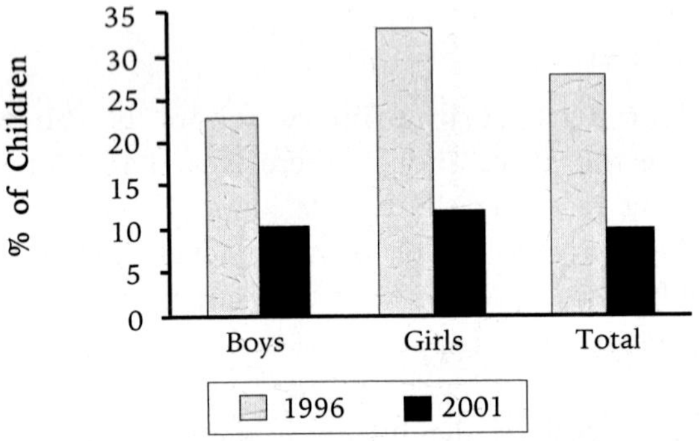

Reasons for Dropout/Being Out of School

Reasons for never attending or currently not attending and drop out are provided by NFHS-II 1998-1999, with some interesting evidences. The NFHS-II survey results indicate that nearly 34 per cent of the boys and 19 per cent of the girls never attended school because of lack of interest in studies. This is also found as one of the most important reasons for dropping out of the school particularly for boys (nearly 50 per cent). It is significant to note that more of boys than girls were not interested in studies. The stagnation of children in a particular class is found to be higher among boys than among girls. Further, classification of lack of interest was probed by the research studies by PROBE Team (1999) and Krishnaji (2001). They found the following responses: (i) what is the use of schooling; (ii) a child can earn some income if he does not go to school; and (iii) a child can do some 'useful' work at home. The reasons for non-attendance like child is required to do household work, work in farm/ business, work outside for wage, cost of education, etc. can be closely related mainly to economic reasons for which the parents do not want their ward to be entered into school. This brings out clearly that the opportunity cost of schooling of the child as well as the financial constraints of the household are mainly responsible for not sending the child to school.

Teacher Position

The role of teachers in education is one of the important determinants of quality of education. It can be explained by pupil-teacher ratio. Across districts, the highest pupil-teacher ratio in all types of schools is found in Raichur and Dharwad while the lowest pupil-teacher ratio is found in Hassan, Tumkur and Kolar (Appendix A-6.12). This reveals clearly that the north Karnataka districts have the highest pupil-teacher ratio indicating low quality of education as against the south Karnataka districts have the advantages of the lowest pupil-teacher ratio. The proportion of female teachers shows an increasing trend in primary education while it has remained more or less constant in case of secondary education. But it is still less than 50 per cent in primary level by the year 2002-03, which needs to be improved in order to achieve gender parity in enrolment.

Infrastructure Facilities Available in Schools

The school infrastructure matters much to motivate both the parents and children to attend the school. For example: girls' education/enrolment affects greatly if there is no separate toilet for girls. Parents do not prefer to send their girls to schools if there is no separate girls' toilet in the school. Teachers particularly female teachers, do not prefer to stay if there is no electricity. Despite the fact that the government has taken various steps continuously to improve the school infrastructure, it is found that more than two-thirds of the schools in the state have no separate toilets for girls and also 50 per cent of the schools have no toilet at all (Appendix A-6.13). More than 55 per cent of the schools have no electricity connection. More than 90 per cent of the schools have no ramps. These are some of the basic facilities for a school to attract children. Though the state has achieved a lot in educational development, it is still far behind in respect of some of these basic facilities.

6.1.7 Financial Requirements for Achieving UEE

In order to curb the major challenges in relation to drop out, teacher position, infrastructures, there is a need for sound financial planning with strategic options, which will also facilitate to attain UEE in the state. Accordingly, the main objective of GoK for elementary education is, "All children aged 6-14 years are enroled by June 2007". The enrolment of the children in the elementary level is expected to be 9.56 millions at the end of 2004 and afterwards it will start declining and it would be 8.33 millions in 2011. The enrolment in classes I to VIII is 9.2 millions in 2003-04. Since the enrolment in private unaided (PUA) schools is increasing at a higher rate and if this trend is assumed to continue (Government 71.70 per cent, PA 11.89 per cent, PUA 16.41 per cent in the year 2003-04), the financial pressure on government will be reduced over the period.

The government of Karnataka in its budget allocations for the year 2003-04 has made the allocation of Rs. 2,139.07 crore for elementary education and Rs. 1,085.50 crore for high school education. As against this, the World Bank's calculation for these two levels for the year 2003-04 was Rs. 2,793 and Rs. 680 respectively for elementary and secondary education. The Majumdar Committee (Government of India, 1999) also made the detailed estimates of the financial requirements for making the elementary education as a fundamental right considering the number of out-of-school children, additional schools and class rooms to be constructed and inputs required for maintaining equity and quality in education. The Committee estimated that at least 8,000 primary schools need to be opened during the next 10 years to accommodate all the children.

According to these estimates, Karnataka would require Rs. 3,939.38 crores additionally of which Rs. 3,333.40 crores for primary and Rs. 605.98 crores for upper primary education by the year 2007-08 (Appendix A-6.14). The state government has to make special efforts to generate the required resources for achieving the 'universalisation of elementary education, For this purpose, community resources and state government's own revenue need to be raised. When all the children would be enrolled the financial need for secondary and higher education would also increase at a faster rate. Hence, the state government needs to make special commitments to raise the required resources in order to achieve universalisation of elementary Education by the year 2007.

6.1.8 Major Findings and Policy Options

The literacy rate in the state has improved over the years but the regional, caste and gender disparities continue to persist, which is a serious concern in the state. The gross enrolment has become more than 100 per cent but the girls are behind the boys and ST GER is less than SC and other communities. Though the net enrolment is much below 100, the dropout rate has declined substantially over the years especially at the lower primary stage. However, the dropouts have not made any improvement. Similar pattern has also been observed in the case of out of school children. Across the districts, in all respect, the north Karnataka districts are positioned at a lower level than the south Karnataka districts, which has come out very clearly. There are no new lower and higher primary schools seemed to have been established from the year 2001-02. But the unaided schools of all types are still coming up in the state. It will result in negative manner to accessibility of the education of the socially and economically backward people, which will nullify the improvement in dropout ratio at the primary level. Though the gender disparity in enrolment is yet to be achieved, the parity index in enrolment in school education has improved over time but across districts south Karnataka districts perform better than the north Karnataka districts. This indicates the low rate of girls' enrolment in the backward districts i.e. north Karnataka. The girls' enrolment in higher general education increased at a faster rate than that of professional education. Girls have crowded out the boys in higher general education, while it is very low in case of professional education. The state spends about 4 per cent of its GDP on education and elementary education gets the highest share. However, the real expenditure per student has not increased significantly during the 1990s. It is also important to note that allocation of resources has remained more or less stagnant for the last 15 years. It could be suggested that government can reduce the allocation of resources in higher education but increase it to the primary level, which will improve the infrastructure facilities and quality of the schools at this level. In this context, it could be suggested that the government should take necessary steps not to open any new schools but to utilise the existing schools optimally. The backward regions like northern part of Karnataka should be given priority. Since the gap in financial requirements of elementary education seems to be a matter of great concern, the role of Central Government and centrally sponsored schemes especially in primary education is necessary and Central Government is also hard pressed because of the fiscal situation in the country. Therefore, the state has to find out appropriate alternative sources to meet the gap. Such type of sources could be the corporate and banking sectors for financing education in the state. Further, planning for education should be an integrated planning rather than a plan for education in isolation. The integration could be primary health care and nutrition, which are significantly correlated to the educational achievements of the children in the state. In order to accomplish for the preparation of integrated planning of primary health care and nutrition along with primary education, there is a need for a strong and sound database with long time series data in detail, rural/ urban, SC/ST, male/female, etc. and in correct form. This will not only help the researchers but also help the government for effective planning. On the whole, the current educational situation in the state is quite satisfactory but still the state has about three per cent of the child population out of school. The dropout rate is high at the higher level of education. In this connection, the state has to make serious commitments to bring out the systematic improvement in the educational sector, which may be regarded as a model state for education.

6.2 Health Infrastructure

Every one wishes to be away from disease, disability and premature death. Substantial evidence is now available regarding the fact that good health is an important contributor to economic growth in any nation. In this background both policy makers and researchers have recognised the importance of investments in health and health infrastructures. Public spending on health and increase in incomes among the poor, seem to be the major determinants of health infrastructures, which would contribute to the better health status of the community. Such an outcome also depends on equitable sharing of provision of health services coupled with life-enhancing activities such as nutrition and education. Therefore, the role of government is very important in order to achieve better health in a country like India. As per the Constitution of India, the provision of health care by the public sector is a responsibility shared by state, central and local governments, although it is primarily a state responsibility in terms of service delivery.

6.2.1 Health Sector in Karnataka State: Review of Current Scenario

As part of the economic reforms, the finances for the health sector in different states seem to have been compressed. As a matter of response to such reduced finances, the reforms within the health sector have been tried out and attempts have been made to find more resources for the delivery of health services both within the health sector as well as outside the health sector. The state had gone for the external assistance in order to upgrade the existing public health care delivery system and increase the efficiency level of the health sector in the state. Accordingly, the World Bank offered a long-term soft loan worth of Rs. 590 crores in 1996-1997 under the Karnataka Health System Project (KHSDP). Nearly 256 secondary level hospitals were upgraded under the KHSDP. The user charge has been introduced in all these secondary level hospitals from 1998. Public-private partnerships have been attempted and few experiments have been carried out to outsource certain components of health care delivery and in some experiments public health care institutions have been transferred to NGOs for the day-to-day management. Risk pooling mechanism is in operation to protect the economically poor and socially vulnerable. A cooperative health plan (Yesashvini) is in operation for the last two years in order to give the financial protection for the low income groups such as farmers and milk vendors for major surgeries. Further, the state had initiated on a pilot basis a community health insurance in order to protect the poor and vulnerable groups like SC/STs.

6.2.2 Public-Private Partnership in Healthcare in Karnataka[4]

The government of Karnataka has embarked on an innovative experiment in involving private sector to operate the poor performing PHCs in partnership with government. As per this, the government will allow reputed medical colleges, NGOs or private sector trusts to come forward and manage PHCs. The primary health centres at Thithimathi in Kodagu district and Gumballi in Chamarajanagar district were the first two PHCs whose management was handed over to a voluntary organisation. Considering the very good outcome of the two PHCs in 2002, the government of Karnataka came up with a new scheme seeking the partnership of the non-governmental organisations, corporate trusts, and private medical colleges to manage up to 100 Category B PHCs with a performance of less than 50 per cent level of indicators. An elaborate procedure was drawn up for contracting out the PHCs with a selection committee headed by the Commissioner of health and

4. Reddy, Ramakrishna M. and Gaurav Arya (2005). *Public-Private Partnerships in Primary Healthcare : Contracting out PHC Facilities for Management*, The POLICY project, Futures Group International, New Delhi.

family welfare as the Chairman to select the NGOs. The public response has been lukewarm and with agitations against contracting out at some places. The response from the NGOs is also not very encouraging because of increased financial burden on the NGOs to manage PHCs with a bad record of performance in the past. Even the medical colleges were not enthusiastic.

An independent evaluation of the project revealed that in principal the scheme is forward looking with a potential. It allows the interested NGOs to operate within the existing public health care system and avoids duplication of facilities. It reduces the burden on state resources by tapping additional resources of the voluntary sector. However, the method of implementation and financial burden towards salaries and drugs, and the bureaucratic approach may act as bottlenecks in the implementation of the programme. The rigid structure of the memorandum of understanding (MoU) does not allow the private sector to run things differently or to introduce efficient management practices. The state government must liberalise the financial constraints and adopt a promotive attitude with a view to attract greater private participation for the ultimate goal of public private partnership in primary health care.

6.2.3 Health Infrastructure as Key Input Indicators in the State

The Government of Karnataka has accorded priority status to health sector over the years and has taken efforts to improve the standard of living of people thereby creating a positive influence on the health and well-being of the citizens of the state. The structural units of health sector are health infrastructure and its related health care financing, which are the key input indicators in the health delivery system. The state is following the national pattern of three-tier health infrastructure in rendering primary health care through primary health centres (PHCs), subcentres, and community health centres to its people by way of implementing various national and state health programme of public health importance through its network of various types of health and medical institutions. In the state level, the Department of Health and Family Welfare plays a vital role in implementing the following healthcare services: (i) Rural Health Component of Minimum Needs Programme, (ii) National Malaria Eradication Programme and National Filaria Control Programme, (iii) National Programme for Blindness Control, (iv) Prevention and Control of the communicable diseases like diarrhoea, kyasanur forest diseases, Japanese encephalitis, etc. (v) School Health Programme, (vi) Nutrition Programme, (vii) Nutrition Education and Demonstration, (viii) Laboratory Services and Vaccine Production Units, (ix) Education and Environmental Sanitation, (x) Health Education and Training Programme, and (xi) Curative Services. Accordingly, a wide network of healthcare institutions with updated infrastructure and providing quality healthcare were established in the state at all levels- primary, secondary, and tertiary. In the availability of health infrastructure, though the state is equally placed with Kerala in terms of total beds per lakh of population at 85.49, the number of hospitals in rural areas is only 25 which are far lower than the other southern states as shown in Appendix A-6.15. While Karnataka is better placed in population covered by an ANM, it has got far lower number of PHCs per CHC at 6.62 as compared to the Indian average of 8.48 as shown in the Appendix A-6.16. While Kerala and Karnataka are far ahead in most of the parameters of health infrastructure, Karnataka is better than Andhra Pradesh in many aspects.

It is also important to note the fact that the Report of the Task Force on Health and Family Welfare (2001) of the Government of Karnataka has categorised the districts of the state into three categories taking into account the disparities in health status of the population (Box 6.2). The seven districts of the northern part of the state have been classified as the

BOX 6.2

Health: Status-wise Classification of Districts

Worse-off Districts	*Intermediate Districts*	*Better-off Districts*
Bidar	Belgaum	Uttara Kannada
Gulbarga	Dharwad	Shimoga
Bijapur	Gadag	Udupi
Raichur	Haveri	Chickmagalur
Bagalkot	Davanagere	Dakshina Kannada
Koppal	Chitradurga	Kodagu
Bellary	Tumkur	Bangalore (Urban)
	Kolar	
	Hassan	
	Mandya	
	Bangalore (Rural)	
	Mysore	
	Chamrajnagar	

Source: *Final Report of the Task Force on Health and Family Welfare* (2001), Government of Karnataka.

FIGURE 6.10

Population per Medical Institution for the Period 1995-1996 to 2000-01

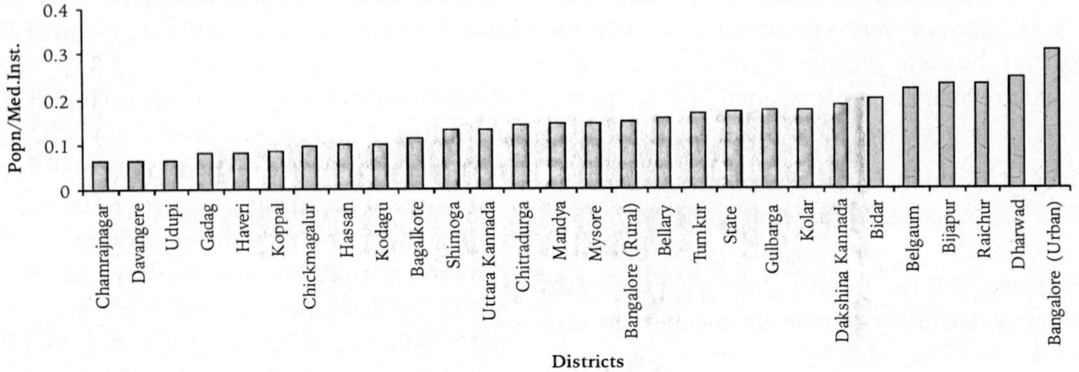

worse-off districts and rest of the four districts of north Karnataka fall under the category of intermediate districts. Thus, it seems that north Karnataka is lagging behind and the need is felt in this part of the state to strengthen the health services to bring these districts on par with other districts of the southern part of the state, which have been categorised as better-off districts.

Taking into account all types of health care institutions in the concerned districts, the average population served per institution was worked out for the period 1995-96 to 2000-01 for the districts of Karnataka as depicted in Figure 6.10.

Most of the districts in the north Karnataka seem to be having more number of people per health care institution as compared to the other districts in the southern part of the state. For example, except the districts of Kolar, Dakshina Kannada and Bangalore Urban, which fall in the southern part of the state, other districts like Bidar, Belgaum, Bijapur, Raichur and Dharwad are the districts of north Karnataka where larger population is served per institution. This may probably indicate the dearth of health care institutions in the northern part of the state.

Similarly, the average bed strength per lakh population was also worked out for different districts of the state as in the Figure 6.11. This indicates the strength or weakness of the healthcare facilities in providing the healthcare services to the community. It can be observed from the Figure 6.11 that 15 districts in the state fall below the state average and out of this, 8 districts happen to be in north Karnataka. Such uneven provision of beds highlights the weak spots of the state as far as provision of such infrastructure facilities across the districts. It can also be observed that in many of the backward districts, the number seems to be quite low as compared to other developed districts.

FIGURE 6.11

Average Beds/Lakh Popn. during 1995-96 to 1999-2000

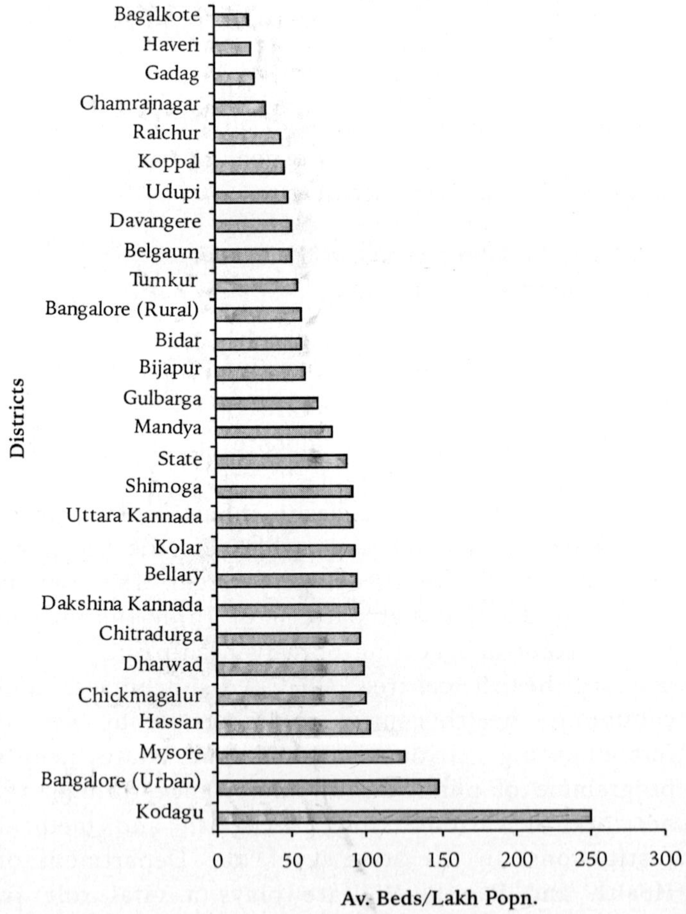

6.2.4 Healthcare Financing

Health care financing is another important input indicator of the infrastructural units in the health sector. Of course, the administration of the health system in the state is financed and managed by both the public and private sectors. Public sector funding includes allocations from Central Government, state governments, and external assistance. Private sector funding is largely by individuals, voluntary organisations and corporate bodies. The private funds flowing into the health sector are estimated as the private expenditure incurred towards health care and this includes the out-of-pocket expenses, and mandatory private insurance expenses namely the ESI, which is financed by contributions from the employees and the employers apart from the private insurance expenses. There are few other state departments, which contribute to the health sector indirectly like water supply and sanitation, nutrition and education, which are discussed in other sections in this chapter.

The interest evinced by *World Development Report 1993* (World Bank, 1993) on treating health expenditure as an investment has been responsible for attracting larger funds for the promotion of health world over. The debate, which was the outcome of this report, has also been responsible for the reforms in general, and in health sector in particular that, could improve the equity and efficiency of resource uses. The report argues for higher allocation of resources in the health sector. However, the resource allocation to health sector is gradually declining in recent years (Appendix A-6.17). The total resources flowing into the state health sector in nominal terms increased from Rs. 714 crore in 1997-98, to Rs. 1,033 crore in 2002-03 at an 8 per cent CAGR (combined average growth rate), which is a low and base level growth rate; whereas at 1993-94 constant prices, the growth rate has been negligible at a CAGR of 5 per cent from Rs. 525 crore to Rs. 656 crore during the same period. Though there is a positive CAGR during the six-year period, the year 2002-03 registered a negative growth rate of 7 per cent. The initial years had registered a higher annual growth rate compared to the last few years. This indicates that the resources allocation to the health sector is gradually on the decline.

It is important to observe the composition of the total resource flows into the health sector in Karnataka state. The main sources of the total resources under the budgetary provisions are Central funds, state funds, and external assistances. There are also non-budgetary resources, which flow directly into health sector and do not get reflected in the annual budget. It includes transfers from Government of India to the registered societies, user fees collected and maintained at the 256 secondary level hospitals, and insurance receipts collected by the Registrar of Cooperative Societies from farmers and milk vendors. The trend in percentage contribution of each of these resources indicates that the Central contribution which was 14 per cent in 1997-98 had increased to 25 per cent in 1999-00 and then had stabilised at 20 per cent (Appendix A-6.17). This resulted in the decline in the state contribution from 74 per cent to 67 per cent over the years, indicating lack of priority attached to the health sector. The contribution of resources through societies and user fees for the health sector seems to be negligible. Though these user charges are not reflected in the budget of the state, it accounts for 0.33 per cent in proportion to total budget allocation of health sector in 2002-03 (Mathiyazhagan, 2004). Further, the inflow of external assistance in the form of aid and grants to this sector had registered a sharp increase in recent years. It increased from 12 per cent in 1997-98 to 19 per cent in 2002-03. Though most of the external assistance is a long-term loan burden, it has created an asset to improve the health system in the state. However, the sustainability of the improved system with the help of external assistance is a huge task of the State Government with low budget allocation to this sector (Mathiyazhagan, 2004).

There has been a substantial increase in the total expenditure in Karnataka state for health and family welfare in nominal terms, but it has increased marginally in real terms. In nominal terms, it accounted for nearly Rs. 708 crore in 1997-98 and it increased to Rs. 1069 crore[5] in 2003-04 (Appendix A-6.18). Total government health expenditure in real terms (i.e., 1993-1994 prices) has registered only a marginal increase from 1994-95 to 2003-04 as compared to nominal terms. It accounted for nearly Rs. 521 crore in 1997-98 which increased to Rs. 638 crore in 2002-03. Out of the total plan allocation, merely 6 per cent was the maximum proportion allocated for the health and family welfare sector of the state during the last 10 years of planning. The budget share of this sector was around 3.63 per cent in 2003-04[6] as compared to 5.62 per cent in 1997-98. The total government allocation to health and family welfare in proportion to gross state domestic poduct (GSDP) reached a maximum of 1.3 per cent for the last 10 years. In fact, it has got reduced to less than one per cent in recent budget allocation for this sector (i.e., in 2003-04) (Appendix A-6.18). This has

5. This amount only refers to the revised estimates of the Budget in 2003-04.

6. The revised estimate of the last years, Budget i.e. 2003-04 is also indicating a decline and accounted only 3.63 per cent.

resulted in an underfunding situation in the health sector at the state level. It could be justified that the per capita health care spending in the state was around Rs. 140 in 1997-98, increasing to Rs. 201 in 2003-04, which is well short of the per capita of Rs. 1,300[7] estimated by WHO to constitute the minimum level of health spending to cover essential interventions in least developed countries like India (WHO, 2001). It implies that total government health care spending has not been kept on par with population growth and epidemiological changes, which increases the need for health care and health infrastructures.

The share of resources to the primary health care is a very important input indicator of health infrastructure as it acts as means to attain better health care output indicators in the state. Indeed, an investment in primary health care services is a better value for money than spending in secondary and tertiary levels. The share of expenditures on primary health care in the state has not increased for the last 7 years. It accounted for 55 per cent in 1997-98 and decreased to 53 per cent in 2002-03 (Appendix A-6.19). The revised estimate of the last year budget indicates 1 per cent increase of share of primary health care services (i.e. 54 per cent in 2003-04). Though there was significant reduction in the share of resources in the secondary level, this same share to the tertiary level had increased in the state. The share of secondary level accounted nearly 20 per cent in 1997-98 and decreased to 18 per cent in 2002-2003. The revised estimates show a decreasing trend (i.e. 13 per cent) of this share in 2003-04. In contrast to this, the share of tertiary level has shown continuous increase in the state. It accounted nearly 26 per cent in 1997-98 and it increased to 34 per cent in 2003-04. It is imperative to note that both expenditure on wages and non-wages had grown considerably over the years in nominal terms, but non-wages had a higher growth with a CAGR of 12 per cent, whereas wages had a CAGR of 7 per cent (Appendix A-6.19). The reduction in percentage of wages to the total expenditure from 65 in 1997-98 to 59 in 2003-04 is justified by the fact that large number of contracted employees had been recruited, thereby reducing the long-term liability of the state. Many of the sanctioned medical positions are still vacant and unless immediate steps are taken to fill up the vacancies in the medical personnel (Class A and B) categories, the state may land up in a situation with lack of quality doctors and other para-medical personnel.

7. It is equal to US$ 30 per person or a minimum of 5 per cent of GDP.

Availability of drugs and medicine plays a significant role in the functioning of efficient health care system at the primary level, which got a significant boost in recent years in the state. It is also evident from the annual budget of drugs and medicine for a PHC which has increased from Rs. 30,000 in 1997-98 to Rs. 50,000 in 1998-99 and further to Rs. 75,000 in 1999-2000 (Mathiyazhagan, 2004). Expenditure towards drugs and chemicals in relation to total health expenditure increased from 3 per cent in 1997-98 to 8 per cent in 2003-04 (Appendix A-6.19). However, the recent household survey results show that there was an acute short supply of drugs and medicine at the PHCs levels in the state (Mathiyazhagan, 2003a and 2004). Though the total share of primary health care resources was more than 50 per cent, the health gains in terms of health indicators is very low in rural areas as total government health care spending is very low. The low level of government health care has also created a situation, where a large proportion of the population depends on private sector and also affects poor income people in the state.

Breakup of health expenditure in the state show that share of urban health services has increased from about 26 per cent in the year 1997-98 to about 31 per cent in 2003-04 (Appendix A-6.20). But the resources devoted to the rural health services have been stagnated at about 31 per cent in the total revenue expenditure for the same period. This may probably indicate that the rural health services have not received higher allocations in the total pool which is likely to affect the health infrastructures and the delivery of health services in rural areas where majority of the population resides. The share of public health has also remained more or less same indicating the lower priority of allocating health expenditures to such an important component of the health sector.

The cost associated with ill-health—including medical bills and indirect cost such as lost income—can be catastrophic for the poor. Indeed, it is reflected in private heath expenditure through out-of-pocket in the state. The rural household in the state spends a high proportion of its income on health. The recent studies reveal that rural households spent nearly 10 to 26 per cent of their total household income in 1993-94 and 2003-04. (Mathiyazhagan 2003a and 2003b). Further, the recent NSSO rounds from 51st to 55th estimations also indicate about 6.10 per cent of the household allocations for medical expenses in proportion to total consumption expenditure in 1999-00. It is also important to note that the out-of-pocket payments are estimated to finance about 60 per cent of health expenditure in the state, which is an important barrier to access services for the poor populations. Further, the analysis from the NSS data (1995-96) in rural areas in the state indicate that nearly 23 per cent cited financial reasons for not availing treatment from government health care unit, which was only 15 per cent during 1986-87. In fact, it also accounts more in the case of people who used private health care providers. It implies that households need to borrow money or sell their assets to face health costs, particularly during the financially catastrophic illnesses. A recent estimate found that nearly 25 per cent of those hospitalised fell below the poverty line because of huge medical costs (World Bank, 2001). One can conclude that ill-health depletes household savings and earnings and impair the capacity of adults and children to work and learn, fostering conditions that create and perpetuate poverty. Therefore, the health care financing system plays an important role in determining access to health care services of the poor in the state. The results indicate that there is a disadvantage situation to the poor in health care financing system in the state as there is a high reliance on out-of-pocket payments for financing health care, which is the worst possible option for the poor and vulnerable people in the state. Furthermore, the public health care system in the states are subjected to centralised controls in health care financing that comprises service delivery, while the private system is largely unregulated and evolving in costly and ineffective directions with a less significant affirmative actions for an active prepayment market mechanism in most of the states in India.

6.2.5 Health Indicators

Health indicators are considered as output indicators of the health infrastructures in the state. A bird's eye view of where the state of Karnataka stands today as far as health status components (some of which, are also considered as indicators of human development) with the country as a whole would give us the performance of Karnataka *vis-à-vis* other states. A look at three indicators should give us an idea of how far Karnataka has progressed in providing basic health facilities/ infrastructures to its people. These are the infant mortality rate, the maternal mortality rate and life expectancy at birth.

The infant mortality rate is a pointer not only to the health status of the population but also to the social and cultural factors that have an effect on health. Throughout the country the infant mortality rate (IMR) has declined in the eighties and nineties (Appendix A-6.21). In Karnataka about 50 out of 1000 infants born die every year (NFHS-2 shows IMR as 51.5 while SRS, 1998 as 58). This is more than the numbers in Kerala, Gujarat, Maharashtra, Punjab, Tamil Nadu and West Bengal. Decline in the infant mortality rate between 1993-90 and 1993 was also higher in Andhra Pradesh, West Bengal and Tamil Nadu than in Karnataka.

The estimate of under-five mortality also indicates that there has been significant reduction in the state. Though the under-five mortality rate (U5MR) reduced from 87.3 to 69 per 1, 000 live births in 1992 and 2001 respectively, it was very high as compared to the national average. The malnutrition is one among the causes for high under-five mortality rate (U5MR) in the state (Mathiyazhagan, 2004). The MMR, women who die of causes linked to pregnancy and child birth, as per the UNICEF estimate shows that they numbered nearly 450 out of every one lakh live births in 1995. This was higher than the national average. The SRS estimates reveal only 195 out of every one lakh population in 1998 (Appendix A-6.21). As compared to all these estimates, the round realities reflect much more maternal deaths especially in the rural areas in the state. MMR for Karnataka is higher than the average for the 15 major states; it is also worse than the figures for Andhra Pradesh, Gujarat, Haryana, Maharashtra, Punjab, Tamil Nadu and West Bengal (Mathiyazhagan, 2004).

Finally, we may place Karnataka on the all-India scale in respect of the life expectancy at birth of its citizens. The International Conference on Population Development (ICPD) had resolved in 1994 to target a life expectancy of 70 by 2005 and 75 by 2015. Against this, Karnataka has achieved a life expectancy at birth of 62 which is slightly higher than the national level of 60. Kerala, Maharashtra, Haryana, Tamil Nadu and Punjab are among the Indian states that are ahead of Karnataka in this respect.

If one looks at some of the input indicators of the health infrastructure in Karnataka and the other southern states, it is interesting to note that Karnataka is lagging behind the states of Kerala and Tamil Nadu. However the state seems to be comfortable with better levels of indicators as far as the state of Andhra Pradesh as well as the situation that exists at the all-India level.

With regard to the some of the health status indicators it needs to be noted that the district-wise information is very scanty in nature. However, based on some studies an attempt is made to present district level IMR, which was computed, based on the census data for 1991. (Rajan and Mohanchandram, 1998) The Figure 6.12 gives us the district-wise IMR. However, the IMR estimates for the state of Karnataka show that there is no clear trend emerging either in favour of north or south Karnataka. However, the highest IMR in the state is found in Bellary district, which happens to be the district of northern part of the state.

6.2.6 *Per Capita Health Expenditure at District Levels*

The public provisioning of health care facilities need to take into account such disparities and future actions in this regard should aim at correcting such imbalances. The health care financing plays an important role in the creation as well as maintenance of such facilities across the districts. In this background, it would be proper to look at public health expenditure in different districts. The per capita expenditure would well capture the disparities in distribution resources across the districts. The Figure 6.13 displays pattern of per capita expenditure on health for different districts in the state.

It can be noted that 10 districts fall below the state average as far as per capita expenditure on health and nutrition is concerned. Out of these 10 districts, 7 happened to be the districts of north Karnataka. Districts with higher state per capita expenditure are 17 out of which only 5 are to be found in the north. The message that one can infer is that health care expenditures in terms of per capita expenditure by and large is highly cornered by the districts of south Karnataka. This would probably support the performance of southern districts with regard to the health care institutions and bed strength for a given set of population as discussed above.

FIGURE 6.12

Infant Mortality Estimaes for Districts of Karnataka as per 1991 Census

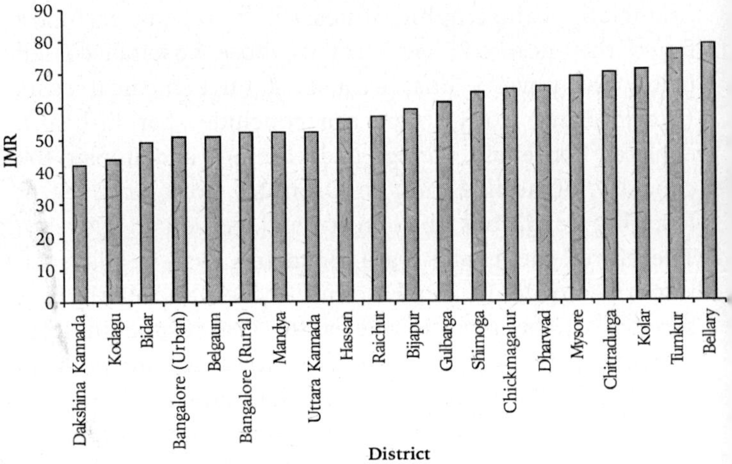

6.2.7 *Major Challenges*

The changing demographic and epidemiological scenario in the state has posed many challenges for the health sector. For example the challenge of HIV with the combination of TB in the state needs immediate

FIGURE 6.13

Per Capita Expenditure on Health and Nutrition for 2003-04

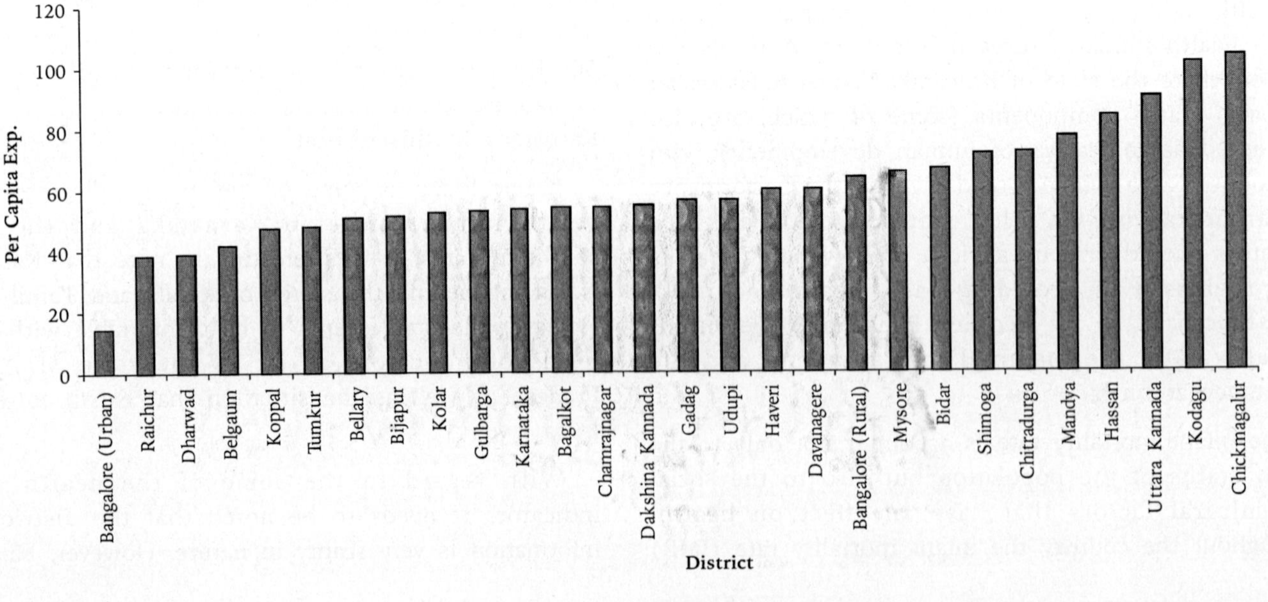

attention. The recurrences of malaria in the state prove that there is need to control and eradicate communicable diseases, especially high incidence of diseases like tuberculosis, malaria and filariasis. Under the National Malaria Eradication Programme, although efforts were made extensively to control and eradicate the disease, the number of positive cases increased six fold between 1991 and 2000 (almost 1,00,000 cases annually). The district-wise prevalence rate of TB is shown in the in the Figure 6.14.

It can be observed that the Bangalore Urban district is topping the list as far as prevalence of TB cases are concerned followed by Belgaum and Gulbarga. There seems to be no clear pattern as far as the distribution of TB cases across the districts. However, the magnitude of the disease can be understood in each district based on the information that is currently available. Similarly the positive cases of HIV have also been increasing in the state. Figure 6.15 gives us HIV positive cases across the districts.

FIGURE 6.14

Prevalance of TB Cases in Karnataka: 2003-04

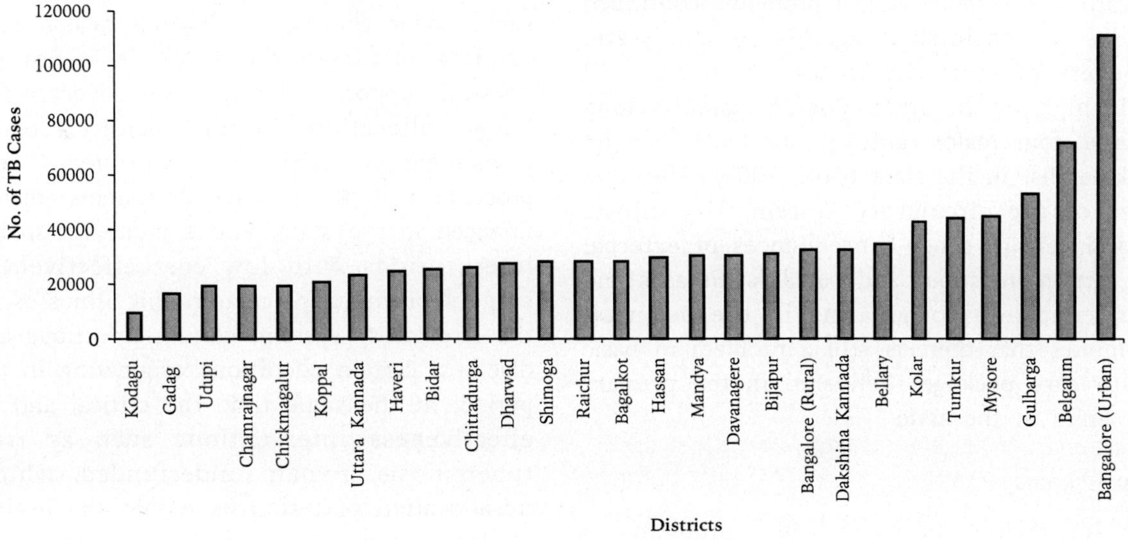

FIGURE 6.15

Number of HIV Positive Cases in Karnataka 2003-04

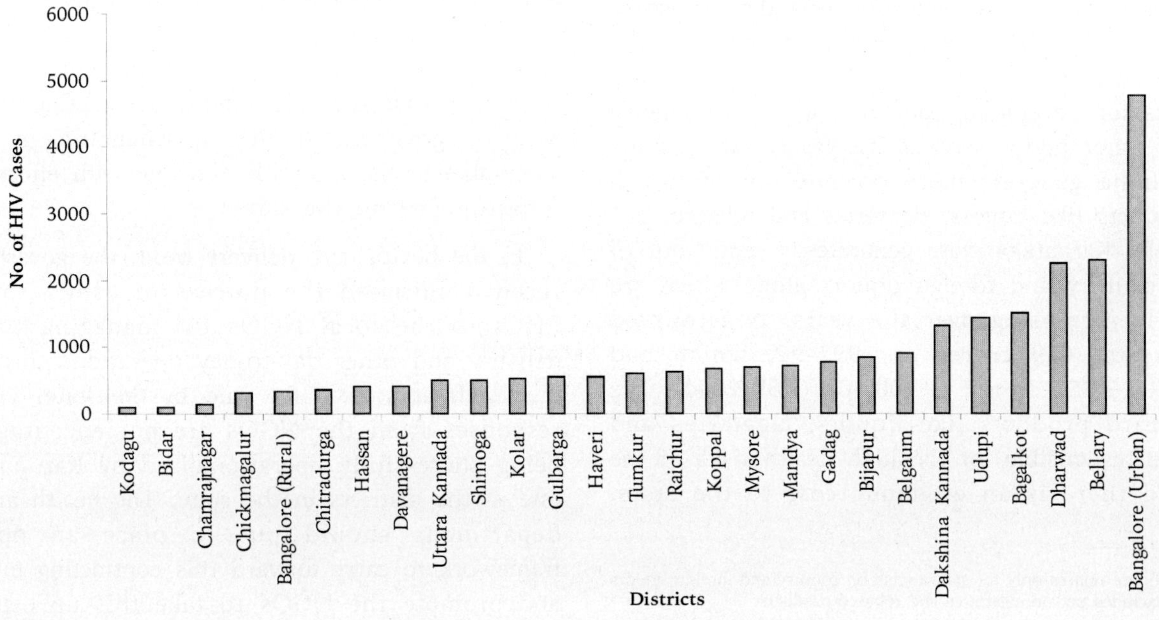

It can be noted that, the Bangalore Urban district is again in lead position as far as number of HIV positive cases are concerned. Next to follow are the districts of Bellary, Dharwad and Bagalkot (Figure 6.17). With regard to both TB and HIV the district Kodag is the least affected one. Majority of districts in north Karnataka are having comparatively larger cases of HIV. Recently, the deadly combination of TB and HIV has been considered to be a major threat and more attention needs to be paid by the authorities in understanding this dimension of the disease scenario for effective design and implementation of intervention strategies.

Despite these remarkable improvements in key health indicators, enormous health problems continued to remain as an unfinished agenda in the state. Absolute levels of mortality in the state are still unacceptably high in the state. For consistently long period of time, four major cause groups have been on top of the killer list in the state (GoK, 2003). They are: (i) diseases of the circulatory system, (ii) injury, poisoning and certain other consequences of external cause, (iii) certain infectious and parasitic diseases and (iv) certain conditions originating in the perinatal period. It implies that there is still a problem in basic public health care packages delivered in the primary health care units in the state.

6.2.8 Policy Options

In order to address the basic health problems in terms of health outcomes, it is often suggested to enhance the allocation of resources in the health sector. It is imperative to note that the basic conclusion on developing countries' revenue-raising capability is clear: it is significantly less than those in industrial countries, and the poorer is the country, the less is the capacity. This limited capacity has important implications for developing countries' ability to finance health and other public services. However, some of the states in India generate more revenue out of health hazard products like liquors, cigarettes and tobacco, etc. For example, Karnataka state generates revenue out of excise on country and foreign liquors alone which are significantly increasing over the years. It accounted nearly for Rs. 419 crores in 1991-92, which had increased Rs. 2,052 crores[8] in 2002-03 (RBI, 2004). The health hazard products like liquors, cigarettes and tobacco are responsible for the high health risks of the people and there is an economic cost to the state. Indeed, it is an excess burden because virtually all taxes create distortions (substitution effects) in economic decision making of the individuals or households that reduce income and production by more than the amount transferred to the government. Therefore, the government should discourage people from the consumption of health hazard products by taxing heavily on these products. An increase of tax revenues from the health hazard products indicates that people are consuming more of these products. It implies that the state government is collecting more and more tax revenue by selling the health hazard products like liquors, cigarettes tobacco, etc. but allocated not even half of the tax revenue of these sources to the health sector over the years. Though health sector is the priority sector in the state, it is not getting any political support and state level advocacy for increased budget allocations in this sector. It results in low investment in health sector and creates several major problems with the way health systems are now run and financed in the state. Public money is spent on health interventions with low cost effectiveness such as surgery or financial catastrophic illnesses, diseases of the circulatory system, certain infectious and parasitic diseases, certain conditions originating in the perinatal period, at the same time the critical and highly cost-effectiveness interventions such as treatment of tuberculosis, remain underfunded, which leads to misallocation of resources within the health sector. It is also an indication that these are the main causes of burden of diseases in the state (GoK, 2003).

The higher spending alone, for any level of income and educational levels in the state will not, necessarily translate into better health. There is a need for good and effective government policies, which reflect a relationship between policy choices and health outcomes in the state. It implies that there is a need to redefine the current role of government health financing in ensuring acceptable levels of health outcome with effective health infrastructures in the state.

In the health care delivery front, the government has recently initiated the process of contracting out of PHCs to the local NGOs for managing the service delivery and other day-to-day operations through their own staff at a fixed fee paid by the state. Though the responses from the NGOs are not encouraging, it is being successfully operationalised by Karuna Trust in one of the districts in the state. The health and finance department should put in place an operational framework to carry forward this contracting out exercise and promote the NGOs to take this up especially in

8. This figure relates only for state excise on country and foreign liquors and excludes tax on cigarettes and tobacco products.

rural areas. A mutually acceptable formula has to be worked out especially in staff deployment and working capital management.

In the healthcare financing front, there is a need for financial protection from the catastrophic illnesses of the socially and economically backward people in the state. All the initiatives undertaken in this regard, is not really benefiting the needy people throughout the state. The universal health insurance scheme by Government of India through four leading insurance companies could be supported by the state government with special subsidies in addition to the Central subsidies for the socially and economically backward people in the state in order to bring all sections of the society into the insurance scheme.

There is a need to reallocate the resources in terms of higher priority to the primary health care services. The role of government in terms of tertiary care should be reduced, which will also help to reduce the wage component of the health care delivery system in the state. In this context, it is suggested to bring all the secondary and tertiary care facilities under the corporate body, which will lead to more allocation for public health and primary health care services with effective health infrastructures in the backward districts in the state.

Introduction of user fees at the secondary and tertiary level hospitals are operating in the state. The resource generated from the user fee is very minimal as compared to the private health provider. It is suggested that the Finance Department should evolve a uniform framework for collecting user fees based on the type of hospitals—CHCs/*taluka* hospital and district hospital. The mechanism of collecting user charges should be strengthened and periodical/annual revisions of user fees as required should be implemented. But, increase in user fee should result in visible changes in the hospital environment and improvement in the quality of care services.

6.3 Nutrition

Nutrition is an input indicator to the health and it is significantly correlated with health and morbidity as the quantity and the type of food that we eat influence our health status. However, still nutrition has not become a part of the primary health care in India and in the state. In a developing country like India, unbalanced diet and adulteration leading to malnutrition, and undernutrition resulting from chronic starvation are the main factors leading to reduced immune system and physical growth and vitamin deficiency diseases (Box 6.3).

BOX 6.3

Ratio of Malnutrition in Children in Karnataka (1998-99)

2:1 – Underweight (44 per cent)

3:1 – Stunted (37 per cent)

5:1 – Wasted (20 per cent)

Source: NFHS, 1998-99.

Every second child is underweight in Karnataka state, 1 in 3 children stunted and 1 in 5 children wasted, which is due to reduction in average per capita foodgrain consumption (NSSO, 1999). Calorie intake of the poor is less than the required quantity as compared to the excess intake by the rich. There is a reported deficit of 300-350 calories and 8-10 grams of protein in the existing diet of pregnant women and nursing mothers (GoK, 2004).

6.3.1 Overview of Nutritional Programmes in Karnataka

Nutrition programmes have generally been focused on improving the nutritional status of children particularly those who are attending *anganwadis* and government primary schools.

BOX 6.4

Overview of Nutritional Programmes in Karnataka

Programme	*Year*	*Coverage and Beneficiaries*	*Component*	*Assistance*	*Objectives*
		Past Programmes			
Mid-day Meals	1963-64 to 1992-93	Govt. primary school children in the age group 5 to 11 years. CARE food benefited nearly 7 lakh children per annum in 53 *talukas*.	Upma was served as ready food, contents—wheat-80 gm, oil-50 gm.	CARE (supplied wheat and oil free of cost) Scheme was closed at the end of 1992-93.	To provide supplementary nutrition and encourage parents to enrol and retain children in school.

Contd. ...

...Contd. ...

Programme	*Year*	*Coverage and Beneficiaries*	*Component*	*Assistance*	*Objectives*
			Past Programmes		
Energy Food Programme	1980-81 to 1992-93	Govt. primary school children in the age group 6 to 13 years. Five units existed in Mysore, Belgaum, Chitradurga, Raichur and Doddaballapur under the programme. Benefited nearly 5 lakh children every year.	100 gm of ready food per child per day was supplied directly to schools.	100 per cent-state govt. UNICEF provided machineries for preparing weaning food in 5 units.	This scheme was started with assistance from Karnataka State Agro Corn Products Ltd. Bangalore as there was gradual reduction in assistance from CARE.
Ksheera Yojana	1994-95	Govt. primary school children studying in class 1 to 4. Implemented in Bangalore.	100 ml. milk.		Nutrition to children.
Akshaya Food Programme	1993-94 to 1996-97	Govt. primary school children studying in class 1 to 4.	Ready food supplied directly to schools.	State government Assistance from Karnataka State Agro Corn Products Ltd. Bangalore.	Started as assistance from CARE completely stopped.
National Nutrition Supplement Programme	1995-96 to 2001-02	Children studying in govt. and aided primary schools with 80 per cent attendance.	Three kg rice per month per child distributed through PDS.	Assistance from Govt. of India through Food Corporation of India.	Induce parents to send children to school.
National Nutrition Supplement Programme	Since 2002-03	Primary school children in aided schools continue to get assistance on records of 80 per cent attendance.	Three kg rice per month per child.	Govt. of India	-do-
Supplementary Nutrition Programme (SNP)	Since 1975	SNP is a major component of ICDS initiated in the year 1975. Selected children between 6 months to 3 years; children in age group 3-6 years attending *anganwadi* centres; pregnant women and nursing mothers.	A. In 183 ICDS projects; SNP-2 days ready to eat food-1 day-egg-3 days-cooked rice Pregnant and nursing mothers are given 1.5 kg of rice and 2.75 gms green gram.	Cost of administrative. expenditure met by Central Government. Cost of Supplementary nutrition borne by the state government. Cost of Amylase-rich energy Food(AREF) under PMGY-borne by the Central Government.	To fill the gap between equired food in terms of calories, proteins, vitamins, minerals, fats, etc., and that is actually available at home through food intake.
Akshar Dasoha Programme (Mid-day-meals)	Initiated in 2001-02	The programme was first initiated in one govt. primary school in every *taluka* of 7 backward districts. In 2002-03 it was extended to all govt. schools in these districts. From 2003-04, children studying in class 1 to 5 in all the govt. primary schools are covered.	The hot cooked food served daily per child is equivalent to 400 calories containing 100 gms rice, 20 gms pulses, 25 gms vegetables, 5 gms salt and 3 gms oil. In addition, each child is supposed to get 2 vitamin sup.	Central government provides free food grains (rice/wheat). Conversion charges are met by the state government.	To improve enrolment, retention rate, child health and performance level of children.
Public Distribution System (PDS)		The coverage of PDS is universal in Karnataka. Comprehensive Tribal Development Programme of GoI, was initiated in 1986 in 23 *talukas* in Mysore, Chickmagalur, Kodagu and Dakshina Kannada.	The beneficiaries under TPDS get foodgrains at lower prices compared to general mass. They also get larger quantities and their PDS basket contains additional commodities. Currently 28 kgs of rice, 7 kgs of wheat and 7 litres of kerosene are given to urban beneficiaries.	PDS is implemented with assistance from Government of India.	The objectives are to ensure availability of basic food for mass consumption and ensure food security for the poor by supplying food-grains and other essential commodities at affordable prices.

Despite the programmes being implemented for a long period of 40 years, the nutritional status of the children and women in the state is not satisfactory. Currently four nutritional programmes are implemented in the state. It includes: National Nutrition Supplement Programme Supplementary Nutrition Programme, Akshar Dasoha Programme, and supply of foodgrains to the poor at subsidised rates under the public distribution system. A brief about these programmes is presented in Box 6.4.

6.3.2 *Overall Scenario of Nutritional Status in the State*

A comparative picture of the nutritional status as reflected in NFHS-1 (1992-93) and NFHS-2 (1998-99) reveals that though there is a decline in the percentage of undernourished children in four year period (Figure 6.16) , the nutritional status of children and women in Karnataka is lower than that in the neighbouring states of Andhra Pradesh, Goa and Kerala (Box 6.5). Severe anaemia is high among children below 3 years (Appendix A-6.22). This indicates that current coverage is not sufficient and SNP should focus intensively on children not attending to *anganwadis*. At present AREF is given as nutritional supplement. But, there is no surety that mothers who take the AREF powder prepare porridge for the children at home.

BOX 6.5

Nutritional Surveys

The nutritional surveys conducted by NNMB in rural areas of the state also reveal that mild and moderate undernutrition is higher in the state.

FIGURE 6.16

State of Malnutrition

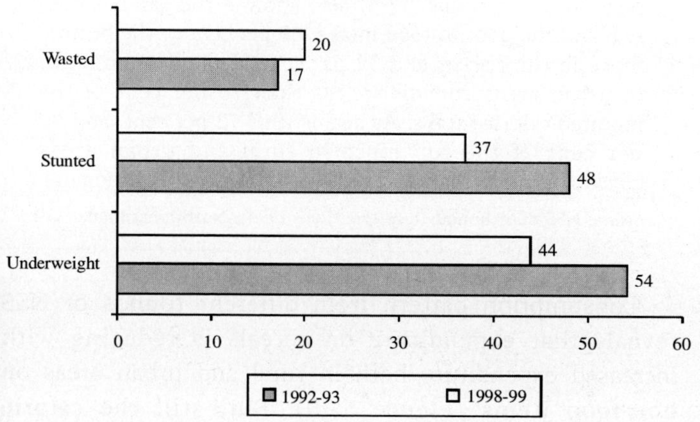

The NFHS-I results indicate that there was a significant variation in malnourishment across districts. Less than 40 per cent of the children (3<6 years) in backward districts of Koppal, Haveri, Raichur, Bellary, Bidar, Bijapur and Bagalkot fall in normal nutritional category. This disparity in the nutritional status among districts indicates the need for enhancing the coverage of nutritional programmes in these districts (Box 6.6). Percentage of BPL population is higher in most of these districts as compared to state average. These districts also rank low in terms of per capita income. Totally 45 per cent of the boys fall in the normal category while 42 per cent of the girls fall in normal category. This could be due to better care and slightly larger share that the boys get from the food basket. The percentage of children with severe malnourishment is also higher as compared to boys. According to nutritional experts, moderate under nutrition may not affect an individual as far as his day-to-day functioning is concerned. But, that needs to be taken as an alarming sign and corrected gradually with proper intervention in the absence of which moderate condition may turn to severe condition. Living conditions, education and social background influence nutritional status of the population. There are evidences of such correlation as revealed in NFHS-I & II (Figures 6.17 and 6.18).

BOX 6.6

Disparities

- Median duration of any breast feeding was longer by two months for male child (NFHS-I) in 1992-93, but no such difference is found in 1998-99.
- Initiation of supplementary food also started at a relatively younger age for boys than female children (NFHS-I).
- Nutritional status of children and women is lower in rural areas.
- Percentage of severely malnourished children higher in backward districts
- Percentage of undernourished children and women with low nutritional status is high:
  - among illiterates,
  - among SCs/STs,
  - among non-working mothers, and
  - in families with low standard of living.

FIGURE 6.17

Undernourished Children by Background Characteristics (Weight for Age)

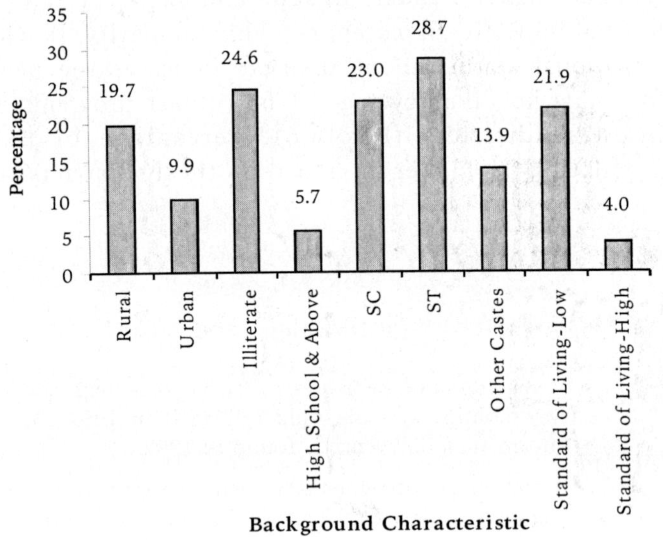

FIGURE 6.18

Percentage of Women with Any Anaemia by Background Characteristics

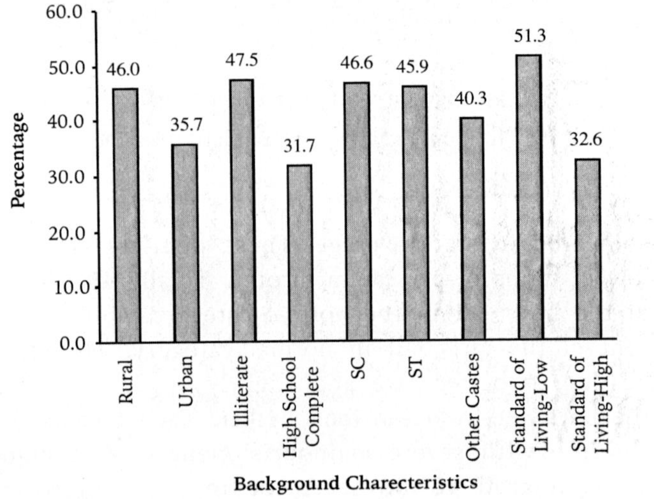

Composition of food plays an important role in nutritional status (Box 6.7). Anaemia is found to be low among those who consume fruits and vegetables. Thirty-nine per cent of the women suffer from mild undernourishment in the state. On the other hand there is also a problem of over nutrition. Nearly 14 per cent of the women have body mass index (BMI) above 25.0 kilogrammes/metres squared (kg/m^2). The percentage of such women may increase in the future, particularly among educated, rich and in urban areas.

BOX 6.7

Nutritional Status

NSS 52nd (1995-96) round results reveal that the prevalence of tuberculosis (TB) is highest among aged in both rural and urban areas and the prevalence of malnutrition diseases is higher among aged in rural areas as compared to other age groups. Malnutrition reduces immunity hence enhancing susceptibility to infections. TB is one of the major infectious diseases linked to nutritional deficiency. Elderly population particularly the poor may find it difficult to take appropriate quantity of food due to dependence on other family members. Unfortunately, we do not have adequate data to estimate the nutritional intake by elderly population and its linkage with their nutritional and morbidity status.

6.3.3 Nutritional Intake in Karnataka

Karnataka ranks fourth in terms of per capita foodgrains production next to Punjab, Haryana and Uttar Pradesh with a average share of 5 per cent in total foodgrain production. But, Karnataka ranks 17th and 18th in terms of average per capita monthly consumption of cereals in rural and urban areas respectively. Per capita consumption of cereals is 11.53 kg in rural and 10.21 kg in urban areas both less than the national average (Box 6.8). Per capita monthly consumption of pulses is one kg in urban area and 0.95 kg in rural area. In terms of average expenditure on consumption also Karnataka ranks 16th in rural and 14th in urban area. Figure 6.21 presents the percentage share of consumption components in total household expenditure.

BOX 6.8

Nutritional Intake

NSS 50th round (1993-94) also showed the gap between rich and the poor in food intake. 69 per cent of the bottom mpce in rural areas and 32 per cent of the bottom mpce in urban areas consumed less than 70 per cent of the required calorie intake. As against this 72 per cent and 90 per cent of the top mpce in rural and urban areas consumed more than 150 per cent of calorie requirements.

Source: NSS 50th Round (July 1993-June 1994), Nutritional Intake.

Consumption pattern from different rounds of NSS reveals that expenditure on cereals is reducing with increased expenditure both in rural and urban areas on non-food items (Figure 6.19). But, still the calorie requirement both in rural and urban areas comes largely from consumption of cereals. Consumption of pulses and pulse products, which are main source of protein is very low accounting for about 3-4 per cent of the foodgrains consumption for bottom mpce class and 8-9 per cent for the top mpce class in both rural and urban areas. Per capita monthly expenditure on *pan*, tobacco and intoxicants is more than the expenditure on fruits, eggs, fish, meat and sugar and higher in rural areas (Rs. 18.23) than in urban areas (Rs. 12.48) constituting around 4 per cent of the total expenditure in rural and 2 per cent in urban areas. Rural households spend Rs.500 per person per month while urban households spend Rs. 911 (1999-00).

FIGURE 6.19

Consumption Pattern as Percentage Share to Total Expenditure: 1999-2000

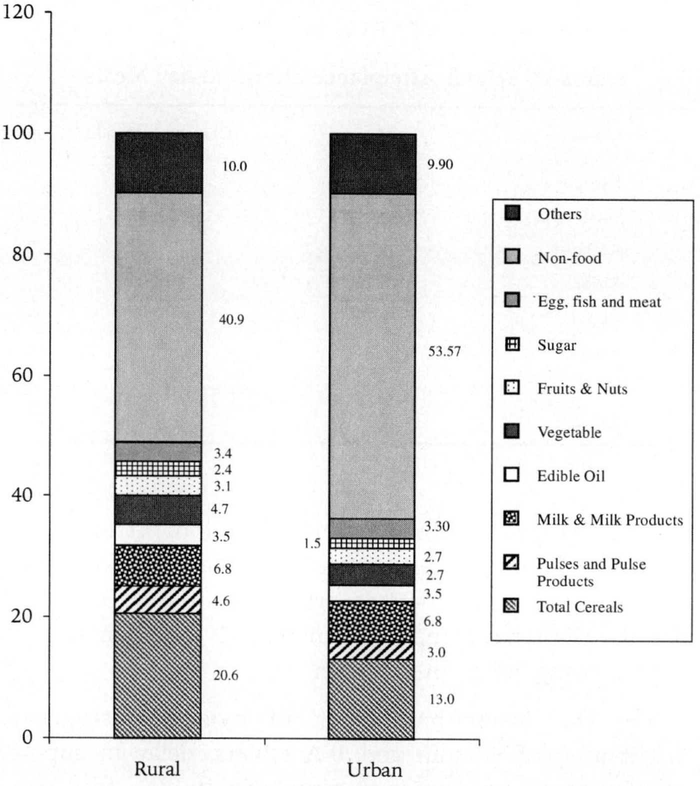

There is a wide disparity in the consumption of foodgrains between the rich and the poor as shown in Figure 6.21. The gap is more so in rural area. Per capita monthly cereals and pulses consumption is 7.43 and 0.49 kg for lowest mpce class and 14.89 and 1.3 kg for top mpce class respectively in rural area. In urban area it is 8.09 kg and 0.59 kg for bottom and 10.27 and 1.36 kg for top mpce class. There is a need to narrow this gap through proper intervention as the poor both in rural and urban areas would need more calories as they are generally engaged in laborious activities or heavy work as compared to the rich and the middle class occupied in sedentary work requiring lesser calories. The factors that affect nutritional status is presented in Box 6.9.

6.3.4 Financing of Nutrition Programmes

All the nutrition programmes of the state receive assistance from Central Government. While SNP and TPDS are part of the Central Government programmes of ICDS and PDS respectively, mid-day meal is a state initiated scheme. Administrative cost of SNP is met under ICDS. Foodgrains are supplied under PDS at subsidised rates, while they are supplied freely under mid-day meals.

BOX 6.9

Plan Expenditure on Nutrition in Karnataka

(Crores)

Seventh Plan	183.39
Eighth Plan	108.38
Ninth Plan	207.35 (A)
Tenth Plan	263.91 (outlay)

- Currently, Karnataka government is not receiving any direct assistance from external agency for nutrition programmes. Assistance from CARE which was available from 1992-93 was stopped. UNICEF assistance was available for establishing machineries for preparing weaning food under Energy Food Programme, which operated till 1992-93.
- SNP is provided @ Rs.1.50 per child and @ Rs. 3.00 per malnourished child, pregnant woman and nursing mother.
- The plan expenditure on nutrition in Karnataka has increased from Rs. 183.39 crore in Seventh Five-Year Plan to Rs. 263.91 crore in Tenth Five-Year Plan (Box 6.10). However, as per the estimates of Directorate of Women and Child Development, the financial allocations made under SNP are not sufficient to provide 300 calories and 8-10 gms of protein per day per beneficiary for 300 days. The requirement and deficit in budget allocation is highlighted below:
    - To increase the coverage of beneficiaries under ICDS as per the Supreme Court Direction (Writ petition No. 196/2001), the requirement of funds to start additional

11,313 *anganwadi* centres is estimated to be 52 crores.

- Under PMGY, AREF is given to children in 0-3 years and malnourished children below 6 years @ Rs. 2 per day.
- Under Akshar Dasoha (mid-day meals), state government bears the conversion charges @ Rs. 1 per child per day i.e. pulses and salt-0.50 paise; oil-0.10 paise; vegetables-0.20 paise; cooking gas-0.20 paise. In addition, Rs. 11.00 per child per year is provided for additional nutrition in terms of IFA, vitamin and deworm tablets.

Karnataka government proposes to cover children studying in 1-10 classes under mid-day meals. At the current enrolment of 70.53 lakh children, the budget requirement would be Rs. 21,459.15 lakhs per year (Rs. 15,516.70 lakhs for meals + Rs. 5,166.61 lakhs for remuneration of cooks + Rs. 775.84 lakhs for provision of deworm tablets and IFA and Vitamin supplements) excluding the one time allocation made towards establishment of kitchen centres and permanent structure for water storage.

BOX 6.10

Positive Institutional Interventions

- To curb leakages in PDS, government has introduced coupon system for rationed commodities.
- Relaxation of norms for increasing number of ration shops in rural areas.
- Mobile fair price shops operate in tribal and remote areas of Mysore, Kodagu, Dakshina Kannada, Raichur and Gulbarga.
- State government has taken the responsibility of transporting the foodgrains from *taluka* level to fair price shops in rural areas.
- Ninety-three proposals have been submitted for the issue of fair price shops to *Stree Shakti* groups (2004-2005).
- Extension of coverage of TPDS: Government of Karnataka has identified 63 lakh BPL families under TPDS for receiving antyodaya and yellow cards (addition of 55.7 lakh families). Government of India had identified 4.9 lakh families under Antyodaya and recently extended the benefits to additional 2.40 families.
- Mid-day meals to be implemented with assistance from *Gram Panchayats* and *Stree Shakti* groups.
- Proposal to extend mid-day meals up to 10th standard.

Programme-wise details of expenditure and coverage are presented in Appendix A-6.23. There is a reduction in the expenditure on SNP and TPDS over the years. This is not desirable as 20 per cent of the population lives below poverty line and there is wide prevalence of chronic and acute under nutrition in the state. (Box 6.10).

6.3.5 Evaluation of the Programmes

Studies and Reports

Akshar Dasoha scheme has resulted in an increase in the attendance by 2.75 per cent in the first month of implementation in 2003-04. There is reported increase in the involvement in school activities (Mid-day Meals Background Note, 2004). In addition 95,000 women working as cooks have benefited from the scheme.

TABLE 6.1

Status of School Attendance after Mid-day Meals

Districts	*Change (per cent)*
Koppal	4.9
Gulbarga	2.1
Raichur	5.8
Bidar	2.4
Bellary	4.6
Bijapur	8.3
Bagalkot	13.5
Total	**5.7**

Source: Hiremath, U.B., 2004.

District-wise improvement in school attendance available for the seven districts, where mid-day-meals was initiated in 2001-02 is presented in Box 6.12. All the districts have reported increased attendance, the impact being more in Bagalkot.

On the other hand lack of hygiene, irregular distribution of vitamin and IFA tablets, delay in supply of foodgrains, limited time available for the headmistress to attend to other activities and diversion of children's attention towards food are some of the drawbacks of the scheme that have been reported.

ICDS: A household survey carried out as a part of the World Bank sponsored study that enquired into the factors that facilitated successful primary school completion (Vimala, *et al.*, 2003) in states of Karnataka, Andhra Pradesh, and Uttar Pradesh, revealed that four per cent of the children (0-5 years) were severely undernourished and nine per cent are severely stunted. The study pointed out that community and teachers appreciated the mid-day-meals programmes in Karnataka. Ninety-nine per cent of the children surveyed, had enrolled either in *anganwadi* or school. Though the status of ICDS was found to be satisfactory as compared to Andhra Pradesh and Uttar Pradesh, preschool education was found to be ineffective. It was also found that *anganwadi* worker (AWW) focused on record keeping, which is one of her major duties. The very purpose of SNP was not served as foodgrains given to pregnant and nursing mothers went to family food basket.

6.3.6 Experiences and Lessons for Corrective Action

- Role of community and *Gram Panchayats* limited: *Bal Vikas Samitis* have been constituted. But they are not functioning regularly. Community participation is limited to demands placed by parents for additional benefits rather than improving the efficiency of the implementation. Nutrition education is imparted only during health camps, which are organised rarely.

- AWW generally keeps record of nutritional status of children and pregnant women. This can be formalised in such a way that the information is collected twice a year and computerised so that regular village level nutritional surveillance is made possible. This would put an additional burden in the first year but, in the subsequent years only additional data is fed. Data can be pooled at one centralised agency. This may lessen the burden of AWW who currently is entrusted with maintenance of 26 registers (birth, death, pregnancy, nutrition, etc.) and also is responsible for organising *Stree Shakti* groups.

- There is absence of continuous monitoring and provision of assistance to severely malnourished children. Since *anganwadi* workers are entrusted with various responsibilities, follow up visits to houses are not made by them. This will not ensure intake of supplementary food as well as vitamin and IFA tablets by children in the age group 3-6 years and by pregnant women.

- Evaluation reports on nutrition programmes should be sent to concerned department at the district level for the perusal of department officials and programme officers.

- Quality of CARE food that was available till 1992-93 is generally appreciated by programme officers. SNP may be continued on the similar lines including pregnant women and nursing mothers as the foodgrains given to these women goes to family food basket.

- Despite of the frequent raids made by the KFCS officials there is rampant illegal operation of PDS in the state. Recently, it was found that 70 per cent of the rice received from FCI, for PDS, mid-day meals and drought relief was stored and sold in black market in Karnataka. State government has ordered for an enquiry, but it gives a clear picture of why the objectives of well laid policies of the government are not reaching the poor, needy and deprived population. Such acts definitely do not comply with the objectives say the Ninth Plan, which states that 'food security at the household level must be the top priority'. Unless there is transparency in distribution and off-take of subsidised foodgrains, the efforts would be futile whatever the government does to increase the coverage (Box 6.11).

> BOX 6.11
>
> **Goals *versus* Financial Constraints**
>
> Tenth Plan goals for nutrition programme in the state include reduction of underweight children by 50 per cent, moderately underweight children by 37.4 per cent and making efforts for substantial improvement in infant feeding practices. Reduction in moderate and severely stunted and acute (wasted) undernutrition, which are higher in the state are not included in the specified goals. This could be because of the shortage of funds. Estimated deficits made by Planning Commission (Tenth Plan) in the allocation and actual requirement for SNP in the state were in the range of 5 per cent to 36 per cent for different components of the programme in 2001. Estimates of the Directorate of Women and Child Development indicate a shortage of 42 per cent of the requirement (i.e 77 crores) for the year 2003-04 to provide recommended nutrition supplement. In such a situation of funds shortage, goals may remain on policy document.

- Quantity of consumption may not largely influence health status as the details for Kerala reveal. The per capita consumption of cereals and pulses is lowest in Kerala as compared to Andhra Pradesh, Karnataka, Goa, Maharashtra and Tamil Nadu, but it has better nutritional and health status compared to these states.

Composition of different varieties in the food, education of the family members, health, water supply and sanitation services significantly influence nutritional status. More than 30 per cent in rural and more than 20 per cent in urban areas in the state do not have access (1991) to safe drinking water. Incidence of waterborne diseases is high in the state. Nutrition programme should be linked to health care, water supply and sanitation services at household level.

6.3.7 *Action Agenda for Nutrition Programmes*

Gradual fall in the rates of malnourishment and IMR indicate that nutrition programmes have made some impact on the nutritional status of the population, though not significantly. The reasons are obscured in the implementation aspects. Relying exclusively on AWW, lack of monitoring of food intake by malnourished and at home children, shortage in supply of nutritious food as per norms, malpractices in PDS limiting its outreach, irregular distribution of additional supplements (vitamin, IFA, deworm tablets) to children, pregnant women and recently to primary school children are some of the drawbacks found widely in the implementation of the programme. Though there were lots of positive institutional interventions taking place in the state, the effectiveness of the nutritional programme is in positive progress (Box 6.12). Unless measures are taken to increase the efficiency in implementation of the programmes, the effectiveness would be minimal or peripheral. To conclude, ensuring food security for the malnourished children, pregnant, nursing mothers and aged from the BPL families and the poorest should be the priority in formulating policies and the task ahead in implementation.

BOX 6.12

Issues and Actions for Nutrition Programmes

Issues	*Action*
· Acute malnutrition has increased and is higher among preschool children who are out of *anganwadi*.	· Present coverage is not effective. Hence, programmes should intensively focus on 0-3 age group: · Ensure distribution as well intake by the recipients. · Continuous monitoring till the child is in normal grade. · Creating awareness on feeding practices among mothers to start supplementary and nutritious food for the child at the age of 4 months.
· Disparities reflected in the higher rates of undernutrition among children and women in rural areas, among SCs/STs, among non-working mothers, among female children, in families with low standard of living and in backward districts.	· Nutrition education/awareness and steps to increase the capacity of vulnerable groups to earn more and have access to food. · Linking nutrition with health care, water supply and sanitation services at community as well as household level. · *Stree shakti* groups to be entrusted with monitoring of - Nutrition programme - Water supply and sanitation - PDS Since majority of members are poor, government may provide incentive for active participation of *Stree Shakti* groups.
· PDS not reaching the needy and the poor. Functioning of PDS is not satisfactory and effective. The general complaint that there is no on-time distribution of PDS continues to exist since the inception to present date. Nearby villagers find it difficult to come often to fair price shops.	· Availability should be ensured on fixed dates of the month. Relaxation of norms for setting up fair price shops may increase the coverage and distribution in the future. · Ensure off-take of foodgrains to be 100 per cent. · Transparency in distribution and proper targeting of PDS. · APL families should be out of PDS coverage. · Involving private sector in storage, transport. · Involving private consumer shops PDS commodities in villages where the number of card holders is less. · *Panchayats* should be empowered to cancel the licence of fair price shops based on the recommendation of *Gram Sabha*.
· Dependence on cereals for calorie requirement and wide gap in consumption of food-grains between rich and the poor.	· Rationed supply of pulses and edible oil at subsidised rates to the poorest landless families only under PDS.
· The higher prevalence of TB	· Elderly constitute nearly 5 per cent of the population in the state. 20 per cent of them i.e. around 5 lakh are likely to be poor and unable to feed and take care of themselves, particularly when they are dependent. This calls for government action to regularly provide food supplements to the needy elderly population.

6.4 Integrated Child Development Services in Karnataka State: A Current Status

The Integrated Child Development Services (ICDS) was started in Karnataka on October 2, 1975 in pursuance of the National Policy for Children of August 1974 evolved by the Government of India. ICDS is a programme for holistic development of children in India and is the largest programme for promotion of maternal and child health and nutrition. The ICDS targets children below 6 years, pregnant and nursing mothers belonging to families below poverty line and living in the disadvantaged areas including backward, rural and tribal areas and urban slums. Children below 6 years constitute 17 per cent of total population in India. Therefore, ICD services are major input indicators of the social infrastructure in the state. As at the end of September 2002, Karnataka had 23,93,882 children below 6 years and takes 5th place in all-India. Six states namely, Orissa (14.7 per cent), Uttar Pradesh (11.9 per cent), Maharasthra (11.5 per cent), West Bengal (9.7 per cent) Karnataka (7.2 per cent) and Madhya Pradesh (6.9 per cent) together account for 61.9 per cent of the country's children below 6 years. It is a multi-sectoral programme and involves several government departments. The programme services are coordinated at the village, blocks, districts, and state and Central Government levels. The welfare of pregnant and nursing mothers and children below 6 years has acquired a prime place in the nutrition, immunisation, health check-up, referral services, treatment of minor illness, nutrition, health education and preschool education. The objectives of the scheme are noble like: a) to lay a firm foundation for proper psychological, physical and social development of the child, b) to reduce infant mortality and morbidity and also maternal mortality rate, c) to improve the nutrition and health status of children below six years, pregnant women and nursing mothers, d) to reduce the school dropout rate, and e) to provide proper health and nutrition education to the mothers to remove ignorance and superstition and develop their capability to look after the health and nutritional needs of the child. The Department of Social Welfare (the Department of Women and Child Welfare in Karnataka) is in charge of this programme and is responsible for the non-health components of the programme, while the health components are taken care of by the Department of Health and Family Welfare Services, whose director is designated as the State Coordinator.

The World Bank evinced keen interest in funding these programmes. Karnataka received assistance under UDISHA for training of the ICDS functionaries at all levels such as the *anganwadi* workers, supervisors and Child Development Project Space Officers (CDPO) further Bangalore is one of the three centres where National Institution of Public Cooperation and Child (NIPCCD) has set up its regional centre. NIPCCD, is an apex organisation for designing training programmes for ICDS functionaries.

The ICDS programme was started in Karnataka on October 2, 1975 with a pilot project at T. Narasipura of Mysore district with just 100 *anganwadi* centres. Since then the programme has expanded to all the revenue *taluks* and 10 urban areas in the state. Now there are 185 ICDS projects (Appendix A-6.24). Out of this, 30 which were originally in the state sector where converted into central sector in 1996-97 by the Government of India and at present all the 185 ICDS projects are operational under central sector only. The number of *anganwadi* centres at present are 40301 of which 36,347 are rural 1,151 are urban and 2,803 are tribal. Out of 185 blocks 166 are in rural, 10 are in urban while 9 are tribal projects. Twenty-seven per cent of beneficiaries belong to SCs and STs while 12 per cent belong to minority community.

6.4.1 Expenditure under ICDS

Under the ICDS, Government of India bears full cost of meeting the administrative expenditure. The expenditure towards supplementary nutrition is borne by the respective state governments. Over the period and also with the expansion of the ICDS programme, the Centre's expenditure under ICDS has gone up many folds. The Appendix A-6.25 provides data on the Centre's releases to Karnataka under ICDS as also the expenditure along with all-India picture from 1992-93 to 2002-03. There is no set pattern in the quantum of release of funds. However for 2002-03, it may be observed that there has been a quantum jump in the amount released from Rs. 7,660.68 lakh in 2001-02 to Rs. 15,041.27 lakh in 2002-03.Under the ICDS(UDISHA) Training Programme, the state received Rs. 0.43 crore, Rs. 1.56 crore, Rs. 2.16 crore and Rs. 2.06 crore respectively for the years 1998-99, 1999-00, 2000-01, and 2001-02.

6.4.2 Supplementary Nutrition Programme

The Supplementary Nutrition Programme, (SNP) is one of the important services under the ICDS package. The cost is borne by the respective state governments. Feeding under the supplementary nutrition programme is provided in *anganwadi* centres to the targeted beneficiaries in addition to what they get at home with an intention to fill in the gap between what is required in terms of calories, proteins, vitamins, minerals, fat, etc. and what is available through their regular intake of food at home. Children in the age group of six months to six years, pregnant women and nursing mothers and adolescent girls in the age group of 11-18 years (in some districts) are provided supplementary nutrition covering all the rural and urban areas in the state. Around 30 lakh beneficiaries are covered each month. Each beneficiary is provided with 300 calories and 10-12 gms of protein as supplements covering 300 days in a year. For children in the age group 0-6 years supplementary nutrition is being given @Rs. 1.50 per beneficiary per day for normal children including transportation charges. In all ICDS projects, malnourished children, pregnant women and nursing mothers are provided with double the quantity of food @ Rs.3.00 per beneficiary per day for 300 days in a year.

TABLE 6.2

ICDS: Number of Beneficiaries under Women Welfare Schemes

Beneficiaries	*1998-99*		*2003-04*	
	Pregnant Women	*Nursing Women*	*Pregnant Women*	*Nursing Women*
SC	46079	53534	47723	56065
ST	5791	18575	5816	19383
Others	141158	154145	140312	158879
Total	**193028**	**226254**	**193851**	**234327**

Source: Department of Women and Child Welfare, Government of Karnataka.

The total expenditure under SNP incurred for women welfare and child development in Karnataka including the non-plan expenditure has increased many folds from Rs. 1,477.11 lakhs in 1990-1991 to Rs. 9,754.95 lakhs Appendix A-6.26. Accordingly, the number of beneficiaries (i.e., pregnant and nursing women) has increased substantially from 1998-99 to 2003-04. The improvement in the coverage under the tribal group is quite striking in both the categories (Table 6.2).

6.4.3 Recent Initiatives by Karnataka Government

Firstly, Karnataka Government had on its own taken many initiatives for improving ICDS in the state. The state government had started supplementary nutrition in 94 projects prior to September 1989, by meeting the expenditure outside the plan as non-plan expenditure. Supplementary nutrition in these 94 projects consisting of 300 calories per day at 8 to 10 grams of protein is provided to women for 300 days in a year.

Secondly, the government of Karnataka has launched a scheme during 2002-03, to provide financial assistance to the families of *anganwadi* workers and *anganwadi* helpers when they die during their services and provide medical relief if they suffer from serious disease ailments. The scheme is eligible to those *anganwadi* workers and helpers who have completed a minimum of one year of service. A sum of Rs. 20,000 per *anganawadi* worker and Rs. 10,000 per *anganawadi* helper have been earmarked for this purpose.

Thirdly, the Government of Karnataka launched 'Kishori Shakthi Yojana' in February 2003 to take care of the urgent need of providing the cover of ICDS to adolescent girls in ICDS projects. The scheme based on Government of India guidelines primarily aims at breaking the inter-generational life cycle of nutritional and gender disadvantage and providing a supporting environment for self-development. The scheme benefits adolescent girls in 38 *talukas* of the state with a budget provision of Rs. 1.10 lakhs to be utilised for training purposes out of ICDS funds. Under the SNP, nutrition is also being provided to these beneficiaries.

Fourthly, in order to regularly monitor and evaluate the training component ICDS, the Government has constituted the State Training Force which would integrate and coordinate all aspects of ICDS training at all levels and recommend changes.

The state government intends to provide buildings for each of the 40,301 *anganwadi* centres, which are presently functioning in status of having a kind of make-shift arrangements. The state has sent a proposal to NABARD seeking assistance under Rural Infrastructure Development Fund (RIDF) and NABARD has given 'in principle' approval to provide a loan of Rs. 25 crore for construction of 1,667 *anganwadi* centres for a period of 2 years. So far, 786 buildings were constructed. Further, Government of India also have given approval for construction of 650 model *anganwadi* buildings at Rs. 1.25 lakh per building. As this unit value was inadequate, the Karnataka government revised and raised the unit cost Rs. 1.42 in hilly and black cotton soil areas and Rs.1.32 lakh in other places. The Government of India would provide Rs. 93,950 for building while the remaining cost Rs. 48,250 would be met by the state government. Government of India has already released Rs. 500 lakh for construction of model *anganwadi* buildings in 2003-04.

6.4.4 Assessment of ICDS in Karnataka and Policy Options

Encouraged by the good response received as also its positive impact, a number of new initiatives have also been taken in the recent years to strengthen the impact of ICDS. These include: a) services for the adolescent girls in the age group of 11-18 years, using the ICDS infrastructure, b) effective involvement of NGOs, and

c) strengthening of monitoring. As far as Karnataka's performance in ICDS is concerned it has been ranked above average. The ICDS has been offering nutritional supplements to *anganwadi* workers, financial assistance for the education of children, health check-up every three months by a primary health centre doctor, etc. A Child Development Project Officer has been appointed in every *taluka* to take care of the *anganwadi* centres. IBM has provided computers in 10 *anganwadi* centres. Early detection of disability, NGO coordination and community-based rehabilitation are some of the other important schemes taken up by ICDS. Karnataka has taken up good reforms like creating a committee for local people who can supervise the *anganwadi* centres. The total immunisation is fairly satisfactory. Despite all these efforts certain areas need more attention and need to be improved. Though IMR has sharply come down, the neonatal mortality is still high. Out of 52 infant mortality 32 are reported to be neonatal mortality. The nutrition for pregnant women and infants needs to be improved. Filling up of all vacant posts at *anganwadi* centres, concentration of immunisation programme in urban slums and remote districts in view of the fact that diarrhoea and acute respiratory infections continue to be major causes of mortality among children, all of these need more involvement and participation.

Another positive impact of ICDS as stated earlier is the decrease in the malnutrition in the pre-school children. In the five-year period 1998-99 and 2003-04, the number of pre-school children with malnutrition has come down by 11,659 to 11,20,428 from 11,32,187. The number of pre-school with normal malnutrition infact has increased by 41,704 in this period but this was offset by sharp improvement in the other categories of malnutrition. Those with severe malnutrition have decreased by 2,151, mild malnutrition decreased by 15,087, and those with moderate malnutrition were reduced by 35,104. Among the districts, malnutrition is highly prevalent in Belgaum, followed by Gulbarga, Bijapur, Kolar, Tumkur and Bagalkot. Districts like Kodagu, Udupi, Chamrajnagar, Chickmagalur and Gadag are relatively better with less number of malnutrition affected pre-school children. Severe malnutrition is high in Gulbarga, Bellary, Koppal and Belgaum. Among the totally malnutrition children of 11,20,428, it is heartening to note that the number of girls are lesser than boys i.e., 5,56,196 and 5,96,968 respectively. This situation is observed in most of the districts except in 6 i.e., Bangalore Urban, Bellary, Chamrajnagar, Dharwad, Gulbarga and Kodagu. But in respect of mild, moderate and severe malnutrition, the number of girls was more than the boys. It implies that there is a widespread hidden hunger in the state. The futuristic policy and measures adopted by the government need to be oriented to correct these imbalances in the levels of nutrition as it is more dangerous than famines. The worst off are children. There is a need for strengthening of the nutrition schemes especially for school children, which could be done by extending the free noon-meal scheme for children up to high schools. Further, there is also need for targeting pregnant women and their children until five years to be covered by a special social security scheme.

6.5 Housing: A Current Scenario in Karnataka

Housing is considered as one of the merit goods because of its inherited utilitarian characters. In fact, housing is unlike any other ordinary consumable goods. Any consumable goods, fulfils particular needs, whereas housing symbolises many aspects of life. It is a replica of human taste, an institution of social order and economic advancement of society. Therefore, housing is considered as one of the important social infrastructures, which helps for overall development of the state. Karnataka is the eighth largest state to face the housing problem with 4.38 per cent share in the total housing shortage of the country. The present order of shortage of 6.62 lakh units in Karnataka is not only very well above the average shortage (4.73 lakh units) per state in the country but also more than the average shortage (6.58 lakh units) per state in southern states (Census, 2001). In all about 7 per cent of the total families are facing the housing shortage in the state by 2001 as against 7.54 per cent in the entire country. The district-wise shortage of housing by rural and urban areas and by source is presented in Appendix A-6.27. The most disturbing reality is the higher incidence of the housing problem in rural areas. Rural areas are facing a total housing shortage of 4.86 lakh families @18,000 units per district (Mahadeva, 2004). The rural housing shortages work out to 73.41 per cent as against 26.59 per cent (or 1.76 lakh units) in urban areas of the state. The most disappointing is the higher incidence of housing shortage in the vulnerable districts. By the year 2001, nine districts can be considered as vulnerable. These nine districts together accounted to half of the housing shortage in the state with 3.36 lakh units or 37,333 units per district, which is certainly more than the state average of 24,519 units per district. Bangalore Urban district topped the higher incidence districts with 0.62 lakh units, followed by Belgaum (0.61 lakh), Mysore (0.37 lakh), Tumkur (0.33 lakh) Gulbarga (0.32 lakh), Bangalore Rural (0.31 lakh), Shimoga (0.29 lakh) Uttara Kannada (0.26 lakh) and Hassan (0.25 lakh). It goes without saying that excepting the case of Bangalore Urban district; the rural areas have had a major contribution to the total housing shortage of the vulnerable districts. The average housing shortage of rural areas of vulnerable districts was in the order of 21,125, which is more than the state average.

Like the problem exists in the other parts of the country, Karnataka also experiences both quantitative and qualitative housing shortage. Also these shortages are referred to as crowd dwelling and dwelling in dilapidated or deficient units. Shortage in quantitative terms arise largely due to an outgrowth in the number of families than the residential housing stock, while the qualitative shortage are the number of sub-standard (life threatening and unsafe) and inadequate housing units largely constructed by poorer and vulnerable sections without adhering to any standard norms or using any standardised building materials. In fact their immediate concern would have been to take some sorts of housing to protect themselves and their belongings. On both counts, the nature of housing shortage in Karnataka is by and large the same, as compared to the national scenario. The total number of families in Karnataka was in the order of 102.32 lakhs as against a total residential housing stock of 100.69 lakhs. The gap that arises on account of the difference between the number of families and housing stock worked out to 1.63 lakhs (1.04 lakh units in rural areas and 0.59 lakh units in urban areas) in the state, which, should be considered as the core housing shortage. In other words, as many as 1.63 lakh families are experiencing crowd dwelling. In this regard, every district in the state has registered an outgrowth in the number of families over and above the residential houses, though the incidence was dissimilar. Especially 6 (Belgaum, Bangalore Urban, Dharwad, Gulbarga, Mysore and Bellary) of the 27 districts have registered a very high growth in number of families and thus contributed for outspread growth largely to the extent of over 56 per cent of the incidence in the state. The average outspread growth in the number of families in these districts works out to 15,333 as against 6,037 per district in the state. This means that the said districts have registered the family growths, which were around 3 folds more than the state average. The difference in the outgrowth in the number of families over residential housing stock was 0.33 lakhs in Belgaum, followed by 0.23 lakhs in Bangalore Urban, 0.12 lakhs each in Dharwad and Gulbarga, 0.08 lakhs in Mysore and 0.07 lakhs in Bellary. Further, it is significant to note that rural areas have largely contributed for the outgrowth in families in excess to residential houses in the state as it accounts to over 64 per cent. Thus the families in excess of houses usually dwell jointly with fellow families of relatives and friends.

The other but a very serious dimension of housing shortage is qualitative. As mentioned earlier, it refers to such dwelling structure by the vulnerable sections, which is not safe. Since non-durable materials are used to construct such unsafe structures, generally they do not ensure dwelling round the year as they subject to fluctuations in climatic conditions. (NBO, 1988). Also these structures fail to ensure even minimum in-house amenities like adequate living space, safe drinking water, sanitation, adequate proper lighting, proper ventilation, privacy, etc. Crowding and unreasonable sharing of available services and filthy environment are the added features of unsafe houses. Karnataka state is registered to have 4.99 lakh unsafe houses at an average of 18,481 houses per district. The incidence of unsafe housing stock is alarming in more than half of the districts. Bangalore Urban district has led the higher incidence of unsafe units with 0.39 lakhs, followed by Tumkur (0.30 lakh), Belgaum (0.28 lakh), Shimoga and Bangalore Rural (0.25 lakh each), Davangere, Kolar and Uttara Kannada (0.21 lakh each) Gulbarga, Hassan, Mandya (0.20 lakh each) and Dakshina Kannada (0.19 lakh). Though the incidence of unsafe houses is equally worse in the other districts, redevelopment or replacement should form the major public action in the state in general and higher incidence districts in particular. Reconstruction is indeed necessary not just to ensure safe dwelling with assured services round the year but to do away with crowded dwelling and to bring about hygienic living environment. Therefore, it may not be an exaggeration to mention that the success in arresting housing shortage in the entire state largely lies in replacing the huge order of existing unsafe houses, especially in the rural areas as they account for over three-fourths of the total housing shortage.

6.5.1 Housing: As a Problem of the Deprived Sections

Scheduled Castes (SC) and Scheduled Tribes (ST) being the major deprived sections in the state, more than half of these families lack agricultural lands (GoK, 2003) and other income generating assets to meet their livelihood and housing requirements. The taller order of asset less over the years has led these sections to heavily depend upon the state actions/interventions including for housing. Housing as one of the basic needs and a socio-political empowering institution, its deprivation among SC/ST families is highly alarming. Being one-fourth in the total number of families, about 14 per cent of the SC/ST families are houseless, which is double the deprivation level of the state. The total housing shortage of SC/ST families is in the order of 3.38 lakh families (2.30 lakh SC families and 1.08 lakh ST families) or a little more than 51 per cent in the overall incidence in the state (Appendix A-6.28). Though the average requirement of housing units per district works out to 12,518 to house the deprived sections, 11 of 27 districts requirement is even more. These 11 districts alone constitute to a total housing shortage of 2.20 lakh units, which works out to 65 per cent of the shortage in the state. Gulbarga has led the higher incidence districts with a total shortage of 0.27 lakh units, followed by Mysore (0.23 lakh), Kolar (0.21 lakh), Belgaum, Belgaum and Bidar (0.20 lakh each), Chitradurga and Davangere (0.19 lakh each), Bangalore Urban (0.18 lakh), Tumkur (0.17 lakh) and Bijapur (0.16 lakh). Twenty thousand housing units being the average requirement, not only these districts need a special district action plans to arrest the incidence but also need to be focused by the state with additional resources to these districts. In fact it is also important to note that similar to that of the state scenario and in a few cases, the problem of housing deprivation among SC/ST families is the problem of the district itself, especially among the vulnerable districts. In other words, major part of the housing problem/shortage is due to large-scale deprivation of SC/ST families. For example, in Gulbarga, around 85 per cent of the district problem is due to huge deprivation level of the SC/ST families, followed by Mysore (62.16 per cent), Tumkur (52.00 per cent) and Belgaum (33.00 per cent).

The problem of housing deprivation among SC/ST families in the state is more of rural in nature as 76 per cent of these families live in countryside. Of the total housing shortage, rural families account for 2.85 lakh units or around 85 per cent. Further, unlike the state scenario, whose problem is more of dilapidated structure, the problem among SC/ST families is equally spread between the over crowding (1.43 lakh units) and dilapidated housing (1.42 lakh units). It only indicates that the problem should be arrested both by increasing the supply of new housing units as well as by reconstructing the existing dilapidated structures with equal emphasis. Since 10,555 housing units are the average requirement per district, the same have to be met at 5,296 and 5,259 units respectively to arrest both overcrowding and dilapidated houses. But while designing any such intervention, it is the need of the hour to lay special emphasis on the most vulnerable districts, which are facing the problem on a huge scale. It is clear from the table that rural families are facing higher order (more than the state average) of overcrowding as well as dilapidated living in as many as 11 districts of the state. For example, in the rural areas of Gulbarga district, about 0.24 lakh SC/ST families are experiencing overcrowding and dwelling in the dilapidated units, which is two folds higher than the state average followed by 0.20 lakh in Kolar, 0.19 lakh in Mysore, 0.18 lakh each in Bidar and Chitradurga, 0.17 lakh each in Belgaum, Bellary, Chamrajnagar and Davangere and 0.16 lakh families in Tumkur. In fact, more than 64 per cent of the total incidence could be arrested if these rural areas are focused in the development interventions. Further, though the incidence of overcrowding and dilapidated dwelling by SC/ST families in urban areas is not as challenging as in rural areas, but still over 0.50 lakh SC/ST families are facing the problem in varying degrees. Especially, dilapidated dwelling by these families needs a special mention, as the incidence is very huge in urban areas. In this regard, Bangalore Urban district needs to be given more attention as it alone account for one third of the dilapidated dwelling in the entire state. That apart, given the growing incidence of deaths due to collapse of dilapidated structure (walls and roofs) during the rainy seasons it is all the more necessary to arrest the incidence of dilapidated dwelling at the earliest.

6.5.2 Existing Potentialities of Housing

Karnataka is one of the lead examples to have created the institutional infrastructure (Appendix A-6.29) in the cooperative, public and in private sectors to promote housing development by supplying the critical inputs (land and finance) for various sections. Karnataka being the first state to give birth to cooperative housing movement, its societies have been into the housing development activities since the first decade of the 20th century. Similarly, a number of public institutions have come into existence to meet the needs from the early sixties and finally private housing finance companies or subsidiaries of commercial banks, insurance sector and private companies have largely come into being since the late eighties. The overall functioning of these institutions including their area of operations and target group is presented in Appendix A-6.29. However, given the needs and nature of the housing problem in the state in general and weaker/deprivation in particular, the existing set of institutions by their designs and operations has a number of deficiencies.

First of all, most of these institutions are urban focused in their operations. As a result, the housing problem of the rural areas has been either left to itself or to the only ambit of the various social housing programmes implemented through local government (*Panchayati Raj* Institutions). Unfortunately, the Rajiv Gandhi Rural Housing Corporation (RGRHC) so called designated agency of promoting housing activities in rural areas is not even free from the urban operations. Similarly, though cooperatives are almost a century old organisations have had only a limited coverage of rural housing operations. It is disappointing to note that out of the total number of 1,589 cooperative housing societies in the state by the year 1995-96, only 219 societies were functioning in the rural areas, which works out to just 14 per cent (NABARD, 1996). If this is the situation with regard to the so-called people oriented institutions (which are supposed to have represented the interest of the common man), it is less said the better with regard to other institutions.

Secondly, given the existing order of deficient housing stock in the state in general and the rural areas in particular, housing development strategies and the existing institutions should have had redevelopment as part of their interventions. But, unfortunately this did not happen. Had redevelopment of the dilapidated stock been a part of the overall development approach, the state would not have faced the present challenge of high order of the incidence. It is important to note that the total requirement of housing units in the state cannot be met only by supplying new units as the same involves displacement of existing habitations, huge resource requirement for development of new settlement with housing services etc. Taking the quality improvement of the poor people, cost advantages and other social benefits into consideration, improvement of the existing bad structure should be the development approach along with the supply of new units especially in rural areas. However, excepting the Karnataka Slum Clearance Board (KSCB) and RGRHC, all the other institutions have aimed only at supplying or facilitating new construction, which would only further distance the dream of quality living of the vulnerable groups, owing to a number of supply constraints.

Thirdly, as is already indicated, the present order of housing problem in the state is largely faced by the poor in general and deprived sections in particular. But the disappointing reality is that the state is not geared up to meet the total housing requirement of these sections. No doubt, that the existing institutions in the housing sector are earmarking certain portion of the development benefits to these sections. But that alone has not been able to meet the total requirement over the years. What was required that considering the housing problem of the poorer sections and the deprived sections beyond the existing (reservation) arrangements. One such alternative could be to have an exclusive housing development institution for the benefit of the poor including the deprived sections, especially in rural areas on the similar lines of KSCB. Such institution can have the resource support of the state, commercial banks and other financial institutions of public sector. Otherwise, it is all the more necessary to make RGRHC as an exclusive institution for rural areas to take up housing development activities (new housing and redevelopment of existing bad stock) for the poor including the deprived sections. But then, it is equally important to make RGRHC as a nodal agency to implement all the social housing commitments of the state.

With this backdrop of supply side constraints, let us now turn towards the individual institutional setup with their functional assessment. In view of the necessities of ensuring orderly residential environment and smooth flow of developed residential lands in the urban areas of the state urban development authorities (UDAs) were created in every district head quarters of the state. These UDAs during 1990s have had acquired land to carry out residential and other infrastructure development (roads including ring-roads, market and commercial complexes) and promote other economic activities. As can be seen in Appendix A-6.30, less than a lakh of residential sites have been distributed to various income groups including the weaker sections. Further, it is significant to note that all UDAs have been financially well managed as they have registered a surplus to the tune of over Rs. 250 crores on an average of Rs. 8.96 crores per UDA. The UDAs in addition to their annual work schedule can initiate other development works out of the surplus generated. Further, notwithstanding the revenue surplus, not all the UDAs in the state are functioning uniformly in terms of executing their responsibilities. Some are functioning very well due to enormous public demand for allotment of residential sites and for other facilities and some are not for non-availability of land in the urban adjacent. In the total land acquired, during the period under review, development authorities in Bangalore Urban district, Mysore, Shimoga and Bellary have had a major share to the tune of over 56 per cent and at an average of 1,978 acres, which was more than the average land acquisition of all the authorities. Similarly in the case of site distribution, Mysore Urban Development Authority (MUDA) has topped the other authorities by contributing almost one–fourth in the total, followed by 18 per cent by the Bangalore Development Authority (BDA). However, in the case of a large number of authorities, the site distribution performance is far below the average of 344 sites per authority and per year. Further, in the total revenue surplus, BDA alone have had more than 50 per cent share. Although, a few authorities have posted a revenue surplus over and above the state average, all the others have to go a long way not only in financial front but also in land acquisition/development and in distribution of residential sites, as their performance is far below the state average. These authorities have got to come out of the red with the help of the increasing financial services for house construction and urban development activities in order to prove their existence and to meet the growing challenges in urban areas.

Following the imposition of social responsibility on commercial banks, there has been a tremendous spread of bank branches across the country including the rural areas. But unfortunately, credit expansion on various socio-economic activities did not corroborate with the branch expansion especially in the neglected sectors. Housing is one such activity, whose credit needs has never been met by the commercial banks in full, despite major networking in rural and semi-urban areas. This is largely due to lowest credit packages for the rural areas, which in turn has increased dependence of the houseless families on the social housing programmes of the state. The position of Karnataka state is not an exception. Of the total number of 4,840 scheduled commercial banks offices, rural and semi-urban areas together account to 3,236 offices (66.72 per cent) in the state (RBI, 2000). During the period under review, the total bank credit limits for housing and actual investment in housing have increased 6-folds each as against a 4-fold increase in the overall bank credit (Appendix A-6.31). Unfortunately, these increases have not brought about the needed change in the rural housing credit needs. It is evident from the fact that rural and semi-urban areas have together account for a total housing investment of Rs. 5.36 crores (Rs. 1.93 crores in rural and Rs. 3.43 crores in semi-urban areas) or 5.50 per cent of the total banks' credit to these areas of the state. These investments (of Rs. 5.36 crores) work out to about 27 per cent of the total housing credit limit of the scheduled commercial banks and the average of the same was as low as Rs. 16564 as against an average deposit of Rs. 4,56,026 per branch office. In other words, the remaining 73 per cent of the housing credit of the banks has been deployed in urban and metropolitan areas, which account to 27 per cent of the total housing problem of the state. This unreasonable deployment pattern of resources in housing cannot justify the existence of the commercial banks in rural areas that too in a big way. Considering the rural segment in the overall housing requirement in the state and commercial banks being the principal household saving mobiliser, it is the need of the hour to over turn the situation by earmarking more credit for housing to rural and semi-urban areas to bring about quality in living standard.

The position of cooperative housing societies (CHSs) as far as housing development in the state is concerned is not different to that of the two major institutions and their performance (UDAs and SCBs). Rather, the apathy is more conspicuous in the case of cooperatives. CHSs having born with a sole motto of supplying critical housing inputs (land and finance) and providing housing for their members, have failed to meet either of them in total. With over 1,700 primary housing societies in the state, the total working capital as well as the loans advanced to housing activities of their members has constantly increased by more than six and nine folds respectively as can be seen in Appendix A-6.31. The same have respectively increased from Rs. 222 crores to Rs, 1,400 crores and from Rs. 57 crores to Rs. 560 crores during the period 1990-91 to 1999-00. Also, housing loans as percentage of the total working capital have increased from 26 to 40 per cent. But, these increases have not brought any major breakthrough, as the coverage of members is very low. It is worth noting that a major segment of the working capital (which is meant for financing of housing activities) of the societies is being invested in the capital market. Had the remaining working capital of these societies been invested for the welfare of the members, the total housing stock in the cooperative could have easily doubled. Therefore, given the large scale of members uncovered on the one hand and the increasing working capital on the other it only reiterate the necessity to step up investment in the creation of housing benefits to the members of the societies.

One of the major changes that have taken place in the housing credit market was the entry of subsidiaries (Housing financial institutions (HFIs) from the late eighties in the country. Commercial banks, insurance companies, and private companies mainly to deploy their resources in a large scale in the housing sector have sponsored these HFIs. Karnataka is the second largest state next to Maharashtra to give birth to a large number of subsidiaries. National Housing Bank (NHB), as apex institution has approved as many as 65 HFIs in the state to mobilise public deposits and invest the same for housing development. The volume of resource mobilisation and the business in terms of loans sanctioned for housing activities are the testimony to the functioning of these subsidiaries. HFIs till March 1999 have mobilised anything more than Rs. 800 crores and lent Rs. 1,005 crores for housing activities of group, community and individuals in the state ((NHB, 1999) are an achievements in themselves, notwithstanding their nature of investment and clientele coverage. This alone should speak of their professional approach, flexible attitude and so on given the various fiscal incentives made available to these institutions (Mahadeva, 2004). However, one of the discouraging notes is the non-shouldering of the social responsibility by these subsidiaries. These subsidiaries owing to their large concentration of housing projects in the urban/metropolitan centres, backward and rural areas, are continued to neglect or have hardly had any investments. In view of the large-scale business potentials in backward and rural areas and for having enjoyed a number of fiscal concessions and incentives there need to be some degree of social responsibility to these housing financial institutions.

6.5.3 Alternative Development Strategies

The housing problem in the state is more of a qualitative than quantitative. People living in the qualitatively challenging or deficient houses have neither repaired them from time to time to improve their quality nor have replaced or rebuilt them owing to their challenging economic condition. This has led to a cumulative accumulation of stock of dilapidated houses over the years. Considering the enormity of the problem, there should have been concrete efforts to arrest the incidence. Unfortunately, neither the empirical research nor public policymaking have recognised this challenging problem for a very long period. Thanks to the Census for having accounted the housing problem in general and dilapidated dwelling in particular for the first time in 1991. Equally important is the problem of overcrowding, which mainly arises due to increasing number families especially in rural areas. Disproportionate supply of new housing units has left a number of families uncovered, which has exerted the pressure on the existing units as well as on the household services. What is still disappointing is the enormity of the problem in both quantitative and qualitative terms among the poverty group and more particularly among the deprived sections. It may not be exaggeration to note that the deprived sections contribute more than half of the housing problem of the state and therefore it should become the state's problem as the most SC/ST families cannot afford a decent house on their own. Finally, given the existing institutional infrastructure in the housing sector, the problem of houseless should have been arrested long back especially in the urban areas. But, over the years, eroded public confidence together with public assistance and the organisational deficiencies as discussed already have contributed to the apathy of these institutions. Therefore to arrest the existing and to meet the growing incidence of the housing problem in the state, the need of the hour is to evolve a need based housing policy as it never been the case in the last 50 years. Such a policy should obviously focus on a major intervention for improvement of rural housing conditions and then to strengthen the existing institutions.

The needbased housing development strategy should primarily have twin objectives to both supply of new housing units as well as replacement or redevelopment of the existing challenging stock especially in rural areas. Since poorer sections are the habitants and considering the social (displacement)/ economic (cost effectiveness) benefits, overriding priority needs to be accorded to redevelopment of dilapidated stock. Mere policy pronouncement to replace the challenging stock alone does not arrest the incidence. Instead, it has to be supplemented with resource reallocation both by the government and by the housing financial institutions. The financial allocation for the implementation of social housing schemes needs to be stepped up in order to cover the hitherto uncovered families. While implementing government housing commitment, there needs to be equal emphasis for redevelopment along the line of new housing units. Besides, government needs to create a favourable environment including fiscal incentives to ensure direct or indirect investment by the housing financial institutions for the redevelopment purposes. Further, no doubt the existing new unit supplying mechanism has a number of constraints including the resource. But to arrest the existing incidence of overcrowding, there is no other alternative but to increase the number of units, which would be a reality with increased financial allocation especially in the social housing schemes. Supplying new housing units alone does not matter but in what quantity is the concern. In future, while drawing any such supplying mechanism, the state should plan for alleviating the existing backlog housing units besides planning to meet the future needs.

If at all the state is serious about mainstreaming the deprived sections and the poorer sections, housing as a basic necessity and socio-political empowering institution has to be ensured to all. However, as in the case of the past, arresting the housing problem on piecemeal basis has to be reversed and the state has to address the problem either by earmarking more than 50 per cent of the total allocation for the housing activities or by setting up a separate financing institution. Because, the existing institutional infrastructure is not in a position to meet the total housing needs of the deprived sections under the existing resource allocation strategy. The proposed strategy though appears to be overlapping and analogous with similar institutions, but the same would go a long way in arresting the housing problem of the deprived sections. Further, mere setting up of an exclusive housing development institution for the deprived sections does not solve their problem. Rather it should have a regular public funding besides the power to mobilise resources from the market with the guarantee of the state to take up additional housing activities from time to time.

No doubt the existing institutional infrastructure in the state is highly urban oriented, although the housing problem is more conspicuous (especially qualitatively) in rural areas. Therefore, it is high time to reorient the RGRHC as a full-fledged institution to administer the housing commitment of the state and to implement all the social housing schemes in the rural areas. RGRHC needs to assess the rural housing needs by source and evolve housing development strategy from time to time, besides taking special housing projects for the most vulnerable groups in the most backward areas. It is also necessary to empower RGRHC to mobilise resources from the market on the guarantee of the state to meet the total housing needs both in the new housing and redevelopment streams in rural areas. Further to supplement the housing activities in rural areas, the housing investment by the commercial banks needs to be stepped up. Similarly, the housing subsidiaries need to be imposed with the social responsibility so as to participate indirectly by subscribing to social housing programmes of the state.

6.6 Water Supply and Sanitation in Karnataka: Current Status

Water supply and sanitation, being the basic requirements of life are considered as main input indicators to the health infrastructure as it plays an integral role in maintaining and promoting health status. Safe and adequate quantity of drinking water supply and sanitation facilities is essential for achieving and maintaining quality life. The wide linkages of water supply and sanitation with health status and thus on productivity and income of people increase the significance for the provision of safe drinking water supply and sanitation services. Considering the significance of safe water supply and sanitation in maintenance and promotion of health and hygiene, both the Central and state governments have taken major steps to create provision of these basic services in both rural and urban areas. Water supply and sanitation programmes have been successful in covering over 84 per cent of the households with safe drinking water supply. But, in the sanitation front the achievement is still insignificant as just around 38 per cent of the households have latrine facility while many other community based sanitation services are absent. The current status of water supply and sanitation services, are explained in terms of service providers, drinking water supply, sanitation, government initiatives on water supply and sanitation and expenditure on water supply and sanitations, in the state.

6.6.1 Water Supply and Sanitation Service Providers

Different agencies are involved in creating the provision of water supply and sanitation services for rural and urban areas. The Rural Development and *Panchayat Raj* Department has the responsibility of providing water supply and sanitation services to rural areas. The rural programmes are being implemented and maintained by the Rural *Panchayat Raj* Institutions—*Zilla Panchayat, Taluka Panchayat and Gram Panchayat.*

The responsibility of water supply and sanitation for urban areas lies with the Karnataka Urban Water Supply and Drainage Board (KUWSDB) along with urban local bodies (ULBs), other than Bangalore city. There are 226 ULBs[9] in the state, out of which 208 ULBs are being covered by the KUWSDB. While the KUWSDB

9. Karnataka has 226 Urban Local Bodies, including 6 Municipal Corporations, 39 City Municipal Councils, 83 Town Municipals, 90 Town *Panchayats*, and 8 Notified Area Committees (Department of Municipal Administration, GoK).

constructs the water supply and sanitation facilities, the responsibility of maintaining these systems is with the concerned ULBs. The responsibility of creating and maintaining water supply and sanitation facilities to Bangalore city is entrusted to the Bangalore Water Supply and Sewage Board. In addition, the Karnataka Urban Infrastructure Development Financial Corporation is also working to augment the financial resources for urban water supply and sanitation programmes.

6.6.2 *Drinking Water Supply*

In the provision of drinking water supply access to adequate quantity of safe drinking water[10] supply is an important issue. While many households lack access to safe drinking water sources, those having access suffer from inadequate quantity of water supply. In order to maintain health and hygiene an individual needs a minimum of 40 litres per capita per day (LPCD) of water. Similarly, quality of water requires attention, particularly in the context of environmental pollution causing contamination of drinking water at source and distribution levels. In Karnataka groundwater is the major source of drinking water in both rural and urban areas as over 90 per cent of 56,682 rural habitations (GoK, 2000) and 40 urban local bodies exclusively depend upon ground water (Puttaswamaiah, 2004).

Access to Sources of Drinking Water Supply

Access of households to different drinking water sources reveals that about 59 per cent of the households have connection to tap water supply in the state (Appendix A-6.32). The other major sources of drinking water are hand pump and open well, respectively at 17 and 12 per cent of households. The percentage of households with tap water connection is high in the state as compared to all India level (about 37 per cent). However, there is a big gap across rural and urban areas in the state as while 78 per cent of urban households have tap water connection, it is only 48 per cent among rural households. Across the districts, in only 13 districts more than 58 per cent[11] of the households have tap water connections as the major source. It includes districts of Bangalore Urban, Bellary, Dharwad, Mysore, Gadag, Kolar, Haveri, Bangalore Rural, Davanagere, Mandya, Koppal, Chitradurga, and Shimoga. Further, in districts such as Belgaum, Chamrajnagar, Gulbarga and Bijapur over 50 per cent of the households collect drinking water from sources other than tap.

Distance of Sources

Location or distance of drinking water sources from the household is another issue that needs to be considered, because sources situated at a long distance consumes larger share of the productive time of households, resulting in loss of productivity. Large number of households in the state reported that their principal sources of drinking water are near to their premises (Census, 2001). In the case of tap water connection relatively more number of households (41 per cent) have the collection point within their premises. However, the scenario differs in rural Karnataka as compared to that of urban, because in rural areas only about 23 per cent of the households have tap water connection within premises, while it is 62 per cent in urban areas. However, all other major sources are close to households in both rural and urban areas indicating improvement in terms of reduction in the distance between households and sources of drinking water.

Adequate Quantity of Drinking Water Supply: Rural Habitations

The Karnataka government has adopted the norm of 55 LPCD of water supply to rural people. In order to provide the adequate level of water supply the following three programmes are being implemented; (i) Borewells with Handpump Scheme (BWS), (ii) Mini Water Supply Scheme (MWS), and (iii) Piped Water Supply Scheme (PWS). Selection of a particular scheme is based on the population size of the village/habitation. Villages/habitations with a population of 1000 and above are provided with one Piped Water Supply Scheme. Villages/habitations in the population range of 500-1000 and below 500 are respectively provided with Mini Water Supply Scheme and Borewell with Handpump. The Government has created 213,132 drinking water supply schemes by the end of 2003 (BWS–1,77,879; MWS-19,541; and PWS-15,712) (GoK-RDPR 2002-03).

In rural Karnataka, over 64.7 per cent of the 56,682 habitations have been provided with more than 55 LPCD of water supply as on March 2003 (GoK-RDPR 2002-03). However, we should note that over 33 per cent of the habitations are yet to be covered with adequate drinking water supply. The district-wise scenario during 2002 reveals that over 50 per cent of habitations in 7 districts namely Belgaum (64.44 per cent), Bellary (57.28 per cent), Dharwad (54.69 per

10. Safe drinking water is generally defined as, water which is sweet and free from odour, colour and organic and inorganic contamination.

11. State's proportion of households with tap water connection is 58.9 per cent.

cent), Gulbarga (62.59 per cent), Kodagu (82.94 per cent)[12], Chamrajnagar (75.18 per cent) and Bangalore Urban (64.79 per cent) have less than 55 LPCD of water supply (DRDP, GoK, 2004).

The problem of inadequate drinking water supply is more acute in drought prone districts like Bellary, Bijapur, Bidar, Bagalkot, Dharwad, Gulbarga, Banglaore Urban, Chitraduga, and Davanagere. Coverage of habitations with adequate drinking water supply has increased from 54 per cent in 1999 to 64.7 per cent in 2003, which increased at an annual rate of 4.51 per cent between 1999 and 2003 (Appendix A-6.33). Although, around 35 per cent of the habitations are partially covered (with less than 55 LPCD), there is no habitations yet to be provided with drinking water supply in the state. However, functioning of the water supply system is important to provide the adequate quantity of water, which is discussed later.

Adequate Quantity of Drinking Water Supply: Urban Areas

Access to and adequate quantity of drinking water is a major issue in urban areas also. Karnataka has experienced significant urbanisation (about 34 per cent of people live in urban areas) as compared to that at all India level (31 per cent) (Census, 2001), which increases the task of providing water supply services to urban people. The KUWS&DB has adopted the adequacy norm of drinking water supply stipulated by the Central Public Health Engineering and Environmental Organisation (CPHEEO), ranging from 70 to 135 LPCD depending upon population.

While Karnataka has 226 urban local bodies, information on the level of drinking water supply is available only on about 208 ULBs from the KUWSDB. The Board has constructed about 240 Piped Water Supply Schemes, 127 Urban Water Supply Schemes and 20 Board Water Supply Schemes to provide drinking water by the end of October 2003. (GoK, 2004). Out of 208 ULBs for which information is available only about 23 per cent of the ULBs have adequate quantity of drinking water supply. All towns in Bangalore Urban, Kolar, Tumkur, Udupi, Chitradurga, Dharwad, Gadag, Haveri, Raichur and Bagalkot districts suffer from inadequate quantity of drinking water supply. Among the municipal corporations in only two corporations, Mysore and Mangalore, people are getting adequate drinking water (Appendix A-6.34).

The progress of the various water supply schemes created by the KUWSDB (Appendix A-6.35), shows that the number of Piped Water Supply Scheme has increased from 216 in 1999 to 240 by end of October 2003, while that Urban Water Supply Scheme raised from 89 to 127 during the same period. However, this increase has not been enough to provide adequate drinking water supply to urban people in many ULBs.

Drinking Water Supply in Bangalore City

Bangalore, the capital city of Karnataka state, is one of the fastest growing cities, with the decadal growth of 41.36 per cent (BWSSB, Annual Report 2001-2002). There is a rapid increase in population from 4.13 million in 1991 to 6 million in 2001, for which provision of basic amenities of life like adequate drinking water, sanitation facilities, etc. are necessary. Bangalore city is provided with the services of filtered water for over 100 years and with sewerage system since 1922.

The level of drinking water supply in Bangalore city lies in the range of 115 LPCD (BWSSB-website). But, this level of water supply is less than the norm of 150-200 LPCD recommended for a city of this size by the CPHEEO (BWSSB, Website). During 1995 Bangalore people were receiving about 145 LPCD of water, but currently it is around 115 LPCD. Hence, inadequate supply of drinking water is an important issue for a large metropolitan city like Bangalore. The sources of drinking water for Bangalore are Cauvery and Arkavathi rivers, and groundwater. River Cauvery is the major source providing over 87 per cent of drinking water drawn from river sources and the dependency on Cauvery is growing with the increased number of water supply schemes (three schemes i.e., Cauvery Water Supply Scheme—I, II and III are completed and IV in progress). In addition to rivers, groundwater is another major source of drinking water in Bangalore. There are over 7,000 borewells maintained by the BWSSB, apart from over 80,000 borewells maintained by private people. An estimation by the BWSSB shows that over 1,03,000 million liters of water per year is extracted from groundwater source, which is about 28 per cent of the total drinking water supply during 2001-02.

6.6.3 Sanitation Services

In the maintenance of health and hygiene, sanitation facilities are as important as that of adequate quantity

12.. Few districts like Kodagu, Dakshina Kannada, Udupi also show higher per cent of habitations with inadequate water supply as per the data of RDPR. But this needs to be looked carefully considering the ground level situation i.e., large number of households having their own drinking water sources, which might not have been accounted for by the RDPR.

and quality of drinking water. Sanitation facilities such as sewerage system, storm water drain, latrines (public or private), and other community sanitation services form an integral part in maintaining hygiene and clean environment. Although, improved sanitation is considered as an essential requirement for socio-economic development and critical to health and well-being, which is an index of human development, significant attention is given in the recent years to sanitation as a major component of health promotion (GoK, 2000). Realising the significance and the necessity of sanitation services, the Karnataka government has taken up various programmes to provide and promote sanitation services in both rural and urban areas.

Availability of Sanitation Facilities

Sanitation facilities, both household and community, are very minimal in the state. Although we do not have information on the level of community sanitation services such as habitations with proper drainage system, non-existence of stagnant water pools, compost pits, etc. data are available on the level of household latrine facility. As per Appendix A-6.36, about 38 per cent of the households have latrine facility at their residence. It is to be noted that household latrines are an important segment of sanitation facilities, particularly for women and children. However, over 62 per cent of the households, including rural and urban, do not have latrine facility. The proportion of household latrines in the state is not much better than that at the all India level, which is about 36 per cent.

Drainage is another important sanitation facility required for carrying out wastewater generated from households and other business establishments, rainwater, etc. to keep rural and urban habitations in hygienic condition. But, around 50 per cent of the households do not have connection to drainage system. This might indicate that drainage system has not been provided in large number of habitations.

Rural Sanitation Services

Availability of sanitation facilities is inadequate in rural areas. While over 82 per cent of rural households lack latrine facilities, more than 64 per cent of the households have no drainage connection for wastewater outlet (Appendix A-6.36). According to the Department of Rural Development and Panchayat Raj, as reported in the Strategy Paper 2000-2005, there is a lack of network of sullage and storm water drains along the streets and also paving of internal roads in rural habitations, which make the streets slushy in monsoon and dirty during summer season (GoK, 2000). Rural habitations also face the problems of compost pits existing close to the residence or inside the village and stagnant water pools, which are the major sources of mosquitoes and other insects. But, there is lack of information on the magnitude of these problems in rural areas.

Under the Central Rural Sanitation Programme (CRSP) just about 1.19 lakh households were provided during the period from 1985-1986 to 1994-95 in the state. But, under the Nirmal Grama Yojana launched recently, the state government has been able to provide additionally 7,53,464 households with latrine facilities within six years during 1994-2000. Besides, the World Bank supported Integrated Rural Water Supply and Environmental Sanitation project has created about 89,000 latrines between 1993 to mid-2000. However, this is still away from covering all the 60 lakh households (Census, 2001). Clearly, the present rate of covering sanitation facilities is grossly inadequate.

Urban Sanitation Facilities

The urban sanitation facilities mainly include provision of underground drainage (UGD) system, waste water treatment plant, garbage collection and disposal, public sanitation facilities like toilet/latrine, etc. Availability of these services is essential in urban areas to maintain and promote health and hygiene due to the high density of population.

Underground Drainage System

The numbers of ULBs provided with UGD system are only 36 out of 226 in the state, excepting Bangalore and the City Municipal Councils around Bangalore. Even in those towns where the UGD system is being provided the percentage coverage of area is relatively less (KUWSDB, GoK, 2003). At the state level 182 ULBs are yet to be provided with underground drainage system. Provision of UGD system in municipal corporations (Appendix A-6.37), apart from Bangalore, shows that none of the 5 municipal corporations have full coverage. As a result, large number of urban people still depend upon soak pits, septic tanks and community latrines, which increases the sanitation related problems.

Wastewater: Management of wastewater is another sanitation service required in urban areas, because of generation of large quantity of wastewater. In 10 towns the average per capita sewage flow is more than 100 litres per day (KUWSDB, GoK, 2003). Mangalore and Bellary ULBs generate the highest per capita of sewage of around 135 litres per capita per day. Wastewater generated needs to be treated to avoid it from polluting water bodies or soil. But, most of the ULBs do not have sewage treatment plants (STPs) to treat the wastewater. For instance, out of 36 ULBs, where UGD system is provided, 9 ULBs do not have treatment plants. Even among other urban bodies where STPs are provided, they are either oxidation plants (in 16 towns) or primary treatment plants (in 6 towns) and secondary and tertiary treatment plants are established in none of the towns. Worst of all, even in majority of the municipal corporations STPs are not provided. For instance, Belgaum and Hubli-Dharwad, which produce an average of 100 LPCD of sewage, do not have treatment plants. Among those ULBs where treatment plants are provided in 4 ULBs, i.e., in Jamkhandi, Bhatkal, Chickmagalur and Ilkal, they are not functioning.

Public Sanitation: Public sanitation facilities such as latrines, toilets, etc. at the common places like bus stand and markets, form another type of sanitation services. But, majority of ULBs do not have these facilities, even wherever it is available the facilities are inadequate and not maintained properly. All this adds to the inadequate sanitation services in urban areas. However, we are handicapped by non-availability of information to assess the magnitude of these problems.

Slums: Slum is an area being low-lying, having ill-sanitary conditions, overcrowded population, and hence a source of danger to public health. In urban areas of Karnataka there were 2,428 slums during 2002, showing the magnitude of the problem. Among the districts, Bangalore Urban has maximum number of slums (366) followed by Gulbarga (179), Shimoga (153) and Bellary (136). All other districts, except Dakshina Kannada, Udupi and Kodagu, have on average more than 50 slums each. The problem of slums is too severe in Class–I cities with 998 slums as on May 3, 2003 according to the Karnataka Slum Clearance Board. Presence of large number of slums in almost all districts indicates the magnitude of additional sanitation, drinking water supply and health problems in urban areas. In all these slums to a larger extent, the drinking water facilities, drainage system, community toilets, roads, etc. are not available.

Over the years, there is a significant increase in the number of slums in the state. During 1998 there were 1,984 slums, which increased to 2,428 in 2002, at a compound growth rate of 5.17 per cent.

Sanitation Facilities in Bangalore City

Increase in population and industrialisation has created more demand for sanitation services in Bangalore city. According to BWSSB, about 80 per cent of the water supplied in the city gets reduced as wastewater, which amounts to about 528 MLD. This wastewater needs to be collected and treated before it is let to the natural drainage system. At present about 38.6 per cent of the geographical area of Bangalore city is covered with sewerage system. This shows that the provision of sewerage system in Bangalore is highly inadequate, as nearly 61 per cent of the total geographical area of 593 sq. kms. is yet to be provided with sewerage system (BWSSB, 2001). It should be noted that the present sewerage system exists in core area of the city, while peripheral areas are being slowly covered. The existing sewerage system of Bangalore city is divided into 3 drainage zones, namely Vrishabhavathi, Koramanagala and Challaghatta and Hebbal. In addition there are three minor valleys namely Kethamaranahalli and Arkavathi, Tavarekere and Kathriguppe. But, the sewers in these valleys are inadequate and their capacity to carry the sewage is also low, which contribute to wastewater stagnation and other related problems.

There are 5 sewage treatment plants in Bangalore to treat the huge of amount of wastewater, i.e., 528 MLD. Out of this about 408 MLD of wastewater is treated in the 5 existing treatment plants. But, the rest of about 120 MLD of wastewater is not currently treated. Besides according to study conducted by TCE Consulting Engineers Limited (BWSSB, 2001), the treatment plants work below their capacity. At the Koramangala and Challaghatta Valley Sewage Treatment Plant the average inflow is about 80 MLD to 100 MLD against the capacity of 163 MLD. Similarly, in the Vrishabhavathy Valley Sewage Treatment Plant during 2000 the sewage inflow was 103 MLD, which is much below the capacity of the plant i.e., 180 MLD. This shows that the STPs are performing less than their capacity.

6.6.4 Expenditure on Water Supply and Sanitation

Government spending is an important input in providing water supply and sanitation services to the population. Public goods like the nature of water supply and sanitation services and inadequate provision of existing services, demand government financing to mitigate the problem. Financial resources for water supply and sanitation are provided by the Central Government, state government and also by the local government organisations (LGOs) in the state, while the state government has the major responsibility. A study in the Institute for Social and Economic Change on the share of expenditure on water supply and sanitation revealed that during 2002-03, the state government contributed about 54 per cent of the total expenditure on water supply and sanitation (rural and urban together), while the Central Government and the ULBs shared respectively about 17 and 29 per cent (Puttaswamaiah and Bhide, 2004).

Total Government Expenditure

The government has spent about Rs. 640 crores during 2003-04 on water supply and sanitation (Appendix A-6.38). The expenditure has increased from Rs. 154 crores in 1991-92 to 640 crores in 2003-04, at an annual growth rate of 14.27 per cent. Allocation of government finance has significantly increased from 1998-99 onwards, which might be due to the external assistance and the government's commitment to provide water supply and sanitation services to people. However, spending as a proportion to the total expenditure of the government is stagnant around 2.5 per cent, except for the three years—1998-99, 1999-2000, and 2001-02 when water supply and sanitation constituted about 3.5 per cent. In fact, the government expenditure on water supply and sanitation started rising from 1994-95 due to the financial assistance from external agencies such as the World Bank.

Although there is an increase in the total amount spent on water supply and sanitation in the state, there is a huge disparity in the allocation for the provision of water supply and for creating sanitation facilities. Both water supply and sanitation are essential for maintaining health and hygiene, but the share of state government expenditure on sanitation is less as compared to that of water supply. Throughout the period of 1991-92 to 2003-04, sanitation constituted about 4.5 per cent of the spending on water supply and sanitation, excepting the years 1996-97, 1997-98 and 2002-03. However, in 2002-03 and 2003-04 there is a significant step up in government spending on sanitation leading to a doubling of the share over the average for the previous four years. In absolute value, there is a significant increase in the amount spent on both water supply and sanitation over the period, particularly on sanitation it has increased at an annual average rate of 42.5 per cent, whereas on water supply the increase is at 14 per cent. However, the increase has not been able to enlarge the share of sanitation, as expenditure on water supply also has increased. In terms of per capita expenditure, spending on water supply and sanitation increased from Rs. 15.5 to Rs. 24 between 1991-92 and 2003-04 (Puttaswamaiah and Bhide, 2004).

Spending on Construction and Maintenance of Assets

Adequate provision of water supply and sanitation services depends upon both creation and maintenance of infrastructure. Government expenditure on creation of assets and maintenance of the assets created has been analysed considering the 'capital expenditure' and 'revenue expenditure', separately for water supply, sanitation. With regard to water supply two stages in the pattern of proportion of revenue and capital expenditure are observed. While the revenue expenditure had the high share up to 1998-99, both revenue and capital expenditures share almost equally between 1998-99 and 2002-03. In the year 2003-04 the capital expenditure accounted for 62 per cent, the highest ever, during the period between 1991-92 and 2003-04. This indicates shift in the state government's priority towards creation of more assets for water supply. But, since the expenditure has shared almost equally between revenue and capital accounts it can be said that the government has given equal priority for both creation as well as maintenance of assets already created for providing water supply in recent years.

The pattern of revenue and capital expenditure on sanitation reveals that most of the spending is in revenue account, barring a few years. The ratio of revenue expenditure was well over 85 per cent, showing the inadequate resources allocated for assets creation in the sanitation sector. Most of the sanitation facilities being public goods essentially require government's investment for better provision of public health services. But, the low percentage of financial resources allocated for the creation of assets shows the scanty attention given by the government for sanitation sector. This might be one of the reasons for lack of sanitation services, particularly in rural areas.

Expenditure across Rural and Urban Areas

There is wide disparity in the expenditure across the rural and urban areas of the state (Puttaswamaiah and Bhide, 2004). For instance, during 2002-03 the government spent about 67 per cent of the total expenditure on water supply and sanitation in urban areas, while the rural areas could get only 33 per cent. There was a sharp decline in the share of amount spent for rural water supply and sanitation between 1999-00 and 2002-03, from 53.5 to 33 per cent.

6.6.5 Government Initiatives on Water Supply and Sanitation

Programmes of Rural Water Supply

The RDPR has implemented different programmes sponsored by Central Government, state government and external agencies (the World Bank, DANIDA, Netherlands, etc.). The state government, having the responsibility, started water supply programmes from the First Five-Year Plan by allocating financial resources. The programmes included are: Accelerated Rural Water Supply Programme, Rajiv Gandhi National Drinking Water Supply Programme, Karnataka Integrated Rural Water Supply and Environmental Sanitation Project, World Bank assisted Integrated Rural Water Supply and Sanitation Project-I, and II, Netherlands assisted Integrated Rural Water Supply and Sanitation Project, and The Dannida assisted Integrated Rural Water Supply and Sanitation Project,

Programmes for Urban Water Supply

The KUWS&DB implements different urban drinking water supply schemes, selected on the basis of population and funding pattern. It includes: Piped Water Supply Schemes, Accelerated Urban Water Supply Programme, and Other Urban Water Supply Schemes.

Sanitation Programmes in Rural Areas

Various programmes initiated by the government for providing sanitation services in rural areas. It includes: Central Rural Sanitation Programme, Nirmala Grama Yojana, School Sanitation Programme, and Swachcha Grama Yojana,

6.6.6 Problems Related to Water Supply and Sanitation

Review of the current status of water supply and sanitation sector revealed that the state has been able to provide water supply and sanitation services to relatively large section of the population. However, problems are still confronting the sector as pointed out in the review. The problems are mainly related to inadequate coverage of services, non-functionality of systems, lack of maintenance, resource problems, etc. These problems are discussed below.

Problems in Water Supply

The problems related to drinking water supply are mainly inadequate coverage of habitations, non-functionality of the systems, lack of maintenance, depleting groundwater level, etc. which are more acute in rural areas.

Inadequate Coverage

Inadequate coverage of water supply service still persists in both rural and urban areas. In rural areas nearly 35 per cent of the habitations are partially covered, while in urban areas the proportion is 77 per cent of the ULBs. This indicates the urgent need of creating adequate provision of water supply systems in the partially covered habitations.

Functionality of Water Supply System

Apart from coverage of habitations for adequate quantity of drinking water, it is essential to see whether the stipulated norm of adequacy is actually realised or not; and the water supply schemes created are functioning or not. Generally, the claim of having covered the habitations with adequate water supply appears to relate to the pumping and distribution capacity created under various water supply schemes rather than the actual service provided to the villagers (GoK, 2002) (Box 6.13). A study conducted by the Directorate of Economics and Statistics (GoK) showed majority of habitations surveyed had less than 55 LPCD of drinking water supply, which is indicative of lacunae in engineering plan, capacity installation and the satisfaction derived by people (Box 6.15). According to the Department of Rural Development and Panchayat Raj (2001) as many as 21 per cent of drinking water borewells, 7 per cent of mini water schemes and another 7 per cent of piped water supply schemes are found defunct. This non-functionality of the systems might be due to lack of maintenance, non-availability of water at the source, etc.

BOX 6.13

Actual Level of Drinking Water Supply in Rural Area (Based on Sample Survey-2001)

- **Borewell with Handpumps**—91.7 per cent of 470 rural habitations had less than 55 LPCD.
- **Mini Water Supply Schemes**—Out of 646 schemes surveyed 91.48 per cent reported less than 55 LPCD.
- **Piped Water Supply Schemes**—86.07 per cent of 977 rural habitations had inadequate water supply (< 55 LPCD).

Source: GoK, *HPC Report*, 2002.

Scarcity of Drinking Water in Summer Season

Level of water supply is severely affected during summer months in both rural and urban areas due to decline in groundwater level and also in availability of surface water. According to the Study on Rapid Sector Assessment in Karnataka (GoK, 2001), supply level of rural drinking water scheme goes down by 50 to 75 per cent of the intended level of the scheme during summer months. The High Power Committee reveals that 13 per cent of the 470 villages based on borewell water supply scheme, 15 per cent of the 646 villages based on mini water supply schemes, and 19 per cent of 977 villages based on piped water supply schemes had irregular water supply (GoK, 2002).

Quantity of water supplied declines in urban areas due to the large quantity of unaccounted for water (UFW) resulted from leakage in distribution system, illegal connections of water supply, etc. Though accurate data is not available on unaccounted for water, the estimates vary between 30-70 per cent in most ULBs. For instance, the UFW is estimated at 60 per cent in Hubli-Dharwad, 51 per cent in Belgaum and Mysore.

Depletion of Groundwater

Depletion of drinking water sources, be they the ground or surface water, adds to further problems, *via* shortage and deterioration of quality, as experienced by more than 95 per cent of rural habitations. A study by the Department of Mines and Geology on fluctuations in groundwater tables across the watersheds during 1999 depicted 56 watersheds as overexploited and critical, attributed to over extraction of groundwater. Kolar, Tumkur, Bangalore Rural, Banglaore Urban, Chitradurga districts have more number of over exploited and critical *talukas*. The drastic decline in the groundwater level, which is again accentuated by the continuous spell of drought for the recent three years, has adversely affected over 50 per cent of villages in majority of *talukas*. This clearly indicates that depletion of groundwater, the major source of drinking water, would affect the availability of drinking water.

Poor Drinking Water Quality

Quality of drinking water is an important issue that needs to be addressed in the provision of drinking water. Drinking water quality is determined by the presence of certain organic and inorganic substances in excess of tolerance limits as prescribed by Bureau of Indian Standards: IS 10500 in 1991 (GoI, 1991). Consumption of poor quality of water has serious adverse impacts on health, like skin and waterborne diseases. For instance, presence of chemicals like fluoride in excess quantity (more than 1.5 PPM) causes dental and bone hazards, while skin rashes result by consuming water with excess brackishness. Similarly, biological or organic contamination of water may give rise to water borne diseases. Drinking water quality is affected mainly due to both natural and man-made factors, while chemical contamination largely caused by natural factors, organic pollution of water occurs mainly in transmission and distribution system due to human errors. Efforts have been made to identify the habitations with drinking water quality problems by establishing established water quality testing laboratories in 18 districts.[13] However, out of 18 only 7 laboratories are functioning and the remaining are not working due to lack of staff (RDPR website).

Groundwater in more than 37 per cent of rural habitations was contaminated from chemicals in excess of prescribed limit, indicating the poor quality of drinking water (Figure 6.20). Habitations in Bagalkot, Bangalore Urban, Bijapur, Chamrajnagar, Chitradurga, Haveri, Mandya, Tumkur, Bellary, Davanagere, Kodagu, Kolar, Raichur and Koppal districts have serious groundwater quality problems, ranging from 50 to 79 per cent (RDPR, 2002). More specifically, excess fluoride in groundwater is a major problem in 14 districts, ranging from 10 to 67 per cent of the total habitations of each district.

FIGURE 6.20

Per Cent of Groundwater Quality Affected Rural Habitations in Karnataka

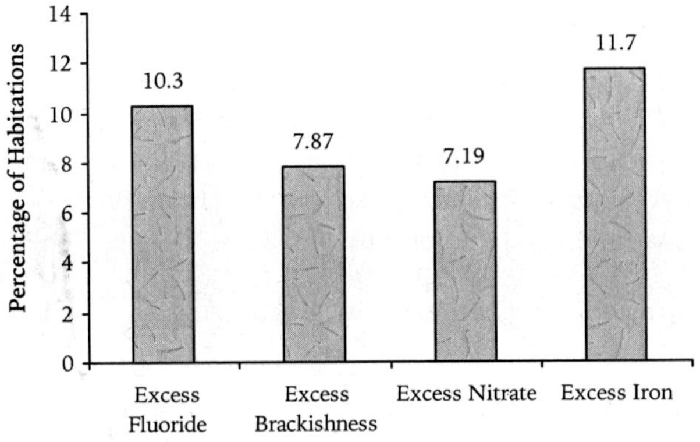

Even urban areas are not free from poor water quality problems in the state. The survey conducted by the High Power Committee (GoK, 2002) reveals that out of 76 towns surveyed for borewell based water supply scheme, 16 per cent reported of unfitness for drinking purpose; 5 per cent of towns reported saltishness, 5 per cent hardness and 3 per cent contamination. Among the districts surveyed by the

13. Bangalore Rural, Tumkur, Kolar, Shimoga, Mysore, Mandya, Mangalore, Belgaum, Gulbarge, Raichur, Dharwad, Bidar, Gadag, Bagalkote, Bijapur, Hassan, Koppal, and Bellary.

HPC, saltishness is a major problem in 33 per cent of towns in Raichur, 20 per cent in Bangalore Rural, 15 per cent of towns in Kolar, while hardness in water was reported in 50 per cent of towns in Shimoga, 40 per cent in Bangalore Rural and 17 per cent in Haveri districts. In Davanagere and Tumkur water was contaminated, in 33 and 12 per cent of towns respectively. Similarly the water quality test for tank based drinking water schemes showed that in 8 per cent of 28 towns surveyed, the quality of water was low with high salt and hardness in water.

6.6.7 Problems in Sanitation Services

Sanitation sector has the problems of inadequate provision of latrine/toilet facilities, drainage systems, public sanitation facilities, etc.

Inadequate Provision of Sanitation Services

Sanitation facilities both household and community level are highly inadequate in the state. While large numbers of households lack latrine facilities particularly in rural areas, the community level services like drainage, wastewater treatment plants, etc. are absent.

When it comes to latrine facility, utilisation is as important as construction to maintain hygiene and safe environment. It is distressing to note that in rural areas many households do not use even the existing latrine facilities for various reasons. According to a study by the Directorate of Economics and Statistics (GoK, 1998), out of 8634 latrines constructed under NGY, 13 per cent were misutilised and 3 per cent non-utilised. It is significant to note that misutilisation of latrines was more in Bijapur (69 per cent), Gulbarga (56 per cent) and Raichur (51 per cent). While in Raichur around 40 per cent of the latrines were found to be in use as bathrooms, in Gulbarga 34 per cent were used for other uses. All these indicate that people have not given much importance to proper use of latrines.

The problem of inadequate provision of sanitation facilities persists in urban areas also. As observed in the current status large number of ULBs are still not provided with underground drainage systems and public sanitation facilities like toilets at public places. Many of the ULBs do not have sewage treatment plant an essential part of wastewater disposal mechanism.

6.6.8 Policy Suggestions

Considering the status of and problems in the water supply and sanitation sector the following points might be considered to resolve the problems and augment the services.

Partially covered habitations, in both rural and urban areas, should be brought under full coverage of water supply. There is overlapping of various water supply and sanitation programmes. It is necessary to avoid overlapping of various programmes and to spread them equally across the state to bring partially covered habitations under full coverage. Drought prone districts should be given high priority to resolve the problem of inadequate water supply. Drinking water quality affected habitations should be taken on first priority basis to provide safe drinking water, through alternative sources or by treating water.

Immediate attention needs to be given towards providing sanitation facilities like drainage, sewerage system to avoid adverse impact on health in both rural and urban areas. In urban planning provision should be given for sewerage system, public toilets/latrines, garbage disposal place, site for sewage/wastewater diversion, STPs, etc. STPs should be provided immediately to those ULBs which are generating large quantity of wastewater on priority basis. Slum development programmes should be given priority to provide basic facilities like drinking water and sanitation to slum dwellers covering all ULBs.

Operation and maintenance is a major problem in both water supply and sanitation system. Hence, importance needs to be given to operation and maintenance activities for efficient working of the system. Waterman should be a trained/qualified personnel also for maintenance of water supply system (both quantity/quality). ULBs can consider privatisation of operation and maintenance of water supply schemes, but by protecting poor and vulnerable groups. In villages, Village Water Supply and Sanitation Committees (VWSCs) can be established, based on the World Bank project experiences, to supervise the operation and maintenance activities of water supply and sanitation schemes.

Maintenance of water quality is an important issue. A single water quality testing agency should be promoted for both rural and urban areas, and it should be informed to people on a transparent basis. A vigilance group has to be created to report on quantity and quality of water supply functioning of the system, etc. for regular and efficient functioning of the system. Water quality awareness camps should be promoted, particularly in rural areas, where groundwater quality is a serious problem.

An integrated institutional system for groundwater conservation and recharging measures needs to be promoted as groundwater is the major source of drinking water. Institutional initiatives need to be promoted for rainwater harvesting in both urban and rural areas. Attention may be given towards dual water supply system in water quality affected areas (i) one for drinking (ii) another for washing, bathing and cleaning purposes. Utilisation of treated wastewater needs to be promoted for purposes like industrial and gardening activities, for which incentives in terms of subsidised price may be given. Beneficiary involvement and participation is essential in the success of any programme. Hence government, community, NGOs based initiatives should be promoted for efficient functioning of water supply and sanitation system in both rural and urban areas. The model of Bangalore Agenda Task Force (BATF) and Infosys in establishing 'pay and use' toilets at public places in Bangalore city may be considered for developing suitable system of government, community based organisations and NGOs participation. This approach can result in reducing the burden on service providers and increase the accountability and responsibility among users.

6.7 Social Security Schemes

Social security scheme is an important component of social infrastructures in India as it provides financial protection for the workers and their dependents, old age pensions and maternity schemes. For the welfare of destitute, handicapped and the elderly without support, several social programmes are being implanted. After a few years of preparation for a social security plan in India with some modifications suggested by the International Labour Organization (ILO) experts, promulgated the Employees' State Insurance (ESI) Act in 1948. It has been operative since 1952 and has provided full comprehensive medical care and cash benefits to the insured and restricted medical benefits to their families. However, Karnataka state implemented the ESI scheme only on 27th July 1958 (ESI, 2003). Concurrently, there were separate schemes for government employees, railway workers and military personnel (Ron, Abel-Smith and Tamburi, 1990). Initially, the statutory and contributory Employees' State Insurance was applied to non-seasonal power-using factories employing 20 or more workers. Later, it was gradually extended to, namely, by geography, by industry, and by wage group. The main schemes working under the national social assistance schemes are National Social Assistance Programme with full financial support of the Central Government, National Old Age Pension Scheme, National Family Benefit Scheme, and National Maternity Scheme. The social welfare programmes under the social security schemes are especially focusing people who are not having any support from family institutions in the state, which may not be helpful to all the needy people in the state. Therefore, there is a need for universal social security schemes at the state level by integrating all the individual social welfare schemes. This can be done through self-help groups, which is widespread in the state. In fact, all the rural development schemes are being implemented with the help of the self-help groups.

6.7.1 Social Security and its Links with Women's Empowerment

Social security has come to be recognised as a crucial sub component of the social sector. This is important considering that the number of female-headed households[14] is increasing every year. The woman has the main responsibility for the economic maintenance of the family in such households. Although the cultural ethos prescribes that the households should be headed by men, labour migration leads to temporary heading of the households by women. Death, desertion by husband or divorce leads to such roles on a permanent basis. The nature of women's household membership is related to her marital status. About 3 per cent of women face divorce or desertion; it is the widows who are much larger in number. Karnataka has accounted for a high incidence of widowhood than it is at the national level (11.2 per cent as against 9.6 per cent in 1993-94 as per NFHS data). The loss of the earning male member on the one hand, and the exploitative labour market where women receive less wages for same or even more work, has led to what is called as feminisation of poverty. Increasing number of widows is falling into what is called as greying feminisation of poverty (Batliwala, 1995). They have no independent economic resources, and get into poverty.

Major categories of women who have to be brought under social security net are those from households below poverty line. There are significant interdistrict disparities in their number or presence. For example, Uttara Kannada, Udupi and Dakshina Kannada districts have reported low presence while it is high in the Hyderabad-Karnataka region. Any discussion about social security for women should take into consideration

14. District and even state-specific data on the magnitude of female headed HHs below poverty line are not available.

human rights as a principle of equality of all human beings. After the UN Convention in 1993 on Elimination of All Forms of Discrimination against Women (CEDAW), Indian Government included measures to bring about gender equality and eliminate discrimination against women. Laws and policies were enacted/passed to ensure this. These laws have ensured equal access and control for women over property and better socio-economic security for them. Many government policies have also been targeting to tackle the existing gender discrimination in the field of political representation, employment, education and health.

6.7.2 *Self-Help as an Approach*

Self-help is defined as a way to deal with problems everyone faces from time to time in their lives—illness, divorce, the death of a loved one, emotional upsets or strains. Mingling with people suffering from similar problems is expected to enable them to cope with their own difficulties and learn to deal with them better. Underlying the self-help is the basic theme: "You are not alone." Self-help movement has mushroomed in the past two decades, especially in the developing nations. Helping is the centre of this approach—how to give help, receive help and to help yourself. Thus, the members would feel less isolated, knowing that others share similar problems, exchange ideas and effective ways to cope with problems, actively work on their attitudes and behaviour to make positive changes in their lives and gain a new sense of control over their own lives. The knowledge base of these groups is experimental, indigenous and rooted in the wisdom that emerges from the struggle with problems in concrete and shared ways. Self-help groups build on the strengths of their members.

Stages in the Formation of SHGs

Generally three stages are identified in the evolution of SHGs. The first is when they are formed. This includes motivation to join the group, developing the group, working with meetings, etc. The second is when the group engages in saving, thrift and internal lending activities. Finally, the group tries to establish linkage with the financial institutions for micro-credit to undertake IGA.

Micro-Finance and SHGs

Micro-finance and SHG approach aim at enabling the twin purpose of income generation and savings, self-employment and empowerment of women. The experience in the state has been positive by showing that the poor women can save and use credit for their daily needs.

Studies are lacking in this context but consultancy type of research projects undertaken in the subject have shown a definite shift in the receptivity of SHG approach in achieving social mobilisation of women besides offering certain economic benefits. At least in few cases there is a shift from loaning pattern for consumption to productive purposes. But there has not been substantial increase in the income levels of members. The institutional mechanisms that are sensitive and responsive to the needs of the poor are present in the rural and urban areas, particularly in the form of local bodies of a decentralised governing system.

6.7.3 *Women's SHGs in Karnataka*

The self-help group approach has come a long way in India, from 1974, when SEWA started mobilising poor women based on their respective trade. The women's movement in the west in the 60s and 70s influenced many countries, India being one of them. The main aim of SHG concept is to improve the economic development of women and to create a facilitating environment for their social transformation, in the light of gender based discrimination in work and the household. Perhaps the first concerted effort to form women's groups in Karnataka was when DWCRA scheme was introduced in the mid-eighties. But earlier to it, an NGO called MYRADA had initiated the concept by forming women's groups in some of its project sites. The reasons lie in the realisation that women's development is an essential prerequisite for overall development. However, this came to be realised only after many schemes were introduced (Appendix A-6.39).

Following the changed situation in the 1990s when the economic agenda trusted private and market sectors as vehicles for growth, the aid agencies also started insisting that the share of the state in development should be participatory. It was also emphasised that such duties like service, delivery and development should be entrusted to the decentralised institutions at grassroots levels.

The Central Government launched the Swarna Jayanthi Gram Swarojgar Yojana on April 1, 1999 emphasising the integrated upliftment of rural households that fall under the BPL line in a span of five years. Even here the SHG approach has been upheld. The scheme was the result of merging of all the direct anti-poverty programmes like IRDP, DWCRA, TRYSEM, etc into one single programme in order to promote holistic self-employment among men and women. A review of the programme has indicated that women form nearly 50 per cent of the total persons assisted in the programme. The programme sought to take assistance of several institutions like the line departments of the government, NGOs, other local organisations and the *panchayat* bodies. Besides these governmental efforts to provide sustained development to women, a number of NGOs have also initiated programmes that encourage SHGs of women and men to be formed (Rajasekhar, 2000). In fact the credit for initiating savings and credit practices among women could be attributed to their efforts. Further, their efforts encouraged many other 'promotional agencies such as NABARD, SIDBI and external donors to start similar programmes on a wider scale' (Rajasekhar, 2002).

A commonly held view is that there is a proliferation of SHGs in the state (besides few other states). While on the one hand, this has been the result of the recognition of the need to empower women and bring them to the mainstream, it is largely also due to the interest taken in the case by political parties/ruling parties/governments. Moreover, it is binding upon the governments that they include a gender component whenever a developmental project is sponsored by external aid agencies. Yet another important emerging dimension is that of the human rights perspective that argues for extending all benefits to women also as human beings and not just as women. Thus, the SHGs have become common ground for almost all development activities. Three self-help group formation programmes currently being implemented in the state are particularly important in the context of their association with the SHG approach. Swashakthi and SGSY are the Centrally Sponsored Schemes while the Stree-Shakthi programme is the state government programme. The three have been in operation more or less since the same time.

6.7.4 Functioning of SHGs in Karnataka: Myth and Reality

The discussion on the operational part of SHGs in the state is divided into three parts, to fall into the stage of preparation or formation of SHGs; stabilisation stage and the functional stage. The first stage is one that includes the processes of dissemination of information, motivation to join the groups, selection of members and the representatives, and laying down the rules. Stage two is when the group stabilises itself by following the rules of working, like meetings, savings and identifying IGA. Finally, the stage when the group is performing well by carrying on the IGA and achieves wider goals like bank linkage, etc. is when it is successfully functioning.

Stage of Formation of SHGs

The Swashakthi programme also resting upon the formation of groups of women has gone ahead very well by achieving required target. The process of formation with all the sub-processes like meeting the villagers (*Gram Sabha*), establishing rapport, motivating them, identifying the members and enlisting them as members—is reportedly good. However, there are also reasons for the relative failure of three types of groups to take off and enable empowerment of women were primarily related to lack of sufficient knowledge about the goals of the programmes themselves. The reasons for this were the following:

- The DWCD (its staff) considered it burdensome to manage many programmes, in the absence of additional staff. The *anganwadi* worker felt that she was overburdened with work.
- Absence of sufficient training to them in the skills of group formation like motivating women, obtaining the consent of the household/husband, confidence-building and awareness about possible benefits—were absent.
- The staff themselves lacked sufficient training, knowledge and resources to carry out their responsibilities.

Barring SGSY and Swashakthi groups, here the analysis concentrates upon the *Stree Shakti* groups. The picture presented generally about the latter is that they are working well and are posing to be models to groups in other states. It is here that one has to separate the political rhetoric from the actual grassroot situation. Undoubtedly, the groups were formed with a lot of enthusiasm in all the 27 districts. Usually a SHG has to progress from being a mere savings and thrift group to the status of being able to obtain an external linkage with a financial institution and loan for starting IGA on a collective basis. The latter is important as an enabling mechanism for achieving self-reliance, the ultimate in sustainable development and empowerment of women.

Stabilisation Stage

The ideal situation for a SHG to come into existence, work and take up an activity to sustain the interests of its members is rare. An important function of a SHG is to ensure economic empowerment to its members. It is a crucial indicator of its capacity to ensure social security to itself and to others. A number of groups have taken up economic activities, but most of them are individual based rather than group based. Whenever they are of the former type, the chances of the head of household (HH's) traditional activity continued or pursued as the activity under the SHG programme are very many. As a family activity, the domination of the male members/ husband in decision making and access to income from the economic activity would be certainly there directly or indirectly.

Collective activities pursued as part of the SHG are again class based. The experiences in this context show that only homogenous surroundings and its groups has taken successfully collective economic pursuits. Single caste villages with a vulnerable community living there have proved to be good examples here.

Migration of members to other villages or to towns on wage work, periodically, affects the functioning of groups. Therefore, the presences of economic activities are strong enough to arrest such migration. Cases are not lacking where the poor women have continued to migrate after taking loan for an activity. It is under such circumstances, when they cannot make use of the loan for IGA, the very poor people agreed to allow the richer members availing of the loan for them.

This advantage of Swashakthi groups lied in its relative autonomy in implementation by the DPMU and carried out by a NGO. The grassroot workers of the latter gave a feeling among the groups that they were more committed. The propaganda for the groups was conspicuous with boards announcing the names of all the *Swashakthi Sanghas* put up near the colonies where the members lived, the training and capacity building exercises carried out for them by renowned trainers like MYRADA, etc. the successful linkages established with the banks for credit facility—all enabled this type of a different feeling.

Capacity building of women at three levels *viz.*, the staff of the line department, representatives of the group and members—is found to be crucial in preparing them towards autonomy in managing the groups in such important work like book-keeping, convening meetings, identifying income generation activity (IGA) activities and so on. Dependency on the *anganwadis* is quite there as a factor in the way of self-reliance by most groups. This is true of the NGO sponsored groups and *Swashakthi* groups too, but the former have taken initiative to train a literate member in bookkeeping, etc. In the government sponsored groups, the members as well as the government's representative are under the impression that it is the work of the latter, and it is like any other government scheme. The participatory nature of the entire exercise is weak here.

Another significant issue here is the external linkage of the groups with the local power structure are the banks, the line departments and the GP. The latter institution is important here since in many cases, a sustained relationship between the two is lacking. Among other reasons, lack of awareness among *panchayat* members about the role of groups seems to be the crux of the problem. In those villages, where the GP has taken interest in the women's groups, SGSY loans and other forms of assistance have reached the latter. GP laments that it cannot control the *anganwadis* (AW).

Physical and material assets, besides human resource potential of most SHGs are another question that needs mention here. The members have expressed the need for a separate place to conduct meetings and not in the house of the representative as is the usual practice now. This is where at least meetings are held regularly. In the latter case the usual practice is to collect contributions to savings in the AW centre itself.

Regular Working with Income Generation Activity

The final stage is when the SHGs mature into units turning out economically productive work with IGA as a result of external assistance. A number of SHGs have reached this stage. What they desire is the formation of a federation of SHGs to establish on a firm footing and work for wider issues. It is here that we have the role for them to get into social security issues and assist the government in its implementation of programmes in the social sector like education and health, in particular.

The emphasis on participatory development in almost all spheres today especially in the context of social sectoral issues has in fact enhanced the role of SHGs in it. Literacy programmes, health issues including immunisation, safe motherhood, etc., water and sanitation projects, tank improvement works, forest management and conservation, environmental programmes, child labour projects, other programmes of women's development like anti-violence—all depend on the strength of the SHG approach in reaching the women. In other words, they provide what is called as the 'critical mass' to enable many tough programmes to reach the needy in both urban and rural areas. We find the action plans of these government programmes containing organisational charts where SHGs of women have a predominant role to play. For example, the JSYS has commissioned a number of tank committees in selected villages. These also include local women also as members–both from land owning and landless HHs. They prepare action plans for each village considering the local situation, availability of raw materials for undertaking IGA, type of IGA to be taken, whether it would suit all those HHs whose livelihoods are linked to the natural resource base. This is true of other projects like watershed programme or sanitation, where women's groups are a mandatory need or aspect of the project. But the studies have shown how the whole concept is understood and adopted as long as a project is in operation after which the SHGs are found to be defunct or poor in performance.

6.7.5 The Way Forward

The need for social security for men, women and children to safeguard life and property needs no emphasis, particularly in the present day society where poverty has come to be recognised for its social and gender aspects. Just as the interest—both academic and policy—in the need to boost women's development both as an escape from patriarchy and gender-based discrimination as well as from the human rights perspective has widened in the recent decades, it has also become broad-based by such expectations of its contributions to the expansion of social sector and in ensuring social security.

Karnataka state has been acclaimed to be one of the pioneers as long as its efforts to design, implement a number of policies and programmes in the realm of women's development and empowerment. These have responded well to the genesis of gender ideology from welfare to equity approaches. Today, therefore women are not only seen to be recipients of fruits of development but also as the carriers of development to men and children too, thereby leading to total development. Women's groups are viewed thus to be the torch bearers of community participation in bringing about development especially social sector development. Social security is in-built in such endeavour.

An analysis of information existing on the subject of SHGs of women in the state especially the ones in rural areas has shown that the achievement has been substantial. Chief among them are:

- There is awareness among all about the concept of self-help groups of women. However, such knowledge is still in terms of savings and internal lending, which the groups are presently up to. This is a useful and significant achievement from the social security point of view that women are economically better with some savings than what they were before.
- Savings have provided them with something to fall back upon during crises periods. Internal lending has been for consumption purposes in most cases. These include purchase of food items, hospital expenses, paying school fees at lower levels of schooling, purchase of petty items for HH, repayment of some other loan, etc.
- Savings have enabled some to go for external loans for IGA. This has enabled income generation, exposure and awareness. If the activity is dairy, arts and crafts or traditional occupations where women are proficient already, and which does not demand any training or skill development, then there is more success in terms of economic returns directly to women's hands. This is also adding to security of the HH and not just the woman concerned.
- Positions in the group have enabled driving home power—political and economic besides social—that is also a form of security against marginalisation. Even otherwise, attending meetings, participating in decision making, knowing about the programmes for women's development, etc. are indicators of power spreading even among members.
- An important aspect of social security through SHG is the fact of being a member in a group itself. Since most of the groups are homogeneous in their constitution, members are identical in their problems. They form a human chain to a address social issues like dowry harassment, alcoholism among husbands and wife beating, other forms of atrocities on women both with in and outside the HH. If the groups are formed by NGOs, then the occasions when the groups take up issues of social cause are not rare. Thus, repayment of loans, lessening of dropouts among girl children and atrocities on women are few examples of where

a group has accomplished the capacity to fight for human and social rights.

- Women heading their HHs are specially benefited if they are in SHGs. But preoccupation with work in the absence of the male and absence of sustained income to contribute to savings on a regular basis are the constraints that these women face in their participation in group activities.
- Homogeneity in membership is found to be having its own advantages. It has encouraged better participation, accountability and transparency in work.

There are a number of negative aspects, which have affected the working of SHGs in ensuring social security, and in promoting development in the socio-economic sectors.

- While these have been discussed in the paper, chief among them is the institutional infrastructural issues like para-extension staff, material and human assets, clarity in work requirements, capacity building at regular intervals, establishing of proper linkages, and viability of IGA.
- Absence of transparency in work has led to development outcomes to go in another direction. The better off have been cornering the benefits like loans. Likewise a limited livelihood opportunity has pushed many poor women to seek job outside by migration.
- Inability to provide loans due to failure to generate external funds is another problem. This again is linked to inadequate savings, which is the result of poverty, migration and insecurity.
- Expectation of bank assistance (loan) has motivated many to join the groups. Often 2-3 women from the same HH are there in a single group. The AW is president or secretary in some groups.
- Likewise a spurt in the number of groups is also expression of expectation from bank.
- Many groups are defunct already (within six months to one year of formation) due to internal rifts on money matters). Inequity in loan disbursement is the cause. Leadership is often unaccountable, selfish and benefits are cornered.

6.8 Conclusion

The social infrastructures such as education, health, nutrition and ICDS programme, housing, water supply and sanitation, and social security have been reviewed. The critical evaluation of all these sub-components of the social sector shows that there is a need for redefined role of government especially in health, education and social security programmes. In case of education, reallocation of resources is needed by giving the priorities to primary education, which will lead to more allocation of resources to provide a quality oriented primary schooling in the state. In the case of health, public health issues need to be given high priority with more allocation of resources to the primary health care services. There is a need for universal health insurance scheme through community participation, which will bring all the people, who are socially and economically backward, in to the main stream of health insurance scheme in the state. In this case, self-help group at the village levels will be endorsed for not only implementing health insurance scheme but also social welfare schemes in the state.

References

Bangalore Water Supply and Sewerage Board (2001-02). *Annual Performance Report*, BWSSB, Bangalore.

Bashir, Sajitha (2000). *Government Expenditure on Elementary Education in the Nineties*, The European Commission.

————.(2002a). *India: Karnataka: Secondary Education and the New Agenda for Economic Growth*, Report No.24208-IN, Human Development Sector Unit, South Asia Region, World Bank.

————.(2002b). *India: Karnataka: Financing Education in the context of Economic Restructuring*, Report No.24208-IN, Human Development Sector Unit, South Asia Region, World Bank.

Batiliwala, Srilatha (1993). *Empowerment of Women in South Asia: Concepts and Practices*, FAO, New Delhi.

Booth Anne (1999). "Survey of Recent Developments", *Bulletin of Indonesian Economic Study*, 35(3), p.3-38.

Census (2001). *Tables on Houses, Household Amenities and Assets*, Registrar General of India, Government of India, New Delhi.

Child Development: The programme provides an integrated approach for... and joint action for Child Development and Women's.... Haryana, universal Himachal Pradesh, Karnataka, coverage of *http://www.nic.in/childdet.htm-38k*.

expresshealthcaremgmt.com. Is the ICDS performing up to the mark? Healthcare Management decided to find out how the Integrated Child Development Schemes for children aged 0-6, is faring in Karnataka.

Gayathri, Devi K.G. (1998a). "Female Enterprise and Male Employment: Thigala Holeyas of Akkahalli", in Simon R. Charsley and G. K. Karanth, (eds.), *Challenging Untouchability: Dalit Initiative and Experience from Karnataka, Cultural Subordination and the Dalit Challenge*, Volume I, Sage, New Delhi.

————. (1998b). "Privilege and Conformity: The Madars of Nuliyur", in Simon R. Charsley and G. K. Karanth (eds.), *Challenging Untouchability: Dalit Initiative and Experience from Karnataka, Cultural Subordination and the Dalit Challenge*, Volume I, Sage, New Delhi.

Gopalan, C. (1984). "Measurement of Under Nutrition–Biological Considerations", *Economic and Political Weekly*, 18, (14).

Government of India (1980). *Integrated Child Development Services Scheme*, Department of Social Welfare.

———.(1986). *An Evaluation of Integrated Child Development Services (1975-85)*, Department of Institutional Finance and Statistics in Karnataka Government Secretariat, Bangalore.

———.(1991). The Bureau of Indian Standards (BIS), IS 10500: 1991.

———. (1999). *Expert Group Report on Financial Requirements for Making Elementary Education a Fundamental Right*, Ministry of Human Resource Development (Chairman: Tapas Mujumdar), New Delhi.

———. (various years). *Selected Educational Statistics*, Ministry of Human Resource Development, Dept of Education.

Government of Karnataka (1998). Directorate of Economics and Statistics.

———. *Annual Report*, Department of Food and Civil Supplies (2000-01).

———. *Manual for Mid-day Meals Programme and Background Note*, Department of Public Education

———. *A Hand Book of Schemes of the Department of Women and Child Development*, Directorate of Women and Child Development (2003-04).

———.(2000). *Agricultural Census 2000-01*, Report on Operational Holdings in Karnataka, Department of Economics and Statistics & State Agricultural Commissioner, Bangalore.

———. (2000). "Rural Water Supply and Sanitation in Karnataka– Strategy Paper", 2000-2005, Rural Development and Panchayat Raj Department, Bangalore.

———.RDPR (2000-02), *Annual Report.*

———.(2002). Annual Report of RDPR Department.

———.RDPR (2001). *Study on Rapid Sector Assessment in Karnataka*, Project Planning Monitoring Unit.

———.(2001). *Towards Equity, Quality and Integrity in Health*, Task Force on Health and Family Welfare, Government of Karnataka.

———.(2002). High Power Committee (HPC) for Redressal of Regional Imbalances.

———. (various years). *Economic Surveys*, Planning and Statistics Dept. Govt of Karnataka.

———. Department of Women and Child Development.

———. (2003). Karnataka Urban Water Supply and Drainage Board, Annual Report.

———. (2004). *Economic Survey 2003-04*, Department of Planning and Statistics.

Hiremath, U.B. (2004). "Akhshar Dasoha for Revolution in Literacy", *Karnataka Vikas*, 45(4).

Census of India, (2001). "Houses, Household Amenities Band Assets", *Series 1*, Registrar General and Census Commissioner, India, New Delhi.

Reserve Bank of India, (2000). *Basic Statistical Returns of Scheduled Commercial Banks in India*, Volume 29, Mumbai.

Institute for Population Sciences (2001). *Karnataka—National Family Health Survey-2*; 1992-93, Mumbai.

Joshi, P.D. (1998). *Changing Pattern of Consumption Expenditure in India and Some Selected States*, National Sample Survey Organisation (NSSO), Ministry of Planning and Programme Implementation, Government of India.

Kanbargi, R. (2002). *Equity in Education in Karnataka*, Education Dept., Government of Karnataka.

Karnatka.com: About State Government–Social Welfare Measures ...1986; Reservations for Women in Karnataka (Panchyat Raj Act 1988). In order to *http://www.karnataka.com/govt/welfare.shtml*

Krishnaji, N. (2001). "Poverty, Gender and Schooling: A Study of Two Districts in Andhra Pradesh", in A.Vaidyanathan and P.R.G Nair (eds.), *Elementary Education in Rural India: A Grassroots View*, pp.131-65, Sage, New Delhi.

Mahadeva, M. (2004a). "Housing Problem and Public Action: Continued Incompatibility-Experience from a Southern State, Review of Development and Change", IX, (1), January–June, Madras Institute of Development Studies, Chennai.

———. (2004b). *Development of Housing Finance: Shouldn't Indian Housing Finance System be Responsive, Savings and Development*, Giordano Dell' Amore Foundation, Italy (Forthcoming).

Mahendra, Dev S. (2003). "Right to Food in India", *Working Paper No. 50*, Centre for Economic and Social Studies, Hyderabad.

Mathiyazhagan, M.K. (2003a). "People's Choice of Health Care Provider: Policy Options for Rural Karnataka in India", *Journal of Health Management*, 1.5 (1): 111-137.

———. (2003b). "Rural Household Characteristics and Health Expenditure in India: An Analysis", *Journal of Social and Economic Development*, 5 (1): 1-25.

———. (2004). *Health Care Financing in Karnataka State: A Case for Government Health Financing under Health Management Trust and Health Insurance Scheme*, Ministry of Health and Family Welfare, Government of Karnataka, Bangalore.

Mayoux, Linda (1998). "Women's Empowerment and Micro-Finance Programs: Approaches, Evidence and Ways Forward", *Discussion Paper*, Milton Keynes, The Open University.

Mishra, K. Vinod, Subrata Lahiri and Norman Y.Luther (1999). *Child Nutrition in India*, International Institute for Population Sciences, Mumbai, India and East West Center, Mumbai.

NABARD (1996). *Statistical Statements Relating Cooperative Movement in India: Part II-* Non- Credit Societies, Mumbai.

Narayana, M.R. (2002). *Collegiate Education in Karnataka State*, Education Dept., Govt. of Karnataka.

National Buildings Organisation (1988). *Housing Needs*, New Delhi.

National Housing Bank (1999). *Report on Trend and Progress of Housing in India.*

National Sample Survey Organisation (2001). *Level and Pattern of Consumer Expenditure in India 1999-2000*, 55th Round, Report No. 457, Ministry of Statistics and Programme Implementation, Government of India.

NFHS. *National Family Health Survey* (1992-93 and 1998-99), International Institute of Population Studies, Mumbai.

Panchamukhi, P.R and Sailabala Debi (2000). *Responsiveness of Various Schemes to Girls Literacy/ Education: Comparative Analysis of Karnataka and Andhra Pradesh*, Conducted by CMDR, Sponsored by Planning Commission, Government of India.

Population Research Centre, Institute for Social and Economic Change and International Institute for Population Sciences (1995). *Karnataka - National Family Health Survey* 1992-93, Bangalore and Mumbai.

PROBE (1999). *Public Report on Basic Education in India*, New Delhi, Oxford.

Puttaswamaiah, S. (2004). *State of Environment Report and Action Plan*, Department of Ecology, Environment and Forest, Government of Karnataka, Bangalore.

Puttaswamaiah, S. and Shashanka Bhide (2004). "A State Level Analysis of Public Expenditure on Provision Of Basic Public Health Services", report prepared for the World Bank Sponsored Project *Restructuring Local Environment Management for Better Health Outcomes: Towards A District Pilot in Karnataka*, Institute for Social and Economic Change, Bangalore.

Radhakrishna, R., K.Hanumantha Rao, C.Ravi and B. Sambi Reddy (2004). "Chronic Poverty and Malnutrition in India", *Working Paper 11*, Chronic Poverty Research Centre and Indian Institute of Public Administration, New Delhi.

Rajan, Irudaya and P. Mohanchandran (1998). "Infant and Child Mortality Estimates", Part-I, *Economic and Political Weekly*, 33, 19, pp.1120-40.

Rajasekhar D. (2000). "Non-Governmental Organisations (NGOs) in India: Opportunity and Challenges", *Journal of Rural Development*, 19 (2): 249-275.

———. (2002). "Impact of Micro-Finance Programs on Poverty and Gender Equality: Some Evidence from Indian NGOs", in Shahra Razavi (ed.), *Shifting Burdens: Gender and Agrarian Change under Neoliberalism*, Kumarian Press, Inc.

Rajasekhar, D., B.P. Vani and K.G. Gayathri Devi (2003). *Role of Local Organisations in Women Development and Empowerment: A Study in Karnataka and Madhya Pradesh States, India*, World Bank Project on Roles of Rural Local Organisations, ISEC, Bangalore, November.

Rao, N.R. and P. H. Rayappa (1993). "Child in Karnataka A Situational Analysis", Conference Paper, Indian Association of Women Studies, Mysore.

Seetharamu, A.S. (2002). *Structure and Function of Education Management Set Up in Karnataka State*, Education Dept., Government of Karnataka.

Sen, Amartya Kumar (1985). *Women, Technology and Sexual Divisions*, UNCTAD & INSTRAW, New York.

Sopher D.K. (1974). "Measurement of Disparity", *The Professional Geographer*, 26/2 (Nov.), 380-92.

State-wise Projects Sanctioned under Integrated Child Development Scheme in India (2002-03), *http://www.indiastat.com.*

Swaminathan, M. (1992). *Handbook of Food and Nutrition*, Bappco Ltd., Bangalore.

Tilak, J.B.G (2002). *Education in Orissa: A Review of Progress, Problems and Perspectives for Future on School Education*, Monograph prepared for UNDP, New Delhi.

Tinker and Bramsen (eds.) (1976). "The Adverse Impact of Development on Women", in *Women and World Development*, Overseas Development Council, Washington D.C.

Thant, Myo (1999) "Lessons from East Asia: Financing Human Development in Human Capital Formation an an Engine of Growth", in Joseph L.H. Tan (ed.), *The East Asian Experience*, Singapore Institute of South East Asian Studies, pp. 202-36.

Women and Child Development Department (2002-03). *Annual Report*, Government of Karnataka.

World Bank (1980). *Recognising the Invisible Women in Development: The World Bank's Experience.*

————. (1993). *The East Asian Miracle Economic Growth and Public Policy*, New York.

————. (2001). *India Raising the Sights: Better Health Systems for India's Poor: Overview*, Health Nutrition, Population Sector Unit, India, South Asia Region, Nov.3.

APPENDIX A-6.1

Growth of Educational Institutions and Enrolment in Different Levels of Education in Karnataka

Levels of Education	Compound Growth Rate in per cent	
	Institutions	Enrolment
Primary Education (1990-91 to 2003-04)	1.79	1.54
Secondary Education (1990-91 to 2002-03)	5.67	2.99
Colleges for General Education (1990-91 to 2000-01)	7.75	15.52
Colleges for Professional Education (1990-91 to 2000-01)	7.88	-2.69

Source: Commissioner of Public Instruction, Government of Karnataka.

APPENDIX A-6.2

Share of Expenditure on Different Levels and Types of Education in SDP in Karnataka

(per cent)

Year	Elementary	Secondary	Higher	Technical	Others*	All Education
1980-81	1.40	0.53	0.44	0.08	0.08	2.54
1990-91	1.63	0.88	0.45	0.09	0.16	3.92
1991-92	1.45	0.84	0.48	0.08	0.12	3.83
1992-93	1.49	0.97	0.42	0.07	0.14	4.07
1993-94	1.58	0.89	0.43	0.08	0.13	3.84
1994-95	1.50	0.88	0.42	0.08	0.15	3.74
1995-96	1.53	0.90	0.39	0.07	0.14	3.77
1996-97	1.50	0.85	0.37	0.07	0.17	3.62
1997-98	1.54	0.90	0.37	0.09	0.17	3.77
1998-99	1.48	0.89	0.35	0.08	0.12	3.66
1999-00	1.62	0.98	0.38	0.06	0.12	4.14
2000-01	1.68	0.94	0.53	0.06	0.12	4.14
2001-02	1.63	0.97	0.41	0.07	0.13	4.03

Note: *: State Resource.

Source: Budgets of GoK and *Economic Survey of Karnataka*, different volumes.

APPENDIX A-6.3

Intrasectoral Expenditure on Education in Karnataka

(per cent)

Year	Elementary	Secondary	Higher	Others	Total
1990-91	52.11	28.43	14.34	5.12	100.00
1991-92	50.11	29.23	16.60	4.07	100.00
1992-93	49.62	32.18	13.88	4.32	100.00
1993-94	52.42	29.39	14.25	3.95	100.00
1994-95	50.89	29.99	14.29	4.83	100.00
1994-95	51.91	30.67	13.25	4.17	100.00
1995-96	52.65	29.97	13.07	4.32	100.00
1996-97	52.05	30.50	12.59	4.86	100.00
1997-98	52.12	31.10	12.23	4.56	100.00
1999-00	52.25	30.94	12.60	4.21	100.00
2000-01	52.29	29.31	16.41	1.99	100.00
2001-02	53.02	31.44	13.22	2.32	100.00

Source: Government of Karnataka.

APPENDIX A-6.4

Per Pupil Expenditure in Education in Karnataka State (Rs.)

Year	At Current Prices			At Constant Prices (1993-94)		
	Elementary	Secondary	Higher Sec.	Elementary	Secondary	Higher Sec.
1980-81	187.47	450.39	1290.36	565.55	1358.66	3892.58
1990-91	472.61	1716.69	6276.13	627.81	2280.46	8337.28
1991-92	651.31	2020.18	8680.21	750.55	2328.00	10002.82
1993-94	837.44	2489.03	7193.82	837.44	2489.03	7193.82
1993-94	837.44	2489.03	7193.82	837.44	2489.03	7193.82
1994-95	874.41	2820.42	8199.58	791.78	2553.89	7424.73
1995-96	1066.63	3201.98	6800.47	875.99	2629.67	5584.98
1996-97	1224.08	3613.36	6992.21	944.74	2788.78	5396.57
1997-98	1342.35	4078.70	7707.74	987.87	3001.62	5672.33
1998-99	1567.60	4628.05	3517.26	1085.55	3204.91	2435.69
1999-00	1873.75	5508.22	4107.45	1270.23	3734.08	2784.48
2000-01	2031.78	5171.08	6338.66	1335.82	3399.81	4167.46

Source: Government of Karnataka and Budget Documents.

APPENDIX A-6.5

Object-wise Expenditure (per cent) for School Education

Items	1991-92	2001-02
Direction, Administration and Inspection	0.68	0.52
Teachers Training and Other Services	0.78	0.36
Textbooks	1.22	0.44
Scholarships and Incentives	2.81	0.65
Examinations	0.38	0.35
Government Elementary and Secondary Schools	85.66	87.05
Grants, Assistance to Non-Government Ele. and Sec. Schools	7.47	3.75
Other Expenditure	1.00	6.87
Total	**100.00**	**100.00**

Source: Commissioner of Public Instruction, Government of Karnataka.

APPENDIX A-6.6

Literacy Rate from 1961 to 2001 in Karnataka

Year	Persons	Males	Females	Gender Disparity Index*
1961	29.8	42.29	16.70	0.47
1971	36.83	48.51	24.55	0.36
1981	46.21	58.73	33.17	0.32
1991	56.04	67.26	44.34	0.25
2001	67.04	76.29	57.45	0.18

Note: *: Estimated by the author.

Source: Census of 1961, 1971, 1981, 1991 and 2001.

APPENDIX A-6.7

Mean, Standard Deviation and Coefficient of Variation of Literacy Rate in Karnataka

Population Category/Estimates	*Total*			*Male*			*Female*		
	1981	*1991*	*2001*	*1981*	*1991*	*2001*	*1981*	*1991*	*2001*
All Population									
Average	45.47	55.23	66.05	57.83	66.49	75.61	32.84	43.57	56.24
Standard Deviation	10.62	10.94	9.52	9.34	9.34	7.83	12.10	12.88	11.60
Coefficient of Variation	23.35	19.80	14.41	16.15	14.05	10.35	36.84	29.56	20.63
Scheduled Caste									
Average	20.54	38.60	-	29.18	50.08	-	11.59	26.69	-
Standard Deviation	5.99	8.92	-	6.64	8.72	-	5.50	9.41	-
Coefficient of Variation	29.17	23.11	-	22.74	17.42	-	47.40	35.25	-
Scheduled Tribe									
Average	20.25	37.35	-	29.48	48.74	-	10.68	25.44	-
Standard Deviation	6.52	11.28	-	8.06	11.82	-	5.56	11.29	-
Coefficient of Variation	32.19	30.21	-	27.34	24.25	-	52.02	44.38	-

Note: Estimated by the author, 2001 Census includes 27 districts as against 20 districts in 1981 and 1991.

APPENDIX A-6.8

Gender Parity Index* of School Enrolment in Karnataka

Year	*Primary G/B Ratio*	*Secondary G/B Ratio*
1980-81	75.74	56.88
1990-91	82.54	62.35
1997-98	90.28	75.90
2002-03	93.38	85.49

Note: *Ratio of girl's enrolment to boy's enrolment.

APPENDIX A-6.9

Gross and Net Enrolment Ratio for Elementary Education in Karnataka

	NER			*GER*		
Year	*Boys*	*Girls*	*Total*	*Boys*	*Girls*	*Total*
1996-97	77.26	67.25	72.28	95.49	87.82	91.67
2002-03	87.21	77.28	82.27	107.78	100.92	104.37

Source: For 1996-97: Human Development in Karnataka, and for 2002-03: author's estimations.

APPENDIX A-6.10

Gross Enrolment Ratio in Elementary Education by Social Groups in Karnataka

Category of Children	*Years*	*Classes I-V*			*Classes V-VIII*		
		Boys	*Girls*	*Total*	*Boys*	*Girls*	*Total*
General	1990-91	113.92	101.70	107.95	67.14	47.15	57.25
	2001-02*	116.80	108.57	112.74	77.73	70.07	73.93
SC	1990-91	120.67	102.86	111.96	63.53	41.56	52.67
	2001-02*	110.42	102.66	106.55	99.29	86.19	92.83
ST	1990-91	92.56	79.92	86.38	47.41	32.83	40.20
	2001-02*	105.97	101.63	103.86	99.84	85.98	93.06

Note: *Provisional.
Source: Selected *Educational Statistics*, various years, MHRD, Government of India.

APPENDIX A-6.11

Student Dropouts (per cent) in Primary Schools in Karnataka

Years	*Lower Primary Schools (I-IV)*			*Total Primary Schools (I-VII)*		
	Boys	*Girls*	*Total*	*Boys*	*Girls*	*Total*
1992-93	24.90	29.40	27.00	43.84	54.22	48.71
1993-94	28.30	34.00	31.00	50.40	55.40	52.70
1994-95	23.40	30.30	26.70	47.10	51.10	49.00
1995-96	16.30	27.40	21.80	49.40	53.20	57.30
1996-97	16.50	23.20	19.70	45.60	48.00	46.80
1997-98	16.90	16.10	16.50	41.34	46.28	43.71
1998-99	14.20	12.30	13.30	38.70	43.30	40.80
1999-00	15.00	12.00	13.50	35.00	38.00	36.50
2000-01	10.00	11.00	10.50	35.00	41.00	38.00

Source: Ramesh Kanbargi (2002) *Equity in Education in Karnataka*, Education Department, Government of Karnataka and *Human Development in Karnataka 1999*, Planning Department, Government. of Karnataka, Bangalore.

APPENDIX A-6.12

Management-wise Pupil-Teacher Ratio in Primary Schools in Karnataka, 2003-04

Districts	*Government*	*Pvt. Unaided*	*Pvt. Aided*	*Total*
Highest P/T ratio				
Raichur	52.15		56.8	47.45
Dharwad		34.96		
Lowest P/T ratio				
Hassan	23.1			22.84
Tumkur		18.71		
Kolar			31.97	
State	**34.46**	**26.06**	**41.92**	**33.21**

Source: Planning Dept., GoK.

APPENDIX A-6.13

Percentage of Schools without Infrastructure, 2003-04

Type of Infrastructure	*Per Cent of Schools Having No Such Infrastructure*
Building	2.05
Common Toilet	49.95
Girls' Toilet	63.07
Electricity	55.52
Drinking Water	21.45
Playground	47.46
Boundary Wall	41.83
Blackboard	5.41
Ramps	90.57
Computer	90.47
Medical Check up	21.90

Source: Planning Dept., GoK.

APPENDIX A-6.14

Additional Requirements of Resources for Universalisation of Elementary Education, Karnataka

(Rs. in Crores)

Items	*Primary*	*Primary*	*Total*
Access and Retention: Non-recurring Costs			
Construction of school with community supervision	1173.50	146.95	1320.45
Provision of school equipments by decentralised procurement	7.93	0.00	7.93
Establishment of new DIETs and upgradation of existing DIETs	900.00	-	900.00
Establishment of cluster centres	4.25	2.26	6.51
Establishment of block resource centres	12.25	149.21	161.46
Sub-total	2097.93	298.42	2396.35
Access and Retention: Recurring Costs			
Teacher salaries	794.57	32.20	826.77
Teacher support material and aids	10.02	8.70	18.72
Maintenance and repair of school infrastructure with the community support	9.04	7.54	16.58
Provision of sustainable replacement/repair/maintenance of school equipment	9.04	7.54	16.58
Salaries of diet staff	43.14	-	43.14
Salaries of block level institutions	3.04	-	3.04
Sub-total	868.85	55.98	924.83
Access and Retention: Special Needs-Non-recurring Costs			
Integrated Education for disabled children	69.36	44.73	114.09
Access and Retention: Special Needs Recurring Costs			
Teachers for disabled children	18.09	9.04	27.13
Access and Retention: Incentives-Recurring Costs			
Free uniforms	72.25	46.60	118.85
Mid-day meals	57.80	37.28	95.08
Scholarships	72.25	46.60	118.85
Teaching and learning equipment for students	46.24	55.92	102.16
Sub total	335.99	240.17	576.16
Curriculum and Textbooks: Non-recurring			
Curriculum and textbook improvement	0.15	8.70	8.85
Teacher training	14.04	-	14.04
Teachers' support and aids	3.01	-	3.01
Community based monitoring supervision and research	4.00	-	4.00
Advocacy environment building and mobilisation	4.00	-	4.00
Classroom observations by resource persons	5.43	2.71	8.14
Sub Total	30.63	11.41	42.04
Grand Total	**3333.40**	**605.98**	**3939.38**

Contd. ...

...Contd. ...

Source: *Expert Group Report on Financial Requirements for Making Elementary Education a Fundamental Right* (Mujumdar Committee), MHRD, 1999.

APPENDIX A-6.15

Health Infrastructure across Southern States in India in 1998

State	*Rural*		*Urban*		*Total*		
	No. of Hospitals	*No. of Beds*	*No. of Hospitals*	*No. of Beds*	*No. of Hospitals*	*No. of Beds*	*Beds per lakh of population*
Karnataka	25	3015	268	35434	293	38449	85.49
Andhra Pradesh	883	10117	2007	35715	2890	45832	68.91
Kerala	1443	44103	597	33096	293	38449	85.49
Tamil Nadu	89	4235	319	44545	408	48780	87.33
All India	**4621**	**122453**	**10416**	**501366**	**15037**	**623819**	**73.71**

Source: *Annual Report of Ministry of Health and Family Welfare*, 2000-01, GoI.

APPENDIX A-6.16

Rural Health Infrastructure among Southern States in India in 1998

State	*Area Covered by a PHC in Radial Distance (km)*	*Area Covered by a Sub-centre in Radial Distance (km)*	*Number of Sub-Centres Per PHC*	*Number of PHCs per CHC*	*Average Population Covered by a ANM*
Karnataka	6.1	2.71	5.09	6.62	3837
Andhra Pradesh	8.02	2.85	7.92	6.45	4466
Kerala	3.43	1.49	5.31	12.00	4748
Tamil Nadu	5.24	2.13	6.05	19.94	4305
All India Total	**6.58**	**2.70**	**5.95**	**8.48**	**4707**

Source: *Rural Health Statistics in India*, 1998; Bureau of Intelligence, GoI.

APPENDIX A-6.17

Trends in Total Resources Flow into Health Sector in the State

Particulars	*1997-98*	*1998-99*	*1999-00*	*2000-01*	*2001-02*	*2002-03*	*CAGR-*
THSR (Current Prices)	714	826	988	1018	1107	1033	8.00
Growth Rates (per cent)	-	16	20	3	9	-7	-
THSR (Constant Prices)	525	570	665	683	728	656	5.00
Central Funds (per cent)	14	9	25	15	18	20	-
State Funds (per cent)	74	75	60	69	63	67	-
External Assistance	12	16	15	15	19	12	-

Note: THSR refers to total health sector resources.

APPENDIX A-6.18

Trends in Total Health Expenditure in the State

Particulars	*1997-98*	*1998-99*	*1999-00*	*2000-01*	*2001-02*	*2002-03*	*2003-04 (RE)*
HE (Current Prices)	708	819	977	1005	1088	1004	1069
HE (Constant Prices)	521	565	657	674	715	638	-
HE as per cent to State's Total Expenditure	5.62	5.50	5.48	5.11	4.95	3.91	3.63
HE as per cent to GSDP	1.04	1.01	1.14	1.06	1.16	1.01	0.82
Per Capita HE in Current Prices	140	160	188	192	206	187	201
Per Capita HE in Constant Prices	103	110	127	129	136	119	

Note: HE refers to health expenditure.

APPENDIX A-6.19

Trends in Total Health Expenditure by Various Classifications in the State

Particulars	*1997-98*	*1998-99*	*1999-00*	*2000-01*	*2001-02*	*2002-03*	*2003-04 (RE)*	*CAGR (per cent)*
Primary (per cent)	55	48	50	49	51	49	54	
Secondary (per cent)	20	23	24	21	19	18	13	
Tertiary (per cent)	26	28	27	30	30	33	34	
Wage (per cent)	70	2	62	60	61	59	61	12
Non-Wage (per cent)	30	38	38	40	39	41	39	7
Drugs and Chemicals as a Non-wage Component to Total HE (per cent)	2.95	5.73	6.15	6.22	6.38	6.87	7.68	

Source: Budget Document, Government of Karnataka

APPENDIX A-6.20

Breakup of Total Health Expenditure

(Rs. in Crore Current Prices)

Periods	*Urban Services*	*Rural Services*	*Medical Edn.*	*Public Health*	*Total Rev-MPH*	*Capital-MPH*	*Total-MPH*	*Total FW*	*Total Exp.*
1997-98	175(24.72)	222(31.36)	75(10.59)	40(5.65)	512(72.32)	68(9.60)	580(81.92)	128(18.08)	708(100.00)
1998-99	251(30.65)	242(29.55)	83(10.13)	40(4.88)	616(75.21)	88(10.74)	704(85.96)	115(14.04)	819(100.00)
1999-00	305(31.28)	273(28.00)	93(9.54)	50(5.13)	721(73.95)	94(9.64)	815(83.59)	160(16.41)	975(100.00)
2000-01	325(32.31)	285(28.33)	112(11.13)	46(4.58)	768(76.34)	72(7.15)	840(83.50)	166(16.50)	1006(100.00)
2001-02	327(30.11)	287(28.42)	127(11.69)	45(4.14)	786(72.38)	79(7.27)	865(79.65)	221(20.35)	1086(100.00)
2002-03	328(32.67)	293(29.18)	126(12.55)	47(4.68)	794(79.08)	43(4.28)	837(83.37)	167(16.63)	1004(100.00)
2003-04@	335(31.51)	317(29.82)	120(11.29)	64(6.02)	836(78.64)	31(2.92)	867(81.56)	196(18.44)	1063(100.00)

Note: @ Revised estimates.

Source: Budgetary Documents of the Government of Karnataka.

APPENDIX A-6.21

Comparison of Health Indicators across Southern States and Countries: 2000

State	*IMR*	*CBR*	*MMR*	*Life Expectancy at Birth*		*TFR*	*CDR*
				Male	*Female*		
Karnataka	**58**	**22.00**	**195**	**64.2**	**65.3**	**2.13**	**7.6**
Andhra Pradesh	66	22.30	154	61.5	64.5	2.25	8.3
Kerala	16	18.20	195	68.6	75.0	1.96	6.0
Tamil Nadu	53	18.90	76	62.3	63.1	2.19	7.9
All India	**70**	**26.10**	**408**	**60.6**	**61.7**	**2.85**	**8.7**
China	35	17.00	55	68.1	71.3	1.9	7.0
Korean Republic	10	16.00	20	69.5	72.1	1.8	6.0
High Income Economies	7	13.00	16	76.8	75.5	1.7	8.0
Medium Income Nations	39	22.00	79	68.5	65.7	3.0	8.0
Low Income Economies	69	26.0	360	57.9	55.4	3.2	10.0
World Average	**55**	**23.0**	**240**	**67.5**	**65.2**	**2.9**	**9.0**

Source: *Annual Report of Ministry of Health and Family Welfare*, 2000-01, GoI, *National Family Health Family Survey* (NFHS-Round II) *State of the World's Children, 2001*, UNCIEP.

APPENDIX A-6.22

Nutritional Status of Children and Women among Selected States: 1998-99

State	*Per Cent of Severely Undernourished Children Weight-for-age Below–3 SD 1992-93*	*1998-99*	*Per Cent of Children <3 Years with Any Anaemia*	*Per Cent of Women with Any Anaemia and and (Severe Anaemia)*	*Per Cent of Women with BMI<18.5 kg/m² (Severe Anaemia)*	*Per Cent of Women with BMI >25.0 kg/m²*
Andhra Pradesh	20	10.3	72.3 (4.4)	49.8 (2.4)	37.4	12.0
Goa	9	4.7	53.4 (2.0)	36.4 (1.0)	27.1	21.2
Karnataka	**19**	**16.5**	**70.6 (7.6)**	**42.4 (2.3)**	**38.8**	**13.6**
Kerala	9	4.7	43.9 (0.5)	22.7 (0.5)	18.7	20.6
Maharashtra	21	17.6	76.0 (4.4)	48.5 (2.9)	39.7	11.7
Tamil Nadu	15	10.6	69.0 (6.9)	56.5 (3.9)	29.0	14.7
All India	20	18.0	74.3 (5.4)	51.8 (1.9)	35.8	10.6

Source: IIPS, NFHS- 1(1992-93) and 2 (1998-99) India and Karnataka.

APPENDIX A-6.23

Expenditure and Coverage under Nutrition Programmes in Karnataka

Programme	*1997-98*	*1998-99*	*1999-00*	*2000-01*	*2001-02*	*2002-03*	*2003-04*
I. Supplementary Nutrition Prog.	3607.95	3249.35	3873.35	4360.58	3794.94	3236.14	-
A. Plan Expenditure (Rs. in Lakhs)							
B. Beneficiaries (in Lakhs)	29.02	28.62	30.99	31.13	31.22	32.73	-
II. Distribution of Foodgrains at Subsidised Rates							
A. Expenditure (Rs. Lakhs)	18469.0	17104.0	30602.4	30875.4	22029.3	19435.4	20942.5
B. Beneficiaries							
a) General	43.22	45.84	49.36	48.87	46.81	48.44	-
b) TPDS	58.18	64.76	62.67	62.83	64.02	63.00	-
III. Akshar Dasoha (Mid-day Meals)							
A. Expenditure (in Lakhs)	-	-	-	-	-	3735.74	13737.5
B. Beneficiaries (in Lakhs)	-	-	-	-	-	16.87	44.40

Source: 1. Department of Women and Child Development, GoK.
2. Planning and Statistics Department Economic Survey 1993-94 to 2003-04, GoK.
3. Department of Food and Civil Supplies, GoK.

APPENDIX A-6.24

Progress of ICDS in Karnataka

Name of the Projects	2000-01		2001-02		2002-03		2003-04
	Karnataka	India	Karnataka	India	Karnataka	India	Karnataka
No. of Operational ICDS	185	4384	185	4608	185	4903	185
No. of *Anganwadi*	40093	475844	40133	545714	40285	600391	40301
No. of Beneficiaries	2840767	29037429	2880394	37509865	3018277	38783760	3385421

Source: Department of Women and Child Welfare, Government of Karnataka.

APPENDIX A-6.25

Centre's Releases and Expenditure under ICDS (Gen.) Scheme in Karnataka

(Rs. in Lakh)

Year	Karnataka		India	
	Released	Expd.	Released	Expd.
1992-93	2123.30	1919.05	32934.39	2722.93
1993-94	3201.45	2582.24	41045.16	32336.28
1994-95	2874.87	3194.23	43481.01	33739.74
1995-96	4153.54	3647.00	56781.46	36842.61
1996-97	4132.23	4100.79	52655.11	43214.16
1997-98	5158.03	5768.69	60870.85	56250.01
1998-99	5709.83	5935.36	79421.08	84406.77
1999-00	5111.35	6424.15	88097.59	93068.63
2000-01	7466.18	6715.49	104653.79	102537.62
2001-02	7660.68	7329.77	122365.19	105572.61
2002-03	10541.29	NA	150497.71	NA
2003-04	10346.92	11605.29	NA	NA

Source: Department of Women and Child Welfare, Government of Karnataka.

APPENDIX A-6.26

Expenditure under SNP in Karnataka

Year	Total Expenditure (Rs.in Lakh)
1990-91	1477.11
1991-92	1778.07
1992-93	2346.75
1993-94	2491.72
1994-95	3683.34
1995-96	5851.00
1996-97	7275.92
1997-98	7685.79
1998-99	6812.41
1999-00	7754.89
2000-01	9170.53
2001-02	8110.17
2002-03	7999.38
2003-04	9754.95

Source: Department of Women and Child Welfare, Government of Karnataka.

APPENDIX A-6.27

Housing Problem of Karnataka by Source in Rural-Urban Areas: 2001

(in Lakhs)

District	Housing Shortage			Rural		Urban	
	Rural	Urban	Total	Crowded	Dilapidated	Crowded	Dilapidated
Bagalkot	0.09	0.06	0.15	0.02	0.07	0.02	0.04
Bangalore (Rural)	0.26	0.05	0.31	0.04	0.22	0.02	0.03
Bangalore (Urban)	0.10	0.52	0.62	0.03	0.07	0.20	0.32
Belgaum	0.49	0.12	0.61	0.26	0.23	0.07	0.05
Bellary	0.16	0.08	0.24	0.04	0.12	0.03	0.05
Bidar	0.16	0.03	0.19	0.03	0.13	0.01	0.02
Bijapur	0.16	0.03	0.19	0.02	0.14	-	0.03
Chamrajnagar	0.16	0.03	0.19	0.03	0.13	0.01	0.02
Chickmagalur	0.16	0.03	0.19	0.02	0.14	-	0.03
Chitradurga	0.17	0.02	0.19	0.03	0.14	-	0.02
Davangere	0.17	0.07	0.24	0.02	0.15	0.01	0.06
Dharwad	0.12	0.10	0.22	0.06	0.06	0.06	0.04
Dakshina Kannada	0.16	0.06	0.22	0.01	0.15	0.02	0.04
Gadag	0.05	0.02	0.07	0.01	0.04	-	0.02
Gulbarga	0.24	0.08	0.32	0.09	0.15	0.03	0.05

Contd. ...

...*Contd.* ...

District	Housing Shortage			Rural		Urban	
	Rural	Urban	Total	Crowded	Dilapidated	Crowded	Dilapidated
Hassan	0.20	0.05	0.25	0.03	0.17	0.02	0.03
Haveri	0.15	0.02	0.17	0.04	0.11	-	0.02
Kodagu	0.09	0.02	0.11	0.01	0.08	0.01	0.01
Kolar	0.20	0.05	0.25	0.02	0.18	0.02	0.03
Koppal	0.09	0.01	0.10	0.02	0.07	-	0.01
Mandya	0.21	0.04	0.25	0.04	0.17	0.01	0.03
Mysore	0.28	0.09	0.37	0.06	0.22	0.02	0.07
Raichur	0.10	0.02	0.12	0.02	0.08	-	0.02
Shimoga	0.22	0.07	0.29	0.02	0.20	0.02	0.05
Tumkur	0.29	0.04	0.33	0.03	0.26	-	0.04
Udupi	0.18	0.03	0.21	0.01	0.17	0.01	0.02
Uttara Kannada	0.20	0.06	0.26	0.03	0.17	0.02	0.04
Karnataka	**4.86**	**1.76**	**6.62**	**1.04**	**3.82**	**0.59**	**1.17**

Source: Computed from *Census of India* (2001), Houses, *Household Amenities and Assets*, Series 1.

APPENDIX A-6.28

Housing Problem of SCs and STs by Source in Rural-Urban Areas: 2001

(Figures in Lakhs)

District	Housing Shortage			Rural		Urban	
	SCs	STs	Total	Crowded SCs/STs	Dilapidated SCs/STs	Crowded SCs/STs	Dilapidated SCs/STs
Bagalkot	0.07	0.03	0.10	0.03/0.02	0.02/0.01	0.01/0.00	0.01/0.00
Bangalore (Rural)	0.08	0.02	0.10	0.01/0.01	0.06/0.01	0.00/0.00	0.01/0.00
Bangalore (Urban)	0.15	0.03	0.18	0.01/0.00	0.03/0.01	0.00/0.00	0.11/0.02
Belgaum	0.12	0.08	0.20	0.06/0.05	0.04/0.02	0.01/0.01	0.01/0.00
Bellary	0.08	0.12	0.20	0.04/0.07	0.03/0.03	0.00/0.01	0.01/0.01
Bidar	0.14	0.06	0.20	0.08/0.04	0.04/0.02	0.01/0.00	0.01/0.00
Bijapur	0.15	0.01	0.16	0.10/0.01	0.03/0.00	0.01/0.00	0.01/0.00
Chamrajnagar	0.06	0.03	0.09	0.02/0.00	0.03/0.02	0.00/0.00	0.01/0.01
Chickmagalur	0.06	0.01	0.07	0.00/0.00	0.05/0.01	0.00/0.00	0.01/0.00
Chitradurga	0.11	0.08	0.19	0.05/0.05	0.05/0.03	0.00/0.00	0.01/0.00
Davangere	0.11	0.08	0.19	0.05/0.04	0.05/0.03	0.00/0.00	0.01/0.01
Dharward	0.04	0.02	0.06	0.01/0.01	0.01/0.01	0.01/0.00	0.01/0.00
Dakshina Kannada	0.05	0.01	0.06	0.00/0.00	0.04/0.01	0.00/0.00	0.01/0.00
Gadag	0.02	0.02	0.04	0.01/0.01	0.01/0.01	0.00/0.00	-/0.00
Gulbarga	0.23	0.04	0.27	0.15/0.03	0.05/0.01	0.01/0.00	0.02/0.00
Hassan	0.09	0.02	0.11	0.03/0.01	0.05/0.01	0.00/0.00	0.01/0.00
Haveri	0.05	0.05	0.10	0.03/0.03	0.02/0.02	0.00/0.00	-/0.00
Kodagu	0.01	0.02	0.03	0.00/0.00	0.01/0.02	0.00/0.00	-/0.00
Kolar	0.15	0.06	0.21	0.07/0.04	0.07/0.02	0.00/0.00	0.01/0.00
Koppal	0.04	0.04	0.08	0.02/0.03	0.02/0.01	0.00/0.00	-/0.00
Mandya	0.05	0.01	0.06	0.00/0.00	0.04/0.01	0.00/0.00	0.01/0.00
Mysore	0.13	0.10	0.23	0.05/0.03	0.06/0.05	0.01/0.01	0.01/0.01
Raichur	0.06	0.06	0.12	0.02/0.04	0.02/0.02	0.01/0.00	0.01/0.00
Shimoga	0.08	0.01	0.09	0.01/0.00	0.06/0.01	0.00/0.00	0.01/0.00
Tumkur	0.12	0.05	0.17	0.04/0.02	0.07/0.03	0.00/0.00	0.01/0.00
Udupi	0.02	0.01	0.03	0.00/0.00	0.02/0.01	0.00/0.00	-/0.00
Uttara Kannada	0.03	0.01	0.04	0.00/0.00	0.02/0.01	0.00/0.00	0.01/0.00
Karnataka	**2.30**	**1.08**	**3.38**	**0.89/0.54**	**1.00/0.42**	**0.08/0.03**	**0.33/0.06**

Source: Computed from *Census of India (2001), Houses, Household Amenities and Assets*, Series 1.

APPENDIX A-6.29

Institutional Infrastructure for Housing Development in Karnataka

Agency	*Year Established*	*Functions*	*Area of Operation and Target Group*
Cooperative Housing Societies (CHS)	1909	To acquire land and develop residential layouts for the members. To finance house construction of the members.	Largely located in urban areas and members of the societies.
Karnataka Housing Board (KHB)	1962	To prepare and execute housing schemes (composite, group housing to multi-storied the satisfaction of the and labour housing. To develop sites and services and satellite towns.	Urban areas andAll means groups (economically weaker sections, LIG, MIG & HIG).
Karnataka Slum Clearance Board (KSCB)	1976	To identify and declare slum areas. To take up socio-economic survey in the identified schemes. To take up environmental improvement and re-developmental of the schemes.To provide new houses and to upgrade existing houses of the slum dwellers. To provide basic amenities (drinking water, toilets, street lights, drains, roads community baths and toilets, etc.).	All slum areas in urban areas and slum dwellers that generally consists of wage related migrants, casual wage cameras, construction workers, etc.
Urban Development Authorities (UDAs)	1998	To prepare dent and action plans for the urban areas. To approach dent and building plans and residential layouts. To provide residential, commercial, industrial and civic amenities. To put up parks and playgrounds. To construct houses for EWS, LIG, MIG, HIG & commercial complex. To develop major infrastructure facilities.	All distinct headquarters and all income groups.
Rajiv Gandhi Rural Housing Corporation Ltd. (RGRHC)	2000	To implement housing programme for economically and socially weaker sections and specially occupation groups. To organise manufacture of bulk procurement of cost-effective materials. To ensure smooth flow of funds and recovery of loans from the beneficiaries.	Rural and urban areas and all poorer sections including SCs/STs.

Source: Compiled from the annual and other reports of the institutions.

APPENDIX A-6.30

Functional and Financial Performance of Urban Development Authorities in Karnataka during 90s

(in Acres and Rs. in Crores)

Devt. Authorities	*Establish-ment Year*	*Planning Area (in Sq. Kilometres)*	*Total Land Acquired*	*Average land Acquired per Year*	*No of Sites Distributed*	*Average Sites Distributed per Year*	*Revenue Surplus (1995-96 to 2000-01)*
Bangalore	1976	8700*	3048.70	305	15622	1562	126.58
Belgaum	1988	182.07	907.22	91	7438	744	4.02
Bellary	1988	NA	1266.35	127	6769	677	0.22
Bidar	NA	NA	122.51	12	864	86	7.51
Bijapur	1988	169.51	193.05	19	7038	704	3.91
Chamrajnagar	1996	Town+27Vill	133.26	13	NA	NA	0.18
Chitradurga	1988	64.80	638.11	64	3029	303	0.67
Chickmagalur	1988	City +21 Vill	309.40	31	753	75	3.08
Davangere	NA	NA	752.24	75	836	84	4.91
Gadag	1998	NA	292.58	29	NA	NA	11.27
Gulbarga	1988	City+32 Vill	644.10	64	6813	681	9.76
Hassan	1988	City+42 Vill	NA	NA	2795	280	36.57
Haveri	1998	NA	NA	NA	NA	NA	0.04
Hospet	1998	NA	NA	NA	NA	NA	0.22
H-Dharward	1987	413.00	166.42	17	6756	676	5.66
Karwar	1988	City +11 Vill	124.00	12	1373	137	0.06
Madikeri	1988	NA	NA	NA	NA	NA	0.04
Kolar	1988	NA	546.56	55	6137	612	6.17

Contd. ...

...Contd. ...

Devt. Authorities	*Establish-ment Year*	*Planning Area (in Sq. Kilometres)*	*Total Land Acquired*	*Average land Acquired per Year*	*No of Sites Distributed*	*Average Sites Distributed per Year*	*Revenue Surplus (1995-96 to 2000-01)*
K.G.F	1988	126.00	60.04	6	82	8	3.43
Koppal	1998	NA	NA	NA	NA	NA	NA
Mandya	1988	City+18 Vill	413.18	42	216	22	2.19
Mangalore	1988	306.00	29.00	3	396	40	0.01
Mysore	1987	495.32	2128.07	213	21713	2171	16.83
Raichur	NA	NA	48.05	5	NA	NA	0.53
Ramnagar	1996	NA	92.32	9	NA	NA	2.14
Shimoga		City Bhadravati Municipal Areas	1473.24	147	2564	256	3.21
Tumkur	1988	75+24 Vill	640.42	64	1565	156	0.71
Udupi	1998	NA	50.00	5	NA	NA	1.23
Total			**14075.82**	**1407.58**	**92759**	**9276**	**251.15**

Source: Compiled from the Annual Reports of the Department of Housing and Urban Development, Government of Karnataka, Bangalore.

APPENDIX A-6.31

Housing Investment by the Scheduled Commercial Banks, Housing Cooperatives and Housing Financial Institutions in Karnataka during 90s

Year	*Scheduled Commercial Banks*			*Cooperative Housing Societies*			*Housing Financial Institutions (HFIs)*	
	Total Bank Credit	*Credit Limit for Housing*	*Actual Investment*	*Total Working Capital*	*Loans Advanced to Housing*	*Per Cent in the Working Capital*	*Savings Mobilised*	*Investment in Housing*
1990-91	92.15	3.20(3.47)	2.86(89.38)	221.90	57.08	25.72	NA	NA
1991-92	104.86	3.50(3.34)	3.06(87.43)	293.82	73.02	24.85	NA	NA
1992-93	107.90	3.76(3.48)	3.39(90.16)	345.19	85.50	24.77	NA	NA
1993-94	128.08	4.23(3.30)	3.82(90.31)	305.30	112.12	36.72	NA	NA
1994-95	153.63	4.61(3.00)	4.21(91.32)	498.79	195.04	39.10	NA	NA
1995-96	200.03	6.07(3.03)	5.47(90.12)	691.79	278.00	40.19	NA	NA
1996-97	232.13	7.01(3.02)	6.35(90.58)	885.58	371.53	41.95	607.75	624.00 (102.67)
1997-98	266.44	9.28(3.48)	8.28(89.22)	1078.71	417.71	38.72	806.65	778.05 (96.45)
1998-99	322.16	13.38(4.15)	11.93(89.16)	1271.74	499.09	39.24	829.40	1005.55 (121.24)
1999-2000	364.69	20.06(5.50)	17.88(89.13)	1399.57	559.83	40.00	NA	NA

Source: 1. IRBI, *Banking Statistics, Banking Statistical Returns*, 1991 to 2000, Mumbai.
2. NABARD, *Statistical Statements Relating to Cooperative Movement in India*, Part II : Non-Credit Societies, for various years, Mumbai.
3. NHB, *Report on Trend and Progress of Housing in India*, June 1999, Mumbai.

APPENDIX A-6.32

Per Cent of Households by Principal Source of Drinking Water (2001)

Sources of Drinking Water	*Karnataka*			*All India*		
	Total	*Rural*	*Urban*	*Total*	*Rural*	*Urban*
Tap	58.89	48	78.43	36.7	24.3	68.7
Handpump	17.11	23	6.19	35.7	43.2	16.2
Tube Well	8.56	9	7.51	5.6	5.7	5.1
Well	12.40	16	6.48	18.2	22.2	7.7
Others	3.04	4	1.4	3.9	4.5	2.2
Per Cent of Households with Safe Drinking Water Supply	84.56	80.00	92.13	78.00	73.20	90.00

Note: Others include tank, pond, river, canal, springs and any other safe drinking water sources include tap, handpump and tube well.

Source: Census, 2001.

APPENDIX A-6.33

Year-wise Coverage of Habitations for Drinking Water Supply in Rural Karnataka

Year	*FC*	*Per Cent to Total*	*PC*	*Per Cent to Total*	*NC*	*Per Cent to Total*	*Total*
1999	30800	54.34	25037	44.17	845	1.49	56682
2000	33135	58.46	23482	41.43	65	0.11	56682
2001	34562	60.98	22120	39.02	0	0.00	56682
2002	36187	63.84	20495	36.16	0	0.00	56682
2003	36714	64.77	19968	35.23	0	0.00	56682

Note: FC = Fully covered, PC = Partially covered, NC = Not covered.
Source: Annual Reports, Department of Rural Development and Panchayat Raj.

APPENDIX A-6.34

Water Supply in Different Municipal Corporation Areas

Name of the Municipal Corporations	*Level of Water Supply (in LPCD)*	*Adequate/Inadequate*
Hubli-Dharwad	100	Inadequate
Gulbarga	86	Inadequate
Belgaum	85	Inadequate
Mysore	141	Adequate
Mangalore	152	Adequate

Note: The Norms fixed for Class I towns is 135 LPCD.
Source: KUWSDB.

APPENDIX A-6.35

Progress under Karnataka Urban Water Supply and Drainage Scheme

Year	*Piped Water Supply Schemes*	*Urban Water Supply Schemes*	*Board Water Supply Schemes*
1999	216	89	20
2000	220	96	20
2001	228	102	20
2002	236	119	20
2003 (up to October)	240	127	20

Source: KUWS and DB.

APPENDIX A-6.36

Per Cent of Households with Sanitation Facilities: 2001

Sanitation Services	*Karnataka*			*All India*		
	Total	*Rural*	*Urban*	*Total*	*Rural*	*Urban*
Type of Latrine within the House						
Pit Latrine	13.38	9.48	20.70	11.5	10.3	14.6
Water Closet	18.64	4.67	44.86	18	7.1	46.1
Other Latrine	5.48	3.25	9.67	6.9	4.5	13.0
No Latrine	62.50	82.60	24.77	63.6	78.1	26.3
Type of Connectivity for Waste Water Outlet						
Closed Drainage	17.26	4.28	41.64	12.5	3.9	34.5
Open Drainage	33.97	31.11	39.33	33.9	30.3	43.4
No Drainage	48.77	64.61	19.03	53.6	65.8	22.1

Source: *Census 2001.*

APPENDIX A-6.37

Level of Underground Drainage System in Five Municipal Corporation Areas (as on 2001)

Name of Municipal Corporation	*Apprx. per cent of Area Covered with UGD*	*Avg. per Capita Contribution of Sewage*	*STP Provided/ Not Provided*
Gulbarga	60	90	Provided
Belgaum	80	100	Not provided
Mysore	80	130	Provided
Mangalore	80	135	Primary treatment provided
Hubli-Dharwad	50	100	Not provided

Note: STP-Sewage Treatment Plant.
Source: KUWSDB.

APPENDIX A-6.38

Expenditure on Water Supply and Sanitation

(in per cent)

Year	*Share of Water Supply*	*Share of Sanitation*	*Total Expenditure (Rs. Crores)*	*WSS Exp. as per cent to Total Exp. of the Government*
1991-92	98.1	1.94	154.08	2.46
1992-93	94.6	5.42	142.31	2.00
1993-94	96.0	4.04	157.18	1.94
1994-95	95.9	4.09	199.98	2.25
1995-96	96.2	3.77	267.64	2.57
1996-97	88.7	11.29	316.48	2.64
1997-98	90.9	9.09	333.58	2.65
1998-99	94.4	5.63	509.63	3.42
1999-00	95.6	4.45	654.88	3.69
2000-01	95.1	4.92	623.21	3.16
2001-02	95.1	4.95	596.59	2.73
2002-03	89.5	10.51	503.73	2.02
2003-04	91.6	8.42	640.84	
Average Annual Growth	14.03	42.5	14.27	

Note: WSS = Water Supply and Sanitation.
Source: Government of Karnataka Budget Documents.

APPENDIX A-6.39

Showing the Progress Relating to *Stree Shakti* Groups

District	*Total No.of SHGs*	*Number of Members*					*Groups with Bank Linkage*
		SC	*ST*	*Minorities*	*Others*	*Total*	
Bangalore (Urban)	2281	10880	1110	997	23996	36983	285
Bangalore (Rural)	5658	22247	3963	3707	69239	99156	832
Bagalkote	1956	9850	3751	4867	31706	50174	788
Belgaum	10100	21336	10128	13451	99933	144848	2343
Bellary	3500	9390	9524	4190	26510	499614	394
Bidar	2066	9815	5497	3451	23463	42226	1077
Bijapur	2983	4661	588	1946	10102	17297	845
Chamrajnagar	3045	11462	2165	670	31156	45453	464
Chickmagalur	2385	7294	1603	2736	19891	31524	416
Chitradurga	3625	13520	7918	1769	30989	54196	995
Davanagere	3358	12846	7695	2920	29158	52619	583
Dakshina Kannada	3352	5170	3222	8452	31328	48172	1396
Dharwad	2081	3023	1990	3253	23502	31768	533
Gadag	2226	3518	2126	4638	18068	28350	615
Gulbarga	6500	28879	5111	6747	48384	87121	4099
Hassan	4493	13740	2154	1143	55853	71890	2004
Haveri	3358	9432	6677	5716	30718	522543	882
Kodagu	648	2299	1063	1323	5606	10291	152
Kolar	6500	22725	8380	3949	50993	91047	477
Koppal	2000	7520	5126	2296	17825	32767	423
Mandya	4780	9789	259	1644	61568	73260	897
Mysore	4785	18736	5996	2512	53351	80595	1356
Raichur	3600	8350	7534	5272	21991	43147	239
Shimoga	2988	7931	1598	2382	25813	37724	259
Tumkur	7230	28819	10986	6632	67032	113469	2995
Udipi	2200	2202	1665	2128	27501	33494	161
Uttara Kannada	1354	1924	530	990	5622	19068	484
Total		**310358**	**113359**	**99779**	**951298**	**1479794**	**25994**

Source: DWCD, GoK March 2004.

Chapter 7

Financial Infrastructure: Banking, Capital Markets and Cooperatives

7.1 Introduction

Infrastructure in general facilitates growth. Financial infrastructure promotes growth through the effective mobilisation of savings into productive capital, and channelises this capital to its most productive uses. There are two different ways this can be done. Capital allocation process can be decentralised or centralised. That is, it can operate through many small investors in the capital markets, or capital can be provided mainly by large banks and other large investors. The distinction between these two approaches is somewhat arbitrary and an economy can combine these two approaches to cater different needs of capital seekers. Increasingly several countries including India is moving towards decentralised allocation process. Along with economic liberalisation, India has also liberalised financial sector to facilitate direct capital allocation process and be consistent with economic liberalisation initiatives. The process of financial sector reform started with abolition of controls on capital issues and further moved forward in allowing capital flows from outside the country under various forms. While many sectors have attracted fresh capital, the major beneficiaries are new economy sectors which consist of information technology (IT), telecommunication, biotechnology and others, where states like Karnataka has benefited significantly. The flow of capital is also influenced by Union Budgets and policies and regulations of various agencies like Foreign Investment Promotion Board, Reserve Bank of India, Securities and Exchange Board of India, Insurance Regulatory Authority of India, etc. The Government of India has initiated several policies to simplify the approval process in allowing setting up of new units with large investments and also providing certain tax incentives for units in IT. Again, these measures have a positive impact on the development of states like Karnataka.

To facilitate financial flows in both centralised and decentralised systems of capital formation and distribution, there is a need for adequate financial infrastructure. Financial infrastructure is not a single element. It includes financial institutions of different types, several facilitating institutions to mobilise capital and regulatory setup that facilitates smooth functioning of the financial system.

Financial institutions are present both at all-India level and state level. Similarly, regulations are centrally framed and administered. Despite such all-India nature of financial infrastructure, there are large differences at state levels. The financial infrastructure of states like Maharashtra and Gujarat is generally perceived to be much developed than other states. Financial infrastructure develops along with other economic development and they are complementary with each other. Economic development creates surplus capital and such surplus capital gets absorbed when the state facilitates further economic development. Financial infrastructure simultaneously develops to facilitate this process of connecting surplus and deficit sector and often it attracts fresh capital from other states, when there are no restrictions on the movement of capital from one state to other state and when such states fail to facilitate economic development. In that process, financial infrastructure facilitates higher economic growth. Mumbai, the financial capital of India, is a good example how economic development facilitates financial infrastructure, which in turn facilitate economic development of the region. In this chapter are analysed the financial infrastructure, their promotion, development and the issues in Karnataka with the all-India perspective. Since macroeconomic policies relating to the financial sector are all centralised, how Karnataka faired in the backdrop of these policies are all discussed.

7.1.1 Financial Flows in Karnataka

Savings and capital formation are critical for economic growth. At the country level, gross domestic savings witnessed an average year-to-year growth rate of 14.15 per cent during the period of 1990-91 to 2001-02. Gross capital formation during the same period has witnessed an average year-to-year growth rate of 11.58 per cent though the growth rates show higher level of volatility. Both savings and capital formation data are not available at the state level. While few states compute data relating to capital formation, many states restrict the data only at capital formation by the state government agencies and institutions. The gross capital formation of the state government segment witnessed an average growth rate of 16 per cent. Similar to all-India growth trend, this series also witnessed volatility.

Several states including Karnataka do not compile capital formation by non-government agencies. Hence, one has to rely on statistics compiled by the Government of India for Annual Survey of Industries. Data complied for Annual Survey of Industries is restricted to organised sector and hence it can give an approximate value. Among the four states compared, the share of capital formation by the registered units of Karnataka is the lowest. While comparable states like Gujarat and Tamil Nadu have reported a share of more than 10 per cent, gross capital formation by the registered units of Karnataka is less than 5 per cent of gross capital formation by the registered units of all states. Though capital formation in Karnataka had also witnessed some growth and consistent with several other states, it is not aggressive.

Financial system/infrastructure essentially consist of commercial banks which constitute the major portion, regional rural banks (RRBs), cooperative banks and micro finance institutions (MFIs), non-banking finance companies, all-India and state-level term lending institutions and the capital market. At the regional level or state level, presence of capital market is not as significant as others. Nevertheless, RRBs and cooperative banks and the SFIs do reflect more regional characteristic features than the others. In this chapter are analysed and discussed, namely: a) financial infrastructure in Karnataka, b) commercial banking and their operations in Karnataka, c) RRBs and their significance in the state, d) role of cooperative banks and MFIs in Karnataka's development, e) recovery performance and overdue position of these institutions, f) Non-banking finance companies, g) all-India and state level institutions like KSFC, KSIIDC, h) capital market with a brief discussion on the Bangalore Stock Exchange and lastly summary and conclusions. Each of these institutions do possess specific characteristic features and cater exclusively to certain segments, for example, in the rural economy RRBs and cooperative sector play a critical role in mobilising savings and capital formation. The last section also identifies the gaps and efforts required on the part of Karnataka to promote and develop financial infrastructure.

7.2 Financial Infrastructure in Karnataka

Financial infrastructure in Karnataka is well developed having all possible financial intermediaries for facilitating smooth business transactions. At the apex it has a branch of the country's Central Bank, namely, the Reserve Bank of India (RBI) with all its core departments relating to note issue, government transactions, public debt, banking transactions, rural credit, foreign exchange management, non-banking financial companies, cooperative banks, RRBs, etc. There is a full-fledged Clearing House managed by the RBI to facilitate day-to-day and intra-day inter bank settlements. Its one of the two note presses is situated at Mysore. There are 78 commercial bank offices functioning in the state. In addition to this, there are 300 urban cooperative banks, 30 state cooperative banks and 602 district cooperative banks operating throughout Karnataka. A number of microfinance institutions are also present to take care of the poorest of poor. There are regional offices of the all-India financial institutions and also the state-level financial institutions like KSFC and KSIIDC. Besides these, there are a good number of non-banking financial companies of all nature existing in the state.

7.2.1 Contribution of Banking and Insurance to Karnataka's SDP

Banking and insurance is an important economic activity and is classified under the services sector. Karnataka possesses a well-developed and more or less balanced financial infrastructure. The net value added by this sector in Karnataka to its NSDP grew rapidly from Rs.1,87,275 lakhs in 1993-94 to Rs.7,02,912 lakhs in 2002-2003 at current prices and contributed 11 per cent to net state domestic product in 2002-03 at current prices and there is a steady trend observed in the past 10 years (see also Appendix A-7.1 and Figure 7.1).

FIGURE 7.1

Contribution of Banking and Insurance to NSDP at Current Prices

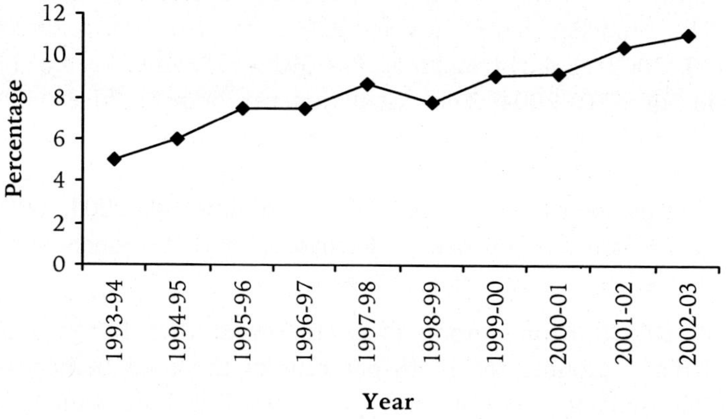

Source: Directorate of Economics and Statistics, Government of Karnataka.

TABLE 7.1

Banking Infrastructure in Karnataka

	Values	*Ranking in All-India**
Contribution of Banking and Insurance to NSDP (Per Cent) 2002-03	10.99	6.45**
Average Population per Bank Office 2003-2004 (No)	11	2
Share in Deposits 2001-02 Commercial Banks (per cent)	5.80	5
Share in Advances 2001-02 (per cent)	6.30	4
Credit–Deposit Ratio as per Utilisation	71.10	4
Per Capita Deposit 2001-02 (Rupees)	12069	6
Per Capita Credit 2001-02 (Rupees)	7212	4
Per Office Deposit 2001-02 (Rupees)	1333	9
Per Office Credit 2001-02 (Rupees)	1324	5

Note: * Excluding smaller states. Data from second row onwards pertain to commercial banks only.
** 2001-02.

Source: Directorate of Economics and Statistics, Government of Karnataka and Reserve Bank of India.

7.3 Commercial Banking in Karnataka

Banking institutions play an important intermediary role in capital formation of the economy. Banks serve as financial intermediaries by matching the demand for credit and the supply of credit. In this process, banks indulge in the 'capital mobilisation' by accepting deposits from the public for specified terms and 'capital allocation' by loaning out these borrowed funds to deserving projects. In this respect, both savings and investment require physical proximity to a bank. Especially in rural areas where banks deliver market credit to small agriculturists, artisans and the like, access to banks services helps in greater deposit mobilisation and faster credit disbursal to borrowers. The greater the deposit mobilised, the greater is the credit available for disbursal into productive activities. Both corporate and retail banking space is required for a banking system to be effective.

Through credit creation, banks allow expansion of economic activity. Banking infrastructure in India is reasonably developed and matured, particularly after liberalising the financial sector. Though public sector banks still dominate the banking industry with its strong 27 banks and a large number of branches network, private sectors banks are showing high level of growth in their activities (Table 7.1).

A unique feature of the financial sector in Karnataka is that it is the home for maximum number of commercial banks in the country. Nationalised banks such as Canara Bank, Syndicate Bank, Vijaya Bank, Corporation Bank, State Bank of Mysore in the SBI group, ING Vysya Bank Limited, Karnataka Bank Limited in the private sector have found their origin in Karnataka. As at the end of June 2004, there were in all 4,851 branches of scheduled commercial banks in Karnataka, which accounted for 7.2 per cent of total such offices in India. Karnataka occupies fifth position. But to judge the appropriate financial infrastructure in terms of the offices of banks, it should be related to population that these offices cater to. In that sense Karnataka is in a better position *vis-à-vis* the other comparable states. The average population per bank office (APPBO) is 11 for the state and Karnataka occupies the third place next to Kerala which has APPBO of 10 and Punjab takes the first place with APPBO of 9 (Table 7.2).

TABLE 7.2

Commercial Bank Branches as on June 30, 2004

Name of State	*No. of Branches*	*APPBO* in '000s*
Karnataka	**4851**	11
Andhra Pradesh	5300	15
Tamil Nadu	4768	13
Kerala	3441	10
Maharashtra	6373	15
West Bengal	4469	19
Uttar Pradesh	8210	21
Gujarat	3677	14
Punjab	2645	9
All India	**67118**	16

Note: * Average population per bank branch.

Source: Report on *Trend and Progress of Banking in India* 2003-04, Reserve Bank of India.

Of the total bank offices in the state, 44.94 per cent is in rural areas, 21.22 per cent is in semi-urban areas, 17.31 per cent in urban and 16.53 per cent in metropolitan areas. In the recent period the number of rural branches has been declining and the branch rationalisation policy adopted by the banks has impacted on the share of rural branches. Karnataka had opened 70 branches in 2002-03 and 54 branches in 2003-04 out of 844 and 641 branches opened at the all-India level respectively.

Karnataka has a good mix of different groups of commercial banks. Therefore, in terms of doing banking business, the state has a good infrastructure and well spread over (Figure 7.2).

FIGURE 7.2

Structure of Commercial Banks in Karnataka

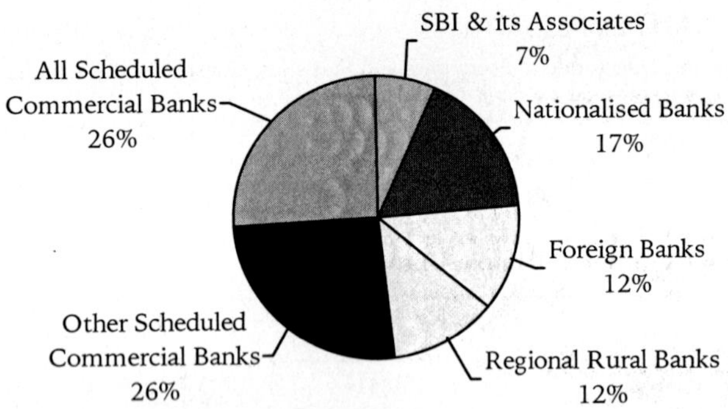

Source: Reserve Bank of India.

It is quite interesting to note that more than 90 per cent of these branches were opened after the first phase of nationalisation of banks in June 1969 (Table 7.3). Likewise 71.5 per cent of the deposits mobilised occurred after June 1969 and 75.4 per cent of credit was deployed in this period. Therefore, nationalisation of commercial banks was a significant turnaround in banking development not only in Karnataka but all over the country.

TABLE 7.3

No. of Offices of Scheduled Commercial Banks Opened after Nationalisation and their Deposits and Credit in Karnataka: March 2002

(Rupees Crore)

	No. of Offices	*Deposit*	*Credit*
SBI and its Associates	753	9507	7631
Nationalised Banks	1733	20085	12552
Foreign Banks	7	624	448
RRBs	1108	2706	2261
Other Scheduled Commercial Banks	446	11202	4448
All Scheduled Commercial Banks	4049	45506	28663

Source: Reserve Bank of India.

7.3.1 Distribution of Commercial Bank Branches

Commercial bank branches are those doing exclusively total banking business. At the end of June 30, 2004, the number of such branches in Karnataka stood at 4,851. The branches have been increasing from 4,770 in June 30, 2002 to 4,814 in June 30, 2003 and further to 4,851 in June 30, 2004. The population per branch office was 11 and this number has been maintained. Although there has been emphasis to open branches in unbanked centres, between June 30, 2003 and June 30, 2004, out of 54 branches opened in Karnataka, only 1 branch was opened in an unbanked centre.

Distribution among districts reveal that Bangalore Urban accounts for 17.48 per cent of the total branches followed by Belgaum (6.73 per cent), Dakshina Kannada (6.48 per cent), Mysore 5.15 per cent, Udupi 4.33 per cent, Tumkur 3.88 per cent and Davangere 2.66 per cent. These 7 districts together account for over 46 per cent of the state's total branches. While Bangalore Urban is strong with all the metropolitan branches of the state, Udupi, Kolar, Belgaum, Hassan, Dakshina Kannada, Tumkur, Chickmagalur and Gulbarga have more rural branches exceeding 100. Dakshina Kannada and Mysore have more urban branches. Districts such as Chamarajnagar, Gadag and Koppal, Bidar, Haveri and Raichur have relatively less number of commercial banks i.e. less than 100 (Appendix A-7.2).

Number of Authorised Dealer Branches

Authorised dealer (AD) branches are those that are authorised to deal with foreign exchange business. Out of 26,377 of AD branches of scheduled commercial banks in India, Karnataka accounts for more than 10 per cent at 2,646 branches and takes the third position. Tamil Nadu takes the first position having 3,446 AD branches followed by Maharashtra with 3,060 AD branches.

7.3.2 Deposits, Advances and Investment of Commercial Banks in Karnataka

In terms of deposits and advances, scheduled commercial banks in Karnataka have mobilised nearly 5.6 per cent (average) of the country's deposits. Its share in all-India quantum has been increased albeit fractionally from 5.4 per cent in 1995-96 to 5.8 per cent in 2001-02. The credit deployed in Karnataka accounts on an average 6.3 per cent of the all-India credit. The state ranks 5th in deposit mobilisation and 4th in credit deployment. In the recent period growth in both deposits and credit have been decelerating which is in tune with all-India phenomenon. (Appendix A-7.3)

7.3.3 Credit-Deposit Ratio and Investment plus Credit-Deposit Ratio

Mere size or quantum of deposits or credit will not reveal the correct picture of banking. Credit-deposit ratio (CD ratio) is one of the ratios to judge the banking development in any state or area. The CD ratios in almost all the states have been witnessing a deceleration in the recent years, which may be attributable to increase in investments of the banks. However, the CD ratio in Karnataka as per utilisation was higher than the sanctioned amount and there is a gradual increase in the CD ratio and this was quite sharp in 2002-03 at 71.1 (Figure 7.3). Since, investment by banks also includes commercial activity such as shares, commercial papers, etc. it is appropriate to take investment plus credit-deposit ratio. As per this, the ratios are higher and also showing an increase. All these ratios in Karnataka are more than the all-India levels (Figure 7.4).

7.3.4 Interstate Comparison

The CD ratios of western and southern regions remained higher than the all-India level. Across states only five states including Tamil Nadu, Maharashtra, Andhra Pradesh, Karnataka and New Delhi had CD ratios higher than the all-India. Tamil Nadu had the highest ratio as per utilisation in 2002-03 followed by Maharashtra and then Karnataka. Even after taking investment also the ratios followed similar pattern, but Karnataka took the fourth position (Figure 7.5).

FIGURE 7.3

CD Ratio as per Sanction and as per Utilisation

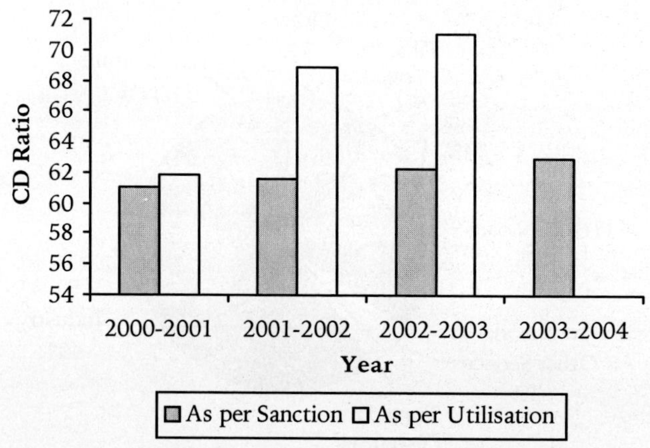

Source: Reserve Bank of India.

FIGURE 7.4

CD Ratio as per Utilisation (Karnataka and India)

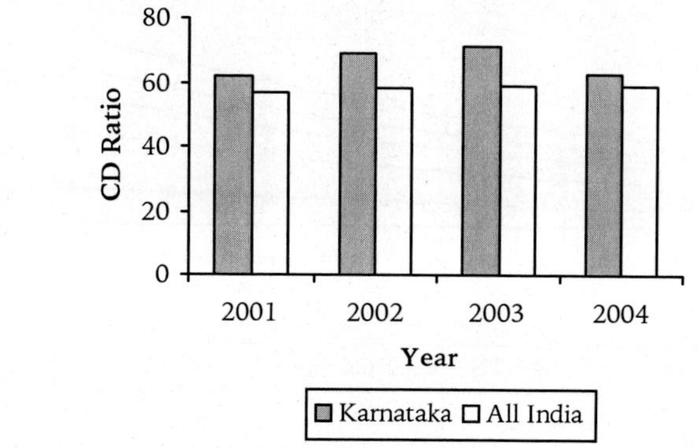

Source: Reserve Bank of India.

FIGURE 7.5

CD Ratio as per Utilisation: 2004 (Select States)

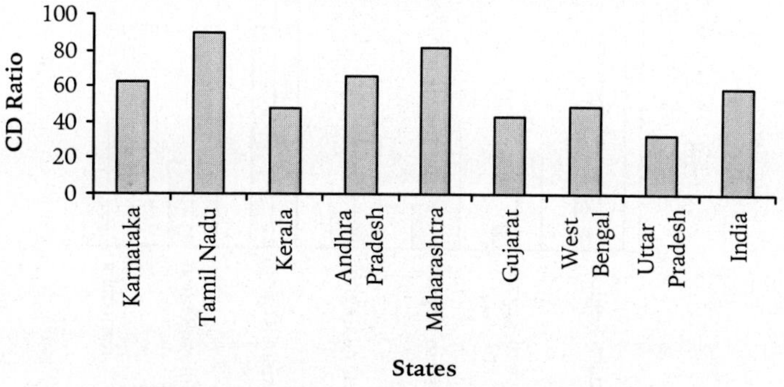

Source: Reserve Bank of India.

7.3.5 Per Capita Deposit and Credit

There is a steady rise in per capita deposit and per capita credit in Karnataka. As compared to the neighbouring states, the state's per capita deposit was lower than Kerala but higher than Andhra Pradesh. Credit was highest once again in Tamil Nadu followed by Karnataka (Figures 7.6 and 7.7).

FIGURE 7.6

Per Capita Deposit

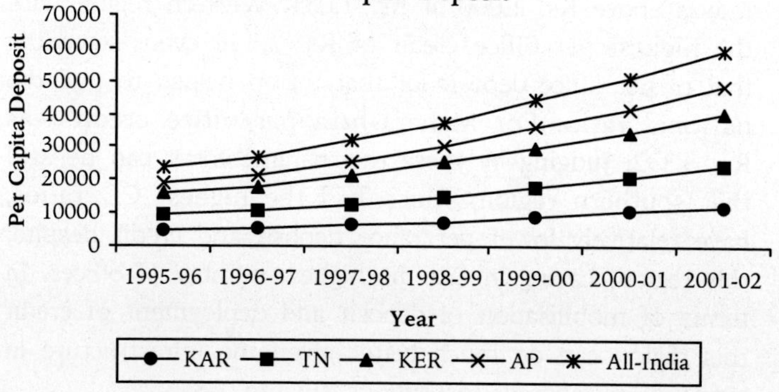

Source: Reserve Bank of India.

FIGURE 7.7

Per Capita Credit

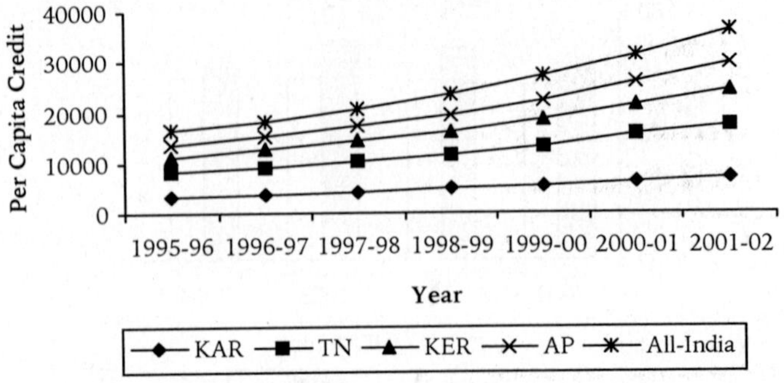

Source: Reserve Bank of India.

FIGURE 7.8

Deposit and Credit per Office (March 2002) (Rs.)

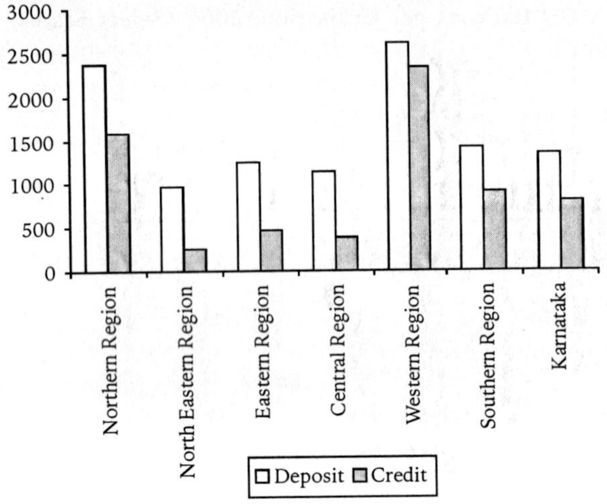

Source: Reserve Bank of India.

The deposits mobilised per office in 2001-2002 was Rs. 1,333 in Karnataka. This ratio was Rs. 1,442 for all-India (Figure 7.8). Across regions this ratio was high at Rs. 2,294 in the Western Region and this was true of the northern region also. For the southern region as a whole it was lower at Rs. 1,221 only. Per office deposit was less than Rs. 1,000 for the southern region (Rs. 900) and for Karnataka, it was still lower at Rs. 796, while for all-India it was above Rs. 1,000 at Rs. 1,031. Western region with the highest per office credit of Rs. 2,338 even exceeding that of per office deposit for that region helped to pull the national ratio. For Maharashtra per office credit was Rs. 3,332. Judging by these two parameters it can be said that southern region, which had the highest CD ratios, have relatively lower per office deposit and credit despite, this region, having in fact the highest number of offices. In terms of mobilisation of deposit and deployment of credit this region can do much better given the infrastructure in terms of number of institutions (Figure 7.8).

7.3.6 Direction of Credit of Scheduled Commercial Banks (SCBs)

More than 41 per cent of the outstanding credit of SCBs in Karnataka has been deployed for industry. Credit to agriculture formed 16.89 per cent below the stipulated level of 18 per cent. At the all-India level, industry got a higher proportion of 49.15 per cent and credit to agriculture on the contrary was far below at 10.69 per cent. The credit outstanding to artisans and village industries was 0.56 per cent for Karnataka and 0.66 per cent for all-India. Other small scale industries received 8.48 per cent of credit in Karnataka and 8.22 per cent in all-India (*Banking Statistics,* RBI) (Figures 7.9 and 7.10).

FIGURE 7.9

Direction of Advances in Karnataka (Credit Outstanding March 1999)

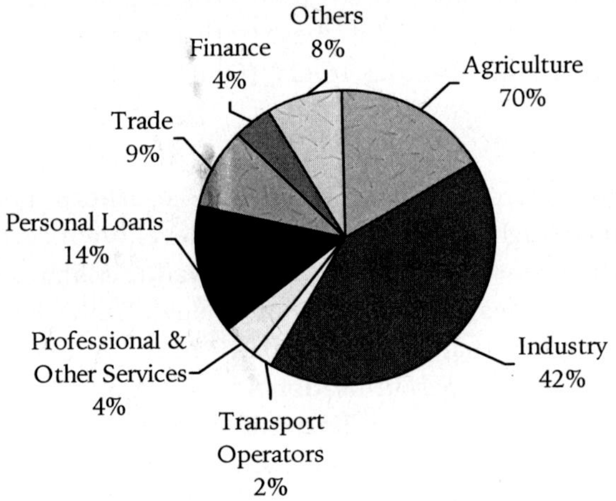

FIGURE 7.10

Direction of Advances All India (Credit Outstanding March 99)

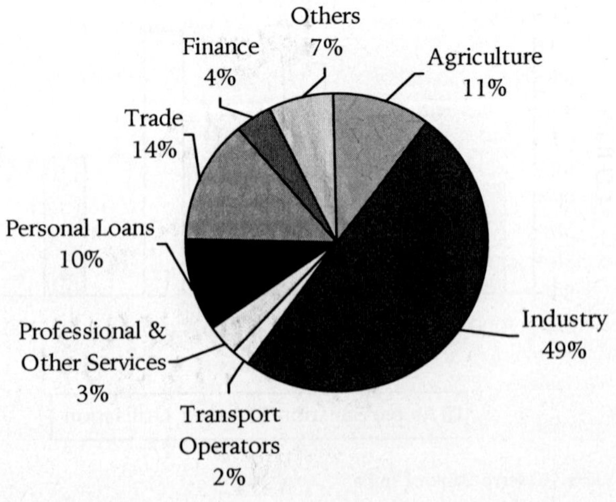

Bank Credit to Small-Scale Industries

The small-scale sector has grown phenomenally during the last three decades and the sector has played and has potential to play a vital role in the fulfilment of our socio-economic objectives, providing large number of employment opportunities while contributing substantially to production of goods and exports of the country.

Small-scale industries in Karnataka as discussed in Chapter 14 have also played a major role in the development of state. Banks have lent Rs. 5,013 cr. for 1,18,694 SSI units and road and transport operators as on March 2002. Karnataka stands at fourth place among the states in getting such assistance from banking system. The top three aie Maharashtra (Rs. 19,051 cr.), Tamil Nadu (Rs. 8,237 cr.) and Delhi (Rs. 5,307 cr.). While the state can claim that its performance is better than many other states but at the same time, the gap between Tamil Nadu and Maharashtra, the two neighbouring states is so large, it gives an opportunity for the state to aspire for higher levels and work towards the same. The number of SSI units is also significantly smaller compared to states like Tamil Nadu.

Bank Credit to Industries

Banking finance to industries at all-India level has gone up from Rs. 1,22,249.40 cr. in 1995-96 to Rs. 2,71,625.70 cr. in 2001-02 registering a compound growth rate of 14.23 per cent. Though Karnataka posted marginally better growth rate (14.8 per cent) over all-India average growth rate, its share on all-India compared to Tamil Nadu and Gujarat is lower. Industries in Karnataka have received a total bank credit of Rs. 16,874.60 cr. in 2001-02 compared to Rs. 20,700.30 cr. by Gujarat and Rs. 29,663.30 cr. by Tamil Nadu. The gap between Maharashtra and Karnataka is also huge. Among different segments of industries, engineering, metal and metal products, electricity and construction are major industrial segments that received banking assistance (Table 7.4).

TABLE 7.4

Commercial Banks' Credit to Industry (Rs. Crore)

Industry	*1995-96*	*1999-00*	*2001-02*	*Growth 1995-96 to 2001-02 in per cent*
All-India	122259.40	213778.70	271625.70	14.23
Karnataka	7380.50	11728.40	16874.60	14.78
Maharashtra	36330.40	66195.40	78963.40	13.81
Tamil Nadu	12830.00	23629.60	29663.30	14.99
Gujarat	8815.50	16074.20	20700.30	15.29

Source: Reserve Bank of India.

Bank Credit to Service Sector

Assistance to service sector has gone up from Rs. 13,621.90 cr. in 1995-96 to Rs. 37,204.90 cr. in 2001-02 registering a growth rate of 18.13 per cent. The state has reported a lower growth rate of 17.77 per cent whereas Tamil Nadu and Maharashtra have reported higher growth rates. In terms of Rupee value, bank credit to the state has increased from Rs. 1,106.40 cr. to Rs. 2,952.40 cr. during this period. Karnataka's share on all-India remains at 8 per cent whereas the service industries in Tamil Nadu has increased their bank credit share from 12 per cent to 13 per cent whereas Maharashtra has increased its share from 21 per cent to 29 per cent during this period. Though the state is trying to project itself as country's service sector capital, the hard fact is there is no major change in the banking credit (Table 7.5).

TABLE 7.5

Commercial Banks' Credit to Service Sector (Rs. Crore)

Service Industry	*1995-96*	*1999-00*	*2001-02*	*Growth 1995-96 to 2001-02 in per cent*
All-India	13621.90	22728.30	37024.90	18.13
Karnataka	1106.40	1923.80	2952.40	17.77
Maharashtra	2850.70	5291.40	10589.70	24.45
Tamil Nadu	1650.60	2587.70	4693.60	19.03
Gujarat	618.10	819.90	1083.70	9.81

Source: Reserve Bank of India.

Bank Credit to Trade

Trading segment heavily depends on bank credit for their operations. About 15 per cent of the total credit of banking systems go for trade finance. Credit flow to this sector for Karnataka is one of the lowest among the comparable states. The state's share has decline from 4 per cent to 3 per cent whereas states like Gujarat, Tamil Nadu and Maharashtra have either improved or retained their share. The growth rate of credit to trade in Karnataka is also one of the lowest among the four states. The gap between Karnataka on the one hand and Tamil Nadu and Maharashtra on the other hand is so large, it will take long time for the state to attract such additional credit. While trade finance for Maharashtra is about 34 per cent, Tamil Nadu accounts for 7 per cent (Table 7.6).

TABLE 7.6

Commercial Banks' Credit to Trade (Rs. Crore)

Bank Credit to Trade	*1995-96*	*1999-00*	*2001-02*	*Growth 1995-96 to 2001-02 in per cent*
All-India	35342.50	71617.90	100872.00	19.10
Karnataka	1460.30	2740.20	3155.80	13.70
Maharashtra	11396.80	22495.70	34250.90	20.13
Tamil Nadu	2603.00	6196.80	6592.20	16.75
Gujarat	813.00	2172.90	3422.90	27.07

Source: Reserve Bank of India.

7.3.7 Rural Infrastructure Development Fund (RIDF)

RIDF was created out of the deposits contributed by the domestic commercial banks on account of shortfall in meeting the sub-target of agricultural lending under priority sector. Out of this corpus created, loans are sanctioned and disbursed to the states for infrastructure development in rural areas. There exists a wide gap between the loans sanctioned and loan disbursed. For Karnataka while this gap was very small up to RIDF VII tranche, from RIDF VIII onwards it is quite wide. But this gap was smaller than the all-India (Table 7.7).

TABLE 7.7

Sanctions and Disbursements under RIDF as on March 31, 2005

(Rs. Crore)

RIDF Tranche	*Karnataka*		*All-India*	
	Loans Sanctioned	*Loans Disbursed*	*Loans Sanctioned*	*Loans Disbursed*
RIDF I	175.68	158.79	1910.54	1760.87
RIDF II	195.21	180.08	2658.88	2397.75
RIDF III	171.29	161.75	2717.71	2453.50
RIDF IV	172.34	166.87	2904.03	2367.03
RIDF V	173.18	164.31	3504.41	2875.33
RIDF VI	301.08	270.90	4539.05	3638.07
RIDF VII	236.77	197.49	4792.52	3370.87
RIDF VIII	231.03	156.89	6039.62	3686.34
RIDF IX	297.18	120.04	5599.00	2147.63
RIDF X	420.96	11.39	8282.75	686.43
Total	**2374.72**	**1588.51**	**42948.51**	**25384.02**

Source: Report on Trend and Progress of Banking in India, 2004-05, Reserve Bank of India, Mumbai.

7.4 Regional Rural Banks

Regional rural banks (RRBs) are important in rural institutional financing in terms of geographical coverage, clientele outreach, business volume and contribution to the development of the rural economy.

TABLE 7.8

Karnataka-based Regional Rural Banks: March 2005

Name of the Bank	*No. of Branches*
Bijapur Grameena Bank	91
Cauvery Grameena Bank	125
Chickmagalur – Kodagu Grameena Bank	50
Chitradurga Gramin Bank	91
Kalpatharu Grameena Bank	79
Kolar Gramin Bank	61
Krishna Grameena Bank	103
Malaprabha Grameena Bank	243
Netravathi Grameena Bank	22
Sahyadri Gramin Bank	29
Tungabhadra Grameena Bank	162
Varada Grameena Bank	31
Vishveshwaraya Grameena Bank	25
Total	**1,112**

Source: Report on Trend and Progress of Banking in India, 2004-05, Reserve Bank of India, Mumbai.

RRBs have a distinct regional character as also socio-economic identity of the issues. Out of 196 RRBs in the country, Karnataka in all has 13 RRBs. At the end of March 2005, there were 1,112 branches of these 13 RRBs (Table 7.8). Malaprabha Grameena Bank is not only the biggest RRB in the state but also of the country. It has 243 branches in Karnataka. Majority of the branches i.e. 79.4 per cent, are in rural areas and another 14.6 per cent are in semi-urban areas. These two together account for more than 94 per cent. About 6 per cent of them are in urban areas and only one branch in metropolitan areas. In the three years ending 2000-01, RRBs have opened 62 branches in banked centres and only one in unbanked centre. Of late, it has been observed that rural branches of RRBs are also declining and on the contrary the urban branches are increasing (Appendix A-7.4).

7.4.1 Deposits, Advances and Investment of RRBs

All the three variables i.e., deposits, credit and investment have registered increases for all the 13 RRBs over a period of time (Table 7.9). This is more so subsequent to the restructuring of RRBs all over the country facilitated by substantial delegation of decision making i.e. deregulation and freedom given to the RRBs, (Figures 7.11 and 7.12). Their advances are both agricultural and non-agricultural. Under agricultural advances, they lend short-term loans (crop loans) both direct and indirect advances. The non-agricultural advances include loans to rural artisans other, industries, retail trade, etc. In the recent years there has been a marginal bias in favour of non-agricultural loans, which may be attributed to the reforms in RRB sector which include *inter alia* delegation of powers of fixing interest rates, etc. (Appendix A-7.5).

FIGURE 7.11

RRB Deposits, Advances and Investment in Karnataka as on March 31, 1996 (Rs. Lakhs)

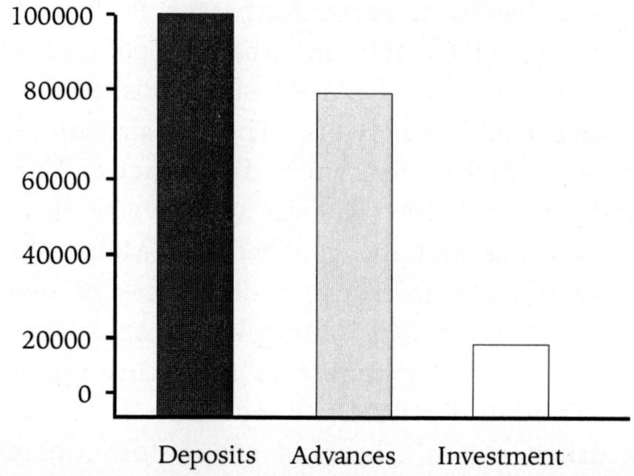

Note: Based on Appendix A-7.5.

FIGURE 7.12

RRB Deposits, Advances and Investment in Karnataka as on March 31, 2002 (Rs. Lakhs)

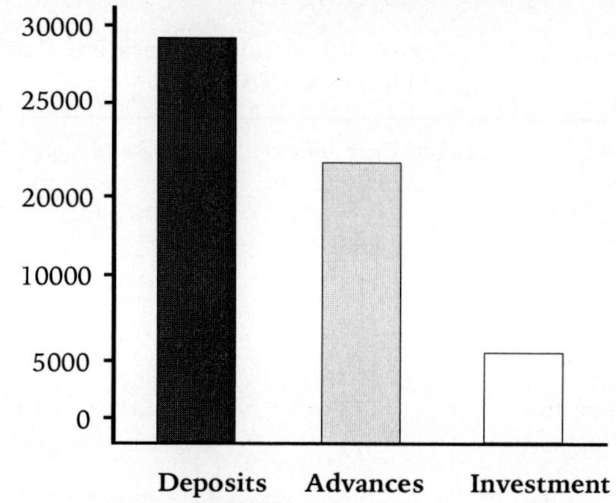

Note: Based on Appendix A-7.5.

Source: State Level Bankers' Committee, Karnataka, June 2004.

TABLE 7.9

Increases in Deposit, Advances and Investment of RRBs 1995-96 and 2001-02

	(Rs. Lakh)
Deposits	179.50
Advances	150.08
Investment	217.21

7.4.2 *Credit-Deposit Ratio of RRBs*

The credit-deposit ratio (CD ratio) of the 13 RRBs in the state was quite high in the year ended March 1996 ranging from 50.57 to 113.89 whereas seven years later in the year ended March 2002, with the sharp shrinkage in credit, this ratio also slided down for all banks except in case of 5 banks. The CD ratio, ranged between 55.17 and 97.47. For all the 13 RRBs put together the CD ratio dipped from 89.20 in 1995-96 to 79.81 in 2001-02. This can be attributed to the sharp rise in investment following the relaxation of norms in their investment activity as reflected in the many fold increase between 1995-96 and 2001-02. Further, in 2002-2003 RRBs were advised to maintain their entire statutory liquidity ratio (SLR) holdings in the form of government and other approved securities by converting existing deposits with sponsor banks into approved securities. Accordingly RRBs in Karnataka in line with all-India trend, expanded their investment in SLR securities. In some banks like the Krishna Gramin bank, the investment at Rs.5,164 lakh was higher than its volume of credit at Rs.5,045 lakh in the year 2001-2002. So also with Chickmagalur Kodagu Gramin Bank, Sahyadri Gramin Bank, and Visveswaraya Gramin Bank. In fact in 1995-96, two RRBs had reported nil investment, i.e., Chickmagalur Kodagu Gramin Bank and the Sahyadri Gramin Bank. But seven years later their investments expanded substantially. These data suggest that RRBs are not keen on lending because of the fear of rise in bad loans and so are shy of risk taking (Appendix A-7.6).

7.4.3 *Financial Performance of RRBs in Karnataka*

Karnataka has a unique distinction in respect of its RRBs. At present all its 13 RRBs are profit making unlike rest of the country (Table 7.10). In the period 1995-96 and 2001-2002, all the 13 RRBs in Karnataka

TABLE 7.10

Number of RRBs Reporting Profit/Loss

Years	*Profit*		*Loss*	
	Karnataka	*All-India*	*Karnataka*	*All-India*
Total No. of RRBs	**13**	**196**	**13**	**196**
31.3.1996	5	51	7	144
31.3.1997	6	46	6	146
31.3.1998	13	125	-	71
31.3.1999	13	162	-	34
31.3.2000	13	166	-	30
31.3.2001	13	170	-	26
31.3.2002	13	168	-	28

Source: Reserve Bank of India.

reported profit in 5 years and loss in 2 years. Whereas in all-India, there are some RRBs, which are still reporting losses. However, one redeeming feature is that the number of loss making RRBs has been declining for the country over a period of time from 144 in 1995-96 to 28 in 2001-02. RRBs in Karnataka have exhibited resilience and improved their overall financial health. The size of profit also increased sharply for all the RRBs. The management of non-performing assets (NPA) was prudent as is reflected in the sharp reduction in the quantum of provisions and contingencies made towards NPAs. But it has to be noted here that this favourable position may not be fully attributable to good recovery of loans and RRBs made this possible by shunning away from advances thereby avoiding any untoward bad loan accounts. (Appendix A-7.6, A-7.7 and A-7.8)

7.5 Cooperative Banking

Cooperatives have been developed in India as important instruments for economic, social and cultural development. Fostering economic development, promoting social justice and strengthening political democracy were the three main ideologies of cooperatives besides minimising the role of private middle men. Cooperative banks with their extensive branch network and localised base play a key role in the development process in general and credit delivery in particular. The cooperative banking system with two broad segments of urban and cooperatives forms an integrated part of the Indian financial system (Figure 7.13).

FIGURE 7.13

Cooperative Banking Structure

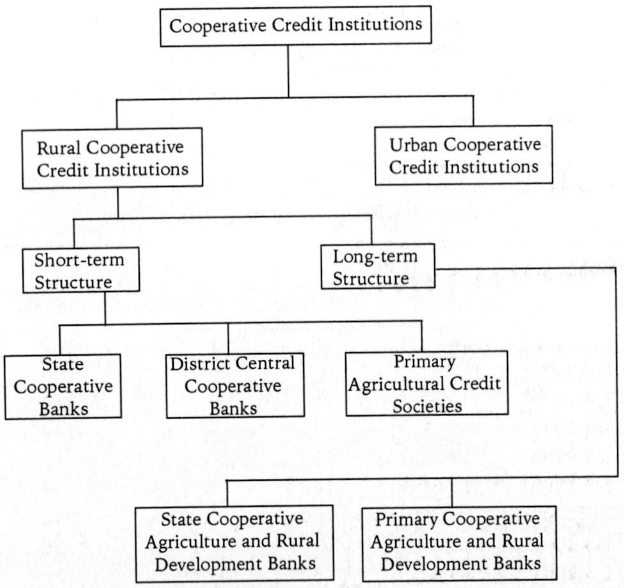

Source: Directorate of Economics and Statistics, Government of Karnataka and Reserve Bank of India.

Cooperative sector in Karnataka has just completed 100 years in 2004. Karnataka has defined its own Cooperative Policy in 1997. Karnataka is one of the few states in the country where, the cooperative sector has gained considerable momentum and made its impact on its economy.

7.5.1 Cooperative Banking Network

Table 7.11 shows the distribution of urban and rural cooperative banks in India. Karnataka is ranked below Maharashtra and Gujarat on urban cooperative banking network whereas it is placed sixth position on rural cooperative banking network. Though size of the state could be a factor for such differences, Karnataka definitely ranks below Gujarat whose size is close to Karnataka's size and the gap between Maharashtra and Karnataka is so large that size differences of two states fails to explain the gap. Mumbai is financial centre for the country and its impact is seen through out the states. Though Karnataka's position is better than many other states, there is scope for considerable improvement in spreading the banking network at rural level. If banking network is an important parameter to measure financial infrastructure development, there is lot more for Karnataka to achieve.

TABLE 7.11

Distribution of Urban and Rural Cooperative Banking Network (No.)

States	*Urban Coop. Banks*	*Rural Coop. Banks*
Maharashtra	670	3826
Gujarat	362	1111
Karnataka	324	646
Andhra Pradesh	169	599
Tamil Nadu	136	763
Uttar Pradesh	78	1316
Madhya Pradesh	77	856
Kerala	65	502
West Bengal	55	274
Rajasthan	44	401
Other States	124	3216
All-States	**2104**	**13510**

Source: Reserve Bank of India.

Taking into account all aspects of cooperative development across the districts in Karnataka, 7 districts namely Udupi, Bagalkot, Dakshina Kannada, Uttara Kannada, Kodagu, Bijapur and Belgaum have high level of cooperative development, while another 7

TABLE 7.12

Loans Disbursed by Cooperative Credit Institutions in Karnataka

(Rs. Crore)

Year	*Short-Term Loan*	*Medium-Term Loan*	*Long-Term Loan*	*Total*
1990-1991	58.65	5.75	58.12	122.52
1991-1992	73.50	3.59	97.21	174.30
1992-1993	195.93	6.34	120.57	322.84
1993-1994	230.00	9.12	134.54	373.66
1994-1995	303.54	24.42	107.15	435.11
1995-1996	450.67	37.95	153.66	642.28
1996-1997	531.35	37.25	168.06	736.66
1997-1998	727.48	57.06	177.58	962.12
1998-1999	823.36	69.13	150.36	1042.85
1999-2000	994.00	82.14	163.19	1239.33
2000-2001	1150.98	48.95	140.62	1340.55
2001-2002	1384.44	32.33	120.00	1536.77
2002-2003	1323.76	30.35	127.57	1481.68
2003-2004	1300.00	28.00	83.44	1411.44

Source: Reserve Bank of India.

districts such as Shimoga, Mysore, Bidar, Bangalore Urban, Hassan and Mandya are all in the category of above normal cooperative development. Majority of the districts, i.e., 11 of them come under the category of normal cooperative development. Only in 3 districts i.e., Chamrajnagar, Chitradurga and Kolar the level of cooperative development is below normal.

Cooperative credit institutions play a critical role for the development of small industries and agriculture. Since rural India is dominantly agriculture and small and cottage industry oriented, the relevant financial infrastructure for rural India is the cooperative credit institutions. Table 7.12 shows the role played by cooperative credit institutions in Karnataka in providing financial assistance. For the full year 2002-03, these institutions have lent Rs. 1481.68 cr. registering a compound growth rate of 22 per cent during the last 12 years.

Though lending by cooperative credit institutions in Karnataka is impressive, a comparison with other states suggest scope for improvement.

Table 7.13 shows deposits raised by urban, state and district cooperative banks and also advances given by them. Consistent with several other measures, Karnataka ranks below the three states both on deposits and advances. Though in terms of size, Karnataka is comparable with Gujarat, the cooperative penetration in Karnataka is about 50 per cent of Gujarat. It is below 20 per cent compared to Maharashtra. The proportion of advances as a percentage of deposits is consistent among the states and also very high. In other words, there is a less chance for the export of capital since these institutions operate mostly within the state.

7.5.2 Financial Health of Urban Cooperative Banks in Karnataka

Urban cooperative banks (UCBs) play an important role as financial intermediaries in urban and semi-urban areas catering to the needs of non-agricultural sector, particularly small borrowers. There were 324 UCBs in Karnataka as at the end of March 2003 which decreased to 300 later in March 2004. These UCBs have 1,052 branches with an addition of 18 extension counters. Karnataka is the third largest state in the UCB category next to Maharashtra (639) and Gujarat (328) and accounts for 15.6 per cent of the country's UCBs of 1,926 (*Report on Trend and Progress of Banking 2003-2004*, RBI).

TABLE 7.13

Deposits and Advances by Cooperative Banks of Select States

(Rs. in Crores)

States	*Deposits Raised by Cooperative Banks*				*Advances by Cooperative Banks*				*Advances as a Percentage of Deposits*			
	Urban	*State*	*District*	*Total*	*Urban*	*State*	*District*	*Total*	*Urban*	*State*	*District*	*Total*
Karnataka	7768	1653	3490	12911	4862	1510	3563	9935	63	91	102	77
Maharashtra	46567	10197	19574	76338	29733	8830	15635	54198	64	87	80	71
Tamil Nadu	3309	2727	6855	12891	2100	1938	6401	10439	63	71	93	81
Gujarat	17068	2846	6813	26727	12364	1936	4818	19118	72	68	71	72
All India	**86037**	**36046**	**67660**	**189743**	**56585**	**32598**	**59035**	**148218**	**66**	**90**	**87**	**78**

Source: Reserve Bank of India, Mumbai.

BOX 7.2

Categories of UCBs

Grade-I	80
Grade-II	58
Grade-III	118
Grade-IV	40

The UCBs come under multiple regulatory structure comprising Registrar of Cooperative Societies of States, Central Government and the RBI. In the recent years UCBs all over the country have been facing problems as their conduct of banking business often poses a number of challenges, especially in terms of high levels of loan delinquency. Apart from their large number, regulatory overlaps have compounded these issues. For regulatory purpose, RBI introduced a new system of grading of cooperative banks in April 2003 based on their CRAR, level of net NPAs, record of losses and compliance with regulatory environment. As per this UCBs have been classified into four categories.[1] According to this grading system, the financial position of 295 UCBs as at end March, 2005 in Karnataka was not considered satisfactory as majority of them come under Grade-II, III and IV. Only 80 were in Grade-I category. In fact Karnataka is having the highest number of UCBs of 118 in III Grade, followed by Gujarat at 87. This grading system means the low grade UCBs would face ban on declaration of dividend, as well as on opening branches, etc.

UCBs under Direction and Liquidation Cancellation of Licence

Reserve Bank of India issues directions under Section 35 A in respect of those UCBs, which are in serious financial difficulty which include restriction on deposit taking, withdrawal of deposits with or without a ceiling, further expansion of loans, etc. There were altogether 84 UCBs in the country which are working under the direction of the RBI as of June 2005. Of this, 16 UCBs are in Karnataka. Out of 214 UCBs under liquidation in India, Karnataka accounts for 26. Under both these categories, majority of the UCBs are in Gujarat (75), Andhra Pradesh (56), Maharashtra (4), and Karnataka (42). Therefore, the higher number of weak banks in Karnataka is a matter of concern.

7.5.3 Analysis on Cooperative Sector in the State

As said earlier cooperative sector in Karnataka has completed 100 years very recently. Born in 1904 the sector has faced many ups and downs. It has many achievements to its credit. It has also many failures in many areas.

The cooperatives in Karnataka have built a good structural network. Their federal structure has brought about both vertical and horizontal linkages among the various constituents. Undoubtedly, the cooperatives in Karnataka enjoy a tremendous support from all political parties in the state. These parties have also subscribed strongly to the ideology of cooperation. Cooperatives in the state have provided excellent support system to the agricultural and rural development programmes. However, as recognised by the New Cooperative Policy in Karnataka in 1997, the patronage extended by the state and its control over the working, decision making and management of cooperatives coupled with the excessive and restrictive legislative measures have led to certain set backs like low member participation and the resultant fall in quality of membership, reduced initiatives in cooperatives, absence of professionalism required for operational efficiency apart from discouraging voluntary formation as well as emergence of new leadership, etc. Therefore, the policy contemplated to create a congenial environment required for promoting voluntary enterprises by withdrawing controls. Some of the key objectives are, inculcating the spirit of cooperation among the people, to ensure that cooperatives are formed and run on democratic principles and also enjoy maximum autonomy at the same time being accountable to members also, to make them efficient deposit mobilisers in self supporting, viable, economic service and business centres, etc. But the implementation of the policy is far from reality. It must be recognised that cooperatives can play a significant role in the rural

---

1. Grade-I: Sound banks having no supervisory concerns.

   Grade-II: Problems banks: (I) CRAR of 1 per cent below the prescribed norms, or (ii) net NPAs of 10 per cent or more, but below 15 per cent, or (iii) incurred a net loss for the previous financial year, or (iv) defaults in the maintenance of CRR/SLR in the previous financial year and/ or there is more or less a continuous default in maintenance of CRR/SLR during the current year.

   Grade-III: Banks meeting any two of the following conditions are classified under Grade III: (I) CRAR of less than below 75 per cent of the minimum prescribed but 50 per cent or above the level required; (ii) net NPA of 10 per cent or more but less than 15 per cent; (iii) incurred net losses for the years out of the last three years.

   Grade-IV: Banks meeting the following conditions are classified under Grade IV: (I) CRAR of less than 50 per cent of the prescribed limit and (ii) net NPA at 15 per cent or more or incurred net losses for the last three consecutive years.

reconstruction and agricultural development in the state, provided there is total commitment by cooperatives, the right leadership and the dedication on the part of the cooperatives.

7.6 Recovery and Non-Performing Assets

7.6.1 NPAs of Commercial Banks in Karnataka

Keeping in view the recommendations of Narasimham Committee on Financial Sector Reforms, a number of measures were initiated to make the financial sector strong, flexible and vibrant. Prudential norms and prudential accounting guidelines of income recognition, asset classification norms and provisioning for bad and doubtful debts were all introduced for the whole financial sector as such. All these norms were progressively tightened and made more and more stringent. At the same time deregulation and greater operational flexibility were also ensured in order to improve the operational efficiency and profitability. Therefore, recovery and management of assets assume greater importance. Reducing the ratio of non-performing assets was the driving force for the banks to operate in the reform period. As a result, there was notable and progressive reduction in the ratio of non-performing assets to advances in response to further measures undertaken, such as improved risk management practices and greater recovery efforts driven, *inter alia* by the recently enacted Securitisation and Reconstruction of Financial Assets and Enforcement of Security Interest Act, 2002.

Since the policies and some of the parameters such as NPA ratio etc., are all at individual bank level, regional level data on NPA management, profitability and income and expenditure of financial sector are not available. But in Karnataka it can be inferred there are no alarming levels of NPAs and not many willful defaulters (Table 7.14). Therefore, with good recovery and prudential lending practices, NPA levels are relatively lower. As per the Karnataka State Level Bankers' Committee (SLBC) (Convener: Syndicate Bank) sources the total-credit outstanding at the end of June 2004 was Rs. 53,195 crore relating to 44,98,067 accounts. Out of this, NPAs were Rs. 4,185.14 crore or 7.86 per cent to bank credit relating to 5,47,475 accounts. So more than 12 per cent of the loan accounts are NPAs in Karnataka. Sectorwise it is the SSI, which is having the highest NPA ratio. Again out of total NPA of Rs. 4,185 crore, 52.52 per cent i.e., Rs. 2,198 crore is the priority sector advances, which in fact have raised the NPA levels in the state. The sectorwise NPA accounts also suggest that priority sector advances account for 82.92 per cent of the total accounts (Figures 7.14 and 7.15).

TABLE 7.14

Sector-wise Breakup of NPAs in Karnataka: June 2004

Sector	*Amount Outstanding Rs. Crore*	*NPA Level Rs. Crore*	*NPA Percentage to Credit*
Agriculture	9872	825	8.35
SSI	3776	704	18.64
OPSA	10942	669	6.11
TPSA	24590	2198	8.93
NPSA3	28605	1987	6.94
Total Credit	**53195**	**4185**	**7.86**

Note: OPSA – Other Priority Sector Advances
TPSA – Total Public Sector Advances
NPSA – Non-priority Sector Advances
Source: State Level Bankers' Committee, Karnataka, June 2000.

FIGURE 7.14

NPA Level in Karnataka (Amount) as End June 2004

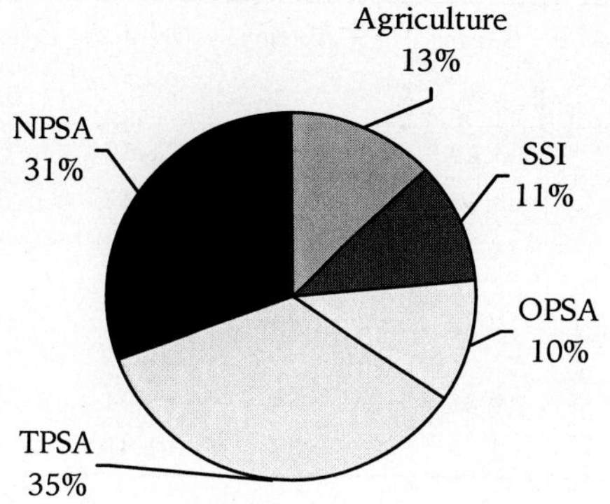

FIGURE 7.15

NPA Level in Karnataka (No. of Accounts) as End June 2004

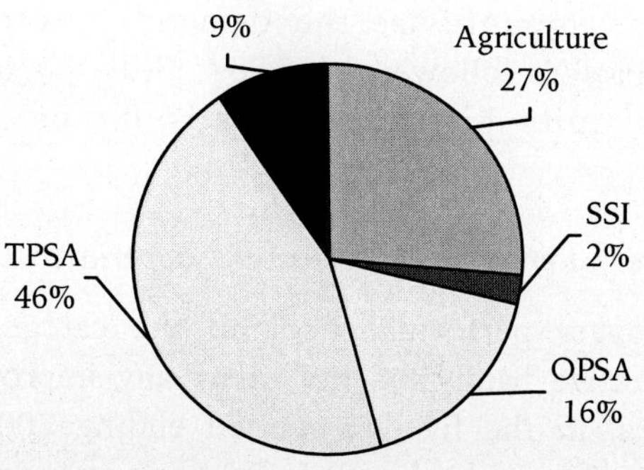

Note: OPSA - Other Priority Sector Advances
TPSA - Total Priority Sector Advances
NPSA – Non-Priority Sector Advances.

TABLE 7.15

Sector-wise Number of NPA Accounts of Scheduled Commercial Banks in Karnataka, June 2004

Sector	*No. of NPA Accounts*	*Amount of NPA (in Crore)*
Agriculture	48.39	19.71
SSI	4.44	16.82
OPSA	30.09	15.96
NPSA	17.08	47.49
Total	**100.00**	**100.00**

Source: SLBC, June 2004.

As for recovery performance of scheduled commercial banks, details are available only in respect of centrally sponsored schemes such as PMRY, IRDP, SGSY and SJSRY. At the end of June 2004, the overdues as percentage of demand was highest in respect of SJSRY followed by PMRY (SLBC, June 2004) (Table 7.16).

TABLE 7.16

Recovery Performance of Commercial Banks

(Amount: Rs. in Crore)

Sector	*Demand*	*Collection*	*Overdues*	*Percentage of Overdues to Demand*
PMRY	105.29	41.01	61.58	60.02
IRDP	0.88	0.61	0.27	30.68
SGSY i. Individuals	31.12	17.58	13.54	43.50
ii. Groups	17.53	13.30	4.23	24.13
SJSRY i. ME	9.85	4.54	5.31	53.90
ii. DWCRA	2.12	0.69	1.43	64.75

Source: SLBC, June 2004.
PMRY: Prime Minister Rozgar Yojana
IRDP: Integrated Rural Development Programme
SGSY: Swarna Jayanthi Gram Swarozgar Yojana
SJSRY: Swarna Jayanthi Shahari Rozgar Yojana
DWCRA: Development of Women and Children in Rural Areas.

However, amount-wise the demand is largest in respect of PMRY, followed by SGSY. Still the overdue position is quite high. Recovery is far below the demand.

7.6.2 Recovery Performance of Rural Cooperative Banks

The recovery performance of all the categories of rural cooperative banks did not show any improvement in Karnataka, in the five-year period ending 2004-2005 which is in line with the all-India phenomenon. Only the PCARDBs improved in 2004-05 (Table 7.17).

TABLE 7.17

Recovery Performance of Rural Cooperative Banks

(in per cent)

Coop. Banks	*2000-01*	*2001-02*	*2002-03*	*2003-04*	*2004-05*
		Karnataka			
State Coop. Banks	84	90	86	82	64
CCBs	69	63	56	53	63
SCARDBs	31	26	22	18	33
PCARDBs	35	29	26	17	60
		All India			
State Coop. Banks	84	82	79	83	—
CCBs	67	66	61	62	—
SCARDBs	56	55	49	44	—
PCARDBs	53	48	44	45	—

Note: SCARDBs – State Cooperative Agriculture and Rural Development Banks
PCARDBs – Primary Cooperative Agriculture and Rural Development Banks
— Not Available.
Source: Report on Trend and Progress of Banking in India 2004-05, Reserve Bank of India and Government of Karnataka.

Among the different institutions of the cooperative banks the recovery performance of state cooperative banks and CCBS was better. But the lower level institutions like SCARDBs and PCARDBs showed not only low recovery but also deterioration year after year. Overall the recovery performance was very good in Haryana (100 per cent), Tamil Nadu (97 to 99 per cent), Chhattisgarh, Punjab, Kerala and Madhya Pradesh all have reported over 90 per cent recovery in respect of state cooperative banks. *(Report on Trend and Progress of Banking in India 2003-04)*.

7.7 Micro-finance Institutions

Discussion on financial infrastructure would be incomplete without a discussion on micro-finance infrastructure. Availability of credit is considered as an important remedy for many of the ills of the poverty. Central and state governments have initiated a large number of programmes and allocated large resources to help rural people. The Reserve Bank of India had issued guidelines to banks in February 2000 for mainstreaming micro-credit providers. An important provision include that microcredit extended by banks to individual borrowers directly or through an inter-mediary would be reckoned as part of their priority sector lending. While the underlying objectives are laudable and substantial progress was achieved, credit flow to the poor, and especially to poor women, remained low. This led to initiatives that were institution led, that attempted to converge the existing strengths of rural banking infrastructure and leverage this to better serve the unbanked poor. Micro-finance allows the poor people to form self-help groups (SHG) and obtain credit for their activities.

The Reserve Bank of India has been supporting the SHG's. Bank linkage programme of National Bank for Agriculture and Rural Credit (NABARD) initiated in 1991-92. The strategy involved forming small, cohesive and participative groups of the poor, encouraging them to pool their thrift regularly and using the pooled thrift to make small interest bearing loans to members, and in the process learning the nuances of financial discipline. Subsequently, bank credit also becomes available to the Group, to augment its resources for lending to its members. NABARD also supports other models of micro-finance such as Grameen, wholesaling funds through NGO-MFIs, etc. During the period April 2003 to March 2004—361,731 new SHGs were financed by banks to a tune of Rs 1,855 cr. by way of loans. Cumulatively, banks have lent Rs 3,904 cr. to 1,079,091 SHGs.

Southern states have made significant progress in micro-finance compared to rest of the country. Among the southern states, Andhra Pradesh and Tamil Nadu take larger stake compared to Karnataka (Table 7.18).

TABLE 7.18

Micro-finance Assistance by Banking Institutions (Rs. in Crore)

State	*No. of SHG Units*	*Financial Assistance*
Andhra Pradesh*	2,43,714	521.26
Tamil Nadu*	62,709	202.67
Karnataka**	1,63,198	551.74
All-India**	16,18,476	6898.00

Source: National Agricultural Bank and Rural Development, Annual Reports of Various Issues.

Note: *March 2002.

** As at end March 2005.

7.8 All-India and State Level Financial Institutions

While banks constitute important source of finance for industrial and non-industrial activities, there are several other intermediaries which actively contribute to the development of the states. All financial institutions are classified into three groups, namely, i) all-India financial institutions, ii) state level institutions and iii) other institutions. The first category includes development banks like IDBI, SIDBI, IIBI, IFCI and IDFC and specialised financial institutions such as Exim Bank, ICICI ventures, IVCF and TFCI and investment institutions like UTI, LIC, GIC and subsidiaries plus refinance institutions like NABARD and NHB. The state level institutions for Karnataka are KSFC, KSIIDC and other institutions include, ECGC and DICGC. Non-banking financial intermediaries operate at two levels. All-India financial institutions like IFCI, IDBI, SIDBI, etc. provide loans to medium and large companies in addition to refinancing state-level financial institutions. Table 7.19 provides data on assistance provided by all-India financial institutions (AIFI).

TABLE 7.19

State-wise Sanctions of Loans by All-India Financial Institutions

(Rs. in Crore)

State	*1998-99*	*1999-00*	*2000-01*	*2001-02*	*2001-02*	*2002-03*	*Cumulative up to 2003*
Karnataka	4449.50	5456.30	6934.10	3978.80	2429.60	1879.30	48225.90
(% on Total)	5.68	5.61	5.98	5.33	6.33	6.54	6.05
Tamil Nadu	7263.50	7679.90	6796.10	4453.00	2718.90	2416.40	64172.20
(% on Total)	9.27	7.90	5.86	5.97	7.08	8.41	8.05
Gujarat	8921.90	12297.60	14947.30	7078.80	3783.10	1929.10	107073.30
(% on Total)	11.39	12.65	12.89	9.49	9.86	6.71	13.43
Maharashtra	23842.30	21630.20	31654.80	19968.80	12854.10	8688.50	192922.80
(% on Total)	30.44	22.25	27.29	26.76	33.49	30.22	24.20
All-States	**78316.5**	**97198.5**	**115982.3**	**74613.1**	**38383.9**	**28746.2**	**797177.9**
	100.00	**100.00**	**100.00**	**100.00**	**100.00**	**100.00**	**100.00**

Source: Report on Development Banking 2002-03, IDBI, Mumbai.

Loans by all-India financial institutions have also stressed the earlier observation that Karnataka's rank is below the two neighbouring states, Tamil Nadu and Maharashtra. Financial assistance to Gujarat was also significantly large for most of the period under study except in 2002-03. Though the share of Karnataka has shown an improvement over the years, it should be noted that the level of assistance by all-India financial institutions has come down over the years and in absolute value, there is a drop in loans sanctioned to Karnataka.

As in many states, Karnataka also has two state-level financial agencies namely Karnataka State Finance Corporation (KSFC) and Karnataka State Industrial Investments and Development Corporation (KSIIDC). Table 7.20 shows the financial assistance of the two agencies over the years. Consistent with the declining trend of financial assistance by AIFI, there is also a decline in the financial assistance of state-level agencies during the last few years. Compared to several other states (Appendix A-7.9), the level of financial assistance of state level agencies of Karnataka has not witnessed any sharp decline. In other words, the state role on financial infrastructure is declining, the good news is it is not showing any major reversal witnessed in states like Gujarat or Maharashtra. However, the Maharashtra state government is creating considerable financial and industrial infrastructure through the State Industrial Development Corporation. It has sanctioned and disbursed a cumulative value of Rs. 7,500 cr. as against Karnataka's figure of Rs. 2,091 cr. Karnataka competes well with other states in getting assistance from other state-sponsored financial agencies like National Small Industries Commission and Khadi and Village Industries Commission along with other states. Consistent with many other evidences, Karnataka ranks below Maharashtra and Tamil Nadu. To sum up, the role of the state-sponsored financial agencies has declined over the years due to reasons like non-performing assets. However, the same agencies have played a major role for development of some of the industrially developed states today.

7.9 Non-banking Financial Companies

NBFCs encompass an extremely heterogeneous group of intermediaries. They differ in various attributes like size, nature of incorporation and regulation as well as the basic functionality of financial intermediation. Non-banking financial companies (NBFCs) are of two types i.e., companies accepting deposits 'A' category and those companies not accepting deposits called 'B' category. In the 'A' category are included Equipment Leasing, Hire Purchase, Investment and Loan. Table 7.21 shows activities of NBFCs at all-India level.

TABLE 7.20

Loans Sanctioned and Disbursed by KSFC and KSSIDC

(Rs. in Crore)

Year	*KSFC Sanction*	*KSFC Disbursement*	*KSSIDC Sanction*	*KSSIDC Disbursement*	*Total Sanction*	*Total Disbursement*
1990-91	246.51	190.71	71.90	49.98	318.41	240.69
1991-92	342.06	246.34	68.83	59.59	410.89	305.93
1992-93	336.25	299.81	69.33	54.96	405.58	354.77
1993-94	354.77	310.01	109.56	66.80	464.33	376.81
1994-95	520.18	432.09	318.05	160.76	838.23	592.85
1995-96	818.81	612.63	380.03	213.51	1198.84	826.14
1996-97	859.84	649.46	313.83	220.54	1173.67	870.00
1997-98	577.36	469.55	203.31	224.49	780.67	694.04
1998-99	371.96	358.97	192.48	193.10	564.44	552.07
1999-2000	340.26	298.49	170.73	117.96	510.99	416.45
2000-2001	440.05	328.78	248.08	150.85	688.13	479.63
2001-2002	303.71	292.42	272.33	187.56	576.04	479.98
2002-2003	340.67	268.28	23.57	88.15	364.24	356.43
Total	**5852.43**	**4757.54**	**2442.03**	**1788.25**	**8294.46**	**6545.79**

Source: Report on Development Banking 2002-03, IDBI, Mumbai.

TABLE 7.21

Activity-wise Distribution of Assets of NBFCs

Activity	*Amount in Rs. Crore*			*Percentage to Total*		
	2001	*2002*	*2003*	*2001*	*2002*	*2003*
Loans & Inter-corporate Deposits	10271	13710	13296	27.3	34.4	35.3
Investments	4344	4334	4338	11.5	10.9	11.5
Hire Purchase	12887	13202	13031	34.2	33.1	34.6
Equipment Leasing	4681	3112	2011	12.4	7.8	5.3
Bills	788	673	450	2.1	1.7	1.2
Other Assets	4663	4802	4583	12.4	12.1	12.2
Total	**37634**	**39833**	**100**	**100**	**100**	**100**

Source: *Trend and Progress of Banking in India*, Reserve Bank of India, Mumbai, 2003-04.

TABLE 7.22

Region-wise Breakup of Number of NBFCs and Deposits of NBFCs (2003-04)

Region	*No. of NBFCs*	*Deposits (Rs. in cr.)*	*Per Cent*
Northern	271	3	2.7
Northeastern	1	2	-
Eastern	21	7634	38.0
Central	83	7752	38.6
Western	63	687	3.4
Southern	436	3482	17.3
Total	**875**	**20100**	**100.0**
Metropolitan Cities			
Mumbai	45	672	3.3
Chennai	318	3162	15.7
Kolkata	18	7625	37.9
New Delhi	108	443	2.2
Total	**489**	**11902**	**59.2**

Source: *Trend and Progress of Banking in India*, 2003-04, Reserve Bank of India, Mumbai.

According to the regionwise data on registered NBFCs, Table 7.22 southern states dominate in number of NBFCs whereas eastern and central regions dominate on deposits. Among the southern states, Chennai contributes 70 per cent of number of NBFCs and 85 per cent of the deposits. Indirectly, it shows that NBFCs role in other states is not significant.

In Karnataka the number of registered NBFCs is very small and it has been declining (Table 7.23). The state accounts for only six per cent of the registered companies and just one per cent of the deposits of the southern region only. The reduction in registered companies is because these companies not being able to comply with stringent regulations, have chose to close their business.

TABLE 7.23

Number of Registered NBFCs and Public Deposits Held by them in Karnataka

Period	*Number of Registered NBFCs*	*Public Deposits (Rs. Crore)***	*Of which RNBC**
End March 2002	35	236.17	5.34
End March 2003	31 (10)	37.65 (24.10)	2.81
End March 2004	26 (7)	35.06 (24.40)	1.62
End December 2004	21	32.44	1.62

Note: * Relates to that of one RNBC: Residual Non-Banking Company.
** Includes deposit amounting to Rs. 185.60 crore relating to Maharashtra Rural Apex Company Ltd. (MRACL) and ICDS, whose registrations have been cancelled and the companies have been closed.
Figures in parentheses relate to Bangalore city only.
Source: Reserve Bank of India.

Recently, venture capital financing particularly for technology oriented firms gained importance in India. Though the level of venture capital financing is

TABLE 7.24

Venture Capital Assistance by Private and Public Sector Venture Capital Funds

(Rs. in Crores)

State	*1992*	*1993*	*1994*	*1995*	*1996*	*1997*	*1998*
Gujarat	22.28	22.94	35.88	48.87	80.03	110.21	159.77
No. of Assisted Units	25	28	40	48	44	49	54
Karnataka	26.77	28.78	50.82	70.78	68.65	104.62	131.26
No. of Assisted Units	46	48	70	83	79	93	106
Maharashtra	36.66	42.95	118.32	162.63	164.66	256.65	292.81
No. of Assisted Units	50	61	115	146	140	161	167
Tamil Nadu	36.79	33.13	57.13	84.11	119.19	153.17	180.24
No. of Assisted Units	61	58	88	102	111	119	121
Total	**191.28**	**317.38**	**425.80**	**572.46**	**672.85**	**1000.05**	**1255.99**
No. of Assisted Units	**284**	**0**	**0**	**0**	**0**	**691**	**728**

Source: Indian Venture Capital Association Year Book: Various Issues.

relatively small in India compared to international levels, this will be critical infrastructure for knowledge-based economy and states. While some of the states like Gujarat initiated venture capital fund much earlier and made substantial progress, states like Karnataka initiated the process recently. Table 7.24 shows the venture capital assistance by both private and public sector venture capital funds over the years.

Though venture capital activity in Karnataka is active, states like Maharashtra, Tamil Nadu and Gujarat leads the show. Since Karnataka has seen as knowledge capital of the country and destination for the many IT services, it is important that the state facilitates financial infrastructure relevant to this sector. Entrepreneurs of knowledge sector are typically first generation entrepreneurs with meagre own capital and limited resources to offer collateral for assistance from traditional financial institutions. Capital market is also of limited use initially in view of small size with which these entrepreneurs promote their ventures. Venture capital institutions of different sizes are right fit in this context.

7.10 Capital Market

Capital markets include both financial institutions as well as institutions facilitating flow of capital directly between the investors and capital seekers. Since financial institutions were discussed in the earlier sections, this section discuss the role played by stock market in mobilising financial resources for the firms operating in Karnataka. Since Karnataka is placed 7th in industrial production among the states of India, capital market activities would also be expected to low compared to other industrially developed states. Karnataka has two stock exchanges namely Bangalore Stock Exchange (BgSE) and Mangalore Stock Exchange (MSE). In that context, it is one of the few states in India, which has two stock exchanges. However, the role of regional stock exchanges has become redundant following increased communication and computational facilities. National Stock Exchange and to an extent Bombay Stock Exchange capture almost all volumes of trading generated in the stock market today.

Capital market activities of Karnataka are relatively low key compared to many other states. The weakness is reflected both in terms of: (a) number of Karnataka based companies approaching capital market, (b) response of people in Karnataka in capital issues, and (c) stock market activities in secondary market. Table 7.25 shows the number of public issues originated by Karnataka-based companies and the figures are also compared with few major states of the country.

TABLE 7.25

Number of Public Issues between 1991-2004

Year	*Karnataka*	*Tamil Nadu*	*Gujarat*	*Maharashtra*	*Total*
1991-92	4	18	12	28	141
1992-93	16	37	131	102	527
1993-94	24	57	131	198	770
1994-95	40	121	195	354	1343
1995-96	45	153	230	420	1391
1996-97	13	47	144	131	753
1997-98	4	3	14	10	62
1998-99	2	1	1	16	32
1999-2000	7	7	3	26	65
Total	**155**	**444**	**861**	**1285**	**5084**
% on Total	3	9	17	25	100

Source: Primary Directory, Bombay Stock Exchange, Various Issues.

The distribution of public issues by firms of Karnataka and other states shows that only 3 per cent of the public issues were originated by Karnataka based firms, whereas states like Gujarat and Tamil Nadu performed shared larger proportion. As in many cases, Maharashtra has dominated the capital market segments too. In other words, there is a close nexus between industrial development and financial markets development and each one complements the other for overall development.

The culture of investing in equity or stock market by the people of the state to an extent determines the number of public issues generating from the states. Equity culture is dominant only in few states in India. States like Gujarat and Maharashtra take the lead. An analysis of responses to public issues (Table 7.26 during the last 10 years shows the share of Maharashtra has significantly gone up over the years and almost two-thirds of response emerged from Maharashtra. A part of this response could be on account of institutional investors who are normally located in Maharashtra. Next to Maharashtra, Gujarat dominates the picture. States like Karnataka has negligible share in the equity market investments. Even such responses are also restricted to Bangalore city despite the fact of having two stock exchanges in the state.

TABLE 7.26

Distribution of Responses (per cent) to Public Issues of Selected States

States	1990-1991	1991-1992	1992-1993	1993-1994	1994-1995	1995-1996	1996-1997	1997-1998	1998-1999	1999-00
Karnataka	**3.12**	**2.63**	**3.29**	**3.05**	**3.29**	**2.94**	**2.77**	**2.76**	**4.46**	**2.47**
Gujarat	27.32	30.31	26.42	24.13	21.64	25.42	10.14	11.70	13.66	15.70
Maharashtra	26.97	23.71	21.25	33.42	30.87	28.90	43.14	54.09	57.03	68.30
Delhi	11.45	10.14	10.47	10.65	12.21	11.20	12.77	8.41	9.49	3.10
West Bengal	6.87	7.08	5.44	6.41	6.47	8.09	8.15	6.54	7.77	2.17
Tamil Nadu	4.46	4.16	4.67	4.46	4.80	5.75	3.71	3.49	5.22	2.27
All States	100	100	100	100	100	100	100	100	100	100

Source: Primary Directory, Bombay Stock Exchange, Various Issues.

The distribution of volume of securities traded in secondary market also confirms cities like Mumbai, Ahmedabad, Delhi, Calcutta and Chennai account for almost the entire volume and cities like Bangalore are reporting meagre trading volume. Table 7.27 shows the distribution of trading volume in select cities.

TABLE 7.27

Distribution of Secondary Market Volume in Select Cities

City	1999-00	2000-2001	2001-2002	2002-2003
Mumbai	44.26	48.35	40.2	40.01
Delhi	17.77	17.03	19.4	18.38
Calcutta	9.85	8.24	9.15	12.03
Chennai	3.88	3.40	3.56	3.56
Ahmedabad	2.66	2.68	2.49	2.28
Hyderabad	2.47	2.30	2.85	3.20
Bangalore	1.42	1.69	2.79	2.52

Source: Securities and Exchange Board of India, Annual Reports, Various Issues.

The absence of equity culture in the state indirectly restricts the regional companies to venture into capital market for raising funds. On other hand, companies in Gujarat and Maharashtra due to high equity culture are more forthcoming in approaching capital market. A comparison of funds raised by Karnataka companies with funds mobilised in Karnataka by firms coming out public issues also shows capital flight from Karnataka to other states.

7.11 Summary and Conclusions

Savings and capital formation are critical for development of economy. State plays an important role in creating necessary environment for development of agriculture and allied activities and industries of different sizes. Financial infrastructure not only mobilises saving but also make them available to those who seek capital. While financial infrastructure *per se* may not bring development but it accelerates development process. In other words economic development and financial infrastructure complement each other for the development of the state. States like Maharashtra and Gujarat are not economically developed but also stand better on financial infrastructure, which in turn attracts large-scale capital formation activities. This chapter presents the current status of financial infrastructure prevailing in Karnataka and compared the same with three important states namely Tamil Nadu, Maharashtra and Gujarat. The choice of Tamil Nadu and Gujarat is primarily on account of size and also relatively improved economic development. Gujarat is also well known for capital market activities, which is an important constituent of financial infrastructure. Since Maharashtra, particularly Mumbai is financial centre or capital of the country and hence infrastructure of the state is benchmarked with Maharashtra.

Studies on financial infrastructure are in general looked into the issue at country level and considered various issues including banking and other institutions, capital markets and regulations relating to financial markets. Many of them are not relevant when financial infrastructure is examined at the state level. Further state-level savings and capital formation are also not available. In view of these limitations, this chapter examined the penetration of institutions relating to financial markets and their performance. The following major conclusions emerge from our analysis:

(a) Financial institutions network particularly banking and cooperatives institutions are fairly good compared to several states and comparable with Gujarat and Tamil Nadu. Compared with Maharashtra, the institutional penetration is low.

(b) Savings and credit data of banking institutions show an interesting picture. While Tamil Nadu and Maharashtra are net importers of capital (savings) from other states, Karnataka's requirement of credit is met by the savings generated within the state.

(c) Capital market activities are seen as an important indicator for the development of financial infrastructure. However, despite having two stock exchanges in the state, neither firms from Karnataka taps capital markets for major funding nor people of Karnataka actively participate in capital market activities.

(d) The trend of reasonable development is seen on non-banking financial institutions including venture capital institutions but Karnataka ranks below Maharashtra, Tamil Nadu and Gujarat.

(e) Developments on cooperative credit institutions also confirm overall satisfactory position compared to several states but Karnataka continues to rank below the three states namely Tamil Nadu, Gujarat and Maharashtra.

(f) Karnataka achieved significant progress on micro-finance institutions but here again it is below to two neighbouring states like Tamil Nadu and Andhra Pradesh.

Overall, financial infrastructure of the state is reasonably good but there is a scope for considerable future development. The state government can play a critical role for the improvement. Some of the measures in this direction are listed below:

(i) In the long-run, the financial infrastructure of the state should attract capital from other states for the economic development of the state, which in turn facilitate the development of financial infrastructure. State needs to develop policies conducive of major capital formation activities in manufacturing, service and agriculture and allied activities.

(ii) Karnataka, particularly Bangalore and Mysore are seen as knowledge centre for the country. The service industry is likely to spread to other major cities and towns of the state. The financial infrastructure needs of the knowledge industry is different from conventional manufacturing and trading sector. The state should play a major lead role in developing or facilitating to develop private agencies to cater this segment. Bangalore should be promoted as 'venture capital centre or hub' for the entire country. Agencies like Karnataka Information Technology Venture Capital Fund should be strengthened to allow large-scale establishment of such service ventures. Since several states are competing to attract such venture, Karnataka should leverage its first mover advantage.

(iii) Knowledge industry requires considerable risk capital. While venture capital funds can provide initial risk capital, once the unit overcome initial phase further expansion requires additional risk capital. Also, venture capitalists need an exit route. Karnataka needs to promote capital market segment exclusive to knowledge sector. Since Karnataka has large number of knowledge workers with high per capita income, it is possible to develop such capital market activities. It is also possible to attract large foreign capital for this segment through organised exchanges. The state can initiate the idea of setting up of an exclusive stock exchange for small knowledge-based companies with international collaboration and fair regulatory practices. Such an exchange need not serve firms of the region alone but should be a centre for the entire nation and over a period for the entire subcontinent.

(iv) In the process of developing knowledge industries, which are normally located in urban areas, one should not loose track of the aspiration and needs of people in rural sector. Though Karnataka is not on the top in micro-finance activities, it has considerable experience in this sector. It is important to strengthen to micro-finance institutions to cover a large number of rural public. While penetration of financial infrastructure is critical in this context, it is equally important to generate necessary business opportunities for the rural people. Business Development Agencies exclusively for rural businesses can be established to identify business opportunities.

Finance and financial infrastructure facilitate growth provided economy creates opportunities. The state has a positive role to play on both—creating opportunities and developing new types of financial infrastructure to leverage such growth opportunities.

Financial infrastructure in any form needs to be on strong and sound lines. For this financial stability is very important. Financial stability has evolved as an increasingly important goal of policy across countries. Although major segments of the financial system operate at the all-India level all policy and decision are all centralised. However, there are a few segments where states do play an important role like the RRBs, Cooperative banks, state level financial institutions, etc. Financial stability applies to these segments also. In view of integration of financial markets and because of the contagion effect, any crisis in any one these sectors would affect the total financial system of the country. The recent episode of the crisis in Madhavapura Cooperative Bank in Gujarat is an eye opener. Therefore and since Karnataka has a strong presence of cooperative banks, the state government also need to pay attention to their financial health by good governance. While the RRBs in Karnataka are doing exceedingly well, much needs to be done in the cooperative banks and also the KSFC and KSIIDC.

Another important aspect of financial infrastructure is in respect of the banking and credit policy which is highly centralised. There is one policy for the whole country which is a mix of many characteristic features—backward states, progressive states and some middle category states, big states, very small states like Goa, etc. One policy will not help all the states and even if it helps it will not help uniformly across the states. This is a debatable issue and needs to be looked at. Further rural credit suffered with the financial sector reforms, which has gradually reduced the number of institutions at the rural level to cater to the needs of the agriculturists and poor farmers. The present government at the Centre is committed to enhance and outreach the rural credit delivery. Many Committees were set up which have gone over the rural credit infrastructure but it is a sad story nothing significant has materialised. There are views that even state governments which once was very close to the villages and agriculture are slowly withdrawing from its developmental work and keeping away from this. Though Karnataka has been the pioneer in the decentralised administration even the *Panchayat Raj* Institution also do not seems to be giving adequate attention to this. These are some of the issues and areas of concern as far as financial infrastructure is concerned where the state of Karnataka needs to deliberate.

References

Reserve Bank of India. *Report on Trend and Progress of Banking in India*, various years.

———. *Annual Report*, various years.

———. *Banking Statistics*, various years.

———. *Statistical Tables Relating to Banks in India*, various years.

———. *Branch Banking Statistics*, various years.

———. *Report on Currency and Finance*, various years

Industrial Development Bank of India. *Report on Development Banking.*

Vasanthakumari, R. M. and C. L. Dadhich (2003). *Impact of Reforms on the Rural Credit System*, RBI Staff Studies, Jan.

Government of Karnataka. *High Power Committee for Redressal of Regional Imbalances*. Accompaniment-3. The Role of Cooperatives in Reducing Regional Imbalances in Karnataka, June 2002.

APPENDIX A-7.1

GDP and Component of GDP at Factor Cost

(At Constant Price)

GDP & Component of GDP	*All India*			*Karnataka*			*Relative Position in*	
	1993-94	*2001-02*	*% Change*	*1993-94*	*2001-02*	*% Change*	*1993-94*	*2001-02*
GDP—Total	**781345**	**1267833**	62	**41079**	**70558**	72	7	7
Agriculture, Forestry & Fishing	241967	305263	26	14613	18459	26	6	5
Industry	205162	337480	64	10744	19516	82	7	7
Mining and Quarrying	20092	28545	42	308	511	66	13	12
Manufacturing	125493	213681	70	7339	12610	72	7	6
Electricity, Gas and Water Supply	18984	30692	62	1006	1590	58	8	8
Construction	40593	64562	59	2091	4805	130	9	7
Service	334216	625090	87	15722	32582	107	7	7
Trade, Hotel, Transport, etc.	150500	296905	97	4492	14125	214	7	7
Banking and Insurance	41665	81726	96	1976	4468	126	5	5
Real Estate and Bus Service	48419	76007	57	2836	4963	75	7	7
Community and Personal Services	93632	170452	82	4531	9327	106	6	6

Source: Central Statistical Organisation website.

APPENDIX A-7.2

District-wise Distribution of Branches of Commercial Banks

Name of District	*R*	*SU*	*U*	*M*	*T*
Bagalkot	68	55	-	-	123
Bangalore (Rural)	66	43	-	-	109
Bangalore (Urban)	49	36	-	743	828
Belgaum	127	113	79	-	319
Bellary	82	43	31	-	156
Bidar	68	12	15	-	95
Bijapur	74	23	27	-	124
Chamrajnagar	34	19	-	-	53
Chickmagalur	109	25	-	-	134
Chitradurga	82	32	-	-	115
Dakshina Kannada	115	41	151	-	307
Davangere	69	23	34	-	126
Dharwad	54	17	116	-	187
Gadag	37	25	16	-	78
Gulbarga	101	35	39	-	175
Hassan	114	52	-	-	166
Haveri	61	35	-	-	96
Kodagu	89	22	-	-	111
Kolar	127	54	-	-	181
Koppal	45	29	-	-	74
Mandya	92	18	19	-	129
Mysore	86	32	129	-	244
Raichur	40	32	23	-	95
Shimoga	79	42	36	-	157
Tumkur	113	37	34	-	184
Udupi	130	44	31	-	205
Uttara Kannada	87	79	-	-	166
Karnataka Total	**2199**	**1018**	**777**	**743**	**4737**

Note: R – Rural, SU – Semi Urban, U – Urban, M – Metropolitan, T – Total.
Source: Reserve Bank of India.

APPENDIX A-7.3

States' Shares of Deposits and Credit

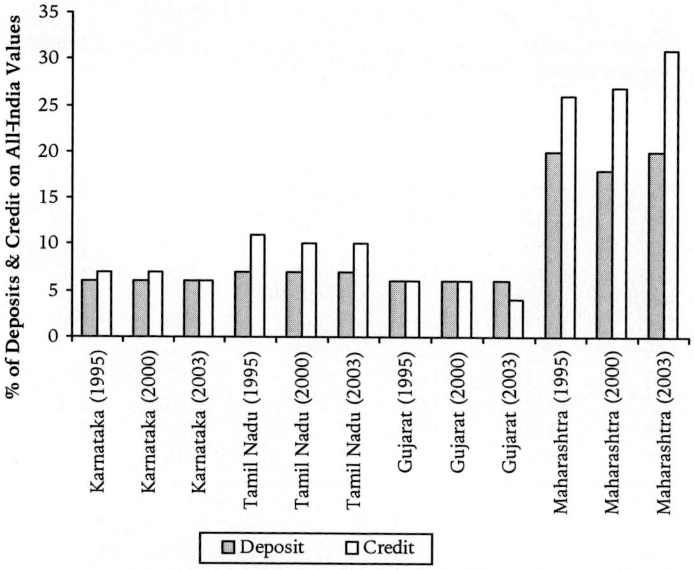

Source: Reserve Bank of India.

APPENDIX A-7.4

Regional Rural Banks in Karnataka—No. of Branches of Regional Rural Banks Functioning as on March 2005

RRBs	*Rural*	*Semi-Urban*	*Urban*	*Metropolitan*	*Total*
Total RRBs	883	162	66	1	1112
Bijapur Grameena Bank	77	11	3	-	91
Cauvery Grameena Bank	102	16	7	-	125
Chickmagalur-Kodagu Grameena Bank	43	7	-	-	50
Chitradurga Gramin Bank	82	8	1	-	91
Kalpatharu Gramin Bank	58	18	2	1	79
Kolar Gramin Bank	50	11	-	-	61
Krishna Grameena Bank	84	12	7	-	103
Malaprabha Gramin Bank	185	29	29	-	243
Nethravathi Gramin Bank	12	8	2	-	22
Sahyadri Gramin Bank	17	10	2	-	29
Tungabhadra Gramin Bank	134	16	12	-	162
Varada Grameena Bank	19	12	-	-	31
Visveshvaraya Gramin Bank	20	4	1	-	25

Source: Reserve Bank of India.

APPENDIX A-7.5

Regional Rural Banks: Deposits, Advances and Investments

(Rs. Lakhs)

Regional Rural Banks	*Deposits*			*Advances*			*Investments*		
	31.3.1996	31.3.2002	31.3.2005	31.3.1996	31.3.2002	31.3.2005	31.3.1996	31.3.2002	31.2.2005
Bijapur Grameena Bank	8746	26781	36221	9343	20911	35209	888	6761	14106
Cauvery Grameena Bank	8552	20264	33953	7185	13179	22357	1495	6589	13913
Chickmagalur Kodagu Grameena Bank	3527	9089	10538	3159	6413	8577	-	5407	3712
Chitradurga Gramin Bank	5721	19130	30653	5100	15180	26532	402	4426	9515
Kalpatharu Gramin Bank	7194	17991	31293	4412	9926	22364	3316	3697	12078
Kolar Gramin Bank	5602	15435	23873	4373	9229	17717	1636	3482	9290
Krishna Grameena Bank	9976	23004	37458	5045	20295	39293	2530	5164	12158
Malaprabha Gramin Bank	21930	68598	100398	24976	55210	89455	2141	11773	33953
Nethravathi Gramin Bank	1141	4752	7293	846	4031	6292	20	522	2295
Sahyadri Gramin Bank	2125	7350	10446	2017	5867	8938	-	2158	5125
Tungabhadra Gramin Bank	19249	48810	71535	17218	47381	71851	7351	11343	21549
Varada Grameena Bank	2135	6203	12881	2299	6046	9721	148	1225	6005
Visveshvaraya Gramin Bank	1496	4805	7457	902	3586	7040	100	980	2465

Source: Reserve Bank of India and NABARD.

APPENDIX A-7.6

Income and Expenditure of Regional Rural Banks in Karnataka

(Rs. Lakh)

Regional Rural Banks	*Income*			*Expenditure*			*Profit/Loss*		
	31.3.1996	*31.3.2002*	*31.3.2005*	*31.3.1996*	*31.3.2002*	*31.3.2005*	*31.3.1996*	*31.3.2002*	*31.2.2005*
Bijapur Grameena Bank	1642	4499	5458	1508	3241	3422	134	1258	2036
Cauvery Grameena Bank	1355	3896	4524	2282	3231	4209	926	666	315
Chickmagalur Kodagu Grameena Bank	498	1446	1393	519	1233	1377	-21	134	16
Chitradurga Gramin Bank	745	3290	3796	975	2739	3130	-230	544	666
Kalpatharu Gramin Bank	756	2624	3700	945	2297	3285	-189	280	415
Kolar Gramin Bank	758	2281	2827	873	1859	2276	-116	494	551
Krishna Grameena Bank	2720 (31.3.1998)	4568	6579	2228 (31.3.1998)	3711	4412	386 (31.3.1998)	423	2167
Malaprabha Gramin Bank	4329	11227	15902	3988	9381	11261	341	920	4641
Nethravathi Gramin Bank	145	812	852	189	698	713	-44	110	139
Sahyadri Gramin Bank	367	1355	1417	360	1049	1117	6	262	300
Tungabhadra Gramin Bank	3271	8687	9441	2996	6314	7331	276	1610	2110
Varada Grameena Bank	386	1309	1475	338	1043	1233	48	205	242
Visveshvaraya Gramin Bank	181	803	1042	190	635	811	-9	146	231

Source: Reserve Bank of India and NABARD.

APPENDIX A-7.7

Provisions and Contingencies as Proportion to Expenditure of Regional Rural Banks

(Rs. Lakh)

Regional Rural Banks	*Provisions and Contingencies*			*Expenditure*		*Provisions and Contingencies as Proportion of Expenditure*	
	31.3.1996	*31.3.2002*	*31.3.2004*	*31.3.1996*	*31.3.2002*	*31.3.1996*	*31.3.2002*
Bijapur Grameena Bank	82	-	775	1508	3241	5.40	-
Cauvery Grameena Bank	880	-	740	2282	3231	38.56	-
Chickmagalur-Kodagu Grameena Bank	31	79	636	519	1233	5.97	6.41
Chitradurga Gramin Bank	-	7	631	975	2739	-	0.26
Kalpatharu Gramin Bank	25	47	407	945	2297	2.64	2.05
Kolar Gramin Bank	-	71	558	873	1859	-	-3.8
Krishna Grameena Bank	-	435	1011	-	3711	-	11.72
Malaprabha Gramin Bank	149	926	2513	3988	9381	3.74	9.87
Nethravathi Gramin Bank	-	4	64	189	698	-	0.57
Sahyadri Gramin Bank	-	43	442	360	1049	-	4.10
Tungabhadra Gramin Bank	101	763	661	2996	6314	3.37	12.08
Varada Grameena Bank	14	61	351	338	1043	4.14	5.85
Visveshvaraya Gramin Bank	-	22	104.35	190	635	-	3.46

Source: Reserve Bank of India and NABARD.

APPENDIX A-7.8

Number of Regional Rural Banks Making Profits and Losses

Years	*Profit*		*Losses*	
	Karnataka	*All-India*	*Karnataka*	*All-India*
31.3.1996	5	51	7	144
31.3.1997	6	46	6	146
31.3.1998	13	125	-	71
31.3.1999	13	162	-	34
31.3.2000	13	166	-	30
31.3.2001	13	170	-	26
31.3.2002	13	168	-	28
31.3.2003	12	156	1	40
31.3.2004	13	163	-	33
31.3.2005	13	NA	-	NA

Source: Reserve Bank of India and NABARD.

APPENDIX A-7.9

Financial Assistance by State Finance Corporation (SFC)

State Finance Corporation	*Sanction*						*Disbursement*					
	1998-99	*1999-00*	*2000-01*	*2001-02*	*2002-03*	*Cumulative up to 2003*	*2003*	*1998-99*	*1999-00*	*2000-01*	*2001-02*	*Cumulative up to 2003*
Andhra Pradesh	282.80	335.20	391.90	390.10	385.20	3704.10	163.20	264.20	282.80	308.50	301.30	3050.40
Assam	2.80	2.60	1.10	-	0.60	117.50	3.80	2.90	3.70	1.70	0.90	113.30
Bihar	3.20	0.90	0.20	-	-	784.20	3.20	1.90	0.90	0.04	0.02	423.40
Delhi	36.50	42.70	266.10	48.80	74.40	955.60	16.50	18.60	84.00	38.90	60.30	512.30
Gujarat	157.90	364.80	282.00	93.90	3.90	4467.50	117.30	328.30	219.50	90.40	22.10	3379.10
Haryana	80.20	48.10	81.50	89.50	40.30	1782.30	78.90	65.50	54.70	72.00	71.40	1523.90
Himachal Pradesh	16.70	15.20	12.10	32.20	-0.30	211.90	16.50	14.80	14.80	23.80	10.10	202.40
Jammu & Kashmir	16.00	20.50	18.90	14.60	10.20	396.50	7.60	16.00	10.90	16.40	9.70	355.90
Karnataka	339.80	336.70	461.40	289.50	331.70	5802.60	353.20	281.80	357.40	288.80	265.10	5374.80
Kerala	200.30	162.10	292.50	160.20	155.60	2432.80	191.10	149.70	226.90	175.90	112.30	1981.50
Madhya Pradesh	101.70	83.00	107.90	98.60	107.00	1154.50	60.50	71.50	73.80	66.10	75.00	1061.00
Maharashtra	62.70	56.00	78.30	23.60	0.20	3687.70	68.00	46.70	50.50	30.40	5.60	2735.50
Orissa	105.30	131.10	131.40	122.30	15.30	1441.50	82.70	82.90	115.00	95.20	29.00	1292.40
Punjab	45.50	50.20	5.20	50.30	8.30	1095.90	59.20	54.80	39.70	50.00	28.90	1059.70
Rajasthan	89.20	198.80	178.20	157.30	192.40	2165.20	96.00	127.90	146.10	128.80	139.90	2032.40
Tamil Nadu	151.50	244.30	279.90	211.00	145.40	4558.70	117.70	172.80	200.20	187.90	126.70	3200.80
Uttar Pradesh	98.90	65.60	107.20	152.70	196.50	3199.90	128.70	69.60	58.40	100.20	124.80	3070.60
West Bengal	73.20	80.00	94.90	144.00	141.70	1074.40	60.60	55.20	68.80	95.90	106.00	970.10
Total	**1864.20**	**2237.80**	**2790.70**	**2078.60**	**1808.40**	**39032.80**	**1624.70**	**1825.10**	**2008.10**	**1770.90**	**1489.10**	**32339.50**

Source: *Report on Development Banking 2002-03*, IDBI, Mumbai.

Chapter 8

Political, Cultural and Social History of the State

8.1 Introduction

Any discussion on development is incomplete without touching the historical roots and the socio-cultural heritage on which as part of a development drive a programme of improving the welfare, equity, and security of the people are being framed. Karnataka has a long strong history of over 2000 years of rulers who on their own interest had played key roles to bring about a variety of socio-economic transformation of the region originally known as *Karnat*.

This chapter is intended to trace those historical, social and anthropological roots of development leading up to the present day state of Karnataka. Tracing only some of the major events and transitions on the dynasties, the cultural, linguistic, religious, social, economic, and institutional development are knitted to provide some clues on the present-day status of development and its future challenges. Sections are developed to provide only the historical transits, rather than providing any analytical model or process of establishing the causalities of development in the state from this historical perspective.

8.2 An Overview of Social History

The earliest reference to Karnataka is found in Paninis work, wherein he has called 'karnadhaka' as the 'gotra' of a people. Allusions to Karnataka as a territory are also found in many *puranas* including the Mahabharata. In the works of the foreign travellers from Greece, China and Persia one finds generous accounts of the rulers and the life of the people of Karnataka, an area that stretched from the river Cauvery to Godavari. Ptolemy's *Geography* (C-130 AD) informs us about the trading connection Karnataka had together with other south Indian states with the Western countries, and China. Pepper, sandalwood, spices, etc. were exported from the harbour of west coast. Foremost among these accounts is the one by Sulaiman (851 AD) who declares the empire of the Rashtrakutas as one of the four great empires of the world.

Many dynasties have ruled over Karnataka. The earliest dynasties that ruled the region were the Nandas and the Mauryas. Chandragupta Maurya or Samprati Chandragupta was believed to have visited Shravanabelagola and spent his last days there. Most distinguished among these dynasties being the Shathavahanas, the Gangas (345 to 1004 AD), the Kadambas (345 to 540 AD), Chalukyas of Badami (540 to 753 AD) and of Kalyana (973 to 1189 AD), Rashtrakutas (753 to 973 AD), Hoysalas (1000-1346 AD), and then the famous Vijayanagara emperors (1336 to 1565 AD). The contemporaries of Vijayanagara in the north were the Bahmanis of Gulbarga and Bidar (1347 to 1489 AD). Scholars point out that for several centuries Karnataka was a meeting point of various religions and philosophies, and a centre of many different styles of art and architecture. In a sense, it was the place where cultures of the North and the South India met and fused. Notably the Hoysala style of art was the product of the combination of the Nagara style of the North and the Dravidian style of South India.

For ages now Karnataka has interacted with various cultures and absorbed them too and developed a culture of her own. Buddhism spread in parts of Karnataka and had a tremendous influence on her different spiritual traditions. Jainism, along with other spiritual cults such as Shaivism, Vaishnavisms had a deep impact on the life, culture and literature here. Truly, Karnataka was a confluence of many religions and philosophies.

Religious reformers such as Sankaracharya, Ramanujacharya and Madhavacharya have a strong following in this land. And Veerashaivism, the unique socio-religious and philosophical movement led by Basavanna in the 12th century Karnataka, was a great gift of this state to the people of this country. It is no exaggeration to say here that the Bhakti movement that spread throughout India had been influenced by Karnataka.

Except about a dozen Ashokan inscriptions and about 100 Shatavahana (mostly fragmentary) inscriptions in northern parts of Karnataka, all in Prakrit language, not much of recorded history of Karnataka is seen before the 4th century AD, when the Kadambas of Banavasi and the Gangas of Kolar (later Talakadu) emerged as ruling dynasties in Karnataka. Both these families had started their rule after revolting against the Pallavas of Kanchi. But it is only two copper plates (the Hirehadagali and the Sakrepatna plates) that speak of Pallava rule and no details of the nature and effectiveness of their administration over this land are known. No doubt in the northern parts, the Shatavahana rule had founded the Buddhist centres of worship at Sannati (in Gulbarga district) on the banks of river Bhima and it appears to have been a flourishing commercial centre too. Wadgaon—Madhavpur near Belgaum was also a small trading town of their times.

Undoubtedly Banavasi was a provincial capital of the Shatavahanas, being ruled by their subordinates, the Chutus, and a Buddhist *vihara* was founded at the place by a Chutu princess, Nagashri around the beginning of the Christian Era. There was also an *agrahara* at Talagunda founded by the Shatavahanas. Chutu Shatakarnis, the Shatavahana feudatories were ruling from Banavasi after the fall of Shatavahanas. The Pallava domination was ended by two indigenous dynasties namely, the Kadambas of Banavasi and Gangas of Talkad, who divided Karnataka between themselves. A young scholar from this *agrahara* had gone to Kanchi, the capital of the Pallavas perhaps to secure a degree at Kanchi, which also had a *ghatikasthana*, a centre where scholarship was recognised by conferring a degree called 'Ghatika Sahasi'. It is this young scholar Mayurasharma son of Bandhushena who founded the Kadamba dynasty in *circa* 345 AD. He gave up his hereditary priestly vocation and took to the life and career of a warrior by a revolt. The Pallavas recognised him as sovereign when he crowned himself at Banavasi.

Various dynasties that ruled and shaped the socio-economic and cultural space of Karnataka are briefly presented in Section 8.3. This is followed by some of the early phases of development in a historical perspective in the following sections.

8.3 The Heritage that Shaped the Economy

8.3.1. The Kadambas of Banavasi

Mayurasharma, this young scholar, was insulted at Kanchi, and being provoked, he revolted against the Pallavas and founded a new royal line of the Kadambas of Banavasi, having this old town as his capital. Banavasi had received Buddhist missionaries from the days of Ashoka and later was a capital of the Chutus. It was a merchant from this town who had built the famous huge monolithic Chaitya (rock-cut shrine) at Karle near Pune. Halasi was a centre of Jainism under the Kadambas.

8.3.2. The Agraharas

An *agrahara* was a settlement of scholarly Brahmins who were invited from far-off places in the north, and later, during Medieval period, such scholars were invited even from Tamil Nadu or Andhra. New *agraharas* were also created by inviting Brahmins from older *agraharas* in Karnataka. The Brahmin scholars in an *agrahara* were to engage themselves in six-fold duties (*shat karmas*) which included the undertaking of spiritual, academic, and charitable acts. They were to be first rate scholars in Vedic studies and also various ancient sciences like astronomy, *vastushastra* (architecture), *ayurveda* and other physical sciences. They guided agriculturists by telling them of the star that brought rain. Various encyclopaedias like *Brihatsamhita* of Varahamihira or *Lokopakara* of Kshemedra were known to them. They could guide people on agricultural practices, identifying water sources, grafting, animal husbandry, veterinary science, *vrikshayurveda* (treating the flora) and even other crafts like carpentry, pottery, smithy, etc. as these Sanskrit texts contained theoretical information on all these.

A 11th century Sanskrit encyclopaedia called *Manasollasa*, ascribed to Emperor Someshwara-III of Kalyana (1127-37) discussed 100 various topics including *vastu* (architecture), painting, textile production (cotton, silk, wool, etc.), jewellery making, carpentry, smithy, cookery (both vegetarian and non-vegetarian), etc., consolidating all traditional knowledge including the technical aspects.

No doubt, technical training was imparted in the various families of craftsmen hereditarily, like the cobbler, carpenter, basket maker, weaver, smith, potter, etc. as all crafts were domestic. But the scholars in the *agrahara* had the theoretical, and at least some of them, even practical knowledge of most of the crafts.

By the 13th century, every holy region of modern times had at least half-a-dozen exclusive *agraharas* settlements like the existence of colleges in our times, and in addition, every town had Brahmins' streets called *Brahmapuris*, and a huge secondary capital of the Kalyana Chalukyas called Ballignve (modern Belgami in Shimoga district) had many *brahmapuris* spread over various extensions. These scholars, well-versed in philosophic schools and worldly sciences, contributed in their own way to the economic development of a region.

While an *agrahara* was founded, fertile or already cultivated land was donated to the scholars, and as the land grant was free from all imposts (*sarvamanya*) or was on a nominal quit rent, they could appropriate the royal income (revenue share) from the lands and pursue their six-fold duties. But there are many instances when they were granted barren or unexplored lands. The donees brought the lands under plough and converted them into fertile fields by cutting trees, levelling the ground and creating tanks or canals. A record from Munirabad says that a Brahmin scholar was granted some village on the banks of the Tungabhadra, and he, like the splitting of the stem of a lotus, created a network of canals and made the whole region fertile during the 12th century. One 'Jalasutradhari' (hydraulic engineer) Singaya Bhatta turned the course of the Pennar river to provide water to Penukonda town during the 14th century (in Vijayanagara times).

The *agraharas* were so numerous and so powerful in public life that there was great intellectual activity in Karnataka and Buddhism, Jainism, Kalamukha, Pashupatha, Natha Pantha, and other Shaiva cults grew in Karnataka. There was intellectual freedom too. Acharya Shankara from Kerala found Karnataka intellectually alive and founded one of his main four Mathas at Sringeri. Acharya Ramanuja, harassed for his thoughts in his home province, Tamil Nadu, could find shelter in Karnataka and could get followers here. Basaveshwara, who had revolted against Vedic Varna system was born in the Bagewadi *agrahara* and he was the son of the chief of that *agrahara*. Acharya Madhwa also could propound his philosophy of dualism here.

8.3.3 The Badami Chalukyas

The Kadambas were overthrown by the Chalukyas of Badami in around 540, and Chalukya Pulakeshin II created a huge empire that extended from the Narmada in the north to the Cauvery in the south. They are remembered for their wonderful rock-cut shrines (caves) at Badami and Aihole and dozens of structural temples at Badami, Aihole and Pattadakal. Aihole had more than 100 temples and Pattadakal has huge monuments, now declared as World Heritage monuments by the UNESCO. They paid much importance to irrigation and Kendur and Banashankari tanks near Badami and over a dozens tanks at a single place called Gudigeri near Hubli are few examples of their wide irrigational activity. There was no practice of *sati* in their times and we come across widows of the royal family like Durlabha Devi, Vinayavati and Vijayanka being active in public life, and the last named being a governor in Konkan and noted Sanskrit poetess. Chalukyan art seen in their hard sandstone temples are wonderful examples of creativity. They started using Kannada in administration and their army, called as "Karnataka Bala", is described as invincible (*ajeyam*) by inscriptions and literary works. They had trade connection with Persia, China and southeast Asia. Hiuen-Tsiang from China visited the court of Pulikeshin II.

8.3.4 The Rashtrakutas

The Gangas in the south (who started ruling almost at the same time when the Kadambas ruled in northern parts of Karnataka) befriended themselves with the Chalukyas and later also the Rashtrakutas of Malakhed who overthrew the Chalukyas in 753 and inherited their vast empire. The Rashtrakutas continued their building activity and the famous Kailasa temple at Ellora (now in Maharashtra) and a cluster of temples at Shirival in Gulbarga district (now in ruins) are some examples of their structures. They had friendly relations with Arabs and overseas trade flourished. (Earlier Pulikeshin II had foiled the efforts of the Arabs to conquer Thana port near Mumbai.) Ports from Mangalore to Broach on the west coast were controlled by them. Emperor Krishna II had an Arab (Tajjika) governor in Konkan during the 9th century. The Arabs and their descendants, the Navayats and the Moplahs became an active commercial group on the coast.

Though practice of *sati* was slowly creeping in, we see a widowed lady being appointed as a Nadagavundi ('tahshildar') in Shimoga district in the place of her deceased husband. The first extant Kannada work

Kaviraja Marga was written in the days of Emperor Amogavarsha (814-78) and great Kannada poet Pampa lived during their times. Jainism flourished in Karnataka under the Rashtrakutas and their subordinates, the Gangas in the south. They founded notable *agraharas* at Kurugodu (300), Shirur (200), Kadiyur (modern Kalasapur, 200), Dandapura (Nargund, 200), Niragunda (120), Hatti Mattur (120), and Handigola (50) etc. to mention only a few, and the figures in parentheses indicate the number of *Mahajanas* or heads of families of scholars in those *agrahara* towns.

Both the Rashtrakutas and the Gangas created irrigation tanks. A piece of land called *bittuvatta* was assigned to a family or more in a village. The persons enjoying this land were entrusted with the responsibility of the upkeep of the irrigation facility, whether desilting the tank, repairing its embankment or maintaining its canals. The flourishing conditions of agriculture and animal husbandry in the Cauvery valley is testified by an inscription of Kirtipura (Kittur) in Mysore district. It says that the small region Punnata during the 6th century was a hub of agricultural activity. Ptolemy, a Greek geographer during second century says that Punnata was famous for beryl export.

8.3.5 The Kalyana Chalukyas

When the Chalukyas of Kalyana overthrew the Rashtrakutas, the two centuries of rule of the Kalyana emperors (973 AD to 1189 AD) and their subordinates like the Hoysalas in the south and the Sevunas (Yadavas) from Devagiri saw the flowering of the economic and cultural life of Karnataka. Of course, the Gangas in the south stopped cooperating with the new imperial Chalukyas power and tried to assert their freedom. The tragic outcome was their annihilation and southern Karnataka or 'Gangavadi' which came under the sway of the Cholas of Tanjore for more than a century (1000 to 1114 AD).

The Chalukyas of Kalyana had to struggle against the Cholas. But they encouraged irrigation, encouraged agriculture more than ever before and industry, especially textile. They raised hundreds of beautiful temples and also created *agraharas*. More urban centres emerged such as Badami, Aihole, Gadag, Betgeri, Hanagal, Rattihalli, Halasi, Belgaum, Managoli, Balliganve, Bagevadi, Bagadage (Bagalkot), Sedam, Kalgi, Itagi, Kukanur, Kuruvatti, Shravanabelagola, Annigeri, Arasikere, Haveri, etc. They grew to be important centres of trade and also of textile weaving. Annigeri had a guild of weavers claiming a membership of 1000 weavers ('Saligasasirvar'). Temples in hundreds in soft soapstone, famous for their intricate carvings were raised at Itagi, Lakkundi, Gadag, Balliganve, Kuruvatti, Dambal, etc., and their feudatories like Kadambas of Goa, Kadambas of Hanagal, Rattas of Saundatti (later Belgaum), Sindhas and others not only created their capital towns, but these towns grew by the raising fine temples, forts and *agraharas*. Hanagal, Halasi, Huli, Deganve, Saptasagara, Sannati, Satti, Rattihalli, Mulgund, Ron, Annigeri, etc. were some such glaring examples. Industrial and plantation (especially of betel leaves, areca, etc.) increased and Mangalore, Bhatkal, Kumta, Goa, etc. had flourishing overseas trade, not to speak of ports in Konkan. Hubli was famous as Eleya Purvahalli for its betel plantations. We hear of 'Tigalas' in a record from Hooli. Rivers like the Varada, Tungabhadra, Malaprabha, etc. were harnessed for irrigation by raising check dams. Ranna speaks of Araghatta or Persian wheel and Basavanna of *yeta* (piccota). One Aditya Bhatta form Pulige on the banks of Tungabhadra had created a network of irrigation canals.

In the south too Cholas were great builders and created many tanks as at Bellandur and Pattandur near Bangalore, Kudlur and Honganur near Chennapatna, and many more in Mysore district area. They founded *agraharas* and raised temples at Malur near Channapatna, Talakadu, Kollegal, Begur near Bangalore, Nandi, Kolar, and other places. They also founded *agraharas*, and such places have the suffix 'mangala'. They gave great fillip to agriculture and economic activity.

8.3.6 The Hoysalas

Later when the Hoysalas threw the Cholas out from Karnataka in around 1116, they continued the work of the Cholas in developing irrigation and paid special attention to irrigation and trade. They created weekly shandys, and many traders from Kerala also settled down in Karnataka and ports like Mangalore, Malpe, and Barkur were their overseas trade outlets. Halebidu, Harihar, Kiruvennagara (near Talakadu), Melukote, and Kodiyala were great centres of textile weaving among other towns in their kingdom. Sheep rearing and blanket weaving were equally widespread in Chitradurga-Davanagere belt.

Unprecedented encouragement was given to irrigation. Ereyanga, father of Vishnuvardhana says that in the days of his father Vinayaditya during 11th century, "who has kept an account of the ponds, streams, tanks he created in Gangawadi?" It was full of water sources. He also created sluices to tanks, records indicate. Vinayaditya also expanded the Dwarasamudra tank and made land grant (*bittuvatta* or *Kattukoduge*) for its upkeep.

The Hoysalas too created wonderful temples at Belur, Halebidu, Mosale, Belavadi, Amritapura, Doddagaddavalli, Arasikere, Kikkeri, Somanathapura, Talakadu, etc. and their number exceeds thousand. Every temple had *agraharas* founded to take care of their services and irrigated lands donated to the scholars of the *agraharas*. Trade routes were created and commercial centres increased. Trade and professional guilds also grew in number and were very powerful. The temples built by the Kalyana Chalukyas and Hoysalas, using polished soapstone are unique pieces of art, known for their intricate art work. A Hoysala record says that tall rocky hills were reduced to be deep tanks due to stone quarrying for temples, and the burden and the frequency of the movement of cartwheels transporting these stones to temples had created new streams and rivulets. All this temple building activity required sufficient economic surplus, outcome of flourishing agriculture, trade and crafts. Malnad was also a rich sources of wealth, not far away from ports on the west coast.

8.3.7 The Vijayanagar Empire

The Vijayanagar Empire founded in 1336 maintained peace and helped growth of prosperity. Vijayanagara decentralised power. New subordinate rulers came into existence. Sonda, Keladi, Ikkeri, Bilgi, Bidanur, Harapanahalli, Kanakagiri, Madhugiri, Chitradurga, Bangalore, Basavapatna, Santebennur, Chikkanayakanahalli, Avati, Srirangapattana, Mysore, Karkala, Mudabidre, Bellary Anegondi, etc. were new capitals which grew as major urban centres. Military roads were created and these helped the movement of merchandise too. Ports on the west coast which were frequented by Arabs, Persians, Chinese and other traders had now European visitors, beginning with the Portuguese (after 1498). Kumble, Ullala, Mangalore, Malpe, Hangarakatta, Basrur, Gangolli, Bhatkal, Kumta, Mirjan, Honnavar, Ankola and Sadashivgad (modern Karwar) were important ports.

The Portuguese conquered Goa in 1510 from the Bijapur rulers. They forced the traders at the ports of Karnataka to sell them goods at the prices they themselves quoted, despite the fact that the strong Vijayanagar empire was well-entrenched in the interior.

The Vijayanagara Empire could not staunchly oppose them for a variety of reasons. Firstly the empire wanted to buy good war horses brought from the Middleeast by the Portuguese, as the Arab traders mostly sold the horses to their co-religionist Muslim rulers in the Deccan like the Bahmani rulers (ruling from Gulbarga from 1347, later from Bidar from 1426) and also to the Adilshahis of Bijapur, (the dynasty being founded in 1489). Secondly, the Vijayanagar empire did not have modern firearms and a navy to encounter the Portuguese.

But the Vijayanagara rulers like Shri Krishnadevaraya welcomed the new comers, bought war horses from them, and foresaw the rich potential of European market for Karnataka's products like rice, textiles, silk, iron ore, teak wood, sandalwood and other forest products like pepper, cinnamon, cardamum, etc., which the Europeans longed to have in addition to precious stones like diamonds and pearls. Being rivals to the Arabs, the Portuguese could help explore wider markets was the expectation which was accurate.

8.3.8 The Portuguese on the Coast

The mutual squabbles among the petty rulers on the coast was another problem that was to the advantage of the Portuguese. In about 1550, the administration of the major parts of the coastal belt was entrusted to the Nayakas of Keladi (later Bidanur). The Portuguese succeeded in having their own factories at Honnavar, Basrur and Mangalore in the 1560s. But European rivals like the Dutch, French, and the English arrived on the scene. The British founded a factory at Kadwad on the Kali in the 1630s and signed an agreement with 50,000 weavers for the interior till Hubli, Gadag and Raibag to supply textile goods. The Portuguese entrenched themselves in Goa, but could not challenge the British forever.

The advent of the Europeans gave greater fillip to trade with the West and the Middle East. Rice, salt, teak, sandalwood, spices, etc. were in demand. Silk weavers from Khandesh migrated to Hubli. Christian converts (by the efforts of the Portuguese) introduced new techniques in carpentry and production of copper and brass vessels. From the new world came groundnut, tobacco, potato, onion, cashew nut, chilly, and a variety of items like papaya, pineapple, tomato, etc. through the Portuguese and this revolutionised agriculture in Karnataka, though after several decades.

Sati prevailed, though not common. Polygamy was not the general practice. Women engaged themselves as sales persons and guards and palanquin bearers in royal households. Trade and warfare provided scope for social mobility. Slavery prevailed, both domestic and agristic, and agristic slaves were mostly the 'untouchables'. Islamic rule gave greater fillip to this practice, and domestic slaves increased in number.

8.3.9 The Muslim Rulers

The Bahmanis built fine Indo-Sarsenic buildings and forts. They strengthened the forts at Kalyana, Raichur, Bidar, Gulbarga and Mudgal. Use of mortar in buildings became more popular. Wonderful monuments were raised at Gulbarga, Bidar and at Ashtur near Bidar. Bidariware developed as a craft. Production of joss sticks and perfumes received fillip. Silk weaving and embroidery work became further popular. Later Bijapur grew as an important city under the Adilshahis and they built fine monuments at Bijapur like Gol Gumbaz and Ibrahim Roza. Shahpur (near Belgaum), Gogi, Shahpur (Gulbarga at) Bagalkot, Belgaum, Khanapur, Sampangaum, Hubli, Mugutkhan Hubli, Raibag, Athani, Bankapur, Ranebennur, etc. further expanded as commercial towns. From Hubli, the Bijapur rulers could reach Kadra by land and from there, through the Kali reach Sadashivgad port. The English increased their trade from Kadwad, a village on the banks of Kali. The Dutch also reached the west coast and for some time competed with the English and the Portuguese. The Portuguese's high-handedness in trade was curbed by Shivappa Nayaka of Keladi (1646-1660) by throwing them out of their factories at Mangalore, Honnavar and Basrur. The Keladi Nayakas (1500-1763) enjoyed the benefits of the rich coastal trade and also of the forest products of the Malnad. Rice from the coast was in great demand in the Middle East, and a particular variety of rice was called "muscati" as it was in great demand at Muskat.

Vijayanagar had systematised land settlement and finalised the revenue called as 'Rayarekhe'. This protected the landowners from harassment. Mohamood Gawan of Bidar, the noble minister (whose *madrasa* or school building at Bidar is famous) also had reorganised revenue system in a rational way. Keladi Shivappa Nayaka (1645-1660) who ruled over the Malnad and coastal region further systematised it in his realm and this is famous as 'Shivappa Nayaka's Sistu' and he brought lot of fallow land under cultivation.

If Vijayanagara encouraged Carnatic music, Bijapur patronised Hindustani music. Ibrahim Adilshah II (1580-1626) had 300 singers in his court. To introduce Hindu music to Muslims he composed *Kitab-e-Nauras* in Urdu containing new songs, and the work begins with an invocation to Goddess Saraswati and Ganapathi. The Sufi saints visiting Gulbarga, Bidar and Bijapur created vast literature and folk songs in Urdu, which is called 'Dakhni Hindi'. Bande Nawaz is one among them. The rule of the Bahmanis, Adilshahis and Haider and Tippu saw the spread of Islam. Mosques in various towns and villages had *madrasas* attached to them to teach the children the three R's and also theology.

8.3.10 The Marathas and the Mughals

The Marathas, beginning with Shivaji started their activities in Karnataka. But his father Shahji had been appointed Jahgirdar of Bangalore by the Bijapur rulers in 1638, after conquering it from Kempegowda family (who had created the new town, Bangalore in 1537 as per the orders of Vijayanagar Emperor, Achutaraya). Bangalore grew as a noted centre of weaving, and so was Doddaballapur (a town created by Hoysala Ballala II and known originally as 'Ballalapura') and Sarjapura. Shivaji built strong forts at Nargund, Ramdurg, Gajendragad, Parasgad, and Sampagon and helped the growth of new towns. Hubli, Gadag, Betgeri, Ron, Gajendragad, Kamatgi, Ilkal, Ramdurg, Shahpur, Hanamsagar, Gudur etc. had flourishing cotton weaving.

Bijapur kingdom was conquered by the Moghuls in 1686. They came till Bangalore in the south and reached Arcot. They forced all Bijapur's feudatories into submission and handed over Bangalore on lease to Chikkadevaraya of Mysore. Chikkadevaraya was an able administrator, who systematised revenue collection. He patronised Kannada poets. He had ordered that on his death (which occurred in 1704) none of his 17 queens should perform *sati*. This was a wonderful example to end the practice, which was slowly vanishing.

Shivaji's successors, the Maratha Peshwas secured the right of collecting *chauth* and *sardeshmukhi* from the six southern Subahs of the Moghuls, and conducted periodic raids in the south, reaching even Srirangapattana, the capital of Mysore.

The powerful Mysore rulers were keen on securing Trichinapally (Tiruchirapalli) in Tamil Nadu, as the controlling of the Cauvery waters for irrigation was important for them. This adventure proved very costly. The Arcot succession wars (Cale called as Carnatic Wars) are famous. The Mysore court turned bankrupt because of this aggression and the demands of the Marathas, and this helped Haider Ali to secure control over the weak Mysore Administration after 1761.

8.3.11 Mysore Rulers, Haider and Tipu

Haider Ali conquered Keladi (1763) and secured immense wealth accumulated in the treasury of this Malnad kingdom and the fertile west coast with flourishing ports, commanding overseas trade. He made use of cavalry for quick movement of the army, used trained mercenaries from all over, followed European techniques of warfare and challenged the British. The rich capital Srirangapatnam with its 1.50 lakh population supported Bangalore's craftsmen, including silk weavers whom Hyder brought from Tanjore. Hyder liquidated many petty rulers like those of Devanahalli, Chitradurga, Harapanahalli, Sonda in addition to Keladi and achieved unification of vast Kannada speaking areas though Marathas in the north and the Nizam (the successor of Mughuls) in the northeast held considerable Kannada speaking territories.

His son, Tipu Sultan, highly innovative, produced rockets, introduced sericulture by bringing experts from Bengal, developed sugar industry with the help of Chinese experts, founded factories to forge guns at Taramandalpeth in Bangalore and at Kanakanahalli (Kanakapura). Channapatna, Kollegal, and modern Ramanagaram grew as centres of sericulture.

8.3.12 British Rule Begins

The British East India Company conquered Mysore kingdom in 1799 after defeating Tipu, retained Malabar, Canara and areas in Tamil Nadu. The princely Mysore state was handed over to the Hindu princely family Krishnaraja Wodeyar III (1799), a boy of five who became the ruler, and Purnaiah, the Dewan. When the Prince came of age, he ran the administration till 1831, (Figure 8.1) and as was found inefficient, the British took over the reigns of Mysore till 1881. Commissioners' Cubbon and Bowring modernised Mysore administration. All-season roads connecting all district headquarters with Bangalore, the new capital from 1831 were laid. Government Kannada and English schools were opened. Bangalore Cantonment, acquired by the British in 1808 helped introducing Western ideas and institutions and also European architecture, technology and medicine.

The region to the north of the Tungabhadra was under of the Marathas till 1818, and British, after its conquest incorporated it in the Bombay Presidency which included old districts of Dharwad, Bijapur and Belgaum, and later North Canara (Karwar in 1862) became part of the Bombay state. Over a dozen Kannada speaking regions remained under the Maratha states like Jamkhandi, Mudhol, Sandur, Ramdurg, Wadgaon and parts of Sangli, Miraj, Miraj Junior, Aundh, Kurundwad, and a Muslim state Savanur together with princely regions like Mysore and Hyderabad. Kodagu (Coorg) was acquired by dethroning the Raja by the British in 1834. The present state of Karnataka was 'distributed' among 20 administrations prior to 1947.

It was during this time (18th century) that a Sufi saint had procured coffee seeds from the Middle East to the Malnad area and the British encouraged the starting of coffee plantations in the 1840s in Kodagu and Chickmagalur-Hassan ghat belt, and these plantations later flourished. Mysore Commissioner Cubbon took special steps to encourage coffee estates. The Abolition of Slavery Act, 1843 by the British government helped to secure freed slaves as labourers in these plantations especially from the Canara district. They were also engaged in construction of roads across the Western Ghats by the PWD.

The first railway line connecting Bangalore with Jolarpet and, further to Madras was opened in 1864. Bangalore-Mysore rail link was opened in 1882, Bangalore-Pune in 1889, and Bombay-Madras connection in 1874, passing through Raichur and Gulbarga. Mangalore was linked with Madras in 1907.

Protestant missionaries started printing in 1830s and 1840s. The Mysore Palace started a press in 1841. The first Kannada newspaper *Mangalura Samachara* was published in 1843 by Basel Mission's Rev. Moegling and printing soon became widespread conveying knowledge faster and providing textbooks to schools. Mangalore, Mysore and Bangalore became notable centres of printing.

8.4. Religious Diversity

8.4.1 The Temples

The earlier form of worship under Hinduism included the forces of nature which however changed under the impact of Buddhism and Jainism's practices of temple worship. This crept into Hinduism—the *Stupas* and *Vihars* being the fore runners of Hindu temples. The age of *Puranas* heralded the dynastic rule of Sathavahans, the Vakatakas and architectural origin of Hindus temple styles. Kings, nobles, ministers, and the rich founded the *agraharas* and built temples in them. Building of temples provided work to thousands of quarry workers, stone cutters, builders and labourers and every temple provided employment to considerable number of men like priests, reciters of *Puranas*, palanquin bearers, flag bearers, fly whisk bearers, cooks, sweepers, the orchestra, the dancing girls, etc. A Hoysala temple at Somnathpur had nearly 60 servants, for whom provision for payment was made by land grants. A temple was also a consumer of goods like foodstuffs, items like coconut, plantains, betel leaves, betel nut, oil for lamps and a large variety of items used in daily services of the temple.

A temple's small tank (*kalyani*) provided drinking water to the village, and some bigger tanks provided water to its flower gardens and at times also to the neighbouring lands. The *aggishte* (perennial ritual fire) supplied fire every morning to the hearths in the village. The temple Basava (a bull maintained in a Shiva temple) helped the insemination of the village cattle. The temple building provided shelter to the homeless ramblers and itinerary traders and travellers. Part of the food offered to the deity was used to feed travellers and mendicants. Recital of *Puranas* and folk songs in praise of the deity were undertaken as means of popular education. If there was a *jatra*, various community groups undertook various duties like whitewashing the building, decorating the premises, etc. like one caste group whitewashing the building, another decorating the premises with green festoons, or a third caste decorating the car (*ratha*), etc. Village corporate bodies (assemblies) met in the temple and disputes too were settled in temple premises. Some donated the first calf born in a house to the temple and temples maintained herds of cattle. Instead of land or cash deposits, sheep were also donated to temple to help perform certain specified services. (The present generation of scholars and artists like singers, dancers or folk performers are mostly descendants of such persons attached to temples.) In coastal Karnataka, temples maintain Yakshagana troupes even today.

The Kadambas and the Gangas, to begin with built many temples and created many more *agraharas*. The Talagunda *agrahara* to which Kadamba Mayurasharma belong came to be expanded with thousands of scholars being settled there. The Ganga structures at Kolar, Talakadu, Narasamangala, Kambadahalli, Shravanabelogola, etc. still exists, some of them being Jaina *bastis*.

The Kadambas (*circa* 345 to 540 AD) created tanks at Chandravalli near Chitradurga and Gudnapur near Banavasi, to mention the known.That they had trade connections with Rome is testified by the Roman coins found at Banavasi. Halasi, Gokarna, Triparvata (Devagiri) and Uchchangi were major towns of their times and undoubtedly they had flourishing ports on the West Coast.

8.4.2 *The Mathas*

Some temples had *mathas* (mutts) attached to them, and a *matha* was a residential school where the teachers and the taught stayed together to engage themselves in academic pursuits. But mostly Brahmin boys were educated here. Later a *mathas* came to have restricted meaning, being described as the resort of ascetics, especially among the Veerashaivas, but teaching continued in these *mathas* also, mostly for the Veerashaivas. The Jain *mathas* also taught boys, but in other castes, the rich engaged private teachers to educate their boys. But technical education was provided in the families of the craftsmen hereditarily.

Temple *jatras* also organised trade fairs and itinerary merchants from far and near came to these *jatras* and people bought their annual needs of clothes, vessels, livestock, etc., at these temporary markets, and novel consumer goods too from far-off places were popularised at these *jatras*.

8.4.3 *Virasaivism*

A consideration of Virasavism is of great importance and relevance to understand the process of social development for two reasons: one, the Veerashaiva movement or traditions highlights certain facts that are true of all great spiritual traditions in this country. Veerashavism developed as both an internal and external critique of the dominant religions and social beliefs and practices of the day, and blazed a new path in the understanding and practice of *adhyatma* or spirituality and social goodness. Two, like many a religious movement in this country, Veerashaivism too, despite its radical spirituality and criticism and rejection of caste system and other social evils, eventually succumbed to the ubiquitous caste principle to become yet another caste, known as the Lingayat community today.

Akka Mahadevi, Basavanna and Allama Prabhu were the leading figures of the spiritual radicalism of the 12th century Karnataka. Akka, through her lifestyle and *vachanas* (composition in poetic prose) proclaimed not merely absolute equality between men and women, but also a state of being beyond sexual dualism which has

FIGURE 8.1

The Wodeyars of Mysore (1800 AD–1831 AD)

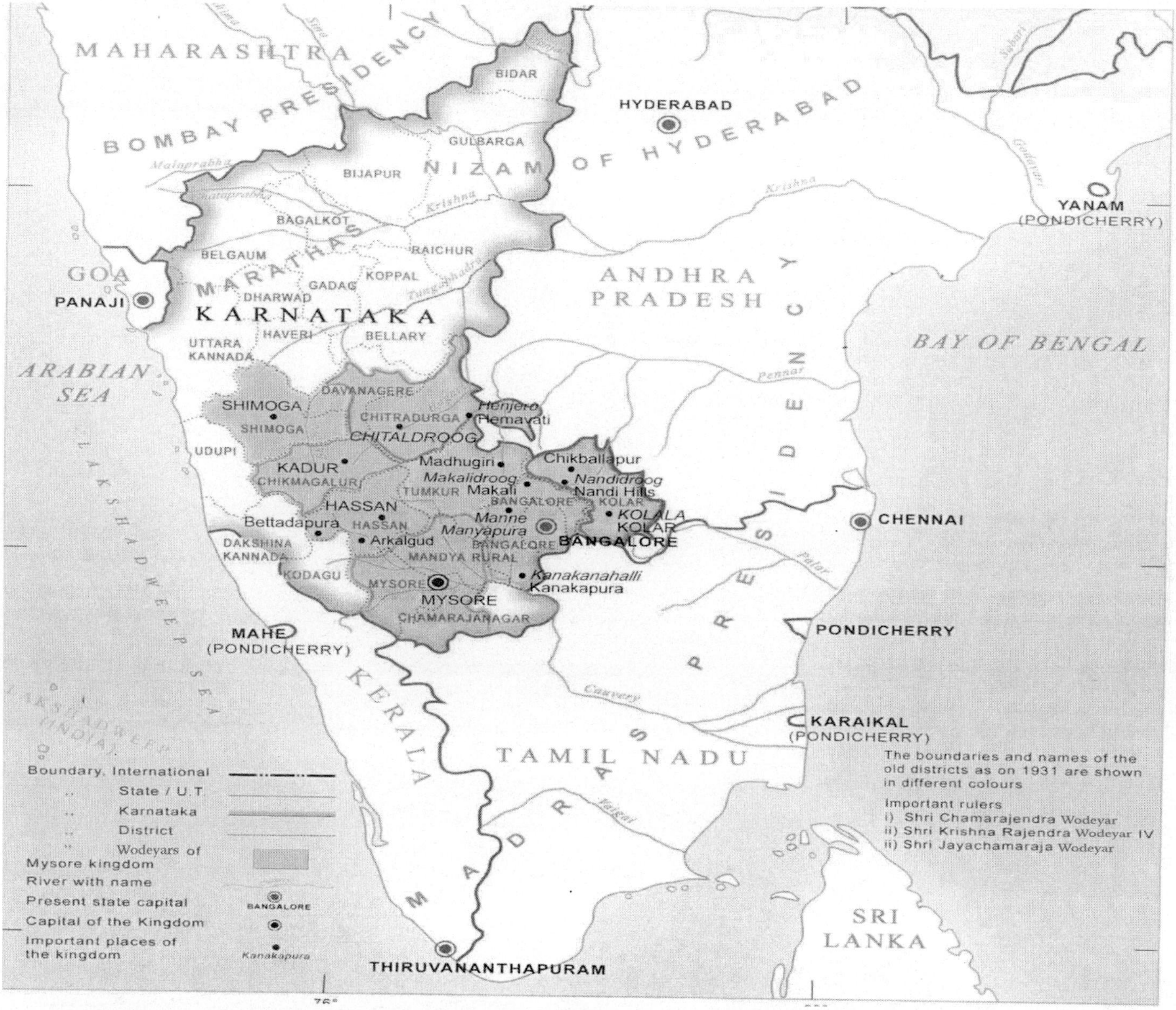

Source: Directorate of Census Operations Karnataka: *A Historical Atlas of Karnataka*.

tremendous psychological and socio-political implications in our culture even today. Allama was a mystic poet, a guru of gurus, who rejected all social symbols, even religious faith in his, what may be called, direct perception or experience of God or Reality. Basavanna of course was a saint with a vision of an egalitarian social order and compassionate life. His teachings drew literally hundreds of thousands of people from the lower castes into the movement. Though born in Brahmin family he rejected the caste system and asserted equality between human beings. He stressed the value of kindness towards all creatures as essential to *dharma*. He was critical of the dominance and exploitative character of temple culture. 'Work is worship' he proclaimed, thus asserting the dignity of labour.

Ironically, it was the reassertion of the caste principle through the King Bijjala (in whose court Basavanna was a minister) that rendered almost a death blow to the revolutionary zeal of the movement. When Basavanna supported the marriage of two children of the *sharanas* belonging to two different castes (the boy belonged to the cobbler community and the girl a Brahmin), King Bijjala, backed by the priestly class and supporters of caste practices, got the parents of the couple killed. The commotion that followed resulted in the murder of the King, after which the King's son unleashed a reign of terror on the followers of Basavanna. And Basavanna himself had to relinquish his ministership and leave the Capital.

Today there are numerous religious centres or what are popularly called Lingayat mutts spread all over the state. These mutts have rendered great services by taking education even to the remote corners of the state. That is something to be appreciated and recognised. However, the mutts do not appear to be so very free of religious dogmatism and rituals of which Basavanna was very critical. There is a need, it is felt, to rediscover and reassert Basavanna's teachings, in order to critique casteism and religious dogmas, and work towards a just and an egalitarian society.

Four centuries later, what is called *bhakti* movement spread all over the country, which shared some of the concerns of the Vachanakaras. The heroes of this movement emerged from all castes, in great numbers especially from lower castes. By and large they all spoke and sang about the importance of *bhakti*, surrender to God in one's pursuit of self-realisation. They all unequivocally spoke against casteism, against all narrow, constricting identities and dogmas that became barriers or obstacles to one's realisation of truth and God.

The great leader Ambedkar though started as an admirer of these *bhaktas* their spiritual radicalism grew critical of them later. For, according to him, the *bhakti* culture of course talked of equality, but it was equality before God, but this attitude did not manifest in the day-to-day social relationship of people. It remained a noble sentiment but could not lead to any structural changes in the Hindu society, nor build a base for an egalitarian society.

8.5 Development of Literature and Culture

8.5.1 Literature and Cultural Historical Roots

This epoch also saw great literary activity in Kannada and Sanskrit. After Pampa came Ranna at the Chalukya court, composing famous epic *Gadayuddha* and many Jaina works. Nagachandra wrote *'Jaina Ramayana'*. Durgasimha *Panchatantra* and Kirtivarma *Govaidaya* on veterinary science in Kannada.

In the Hoysala court lived Kannada poets like Harihara (work *Girijakalyana*), Raghavanka (*Harischandra Kavya*), Janna (*Yashodhara Charite*), Rudrabhatta (*Jagannatha Vijaya*) and Keshiraja (*Shabdamanidarpana*), to mention the most important ones.

During Kalachuri usurpation at Kalyana (1162-84), grew vibrant Vachana literature in poetic-prose, spearheaded by Basaveshwara, Allamaprabhu and Akkamahadevi with the message for disregarding caste barriers and stressing toiling or bread-labour with the slogan *Kayakave-Kailasa*, the message of hard work to produce real wealth through respect for all professions. Though the socio-religious movement of Basaveshwara received a setback, the message that bread-labour was service to God was not forgotten, helping the land to be prosperous by dedicated labour.

At the Kalyana court came to be written Sanskrit works like *Manasollasa* an encyclopaedia, which also propounded fine arts like music and dance. Even royal ladies like Savaladevi (Kalachuri Bijjala's daughter-in-law), Chandaladevi, Queen of Emperor Vikramaditya (1076-1127) VI and Shantaladevi, Queen of Hoysala Vishnuvardhana (1108-1141) were accomplished dancers, also well-versed in music. This encyclopaedia by Emperor Someshwara III has technical details of all arts and crafts, as already seen.

Sharngadevas at Sevuna court (Devagiri) composed *Sangita Ratnakara* in Sanskrit, and *Manasollasa* further improved the theories on music and also speaks of variety of musical instruments. The tradition continued later by Vijayanagara empire. Art, literature, music, dance scholarship flourished and so did agriculture, crafts and trade. Chalukya-Hoysala epoch, an era of all-round cultural progress, was supported by flourishing economic conditions.

The invasions of the Delhi Sultans army created a political vacuum in South India with the destruction of the power of the Sevunas or Yadavas of Devagiri (Daulatabad), the Kakatiyas of Orangal and the Hoysalas of Halebidu, who were all subordinates of the Chalukyas of Kalyana, and they later had become independent after the fall of the Chalukyan empire in 1189. But all these powers, by creating irrigation facilities had improved agriculture. By raising hundreds of beautiful centres of worship and providing lands for their maintenance, created jobs for thousands. Many temples became centres of pilgrimage, help creating new towns like Itagi, Melukote, Kudalasangama, Harihara, Hanagal, Halasi, Gokarna. Dhareshwar, Raibag, Sapatasagar, Udupi, Bagewadi, Gadag, Lakkundi, Soratur, Sedam, Kalgi, Annigeri, Balliganve, Kalyana, Arasikere, Basaralu, Kikkeri, Shravanabelagola, Hiremagalur, Vastare, Belgaum, Saundatti, Banavar, Halebidu, Asundi, etc. and became important commercial and also industrial centres.

Jainism was weakened because of the spread of Veerashaivism in northern Karnataka, Srivaishnavism in southern Karnataka and Vaishanavism propounded by Madhwacharya on the west coast. But as a political power, the Jainas were strong on the west coast during Vijayanagar times, raising monument at Karkalla, Mudabidre, Bhatkal and Bilgi. (It is very difficult to explain how the Udupi Vaishnavas became dominant in hotel industry and Hassan Srivaishnavas took to bread baking in our own times, and also Tamil Advaitins or Iyers started hotels by the close of the 19th century and the beginning of the 20th century and dominated the field for some decades. Their traditional profession was no longer lucrative and rivalry in that field was strong, can be one explanation.)

Forts built by these rulers at strategic places where hundreds of soldiers were posted also gave rise to new towns like Bidar, Raichur, Shahpur (Sagar), Mudugal, Bagalkot, Ballalarayanadurga, Mulluru, Niragunda, Hosadurga, Narasimhagad (Jamalabad), Betamangala, Nagamangala, etc. Various craftsmen and traders migrated to these new centres and towns grew in size, giving fillip to economic activity.

8.5.2 Conservation of Cultural Tradition

Karnataka which has innumerable tanks, beautiful temples, churches and European architectural speculations and mosques with the excellent domes, arches and minerates and towns of historical importance also has many sites of pre-historic period and most of them situated in the river valleys. Places like Hunasagi, Budihal, Pikhlihal, Kibbanahalli, Nittur, Anagavadi, Khad, Nyamati, Balehonnur, Uppinangadi, Hirakal, Tamminahal, Savalgi, Pattadakal, Talkad, Ingaleshwar, etc. are noted prehistoric sites of Karnataka. The *ragi* grain was found commonly in prehistoric sites of Africa and Karnataka.

Of the 14 Ashokan rock edicts found in Karnataka, 2 each at Nittur and Udagolam in Bellary district, 1 at Maski in Raichur district, 1 each at Brahmagiri, Jattinga Rameshwara and Siddhapur in Chitradurga district, and 4 at Sannatti in Gulbarga district testify the glorious existence of the Mauryan Empire. It is interesting to note that Emperor Ashoka's name occur for the first time in Maski minor rock edict, wherein his familiar ephithet *Devanampiya Piyadasi* is accompanied with his personal name Ashoka. At Banavasi a horse shoe shaped stupa has been discovered. Sannati had many Buddhist stupas of their times with beautiful sculptures on them.

The Vijayanagara Empire encouraged all religions and languages of south India and undertook irrigation works on a wide scale. The court of Sri Krishnadevaraya comprised of *Asthadiggajas* or poets drawn from all the eight directions. The Royal Court was visited by celebrated foreign travellers like Domingo Paes, Nicolo County, Abdul Razak, Nuniz witness account of the grandeur and richness of the Vijayanagara Empire. Hinduism was revived by great saints and *rishis*.

The Hindu sect produced great men. The Advaita school had great men like Vidyaranya and his brother Sayanacharya. The Sringeri *Matha* came to be highly patronised by Vijayanagara rulers. A commentary on the Vedas was commissioned to be written by Emperor Bukka (1356-77) and the work in several volumes was completed in the days of Harihara II (1377-1404), and this commentary, *Vedarthaprakasha* was the work of several scholars under the guidance of Sayanacharya, popularly known as *Sayana Bhashya*.

To conserve traditional learning of India works like *Ayurveda Sudhanidhi* (on the Indian science of healing), *Alankara Sudhanidhi* (on rhetorics), *Yajnyatantra Sudhanidhi* (on the techniques of performing sacrifices),

Subhashita Sudhanidhi (on traditional 'quotable' statements), *Prayaschitta Sudhanidhi* (on religious expiatory rites) and *Purushartha Sudhanidhi* (on the four-fold duties of the Hindus) all in Sanskrit, came to be compiled by Sayanacharya. This was found necessary as all such information was under threat of annihilation or open to misinterpretation unless codified.

The Dwaita philosophy propounded by Madhwacharya (1236-1317) had its original seat at Udupi, but some of his close disciples like Madhava Tirtha, Narahari Tirtha and Akshobhya Tirtha had lived at Anegondi near Hampi. Later Maadhwa scholars like Teekacharya, Sripadaraya and Vyasateertha were associated with the capital and the second one was very close to the Emperor Saluva Narasimha (1491-1501) and the third one to Emperor Krishnadevaraya (1509-1529). There also lived famous saint poets in Kannada who upheld the concept of intense *Bhakti*, propounded by Madhwacharya's teachings like Purandara Dasa and Kanaka Dasa, great composers of devotional songs and also renowned vocalists of repute. Kumara Vyasa and Ratnakaravarni were great poets of the time, the latter being a Jaina.

Veerashaivism, after its setback during the 12th century, came to be revived at Hampi by the 101 Viraktas like Tontada Siddalinga Yati, Kallumathada Prabhuva, Chamarasa, etc. The Vachanas of the Sharanas were collected under the title called *Shunya Sampadane*, subject-wise. Veerashaiva Mathas were spread widely in the empire, fed the poor under the concept of *dasoha*. They also became centres of learning. Vijayanagar officers like Lakkanna Dandesha and Jakkanna Dandesha and rulers like Keladi Nayakas patronised Veerashaivism.

The later emperors of Vijayanagar like Krishnadevaraya and his successors were followers of Srivaishnavism, and patronised the religion. Portuguese traveller Barbosa vouches for the religious tolerance in the empire.

The empire repaired all old temples, provided all temples in south India with huge protective *prakaras*, tall *rayagopuras* and huge artistically wrought Kalyanamantapas including those temples in Andhra like Srishailam or Tirupati or in Tamil Nadu like Kumbhakonam or Chidambaram.

They also raised strong stone forts to protect them from gun attacks. Thus construction work provided jobs to thousands. Hampi grew as a great capital with fine monuments. They also undertook extensive irrigation works. One Madhavamantri built a dam across the Cauvery near Talakadu. A dam raised across the Haridra near Harihar by Devaraya I was damaged. A decade later it was rebuilt. The highly devastating Durgadevi famine which is believed to have lasted 12 years from 1398 gave fillip to more irrigation works. Bukka, Devaraya I and Krishnadevaraya toiled to provide not only drinking water to Hampi, but also water for irrigation in the empire by various fantastic irrigation projects. An inscription at Hampi in Kannada tells us that a noble mother, while feeding milk to her child dinned into its ears that he should build tanks, sink wells, create temples and such public works. This was the spirit inculcated in the young.

One minister of Achutaraya (1529-1541) called Bayakara Ramappa has created 16 tanks to the south of Hampi, all in the name of his close relatives. The famous Magada at Masur is a Vijayanagar creation later renovated by the Adilshahs. Innumerable tanks of the Vijayanagara rulers named after them dot the length and breadth of south India like Bukka Sagaram, Devarayasamudra, Krishnaraya Sagara, Sadashiva Sagara, etc. The feudatories also followed their example. European travellers who have visited the empire praised it for its greenery, the variety of crops, abundance of domestic animals and huge stocks of merchandise in its markets, their cheap price and the teaming flourishing population. This was not only due to natures bounty, but also due to state policy.

Social mobility was evidenced in the army organisation and the appointment of subordinate rulers like Bedas (Nayakas of Chitradurga, Kanakagiri or Harapanahalli), Vokkaligas at Bangalore or Avati, the Baligas at Channapatna or Madhurai and Lingayats at Keladi. The army officers also were from various castes. There are herostones, commemorating the death of the so-called untouchable soldiers.

Fine arts and music were at the height of patronage. Vidyaranya, Ramaamatya, Purandara Dasa and Kanada Dasa popularised Carnatic music. Dancing girls were provided to temples, and Dasara was a special occasion to demonstrate their talents, highly praised by foreign visitors like (Persian) Abdur Razzak.

Though the empire was destroyed (in 1565), its artistic and cultural traditions were continued by its subordinates that outlived the Empire like the rulers of Madurai, Tanjore, Chitradurga, Keladi and Mysore and Mysore Dasara is reminescent of the similar festival at Hampi.

The activities of the European seamen increased and trade continued though Goa lost its commercial importance for long as its proximity to capital, Vijayanagar was no longer there.

8.5.3 *About Kannada Culture*

Kannada culture has a unique identity of its own, yet, like all other cultures, Kannada has borrowed richly from other cultures as well. For, no culture develops in vacuum. The Tamil, Marathi and Telugu speaking people and their culture have contributed a lot to Karnataka just as Kannada has had a significant influence on other cultures. Also, Karnataka has absorbed and made its own influences from Jainism, Buddhism and Islam.

In modern times, the spread of education, introduction of printing, activities of the Christian missionaries and spread of liberal and democratic ideas were mainly responsible for the renaissance in Karnataka.

Christian missions started English schools in many parts of Karnataka in 1830s. And between 1840 and 1854, all the district headquarters in Mysore state came to have English schools. The Department of Education was founded in the princely state in 1858, and by 1881, the state had about 2,087 schools. College education too spread rapidly. Central College in Bangalore (1870), Maharaja's College (1869), Government Arts College (1869) and St. Aloysius College (1879) in Mangalore, St. Joseph's College (1882) in Bangalore, and Mysore University in 1916. The college and university education created a new awakening. Exposure to liberal ideas of the West and a rigorous rethinking on Indian cultures saw the rise of modern nationalism and a longing for social changes, emancipation of women and eradication of untouchability and such emancipatory ideals.

Starting of printing press hastened the process of modernisation as also the rediscovery of regional literature. The first book in Kannada came out in 1817, Kannada Bible (1820), Kannada newspaper (1843), and ancient Kannada works such as *Jaimini Bharatha* (1848) and *Basava Purana* (1850).

In the same period, Mysore state also witnessed a spurt of development in the art and theatre field. And the state witnessed establishment of institutions oriented towards radical, social and spiritual changes, such as Brahma Samaj in Mangalore (1870) and Bangalore (1864), Theosophical Society (1884) in Bangalore, Arya Samaj both in Mangalore (1919) and Bangalore (1894), Ramakrishna Mission (1904) and the Indian Progressive Union of Bangalore (1904).

8.5.4 *Cultural Development*

Karnataka's cultural heritage is rich and varied. Karnataka's history of about two 2000 years reveals a profuse growth of its language, literature, art and culture. The famous king and Kannada poet Nrupatunga in the ninth century described Karnataka as a vast land stretching from the river Godavari in the north to Cauvery in the south. The land was ruled by the array of distinguished dynasties like the Shatavahanas, Kadambas, Gangas, Chalukyas of Badami, Rashtrakutas, Hoysalas, the Chalukyas of Kalyani, the royal families of Vijayanagar, Hyder Ali, Tipu Sultan and the Wodeyars of Mysore and the Bahamani kingdoms of the Deccan. The art, sculpture, literature and painting were patronised during the rule of the famous kings of these dynasties. Karnataka's culture reached its zenith in Vijayanagar Empire.

Karnataka is surrounded on three sides by areas speaking Dravidian languages i.e. Tamil, Malayalam and Telugu and areas of Aryan languages like Marathi and Konkani in the North and Northeast. Due to the expansion or shrinking area, Karnataka's culture came under the influence of both Dravidian and Aryan. Under the British rule, Kannada speaking areas had been torn asunder. Under the linguistic reorganisation of the states, Kannada speaking areas of erstwhile Bombay state, Madras state, Hyderabad state and Coorg were merged with the erstwhile Mysore state in 1956. From 20 unity big and small, where Kannada was being spoken, these five regions had emerged (after mergers) soon after Independence. Kannada became the official language of the new Mysore state, which was renamed as Karnataka in 1973.

The greatest saints, philosophers and poets of this land, with their extraordinary range of vision and through their preachings moulded the beliefs and culture of Kannadigas in the 8th, 12th and 13th centuries. The names of some of those great personalities who made great impact on the people are Adi Sankaracharya, Ramanujacharya, Basavanna, Akka Mahadevi and a host of Shivasharanas, Haridasas, Kanakadasa and Purandaradasa.

An attempt is made here to present a bird's eye view of Kannada literature and fine arts i.e., music, dance, sculpture, etc. through many centuries.

FIGURE 8.2

Kannada Speaking People under Different Administrative Units: 1912

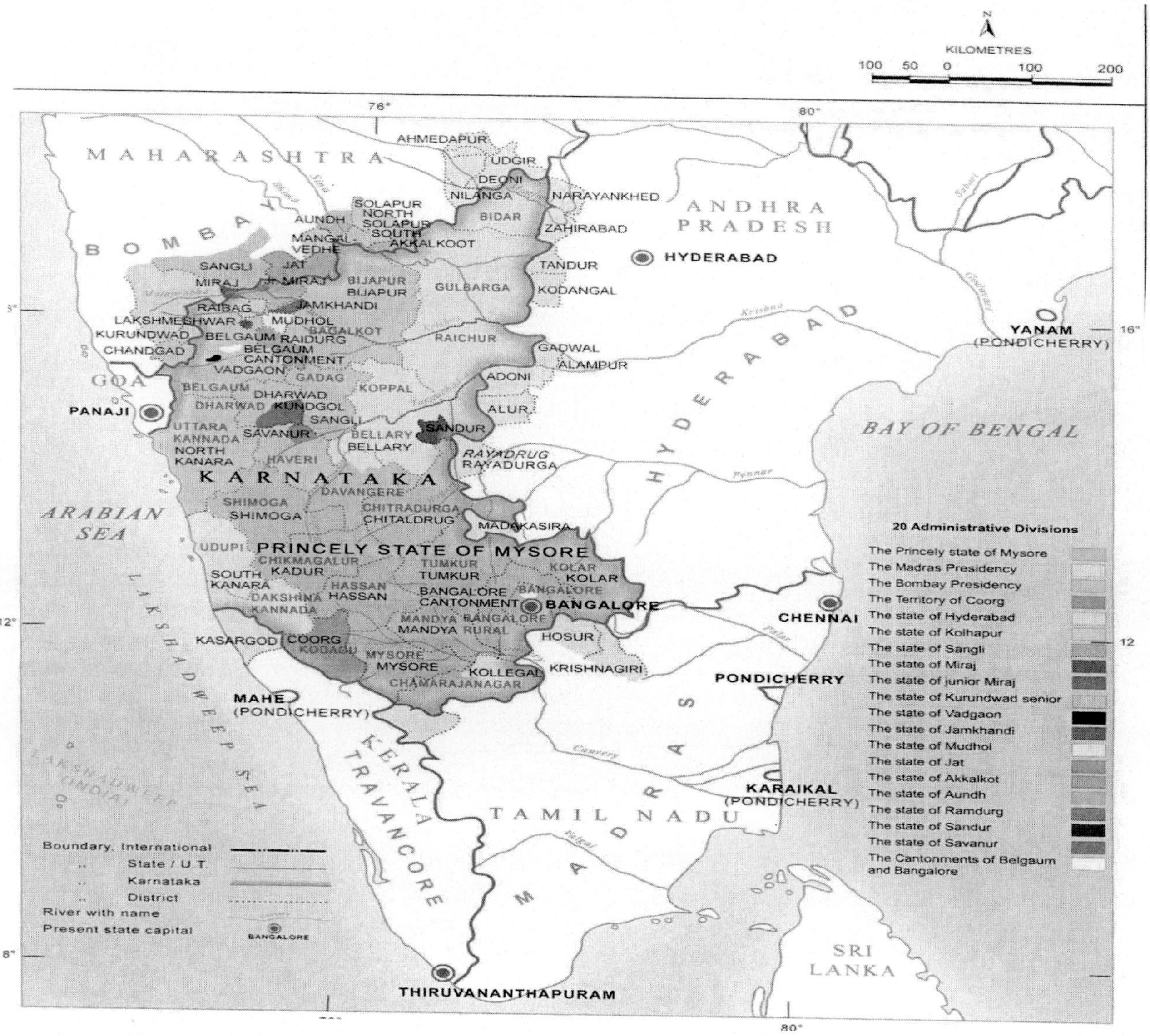

Source: Directorate of Census Operations Karnataka: *A Historical Atlas of Karnataka.*

8.5.5 Kannada Literature

Language and literature are important components of any culture, Kannada literature has a rich glorious past; its history going back to at least 1500 years. The oldest available literary work of Kannada is a book of poetry known as *Kavirajamarga* produced in the ninth century. Karnataka gave birth to numerous great poets of Kannada. The epic verse of a few poets could be comparable to those of Valmiki or Homer. The magnificent works of Kumar Vyasa, Lakshmisha, Shadakshari, Harihara, Raghavanka and Ratnakaravarni could match the best in the world's literature. The contribution of the great litterateurs, poets like Pampa, Ponna or Ranna of the 10th century, Vachanakaras of the 12th century, Sarvajnya, Purandaradasa and Kanakadasa of the 16th century enriched Kannada literature.

The influence of western literature and thought ushered in a new renaissance ('Navodaya Movement'). Among the many who contributed in this sphere, names of a few distinguished personalities could be mentioned—B.M. Sreekantayya, D.V. Gundappa, Masti Venkatesh Iyengar, Kuvempu, Bendre, Karanth followed by Kailasam, Sriranga, Anakru, Gokak and Adiga. In the post-Navodaya period, many literary figures contributed and enriched Kannada literature. Thereafter, Navyotthara Sahitya or Bandaya Sahitya or Dalitha Sahitya emerged. Feminist movement in Sahitya brought many women writers like Triveni, Indira to the forefront.

From the above it can be seen that many great literary figures including those who contributed to Vachana Sahitya or Dasa Sahitya hailed from north Karnataka, in the earlier periods. In fact the first renowned Kannada poetry work was produced in north Karnataka by the ninth century king Nrupatunga who ruled from Malakhed, which is now a part of Gulbarga district. From Navodaya movement and onwards, majority of literary figures are from south Karnataka.

8.5.6 Kannada—Evolution of the Language

An earlier reference to Kannada language can be found in the *Linguistic Survey of India* (1927, reprint 1967) by Mr. G.A. Grienson (Table 8.1). It mentions Kanarese, Kodagu, Tulu as languages of the Dravida group. It found that a large number of Kanarese speakers were found within the Bombay Presidency. This language was also found in Madras, the Nizam Dominions, Mysore and Coorg. The true centre of the Kanarese speaking people is Mysore. The character used for writing and printing Kanarese is clearly connected with that employed for Telugu, but the language itself possesses greater affinity to Tamil. The ancient Kanarese alphabet known as the *Hala-Kannada* which was the same as that in contemporary use for Telugu, dates from the 13th century, but since then, there has arisen a marked divergence between the two characters, which has increased since the introduction of printing in the course of the 19th century. The curved form of the letters is a marked feature. Up to the 16th century Kanarese was free from any admixture of foreign words, but since then, the vocabulary has been extensively mixed with Sanskrit. During the supremacy of Haider Ali and Tipu Sultan, Urdu words were largely imported into it from Mysore, and it has also borrowed from Marathi. On the northwest and from Telugu on its northeast. Dialects of Kanarese are Badaga, Kurumba and Golari. The first two are spoken in the Nilgiri Hills. The Badaga tribe, called by our early historians the Burghers, speak a language, which closely resembles old Kanarese. Kurumba or Kurumvari is the dialect of the forest tribe of Kurumbas or Kurubas, and is said to be a corruption of Kanarese with an admixture of Tamil. The Golars or Golkars are a tribe of nomadic herdsmen and the holiyas are a caste of leather-workers and musicians, both hailing from the central provinces. They both speak the same dialect of Kanarese, which is called indifferently Golari or Holiya (Figure 8.2).

TABLE 8.1

Dravida Group

Languages	*Survey*	*Census of 1921*
Tamil	15272856	18779577
Malayalam	5425979	7497638
Kanarese	9710832	10374204
Kodagu	37218	39995
Tulu	491728	592325
Toda	736	663
Kota	1201	1192
Total	**30940550**	**37287515**

Source: Linguistic Survey of India: G.A. Greenson, Vol. 1, Part I, Introduction, 1927.

Kanarese	*Survey*
Standard	9,666,163
Badaga	30,656
Kurumba	10,399
Golari, Others	3,614
Total	**9,710,832**

Source: Linguistic Survey of India.

Kodagu or Coorgi, the main language of Coorg is described as standing midway between old Kannada and Tulu. Tulu, immediately to the southwest of Kanarese, is confined to a small area in or near the district of South Kanara in the erstwhile Madras Presidency. It is a cultivated language, but has no literature. It uses the Kannada character. The remaining languages of the Dravida group are Toda and Kota, both by wild tribes in the Nilgiri Hills. By some they are considered to be dialects of Kanarese.

8.5.7 Language Diversity in Karnataka

In Karnataka, 96.54 per cent of the population speaks the 18 scheduled languages and 3.46 per cent speak 47 unscheduled languages specified in the Eighth Schedule of the Constitution. These percentages are more or less similar to the all-India pattern. Among the scheduled category Kannada occupies 66.22 per cent in the state. Urdu and Telugu have 9.96 per cent and 7.39 per cent respectively followed by Tamil 3.84 per cent and Marathi 3.65 per cent. These five languages account for over 91 per cent of the scheduled languages spoken in the state (Figure 8.3 and Figure 8.4). In Karnataka the percentage of scheduled languages across the districts suggest that in most of the districts it accounts for over 99 per cent whereas in Dakshina Kannada it is 54.96 per cent, Kodagu 74.60 per cent, Chickmagalur 94.06 per cent and Bangalore 98.98 per cent.

FIGURE 8.3

Number of Persons in the Scheduled Languages

Karnataka

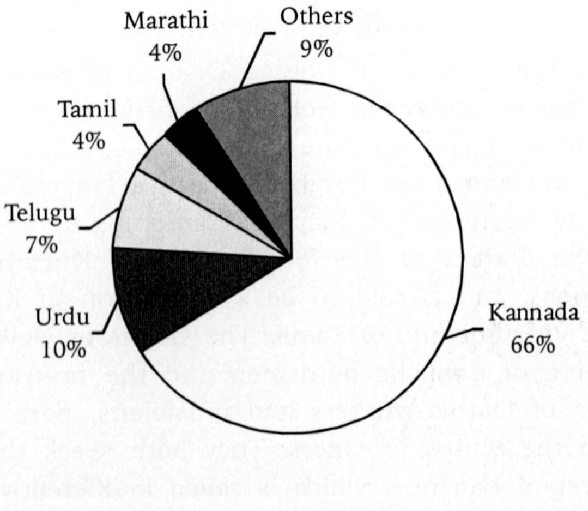

Source: Census of India.

FIGURE 8.4

Number of Persons in the Scheduled Languages

All India

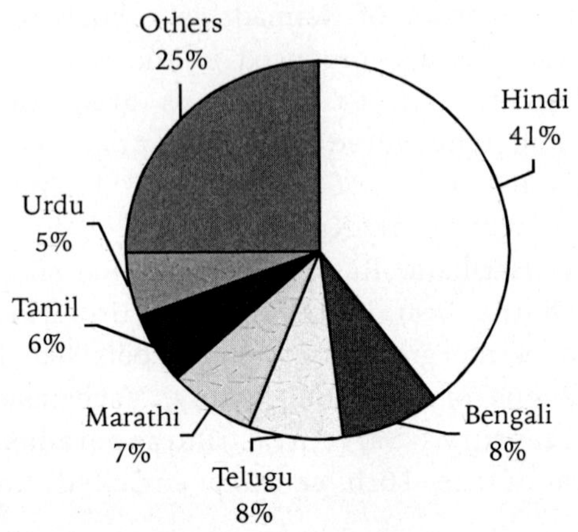

Source: Census of India.

Among the non-scheduled languages, Tulu occupies the prime place with the largest share of 88.70 per cent followed by Coorgi 6.19 per cent (Figure 8.5).

FIGURE 8.5

No. of Persons in the Non-Scheduled Languages: Karnataka

Major Languages

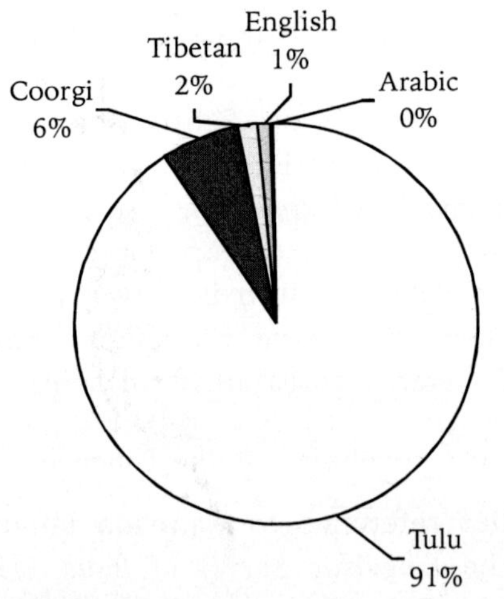

Source: Census of India.

8.5.8 Archaeology

Karnataka has the second largest number of inscriptions in the whole of India. Beginning from the Asokan edicts (BC 300) to the inscription of the kings of Vijayanagar, they are legions. In the field of art and architecture, Karnataka has its own contribution. The beginning of Chalukya architecture and sculpture is seen in the exquisite carvings of Badami, Aihole and Pattadakal temple complex as cradles of temple architecture. Hoysala style of architecture is found in the temples at Belur, Halebidu and Somanathpura. The architectural work here bears testimony to the aesthetic attainment of the rulers and their people. Each dynasty had shown interest in developing its own architecture and the monuments/sculptures built by them are known as Rashtrakuta style/Ganga and Chola style/Kalyani Chalukya style/Vijayanagar style of architecture. Forts spread over the nooks and corners of Karnataka are gigantic monuments to the architectural skill of the builders of Karnataka. Muslim rulers too built unique monuments like Gawaris Madrasa at Bidar, Ibrahimrosa and Golgumbaz at Bijapur. The Gomata monolithic is another example of outstanding sculpture. Modern architectural monuments can be seen in Churches, Vidhana Soudha and many modern buildings.

8.5.9 Music, Dance and Drama

Karnataka is popularly known as the birth place of Indian music. Carnatic music originated in this land. The most unique feature of Karnataka is that Karnataka and Hindustani styles of music prevail side by side. Karnataka has produced outstanding talented personalities. It may appear paradoxical that some of the great stalwarts of the Hindustani tradition are from North Karnataka. Mallikarjuna Mansoor, Bhimsen Joshi, Rajguru, Gangubai Hangal, to name a few are top-notch artistes in the Hindustani style. Even in Karnataka music, under the patronage of the Mysore Wodeyars, Sadashivaraya, Muthaiah Bhagavatar and Vasudevacharya composed hundreds of *Keerthanas* of exquisite beauty. The old Mysore is known as the beehive of Veenakaras. Veene Sheshanna, Bidaram Krishnappa (vocalist), and T. Chowdiah (with his seven-stringed violin), were the stalwarts.

Bharathanatyam has grown strong roots in Karnataka and the Hoysala queen, Shantala Devi herself is believed to be a great exponent in this art. Later the Mysore kings patronised this art and there were great performing artistes attached to the palace. Nowadays, a number of schools (i.e., teaching) institutes have sprung up. In the field of dance, Yakshagana is both a folk and the elite art that is flourishing especially in Dakshina and Uttara Kannada district.

There is again a lot of enthusiasm generated in the theatre movement. Kailasam and Sriranga are pioneers of the changing theatre scheme. In the recent past, Karnad, Karanth and Kambara have turned out exquisite plays.

8.5.10 Academies

Ten academies *viz.*, Karnataka Sahitya Academy, Karnataka Lalitha Kala Academy, Karnataka Sangeeta Nritya Academy, Karnataka Nataka Academy, Karnataka Urdu Academy, Karnataka Janapada and Yakshagana Academy, Karnataka Tulu Academy, Karnataka Konkani Academy, Karnataka Kodava Academy and Karnataka Patrika Academy were constituted in different years during the period from 1954-55 to 1980-81 and made autonomous bodies with a view to foster the development of literature, music, dance and drama and literay activities. These academies function under the control of the Directorate of Kannada and Culture except the Patrika Academy functioning under the Information Department. Each of these academies has a Chairman/President and members who are renowned figures in the perspective fields, nominated by government for a stipulated period. These academies plan their own schemes and hold programmes. Under the plan schemes, the activities of various academies are encouraged and supported by the government financially too. In the second Five Year Plan, construction of central national theatre at Bangalore and nine national theatres at district headquarters was taken up. In order to encourage the artists and drama writers, grants were awarded to institutions of fine arts and prizes were given to writers to publish the connected literature from time to time.

But Karnataka is the home of speakers of many languages like Tamil, Telugu, Marathi, Urdu, Konkani, Kodava and Tulu. Konkani and Tulu are found mostly on the coastal belt. One may be surprised to know speakers of many of these languages have contributed to Kannada culture and mainly to Kannada literature. For example, poet Bendre spoke Marathi; K.K. Rai, Tulu; Masti, Tamil, Karnad and Govinda Pai, Konkani; N. Kasturi, Malayalam; Nisar Ahmed, Urdu and Ta.Ra.Su. (T.R. Subba Rao, Telugu), B.M. Idinabba speaks Beary dialect.

The Sahitya Academy awards prizes to the best literary works, gives subsidy for organising seminars on Kannada literature. It arranges workshops to young/budding Kannada writers on all literary forms.

The Nataka Academy conducts drama festivals at various district headquarters and at Bangalore, besides arranging seminars and workshops on stage-craft. The academy helps the institutions/associations for arranging drama festivals/ seminars. It also provides scholarships to students studying in National School of Drama in New Delhi and other places. It runs a repertory at Mysore.

The Karnataka Lalit Kala Academy arranges exhibitions of paintings and extends financial aid to art institutions and awards prizes to artists.

The Sangeetha Nritya Academy gives aid to the institutions and associations for conducting programmes of music, dance, etc. It also conducts music and dance festivals at various places in the state.

The Janapada and Yakshagana Academy promotes this art and literature and gives financial assistance to institutions and associations, which arrange folk-art festivals from village *panchayat* level to district level.

The Urdu Academy promotes Urdu literature and encourages writers and poets by giving subisides.

Similar is the functions of Kodava, Tulu and Konkani academies to foster literary and cultural activities in these local languages.

The state government gives a monthly pension and honorarium to eminent persons who have rendered great service in the field of literature, music, dance, fine arts and folklore, drama, etc. as financial aid, on the recommendations from the respective academies.

BOX 8.1

Nurturing the Cultural Heritage

- Entire Vachana Sahitya will be made available in CDs; CDs of 1,000 Vachanas with musical tunes will be brought out
  - 'Kalagrama' to house all arts under one roof.
- Constructive programmes to commemorate birth centenary celebrations of Rashtrakavi Kuvempu. The period from December 29, 2003 to December 28, 2004 is declared as 'Vishwa Manava Varsha'. 'Jaya Bharatha Jananiya Tanujathe' is declared as "State Song" (Nadageethe). English version of Sri Ramayana Darshanam has been published. Postal covers with photograph of Sri Kuvempu released.
- Birth centenary of Dr. Roerich, an artist of international fame, celebrated at Chitrakala Parishat on October 23, 2004. Protected Mansion of Dr. Roerich is kept open for public view. Arrangement for exhibition of his masterpieces and other artefacts all over the state.
- Cultural Directory:
  - Computerised information data of all the folk artistes and other noted artists in the state.
  - Computerised data with full information besides pictures of more than 3,000 historical monuments and all the museums of Karnataka with reference to Archaeological Directory.
  - One lakh NSS students in the protection of monuments, to instil a sense of pride and respect among the youth, about our heritage.
- Karnataka Rajyothsava Celebrations November 1, 2004.

TABLE 8.2

Initiatives taken by the Government to Provide Proper Environment to the Artists

Details	*Nos.*
Zilla Ranga Mandirs	12
Open Air Theatres	233
Arts Schools	7
Cultural Training Centres	4

In order to provide facilities and proper environment to the artists in different fields, government have constructed *Ranga Mandiras* and 'open air theatres' and provided arts schools and cultural training centres at various places in the districts (Table 8.2).

TABLE 8.3

Award Winners in Different Fields

Sl. No	*Awards*	*State*
1	Jnanpita Award–1967-1998	7
2	Central Sahithya Academy Award 1953-2000	48
3	Pampa Award–1987-2003	17
4	Dana Chintamani Attimabbe Award 1955-2004	10
5	Janapada Shree Award Winner 1994-2004	11
6	T S R Award 1993-2000	8
7	Janapada Tagnya Award 1986-2000	42
8	Karnataka Shilpakala Academy Award Winners –1996-2000	26
9	Jakanachari Award – 1995-2004	10
10	Sri Karnataka Purandara Award 1991-2004	14
11	State Sangeetha Vidwan Award Winners – 1993-2004	12
12	T. Chowdaiah Award – 1995-2004	10
13	Santa Shishunal Shariff Award 1995-2004	10
14	Natyarani Shantala Award 1995-2004	10
15	Karnataka Sahitya Academy Award 1995-2003	44
16	Karnataka Ratna Award 1992-2004	5
17	Basava Puraskara 2000-2004	4
18	Varna Shilpa Venkatappa Award 1994-2004	11
19	Gubbi Veeranna Award 1994-2004	11
20	Karnataka Sangeetha Nritya Academy Awards 1995-2003	384
21	Karnataka Shilpa Kala Academy Awards 1995-2004	53
22	Karnataka Urdu Academy Awards 1987-2003	50
23	Karnataka Lalitha Kala Academy Awards 1996-2002	145
24	Karnataka Tulu Sahitya Academy Awards 1995-2003	47
25	Karnataka Konkani Sahitya Academy Awards 1995-2004	57
26	Karnataka Janapada and Yakshnagana Academy Awards 1980-2004	547
27	Karnataka Nataka Academy Awards 1959-2003	494
	• Fellowships 1989-1993	50
	• Puraskara 1990-1994	51
	• Paddanna Awards 1998-2001	51
28	Karnataka Kodava Sahitya Academy Awards 1995-2002	68

Source: High Power Committee for Redressal of Regional Imbalances, June 2002, and Department of Kannada and Culture, Government of Karnataka.

8.5.11 Awards

As mentioned earlier, awards are given to the best writers and artists in different fields based on the recommendations of the concerned academies and of the Department of Kannada and Culture. Table 8.3 provides the number of award winners from Karnataka.

8.5.12 Rajyothsava Awards

Rajyothsava awards are given every year right from 1966 in recognition of the good work done by the scholars and artists in different fields of culture. As many as 1,210 Rajyothsava awards have been given upto 2000 AD. Appendix A-8.1 gives the district-wise details of Rajyothsava awards for the years 1995-2001, whereby 401 scholars were given these awards in this period in Karnataka.

8.6 History of Socio-Economic Development

8.6.1 Tanks and their Maintenance

One interesting ninth century example on irrigation from near Nargund is worth noting. The villagers built a tank called Kanthamagere. If there were to be marriage in a family of Brahmin in the village, the family was to contribute three gold coins and in the case of a thread ceremony two coins; and in the case of a marriage in a non-Brahmin family, the contribution was to be one coin. These contributions were to create a corporate fund out of which the cost of upkeep of the tanks had to be met, and all judicial fines imposed for crimes committed in the village were added to the same fund, and the corporate assembly looked after the village tank. In some places the administrative bodies of temples did the job where money was deposited for the purpose. Village assemblies (*oora samudaya, oora samastaru,* etc.) generally supervised the local irrigation facility.

For various services in temples, individuals deposited money and out of the interest accrued on such deposits, lighting of lamps, feeding certain number of guests on certain specified days or meeting the expenses of a festival were among such services. The amounts so deposited were advanced to traders and thus temples served as bankers too.

8.6.2 Village Organisation

A village when it grew in size with increased commercial activity came to be recognised as a town by the state, by starting a weekly shandy at the place, and a leading merchant was appointed Pattanswamy or Pattanashetty who was authorised to collect tolls on merchandise brought for sale to the shandy and provide visiting traders a place to spread their ware and provide shade, water, and also fodder to the pack animals. He was to function like a mayor in the town, and in urban areas merchants associations or guilds dominated over other guilds of weavers, potters, oil-mongers smiths, and other craftsmen. *Sheni, Nigama, Kottali, Nikaya,* etc. were the names of guilds, and under the Badami Chalukyas even the *malekaras* (Garland makers) and cobblers of Badami had their guilds, and we also come across guilds of *uguraru* (pluckers of betel leaves), *gale* (pluckers of fruits from orchards) and *Panchalaru* (smiths) in records.

Villages had the assemblies of agriculturists described as *Gavundaprajes* (*Gramavriddhas* of Kautilya's text), and a Ganga record from a village (of the 5th century) speaks of 12 *Prajegavundas* form a village who constituted the village assembly. Talakadu initially had 25 such *Gavundaprajes* (representing agricultural sections) to which in course of time, oil-mongers, merchants and other professionals joined to form the town assembly during subsequent centuries when the town was further urbanised.

Every caste had its assembly or a guild of each profession and if more than one caste followed a common profession like weaving, they formed a joint guild. They had their own rules regarding quality of the product, price and other matters of common interest. The merchant guilds had their own army to safeguard their caravans of pack animals like bullocks or asses. Aihole-500 is described as a powerful federal guild of merchants having influence over the whole of south India and even Southeast Asia. The guilds accepted deposits and lent money to members, and served as banks.

8.6.3 Agriculture

Cereals like rice, wheat, *ragi* and *jowar*, and leguminous crops like green gram, black gram, *kulti* and bengal gram, oil seeds like sesamum, safflower and gingeley, cash crops like cotton and sugar cane, plantation crops like betel leaves, areca and coconut were raised. Orchards and flower gardens too existed. Ginger, turmeric, cumin, coriander, etc. were cash crops. The Portuguese during the 16th century introduced potato, tobacco, groundnut, cashewnut, onion and chillies as new crops. Pepper, cardamum, soapnut, honey, wax, gum, myrabalon, medicinal herbs etc., were forest products, mostly gathered by forest dwellers and tribals. Traders paid shop tax and tolls at various points of transit. Land revenue was one of the important sources of state income. Irrigated land had higher rates and so did plantation crops. Salt pans and toddy trees were also taxed. Textile production was a major industry and cotton piece goods were major items of export from India. Gunny bags and woollen blankets were also woven. Pattegars wove silk cloth, mostly from imported yarn. Women in all households spun at *charkha* and earned as much as farm labourers. Production of jaggery, salt, lime, etc. were other professions. Animal husbandry was popular and there was an exclusive castes tending cows called Gollas and those raising sheep were the Kurubas. Between 7th and 10th centuries cows were brought on large scale and were donated in herds, as testified by *gosasa* (*gosahasra*) stones found all over, especially in north Karnataka. Buffaloes were also raised. Donating cows was considered a meritorious act. Pigs, buffaloes, fowls, goats, etc. were other domesticated animals. The state purchased *ghee* on a large scale and stocked it for military purpose.

8.6.4 Industries and Trade

Towns had exclusive streets of various craftsmen like weavers (like Bangalore's Aralepete), potters (like Kumbarpete), salt makers (Upparapete), milkmen (Gollarapete), etc. and also streets of traders with shops. A town like Barkur had Javalikeri (for cloth merchants) or Manigarakeri (for jewellers). Rural settlements adjacent to a big village or town like Kumbarakoppa (potters' hamlet) or Sunagarakoppa (of lime makers) also existed. Place names like Uppuru, Upponi, Uppala, Uppinapattana or Uppinangadi on the coast indicate places known for their production/sale of salt. Even in the interior, near Chickamagalur is Uppavalli known from ninth century records, where rock salt was mined. Brahmavar, once an *agrahara* (Brahmapuri) had its Salikeri (weaver's settlement) outside the town. Every village, generally had a Holegeri, a settlement of people who were engaged in the so-called 'impure professions' like flaying the dead animals, tanning and manufacturing footwear. They were mostly 'untouchables'.

The mighty empire of the Rashtrakutas (753 to 973 AD) was described as one of the four great empires of the world by the Arab traveller Suleiman in 851. (The other three were the Arabian, Eastern Roman and the Chinese empires.) They had inherited this by overthrowing the Chalukyas of Badami, and Malakhed (in Gulbarga district) was their new capital. The Gangas in the south remained friendly with them and resisted the efforts of the Pallavas of Kanchi in securing a foothold in Karnataka.

8.6.5 Modern Industries

The American Civil War in the 1860s saw the 'Cotton Boom' in North Karnataka, popularising cotton cultivation on an unprecedented scale and ginning units increased in number. After the declining of the 'Cotton Boom', cotton cultivation continued on a larger scale than the pre-boom days and textile mills were opened at Bangalore (Mysore Mill in 1884 and Binny in 1887), Bharat Mill in Hubli in 1898, Gokak Mill (in 1889 by producing hydroelectric power and Gokak Falls in 1887-7kW), and a similar mill at Gulbarga in 1884. Davanagere also saw opening of textile units. Tile factories were found in Mangalore. Gold mining was started in KGF in 1886, and major Hydro-Electric Project at Shivasamudra in 1902, supplying power to KGF and also to Bangalore in 1905. This was the dream project of Sir Sheshadri Iyer, who became the *Dewan* of Mysore in 1883 after the rendition of power to the Mysore Maharaja in 1881.

Swadeshi movement (1907-08) gave fillip to local small scale units and *Khadi* production and village industries. A ceramic unit was founded at Khanapur in 1907. Mysore Economic Conference (1911) created a favourable atmosphere for the founding of new industries. It also pinpointed the industrial possibilities in the state.

Later Mysore *Dewans* like Sir M. Vishveshwarayya (1912-1918) and Sir Mirza Ismail (1926-1941) paid attention to the all-round development of Mysore by also starting industries under state sector like Mysore Chrome Tanning Company (1908) or the Sandal Oil Factory (1915). Sir Mirza also started several units including the Mysugar of Mandya or Mysore Paper Mill at Bhadravati. The Mysore University was founded in 1916, Bangalore Engineering College in 1917, Mysore Bank in 1913 and School of Agriculture (which later became a college and UAS in our own times). Founding of the Indian Institute of Science in 1911 was a great boon.

West Coast saw banking flourishing and Bombay-Karnataka nourished cooperative movement beginning with a small society founded as early as in 1904 at Kanaginahal near Gadag.

The two World Wars helped expansion of Indian industries and the need for self-reliance was cleanly felt.

8.6.6 Ruination of Industries

The Industrial Revolution in England almost ruined flourishing textile and gunny weaving industry in the state. Salt monopoly of the Government threw the salt makers out of job (both on the coast and the interior) and some of them took to building construction work. Rubber gave a blow to leather workers and kerosene oil to the oil-mongers who produced non-edible lamp oil. Karnataka, known for its flourishing iron and steel units from prehistoric times (beginning with Hallur in 1500 BC) could not face the competition from Bermingham products (Buchanan, in 1800, speaks of quality steel produced at Magadi and lists many more such centres). Lakhs of women spinners of yarn including those from the scheduled castes were thrown out of job. Loss of economic power led to the social degradation of women. Unemployment and resultant starvation deaths were in lakhs, and added to this were the death due to famines in 1866 and 1876-1878, followed by the deaths caused by epidemic plague in 1887-88. That apart, Karnataka, like India, became a raw material growing land and cotton export from Kumta port to England was a notable development. Pressure on land increased with vanishing of industries and crafts.

8.6.7 Spread of Education

After the establishment of British rule in Karnataka, various administrations themselves starting or encouraging the finding of schools with prescribed syllabus, etc. was evidenced. The Christian missionaries also took up the task of opening schools. Their schools, popularly called *koolimatha* or *aygala matha* in villages or towns, were run by private teachers who were paid, by the parents, in cash and kind and also on occasions of festivals. Bangalore alone had 18 such schools during the 19th century. But people of the lower castes could not attend them, nor could think or afford this 'luxury' of schooling.

The Mysore ruler, Krishnaraja Wodeyar III opened Raja's school in Mysore in 1833 to teach English and it became Maharaja's high school (and also college later). But he was not the ruler then, still he encouraged learning and fine arts. But Wood's Despatch of 1854 made the Mysore Government headed by the Commissioner to take serious steps in the direction. A Director of Public Instructions was appointed. In addition to primary schools, a government high school was started in Bangalore in 1858. The protestant missionaries started high schools later at Bangalore, Mysore, Tumkur, Shimoga and Hassan. There were 81 primary schools in the state with 4,471 pupils in 1867-1868. By 1900-1901, the number were 1,946 schools and 65,493 pupils (including 13,375 girls), and in 1940-41 number of schools rose to 6,505 and pupils 2,74,454 (with 35,291 girls). At the time of states reorganisation (1956-57) there were 12,553 schools with 8.60 lakh pupils which included 2.93 lakh girls. The Mysore University was founded in 1916, and there were 2 degree colleges at Mysore and Bangalore in addition to 6 intermediate colleges and 2 engineering colleges and 1 agricultural college and 1 medical college by 1956, in the erstwhile Mysore state. Bangalore cantonment had St. Joseph's College and many Anglo-Indian high schools.

In the Bombay-Karnataka area, 2 Marathi schools were opened, 1 at Dharwad and 1 at Hubli by the Bombay Native School and Book Society. But British officer called Russel realised that Kannada was the language of the area and opened Kannada schools one each at Hubli and Dharwad on his own initiative soon after. Before 1826, there were 270 private schools (*koolimathas*) in the region. A Board of Education was started in 1840 by the state government and in 1855 it was transferred to the Education Department. There were in the region 34 local language schools in 1854-55. The Basel Mission started a high school at Dharwad and the Government Sardar's English School was started in Belgaum in 1855 which later became a high school. The native states like Jamkhandi, Ramdurg, Mudhol, Savanur, etc. also started English schools. By 1881 there were 870 schools (both government and aided) in the whole region including the small princely states with 47,751 pupils. By 1902-03 the number of schools rose to 1,309 with a strength of 76,094 and in 1955-56, the figures were 6,086 schools with 6,32,000 pupils. There were colleges at Dharwad and Belgaum with an engineering college at Hubli and degree colleges were opened at Bagalkot and Bijapur before states' reorganisation and an Agricultural College at Dharwad. Hubli had an engineering college also. Basel Mission had opened high school at Dharwad, and the London Mission another high school at Belgaum during the 19th century. The government training schools founded at Belgaum later shifted to Dharwad gave great fillip to learning and scholarship.

The small region of Kodagu is educationally advanced. Two Anglo-vernacular schools were started at Madikeri and at Virajpet in 1834 and by 1874-75, there were 44 schools in Kodagu, and by 1912, the number of primary schools rose to 117 with 8,715 pupils and by 1946-47 the figures were 127 schools with 13,907 pupils. By 1956-57, the total number of schools were 221 with a total strength of 28,000. A high school was started in 1879 at Madikeri. After Independence, a government college was opened at Madikeri.

The Hyderabad-Karnataka region education was mostly under the initiative of religious men like *pandits* and *maulvis*. It was in 1859 that government issued orders to start one Persian and one vernacular school at every *taluka*. Excluding the Bidar district, there were 591 primary schools with 31,138 pupils in the Kannada region in 1920-21 and by 1956-57, the number of schools rose to 2,092 and 1,30,000 pupils. There was an Intermediate College at Gulbarga started just before Independence.

Bellary and Dakshina Kannada (in former Madras presidency) were rather educationally advanced. The Basel Mission and the Catholic Missions took steps to open English schools in Mangalore and Udupi in the 1830s and the 1840s. The Madras Elementary Education Act, 1863 helped to spread the network of government schools and if there were 557 schools with 9,956 pupils in Dakshina Kannada, their numbers rose to 1,211 in 1931-32 with 44,223 pupils. By 1946-47, schools numbered 784 and pupils totalled 53,970. In 1956-57 there were 1,153 schools with 1,66,846 pupils including 67,565 girls. Bellary district was also part of Madras Presidency and the Madras Elementary Education Act of 1863 helped spread of education in the region. The London Mission was also active here. The number of schools in the district was 188 in 1881-82 with 6,986 pupils, and 1921-22, their number rose 775 schools and 60,266 pupils. On the year of Independence, the figures were 1,249 schools and 1,69,946 students and in 1956-57, there were 1,298 schools and 1,74,000 pupils. District local boards played a prominent part in spreading high school networks in the Madras region. Dakshina Kannada had four colleges by 1956 (of which one was for women) with one polytechnic and Bellary had one private college.

Colleges were opened at Mangalore (1869), Bangalore (1870) and Bellary (1869). One at the last named was later shifted to Anantpur. The Maharaja's College of Mysore (1894), Maharani's at Mysore (1901) St. Aloysius College at Mangalore (1879), St. Joseph's College at Bangalore (1882) were other degree colleges. Karnatak College was started at Dharwad and the Lingaraj College in Belgaum later: Belgaum saw the opening of a Law College in 1937.

8.7 Social Movements

8.7.1 Backward Classes' Movement

Spread of education provided some employment avenues in government. But most of the government jobs were cornered by Brahmins. This led to the Backward Classes' Movement, and community organisations came to be founded like the Veerashaiva Mahasabha in 1904 and the Vokkaligara Sangha in 1907, and the Praja Mitramandali in 1917 in Mysore state and the Brahmatetara Parishat at Hubli in 1920. These movements popularised the clamour for education, opened hostels, later educational institutions, and even our own times we see caste associations running colleges including medical, engineering and in other technical faculties. It was the Lingayats who led the KLE Society, Belgaum, and various Veerashaiva Mathas also took lead in this matter. This Christian missions beginning with the Basel Mission (in Mangalore and Dharwad), London Mission in Belgaum, Bellary and Bangalore and the Wesleyans in Mysore and Bangalore played their useful part in spreading education and especially teaching English as already observed. The Catholics also did not lag behind.

8.7.2 Freedom Movement

Anti-British uprisings of Dhondia Wagh (1800-1801), of Koppal (1819), Bidar (1820, Deshmukh Rebellion), Kittur in 1824 and 1829 (led by Sangolli Rayanna), Nagar uprising (1830-31) and the 1857-58 uprisings helped the British to know the needs for improving roads and communication facilities and tighten the administrative machinery. In fact, the need for a Representative Assembly in Mysore was felt in the background of revolts as suggested by Commissioner Gordon in 1878, and it was started in 1881.

Congress did influence Karnataka and there were strong stirrings in 1906-07 during Swadeshi Movement in Karnataka. Tilak organised the branches of the Home Rule Leagues in Karnataka too (1916). The Non-cooperation movement saw nearly 70 arrests in British Karnataka (in Presidencies) and the famous Dharwad Firing, killing three. The Belgaum Congress of 1924 was a historic event, presided over by Mahatma Gandhiji, who also later took up the cause of eradication of untouchability. In 1934 and 1936 he toured the state and collected donations for Harijan Sevak Sangh. Many temples and wells were made accessible to the untouchables during his tours. In 1930-34, Civil Disobedience Movement was evidenced in British Karnataka including Kodagu and thousands went to jail. In 1937, according to the Federal Act, elections were held for Bombay and Madras Presidencies and Congress secured a majority in Karnataka Constituencies too. But all this was in the British Presidency regions. The Congress had also strongly propounded *khadi* and village industries. Thousands of poor people earned their livelihood by spinning, dying, weaving, soap making, footwear making, etc. under the Karnataka Village Industries Association.

In Mysore, Congress was pressing for responsible government and Shivapura Congress Session in April 1938 was a landmark. The Vidurashwatha Firing against Flag Satyagraha on April 25 (1938) was a turning point. The Arya Samaj and the Hindu Maha Sabha created awakening in Hyderabad area and Hyderabad State Congress was started in 1938. The Quit India Movement was evidenced like a volcanic eruption in all districts and 15,000 persons were jailed.

The movement for Unification of Karnataka went hand-in-hand with freedom movement. Alur Venkata Rao was the Harbinger of the movement. When India became free in 1947, Kannada-speaking regions came under five units instead of 20. (The five units were Bombay, Madras, Mysore, Hyderabad and Kodagu.) Responsible Government was founded in Mysore in 1947 October, and in Hyderabad in September 1948.

8.7.3 Moves against Regional Imbalances

Krishnaraja Wodeyar IV (1902-1940) was an enlightened ruler called as Rajarshi. He not only stood by the Dewans who wanted industrial expansion but also expansion of irrigation. He relentlessly fought for raising the K R Sagar Dam. Music, arts and scholarship flourished under his leadership. Scholarship and creative literature also grew. He founded the Kannada Sahitya Parishad in 1915.

The Mysore state under the rule of the British Commissioners in 1831-81 and after rendition (1881) under able *dewans* like Rangacharlu, Sheshadri Iyer, Visveswarayya and Mirza Ismail saw growth of education, infrastructure including production of cheap hydro-electricity (1902), expansion of irrigation and industrial growth mainly under state enterprise. It provided a potential nucleus for growth of the new state. The Mysore court also encouraged learning and fine arts, especially under Krishnaraja Wodeyar IV (1902-40). The centre also founded industries in Bangalore as a result.

Dakshina Kannada, Kodagu and Bellary, though under the British had learnt long back that they could not depend upon the government alone for development. Fisheries was a boon to Dakshina Kannada. Voluntary effort in cooperative movement, road transport, banking and education helped their growth. Manipal is a unique example in matters of educational advancement. But Bellary lacked much of popular initiative though it was culturally advanced especially in histrionic talent. Improved irrigation has helped outsiders to reap the benefit in Bellary district.

Bombay-Karnataka area suffered as in the Bombay Presidency, the Marathi and Gujarati population always had an upper hand in 'sharing the cake'. But Veerashaiva community took big initiative in starting the K.L.E. Society. In cooperation too the area was advanced. Dharwad was a cultural centre that grew to be so without royal patronage. The Vidyavardhaka Sangha (1870) and the Teachers' Training College were a boon. Alur Venkatarao was a prominent active public figure. Hindustani music had fine patronage here. Uttara Kannada (Karwar) suffered due to lack of infrastructure. Princely centres like Jamkhandi, Kundgol, Shahpur, etc. proved to be centres of education and culture.

Hyderabad state which was vast with many rivers and rivulets, lacked in transport facility, irrigation, and was educationally backward. The feudal atmosphere hampered peoples' initiative. It was a dry area in the rain shadow like Bijapur.

The Kodava community in Kodagu joined the army. They also came into contact with European coffee planters. Despite its secluded nature Kodagu emerged as a modernised region.

8.8 Social Mobilisation

8.8.1 Backward Class/Non-Brahman Movement

Historically speaking and notably the backward caste movement in India could be traced to Jyotirao Phule (1827-1890) of Poona. By the time he was 20 years old, he was a politically awakened young man with a social vision. He started a school for girls in 1851. He was of a firm belief that education was necessary for the social and economic upliftment of the poverty-stricken lower castes, and the general progress of the country. He believed in the oneness of human beings and their equality before God. He established the *Satya Shodak* Samaj (1873) to propagate his egalitarian ideals.

Phule's efforts had its effect and from the 1870s, "depressed classes" began to be used as a term to identify the most socially and economically disadvantaged sections of the population on whose behalf action was needed. But it was a term that embraced very large number of hitherto separate and often diverse castes. The terms such as 'untouchable', 'scheduled castes', 'Dalit' came later into the social processes and its discourses.

Down south, the period 1907 to 1920 saw an awakening among the major non-*Brahmin* communities in Madras and the princely state of Mysore. The Vokkaligara Sangha was formed in 1906, the Lingayat Education Fund in 1909, and the Central Mohammedan Association in 1909. During that time 'backward' meant all castes except the Brahmins. Later, following the formation of the South Indian People's Association (1916) in Madras, in 1917, Praja Mitra Mandali was formed in Mysore state. It was all by no means a mass movement in favour of structural changes or the upliftment of lower castes, but more oriented towards reservation of seats in educational institutions and government jobs. The non-*Brahmin* communities in their demand for reservations in education and government services, built a kind of alliance with Dalits, but with no special provisions for the Dalits who were the most backward castes, and it would not until 1940, when Dalits would be offered political reservations.

In June 1918, a deputation of non-Brahmin leaders submitted a memorandum to the Maharaja of Mysore about the backward condition of the vast majority of his subjects, and the need to ensure 'a just balance of all interests' and provide reservation and special treatment to the affected groups. The Maharaja assured the deputation that the state would 'carefully and sympathetically' consider their grievances. In August 1918, a Committee headed by Sir Leslie Miller, the Chief Justice of the Chief Court, was formed to investigate the preponderance of the *Brahmin* community in the public service, to recommend changes in the existing rules of recruitment to the public service, to suggest facilities to encourage higher and professional education among the members of the backward communities and any other special measures to enable their growth.

In 1919, the Miller Committee submitted its report and recommended reservation of jobs in public service for backward classes, starting of more schools in the rural areas with reservations for backward castes, starting of hostels and increase in scholarship for students from backward classes. In effect, the committee recommended only general provisions for *non-Brahmins* with the aim that within 7 years they were to get 50 per cent of higher level appointments and two-thirds of lower level ones, but with no special provisions for Dalits. Subsequently, the government approved the report and passed the order in 1921. There was of course opposition to the report which reflected what is generally seen as a conflict between the principle of merit and the principle of social justice which incidentally continues to be expressed by certain classes against reservation policy even today.

However, in seven years time, the reservation policy did not succeed to the extent the committee had intended and expected, though the Lingayat and Vokkaliga communities had used the opportunity well to march ahead in comparison to the dalits.

As per Dushkin study, the percentage of *Brahmins* and non-*Brahmin* communities in gazetted posts in 1918, 1936, 1942, 1949, 1956 are given below in Table 8.4.

TABLE 8.4

Communities in Gazetted Posts

Community	*1918*	*1936*	*1942*	*1949*	*1956*
Brahmin	64.86	61.32	54.57	41.29	34.90
Christian	15.14	8.15	7.86	5.53	5.75
Muslim	4.32	7.24	7.51	6.79	5.37
Lingayat	1.89	5.00	5.78	9.65	12.74
Vokkaliga	1.08	2.52	3.82	8.47	9.80

Source: Table-18, P-249 of Dushkin study.

The reservation policy during the 1920s, 1930s and 1940s led to a situation wherein the non-*Brahmin* caste groups and communities, dominated by Lingayats and Vokkaligas, engaged in political opposition to the dominant *Brahmins*, manoeuvring for a share of the pie. The depressed classes, especially the Dalits, hardly had a voice in the matter, except for one Murugesan Pillai who expressed the fear that by being clubbed with the non-*Brahmin* groups all lower castes and their grievances would be swamped. He also expressed the doubt if the Depressed Classes should continue as part of the uneasy non-*Brahmin* alliance at all.

8.8.2 Dalit Movement in Karnataka

In 1920s a vigorous Dalit movement emerged under the dynamic leadership of Ambedkar in Maharashtra, and it was radically different from the Periyar's *anti-Brahmain* movement in Madras, though they shared certain common concerns in favour of the depressed classes. Karnataka had no leader of the stature of either Ambedkar or Ramaswamy Periyar, no significant political struggle such as the Mahad Tank Satyagraha or the burning of portions of Manu Dharmashastra (1927). After its beginning in Bombay (1920s), it took nearly 50 years for a distinct Dalit identity and Dalit movement to emerge in Karnataka.

The emergence of Dalit movement in Karnataka in the late 1970s was marked by three significant developments:

- One, Dalits breaking away from the alliance and stranglehold of the Congress-party-based politics.
- Two, the coming together of Dalits from three (not entirely) different political streams, namely, Marxism, Ambedkarism and Lohiaism to form a united Dalit Sangarsh Samithi (DSS) in 1977.
- Three, the emergence of *bandaya* or protest literature which both challenged the mainstream Kannada literature 'trapped' in *Brahminical* cosmologies, and curve out a distinct identity and character of its own.

In many ways the *bandaya* or Dalit literature in Karnataka paralleled a similar though earlier growth of Marathi protest literature in Maharashtra. An event associated with the late B. Basavalingappa deserves a special mention here for its political and cultural significance. Basavalingappa represented Dalit anger and radicalism within the Congress establishment. He was a minister during Devaraj Urs period (1972-1980), and was responsible for abolishing the carrying of night soil. Once, while giving a fiery speech against the caste system, he termed the mainstream Kannada literature as *boosa* (cattle feed). This remark created quite a stir and controversy throughout the state, as also it inspired and ignited the minds of many a young Dalit (for instance, Siddalingaiah and company, who were all to become notable activists) to take up Dalit issues with a revolutionary zeal.

The DSS was spearheaded notably by Siddalingaiah, Devanoor Mahadeva, Krishnappa and Baragur Ramachandra. Dalit activists emerged from villages, from agricultural labourers' families, from the working class in the public sectors, from the teaching community, and then there were the young college-educated and college-going men and women fired by a new vision of a casteless society and a just social order. Their politics was also naturally marked by social rage against not only the inhuman caste practices but also all forms of oppression, exploitation and injustices. And within a decade there were about two lakh members with branches of DSS spread across the state.

The DSS struggle was driven and defined by their demand for structural rights (issues related to land and property); right to social space (right to enter and use public spaces); right to cultural space (in the field of art, music, theatre and literature).

In other words, it was no utopian politics but politics rooted in reality and issue based, issues related to land in villages and tribal areas, wages and working conditions, atrocities against women and Dalits, police atrocities, legal and political rights of Dalits and so on. Dalit activists intervened wherever harassment or atrocities against Dalits occurred. They held meetings, demonstrations and street plays to highlight issues related to bonded labour, rape and exploitation of women, cruelties of landlordism and caste system and so on. By mid-1990s, DSS had become a significant voice and a cultural force throughout the state. The rather aggressive yet creative *bandaya* literature and their professional journalism raised politically and philosophically significant and profound issues and questions with regard to society, culture, religion and politics. In other words, their works posed a challenge to the dominant narratives and discourses of society.

Remaining outside party politics, DSS built alliances and interacted with women's movement groups, other minority groups (Muslims, Christians), and civil liberty groups in developing a critique of all forms of violence and injustices suffered by landless labourers, workers, women, minorities and the economically disadvantaged and marginalised sections of the society. For some time, DSS also supported Kanshi Ram's Bahujan Samaj Party (BSP), but withdrew its support once BSP aligned itself with the BJP. Though it's a fact that the BJP, over these years, has successfully incorporated the support and participation of sections of Dalits for the construction of Ram temple in Ayodhya, and their Hindutva ideology in general, DSS continues to be critical of BJP's Hindutva and the chauvinism of groups like RSS and Shiva Sena. Their criticism is that these chauvinistic ideologies not only sideline the real and crucial issues of poverty, exploitation and social injustice, they also succeed in breaking the solidarity of Dalits and dividing them into further splinter groups.

In Karnataka today, ironical as it may sound, the increase in atrocities on the Dalits has been a direct result of the increasing assertion of their equality.

The DSS continues to be active and continues to intervene (often in alliance with civil liberty groups) whenever and wherever there are instances of exploitation and victimisation of Dalits. But DSS is no more a massive cultural organisation that it was some years ago, though it remains to be a voice and force to be reckoned with. Electoral politics, Dalits entering party politics and fights within groups for political seats and incorporation of Dalits into government sponsored programmes and institutions have led to a confusion of priorities, and weakened their solidarity for a common cause. Also the incomplete debate on the social implication of Gandhian ideals and Ambedkar's ideas today, the ongoing debate on modernity and globalisation, strategies and methods to be employed for developing a new cultural politics for dalits today, have also created ideological differences and clashes within the group. This is understandable given our rapidly changing world and the complexity of our situation.

BOX 8.2

Atrocities on Dalits

- On 3rd November 1991 in a village of Gulbarga, Malkappa was made to eat human excreta for his refusal to cut firewood.
- In Harathi village of Kolar when Kannappa, a Dalit of Kataganahalli refused to obey the orders of the upper caste to go round Harathi village beating a drum to make a public announcement, he was forced to eat human excreta (1994).
- In Alagi, another village of Gulbarga, when the Dalits refused to cut buffaloes for the Laxmi Devi festival of caste Hindus, three of their leaders were murdered in June 1992.
- The caste Hindus of Tippalapura village in Hunsur Taluka ostracised Dalits for discontinuing the age-old practice of carrying food from the former's houses during festivals (1992).
- Four caste Hindus were killed and 12 others were injured in police firing following a dispute over the entry of Dalits into restaurants run by caste Hindus in Raichur (1992).
- Gurulingappa of Shammur village in Gulbarga was murdered on October 2, 1993 for buying five acres of land (1994).
- Thimmaraju, a Dalit Coordination Committee activist was killed by a gang of 18 persons for opposing the alleged grabbing of 257 acres of land belonging to the *Harijan Shakahara Sangh* in Kadugodi Bangalore (1995).

8.8.3 Empowerment of SC/ST

In fact, Karnataka, as a region, has had a unique history in this respect. The southern part of what is now called as unified Karnataka state was known as the princely state of Mysore. Wadeyars, the most benevolent rulers of Mysore, ruled it. So, much before Independence, the old Mysore enjoyed the reputation of being one of the well administered and most progressive regions of the country. A modern system of education was introduced in Mysore as early as in 1833. The foresight and progressive attitudes of the government of old Mysore were a model for other Indian states in political as well as social matters. The Representative Assembly of Mysore dates back to 1881, when even the Presidencies did not have such bodies. Thus, unlike some other regions elsewhere in the country, the princely state of Mysore was functioning in a different mould. It had initiated major programmes in the cause of the betterment of even the lowest of the low. Of such programmes, the most successful was the programme of education to lower castes. By 1904-05, there were 76 schools, 37 government schools, 36 government–aided mission schools, and three unaided. In 1915, there was a famous test case in which the government ordered a school master in the Sringeri Jahagir to admit untouchables; there was protest from both caste Hindus and Muslims who withdrew students, but C. R. Reddy, the then administrator of schools, prevailed upon the Maharaja that education was everyone's right. In 1919, the order was generalised to allow *Panchamas* into all schools; again, in spite of the protest the Maharaja stood firm. By 1920s, a small section was making a limited entry into government employment: statistics showed that there were 165 Dalits in 1918 of a total of 4,234. The Maharaja Krishnaraja Wodeyar was quite liberal in social reforms. It was during his regime that the Miller Committee as referred to earlier was appointed in the year 1918 to study the problems of the backward classes. The Millers Committee came out with the recommendations of giving reservation to the backward classes while making appointments to administrative posts in the princely state of Mysore. But not less than a person like M. Vishveswaraiah, a great *Dewan* of *Maharaja*, opposed this policy of the princely state of Mysore. Finally he even resigned from his post in protest against the enlightened move of the Maharaja Wodeyar. However, in such appointments only two major communities'—the Lingayats and the Vakkaligas—became the significant beneficiaries. The rest of the communities like untouchables and Muslims were to wait until some special provisions were made in their favour in the form of the Mysore Act of 1940, according to which 67 and 30 of the 310 seats were reserved for the minorities and the depressed classes respectively; the position thus was set for the post-Independence situation in which Dalits would be constitutionally and legally guaranteed a share as scheduled castes. This should no doubt be considered as an amazing concern of the princely state of Mysore shown towards the backward classes, minorities and the depressed classes.

Further, as a civil society, Karnataka region has witnessed volcanic revolts against its traditional and unjust social order of the caste system. This could happen much before the emergence of the Western liberationist trends. As far back as 12th century AD, Basaveshwara, the Prime Minister of Kalyana—the kingdom under the rule of King Bijjala in northern Karnataka, had ridiculed the discriminatory treatments based on caste and untouchability. As a mark of challenge to such wicked practices of Hinduism he founded the Veerashaiva Dharma, a new religious movement which drew disciples from every stratum of the society including the outcastes. His close untouchable followers like Samagara Haralayya, Dhor Kakkayya, Madar Channayya had a unique role and place in his movement. The main objective of Basaveshwara's movement was to establish a right relationship between man and man, and, God and religion. So throughout his life he struggled to bring in a just social order. But, in course of time, Veerashaivism as a revolutionary movement lost its fire. It gave rise to many minor creeds later to be turned as a narrow parochial monasteries without any open door practices. In the subsequent centuries the onslaughts of saint poets like Purandaradas and Kanakadas were also not sufficient to shake the formidable foundation of a caste based society. Equality before God did not seem to translate into social equality or equality of all men.

However, with the advent of the British rule in India slowly the social circumstances in Karnataka started changing too. The British rule gave rise to many revolutionary changes in the domains of society, economy and polity. Karnataka acted well in time in response to these revolutionary changes with the hope of ushering in an era of liberty, equality and fraternity. The benevolent rulers of Karnataka, as stated above, were always aware that the untouchable and backward communities, being socially oppressed over centuries, deserved special state sympathy.

So from time to time, if not in the human rights or legal sense of the term, at least from humanistic point of view, care has been taken towards the development of these downtrodden sections of the society. This legacy, with added support from the new constitutional spirit of justice—social, economic and political—is continuing even more vigorously in a new context created by the circumstances of freedom and democracy. Apart from adhering to what is popularly known as constitutional provision of Protective Discrimination Policy which provides for reservation of seats in the Lok Sabha, the Legislative Assemblies of the states, the government jobs and the higher, technical and professional institutions, the state has committed itself to remove social and economic disparities in many other ways. Keeping in view the nature of problems faced by the SC/STs in the state, the policy measures have been formulated, evaluated and reformulated. There have come up plenty of schemes and programmes to vehemently address both persisting and emerging contexts of deprivation. In the complex era of revolutionary trends like industrialisation, transport and communication, consumerism, liberalisation and globalisation things have been proving to be very difficult to cope with for the vulnerable sections of the society. Due to these processes, the SC/ST communities in particular have been put to greater strains. Hence, they are continuing to be victims of acute poverty characterised by malnutrition, ill health, illiteracy, unemployment, ignorance and above all imposed social restrictions in the face of persisting system of caste and untouchability. However, by using its strength of political power the state government of Karnataka has been doing its best to address these issues.

8.8.4 Constitutional Interventions

After the Poona Pact (1933), under the guidance of Gandhiji, Harijan Sevak Sangh was established and it became a major national campaign for the removal of untouchability from 1932-36. And Gandhiji himself set out on a countrywide tour and covered 12,500 miles, to promote the *Harijan* cause. The Sangha had three-fold tasks:

One, to open public wells, *dharmashalas*, roads, schools, temples and burning *ghats* for the *Harijans;*

Two, moral and spiritual upliftment of the *Harijans*, along with legal reforms for the amelioration of their condition; and

Three, service in the cause *Harijans* by caste Hindus as an act of penance and self-purification.

Ambedkar, who had agreed to be an executive member of the Sangh, resigned on the ground that the Sangh's activities were geared towards only the 'removal of untouchability' in order to reform Hinduism and not the total eradication of caste system or *chaturvarnya*. Further, he took exception to the fact that the leadership of the Sangha was solely in the hands of caste Hindus when it ought to be in the hands of untouchables if any genuine change had to take place in the social structure of the Hindu Society.

Karnataka, however, was in the forefront of the Harijan Programme. Branches of the Sangh were started in Bijapur, Belgaum, Karwar, Mangalore, Coorg and Bellary, with Hubli as the headquarter. When Gandhiji toured Karnataka he witnessed a great enthusiasm everywhere.

The *Harijan* programmes ranged from activities such as opening of temples for *Harijans* and *Harijan bhajans* to exhortations against drinking alcohol, meat eating and animal sacrifice, from reservation of seats for *Harijans* in legislatures to starting schools, hostels, medical clinics for untouchable students.

On 16 June 1935, a 'conference of workers in the *Harijan* cause' was organised in Mysore. The conference, presided over by Jawaharlal Nehru, passed a resolution with an appeal to the government to give agricultural lands and sites for houses and drinking water facilities for Harijans, to increase grants for hostels, scholarships and preferential appointments in government services.

The intentions of the Gandhian Harijan Sevak Sangh were undoubtedly high but the achievement was minimal and did not trouble the deep structure of Hindu society. Acquisition of land and breaking with bonded labour that would have empowered the *Harijans* remained a distant dream. The entire mobilising effort of the sangh was from the top down, mobilising the middle classes and upper castes to act for the downtrodden and not enable Dalits to organise themselves. So, against such Gandhian programmes and efforts of similar bodies for the upliftment of Dalits which failed to bring about any fundamental change in the caste system or the traditional caste duties within the *jajamani* system, which did not led to any genuine empowerment of the Dalits, Ambedkar was to come up with the inspiring slogan; "educate, agitate, organise" and launch his self-help, self-elevation and self-respect movement to instigatge and inspire Dalits to become self-dependent and work towards their own upliftment.

Now, without either glorifying or dismissing the importance of the *Harijan* programmes in Karnataka, as a matter of fact, it should be admitted that despite the absence of an Ambedkar or Periyar here, the social and material condition of the *Harijans* in 1937 in Karnataka was upward looking compared to the conditions of the lower castes in several other states. Men like Kudmul Ranga Rao of Mangalore (death 1931) or Gopala Swamy Iyer in Mysore state (ed. 1943) had exclusive work for the Dalits with all humility. It had set in motion the philosophy of equalitarianism and social mobility of Dalits which would have far reaching consequences in future.

The most backward castes namely Holeyas and Madigas who were styled as Panchamas, then as depressed classes, were now either referred to as *Adi-Karnatakas* and *Adi-Dravidas* or *Harijans*. And the *Harijans* movement was largely led by Gandhian Congressmen. Members of groups such as Adi-Karnataka Abhivruddhi Sangham and Adi-jambara Abivrudhi Sangham (Murugesaram Pillai) were not too happy with the turn of events. The government was not sympathetically disposed towards the problems and aspirations of the *Adi-Karnatakas*. Yet they clung to a beneficent Princely state for the lack of any other alternative. And now, quite ironically and helplessly they accepted an alliance with Brahmins and other 'minority castes', since the large peasant based non-Brahmin castes such as Vokkaligas and other middle castes were least sympathetic to their cause and in point of fact quite oppressive.

Eventually, their loyalty to a beneficient autocracy was rewarded when the Government of Mysore Act of 1940 reserved 67 of 310 seats for minorities and of these 30 for the depressed classes and later followed by removal of Civil Disabilities Act, 1943. This set a position in favour of Dalits who would constitutionally and legally be guaranteed protection and a share as 'Scheduled Castes'.

8.8.5 The Outlawing of Untouchability and Other Constitutional Measures in Favour of Dalits

> The Constitutional provisions for the amelioration of the Scheduled Castes and Scheduled Tribes include Article 46, Articles 330, 332, 334, 335, 338, 341 and 342. Article 15 is on equality in citizenship that 'the State shall not discriminate against any citizen on grounds of religion, race, sex, place of birth or any of them'.

There was both a poetic and historic justice done when Dr. Ambedkar was appointed as the Chairman of the Drafting Committee of the Indian Constitution. With the adoption of the Indian Constitution in 1950, the practice of the untouchability was abolished. The key Article 17 declared: " 'Untouchability' is abolished and its practice in any form is forbidden. The enforcement of any disability arising out of 'untouchability' shall be an offence punishable in accordance with law."

While Article 14 upheld the basic democratic principle of equality, Clause 3 of Article 16 sought to fulfil the aims of the principles enunciated in the Preamble and in Articles 36 to 51 of the Directive Principles of State Policy to establish a Welfare State in which social justice prevails. Specifically Article 46 made Scheduled Castes and Scheduled Tribes the particular wards of the state and exhorted the states to "promote with special care the educational and economic interests of the weaker sections of the people, and, in particular of the Scheduled Castes and Scheduled Tribes. It shall protect them from social injustice and all forms of exploitation."

An amendment to Article 15 the following year, further protective measures were ensured for Dalits. The Clause said for any citizen it is illegal to subject anyone to any disability, liability, restriction or condition with regard to a) access to shops, public restaurants, hotels and places of public entertainment; or b) the use of wells, tanks, bathing *ghats,* roads and places of public resort maintained wholly or partly out of state funds or dedicated to the use of the general public.

Four years later, in 1955, The Abolition of Untouchability Act was passed. This Act lasted for 20 years, but with no substantial change in the caste relations, particularly in the agricultural sector. Atrocities against Dalits never seem to abate. An amendment to the Act was added in 1976, and it was renamed The Protection of Civil Rights Act 1976, state governments were given power to institute enquiries and punish or impose appropriate penalties on those who violate the law. In the new amendment, any case of insult to Scheduled Castes and forcing them to do scavenging, sweeping, removing carcasses, flaying animals, were added to the forbidden list. To the list of hotels and eating-places were added laundries and hair-cutting saloons as places where discrimination in service was not to be permitted. Violation of this law now merited not 6 months but a minimum of 2 years of imprisonment.

- Kilavenmani in Tamil Nadu where 42 Dalits, mostly women, children and elders, were killed on 25.12.1968.
- Belchi in Bihar where 11 Dalits along with 2 OBC members coming within the category of Vishal *Dalit* were killed on 27.5.1977.
- Pipra in Bihar where 14 Dalits were killed and 26 houses burnt on the night between 26.2.1980 and 27.2.1980.
- Nonki-Nagawa in Bihar where 19 Dalit persons were killed on the night of 11.8.1988 and 12.8.1988.

The Constitutional provisions for the Schedules Castes and Tribes may be grouped into three categories: Protective, Developmental and Preferential. The Protection of Civil Rights Act 1977, and the Scheduled Castes and Schedules Tribes (Prevention of Atrocities) Act, 1989 fall under the protective measures. Programmes for their educational and economic development under the Central and state sectors, the 'special component plan' of the Central and the states, special Central assistance and formation of SC Development Corporation fall under the second category. Reservations in education and employment preference (positive discrimination) in various other areas constitute the third type of measures.

The Central Ministry is the nodal ministry for overall policy, planning and coordination of programmes for the development of SCs and STs. From the start of the Sixth Five-Year Plan in 1980, its objective has been to bring about economic development and educational upliftment of SCs/STs, and to remove social discrimination. All other relevant central ministries such as the Ministry of Human Resources Development, Department of Women and Child Development, and the Ministry of Health and family Welfare necessarily include the 'special component plan' in favour of SCs and STs within their general plans and activities.

In the state of Karnataka, as in other states, the Department of Social Welfare, in particular Karnataka SC/ST Development Corporation (1975), in coordination with the Ministry of Welfare at the Centre, is geared towards the development of SCs & STs. Under the Special Component Plan there are various schemes for SCs and STs, which may be generally enumerated thus:

- The development of agriculture, horticulture, animal husbandry, dairying and small-scale industries.
- Promotion of education and training. Scholarship and freeship.
- The sinking of borewells and supply of free pumps.
- Assistance for self-employment and training in skills such as weaving, rickshaw driving, radio and TV repair and computer training.
- Assistance to help with the electrification of houses and with rebuilding after houses are burnt down or otherwise destroyed by natural disasters.
- Financial assistance to the victims of atrocities.

Karnataka has the largest list of SCs that include Tamil and Telugu speaking communities, but all of them are not necessarily 'untouchables'. Generally, in Karnataka, 'Holeya' and 'Madiga' are seen as 'real' untouchables, equivalent to 'Mahar' in Maharashtra, 'Dhed' in Gujarat, 'Mala' in Andhra, 'Paraihan' in Tamil Nadu. The Holey and Madiga are also referred to as the "right hand" (*Balagai*) and "left hand" (*Edagai*), a division within the caste. The long history of antagonism between them, which continues to this day, has often led to controversies in the reservation policy and other socio-political schemes.

There are of course several other castes other than Holeya and Madiga, who remain backward and who are discriminated against though not always and everywhere in the state. They are Koracha, Korma, Handi jogi, Bhovi and Bhanjara. Further, though STs are often clubbed with SCs in policy matters, unlike SCs, STs are more unevenly spread in the state. Much of STs live in scheduled areas and a set of special provisions apply for them.

In the last 50 odd years the triple provisions for the protection and development of SCs and STs have brought about substantial changes in the condition and position of the lower castes in our society, which wouldn't have been possible without these provisions and the policy of positive discrimination. As a matter of fact, the livelihoods and careers of millions of SCs and STs have improved and continue to depend upon the continuity of the various schemes meant for their development. Yet, it must also be admitted that these schemes have been marginal considering the vast population of the SCs and STs. The enormous funds that have been poured into various schemes should have, strictly speaking, brought about a radical shift in the lives of these low castes. But these funds have not always reached the target population. And the disappearance of caste practices or casteism envisioned by our philosophy and politics of positive discrimination has remained an incomplete project.

The reservation policy is reviewed and renewed every 10 years. And every new commission for SCs/STs has favoured preferential treatment of SCs/STs and recommended reservation of more number of seats and jobs for SCs/STs (Havanur Commission—Karnataka (1975), Mandal Commission, etc.). This has been inevitable considering the vast sections of marginalised people in the country. However, in some ways, the reservation policy has alienated the non-Dalits (especially the middle and upper middle classes) from the politics of social justice. The pejorative remark "sarkari Brahman" about Dalits and the anti-mandal riots, to mention only two instances, were an expression of their resentment towards reservation policy and indifference to the issues of equality and social justice. Added to this the politics of power and antagonism within and between the lower castes, especially between the Holeya and Madiga groups in Karnataka, and the indifference of the 'liberated' SCs towards their own brethren, and the cooption of prominent Dalit leaders have not helped the cause of the Dalits.

It is clear and evident that constitutional measures, reservation policy and other such schemes in themselves are not enough to secure equal rights and render social justice for the dalits. Civil society intervention and a cultural politics for social justice and dignity become an absolute necessity to carry forward the struggle for the realisation of a just social and political order. It is in answer to this deep-felt need that Dalit movement and NGOs emerged all over the country.

8.9 The Concept of Karnataka State

After the fall of Tipu Sultan in 1799, the princely area of Mysore had fallen in the hands of British and before the first part of the 19th century the whole of Karnataka came under the total control of the British. There were several uprising against the British rule: Dhondji Wagan (1800), Kittur Chennamma (1824), Sangoli Rayanna (1829), the Coorg uprising under Chikkaviraraja (1834).

The countrywide uprising of 1857 had its echo in Karnataka, too. The princes of Surapur and Nargund, the Bedas of Halagali, and Desais in Dharwad led by Mundargi Bhimrao revolted against the British in 1857-1858. There were uprising in Supa and Khanapur *talukas* in 1958-59 in which the Siddhis had also joined. The British did put down the revolt, but gained complete control over the land only by 1859.

With the rise of modern nationalism and the people of Karnataka taking an active part in freedom struggle all through, as early as 1916, a demand for a separate province/state for Kannada speaking people had already arisen. The Congress Party recognised the demand by forming a separate unit of the Party (K.P.C.C.) in 1920. The Karnataka Unification Conference was held at Belgaum in 1924, presided over by Siddappa Kambli, the leader of the *Brahmanetara Parishat.* The demand gathered momentum over the years. In 1938, the Madras and Bombay legislatures even passed a resolution which saidsteps may be taken for the creation of a new province to be called Karnataka by amalgamating all the predominantly Kannada speaking areas under one autonomous administration. In 1946, Sardar Vallabhai Patel, speaking at Karnataka Unification Conference (Fgiure 8.6) held at Bombay, assured that a united Karnataka

FIGURE 8.6

Karnataka Unification

Note: Composition of Karnataka:

- Mysore State, including Bellary district.
- Areas from Bombay: Belgaum except Chandgad *taluka;* whole of Dharwad, Bijapur and North Kanara districts.
- Areas from Madras: South Kanara district except Kasargod *taluka* and Amindivi Islands; Kollegal *taluk* of Coimbatore District.
- Areas from Hyderabad: Gulbarga district except Kodangal and Tandur *talukas;*
- Raichur district except Alampur and Gadval *talukas;* Bidar, Bhalki, Aurad and Humnabad *talukas* from Bidar district.
- Whole of Kodagu.

Source: U. Kamath, Suryanath (2002). *A Concise History of Karnataka (from Pre-historic Times to the Present)*, Jupiter Books, Bangalore, July.

would be formed, but the people have to wait. After Independence, in 1951, the death of Potti Sriramulu hastened the formation of Andhra state. The demand for Karnataka state remained unfulfilled. It was indeed a genuine and legitimate demand, for the Kannada speaking people were scattered and marginalised in different provinces. They wee subjected to 20 different administrations in the princely state of Mysore, the Madras Presidency, the Bombay Presidency, the territory of Coorg, the cantonment of Bangalore, Belgaum under the Central Government and so on. The movement for unification became all the more strong after Independence.

In response to Akhanda Karnataka Rajya Nirmana Parishat's aggressive agitation and such similar protests in other parts of the country, the Government of India set up the States Reorganisation Commission in 1953. The Committee recommended the division of the whole of the country into 14 major states (and a few small strategic states) considering the linguistic and cultural homogeneity as one of the principles.

Fazal Ali Commission recommended the founding of United Karnataka, which came into existence in November 1, 1956. This amalgamation of different provinces/districts was not an easy task. To the whole of the old princely state of Mysore were added Kannada speaking areas/districts from Bombay Presidency, Madras Presidency, the Hyderabad state and the whole of Coorg. Bellary district had already been merged with Mysore state in 1953. This Unified state was renamed as *Karnataka* on November 1, 1973, under the Chief Ministership of Sri Devaraj Urs. It then had 19 districts. Bangalore district was created in 1980. Seven more districts were carved out in 1997 (Figure 8.7).

At the time of Karnataka state formation, the state's population in (1951 census) was 1.94 crores with a literacy rate of 18.7 per cent (with 28.8 per cent males 8.8 per cent females). Per capita income was Rs. 230, income from agricultural sector was Rs. 3,000 crores, total foodgrain production was 32.80 lakh tonnes in a total cultivable area of 98.64 lakh ha. Irrigation facility was 7.4 per cent, road mileage was 43,183 km, and total railway length 2,595 km. It had 7 cities with a population over 1 lakh, namely, Bangalore (11.00 lakhs in 1956), Mysore (3.16 lakhs), KGF (1.74), Hubli (1.52) and Belgaum (1.21). It had a total of 20,164 primary schools, 1,565 middle schools and 548 high schools and 61 colleges and polytechnics. It had a sound infrastructure for growth and even before 1956, Central Government had started many industrial units like HAL, ITI, HMT, BEL, etc. in Bangalore.

But development was not uniform in all regions, for apparent political reasons, as already seen.

8.10 Voluntarism and Decentralised Governance

8.10.1 The Role of NGOs

Panchayati raj and NGOs have played a tremendous role in the empowerment of SCs/STs and especially women.

There are literally thousands of NGOs spread across the country, some of them working in even remote villages. And there are NGOs of all kinds: ranging from those funded by foreign agencies, government departments and local sources. Enormous amount of funds that run into several hundred crores coming from several sources into NGOs always do not reach the target population. In the last decade or so the development activists/experts with high salaries have become an elite class of their own and they tend to see their work more as a profession to be pursued rather than a social commitment. Also today, many a government programme/schemes (some of them funded by World Bank, Asian Development Bank, etc.) are increasingly being implemented through NGOs. This had led to cooption of NGOs into the government process which is plagued by corruption and vested interests.

> A survey conducted in 1991 (Prasad) found 786 bonded labourers in 120 out of 298 surveyed villages. The survey documented the castes of 731 out of the 786—690 were Dalits, 21 belonged to other lower castes, 11 from dominant castes and 9 were STs, and 19 were women. About 147 bonded labourers were between 11 and 15 years of age, 35 below the age of 10. Over 300 were below the age of 20.

But all this cannot distract us from the fact that over the last three decades or so NGOs have played an instrumental role in the conscientisation of the SCs, STs and women in their struggle for equality, social justice and dignity. By taking up issues of bonded labour, caste prejudices and cruelties, wages and working conditions, rape and violence against women, legal reforms, adult education and so on have affected a radical change in the political consciousness of the disadvantaged and marginalised section of the country. Their socio-economic programmes, especially self-help groups for women have significantly empowered the lower castes and women.

The non-hierarchical and participatory approach of the NGOs has done wonders in promoting decision making and direct participation of people in their socio-economic development. This participatory approach has substantially increased the efficiency and sustainability of several projects. For instance in projects in areas like rural water supply and sanitation, watershed development and drought prone areas which focus on the problems of people living in dire conditions. This method or model or democratic practice could be replicated in local bodies or decentralised political structures with great benefit.

Self-help groups as a mechanism to tackle the crucial problem of rural credit was initiated by NGOs. Self-help groups (SHG) were originally devised as informal support system for the very needy who could not access funds for consumption and production purpose because of poverty and vulnerability. By forming self-help groups women come together to pool resources and provide mutual support in times of distress; also take up economic projects to earn money and improve the quality of their lives. The utilisation and repayment of loans have been almost 100 per cent successful. Now financial institutions have stepped into fund self-help groups in their projects. SHGs have been a tremendous success and have already sown the seeds of genuine political and gender empowerment.

8.10.2 Panchayat Raj—Towards Decentralisation

Panchayat system has been a natural extension and expression of the democratic principles of the state. Much before Independence Gandhiji spoke of 'Village *Swaraj*', of villages as autonomous self-governing units. Incidentally, Karnataka has a long history of *Panchayats* at the village level. Mention must be made here of the two statutes, namely, Mysore Village Panchayats Regulation and the Mysore District Boards Regulation of 1926, both of which were in force till after independence.

> BOX 8.3
>
> **Types of NGOs**
>
> NGOs are principally of three types:
>
> - One, those which concentrate mainly on relief and welfare activities.
> - Two, those which focus mainly on community development and act as mobilisers in the community.
> - Three, NGOs which have evolved from people's movements in the area of human rights, women and *Dalit* rights, social justice and so on.
> - There are several NGOs such as MYRADA and others working in Karnataka in the area of rural development. They have built partnership with government agencies in the implementation of several of the development projects. NGOs, notably MYRADA has been able to take the lead in the state in promoting innovative community-based initiatives and building local level structures which the Karnataka government takes advantage of while implementing its many schemes.
>
> *Source:* Directorate of Kannada and Culture, Government of Karnataka.

After Independence, the concept of *Panchayats* was given due weightage and enshrined in the Constitution of India. Article 40, one of the Directive Principles, states that: "...the state shall take steps to organise village *Panchayats* and endow them with such powers and authority as may be necessary to enable them to function as units of self-government."

Karnataka has been a pioneering state in both implementing and further developing the *Panchayat Raj* in the country. In 1959, the state brought into effect the Mysore (Karnataka) Village Panchayats and District

FIGURE 8.7

The Karnataka State Formation of New Districts from 1973 to 1997

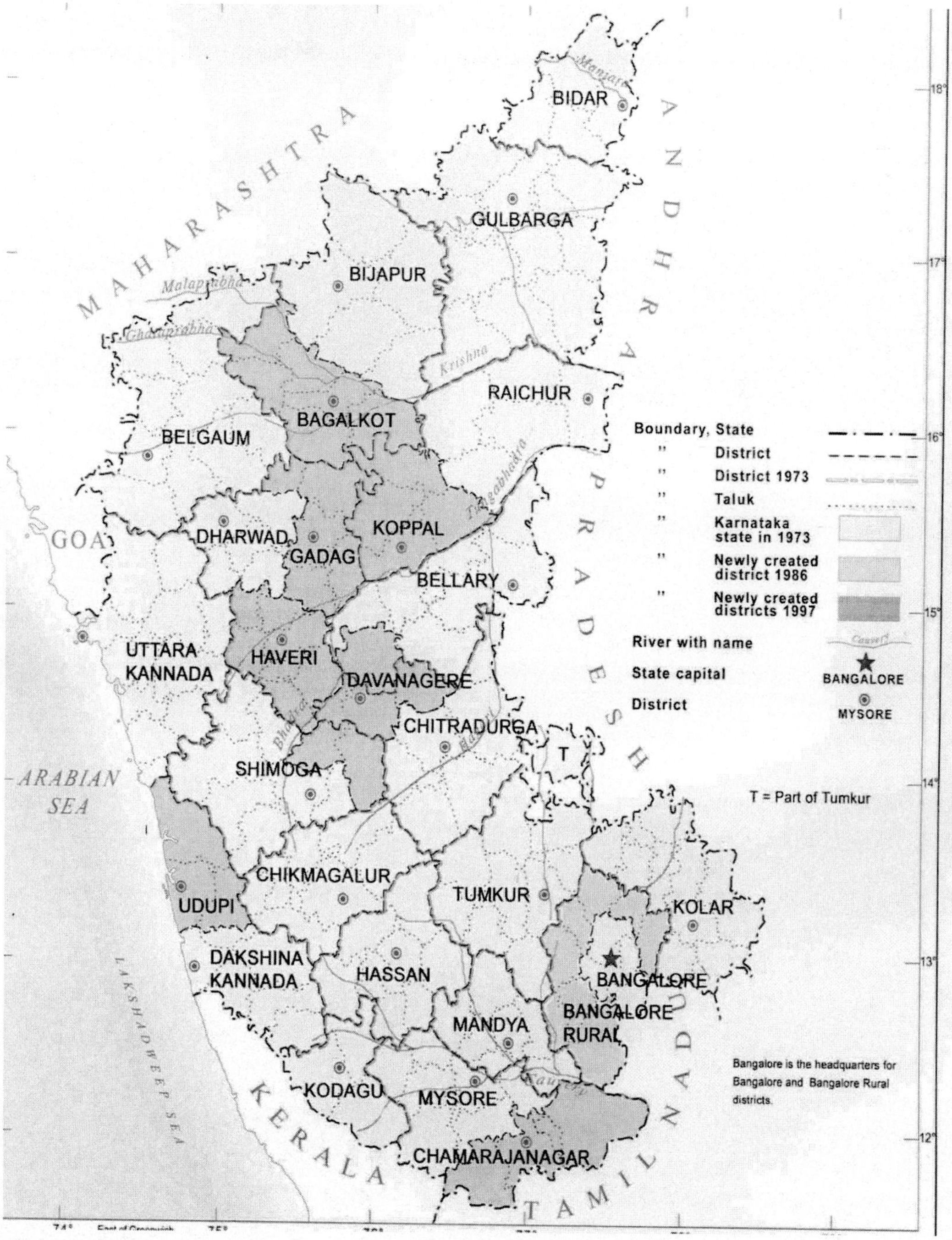

Source: Directorate of Census Operations, Karnataka, *A Historical Atlas of Karnataka.*

Boards Act, under which a three-tier *Panchayat Raj* structure, comprising village *Panchayats, Taluka* Development Boards and District Development Councils were set up. The *Panchayat Raj* experiment was carried forward further in 1983 with the enactment of a legislation that transferred a wide range of functions of the government to *Zilla Parishads* and *Mandal Panchayats*. And the *adhyakshas* of *taluka* and *Zilla Panchayats* were made chief executives.

Ten years later, in tune with the changes mandated by the 73rd and 74th Amendments to the Constitution (1992), the state passed The Karnataka Panchayat Raj Act in 1993. The Act provides for an elected three-tier structure at the village (*Gram Panchayat*), block(s), and district (*Zilla Panchayat*) levels. The *Gram Sabha* is the foundation for this three-tier structure. The *sabha*, which consists of all persons on the electoral roll in a village, meets twice a year to review the accounts and performance of the *Gram Panchayat* and identify beneficiaries for various development programmes.

Gram Panchayat

It is the *Gram Panchayat*'s responsibility to maintain drinking water and rural sanitation schemes, construct and maintain village roads and drains, construct primary school buildings and maintain village libraries and reading rooms.

There are about 5,640 *Gram Panchyats* in the state.

Apart from statutory grants, the *Panchayats* has some sources of revenue from taxes on buildings, entertainment and markets.

Taluka Panchayat

The important functions of this *Panchayat* are the maintenance of rural water supple and sanitation schemes, the establishment and maintenance of primary schools, the implementation of poverty alleviation, primary health and family welfare programmes and the maintenance of health and *anganwadi* centres. The *Panchayat* is not empowered to raise its own funds but depends upon government grants for its activities.

There are about 175 *Taluka Panchayats*.

Zilla Panchayat

The *Panchayat* prepares the district plans and integrates it into the plans of *Taluka Panchayats*. Each *Panchayat* has five committees: one each for finance, audit and planning, social justice, education and health, agriculture and industry, with one general standing Committee.

The *Panchayat* does not generate revenue of its own but depend upon the statutory and discretionary grant from the government for its various programmes.

In all three *Panchayats* the statutory reservations are as follows:

- For SCs and STs, a minimum of 15 per cent and 3 per cent of seats respectively.
- For OBCs, 33 per cent of the total seats.
- For women, 33 per cent of the seats in each category.

8.11 Political Participation and the Question of Women's Empowerment

The oppression of women over thousands of years have two significant sides to it: one, the denial of equal rights, self-autonomy and dignity to women; two, the great loss of women's intelligence and skills in the process of human development. But freedom movement had helped thousands of woment cross the threshold and participate in public life by participating in processions, meetings and even court arrest and suppest imprisonment.

In the modern world, however, women's entry into and participation in public spaces, women's movement and writings have initiated radical changes in the production and structures of knowledge and power.

The UNDP and the Human Development Reports (1995) have aroused the conscience of the world and advocated radical reform of attitude and behaviour patterns in gender relations. Today the governments and societies the world over have become increasingly sensitive to the great mistake of excluding women, who form half the population of the world, while formulating strategies for human development and in the processes which determine developmental directions and priorities.

In India, the entry of women in the freedom struggle (1930s) may be seen as the beginning of women's entry into public space and their participation in decision making in public sphere. But after Independence, women's political participation did not grow to the expected extent.

Even today, few women are represented in political organisations and decision making processes. The labour movement, under male leadership, continues to be male dominated. The same could be said of mass organisations such as Peasant Federation, Raitha Sangha (Karnataka), Civil Society Associations, including Dalit organisation. For that matter, even in political parties the representation of women is quite low. In the recent Lok Sabha elections (2004), very few women stood for elections. And in the Cabinet run by the Congress Party that swears by Women's empowerment there are hardly any women. Women's Reservation Bill (1996) hangs in suspense.

What needs to be understood here is that the representation of women in power-structures and decision making processes and their empowerment connotes not only control over resources: human, financial and physical, but also the right to their own beliefs, values and attitudes. This implies too the right and freedom to participate and influence the political processes which affect society and individual lives.

The *Panchayat* system with 33 per cent seats reserved for women in the three-tier structure, including reservation of seats for women for the post of Chairperson and Vice chairperson has initiated considerable changes in the power structure of the local bodies.

BOX 8.4

Women's Representation in Rural Local Bodies in Karnataka under Panchayat Raj Act, 1993

The share of female *Gram Panchayat* members among those below 30 years of age is 28 per cent, at the *taluka* and *zilla* levels the percentage work out to 37 per cent and 34 per cent respectively. Evidently, younger generation women are showing interest in PRIs.

The overwhelming majority (68 per cent) of women members at all the 3 levels of the PR system are married. However, single women like widows, divorcees and *devadasis* have also attained positions of power.

In all 17.7 per cent of women members are illiterate. Illiteracy among female members is higher at the *Gram Panchayat* level. However, it is promising to observe that 17.4 per cent of the members at the *Zilla Panchayat* level are graduates.

Data show domination of backward castes among women representatives (35.3 per cent at the GP level, 34.6 per cent at the TP level and 46.4 per cent at the ZP level).

Mention must be made here of Karnataka's pioneering efforts in this radical political process. The Karnataka Panchayat Raj Act, 1985 was an historic attempt at decentralisation of power and bring women representatives into the local self-government institutions. This Act has had tremendous effect on rural women in the state by legitimising, not only the entry of women in greater numbers into these hitherto male-dominated public space, but also by giving them functional decision-making powers, no matter how limited and constrained, over public resources.

This process of radical change in the position of women has been further strengthened by legislative Acts such as Equal Remuneration Act (1976), Dowry Prohibition Act (1984), Devadasi (Prohibition of Dedication Act), and the formation and activities of Department of Women and Child Welfare (1975), the Women's Development Corporation (1987), and self-help groups in the rural sector, etc.

But all this should not make us blind to the ground realities. Reports of exploitation, harassment, marginalisation of women in decision-making process, and violence against women show most forcefully that legislations or political measures are not enough, rather they are only jobs half done, and that this huge task of the empowerment of women is an incomplete project and it needs to be carried forward with greater rigour and dedication.

Today, Karnataka boasts of having more than 40 per cent of women representatives in the *panchayats*. And a considerable number of Dalit women as chairpersons and vice chairpersons in the *Zilla Panchayats*, but a close look at the ground realities reveals a complex picture plagued by many problems due to the patriarchal attitudes and values.

- In most cases, women have been elected as proxy candidates to stand in for powerful men backers.
- Women's ability to articulate women's issues, especially issues of injustices towards Dalit women, is found to be weak.
- Since the structure of social power is controlled by men, women even when they get elected to position of authority, have no power. Power remains gendered.
- A recent report (V. Vijayalakshmi, 2002) reveals that consultations and decisions on crucial issues are taken by men (sometimes with individuals who are not elected members) and the decisions are not communicated to women. More than 90 per cent women did not/could not carry out the functions of the Panchayats. Nearly 90 per cent women perceived their status in the *Panchayats* as 'low', with no real authority and power.
- Active participation and exercise of power by women of courage is often met with intolerance,

intimidation and harassment. There have been instances of backlash from men by way of engineering no confidence motion against such women.

Despite these facts it must be said that there are several cases of women in *Panchayats* who have stood up to their beliefs and values and performed their given tasks with courage and determination. This is of course true in all other sectors as well. However, the political participation and empowerment process cannot be reversed. It is an ongoing process, fraught of course with constraints and problems that needs to be overcome.

BOX 8.5

A Story of Courage

Generally politically active women and their works are viewed with suspicion and not tolerated. In 2002, in a *Gram Panchayat*, no-confidence motions were moved on three occasions against a woman president. Certain men and vested groups made false allegations against her. However, on all three occasions the woman-president managed to get the required number of votes to defeat the no-confidence motions. It was a triumph of her courage and commitment to the cause of the *Panchayat*.

8.11.1 Some Government Initiatives

Karnataka Mahila Abhivrudhi Yojana (KMAY)

The KMAY earmarks one-third of the resources under all schemes and programmes of various government departments for women. This is done with the hope of giving women greater access to government programmes. From 1993-94, 11 departments have been earmarking one-third of their financial resources for the developmental programmes for women.

The Mahila Samakhya

The Mahila Samakhya is a pilot programme of the Department of Education, Ministry of Human Resource Development, Government of India. It was born out of the emphasis given in the New Education Policy of 1986 to the need for education programmes to play a 'positive, interventionist role' in bringing about women's equality. The programme was launched in Gujarat, Karnataka and Uttar Pradesh.

Despite the many educational and developmental programmes undertaken by the government over the past four decades, women remain exploited and oppressed. The worst affected are the poor, rural women who are the most powerless group of all. They play no role in designing the welfare and development schemes but must remain their passive 'beneficiaries'. The objective of Mahila Samakhya is to reverse this process.

The basic strategy is the building of village level collectives or 'sanghs' which are not merely activity oriented but which enable women to improve their self confidence and recognise their own strengths.

Mahila Samakhya also sees education as a dynamic process of learning, where women receive meaningful information, engage in critical reflection and act as a collective to change the material and social conditions of their existence.

Devadasi Rehabilitation Project

The Project was set up in 1991 by the Karnataka State Women's Development Corporation to eradicate *devadasi* system prevalent in the state, especially in Belgaum. It was much more than economic rehabilitation, and called for the full involvement of the *devadasi* women. These women were organised into self-help groups to discuss the evils of the system and ways overcoming their problems. The issues were also discussed at *Gram Sabha* and *Panchayat* meetings. Eventually ex-*devadasis* came together to form an organisation of their own. The coming and working together of the community, affected women, government and NGOs contributed effectively to the success of the project.

BOX 8.6

Some Women's Organisations

Vimochana: The group's main focus has been domestic violence and sexual harassment at the workplace. They have been working in and around Karnataka for the last 17 years, mostly to protest and defend the rights of women wherever and whenever they have been violated. They have reached out to women who are victimised for dowry and either killed, driven to suicide or are forced to leave violent home situations, women who are victims of rape, sexual harassment, wife beating, of bigamous husbands or desertion, etc. The various activities of Vimochana include holding public meetings, poetry readings in parks and organising women's film festivals.

Women's Voice: The women slum dwellers have organised themselves into a community movement, Women's Voice, which fights for decent amenities and against the government's slum clearances for the last 22 years. In 1993 they initiated a rally of 100,000 of the urban poor.

Hengasara Hakkina Sangha: An organisation which builds capacities of NGOs and community-based organisations by providing training on women's rights, legal aid, etc.

State Commission for Women

Established in 1996, It is a statutory body especially formed in order to investigate and examine matters related to the safeguards provided for women under the Constitution. The commission is empowered to facilitate redressal of grievance of women as a result of their marginalised/unequal status.

TABLE 8.5

Some Key Statistical Indicators

(in per cent)

Below Poverty Line (1993-94)	*Rural*	*Urban*	*Combined*
All-India	37.27	32.36	35.97
Karnataka	29.88	40.14	33.16
Literacy in Karnataka	*1991*		*1996*
Male	67.3		73.7
Female	44.3		52.6
	1961		*1991*
SC-Male	14.87		49.69
SC-Female	3.04		25.95
ST-Male	13.24		47.95
ST-Female	2.81		23.57
Adult Literacy	*1981*		*1991*
	43.5		50.94

Source: For below poverty line (1993-94) it is the National Sample Survey for the respective year.

For literacy in Karnataka, it is both Census of India and NSS for the respective year.

8.12 The Way Forward

The state both at the Centre and the state level need to carry forward the politics of positive discrimination. Given the fact that more than 35 per cent of our population live below poverty line and the discrimination of and atrocities against Dalits and women never seem to stop, the stat's intervention in this matter both to protect and empower them through legal measures and constitutional provisions become inevitable.

In the context of globalisation the role of the state has become very critical. Profit and expansion are driving forces of the market forces. The fear that unchecked the transnational corporate world would eventually begin to take control over the world's resources and marginalise the role of governments is not unfounded. The state is accountable to people; the removal of poverty, inequality, and social justice remain to be its cardinal principle and responsibility.

While the state have to be made to live up to the ideals for which it came into existence, it would be rather naïve to let the fate of the people depend entirely on the state and its policies. In this context, the roles of civil society Groups and NGOs have become doubly important and even critical, especially to the cause of the oppressed and the marginalised sections of the society. Also, only civil society politics can critique and keep under check and possibly prevent the excesses of both the state and the corporate world.

NGOs: NGOs do represent today a truly non-party political process on a massive scale and they have contributed tremendously towards the empowerment of the lower castes and women. The implication of this huge experiment and process for the next two or three decades needs to be critically analysed and reassessed if only to bring into focus the problem areas and priorities of the disadvantaged and marginalised sections in our rapidly changing world today. The criticism that NGOs have become parallel governments with no accountability cannot be completely ignored. But in this matter, people involved in the process are the better judges and the decision to support, reject or change things lies with them.

Panchayat: The budget allocation for each *Panchayat* has considerably increased every five years. Ideally funds should be allocated as block rather than sectoral grants. There is a need to integrate the three-tier efforts and promote an integrated area planning, starting from the *Gram Sabha*. And the larger social goals and needs to be kept in mind by the local community while formulating village and block level plans.

Reservation of seats for women, SCs, STs and OBCs in *Gram Panchayat* is fraught with problems (women-43.8 per cent, SCs-22 per cent, STs-9 per cent, OBC's-35 per cent). They also have reservations for the post of chairpersons and vice-chairpersons of *Gram, Taluka* and *Zilla Panchyat*. There have been many instances of the dominant castes (often landlords and castes like Vokkaligas, Lingayats, Bunts) both inside and outside *Panchayat*, harassing and preventing reserved candidates, especially women, from contesting in the election for this high post. More than the government or police intervention in this matter, the intervention of people themselves would be truly a triumph of *Panchayat Raj*.

It is found that there is a large-scale misuse of funds and abuse of power in the *Panchyats*. It appears that most representatives are not seriously concerned or worried about these corrupt practices, rather they are interested in getting maximum benefit for themselves out of their position, irrespective of their level of involvement. With large funds flowing into these *Panchayats*, especially *Taluka* and *Zilla Panchayat*, the representatives are more concerned about their share of the bribe and commissions. Evidently this corrupt practice is not confined to the *Panchayats* alone. It is almost endemic in this state and country. The only effective way to change this or keep it under check would be for people to become alert and keep vigil over the activities of the *Panchayat*.

Dalits: The debate on the implications of modernity and globalisation for SC/STs, women and other economically disadvantaged and marginalised people is of crucial importance today. Vocal sections of Dalits and feminists argue that there is no alternative but to use the forces of modernity and globalisation for the advantage and benefit of the poor and marginalised. In fact, modernity, they would argue, in comparison with traditional institutions and practices, is liberative and ought to be appropriated to our benefit. There is also a significant section of Dalits who believe that while the 'new capitalism' has its charm and apparently liberative potential, it is ultimately destructive and would marginalise huge sections of society. In other words, the new capitalism with its corporate world and their global reach is driven by profit motive and power. It would be naïve to believe that globalisation would help realise our socialist ideals. In fact the whole process is geared towards increasing control and power over land, water and natural and human resources, which could only reduce SC/STs to marginalised existence.

Both appear to be extreme positions. A middle path is possible. Dalits cannot reject modernity much less be naïve as to believe that modernity *per se* could be liberative. They have a right to a life of security, comfort and dignity. At the same time, their voice against all forms of oppression and violence needs to be kept alive.

References

Directorate of Information (1957). *Mysore Rajyada Anki Amshagala Kaipidi* (Kannada), Directorate of Information, Bangalore.

Fernandes, Walter (1996). *The Emerging Dalit Identity—The Re-assertion of the Subalterns,* Indian Social Institute, New Delhi.

Government of Karnataka (2002). High Power Committee for Redressal of Regional Imbalances, June.

Kuppuswamy (1978). *Backward Class Movement in Karnataka,* Bangalore University, Bangalore.

Muthanna, I.M. (1997). *Karnataka: History, Administration and Culture.*

Nagaraj, D.R. (1993). *The Flaming Feet—A Study of the Dalit Movement in India,* South Forum Press in association with Institute for Cultural Research and Action (ICRA), Bangalore.

National Institute of Advanced Studies (1998). *Status of Rural Women in Karnataka,* Bangalore.

Nilakanta, Sastri K.A. (1955). *A History of South India.* Government of Karnataka (1999). *Human Development in Karnataka 1999.* Planning Department.

Omvedt, Gail (1994). *Dalits And Democratic Revolution—Dr. Ambedkar and the Dalit Movement in Colonial India,* Sage Publications, New Delhi.

Simon, R. Charsley and G.K. Karanth (eds.) (2003). *Challenging Untouchability—Dalit Initiative and Experience from Karnataka,* Sage Publications, New Delhi.

Suryanath, U. Kamath (1980). *A Concise History of Karnataka,* Archana Prakashana, Bangalore.

———. (ed.) 1982-83. *Karnataka State Gazetteer,* 2 vols. (ed.) 1995. *A Handbook of Karnataka* (Gazetteer Dept.).

———. (2002). *Karnataka A Handbook,* Kannada Sahitya Parisha.

Vijayalakshmi, V. and B.K. Chandrashekar (2002). "Authority, Powerlessness and Dependence: Women and Political Participation", *Working Paper 106,* Institute for Social and Economic Change, Bangalore.

Yadav, Manohar (2003). *Socio-Economic Survey of Scheduled Castes and Scheduled Tribes in Karnataka: A Critical Analysis,* ISEC, Bangalore.

APPENDIX A-8.1

District-wise Details of Rajyothsava Awards for the Years 1995-2001

District	*1995*	*1996*	*1997*	*1998*	*1999*	*2000-01*	*Total*	*% Share in the State*
Bangalore (Rural)	2	1	2	1	-	3	9	3.46
Bangalore (Urban)	6	4	9	3	6	17	45	17.31
Chitradurga	1	-	1	-	-	1	3	1.15
Davanagere	1	1	-	3	2	-	7	2.69
Kolar	2	4	1	2	5	2	16	6.15
Shimoga	2	2	1	3	3	2	13	5.00
Tumkur	14	1	1	2	7	2	27	10.38
Bagalkot	1	1	4	2	-	-	8	3.08
Belgaum	-	4	-	2	1	3	10	3.85
Bijapur	2	1	-	5	1	2	11	4.23
Dharwad	7	1	2	3	-	2	15	5.77
Gadag	2	1	-	-	-	1	4	1.54
Haveri	-	-	-	-	1	-	1	0.38
Uttara Kannada	-	1	2	2	1	2	8	3.08
Bellary	1	2	1	2	2	1	9	3.46
Bidar	-	-	1	1	-	1	3	1.15
Gulbarga	1	1	2	1	2	1	8	3.08
Koppal	-	-	1	-	-	-	1	0.38
Raichur	1	-	1	1	1	1	5	1.92
Gulbarga Division	3	3	6	5	5	4	26	10.00
Chamrajnagar	-	-	-	2	1	-	3	1.15
Chickmagalur	1	1	-	-	1	1	4	1.54
Dakshina Kannada	-	1	1	3	3	3	11	4.23
Hassan	1	2	2	3	-	1	9	3.46
Kodagu	-	1	1	1	-	-	3	1.15
Mandya	3	3	2	3	2	1	14	5.38
Mysore	2	3	4	3	3	6	21	8.08
Udupi	-	1	1	1	1	2	6	2.31
Mysore Division	7	12	11	16	11	14	71	27.31

Source: Directorate of Kannada and Culture.

Chapter 9

Social Sector Development

By the very wider meaning of 'development'—unlike in mere 'growth'—is implied a social and economic transformation that represents an inclusiveness rather than social exclusion of the marginalised and the weaker sections of a society. This chapter takes a look at the efforts and processes of those sections of population that were historically subject to social exclusion: the Scheduled Castes and Tribes, and women. The state of Karnataka has enjoyed the fair reputation for a long time now for having been one of the more 'progressive' states in this respect. Yet, as the different sections in this chapter makes a point the challenge is daunting.

9.1 The Socio-economic Status of Scheduled Tribes in Karnataka

One of the groups more vulnerable to exploitation is Schedule Tribes[1] (STs), which is heterogeneous with different social and cultural identities. The STs constitute around 8.6 per cent of the population in the country. Historically, such differences have not only segregated STs from the mainstream society but also excluded them from getting the benefits of developmental programmes. They live in different geographical areas with many clans and nomadic bands. The lifestyle of tribes is highly influenced by their close dependency on the forest for cultivation, collection of forest produce and hunting. Apart from this, they focus on mixed cropping strategies coupled with shifting cultivation, risk aversion and ecological adaptation.

In Karnataka, tribals belong to Dravidian language family who speaks 9 different unrecognised languages. There are 49 major tribal groups dominated mainly by Adiyan, Bhil, Gond, Irular, Koya, Kuruba, Thoti, and Yerava in the state.

According to Census 2001, there are 34.6 lakhs tribes in the state, constituting 6.6 per cent of the total population (Appendix A-9.1). There are 7.39 lakh tribal households of which, 5.8 lakh (78.3 per cent) live in rural areas. Around 70 per cent of tribal population are concentrated in five districts of the state *viz.* Bellary, Bidar, Chitradurga, Mysore, and Raichur (Figure 9.1). Chitradurga has the highest density of tribal population in Karnataka. Interestingly, gender gap among tribal communities in Karnataka decelerating

FIGURE 9.1

Percentage Change in STs of Karnataka during 1991 to 2001

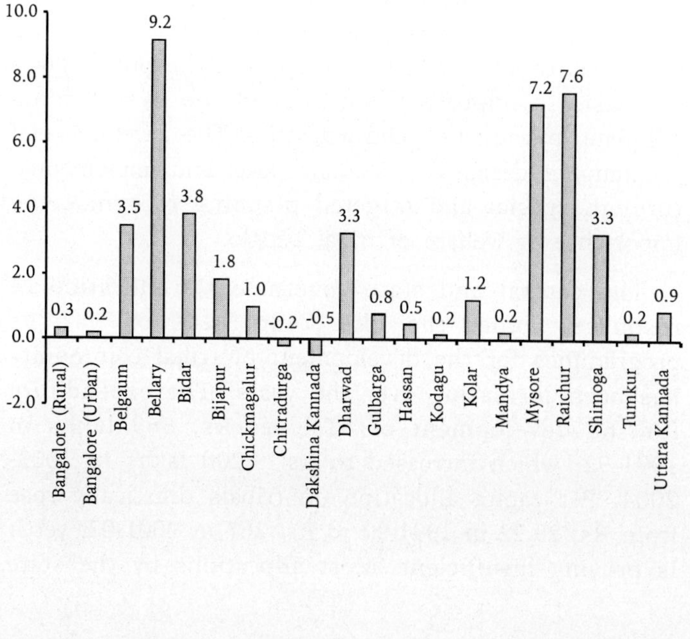

1. The STs were identified on the basis of certain well-defined criteria including the traditional homeland of a definite geographical area, distinctive culture including shyness of contact, occupational traits such as pre-agricultural modes of cultivation and general lack of development. However, Constitution of India in Article 366 (25) defined Scheduled Tribes as "such tribes or tribal communities or parts of or groups within such tribes or tribal communities are deemed under Article 342 to be ST for the purpose of this Constitution" (Government of India, 1960). However, this chapter uses STs or tribal or tribes refer to the various tribal communities.

from 39 in 1991 to 28 in 2001. Further, Dakshina Kannada district registers more females than males (Figure 9.2). The tribes who live in the interior or remote areas and in the close vicinity of forests and hills are the poorest and vulnerable to exploitations. In recent times, non-tribal people have slowly driven away the tribals from fertile plains. The child, infant and maternity mortality rates are found to be high among tribal communities due to indigenous medical practices and non-availability of health centres.

FIGURE 9.2

Demographic Changes in STs of Karnataka between 1991 and 2001

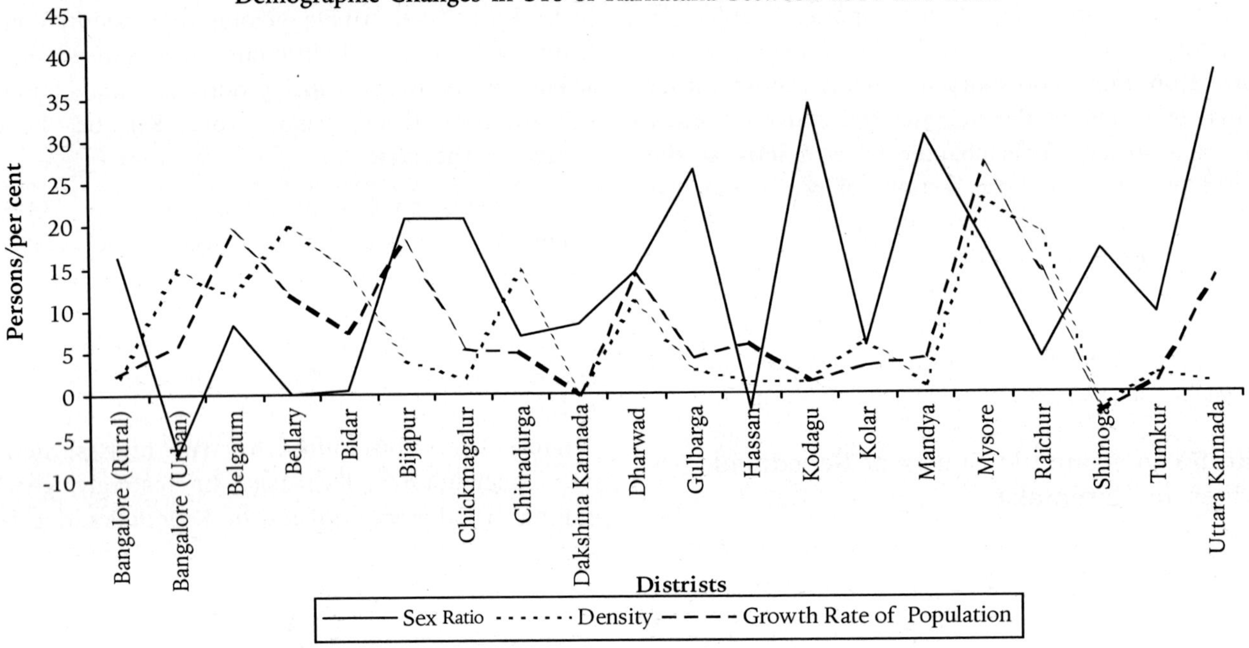

Since Independence, both central and state governments have launched a series of developmental programmes for the upliftment of tribals. The notable among them is designing specific policy goals and objectives of the Directive Principles. The policy gives emphasis to improve the quality of life by providing adequate infrastructure and amenities. The developmental programmes designed at national level and implemented through special and targeted planning recognise the importance of welfare of tribal people.

The central and state government's allocation of resources under the Five Year Plans on various programmes for the development of tribal community has been increasing over the years. The expenditure for the development of STs was Rs. 569 lakhs in 1991-92; which increased to Rs. 9,200 lakhs in 2003-2004. Per capita allocation on tribals drastically rose from Rs. 29.72 in 1991-92 to Rs. 267 in 2001-02, yet it is proving insufficient. Most allocations by the state government are meant for providing social and economic services to STs, which is declining over time. On the other hand, the expenditure under the heading of welfare of STs[2] constitutes major part of the total capital expenditure allocated for the upliftment tribal community (Appendix A-9.2). The overall budget allocations has been growing drastically in the recent past due to the implementation of many effective safeguard measures through developmental programmes. However, the developmental programmes failed to bring desired improvement in the social and economic status of tribal community in Karnataka.

In this context, this section attempts to review the development of STs in Karnataka mainly to identify the loopholes in the existing programmes and propose alternative policy suggestions for improving their social and economic status based on limited source of data.[3]

2. In fact, welfare of STs mainly contributes expenditure on grants to *Zilla Panchayats* and *Gram Panchayats*, Special Central Assistance to TSP, Education and Housing.

3. The main sources of data are Census, NSS, Reports of various expert groups, field based empirical studies and Annual Reports of the Departments. Unfortunately, all these sources have their own limitations. Census being an important source of data for demography, Agriculture Census, Housing and Amenities and so on, but the information is available only once in a decade. Likewise, NSS Quinquennial Survey is another important data source, which is available once in five years. However, the information available is not in absolute terms for all parameters but only in percentages. Expert Group Reports constituted by the public authorities and field based empirical studies by the researchers, investigations are generally specific based and incomplete. Finally, Annual Reports provides the schemes under implementation and budget allocations for couple of years.

The rest of this section in the chapter is organised as follows: subsection 9.1.1 examines the overall development policies and programmes in Karnataka; subsection 9.1.2 discusses the present status of tribal community across different sectors; and subsection 9.1.3 provides policy suggestions towards a sustainable development of the tribal community in the state.

9.1.1 Policies and Programmes

Recognising that the STs count among the most deprived and marginalised sections of Indian society, a host of welfare and developmental measures have been initiated for improving their social and economic status in the society. In this regard, particular reference can be made to the tribal subplan approach, which came into existence as the main strategy from the Five-Year Plans. Since Independence both the government of India and the government of Karnataka have launched a series of development programmes for the upliftment of the tribals in the state. Broadly speaking, the programme structure comprises: (i) policy goals and objectives in the shape of Directive Principles in Article 46; (ii) the legislative and physical infrastructure in the fifth and sixth Schedule; and (iii) financial support under Article 275 for funding schemes that promote tribal development and welfare. In addition, attempts have also been made to design many policies to improve the quality of life and provide infrastructure and amenities to generate economic assets, and ensure access to inputs. The national programmes that are implemented by the state government recognise the importance of an all-round development of tribal people through special and targeted planning. Appendix A-9.3 gives list of major policies to safeguard STs in India in general and Karnataka in particular.[4] It is increasingly felt that the provisions of the Constitution have not been operationalised adequately to the benefits of STs. There is need to work on these provision more closely and even intensively.

9.1.2 Status of STs in Karnataka

The public interventions for the development of the STs have been proved to be inadequate over the years, causing a number of serious problems in maintaining quality of life. Landlessness continued to be a major problem, which is challenging STs in maintaining even a minimum level of livelihood.

Landlessness

The importance of land as a means of livelihood need not be overemphasised in an agrarian and rural based society. The livelihood and survival of tribals depends on agriculture and forestlands. But, growing incidence of the landlessness paved the way for higher level of poverty, as minimum critical level of access to resources determines the intensity and extent of poverty. Appendix A-9.4 depicts that the operational landholding of tribal communities largely falls in the category of semi-medium (2.01 to 4 hectares) and medium (4.01 to 10 hectares). Over time, the land base of these groups is declining sharply and number of marginal and small farmers is increasing substantially. According to Census 2001, 56.4 per cent of STs are left without any assets in rural areas and 30.7 per cent in urban areas. However, landholding among tribals has increased during 1993-94 to 1999-2000 both in rural and urban areas. There is a decline in landless tribals from 38.8 per cent in 1993-94 to 26.1 per cent in 1999-2000 (Appendix A-9.6). Although it is a good sign, it is not sufficient as compared to other communities. The legal status of the tribal land is complex and landholding is based on mainly individual ownership (*patta*), usufructuary rights to common property resources (CPR) and encroached lands. However, land alienation is the major problem confronted by the tribals in the state. This is because non-tribals are manipulating the records and grabbing the lands from tribal community, as they are fertile and productive. The economic status of the tribes declines due to growing landlessness. Therefore, protecting the tribal ownership of lands is an inevitable policy option to improve their status.

Agriculture and Allied Activities

Tribals operate over 6 per cent of the operational area in the state that constitutes about 11 per cent of the total operational holders. By and large, they are marginal and small farmers. Agriculture is mainly monsoon based due to topography of the tribal areas, which has been scattered with forests. Therefore, tribal farmers are suffering from frequent drought and crop failure in most of the years. The Department of Agriculture provides incentives by supplying diesel pump sets, sprinkler sets, agricultural implements, plough bullocks, 60 per cent subsidised loan to the eligible farmers. They are also given assistance for the construction of water storage tanks. The state government has spent Rs. 31 lakhs in the year 2002-03 for implementing various schemes from which 1,086 tribal farmers are benefited.

---

4. For more discussion on government policies and programmes and its implications, also refer Sankaran (2000), Srivastava (2000) and Singh (2000).

(a) Animal Husbandry and Dairying

The Department of Animal Husbandry and Dairying helps tribals in generating income and increasing nutrition level. Since Ninth Five-Year Plan, the following measures have been taken up for benefiting tribals. White Revolution has increased productivity through cross breed programme relating to cattle herds by means of artificial insemination and embryo transfer technology in the tribal areas. Tribals have been given short-term training on live stock management and fodder cultivation. To meet the growing demand for the meat, local breed has been upgraded in case of goat, pig, rabbit and sheep. Besides, facilities are extended in the form of mobile veterinary clinic to reach and serve regularly in remote tribal areas of the state. Majority of the programmes implemented by the Department of Animal Husbandry is generating income to the tribals. In addition, tribals are supplied with milch cows, she buffaloes, sheep units, piggery units, etc.

(b) Horticulture

Horticulture is one of the important land based activities for the tribals in Karnataka. It covers an area of 12.71 lakh hectares in 1991-92 and rose to 15.6 lakh hectares in 2002-03 with a production of about 107 lakh tonnes from 90 lakh tonnes. Tribal sub-plan during the Ninth Five-Year Plan covers production of planting materials like fruit orchards, which is the thrust area for horticulture development in the state. However, under horticulture programmes, assistance is being given for establishment of half-acre coconut garden, one-acre mango or other fruit orchard and so on with the facility of drip irrigation. The main objective of the scheme is to minimise the utilisation of water in the cultivation of agricultural crops by adopting water saving devices for irrigation. It amounts to Rs. 28 lakhs during 2002-03 benefiting around 800 tribal farmers.

(c) Forestry

The tribal population is concentrated in and around the forest areas. The total geographical area of the state under forests is 0.39 lakh sq. kms in 2002-03. Due to deforestation and land grabbing, area under forests declined from 20.3 per cent in 1991-92 to 19.3 per cent in 2002-03. The forests are classified as reserved (28,611 sq.km), protected (3,932 sq.km), unclassified (5,748 sq.km), village (124 sq.km) and private (309 sq.km). The percentage of forest area in the state is 19.3 per cent, which is less than the all-India average of 33.5 per cent. Forest plays an important role for fodder, timber, medicinal plants and saleable minor forest produce. The life and culture of the tribals are closely linked with the forests. Government of Karnataka distributed seedlings for planting in private lands under Farm Forestry Programme with the help of village forest committees and self-help groups. Main activities of the Forest Department are to meet the demands of tribals in respect of raw material requirement like timber, firewood and minor forest produce. The Karnataka Forest Department is implementing the forestry and environment project for eastern plains over a period of five years. It covers 141 *talukas* in 23 districts of the state. The afforestation covers remain around 31.98 lakh hectares since 1991-1992, which comes under reserved forests and government lands. Participation of village community in regenerating and managing degraded forest areas is the cornerstone of government policy. Since tribals reside mostly in forest areas, institutional arrangements have been set up to get adequate representation of tribal members from 3,100 village forest committees. Likewise, main objective of the India Eco-development Project is to improve the capacity of protected area management to conserve biodiversity and increase the opportunities for local people so as to reduce negative impact on protected area. During 2003-04, Rs.750 lakhs is earmarked for protected area management, Village Eco-development Programme, environmental education and awareness campaign. The STs are given special assistance for the establishment and maintenance of social security plantation under forest department. Under the Tribal Sub-Plan (TSP), schemes such as raising of social security plantations, supply of bamboos and canes are implemented for the benefits of the tribal population.

(d) Common Property Resources

Tribals in Karnataka considered forests as common property and have a strong sense of affinity to the forest as their congenital boundary. The forests to the tribes have been their heart and soul as they depend on it for livelihood and spend most of their time in it. The legal status of tribal constitutes usufructuary rights i.e. right to collect fruits, leaves, waste wood and timber, etc. and the common property lands used for grazing. In addition, tribals cultivate a considerable amount of encroached land. Encroached land is divided into two categories: government land and other category of forestland on hill slopes. The law entitles ownership to tribals who have cultivated non-objectionable government land continuously for a decade. Some of the policies that guide the state government on land allotments for tribals may be acquired by the state at any time without appropriate or corresponding compensation. On the whole, the tribal population access to the common property rights is not clearly defined in the state.

Indebtedness

It is very difficult to assess the incidence of indebtedness among the tribes. Most of the tribals do not have access to banks in their area and even if it is there in some places, they do not have the working knowledge to operate and avail the banking services. It is evident from the Census 2001 that about 78 per cent of rural and 69 per cent of urban households have not availed banking service at all in the state (Appendix A-9.5). Moneylenders continue to play a predominant role in meeting the financial needs of the tribals and charge high rate of interest on loans. The repayments of such borrowings are realised through foodgrains in most cases. In order to safeguard the tribal from exploitations, government should implement the enforced rules and regulation strictly against them. Nevertheless, tribes are happy with the limited access to means of production, consumption in their day-to-day operations.

Employment Status

Although labour is the main asset for most of the distressed, broadening productive employment is crucial for balanced economic growth, elimination of poverty, social justice, income distribution, social stability, and peace. Nevertheless, in most parts of the country the level of unemployment and under employment remain high and Karnataka is no exception. The National Sample Survey (NSS) depicts that self-employment is enlarging among tribals in urban area as against rural Karnataka during 1993-94 and 1999-00. During the same period, dependence on agriculture is increasing in rural areas; may be due to non-availability of their traditional works. Urban tribals mainly depends on self-employment than wages and salary. Working women are growing in both rural areas as against males who are sinking under usual principal status[5] (UPS). In the case of current daily status (CDS), both males and females are growing over the years (Appendix A-9.6). Female participation rate is growing both under UPS and CDS in both rural and urban areas in Karnataka. It increases male unemployment, which indirectly show the way to child labour. However, to help growing unemployed ST candidates, many programmes have been made to train the unemployed tribals in the state. One of the provisions made at district sector is to give three months training in light motor vehicle (LMV) driving and autorickshaw driving and a sum of Rs. 150 to urban areas students and Rs. 300 to rural area student as stipend. And, Navachethana Scheme gives training in information technology (IT) in reputed training institutions. The main objective of TSP is to lay down policies, which will protect tribal culture, promote tribal welfare and to provide the tribal habitats with the basic minimum infrastructure.

Furthermore, five Integrated Tribal Development Projects (ITDP) are functioning in the districts of Mysore, Chickmagalur, Madikeri, Dakshina Kannada and Udupi. To alleviate poverty among STs, various income generating and employment-oriented development schemes are being implemented in the state. Swarnajayanti Gramswarozogar Yojana, Jawahar Gram Samridhi Yojana, Indira Awaas Yojana and Employment Assurance Scheme are the important poverty alleviation programmes implemented in Karnataka. Further, there are Integrated Tribal Development Programmes (ITDP) and non-ITDP that aims at alleviating poverty among tribals.

Under small-scale industries development programmes, training is given in various craft makings. After training tribals are being provided with living-cum-work sheds. Moreover, Department of Sericulture gives assistance for construction of silk rearing house. In addition, the Department of Rural Development generates employment for better standard of living of the tribals. However, most of the tribals remain below the poverty line and they are unemployed or under employed. In addition, forest protection measures prevent tribals from cultivation in and around forest. Shortage of minor forest produces limits their consumption and the available market surplus. Under these circumstances, tribals are coerced to migrate and take up employment in tertiary sector. As a consequence, tribals became bonded labourer or bankrupt. Therefore, the government has to rehabilitate and bring tribals into mainstream.

---

5. In India, NSS data captures the employment situation in an agrarian and unorganised economy using three concepts, namely, usual principal status (UPS), current weekly status (CWS) and current daily status (CDS). These three concepts are based on three different reference periods for ascertaining the actual status of a person. Under the UPS criterion, the reference period is one year and the activity status of a person is working or unemployed or out of labour force on the basis of activity pursued by him for a relatively longer time during the previous year. In the CWS approach a person, is considered as working or unemployed or out of labour force if the person was engaged in work related activity for at least one hour on any one day during the week, preceding the date of survey. Under the CDS concept, the unit of classification in half-a-day daily. In this approach, the person days are distributed by activity category during an average week.

Income

Adequate level of income and wealth indicate feasibility of leading a decent life. Agriculture, forestry and wage labour are the main source of income for tribals in Karnataka. Although tribals mainly depend on agriculture, they involve in traditional occupations like gleaning, hunting for consumption especially on festive occasions, and collect minor forest produce. However, collection of forest products is declining due to high degree of deforestation. A few tribes own lands while a large number of them are bonded slaves for moneylenders, landlords, contractors and a small proportion of tribes are labourers in plantations, and other enterprises. Due to decline in output from forest produce, tribals are increasingly depending on agriculture and construction, which provides seasonal employment. Tribals are underpaid, despite minimum wage fixed by the government. Though modern markets have come into existence, mobile traders, salesmen and others visit tribal villages during harvest and purchase the produce on the spot against their saleable items at lower than existing market rates. On the whole, it is very difficult to account tribal household income in money terms but most of the tribals falls below the poverty line.

Poverty

Scheduled Tribes in Karnataka suffer from large-scale poverty and deprivation. State sponsored development programmes over the years seem to have hardly contributed to contain poverty and deprivation. The monthly average per capita consumption is Rs. 404.28 in rural and Rs. 634.2 in urban areas. The proportion of poor among the tribal population is 24.78 in rural and 50.93 in urban areas. The relative inequality in consumption distribution is 17.71 in rural and 33.5 in urban areas. This structure indicates that the incidence of poverty and inequality is relatively high in urban areas. Nutritional status[6] is another indicator of deprivation and poverty. It is evident from Appendix A-9.7 that the weight-for-age and height-for-age nutritional index for children is relatively high among tribals in Karnataka in 1998-99. In other words, tribals are considerably behind compared to other sections of the society in Karnataka. However, tribals in Karnataka are better off compared to tribals in India. The NSS data reveals that around 70 per cent of the tribals are spending below Rs. 420 per month in rural whereas it is 43.5 per cent in urban. Interestingly, monthly per capita expenditure has increased over the period 1993-1994 to 1999-00. The infant, child and under five mortality rates[7] are other indicators of deprivation. The infant and child mortality rates can be considered as indicators inversely related to quality of life in the society. All the indicators recorded highest deprivation among tribal compared to other communities in Karnataka. On the whole, 50.9 per cent of urban and 24.8 per cent of rural tribals are living below poverty line. One of the reasons for such an outcome is that the policy gives less emphasis to human resource development. The government has taken several initiatives to improve their participation in economic activities and reduce poverty among the tribals. Need-based policies in areas such as education, health, and sustainable development are very essential to improve the living conditions of the tribals.

Educational Status

Literacy is an important index of educational development and one of the fundamental prerequisites to achieve cultural, economic and social progress. It creates awareness among the tribals and increases knowledge, which contributes to their economic development. Moreover, it brings a sizeable section of the tribal population to the mainstream. There has been a substantial increase in the literacy rates of STs during the last couple of decades but the gap between general population and the STs are widening. The public commitment to promote the educational interests of STs has yielded only a little benefit. However, partly they themselves are responsible for the situation because of the reason that majority of rural tribes felt education does not fetch a basic livelihood or a decent living. Added to this, lack of capital and other economic resources pave the way for child labour. Further, the literacy[8] rate among the STs accounted to be 36 per cent in Karnataka in 1996 whereas in rural it was 33 per cent. As usual female literacy is lower than the male counterpart in the state. Besides, adult illiteracy

6. Nutrition can be examined in terms of anthropometric measures like weight-for-age, height-for-age and weight-for-height. Given information on these indicators an assessment of the nutritional status is made by comparing with the respective median for the international reference population recommended by the World Health Organization and expressed in units of standard deviation. If the estimate for any of these measures fall short of the reference median by more than two (three) standard deviations, it indicates undernourishment (severe undernourishment).

7. The mortality estimates are not rates, but are probabilities, calculated according to the conventional life table approach. The probabilities are expressed as a proportion of 1000 live births/1000 children aged one. Infant mortality is the probabilities of a child dying before his first year birthday. Child mortality indicates the probability of the child dying between the first and the fifth birthday. Lastly, under-five mortality is the probability of dying between birth and exact age five.

8. A literate person is on who can both read and write a simple message in any language or dialect.

FIGURE 9.3

Education Levels by Gender in Karnataka: 1993-1994 and 1999-2000

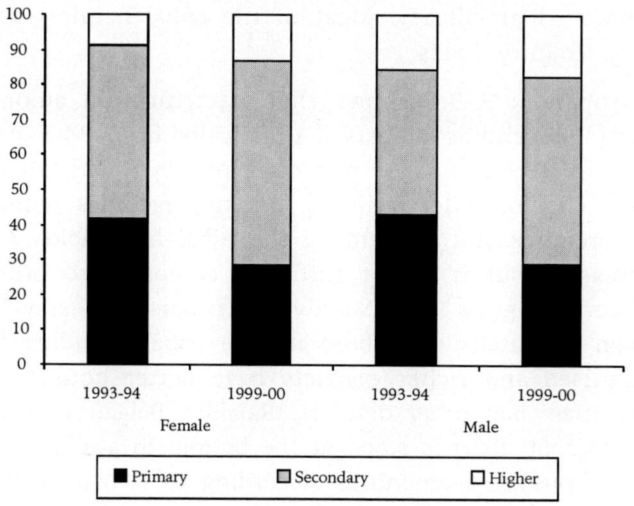

Source: National Sample Survey of Respective Rounds.

in rural and females illiteracy in urban is growing during 1993-94 and 1999-00 (Figure 9.3). Similarly, female literate level is increasing up to secondary school education in rural areas whereas it increases up to secondary and higher education level in urban areas. Likewise, male education beyond primary level is also increasing in both rural and urban areas over the same period (Appendix A-9.6). Nevertheless, high levels of absenteeism and alarming dropout rates contribute to slowdown in the progress of education in tribal areas.

Further, both boys and girls dropouts are lowest in Dakshina Kannada district in the state. On the contrary, Gulbarga and Raichur districts register the highest dropout rate (Government of Karnataka, 2001). To overcome this, several innovative policy interventions such as appointment of local women as teachers, micro level planning, etc. have been implemented at grassroots level to improve literacy and reduce dropout rates in the state.

In Karnataka, both the Departments of Education and Social Welfare Department have paid considerable attention on education in the tribal areas of the state. Social Welfare Department is playing crucial role in providing special schools for educational progress of the STs. There are 120 *ashram* schools benefiting 6,900 ST children at primary level. The government provides uniforms to students, Rs. 350 per boarder of hostel and Rs. 100 per annum for books. There are 104 pre-metric hostels run by the government providing boarding and lodging facilities to ST students. They provide stationery, books, uniforms and boarding expenditure of Rs. -400 per month for each student. An amount of Rs. 264 lakhs was spent for these purposes during 2002-03 that benefited 49,700 ST students.

Besides, voluntary agencies run hostels for the pre-metric students. There are 1,221 students studying in 24 grant-in-aid hostels. These students get Rs. 350 per month as boarding charges. Further, students from I to VII standard are given monetary incentive of Rs. 75 per annum and Rs.100 per student studying in VIII to X. In order to encourage ST students to fair well in public examination and to create a sprit of healthy competition among students merit scholarships are awarded for those who score above 60 per cent. In the same way, scholarships are sanctioned for higher education depending on the requirements.

Health Status

Health status of a community is an important indicator of its well-being. The delivery of primary health care is the foundation of rural health care system. Realising this, Karnataka has a wide institutional network providing health services both in rural and urban areas. The main objective of the Health Policy of both the central and state is to provide preventive and curative health care to all sections of the society including the tribals in remote and inaccessible areas. Attempts have been made during Seventh and Eighth Five Year Plans to provide health care at the doorsteps of the tribals by starting more numbers of subcentres (SC), primary health centres (PHC) and community health centres (CHC). Further, it was decided to establish one PHC for 20,000 populations and one SC for 3,000 population in tribal areas where as one CHC per 4 PHCs or for every 80,000 to 1.2 lakh population. Recently, to provide health for all in tribal areas, all the PHCs have been given ambulances. PHCs and mobile health units are functioning in the tribal area to take care of the health problem of the tribals. In addition, NGOs are also involved in these education-related programmes

Housing Status

Housing for tribals was not given proper attention in Karnataka. Majority of the tribals does not own a house or a land for constructing a house. The existing houses for tribals are very small without ventilation and located mostly in unhealthy surroundings in unauthorised or illegal sites in forest or government lands. According to Census 2001, about 60 per cent of household does not have drainage and bathroom facilities, 80 per cent do not have latrine facility in

Karnataka. Similarly, one-fourth of the tribal households do not have separate kitchen. Added to this, Appendix A-9.8 reveals that tribal household having an own house decelerates between 1991 and 2001 in Karnataka. In urbanised districts like Bangalore Urban and Kodagu, about 60 per cent of the tribals are houseless. Thus, homeless poor is considered an important component of the package of basic minimum services of the state. In fact, to improve the quality of tribal life, government decided to help the qualified tribals to construct well-ventilated and hygienic houses in authorised land. There are programmes for the distribution of house sites for poor in rural and urban areas. Under Ashraya Scheme, free sites are distributed and houses are being constructed for the tribals throughout the state. Besides, houses are also being constructed under Ambedkar Housing Scheme, Rs. 20,000 is paid as subsidy for tribals whose annual income is below Rs. 11,800. Similarly, Indira Awas Yojana named as Integrated Rural Housing aims at providing houses for those who are below the poverty line.

Infrastructure Status

Tribal villages do not have proper roads, electricity and drinking water facilities. It is impossible to bring economic, social and cultural changes among tribal community without proper infrastructure. As stated rightly by United Nations Centre for Human Settlements (1996), "Provision of infrastructure like safe drinking water, electricity, safe disposal of human waste are obviously central to good housing and living conditions, and to health." The government has recognised the fact that proper roads, electricity, and safe drinking water are highly essential without which the benefits of development programmes can reach remote tribal villages. Most of the tribal hamlets are using country roads.

FIGURE 9.4

Household Amenities among STs in Karnataka: 1991 and 2001

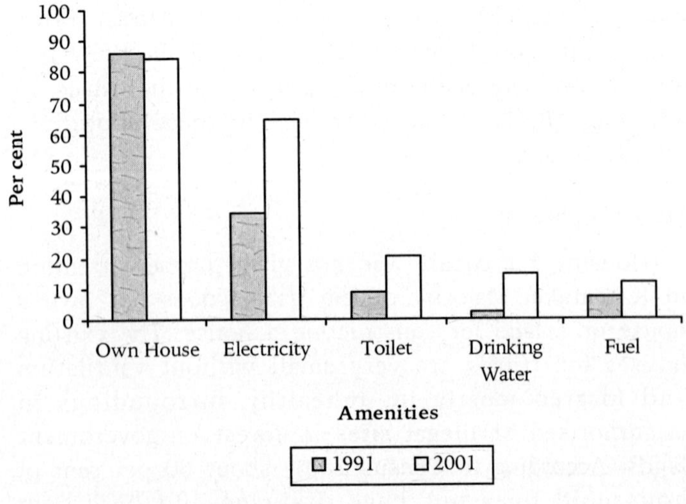

Note: Based on Appendix A-9.8.

Appendix A-9.8 shows that electrification among tribal households increased drastically from 34.5 per cent in 1991 to 64.7 per cent in 2001. Likewise, availability of toilet facilities, drinking facilities within the premises and fuel among the tribal households are increasing but it is not sufficient compared to other sections (Figure 9.4). Mainly the tribals who stay in urban Karnataka contribute it. The tribals residing in urbanised and richer districts have better household amenities than other districts. Raichur, Belgaum, Bidar and Bijapur districts stood at the bottom in availing the basic household amenities According to Census 2001, around 27 per cent in rural and 14 per cent in urban households do not have drinking water available nearer to their premises. Nearly, 35 per cent of tribal household does not have electricity facility in Karnataka. It is also found that about 40 per cent of rural and 19 per cent of urban households do not have electricity (Government of India, 2001).

The houses are being electrified by sanctioning supplementary financial assistance at Rs. 500 per house. Tribal houses and/or street lights are electrified using Baghya Jyothi Scheme. Safe drinking water is another crucial problem faced by the government because of very low subsoil water in the state. As a result tribal people carrying drinking water from far places. The government has been fixing norms to provide 40 litres of safe drinking water per person per day. Under TSP, the government provides borewells with hand pump for 350-tribe villages. The mini water scheme is implemented in 350 to 700 villages and the rest of the villages are connected with piped water supply schemes.

Status of Women

Scheduled Tribe women constitute about 49 per cent of the total tribal population. According to 2001 Census, the sex ratio amongst Scheduled Tribe population is 966 females for 1000 males. The females are the most neglected section of the society. They contribute substantially to family income through household affairs and participation in agriculture. They constitute major part of the working labour force in farming and collection of minor forest produce. Further, women take up wage labour whenever available and some time they work at nights during harvest seasons. Nevertheless, women in general are underpaid than men for the same labour time. Among all the tribal groups, women are associated with household rituals and men represent the household in public affairs.

Although women are members of tribal committees they are not encouraged to attend the meetings or participate in the proceedings. Barring to few instances, women do not have access to resources such as land, credit, training and counselling that would improve their standard of living. The provision of representation of women in the institution of local governance thanks to Karnataka's Panchayat Raj Act (1993) did not result in equal sharing of power, because of social hierarchy. Women are given much respect in all the tribal rituals. In order to increase school going habits at an early age, 70 women welfare centres are instituted to benefit 3,288 ST children in the state. Added to this, the children in these centres are provided mid-day meals at Rs. 1 per day and two sets of dresses annually in pre-primary schools.

As discussed above, women are burdened with various responsibilities. Apart from being engaged in domestic activities, they also play a major role in economic activities. They are mostly engaged in different agricultural related activities, collection of forest produce including firewood and in marketing their surplus agricultural and forest produces. They work more than men in all the socio-economic activities and are more concerned about the maintenance and the economic well being of the family as against men. Reflecting the recommendations of the various Five Year Plans, tribal women are encouraged to involve in crafting works such as bamboo and cane work, rope making, tailoring, weaving, honey extraction, etc. through financial assistance, technical knowledge, and providing necessary tools and raw materials. The emphasis is needed mainly in three areas: long-term strategy concentration on women's reproductive health, education and basic infrastructure, micro-level strategy based on local resources, and livelihood systems approach, which generates income through multiple activities.

Non-government Organisations

Non-government organisations (NGOs) have been playing a very important role in sharing the responsibility of the government in making the services available to tribals who live in remote and inaccessible areas. NGOs are more effective in bringing the most desired social change and development by virtue of their direct contact and linkages with the tribals. There are few NGOs who have played a significant role in mobilising support for the tribal people, in extending counselling and providing services like education, health, nutrition, women and child development, awareness generation and techno-vocational training. NGOs have created awareness among tribals about their rights and potentials, apart from safeguarding them from social and economic exploitation. The Karnataka's Panchayat Acts 1983 and 1993 provide reservation of seats in local government to ensure equal opportunity for women to participate in politics. However, it is not providing them effective participation. NGOs are also increasing advocacy, training, and counselling for tribal representation to increase their participation in local governance. Realising the facilitating role of the NGOs, the government of Karnataka is financing some of their programmes. Likewise, considering their work and commitment to the development of tribal population, the NGOs can be considered as a parallel agency as against government in the implementation of the development programmes for tribals.

Atrocities

Atrocities are punishments given to tribals or weaker communities by higher castes or non-scheduled castes. They have undergone suppression and exploitation over centuries. They are vulnerable to looting, arson, rape, social boycott, stoppage of work, shower of abuses, and humiliating treatment. The reasons for atrocities are many and the methods through which the acts of atrocities carried on are also varied. Many times, tribals are adjusting their lifestyles and livelihood according to the whims and fancies of the richer communities. Besides, oppressive features like poverty, illiteracy, ignorance, unemployment, and above all voicelessness continue to mar the life of STs everywhere. Unfortunately, this has been turned out to be a distant goal even after five decades of development planning. In the recent past, allegations of atrocities received from the members of the ST are inquired properly by the police officers of the district and also by the offices of the Directorate of Civil Rights Enforcement Cell. In spite of this, number of cases registered under the prevention of Atrocities Act is more than thousand during the year 2000 and it registers an alarming rise over the years.

9.1.3 The Road Ahead: STs in the New Millennium

During the planning era, the government of Karnataka has implemented several innovative programmes for improving the welfare of the tribal community. Both central and state governments have attempted to improve social and economic status of tribes, to prevent them from exploitation and to uplift them to join the mainstream society by implementing a package of policy measures. Yet, the benefits of the development programmes could not reach the community. Measures that would promote a comprehensive approach and remove the rigidities in the channels through which the services are delivered should be reinforced.

Landlessness

- Provide agricultural land and residential sites for all the tribal households. The legal status of tribal lands holdings should be made clear and effective.
- Computerising the forestland and CPR to protect lands from non-tribal encroachments. Enforce vigorous punishments for such encroachments.

Agriculture and Allied Activities

- They should be motivated to have additional rainwater harvesting to protect themselves from regular monsoon failures.
- Provide training in modern agricultural implements and motive them to go for commercial crop cultivation.
- Establish mobile marketing yards to visit all the major villages to procure the tribal produce.
- Focus horticulture and forest policies on area expansion, supply of plant and effective protection.

Educational Attainment

- Tribal education should be viewed as a long-term strategy and embedded in a meaningful policy framework. It is an important social resource and a means of reducing inequality in the society. More emphasis should be given to quality of education that makes tribal communities economically effective and independent. In addition, education centres libraries and resource centres that provide access to knowledge could be established.
- There are two main functional problems in delivering a quality education to the tribal community: (a) teachers are not regular to their duties; and (b) unsuitable school timings. Therefore, government must ensure that teachers are regular to the schools and school timing is suitable to the requirement of region specific economic activity rather than following a directive from the state. Doing so will help in reducing school dropout ratio.

Employment, Income and Poverty

- Government policies that benefited tribals and improved their position in the workforce have to be further strengthened or adjusted to meet the changing position of tribals. For instance, the state's reservation policies for SC/ST have to be defined separately for each group.
- The proposed plans should emphasise creation of additional income yielding activities through family-based economic activities. Besides, strictly instructing the contractors to hire local tribal people in building the infrastructure in tribal areas, as such arrangement provides them employment opportunities.
- The creation of exclusive markets to enable producers and traders in the rural areas to sell their wares can be considered.
- Provide employment guidance and free housing facilities for all deserving migrant tribals for at least six months period.

Demography and Health

- The tribals in Karnataka are suffering from many chronic diseases, namely diarrhoea, dysentery, guinea worm, and skin diseases, due to unsafe drinking water and lack of drainage system. All these diseases are preventive in nature if government takes necessary action. Besides, many tribal peoples consume indigenous medicines in their day-to-day life for both chronic and acute disease, which may not be effective and lead to further health complications.
- Often, government hospitals are not well equipped with adequate number of doctors and medicines. Majority of the tribal patients are not given proper attention. Hence, government should educate tribals to have modern medicines through NGOs and create awareness among tribals with popular personalities using mass media. Besides, the doctors must be made to be accountable to attend dispensaries regularly in the tribal areas. Furthermore,

provide safe drinking water and sanitation facilities to all tribal villages in the state.

- It is inevitable to create awareness about education, nutrition, health practices, hazards of teenage pregnancies, maternal and child health and family welfare programmes through appropriate disseminating mechanism and mass media.

Financial Facilities

- Considering the high scale of deprivation among tribes, it is necessary to increase public resource allocations to meet the economic and social need of the tribes. Given growing incidence of economic crisis, easily accessible and need based financial assistance must be extended by the government owned financial institutions. Besides, financial institutions must be encouraged through proper incentive mechanism to extend adequate institutional credit that would ensure social and economic justice for the tribals.

Non-Governmental Organisations

- NGOs should be fully utilised in the implementation of many tribal programmes, because their local base and rapport with the tribal people will strengthen the effective implementation of the programmes.

Social Security

- Policy imperatives for the state government include an early review and revision of the Old Age Pension schemes, extension of social assistance to cover everyone below the poverty line and provide incentives to the children to look after their aged parents. In addition, free old age homes need to be established exclusively for the tribals.

Equality for Women

- Efforts should be put in designing specific programmes for tribal women. Women's group should be formed in tribal settlement and there should be a network of these groups. These groups can comprise of both tribal and non-tribals, as the latter have the potential for marketing the produce in the urban centres. Leadership capacities of the tribal women should be strengthened.
- Amendments to legislations on property rights should be passed whereby tribal women can become joint owners of properties and assets earned by the husbands. SHGs and other village level committees and *Gram Panchayats* can work towards arresting gender specific measures that push tribal women into poverty and protect women's economic interests.

Atrocities

- More protection against harassment and exploitation in the workplace must be provided as tribals fail to report such behaviour due to lack of safety and security.

Disparities

- Districts with pronounced tribal inequalities need comprehensive programmes to take care of immunisation, awareness against female infanticide, improving educational attainment levels through higher female literacy, educating parents about the benefits of schooling for girls and increasing the per capita income to reduce the wage differential between tribals and non-tribals.

General Policies

- Area specific micro-level policy interventions must be designed on the basis of locally available resources and the problem specific to the region. The government policies must be culture friendly and the implementation of the programmes should be properly monitored involving tribal committees or tribal *Panchayats*.
- Create awareness among tribal peoples about the importance of education, health, infrastructure, and government polices. They should also provide basic amenities such as safe drinking water, housing electricity to all poor tribal families at their doorsteps.

9.2 Scheduled Caste in Karnataka: Analysis of Status

Scheduled Castes in Karnataka present a complex and mixed story of development. Their literacy, health and nutritional status, and overall living condition as such have improved considerably. Yet, they show poorly in terms of other development indicators. Poor housing conditions, landlessness, child and girl problems, social stigma of untouchability and such other social disabilities have made the Scheduled Caste people the victims of all forms of discrimination and deprivation—caste, class and gender.

Presently there are several schemes and programmes designed in the cause of the upliftment of Scheduled Castes. During the Sixth Plan Period the state started making strategic interventions through what is popularly known as Special Component Plan (SCP). Special Central Assistance (SCA) was also given to the states and union territories to help them move out of the state of abject poverty. Some schemes and programmes are oriented to generate income and employment opportunities. Due to the introduction of decentralised governance at grassroots levels their political empowerment has also been taking place. This is how the state's special concern and care are for attempting towards their overall improvement. But how far it has been real for them to experience such state sponsored benefits and whether there has been any improvement at all seen from the aspects of their livelihood and income position, and health and educational achievements is a question that is still open for probe. This section is an attempt in that direction.

9.2.1 Growth of Scheduled Caste Population

The trend with respect to the growth of the population of Scheduled Caste in Karnataka does not indicate to be in tune with regular demographic directions. The past few decades show that there has been quantum jump in the growth of population of Scheduled Caste in Karnataka. For the decade from 1971 to 1981 the population of Scheduled Caste increased from 13.14 per cent to 15.05 per cent to 16.20 per cent by 2001. In terms of decadal growth variation, the SC population in Karnataka grew by 45.33 per cent during 1971 to 1981, the highest ever-recorded growth rate, and by 31.70 per cent between 1981 and 1991. From 1991 to 2001 it has grown by only 16.21 per cent. On the whole, there is a declining trend in the growth rates.

As far as the degree of the rural and the urban concentration of the Scheduled Caste population in Karnataka is concerned, the 1991 Census reveals that 76.60 per cent of the Scheduled Caste was in rural areas and about 23.40 per cent in urban areas. The 2001 Census reports a lower per cent i.e., 74.93 per cent of the Scheduled Caste in Karnataka belonging to rural areas and consequently a higher proportion of 25.07 per cent in the urban areas. As against these, for the state as a whole, the total number of persons, who lived in rural and urban areas in 1991 constituted 69.08 per cent and 30.92 per cent, and 66.01 per cent and 33.99 per cent respectively during 2001.

If we look at the district wise-concentration of SC population in Karnataka, according to 2001 Census, Bangalore (Urban) district (9.94 per cent) ranks first in sharing the largest number of the Scheduled Caste, followed by the districts of Gulbarga (8.38 per cent), Mysore (8.24 per cent), Kolar (7.84 per cent) and Chitradurga (7.82 per cent). At the other end Kodagu (0.79 per cent) district shared the smallest portion of the SC population in the state.

9.2.2 Land Ownership and Employment

The employment situation of Scheduled Caste in Karnataka presents a grim picture. About 54 per cent of them are accounted to be landless agricultural labourers. According to 1981 Census, the Scheduled Caste dependent on landless agriculture labour were reported to be 46.24 per cent. Subsequently this dependence further increased. In 1991and 2001, the landless agriculture labourers among Scheduled Caste were accounted to be 49.87 per cent and 53.7 per cent, respectively. It means their presence in other sectors has been either decreasing or that, they have not been encouraged to make impressive shift towards other sectors. Despite different efforts, the presence of Scheduled Caste in primary sector continues, but mainly without assets. Presently, their employment shares in secondary and tertiary sectors make up only for 9.8 per cent and 12 per cent respectively. It should also be noted that even in agriculture and allied fields, the work opportunities are very uneven and irregular.

The situation with respect to owning land is also very precarious. Their holdings appear to be highly fragmented and chaffed off into smaller bits. Thus they prove to be hardly useful for cultivation in the real sense of the term. The Scheduled Caste in Karnataka own only 8 per cent of the total state's agricultural land. But due to fragmentation, from 1991 to 2001 their operational holdings in marginal size class have grown up from 45 per cent to 52 per cent. Despite land reforms and land purchase measures of the government of Karnataka, during the period from 1991 (9.95 hectares) to 2001(10.71 hectares), the area of operational holdings by Scheduled Caste has grown up only by 6 per cent. However, according to some micro studies, there is also a doubt about the quality of land that the Scheduled Caste got as a result of land reforms efforts in Karnataka.

Further when we look at land ownership pattern among Scheduled Caste from gender lens, for the year 2001, only 15 per cent of the SC women have been reported as proper cultivators as against 24 per cent of their men. Also, 69.31 per cent of SC women accounted to be landless agricultural labourers as against 43.16 per cent of their men in Karnataka.

According to NSS Survey 1999-2000, in the category of households earning from pension, the Scheduled Caste households constituted 27 per cent, whereas all other households in this respect constituted 44.6 per cent. Among the households earning from non-agricultural enterprises, the Scheduled Caste constituted only 10.9 per cent, but OBC and other households constituted 47.5 per cent and 38.8 per cent respectively. Hence, economic independence as such from the viewpoint of either sharing opportunities or earning from more rewarding sources still remains to be achieved by the Scheduled Caste in Karnataka.

9.2.3 Levels of Income and Expenditure

Given the disadvantageous position of Scheduled Caste in sectoral location of earning, one cannot expect their income position to be on par with others in the state. Therefore, compared to all other social and religious groups, the per household annual and the per capita income of Scheduled Caste are very low in Karnataka.

The NCAER Survey conducted in the year 1994 presents some facts relating to this situation. It reports that, the per household annual income and per capita income of Scheduled Caste in rural Karnataka was Rs. 16,579 and Rs. 3094, respectively. On the other hand, the per household annual income and the per capita income of Hindus was Rs. 27,801 and Rs. 4897 and those of Muslims was Rs. 23,661 and Rs. 3681, respectively. The average household and per capita income for the entire state was Rs. 27,372 and Rs. 4769 respectively. Both per household and per capita income of Scheduled Caste were 40 to 45 per cent less than the per household and per capita average income in the state. According to the NSS 55th Round of Survey, during the year 1999-00, the monthly per capita expenditure (MPCE) among Scheduled Caste in rural Karnataka was Rs. 419 whereas among OBCs and others it was Rs. 507 and Rs. 560 respectively. For all rural groups in Karnataka the average MPCE was Rs. 500. In urban Karnataka the average MPCE of Scheduled Caste was Rs. 593 whereas for OBCs and others it was Rs. 829 and Rs. 1044 respectively. For all groups in urban Karnataka the average MPCE was Rs. 911. This means compared to all groups, the MPCE of Scheduled Caste was the lowest both in rural and urban areas of Karnataka.

9.2.4 Literacy and Educational Levels

Education and literacy levels are considered to be decisive among the various determinants of quality of life of people and of social development. Awareness with respect to health and hygiene maintenance, better avenues of livelihood, etc. follow from the degree of literacy and education. The level of literacy and education among the Scheduled Caste in Karnataka has been increasing over the years. According to 1981 Census, the literacy rate among Scheduled Caste in Karnataka was 27.62 per cent. It increased to 38.06 per cent in 1991. For the state in general, the literacy rate for these respective years was 46.21 per cent and 56.04 per cent. According to 2001 Census, the average literacy rate for all the people in general in the state has been reported to be 67.04 per cent. For Scheduled Caste, the literacy rate improved substantially to 52.9 per cent. So, the number of illiterates among the Scheduled Caste has become less than 50 per cent.

The female literacy rate among Scheduled Caste in Karnataka, according to 1981 Census, was 11.55 per cent, but in the year 1991 it more than doubled to 25.95 per cent and in 2001, it registered a quantum jump to 41.7 per cent. The average female literacy rate in the state during these respective years was 33.17 per cent and 44.34 per cent.

However as per the estimates from NSS Report No. 473, 1999-00, the male and female literates among Scheduled Caste in rural Karnataka constituted 55.2 per cent and 32.5 per cent respectively. As of 2001, these are much higher at 63.8 per cent and 41.7 per cent respectively. In urban Karnataka the male and female literates among them constituted 74.6 per cent and 56.8 per cent. But the literacy rate at the level of graduation and above among Scheduled Caste in rural Karnataka was only 1.2 per cent for males and zero per cent for females. The fact that the females among Scheduled Caste are yet to receive required encouragement to educate themselves at higher levels remains a major concern.

9.2.5 School Dropouts and the Reasons

The drop out rates among the children belonging to the Scheduled Caste in Karnataka prove to be higher for all ages. During 2001, in the age group 6-7 the average drop out rate for these children was reported to be 15.8 per cent as against 9.3 per cent among others children. In the age group 13-14 the average drop out rate among SC children was 29.6 per cent whereas among all children it was 17.8 per cent. Viewed from gender disparities, the girls belonging to Scheduled Caste appear to be dropping out more in number than all girls. In age group 6-7 the drop out rate of SC girls was 16.3 per cent, whereas for all girls it was 11.5 per cent. Similarly in age group 13-14 the respective drop out rate for SC girls and all girls was 39 and 21 per cent.

The reasons for dropouts are varied. But poverty appears to constitute the prime reason for the drop outs. According to SC/ST Survey 1996, about 58.37 per cent of the dropouts take place due to circumstances created by poverty. Household work, where often females are affected, constitutes the next important reason why 22.90 per cent of candidates opt out of schooling process. But it is disturbing to note that 6.22 per cent of dropouts occur due to discriminatory treatment meted out to the enrolled Scheduled Caste students at different levels of their education.

9.2.6 Housing, Drinking Water and Sanitation

According to 2001 Census, while 30.64 per cent of the houses among Scheduled Caste in rural Karnataka were counted as good, 61.75 per cent and 7.61 per cent were enumerated as liveable and dilapidated. Among rural non-SC houses, on the other hand, while 37.50 per cent were reported as good, 57.12 per cent and 5.38 per cent were counted as liveable and dilapidated. Among urban SC houses, 45.88 per cent were reported as good and 47.88 per cent and 6.86 per cent were reported as liveable and dilapidated, respectively. The respective proportion of good, liveable and dilapidated among the non-SC houses in urban Karnataka was enumerated to be better—60.21 per cent, 36.94 per cent and 2.85 per cent respectively. It suggests that the housing situation of Scheduled Caste in both rural and urban Karnataka continues to be below the average housing situation.

The 2001 Census also reports that, while 88.44 per cent of the SC households in rural Karnataka have access to safe drinking water, only 78.63 per cent of the non-SC households enjoyed such access. Further, the SC households with latrine facility accounted for 21.18 per cent as against 40.80 per cent of the non-SC households in Karnataka. While 32.77 per cent of the rural SC households have bathroom facility, about 51.72 per cent of the non-SC households have this provision. Almost 81.48 per cent of the non-SC and 62.36 per cent of the SC households in urban Karnataka possess own bathroom facility most often attached to their houses. In brief, the housing situation for this social group is extremely bad.

9.2.7 Electricity Connections

As far the situation with respect to electricity connection is concerned there seems to be lot of improvement taking place since last 10 years. In 1991, in rural Karnataka, about 28.23 per cent of SC households were reported to have had electricity connections. Among non-SC rural households about 44.81 per cent were reported with electricity connections available to them. By 2001 about 64.47 per cent of the SC households and 74 per cent of the non-SC households were reported to have electricity facility. Similarly, during 1991, the urban SC and non-SC households with electricity connections were counted to be 54.05 per cent and 78.92 per cent respectively. In the year 2001, the position of both the urban SC households and non-SC households further improved to constitute 80.51 per cent and 91.92 per cent respectively.

9.2.8 Health and Nutritional Levels

According to NFHS 1992-93, the neonatal mortality rate for children of Scheduled Castes (63.80) was higher than others (46.70). Post-neonatal mortality rate was also higher among SC children (34.60) compared to others (23.90). And while infant mortality for SC children for the same year, was reported to be 98.40, for other children it was 70.60. After 10 years this situation has improved considerably.

According to NFHS conducted during the year 1998-1999, the neonatal mortality rate for SC children was reduced to 46.90 and for others it came down to 39.60. In case of post neonatal mortality for both SC children and others, the reduced rate was reported to be 23.00 and 16.80 respectively. Also infant mortality for SC children, after 10 years has come down to 69.90, whereas for other children it came down to 56.40.

As per the NFHS 1998-99 report, only 55.7 per cent of the SC women consume milk or curd as against 78 per cent of the OBC and 83.1 per cent of other class women. Also SC women who consume fruits constitute only 39.8 per cent as against 54.2 per cent of OBCs and 62.2 per cent of others. In terms of other food items like pulses, beans or green leafy vegetables too, the SC women show low levels of consumption as against OBCs and others. Therefore, substantial differentials become visible in nutritional status of women as seen in terms of their mean height and weight-for-height or body mass index (BMI). About 11.3 per cent of SC women were reported to be below the mean height, as against 9.2 per cent of the OBC women and 9.4 per cent of other women. Also about 44.2 per cent of SC women were counted to be below the BMI as against 40.1 per cent of the OBC women and 32.8 per cent of other women. As far as weight for children in Karnataka is concerned, about 23 per cent and 52.80 per cent of SC children were reported to be below 3SD and 2SD respectively. Among OBC children however, 12.20 per cent and 40 per cent were reported to be below 3SD and 2SD. And among other children, in this respect, 15.60 per cent and 41.30 per cent were reported to be below 3SD and 2SD.

9.2.9 Poverty and Public Distribution System

According to *Economic Survey of Karnataka, 2003-04*, the proportion of the poor population among both the Scheduled Castes (26.87 per cent) and the Scheduled Tribes (24.78 per cent) in rural Karnataka was more than the state average (18.08 per cent). In the urban context while the proportion of the poor population among Scheduled Castes was 47.50 per cent, among the Scheduled Tribes it was 50.93 per cent, against the state average of 25.83 per cent. Among the OBCs while the proportion of the poor population in rural and urban areas was 16.15 and 29.09 per cent, the proportionate share of the rural and the urban poor among others was 12.11 per cent and 16.81 per cent respectively. Hence, for both these categories the proportion of poor population was less than the state average. Keeping in view these figures, the Economic Survey concludes that "nearly half of these two social categories are poor whereas it is only a sixth for other households." Fixing annual income of Rs. 11,000 as a criteria to define poverty line among SC/Scheduled Tribes in the state, the SC/ST Survey 1996, carried out by the government of Karnataka, reports that about 92.6 per cent of the Scheduled Castes and 93.10 per cent of the Scheduled Tribes in the state fall below the poverty line. This of course could be substantiated by the information with respect to the number of green ration card holders among the SC/ST households in the state.

As anywhere else in India, the government of Karnataka has been implementing targeted public distribution system. Different types of ration cards—Green, Yellow, Saffron and so on are given to the people based on their economic backgrounds. Green cards are given to the BPL families and each one of these families is eligible for 20 kgs of rice and 5 kgs of wheat per month at subsidised price. According to SC/ST Survey 1996, in rural Karnataka about 93.95 per cent of the SC households and 91.01 per cent of the ST households possess green ration cards. And in urban set up, those SC and ST households, constituted 49.09 per cent and 42.62 per cent, respectively. The rest among both the categories of households owned other types of ration cards.

9.2.10 Panchayat Raj Institutions and Political Empowerment

Due to the provisions of Karnataka Panchayat Raj Act 1993, both membership and executive positions—have been reserved for Scheduled Caste in proportion to their population in the state, at all the levels of *Panchayat Raj* System. This has led to the political empowerment of Scheduled Caste at grassroots level in Karnataka. In the year 1995-96, the representation of Scheduled Castes in *Gram Panchayats* (GP), *Taluka Panchayats* (TP) and *Zilla Panchayats* (ZP) constituted 22.2 per cent, 18.0 per cent, and 18.0 per cent respectively. During the same year, about 7372, 251 and 63 SC women members represented to GP, TP, and ZP, respectively. But the quantum of SC representation dropped during 2000–2001 to be 18.57 per cent, 17.91 per cent, and 17.75 per cent respectively. In the same year, the SC Presidents and Vice-Presidents in G.P., T.P. and Z.P. were reported to be 18.25 per cent and 18.25 per cent, 18.29 per cent and 18.29 per cent and 18.52 per cent, and 18.52 per cent respectively.

Very often Scheduled Caste candidates have proved to be 'namesake representatives'. Some of the micro studies have proved that it is upper and dominant caste local elite or leaders who had a say in the selection and election of candidates for the *Gram Panchayats*. Political empowerment as such in reality turns out to be yet a far-off dream for the Scheduled Caste.

The fate of the SC women members was also the same as their menfolk. Sometimes some of the SC women members had a chance to become Presidents or Vice-Presidents wherever reservation to such positions occurred but their functioning was mostly controlled by local upper caste leaders and to some extent also by their male members. Therefore, in case of SC women members too, questionable authenticity continues as far as their political empowerment is concerned.

9.2.11 State Interventions, Budget Allocations and Expenditures

The Department of Social Welfare, Government of Karnataka, has been implementing about 68 schemes, 36 of them being under state sector and 32 under the district sector. In addition, there are 31 schemes being implemented under Non-Plan projects. Some programmes, specially designed to commemorate the

Ambedkar Centenary Celebrations, are also being implemented. Further, many schemes are also being implemented under Special Component Plan by several development departments.

For the past five years (1999-2000 to 2003-04) a total of Rs. 1,59,125 lakhs has been allocated in the state's budgets for various schemes and programmes meant for Scheduled Castes in Karnataka. Of which 90 per cent has been actually released and 100 per cent of which has been spent.

During the year 2002-03 an amount of Rs. 20,690 lakhs was made available to spend on various planned schemes and programmes, including the amount to be allocated for SC/ST Development Corporation and Civil Rights Enforcement Directorate. An amount of Rs. 11,499 lakhs was also made available under the Non-Plan. Up to January 2003, a total amount of Rs. 11305 lakhs was spent on planned schemes and Rs. 7709 lakhs was spent on Non Plan activities. Under Special Central Assistance to Special Component Plan a budget provision of Rs. 3203 lakhs was made and out of which Rs. 970 lakhs was spent. In total, for the year 2002-03, an amount of Rs. 66,740 was earmarked for the various activities of the Special Component Plan.

Broadly the schemes and programmes can be classified into two categories *viz.*, Employment and Income Generation Schemes or Poverty Alleviation Schemes and Minimum Needs Programmes. Some productive programmes have been designed to help the Scheduled Castes to come up economically, say, by taking up self-employment through small-scale industries or allied agricultural activities like animal husbandry, silk worm rearing, etc. The minimum needs programmes aim at improving quality of life by providing free education, health care, housing, and water supply to the rural and urban poor and the landless amongst the Scheduled Castes.

9.2.12 Caste based Violence and Atrocities

Caste, like race is exploitative, discriminatory and anti-developmental. The discriminatory nature of caste as well as race is duly recognised by the Indian Constitution. Article 15 (which outlaws discrimination on grounds of religion, race, caste, sex or place of birth) and Article 17 (which in effect bans the existence of caste based discrimination and its effects of untouchability as racial discrimination) are instances in point. In effect, however, the rights and guarantees enshrined in the Constitution are often being eroded.

The Indian Government has passed two Legislations namely, Protection of Civil Rights Act (PCRA) 1955 and Prevention of Atrocities against Scheduled Caste/Tribe in 1989 to enable the Dalits to enjoy human rights on par with other sections of Indian society. This is a positive factor for the potential to dispense justice to the Dalits. Crime against Dalit women, torture and atrocities are indicators of social disharmony. Although the state of Karnataka does not have a high incidence of atrocities as in a few other states in the country, it is high enough to cause alarm (Appendix A-9.9, A-9.10 and A-9.11).

9.3 Gender Issues in Karnataka Development

With the universal adoption of CEDAW (Convention on the Elimination of the Discrimination of Women) and CRC (Convention on the Rights of the Child), there has been growing recognition of the vital relationship between the two areas for public action. The challenge, however, will be to ensure that rights are incorporated harmoniously into development frameworks, explicit targets are set and processes of accountability established from the community upwards.

Gender bias has been recognised as a major hindrance in combating poverty as well as reducing gender inequity within society. It affects a woman's access to and control over resources, her active participation in society and her ability to exercise her rights. The adverse sex ratio and the continuing downward trend underscore the alarming extent of this disparity. It is seen in differential participation and completion levels of primary education between boys and girls and literacy between men and women. Economic, political and social empowerment of women is essential to guarantee women's equal opportunities to development. Therefore, women need to be mobilised and the developmental programmes should aim at building women's capacities into their design. The gender concerns need to be mainstreamed across different ministries through Inter-Ministerial mechanisms.

In India, the violation of human rights of the marginalised sections, which includes the Scheduled Castes and Scheduled Tribes and the women, is very common. This situation demands for special efforts from the government to ensure the realisation of their Constitutionally guaranteed rights. The descent based discrimination results in disproportionate power, privilege and status and rewards to the particular privileged group. Keeping these burning issues in mind, this section examines the gender specific development perspectives in Karnataka.

9.3.1 Women and their Development in Karnataka

This section takes stock of the situation of women in respect of these indicators of development in the context of Karnataka.

i) **Education:** Karnataka's performance in literacy level looks satisfactory when compared with the national average. However, the gender gap in literacy still persists in spite of the conscious efforts to bridge this. Over the last decade, i.e., between 1991 and 2001 this gap has been reduced from 24.84 per cent to 19.20 per cent.

The enrolment of girls has increased from 28 per cent in 1951 to 43 per cent of total in 1991 at the primary level, for middle schools it has increased from 16 per cent to 39 per cent, and for secondary and senior secondary schools from 13 per cent to 35 per cent. The dropout rate has declined from 71 per cent in 1961 to 56 per cent in 1995 at the upper primary level.

ii) **Health:** Health is a function, not only of medical care but also of the overall integrated development of society-cultural, economic, education, social and political. Each of these aspects has a deep influence on health that in turn influences all these aspects. In the health sector, a look at four basic indicators of gender ratio, the infant mortality rate, the maternal mortality rate and life expectancy at birth would give us an idea of how far Karnataka has progressed in providing basic health facilities to its people.

iii) **Gender Ratio:** In Karnataka, there are 964 women for every 1000 men according to the 2001 Census and the sex ratio in fact declined from 963 in 1981 to 960 in 1991. However, Karnataka stands above the national average of 933 women per 1000 men in 2001.

iv) **Infant Mortality Rate:** In Karnataka about 50 out of 1000 infants born, die every year as per the Census data (The NFHS-2 shows IMR as 51.5 while SRS, 1998 as 58.) This is above the national average of 70 per 1000 infants.

v) **Maternal Mortality Rate:** The maternal mortality rates are not readily available for making comparison among states. The computation of the ratio also suffers from serious deficiencies. Anaemia, haemorrhage, eclampsia, obstructed labour, infection, and abortion are found to be major causes of maternal deaths (80 per cent) in the country. UNICEF has made a comparison of maternal health statistics throughout the country and pointed out that 450 out of one lakh women die of causes connected to pregnancy and childbirth in Karnataka. Recent estimates of maternal mortality rates for Karnataka by SRS (1988) indicates 195 deaths out of one lakh.

vi) **Life Expectancy at Birth:** The expectation of life at birth for both men and women which was 42 in 1951 improved 30 years later to 60.6 for men and 63.61 for women in 1991. As per the projections made by the Technical group on Population projections by the Registrar General India, it will be 67 for females by 2011. Further according to the Annual Report of Health and Family Welfare 2000-01 Government of India, the life expectancy of birth in 2000 in Karnataka was 65.3 for females, which was lower than Kerala but higher than all-India (61.7), Andhra Pradesh (64.5), and Tamil Nadu (63.1). The International Conference on Population Development (ICPD) had resolved in 1994 to target a life expectancy of 70 by 2005 and 75 by 2015. (SRS data-Abridged Life Tables 1981-1985 and 1991-1995.)

9.3.2 Atrocities against Women

India is one of the few countries where males outnumber females significantly and this imbalance has increased over time. There seems to be a consensus that higher female mortality between ages one and five and high maternal mortality rates result in a deficit of females in the population. Chatterjee (1990) estimates that deaths of young girls in India exceed those of young boys by over three lakhs each year and every sixth infant death is specifically due to gender discrimination. Of the 15 million baby girls born in India each year, nearly 25 per cent do not live to see their 15th birthday.

The Indian Constitution grants women equal rights with men, but strong patriarchal traditions persist, with women's lives shaped by customs that are centuries old. In most Indian families, a daughter is viewed as a liability, and is conditioned to believe that she is inferior and subordinate to men. Sons are idolised and celebrated. Exposure to and interactions with the outside world are instrumental in determining the possibilities available to women in their daily lives. The situation of women is affected by the degree of their autonomy or capacity to make decisions both inside and outside their own household.

In India, about 6,000 dowry related murders are committed each year. This reality exists even though the Dowry Prohibition Act has been in existence for 33 years, but there are virtually no arrests or punishments under the Act. Since those giving as well as those accepting dowry are punishable under the existing law, no one is willing to complain. It is only after a 'dowry death' that the complaints become public. It is estimated that the average dowry today is equivalent to five times the family's annual income and that the high cost of weddings and dowries is a major cause of indebtedness among India's poor. Despite every stigma, dowry continues to be the signature of marriage. Says Rainuka Dagar, "It is taken as a normative custom and dowry harassment as a part of family life."

Sexual crimes against women are on the rise. In India, sexual harassment, molestation and rape of women are common. Relatives and close acquaintances of the victim are committing most of these sexual crimes. Sexual crimes against psychiatric patients are also increasingly being reported.

The Table 9.1 compares the state of Karnataka with three states reporting highest and lowest incidences of crimes against women in the country. In the country, the state of Karnataka occupies the 12th place in terms of number of cases reported (Appendix A-9.12).

Table 9.2 compares the city of Bangalore with three cities reporting highest and lowest incidences of crimes against women in the country. In the country, the city of Bangalore occupies the 9th place in terms of number of cases reported (Appendix A-9.13).

TABLE 9.1

Atrocities on Women: A Comparison with Other States

State	*Population (in Lakhs)*	*Incidences of Atrocities against Women*					
		Rape	*Kidnapping & Abduction*	*Dowry Deaths*	*Cruelty by Husband and Relatives*	*Total*	*Rank*
Uttar Pradesh	1660.53	1958	2879	2211	7365	14413	1
Rajasthan	564.73	1049	2165	376	5532	9122	2
Maharashtra	967.52	1302	611	308	6090	8311	3
Karnataka	527.34	293	271	220	1755	2539	12
Goa	13.44	12	6	2	11	31	26
Nagaland	19.89	17	6	0	0	23	27
Sikkim	5.4	8	2	0	0	10	28
***All India**	**10270.15**	**16075**	**14645**	**6851**	**49170**	**86741**	—

Note: * All India total includes union territories also.

Source: National Crime Records Bureau.

TABLE 9.2

Atrocities on Women in Bangalore City *vis-à-vis* Other Cities

City	*Population (in Lakhs)*	*Rape*	*Kidnapping & Abduction*	*Dowry Deaths*	*Cruelty by Husband and Relatives*	*Total*	*Rank*
Delhi	127.91	326	820	84	108	1338	1
Hyderabad	55.34	37	39	24	746	846	2
Ahmedabad	45.19	39	117	7	530	693	3
Bangalore	56.87	40	56	40	229	365	9
Kochi	13.55	10	1	0	62	73	33
Madurai	11.95	2	18	12	24	56	34
Coimbatore	14.46	4	10	5	28	47	35
All Cities	1046.23	1261	2278	556	6167	10262	—

Note: * Incidence of atrocities not recorded in three cities out of 35, namely Jamshedpur, Dhanbad and Asansol.

Source: National Crime Records Bureau.

Table 9.3 gives the incidences of crimes against women in Karnataka from 1999 to 2001 and compares the percentage variation in crime against women between 2000 and 2001. As suggested earlier, the crimes against women are on raise in the country and Karnataka is no exception to it. A significant increase in number of cases registered under rape, dowry death, torture, molestation and sexual harassment is apparent.

TABLE 9.3

Crime against Women in Karnataka 1999–2001

Crime Head	*No. of Incidences*			
	1999	*2000*	*2001*	*% Variation in 2001 over 2000*
Rape	301	281	293	4.27
Kidnapping and Abduction	630	336	271	-19.35
Dowry Death	217	213	220	3.29
Torture (Cruelty by Husband or Relative)	1560	1688	1755	3.97
Molestation	1501	1568	1665	6.19
Sexual Harassment (Insulting Modesty)	147	76	81	6.58
Importation of Girls	0	0	0	0
Sati Prevention Act	0	0	0	0
Immoral Traffic (P) Act	1225	1337	1356	1.42
Indecent Rep. of Women (P) Act	1	0	0	0
Dowry Prohibition Act	361	392	361	-7.91
Total	**5943**	**6841**	**6002**	**-12.26**

Source: State Crime Records Bureau, Karnataka, Government of Karnataka.

The proportion of crimes against women to total IPC crimes in the state is given in Table 9.4. It shows a marginal decrease in 2000 and an increase again in cases is reported in the year 2001.

TABLE 9.4

Proportion of Crimes against Women to Total IPC Crimes

Year	*Total IPC Crimes*	*Crimes against Women*	*% Total*
1999	110559	4356	3.93
2000	109410	4162	3.80
2001	109098	4285	3.93

Source: State Crime Records Bureau, Karnataka, Government of Karnataka.

It is very threatening to note that the rape of minor girls is alarmingly high in number. Majority of rape victims are in the age group 16 to 30 (Table 9.5).

TABLE 9.5

Victims of Rape

Age Groups	*Year*		
	1999	*2000*	*2001*
Below 10	24	28	24
10–16	46	39	63
16–30	210	191	185
30 and above	21	23	21
Total	**301**	**281**	**293**

Source: State Crime Records Bureau, Karnataka, Government of Karnataka.

9.3.3 The Role of State and Non-State Actors in Checking Atrocities against Women

The Constitution of India guarantees equality and prohibits discrimination. But the expression 'equality' and 'discriminations' are not defined and are left to the interpretation of the courts. The judiciary in a number of decisions has struck down the discriminatory provisions of law and rules. The Supreme Court of India and various High Courts have upheld the equality principles and 'substantive equality' principles have been used to interpret the term 'equality' in many cases. It has held that the equality clause in the Constitution does not speak of mere formal equality before law but embodies the concept of real and substantive equality which strikes all the inequalities arising on account of vast social and economic differentiation and is thus consequently essential ingredient of social and economic justice.

Despite the Constitutional mandate of equal legal status for men and women, the same is yet to be realised. The *de jure* laws have not translated into *de facto* situation for various reasons *viz.*, illiteracy, social practices, prejudices, cultural norms based on patriarchal values, poor representation of women in policymaking, poverty, regional disparity in development, lack of access and opportunity to information and resource. The government in many of its initiatives through the National Empowerment Policy of Women, 2001, Gender Budget, Women Component Plan, and various schemes has attempted to bridge the gap between the promise in the Constitution and the Convention and the *de facto* situation.

Several initiatives have been introduced and being pursued at the state, judiciary, civil society and citizen groups. The government has taken various positive steps towards gender equality. The Constitution guarantees right to equality (Article 14, 16), right to life (Article 21) guarantees right to equality and equal protection before the law (Article 15) and provides for discrimination in favour of women (Article 15(3) and 16(4)). The government invoking these provisions have introduced various special measures. Many laws have been enacted to enable women enjoy the fundamental rights guaranteed in the Constitution. Some of them have been highlighted in the initial report. These laws are under constant review and are amended whenever the situation warrants. The Department of Women and Child Development and the National Commission for Women have been monitoring these laws and have suggested many amendments to the discriminatory provisions, some of which are accepted by the government and others are being processed at various stages and are pending consideration. Several Acts like The Indian Divorce Act, The Indian Succession Act, The Marriage Act (Amendment) 2001, the Pre-Conception and Pre-Natal Diagnostic Techniques (prohibition of sex selection) Act, 1994 (PNDT), The Medical Termination of Pregnancy Act, etc., which were discriminatory to women have been amended during the last three years. Attempts are being made to introduce new laws on domestic violence, 'Protection from Domestic Violence Bill, 2002' and pass the Constitutional Amendment Bill providing for one-third reservation for women in the Assemblies and Parliament.

Special courts have been set up to deal with the offences against women and fast track courts have been established to ensure speedy trial of undertrials. Specialised courts *viz.*, family courts, about 84 in numbers, have been established in 18 states and union territories, since the year 1984 to deal with the issues pertaining to family matters *viz.*, marriage, divorce, child custody, guardianship, maintenance, etc.

The National Commission for Women, (NCW) a statutory body, established in the year 1992, has a mandate to safeguard the rights and interest of women by ensuring Constitutional guarantees of equal status to women; to review the existing legislation and monitor its effects on women; to recommend suitable amendments; and to provide a forum for women for redressal of their grievances. It pursues its mandate through various activities *viz.*, investigation into individual complaints of atrocities, denial of rights, and sexual harassment of women at workplace, conducting *parivarik/mahila lok adalat*, (alternate dispute resolutions) legal awareness programmes/camps, review of women specific and women related legislation.

Similarly many states have enacted State Commission Act. State Commission for Women has been constituted in 20 states out of 28 states and union territories. The government is persuading the other states and union territories to establish the State Commission for Women.

The Protection of Human Rights Act, 1993 provides for Constitution of a National Human Rights Commission and State Human Rights Commissions for better protection of Human Rights and enforcement of the same. It is empowered to deal with all cases of human rights violations by pubic servants which includes women also.

The National Commission for Backward classes, National Commission for Schedule Caste and Schedule Tribes also has powers to adjudicate on individual complaint for violation of rights of an SC/ST person.

Article 51 of the Constitution, imposes an obligation on the state to foster respect for International Law and Treaty Obligation, However, the treaty provisions cannot be invoked without the same being incorporated through enabling legislation. Though CEDAW has not been incorporated, the judiciary and its proactive role have paved the way to use the principles of the treaty in many judgements.

The Central Government has committed to take a lead to introduce Legislation for one-third reservation of women in Parliament and the State Assembly and to introduce the legislation on domestic violence and gender discrimination and to amend discriminatory laws and enact new legislations that give women equal rights of ownership of assets like house and land. It further has committed to ensure 1/3rd of the funds that flows into *panchayats* should be earmarked for programmes for development of women and children and promises to involve rural women assume responsibilities for all development schemes relating to drinking water, education, health, etc.

Civil society organisations have been active in monitoring state compliance to eliminate discriminatory laws and promoting an effective delivery of justice for women. Advocacy, lobbying, and networking are their major strategies. They are also cooperating with the government in drafting laws on women's rights. However, these have not been effective enough to bring any positive impact in women's lives.

9.3.4 An Analysis of the Condition of Women in Urban Karnataka

The problems erupting as a consequence of urbanisation as part of development agenda have been on the rise over the years. Urban poverty as a consequence of globalisation, industrialisation, migration and partial programmes by the successive governments that benefit a certain section of the population are some of the issues that need to be looked. This is especially in the light of the repercussions that these processes have on the condition of women.

Till about 1980, the emphasis of the Five-Year Plans was on housing. With the Sixth Plan schemes for shelter and poverty alleviation were announced for the urban poor. The Eighth Five-Year Plan recognised the significance of urban centres as beneficial for the country's economy. There was increasing emphasis on urban poor and the adversities faced by them due to lack of proper sanitation, electricity, safe drinking water, inadequate housing facility to accommodate the increasing urban population, rise in slum settlements, unemployment, and the resultant increase in urban poverty.

One of the worst affected section of population is the women. Developmental programmes whether in rural or urban areas have no specific or dedicated plans for women. Women are most affected by poverty since the responsibility of meeting the day-to-day needs of the household rests with them. In an all-India scenario the literacy of women is at the appallingly low level of 39.42 per cent. The lack of health facilities in rural areas has made the maternal mortality rate of rural women between 15-45 particularly high at 12.5 per cent. India's MMR rate is 50 times that of developed countries. The Indian Council for Medical Research (ICMR) records reveal that up to the age of 35 more women than men die at every age level.

The indicators that highlight the status of women in urban Karnataka indicate a positive trend. The state has registered an increase in the sex ratio from 960 in 1991 to 964 (no. of females per 1000 males) in 2001. Udupi with 1127 has the highest sex ratio whereas Bangalore with 906 has the lowest. In urban areas in total there has been an increase in the sex ratio from 930 in 1991 to 940 in 2001.

The overall literacy rate has gone up from 56.04 per cent in 1991 to 67.04 per cent in 2001 in the state. The increase in female literacy rate by 13.11 per cent has gone up as well from 44.34 per cent in 1991 to 57.45 per cent in 2001 and was much faster than that of 9.03 per cent in the male literacy rate from 67.26 per cent in 1991 to 76.29 per cent in 2001. Despite the increase in the rate of female literacy in Bangalore the sex ratio shows a reverse trend i.e. the ratio of women per men is the lowest. These are such revealing figures, Bangalore that is considered to be the hub of commercial activity and economic growth has the lowest sex ratio in the state. The possible explanation for this could be that population of male migrants in search for livelihood is quite high and the other is that as a result of sophisticated techniques, sex detection has become easier and female feoticide is increasing. The sex ratio is adverse in all districts except Udupi, Dakshina Kannada and Hassan districts. It is interesting to note that except Bangalore, districts with high literacy rates such as Udupi, Dakshina Kannada, Uttara Kannada, Hassan and Kodagu have higher sex ratios (Table 9.6).

TABLE 9.6

State and District-wise Urban Literacy Rate

State/Districts	*Combined*	*Male*	*Female*	*Gender Gap*
Karnataka	**81.05**	**86.85**	**74.87**	**11.98**
Belgaum	80.87	88.60	72.75	15.85
Bagalkot	71.62	82.15	60.82	21.33
Bijapur	75.28	84.25	65.87	18.38
Gulburga	71.28	80.22	61.70	18.52
Bidar	76.18	84.23	67.42	16.81
Raichur	67.63	76.29	58.50	17.79
Koppal	69.79	80.09	59.18	20.91
Gadag	74.55	84.83	63.94	20.89
Dharwad	80.60	87.27	73.59	13.68
Uttara Kannada	86.14	91.61	80.51	11.1
Haveri	75.30	81.79	68.43	13.36
Bellary	70.97	79.49	62.08	17.41
Chitradurga	81.66	87.60	75.39	12.21
Davangere	78.02	83.62	72.06	11.56
Shimoga	86.78	88.63	78.76	9.87
Udupi	89.13	93.42	85.03	8.39
Chickmagalur	83.19	88.00	78.16	9.84
Tumkur	81.74	87.00	76.12	10.88
Kolar	79.36	84.96	73.57	11.39
Bangalore (Urban)	85.66	89.51	81.40	8.11
Bangalore (Rural)	76.27	81.92	70.12	11.8
Mandya	78.72	84.32	72.91	11.41
Hassan	84.74	89.56	79.74	9.82
Dakshina Kannada	89.06	93.64	84.53	9.11
Kodagu	89.85	93.21	86.31	6.9
Mysore	82.48	87.45	77.34	10.11
Chamrajnagar	71.41	78.03	64.57	13.46

Source: Population Census, 2001.

The female infant mortality rates according to 1991 figures indicate the state figure to be 72 per 1000 in 1991 for the entire state; 24 per 1000 in urban areas. For the state as a whole 12.3 per cent of women's deaths take place between the age of 15 and 24 years as against 5.9 per cent for men. The maternal morbidity rates in the state continue to be higher than the national average. Even the rates of female work participation are very low at 29.39 per cent as compared to 53.9 per cent for men.

All these figures and analysis indicate that even though the trends are showing a positive picture, the various indicators that highlight the status of women like health, literacy, sex ratio, work participation, etc. have not shown a proportionate improvement *vis-à-vis* the increase in the population figures. In case of urban poverty the situation becomes more complex for women. They go out to work for wages and contribute to the family income and at the same time manage the basic needs at the home front as they are the primary collectors of water and managers of sanitation, waste disposal and environmental management, and also bear a primary responsibility in household chores. Even the rates of crime against women (number of crimes against women per lakh of population) are on the rise in the urban areas even though the figures do not look alarming at first sight (1.63 during 2001). This rate needs to be viewed with caution since a sizeable number of crimes against women go unreported due to the social stigma attached to them. Bangalore city accounted for 20.96 per cent of all crimes against women in the state, followed by Mysore city (8.38 per cent), and Gulbarga (5.86 per cent).

The situation becomes more alarming in case of Scheduled Caste and Scheduled Tribes. Of the total Scheduled Caste population of the state 25.06 per cent are in the urban areas. Out of urban population of Scheduled Castes 48.5 per cent are women. The percentage of Scheduled Tribes in urban Karnataka is 15.28 per cent of which 48.97 per cent are women. A majority of the Scheduled Caste and Tribes population is found employed in the unorganised sector such as construction workers, domestic help and vendors. This segment of the urban population is vulnerable to exploitation by the employers, enforcement agencies, violence, riots, etc. Amongst this group, the women and children are the major sufferers. In all cases of caste conflict, Dalit women are the first victims.

The governments at the centre and the state level have made several provisions for the welfare of women *per se* and to improve their current status like the Karnataka Mahila Abhivrudhi Yojana (KMAY) which makes intersectoral allocations for women. The KMAY earmarks one-third of the resources under all schemes and programmes of various government departments for women. In the last four years the performance of the programme has shown improvement. An overall financial achievement in relation to the earmarked budget (one-third) under various schemes of government departments, which was 69 per cent in 1997-98, has reached 81 per cent in 2001. (Government of Karnataka, 2002).

Many other programmes run by Asian Development Bank, World Bank and non-government organisations are also looking at the whole question of women in development. According to an eminent social economist Professor Naila Kabeer, "if gender inequality is part and parcel of the processes of poverty and discrimination in a society, it must constitute the part and parcel of the measures to eradicate these conditions." She stresses on increased accessibility for the women to rapid employment outside agriculture in order to reduce household poverty.

The Asian Development Bank is assisting the Government of Karnataka in supporting women in slum areas by helping them establish self-help groups as an avenue to discuss and solve mutual problems and issues, provide access to credit facilities, and learn new skills. Under a component of the Karnataka Urban Development Project, which ADB started financing in early 1996, the efforts have been substantially improving the health and living conditions of more than 30,000 slum residents, 65 per cent of whom are women and children. Besides establishing self-help groups and conducting vocational training, the Project is also providing slum areas with improved drainage, low-cost sanitation, community centres public health, and conducting hygiene campaigns.

In implementing the Project, both ADB and the state government's executing agency, the Karnataka Urban Infrastructure Development and Finance Corporation (KUIDFC), recognised that women should be empowered to participate in decision making at the micro level to bring about constructive changes in the living conditions of the urban poor. With the help of non-government organisation (NGO) workers, adult classes and street plays are being conducted to sensitise the people to social issues, such as alcoholism and HIV/AIDS. Through constant motivation and non-formal education, women started forming groups. As they have become more united, the concept of *sangha* (self-help) groups emerged. In Mysore for example, the self-help groups in the Ghandhinagar slum are lobbying against and creating awareness of alcoholism through women. Similarly in Ghousinagar, a big slum in eastern Mysore, women started to come together and discuss their mutual problems and issues. Through a collective voice, the women were able to get the local municipality to improve water supply, install community taps, and clean the roads and drainage systems.

Through the ADB loan, some 6,000 units of low-cost sanitation (LCS) toilets were built in the slum areas in Mysore and another 2,000 units are in the pipeline. An additional 7,000 units are being built in the other three towns.

The training, savings, and access to credit facilities have helped increase the incomes and confidence of poor women in some slum areas in Karnataka. Of equal importance, the Project has increased awareness on health, sanitation, and improved community participation (Box 9.1).

BOX 9.1

Community Participation

An interesting example which can be picked up and replicated in towns of Karnataka is from Andhra Pradesh. The Municipal Corporation of Hyderabad (MCH) under the auspices of the DWCUA (Development of Women and Children in Urban Areas) programme has arranged for a unique incentive for groups of 10 or more poor urban women to establish self-employment ventures. The Corporation also has recently introduced a Community Contracting Scheme. Which has allotted 14 sanitation units for sweeping and garbage lifting to women's groups on the same terms and conditions as apply to private contractors. The women's groups no longer operate through middlemen but are direct contractors to the Corporation. They have grouped themselves into Thrift and Credit Societies and save part of the amounts received from MCH each month. The scheme is running very successfully. The MCH also encourages the public to take up door-to-door collection of garbage in their area by the appointment of their own sanitation workers. MCH provides a tricycle free of cost to a colony/group of houses, which engages a ragpicker to collect garbage from their doorsteps every day and pays him at the rate of Rs. 10 per household. By adopting this scheme, the people get a garbage free locality and a poor ragpicker gets employment. This scheme is called Voluntary Garbage Disposal Scheme (VGDS) and so far 550 such VGDS units are operating in Hyderabad.

Source: Nagari (2000). *Tenth Meeting of the Urban Think Tank*, Flow and Utilization of Urban Poverty Funds, February 25, Hyderabad, Andhra Pradesh.

No longer can urban development programmes restrict themselves to issues of infrastructure and urban planning, without addressing issues such as the need for community participation and the complex linkages between poverty alleviation, environmental management and the gender component. Also important is the need to establish industrial townships along with the diversification of economic base of the existing towns. Simultaneously, much is required to be done for improving the living conditions in the metropolises themselves so that the increasing concentration of population into these areas does not result in the growth of slums and squalors.

9.3.5 Women and Employment

Education, work and employment are closely related to both empowerment and development. The historical gender division of labour has largely been based on the social and cultural practices embedded in society, which has always been disadvantageous to women. The official statistics have invariably recorded lower work participation rates for women when compared to men. The official definition of work does not cover all working women, as most of them are engaged in work not officially defined as work. Contrary to belief, there exist a higher percentage of women who work when compared to men. They are often engaged in more arduous and long hours of work. Thus, it is important to redefine work to include women and create equal opportunities for work and employment, which draws on the capabilities of both men and women.

Of the 52.7 million population of the state, 23.5 million persons or 44.6 per cent of the total population of the state are reported as workers and 29.2 million persons or 55.4 per cent of the population are non-workers. The work participation rate, which stood at 42.0 per cent in 1991, has risen to 44.6 per cent in 2001. Karnataka witnessed a decennial population growth of 17.2 per cent during 1991-2001, while percentage of workers grew at a rate of 24.5 per cent.

The work participation rate in rural areas (49.2 per cent) is considerably high as compared to urban areas (35.7 per cent). The male work participation rate has increased from 54.6 per cent in 1971 to 56.9 per cent in 2001. The female work participation rate has shown an increasing trend since 1971. It has almost doubled during the last 40 years, i.e., from 16.8 per cent in 1971 to 31.9 per cent in 2001. During 1991-2001, the male work participation rate has increased from 54.1 per cent to 56.9 per cent, and that of the female work participation rate increased from 29.4 per cent to 31.9 per cent. Tumkur district has registered highest work participation rate of 51.0 among all the districts of the state. The other two districts, which had a work participation rate of 50 and more, are Hassan and Dakshina Kannada. Chamrajnagar, a newly formed district from the erstwhile Mysore district, has registered the highest male work participation rate of 61.7. Bidar is the only district in the state, which has registered a male work participation rate of less than 50 per cent. Dakshina Kannada district with a female work participation rate of 41.7 stands first among all the districts of the state.

The female work participation rate in spite of increase is considerably lower than the corresponding rate for males. In rural areas the proportion of workers is higher than in urban areas in respect of persons, males and females. Bidar district of Hyderabad-Karnataka area has registered the lowest work participation rate in respect of persons (37.2) and males (47.6) while in case of females Bangalore district with 18.3 has the least work participation rate among all the districts of the state.

Of the 23.5 million workers, 19.3 million persons or 36.7 per cent of the total population are main workers and the rest—4.2 million persons or 7.9 per cent are marginal workers. A comparison of the workers across sex shows that both the rural and urban areas have a high proportion of male main workers as compared to female main workers. A closer look at the figures reveal that the male workers in urban area were almost four times to that of female workers, while in rural areas it was twice the number of female workers. The marginal workers of females in rural areas were more than twice that of males but in the urban areas the percentage of male marginal workers is slightly higher than that of females.

The work participation rate of males as main workers is highest in Kodagu district followed by Dakshina Kannada. In comparison the percentage of marginal male workers is highest in Chamrajnagar 10.1 and for the females it is Tumkur with a record of 15.5 per cent.

The proportion of main workers among males and females is 51.9 per cent and 20.9 per cent respectively in the state showing a wide gap in employment among males and females. However the number of women joining the labour force as main workers has increased during 1981-2001. The data on main workers also shows a small decline in the percentage of males and females in most districts. However one needs to take notice of the fact that the decline in the work participation rates has been considerably high for the districts of Gulbarga, Koppal, Raichur, Bidar, Bijapur and Bagalkot (between 4 per cent and 9 per cent). The fall in the work participation rates though reflected in the figures in relation to the male main workers, it is comparatively much higher for the female main workers in this district driving home the point that when the dry belts—North Karnataka reel under drought, the impact on the employment opportunity for women is further reduced.

The above districts, which recorded a steep fall in the work participation of women main workers, have correspondingly recorded a higher percentage of marginal workers in comparison to the male figures. In addition to these districts Bellary, Gadag, Mandya, Hassan, and Belgaum also showed marked differences in the percentage of female marginal workers in comparison to males in the 2001 Census. While there has been an upward trend in work participation rates of main workers with respect to men in the period of 1991-2001.

Proportion of main workers in rural areas has declined from 41.6 per cent in 1991 to 38.7 per cent in 2001, while in urban areas it increased from 31.4 per cent to 32.9 per cent during the same period. The proportion of marginal workers in the total population has more than doubled during 1991-2001. It has increased from 3.5 per cent in 1991 to 7.9 per cent in 2001. Every 13th person in the state is a marginal worker. The proportion of marginal workers to the total population is significantly higher in rural areas (10.5 per cent) than that in urban areas (2.8 per cent). In rural areas the proportion of female marginal workers exceeds that of male marginal workers. In urban areas the proportion of male marginal workers slightly exceed that of females.

The purview of women's employment need to be expanded beyond formal employment and cannot be discussed by merely focusing on formal employment. The New Economic Policy, and subsequently, the liberalisation of the economy which promised greater employment opportunities for women has in fact adversely affected women. The past decade has been marked by the growth of the unorganised sectors characterised by increased hours of work, low remuneration, and poor working conditions.

A careful analysis of women's labour clearly shows that most of their work is invisible and unrecognised.

They either engage in activities that are normally not classified as productive, or alternatively, they perform tasks in other related productive work that are lower in hierarchy and are given a very low economic and social value. In urban areas, women engage in petty businesses like selling flowers, fruits, vegetables, bangles, etc. They are also seen in the unorganised sectors like the garment industries, electronic assembling units and other industries that have sprung in the outskirts of the cities known as the export free zones. Women are also active as domestic servants catering to the service needs of the middle and upper classes. A large number of rural women have migrated to urban areas and are working in brick kilns, road and building constructions, and other informal sectors. Most often these women are not categorised as workers and their contribution to the economy is not recognised.

The gender bias in the labour market, both formal and the informal sector is pronounced and stark. The wage differentials between men and women are visible, with women having a higher rate of unemployment compared to men. Moreover, women are over represented in the informal sector which is characterised by job insecurity, long working hours and low wages. Over the years, the informal sector has grown both in rural and urban areas.

Women in Government Sector: As on 21st March 1998, the total number of posts that were sanctioned in the state public services was 5,58,077. Of the sanctioned posts, only 83.28 per cent were filled. An analysis of the employment in the government sector reveals that for every 100 government employees, only 24 are women. Further, a group-wise distribution shows that 85.90 per cent of the women employees are concentrated in-group 'C'. The percentage of women in the government sector in the year 1994 was 17.22 per cent, which has increased to 24.39 per cent in 1998. The corresponding percentages of women employees in the same year 1998 in group A and group B were merely 1.42 per cent and 1.71 per cent respectively (Table 9.7).

Out of the 104 government departments/institutions/offices, there are 47 centres that do not have even a single woman officer in Group A. Another 32 centres have no women officer in the B category. There are a total of 27 centres that do not have a single woman officer neither in category A or category B. The above data clearly reflects the acute need of greater representation of women in decision-making processes.

Available statistics reveal that in December 2001, of the total 18,63,190 posts, in the government, semi-government, local self-administration and private sectors, 5,75,878 were women.

On the contrary as high as 47.6 per cent of those employed in the NGO sector are women in South India including Karnataka (Voluntary Health Association of India, 2000). The NGOs must work further to increase the representation of women in their sector, which will be a stepping-stone in the direction of women's development.

According to a Bangalore-based study in 1990 by Sharif (National Profiles on Women, Health and Development, Page 128), women on an average take about 1 hour 55 minutes to travel to their workplace from home and spend about 9 hours 36 minutes daily outside their homes. In spite of these long working hours, the familial responsibility of women is not reduced. Specifically, Karnataka, which takes a lead role

TABLE 9.7

Women in State Public Services: 1998

Group	*Sanctioned Posts (Nos.)*	*Posts that were Filled*						*Percentage of Women to the Total Sanctioned Posts*	
		Men		*Women*		*Total*			
A	16691	11492	(87.73)	1608	(12.27)	13100	(78.49)	1608	(1.42)
B	15506	18342	(90.43)	1941	(09.57)	20283	(79.52)	1941	(1.71)
C	429047	262973	(72.98)	97369	(27.02)	360342	(83.99)	97369	(85.90)
D	86833	58606	(82.49)	12437	(17.51)	71043	(81.82)	12437	(10.97)
Total	**558077**	**315413**	**(75.61)**	**113355**	**(24.39)**	**464768**	**(83.28)**	**113355**	**(100)**

Note: Figures in parentheses denotes percentages.

Source: Government of Karnataka.

in the IT industry, should identify qualified women and encourage their participation in the development of information technology.

Women in Unorganised Sector: According to the 2001 Census, as high as 53 per cent of women and 42 per cent of men are engaged in the unorganised sector. This includes agriculture, cattle rearing, forestry, fishery, horticulture, mines and stone quarrying, cottage industry and allied activities, construction, trade and commerce, etc. Women engaged in these activities have periodic employment and have relatively large periods of unemployment. This sector is also characterised by long hours of work, job insecurity, poverty, credit, bonded labour, migration, low wages, illiteracy and malnutrition.

Majority of the women in the unorganised sectors are poor and belong to the backward castes, Scheduled Castes/Tribe. These women are economically weak, socially disadvantaged and educationally backward. The social security programmes and regulations undertaken by the government remain elusive to workers in the unorganised sectors. The organised sector comprise of only 8 per cent, as against 62 per cent that constitute the unorganised workers. Although they contribute more than 60 per cent to the national economy, yet social security is far beyond their reach. Within the unorganised sector, there are many activities where women are predominantly engaged (Box 9.2).

BOX 9.2

Women Engaged in Different Unorganised Sector

i. **Sericulture:** Karnataka has the advantage of being a pioneer in this field. Most of the activities being done within the house, many women find it convenient to engage in this activity and they perform 60 per cent of the tasks—predominantly the tasks that are non-mechanised involving long hours of labour and low wages.

ii. ***Beedi* Manufacturing**: This is another activity where men constitute only 5 to 10 per cent of the workforce and the rest are women and children. However, the industry is facing problems in terms of lower sales and many of the *beedi* companies have migrated to other states where wages are low. This has impacted adversely many households and women in particular.

Some the *beedi* companies also enjoy the concession offered by the government but do not give any benefit like bonus to the workers. There are other problems which the women workers face such as hardships, in collecting the raw materials, poor quality of *beedies* because of poor raw materials, and the resultant downfall are all adjusted against the payment and women face a loss apart from low wages.

iii. ***Agarbatti*:** Being a household activity women are largely engaged and according to some estimates about 2 lakh women are working in this sector. Because of continuous sitting posture, women are prone to backaches, etc.

iv. **Flower Industry**: It is a powerful women industry and at all levels women are in the forefront and control even the market.

v. **Embroidery**: A source of self-employment and hence an individual activity. But the market linkages are weak and women do not get minimum wages. There is a need to address these along with training in skills, etc.

vi. **Metal Industry**: Mainly making decorative pieces, which fetches good income. Since the middle-men play a major role, women are not paid well for the hard work involved in this.

vii. **Bamboo Weavers**: Women belonging to the 'Medara' ethnic group are skilled in the art of bamboo basket weaving. But here again, women are exploited and further the industry faces competition from plastic products, lack of adequate credit, and lack of training etc.

viii. **Consumer Industry:** Household activities like making *papad*, pickles, *sambar* powder, etc., and lakhs of women are engaged in this industry but this sector requires development of market linkages, credit assessment and its availability, publicity by *Panchayats*, etc.

ix. **Women Potters:** Many rural women are engaged in pottery making but many women lack adequate knowledge and therefore need training, market facilities, and publicity etc.

x. **Dairy Industry:** Women have a bigger role in milk production. This has very high potential and prospects to women, particularly in the Milk Producers Associations at the village level. It has helped many women to become economically independent. But some of the industry related problems like absence of veterinary centres at the *taluka* levels, indefinite supply of cattle feed, non-availability of proper and timely veterinary service, and non-availability of local markets for milk products need some attention.

xi. **Arts and Crafts Industry:** Wood and Clay toys, wooden dolls, sandalwood idols, oil paintings, stone and metal carving, etc. bring about economic independence for women. The Viswa Programme of the Government, which was very useful for freely training women in this profession has since been stopped and this needs revival.

FIGURE 9.5

Workers in Unorganised Sectors

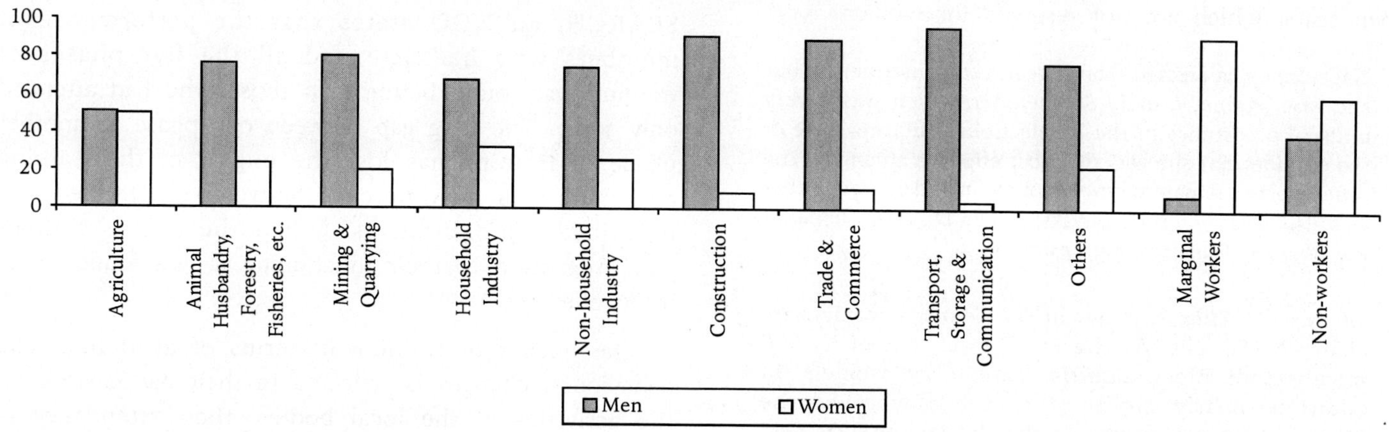

9.3.6 *Women and Governance in Karnataka*

Article 40 of the Constitution had envisaged, "the State shall take steps to organise *village Panchayats* and endow them with powers and authority as may be necessary to enable them to function as units of self-government." This is far from complete and achieved. Notwithstanding in these shortcomings, the women's movement, which gathered strength after 1970s, has led to progressive legislation and positive changes and spurred on by the participation of women in local self-government (Box 9.3).

BOX 9.3

Reconstitution of *Panchayat Raj* Institution

The Karnataka Government proposed to re-constitute *Panchayat Raj* Institutions to enable them to play an effective role in rural development and the government introduced a Bill in the State Assembly in August 1983 to this effect, based on the recommendations of Ashok Mehta Committee. This Bill was referred to the Joint Select Committee of the Legislature, which got its acceptance from the President of India in July 1985. The Act known as the Karnataka Zilla Parishads, Taluka Panchayat Samitis, Mandal Panchayats and Nyaya Panchayats Act, 1983 was revolutionary as it provided the maiden opportunity by reserving 25 per cent of seats for women, including SC and ST women to participate in *Panchayat Raj* Institutions thereby enhancing women's political participation.

The large entry of women in the sphere of governance was unprecedented in the country and created a stir within Karnataka and other parts of the India. Though the Constitution of India provides for the government to make special provisions to safeguard the interests of women as detailed in Article 15 (3) and Article 39, it has not made any provision for reservation for women in respect of jobs and political offices. However, the 73rd and 74th Constitutional Amendments passed in 1992 mandated reservation of one-third seats for women in *Panchayat Raj* Institutions in rural areas and in *Nagara Palika* and Municipalities in towns and urban areas.

Karnataka enacted this affirmative action in 1993 by providing 33 per cent reservation for women in the *Panchayat Raj* Institutions as well as in the position of presidents and vice-presidents. This applied even to backward classes, Scheduled Castes, and Scheduled Tribe and in general to women. This Act provided opportunity for thousands of rural women to become leaders. It was a stepping stone towards equality between men and women. One has to note that more women not only from the general category but also from backward, Scheduled Castes and Scheduled Tribe have been elected to these institutions. (Appendix A-9.14)

As a result of the 73rd and 74th Amendment, around 40 per cent of the seats has been occupied by women in the PRIs and this has prompted the state to be sensitive to issues of poverty, inequality and gender injustice. Women have gained a sense of empowerment by asserting control over resources, officials, and most of all, challenging men (Jain, 1980; Anveshi, 1993). Women have gained self-confidence through their participation in local bodies and they are sincere in carrying out their work, which gets recognised and gives them opportunity to contest the forthcoming elections. Appendix A-9.15 shows the marginal increase in the number of women being elected to the three tiers of the PRIs from the earlier term. It is evident that women are contesting and winning elections even from open seats, which are not reserved for women.

Nagamma was elected from a reserved constituency, but she won against a male SC member, which was a very unusual occurrence in the PR elections. Villagers were of the opinion that she was the most effective among all the other elected female members of the mandal, a view that was also shared by the Adhyaksha (Jain D. 1996. *Panchayat Raj: Women Changing Governance*).

Of the 475-*Zilla Parishads* in the country, women are chairing 158 ZPs. At the Block level, out of 51,000 members of Block samitis, 17,000 are women. In addition, nearly one-third of the Mayors of the Municipalities are women. In the elections to PRIs held between 1993 and 1997, women have achieved participation even beyond the mandatory requirement of 33 1/3 per cent of the total seats in states like Karnataka (43.45 per cent), Kerala (36.4 per cent) and West Bengal (35.4 per cent). However, the all India figures for women show that their representation in 2001 is still low.

Source: *Tenth Five-Year Plan*-Planning Commission, Government of India.

Lack of information and formal education prevent women from participating effectively in governance, which robs them of self-esteem and confidence. To reverse this, women have to come together to share their experiences. These kinds of exercises are being carried out by NGOs in Karnataka to motivate them to be effective participants in local governance. Listening to the true stories of other women representatives have made them think and act fearlessly in carrying out their job.

Large number of women in Karnataka have been elected to the local bodies because of reservation. Most of them were first timers, illiterate with little political awareness or sense of their new roles. They had no understanding of their responsibilities and duties to be performed, or whom they could approach for solutions to problems. They did not have an idea about developmental programmes, GP activities, *Panchayat* procedures, etc. It was therefore essential to provide them with inputs that would equip them to tackle the problems and help them function effectively. Training was thus considered absolutely essential.

State run administrative training institutions and NGOs have charted out programmes to train and build capacities of elected women representatives to equip them to perform their duties better. These training were carried out in phases and at places, which were not convenient for all women representatives to participate.

Studies carried on the impact of training by SEARCH, an NGO states that the performance of members who had attended all the five phases of training was found better than those who had attended only some. The long gap between one phase to another phase of training has lost the impact of the training and there was no difference between the trained and untrained representatives. When the course content was in relation to their functioning it was found to be more effective.

The impact of training in terms of attitudinal and behavioural changes is reflected in their participation in the activities of the local bodies, their attendance at meetings, contacting officials, transformation in their gender roles and their level of empowerment. Those women elected through the local bodies need specific kinds of support, which go beyond technical training. They need support to build solidarity amongst women, through strengthening links between women's organisation and elected bodies. Some of the NGOs are trying to bring the elected women representatives of the PRIs together to discuss their problems and exchange of ideas. Singamma Sreenivasan Foundation is an NGO which has tried to federate elected women representatives in order to empower and enable them in macro policy planning. This collective could bargain for their power within the political system.

Government of Karnataka has launched an experimental satellite broadcasting programme in collaboration with ISRO to broadcast programmes to 17 districts in the state which would enable elected women representatives to organise video-conferencing among villages, *talukas* and districts with anybody anywhere in the country. Computerisation of *Panchayats* enhances women to access administrative data, various programmes and number of beneficiaries, status of applications for power and water connections, etc. at their *Panchayat* office without running around to *taluka* and district headquarters.

Research, action and advocacy strategy of Gender Studies Unit of National Institute of Advanced Studies was able to lobby and advocate for amendments to the Karnataka Panchayati Raj Act which have enabled women in particular to participate effectively. First was the removal of the 'toilet rule', which had prevented many aspirants from the weaker sections especially women who did not have access to resources to construct toilets in order to be a contestant/elected representatives. The enhancement of honorarium and sitting fees for the members have helped particularly those women who lack resources to travel, provide child-care, and are engaged in wage labour. The rotation of seats have hindered their effective participation, duration of 20 months for the presidents and vice-presidents of *Taluka* and *Zilla Panchayats* was a short period to fulfil the tasks that were being carried out. Now the duration has been increased from 20 to 30 months, which would facilitate to continue and fulfil their commitments to their constituencies. Being part of the working group constituted by the government of Karnataka had helped to incorporate recommendations that would facilitate women's effective participation in decision making.

Strategies of government and the NGOs intervention to empower women have helped many of them to challenge the hurdles faced for effective performance of their duties. There is the need for the federations of these elected representatives to network with each other effectively to make their way into the political party's decision making spaces. So far no information about the federation being formed by the members of the municipalities or *nagara palikas* in the state. Most of the studies are being carried out in the area of PRIs than on women elected representatives in the urban governance.

9.3.7 Government Initiatives

To facilitate the economic development of women in Karnataka, the state government through the Department of Women and Child Welfare and The Women Development Corporation have implemented various schemes and programmes.

The government has initiated vocational training for women through the Department of Women and Child Development, Karnataka State Women Development Corporation, Karnataka State Social Welfare Advisory Board, etc. After training, these women are provided with financial assistance by NABARD and nationalised banks and sometimes by the Department of Rural Development and *Panchayati Raj*.

The formation of SHGs under the Swarna Jayanthi Gram Swarozgar Yojana Programme has been very successful. These women are provided with both training and credit programmes for their overall development.

Swashakthi Programme: The Central Government's 'Swashakthi' programme aims to strengthen and create a conducive environment for social change. This programme is executed in 7 districts (Gulburga, Raichur, Koppal, Bellary, Chitradurga, Tumkur, and Kolar) to empower women to mediate for social change through self-help groups involving 42,000 women. The Swashakthi programme will operate through the local voluntary associations for a period of 5 years. It has been projected that at the completion of this programme, the self-help associations would have acquired the strength to earn and manage their income-generation activities. With the help of their savings, they are expected to take advantage of women's loan disbursement facility. The programme envisages also bringing about an improvement in women's health, increasing capability to face and resolving problems with greater self-confidence and independence. After reviewing the success of the Swashakthi programme in the state, it is recommended that this programme be extended to the remaining backward districts.

Stree Shakthi Programme: The National Perspective Plan for women aims at the economic development and integration of women into the mainstream economy, keeping in view social justice and equity. The all-round development of women is to be achieved by treating them not merely as providers and producers but also as individuals with a right to human dignity. Hence, there has been a shift in focus from welfare to empowerment.

The Stree Shakthi Programme, launched in 2000-01, aims at empowering rural women through the formation of self-help groups (SHGs). NGOs are actively involved in organising rural women into self help groups, extending development services of various departments to these groups mobilising savings and providing banking linkages for credit and lending. The self-help groups, thus formed, are eligible for availing the benefit of a revolving fund of Rs. 5,000 per group which is a grant from government, six months after the formation. By the end of October 2003, 97,435 self-help groups have been formed with 14.06 lakh members who have mobilised savings of Rs. 146.44 crores, 81,128 groups have opened accounts in banks. Training has been imparted to 73,893 women members involving and expenditure of Rs. 5.36 crores, on gender, equity, book keeping, credit management, social issues, monitoring and evaluation, maintenance of records etc. During the current year as at the end of October 2003, Rs. 31.31 crores have been spent (Box 9.4).

BOX 9.4

Highlights of Achievements

- Revolving fund of Rs. 11.00 crores released to 22053 Stree Shakti self-help groups.
- Rs. 69.70 lakhs spent for training to SHG members.
- Assets in 20 community blocks created.
- Attendance scholarship worth Rs. 85.10 lakhs awarded to 23,000 rural girls.
- Rs. 27.55 lakhs spent to run hostel for girls benefiting 645 rural girls.
- Rs. 18.50 lakhs spent by 36 *Santhwana* centres benefiting 3040 women victims of atrocities.
- 288714 pregnant women, 295033 nursing mothers, and 3420 adolescent girls given supplementary nutrition.
- 33 per cent of the total budget allocation earmarked in 25 departments covering 220 beneficiary oriented schemes.
- 30 per cent reservation in direct recruitment.
- 520 deserted and destitute women provided shelter in 8 state homes and 11 reception centres.
- Rs. 69.06 crores spent towards women's development programmes by the Department of Women and Child Development and Karnataka State Women's Development Corporation.

Source: *Times of India*, Bangalore, March 8, 2005.

The Dharmadhikari of Dharmasthala has trained the women of Belthangadi to produce hundreds of articles like soap, phenyle, turmeric powder, *masala* powder, and other essential items. These products are marketed with the assistance of the temple. Women take a lead role in production as well as in marketing. Prices are maintained lower than the market price as the middlemen are eliminated. Care is taken to maintain the quality. More than a 1000 Stree Shakti women are employed here.

In the background of the success of Stree Shakthi Scheme, the state government has not only resolved to strengthen this programme but also intends to increase its financial assistance. The state government has released Rs. 21 crores for the revolving fund and for training to the Stree Shakthi programme. The programme envisages providing complete training to more members of the self-help groups to take up self-employment based on local raw materials. The training programme, also aims to study the market and institute mechanisms to market the finished goods. Innovations and improvisation of the products are also part of the expansion of the programme.

Fisheries: The state government has allocated some funds to encourage fisherwomen to become members of their cooperatives. From 1994-95 to 1998-99 government had allocated funds and encouraged 950 fisher women to become members of fishing cooperatives (coastal area-5, other areas-4). Though there are lot of fisher women in the interior areas, only 110 of them received this benefit. This programme was able to give membership to only few fisher women; it shows that the programme was not able to widen its scope. More funds have to be allocated for this programme, as it is very encouraging/stimulating.

Among those districts where women's literacy rate is very low, four of the districts have a larger number of fisher women (Chamrajnagar–5800, Koppal–3750, Bellary–2990, Mysore–1637). In these districts this programme has to be extensively carried out. Majority of the fisher women are found in the following districts: Uttara Kannada (13,266), Udupi (10,926), Dakshina Kannada (6919) and Bangalore Rural (4275), hence programmes related to fisheries development had to be formulated and implemented, which will be important from the point of women's empowerment.

There are other districts: Mandya (47,517 fisher women, of whom 98 are engaged in the fishing related activity), Kolar (39,880 of whom 1,345 are engaged), Mysore (38,374–1637), Hassan (18,822–450) and Shimoga (13,599–889) where the percentage of fisherwomen are less compared to the coastal districts and among them doing the concerned activity is very less, hence these kinds of programmes have to be implemented even in these districts to enhance their development.

TABLE 9.8

Fisheries Department Programmes

Programmes	*Financial (Rs. in Lakhs)*		*Physical (in Nos.)*	
	Target	*Achievement*	*Target*	*Achievement*
Fish Rearing in Uncultivable Lands.	6.00	3.90	20	13
Fish Marketing	1.50	0.92	120	74
Support to Register as Members in Fishing Cooperative Societies.	0.50	0.37	1000	730
Matsyavahini	1.00	0.25	4 Grps	1 Grp.
Finance for Rearing Ornamental Fishes	1.00	0.10	10	1

Dairy Industry: Another important initiative taken by the government is the establishment of the Women's Milk Producers' Associations through the STEP programme. A large number of women are formally and informally associated with milk production in the state. The state government, in the year 2001-02 extended the child labour rehabilitation scheme to include 50 young girls. In the current year, 37 schools in 26 districts have been started for girl child labourers and this programme, which was initially conceived for 6 months, is now extended to 1 year.

BOX 9.5

STEP

Karnataka occupies the third place in the country in milk production. In the Women's Cooperative Milk Producer's Associations which will be established under the STEP plan, all the members, the Administrative Committee and the staff must be all women. In this set up women have the complete rights to review all administrative and business decisions. In Karnataka, there was a plan to establish 400 Women's Milk Producer's Associations under a 13 member-milk-federations. But only 369 associations, 20,000 poor women have been identified and 989 lakhs have been spent.

The Federation of Bangalore Urban and Rural Milk Producer's Cooperative Associations has established 35 Women's Producer's Cooperative Associations and it is foremost in the field. The number of those who have profited from this is also considerable.

The Women Milk Producer's Cooperative Associations of Bangalore Urban and Rural, Hassan, Kolar, Tumkur, Chikballapur, Mangalore, Kodagu, Mandya and Mysore districts are developing in a significant manner.

Along with it, these cooperatives are initiating community programmes and awareness camps for rural women about health, nutrition, hygiene, awareness about law, removal of sexual discrimination are also catching up.

To promote the poor and disadvantaged rural women, the government is distributing a sum of Rs. 70,000 directly and Rs. 1,30,000 indirectly, that is, a total of Rs.2 lakhs for each association as an aid under planned expenditure.

In conclusion, it can be said that women will cut a niche for themselves in the coming years to play an important role in the white revolution that is taking place

Source: Federation of Karnataka Milk Producers' Association, Bangalore.

9.3.8 Challenges Ahead Suggestions for Ways Forward

One area of concern for the state is about enforcing equality and non-discrimination against private individuals, organisations and enterprises. There is a demand from the women's groups for an anti-discriminatory law providing for remedy and redressal and penal action and sanctions against discriminatory practices. The suggestion made by the Committee in the concluding comments for such an enactment in the initial report is in consideration of the government.

The policies and plans for alleviation of poverty need to be more sensitive to the needs of the women. Despite provisions for alleviation of poverty in urban areas in every Five-Year Plan are made ever since independence, the rate of growth in the urban population outgrows the provisions made for its accommodation in terms of housing, water supply, sanitation, electricity, employment, etc. there is a wide gap between the demand and supply. A serious revaluation of the policies and plans is required to overcome the rising urban poverty. An assessment of regional variations in terms of population, density of population, growth rate and its mapping against the provisions made, to incorporate the increased population, are required for urban development in the right direction.

Recommendations for Welfare of Women in Urban Karnataka

- Constitution of a neighbourhood watchdog committee for looking into the safety of women in the slums and squatter colonies.
- The Unorganised Workers' Bill Karnataka needs to be passed in order to enable social welfare funds for the unorganised workers and for regulation of their employment conditions like health, safety and job security. This would regulate the working hours, standardisation of wages, overtime benefits, maternity benefits, insurance, pension, insurance, etc. This would benefit the women workers in a substantial way and rid them of exploitation at work.
- Providing alternative housing for the slum dwellers within the limits of the city and not in the outskirts, which restricts their employment opportunities.
- Literacy programmes for women especially Dalit women by involving them in the formulation of strategies for development.
- Formation of self-help groups of women in the slums to make a collective platform and push their demands for proper sanitation, housing, safety, water facility, child care facilities, schools in the vicinity for the children so that the girl children do not have to drop out because of the distance factor.

Strategies for Women in Employment Sector

Gender equality is essential for equitable and sustainable development. An initial step to achieving gender parity is to make a critical analysis of the governmental policies from a gender perspective. All such existing policies need to be effectively implemented, forging partnerships between the government and civil society to address gender issues. Each department must set up monitoring mechanisms as a means towards effective implementation of governmental policies. Gender sensitisation of the decision makers and bureaucrats are an integral part of engendering the governmental organisations.

There is an urgent need to collate and generate gender-disaggregated data that would not only feed into the existing human development indicators but also move beyond and capture more authentically gender inequality, as it exists in society. There is a need to set the trend of generating data on more sensitive indicators of gender development in the state. One of the major constraints in gender analysis and therefore in effective policymaking is non-availability of reliable sex-disaggregated data. The state's exercise of preparing the HDR Report has a significant effect which was instrumental in terms of both collation/compilation of gender related data for purposes of index construction as also the normative value of sensitising the need for more reliable data at the district and local levels, including the training of data providers.

In the organised sector, in order to encourage women the following steps are needed:

- to increase the representation of women in all categories, (33 per cent reservation for women in government and semi-governmental offices at all levels);
- an incentive of a tax rebate to private organisations, which employ more than 51 per cent of women;
- the government to amend their rules/Acts in such a way that it makes it mandatory for these organisations used for housing the basic infrastructure of the government to reserve at least 50 per cent of the jobs for women;
- the available vacant positions are filled by women alone;
- women need to be trained for taking up jobs in private organisations and NGO sectors; talented women have to be provided part time-jobs, leave, provident fund and other facilities;
- to enhance the participation of women in information technology industry and to impart training to young women in information technology to occupy the lower middle and lower rungs in the IT industry;
- special encouragement has to be given to the handicapped women to increase their participation in the IT industry;
- the media should be effectively used to disseminate information about the multiple responsibilities of working women, so that the family understands their burden and to create a conducive environment for them;
- women from rural background should be provided with reservation quota in employment and educational and vocational training institutions to promote entry of women in sports.

In the unorganised and informal sectors, the loopholes and problems, which have been identified, need to be looked into and specific measures are required to reduce the anomalies.

- Introduction of new technologies leading to transformations in the fields like agriculture, horticulture, animal husbandry, *khadi* and village industries, arts and crafts, weaving, forestry, silk spices production has to become an integral part of the stree shakthi programme.
- Marketing of the products created by women must transcend local boundaries and aim to compete in the global market.
- Encourage entrepreneurs and self-help groups in the state, to set up independent production units. The government should seriously review and extend economic and technical assistance to these women.
- Provide credit to poor women by simplifying procedures and making the banks people-friendly.
- There is already a RBI directing to banks to lend five per cent of their total credit to women. Karnataka State Bankers *samithi* had changed the rules and regulations keeping in view of the women's welfare, yet some of the banks do not give loans easily to women. Government has to look into this matter.
- Government has to take necessary steps to give facilities to the self-employed women by giving technical advise and render help in marketing.

Networking

- More programmes must be introduced, to develop the skills of women in these cooperatives.
- A local network including all cooperatives engaged in economic activities has to be developed to give a boost to the cooperative sector.
- Awareness camps disseminating information for self-employment must be organised in a big way.
- Every *Gram Panchayat* and every library in urban and rural areas must have relevant literature about these self-employment activities.
- Assist women voluntary associations and other organisations to strengthen the cottage industry.
- Assist women to market the art and craft articles that are produced by them by establishing temporary marketing complexes, like 'Delhi Haat' in Delhi and 'Gramashree' in CAPART.
- The State Women's Development Board has taken the initiative to establish a similar complex at Koramangala, Bangalore. Similar complexes need to be established in all-important cities of the state. This will play an important role both in eliminating the middlemen and subsequently, increasing the income of women.
- It is recommended that the state government adopt the model of the income generation programme of Dharmasthala, where women manage both the production and marketing of products and assist women to establish such models at the *hobli* levels.
- To help women in the unorganised sector, Karnataka state should, on the model of Bank of Bangladesh, establish a cooperative bank and lend money to rural agricultural labourers.
- The newly established bank should organise workshops on social subjects like health, nutrition, etc. and increase awareness of its members.
- Banks lend to women at an interest rate of one per cent lower than the usual rate of interest. In addition, the other conditions for giving loans must also be simplified for women. Preference must be given to women headed households, while disbursing loans.

Access to Other Facilities

- All women in the unorganised sector have to be registered and a database on their working conditions needs to be generated.
- On the basis of this information, a plan has to be drawn to introduce reforms in various aspects like their wages, promotion, leave, health, etc.
- It must be mandatory to absorb these women who have been registered, for employment as and when they are created.
- The responsibility of strictly implementing this rule must rest with some good local women's organisation under the chairmanship of the Department of Women and Child Development.
- A separate section in the Department of Women and Child Development must monitor the facilities offered to the women in the unorganised sectors.
- Social security schemes like landless labourers collective insurance scheme, national old age pension scheme, national family benefit scheme, national maternity allowance, etc. must be extended to the workers in the unorganised sectors.

Strategies for Women in Governance and Decision Making

- The sex segregated data of elected representatives of the municipalities and *Nagara Palikas* (urban governance bodies) to be made available, similar to that of PRIs.
- There is lack of literacy, education, information dissemination and their economic dependence. Providing information alone is of no use without proper support structures and awareness on how to use it.
- Efforts in the areas of their rights as citizen need to be made, so as to enable them to face various kinds of discrimination, which often takes violent and physical forms.
- There is a need to reorient the male members of the family and society as they have manipulated and dictated their power to take decisions in their favour.
- Timings of meetings need to be decided unanimously, by all members, to ensure that they are held at a time convenient for women.

- Minimum representation of women in the political parties should be made for creating the space for a greater number of women in the party's decision making area. This would enable them to participate actively and influence party decisions in favour of women.
- A minimum code of conduct such as abstaining from drinking and use of abusive language, etc. should be fixed.
- To enable women's effective participation, the government should take certain facilitative measures such as, child care facilities and financial assistance.

References

Anveshi, Hyderabad (1993). "Reworking Gender Relations, Redifining Politics: Nellore Village, Women Against Arrack", in EPW, January, pp.16-23.

Basu, S.K. (1993). "Health Status of Tribal Women in India", *Social Change*, Dec.

Census of India (1991a). *Final Population Total*, New Delhi: Registrar & Census Commissioner.

———. (1991b). *Tables on Houses and Household Amenities*, Director of Census of Operations, Bangalore.

———. (2001a). *Final Population Totals*, Series 30, Directorate of Census of Operations: 1-93, Bangalore, pp. 1-93.

———. (2001b). *Tables on Houses and Household Amenities*, CD No.00-036-2001-CEN, Director of Census of Operations, New Delhi.

Chatterjee, Meera (1990). "Indian Women: Their Health and Economic Productivity", *World Bank Discussion Papers 109*, Washington D.C.

Government of India, (1960). *The Adivasis*, Ministry of Information and Broadcasting, New Delhi.

———. (2000). *Crimes in India*, National Crimes Record Bureau, Ministry of Home Affairs, New Delhi.

———. (2001). *Tables on Houses, Household Amenities and Assets for Scheduled Tribe*, Registrar & Census Commissioner, New Delhi.

———. (2002). *10th Five-Year Plan 2002-07: Sectoral Policies and Programmes*, Vol.2, pp. 443-473, New Planning Commission, Delhi.

Government of Karnataka. (1996). *Agricultural Census 1995-96*, Part-I, Directorate of Census Operations, Bangalore.

———. *Manpower Profile Karnataka*, 2000-2001.

———. *Men and Women in Karnataka.*

———. *Women's Task Force Report.*

———. *A Report on Task Force on Women Empowerment.*

———. (2002). *High Power Committee for Redressal of Regional Imbalances*, Department of Planning and Statistics, pp. 421-484, Bangalore.

———. (2003a). *Annual Report 2002-03*, pp. 1-82, Department of Forest, Bangalore.

———. (2003b). *Annual Report 2002-03*, pp. 4-76, Department of Social Welfare, 6 Bangalore.

———. (2004). *Economic Survey 2003-04*, Department of Planning and Statistics, pp. 4-76, Bangalore.

Jain, Devaki (1980). "Manipur: Night Patrollers in Women's Quest for Power", Vikas Publishing House, New Delhi.

Mandelbaum, David G. (1970). *Society in India: Change and Continuity*, Vol.1, pp. 208-210, California University Press, Berkeley.

Mohanty, P.K. (2000). "Development of Scheduled Castes and Scheduled Tribe in Independent India: Leads and Lags", *Journal of Rural Development*, 19(4): 535-572.

NSS (1997). *Employment and Unemployment Situation Among Social Groups in India 1993-94*, 5th Quinquennial Survey, 50th Round, Department of Statistics, Delhi.

———. (2001). *Employment and Unemployment Situation Among Social Groups in India 1999-2000*, 6th Quinquennial Survey, 55th Round, Ministry of Statistics and Programme Implementation, Delhi.

Sankaran, S.R. (2000). "Welfare of Scheduled Castes and Scheduled Tribe in Independent India: An Overview of State Policies and Programmes", *Journal of Rural Development*, 19(4): 507-533.

Singh, Syam Nand (2000). "Impact of Reservation Policies for Tribals in India", *Journal of Rural Development*, 19(4): 603-623.

Srivastava, B.N. (2000). "Working of the Constitutional Safeguards and Protective Measures for the Scheduled Castes and Scheduled Tribe", *Journal of Rural Development*, 19(4): 573-602.

United Nations Centre for Human Settlements (UNCHS), (1996). *An Urbanising World.* Oxford University Press, New York.

Raghuram, Shobha (2002). *The Position and Condition of Women in India.*

Kabeer, Naila (1994). *Reversed Realities, Gender Hierarchies in Development Thought*, Verso.

Voluntary Health Association (2000). *National Profile on Women, Health and Development*, Voluntary Health Association of India (VHAI) and World Health Organization.

World Bank, (1991). *Gender and Poverty in India*, The World Bank, Washington, DC.

APPENDIX A-9.1

Demographic Distribution of Scheduled Tribes in Karnataka: 1991 and 2001

District/s	Population ('000)		Per Cent to Total Population		Sex Ratio (Per '000 Male Population)		Density (Per Sq. Km)		Proportion of Urban Tribals to Tribals	
	1991	2001	1991	2001	1991	2001	1991	2001	1991	2001
Bangalore (Rural)	49.3	61.6	2.9	3.3	935	952	8	11	9.6	11.7
Bangalore (Urban)	53.6	86.0	1.1	1.3	920	913	24	39	72.8	79.0
Belgaum	83.1	243.5	2.3	5.8	971	980	6	18	21.5	12.6
Bellary	166.7	364.6	8.8	18.0	985	985	17	37	22.3	22.8
Bidar	104.2	182.2	8.3	12.1	949	950	19	33	5.5	6.6
Bijapur	39.5	110.2	1.4	3.2	961	982	2	6	13.8	11.9
Chickmagalur	26.5	41.0	2.6	3.6	973	994	4	6	7.5	9.3
Chitradurga	318.4	475.9	14.6	14.4	951	958	29	44	13.5	13.5
Dakshina Kannada	106.2	104.5	3.9	3.5	996	1005	13	12	11.2	13.6
Dharwad	105.1	252.0	3.0	6.3	932	946	8	18	19.9	18.3
Gulbarga	106.9	154.2	4.1	4.9	952	979	7	10	11.2	12.7
Hassan	16.6	26.5	1.1	1.5	991	989	2	4	10.3	8.5
Kodagu	40.3	46.1	8.2	8.4	961	996	10	11	3.5	2.6
Kolar	153.0	205.7	6.9	8.1	967	973	19	25	6.9	7.6
Mandya	11.9	17.2	0.7	1.0	947	978	2	3	20.5	21.5
Mysore	102.1	377.5	3.2	10.5	969	986	9	32	23.9	18.1
Raichur	180.3	441.6	7.8	15.4	984	988	13	32	9.4	7.9
Shimoga	74.1	56.0	3.9	3.4	952	969	7	5	13.1	22.2
Tumkur	167.6	193.8	7.3	7.5	952	962	16	18	10.7	12.3
Uttara Kannada	10.2	23.8	0.8	1.8	948	985	1	2	10.8	20.2
Karnataka	**1915.7**	**3464.0**	**4.3**	**6.6**	**961**	**972**	**10**	**18**	**14.9**	**15.3**

Note: Newly created (7) districts have been adjusted to the previous list of distrists (20) as follows: Bagalkot is included in Bijapur; Davangere in Chitradurga; Udupi in Dakshina Kannada; Gadag and Haveri in Dharwad; Chamrajnagar in Mysore and Koppal in Raichur whereas other districts remain the same.

Source: Census of India (1991a) and Census of India (2001a).

APPENDIX A-9.2

Sector-wise Allocation of Resources for Scheduled Tribes in Karnataka: 1991-92 to 2003-04

(Rs. in Lakhs)

Sector	1991-92	1994-95	1997-98	2000-01	2001-02	2002-03 RE	2003-04 BE
A. Revenue Expenditure							
I. Social Services	85.46	507.86	69.77	1294.69	8734.43	8181.69	8361.90
	(98.2)	(98.6)	(96.6)	(99.8)	(87.8)	(83.7)	(82.2)
(a) Education, Sports, Arts, and Culture	0.00	0.00	57.33	464.94	572.66	475.00	283.82
	(0.0)	(0.0)	(100.0)	(100.0)	(100.0)	(100.0)	(100.0)
(b) Health and Family Welfare	1.32	1.32	2.39	3.06	3.45	3.26	5.06
	(0.0)	(0.0)	(0.0)	(0.0)	(0.0)	(0.0)	(0.0)
(c) Water Supply and Sanitation	80.00	0.00	0.00	0.00	0.00	0.00	0.00
	(100.0)	(0.0)	(0.0)	(0.0)	(0.0)	(0.0)	(0.0)
(d) Information and Broadcasting	2.00	3.00	0.00	0.00	0.00	0.00	0.00

Contd. ...

...Contd. ...

Sector	1991-92	1994-95	1997-98	2000-01	2001-02	2002-03 RE	2003-04 BE
	(100.0)	(100.0)	(0.0)	(0.0)	(0.0)	(0.0)	(0.0)
(e) Welfare of Scheduled Tribe	1.75	499.51	1.51	810.01	8140.02	7678.43	8068.37
	(89.6)	(98.8)	(100.0)	(100.0)	(87.0)	(82.6)	(81.7)
(f) Labour and Labour laws	0.39	4.03	8.55	16.66	18.30	25.00	4.65
	(100.0)	(100.0)	(100.0)	(100.0)	(100.0)	(100.0)	(100.0)
II. Economic Services	3.62	61.01	84.33	0.69	41.42	14.00	0.00
	(100.0)	(100.0)	(100.0)	(0.0)	(100.0)	(100.0)	(0.0)
(a) Agricultural and Allied Activities	3.39	61.01	84.33	0.00	41.42	14.00	0.00
	(100.0)	(100.0)	(100.0)	(0.0)	(100.0)	(100.0)	(0.0)
(b) Cooperation	0.23	0.00	0.00	0.00	0.00	0.00	0.00
	(100.0)	(0.0)	(0.0)	(0.0)	(0.0)	(0.0)	(0.0)
(c) Irrigation and Flood Control	0.00	0.00	0.00	0.69	0.00	0.00	0.00
	(0.0)	(0.0)	(0.0)	(0.0)	(0.0)	(0.0)	(0.0)
Total	**89.08**	**568.87**	**154.10**	**1295.37**	**8772.40**	**8192.43**	**8356.84**
	(98.3)	**(98.7)**	**(98.4)**	**(99.7)**	**(87.9)**	**(83.7)**	**(82.3)**
B. Capital Expenditure	480.38	0.00	7.48	0.00	477.40	291.00	844.00
	(100.0)	(0.0)	(100.0)	(0.0)	(100.0)	(100.0)	(100.0)
(i) Welfare of Scheduled Tribe	480.38	0.00	0.00	0.00	477.40	291.00	844.00
	(100.0)	(0.0)	(0.0)	(0.0)	(100.0)	(100.0)	(100.0)
(ii) Cooperation	0.00	0.00	0.00	0.00	0.00	0.00	0.00
	(0.0)	(0.0)	(0.0)	(0.0)	(0.0)	(0.0)	(0.0)
(iii) Roads and Bridges	0.00	0.00	7.48	0.00	0.00	0.00	0.00
	(0.0)	(0.0)	(100.0)	(0.0)	(0.0)	(0.0)	(0.0)

Note: (1) RE refers to revised estimates and BE for budget estimates.
(2) Figures in the parentheses are percentage of plan receipts/expenditure to total receipts/expenditure.

Source: Various volumes of *Detailed Estimates of Expenditure*, Budget Documents, Bangalore: Government of Karnataka.

APPENDIX A-9.3

Chronology of Major Policy Initiatives for Scheduled Tribes

Five-Year Plan	Policies
Second (1956-1961)	· Protection of Civil Rights Act and Untouchability (Offences) Act 1955.
	· Adoption of 'Panchsheel'-the five guiding principles of the process of tribal development (1956).
	· Opening of Multi-purpose Tribal Development Blocks (1961)—for intensive development of tribals.
Fourth (1969-1974)	· Introduction of Special Strategies of Tribal Sub-Plan (TSP) and Special Central Assistance to TSP to ensure flow of population—proportionate funds from other developmental sectors for tribals (1974).
Fifth (1975-1979)	· Protection of Civil Rights (Amendment) Act 1976.
Sixth (1980-1985)	· The National Health Policy, 1983—to improve the tribal health especially through detection and treatment of endemic and other diseases specific to tribals.
	· Poverty alleviation programmes for at least 50 per cent of tribal families to cross poverty line and expansion of infrastructure facilities in tribal areas (1985).
Seventh (1985-1990)	· The National Policy on Education 1986 (revised in 1992)—to improve the educational status of tribes who live in far-flung remote areas and remain isolated.
	· Prevention of Atrocities Act 1989.
	· Setting up of special financial institutions: Tribal Cooperative Marketing Development Federation (1987) and National Scheduled Castes and Scheduled Tribe Finance and Development Corporation (1989).
Eighth (1992-1997)	· The National Nutrition Policy, 1993—to improve the nutrition level among tribal women and children.
	· Ensure participatory development of Scheduled Tribe at the grassroot levels involving *Panchayat Raj* Institutions (PRIs) and *Gram Sabhas* as per the 73rd and 74th Amendment of the Constitution (1993) and the Panchayats (Extension to the Scheduled Areas) PESA Act (1996).

Contd. ...

...*Contd.* ...

Five-Year Plan	*Policies*
Ninth (1997-2002)	· A major shift in the approach from 'Welfare' to 'Development' and to 'Empowerment of Tribals' (1997). · Setting up of an exclusive Ministry of Tribal Affairs (1999) and Instituting a separate National Scheduled Tribe Finance and Development Corporation (2001).

Source: Government of India (2002).

APPENDIX A-9.4

Distribution of Area and Number of Operational Holdings of Scheduled Tribes by Size Classes in Karnataka: 1990-91 and 1995-96

Size Classes	*Area of Operation Holdings ('000 Hectares)*		*Number of Operation Holdings ('000)*	
	1990-91	*1995-96*	*1990-91*	*1995-96*
Marginal	52 (8.5)	66 (10.0)	98 (34.6)	123 (36.8)
Small	125 (20.3)	149 (22.5)	86 (30.4)	102 (30.5)
Semi-Medium	172 (28.0)	196 (29.7)	62 (21.9)	72 (21.6)
Medium	186 (30.3)	185 (28.0)	32 (11.3)	32 (9.6)
Large	79 (12.9)	65 (9.8)	5 (1.8)	5 (1.5)
All Sizes	614 (100)	661 (100)	283 (100)	334 (100)

Notes: (1) Figures in parentheses are percentages to total.

(2) Farmers who hold below 1 hectare of land are called as marginal farmers, between 1 to 2 hectares are small farmers; 2.01 to 4 hectares are semi-medium farmers; 4.01 to 10 hectares are medium farmers and above 10 hectares are large farmers.

Source: Government of Karnataka (1996).

APPENDIX A-9.5

Non-Availability of Houses, Household Amenities and Assets for Scheduled Tribes in Karnataka: 2001

Item	*Area*		*Total Households*
	Rural (5,78,452)	*Urban (1,60,746)*	*(7,39,198)*
Non-availability of Good and Liveable House	42,694 (7.4)	9,347 (5.8)	52,041 (7.0)
Non-availability of Permanent House	2,15,498 (37.3)	1,07,549 (66.9)	3,23,047 (43.7)
Non-availability of Assets	3,26,297 (56.4)	49,353 (30.7)	3,75,650 (50.8)
Non-availability of Drinking Water	1,54,927 (26.8)	22,476 (14.0)	1,77,303 (24.0)
Non-availability of Separate Kitchen	1,53,851 (26.6)	30,536 (19.0)	1,84,387 (24.9)
Non-availability of Electricity	2,27,854 (39.4)	30,219 (18.8)	2,58,073 (34.9)
Non-availability of Drainage Facility	4,08,640 (70.6)	41,317 (25.7)	4,49,957 (60.9)
Non-availability of Latrine Facility within the House	5,22,430 (90.3)	67,015 (41.7)	5,89,445 (79.7)
Non-availability of Bathroom Facility within the House	3,73,701 (64.6)	52,397 (32.6)	4,26,098 (57.6)
Banking Services Not Availed	4,49,977 (77.8)	1,10,299 (68.6)	5,60,276 (75.8)

Note: (1) Figures in parentheses are percentages to total.

(2) Assets includes radio or transistor, television, telephone, bicycle, scooter, motor cycle, moped, car, jeep, and van.

(3) Electricity excludes lighting through electricity and solar energy.

(4) Drinking water means availability of water either through tap or hand pump within or near premises.

Source: Government of India (2001).

APPENDIX A-9.6

Status of Scheduled Tribes in Karnataka: 1993-94 and 1999-2000

(in Per Cent)

	Rural		*Urban*		*Total*	
	1993-94	*1999-00*	*1993-94*	*1999-00*	*1993-94*	*1999-00*
1. Employment						
1.1. Self-employment	37.0	36.2	21.1	31.4	29.1	33.8
1.2. Rural Labourer	51.7	54.9	41.0	25.8	46.4	40.4
1.3. Workers employed-Usual Principal Status						
1.3.1. Females	31.5	63.7	16.5	23.7	24.0	43.7
1.3.2. Males	60.6	42.2	56.1	52.9	58.4	47.6
1.4. Workers Employed-Current Daily Status						
1.4.1. Female	30.6	34.9	17.3	22.7	24.0	28.8
1.4.2. Male	57.4	58.3	51.6	49.1	54.5	53.7
2. Land Possessed (in hectares)						
2.1. No Land	31.2	4.8	46.3	47.3	38.8	26.1
2.2. Between 0.01 to 0.40	24.1	48.7	13.3	18.3	18.7	33.5
2.3. Between 0.41 to 1.00	17.6	23.8	15.1	12.7	16.4	18.3
2.4. Above	27.1	22.7	25.3	21.7	26.2	22.2
3. Average Monthly per Capita Expenditure (in Rupees)						
3.1. Up to Rs. 420	91.7	70.3	76.3	43.5	84	57
3.2. Above Rs. 420	8.3	29.7	23.7	56.5	16.0	43.1
4. Adult Illiterates						
4.1. Adults	46.1	51.1	23.3	20.6	34.7	35.9
4.2. Female	82.9	74.5	41.9	61.7	62.4	68.1
5. Female Literate						
5.1. Primary	7.9	10.2	15.5	9.4	11.7	9.8
5.2. Secondary	4.2	10.0	23.7	30.4	14.0	20.2
5.3. Higher	0.8	0.4	3.9	8.5	2.4	4.5
6. Male Literate						
6.1. Primary	24.0	17.2	25.6	16.1	24.8	16.7
6.2. Secondary	13.3	22.5	33.7	39.0	23.5	30.8
6.3. Higher	2.6	5.1	15.3	14.8	9.0	10.0

Note: (1) Wage and salary labourers in urban areas are treated under rural labourers.

(2) Monthly per capital expenditure of Rs. 455 in 1993-94 and Rs. 420 in 1999-2000 in rural areas and Rs. 410 in 1993-94 and Rs. 425 in 1999-2000 in urban areas are treated as below Rs. 420, due to non-availability of uniform data.

Source: NSS (1997) and NSS (2001).

APPENDIX A-9.7

Nutritional Status of Scheduled Tribe Children in Karnataka: 1998-99

Item	*Scheduled Tribes*	*Scheduled Castes*	*OBCs*	*Karnataka*	*Scheduled Tribes in India*
		Weight-for-age			
Percentage below–3 SD	28.7	23.0	12.2	16.5	26.0
Percentage below–2 SD	55.7	52.8	40.0	43.9	55.9

Contd. ...

...*Contd.* ...

Item	*Scheduled Tribes*	*Scheduled Castes*	*OBCs*	*Karnataka*	*Scheduled Tribes in India*
		Height-for-age			
Percentage below–3 SD	22.1	17.9	12.7	15.9	27.6
Percentage below–2 SD	41.2	43.7	34.4	36.6	52.8
		Weight-for-height			
Percentage below–3 SD	1.6	6.8	2.5	3.9	4.4
Percentage below–2 SD	21.0	21.0	15.1	20.0	21.8

Note: OBCs stands for Other Backward Communities and SD for Standard Deviation.

Source: Government of Karnataka (2004).

APPENDIX A-9.8

Distribution of Household Amenities among Scheduled Tribes in Karnataka: 1991 and 2001

(in Per Cent)

District	*Owned House*		*Electricity*		*Toilet Facility*		*Drinking Water*		*Cooking*	
	1991	*2001*	*1991*	*2001*	*1991*	*2001*	*1991*	*2001*	*1991*	*2001*
Bangalore (Rural)	91.3	84.6	41.4	78.9	4.7	26.1	1.4	12.8	2.9	10.9
Bangalore (Urban)	69.0	44.6	61.1	88.9	53.1	78.6	11.5	46.6	60.1	74.7
Belgaum	85.1	87.6	43.3	63.9	6.1	8.7	2.6	9.6	6.6	7.0
Bellary	91.4	88.4	21.8	61.6	2.6	15.0	1.5	10.1	1.0	5.5
Bidar	94.9	93.9	31.8	66.8	2.7	10.8	1.1	13.2	1.2	4.0
Bijapur	82.7	86.7	26.4	60.6	3.4	8.7	2.7	11.8	2.2	4.6
Chickmagalur	68.6	70.5	22.3	59.1	12.4	29.1	1.8	16.0	2.7	9.5
Chitradurga	91.8	90.0	35.9	71.1	4.9	13.6	1.1	10.7	2.1	5.4
Dakshina Kannada	91.9	92.3	13.2	45.6	7.7	30.8	1.1	7.3	2.6	7.4
Dharwad	82.7	85.9	43.5	70.0	8.9	16.0	3.0	14.9	6.7	8.6
Gulbarga	84.0	88.5	24.0	49.3	8.4	12.5	5.4	11.0	5.7	5.8
Hassan	83.8	81.2	39.0	74.4	8.5	21.7	3.0	21.0	6.6	13.4
Kodagu	39.4	42.8	13.2	28.8	9.9	30.0	0.9	9.0	0.9	3.8
Kolar	93.7	90.8	40.6	77.2	4.7	17.7	1.3	10.6	2.1	6.0
Mandya	85.9	76.8	24.7	60.8	5.5	22.5	2.3	19.4	3.2	11.3
Mysore	89.2	89.4	26.2	57.7	13.0	18.7	4.0	20.6	8.2	10.3
Raichur	90.9	91.6	16.9	49.5	1.7	5.5	1.0	5.7	1.0	1.5
Shimoga	85.6	78.5	47.0	68.8	10.7	34.3	3.2	19.1	5.7	18.4
Tumkur	91.3	87.6	42.1	71.3	5.2	17.7	1.5	12.9	2.6	7.2
Uttara Kannada	88.7	81.0	31.6	70.8	11.1	19.4	2.4	15.1	4.7	13.5
Karnataka	**86.3**	**84.4**	**34.5**	**64.7**	**8.9**	**20.3**	**2.3**	**14.8**	**6.7**	**11.8**

Notes: (1) Cooking refers to making use of electricity, gas, biogas and kerosene as fuel in domestic activities.

(2) Drinking water refers to water availability either by tube well or hand pump or tap within the premises.

Source: *Census of India* (1991b) and *Census of India* (2001b).

APPENDIX A-9.9

Incidence and Rate of Crime Committed against Scheduled Castes during 2001

State/UT	*Incidence*	*Percentage Contribution to All-India Total*	*Population (in Lakhs)*	*Rate of Total Cognizable Crimes (in Per Cent)*	*Rank**	*Rank***
(1)	(2)	(3)	(4)	(5)	(6)	(7)
States						
Andhra Pradesh	2933	8.8	757.28	3.9	5	4
Arunachal Pradesh	0	0.0	10.91	0.0	-	-
Assam	6	0.0	266.38	0.0	27	23
Bihar	1303	3.9	828.79	1.6	12	8
Chhattisgarh	501	1.5	207.96	2.4	9	11
Goa	1	0.0	13.44	0.1	24	28
Gujarat	1242	3.7	505.97	2.5	8	9
Haryana	229	0.7	210.83	1.1	16	13
Himachal Pradesh	110	0.3	60.77	1.8	11	17
Jammu & Kashmir	10	0.0	100.70	0.1	23	21
Jharkhand	158	0.5	269.09	0.6	18	15
Karnataka	**1621**	**4.8**	**527.34**	**3.1**	**7**	**7**
Kerala	499	1.5	318.39	1.6	13	12
Madhya Pradesh	4212	12.6	603.85	7.0	2	3
Maharashtra	625	1.9	967.52	0.6	17	10
Manipur	0	0.0	23.89	0.0	-	-
Meghalaya	0	0.0	23.06	0.0	-	-
Mizoram	1	0.0	8.91	0.1	22	27
Nagaland	1	0.0	19.89	0.1	26	26
Orissa	1734	5.2	367.07	4.7	4	6
Punjab	134	0.4	242.89	0.6	19	16
Rajasthan	4892	14.6	564.73	8.7	1	2
Sikkim	6	0.0	5.40	1.1	15	22
Tamil Nadu	2336	7.0	621.11	3.8	6	5
Tripura	2	0.0	31.91	0.1	25	25
Uttar Pradesh	10732	32.0	1660.53	6.5	3	1
Uttaranchal	168	0.5	84.80	2.0	10	14
West Bengal	10	0.0	802.21	0.0	28	20
Total (states)	33466	99.9	10105.62	3.3	-	-
Union Territories						
A & N Islands	0	0.0	3.56	0.0	-	-
Chandigarh	3	0.0	9.01	0.3	20	24
D & N Haveli	0	0.0	2.20	0.0	-	-
Daman & Diu	0	0.0	1.58	0.0	-	-
Delhi	19	0.1	137.83	0.1	21	18
Lakshadweep	0	0.0	0.61	0.0	-	-
Pondicherry	13	0.0	9.74	1.3	14	19
Total (UTs)	35	0.1	164.53	0.2	-	-
Total (All-India)	**33501**	**100.0**	**10270.2**	**3.3**	-	-

Note: 1.*Rank on the basis of Rate of total cognizable crimes (Col 6.) 2. ** Rank on the basis of percentage share (Col 7.)

APPENDIX A-9.10

Incidence and Rate of Crime Committed against Scheduled Tribes during 2001

State/UT	Incidence	Percentage of Contribution to All-India Total	Population (in Lakhs)@	Rate of Total Cognizable Crimes (in per cent)	Rank*	Rank**
(1)	(2)	(3)	(4)	(5)	(6)	(7)
States						
Andhra Pradesh	512	8.2	757.28	0.7	11	4
Arunachal Pradesh	72	1.2	10.91	6.6	2	13
Assam	0	0.0	266.38	0.0	-	-
Bihar	47	0.8	828.79	0.1	20	14
Chhattisgarh	486	7.8	207.96	2.3	5	5
Goa	0	0.0	13.44	0.0	-	-
Gujarat	309	5.0	505.97	0.6	12	7
Haryana	0	0.0	210.83	0.0	-	-
Himachal Pradesh	4	0.1	60.77	0.1	19	20
Jammu & Kashmir	0	0.0	100.70	0.0	-	-
Jharkhand	282	4.5	269.09	1.0	10	8
Karnataka	276	4.4	527.34	0.5	13	9
Kerala	83	1.3	318.39	0.3	15	12
Madhya Pradesh	1535	24.7	603.85	2.5	4	1
Maharashtra	238	3.8	967.52	0.2	16	11
Manipur	0	0.0	23.89	0.0	-	-
Meghalaya	0	0.0	23.06	0.0	-	-
Mizoram	10	0.2	8.91	1.1	8	16
Nagaland	310	5.0	19.89	15.6	1	6
Orissa	734	11.8	367.07	2.0	6	3
Punjab	0	0.0	242.89	0.0	-	-
Rajasthan	1023	16.5	564.73	1.8	7	2
Sikkim	6	0.1	5.40	1.1	9	19
Tamil Nadu	9	0.1	621.11	0.0	21	17
Tripura	0	0.0	31.91	0.0	-	-
Uttar Pradesh	254	4.1	1660.53	0.2	18	10
Uttaranchal	18	0.3	84.80	0.2	17	15
West Bengal	2	0.0	802.21	0.0	22	21
Total (states)	6210	99.9	10105.62	0.6		
Union Territories						
A & N Islands	1	0.0	3.56	0.3	14	22
Chandigarh	0	0.0	9.01	0.0	-	-
D & N Haveli	6	0.1	2.20	2.7	3	18
Daman & Diu	0	0.0	1.58	0.0	-	-
Delhi	0	0.0	137.83	0.0	-	-
Lakshadweep	0	0.0	0.61	0.0	-	-
Pondicherry	0	0.0	9.74	0.0	-	-
Total (UTs)	7	0.1	164.53	0.0		
Total (All-India)	**6217**	**100.0**	**10270.2**	**0.6**		

Note: 1. * Rank on the basis of rate of total cognizable crimes (Col 6.).

2. ** Rank on the basis of percentage share (Col 7.).

3. @ Based on Census 2001.

APPENDIX A-9.11

Share and Variation of Crimes Committed against SC/ST

Year	Crimes		
	Total	Against SC/ST	Percentage
2000	109410	1205	1.10
2001	109098	1749	1.60

Source: National Crime Records Bureau.

APPENDIX A-9.12

State-wise Incidence of Crimes Committed against Women during 2001

State/UT	Population (In Lakhs)	Rape			Kidnapping and Abduction			Dowry Deaths			Cruelty by Husband and Relatives		
		I	R	P	I	R	P	I	R	P	I	R	P
Andhra Pradesh	757.28	871	1.2	5.4	765	1.0	5.2	420	0.6	6.1	5791	7.6	11.8
Arunachal Pradesh	10.91	33	3.0	0.2	55	5.0	0.4	0	0.0	0.0	11	1.0	0.0
Assam	266.38	817	3.1	5.1	1070	4.0	7.3	59	0.2	0.9	1248	4.7	2.5
Bihar	828.79	888	1.1	5.5	518	0.6	3.5	859	1.0	12.5	1558	1.9	3.2
Chhattisgarh	207.96	959	4.6	6.0	171	0.8	1.2	70	0.3	1.0	840	4.0	1.7
Goa	13.44	12	0.9	0.1	6	0.4	0.0	2	0.1	0.0	11	0.8	0.0
Gujarat	505.97	286	0.6	1.8	857	1.7	5.9	67	0.1	1.0	3667	7.2	7.5
Haryana	210.83	398	1.9	2.5	297	1.4	2.0	285	1.4	4.2	1513	7.2	3.1
Himachal Pradesh	60.77	124	2.0	0.8	105	1.7	0.7	10	0.2	0.1	317	5.2	0.6
Jammu & Kashmir	100.70	169	1.7	1.1	504	5.0	3.4	13	0.1	0.2	50	0.5	0.1
Jharkhand	269.09	567	2.1	3.5	279	1.0	1.9	217	0.8	3.2	484	1.8	1.0
Karnataka	**527.34**	**293**	**0.6**	**1.8**	**271**	**0.5**	**1.9**	**220**	**0.4**	**3.2**	**1755**	**3.3**	**3.6**
Kerala	318.39	562	1.8	3.5	97	0.3	0.7	27	0.1	0.4	2561	8.0	5.2
Madhya Pradesh	603.85	2851	4.7	17.7	668	1.1	4.6	609	1.0	8.9	2562	4.2	5.2
Maharashtra	967.52	1302	1.3	8.1	611	0.6	4.2	308	0.3	4.5	6090	6.3	12.4
Manipur	23.89	20	0.8	0.1	62	2.6	0.4	0	0.0	0.0	5	0.2	0.0
Meghalaya	23.06	26	1.1	0.2	11	0.5	0.1	0	0.0	0.0	4	0.2	0.0
Mizoram	8.91	52	5.8	0.3	1	0.1	0.0	0	0.0	0.0	16	1.8	0.0
Nagaland	19.89	17	0.9	0.1	6	0.3	0.0	0	0.0	0.0	0	0.0	0.0
Orissa	367.07	790	2.2	4.9	434	1.2	3.0	294	0.8	4.3	1266	3.4	2.6
Punjab	242.89	298	1.2	1.9	324	1.3	2.2	159	0.7	2.3	1128	4.6	2.3
Rajasthan	564.73	1049	1.9	6.5	2165	3.8	14.8	376	0.7	5.5	5532	9.8	11.3
Sikkim	5.40	8	1.5	0.0	2	0.4	0.0	0	0.0	0.0	0	0.0	0.0
Tamil Nadu	621.11	423	0.7	2.6	607	1.0	4.1	191	0.3	2.8	815	1.3	1.7
Tripura	31.91	102	3.2	0.6	35	1.1	0.2	16	0.5	0.2	227	7.1	0.5
Uttar Pradesh	1660.53	1958	1.2	12.2	2879	1.7	19.7	2211	1.3	32.3	7365	4.4	15.0
Uttaranchal	84.80	74	0.9	0.5	126	1.5	0.9	56	0.7	0.8	301	3.5	0.6
West Bengal	802.21	709	0.9	4.4	695	0.9	4.7	265	0.3	3.9	3859	4.8	7.8
Total (States)	**10105.62**	**15658**	**1.5**	**97.4**	**13621**	**1.3**	**93.0**	**6734**	**0.7**	**98.3**	**48976**	**4.8**	**99.6**
Union Territories													
A & N Islands	3.56	3	0.8	0.0	2	0.6	0.0	0	0.0	0.0	9	2.5	0.0
Chandigarh	9.01	18	2.0	0.1	50	5.5	0.3	3	0.3	0.0	36	4.0	0.1
D & N Haveli	2.20	6	2.7	0.0	2	0.9	0.0	0	0.0	0.0	4	1.8	0.0
Daman & Diu	1.58	0	0.0	0.0	3	1.9	0.0	0	0.0	0.0	4	2.5	0.0
Delhi	137.83	381	2.8	2.4	964	7.0	6.6	113	0.8	1.6	138	1.0	0.3
Lakshadweep	0.61	0	0.0	0.0	0	0.0	0.0	0	0.0	0.0	0	0.0	0.0
Pondicherry	9.74	9	0.9	0.1	3	0.3	0.0	1	0.1	0.0	3	0.3	0.0
Total (UTs)	164.53	417	2.5	2.6	1024	6.2	7.0	117	0.7	1.7	194	1.2	0.4
Total (All-India)	**10270.15**	**16075**	**1.6**	**100.0**	**14645**	**1.4**	**100.0**	**6851**	**0.7**	**100.0**	**49170**	**4.8**	**100.0**

Note: I: Incidence R: Rate of Total Cognizable Crimes P: Percentage contribution to all-India.

Source: National Crimes Record Bureau.

APPENDIX A-9.13

Crimes against Women in Cities

State/UT	*Population (In Lakhs)*	*Rape*			*Kidnapping and Abduction*			*Dowry Deaths*			*Cruelty by Husband and Relatives*		
		I	*R*	*P*	*I*	*R*	*P*	*I*	*R*	*P*	*I*	*R*	*P*
Cities													
Agra	13.21	66	5.0	5.2	131	9.9	5.8	62	4.7	11.2	327	24.8	5.3
Ahmedabad	45.19	39	0.9	3.1	117	2.6	5.1	7	0.2	1.3	530	11.7	8.6
Allahabad	10.50	7	0.7	0.6	39	3.7	1.7	7	0.7	1.3	64	6.1	1.0
Amritsar	10.11	7	0.7	0.6	23	2.3	1.0	7	0.7	1.3	72	7.1	1.2
Asansol	10.91	NR	NR	NR	NR	NR	NR	NR	NR	NR	NR	NR	NR
Bangalore	56.87	40	0.7	3.2	56	1.0	2.5	40	0.7	7.2	229	4.0	3.7
Bhopal	14.55	75	5.2	5.9	45	3.1	2.0	12	0.8	2.2	123	8.5	2.0
Chennai	64.25	28	0.4	2.2	0	0.0	0.0	13	0.2	2.3	111	1.7	1.8
Coimbatore	14.46	4	0.3	0.3	10	0.7	0.4	5	0.3	0.9	28	1.9	0.5
Delhi (City)	127.91	326	2.5	25.9	820	6.4	36.0	84	0.7	15.1	108	0.8	1.8
Dhanbad	10.64	NR	NR	NR	NR	NR	NR	NR	NR	NR	NR	NR	NR
Faridabad	10.55	11	1.0	0.9	37	3.5	1.6	9	0.9	1.6	53	5.0	0.9
Hyderabad	55.34	37	0.7	2.9	39	0.7	1.7	24	0.4	4.3	746	13.5	12.1
Indore	16.39	50	3.1	4.0	33	2.0	1.4	21	1.3	3.8	100	6.1	1.6
Jabalpur	11.17	64	5.7	5.1	15	1.3	0.7	12	1.1	2.2	39	3.5	0.6
Jaipur	23.24	28	1.2	2.2	155	6.7	6.8	16	0.7	2.9	338	14.5	5.5
Jamshedpur	11.02	NR	NR	NR	NR	NR	NR	NR	NR	NR	NR	NR	NR
Kanpur	26.90	47	1.7	3.7	176	6.5	7.7	64	2.4	11.5	356	13.2	5.8
Kochi	13.55	10	0.7	0.8	1	0.1	0.0	0	0.0	0.0	62	4.6	1.0
Kolkata	132.17	19	0.1	1.5	78	0.6	3.4	6	0.0	1.1	207	1.6	3.4
Lucknow	22.67	39	1.7	3.1	107	4.7	4.7	27	1.2	4.9	304	13.4	4.9
Ludhiana	13.95	34	2.4	2.7	42	3.0	1.8	9	0.6	1.6	233	16.7	3.8
Madurai	11.95	2	0.2	0.2	18	1.5	0.8	12	1.0	2.2	24	2.0	0.4
Meerut	11.67	6	0.5	0.5	51	4.4	2.2	9	0.8	1.6	151	12.9	2.4
Mumbai	163.68	127	0.8	10.1	12	0.1	0.5	18	0.1	3.2	198	1.2	3.2
Nagpur	21.23	39	1.8	3.1	51	2.4	2.2	7	0.3	1.3	218	10.3	3.5
Nasik	11.52	9	0.8	0.7	9	0.8	0.4	3	0.3	0.5	99	8.6	1.6
Patna	17.07	17	1.0	1.3	7	0.4	0.3	40	2.3	7.2	97	5.7	1.6
Pune	37.56	56	1.5	4.4	28	0.7	1.2	2	0.1	0.4	147	3.9	2.4
Rajkot	10.02	5	0.5	0.4	38	3.8	1.7	3	0.3	0.5	199	19.9	3.2
Surat	28.11	11	0.4	0.9	37	1.3	1.6	20	0.7	3.6	132	4.7	2.1
Vadodara	14.92	3	0.2	0.2	32	2.1	1.4	0	0.0	0.0	90	6.0	1.5
Varanasi	12.12	17	1.4	1.3	17	1.4	0.7	15	1.2	2.7	58	4.8	0.9
Vijayawada	10.11	25	2.5	2.0	48	4.7	2.1	2	0.2	0.4	520	51.4	8.4
Vishakhapatnam	13.29	13	1.0	1.0	6	0.5	0.3	0	0.0	0.0	204	15.3	3.3
Total (Cities)	1046.23	1261	1.2	100.0	2278	2.2	100.0	556	0.5	100.0	6167	5.9	100.0

Source: National Crimes Record Bureau.

APPENDIX A-9.14

District/Category-wise *Gram Panchayat* Elected Representatives in Karnataka: 2000

District	*General*			*OBC 'A'*			*OBC 'B'*			*SC*			*ST*		
	T	*WR*	*% Women*	*T*	*WR*	*% Women*	*T*	*WR*	*% Women*	*T*	*WR*	*% Women*	*T*	*WR*	*% Women*
Bagalkote	1072	412	38.43	669	326	48.73	171	17	9.94	423	193	45.63	170	164	96.47
Bangalore (Rural)	1331	519	38.99	933	440	47.16	230	12	5.22	734	315	42.92	251	230	91.63
Bangalore (Urban)	576	233	40.45	457	213	46.61	114	10	8.77	444	181	40.77	116	112	96.55
Belgaum	3357	1265	37.68	1907	875	45.88	515	94	18.25	912	547	59.98	562	498	88.61
Bellary	904	358	39.60	716	350	48.88	189	15	7.94	573	249	43.46	381	229	60.10
Bidar	817	329	40.27	664	339	51.05	174	13	7.47	572	240	41.96	283	182	64.31
Bijapur	1262	493	39.06	840	396	47.14	213	22	10.33	641	275	42.90	209	201	96.17
Chamrajnagar	654	255	38.99	521	237	45.49	122	18	14.75	468	196	41.88	157	128	81.53
Chickmagalur	757	323	42.67	553	295	53.35	169	5	2.96	467	248	53.10	235	226	96.17
Chitradurga	722	292	40.44	734	352	47.96	182	8	4.40	661	285	43.12	532	258	48.50
Dakshina Kannada	1438	551	38.32	766	364	47.52	202	26	12.87	273	209	76.56	248	209	84.27
Davangere	885	367	41.47	751	382	50.87	213	8	3.76	664	300	45.18	398	251	63.07
Dharwad	809	310	38.32	426	215	50.47	126	12	9.52	156	128	82.05	129	127	98.45
Gadag	626	240	38.34	379	184	48.55	105	7	6.67	237	125	52.74	109	106	97.25
Gulbarga	1627	662	40.69	1337	660	49.36	340	16	4.71	1279	536	41.91	438	350	79.91
Hassan	1385	556	40.14	903	463	51.27	249	7	2.81	652	314	48.16	262	258	98.47
Haveri	1156	454	39.27	681	357	52.42	207	12	5.80	378	225	59.52	245	206	84.08
Kodagu	462	187	40.48	289	154	53.29	96	2	2.08	194	103	53.09	142	104	73.24
Kolar	1325	548	41.36	1144	608	53.15	306	5	1.63	1167	487	41.73	430	294	68.37
Koppal	866	332	38.34	564	269	47.70	140	13	9.29	340	162	47.65	191	138	72.25
Mandya	1655	628	37.95	963	449	46.63	230	22	9.57	502	253	50.40	230	230	100.00
Mysore	1460	558	38.22	1033	464	44.92	239	18	7.53	782	343	43.86	298	245	82.21
Raichur	917	355	38.71	711	331	46.55	177	24	13.56	521	224	42.99	347	194	55.91
Shimoga	889	316	35.55	630	340	53.97	205	1	0.49	507	301	59.37	264	255	96.59
Tumkur	1867	715	38.30	1319	633	47.99	325	14	4.31	938	421	44.88	483	325	67.29
Udupi	1150	433	37.65	588	274	46.60	155	23	14.84	169	147	86.98	176	148	84.09
Uttara Kannada	1082	424	39.19	601	311	51.75	179	11	6.15	257	211	82.10	213	205	96.24
State	**31051**	**12115**	**39.02**	**21079**	**10281**	**48.77**	**5573**	**435**	**7.81**	**14911**	**7218**	**48.41**	**7499**	**5873**	**78.32**

Note: Election not held in the 11 *Gram Panchayats* i.e., Mandya (2), Uttara Kannada (3), Bellary (3) and Bidar (3) T: Total, WR: Women Reserved.

Source: State Election Commission and RDPR.

APPENDIX A-9.15

Percentage of Elected Women Representatives in PRIs in the Elections 1994 and 2000

	GP		*TP*		*ZP*	
Districts	*1994*	*2000*	*1994*	*2000*	*1994*	*2000*
Bagalkote	-	44.39	-	41.41	-	38.46
Bangalore (Urban)	44.66	43.88	39.13	41.18	38.89	41.18
Bangalore (Rural)	43.22	43.58	39.86	41.01	39.47	39.47
Belgaum	43.51	45.21	37.28	38.33	35.53	35.53
Bellary	42.38	43.47	40.15	41.96	39.47	37.50
Bidar	42.60	43.94	40.19	42.57	37.93	34.62
Bijapur	42.74	43.82	37.17	39.52	36.67	37.50
Chamrajnagar	-	43.39	-	40.74	-	42.86
Chickmagalur	48.99	50.30	43.81	48.54	39.39	40.00
Chitradurga	41.58	42.21	40.70	41.74	39.96	38.71
Dakshina Kannada	43.52	46.43	39.81	40.00	34.55	38.71
Davangere	-	44.93	-	41.74	-	41.94
Dharwad	43.64	48.12	42.74	50.00	35.82	44.44
Gadag	-	45.47	-	48.48	-	41.18
Gulbarga	44.30	44.29	39.71	41.41	34.55	34.55
Hassan	44.64	46.31	39.16	41.73	35.14	37.84
Haveri	-	47.02	-	43.12	-	41.38
Kodagu	44.97	48.12	39.58	41.30	37.04	34.62
Kolar	44.25	44.42	43.01	43.09	38.00	38.30
Koppal	-	43.50	-	39.76	-	39.13
Mandya	44.22	32.18	38.10	41.67	35.90	38.46
Mysore	42.09	42.71	38.68	40.79	34.38	36.59
Raichur	41.87	42.20	41.54	40.19	35.19	37.93
Shimoga	48.20	48.62	41.89	47.47	36.59	37.04
Tumkur	42.38	42.74	39.41	41.03	37.04	36.54
Udupi	-	45.80	-	38.64	-	41.67
Uttara Kannada	47.04	49.83	46.34	54.47	36.84	37.14
State	**43.59**	**44.32**	**40.21**	**42.24**	**36.45**	**38.09**

Source: State Election Commission and RDPR.

Chapter 10

Regional Dimensions of Development in Karnataka

10.1 Introduction

Karnataka is one of the above national average states of India, facing inter-regional and intra-regional disparities since its reorganisation in 1956. Many historical and economic factors are responsible for these disparities along with the influence of regional diversities seen across the four major regions of the state (Southern Maidan, Northern Maidan, Malnad and coastal). The old Mysore state, which comprised most of the southern parts of present Karnataka state, had dynamic rulers and administrators, which led to the development of the region, prior to the State Reorganisation.

At the time of State Reorganisation in 1956, many Kannada speaking regions which belonged to the then neighbouring states were integrated and the new enlarged state of Mysore (now Karnataka) was established. Present Karnataka consists of 27 districts and 175 *talukas*. Till recently there were 19 districts, some of the districts were bifurcated now and new districts were formed. Though this integration fulfilled the aspiration of both Kannada speaking people and their leaders, it brought in numerous economic problems along with it. The newly integrated areas presently known as Hydrabad-Karnataka, Bombay-Karnataka were substantially neglected by the erstwhile states to which they belonged before reorganisation. The *Malnad* region and northern coastal areas were also lagging behind in spite of their rich natural and capital resources base.

Karnataka has prominent regional diversity as well as regional disparity. There is diversity in natural resources like, the soil type, climate, rainfall, minerals, rivers, forests, coastal zone, hills and so on. There is also disparity caused by the socio-economic policies pursued in the past and present. Concerted efforts have been made since the inception of the Second Five-Year Plan to reduce regional disparities in Karnataka. However, there is still a general concern about relative backwardness of some districts belonging to these regions. In fact such regions have made considerable progress in absolute terms. But their relative position shows little change. This has led to discontentment among the people of these regions. There are severe allegations that their regions have constantly been neglected.

Many times it is alleged that the old Mysore area is fully developed while the areas which joined new Karnataka remained backward. About this the High Power Committee on Redressal of Regional Imbalances (HPC) in 2002 expressed, "While Mysore-Karnataka has for historical reasons registered relatively a higher level of development, this is not so in respect of intra-Mysore-Karnataka region. There are disparities from one district to another and also from one *taluka* to another. Similarly, if we take Hydrabad-Karnataka or Bombay-Karnataka region, it cannot be asserted that the entire region has not registered any development at all. Very substantial improvements in output, income and infrastructure have taken place between 1956 and 2000. But due to lower base with which they started in 1956 and for historical reasons, the relative development registered through the Annual and Five-Year Plans and also Externally Assisted Projects implemented in those areas, and the rates of growth have not been adequate to reach the Mysore-Karnataka level, though the increases in output and income have escalated several-fold."

The natural resource diversities are often disadvantageous for harmonious development of all the regions of the state. Most of these natural constraints have to be accepted as such. Apart from the diversity factors, there are severe disparities which emerged as a consequence of alarming rise in the growth of population, unemployment, low literacy rate, low productivity, lopsided concentration of industries and infrastructure and modern civic amenities in few metropolitan centres.

With the introduction of Five-Year Plans, the state accorded greater importance to regional perspectives underlying the importance of local needs in general and development of potentialities of the backward areas in particular. Attempts were made to track relative levels of development attained by different districts and to evolve planning machinery at the district level, with a view to bring harmonious state of development.

This chapter goes into a brief history of regional dimensions of the state, its development and future challenges. Sectoral, human and social developments are viewed in a regional framework, taking administrative divisions (synonymous to the regions referred in the context of political economy of development) as the spatial units. Issues of regional variations over time and space are analysed. After a review of policies and implementation strategies in the past, vision and strategies for the future are presented.

10.2 Karnataka *vis-à-vis* Other States

The relative position of Karnataka among the Indian states in respect of the parameters chosen by Kurian (2000) for analysing the regional disparities presents a mixed picture. In terms of demographic parameters: population growth, sex ratio and urbanisation, the state displayed a favourable picture compared to the national average. However, its per capita income below the national average, were sources of concern. Although the percentage share of poor in Karnataka (33.2 per cent) was below the national average (36 per cent) in 1993-1994, it did not compare well with many other states like Andhra Pradesh, Gujarat, Haryana, Kerala and Punjab. Analysis of state government expenditures: developmental and non-developmental, an important public policy instrument for economic and social development, between two points of time: 1980-81 and 1995-96, revealed that Karnataka had more than doubled the per capita development expenditure in real terms. This was also true of the per capita non-development expenditure in the corresponding period. While both development and non-development expenditures increased in real terms, the growth in the latter was faster. In other words, the relative importance of development expenditure has come down in 1995-96 as compared to 1980-81, which may be surmised to have a negative bearing on reducing regional disparities.

The share of Karnataka in private investment proposals from 1991 to 1998 stood at 5.6 per cent thus occupying the 7th position in the country. Its share in cumulative financial assistance disbursed by AFIs up to March end 1997 stood at 6.1 per cent or 6th position in the country. This remained at 6.1 per cent but with 5th position in the country in the year 2000-01.[1]

10.2.1 Interdistrict Disparities in Development in India

Centre for Monitoring Indian Economy (CMIE) had prepared a relative index of development at the all-India district levels. CMIE selected a few indices of development. Based on these indices relating to 427 districts interdistrict disparities were examined. Relative index of development pertaining to 409 districts of India are estimated. The average level of development of the groups of districts based on the relative level of development of the states and their coefficient of concentration, the relative position of the states and their coefficient of variation on interdistrict disparities are shown in Table 10.1.

A cursory look at the last row of Table 10.1 shows that interdistrict disparities are very wide in India. The coefficient of variation, which is a good measure of disparities, was as high as 72.14 per cent in 1993. The average level of development taking all districts into consideration was 88.08-index value.

As may be seen from the Table 10.1, there are 10 states, which have recorded above national average index values. However, the position of Jammu and Kashmir is not very convincing. Karnataka recorded an above average index value (111.85) thus occupied the 5th position among the states of India in terms of district level development. Karnataka also recorded lower level of disparities as measured by coefficient of variation compared to states like Maharashtra (116.89) and West Bengal (114.34).

It is equally important to observe that the level of interdistrict disparities varies from state to state. In general, backward states like Bihar, Himachal Pradesh, Madhya Pradesh, Orissa, Uttar Pradesh, have recorded very low coefficient of variation indicating low level of 'interdistrict disparities'. On the contrary, developed districts like Maharashtra, West Bengal, Jammu and Kashmir (not sure whether really developed), Tamil

1. For details see, IDBI, *Report on Development Banking in India*, 1999-2000, Table 3.6.,p.15. Also see Chapter 22 of Hemlata Rao (1984) Report.

Nadu and so on have shown very wide regional disparities. Among the developed states only Punjab and Kerala have low levels of disparities. This is brought forth by the coefficient of variation given in Table 10.1. A careful look at the table reveals that while reduction in regional disparities is desirable, a lower level of regional disparities does not ensure the optimum level of prosperity and welfare. The backward states have low regional disparities because a large number of districts are backward in these states and average level of development is far below the average of the country. Rather, this only reveals equal distribution of poverty. On the contrary, developed states have wider disparities, but their average level of development is also high. Interstate disparities are revealed by the state average index of development and the coefficient of concentration.

TABLE 10.1

Intradistrict Disparities in the Levels of Relative Index of Development (Summary Measures)

States	*District Average*	*Variation Coefficient of %*	*Standard Deviation*	*Coefficient of Concentration %*
Bihar	42.90	38.48	16.51	48.70
Rajasthan	63.33	41.64	26.37	71.90
Assam	65.11	46.49	30.27	73.92
Orissa	66.54	19.89	13.23	75.54
Madhya Pradesh	70.18	39.49	27.71	79.68
Uttar Pradesh	70.48	39.35	27.73	80.02
Himachal Pradesh	75.00	36.47	27.36	85.15
Andhra Pradesh	92.04	54.51	50.17	104.50
West Bengal	94.25	114.34	107.76	107.00
Maharashtra	99.63	116.89	116.46	113.12
Gujarat	106.79	42.74	45.64	121.24
Jammu & Kashmir	111.43	75.98	84.66	126.51
Karnataka	111.85	47.92	53.60	126.99
Kerala	113.57	24.84	28.21	128.94
Tamil Nadu	126.70	68.72	87.07	143.85
Haryana	150.69	41.59	62.67	171.09
Punjab	200.17	22.43	44.90	227.26
All States	**88.08**	**72.14**	**63.54**	**100.00**

Source: Computed from *Profiles of Districts*, November 1993, Economic Intelligence Service, CMIE, Bombay.

An ideal situation is one found in Punjab, where not only the average level of development is very high but also the level of interdistrict disparity is very low. Country should strive to achieve this type of growth with equity. Karnataka holds a comfortable position as for as the district level of development and the level of disparities are concerned when compared with most of the major states.

10.3 Interdistrict Disparities in Karnataka

Against this background, micro view of disparities in Karnataka at the district level in respect of per capita income, overall backwardness, poverty and human development are presented, followed by a discussion on changes in the sectoral composition of state/districts' income since 1980-81.

Regional disparities can be assessed on the basis of the index values of development. Levels of development can be measured either in terms of monetary index like per capita income or on the basis of physical indicators of development and a composite index. Districts of Karnataka state are identified according to differential levels of development with the help of both types of indices.

10.3.1 Backward Areas in Terms of Per Capita Income

Government of Karnataka (2002) has used per capita income measure as initial point to measure the trend in disparities across the *talukas* and districts in Karnataka. To get such an overview, HPC[2] presented the per capita income, district-wise, at four different points of time: 1970-71, 1980-81, 1993-94 and 1997-98. According to them, the average per capita income in Karnataka increased from Rs. 685 in 1970-71, to Rs. 13,621 in 1997-98 (at current prices). All the districts in Karnataka registered a growing trend in their per capita incomes. The Committee also brought forth the following points relevant for the analysis of regional disparities:

a) In 1970-71 and 1980-81 per capita income in nine districts was above the state average. This number was reduced to eight districts in 1993-1994 and further to six districts in 1997-98. Region-wise categorisation of these districts in per capita income above the state average is shown in Table 10.2. It is obvious that the districts, which had their per capita income above the state average, belonged mostly to south Karnataka.

b) Relative ranks of backward districts: Bidar, Gulbarga, Raichur, Bellary and Uttara Kannda

2. Government of Karnataka, *High Power Committee on Redressal of Regional Imbalances*, (June 2002) Table 4.5, p.72.

of north Karnataka and Shimoga, Chickmaglur and Tumkur of south Karnataka deteriorated over the years.

c) Districts, which managed to steadily improve their ranks, were Belgaum and Dakshina Kannada only.

TABLE 10.2

Number of Districts above State Average in Per Capita Income

Year	Number of Districts		
	South Karnataka (15)	*North Karnataka (12)*	*Total (27)*
1970-71	6	3	9
1980-81	7	2	9
1993-94	7	1	8
1997-98	6	0	6

Note: Figures in parentheses are total number of districts in the region.
Source: Directorate of Economics and Statistics, Government of Karnataka.

HPC concluded that, interdistrict disparities in per capita income across the districts seemed to be narrowing between 1970-71 and 1993-94, but widened between 1993-94 and 1997-98, as is also evident from the values of coefficient of variation computed for the different time points under reference (Table 10.3).

In the recent periods, on the whole, the per capita incomes improved across all the districts in the state, as can be seen from Table 10.3. As noted by HPC (2002) in respect of regional variations, several districts, relatively more so in north Karnataka the situation has worsened as can be seen from Table 10.4. By the year 2001-02, the state average per capita income increased from Rs. 6,655 in 1991 to Rs. 11,484 (in constant 1993-94 prices). But the relative rankings of the districts also remained fairly the same with all the 12 districts of north Karnataka below the state average.[3] The Composite Development Index for the year 2002-03

TABLE 10.3

District Per Capita Income in Karnataka: 1970-71, 1980-81, 1993-94 and 1997-98 (at Current Prices)

(in Rupees)

Districts	*1970-71*	*Rank*	*1980-81*	*Rank*	*1993-94*	*Rank*	*1997-98*	*Rank*
Districts in South Karnataka								
Bangalore	699	9	2100	2	12646	1	25740	1
Bangalore (Rura)					8865	5	12215	9
Chickmagalur	1176	2	1858	3	11134	3	17609	4
Chitradurga	674	12	1622	7	7076	13	10989	13
Kodagu	786	6	1701	5	9746	4	20167	3
Hassan	674	10	1381	14	7333	12	12346	8
Kolar	1851	1	3069	1	12540	2	24623	2
Mandya	481	18	853	19	8181	9	10013	16
Mysore	607	13	1592	8	7612	10	11081	12
Shimoga	742	8	1459	10	8416	7	14576	5
Dakshina Kannada	968	3	1800	4	8712	6	13970	6
Tumkur	514	16	1172	17	6559	16	9011	18
Districts in North Karnataka								
Belgaum	559	15	1399	12	8292	8	13377	7
Bellary	797	5	1579	9	6958	15	12200	10
Bidar	503	17	1329	15	5405	20	7861	20
Bijapur	479	19	971	18	6355	18	10049	15
Dharwad	586	14	1283	16	7051	14	10397	14
Gulbarga	622	11	1381	13	6489	17	9516	17
Uttara Kannada	751	7	1447	11	5976	19	8688	19
Raichur	869	4	1662	6	7074	11	12019	11
States	**685**		**1520**		**8190**		**13621**	
C.V.(%)	42.31		30.17		24.86		37.7	

Source: HPC (June2002) Table 4.5, p.72. Data taken from *Economic Survey of Karnataka* (for concerned years), Government of Karnataka.

3. As indicated by the rank correlations. Even the coefficient of variations has not improved over the years.

TABLE 10.4

Number of Districts below State Average in Per Capita Income and Composite Index of Development

Region/Divisions	Per Capita Income 1990-91	Per Capita Income 1998-99	Per Capita Income 2001-02	CDI 2002-03
Hyderabad-Karnataka-Gulbarga (5)	5	5	5	4
Old Bombay Karnataka-Belgaum (7)	6	5	7	4
North Karnataka (12)	11	10	12	8
Bangalore (7)	4	5	4	4
Mysore (8)	4	4	3	2
South Karnataka (15)	8	9	7	6
State Level (27)	19	19	19	14

Note: Figures in parentheses are number of districts in the divisions.

Source: Directorate of Economics and Statistics, Government of Karnataka.

TABLE 10.5

Per Capita Income at District Level (in Rupees at 1993-94 Prices)

Districts	Per Capita Income 1990-91	Per Capita Income 1998-99	Per Capita Income 2001-02	Rank 1990-91	Rank 1998-99	Rank 2001-02
Belgaum	6806.70	10008.50	9923.97	8	10	13
Bijapur	5285.52	7292.74	8279.32	18	24	23
Bagalkot	5284.36	9755.58	10470.53	19	12	12
Dharwad	5224.40	10872.44	11067.31	20	7	9
Gadag	5221.28	7247.72	9712.18	22	25	14
Haveri	5221.42	7513.85	7790.45	21	22	24
Uttara Kannada	6402.55	9947.54	10815.37	10	11	10
Belgaum Division	5872.26	9217.23	9747.11			
Bellary	6571.76	10872.70	10804.53	9	6	11
Bidar	5162.80	6395.85	6889.22	24	27	27
Gulbarga	5837.17	7443.28	7761.40	15	23	25
Raichur	4951.00	6458.36	6906.74	26	26	26
Koppal	4953.23	7575.57	9420.66	25	21	16
Gulbarga Division	5622.51	7853.43	8333.72			
Bangalore	10543.21	18453.99	20435.11	2	2	1
Bangalore-Rural	10502.82	9239.61	14527.00	3	13	4
Chitradurga	5823.86	8122.59	9281.51	16	18	18
Davangere	6288.87	8374.31	9134.69	11	17	20
Kolar	4454.78	7900.91	8665.12	27	20	21
Shimoga	7028.78	11084.41	11131.56	7	5	8
Tumkur	5193.91	8778.09	8508.90	23	16	22
Bangalore Division	7686.23	12158.00	13752.29			
Chickmaglur	7667.11	10152.59	12212.37	5	9	6
D. Kannada	7660.63	21952.60	18437.59	6	1	2
Udupi	7927.63	10862.13	14024.51	4	8	5
Hassan	5311.10	8037.64	9426.01	17	19	15
Kodagu	11850.25	15758.59	17530.36	1	3	3
Mandya	5927.89	8875.81	9146.16	14	15	19
Mysore	5950.05	11378.60	11573.79	12	4	7
Chamrajnagar	5944.13	9033.79	9378.53	13	14	17
Mysore Division	6750.61	12046.50	12395.64			
North Karnataka	5769.95	8645.96	9150.16			
South Karnataka	7304.29	12114.12	13226.17			
State	**6654.92**	**10635.14**	**11483.71**			
C.V.	0.29	0.36	0.31			

Source: Directorate of Economics, Government of Karnataka.

indicate that almost half of the districts (likewise the *talukas* also) remain relatively backward in Karnataka. They are mainly from Hyderabad-Karnataka region (eg., Bidar, Koppal, Raichur and Gulbarga), three districts of old Bombay state (Haveri, Bagalkot, Bijapur) and five districts of South Karnataka (Kolar, Mandya, Chitradurga, Tumkur, and Chamrajnagar).

10.3.2 Poverty and Inequality in Karnataka

Poverty is a multidimensional concept. It reflects lack of entitlements, an inability to buy things that are essential for a minimum and dignified life. There can be debates about what the minimum things are. Taking income as a criterion to define poverty, we find for the country as a whole that 27 per cent in rural and 24 per cent in urban areas to be below poverty line. Discussions regarding the state level poverty and the human development indicators are already discussed in Chapter 1 along with the comparison with other states. Here, it is essentially the regional dimensions of poverty, inequality and HDI that are presented.

Poverty indicators across the rural and urban Karnataka as per the Planning Commission's official estimates reveal that the poverty in Karnataka during 1999–00 was 16.8 per cent in rural and 24.6 per cent in urban. However, the cheerful fact is that poverty is declining over the period. Rural poverty fell from 55.1 per cent in 1973–74 to 16.8 per cent in 1999–00 (Table 10.6). Urban poverty fell from 52.5 per cent in 1987–88 to 24.6 per cent in 1999–00. It is also seen that the decline is much greater in the rural than the urban areas.

TABLE 10.6

Trends in Poverty

Year	*Karnataka*			*All-India*		
	Rural	*Urban*	*Combined*	*Rural*	*Urban*	*Combined*
1973–74	55.1	52.5	54.5	56.4	49.0	54.9
1977–78	48.2	50.4	48.8	53.1	45.2	51.3
1983*	36.3	42.8	38.2	45.7	40.8	44.5
1987–88	32.8	48.4	37.5	39.1	38.2	38.9
1993–94	29.9	40.1	33.2	37.3	32.4	36.0
1999–00	16.8	24.6	19.0	26.8	24.1	26.1

Note: Refers to calendar year 1983.

Source: Indian Planning Experience, A Statistical Profile, Planning Commission, Govt. of India for the years 1973–74 to 1993–94 and for the year 1999–00; Angus Deaton and Jean Dreze (2002). "Poverty and Inequality in India: A Re-examination", *EPW*, Sep 7.

Poverty estimates below the state level are usually not available due to the limitations of survey sample sizes. Many states conduct household surveys on a matching basis with NSSO and Karnataka is one among them. For the first *Karnataka Human Development Report* (1999), Karnataka government pooled the state and Central samples for the 50th NSS Round (1993–94) to estimate poverty at the district level. Using the same steps Murgai *et al.* (2003) updated these estimates to 55th NSS Round (1999–2000). Based on their work, the district poverty estimates are given in Table 10.5. Estimates for rural and urban areas are separately not available due to small size of the sample.

Income inequality and poverty are significant areas of concern for social and economic policy. Income inequality measures indicate underlying structural problems that can lead to constrained economic growth, human suffering or social unrest. A high-income inequality implies that a segment of the society does not participate equally in socio-economic life.

Following observations can be made based on Table 10.7.

- Northern districts are poorer than rest of the state.
- Even though Raichur is the poorest district as per head count ratio, depth of poverty, measured through poverty gap index, is greater in Kolar.
- Poverty in Chickmagalur is almost negligible. Only 2.3 per cent are poor in that district.
- Districts better developed in terms of Human Development Indicators, such as Bangalore (U), Dakshina Kannada, Bangalore (R), Kodagu, Shimoga, etc. have low incidence of poverty i.e., less than 10 per cent.
- The most commonly used measure of income inequality, the Gini Index (also known as the index of income concentration) indicated a decline in household income inequality of 6.2 per cent from 1983 to 1999–00 in rural parts of Karnataka.
- Inequality in urban areas is much higher than rural areas. Urban parts indicate a decline of only 1.3 per cent from 1983 to 1999–00.
- Further disaggregation by occupational group indicates that in rural areas inequality is high among self-employment in non-agriculture and others.

TABLE 10.7

District-wise Poverty Ratios and Human Development Index

Districts	*1999-00*		*2000-01*
	Head Count Index	*Poverty Gap Index*	*HDI*
Bangalore (Urban)	9.9	1.5	0.99
Bangalore (Rural)	5.2	0.7	0.73
Belgaum	17.9	3.2	0.60
Bellary	33.1	6.0	0.37
Bidar	30.4	5.2	0.22
Bijapur	32.1	6.8	0.18
Chickmagalur	2.3	0.4	0.46
Chitradurga	16.3	2.8	0.46
Dakshina Kannada	7.4	1.7	0.91
Dharwad	21.4	4.2	0.34
Gulbarga	26.8	4.9	0.08
Hassan	11.5	1.5	0.26
Kodagu	4.9	0.6	0.71
Kolar	41.9	10.3	0.32
Mandya	16.6	2.8	0.28
Mysore	15.5	2.0	0.42
Raichur	45.6	6.3	0.16
Shimoga	8.1	1.4	0.71
Tumkur	18.5	2.7	0.48
Uttara Kannada	6.7	1.4	0.49

Source: Murgai *et al.* (2003), HDI is based on per capita income, literacy levels and IMR for the 2001.

TABLE 10.9

Inequality between Occupational and Social Groups: 1999–2000 Occupation Communities

	Karnataka	*All-India*
Rural		
Self-employed in Non-agriculture	0.274	0.255
Agricultural Labour	0.197	0.222
Other Labour	0.237	0.257
Self-employed Agriculture	0.235	0.253
Others	0.267	0.293
All	0.245	0.266
SC	0.216	0.238
ST	0.177	0.248
OBC	0.234	0.250
Others	0.255	0.269
All	0.245	0.266
Urban		
Self-employed	0.306	0.350
Regular Wage/Salary Earning	0.314	0.312
Casual Labour	0.232	0.300
Others	0.344	0.362
All	0.321	0.347
SC	0.280	0.279
ST	0.335	0.326
OBC	0.309	0.325
Others	0.316	0.345
All	0.321	0.347

Source: *Economic Survey of Karnataka*, 2003–04.

TABLE 10.8

Gini Ratio for Per Capita Consumption Expenditure

Year	*Karnataka*		*All-India*	
	Rural	*Urban*	*Rural*	*Urban*
1983	0.303	0.334	0.298	0.330
1993–94	0.269	0.315	0.282	0.340
1999–00	0.241	0.321	0.258	0.341

Source: *National Human Development* Report, 2001.

- In urban areas, casual labour group witness very low inequality.
- Among the social groups, inequality is much lower in socially backward groups such as SCs and STs in rural areas.
- Compared with the national level indices, better situation exists only in respect of non-agriculture self-employed workers in rural areas, and regular wage earners, SCs and STs in the urban areas. In respect of all the other types, Karnataka figures are lower than those of the national averages.

The onus therefore lies, to a greater extent on devising specific poverty alleviation programmes that cater to the needs and situations obtaining in relation to such specific groups, social or occupational.

Poverty Alleviation Programmes

Having thrown light on the magnitude of the problem of poverty and inequality in Karnataka, though briefly, one may examine the steps taken by both governmental and non-governmental entities to redress the problems. The Governmental interventions are through both state (Box 10.1) and the Central Government Schemes (Box 10.2)

BOX 10.1

Major Poverty Alleviation Programmes of Karnataka Government

Social Security Programmes and Poverty Alleviation Programmes:

i) Financial assistance of Rs.125 per month to the disabled

ii) Old age pension at the rate of Rs.100 per month to elderly persons aged 65 years and above and who are without any means of support.

iii) Destitute Widows—Financial assistance of Rs.100 per month.

iv) Maternity Allowance of a lump sum amount of Rs.500 in the duration of 2-8 weeks before delivery for the first and second child for both prenatal and postnatal period of 3 months.

v) Stree Shakti Programme aims at empowering rural women through the formation of SHGs (For details see Chapter 6).

vi) Balika Samrudhi Yojana–Girl child born on or after August 15, 1997 (in BPL category) would get a one-time post delivery grant of Rs.500.

vii) Financial assistance to children in difficult circumstances i.e., children of ex-prostitutes, *devadasis* and prisoners for pursuing education.

viii) Udyogini–Subsidy is provided to women to take up business and trading activities at a unit cost of Rs.50,000.

ix) Santwana: Assistance to women who are victims of various atrocities.

x) Constitution of Welfare Fund for *Anganawadi* workers and helpers.

xi) Many assistance oriented schemes have been in force for the welfare of disabled like providing telephone booths, monthly maintenance of Rs.125 per person, per month, many self-employment programmes 'Aadhara', etc.,

xii) A pilot poverty alleviation project in *Bangalore* Mahanagara Palika for urban poor.

xiii) Mid-day meals for primary school children, Akshara Dasoha.

xiv) Many women empowerment schemes—'Stree Shakti'.

xv) Several initiatives to improve economic opportunities and also reduce poverty among the socially underprivileged.

BOX 10.2

Important Poverty Alleviation and Employment Generation Programmes of the Central Government

1. Pradhan Mantri Gramodaya Yojana (PMGY) launched in 2001-02 in all states and union territories for achieving sustinable human development at the village level .
2. Swarnajayanthi Gram Swarozgar Yojana (SGSY) launched in April 1999 is the only self-employment programme.
3. Sampoorna Grameen Rozgar Yojana (SGRY) was launched in September 2001 with an objective of providing additional wage employment in the rural areas along with food security and creating social and economic infrastructure in rural areas.
4. Rural Housing Schemes such as Indira Awaas Yojana (IAY) essentially aims at providing dwelling limits, free of cost, to the poor families of SCs and STs, freed bonded labourers and non-SC, ST below poverty line in rural areas.
5. Pradhan Mantri Gram Sadak Yojana (PMGSY) launched in December 2000 is being executed by all states and Union Territories to provide road connectivity to 1.6 lakh unconnected habitations with population of 500 persons or more in rural areas by the Tenth Plan period.
6. Drought Prone Areas Programme (DPAP), Desert Development Programme (DDP) and Integrated Wastelands Development Proglramme (IWDP) were launched between 1973-74 and 1989-90. These programmes which were implemented as sector programmes till 1994-95 are being implemented on watershed bases from April 1995.
7. Antyodaya Anna Yojana (AAY) launched in December 2000 under which one crore of the poorest among the BPL families covered under targeted PDS are identified and foodgrains are distributed to them on a highly subsidised rates.
8. Swarna Jayanthi Shahari Rozgar Yojana (SJBRY). It is essentially an urban poverty alleviation programme initiated in December 1997 wherein these two special schemes namely, the Urban Self-Employment Programme and the Urban Wage Employment Programme. This is funded on a 75:25 basis between the Centre and the states.
9. Valmiki Ambedkar Awas Yojana (VAMBAY) was launched in December 2001 to ameliorate the conditions of the urban slum dwellers living below the poverty line without adequate shelter.

10.3.3 Disparities in General Backwardness

The above salient points together with the discussion on the growth and variation in per capita income across districts in Karnataka are useful in appreciating the regional disparities. But they do not throw light on the growth and variations across the districts in the sectoral development like agriculture, industry, transport, social services, etc. Therefore reference has to be made to the physical level of development registered in different districts covering various sectors and sub-sectors. Computing a composite index of development of different districts may capture this. The composite index of development presented for the districts for different time points, (Table 10.10) helps understand the nature of regional disparities from this perspective.

Between 1960-61 and 1998-99, Belgaum, Bidar, Bijapur, Chickmagalur, Kodagu, Gulbarga and Kolar districts have been pushed to lower ranks compared to what they enjoyed in 1960-61. Relative ranks of Bangalore, Belgaum, Chitradurga, Hassan, Mandya, Mysore, Raichur and Tumkur have improved in the corresponding period. It is to be noted, however, that the relative degree of backwardness or that of development can vary from period to period in so far as the development effort has not been stagnant.

10.3.4 Indicators of Backwardness

An effective tackling of the problems of backwardness and regional imbalances requires proper identification and delineation of backward areas with appropriate indicators which indeed is a complicated exercise. In Karnataka several studies are made in this direction by the State Planning Department, various committees and individual scholars.

Dwelling upon the indicators of development, the Third Five-Year Plan document noted: "For assessing

TABLE 10.10

Composite Index of Development of Districts in Karnataka: 1960-61, 1971-72, 1976-77 and 1998-99

Districts	*1960-61*		*1970-71*		*1976-77*		*1998-99*	
	Development Index	*Rank*	*Development Index*	*Rank*	*Development Index*	*Rank*	*Development Index*	*Rank*
Districts in South Karnataka								
Bangalore	218.00	2	206.26	1	206.42	1	209.00	1
Bangalore (Rural)	218.00	2	206.26	1	206.42	1	76.50	13
Chickmagalur	123.74	7	92.66	12	84.56	16	75.80	15
Chitradurga	100.24	11	104.00	9	107.02	7	83.54	6
Kodagu	124.15	6	107.79	7	103.44	8	72.80	17
Hassan	90.03	13	87.21	13	86.22	14	81.02	9
Kolar	136.53	4	129.96	4	107.55	6	79.11	10
Mandya	114.70	10	111.96	6	112.94	4	91.16	5
Mysore	124.60	5	123.35	5	112.09	5	92.59	4
Shimoga	180.15	3	141.07	3	118.05	3	94.22	3
Dakshina Kannada	230.21	1	187.04	2	172.86	2	119.21	2
Tumkur	84.52	5	83.47	16	88.64	13	77.44	12
Districts in North Karnataka								
Belguam	91.12	12	95.06	11	91.89	12	75.96	14
Bellary	89.23	14	83.90	15	100.09	10	78.76	11
Bidar	64.28	17	86.85	14	85.86	15	69.22	19
Bijapur	71.66	16	77.38	18	79.99	17	71.14	18
Dharwad	118.54	8	103.19	10	98.74	11	82.28	8
Gulbarga	60.10	19	63.19	19	66.83	19	66.44	20
Uttara Kannada	118.24	9	106.17	8	102.05	9	82.30	7
Raichur	63.04	18	80.53	17	76.34	18	73.17	16
State	**100.00**		**100.00**		**100.00**		**100.00**	

Note: Composite Index of Development computed using 22 common indicators.
Source: For 1960-61, 1971-72 and 1976-77: Five-Year Plans of Karnataka. For 1998-99: HPC FRRI estimates.

levels of development in different regions, indicators of development based on agricultural production, industrial production, investment, unemployment, electricity consumption, irrigated area, value of output by commodity producing sectors, level of consumption expenditure, road mileage, primary and secondary education and occupational distribution of population are useful."[4] Further the plan document mentions, "As a comprehensive indicator of economic progress, estimates of State income are of considerable interest in studies of development in different States and regions..." Later on the state Government also reviewed the recommendations of the Pande Committee[5] for the identification of backward regions.

Karnataka's Fifth and Sixth Five-Year Plans, for the first time, made use of an exercise to measure backwardness of districts in Karnataka at four points of time: 1960-61, 1970-71,1974-75 and 1976-77. This exercise identified 22 indicators of development,[6] broadly relating to four typologies: demographic and occupational pattern, land utilisation and agricultural development, industrial development, and infrastructure facilities, to compute a Composite Index of Development. The latest official efforts to identify backward regions on the basis of composite index of development was made by the HPC (2002). The Committee selected 35 indicators for this purpose. Invariably the indicators represent agriculture, industry, services including banking, infrastructural facilities and social developments.

As can be viewed from Table 10.10, in 1960-61, six out of eight districts (then existing) from north Karnataka were below the state average. In 1998-99, all the eight districts of north Karnataka are below, indicating worsening of regional variations. However, HPC opined that for a proper formulation of policy for bringing down regional disparities, it is very important to analyse not only the aggregate level performance of districts but also the sectoral development pattern and dimensions of backwardness. The HPC also felt that variations in per capita income across districts and poverty ratios, though useful in appreciating the regional disparities in Karnataka do not throw light on the growth and variations in the sectoral development like agriculture, industry, transport, and social services of the districts. In order to capture this dimension, the Committee also used a composite index based on physical variables, which were given different weights based on their relative contributions to SNDP.

HPC divided the districts on the basis of north and south zones and by administrative divisions. Within north Karnataka, while relatively better off districts like Belgaum, Dharwad and Uttar Kannada have shown a decline in their relative levels of development, the districts of Raichur, Gulbarga Bidar, and Bellary have improved their positions by recording higher index values. It is rather disheartening to find that in the southern Karnataka almost all the districts have recorded a lower index value in 1998-99 compared to the previous benchmark years. There appears to be continuous fall in the index values of relatively better off districts. This trend is not very healthy. It may show a decline in the extent of regional disparities but if this narrowing down of disparities is at the cost of developed districts it is not good for the development of the state.

However, in spite of several Five-Year Plans the disparities have remained at significant levels. But it should be remembered that there has been good progress in terms of socio-economic development of the lagging regions. The absolute level of growth as well as development of the backward regions have been significant, only in relative terms the rankings have not shown much change.

---

4 Government of Karnataka, *Third Five Year Plan*, Bangalore.

5. Government of India (1968). *Identification of Backward Regions*, (Pande Committee, New Delhi).

6. Planning Department, Karnataka:
Density of population
Proportion of urban population to total population
Proportion of non-agricultural workers to total workers
Percentage of net area sown to total area
Double cropped area as per cent of net area sown
Per cent of net area sown to cultivable land
Per hectare yield in cereals
Per hectare yield in pulses
Per hectare yield in oil seeds
Number of industrial establishments as per cent to State total
Net area irrigated as per cent of net area sown
Number of vehicles per lakh population
Road length in km.100 sq.kms area
Number of bank offices per lakh population
Value of turnover per regulated market
Percentage of literate to total population
Number of schools per lakh population
Number of university educational institutions per lakh population
Number of health units per lakh population
Number of hospital beds per lakh population
Percentage of village and towns electrified
Number of irrigation pump-sets as percentage of state total.

10.4 Regional Variation in Resource Allocations

Causes for regional disparity and variations can be many. Among them, resource allocation to the districts is generally referred as the primary one. In Karnataka, funds are allocated according to the Second State Finance Commission's awards to the districts, *talukas* and villages based on a formula (Table 10.21). Additionally, there may be projects and schemes approved by the Planning Commission having some weight on regional development and reduction of disparities.

Between the years 1998-99 and 2003-04 (Appendix A-10.1), the per capita total plan and non-plan transfers increased very marginally from Rs. 758 to Rs. 857 as a state average. But considerable amount of variations between the districts is visible over the years. For instance, in 2003-04, 12 districts received less than the state average of total allocations on per capita basis. They are Tumkur, Mandya, Gulbarga, D. Kannada, Bijapur, Belgaum, Shimoga, Mysore, Kolar, Hassan, Bellary, and Bangalore Urban. Of these 5 are from north Karnataka, and 7 from south Karnataka. The rankings of the districts in terms of their per capita allocations (be it on plan or non-plan), reveal that over the years, the overall pattern of regional variations has not changed much. Barring Bangalore Urban, districts like Bellary, Belgaum, Gulbarga and Tumkur have been consistently ranking lowest.[7] Furthermore, over the years there is some degree of uniformity in the rankings of the districts for plan and also the total allocations, which is not the case with non-plan allocations. This is a bit surprising.[8]

However, over the years, there seems to be an increase on non-plan allocations in general, but not so on plan expenditures, rather decreases in several districts. More striking is the fact that the variations in the non-plan allocations have gone up substantially between the districts, but improved marginally on the plan allocations.[9] Above all, non-plan allocations have been fluctuating quite significantly over the years over the sectors.[10] These factors may be aggravating the regional disparities in terms of performances.

A close examination of sector-wise allocations to the district, *taluka* and *Gram Panchayats* (Appendix A-10.2) indicates that:

- Resources allocations are prioritised as education, health and family welfare, social welfare followed by others.
- Allocations on rural development under plan schemes however, are generally higher than under non-plan.
- No significant disparity in resource allocations between the districts from north or south Karnataka. For instance, under non-plan allocations for education in 2003-04, as many as 4 districts out of 12 from North Karnataka received below the state average of Rs. 426 per capita, where as, 7 districts out of 15 from south Karnataka received lower allocations.
- The regional variations and disparities in allocations seem to have marginally gone up on non-plan allocations (Table 10.11).
- Finally, referring to causality, one does note see any strong relationships between the pattern of resource allocations and the performances as measured by either per capita income or composite indices of development (Table 10.12).

TABLE 10.11

Coefficient of Variations in Resource Allocations between Districts on Various Schemes

	Under Plan Schemes		*Under Non-Plan Schemes*	
	1998-99	*2003-04*	*1998-99*	*2003-04*
Education	0.36	0.46	0.60	0.75
Health and Family Welfare	0.33	0.31	0.56	0.71
Water Supply and Sanitation	0.43	0.39	0.58	0.78
Social Welfare	0.30	0.29	0.55	0.68
Rural Development	0.32	0.31	0.53	0.66
Total	**0.30**	**0.28**	**0.56**	**0.70**

Source: Own calculations on the data from Budget documents of Government of Karnataka.

7. Some variations are however seen in plan and non-plan allocations, making some districts still worse off in one or the other categories. For instance, when it comes to plan allocations, districts like Dharwad and Mysore show at the lowest category. Likewise, under non-plan allocations, Bellary and Gulbarga have received the lowest ranks in 2003-04.
8. The rank correlations on these over the years reveal this significantly. Non-plan allocations being more of the category of committed expenditures are expected to show more consistent and uniform patterns on per capita allocations.
9. For details see coefficient of variations in Table 10.12.
10. This fact is revealed by the fluctuating standard deviations over the years (Table 10.11).

TABLE 10.12

Correlation Coefficients between Resource Allocations and Performance Indicators

	Under Plan Schemes			Under Non-Plan Schemes		
	Per Capita Income		Composite Index of Dev.2001-02	Per Capita Income		Composite Index of Dev.2001-02
	1998-99	2001-02		1998-99	2001-02	
Education	0.108	0.018	0.200	-0.017	0.291	0.308
Health and Family Welfare	0.406	0.493	0.323	0.078	0.419	0.464
Water Supply and Sanitation	0.332	0.337	0.374	0.059	0.349	0.361
Social Welfare	0.130	0.188	0.118	0.168	0.424	0.445
Rural Development	-0.140	0.128	0.188	-0.092	0.363	0.374
Total	**0.090**	**0.251**	**0.292**	**0.004**	**0.323**	**0.341**

Source: Own calculations on the data from Budget Documents of Government of Karnataka.

10.5 Regional Dimensions of Human Development

10.5.1 The Vision

The *Vision 2020* Document of the Planning Commission (2004) and the *National Human Development Report of 2001* (GoI, 2001) and Millennium Document of World Bank (World Bank, 2004) refer to various elements of human development as part and parcel of targets for regional development. Education, health care, quality of life, minimum employment and income are some of them.

For instance, the *Vision 2020* Document of the Planning Commission (2004) sets out the millennium target as:

- Delivering literacy as a right to all.
- Hundred per cent enrolment in primary schools by the year 2020.
- Targeting 10 million job creations per year, perhaps thereby also meaning regional balance.

The specific goals set out on health care by the Indian Planning Commission in the Tenth Five-Year Plan are:

- Reducing infant mortality to 45 per 1000 live births by 2007 and to 28 by 2012.
- Reducing maternal mortality ratio to 2 per 1000 live births by 2007 and to 1 by 2012.
- Achieve zero level increase of HIV/AIDS prevalence by 2007.
- Halve the morbidity and mortality rates by 2010.

Clearly all these are very tall orders of goals, equally challenging is attaining at the regional levels. It may be useful to review the performance on these in Karnataka.

10.5.2 Education: Provisioning, Access and Performance

Karnataka has shown a remarkable improvement in the overall literacy rates, going from 29.8 per cent in 1961 to 65.84 per cent by 2001. But the regional disparities and variations are quite striking, with Dakshina Kannada district ranking highest (with 83.47 per cent) but Raichur district being the lowest (with 49.54 per cent).

One of the best indicators on provision of education is the number of children enrolled in the 6-14 age group. In the year 1990-91 this was about 72 at the state level, which rose to 97 in 1998-99 and further to 109 by 2002-03.[11] Though there is a uniform improvement in the enrolment rates across the districts except for some districts of southern Karnataka (such as Chamarajnagar, Hassan or Mandya, which have shown some declines), regional level variations are visible. Districts from north Karnataka such as Belgaum, Dharwad, and Gulbarga and Mysore from south Karnataka have shown remarkable improvements. Surprisingly enough, the south Karnataka region seems to have continued with low rates of school enrolments. Thus, worsening of the regional disparity is visible on the pattern of enrolment in the recent period. As can be seen from Table 10.13, in many respect regional variations are equally visible in both north and south Karnataka, substantially higher in south Karnataka. The

TABLE 10.13

Number of Districts below State Average in Provisioning of Educational Services (2002-03)

*Region/Divisions**	*Gross Enrolment Ratio*	*Primary Inst. per Lakh Child Popl.*	*Teacher/ Pupil Ratio*	*Sec. Schools per Lakh Popl.*
Hyderabad-Karnataka-Gulbarga (5)	1	5	5	4
Old Bombay Karnataka-Belgaum (7)	2	6	6	3
North Karnataka (12)	3	11	11	7
Bangalore (7)	5	2	1	1
Mysore (8)	6	5	0	3
South Karnataka (15)	11	7	1	4
State Level (27)	**14**	**18**	**12**	**11**

Note: * The figures in parentheses stand for the number of districts in the Division,

Source: Directorate of Economics and Statistics, Government of Karnataka.

11. Such averages above 100 in 2002-03 are attributed to the fact that many children below the age 6 were also enrolled.

'number of primary schools per lakh of children in the age group 6-14,' also seems to have gone up uniformly in almost all districts, with the state average itself having gone up from 425 per lakh of children in 1990-91 to 677 in 2002. But the districts of north Karnataka still lack this facility in a significant way, also in terms of availability of teachers.

FIGURE 10.1

Association between Education Provision Index and Composite Development Index 2002

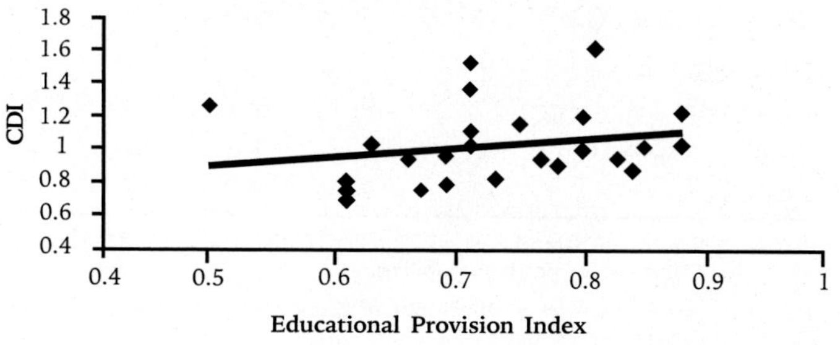

Figure 10.1 shows the Composite Indices of Overall Development and Educational Provisioning at the district levels (Appendix A-10.3). The links seem to be very poor. The districts, which have remained low in educational status, continue to remain low even over the years. No major transition from low to higher levels of educational provisioning seems to have taken place in Karnataka, leaving the pattern of regional disparity a continual phenomenon in the state. In terms of the composite educational provisioning, as many as 10 districts of north Karnataka (5 each from the 2 Divisions) have remained much below the state average. Thus, educational backwardness in provisioning is the major telling story in north Karnataka. But, low rates of enrolment in south Karnataka is also a matter of concern.

As much as provisioning, access to education also has some distinct regional pattern in the state. The 'number of teachers per pupil' has gone up, more uniformly across the state. But about 12 districts are below the state average over the last decade. Likewise, viewed from the 'number of students per classroom', in 2002-03 about 14 districts were having lesser access to class rooms than the state average.

One notices a distinct pattern of correlation between many of these access patterns with the overall development. As can be seen from Table 10.14 and Table 10.15 with many such access indicators taken together it can be concluded that:

- A very high correlation is visible between the levels of development and access to such facilities in the field of education.
- There is still a very high degree of disparity among the districts in access to educational facilities. Invariably the districts from north Karnataka have much less access to these facilities.

TABLE 10.14

Access to Educational Facilities: 2002-03

	State Average	No. of Districts below State Average	
		In North	In South
Percentage of Schools with Common Toilets	15	10	5
Percentage of Schools with Girls Toilets	18	9	9
Class Room/Student Ratio	11	10	1
Percentage Female Teachers	18	10	8
Percentage of Habitations with Schools within	7	1	6
Percentage of Habitations with Schools within 1 Km (but not in)	18	12	6
Percentage of Habitations with Schools beyond 1 Km*	7	1	6
Percentage of Schools with only One Teacher*	11	2	9

Note: * These are the districts more than state average.

Source: *Education at a Glance*, 2002-03, Commissioner Public Instruction, Government of Karnataka.

TABLE 10.15

Regional Disparity in Access to School Facilities

Region/Divisions	No. of Districts in Terms of Percentage of Primary Schools with Access Less than the State Average (2002-03)			
	Own Building	Electricity	Drinking Water	Toilets
Hyderabad-Karnataka-Gulbarga(5)	3	5	3	5
Old Bombay Karnataka-Belgaum (7)	4	2	3	5
North Karnataka (12)	7	7	6	10
Bangalore (7)	3	4	5	3
Mysore (8)	1	1	1	2
South Karnataka (15)	4	5	6	5
State Level (27)	**11**	**12**	**11**	**15**

Note: Figures in parentheses are number of districts in the Division.

Source: *Education at a Glance*, 2002-03, Commissioner Public Instruction, Government of Karnataka.

The attainment of education can be viewed, in addition to number of children enrolled, by other indicators such as extent of children out of school, literacy rate (in particular female literacy), extent of SC/ST enrolments and so on. It is observed that the tendency to be out of schools seems to be highly correlated to the level of over all backwardness (with a correlation coefficient being 0.64). As can be seen from a summary Table 10.16 and Appendix A-10.4, a large number of districts are lagging in SC/ST enrolments, spread over both north and south Karnataka, mainly linked to overall backwardness.

TABLE 10.16

Regional Disparity in Performance of Educational Sector

Region/Divisions	*No. of Districts below State Average in (2002-03)*			
	Share of SC Enrolment	*Share of SC Girls in Total SC Enrolment*	*Literacy (%)*	*Female Literacy (%)*
Hyderabad-Karnataka-Gulbarga (5)	1	3	5	5
Old Bombay Karnataka-Belgaum (7)	5	4	3	4
North Karnataka (12)	6	7	8	9
Bangalore (7)	0	0	3	3
Mysore (8)	5	4	3	3
South Karnataka (15)	5	4	6	6
State Level (27)	**11**	**11**	**14**	**15**

Note: Figures in parentheses are number of districts in the division.

Source: *Education at a Glance*, 2002-03, Commissioner Public Instruction, Government of Karnataka.

On the whole, both in terms of provisioning, access and performance of education system in the state, the regional disparity seems to be persisting, lot more with provisioning, better in performance.

10.5.3 Healthcare Provisioning and Outcomes

Health care is yet another aspect of human development. Both provision of health care and the performance in the state over the last one decade reveal similar patterns of regional disparity, but more conspicuously in north Karnataka (Table 10.17). Viewed from the Composite Indices of Health Care Provisioning, districts from north Karnataka seem to be lagging much behind. Moreover, the correlation between Composite Indices of Overall Development and Healthcare (0.52 in 2002-03) seems to be much higher than with that of education (0.23 in 2002-03).

TABLE 10.17

Regional Disparity in Healthcare Provisioning

Region/Divisions	*No. of Districts below State Ave. in (2002-03)*				
	Composite Index of Health Provisioning	*No. of PHCs*	*Beds in PHCs**	*No. of Med. Inst.**	*Hosp. Beds**
Hyderabad-Karnataka-Gulbarga (5)	5	3	4	4	4
Old Bombay Karnataka-Belgaum (7)	6	3	4	4	5
North Karnataka (12)	11	6	8	8	9
Bangalore (7)	0	1	1	3	3
Mysore (8)	1	0	0	0	3
South Karnataka (15)	1	1	1	3	6
State Level (27)	**12**	**7**	**9**	**11**	**15**

Note: Figures in parentheses are number of districts in the Division.
*All data are per lakh population.

Source: *District at a Glance*, Directorate of Economics and Statistics, Government of Karnataka.

Just as much as provisioning and access, a large number of districts from north Karnataka are lagging far behind in health related outcomes (Table 10.18). As far as birth rates are concerned, 10 out of 12 districts are having higher rates than the state average of 22.4 in 2001-02. Likewise, as against the state average of crude death rate of 7.5 per 1000 lives, it is as high as 9.2 in Bijapur district (but also as low as 6.0 in Dakshina Kannada district).

TABLE 10.18

Regional Disparity in Performance of Health Sector

Region/Divisions	*No. of Ditricts above State Average in (2001-02)*		
	Crude Birth Rate	*Crude Death Rate*	*IMR*
Hyderabad-Karnataka-Gulbarga (5)	5	4	5
Old Bombay Karnataka-Belgaum (7)	5	6	6
North Karnataka (12)	10	10	11
Bangalore (7)	0	1	1
Mysore (8)	0	6	6
South Karnataka (15)	0	7	7
State Level (27)	**10**	**16**	**17**

Note: Figures in parentheses are number of districts in the Division.

Source: High Power Committee on Redressal of Regional Disparities, Government of Karnataka.

It may also be noted that the *Karnataka Human Development Report* 1999, the Task Force on Health and

Family Welfare (2001) and the HPC (2002) all have pointed out the extent of regional variations in provision of health care in the state. Invariably all these reports found that a substantial portion of PHCs is functioning with only one doctor and this deprivation was found more pronounced in northern than southern districts. In addition, HPC (2002) has also looked into the extent of regional variations in respect of health care access and deliveries such as: Unsafe baby deliveries; extent of malnutrition in children below age 5; unsafe drinking water; adequacy of drinking water; number of doctors, beds, etc. According to the Health Infrastructure Index (linking number of doctors, number of beds and quantum of drinking water supply, etc), HPC (2002) observes that the overall picture on status of health is such that as many as 119 *talukas* in the state were below the state average, of which about 39 of them were identified as most backward. At the state level as many as 50 per cent of children were found to be malnourished, with as many as 7 districts much worse than the state average (HPC, pp. 121). At the State level about 35 per cent of deliveries were found to be conducted in unsafe conditions. With such indicators, the number of districts worse than the state average health infrastructure index is 12. Many of the affected districts are from north Karnataka only.

On the whole, as far as developments in health care is concerned, three observations can be made: first, compared to the educational sectors, the regional disparity in health care is much less; second, lower orders of disparity in provisioning of health care are observed than in education or even in performance in health care; third, much larger variations in health care delivery or performance are visible than in delivery of education.

10.5.4 Status of Livelihood

One can view human development also from several angles of quality of livelihood. Provision of drinking water and its quality, its access in terms of distance to fetch are some of the most burning issues in quality of life. As far as provisioning of safe drinking water is concerned, the situation in the state across the regions and districts seems to have improved considerably between 1990s and 2000s (Appendix A-10.5), to cover almost 97 per cent of households by 2001. Only 10 districts (of which 8 are from north Karnataka) are below the state average in 2001, that too very marginally, rather almost negligibly lower. However, there is quite a bit of variation in the degree of actual access to drinking water (in terms of LCPD per day per person) within the district and among the districts and among the disadvantaged section of the people (Table 10.19). For instance, at the state level, the percentage of habitations with less than 20 LCPD of water supply were 51.3 per cent, which declined to 21.9 per cent in 1998-99 and to 7.2 per cent in 2003-04, indicating major improvement in the distress situation. On the other hand, just 36.5 per cent of habitations received above 55 LCPD of water by 2003-04. Half the number of districts (6 out of 12) of north Karnataka are reported worse than the state average, whereas only 6 out of 14 districts from south Karnataka did not get this high rates of water supply (Appendix A-10.5). Therefore, as far as regional variation in access to drinking water supply is concerned, the situation seems to be the same across all the regions, more serious in north Karnataka.

TABLE 10.19

Percentage of Habitations in the State with Different Average LCPD of Drinking Water Supply

Access to Water	*1990-91*	*1998-99*	*2003-04*
With less than 20 LCPD	51.3	21.9	7.2
In the range of 20-40 LCPD	9.9	9.8	20.2
In the range of 40-55 LCPD	38.8	13.9	36.0
Above 55 LCPD		54.3	36.5

Note: This is for greater than 40 LCPD, as the breakups for 40-55 and >55 were not available.

Source: Rural Development and Panchayat Raj Department, Government of Karnataka.

Likewise, in terms of the 'ease' of fetching water, public health provisioning of availability of latrine, bathrooms and drainage (Table 10.20), the regional variations are still persisting in the state, significantly more in north Karnataka.

TABLE 10.20

Number of Districts below State Average in Terms of Share of Households Having the Facilities (2001)

Region/Divisions	*Within House/Premises*			
	Drinking Water	*Bathroom*	*Latrines*	*Closed Drainage*
Hyderabad-Karnataka-Gulbarga (5)	5	5	5	4
Old Bombay Karnataka-Belgaum (7)	5	4	5	6
North Karnataka (12)	10	9	10	10
Bangalore (7)	5	2	2	5
Mysore (8)	4	1	3	5
South Karnataka (15)	9	3	5	10
State Level (27)	**19**	**12**	**15**	**20**

Note: Figures in parentheses are number of districts in the Division.
Source: *Population Census*, 2001.

Recently, Karnataka Government has completed a major study on the *Status of Environment* (2004). Among many other regionally specific issues they have identified the critical regions of the state requiring immediate attention to improve the environment and quality of life. According to them, about 37 per cent of the habitations are badly affected by poor quality of water. Six districts of Belgaum Division, three districts of Gulbarga Division, five districts of Bangalore Division and four districts of Mysore Division are badly affected. Districts such as Dharwad have been affected by both decline in groundwater and inadequate supply. Chamrajnagar and Haveri are suffering from both inadequate and poor quality of water. Districts identified as 'hotspots' in terms of inadequacy, poor quality and decline in groundwater supply are Bellary, Bangalore, Bijapur, Tumkur, Kolar and Chitradurga. The same report also brought out another important fact of life, namely about status of slum dwellings in the state. The total number of slums in the state are estimated to be about 2,428, of which other than Bangalore, districts such as Tumkur, Mysore, Shimoga, Belgaum, Bellary, Bagalkot, and Gulbarga have more than 100 each. Certainly, one can easily infer about the quality of life among those dwellers to be very poor.

10.6 Towards Redressal of Regional Imbalances

10.6.1 Constitutional Vision

The Constitution of India under Articles 38 (2) and 39 (a) (b) (c) reflect among other things, the concern towards:

(a) Securing equity not only amongst individuals but also amongst groups of people residing in different areas or engaged in different vocations.

(b) Ensuring through proper policies that operation of the economic system does not result in any common detriment.

Several committees such as Pande Committee in 1968 and Wanchoo Committee in 1968 at the national level made specific recommendations to take up area plan approach in planning. The National Committee on the Development of Backward Areas (NCDFBA), 1981 surmised that areas identified as backward must have three key characteristics: (1) they must have potential for development; (2) there must be some inhibiting factor which prevents this potential from being realised; (3) there must be a need for spatial programmes to remove or mitigate the inhibiting factor to realise the full potential for development. Above all, for achieving the transition from the state of backwardness to the more developed state, a minimum critical effort is needed to overcome the inertia of the underdeveloped regions. The problem of regional disparities and backwardness is sought to be tackled in several ways, of which the more important measures are:

- Backwardness is to be recognised as a factor to be taken into account in resource transfer.
- Special Areas Development Programmes and employment generating schemes are to be formulated and implemented directing them at Backward Area Development.
- Initiate measures to promote private investment in backward areas. and
- Formulate policies to promote equalisation of the physical facilities or services of any region or district with that of the average facility enjoyed by the people in the developed are better off districts, generally represented by the average level in the state.

Karnataka also endorsed the above and in the past pursued a policy of reducing regional disparities. By the early 70s, the problem of regional imbalance had come to the fore more prominently. Area Planning Divisions were set up in almost all the states. Policies had been formulated in Karnataka and in the country as a whole, since the Third Five-Year Plan to tackle the problems of backward regions and regional disparities both at the regional and district levels. However, the efforts made so far to develop strategies appropriate to the needs of these backward areas have been far from adequate.

To begin with, some sort of uniform approach was introduced across the country in different districts and blocks. Examples are the launching of the anti-poverty programmes particularly the Integrated Area and Rural Development Programmes. Every block so identified in the country was sanctioned the same outlay in the past irrespective of the number of poor in the block. The norms regarding proportion of outlay on primary, secondary and tertiary sectors were also uniform for the whole country. Consequently the poor in the more backward areas lagged behind despite the launching of the anti-poverty programmes. It was then realised that there is a need for a more decentralised approach to formulate policies and programmes so that every region can visualise and adopt measures appropriate to its socio-economic characteristics and physical endowments.

A policy of reducing regional inequalities, for its translation into a programme on action, necessitates at the outset identification and delineation of backward regions or districts or more preferably backward *talukas*. An analysis of the causes of backwardness in specified *talukas* provides a logical base for devising region or areas—specific strategies, policies and programmes of development. Backward regions do need a preferential treatment and this cannot be over- emphasised.[12]

10.6.2 Initial Approaches in the State

One of the main objectives of reorganisation of the states in 1956 was to provide sufficient opportunities for regions with common historical, cultural, linguistic and social backgrounds to come together as a state and to move onto a path of regionally balanced development. In terms of natural resources, human capital, and income opportunities significant regional imbalances were then visible in Karnataka among the regions that came together at that time.

Some of the major steps taken by the governments in Karnataka since 1956 are summarised in the Box 10.3, which are noteworthy. The instruments used were: improved resource allocations, and legal and institutional changes on governance, accountability, etc. Certain specific steps and targets set out were:

- Identification of backward areas and drought prone areas.
- Introduction of special component plans for the above areas.
- Creation of four Area Development Boards.

Initially, as many as 14 districts were identified as drought prone in the state, many of them from north Karnataka. Likewise, the Irrigation Commission identified 12 districts and 88 *talukas* as hit by draughts, requiring special allocations under the plans. Four Regional Area Development Boards were established with the sole objective of regionally balanced development in the state. A three-tier PRI system was established in the entire state after the implementation of 73rd and 74th Constitutional Amendments. The HPC made strong recommendations on setting aside Rs. 16,000 crores exclusively to plan for redressal of regional imbalances in 8 years.

10.6.3 Some Lessons

Redressal of regional imbalances has remained still a difficulty task. Invariably, the Regional Development

BOX 10.3

An Overview of Attempts and Steps in Reducing Regional Disparity

Steps Undertaken	*Main Activity/Achievements*	*Time Period*
Fact Finding Committee	Assessment of levels of development among the Kannada speaking areas to be integrated subsequently.	1954.
Setting up of Regional Development Boards	Hyderabad-Karnataka Area Dev. Board; Malnad Area Dev. Board; Bayaluseeme Area Dev. Board, Border Area Dev. Board: All of them are granted special grants for redressing regional imbalances.	At various times starting from 1991.
Committee of Secretaries	To examine if there are any discriminations in allocating resources between north and south Karnataka. The report did not find any evidence on this.	1999.
Plan Allocations	Starting from Fifth Plan, and more so with the Sixth Plan, a scheme of weightage for resource allocation was implemented with almost 50 per cent weightage on backwardness.	1974 onwards.
State Finance Commission	The Finance Commission allocated resources for the districts after developing a formula for allocations to ZP, TP and GPs in the state.	1996.
Panchayat Raj Institutions	After the 73rd amendment of the Constitution, the state has introduced a three-tier decentralised governance with ZP, TP and GP to formulate plans and action programmes to reduce regional imbalances based on the principle of decentralisation.	Since 1993.
High Power Committee	This Committee was established in 2000 and the report was submitted in 2002, with recommendations to redress regional imbalances and also reduce the regional deprivations.	2002.

12. Precisely this was recommended by HPC (2002) of D. M. Nanjundappa. See also Rao (1984).

Boards established with a view to reduce the imbalances functioned more as departments making special allocations for road and bridges, education, health care, drinking water supply, etc. with much less involvement of the people. Unfortunately, quite often, the actual allocations did not follow any agreed formula. Secondly, in several situations the allocated funds are not fully used. Thirdly, in most cases, the allocations on road works dominate, rather than on matters of development. At the same time, the *Gram Panchayats* have very limited resources to deal with the problems of imbalances.

What are the root causes for the persistence of regional imbalances in development? This is a common question to ask. Is public allocation of resources the only answer? The analysis of resource allocations and performances of some of the major sectors and activities relevant at the regional levels clearly indicate that unless the overall development is targeted as the primary drive, by investing only on some selected demonstrative activities one does not attain the expected regional balance. Secondly, much of public provisioning does not reach the designated site and people. For this, concerted efforts on employment, empowerment, investment on reduction in hardship and improvement in quality of life are to be combined. Then the efforts will have to come from all sections of the society.

With the changed economic policies of liberalisation, marketisation and restructuring of fiscal instruments, one may not find very strong answers to redress regional disparities based on measures of only public interventions. The people have also come to the realisation that the 'state' by itself can not deliver all that can be put under development.

10.7 Regional Development Policies in Karnataka

10.7.1 Policies Implemented during Various Five-Year Plans

The focus on backward-area development was addressed substantially during the Fourth Plan period, manifesting itself in its policy objectives for agriculture, where along with maximisation of production, the remedying of imbalance was given equal prominence. This period was also marked by placing emphasis on the incidence of poverty across the state. All these developments resulted in starting of various programmes like Special Programmes for Dry Land Areas, Drought–Prone Area Programme, the Integrated Hill Area Programme and Integrated Development of Tribal Areas Programme.

Another important policy measure which exerted its impact though not in a direct manner on the development of backward areas was the one which envisage tackling the problems of the target groups in the community through enhancing their development opportunities and incomes. Special programmes introduced to tackle the problems of small/marginal farmers and agricultural labourers (e.g., TRISEM, RLEGP) may be cited as examples in this respect. It is noteworthy that on this vexed problem of regional imbalance/backwardness, government of Karnataka took certain initiatives and measures, thanks to the policy guidelines put out by the State Planning Department.

As in the case of the Five-Year Plans of the country, a growing concern for regional imbalance may be seen in the Fifth Five Year Plan (1974-1979). Mysore State Draft Fifth Five-Year Plan stated as "The plans of the state so for have laid emphasis on overall development through an aggregate and sectoral strategy than on regional planning with a bias towards a redressal of the peculiar problems and deficiencies of the various regions. Imbalances noticed among the districts are due to differences in resource—endowment, socio-economic institutions and responsiveness to developmental opportunities. Further, it must be noted that very highly backward areas got added when the state was reorganised and this explains why the process of reducing regional imbalances has been slow. Along with the shift in strategy from emphasis on higher growth rate to growth with more of employment the state shall move forward bringing about reductions in regional disparities, prevention of concentration of economic institutional innovation."

In fact, it formally stated that the state should make deliberate efforts at reducing imbalances as one of the objectives within the nine enumerated objectives.

The Sixth Five-Year Plan of Karnataka continued this exercise and approach and it came to the conclusion: "The approach and policies outlined in the foregoing have reduced the regional imbalances to a considerable extent.... It is to be noted that the imbalances still persist. It is to be hoped that the two-tier planning process which has been introduced very recently coupled with other programmes will help in achieving the regional balance in a reasonable period of time. The problem of regional balance is a long run problem and the policies outlined above have to be pursued continuously. However, the concept of perfect regional imbalance is an utopian concept and it is difficult to achieve. The reasonable objective should be one of achieving higher standard of living, especially, for the subsistence population living in rural areas.... Intensive block planning was proposed to be done brining together all plan schemes, special programmes including Employment Affirmation Scheme. This should facilitate proper integration of the schemes under an area approach with the block as the unit. The extension of the two-tier planning process to the block level, the lowest tier, bringing within it the cluster of villages approach, is expected to help in reducing intra-district imbalances substantially."

Karnataka government also started decentralised planning at the district level in 1978. In addition to identifying the district sector and state sector schemes separately, the state put into operation criteria for allocating financial resources giving a weightage of 50 per cent for backwardness as measured by agricultural output, irrigation, industrial output, roads and railway facilities, financial infrastructure, medical and health facilities, unemployment, power supply, problems of weaker sections (Box 10.4). Special problem areas like Malnad and drought prone areas (substantially from Hyderabad-Karnataka and old Bombay Karnataka regions) are to be allocated special funds.

It is indeed a sad commentary on the sincerity of the efforts by the state government in reducing regional imbalance in so far as clear policy guidelines and/or determined efforts in this direction are conspicuous by their absence since the Seventh Five-Year Plan.

To revive the concern and interest of the state government in evolving a regional development policy, the State Planning Board subsequently brought out a paper on An Approach to the Ninth Five-Year Plan of Karnataka: Some Suggestions (authored by the then Deputy Chairman, State Planning Board, Dr. D.M. Nanjundappa). It suggested that the criteria for distribution of plan funds should be revised with a view to facilitating further weightage being given for the relatively backward districts, measured in terms of per capita income and supplemented by a comprehensive development index built on indicators of backwardness.

BOX 10.4

Sixth Plan Strategies on Allocations

Indicator	*Weightage (%)*
Population	50
Agriculture backwardness as measured by the value of agricultural output per hectare	5
Backwardness in irrigation as measured by the proportion of irrigated area to net area sown	5
Backwardness as measured by the value of industrial output	5
Backwardness in communication as measured by road and railway mileage, for 100 sq.km/lack population	2½
Backwardness in financial infrastructure as measured by size of population served by each commercial and cooperative bank	2½
Backwardness in medical and health facilities as measured by the number of hospitals per 1000 population/bed population ratio	5
Backwardness in power supply:	
(a) as measured by the proportion of villages electrified 2½	5
(b) as measured by per capita consumption power 2½	
Problems of weaker section:	5
(a) as measured by the proportion of SCs/STs in population 2½	
(b) as measured by the proportion of landless agricultural labour 2½	
Local tax effort	5
Special problems of Malnad area and drought prone areas:	
(a) As measured by the area under forest 2½	5
(b) As measured by the rural population of drought prone area 2½	
Incidence of unemployment measured by the proportion of registrants at the Employment Exchange (with appropriate adjustment wherever necessary)	5

Source: Plan Documents, Government of Karnataka.

It further added that in formulation of the Tenth Plan the routine approach of district allocation on the basis of an objective criteria now followed may have to be supplemented by equalisation grants. In other words, instead of relying only on the finances provided, efforts should be made to equalise the level of services obtaining in the backward districts in comparison with the state average and also reduce interdistrict disparities. This is to be achieved by looking into the actual physical level of various services including social and infrastructural, and make a more effective dent on regional disparities. *The Panchayat Raj* Institutions are to be fully involved in the formulation and implementation of schemes of all sectors within the district and also the utilisation of equalisation of grants for achieving better interdistrict balance in the matter of development.

TABLE 10.21

Second Finance Commission's Awards

Criteria	*Weightage (%)*
Proportion of Rural Population	28.31
Proportion of Rural Area	28.31
Road Length per 100 sq.km.	9.44
Illiteracy Rate and No. of Persons Per Hospital Bed	18.88
Total Weight	84.94
Rounded Off to	85.00

Source: Second Finance Commission, Government of Karnataka.

10.7.2 Development Boards

While discussing the approaches to regional imbalance, specific to Karnataka, one cannot ignore the setting up of Area Development Boards in 1991 and thereafter. Regional Development Boards are the initial responses to the felt need for realising the objective of regional development. They were visualised as long back as 1981 for evolving a plan for backward area development in the context of the most backward regions of the state, *viz.*, Hyderabad-Karnataka region. Subsequently, other Development Boards also emerged. *Panchayats* System, though existing then, could not be effectively used for balanced regional development. It is only after the passage of the Constitution (73rd Amendment) Act 1992 that the decentralised decision making set up in terms of *Panchayats*, effectively involving participation of the people in planning and implementation of the programme, received a Constitutional status. Such institutions have started functioning effectively in different parts of Karnataka by the mid-90s.

Karnataka Government established from 1991 onwards four Regional Development Boards under different Acts for the purpose of taking special initiatives for development of different regions. These Boards are:

i. Hyderabad-Karnataka Area Development Board (HKADB) established in 1991, but functioning with effect from 1992, covering the then 4 (currently 5) districts of Hyderabad-Karnataka, consisting of 39 assembly constituencies.

ii. Malnad Area Development Board (MADB), was established in 1991, but it started functioning only with effect from 1993, covering 13 districts of Malnad area consisting of 71 assembly constituencies.

iii. Bayaluseeme Area Development Board (BDB), was established in 1994, and it started functioning with effect from 1995, covering 12 districts consisting of 76 assembly constituencies.

iv. Border Area Development Programme, which started functioning with effect form 1991, covers 15 boarder districts consisting of 52 constituencies along the border of Maharashtra, Goa, Andhra Pradesh, Kerala and Tamil Nadu.

The Acts provide for each of the Boards a separate Charter, which specifies the Constitution of the Board, broad objectives, governance, mode of functioning, etc. More specifically they 'provide for establishment of a Development Board' for each of the specified regions, 'which shall prepare annual plan containing programmes and projects for development of the area, supervise the implementation of projects and programmes and monitor and evaluate the implementation of its plan'.

Each of the Boards comprises Members of Parliament (MPs), Members of Legislative Assembly (MLAs), Members of Legislative Council (MLCs), representing a part or whole of the area, whose constituencies lie within the jurisdiction of the Board, Presidents of *Zilla Panchayats*, Divisional Commissioners (DCs) and Deputy State Government, from amongst whom, a specified number of persons are from SC and STs. Secretary and the Chairman of the Board are appointed by the government. Nominated members have a term of office for a period of three years whereas MLAs have a term of office of five years.

The High Power Committee (HPC) of Government of Karnataka for Redressal of Regional Imbalances, under the Chairmanship of Prof. D.M. Nanjundappa, commissioned a short period evaluation study of Regional Boards of Development in Karnataka, by CMDR. The study brought out that none of the Boards has strictly adhered to either the guidelines or their own Charters in respect of holding of meetings, allocation of funds, implementation, supervision, monitoring of the progress of the schemes, etc.

According to the Acts, the Boards are expected to prepare every year an annual plan for the development of the sub-regions of the area and forward the same to the state government for its approval. Most often, the original plans submitted by the Boards have been found to have undergone changes in the light of the funds received from the state government. This deviation of the actual plans from the original plans may be attributed among other things to the absence of a strong database about the respective regions. MLAs' list of work proposals (which is generally prepared without systematic consultations with all the other members of the Board also) is itself taken as the main database, though under the Act (e.g. Chapter III.16 of Karnataka Act No.35 and 36 of 1991), all the relevant information can be obtained by the Boards from *Zilla Parishads* or any department of the state government. The HPC expressed, "The Boards have missed a great opportunity of developing a strong databank, which would have helped their planning process."

The Boards have particularly depended upon *Zilla Parishads* through which more than 70 per cent of the works of the Boards have been got implemented. *Zilla Parishads* are already loaded with implementing their own respective developmental activities, which are similar in nature to those of the Boards. This seems to have introduced an element of duplication of responsibilities in actual implementation. Existence of multiple agencies for implementation is found to have created its own problems for coordination of the roles of different agencies. Each agency, particularly *Zilla Parishad* seems to have assigned greater priority to its own programmes rather than the programmes of the Board, for obvious reasons. In some cases, members of *Zilla Panchayats* and *Taluka Panchayats* were not even aware of the Board's programmes.

For all the three regional boards taken together (*viz.*, HKADB, MADB and BDB), the government of Karnataka released a total of about Rs.802 cores till the year 2001. The Boards were set up mainly for the purpose of developing the area covered by the respective boars. But the flow of funds has drastically reduced over the last several years. However the budget for the year 2005-6 has made a provision to increase the funds. According to the budget proposal 60 crores is allotted to Hydrabad-Karnataka Board, Rs. 20 crores to Malnad Board, Rs. 9 crores to Maidan Board (Byluseeme) and Rs. 5 crores to Border Area development Board. Thus, the overall allocation to Area Development Boards has gone up from Rs. 42.5 crores in 2004-05 to Rs. 94 crores in 2005-06.

In sum the HPC concludes that the Boards are found to be functioning according to their own style, not so much in line with the Charters and Guidelines. An element of *ad hocism* is witnessed at different stages of Boards' activities. Choice of the works does not seem to be very much consistent with the real needs of the people. Correction of regional imbalances does not seem to be the explicit focus of Boards activities. Quality of works is the casualty on account of lack of systematic supervision and monitoring. People do not seem to have been involved at different stages of planning, implementation, supervision and evaluation of the works. All the same, it should be admitted that Board's have added some infrastructure to the existing ones in the form of roads and bridges, school building, primary health centers, check dams, drinking water supply facilities, etc. Multiplication of agencies of implementation has added difficulties of their coordination. The role of institutions under the *Panchayat* System and that of the Boards do not seem to have been properly integrated.

10.7.3 Need for Alternative Strategies for the Development of Backward Regions

It is by now well recognised that backward regions in general lack basic social and economic infrastructure and this infrastructure bottleneck becomes responsible for the under utilisation of the development potential of the region. However, infrastructure backwardness is not uniform among all the backward regions. The need for different types of infrastructure may vary from region to region. A uniform policy for different types of backward region is not suitable. In fact, differential strategies *or* flexibilities are needed for the development of differentially endowed and differentially developed regions. Some regions may be very well endowed with social infrastructure and may be lacking in economic infrastructure or infrastructure essential for the development of productive sectors. In some other regions, capital inflow may not be very difficult but because of lack of social overheads, capital may be shying away. What proportion of resources should be allotted for social infrastructure, economic infrastructure, financial infrastructure and for directly productive activities should be guided by the regional situation in terms of availability of infrastructure need, resources and development potential.

Secondly, mere allocation of resources does not help the region to grow. For proper development, a comprehensive plan of action for monitoring is required. In this development endeavour, participation of local population is very important. Local participation does not mean mere representation in some administrative bodies. It is of no use to have dummies in the name of local participation. What is required is to enthuse local people (all sections) to come forward and take part in the development programmes. Partnership with the local communities in both the design and implementation is the strategy of the day.

Thirdly, backward area development should not be mixed up with 'poverty alleviation' programmes. Regional development has the 'area dimension', while poverty programmes have 'individual' dimensions. While reduction in poverty leads to prosperity, it may not ensure regional development. In a particular year by transferring more money in the form of grants and loan and subsidies it may be possible to show higher per capita income. But they do not really result in development of the region. Just by giving employment of purely temporary nature people cannot be helped. What is important for the reduction of poverty is the creation of gainful employment opportunities to local people. This can be done only when local resources are tapped most usefully. As mentioned above, special allocations on the lines shown in Box 10.4 for area development be made separately.

Fourthly, in order to bring out the hidden potential, investment in productive non-farm sectors like horticultural processing, rural marketing, and services (including IT and BT) and artisanships need to be made. This in turn requires policies of attracting capital and investors from within the region and from outside. This is a matter of public-private-partnership. It is rather too optimistic to think that policies such as 'tax concessions', 'tax holidays' or subsidies will attract private investments and help improving backward regions. These may be important, but the entrepreneur looks for investment atmosphere, which includes good socio-economic infrastructure. If an investor is sure that in a particular region transport network is very good, power is not a problem, access to information and communication is available and at the same time, the members of the families of the employees can have good education and health facilities, good recreation centres and above all if he is sure that for his product there is proper backward and forward market linkages within the region he will come forward to invest. Therefore, a comprehensive regional development plan should commence with providing good private and local investment climate rather than focusing of fiscal incentive schemes.

Fifthly, in a country like India, backwardness of a region is also due to predominance of rural sector. Most of the villages are scattered and economically unviable to promote any one activity. To overcome this shortcoming, cluster of villages as Rural Growth Centres need to be formed and within the cluster investment climate should be created in such a manner that each cluster eventually emerges as a small town, which in turn grows and takes the size of a city. Each region can be divided into several clusters of villages and policies to promote growth and development may be formulated. What is needed is to take up a comprehensive programme, touching upon all aspects of backwardness under the command of only one agency. This will definitely provide a concrete solution to the problems of backward regions.

In brief, there is urgent need for formulation of differential strategies of development for differentially developed regions. Thus the aggregate as well as the sectoral planning should suit the clearly identified regional needs, potentials, priorities, of course, within the general constraint of national objectives and priorities. Such a plan based on regional requirements directly benefits the local people, kindles enthusiasm among the masses and stimulates local participation. Thus an ideal plan strategy is one that integrates the sectoral plans with spatial plans. Once the strategy is drawn the next issue pertains to drawing up an execution plan.

Based on the above five prone strategies, and also the recommendations of Nanjundappa Committee (HPC, 2002), for purpose of formulating development strategies, following categories of *talukas* can be considered (Rao, 1984):

a) consisting of developed *talukas* with all the three productive sectors (agri., industry and services) developed;

b) consisting of developed *taluka* with all the three productive sectors remaining backward;

c) consisting of developed *talukas* with one of the productive sectors developed;

d) backward *talukas* with all the three productive sectors as backward;

e) average *talukas* with developed productive sectors; and

f) backward *talukas* with one of the productive sectors as developed

The group A consisting of *talukas* with very high level of development and with multi-dimensional development, does not require any special efforts of the government. The present levels of plan efforts are adequate to maintain the rate of growth in future. *Talukas* coming under this category have reached a stage, where they can attract private entrepreneur and capital automatically. The already well developed, economic, financial and social institutional network act as incentives for the entrepreneurs, skilled labour, capital and technology to flow into such regions.

In order to develop the *talukas* coming under Group 'B' and Group 'C' having developed infrastructure but backward productive sectors, the present plan strategies need to be slightly modified. In such *talukas*, more concentrated efforts are required to promote the productive sector. While doing this, development potential of the region needs to be evaluated, so that the goals of economic efficiency are not jeopardised.

The *talukas* falling under Group 'D' are the special category of *talukas*, where the present plan strategies are not only inadequate but need a totally new orientation. These *talukas* not only need to be recognised as priority *talukas* in the development schemes of the state but also require special attention. The new strategy should be based on intensive survey of the region's resource inventories, assessment of the development potentials and study of feasibility of different economic schemes suitable to different *talukas*. Once, this spadework is done, sectoral development plan with an integrated approach needs to be formulated. What is needed here is the organisation of economic activities at all levels and sectors interacting upon one another so as to produce on aggregate growth rate which will help to remove the bottlenecks in the backward regions.

In *talukas* falling under the Groups F and G special attention should be paid on the development of economic infrastructure, financial institutions and providing health and education facilities.

10.8 Future Vision, Options and Possibilities

The policies highlighted in the previous section need to be implemented within the framework of decentralised development. After the major shift in the development strategy, switching from centralised to decentralised framework, under the 73rd and 74th Amendments to the Constitutions, devolution of decision power and economic instruments in respect of as many as 29 functions and activities have been transferred to *zilla, taluka* and *gram panchayats*. They have also been empowered to raise their own resources. They have been supported by several line departments such as Education, Health, PWD, Women and Child Welfare, Water Resources, etc. Significant amount of training and empowerment have already been parted to their members, communities and officials of the line departments by RDPR. Therefore, the first charge on bridging the regional disparity can begin from the Village, *Taluka* and *Zilla Panchayats*. They will be the first and best judges on identification of the gaps, deprivations and remedial solutions acceptable to the communities. An Activity mapping be prepared on all the 29 functions identified for the *Panchayat Raj* Institutions in terms of their capabilities, capacities for their effective implementations and monitoring. These functions should be so regrouped as to internalise the policies listed earlier. For instance, the *zilla panchayats* can concentrate on both promoting public-private partnership and attracting industrial hubs. The *Taluka Panchayats* can take up implementing public-private partnerships with *taluka* level growth centers. The *Gram Panchayats* should concentrate on internalising the local talents in promoting employment and artisanships. They can easily involve the SHGs and other NGOs on some of these functions.

It is in this context that the role of civic societies is also found to be extremely relevant. Though a large number of activities are identified for the *panchayats*, to the extent they have to deal with the society, there is a need for involving other institutions as well. The concept behind the evolution of such institutions is the principle of 'participation'. Viewed on these lines, the role of NGOs and government supported organisations such as self-help groups like Stree-shakti, Swashakti (under a promotive scheme of Department of Women and Child Welfare), Water User Associations, Village Protection Committees of JFM, etc. and cooperative banks and certain segments of corporate bodies and hubs are important as civic society agents, regulators, monitors and implementers. Already there are a large number of NGO organisations in Karnataka, directly working on water resources, health, education, sanitation, poverty and women development. But majority of them are concentrated in four or five prominent or well developed districts such as Bangalore, Kolar, Belgaum, and Gulbarga. Further, they concentrate mainly on health and family welfare and empowerment of women, leaving out water, sanitation or poverty and employment. This public-private partnerships should spread to all the districts. At present, there are no clear constitutional provisions, though Karnataka has enacted several legal Acts to implement such moves. Establishment of Water User Associations and VWSSCs can be cited as some examples. But, there are more opportunities to expand this scheme of thinking.

Recently, Karnataka has taken some further strides in bringing both the public and private agencies to come together to address themselves to several aspects of social and economic developments. Establishment of Village Water Supply and Sanitation Committee (VWSSC) (as a new Institution of Karnataka Integrated Rural Water Supply and Sanitation Project KIRWSESP) or, Village Forest Protection Committees (VFPC) (under Joint Forest Program) are some examples. Since 1993, out of 1,104 villages under KIRWSESP, as many as 239 schemes covered in Phase–I and 727 schemes covered in Phase-II have been handed over to VWSSCs for operation and maintenance. With as many as one lakh self-help groups in the state, well spread in almost all the districts, there is a good opportunity to address to women and empowerment related regional issues.

Finally, there is a need to prioritise various concerns of development within a framework of regionally balanced growth. Here one has to be guided by some of the regionally relevant factors and variables, unlike the usual selective indices of development. For this purposes, the extent of regional variations in the composite indices (both as aggregate and by components) across the districts and the four regions can be used as a tool.

At present allocation of resources does not seem to be in response to any major disparity among the regions or districts. When it comes to poverty levels, the regional variations are quite wide and uncorrelated with the measures of regional developments (Table 10.22). They seem to have increased between 1993-94 to 1999-00 period. While provisioning of educational facilities are better spread over the districts, the same can not be said about access or performances. Provisioning of health facilities seem to be more diversified than the educational facilities. Overall quality of life seems to be regionally more unbalanced as compared to the composite levels of development. As compared to plan allocations, Non-plan resource allocations seem to be going quite widely across the districts. Therefore, an amendment to the allocation criteria shown in Box 10.4 can be to provide weightage for measures of regional variations. Then, as can be viewed from Table 10.22 the priorities shall be poverty reduction, health care, quality of life and infrastructural development and education.

TABLE 10.22

Prioritising Regional Development

Matrix of Regional Disparity		*Data Used*	*Coefficient of Variation*
Quality of Life: 2001		All	0.28
		SC	0.33
		ST	0.28
Education (Provision of Services)	Provisioning	1990-91	0.14
		1998-99	0.13
		2002-03	0.13
	Access	2002-02	0.26
	Performance	2002-03	0.29
Healthcare	Provisioning	1009-91	0.31
		1998-99	0.28
		2002-03	0.30
Resource Allocation (Plan)		1998-99	0.26
		2003-04	0.22
Resource Allocation (Non-Plan)		1998-99	0.53
		2002-03	0.67
Poverty		1993-94	0.40
		1999-00	0.66
Per Capita Income		1990-91	0.27
		1998-99	0.33
		2001-02	0.28
Composite Index of Development		2001-01	0.23

Note: All the attributes are based on composite indices derived from factor analysis.

References

Balasubramanian N. and Ramakrishna Panigrahi (2003). "A Measure of Inequality Of Human Development for Funding and Management: Case Study of Karnataka State, India", *ICFAI Journal of Applied Economics*, Vol. II (2): 46-66.

Dennison, Edward (1961). *The Sources of Economic Growth in The United States And the Alternative before Us*, Committee for Economic Development, New York.

Government of India (2002). *National Water Policy*, Ministry of Water Resources.

Government of Karnataka (2002). *High Power Committee for Redressal of Regional Imbalances*, Final Report, June.

————. (2001). *Task Force on Health and Family Welfare.*

————. (2004). *State of the Environment Report and Action Plan-2003*, Department of Forests, Ecology and Environment.

Hutchins, R. M. (1970). *The Learning Society*, Penguin Books.

Iyengar, N. S., M. B. Nanjappa and P. Sudarshan (1981). "A Note on Inter District Differentials in Karnataka development", *Journal of Income and Wealth*, 5(1):79-83.

Kadekodi, G. K. (2000). "*Regional Disparity Revisited: The Case of Karnataka*", CMDR *Monograph Series No.31.*

Kalam, Abdul A.P. J. and Y.S. Rajan (1998). *India 2020: A Vision for the New Millennium*, Viking Press, New Delhi.

Kamath, S.U. (1982). *Karnataka State Gazetteer*, Government of Karnataka, Bangalore.

Kurian N. J. (2000). "Widening Regional Disparities in India: Some Indicators", *Economic and Political Weekly*, February: 538-55

Murgai, R., M. H. Suryanarayana, and A. Zaidi (2003). "Measuring Poverty in India: the Regional Dimension", *Economic and Political Weekly*, January 25: 404-408.

National Council of Applied Economic Research (2001). *South India Human Development Report*, New Delhi.

Ostrom, Elinor (1990). *Governing the Commons: The Evolution of Institutions of Collective Action*, Cambridge University Pres, New York.

Ostrom, E., J. Walker and R. Gardner (1992). "Government with and without a Sword: Self-governance is Possible", *American Political Science Review*, 86(2): 404-17.

Planning Commission (2001). *National Human Development Report*, Government of India.

———. (2004). *Vision 2020*, Government of India, Academic Foundation, New Delhi.

Rao, Hemlata (1984). *Regional Disparity and Development in India*, Ashish Publications, New Delhi.

Sen, Amartya (1992). *The Concept of Well Being*, Oxford University Press, New Delhi.

Solow, Robert (1957). "Technical Change and Aggregate Productivity Function", *Review of Economic Studies*, (39): 312-20.

Suryanarayana, M.H. (2004): "Measuring Poverty and Policy Targeting in Karnataka: The Regional Dimension", *mimeograph.*

Ul-Haq, Mahbub (1998). *Reflections on Human Development*, Oxford University Press, Second ed. New Delhi.

UNESCO (1990). World Conference on Education for All: Meeting Basic Learning Needs, Jomtion.

World Bank (2004). *Attaining the Millennium Development Goals in India: Role of Public Policy and Service Delivery*, Washington.

APPENDIX A-10.1

Per capita Transfers to Rural Local Bodies

District	*Plan*		*Non-Plan*		*Total*	
	1998-99	*2003-04*	*1998-99*	*2003-04*	*1998-99*	*2003-04*
Belgaum	234.48	200.00	248.22	240.01	482.70	440.01
Bijapur	282.21	223.01	342.48	342.90	624.69	565.91
Bagalkote	279.05	210.09	242.41	839.85	521.46	1049.94
Dharwad	201.24	172.30	231.65	816.28	432.89	988.58
Gadag	269.02	232.22	987.99	1526.05	1257.01	1758.27
Haveri	271.71	228.84	795.12	816.34	1066.83	1045.18
Uttara Kannada	424.47	362.36	1121.53	700.81	1546.00	1063.18
Belgaum Division	266.37	220.54	453.93	605.69	720.30	826.23
Bellary	277.47	216.34	602.87	216.47	880.35	432.81
Bidar	327.33	272.34	959.01	1140.58	1286.34	1412.92
Gulbarga	297.39	214.77	184.93	230.73	482.32	445.50
Raichur	277.12	246.22	607.16	774.17	884.29	1020.39
Koppal	287.40	265.89	592.63	1707.59	880.04	1973.48
Gulbarga Division	293.13	236.10	521.16	652.10	814.29	888.19
Bangalore (Urban)	60.42	49.26	105.97	141.35	166.39	190.60
Bangalore (Rural)	353.73	286.87	490.30	715.48	844.04	1002.35
Chitradurga	387.22	316.76	1146.09	718.63	1533.31	1035.39
Davanagere	209.02	264.03	471.32	693.76	680.34	957.79
Kolar	325.96	242.07	686.26	485.07	1012.22	727.14
Shimoga	443.42	269.87	479.82	545.01	923.23	814.88
Tumkur	348.81	255.85	298.50	275.87	647.31	531.72
Bangalore Division	244.61	188.61	408.98	398.01	653.59	586.63
Chickmagalur	456.85	369.01	677.78	2204.37	1134.63	2573.38
Dakshina Kannada	245.31	213.32	468.72	616.62	714.03	829.94
Udupi	243.49	221.24	976.40	1557.71	1219.88	1778.95
Hassan	379.95	299.12	471.17	351.38	851.12	650.50
Kodagu	491.71	408.77	1177.62	1869.48	1669.34	2278.25
Mandya	306.76	259.45	385.78	596.58	692.53	856.03
Mysore	236.68	193.90	170.40	472.02	407.08	665.91
Chamarajanagar	315.61	335.30	504.59	1913.18	820.21	2248.48
Mysore Division	308.62	262.26	504.15	961.29	812.77	1223.55
North Karnataka	277.70	227.22	482.39	625.62	760.09	852.84
South Karnataka	270.11	217.26	446.88	617.14	716.99	834.40
State	**273.31**	**221.48**	**461.87**	**620.73**	**735.17**	**842.21**

Source: Karnataka Budget Documents of various years, Government of Karnataka.

APPENDIX A-10.2 a

Transfers to Rural Local Bodies: 1998-99

District	*Education*		*Health and Family Welfare*		*Nutrition*		*Water Supply and Sanitation*		*Social Welfare Programmes*		*Rural Development*		*Others*	
	Plan	*Non-Plan*	*Plan*	*Non-Plan*	*Plan*	*Non-Plan*	*Plan*	*Non-Plan*	*Plan*	*Non-Plan*	*Plan*	*Non-Plan*	*Plan*	*Non-Plan*
Belgaum	25.42	165.23	20.92	27.04	10.65	4.00	33.66	0.22	37.97	11.47	86.72	6.33	19.13	33.93
Bijapur	38.67	229.28	22.56	29.94	7.02	10.91	28.60	0.17	36.39	12.42	126.28	10.22	22.70	49.54
Bagalkote	37.70	155.30	20.35	23.76	6.29	5.27	31.03	0.26	39.84	13.64	116.99	7.32	26.86	36.86
Dharwad	23.41	141.44	16.80	22.61	8.62	5.17	26.49	0.65	28.26	20.64	79.48	8.20	18.18	32.93

Contd. ...

...Contd. ...

District	Education		Health and Family Welfare		Nutrition		Water Supply and Sanitation		Social Welfare Programmes		Rural Development		Others	
	Plan	Non-Plan	Plan	Non-Plan	Plan	Non-Plan	Plan	Non-Plan	Plan	Non-Plan	Plan	Non-Plan	Plan	Non-Plan
Gadag	23.99	610.18	18.39	99.48	1.90	17.57	28.22	1.07	40.08	42.74	134.89	26.53	21.55	190.42
Haveri	22.69	529.08	18.27	87.25	8.81	11.68	32.42	0.41	36.59	43.32	136.51	18.52	16.43	104.87
Uttara Kannada	62.32	737.03	30.50	111.61	9.15	21.21	59.75	0.82	49.92	54.65	162.04	30.20	50.78	166.01
Belgaum Division	31.45	295.48	20.91	46.26	8.32	8.71	33.45	0.41	37.83	22.82	111.22	12.27	23.18	67.99
Bellary	37.14	406.44	17.56	57.66	6.88	6.39	23.73	0.46	46.05	31.89	118.51	16.58	27.60	83.46
Bidar	32.49	672.95	19.79	72.60	0.00	19.06	38.24	0.56	64.85	44.97	140.80	26.74	31.17	122.13
Gulbarga	36.32	117.13	20.02	18.38	3.34	2.99	30.92	0.14	52.90	8.84	126.87	7.05	27.02	30.40
Raichur	26.52	423.03	13.60	57.07	11.40	4.23	31.07	0.62	48.53	22.87	116.81	15.98	29.20	83.36
Koppal	31.58	448.36	16.25	53.46	8.79	17.12	34.01	0.53	46.09	22.54	122.63	9.92	28.07	40.70
Gulbarga Division	33.59	361.54	17.87	46.46	5.64	8.25	30.96	0.41	51.73	23.64	125.02	14.12	28.31	66.75
Bangalore (Urban)	6.22	71.03	5.44	9.87	2.21	2.69	11.00	0.07	10.07	4.80	21.17	2.13	4.31	15.39
Bangalore (Rural)	46.50	317.63	33.36	44.35	11.48	4.92	45.73	0.55	49.60	22.52	134.66	12.35	32.41	87.98
Chitradurga	42.31	986.44	23.24	54.40	5.68	6.95	40.58	0.59	76.88	31.48	169.69	10.81	28.85	55.41
Davangere	23.55	331.62	10.85	30.37	8.69	6.63	17.68	0.26	46.79	22.96	86.04	15.13	15.42	64.35
Kolar	39.09	495.85	18.57	53.62	9.96	15.97	33.20	0.46	48.56	25.26	153.04	17.32	23.55	77.78
Shimoga	58.55	298.77	24.83	54.97	6.26	9.44	77.08	0.56	75.45	26.00	165.07	13.70	36.17	76.38
Tumkur	44.25	199.30	29.24	25.97	8.77	11.12	48.01	0.35	47.82	17.65	140.97	7.94	29.75	36.17
Bangalore Division	29.74	295.38	17.28	31.54	6.46	7.30	31.98	0.32	39.87	17.19	99.80	9.15	19.48	48.09
Chickmaglur	54.94	439.50	29.25	76.17	11.25	7.41	56.43	0.98	62.73	34.76	204.20	22.28	38.06	96.68
Dakshina Kannada	33.29	311.10	24.69	48.00	8.96	13.88	40.18	0.28	50.28	24.38	74.00	12.03	13.91	59.06
Udupi	29.20	625.91	26.31	100.55	0.00	28.79	42.90	0.86	44.13	60.02	82.78	27.68	18.16	132.58
Hassan	56.26	349.09	22.53	42.29	7.82	5.43	49.78	0.36	48.88	20.35	167.47	12.90	27.20	40.75
Kodagu	40.45	847.05	40.28	97.72	6.20	26.05	84.97	0.98	71.18	63.37	197.45	16.40	51.20	126.05
Mandya	27.23	268.91	29.87	27.11	11.52	4.55	66.63	0.17	45.39	17.96	94.08	11.23	32.03	55.85
Mysore	25.72	99.38	20.01	18.18	6.98	5.57	27.46	0.22	47.31	14.57	92.86	3.72	16.35	28.75
Chamrajnagar	26.49	351.49	25.83	35.31	7.29	16.71	34.81	0.31	74.45	28.27	126.73	10.64	20.01	61.87
Mysore Division	35.42	339.61	25.54	47.44	7.69	11.33	46.16	0.43	52.10	27.80	117.72	13.06	23.99	64.49
North Karnataka	32.36	323.45	19.63	46.34	7.18	8.51	32.40	0.41	43.71	23.17	117.06	13.05	25.35	67.46
South Karnataka	32.00	312.99	20.57	37.87	6.95	8.91	37.63	0.36	44.74	21.42	106.94	10.70	21.28	54.62
State	**32.15**	**317.40**	**20.17**	**41.45**	**7.05**	**8.74**	**35.42**	**0.38**	**44.31**	**22.16**	**111.21**	**11.69**	**23.00**	**60.04**

APPENDIX A-10.2 b

Transfers to Rural Local Bodies: 2003-04

District	Education		Health and Family Welfare		Nutrition		Water Supply and Sanitation		Social Welfare Programmes		Rural Development		Others	
	Plan	Non-Plan	Plan	Non-Plan	Plan	Non-Plan	Plan	Non-Plan	Plan	Non-Plan	Plan	Non-Plan	Plan	Non-Plan
Belgaum	4.21	160.78	31.24	17.45	9.76	5.25	27.01	0.08	37.66	14.73	75.33	8.41	14.78	33.31
Bijapur	8.54	227.95	29.90	26.43	6.88	8.56	26.64	0.24	34.49	18.15	96.20	14.09	20.37	47.48
Bagalkote	9.50	566.84	20.74	77.61	6.85	13.67	25.51	0.58	36.21	47.75	88.88	27.40	22.41	106.00
Dharwad	6.31	509.50	15.87	73.29	8.55	13.86	25.49	0.68	32.51	49.46	66.01	25.46	17.56	144.04
Gadag	10.46	1001.78	30.12	160.76	2.43	23.83	16.33	0.64	47.36	112.42	100.13	40.97	25.38	185.66
Haveri	8.22	522.14	27.15	76.36	7.20	10.82	29.67	0.67	36.91	65.38	103.52	27.45	16.17	113.51

Contd. ...

Contd. ...

District	Education		Health and Family Welfare		Nutrition		Water Supply and Sanitation		Social Welfare Programmes		Rural Development		Others	
	Plan	Non-Plan	Plan	Non-Plan	Plan	Non-Plan	Plan	Non-Plan	Plan	Non-Plan	Plan	Non-Plan	Plan	Non-Plan
Uttara Kannada	10.87	525.03	38.77	48.51	9.64	24.81	47.87	0.60	44.77	31.46	169.06	17.60	41.38	52.80
Belgaum Division	7.26	401.76	27.85	53.61	7.97	11.58	27.83	0.39	37.63	38.33	91.87	19.20	20.13	80.81
Bellary	10.42	120.14	24.51	22.69	7.78	5.78	17.87	0.53	39.45	20.37	97.05	8.29	19.26	38.67
Bidar	11.23	766.55	29.43	95.88	0.00	21.34	47.68	0.64	52.72	85.07	107.04	31.07	24.25	140.03
Gulbarga	6.83	142.53	18.31	18.10	3.43	4.05	26.78	0.14	38.95	18.70	99.22	8.56	21.26	38.65
Raichur	5.43	543.47	19.30	66.57	13.64	5.87	29.46	0.63	45.79	31.37	108.90	22.89	23.69	103.38
Koppal	7.11	1257.25	20.80	89.08	8.33	31.92	50.55	0.72	56.21	89.55	100.92	45.45	21.98	193.61
Gulbarga Division	8.08	446.61	21.87	48.72	6.21	10.98	31.64	0.46	44.60	40.67	101.88	19.20	21.82	85.46
Bangalore-Urban	2.43	94.00	5.16	11.64	2.14	3.23	10.63	0.07	9.32	8.10	15.64	4.58	3.93	19.72
Bangalore-Rural	4.77	478.44	36.66	59.07	12.20	6.86	46.10	0.59	45.35	42.89	115.14	21.54	26.66	106.09
Chitradurga	10.24	470.00	26.66	59.88	5.65	12.38	48.05	0.64	72.87	53.74	130.38	23.50	22.90	98.49
Davanagere	6.05	490.91	23.57	45.98	7.79	9.37	36.30	0.27	49.60	39.30	118.45	20.80	22.27	87.13
Kolar	4.51	318.03	14.72	45.54	10.08	11.98	31.83	0.22	48.12	33.89	113.39	13.80	19.43	61.60
Shimoga	12.33	379.60	23.51	33.42	6.76	6.91	34.94	0.20	50.04	35.32	121.70	16.03	20.58	73.53
Tumkur	3.64	181.58	30.63	17.98	8.00	11.46	36.36	0.13	39.43	19.76	118.38	9.98	19.39	34.99
Bangalore Division	4.95	267.76	18.18	30.89	6.24	7.54	28.15	0.23	34.80	25.69	81.15	12.33	15.14	53.57
Chickmaglur	16.79	1589.16	38.62	142.57	10.53	52.78	42.03	1.09	65.24	118.76	163.28	61.47	32.52	238.53
D. Kannada	4.90	416.55	30.39	46.01	9.96	23.64	31.01	0.51	51.50	41.83	74.51	15.47	11.05	72.62
Udupi	7.99	1093.07	29.35	114.14	0.00	43.86	42.56	0.92	46.15	88.64	78.76	43.88	16.43	173.22
Hassan	9.50	206.78	28.08	27.23	7.88	11.36	61.26	0.36	42.80	34.90	124.28	14.08	25.31	56.67
Kodagu	16.36	1186.77	44.21	195.79	7.11	21.64	67.77	2.19	69.23	144.64	159.94	66.87	44.15	251.58
Mandya	12.37	435.11	28.25	52.62	11.86	7.83	47.61	0.38	47.74	31.26	84.59	17.96	27.03	51.42
Mysore	3.09	331.85	23.84	38.36	8.71	7.83	23.37	0.21	47.58	30.82	73.95	13.36	13.36	49.58
Chamarajanagar	6.67	1582.30	31.89	90.93	8.48	13.83	60.73	0.99	75.52	77.54	122.44	24.61	29.57	122.99
Mysore Division	8.38	686.31	29.72	69.84	8.35	20.28	42.44	0.62	52.27	56.99	99.57	25.80	21.54	101.44
North Karnataka	7.61	421.02	25.28	51.51	7.21	11.33	29.47	0.42	40.62	39.34	96.17	19.20	20.85	82.81
South Karnataka	6.28	430.59	22.67	46.04	7.06	12.50	33.70	0.38	41.60	37.86	88.32	17.57	17.63	72.19
State	**6.85**	**426.54**	**23.78**	**48.36**	**7.13**	**12.00**	**31.91**	**0.40**	**41.18**	**38.49**	**91.64**	**18.26**	**19.00**	**76.69**

Source: Karnataka Budget Documents of various years, Government of Karnataka.

APPENDIX A-10.3

Provisioning of Educational Services

District	Gross Enrolment Ratio			Primary Institutions per Lakh Population in the Age Group 6-14			Number of Secondary Institutions per Lakh Population			Pupil Teacher Ratio			Share of Girl Enrolment in Total			Education Provisioning Index		
	1990-91	1998-99	2002-03	1990-91	1998-99	2002-03	1990-91	1998-99	2002-03	1990-91	1998-99	2002-03	1990-91	1998-99	2002-03	1990-91	1998-99	2002-03
Belgaum	67.43	93.85	127.64	320	498	519	10	14	14	49	60	41	0.45	0.47	0.46	0.21	0.45	0.56
Bijapur	61.68	97.34	115.50	331	494	453	10	16	16	53	41	44	0.43	0.46	0.53	0.21	0.49	0.58
Bagalkot	61.53	84.27	109.74	330	463	407	10	14	15	53	35	45	0.43	0.51	0.47	0.21	0.53	0.49
Dharwad	66.34	102.56	129.96	266	348	286	12	13	11	57	51	80	0.46	0.47	0.47	0.25	0.38	0.37
Gadag	66.53	91.93	112.37	266	419	428	12	17	18	57	37	39	0.46	0.48	0.48	0.25	0.54	0.57
Haveri	66.62	60.66	107.65	267	466	473	12	16	16	57	27	41	0.46	0.44	0.49	0.25	0.49	0.55
Uttara Kannada	77.23	100.07	108.46	629	1014	1089	15	17	18	41	28	28	0.47	0.48	0.49	0.42	0.71	0.77

Contd. ...

Contd. ...

District	Gross Enrolment Ratio			Primary Institutions Per Lakh Population in the Age Group 6-14			Number of Secondary Institutions Per Lakh Population			Pupil Teacher Ratio			Share of Girl Enrolment in Total			Education Provisioning Index		
	1990-91	1998-99	2002-03	1990-91	1998-99	2002-03	1990-91	1998-99	2002-03	1990-91	1998-99	2002-03	1990-91	1998-99	2002-03	1990-91	1998-99	2002-03
Belgaum Division	66.58	90.65	117.94	338	517	510	11	15	15	51	41	42	0.45	0.47	0.48	0.24	0.50	0.55
Bellary	68.38	90.93	106.59	297	419	485	9	10	11	43	44	38	0.42	0.46	0.47	0.22	0.38	0.46
Bidar	65.95	100.78	114.87	310	378	353	15	19	18	47	37	42	0.40	0.46	0.49	0.28	0.54	0.55
Gulbarga	56.31	96.18	122.05	327	438	402	8	14	10	49	44	51	0.39	0.45	0.48	0.17	0.44	0.44
Raichur	46.76	64.95	111.15	288	405	410	6	9	11	59	37	54	0.39	0.41	0.45	0.05	0.31	0.41
Koppal	46.79	78.58	112.41	288	431	391	6	10	11	59	43	52	0.39	0.45	0.48	0.05	0.37	0.43
Gulbarga Division	57.70	88.17	114.62	306	417	410	9	13	12	49	41	47	0.40	0.45	0.47	0.16	0.41	0.46
Bangalore	72.86	88.59	106.80	245	529	183	10	14	16	49	37	35	0.47	0.50	0.51			
Bangalore (Rural)	72.66	123.39	101.24	668	1195	925	11	18	17	56	31	28	0.46	0.48	0.47	0.30	0.81	0.71
Chitradurga	70.84	101.69	104.15	430	704	738	14	21	20	52	35	33	0.46	0.48	0.47	0.34	0.66	0.67
Davanagere	71.43	99.11	112.72	445	533	398	13	19	21	49	37	46	0.45	0.48	0.49	0.33	0.57	0.56
Kolar	73.23	84.17	107.01	578	815	821	9	14	14	49	31	31	0.45	0.48	0.47	0.32	0.60	0.63
Shimoga	74.35	93.25	106.81	559	810	814	13	19	19	47	38	31	0.47	0.52	0.49	0.37	0.66	0.69
Tumkur	76.13	88.79	99.15	605	922	966	17	21	21	47	26	29	0.46	0.49	0.48	0.43	0.76	0.74
Bangalore Division	73.20	94.44	105.54	467	747	609	12	17	18	49	33	33	0.46	0.49	0.49	0.35	0.68	0.67
Chickmagalur	72.20	93.12	106.50	655	960	976	14	20	20	38	25	27	0.49	0.48	0.47	0.45	0.77	0.78
Dakshina Kannada	104.73	102.26	115.91	329	459	389	12	16	15	59	44	37	0.47	0.50	0.47	0.36	0.55	0.54
Udupi	105.19	132.54	91.34	330	452	335	12	15	17	59	54	35	0.47	0.41	0.48	0.36	0.48	0.53
Hassan	68.37	86.38	95.43	698	1031	1059	16	21	21	40	25	26	0.47	0.50	0.50	0.43	0.79	0.79
Kodagu	81.92	100.81	114.32	450	550	604	16	19	16	45	33	31	0.47	0.48	0.48	0.52	0.67	0.69
Mandya	71.17	93.59	100.75	500	747	760	9	17	18	45	36	31	0.45	0.47	0.49	0.28	0.61	0.68
Mysore	64.67	99.23	128.88	400	610	615	10	15	15	49	39	36	0.47	0.48	0.49	0.27	0.53	0.62
Chamarajanagar	64.87	83.96	93.78	401	553	579	10	13	14	49	34	33	0.47	0.47	0.48	0.27	0.54	0.58
Mysore Division	77.77	98.62	107.15	470	682	671	12	17	17	48	36	32	0.47	0.47	0.48	0.35	0.61	0.65
North Karnataka	62.80	89.54	116.42	324	473	465	10	14	14	50	41	44	0.43	0.46	0.48	0.20	0.45	0.50
South Karnataka	75.05	96.06	106.15	468	722	632	12	17	17	49	34	32	0.47	0.48	0.49	0.35	0.64	0.66
State Average	70.00	94.91	110.97	405	579	554	11	16	16	49	38	37	0.45	0.47	0.48			
Coefficient of Variation	0.19	0.08	0.09	0.35	0.37	0.36	0.25	0.21	0.21	0.12	0.25	0.30	0.06	0.05	0.02	0.38	0.24	0.20

Source: Directorate of Economics and Statistics, *Karnataka At A Glance*, Government of Karnataka, (various issues) and Commissioner Public Instruction, Government of Karnataka.

APPENDIX A-10.4

Access and Performance Indicators in Education: 2002-03

District	Share of Girl Enrolment	Percentage of Children out of School	Share of SC Enrolment to Total	Share of ST Enrolment to Total	Share of SC Girls to SC Enrolment	Share of ST Girls to ST Enrolment	Literacy Rate (2001)	Female Literacy Rate(2001)
Belgaum	46.38	6.80	13.00	5.74	46.47	47.49	64.42	52.53
Bijapur	53.12	13.10	19.36	1.78	43.65	45.98	57.46	46.19
Bagalkot	47.13	11.03	17.97	5.13	46.35	47.20	57.81	44.10
Dharwad	46.75	7.20	9.94	4.78	47.66	49.62	71.87	62.20
Gadag	48.04	9.23	15.98	5.92	48.26	49.13	66.27	52.58
Haveri	49.13	8.93	13.12	8.77	47.51	49.24	68.09	57.60
Uttara Kannada	49.06	7.15	9.02	2.00	49.25	53.54	76.59	68.48

Contd. ...

Contd. ...

Districts	*Share of Girl Enrolment*	*Percentage of Children out of School*	*Share of SC Enrolment to Total*	*Share of ST Enrolment to Total*	*Share of SC Girls to SC Enrolment*	*Share of ST Girls to ST Enrolment*	*Literacy Rate (2001)*	*Female Literacy Rate (2001)*
Belgaum Division	48.31	8.69	14.23	4.89	46.31	48.30	64.96	53.51
Bellary	46.63	13.17	20.18	18.12	45.57	45.80	58.04	46.16
Bidar	48.95	5.90	23.85	8.62	49.46	49.97	61.98	50.01
Gulbarga	48.14	16.23	23.93	4.04	48.22	33.61	50.65	38.40
Raichur	44.87	15.92	19.33	19.55	43.86	43.72	49.54	36.84
Koppal	47.56	16.31	15.62	10.99	43.87	44.46	55.02	40.76
Gulbarga Division	47.36	13.88	21.38	10.94	46.91	43.97	54.32	41.88
Bangalore	51.07	2.07	21.38	3.50	53.34	52.49	83.91	78.98
Bangalore (Rural)	47.39	3.80	19.44	4.70	48.18	46.07	65.00	55.12
Chitradurga	47.43	7.98	25.17	18.73	48.13	49.29	64.88	54.62
Davanagere	48.94	7.35	22.26	13.02	48.28	49.43	67.67	58.45
Kolar	47.15	5.07	27.94	8.05	48.98	48.46	63.14	52.81
Shimoga	48.98	4.34	32.24	6.40	48.73	48.48	74.86	67.24
Tumkur	48.01	4.84	21.03	8.04	48.10	47.81	67.19	57.18
Bangalore Division	48.87	4.34	23.66	7.70	49.81	49.14	72.40	64.30
Chickmagalur	47.12	5.79	26.60	4.27	47.50	52.22	72.63	64.47
Dakshina Kannada	46.98	2.62	7.43	4.08	47.07	49.02	83.47	77.39
Udupi	47.95	1.42	6.52	8.41	47.84	26.68	79.87	74.02
Hassan	49.75	3.95	21.62	2.03	48.24	48.88	68.75	59.32
Kodagu	47.65	2.61	12.09	7.15	52.90	38.94	78.17	72.53
Mandya	48.78	3.00	14.07	1.28	51.00	51.90	61.21	51.62
Mysore	49.27	4.37	17.87	9.98	46.21	46.03	63.69	55.81
Chamarajanagar	47.96	8.11	28.09	13.88	48.48	48.78	51.26	43.02
Mysore Division	48.37	3.89	16.37	6.10	48.04	44.55	69.40	61.58
North Karnataka	47.88	10.93	17.45	7.62	46.64	45.50	59.64	47.69
South Karnataka	48.68	4.17	20.87	7.09	49.28	47.63	70.90	62.94
State Average	**48.16**	**7.51**	**18.81**	**7.75**	**47.87**	**46.86**	**65.84**	**55.94**
Coefficient of Variation	0.02	0.67	0.33	0.64	0.03	0.04	0.14	0.21

Source: *Education at a Glance 2002-03*, Commissioner Public Instruction, Government of Karnataka.

APPENDIX A-10.5

Share of Households having Access to Safe Drinking Water

District	*1991*	*2001*
Belgaum	64.23	96.00
Bijapur	73.30	98.00
Bagalkot	73.30	96.00
Dharwad	81.51	89.00
Gadag	81.51	93.00
Haveri	81.51	98.00
Uttara Kannada	30.20	94.00
Belgaum Division	68.10	95.19
Bellary	84.21	96.00
Bidar	60.47	98.00
Gulbarga	62.99	97.00

Contd. ...

...Contd. ...

District	*1991*	*2001*
Raichur	65.41	87.00
Koppal	65.41	97.00
Gulbarga Division	68.04	95.12
Bangalore	86.51	99.00
Bangalore Rural	81.97	99.00
Chitradurga	88.11	100.00
Davanagere	88.11	99.00
Kolar	89.78	99.00
Shimoga	66.25	96.00
Tumkur	80.79	99.00
Bangalore Division	84.16	98.82
Chickmagalur	69.46	93.00
Dakshina Kannada	20.01	96.00
Udupi	20.01	97.00
Hassan	79.53	98.00
Kodagu	44.83	91.00
Mandya	71.16	99.00
Mysore	82.70	98.00
Chamarajanagar	82.70	99.00
Mysore Division	62.50	96.99
North Karnataka	68.08	95.16
South Karnataka	73.33	97.90
State Average	**71.68**	**97.00**
Coefficient of Variation	0.28	0.03

Source: *Census of India*, various years.

Chapter 11

Politics, Governance and Service Delivery in Karnataka

"The emerging vision is one of a State that needs to do both more and less. It should be more engaged in providing essential public goods and services such as health care, education and basic infrastructure. It should be less involved in the direct provision of economic goods or in the stifling regulation of the private sector. It should be more accountable and responsive to its citizenry. It should be cleaner, more transparent, more efficient and more effective" (Pradhan, 2002).

11.1 Introduction

Many governance reforms have been initiated in Karnataka in recent years to improve the quality of governance and service delivery. Governance reforms such as privatisation of Government activities (disinvestment outsourcing public private partnership and rightsizing) are initiated to improve the operational efficiency and productivity in administration. Transparency in administration and procurements (right to information, simplification of procedures and single windows) are adopted to minimise resource mis-utilisation and corruption. Anti-corruption institutions (*lokayukta*), citizen charters and people's forums (water and electricity *adalats*) are strengthened to ensure administrative accountability. Sound recruitment, promotion and transfer policies are introduced to minimise political interference in administration. Information communication technology (ICT) is increasingly used in administration to empower citizens with information and speedy delivery of services. Democratic decentralised and stakeholders' institutions (education, health, watershed and forest committees) are strengthened to reflect peoples' voice and needs in governance. Fiscal reforms are also initiated for effective utilisation of resources to prevent the crisis of the type that many other states are facing. At the same time civil society organisations including non-governmental organisations (NGOs) and corporate sector are collaborating with the government to improve the quality of governance and service delivery.

Keeping this in view, this Chapter mainly focuses on the implications of governance reforms on service delivery and the role of development politics (state and civil society) in facilitating reforms in Karnataka. The first section deals with the significance of governance reforms on service delivery and governance issues in Karnataka. The second section focuses on governance initiatives in Karnataka for the past decade by critically reviewing recommendations of various committee reports and policy initiatives. The third section reviews the implications of governance reforms (privatisation, transparency, ICT, anti-corruption institution and participation) on service delivery in terms of efficiency (speedy delivery, cost reduction and accessibility of service), accountability, and equity (benefits for disadvantaged groups and areas/regions). The fourth section deals with the role of state and civil society (including corporate sector and international development agencies) in promoting governance reforms in Karnataka. Finally the chapter comes with the policy perspectives. The analysis in the chapter is based mainly on the government documents, newspaper reports and interviews.

11.2 Significance of Governance Reforms on Service Delivery

Ensuring good governance so as to promote security to life and property and to provide adequate quantity and quality of goods and services at a lesser cost to the satisfaction of the people including the disadvantaged groups (such as SC, ST, backward class and minorities) has been a central issue for many governments in recent years. People's expectations from the government are very high and they do change the governments quite often to get the best services and comforts. For instance, defeat of 50-70 per cent of incumbent governments and sitting legislators in elections reflect this trend. Even the people do not hesitate to protest against the government and ruling elite to get better quality of services (increasing number of protest and radical movements reflects this trend). On the other hand, government's resource crunch and poor performance make it increasingly difficult for the government to meet even the basic needs of the people such as water, sanitation, health, education and so on. Government has limited resources and skilled manpower to serve the poor in remote rural areas (Sangita, 2001). Besides this, the outcomes from the government spending of available resources are not on the expected lines. Wastage and leakages in the execution of projects and their poor maintenance escalate the cost of goods and services provided by the government. Even these services are of poor quality and not in tune with the preferences of the people.

Non-transparent and centralised decision making, obsolete laws and complex procedures, bloated and unmotivated bureaucracy, political interference in the day-to-day administration and corruption further affect the quality of public services. Governments have been introducing new mechanisms, techniques, principles and practices in administration to promote good governance, although some of these reforms are influenced by developments like globalisation, economic reforms, revolutionary changes in ICT and public administration discipline (Sangita, 2001).

11.3 Governance Issues in Karnataka

The important governance issues in Karnataka are increasing expenditure on bureaucracy on the one hand and the need to provide basic services and infrastructural facilities for overall development of the people on the other.

11.3.1 Growth of the Government

The Indian state has grown 5-6 times over the years, although it is not uniform across the levels and types of government (central, state, local and quasi). The growth of manpower has doubled at the Central Government level from 15.14 in 1951 to 34.10 lakh employees in 1991 which however declined slightly to 32.73 in 2000 (Table 11.1). While increase was 3 to 4 times at the state and local government levels and 19 times in quasi governments up to 1996, (from 3 lakhs in 1951 to 64.58 lakhs in 1996) but there was a drastic slowdown in 2000 to 63.26 lakh. Similarly, there was a five-fold increase in the strength of the Indian Administrative Service (IAS), which takes major responsibility in the governance of the country. Its strength had gone up to 5,000 in 2000 from 957 in 1951.

Similar trend was seen in Karnataka where a little less than three-fourths of employment in the organised sector came from government as against 28.3 per cent

TABLE 11.1

Staff Strength at the Centre, State, Quasi and Local Governments in India: 1951-2000

Year	*Central Government*		*State Government*		*Quasi Government*		*Local Government*		*Total*
	Number (in Lakh)	*%*	*Number (in Lakh)*	*%*	*Number (in Lakh)*	*%*	*Number (in Lakh)*	*%*	*(in Lakh)*
1951	15.14	35.49	18.45	43.25	3.00	7.03	6.05	14.18	42.64
1956	18.58	35.49	22.65	43.27	3.68	7.03	7.43	14.19	52.34
1961	20.9	29.64	30.14	42.75	7.73	10.96	11.73	16.63	70.50
1966	26.36	28.10	37.23	39.69	13.18	14.05	17.01	18.13	93.78
1971	27.71	25.82	41.52	38.69	19.29	17.97	18.78	17.50	107.30
1976	30.47	22.87	48.97	35.75	33.92	25.46	19.85	14.9	133.21
1981	31.95	20.63	56.76	36.65	45.76	29.55	20.37	13.15	154.84
1986	33.48	18.94	64.78	36.64	56.73	32.09	21.79	12.33	176.78
1991	34.10	17.89	71.12	37.31	62.22	32.64	23.13	12.13	190.57
1996	33.66	17.32	74.14	38.15	64.58	33.23	21.92	11.28	194.30
2000	32.73	13.99	74.60	31.90	63.26	27.05	22.26	27.05	200.88

Source: Dr. K.N. Reddy, "Absorption of Manpower in Government: 1951-74", *Manpower Journal*, June 1976, p.61; *Economic Survey*, Government of India.

in the private sector in 1986-87. The employees in the government have doubled in numbers within 20 years (1967-87). The total number of employees in government including local bodies and public undertakings (PUs) was 5.1 lakhs in 1967. There was a steady increase in the size of the government. The total strength of government employees was 1.79 lakh in 1972 excluding local bodies and PUs. It rose to 6.03 lakh in 2002 (Appendix A-11.1).

Among the different groups of employees, increase in Group B was significant. The main reason for increase of Group B posts was due to considerable expansion in the activities of certain departments coupled with the upgradation of a number of posts. However, the decline in Group D is due to conversion of many posts to Group C. On the other hand, in public sector, there were 1.59 lakh employees in 1987-88 as against 1.61 in 1991-94 (Sangita, 1998) (Table 11.2).

TABLE 11.2

Group-wise Details of Employees in Karnataka

Year	*In Percentage*				*Total*
	A	*B*	*C*	*D*	*(in hundreds)*
1993-94	2.97	5.10	70.89	21.04	4177
1994-95	2.83	5.22	74.15	17.80	4236
1995-96	3.12	4.96	76.01	15.91	4519
1996-97	2.91	4.74	77.44	14.91	4703
1997-98	2.82	4.37	77.52	15.30	4648
1999-00	3.15	5.15	78.58	13.12	4892

Source: Statistical Abstract of Karnataka, 1998-99.

The growth in other categories of officials was also quite significant. For instance, the strength of the secretaries to the government departments doubled during 1958 and 1985 and likewise in respect of the other categories of secretaries also which increased substantially (Table 11.3).

TABLE 11.3

Year-wise Strength of Secretaries in Karnataka

Year	*Secretaries*	*Addl. Secretaries*	*Joint Secretaries*	*Deputy Secretaries*	*Under Secretaries*	*Total*
1958	14	0	0	6	45	65
1968	14	1	3	29	67	114
1978	19	4	9	48	112	192
1985	28	6	11	59	162	266

Source: Compiled from the *Annual Reports*, Government of Karnataka.

Even the same trend is evident, if one looks at the increase in government servants per thousand population and expenditure on salaries over these years. Government employees per thousand population had gone up to 9 in 1972-73 from 6 in 1959-60. However, it was 10.85 in 1989, which is somewhat closer to the all-India average of 11.24. In other words, in terms of the standard measure, the size of bureaucracy in Karnataka is not very high as compared to the states like Maharashtra (14.53), Jammu and Kashmir (20.45), Orissa (12.39), Punjab (16.23), Rajasthan (13.18) and Tamil Nadu (13.59) (Sangita, 1998).

Further, on closer examination we find that the number of employees per 1000 population in some departments was slightly lower in Karnataka. In 1991-92, it was 1.4 in Health and Family Welfare, 3.76 in Education and 1.18 in Police Department (Sangita, 1998). Education constitutes 40 per cent of the total government workforce in 2002 (Appendix A-11.1) with Home (13.2 per cent) and Health (11.96 per cent) following it.

Salaries constituted 31.0 per cent of the total revenue expenditure in 1970-71. The percentage had gone up to 34.8 in 1991 and it had come down to 27.69 in 2002 (Table 11.4). The revision of pay scales in 1991 and 2000 was mainly responsible for increased percentage. This is slightly higher than the safety limit of 25 per cent. In other words, expenditure on salaries was Rs. 263 crores in 1980-81 as against Rs. 702.19 crores in 1986-87 (Sangita, 1998; KARC, 2001) (Appendix A-11.2).

TABLE 11.4

Expenditure on Salaries as Proportion to Revenue and Total Expenditure

Year	*% of Revenue Expenditure Karnataka*	*% of Total Expenditure Karnataka*
1981	31.80	23.73
1986	23.80	22.88
1991	34.80	—
1996	25.49	23.07
2000	27.25	23.09
2002	27.69	22.48

Source: Compiled from the *Annual Reports*, p. 66; *India Fourth Pay Commission*, 1986, p. 66; *Karnataka Fourth Pay Commission*, 1993, p. 50.

The per capita expenditure on salaries in public sector undertakings (PSUs) has doubled from Rs. 21,901 in 1987-88 to Rs. 57,846 in 1993-94. Most of the PSUs were incurring huge losses which was around 35.17 crores in 1990-91 out of the total investment of Rs. 6,948.63 crores. The accumulated loss of 78 PSUs was around Rs. 993 crores (Rao, 2001). Nine of them have been declared sick and another 4 under liquidation (Rajiv, 2004).

The State Legislative Committee on Public Undertakings (PUs) recommended for privatisation of PSUs (including disinvestment, merger and sale of unproductive assets). It also suggested for appointment of Managing Directors (MDs) of 45 years of age with specific purpose, standards and reasonable degree of freedom to operate. The MDs as far as possible, are to be promoted from among those whose careers are linked with the organisation activities. The productivity of the government servants in Karnataka appears to be low. On an average, the government servant works two hours in a day (Sangita, 1998; Third Pay Commission and KARC, 2001).

11.3.2 State Finances

State finances are not encouraging both in terms of revenue and expenditure side. Growth in tax revenues was low; non-tax revenues were stagnant; the salary bill was pushed upwards by the Fifth Pay Commission award; loss-making public enterprises were a growing drain on the state finances. Besides this, weak fiscal position of the state's local bodies and unmerit subsidies are also causes of concern. The ratio of tax revenue to gross state domestic product (GSDP) has fallen from 9.3 per cent in 1990-91 to 8.2 per cent in 1999-00. The ratio of non-tax revenue to GSDP has shown a decline from 2.2 per cent in 1990-91 to 1.17 per cent in 1999-00, mainly due to low and declining cost recoveries from non-merit public services and poor performance of the public enterprises. Implicit subsidies due to uneconomic pricing of irrigation and drinking water supply, higher and technical education and urban health services amount to about 1.2 per cent of GSDP. Cost recovery in irrigation in the state is only a fraction of the corresponding figures prevailing in the neighbouring states. (Rao, 2001; Khuntia, 2003). At the same time, the non-plan expenditure accounts for 70.72 per cent as against 73.90 and 74.50 per cent for neighbouring and all states respectively as shown in the Table 11.5 (NHDR, 2002) and (Figure 11.1).

11.3.3 Problems of Service Delivery

Karnataka's rank in terms of Human Development Index (in terms of life expectancy, infant mortality rate, and literacy), position has slipped to 7 in 2001 from 6 in 1981 as shown in the Table 11.6 while Tamil Nadu improved it to 3rd position from 6th during the same period (Figure 11.2).

TABLE 11.5

Karnataka's Status in Regard to Public Spending (%) 1998-99

	Karnataka	*Neighbouring States*	*All-India*
Plan	29.28	26.10	25.49
Non-plan	70.72	73.90	74.51
Revenue	85.95	87.88	86.48
Capital	14.05	12.13	13.52

Source: NHDR 2001: 286.

FIGURE 11.1

Karnataka Status in Regard to Public Spending: 1998-99

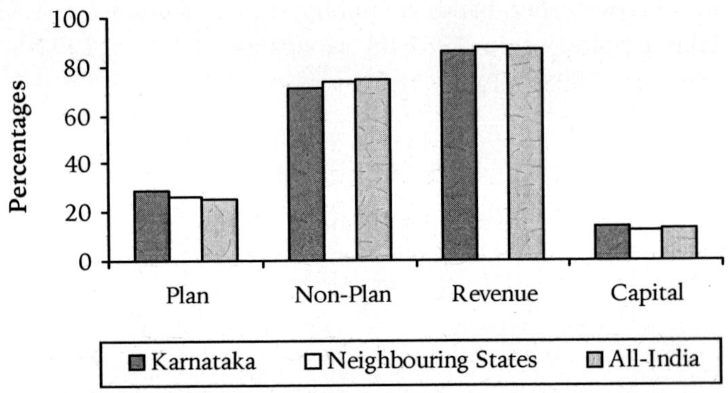

TABLE 11.6

Human Development Index for Indian States

States/UTs	1981		1991		2001	
	Value	*Rank*	*Value*	*Rank*	*Value*	*Rank*
Andhra Pradesh	0.298	9	0.377	9	0.416	10
Assam	0.272	10	0.348	10	0.386	14
Bihar	0.237	15	0.308	15	0.367	15
Gujarat	0.360	4	0.431	6	0.479	6
Haryana	0.360	5	0.443	5	0.509	5
Karnataka	**0.346**	**6**	**0.412**	**7**	**0.478**	**7**
Kerala	0.500	1	0.591	1	0.638	1
Madhya Pradesh	0.245	14	0.328	13	0.394	12
Maharashtra	0.363	3	0.452	4	0.523	4
Orissa	0.267	11	0.345	12	0.404	11
Punjab	0.411	2	0.475	2	0.537	2
Rajasthan	0.256	12	0.347	11	0.424	9
Tamil Nadu	0.343	7	0.466	3	0.531	3
Uttar Pradesh	0.255	13	0.314	14	0.388	13
West Bengal	0.305	8	0.404	8	0.472	8
All-India	**0.302**	**0**	**0.381**	**0**	**0.472**	**0**

Source: National Human Development Report 2001, Planning Commission, 2002, GoI.

FIGURE 11.2

Human Development Index for India

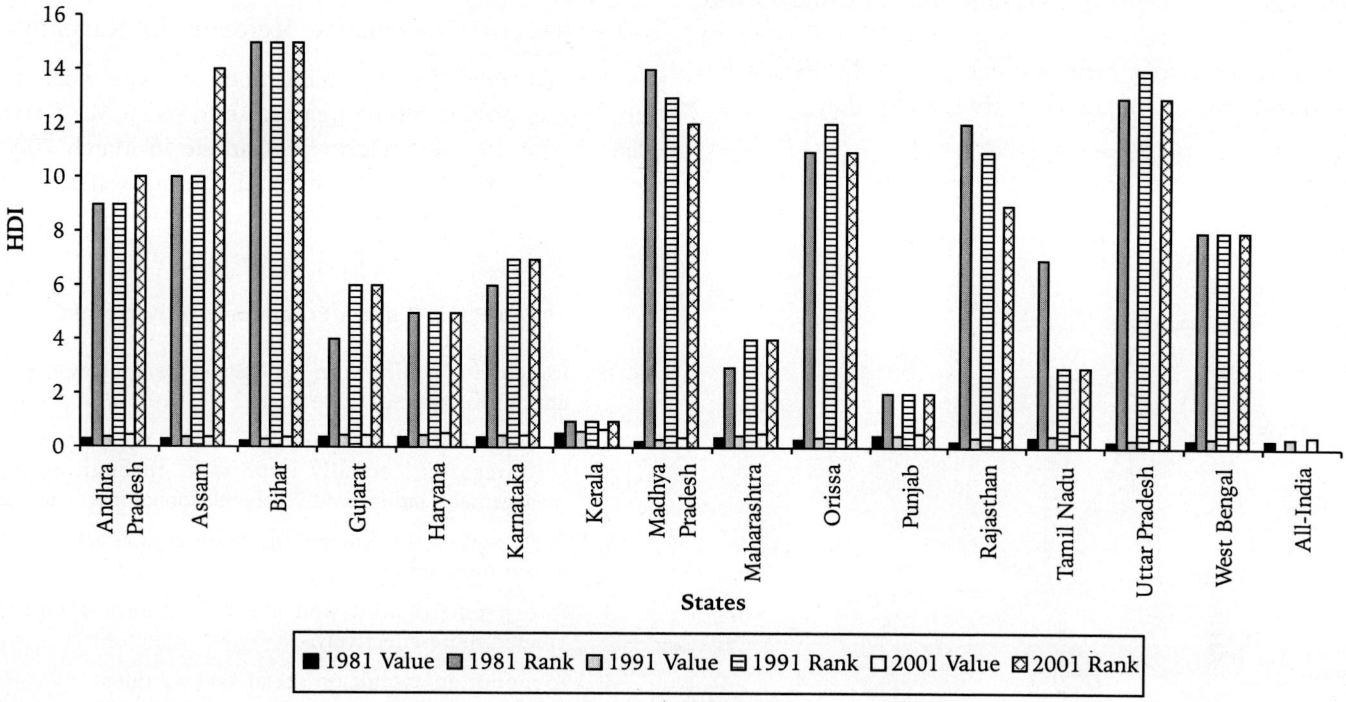

Besides this, service delivery system in most of the sectors has not been satisfactory (Paul, 1995; Paul and Sekher, 2000). The Government institutions are not effective in delivering the goods and services to the poor. For instance, no candidate was qualified in IAS preliminary examination during 2001 in spite of imparting training to 60 candidates for 12 months. Similarly, the institution meant for the development of backward castes, failed to produce desired results, in spite of spending huge money for the same purpose (KARC, 2001: 143). The success rate of the SSLC level in the municipal corporation school is far below the (20-25 per cent) 50 per cent at the state level (KARC, 2001: 71-2).

Non-enrolment of children to schools is relatively high (6 out of 14 children do not enrol and dropout rate is very high (around 35 per cent). Transition rate from higher primary schools to high school is also low (only 25 per cent). Further, Karnataka's per student expenditure on education is far less than that of the neighbouring states—Tamil Nadu, (Rs. 298), Maharashtra (Rs. 313) and Kerala, (Rs. 368). Karnataka had spent 3.20 per cent of its SDP on education in 2001. Karnataka provides primary school for every 300 population as against 200 suggested by the Central Government (KARC, 2001: 68). The teacher and student ratio remains 43 students per teacher (KARC, 200: 68). Literacy rate in the state has increased from 30 per cent in 1967 to 63.42 per cent in 1996 and to 67.04 per cent in 2001. However, regional disparities are very high with Raichur district recording 36 per cent as against 76.3 per cent for Bangalore (KARC, 2001: 68).

The funds earmarked for the poor are not reaching them. Leakages and wastages in poverty alleviation, food and social security programmes such as old age, widows and disabled persons are very high. Ten to 15 per cent of the scholarship amount is not reaching the targeted beneficiaries identified by the Social Welfare Department. Delays, irregularities and non-receipt of scholarships are very common (KARC, 2001: 138). Non-poor are the major gainers of the food security programme. Bogus and ineligible ration cardholders are higher rather than the poor households (112.72 lakh card holders as against 81.78 lakh households in 2001) (KARC, 2001: 179). Irregular functioning of fair price shops, non-display of stocks and non-functioning of vigilance committees are all coming in the way of the poor in availing the benefits (KARC, 200: 182).

The phenomenon of speed money and corruption has become one of the major issues in administration (Sangita, 1995), although Karnataka is less corrupt For instance, according to survey done by a leading magazine *India Today*, (November 24, 1997), Karnataka's corruption was estimated at 6 per cent along with Tamil Nadu, Maharashtra, Gujarat, Haryana and Orissa. Bihar has the highest percentage of 10 followed by Uttar Pradesh 8 per cent. As per the study, Kerala has the lowest rate of 3 per cent (Figure 11.3).

FIGURE 11.3

Corruption Graph

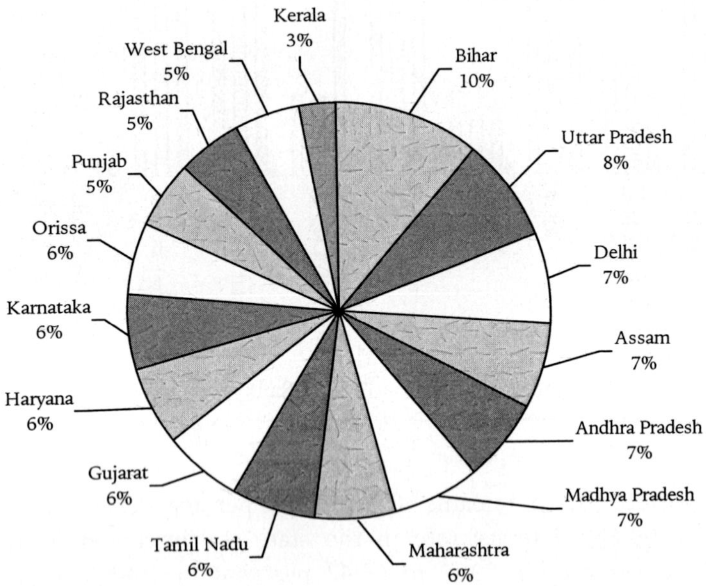

It is believed that 20 to 30 per cent of illicit money is siphoned-off from government contracts and purchases due to lack of transparency and excess of discretionary powers. Corruption at the grassroot level administration has become a way of life. In rural areas nothing moves without speed money in public offices. People are compelled to pay bribes to get government services and facilities such as certificates, licence, *khata* transfers, building plan approvals, and registration of properties and admission in schools and hospitals. Approval of sub-standard works (roads, buildings and hospitals) and procurement of poor quality of goods (medicines, materials, agricultural inputs) and their implementations are very common. Stealing of power, water (through unauthorised connections) and essential items (of public distribution system) and encroachment and misuse of government properties are very frequent. Misappropriation of funds meant for rural development and weaker sections have been reported widely (Sangita, 2003). Corruption in the state has been institutionalised and rates have been fixed for various services. The *Lokayukta*'s recent raids had resulted in the unearthing of 15 scams involving public money to the tune of Rs 1,000-1,500 crores (Sangita, 2003).

11.4 Recent Governance Reforms in Karnataka

Immediately after State Elections in September 1999, the new government headed by Sri S.M. Krishna launched a 10-point reform programme in March 2000 to promote all round development of the state (Box 11.1).

BOX 11.1

Ten-Point Reform Programme in Karnataka

1. To achieve a minimum of 7-8 per cent growth per annum for the next five years.
2. To expand the state's infrastructure, through more resources but, equally important, through better management and innovative organisational mechanisms.
3. To strengthen the foundations of agriculture and give it a new momentum.
4. To expand irrigation and utilise irrigation potential created more effectively.
5. To mount an assault on social backwardness.
6. To give top-most priority to eradicate poverty, empower women, and provide food and nutritional security for vulnerable sections.
7. To bring into the mainstream the backward regions, particularly the north, into the development process.
8. To provide a conducive climate for new investments.
9. To develop a fiscal system that serves the needs of the poor, a pattern of public expenditures that addresses pressing socio-economic concerns and that keeps the state away from a debt trap.
10. To provide the people of Karnataka with a transparent, responsible, responsive and decentralised government.

In his 2001 Budget Speech, the Chief Minister of Karnataka identified reforms in the key areas such as infrastructure and social sectors, governance and agricultural development. The reforms are aimed to create necessary conditions for the eradication of poverty through economic growth with equity (Khuntia, 2003). At the same time, the state government is determined to restore fiscal balance, improve the standards of physical and social infrastructure in the state and ensure competitive advantage for the private sector (Khuntia, 2003). Karnataka has been spending more on irrigation agriculture and social sector. The expenditure on these sectors was slightly higher in comparison to neighbouring and the other states as shown in the Table 11.7.

TABLE 11.7

Percentage of Sectoral Composition of Actual Plan Expenditure: 1997-98

	Karnataka	*Neighbouring States*	*Central Government*
Agriculture and Irrigation	36.29	21.06	3.60
Rural and Social Sector	40.21	41.21	23.40
Social Sector	32.31	25.23	14.80
Infrastructure	23.50	37.73	73.00

Source: NHDR 2001: 287.

FIGURE 11.4

Karnataka Status in Regard to Public Spending on Various Sectors: 1997-98

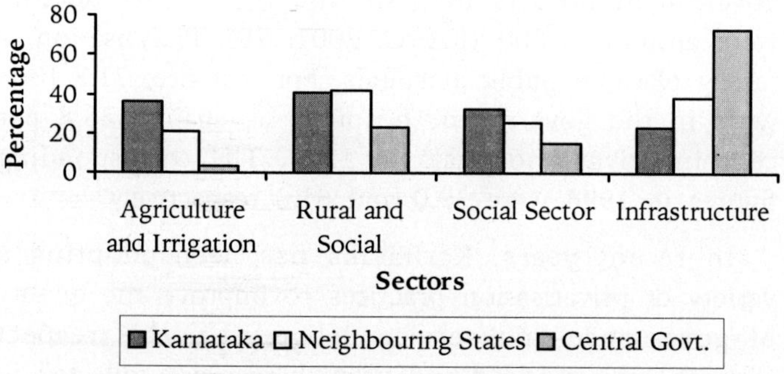

Despite the economic difficulties, the government has succeeded in increasing expenditure in the priority areas like social sectors and human capital formation from Rs. 4,578 crore in 1999-00 to Rs.5,021 in 2000-01 and to Rs. 5,211 crore in 2001-02, an increase of 13.8 per cent in just two years. The government is targeting a growth of at least 10 per cent in each of these categories in the years to come (Khuntia, 2003) (Tables 11.8 and 11.9, Figures 11.5 and 11.6).

TABLE 11.8

Percentage of Public Spending on Education and Health: 1997-98

	Karnataka	*Neighbouring States*	*Central Government*
Education	2.92	2.74	0.50
Health	1.01	1.13	0.25

Source: NHDR 2001: 291.

FIGURE 11.5

Public Spending on Education and Health: 1997-98

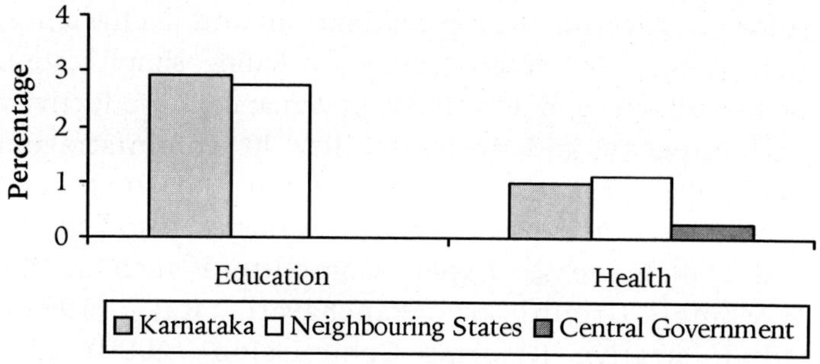

TABLE 11.9

Percentage of Composition of Public Spending—Some Critical Ratios : 1998-99

	Karnataka	*Neighbouring States*	*All-India*
Public Expenditure Ratio	16.48	16.29	-
Development Expenditure Ratio	67.05	62.97	61.76
Social Sector Expenditure Ratio	35.41	34.56	33.07
Education Expenditure Ratio	17.94	17.29	17.39
Health Expenditure Ratio	06.02	06.77	05.78
Amenities Expenditure Ratio	04.79	04.22	04.53
Other Social Expenditure Ratio	06.90	06.29	05.38

Source: NHDR 2001: 290.

FIGURE 11.6

Composition of Public Spending—Some Critical Ratios: 1998-99

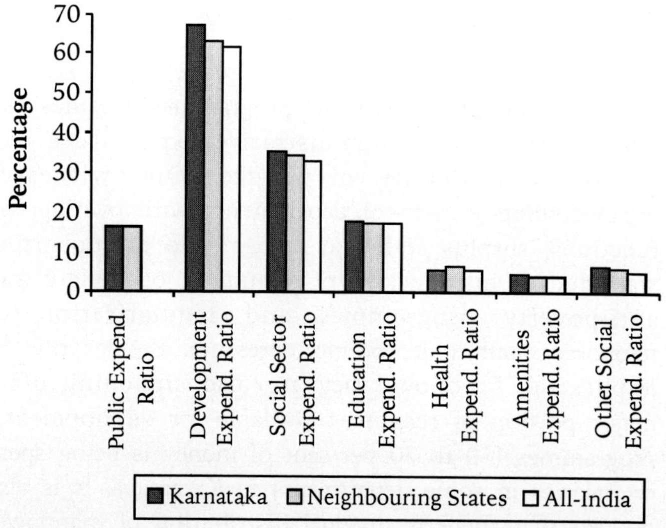

11.5 Governance Reforms and Service Delivery

This section deals with the ongoing governance reforms and their implication on service delivery. The reforms covered are: privatisation and rightsizing, transparency and accountability (including simplification of procedures and electronic governance), productivity and integrity and accountability in administration (transfers, *Lokayukta* and citizen charter) and decentralised and participatory governance (rural, urban and stakeholders). Expert Committees such as the Working Group on Panchayati Raj (1999), Administrative Reforms Commission (2000), Tax Reforms Commission (2000) and Revenue Reforms Commission (2002) were appointed to make administration efficient, effective, transparent, responsive, and accountable. Eight task forces are constituted on agriculture, education, health, infrastructure, urban development and bio and information technology which comprise of eminent persons drawn from professional, private and civil society organisations in 2000 to meticulously study and give recommendations for the promotion of all round development of the state.

11.5.1 Privatisation and Rightsizing

Privatisation promotes efficiency by exposing services to high degree of public competition for ultimate benefit of the consumers. Privatisation also helps to attract specialised talent from outside the government. Outsourcing enables the government to hold the private companies accountable for their performances and delivery of services, which in turn would improve efficiency and reduce costs and the surplus staff (KARC, 2001: 419).

Rightsizing, rationalisation and reduction of staff or reorganisation of departments/programmes/schemes can help to reduce the administrative expenditure and improve the quality of service. One witnesses mushrooming growth of departments with overlapping functions, surplus staff and higher ratio of supporting staff due to introduction of a number of welfare and anti-poverty programmes and regularisation of temporary staff under political pressure. Besides this by duplicating functions they are also siphoning off a major portion of resources available for developmental programmes (50 to 70 per cent of money is being spent on salaries in some departments in Karnataka. It is also noticed that there is unequal distribution of manpower across the departments and state and district governments. For instance, the staff strength in block and villages level organisations is not commensurate with their respective responsibilities.

Privatisation has become quite popular in Karnataka. It is going in a big way in the education and health sectors for quite some time. For instance, the ratio of government to private school was 96.19 in 1969, which has gradually come down to 85.84 per cent in 1998 (KARC, 2001: 68). Fifteen per cent of primary schools and 65 per cent of high schools are under private management (KARC, 2001: 70) Similarly, the proportion of government and private managed professional colleges were 65 and 35 per cent respectively in 1991. But now it is the other way round i.e., 40 and 60 per cent respectively in 2003.

Privatisation is also evident in health sector: 35 per cent out of 17,000 practising doctors in Karnataka were government doctors in 2001 and the private doctors were around 11,000 (KARC, 2001: 75). Privatisation is taking place in public hospitals. For instance, 71.2 beds were in the government hospitals as against 28.8 per cent in private hospitals in 1973. The corresponding figures in 1996 were 39.0 and 61.0 respectively.

In recent years, Karnataka has been adopting a variety of privatisation practices to improve the quality of governance and service delivery. In this respect services are privatised and user charges are collected in major hospitals. Two PHCs are now being run in collaboration with NGOs where they have also been given the permission to raise additional funds for recurring expenses of PHCs. (KARC, 2001: 416). The government hospital in Raichur was privatised. Privatisation is much more visible in urban areas.

Privatisation is also encouraged through competition by opening-up service providers to multiple actors in the place of single supplier in Karnataka. It is in this connection, the Karnataka State Road Transport Corporation (KSRTC) was divided into Bangalore Metropolitan Transport Corporation (BMTC in 1997), North West Karnataka Road Transport Corporation (NWKRTC) (1997), and North East Karnataka Road Transport Corporation (NEKRTC) (2000) to improve the quality of service delivery in the field of public transportation. Similarly the Electricity Board has been corporatised and generation has been separated from transmission and distribution. Four new distribution companies are constituted—for Bangalore Mangalore Hubli-Dharwad and Gulbarga regions to supply electricity in the respective region of the state.

Bangalore is the first city, where activities like collection and disposal of solid waste management, maintenance of street lights and water supply are privatised. Government activities are also outsourced for cleaning of roads, transport of solid waste, parking of vehicles and so on, although similar initiatives were taken in education, health, power and other sectors. Autonomy to the managers for producing results has also been stipulated as a part of privatisation. The government has already taken a decision to appoint doctors on contract basis for the PHCs (KARC, 2001: 401). Chief executives in organisations like Bangalore Development Authority (BDA), BWSSB and BMTC are given autonomy to the executives to achieve the targets.

The KARC (2001) has suggested a number of reforms after the functional review of 11 major departments. They include: reduction of departments and surplus staff after rationalisation of roles, outsourcing of government activities and de-layer of file circulation in the Secretariat. It has found the phenomenon of proliferation of quasi-governmental agencies (public enterprises and government-financed societies) and multiple departments and schemes with overlapping functions. It has identified 3,331 schemes of which 154 are sponsored and 81 are Central Plan Schemes. There are 658 schemes in the ZP sector (both plan and non-plan) and the remaining are in the state sector (Table 11.10). Most of these schemes have similar sounding names as well as similar objectives and purposes and are purely meant for salary and other administrative costs. Similarly, it has identified surplus staff and recommended for their abolition.

TABLE 11.10

Details about the Number of Schemes in Karnataka (Category-wise)

Category (Rs. in Lakhs)	*No. of Schemes*	*Percentage*
Less than 1 lakh	166	6.21
1-2 lakhs	95	3.55
2-5 lakhs	229	8.57
5-10 lakhs	295	11.04
10-50 lakhs	704	26.34
50-100 lakhs	298	11.15
More than 100 lakhs	886	33.15
Total	**2673**	**100.00**

Source: Compiled from KARC.

The KARC has also recommended for outsourcing of the housekeeping services like cleaning of offices, sanitation, gardening, security, etc. The committee felt that the upkeep of government offices has never evoked any sense of appreciation either from the government employees or from the visitors. It is difficult for the government to exercise adequate control over the housekeeping employees. The government is not getting adequate returns from the investment made in terms of salaries, pensions, etc. to those employees engaged in housekeeping (KARC, 2001: 416).

The KARC stressed the need for outsourcing of catering, dietary and security services in the government offices, (food, tea, coffee and other beverages and security) jails and student and welfare hostels (dietary services) to reduce pilferage and wastage and provide better quality food at a reasonable prices. The committee has also recommended for outsourcing of various services in departments like sericulture (soil testing, infection and distribution of chemicals), industry (industrial promotion, conduct of exhibitions, research and so on) and agriculture (seed production and distribution, supply of machineries and equipments, fertilisers and pesticides and storage facility). (This would facilitate to abolish many posts and thereby substantial savings (KARC, 2001: 416.) The committee also suggested for the abolition of vacant posts. Some of these recommendations were accepted by the government. The posts of Divisional Commissioners were abolished and plans are drawn for abolishing the remaining posts in other departments.

Public-private partnership is also popular in Karnataka. The Bangalore Agenda Task Force (BATF), which has been discussed elsewhere, is testimony in this regard. The main aim is to make Bangalore, the best city in India by 2004 AD by upgradation of managerial and financial capacities of civic administrative stakeholders.

The state government has taken many initiatives to improve the performance of PSUs and constituted the following committees. They include: Committee to Evaluate State Government Policies towards PSUs (1998), formation of Cabinet Sub-Committee on PSUs (1998), and Public Restructuring Commission (PRC) (2000). Besides this, High Power Committee under the chairmanship of Chief Secretary (2000) Department of Disinvestment and Public Sector Enterprise Reforms (2002) in the place of Karnataka State Bureau of Public Enterprise (KSBPE) to oversee the reform process have been constituted.

As a result of these efforts, privatisation has been extended to PSUs through closure or disinvestment. Out of 100 loss-making units, 20 were closed (which resulted in loss of jobs for 10,000 employees), another 20 were disinvested, 40 were restructured and in another 40 voluntary retirement scheme was introduced (Rajiv, 2004).

11.5.2 Transparency and Simplification of Regulations and Procedure Transparency

Dissemination of information provides transparency and empowers the citizens to ensure accountability and prevent the corruption in administration. In fact, administrative delays and corruption are due to complex and non-transparent administrative procedures (Sangita, 1995). In many developing countries including India, regulations are often complex and some times inconsistent. Weak implementation of laws and regulations results in the flouting of rules and corrupt practices. Such violations are more where administrators enjoy vast discretionary powers. Sound regulations, simple and transparent administrative procedures and effective communication can help achieve good governance and service delivery. First, rationalisation and simplification of the vast number of regulations and procedures cut short delays and minimise corruption. Secondly, new regulations and laws are essential to ensure accountability and supply of quality goods and services by the private and public sector without harming the interest of the larger society. In this regard, regulatory authorities, consumer laws and laws relating to child labour, environment pollution and so on are to be strengthened to prevent both market and state from human rights violations. Removal of obsolete laws and discretionary powers, simplification of procedures to avoid administrative bottlenecks and constitution of single windows ensures speedy disposal of cases. Similarly, transparency and e-governance also ensure efficiency in administration. In this connection many initiatives have been taken in Karnataka. They include de-layering of files in the Secretariat, single file and single window system have been introduced in the Secretariat and the Electricity Regulatory Authority has come into existence.

Transparency and publicity have received prominent place in Karnataka's reforms. Two major Acts, in this regard are: Transparency in Public Procurement (2000) and Right to Information Act (2000). All government departments strictly maintain transparency in tendering and procurement of the materials, etc. A cell in the Finance Department was established to provide guidance on the Act (Beschel, 2003: 250). Besides this a website has been launched to update the latest circulars and amendments.

The implementation of the Right to information Act has progressed since July 2002. Appellate Authorities in the departments are appointed for disclosure of information including *suo motu*. Efforts are made to bring awareness among the government bodies and citizens about the Act through periodical review and training. For instance, the incorporation of module on Right to Information in the satellite-based training for GP members is one such instance. As a result of this Act, the information flow cycle time in the Bangalore Mahanagara Palike has come down drastically from 48 days to 48 hours. Similarly, now the tenders are being quoted at a price between 15-20 per cent, which is lower than before.

Transparency has also brought in financial administration to ensure accountability. Karnataka is the first state to fall in line with the Government of India policy of putting financial accounts on the Internet on monthly basis. The computerisation of treasuries enabled prompt and timely financial management and prevention of any abuse as noted by Subhash C. Khuntia, 2003.

The BMP has introduced fund based accounting system (FBAS) to bring transparency and accountability in BMC spending and accounting. As part of this, complete financial information about budget allocation, expenditure, and revenue collection and progress of works are given to the corroborators/ward members and citizen for assessing the quality of works.

11.5.3 Simplification of Laws Regulations and Procedures

Recently many changes have been brought in the administrative methods and procedures on the basis of Tax and Administrative Reforms Commissions and *Lokayukta*'s suggestions. An Official Committee has been set up to guide the simplification of rules, acts and procedures. All departments were asked to list out their various enactments for making procedures simple and citizen-friendly. Single file and desk officer systems, and level jumping in the scrutiny of files, have been adopted by most departments in the Secretariat to speed up decision making on the suggestions of KARC (GSAP, 2003: 7).

Similarly, rationalisation of taxes and simplification of procedures in Commercial Taxes, Road and Transport (RT), and Stamps and Registration (SR) Departments were undertaken for better tax compliance on Tax Reforms Commissions' (TRC) suggestions. Policy initiatives have also been under consideration for introduction of the VAT and abolition of the turnover entry and sales tax. Initiatives such as abolition of stamp paper, rationalisation of stamp duty and creations of Central Valuation Committee were taken up to prevent irregularities in the SR Department.

The BMP has simplified the procedure regarding trade licences, permits, building plans approvals and payment of property taxes. In this regard, simplified booklets explaining the procedures are brought out. Birth and death certificates are also computerised in BMP. BMP is planning to introduce the online payment of property taxes, customer complaint system, solid waste management monitoring system and e-procurement system.

Changes are also affected in government offices to control mal-administration and corruption on the basis of *Lokayukta*'s suggestion. Administrative procedures such as the formats for inpatients and outpatient admissions, display of stocks in hospitals, new procedures in RTOs' and Sub Registrars and other offices to prevent corruption can be mentioned in this regard (Sangita, 2003).

Government has also introduced reforms in industrial sector for facilitating investment in the state. The Government simplified procedures by developing a single, new common application form to replace 16 existing forms for establishing a business. The number of registers and returns currently required to be maintained and submitted by industries has been reduced from 24 to 4. A number of 'single windows' for separate industries are being amalgamated, and procedures for receiving approvals for building permits are being streamlined by the introduction of a common building code. The Government is also making serious efforts to tackle the problem of the 'inspection raj' by introducing computer-generated random sampling and other improvements in transparency.

11.5.4 E-Governance (Speedy Delivery and Better Access)

e-governance not only reduces paper work, but also facilitates speedy communication and effective coordination. This ultimately reduces red-tapism and corruption in providing better service at a lesser cost (Meena, 2002; Sangita and Bikash, 2004). Accessibility of information through websites and internet enables people to participate in formulation, implementation and monitoring of government policies. First the accessibility of information on websites enables citizens to improve the quality of life. For instance, displaying the information about the market prices of agricultural commodity helps the farmers to get the competitive prices. Secondly, the information also helps to correct the government functioning and redress the grievances. People can lodge complaints regarding the non-functioning of the borewells, non-attendance of the teachers to the district administration through internet.

Most of the government departments in Karnataka have computerised their activities to provide responsive and transparent administration. Karnataka is the pioneering state in the use of ICT in administration. It established a computer centre as early as 1971 to undertake computerisation in government departments. The government is planning to establish a 'Centre for e-governance' to provide guidance and technical support for speedy and effective use of ICT for the benefit of the common man. The important projects undertaken by the government are: Bhoomi, Khajane Kaveri and Mahithi/service centres (Box 11.2).

BOX 11.2

Bhoomi (Computerisation of Land Records)

Two crore rural land records belonging to over 67 lakh farmers have been computerised in Karnataka through Bhoomi Project. Citizens can obtain land records with ownership and crop details to obtain loans from banks through 177 government kiosks. This facility has helped the farmers not only to secure land records speedily without speed money and middlemen but also save time and money for visiting government offices where they are harassed by corrupt officials. Now, the farmers can obtain copy of their land records (details of rights, tenancy and crops) within 30 minutes by paying Rs.15.00 as against 3-30 days under the earlier manual system.

Nearly 66 per cent of the people were able to utilise the Bhoomi kiosks without any assistance. Seventy-eight per cent of the users found the system to be very simple. Nearly 79 per cent of users of Bhoomi kiosks did not have to meet officials except the counter staff and it provided only error free documents to nearly 74 per cent with a minimal waiting time 10 minutes for the users 79 per cent. The most redeeming features is that corruption and bribery was restricted and 66 per cent of them reported that they did not indulge in paying bribes. (Chawla, 2001), *http://www.bangaloreit.com/html/egovern/Bhoomifrm.html.*

Computerisation of land registration in Karnataka known as Kaveri has facilitated the speedy registration without intermediaries and speed money. Indeed, earlier the execution of sale deeds registration involved enormous manual labour and time. The 225 treasuries all over Karnataka have been connected with computer network under a project known as Khajane. These treasuries have been in turn connected to around 4,500 rural local governments (*Zilla Panchayats* (ZPs), *Taluka Panchayats* (TPs) and *Gram Panchayats* (GPs)). This has facilitated the treasury to handle over Rs. 20,000 crores annually and serving 4.7 lakh clients speedily without irregularities (in fact Rs. 300 crores of money was illegally drawn from the treasury by seven CMCs around Bangalore).

Government has decided to set up 7,500 *mahithi* centres (IT kiosks) throughout Karnataka to provide services such as issue/registration of birth and death certificates, collection of taxes, information about the government schemes and so on. As a part of this, 15 such centres have been located in different parts of Bangalore to facilitate payment of taxes (property and vehicle) and bills (electricity, telephone and water and other payments) (*The Hindu,* 2004).

Various e-governance initiatives are under implementation in most of the Departments such as Commercial Taxes, Transport, Sericulture, Agriculture, Urban Development, Police, and so on. For instance, police department prepared a comprehensive computerisation plan in 2000. Similarly, the computerisation of admissions in the professional course in Karnataka has been a success story over the past few years (Box 11.3).

BOX 11.3

Computerisation of Admissions in Professional Colleges

The Common Entrance Test (CET) is conducted in the most transparent way. Above a lakh students appear for the CET every year including 25-30 per cent students from outside the state. Computerised counselling is being done every year for admitting students to professional courses in engineering, medical, dental courses. The results are announced on the internet and the admission to various colleges is carried out through sophisticated computerised system. Every student gets to see a menu of courses and colleges and gets a chance to choose. Students with highest rank get to choose their favourable college and course on the basis of merit. In addition, a computerised system for recruitment, posting and transferring government teachers is under implementation (*Economic Times, indiatimes.com*).

The application of ICT in *Lokayukta's* office has established the links with the district head quarters and facilitated the speedy disposal of petitions. The internal networking has also helped to provide accurate and complete information to take quick decisions and reduce duplication of work. As a result of e-governance, there is a qualitative and quantitative improvement in the quality of governance and service delivery as shown in the Box 11.4.

BOX 11.4

Governance Projects and Service Delivery (Efficiency, Accountability and Equity) in India

Nature of e-Governance Project	*Type of Government Application*	*Efficiency (Time/Effort/Money for Getting Job)*		*Accountability (Transparency/Speed Money/ Wastage/Harassment)*		*Empowerment (Participation/ Accessibility/ Equity)*	
Kaveri in Karnataka	Valuation of property	Few days	5 minutes	Middlemen, Harassment Rs. 50 to 500	Reduced	Secrecy/ discretion	Information on access
Kaveri in Karnataka	Land registration	7-15 days	2-3 hours	2-5% of the value	Minimised	Ambiguity	Display
Bhoomi, Karnataka	Obtaining land title certificates	3-30 days	5-30 minutes	Rs. 50-500	Rs. 15	Secrecy	Transparency
Khajane in Karnataka	Networking of treasuries local bodies	Red tapism/ delays/ procedures	Speedy/ transactions/ reduction of cost/time/staff	Absence of accountability	Transparency/ less corruption	Delay	Speedy payment of bills
CET Karnataka	Computerisation of admissions	Manual processing of applications	Computerised dealings	Absence of accountability	Transparency/ no manipulation	Irregularities	Admissions based on ranking

Source: Compiled from different sources.

11.5.5 Integrity and Accountability in Administration

Sound personnel policies not only attract and retain competent and committed persons but also improve their productivity and morale. Open selections on the basis of merit by an independent agency and attractive emoluments induce competent persons to apply and get selected. When nepotism or cronyism exists, it is difficult to motivate the staff to perform well. Merit based recruitment and promotion is associated with less corruption and fewer delays as noted by the World Bank (World Bank, 2000: 100). Sound promotional and career development system improves productivity. Similarly, reward and penalisation of personnel on the basis of personal evaluation system enhances accountability. Countries that have greater meritocracy in recruitment and promotion have much higher degrees of government capability. Meritocracy is undermined both by politicisation and by low public sector wages. This is important in the Karnataka context, because politicisation and pre-mature transfers are undermining meritocracy and leading to general lowering of morale.

Government has taken many initiatives to promote integrity and accountability in administration. They include: transparency in recruitment and transfers (streamlining of transfers), strengthening of *Lokayukta* institution, introduction of regulatory authorities, citizen charts and public hearings (water *adalats*).

11.5.6 Transparency in Recruitment and Transfers

Transparency was introduced in the recruitment and posting of primary school teachers in 1993 to prevent irregularities and corruption. Teacher's recruitment constitutes around 25-40 per cent of the state government's recruitment and which is known for malpractices. Prior to 1993, the recruitment of teachers in the government primary school was done through the District Selection Committees (DSC) which conducted interviews. However this system was replaced by the marks secured in the qualifying examination in 1993. In spite of this, influence and money played a significant role in the postings of the teachers. In 1997, the centralised computer counselling system was introduced to minimise the recurrence of such problems. Teachers are invited based on merit and reservation ranking to select schools for posting themselves. Appointments and postings are issued on the spot. Nearly 29,300 teachers were appointed in 1998 in this manner (GoK, 1999).

11.5.7 Streamlining of Transfers

Frequent transfers affect service delivery and also provide scope for political interference and corruption. Karnataka is also known for highest rate of transfers and an average tenure of a district officer is less than a year (Sangita, 1997). During the first year of Krishna government (2000-01) transfers were the highest—54,000 approximately. Similarly transfers were the highest (58,000) in the first year of Veerappa Moily Government during 1992-93. Major departments, including PWD, police, irrigation, commercial taxes, public instruction, agriculture and forestry accounted for 67 per cent of all transfers in 2000-01. In addition, Group C workers, including teachers, health workers and others accounted for 73 per cent of transfers recorded in 2000-01 (Chand, 2003: 268).

The government introduced New Transfer Policy in 2001 on the basis of KARC recommendation. A detailed set of guidelines was issued in 2001 and cadre management authorities were set up to regulate transfers. Restrictions have been placed on the quantum and period of transfer. Transfers are limited to not more than five per cent of the cadre strength. Restrictions including forfeiting of transfer allowances to those who obtain transfers through recommendations are imposed. Besides this, computerised counselling system has been introduced to make transfers transparent and rational in departments like education, where transfers accounted maximum. These measures have brought down the rate of transfers drastically. The number of transfers in the first year (2000-01) of its introduction fell to 16,798, a drop of more than 69 per cent (Chand, 2003:268). While transfers accounted around 5.3 per cent of the total sanctioned strength (about 34,000 transfers) in 2002-03. Most departments succeeded in limiting transfers to less than 5 per cent, except education where 8.8 per cent of teachers were transferred.

11.5.8 Lokayukta and Service Delivery

Lokayukta's interacting with the common man through district visits, inspection of public places and departments known for malfunction and administrative corruption have helped to ensure administrative accountability and better service delivery (Box 11.5). With the pro-active role of *Lokayukta*, the gvernment hospitals had become a little more 'sanitation friendly' and the attendance of doctors has improved. *Lokayukta*'s raids on offices like RTO, Sub Registrars and others have helped to improve the quality of service (Sangita, 2003).

BOX 11.5

Karnataka *Lokayukta* and Service Delivery

The Karnataka *Lokayukta* Institution (*Lokayukta* and *Upa-Lokayukta*) has emerged as the most powerful instrument in the country today (in terms of powers, staff and budget) to tackle both political and administrative corruption. It has been entrusted with the powers of the erstwhile Vigilance Commission and the Anti-Corruption Bureau when *Lokayukta* institution (LI) was established in 1986. *Lokayukta* can investigate the allegations against the highest public officials of the sate including Chief Minister, ministers, MLA's, chief secretary, secretaries, and other public officials of the sate-funded organisations. The highest judicial officials of the country like the Supreme Court and High Court judges are appointed as *Lokayukta* and *Upa-Lokayukta* to give a strong foothold to LI. It is supported by diverse technical staff (judicial, police, administrative, engineering, financial and others) to carry out its responsibilities competently and independently (its staff strength and budget support is 5-10 times bigger than the LI in other states). Ever since the present *Lokayukta* assumed office on 2nd July 2001, a number of initiatives have been taken to promote good governance. Instead of waiting for complaints, *Lokayukta* has been interacting with the common man and inviting complaints by visiting district and *taluka* headquarters. It has been inspecting public places and departments known for malfunction and administrative harassment of the poor. It has been conducting a number of raids against government institutions known for corruption. Erring officials have been encouraged to accept their mistakes and reform. The complaint procedure has also been simplified and computerised to ensure better access to the common man. Similarly, online facility for lodging complaints from remote places have been provided and steps have been taken to strengthen the *Lokayukta* police stations by appointing senior level officers. Besides, the proceedings of *Lokayukta* are made open and transparent to the extent possible and competent persons have been appointed in honorary capacities. Systematic changes have been suggested in administrative procedures to prevent corruption.

Lokayukta has undertaken district visits to listen to the grievances of the common man and find solutions on the spot instead of formal complaints which villagers normally avoid due to ignorance, illiteracy, distance and complex complaint procedure. This is reflected by the 2,400 solutions on the spot provided by the *Lokayukta* and his staff for the 3,584 complaints received (60-70 per cent) through public hearings. There were about 100-125 public hearings during 2001-03 when the *Lokayukta* toured all the districts of the state for about 74 days. District visits alerted the administrators to clear all administrative grievances before the arrival of *Lokayukta*. Wide publicity just two days prior to the *Lokayukta*'s visit in the local newspapers encouraged 50-150 people to attend the public hearings along with complaints that were registered. The presence of the aggrieved party and the district officers has facilitated the *Lokayukta* and its staff to examine and disposed off 150 to 200 cases on the spot after asking explanations from the concerned officers.

Lokayukta also inspected the public places to assess the quality of service delivery and the extent of malfunctioning and corruption that are responsible for people's grievances. During 2001-2003, the *Lokayukta* inspected 59 hospitals, 58 municipalities, 55 *taluka* offices, 50 *Taluka Panchayats*, 27 hostels, 21 sub-registrar offices, and 24 other offices like Anganwadi centres, drought prone areas, RTOs, and so on. These inspections brought to light many incidence of mal-administration and corruption encountered by the common man, such as the absence of doctors and non-availability of medicines in government hospitals, the harassment of the poor at the hands of paramedical staff, exhortations of bribes from the patients and so on. Poor who depend on public services were the major losers due to the rent-seeking activities of the staff. This is also the case with the government's anti-poverty and welfare programmes. Only 15 to 30 per cent of the programme money reached the beneficiaries. The poor who are employed in these works as wage labour were rarely paid the specified wages. Houses meant for them were non-existent under some *Taluka Panchayats*. Accounts for Rs 2.5 core towards SC/ST was not available in one of the CMC raided by *Lokayukta*.

All these initiatives have resulted in changing the people's perception towards corruption. Now the *Lokayukta* is a household name in most parts of Karnataka. This institution was not much known earlier. The credibility of this institution has gone up with in a matter of two years reflected in the three-fold increase of complaints (complaints rose from to 8,850 in 2002 from 1,745 in 2001). Informal complaints accounted for 3,074 in 2001 and 4,940 in 2002 respectively. Secondly, there is an improvement in the hospital services after the *Lokayukta* visits.

Regulators for major public utilities need to be in the place for privatisation to succeed. The productive efficiency of the organisation will greatly enhance by the presence of well-developed and well-administered regulatory framework. Recognising this, the state government has set up a regulatory commission for electricity. It has already issued its first two tariff orders.

11.5.9 Citizens'-Charter, Online Complaint and Public Hearing

Karnataka government has also introduced many other reforms such as Citizens' Charter, Public Hearing and Online Complaints System to ensure administrative accountability. Most of the departments have brought out Citizen Charters to provide time-bound specifications of services, sanctions and approvals. These charters also help to check corruption. The Citizens' Charters at *Taluka* Office list out the services delivered in the office with the specific procedures to be followed, documents required and time limits for implementation/issue of documents/licences. The police department proposes to conduct a public user survey of its Citizens' Charter, which was launched in 2000.

The implementation of Citizens' Charter in Karnataka is not very encouraging like in any other parts of the country. One of the key elements of Citizens' Charter is information and openness that is missing in majority of cases. Those departments and institutions, which have published Citizens' Charters, have not taken steps to disseminate the contents to the public. In fact, it was noticed that a majority of staff members were ignorant about the Charters published by their own departments. This is more so with the citizens. Citizens' Charters are not made available to the public even though it is mandatory to supply them free of cost. A study conducted elsewhere reveals that some departments did display the contents of the Charter on the notice boards of their offices. However, Charters were brief and failed to provide information necessary for the citizens to redress their grievances (Muralidharan, 2002).

The BWSSB has initiated reforms to improve the customer services. They include: telephone voice records of complaints, handling e-mail complaints, public grievances committee and water *adalats*. BWSSB has launched its online complaint management system (OCMS) 2003 to enable quick response to citizen's complaints regarding irregular water supply, clogged manhole, and leakage in supply system. Consumers can lodge a complaint from anywhere along with the details of their connection. Soon after registration, the complaint will be forwarded to the concerned engineer of the area and the complainant will get feedback on the status of the registered problem every eight hours, which will be updated on the website.

The unique feature of OCMS is fixing of exact time frame to solve each of the problem as follows: contaminated water (immediate), water supply (48 hours), water leakage (24 hours), illegal tapping (12 hours), billing errors (24 hours), open manhole, (24 hours), non-functioning of ECS (24 hours), non-cooperation of staff (3 days), delay in getting fresh connection (7 days) (*http://www.deccanherald.com/deccanherald/jun142004/c5.asp; Deccan Herald*, 2004; Change Management Forum, 2002: 6).

Initiatives have also been taken to involve citizens participation in the preparation, review and evaluation of the budgets of both urban and rural local governments. An Act known as The Karnataka Local Fund Authorities Fiscal Responsibility Act, 2003, has been brought in this regard. It mandates a Medium Term Fiscal Plan (MFTP) for the local fund authorities and lays down the principles for financial management. This Act seeks to foster a process of public engagement with the fiscal policies, resulting in feedback on the performance through a 'social audit'. BDA has consulted citizens for its budget exercise to service 12 residential layouts between 1997-2001 (Baindur, 2001). Similar practice known as social auditing is adopted in PRIs for monitoring, which has been discussed elsewhere.

11.6 Decentralised Governance and Participative Reforms

11.6.1 Decentralised Governance and Service Delivery

Participative models increase the citizens' direct participation in deliberations of public policy, formulation, implementation and monitoring. Decentralised democratic governance creates new incentives that can induce efficiency, effectiveness and responsiveness. In other words, decentralised governance creates incentives such as, increased competition among levels of government, increased local control over resources, increased decision making authority, increased targeting of services to local needs and desires and increased transparency for improving efficiency (Brinckerhoff, 2000: 601). For instance, transfer of powers and responsibilities along with resources to PRIs resulted in selecting schemes, designing projects and to spend money according to the local needs. Ultimately maintenance and sustenance of such projects and schemes under decentralised governance appeared to be very high (Sangita, 2001).

Democratic decentralisation and participative management also contribute towards better compliance and enforcement with low cost, since decisions regarding selection of schemes and design of projects are taken in consultation with the various stakeholders in the organisation. This is particularly so in the management of community property resources like forests and water tank where law enforcement and punitive regulations are minimal. Democratic institution's monitoring mechanisms also help to improve the administrative efficiency. Regular monitoring by elected representatives (monthly review and surveys) help to assure that the policies and programmes serve the intended purposes. Further, the increased transparency and accountability that result from the civil society oversight enhances efficiency by decreasing the potential for diversion of resources due to patronage or corruption (Brinkerhoff, 2000: 604).

11.6.2 Rural Decentralised Governance and Service Delivery (Panchayat Raj)

Karnataka is one of the states, which has laid a strong foundation in recent years for decentralised governance in India. It was the first state to devolve maximum powers and responsibilities along with resources to PRIs to undertake development activities under 1983 PR Act (which came into operation in 1987). Under this, PRIs emerged as local self-governments with autonomy to plan and implement all development programmes including centrally planned schemes like IRDP. Elected head of ZP was given the status of a State Minister and the senior most IAS officer of the district was placed under his/her overall control. Reservation was given to women and other weaker sections to have control over development plans and improve the livelihood of the people. State Finance Commission (SFC) was constituted to devolve financial resources to local governments. State Panchayat Council with ZP presidents under the chairmanship of Chief Minister was constituted on the lines of NDC to strengthen the links between State and PRIs (Sangita, 1987). Because of these reasons, Karnataka's experiment was acclaimed widely (Table 11.11). In fact, many features of Karnataka PR are incorporated in the 73rd Constitutional Amendment. However, this revolutionary experiment could not sustain in the absence of original architects and the change of the ruling elite.

Three-tier structure of PR system (ZP, TP and VP at the district, *taluka* and village levels respectively) in the place of the earlier two-tier structure (ZP and *Mandal Panchyat*) came into existence in 1993 on the basis of 73rd Constitutional Amendment. Many changes have been introduced to improve the autonomy, capacity and accountability of PRIs and participation and empowerment of the people in governance to improve the quality of service delivery.

TABLE 11.11

Performance of Village Level *Panchayats* 1997-98

(in per cent)

	Karnataka	*Neighbouring State*	*All-India*
Own Tax/Own Revenue	86.02	80.41	3.60
Own Revenue/Total Revenue	12.90	20.47	23.40
CS Expenditure/Total Expenditure	23.51	28.12	14.80

Source: NHDR 2001: 292.

11.6.3 Autonomy (Political, Administrative and Financial)

PRIs in Karnataka are emerging as units of local self-governments just like Kerala and West Bengal for promoting the development. PRIs enjoy political, administrative and financial autonomy in many respects, although it is far behind the earlier system. Firstly, the state government in order to improve the functioning of PRIs has constituted from time to time many experts to associate with various finance committees. They include Krishnaswamy 1987, P.R. Nayak 1987, R.M. Honnavar 1989, G. Thimmaiah1996 and N. Viswanathan 2002. Secondly, Karnataka and Sikkim were the first states to transfer all major responsibilities along with resources (central and state plan schemes and other resources) to PRIs (Pal, 2000). Many centrally sponsored programmes have been transferred to PRIs, which hitherto was not done by many states. All 29 functions as mentioned in schedule and resources are transferred to PRIs (assigns 30 specific subjects to VPS, 28 to TPs and 28 ZPs). PRIs can prepare plans for subjects like agriculture, animal husbandry, primary and secondary education, public health, rural roads and housing, women and children, social welfare, public distribution, public libraries and so on. GPs can undertake regulatory functions such as issue of licences, approval of building plans, and maintenance of common properties, assets and buildings. They can provide basic services such as drinking water and sanitation and maintain village roads, buildings and streetlights.

Thirdly, the elected head of the ZP is given the status of a minister and entrusted with the executive powers. The chief executive officer who controls the district level departments works under the over all supervision of the elected ZP President.

Fourthly, many initiatives have been taken to minimise the interference of the state government in PRIs particularly in holding of elections. Powers such as demarcation of constituencies and reservation of seats are transferred to SEC from the DC. This was very essential to conduct free and fair elections and enjoy the trust of all political parties. In fact, there were allegations against the ruling party for demarcating constituencies and reserving seats to the advantage of the ruling party.

Fifthly, financial resources accounting 30-35 per cent of state's resources are transferred to the PRIs on the basis of SFC recommendations. For instance, the government had released 33.61 per cent (2,691 crores) to PRIs and 3.61 per cent (about Rs. 290 crores) to urban bodies in 2002. In fact, it was slightly higher in the earlier system (37.22 per cent in 1987-88 and also higher than the FCs recommendation (Sivanna, 2002). The state grants to GPs for maintenance has been increased over the years. The average state grant to GP has increased from Rs. 1 lakh to Rs. 2 lakh in 1999 and again to Rs. 3.5 lakh in 2001. The income of GP has gone up to Rs. 6.00 lakh and further more to Rs. 7.50 lakh as the state government has announced an additional grant of Rs. 1.5 lakh, while presenting the 2003-04 Budget (Babu, 2004). The GPs are given powers to levy tax on property, water, vehicles, entertainment, advertisement and so on. Even they can collect fees from markets, cattle grounds, and bus stands. Both VP and TP get proceeds from cess on land revenue. GP can also acquire, hold and dispose off property, both movable and immovable. However ZP and TP have no such powers.

In spite of these provisions, PRIs in Karnataka are not fully autonomous. Firstly the constitution of parallel bodies outside the PRIs' purview undermines the autonomy of PRIs. Village level committees such as educational committees, Village Forest Committees (VFCs), Water Users Association can be mentioned in this regard. Even development activities under taken under Member of Parliament, Local Area Development Scheme (MPLADS), MLA funds and regional boards (such as Hyderabad Development Board (HDB), and Malnad Development Board (MDB), etc., also undermine the importance of PRIs. In addition, the association of MLAs, MLCs, and MPs with PRIs with voting rights also undermine the autonomy of the PRIs.

Secondly the elected heads have no control over the administrative heads, although the heads of ZP and TP are designated as executive heads. State minister status enjoyed under the earlier Act has not been restored to the ZP President, in spite of expert committees' recommendation. Even the staff is not under the control of the PRIs. The elected leaders have no power to take action against the erring officials although ZP president in earlier system initiated confidential reports of CEO (chief secretary). In fact, PR Nayak committee has suggested for transfer of group C and D staff to PRIs. Besides this, the administrators have been given overriding powers over PRIs to prevent wrong doings. CEO can withhold the resolutions passed by the ZP, if it violates the rules. However, the supervisory control of the GPs has been removed from the administrative control of the Assistant Commissioner through the recent amendments. The VP president has no financial powers, although ZP and TP presidents are given such powers.

Thirdly, the PRIs are also not considered to be financially fully autonomous. They completely depend upon Central and state government grants. For instance, they constitute around 77 per cent of the total revenues of GPs. While GPs own tax and non-tax revenue constitute 20 per cent and 3 per cent respectively, (Babu, 2002), (Figure 11.7 and Table 11.12). The average internal resource mobilisation per capita ranges from Rs. 7.66 to 15.20 in Karnataka. Added to this, most of these funds are tiedup grants on which GPs have little freedom to spend according to the local needs. For instance, 57.77 per cent of GP income and expenditure is under JRY funds provided by the Central Government. In some GPs, it constitutes around 80 per cent (Sivanna, 2002). Besides, ZP and TP have no taxation powers (except the 3 per cent surcharge on stamp duty for TP). They entirely depend upon state and central grants (Babu, 1999).

FIGURE 11.7

Performance of Urban Local Bodies: 1997-98

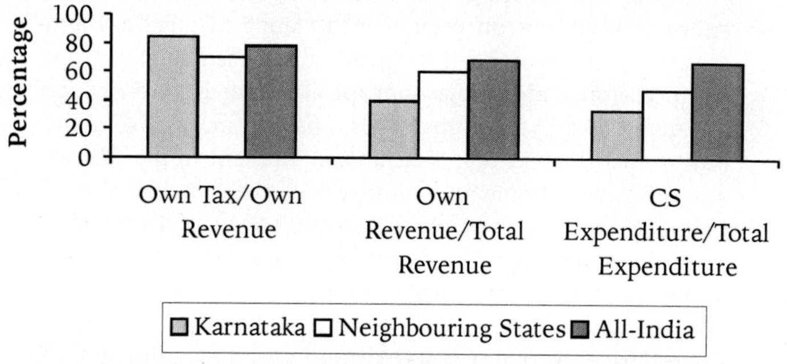

TABLE 11.12

Performance of *Panchayats*—All Tiers: 1997-98

(in per cent)

	Karnataka	*Neighbouring States*	*All-India*
Own Tax/Own Revenue	86.02	77.40	55.67
Own Revenue/Total Revenue	0.80	6.76	3.5
CS Expenditure/Total Expenditure	9.77	17.23	7.43

Source: Government of India (2001). *National Human Development Report* (NHRD).

Capacity of the PRIs

Autonomy is meaningful, if the PRIs have the required capacity (political, administrative technical and financial) to translate powers into concrete action. This ultimately depends upon the distribution of activities among the three tiers and their effective horizontal and vertical linkages, and the capacity of officials and non officials manning these institutions. Karnataka has taken major initiative in this regard. A detailed activity mapping is presented in the Box 11.6. There is no clear division of responsibility among the tiers in overlapping functional areas.

BOX 11.6

Activity Mappings: A Step Forward for PRIs

Karnataka government has a progressive record for strengthening PRIs. State government has come out with activity mapping wherein specific responsibilities were identified at three levels. A particular job/responsibility has been given to a particular level. The essence is that what is appropriate at a given level of PRIs, should be done at that level and not simply at upper level. Hence, the overlapping can be avoided. Important tasks have been identified for every level so that services can be made effective. Plan formulation, implementation, budgeting, evaluation and monitoring responsibilities are distributed among them according their competence and reliability.

For instance, the responsibility of enrolment of school age children, maintaining school building and playgrounds, exercise vigilance on regular attendance of teachers and students and report to the concerned, assessment for drop-out position and initiate appropriate measures to reduce are given to GP; ZP is made responsible for assessing the requirements of schools, teachers, equipment in the district and plan for them; and monitoring the functioning of primary and upper primary schools are vested to *taluka* level. Similarly, identification of schemes and locations for water supply, maintaining water supply schemes rest entirely with GP. ZP is entrusted with the responsibility of formulation of major water supply schemes, approval of schemes proposed by TPs and GPs, establishing water testing laboratories and award contracts for the execution of major schemes coming outside the TP and GP plans. With regard to health care, the ZP is responsible to provide physical infrastructure, coordination of communicable diseases programmes, school health programmes, IEC campaigns and planning of rural sanitation programmes. The specific activities identified for the GP include chlorinating of village tanks and wells, spraying of DDT, construction of sanitary latrines, cleaning of roads and drainage, formation of village health committees, and mobilisation of people for family planning and immunisation camps. GPs are also responsible for supervision of the activities of ANMs and *anganwadi* workers. They are supposed to report the outbreak of epidemics and helping emergency medical relief services.

BOX 11.7

Capacity Building

Ability to discharge the responsibility is enhanced. Effective training facilities to the elected representatives, officials are made available. Satellite based training centre has been established. Scientific training curriculum and modules were prepared for relatively lower educated and inexperienced persons to enable them efficient delivery.

PRIs teams are visiting many places within and outside the state to outreach their knowledge.

Weaker sections failed to ensure effective command in facilitating services and to establish accountability.

11.6.4 Participation and Empowerment

The PRIs are made accessible to the people including the disadvantaged groups to participate in the governance and improve their livelihood systems. Firstly, the establishment of small PRI structures/units nearer the people (6,000 and 400 population for GP and ward respectively) motivates them to participate in the election of good leaders and selection of relevant policies (Box 11.7). High turnout in PR election reflects this trend. For instance, the voter turnout was 68.6 per cent in ZP and TP elections in 1995 and 53.5 per cent in 1993 GP elections (Chandran, 2000: 140). This percentage is always higher than the state and national elections (40-55 per cent), notwithstanding the GPs' low percentage due to the non-partisan elections (absence of political parties in the GPs elections). Secondly, the small units enabled people to assess the performance of the leaders very closely and thereby selection of good leaders, if the elections are held free and fair. The defeat of highest number of non-performing leaders in GP elections reflects this trend. For instance, 30 to 40 per cent members are elected in 1999 GP elections. A large per cent of them got elected for the first time. This is true, wherever, the elections are conducted free and fair and the influence of elite is less due to strict watch of the civil society and vigilance of the political parties. Elite capture (leaders with the money, communal and muscle power) is very common in the absence of such forces. Unanimous election of 30 per cent of the total membership of 80,627 in 1993 GP elections reflects this trend. Similarly, 27.7 per cent got elected unopposed in the recent elections. The local elites and community elders and influential leaders chose most of them.

Thirdly, the constitution of *Gram Sabha* and Ward Committees' meetings provide information about the intended activity to the people to select relevant schemes. These meetings also help people to elect the beneficiaries and localities on the basis of merit and thereby prevent the non-poor and undeserved from availing the benefits. These meetings also help the citizen to assess the extent of fulfilment of the promises and commitments made in the earlier meetings. Such monitoring also minimises corruption, since expenditure is placed before the meetings. These mechanisms helped to ensure the accountability.

Fourthly, reservation of seats and capacity building through the training and competitive political parties and active civil society has empowered the disadvantaged groups (women, SC/STs and OBCs). Reservations of seats and positions in PRIs for women and backward castes in Karnataka enabled these groups to be present in PRIs in big number. Women accounted for 46.7 (37,689) per cent in *Gram Panchayats* in 1999. It was 40.2 (1,343) and 36.45 (335) per cent respectively at the TP and ZP levels respectively. It is the case with other disadvantaged groups. SC/STs constituted around 32.20 per cent in GPs and 23.67 and 23.06 per cent in TPs and ZPs respectively in 1999. The corresponding figure for OBC was 33.24, 33.32, and 33.30 respectively (Sivanna, 2002).

This representation has helped the disadvantaged to articulate their views in governing councils for improving their livelihoods and their awareness is very high due to the presence of political parties and civil society.

BOX 11.8

Achievement in People's Participation

Participation of fairly good improved representation but participation of poor less effective and responsiveness low.

Representation of the poor

The actual representation of the poor was lacking. The weaker sections have voice to the power structure and have an opportunity to take part in development activities though efficiency is less.

Participation by the poor

The poor, the disadvantaged and women enormously enhanced opportunities for participation. Many of the dominant casts can benefit from the OBC provisions and not all women representative will be poor or low caste.

Women representation is higher than that of their reservation (46.6 per cent) but they came from the dominant and higher castes. Social and gender exclusion common. Men are still dominating the activities of women. Elite capture remain problems. *Gram Sabha* and Ward Sabha are not held consistently. Participation mechanism should be strengthened.

Studies pointed out that reservation has improved the awareness and perception levels of women and it has created an urge in them to participate in the governance (Box 11.8). Twenty-five per cent of the women members found visible change in their status within the family after they have been elected. About 60 per cent of women said that they would encourage women to contest election. The same per cent is contemplating to contest election. In an all women GP of Mydolalu in Karnataka it was found that the women were performing better than men in promoting all round development. Interestingly, all women in this GP got elected for the first time and had no previous experience.

However some studies did not agree with this view. They pointed out that their articulation capacity is very weak and played no effective role in council meetings and remained silent or participated as directed by others (Blair, 2000). Scholars attributed the following reasons for their ineffective articulation. Firstly, women are elected as proxies for male family members or elites. This *de facto* politics negatively affected women's political participation and also the scope of addressing gender interest (Vijayalakshmi, 2002). This is more so in the case of tribal women. The wide disparities in social and economic conditions of STs and their marginal position in the development process are major constraints in their participation in the governance (Vijayalakshmi, 2001). Thirdly, gender and other social differences hindered in exercising their power effectively as political representatives. Many women did not perceive their position as a personal achievement, it was rather seen as involving their husbands, patrons and other prominent men. They owe their position to political contacts and economic position of their male family members. Fourthly women representatives were seen less favourable in terms of knowledge, political skills, ability to learn and in their orientation to activities of the public sphere (Vijayalakshmi, 2003).

Sampoorna Grameen Rozgar Yojana (SGRY) is a wage employment scheme introduced by Government of India with an annual outlay of Rs.10,000 crores in 2001. The programme came into existence after merging the two schemes of Employment Assurance Scheme and Jawahar Gram Samridhi Yojana. The objectives of the programme are to:

- provide additional wage employment in all rural areas and thereby provide food security and improve nutritional levels; and

- create durable community, social and economic assets and infrastructural development in rural areas.

The SGRY programme consists of two components which are released in instalments: the cash component is on the basis of cost sharing between the Centre and the states in the ratio of 75:25, while the foodgrains are being provided to the states at free of cost. The cash and foodgrains under the programme will be available in two streams. First stream being implemented at the district and intermediate *panchayat* levels, while the second stream implemented at the Village *Panchayat* level wherein 50 per cent of the total grants are earmarked.

During the year 2002-03, the total cash allocation was Rs. 9,281 lakhs under the second stream. Out of actual available funds of Rs. 12,015 lakhs, 95 per cent of the amount was spent. As far as the physical achievement is concerned, the official records states that 276 lakh of person days were achieved as against the target of 120 lakh person days.

However, the field data shows a different picture. The data collected from 5,212 out of 5,665 *Gram Panchayats* in Karnataka for 2002-03 show that the SGRY grants in all the 5,212 GPs amounted to Rs.194.61 crores (inclusive of opening balance of previous year and interest amount), of which, cash component consisted of 54 per cent. With regard to the expenditure pattern, the proportion of expenditure on the construction of roads and sanitation, and buildings was close to 72 per cent in the state. In contrast, the proportion of expenditure on employment intensive works relating to water and soil conservation was only around 5 per cent. The data, thus, show that the employment potential of the works for which most of the SGRY expenditure was incurred was less and cast doubts on the figures on person days of employment provided by the government.

11.6.5 Accountability and Service Delivery

Studies unravelled that the decentralised governance ensures greater accountability and transparency in delivery of the services at the grassroots level (Aziz, 1994). The experience of *Panchayat* election shows that election became a powerful mechanism for accountability even though intimidation and vote buying are the hallmarks of election scenario in India. This is because if the elected leaders do not work devotedly for the upliftment of rural society, they will not be able to win the election next time (Blair, 2000). The defeat of large percentage of sitting members in PR elections as discussed earlier reflects this trend. Studies even mentioned that the accountability of officials to the elected representatives has increased. Responsible officials (like PHC medical officer, agricultural and veterinary officer, etc.) can be asked for their presence in the PRIs meetings. In the meeting an officer may be asked/questioned for his/her performance.

> BOX 11.9
>
> **Responsiveness for Service Discharge**
>
> The commitment and willingness of local administration increased to serve the public. The development project outputs of the *panchayats* were quite congruent with the perceived needs expressed by the citizens.
>
> Responsiveness to the specific needs of the poor and the vulnerable was quite low. Commitment and willingness to serve the public improved.
>
> At GP level, the councils systematically prevented funds from reaching the SCs/STs. The implementation of specific poverty programmes and the requirement to spend 18 per cent of development funds on the Scheduled Castes were widely distorted or flouted by the council leaders and the bureaucrats.
>
> Benefits not distributed equally among socio-economic groups.

Some studies did not agree with this view that the accountability is one of the weakest aspects of the *panchayat* system. The ineffective accountability and non-responsiveness of elected representative is a major problem in delivering quality services (Box 11.9). For instance, Panchayat representatives have not been responsive to their constituents and have not acted in their interests (Inbanathan, 2002). The following reasons are attributed for non-responsiveness. Firstly PRIs have no recall mechanism to ensure greater accountability. The elected members have no regular and frequent communication with their voters. Voters have very rare chance to ask questions if their members are not functioning according to their desires. Secondly the ethical values of leaders are very low. Many leaders perceive that the official positions in PRIs bring prosperity. Attitude of gaining benefits from their tenure as *Panchayat* members is not seen as a morally abhorrent activity, but as perfectly acceptable convention. Thirdly, the elected representatives considered that they are answerable to their sponsors/local elites and not to the local people/ electorate. It was the husbands who took the *Panchayat*-related decisions, but the women were apparently accountable. This is because that a large percentage of members were elected through the intervention and support of the local leaders or village elites, (Inbanathan, 2002).

Many initiatives have been taken to ensure accountability of leaders to people and reducing corruption. Holding of *Gram Sabha* (GS) meetings have been made mandatory. *Ward Sabha* for 400 population was constituted in 2003 to ensure effective control over the officials. Social audit (*Jamabandhi*) has been introduced to monitor the progress of various works executed. In a study, it was found that the social auditing was made by the administrators particularly GP Secretaries who are responsive and accountable to the citizen with respect to their scheduled tasks and responsibilities (Sivanna and Babu, 2004). It has ultimately resulted in responding to the demands of stakeholders and ensuring effective delivery of services (Boxes 11.10 and 11.11).

BOX 11.10

Strengthening of Leadership at the Grassroots Level

Political leadership improved, young star and well-educated leadership comes to the fore in the PRIs. Opportunity for leadership from downtrodden has increased.

However some studies found that the GS meetings were not held regularly. The attendance in these meetings was thin and declined over the years. Moreover, meetings were mechanical without any seriousness. GS meetings have been reduced to a meaningless ritual primarily aimed at rubber-stamping decisions about work undertaken. Thus many meetings were conducted on paper and signatures were obtained subsequently without full consultations with the *Gram Sabha* (Aiyar, 2004). In many villages, members do not feel enthusiastic for holding meetings, because of the fear of harassment from citizens (Aziz *et al.*, 2002).

BOX 11.11

Accountability Promotion

Little improved but lagging behind the expected level.

Accountability in education and health departments increased.

Accountability of elected members and officials remain in conflicts.

PRIs have no powers for hire or fire staff.

Mechanisms should strengthen.

Enhancing transparency.

Though enhanced to some extent, mechanisms are weak.

Primary process for transparency evolved but may take more time to ensure effective mechanisms.

11.6.6 Corruption and Transparency

Though scholars have raised the issue that the PRIs have increased the corruption, and there is no proper evidence about it. Study finds that decentralised governance enhances greater transparency and reduces the incidence of grand corruption at the grassroots level (Aziz, 1994). Another study found that corruption among PRIs functionaries was minimal where medias, and civil society were effective. The rent seeking is more in areas where institutions like *Grama Sabha*, media and civil society organisations are non-functional (Inbanathan, 2001). However some studies found that the representatives are using their positions for personal gains rather than the public interest. A significant proportion of the representatives could be accused of shirking their responsibilities and they were also found guilty of corrupt practices.

In order to ensure the accountability and reduce the corruption in PRIs, the Working Group on Decentralisation has suggested that an ombudsman institution at the state/district level should be constituted. It can conduct investigation and enquiries regarding allegations and about the wrongdoings. The group suggested that the easy accessibility of information to the public through publication and display of information should be provided. It has also underlined the importance of the Citizen Charters for PRIs specifying the services, categories, standards, periodicity, time limit and so on.

TABLE 11.13

Comparative Picture of Corruption in Different States

Bihar	5.8	Very corrupt
Uttar Pradesh	4.2	Very corrupt
Delhi	3.6	Very corrupt
Assam	3.5	Very corrupt
Andhra Pradesh	3.4	Corrupt
Madhya Pradesh	3.4	Corrupt
Maharashtra	3.3	Corrupt
Tamil Nadu	3.3	Corrupt
Gujarat	3.2	Less corrupt
Haryana	3.2	Less corrupt
Karnataka	3.0	Less corrupt
Orissa	3.0	Less corrupt
Punjab	2.7	Honest
Rajasthan	2.7	Honest
West Bengal	2.6	Honest
Kerala	1.4	Honest

Source: *India Today*, November 24, 1997.

It is found that capacity building of PRIs functionaries is much in an advantageous position. Representatives have taken many innovative measures in mobilising local resources for delivering the effective services. As it can be seen from Boxes 11.12 and 11.13 that the activities of Belandur and Kinnigoli GPs are successful in mobilising the resources and promoting the development in their areas.

BOX 11.12

Experience of Belandur *Gram Panchayat* in Bangalore District

The Belandur *Gram Panchayat* has underground drainage system and garbage collection facilities. The villagers don't have water problem. There is no distributional discrimination between the rich and the poor. The *Panchayat* ensures equal quantity of water to every household. It has provided mini water schemes with 5 overhead tanks to every ward. The member residing in ward takes the responsibility for maintenance of water supply facilities. Besides this, there are 5 employees who have been employed by the GP for maintenance of drinking water supply. GP has made bye-law for fair delivery of water to all households. A penalty of Rs. 2000 can be levied for illegal water connection or the regular connection may be disconnected for a period of six months. About Rs. 25 lakh has been spent for the construction of drainage system. Toilets are being constructed for all the households, including those living below the poverty line. There is no evidence of open defecation in the *Panchayat* area. In 2001-2002, about 365 toilets were constructed in this *Panchayat* under different schemes. GP took a mandatory decision that it will construct more than 40 latrines in a year. Hundred per cent water tariffs are collected from the people. It is important to mention that the annual income of the *Panchayat* is more than 1.7 crores. Factors that play crucial role to make success of the activities of this *Panchayat* are many. However, the important factor is the quality of leadership as provided by the president of the *Panchayat* and his team.

BOX 11.13

Experience of Kinnigoli *Gram Panchayat* in Dakshina Kannada

This *Panchayat* demonstrated that water supply schemes can be maintained by collecting tariffs from the households. The scheme comprises a borewell as the source of water that feeds 5,000 litres capacity overhead tank. There are nearly 100 pipe connections to individual houses. The total cost of the system has been estimated at Rs. 7 lakh. The people of this *Panchayat* raised Rs. 70,000 against the 10 per cent as desired by the Sector Reforms Schemes. The *Panchayat* ensured regular water supply to all the households. The *Panchayat* expected to levy and collect a one time advances charge of Rs. 1000 for each connection but failed to collect the water charges. It was decided to levy a higher rate on higher incremental consumption. A new tariff formula was devised for the Guttakaadu scheme based on monthly consumption. The formula is, a family consuming 3 Kls of water would pay Rs. 50, the same rate is applicable up to 10 Kls. When a family is consuming 15 Kls they would pay Rs. 100 and for 30 Kls, they would pay Rs. 350. For implementing such a tariff system the *Panchayat* has put water flow meters on each of its pipe connections to the 113 houses. To keep a proper account of electric power consumed by the submersible pump, *Panchayats* got a separate electric meter. The system is working very well and the cost collection rate is 100 per cent.

Source: Deccan Herald, April 19, 2003.

Participative Management (Stakeholders Committees)

Participative management structure can be classified into two groups on the basis of composition and values, *viz.*, citizen groups and user groups or deliberative councils. User groups or stakeholders organisations are established in recent times as advisers, collaborations and watchdogs to improve the administrative efficiency. For instance, in many Scandinavian countries, law established User Boards since 1990, although they have the long tradition of managing the schools by citizen organisations. They are very popular in the management of schools. In these cases parents are given powers to influence the strategic matters but not operational matters though they are asking for such powers. In India, similar committees/user groups for the management of irrigation, common property resources, health, educational and other systems have been formed. Deliberative Councils, similar to user groups are constituted with the stakeholders like industrialists, business persons, exporters and administrators to advise on policy issues. These organisations enhance the quality of administration, particularly in responding to the needs and the problems of the stakeholders.

Community participation has transformed the functioning of schools in the state. Parents have now become stakeholders in the efficient management of schools through School Betterment and Monitoring Committees resulting in better student performance and reduced teacher absenteeism. Awareness: 33 per cent of in sample size was not aware of the educational committees. Out of this, hardly 10 per cent participate regularly in the meetings (KARC, 2001: 69).

Participatory institutions like village forest committees (VFCs), water users' associations are coming in big numbers to promote the development and the welfare. For instance, 3,066 VFCs have been constituted in Karnataka covering 10.78 per cent of the total forest area. This has resulted in stopping of illegal cutting and smuggling the wood and protection of forests from fires, grazing, encroachment and so on. Improvement in activities such as forest stocks, water tables and water levels in tanks have also been observed (Box 11.14). Plantation diversification has taken place. Biomass needs of the poor, particularly of women has been met. Access to fodder, fuel and timber has also improved. Collection of NTFP has increased. Women's wages have been on par with those of men (Sangita, 2003: 5).

The main limitations of deliberative and user groups are its implications on poor and decentralised governance. Users groups may strongly represent and articulate their group interests at the cost of public interest. Secondly, they may undermine the significance of decentralised democratic institutions like PRIs by encroaching in their functions. However, the Parparticipative Management Model suffers from some constraints. Absence of commitment and competent leaders and the politicisation of administration is the main constraints for promoting good governance in many developing countries. Leaders in these countries are yet to be familiarised with the state-craft. Elite control and domination over democratic institutions hurt the interests of the poor, notwithstanding the increase of their representation in the political activities. Politicisation of postings and transfers are also identified major hurdles in promoting the administrative efficiency. However, these hurdles have been overcome by the empowerment of vulnerable groups through regular elections and effective involvement of civic society organisation and political party (Manor, 1998).

BOX 11.14

Halkar Village Forest *Panchayat* (VFC) in Uttara Kannada: Survived for Eight Decades

Village forest *Panchayat* in Halkar has been able to protect the 200 acres of village forest adjacent to Kumta Town, for the last 8 decades in spite of many threats from the government, political leaders and other vested interest groups. Village forest *Panchayat* was established in 1929 on the basis of Village Forest Act, 1927 (Bombay Forest Manual Section 27). All households owning land and cattle are members in the GB. Nine members representing different caste groups are elected for two year term and they, in-turn, elect a President and Secretary. GB and MC meetings are held regularly to design and modify rules governing development and withdrawal of forest products and monitor. A household has to pay Rs.15 towards membership fee. Such households are entitled to collect fuelwood, fodder, and dry twigs in a specified manner. MC maintains records of meetings and accounts. It is also vested with powers to harvest and use the products for raising money. They can invest resources for the development of forest and meet administrative and community expenditures. It is also vested with authority to appoint guards and penalise the violators.

The constitutional status, holding of regular elections, proportional representation and active civil society is mainly responsible for the survival of the institution. The tenurial rights over the forest and forest products are provided by the constitution (Village Forest Act, 1927). This has helped the VFC to exclude the outsiders including the government from encroachment. This constitutional status has helped the Halkar *Panchayats* to function as an independent institution for the last eight decades. When Karnataka government decided to merge the village forest with the FD on the basis of Karnataka Forest Act 1963 and the *Karnataka Forest Manual*, 1976, the villagers approached the Karnataka High Court in 1979 against this order and got a verdict in their favour in 1989. In recent times, it prevented the local MLA from acquiring a part of the village forestland adjacent to Kumta town for housing construction.

In fact, the villagers discouraged several such attempts from the government and vested interests in the past. People are interested to occupy this forestland since it is adjacent to the Kumta town. The second important factor is that the elections were held regularly in the presence of the *tahsildar*. Thus, the leadership was changed frequently. There were instances where villagers took delegations to the *tahsildar* for holding the elections and general body meetings whenever they failed to do so. Even they approached the higher-level officials, whenever the lower level officials interfered in day-to-day management of the VFC. For example, they approached the higher officials when they were prevented to sell/auction the tree products and stones to outsiders. Thirdly, all the caste groups are represented in the executive body. Fourthly, rules regarding development conservation, protection, harvesting, punishment and penalties are formulated in consultation with the general body.

Source: Sangita, 2003.

BOX 11.15

Bangalore Agenda Task Force

The government of Karnataka in order to make Bangalore a world class city by 2004 AD has constituted the Bangalore Agenda Task Force (BATF) in 2000. The government has set the goals for upgradation and enhancement of the managerial and financial (augmentation of finances) of various civic bodies to provide high-quality infrastructure and public services to improve the quality of life of individuals and communities. The key areas for initiative identified in this regard are: road and traffic infrastructure; health and sanitation; new knowledge technologies; citizen-centric initiatives and public-private partnership *(www.onlinebangalore.com/gove/baag/banagend.html)*.

BATF with 15 representatives from government, NGOs and corporate sector came into existence in 1999. Its main task is to be a catalyst for realising the city's potential. It has normally an advisory role. It works with 7 civic stakeholders (BMP, BDA, BWSSSB, Police, BMTC, BESCOM, BSNL). Stakeholders set the targeted goals based on citizen feedback and BATF aids them in implementation, wherever desired. In addition BATF undertook some projects on its own initiative to build credibility with the stakeholders and showcase best practices (BATF Partnership, 2000-2002, 2003).

Stakeholder Achievements

1. The BMP property tax collection had gone up from to Rs. 100 crores to Rs. 200 in within 3 years.
2. BDA becomes financially vibrant and develops quality city infrastructure with no burden on the citizens. 40,000 sites allotted in the last 3 years.
3. Bangalore police creates professional, innovative solutions to address the city's traffic problems through one-ways.
4. Public sanitation measures through 23 clean public toilets built with private contribution; solid waste management initiatives are taken.
5. A pathbreaking fund based accounting system for the BMP involving over Rs. 1.7 crores and 300,000 man-hours which allows accurate user cost tracking, asset-liability and budgetary control.
6. City beautification measures through standardised bus shelters, road signage and adopt a park scheme of the BMP.
7. Putting the citizens' interest first—many stakeholders have been driven by the mantra of citizen friendly measures be it *khata* reform, easy plan, *samavesha* camps, bill payments, citizen charter, etc.

11.7 Urban Decentralised Governance and Service Delivery

Many governance reforms have been introduced to improve the quality of governance and service delivery in the urban areas. They include, devolving of powers and resources to the urban local bodies under 74th Constitutional Amendment (1992), public-private partnerships, participation and transparency and accountability. This section mainly deals with governance reforms in Bangalore city.

11.7.1 Bangalore Mahanagara Palike (BMP)

The BMP has initiated a number of reforms in the last three years with a vision of making Bangalore the best city in the country. Bangalore has to act as an engine of growth for Karnataka and the following are the key areas of concern for reforms. They are: infrastructure upgradation; improving the physical quality of life; and capacity building of the organisation—administrative, legal and financial reforms.

11.7.2 Public-Private Partnership (Bangalore Agenda Task Force)

The Bangalore Agenda Task Force (BATF) is one of the most exciting and fruitful experiments in public-private partnership, which perhaps is the first ever in independent India. BATF including eminent persons from corporate sector, professionals and academics have participated in a big way in defining the agenda for development of the Bangalore city. They have initiated a lively public debate focusing on the priorities of the citizens of Bangalore and have organised periodical seminars and conferences to declare the way forward for various stakeholders in the city (Box 11.15). It has generated a sense of involvement among citizens in the work of various agencies involved in the development of the city (BATF Partnership, 2000-2002, 2003).

The implications of the partnership are seen in the areas such as urban infrastructure development, health and sanitation.

11.7.3 Health and Sanitation

The partnership has resulted in defining a new approach to health and sanitation issues in the city. It has resulted in fundamental change in the way solid waste is being handled in the city. The introduction of door to door collection of garbage in Bangalore city, as part of the Swachha Bangalore Campaign has been one of the most successful initiatives in the field. BATF also created a helpline to register citizens complaints on garbage collection enabling close monitoring of this function. The BATF is involved in the facilitation of scientific plans for sanitary landfills for the city.

11.7.4 Urban Infrastructure

With the partnership of BATF and good governance practices, the BDA has developed infrastructure facilities like ring roads, flyovers, grade separators, parks and lakes and other infrastructure facilities at a cost of Rs. 300-400 crores without any assistance from the state government and other civic bodies (BDA, 2004: 32). These projects are completed within 18 to 24 months, which is a rare phenomenon. Despite the odds BDA had fought and recovered 175 acres of property worth of Rs. 700 crores (BDA, 2004: 32). It acquired over 5,000 acres of land without litigation and developed 4 new layouts (Box 11.16). BDA distributed 40,000 residential sites during the last 4 years (2000-04) as against 3,400 sites during 1990-1999 (2100 sites in 1994 and 1,300 in 1999) (BDA, 2004: 32) (Appendix Table A-11.3). It has also planned another layout (Arakavathi) on 2,000 acres of land for developing 50,000 residential sites for which 3 lakh applications were received in June 2004 (*The Hindu*, 2004).

BOX 11.16

Bangalore Development Authority

The Bangalore Development Authority transformed itself from being one of the most despised government bodies to one of the most efficient and respected one within four years by adopting good governance practices. At one point of time, government was planning to wind up the organisation due to its inability to finance itself and failure to perform its goals. Now it is highly appreciated urban body useful for utility by the citizen of Bangalore. For distributing 4,000 house sites, and creating infrastructure and people friendly transparent administration (BDA, 2004: 32). It has been awarded LAA+(SO) rating for its finances by the Indian Credit Rating Agency (ICRA), an independent and professional investment and credit rating agency. BDA is the first state government agency in the country to obtain this rating without government guarantee for raising funds up to Rs. 100 crores by floating bonds.

The BDA was established in 1976 to ensure an orderly development of city for comfortable living. It is mainly responsible for the overall planning, development and maintenance of urban infrastructure and residential layouts and distribution of sites in Bangalore.

The BDA's budget has grown in strength from Rs. 363.12 crores in 2000 to Rs. 1,154.31 crores in 2004. The expenditure on establishment as a percentage of the budget has come down to 7.1 to 2.11 per cent during this period.

The waiting period of 10 long years to obtain an absolute sale deed is now reduced to nil and the deed is issued as soon as full payment of the site value is made by the allottee. In order to clear the backlog, absolute sale deed *samavesha* have been organised regularly to issue sale deeds *en-masse*. Nearly 70,000 sale deeds have been distributed in *Samavesha* organised in the past 4 years. The possession certificate and *khata* are given as soon as the registration of the property is completed.

Source: BDA, 2004.

11.7.5 Citizen Friendly Initiatives

Over the last 3 years BMP with BATF has undertaken a number of citizen-friendly initiatives like the introduction of the Sarala Khata Scheme (SKS). The BMP officials claim that the citizens' response has been very good for SKS. In 2002-03, about 2000 khata booklets were sold. This number was much higher in the previous year (BATF Partnership 2000-2002, 2003). SAS scheme is also very successful. Out of 4 lakh properties in the city, 2.3 lakh property owners opted for the SAS in the first year. Subsequently another 60,000 owners have used this facility. As a result of SAS, the BMPs tax collections has doubled within 3 years (Rs. 113 to Rs. 200 crores in 1999-00 and 2002-2003 respectively (Box 11. 17). The success of this approach has led it to being made compulsory in all cities in Karnataka (Change Management Forum, 2002: 3). In fact the improved tax collection enabled the BMP to repay the first instalment of Rs. 0.25 billion towards the municipal bonds (*Urban Finance,* 2004).

BOX 11.17

Sarala Khata Scheme: An Innovative Approach

Many innovative changes are introduced in BMP to simplify the procedures to provide services speedily and prevent corruption. For instance, Sarala Khata Scheme (SKS) and the Self-Assessment Scheme (SAS) can be mentioned in this regard. Under SKS the number or documents required for obtaining a *Khata* are reduced; the application forms are simplified; the rates of taxation are made transparent; and the *Khatas* are issued within a specified time schedule (*Khata* is an account of assessment of a property recording details such as size, location and built-up area for the purpose of payment of property tax. It is a very important document for all property owners as it is required for many transactions such as obtaining trade licences, bank loans, etc.). SKS was introduced in 2001 and a booklet containing information explaining the procedure was brought out for the benefit of the taxpayers. The BMP has also simplified procedures for obtaining building plan approvals and trade licences. A simple and comprehensive manual (containing full information on procedures, fee structure, steps to calculate the fees, required permissions, as well copies of application forms) has been prepared in this regard. On similar lines, procedures are simplified and manual is prepared for obtaining trade licences.

11.8 Governance Reforms and Outcome

In this section, an attempt has been made to discuss the implications of governance reforms on outcomes (service delivery), although it is difficult to establish causal relations without systematic study. The governance reform measures have already shown results in some of the public utilities in Bangalore such as BMC, BDA, BWSSB, BMTC, and BSNL as shown in the earlier boxes. By limiting manpower and outsourcing its activities, the efficiency levels in BWSSB had gone up from 78 per cent to 82 per cent and further to 95 per cent. While BDA's per capita productivity went up from Rs. 21 lakhs to Rs.1 crore, salary as percentage of budget dropped from 7 per cent to 3 per cent.

The privatisation of maintenance of streetlights by contractors in BMP resulted in increase in efficiency level to 95 per cent as compared to 45 per cent earlier. It helped to avoid pilferage in material use and minimum energy loss (*Urban Finance*, 2004). The privatisation of power sector has led to increased efficiency, most noticeable is a speedier compliance of customer grievances. This is evident from the satisfaction levels of the people. Ninety-seven per cent of households are satisfied with the behaviour of BSNL staff in Bangalore.

Similarly, public-private partnership has helped in mobilising the additional resources in Bangalore. Under Swachha Bangalore, there was collaboration between sanitation staff and citizens for efficient collection and management of domestic waste. Similarly under Nirmala Bangalore 30 out of 100 'pay and use' toilets were constructed with the support of corporate sector. Funds to the tune of Rs. 35 lakhs for each toilet was donated by the corporate sector. On similar lines 12 police stations were developed at the cost of Rs. 35 lakh each.

The e-governance projects like Bhoomi and Khajane has made governance more transparent and citizen-friendly. Studies on 'Bhoomi' project in Karnataka found that the speed money for obtaining the land records was eliminated after computerisation. Hundreds of crores of money was transacted in the form of bribe which was put to an end after the computerisation of land records under Bhoomi project. The farmer can have his/her land record on payment of Rs. 15.00 from the village kiosk. This saves the farmers' time and money and also from avoidable harassment. They have easy access for tenancy land records (Chawla, 2003). The common entrance test (CET) for admission to professional courses in Karnataka is more transparent and efficient (Krishna, 2003). Corruption and harassment of the common man has declined in registration deeds after the introduction of Kavery software. Moreover, it has ensured the speedy delivery of documents and better access to information for the citizen through kiosks. The farmers of Karnataka have paid more than Rs. 19 crores in terms of user fee for getting their land records (Chawla, 2004).

Decentralised governance ensured effective delivery of services like education, health care and poverty elimination programmes in Karnataka (Aziz *et al.*, 2002; Crook and Manor, 1998; Sivanna, 2002). The weaker sections' power over resources has increased through *panchayats* (Box 11.18). It has been found that many SCs, STs and women beneficiaries under different schemes who crossed the poverty line, have experienced upward occupational mobility and many of them started repaying their loan (Aziz *et al.*, 2002).

BOX 11.18

Efficiency in Service Delivery

Did little to directly help pro-poor growth, or equity. Human development and spatial equity indirectly benefited from funding allocations and development programmes.

Owing to mobilisation of own resources of PRIs many development works are less effective, particularly welfare of downtrodden. Sectors like education and health improved a lot. Attendance both teachers and pupil increased. Public health facilities increased. About 26 per cent in rural and 46 per cent in urban case of access to Government health care facilities. Availability of doctors and paramedics in medical centres, respectively, 74 per cent and 93 per cent. Satisfactions with the behaviour of doctors are found highest (31 per cent) in the state compared with other states. Primary schools are accessible within 1 km for 67 per cent villages and 81 per cent urban households. A relatively higher percentage of households (26 per cent) in the state viewed their satisfaction with the behaviour of teachers.

State Government tries to ensure that up to 20 per cent of the development expenditure is spent for the upliftment of downtrodden but only 13.75 per cent of amount is being spent. Pro-poor outcomes were in fact a product of the synergy between local and central factors.

Centrally funded poverty relevant programmes were implemented in cooperation with *Panchayats* and given a strong ideological and organisational impetus at the local level from the commitment of local employees and political activities.

A review conducted by the Government of Karnataka observes that the functioning of school and health facilities improved considerably under the PRI setup. There has been significant improvement in the area of medical and public health facilities and the supply of drugs (Government of Karnataka, 1989). Another study found that the attendance of doctors and paramedical staff improved considerably under the constant monitoring of local leaders in many PHCs and hospitals of Karnataka (Sekher, 2003). *Panchayats* played a positive role in improving the quality of health care services by ensuring regular attendance of health care functionaries as well as by exerting moral pressure on the staff not to avoid their regular duties. The utilisation of resources which has been transferred to the PRIs is much better than it used to be under line departments. Developmental works are being executed more speedily and field staff are better controlled under PRIs (Meenakshi, 1994).

Reforms are also responsible for the improvement of the state revenues. State revenue increased from 12.90 per cent of GSDP in 1999-2000 to 13.53 per cent in 2000-01 (a growth of 15 per cent). The state's own-tax revenue grew by 17 per cent. This ultimately (revenue growth and tight expenditure control) resulted in the decline in revenue deficit in 2000-01 from 2.42 per cent of GSDP to 1.77 per cent of GSDP (Khuntia, 2002).

Also there is an improvement in non-tax revenues through the measures like cost recovery for instance, irrigation rates were hiked 2.5 times in 2000-01 and public transport (bus) rates have been automatically indexed to salary and fuel costs. And in 2001-02, the Bangalore Water Supply and Sanitation Board increased water rates by 50 per cent. The recovery from irrigation charges is estimated to have increased from Rs.18 crore in 2000-01 to Rs.25 crore in 2001-02 (Khuntia, 2003).

The tax to GSDP ratio has already improved from 8.1 per cent in 1999-00 to 8.6 per cent in 2000-01 and is expected to improve to 8.9 per cent in 2001-02. Implementation of tax reforms in the coming years and better administration and enforcement of taxes are also expected to further improve the revenue productivity and the tax GSDP ratio which is predicted to rise to 9.5 per cent in 2003-04). Salaries as proportion to GDSD which was 4.4 per cent in 1996-97 had risen to 4.8 per cent in 1999-00 as a result of the pay hikes associated with the Fifth Pay Commission. However, by 2001-02 salaries had fallen back again to 4.4 per cent of GSDP (Khuntia).

This is also evident from the satisfaction levels of citizens of Bangalore with services provided by various public utilities. According to a study carried by the Public Affairs Centre, there is an improvement in the satisfaction levels of citizens over the years as shown in the Figures 11.7 and 11.8.

FIGURE 11.8

Improvements in Satisfaction: Public Service in Bangalore

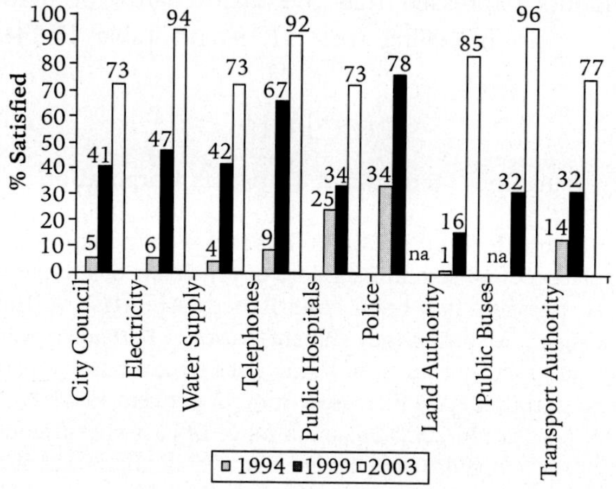

Source: Public Affairs Centre, Government of Karnataka.

In 2003, citizens were reported to be highly satisfied with the services provided by the BMTC, BESCOM and BSNL as reflected in the satisfaction levels in excess of 90 per cent (Figure 11.7). However, these three agencies in 1999 recorded lower satisfaction levels of only 32 per cent, 47 per cent and 67 per cent respectively. Two noteworthy aspects of improvement in quality of public services relate to problem incidence, which has dropped dramatically across all service providers with the exception of the city corporation.

FIGURE 11.9

Trends of Services in Bangalore

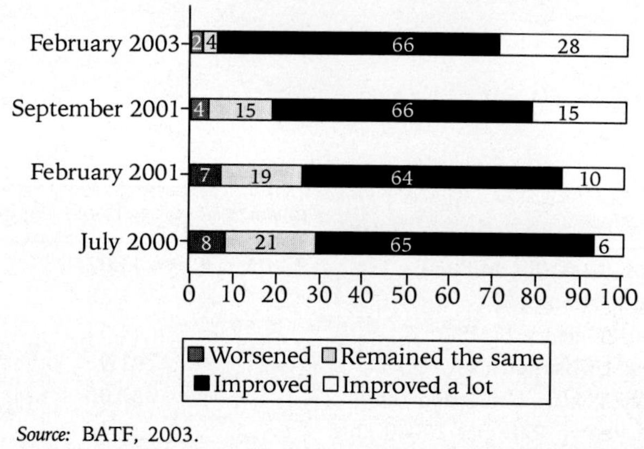

Source: BATF, 2003.

The problem of incidence of slum households with the police dropped from 75 per cent in 1999 to 18 per cent in 2003 and for general households the most dramatic drop was in the case of the BDA where the problem incidence dropped from 66 per cent to 15 per cent. Similar results are also obtained at the state level surveys regarding delivery of services. For instance, a recent state-wide survey on Karnataka's roads, (the first such survey conducted in India, and probably Asia) 72 per cent of the respondents expressed that the maintenance of roads in the state was improving (Box 11.19 and Table 11.14).

BOX 11.19

Bangalore Metro Road Transport Corporation

A mammoth fleet of 3,625 buses for a metropolitan population of 60 lakh in Bangalore of which one bus for every three persons has been constituted. About 7 million passengers use public (government) buses in Karnataka every day. On-time departures for Karnataka's largest bus company on main routes have increased from 92 per cent in 1998-99 to 99 per cent in 2002-03, and a range of customer-friendly initiatives adopted. There has been an overall improvement in key parameters like vehicle utilisation, rate of breakdowns in BMTC has come down, etc., which not only helped the Corporation turn out Rs. 7.8 crore loss in 1997-98 into Rs. 34 crore profit in 2002-03, but also raised levels of customer satisfaction. Significantly, BMTC also got the highest satisfaction rating of 93 per cent from slum households (who would use its services more than general households), compared to satisfaction ratings of 65 per cent that they have given for the City Corporation and 64 per cent for the police (PAC, 2004). In the past 3 years there has not been any of strike or dislocation at work reported symbolising reliable and regular transport services. Ensuring punctual operations the BMTC has brought down cancellations from 15 per cent to 4.1 per cent. For bringing about transparency a unique testing procedure was evolved for recruitment of drivers. Emission testing meters have been installed in all the depots. No transport vehicle older than 15 years would be allowed to ply within the metropolitan area of Bangalore.

11.8.1 Governance Reforms and Disadvantage Groups

Privatisation adversely affects the interests of the vulnerable sections and backward regions in having access to Government resources and employment. The basic services like water and electricity provided by the private organisations and contractor may not be available to the disadvantaged, and backward regions, as they do not have minimum ability to pay. Even their number in government employment may also come down with the shrinking of state authorities. Such a situation may lead to social tensions, which are manifested in the form of radical movements over sharing resources and jobs (sons of the soil and *mandal* agitation) in the past. However some scholars do not agree with this view. According to them, privatisation benefits poor.

The implications of reforms on poor appears to be not very encouraging in some areas. For instance, in spite of BWSSB's all-round performance, the availability of water to the poor and low-income group is very low. In a study of five slums in Bangalore, it was found that the water consumption was only 25 per cent of the city average which, was less than half the water norm fixed by public health engineers (Subramaniam, 1998). One-third of the population has only partial or no access to water (Benjamin, 2000). In another study, it was estimated that more than half of Bangalore's population depends upon public fountains and many of which supply contaminated water due to

TABLE 11.14

Performance of KSRTC

Indicators	*1996-97*	*1997-98*	*1998-99*	*1999-00*	*2000-01*	*2001-02*	*2002-03*
Profit/Loss (Rs. Million)	-94.05	-33.07	-55.59	-16.19	-10.82	38.64	61.08
Cancellations (%)	-	7.80	6.20	6.20	4.80	2.40	2.30
Fuel Efficiency (KMPL)	-	4.55	4.74	4.7	4.67	4.88	5.04
Fleet Utilisation (%)	-	91.90	94.20	93.40	93.60	94.50	95.40
Daily Vehicle Utilisation (km)	-	327.00	333.00	333.00	341.00	360.00	362.00
Breakdown Rate per 10000 kms.	-	0.18	0.17	0.21	0.17	0.12	0.09
Rate of Accidents per Lakh kms.	-	-	0.16	0.16	0.16	0.16	0.15
Absenteeism (%) Drivers	-	-	-	-	9.20	6.50	6.00
Absenteeism (%) Conductors	-	-	-	-	11.50	8.20	7.90
Load Improvement, Mysore Mallige							
a) Mysore Mallige (%)	-	-	-	-	-	85.00	90.00
b) Rajahamsa	-	-	-	-	-	80.00	85.00
c) Airavatha	-	-	-	-	-	-	75
Monthly Pollution Checks (Buses)	-	-	-	-	-	49890	48963
Buses Compliance with Test (%)	-	-	-	-	-	98.77	96.89

Source: Karnataka Road Transport Corporation, Respective Annual Reports.

FIGURE 11.10

Karnataka's Status in Terms of Frequency and Source of Water Supply

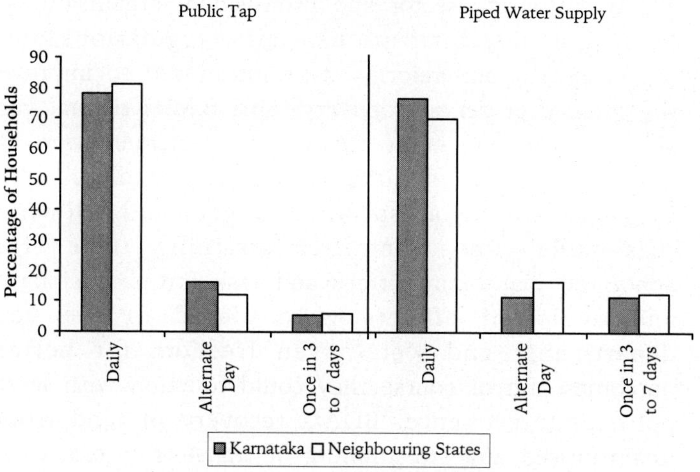

Source: Samuel *et al.*, 2004.

FIGURE 11.11

Public Drinking Water Facilities

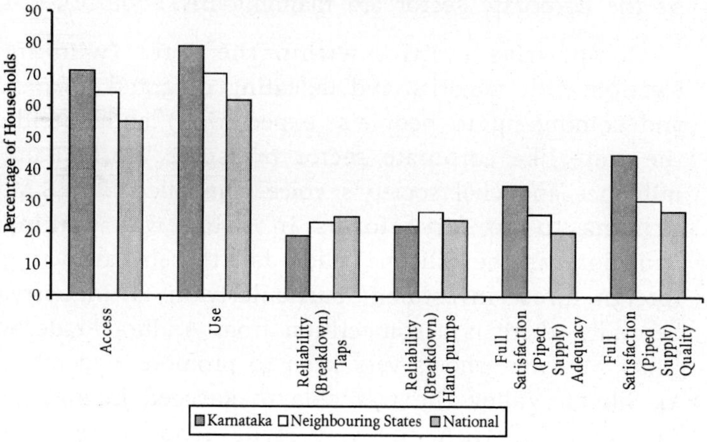

Source: Samuel *et al.*, 2004.

poor maintenance and broken pipes (TARU, 1998). Two out of five slums (studied in 1996) had no water supply. Most get water from public fountains (Loes-Schenk, 1996).

Access to other services such as toilets is also bad. An official report for 1994 stated that there were 113,000 houses without any latrines while 17,500 had dry latrines (Solomon, 2000: 39). In another study of 22 slums (Loes-Schenk, 1996), 9 had no latrine facilities. Most of the women were forced to use open fields to defecate, in 12 slums, women reported facing harassment, and in 9 slums women reported that they have to walk longer distance to reach an open space. Many women and children suffer from diseases due to contaminated water or inadequate supply of water. Infant mortality rates in Bangalore slums were much higher

FIGURE 11.12

Government Health Care—Access, Use, Reliability and Satisfaction Levels

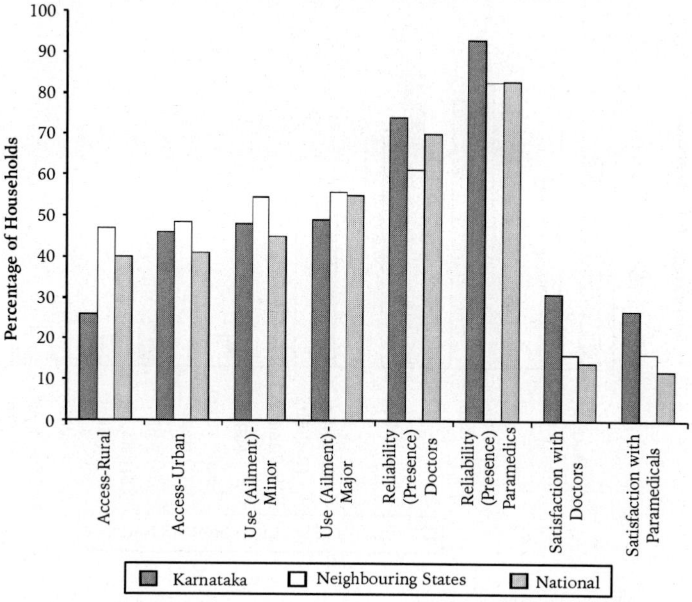

Source: Samuel *et al.*, 2004.

FIGURE 11.13

Government Buses - Access, Use, Reliability and Satisfaction Levels

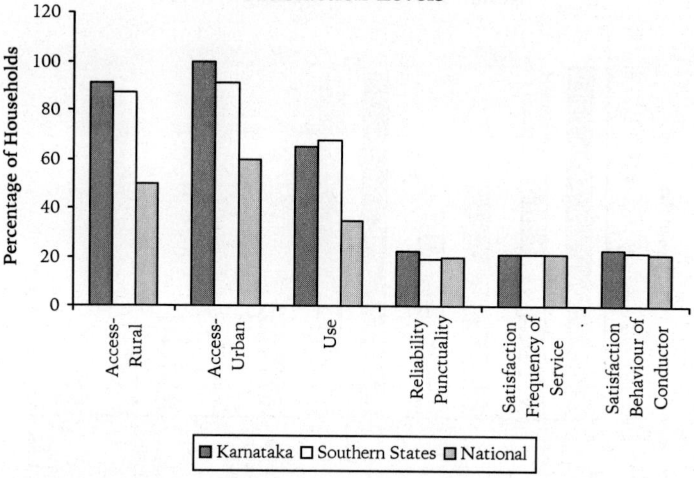

Source: Samuel *et al.*, 2004.

than the state average (Solomon, 2000). Concerns were also expressed regarding the implications of two to three fold increase of water and electricity charges and bus fare for the last three years especially on the poor (Figures 11.10 to 11.15). Privatisation is also helping the poor in different arena. Privatisation of professional education is helping to accommodate more number of students from the disadvantaged groups and cross subsidise their fees as well. The higher allocations of budget health, education, welfare and anti-poverty programmes by having effective decentralised governance can help serve better.

FIGURE 11.14

PDS - Access, Use, Reliability and Satisfaction Levels

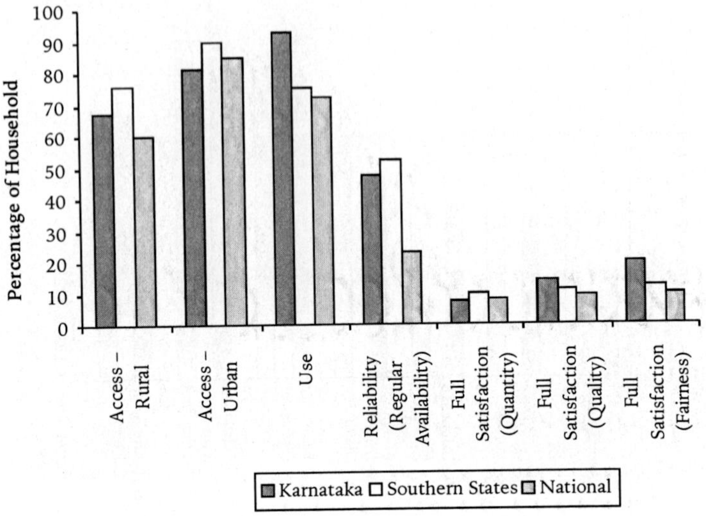

Source: Samuel *et al.*, 2004.

FIGURE 11.15

Government/Aided Primary Schools - Access, Use, Reliability and Satisfaction Levels

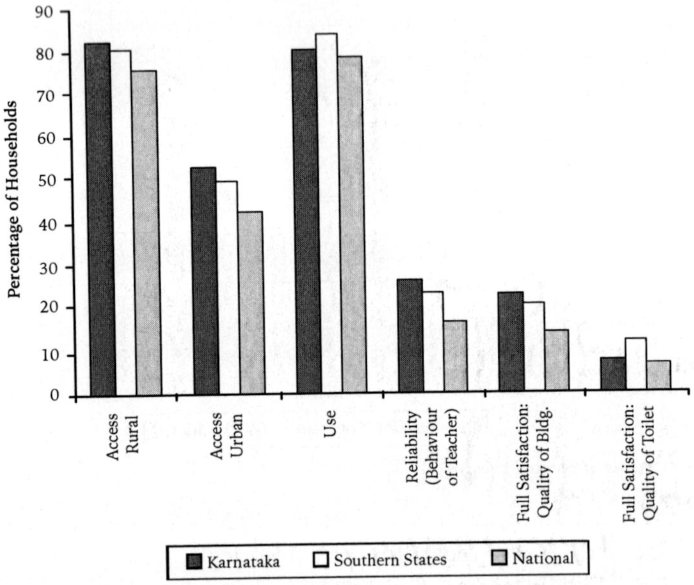

Source: Samuel *et al.*, 2004.

11.8.2 Development Politics and Governance Reforms

Competent and committed political and administrative leadership, synergy between state markets and civil society are mainly responsible for governance reforms. Under the leadership of Shri S.M. Krishna major initiatives have been taken to popularise governance reforms as mentioned in the beginning of the chapter. Administrative and tax reforms and working groups and task force committees were constituted with the representatives of Government, NGOs, corporate sector and professional organisations. Many policies, institutions (laws, regulations and organisations) and reforms were introduced to improve the quality of service delivery. Shri S.M. Krishna was able to overcome many barriers in implementation of governance projects through a focused and strategic approach aiming at specified targets and allowing reasonable time frame for attaining them. He appointed many committees and task forces. Visionary and dedicated officers were placed in the key departments and were given freedom for better outcomes and of course they could function with least political interference. BDA's recovery of land from unauthorised and streamlining of transfers is one such instance in this regard. He encouraged the participation of private and NGO sector particularly young professionals in the development (10 young urban planning professionals with the funds provided by the corporate sector are manning BATF office).

Competitive politics within the state (winning election with majority and defeating of grand alliance and coming up to people's, expectation) and outside the state like corporate sector pressure, World Bank influence and civil society's voice compelled Shri S.M. Krishna to go for reforms in a big way making Bangalore as the Silicon Valley and thereby attracting foreign direct investment particularly in IT industry. Secondly, there is a competition from Andhra Pradesh. Chief Minister who is very keen to promote Hyderabad as Silicon Valley (he was able to succeed in making President of USA to visit Hyderabad instead of Bangalore in March 2000 and his invitation of IT industry to Hyderabad with attractive incentives and so can be mentioned in this regard). Thirdly, the corporate sector is demanding many concessions such as lower taxes, disinvestment, postponement of the introduction of VAT and better infrastructural facilities and good governance for more investments in the state in spite of the opposition from the state government employees and civil society organisation. Representatives from the commerce and industry raised their objection through various fora in this regard. Fourthly, the urban based civil society organisations played a significant role in promoting the reforms. Organisations like Public Affairs Centre have been publishing survey reports about the performance of the government utilities and exercising the pressure on the government for better service delivery. Even many other NGOs like Janaagraha joined this movement and influenced the government for carrying out reforms in Bangalore. Fifthly, the World Bank is also pushing through the reforms as a part of its projects in the state. Reforms need to continue under any circumstances.

References

Advani, Shalini (2003). "Experience of Schooling", *Economic and Political Weekly*, December 6: 5169-5170.

Aloysius, Prakash Fernandes (2004). "NGOs and Government in Collaboration for Development of Karnataka", *IIPA Publication Series 13*, Indian Institute of Public Administration, Karnataka Regional Branch, Bangalore.

———. (2002). "Fixers, Patronage: Fixing and Local Governance in Karnataka", *ISEC Working Paper No.112*, Institute for Social and Economic Change, Bangalore.

Aziz, Abdul *et al.* (2002). *Decentralised Governance and Planning: A Comparative Study in Three South Indian States*, Macmillan, Delhi.

Babu, M. Devendra (2001). "Governance, Planning and Development: The Case of PRIs in Karnataka", *Indian Journal of Regional Science*, XXXIII (1): 83-97.

———. (2002a), "Eleventh Finance Commission's Recommendations and the Local Bodies: Impact Across the States", *Management in Government*, Vol. XXXIV (2), July-September: 1-18.

———. (2002b). "Report on the Karnataka State Finance Commission: Status and Implications", *The Indian Journal of Economics*, Vol. LXXXII (326) January, 403-420.

Baldev, Raj Nayar, (2000). "The Limits of Economic Nationalism in India: Economic Reforms under the BJP Led Government, 1998-99", *Asian Survey*, 40(5): 792-815.

Bandyopadhyay, D. (2003). "The Caucus and the Masses: West Bengal Panchayat (Amendment) Act, 2003", *Economic and Political Weekly*, November 15: 4825-4827.

Bangalore Agenda Task Force Partnership: 2000-2002, Summit 2003, Bangalore Forward, The 5th Summit, February 15, 2003.

Bangalore Development Authority, *Brochure*, various issues Bangalore.

Beschel Jr., Robert P. (2002). "Civil Service Reforms in India: Perspectives from the World Bank's Work in Three States", in Stephen Howes, Ashok K. Lahiri & Nicholas Stern (eds.), *State Level Reforms in India: Towards More Effective Government*, pp. 233-255, Macmillan, Delhi.

Blair, Harry (2000). "Participation and Accountability at the Periphery: Democratic Local Governance in Six Countries", *World Development*, Vol. 31 (1).

Brinckerhoff (2000). "Democratic Governance and Sectoral Policy Reform: Tracing Linkages and Exploring Synergies", Pergamon, Great Britain, *World Development*, Vol. 28(4), 601-615.

Chand, K. Vikram (2002). "Contemporary Governance in India: Islands of Success and Beyond", in Stephen Howes, Ashok K. Lahiri and Nicholas Stern (eds.), *State Level Reforms in India: Towards More Effective Government*, pp. 256-266, Macmillan, Delhi.

Chandran, T.R. Satish (2000). *Karnataka, in Status of Panchayati Raj in the States and Union Territories of India 2000*, George Mathew, (ed.), Concept Publishing Company, New Delhi.

Change Management Forum: For Sustainable Urban Water and Sanitation in India: Experience Sharing Study Tour, Bangalore, 11-12, February, 2002 pp. 1-12.

Chawla, Rajeev and Subhash Bhatnagar (2001). "Bhoomi: Online Delivery of Land Titles in Karnataka, India", World Bank, *www1.worldbank.org/publicsector /egov/ servdel.htm*

Crook, Richard and James Manor (1998). *Democratic Decentralisation in South Asia and West Africa: Participation Accountability and Performance*, Cambridge University Press.

Deccan Herald (2004a). "Water Supply To New Wards: BWSSB Sets Fresh Deadline, June 14", *http://www.deccanherald.com/deccanherald/jun142004/c5.asp*

Deccan Herald (2004b). "BWSSB to e-solve City's Water Problems", June 29, *http://www.deccanherald.com/deccanherald/jun292004/c1.asp*

George Mathew *et al.*, (2000). *Status of Panchayati Raj in the States and Union Territories of India*, Concept Publishing Company, New Delhi.

Government of Karnataka (2002). *Report of the Working Group on Decentralisation*, Department of Rural Development and Panchayat Raj Bangalore. March.

———. (1999). *Human Development in Karnataka*, Planning Department, UBS Publishers, Bangalore.

Jayaramu, P.S. (2001). "The Krishna Government: Achievements and Challenges", in Arun P. Bali (ed.), *Refashioning the New Economic Order–Karnataka in Transition*, Rawat Publications, New Delhi.

Inbanathan, Anand (2001). "Representation and Accountability in Local Government: The Panchayats of Karnataka", *ISEC Working Paper No.96*, Institute for Social and Economic Change, Bangalore.

———. (2002). "Fixers Patronage: Fixing and Local Governance in Karnataka", *ISEC Working Paper No.112*, Institute for Social and Economic Change, Bangalore.

Karnataka Administrative Commission Executive Report (2001).

Karnataka Administrative Reforms Commission (KARC) (2001). *Good Governance: New Work Culture, Transparency, Accountability, Professionalism, Simplification of Procedures, Maximum Efficiency, Minimum Cost, Prompt Delivery of Services*, Government of Karnataka.

Khuntia, Subhash C. (2002). "Fiscal Reforms: The Experience of Karnataka", in Stephen Howes, Ashok K. Lahiri and Nicholas Sterm (eds.), *State Level Reforms in India Towards More Effective Government*, Macmillan, Delhi pp. 212-232.

Loes-Schenk, Sanbergen (1996). "Women, Water and Sanitation in The Slums of Bangalore: A Case Study of Action Research", in H. Schenk (ed.), *Living in Bangalore's Slums*, forthcoming.

Manor, James (1998). *Democracy and Decentralisation in South Asia and West Africa: Participation.*

Meenakshi, Sundaram (1994). *Decentralisation in Developing Countries*, Concept Publishing Company.

Menon, Parvathi (2001). "The Ongoing Process of Corporatization of Water Supply in Bangalore Has Important Implications", *Frontline*, 18 (13), June 23-July06. *(http://www.flonnet.com/fl1813/18130880.htm)*

Muzaffar, Assadi (2004). "Karnataka Elections: Shifts, New Trends and the Congress Defeat", *Economic and Political Weekly*, September 18: 4221-4228.

Singh, Nirvikar (1997). "Governance and Reform in India", *Journal of International Trade and Economic Development*, 6(2): 179-208.

———. (2002). "Miracles and Reform in India: Policy Reflections", *Asian Survey*, 42(5): 708-722.

Pal, Mahi (2004). "Panchayat Raj and Rural Governance: Experiences of a Decade", *Economic and Political Weekly*, January 10: 137-143.

———. (2004), "Voluntary Sector and Credibility Issues", *Economic and Political Weekly*, June 26: 2677-2679.

Planning Commission (2002). *National Human Development Report 2001*. Government of India.

Paul, Samuel *et al.* (2004). "State of India's Public Services: Benchmarks for the States", *Economic and Political Weekly*, February 28: 920-933.

Pradhan, Sanjay (2002). "Reforming Government: International Experience", in Stephen Howes, Ashok K. Lahiri and Nicholas Stern (eds.), *State Level Reforms in India: Towards More Effective Government*, pp. 59-76, Macmillan, Delhi.

Public Affairs Centre (2004). Government of Karnataka.

Rajasekhar and R.R. Biradar (2002). "People, Government and the NGOs", *ISEC Working Paper No.112*, Institute for Social and Economic Change, Bangalore.

Rajasekhar, D. (2000). "Non-Governmental Organisations in India: Opportunities and Challenges", *ISEC Working Paper No.66*, Institute for Social and Economic Change, Bangalore.

Rajeev, Meenakshi (2004). "Reforms in State Public Enterprises in Karnataka: A Review" *Working Paper 148*, Institute for Social and Economic Change, Bangalore.

Raju, K.V. (2000). "Participatory Irrigation Management in Andhra Pradesh: Promise, Practice and a Way Forward", *ISEC Working Paper No.65*, Institute for Social and Economic Change, Bangalore.

Rao, M. Govinda (2001). "Fiscal Situation in Karnataka: Problems and Challenges", in Arun P. Bali (ed.), *Refashioning the New Economic Order–Karnataka in Transition*, Rawat Publications, New Delhi.

———. (2002), "State Finances in India: A Critical Review", *ISEC Working Paper No.113*, Institute for Social and Economic Change, Bangalore.

Roy Chowdhury, Supriya (2003). "Old Classes and New Spaces: Urban Poverty, Unorganised Labour and New Unions", *Economic and Political Weekly*, December 13: 5277-5284.

Sangita S.N. (1987). "Panchayati Raj Experiment in Karnataka", *Kurukshetra*, December.

———. (1989). "The *Lokayukta* Institution (Ombudsman) in Karnataka: A Trend Setter for Three Tier Structure Ombudsman in India", *Indian Journal of Public Administration*, 35(4), OctoberDecember.

———. (1990a). "Panchayati Raj Systems in Karnataka: A Need for Change", *Panchayat Sandesh*, June.

———. (1990b). "Self Employment Programmes for Rural Youth: The Role of Non-Governmental Organisations (NGOs)", *Management Review*, 5 (5), JulyDecember.

———. (1995). "Institutional Arrangement for Controlling Corruption in Public Life: Experiences from Karnataka", *The Indian Journal of Public Administration*, 41 (1), Jan.-March.

———. (1998). "Effective and Responsive Administration in Karnataka", *ISDA Journal*, 8 (4), October-December.

———. (2000). "Corruption in Administration Causes and Consequences, Corruption at the Grassroots", in N. Narayanaswamy, *et al.*, (eds.) Concept Publishing Company.

———. (2001). "Administrative Reforms for Good Governance in Karnataka: An Overview", paper presented at the seminar on *Administrative Reforms for Good Governance in Karnataka*, Seminar.

———. (2001). "Decentralisation and Good Governance" paper presented at the All India Political Science Conference, Nagarjuna University, Guntur.

———. (2002). "Administrative Reforms for Good Governance", *The Indian Journal of Political Science*, 63 (4), December.

———. *Governance and Service Delivery in Karnataka: Initiatives and Outcomes* (forthcoming).

———. "Decentralisation for Good Governance & Sustainable Development", *ISEC Working Paper* in progress.

———. (2003a). "*Lokayukta* and Good Governance in Karnataka: An Overview", paper presented at the *Lokayukta* and Good Governance in Karnataka Seminar on 28th June.

———. (2003b). *Institutions for Self-Governance of Community Forestry Resources: Experiences from Three Indian States*, IDPAD Project Report, March.

Sangita, S.N. (1987). "Panchayati Raj Experiment in Karnataka", *Kurukshetra*, December.

Sangita, S.N. *et al.* (1996). "Ethics in Superior Civil Service in India-Recruitment and Training", *Indian Journal of Public Administration*, Vol. 42 (4): Oct.-Dec.

Sangita S.N. and Bikash Chandra Dash (2005). "Electronic Governance and Service Delivery in India: Theory and Practice", *Working Paper*, ISEC, Bangalore (forthcoming).

Sekher, Madhushree (2002). "Tackling Society's `Detritus': Stakeholder Partnerships and Urban Service Delivery in India", *ISEC Working Paper No.101*, Institute for Social and Economic Change, Bangalore.

Sekher, T.V. (2003). "Sensitizing Panchayats on Health Issues Through Television: Experiences of a Pilot Project", *Working Paper No.133*, ISEC, Bangalore.

Sivanna, N. (2002). "Process and Performance in Panchayats" in Abdul Aziz *et al.*, (eds.), *op. cit.*

Smitha, K.C. and S.N. Sangita. *Urban Governance and Service Delivery* (forthcoming).

Solomon, Benjamin (2000). "Governance, Economic Settings and Poverty in Bangalore", *Environment & Urbanisation*, 12(1), April.

———. (2000). "Governance, Economic Settings and Poverty in Bangalore", *Environment & Urbanisation*, 12, (1): 39.

Subramanium, D.K. (1985). "Consumption Analysis of Bangalore Water Supply" in V. Vyasulu and A. Reddy (eds.), *Essays on Bangalore*, Karnataka State Council for Science and Technology, Indian Institute of Science.

TARU (1998). *Bangalore Water Supply and Sewerage Master Plan: A Situation Analysis*, New Delhi, December.

Urban Finance 2004. "Best Practices by Urban Local Bodies in India: A Study of Karnataka", 7 (2), June.

Vijayalakshmi, V. (2002). "Gender Accountability and Political Representation in Local Government", *ISEC Working Paper No.102*, Institute for Social and Economic Change, Bangalore.

———. (2003). "Accountability and Governance: Local Government in Kerala and Karnataka", *ISEC Working Paper No.125*, Institute for Social and Economic Change, Bangalore.

Vijayalakshmi, V. and B.K. Chandrashekar (2000). "Gender Inequality, Differences and Identities: Women and Local Governance in Karnataka", *ISEC Working Paper No.72*, Institute for Social and Economic Change, Bangalore.

Vyasulu, Vinod (2004). "Transformation in Governance Since 1990s: Some Reflections", *Economic and Political Weekly*, June 5:2377-2385.

Vyasulu, Vinod and A. Reddy (ed.), *Essays on Bangalore*, Karnataka State Council for Science and Technology.

World Bank (2003). *World Development Report 2004*, Washington.

APPENDIX A-11.1

Staff Strength in Government Departments, Karnataka: 1972-2002

	Departments	1972		1986		1993		2002	
		No. of Employees	In per cent	No. of Employees	In per cent	No. of Employees	In per cent	No. of Employees	In per cent
1	Legislature Secretariat	-	-	589	0.12	640	0.14	-	-
2	Secretariat (Government)	-	-	3,774	0.79	3,685	0.78	-	-
3	Law & Parliamentary	6,415	2.30	10,267	2.14	13,288	2.83	15461	2.47
4	Personnel & Administrative-Reforms	-	-	1,720	0.36	1,170	0.25	9030	1.44
5	Finance	-	-	12,583	2.62	15,134	3.22	16620	2.66
6	Food & Transport	-	-	3,584	0.75	4,064	0.87	2452	0.39
7	Information, Tourism & Youth Service	-	-	2,975	0.62	3,179	0.69	2334	0.37
8	Industries & Commerce	-	-	9,358	1.95	8,633	1.84	10859	1.74
9	Education	1,01,104	36.10	2,01,693	42.01	165,393	32.27	247943	39.66
10	Health & Family Services	34,732	12.40	53,502	11.14	60,158	12.83	74779	11.96
11	Home	31,687	11.30	53,422	11.13	58,381	12.45	82497	13.20
12	Agriculture & Horticulture	9,456	3.40	18,631	3.88	21,955	4.67	18133	2.90
13	Revenue	17,624	6.30	27,894	5.18	28,544	6.09	24312	3.89
14	Animal Husbandry & Veterinary	14,396	5.50	22,099	4.6	25,952	5.53	16990	2.72
15	Public Works, CADA, Elec. & Irrigation	14,507	5.20	27,193	5.64	22,976	4.9	37601	6.02
16	Rural Development & Panchayat Raj	-	-	2,264	0.47	1,001	0.21	13868	2.22
17	Cooperation	-	-	8,811	1.83	8,624	1.84	7819	1.25
18	Social Welfare & Labour	-	-	17,051	3.5	17,187	3.66	20784	3.32
19	Housing &Urban Development	-	-	830	0.17	957	0.2	717	0.11
20	Institutional Finance & Statistics	-	-	1,697	0.35	2,069	0.44	1218	0.19
21	Planning	-	-	150	0.03	201	0.04	-	-
22	Others	50,035	17.80	-	-	5,688	1.213	21782	3.49
	Total	**178,852**	**100.0**	**278,394**	**100.0**	**468,879**	**100.0**	**603,417**	**100.0**

Note: Others include Governors Secretariat, Women, Child, Disabled, Welfare and Legal Departments.

The gaps in columns are due to the non-existence of the functionaries in that period which would have been otherwise merged with the major functionaries.

Source: Compiled from Annual Administrative Reports and KARC, 2001.

APPENDIX A-11.2

Details of Plan and Non-Plan Expenditure and Percentage of Salaries and Schemes: 2001-02

	Budget							
	Plan	*% to Total*	*Non-Plan*	*% to Total*	*Total*	*% to Total*	*% of Salary*	*% of Schemes*
Irrigation	111941.00	26.23	45815.15	4.79	157756.15	11.41	8.42	91.24
Public Works	14728.28	3.45	42888.85	4.49	57617.13	4.17	18.42	81.48
Health & Family Welfare	39723.88	9.31	46407.01	4.86	86130.89	6.23	33.02	66.98
Education	31066.94	7.28	82198.77	8.60	113265.71	8.19	28.67	71.33
Agriculture & Horticulture	19685.95	4.61	10282.69	1.08	29968.64	2.17	19.89	80.11
Animal Husbandry & Fisheries	4185.60	0.98	4314.09	0.45	8499.69	0.61	17.70	82.30
Forest, Ecology & Environment	12373.02	2.90	16411.09	1.72	28784.11	2.08	30.14	69.86
Social Welfare Department	32278.39	7.56	972.79	0.10	33251.18	2.41	2.48	97.52
Women & Child Development	5273.00	1.24	5277.24	0.55	10550.24	0.76	20.70	79.30
Information, Tourism & Youth Services	2951.00	0.69	3783.73	0.40	6734.73	0.49	23.51	76.49
Rural Development *Panchayati Raj*	39035.52	9.15	8411.00	0.88	47446.52	3.43	2.52	97.48
Commerce and Industries	21364.00	5.01	17416.86	1.82	38780.86	2.81	15.78	84.22
Cooperation	2413.23	0.57	7332.11	0.77	9745.34	0.70	37.55	62.45
Kannada & Culture	1073.00	0.25	2807.94	0.29	3880.94	0.28	44.69	55.31
Housing	31741.86	7.44	2171.33	0.23	33913.19	2.45	0.02	99.98
Urban Development	34379.00	8.06	1168.58	0.12	35547.58	2.57	1.95	98.05
Labour	1903.20	0.45	3580.61	0.37	5483.81	0.40	63.95	36.05
Finance	2308.00	0.54	29726.38	3.11	32034.38	2.32	43.42	56.58
Dept. Personnel & Administrative Reforms	4773.00	1.12	213834.12	22.37	218607.12	15.81	4.67	95.33
Revenue	1224.00	0.29	36344.82	3.80	37568.82	2.72	50.13	49.87
Law Department	56.00	0.01	17528.79	1.83	17584.79	1.27	68.36	31.64
Home and Transport	2906.00	0.68	93182.01	9.75	96088.01	6.95	71.33	28.67
Food & Civil Supplies	1013.77	0.24	31431.57	3.29	32445.34	2.35	6.51	93.49
Planning	519.58	0.12	2052.62	0.21	2572.20	0.19	45.41	54.59
Energy	3805.00	0.89	230326.88	24.10	234131.88	16.94	92.30	7.70
Information Technology	1097.00	0.26	0.00	0.00	1097.00	0.08	0.00	100.00
Infrastructure	2870.00	0.67	46.67	0.00	2916.67	0.21	0.02	99.98
Total	**426689.22**	**100**	**955713.70**	**100**	**1382402.92**	**100**	**18.05**	**81.90**

Source: Compiled from *KARC Committee Report*, 2001, p. 44.

APPENDIX A-11.3

Performance of Bangalore Development Authority

Items	2000	2001	2002	2003	2004
1. Land Acquired and Utilised (Acres)	530	1550	1850	1348	-253*
2. Illegal Land Acquired (Acres)	-	-	-	175**	-
3. Property Recovered (Rs. Crores)	-	-	-	700$	-
4. Sites Allotted (No.)	10,000	15,000	15,000	10,000@	-
5. Sale Deeds Issued (No.)	7940	15691	13805	16620	2838@@
6. Revenue Collection (Registration Fees)	155.80	365.32	565.14	383.57	-
7. Revenue Collection (Stamp Duty)	672. 99	2376.11	3656.87	3281.33	-
8. No. of Documents Registered	-	-	-	-	-
9. Capital Receipt	87.79	368.28	533.04	639.89	587.81
10. Revenue Receipt	24.40	39.43	45.80	46.12	52.07
11. Capital Expenditure	133.90	263.57	512.85	728.03	793.37
12. Revenue Expenditure	49.86	75.04	31.96	43.50	41.58
13. Growth of Budget (%)	3.43	3.66	2.19	2.11	2.26

Note: * - Up to March 2003
** - From 2001-03
$ - From 2001-03
@ - From 2003-04
@@ - Up to May 2004

Source: Bangalore Development Authority.

Chapter 12

Karnataka State Finances

12.1 Introduction

State governments in the Indian Federation have been assigned important functions and responsibilities by the Indian Constitution. State governments have access to their own sources of revenue and are entitled as well for a share in central taxes and other transfers. State finances have become a subject of serious concern in the recent years due to the mounting fiscal distress experienced by them caused by deceleration in the resource growth and an unbridled growth in expenditure, more so of the revenue expenditure.

Karnataka for long has proved to be a fiscally prudent state in comparison with many other states in the country. The state experienced a sharp deterioration in its fiscal situation after the mid 1990s into early years of 2000, however, there has been a very good recovery as indicated by the growing revenue surpluses, declining fiscal deficits achieved in the revised and budget estimates in the last two years. Going by the recent improvements in the fiscal marksmanship the state has been experiencing in the recent years, it is hoped that the accounts would be close to the budget and revised estimates. A significant aspect to be noted is that the state, has been one of the early birds in announcing fiscal reforms in the country by passing the Fiscal Responsibility Act[1] and adopting a Medium Term approach to achieve fiscal recovery.

The state has certainly been on the path of recovery and being on the reform path does not however absolve the state from fiscal problems as yet: there are serious concerns such as high outstanding debt as per cent of gross state domestic product, high incidence of off budget borrowings, large interest payment and subsidy especially power sector liability, sharp rate of growth of pension expenditure.

Against this background, Chapter 12 has made an attempt to discuss the trends, reform initiatives, issues and concerns regarding Karnataka state finances. The Chapter is presented in seven sections. As a prelude to the discussion on Karnataka state finances, an attempt is made in section two to understand the fiscal position of Karnataka among the other major states in the country. Issues concerning government revenue, such as the adequacy, elasticity and buoyancy, central transfers, value added tax (VAT) are discussed in section three. Trends and issues relating to the manner in which government monies are spent as under various meaningful categories are elaborated in section four. Karnataka's debt related issues such as the magnitude of its increase, and contingent liabilities are dealt with at length in section five. Fiscal decentralisation issues are presented in section six. The last section highlights the conclusions and policy implications.

12.2 Fiscal Indicators

12.2.1 Fiscal Indicators in Karnataka

Karnataka has proved to be a fast reforming state that has been trying to implement reforms as and when mooted at the national level. The fiscal position in the state compares well with the southern states as well as all states' average. This gets very well depicted from the information on various fiscal indicators presented in Tables 12.1 and 12.2. Fiscal and revenue deficit size have been lower than the other states at all the time points with an exception of 1999-00.

1. Fiscal Responsibility Act has been enacted by five states in the country—Karnataka, Kerala, Punjab, Tamil Nadu, and Uttar Pradesh.

TABLE 12.1

Fiscal Deficit in Southern States

(Per Cent to NSDP)

Years	*Andhra Pradesh*	*Karnataka*	*Kerala*	*Tamil Nadu*	*States*
1990-91	3.2	2.7	6.6	4.1	3.3
1991-92	2.9	3.2	4.4	3.6	2.9
1992-93	3.8	4.4	3.5	4.1	2.8
1993-94	3.4	3.4	3.9	2.6	2.4
1994-95	3.8	3.3	3.8	2.4	2.7
1995-96	3.4	2.9	3.7	1.8	2.6
1996-97	2.8	2.3	5.0	3.1	2.7
1997-98	3.7	2.5	4.4	3.3	2.9
1998-99	5.5	4.1	5.3	4.5	4.2
1999-00	4.5	5.0	8.0	4.7	4.7
2000-01	5.8	4.5	6.1	4.0	4.3
2001-02	5.0	6.0	4.7	3.6	4.2

Source: Reserve Bank of India State Finances: A Study of Budgets: Various Issues.

The state also reveals a better picture, although there are signs of deterioration across all the states, both on revenue and expenditure fronts (Table 12.2). The deterioration issue is addressed later in the Chapter. Revenue deficit as a proportion of gross fiscal deficit (GFD) is lower than all states' average for all the time points presented. Further, the state has a better capital outlay level in the GFD. The other important expenditure indicators such as the proportion of interest payments in the revenue expenditure and that of non-development expenditure in the aggregate disbursements also place Karnataka in a better position.

On the resource front, while Karnataka has all along performed better than the other states in terms of tax revenue as a proportion to revenue expenditure, that of non-tax revenue does not compare favourably with other states.

These so called favourable trends observed in the state should however, not lead to complacency as the state is not completely out of fiscal stress and still has a number of issues to address, especially on the expenditure front such as high burden on account of committed expenditure and inadequate social and economic infrastructure investments. On the revenue front, the small yield on account of non-tax revenue is a cause for concern.

12.2.2 Karnataka State Finances

Trends in Deficits

Fiscal imbalances in the Karnataka state finances as indicated by the fiscal, primary and revenue deficits are not of recent origin. Figure 12.1 depicting the trends in these deficit levels as a proportion to GSDP from 1980-81 reveal that although fiscal and primary deficit levels were high in 1984-85, they were on the decline until 1990-91. They have revealed some fluctuations but were on the increase, during the decade of nineties.

The state on the other hand had a comfortable position on the revenue account. Revenue receipts were more than revenue expenditure as a result there was revenue surplus. This situation continued until 1983-1984, after which the state government has been having

TABLE 12.2

Karnataka's Major Fiscal Indicators

Fiscal Indicators	*1990-95 (Average)*		*1999-00 (Accounts)*		*2000-01 (Accounts)*		*2001-02 (Accounts)*		*2002-03 (Accounts)*		*2004-05 (Budget Estimates)*	
	Karnataka	*All States*	*Karnataka*	*All States*	*Karnataka*	*All States*	*Karnataka*	*All States*	*Karnataka*	*All States*	*Karnataka*	*All States*
RD/GFD	11.2	29.8	54.4	60.1	44.1	61.1	56	61.7	50.1	54.0	-13.9	39.1
Capital Outlay/GFD	85.9	49.9	41.6	25.6	46.1	33.5	35.9	33.6	55.6	35.8	98.8	54.2
Non Development Expenditure/ Aggregate Disbursement	24.5	27.3	30.3	35.1	28.9	34.4	28.8	36.6	30.1	36.1	36.8	36.2
Interests Payments/ Revenue Expenditure	11.1	13.6	13.2	17.7	14.3	18.1	14.4	19.9	17.5	20.9	15.4	21.7
State Tax Revenue/ Revenue Expenditure	58.6	44.9	50.8	42.1	54.2	43.1	53.0	40.9	55.5	42.4	60.6	44.4
States NTR/Revenue Expenditure	12.7	14.8	10.6	11.2	9.9	11.2	5.9	10.3	6.8	10.7	17.6	11.9

Note: RD = revenue deficit; GFD = gross fiscal deficit; NTR = non-tax revenues.

Source: RBI State Finances: A Study of Budgets: Various Issues, Mumbai.

mounting revenue deficits, with the exception of two or three years in between. The increase has been very sharp from 1998-99, an impact of the pay revision effected by the Fifth Pay Commission.

FIGURE 12.1

Deficits in Karnataka

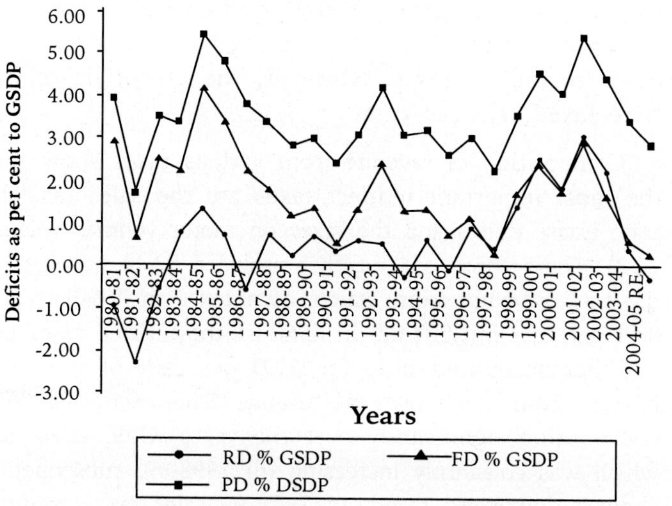

Source: Computed on the basis of data published in *Accounts at a Glance: 1960-2005*, Government of Karnataka.

Fiscal deficit too experienced some improvement during the period 1993-94 to 1997-98 wherein the deficit was on the decline. However, the state has fallen back in to high fiscal deficit level from 1998-99 onwards. The deficit reached an alltime high of 5.36 per cent in 2001-02. The various reform measures introduced in the state on the fiscal front ever since seem to be gaining positive results with the state reducing revenue deficit to a considerable extent as per 2003-04 actuals and achieving revenue surplus in the estimates of 2004-05 and fiscal deficit as a per cent of GSDP being on the decline.

12.3 Tax and Non-Tax Resources of Karnataka

12.3.1 Resource Position

The Karnataka state has made significant efforts to rationalise and simplify the tax and non-tax resources since 1996-97. There has been some improvement in the state's budgetary resources in the last three years. This section examines the state's tax and non-tax revenue resources and the policies pursued to rationalise the tax and non-tax revenue system.

Karnataka derives its finances mainly from the following sources:

- state's own taxes,
- state's own non-tax revenue,
- public debt and other capital resources,
- share in the divisible pool i.e. through central transfer of resources from the divisible pool,
- grants from the centre,
- public account, and
- contingency account.

The first two items of resources are crucial from the point of mobilising resources as per the fiscal policies framed by the state itself. These resources are entirely at the command of the state.

12.3.2 Composition and Trends in State's Own Tax Resources

The taxes levied, collected and appropriated by the state can be put under two categories:

i. commercial taxes, and

ii. non-commercial taxes.

The first category of taxes mainly consists of sales tax, (including turnover/RST), entry tax, agricultural income tax, and profession tax, entertainment tax, betting tax, luxury tax, and so on. These details are presented in Appendix A-12.1. The non-commercial taxes come mainly from items like, state excise, taxes on motor vehicles, stamps and registration fees, land revenue, electricity duty, forest development tax, health cess, and education cess. These are shown in Appendix A-12.2.

12.3.3 Trend and Composition of State's Own Taxes

Direct Taxes: Karnataka, like any other states or even like the Centre depends very heavily upon indirect taxes for its revenue. Till 1960-61 direct taxes contributed significantly to the total revenue from state's own taxes. The share of direct taxes fell consistently to reach less than 1 per cent level by 2002-2003. It is interesting to note that the percentage share of agricultural income tax (AIT) and land revenue (LR) in the total revenue from state's own taxes was 3.03 per cent and 18.02 per cent respectively during 1960-61. Thus, these two taxes, which fall on the agricultural sector, together contributed as much as 21.05 per cent to the total revenue from state's own taxes. Their share has gradually fallen over the years. In 1970-71 the share of agricultural income tax and land revenue was 1.54 per cent and 4.64 per cent level respectively. That is, together their share fell from 21.05 per cent in 1960-61 to just 6.18 per cent in 1970-71. In 1980-81 the revenue from these two taxes put together constituted only 3.73 per cent. The same trend continued in 1990-91. The relative contribution of AIT and LR declined to an insignificant level of just 0.027 and 0.518 percentage respectively in 2001-02 and in 2004-05 (BE). Agricultural income tax accounted for .014 per cent and land revenue accounted for 0.549 per cent only. Thus, these two together contributed a negligible 0.56 per cent in 2004-05 to the state's own tax revenue. Agricultural income tax is mobilised mainly from plantation crop in Karnataka.

Professional tax is another source of direct tax, which was introduced in April 1976 in the state. Initially its contribution was as low as Rs. 3.43 crores only and this source accounted for 1.27 per cent of the state's own revenue. However, it has grown in importance over the years. During 1980-81 yield from this tax was Rs. 7.40 crores and according to the budget estimates for the year 2004-05 it was expected to contribute Rs. 272.00 crores. Major portion i.e. around 96 per cent of this comes from the salaried class.

The state has already taken advantage of the raising of the Constitutional ceiling to revise tax rates and to widen the tax base. Revenue growth has therefore picked up from 9.66 per cent in the eighties to 14.49 per cent in the nineties.

FIGURE 12.2

Percentage Composition of Commercial Taxes in 2001-02

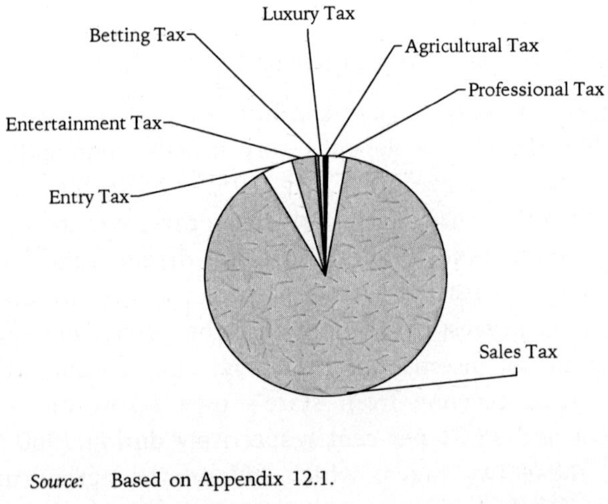

Source: Based on Appendix 12.1.

A study undertaken at ISEC[2] recommends for widening of the tax base by removing the ambiguities in the definition of profession. The existing tax slabs and rates need to be rationalised. The tax can be made more productive if the exemptions and concessions are re-examined and rationalised. As the service sector is expanding and growing at a faster rate this tax can become an important source of state direct tax.

Indirect Taxes: Karnataka occupied third place among states in terms of collection of per capita sales tax. The effective tax rates on many commodities had been in double digits. However, the essentials of life were taxed at 2 per cent.

Composition of revenue from various taxes show that the most important indirect taxes are the sales tax, the state excise duties and the taxes on motor vehicles (Figure 12.2). These three put together provided 83.14 per cent of the total revenue from state's own taxes in 1990-91 and 83.1 per cent in 2001-02. In 1960-61 these three taxes put together accounted only for 61.0 per cent of the total revenue from state's own tax revenue. State excise has been contributing significantly over the years while sales tax, which was constantly increasing till 1998-99, subsequently showed downward trend. In 1998-99 sales tax accounted for 61.43 per cent of state's own taxes and the same declined to 52.43 per cent in 2002-03. However, as is seen from Table 12.3, during the years 2003-04 and 2004-05 there has been a slight improvement as its relative contribution reached a level of 53.5 and 54.215 per cent respectively. Despite these changes in the relative position, sales tax continued to be the major source of revenue. This trend may be seen from Table 12.3. The three taxes namely sales tax, state excise and motor vehicle tax accounted for 54.21 per cent, 17.6 per cent and 6.485 per cent respectively in 2004-05 (BE).

Major portion of commercial taxes come from sales tax. Table 12.3 presents percentage composition of commercial taxes in Karnataka since 1990-91 to 2004-05 (BE). Sales tax accounted for, on an average about 90 per cent of the total commercial taxes. The relative share of sales tax in the total commercial taxes has gone down marginally during the past 15 years from 88.44 per cent in 1990-91 to 86.52 per cent in 2004-05 (Table 12.4). Sales tax is the most important component of commercial taxes. As may be seen from Table 12.4, this single tax accounted for 86.52 per cent in 2004-05(BE). However, it has slightly declined in its relative importance over the years. Contribution of this tax was about 88 per cent in 1990-91. The same became 86.5 per cent in 2004-05. This is followed by entry tax, which accounted for 8.42 per cent in 2001-02. The entertainment tax is the third important commercial tax contributing less than 2 per cent to the total commercial taxes.

2. Devendra Babu (2000). *Profession Tax Base: A Study in Karnataka State*, ISEC Bangalore, *mimeograph.*

TABLE 12.3

Commercial Taxes as Per Cent of Own Tax Revenue

Year	*Agricultural Tax*	*Professional Tax*	*Sales Tax*	*Entry Tax Tax*	*Entertainment Tax*	*Betting Tax*	*Luxury Tax*	*Commercial Tax*	*Own Tax Revenue*
1990-91	0.310	1.725	56.469	2.808	1.801	0.497	0.277	63.888	100.000
1991-92	0.313	1.651	57.004	2.829	1.666	0.297	0.269	64.030	100.000
1992-93	0.351	1.971	57.324	3.546	1.602	0.321	0.338	65.454	100.000
1993-94	0.236	2.046	59.751	3.480	1.555	0.236	0.306	67.609	100.000
1994-95	0.392	2.154	58.419	2.728	1.097	0.328	0.383	65.500	100.000
1995-96	0.943	2.005	56.020	3.192	0.854	0.255	0.394	63.664	100.000
1996-97	0.685	2.070	60.858	3.458	0.593	0.205	0.541	68.410	100.000
1997-98	0.469	1.606	59.714	3.655	0.862	0.142	0.509	66.958	100.000
1998-99	0.699	1.646	61.431	3.934	0.810	0.170	0.607	69.296	100.000
1999-00	0.449	1.715	60.473	4.359	0.776	0.154	0.582	68.508	100.000
2000-01	0.260	1.676	59.566	5.231	0.561	0.158	0.737	68.188	100.000
2001-02	0.027	1.697	53.479	5.055	0.497	0.139	0.805	61.698	100.000
2002-03	0.013	1.726	52.430	4.948	0.439	0.129	0.789	60.473	100.000
2003-04 (RE)	0.008	1.782	53.502	5.309	0.336	0.376	0.658	61.972	100.000
2004-05 (BE)	0.014	1.818	54.215	5.138	0.256	0.587	0.627	62.656	100.000

Note: RE = Revenue estimate.
BE = Budget estimate.

Source: Website of Finance Deparment, *Accounts at a Glance* for 1960-2005, Government of Karnataka.

Table 12.3 shows that the commercial tax has an average share of about 66 per cent (average for 15 years) in the total own taxes. In 1990-91 commercial taxes accounted for about 63.88 per cent of total own tax revenue and the same declined to about 61 per cent in 2001-02. However, the RE and BE for the years 2003-04 and 2004-05 show an increase in its share. The composition of tax revenue is very important from the point of policy formulation.

Non-commercial taxes as percentage of own tax resources as given in Table 12.5 shows that the share of motor vehicles and excise have remained in the last few years at their average of about 6.6 per cent and 17 per cent respectively. The shares of stamps and

TABLE 12.4

Composition of Commercial Tax Revenue (Percentage of Total Commercial Tax)

Year	*Agricultural Tax*	*Professional Tax*	*Sales Tax*	*Entry Tax*	*Entertainment Tax*	*Betting Tax*	*Luxury Tax*	*Total Commercial Tax*
1990-91	0.485	2.700	88.387	4.395	2.820	0.779	0.434	100.000
1991-92	0.488	2.579	89.027	4.419	2.603	0.464	0.421	100.000
1992-93	0.536	3.012	87.580	5.417	2.448	0.491	0.517	100.000
1993-94	0.350	3.026	88.376	5.148	2.300	0.348	0.452	100.000
1994-95	0.599	3.289	89.189	4.164	1.675	0.500	0.585	100.000
1995-96	1.481	3.150	87.993	5.014	1.342	0.401	0.619	100.000
1996-97	1.002	3.027	88.960	5.054	0.867	0.299	0.791	100.000
1997-98	0.700	2.398	89.182	5.459	1.288	0.213	0.760	100.000
1998-99	1.008	2.375	88.649	5.677	1.170	0.245	0.876	100.000
1999-00	0.656	2.503	88.272	6.363	1.133	0.224	0.849	100.000
2000-01	0.381	2.458	87.355	7.671	0.823	0.232	1.080	100.000
2001-02	0.043	2.751	86.678	8.194	0.805	0.226	1.304	100.000
2002-03	0.021	2.854	86.700	8.182	0.726	0.213	1.305	100.000
2003-04 (RE)	0.012	2.876	86.332	8.567	0.543	0.607	1.062	100.000
2004-05	0.023	2.902	86.529	8.200	0.409	0.936	1.001	100.000

Source: Same as in Table 12.3.

registration have increased significantly from 7 per cent in 2000-01 to 10.4 per cent in 2004-05. Except state excise and motor vehicle tax as is revealed from Table 12.5 all other non-commercial taxes contribute less than 1 per cent to the total state's own tax revenue.

In spite of satisfactory growth, indirect taxes had been a source of inefficiency and relative price distortions. This necessitated switching over to a more rational and simple VAT system.

12.3.4 Growth Trend

The ratio of each tax to GSDP is given in Tables 12.6 and 12.7. Commercial tax had an average share of about 6.0 per cent. Under the non-commercial taxes,

TABLE 12.5

Non-Commercial Taxes as Per Cent of Own Tax Revenue

Year	*State Excise*	*Taxes on Motor Vehicles*	*Stamps and Registration*	*Land Revenue*	*Elect. Duty*	*Forest Development*	*Health Cess*	*Education Cess*	*Own Tax Revenue*
1990-91	18.425	8.251	6.187	0.659	2.260	0.220	0.091	0.020	100.000
1991-92	17.596	7.843	7.103	0.592	2.626	0.171	0.028	0.011	100.000
1992-93	16.635	7.118	7.243	0.542	2.771	0.194	0.029	0.014	100.000
1993-94	16.763	6.814	6.318	0.422	1.854	0.201	0.013	0.006	100.000
1994-95	16.634	6.784	8.684	0.461	1.625	0.261	0.039	0.012	100.000
1995-96	15.552	8.647	10.173	0.542	1.185	0.196	0.024	0.016	100.000
1996-97	14.631	5.648	8.454	0.798	1.846	0.197	0.006	0.010	100.000
1997-98	13.470	6.929	9.504	0.695	2.186	0.135	0.015	0.107	100.000
1998-99	14.478	5.571	7.894	0.547	2.020	0.120	0.033	0.040	100.000
1999-00	15.691	5.795	7.306	0.500	2.009	0.098	0.048	0.045	100.000
2000-01	16.844	5.549	7.057	0.477	1.793	0.075	0.017	0.011	100.000
2001-02	20.064	7.230	8.678	0.503	1.739	0.069	0.020	0.010	100.000
2002-03	19.101	6.163	10.173	0.544	1.570	0.068	0.009	0.006	100.000
2003-04 (RE)	18.100	6.792	10.453	0.563	1.924	0.114	0.010	0.072	100.000
2004-05 (BE)	17.601	6.485	10.697	0.549	1.834	0.104	0.000	0.075	100.000

Source: Same as in Table 12.3.

TABLE 12.6

Commercial Taxes as Per Cent of GSDP

Year	*Agricultural Taxes*	*Professional Taxes*	*Sales Taxes*	*Entry Taxes*	*Entertainment Taxes*	*Betting Taxes*	*Luxury Taxes*	*Commercial Taxes (2-8)*	*Own Tax Revenue*
1990-91	0.031	0.172	5.644	0.281	0.180	0.050	0.028	6.386	9.995
1991-92	0.030	0.160	5.509	0.273	0.161	0.029	0.026	6.188	9.665
1992-93	0.033	0.185	5.377	0.333	0.150	0.030	0.032	6.139	9.380
1993-94	0.021	0.182	5.330	0.310	0.139	0.021	0.027	6.031	8.920
1994-95	0.033	0.183	4.958	0.232	0.093	0.028	0.033	5.560	8.488
1995-96	0.084	0.180	5.019	0.286	0.077	0.023	0.035	5.704	8.960
1996-97	0.056	0.170	4.989	0.283	0.049	0.017	0.044	5.608	8.198
1997-98	0.039	0.134	4.986	0.305	0.072	0.012	0.043	5.591	8.350
1998-99	0.054	0.126	4.706	0.301	0.062	0.013	0.047	5.309	7.661
1999-00	0.036	0.138	4.869	0.351	0.062	0.012	0.047	5.516	8.052
2000-01	0.022	0.144	5.111	0.449	0.048	0.014	0.063	5.850	8.580
2001-02	0.002	0.153	4.814	0.455	0.045	0.013	0.072	5.554	9.002
2002-03	0.001	0.152	4.617	0.436	0.039	0.011	0.070	5.326	8.807
2003-04 (RE)	0.001	0.177	5.307	0.527	0.033	0.037	0.065	6.147	9.920
2004-05 (BE)	0.001	0.184	5.481	0.519	0.026	0.059	0.063	6.334	10.110

Source: Same as in Table 12.3.

TABLE 12.7

Non-Commercial Taxes as Per Cent of GSDP

Year	*State Excise*	*Taxes on Motor Vehicles*	*Stamps and Registration*	*Land Revenue*	*Electricity Duty*	*Forest Development*	*Health Cess*	*Education Cess*	*Own Tax*
1990-91	1.84	0.83	0.62	0.07	0.23	0.02	0.01	0.00	10.01
1991-92	1.70	0.76	0.69	0.06	0.25	0.02	0.00	0.00	9.66
1992-93	1.56	0.67	0.68	0.05	0.26	0.02	0.00	0.00	9.38
1993-94	1.56	0.63	0.59	0.04	0.17	0.02	0.00	0.00	9.28
1994-95	1.49	0.61	0.78	0.04	0.15	0.02	0.00	0.00	8.95
1995-96	1.46	0.81	0.95	0.05	0.11	0.02	0.00	0.00	9.38
1996-97	1.29	0.50	0.75	0.07	0.16	0.02	0.00	0.00	8.85
1997-98	1.20	0.62	0.85	0.06	0.20	0.01	0.00	0.01	8.94
1998-99	1.14	0.44	0.62	0.04	0.16	0.01	0.00	0.00	7.91
1999-00	1.27	0.47	0.59	0.04	0.16	0.01	0.00	0.00	8.12
2000-01	1.45	0.48	0.61	0.04	0.15	0.01	0.00	0.00	8.63
2001-02	1.87	0.67	0.81	0.05	0.16	0.01	0.00	0.00	9.31
2002-03	1.77	0.57	0.94	0.05	0.15	0.01	0.00	0.00	9.25
2003-04 (RE)	1.80	0.67	1.04	0.06	0.19	0.01	0.00	0.01	9.92
2004-05 (BE)	1.78	0.66	1.08	0.06	0.19	0.01	0.00	0.01	10.11

Source: Same as in Table 12.3.

TABLE 12.8

Tax GSDP Ratio

Years	*GSDP*	*T/Y Ratio*
1990-91	23332	10.01
1991-92	30008	9.66
1992-93	33026	9.38
1993-94	42739	9.28
1994-95	50535	8.95
1995-96	58861	9.38
1996-97	70360	8.85
1997-98	76790	8.94
1998-99	90623	7.91
1999-00	96179	8.12
2000-01	105396	8.63
2001-02	109461	9.31
2002-03	118540	9.25
2003-04	130678	9.92
2004-05 (BE)	147956	10.11

Source: Same as in Table 12.3.

the share of motor vehicles and state excise has remained constant at their average level of about 0.6 per cent and 1.7 per cent respectively. However, the overall tax GSDP ratio (Table 12.8) has deteriorated from 10.01 per cent in 1999-91 to almost 9.25 per cent in 2002-03, and the budget estimates for 2004-05 expects it to be around 10.11 per cent. In Karnataka, on an average total tax GSDP ratio has been around 9.5 per cent since 1990-91.

An analysis of the state's revenue receipts during the last decade indicates that the total revenue receipts (tax and non-tax) of the state are growing at an average rate of 14.38 per cent.

As may be seen from Appendix A-12.1, states own taxes, which were Rs. 10963.88 crore in 2002-03 is expected to increase to Rs. 14957.90 crore. The commercial tax revenue showed an annual average rate of growth of 14.3 per cent (Table 12.9) in the last 15 years. While the same for the last decade 1990-91, 1999-00 was around 16.4 per cent.

The annual average rate of growth was the highest (Table 12.9) for entry tax and it was 20.15 per cent during the past 15 years (1990-91 to 2004-05). Even the annual compound rate of growth was around 19.09 in the same period. The annual average growth rates and the compound growth rates are displayed for both commercial and non-commercial taxes in Tables 12.9 to 12.11.

TABLE 12.9

Annual Growth Rate of Commercial Tax Revenues and GSDP

Year	*Agricultural Tax*	*Professional Tax*	*Sales Tax*	*Entry Tax*	*Entertainment Tax*	*Betting Tax*	*Luxury Tax*	*Commercial Taxes (2-8)*	*Own Tax Revenue*	*GSDP at Current Prices*
1991-92	25.450	19.041	25.538	25.302	15.044	-25.776	20.898	24.636	24.359	28.613
1992-93	19.735	27.521	7.413	33.853	2.711	15.563	34.187	9.188	6.814	10.057
1993-94	-17.035	27.706	28.275	20.794	19.440	-9.749	11.164	27.119	23.066	29.410
1994-95	86.681	18.477	10.003	-11.818	-20.644	56.459	41.030	9.001	12.511	18.241
1995-96	195.660	14.459	17.906	43.880	-4.251	-4.128	26.598	19.508	22.955	16.476
1996-97	-20.511	12.916	18.810	18.475	-24.084	-12.324	50.048	17.518	9.365	19.536
1997-98	-23.982	-13.783	9.076	17.519	61.637	-22.693	4.614	8.805	11.166	9.139
1998-99	61.398	10.985	11.398	16.533	1.791	29.025	29.127	12.067	8.284	18.014
1999-00	-28.247	16.198	9.802	23.604	6.824	0.934	6.879	10.271	11.541	6.131
2000-01	-32.529	14.144	15.013	40.113	-15.605	20.185	47.803	16.220	16.765	9.583
2001-02	-88.799	10.339	-2.170	5.304	-3.548	-4.059	19.024	-1.406	8.964	3.857
2002-03	-49.810	7.756	3.874	3.698	-6.356	-2.042	3.936	3.848	5.952	8.294
2003-04 (RE)	-24.242	28.224	26.707	33.235	-4.801	263.366	3.556	27.246	24.169	10.240
2004-05 (BE)	115	17.718	16.929	11.664	-12.196	79.836	9.998	16.664	15.391	13.222
AA Growth	15.626	15.121	14.184	20.154	1.140	27.471	22.062	14.335	14.379	14.325

Note: AA=Annual average rate of growth.

Source: Same as in Table 12.3.

TABLE 12.10

Annual Growth Rate of Non-Commercial Taxes in Karnataka

Year	*State Excise*	*Taxes on Motor Vehicles*	*Stamps and Registration Fees*	*Land Revenue*	*Electricity Duty*	*Forest Development Tax*	*Health Cess*	*Education Cess Tax*	*Own Tax Revenue*	*GSDP at Current Prices*
1991-92	18.765	18.209	42.785	11.784	44.470	-3.314	-62.264	-30.435	24.359	28.613
1992-93	0.982	-3.060	8.917	-2.271	12.738	20.968	11.250	37.500	6.814	10.057
1993-94	24.012	17.809	7.340	-4.231	-17.659	28.000	-46.067	-50.000	23.066	29.410
1994-95	11.642	12.014	54.656	23.086	-1.415	45.573	252.083	131.818	12.511	18.241
1995-96	14.959	56.717	44.039	44.388	-10.303	-7.513	-23.669	70.588	22.955	16.476
1996-97	2.886	-28.568	-9.114	61.169	70.373	10.058	-75.194	-35.632	9.365	19.536
1997-98	2.349	36.396	24.970	-3.150	31.634	-23.989	206.250	1123.214	11.166	9.139
1998-99	16.383	-12.946	-10.056	-14.760	0.043	-3.353	133.673	-59.562	8.284	18.014
1999-00	20.893	16.037	3.226	1.921	10.930	-9.330	63.319	24.549	11.541	6.131
2000-01	25.340	11.809	12.784	11.438	4.191	-10.026	-58.824	-71.014	16.765	9.583
2001-02	29.795	41.957	33.994	14.782	5.676	-1.026	30.519	0.000	8.964	3.857
2002-03	5.930	-5.148	30.443	20.327	0.490	10.815	-50.746	-29.000	11.271	8.294
2003-04 (RE)	12.036	30.292	21.489	22.463	44.882	98.128	37.374	1216.901	18.233	10.240
2004-05 (BE)	12.211	10.179	18.079	12.534	10.000	4.993	-100.000	19.786	15.391	13.222
AA Growth	14.156	14.407	20.254	14.249	14.718	11.427	24.439	167.765	14.335	14.344

Source: Same as in Table 12.3.

In terms of growth performance, Karnataka has fared well. During the period 1990-01 and 2004-05 as may be seen from Table 12.11 the compound growth of AIT was negative (-12.28). Total commercial taxes recorded

13.01 per cent growth. The compound growth of sales tax was 12.80 per cent in past 15 years. During the same period GSDP recorded a compound growth of 13.46 per cent (Table 12.11). The growth rate of luxury tax was the highest as it was around 23 per cent.

State excise has recorded 13.59 per cent growth during the same period. Total states' own tax revenue has recorded an impressive growth of 13.44 per cent (Table 12.12). Among the non-commercial taxes as may be seen from Table 12.12, state excise recorded the highest compound growth between 1990-2004 followed by motor vehicle tax.

During 1990-91 and 2004-05, the buoyancy recorded a decline. The buoyancy coefficient of commercial taxes as displayed in Table 12.13 was just 0.955 and that of sales tax it was 0.942 only. Own tax revenue had unit buoyancy. Direct taxes, in particular, the revenues from land revenue and agricultural income tax were not at all buoyant. Other commercial and non-commercial taxes also recorded very low buoyancy coefficients.

The above analysis of the composition, growth trend and buoyancy highlight the need for improving the state tax system.

TABLE 12.11

Compound Growth Rates of Commercial Taxes

Year	*Agricultural Income Tax*	*Professional Tax*	*Sales Tax*	*Entry Tax*	*Entertainment Tax*	*Betting Tax*	*Luxury Tax*	*Commercial Tax (2-8)*	*GSDP*
1990-91 to 2004-05	-12.28	12.58	12.80	19.09	-.40	10.35	22.62	13.01	13.46

Source: Same as in Table 12.3.

TABLE 12.12

Compound Growth Rate of Non-Commercial Taxes in Karnataka

Year	*State Excise*	*Taxes on MotorVehicles*	*Stamps and Registration Fees*	*Land Revenue*	*Electricity Duty*	*Forest Development Tax*	*Health Cess*	*Education Cess Tax*	*Own Tax Revenue*
1991-2005	13.97	11.65	16.63	12.92	11.43	4.57	4.24	22.76	13.44
1985-1999	13.59	11.34	17.90	-	3.10	-	-	-	-

Source: Same as in Table 12.3.

Growth in state's own tax revenue has been much more rapid than the growth in its SDP and per capita income during sixties and seventies. Between 1960-61 and 1970-71 and 1980-81 for every 1 per cent increase in state income there has been an increase of 1.6 per cent in the state's own tax revenue but between 1980-81 and 1990-91 for every 1 per cent increase in SDP there has been 1.3 per cent increase in revenue from state's own taxes.

12.3.5 Tax Reforms and Revenue Policy Measures in Karnataka

The Karnataka government has periodically undertaken reform of its tax structure. At least once every decade, expert commissions have given reports suggesting fiscal improvement measures. The Karnataka Taxation Review April 1982 Committee did an in-depth study of different

TABLE 12.13

Buoyancy of Important Taxes: 1990-91 & 2003-04 and 1985-86 & 1998-99

Year	*Sales Tax*	*Commercial Taxes (2-8)*	*State Excise*	*Taxes on Motor Vehicles*	*Stamps and Registration Fees*	*Land Revenue*	*Own Tax Revenue*
1991-2005	0.942	.955	0.979	.831	1.187	.939	.973
1985-1999	1.090	-	0.92	0.77	-	-	1.001

Source: Same as in Table 12.3.

state levies. Again, in May 1991, the Commission on state finances made a series of recommendations covering the entire spectrum of state finances, including taxation. Another Tax Reform Commission was appointed in 2000. The Commission gave its first report in February 2001 and the final report in October 2001. The Revenue Reform Commission was appointed subsequently.

All the committees and commissions, appointed so far in the state have expressed that the tax system should be simple and transparent; it should be designed mainly to raise revenue for the government in a fair and equitable manner. A simple tax system should have only a few tax rates and very few exemptions. To achieve the objective of simplicity, exemptions based on forms or uses of commodities or nature of purchasers will have to be eliminated. The best practice approach to reforming the consumption tax system in the state is to broaden the base of the tax, simplify the tax structure and reduce rate differentiation. Changes in the tax structure should be planned rather than *ad hoc*. In a properly calibrated tax system, there is no case for giving exemptions or changing the rates of tax or expanding incentives and concessions through notifications throughout the year. Such a possibility should be abolished by the legislature.

Both the reports of this Tax Reform Commission (2001) are very important. This report takes into consideration the federal structure, the transformations that have occurred in the state's economy and in governmental priorities as a consequence of the liberalisation process of the last decade, and the prevailing economic situation in the state while making its recommendations.

The Commission found that for Karnataka, as a whole, tax buoyancy has fallen over the years from 1.082 (in 1993-94) to below unity 0.874 (in 1998-99). Growth rates for the nineties have been below those in the eighties for major revenue earners like sales tax, state excises and motor vehicles tax.

Slowing down of sales tax growth is attributable to increase in the quantum of consumption that escapes the tax net through exemptions and concessions, particularly on account of incentives given for fresh industrial investment. The efficacy of such deferrals and waivers in promoting industrialisation and increasing employment is questionable.

Revenue from state excise duties (which constitute for most states the second most important revenue source after sales tax and related commodity taxes) has been affected during the nineties by popular hostility towards the excise lobby. Neighbouring states like Andhra Pradesh adopted to go dry for some years and similar pressure was also felt in Karnataka. Several factors led to instability in the revenue collection from this source and reduced the annual growth rate.

High tax rates (effective) are attributed for low buoyancy of taxes in the state. And this has led to the perception that Karnataka is a highly taxed state. The Commission confirmed that the effective tax rates in Karnataka are higher than those prevailing in the neighbouring states. Therefore the Commission came out with major reforms, which extended all the way from tax structure to improvement in tax administration.

The focus was on widening tax base of all major and minor taxes. The Commission advocated reforms in the tax administration, tax rates, policies relating to exemptions and concessions, grouping of commodities so that tax slabs and categories can be in line with the requirements of both vertical and horizontal equity (Box 12.1).

BOX 12.1

Tax Reforms Commission

The Tax Reforms Commission suggested measures to rationalise sales tax system keeping in mind the requirements for the proposed changeover to VAT. The Commission has developed a road map for making the transition to value added taxation and recommended immediate measures for rationalisation of sales tax in preparation for the eventual change. It has also considered in detail, reform measures to be adopted in respect of non-judicial stamp duties and registration fees, motor vehicles tax, profession tax and entertainment tax. It has analysed the rationale for and the structure of state excise and developed estimates of probable tax evasion. It has also suggested measures for quality control of potable liquor. The Commission has also laid down the framework for improving governance in taxing departments and made suggestions for reform in two areas—motor vehicles taxation and the administration of non-judicial stamp duties.

The main recommendations of the Tax Reforms Commission have been progressively introduced by the government and have begun to yield dividends in terms of increased tax revenues *vis-à-vis* MTFP projections.

Sales Tax Reform

To achieve the goals set out in the Medium Term Fiscal Plan, the revenue productivity of the tax system in general and sales tax in particular need to be increased appreciably. The MTFP assumes that for every 1 per cent increase in state domestic product, revenue from sales tax will increase by 1.2 per cent. This calls for significant improvement in buoyancy by 0.3 percentage points within a short time; to achieve this, reforms are imperative. Detailed analyses of sales tax systems in states bring out the conclusion that the best way of solving the problem of distortion and improving revenue productivity is to transform the prevailing sales tax into a destination based consumption type VAT at the state level.

Recent deceleration in the growth rate of the tax, decline in buoyancy and falling revenue-GSDP ratios, all point towards considerable scope for improving revenue productivity in the state. At the same time, it is common knowledge that the structure of nominal tax rates in the state when cumulated over the sales tax, turnover tax or RST, entry tax and the infrastructure cess, is higher than in many states. Thus, in spite of having higher nominal tax rates, increase in revenue productivity in Karnataka has been found to be lower than in many states. Therefore, improvement in revenue productivity cannot be achieved by increasing nominal tax rates; restructuring them to induce better tax compliance can only do it. This calls for broadening the base, reducing rates, minimising rate differentiation and simplifying and rationalising the tax system to promote tax compliance. In designing tax rates it is essential to keep in mind tax rates prevailing in neighbouring states to prevent significant diversion of trade. The Committee of state finance ministers had fixed floor rates of tax in respect of different commodities. It is important to implement these in right spirit.

As already mentioned, the government's attempt in the case of commercial taxes has been to adopt an economic rationale for taxation. Efforts have been made to ensure that the rate structure is simple, exemptions are few and specific and the tax base is wide. The state is prepared for the introduction of VAT from 1st April 2005 although sufficient ground was prepared to introduce it two years earlier itself from April 2003.[3] In preparation, tax rates are being rationalised by reducing the number of slabs from 14 to 7 in sales tax. The bulk of the 600 scheduled commodities would be brought under four basic rates, 4 per cent, 8 per cent, 12 per cent and 16 per cent respectively. Two special rates of 17.5 per cent and 25 per cent are being abolished and only three special rates of 1 per cent, 20 per cent and 28 per cent would be retained for a small group of commodities including bullion and spices, diesel, tobacco products and petrol. As a measure to ensure a level-playing field for domestic industry, a special entry tax for high value commodities will be introduced as in Tamil Nadu and Andhra Pradesh. This is expected to reduce trade diversion, improve domestic commerce and enhance sales tax revenues. It is felt that the net effect of rate rationalisation and reduction of concessions will lead to improvement in the buoyancy of commercial taxes from the current levels of 1.04 to 1.1. In projecting the commercial tax revenues for the medium term however, a buoyancy of 1.075 has been adopted in order to cover for the initial revenue dampening effect of VAT.

3. State has switched over to VAT System from 1st April 2005.

State Excise Duties

In 2003-04 the government initiated radical change in excise policy by canalising IML through the Karnataka State Beverages Corporation Limited (KSBCL) and rationalising the excise duty structure. As a result IML revenues in 2003-04 have more than doubled and 'seconds' have been curbed. Thus sales tax on rectified spirit and liquor was merged with state excise. The Budget for 2005-06 proposes to bring even molasses under a similar scheme and exempt molasses from tax under VAT and levy an equivalent excise duty on rectified spirit manufactured out of molasses. A similar model is also envisaged for the arrack trade, which is highly cartelised and impervious to market forces. The administered price mechanism for rectified spirit and arrack will be dismantled and government will only notify the maximum retail price. Arrack manufacture will be liberalised and the duty structure on arrack simplified to eliminate 'seconds'. Rectified spirit will be fully canalised through KSBCL. Over the medium term, efforts will be made to canalise even arrack through KSBCL. The historical buoyancy of excise has been about 1.05. If the reforms are implemented fully, the buoyancy may go up to 1.1 resulting in considerable revenue growth. For the MTFP projections however buoyancy, as said earlier, has been assumed conservatively at 1.075.

Stamp Duties and Registration Fees

All levies falling under the broad heading of stamp duties and registration fees in the state budget are based on different taxation principles. The rationale for judicial stamp duties differs from that for non-judicial duties. Because both employ a similar technique of tax collection, however, they are clubbed together and accounted for under the same head of account. The reform commission felt that as a first step, in Karnataka, overhauling of the tax schedule for stamp duty was needed to eliminate low revenue-earning items, which inconveniences day-to-day transactions of a large number of people. Substantial relief could then be extended at little cost to the department and attention directed to better enforcement of buoyant sources of taxation.

Far-reaching reforms in stamps and registration have been initiated by abolition of stamp papers and by reduction of stamp duty rates by almost 20 per cent and registration charges by 50 per cent. Stamp revenues have shown high average growth of 17.5 per cent in the period 1999-2000 to 2003-04. In 2002-03 and 2003-04 itself, collection of stamps duty have grown by 23 per cent and 15 per cent respectively. That rate reduction has not dampened growth very much is an encouraging sign. A Central Valuation Committee, which was set up in 2003-04, has now notified revised guideline values for registration of properties in Bangalore city. Similar revision in other major cities were planned to be implemented by December 2004. This is expected to raise revenues by another 15 per cent. Accordingly stamp duty rates will be progressively reduced so that higher revenues can be collected by better compliance and enforcement without burdening the consumer. Guideline value revision and rationalisation will be taken up for CMCs in 2005-06 and for TMCs in 2006-2007. With rationalisation of stamp duty rates, all industrial exemptions now stand withdrawn. The historical buoyancy for stamps has been about 0.8. With the proposed reforms, a buoyancy of 1.1 has been targeted for the MTFP period.

Rationalisation in motor vehicle taxes has been implemented by repeal of the Contract Carriages (Acquisition) Act, 1976 and by encouraging private sector participation in public bus routes. Steps have been taken to create a level playing field for private operators by aligning the tax rates imposed on SRTCs with others. MVT has had a historical buoyancy of 0.75. With reforms, the average buoyancy has improved to about 1.005. A comprehensive computerisation programme has been launched and a database of vehicles in the state will be prepared to enforce better compliance and to enable introduction of rate slabs and a pollution tax in 2005-06. A desired buoyancy of 1.025 has been adopted for the projection period.

12.3.6 Non-Tax Revenues

The total non-tax revenues consist of state's own non-tax revenue and grants from the Centre. State's own non-tax revenue consists of interest receipts, dividends and profits and non-tax receipts from general, social and economic services. Grants from the Centre consist of plan grants, statutory grants and grants *in lieu* of tax on railway passenger fare, etc. These transfers are discussed in another section of the Chapter.

Even though as a proportion of total revenue, the importance of non-tax revenue has declined over the years, it is still an important source of revenue to the government. The performance of non-tax revenue is very disappointing. Return from public sector has been a cause of concern. Public sector units loss has been increasing continuously. This source is in urgent need of reforms.

Non-tax revenues have long been underemphasised and estimated mechanically. The user charge enhancements in cooperation, tourism and mines and geology have led to increased collections in 2003-04. The Tax Reforms Commission (TRC) has submitted its final report on non-tax revenues and the recommendations are under consideration. The current trends in non-tax revenues are encouraging. Forest revenues have grown at an average of 8 per cent over the last 4 years. Mineral revenues have grown at 12 per cent, cooperation revenue at 16 per cent and irrigation charges at about 20 per cent. The key areas of reform as also suggested by the TRC are in irrigation charges, road tolls and forest revenues. An implementable programme as suggested below will be taken up over the medium term:

- Rate enhancement in IBs and circuit houses across the state. Unused space in these IBs will be handed over to KHB or any suitable agency for commercial exploitation. Hospitality functions in major city IBs will be outsourced.
- Appropriate legal amendment to continue tolling in state highways beyond recovery of capital cost for maintenance funding. Provision to toll MDRs and ODRs so that maintenance becomes self-sustaining. Lease out roadside land for facilities. Explore possibilities of introducing a betterment levy on all roadside facilities.
- Increase water rates in irrigation by linking them to full recovery of maintenance costs. Treat use of stored water for power generation as non-agricultural use and charge higher rate. Explore possibility of levying user charges on ground water used for commercial purposes.
- Enhance rates for both in and out patients in all government hospitals located in cities.

- Merge the three forest corporations and implement Revenue Reform Commission's recommendations for enhanced and new user charges, seignorage and product pricing (except for head load fines).

The above reforms are expected to ensure enhanced revenues in forests, mines, irrigation and health. The medium term projections for these key non-tax revenues have been assumed at an annual average growth of nine per cent. The government has banned online and Internet lotteries, which are widely seen as social evils. While this will entail immediate loss of captive revenue, it is expected that savings in disposable income to those who gamble on such lotteries will find its way into increased commodity consumption and thereby compensate partly, the losses over the medium term.

Karnataka's intentions to overhaul the entire revenue system are praiseworthy. The Tax Reform Commission has done real good work in examining all aspects of revenue resources, tax, non-tax and other sources in the minutest details and has come out with practical rational measures of reform. The state has implemented many of the suggested recommendations and the results are showing up in the recent years.

In addition to the issues that relate to state's tax and non-tax revenue, central transfers assume a considerable importance in shaping the state finances in a federal set up. The following discusses the recent trends in central transfers to Karnataka and its implications for the state finances.

12.3.7 Central Transfers to Karnataka

It is common in a federal country that there exist vertical and horizontal fiscal imbalances. The former refers to the differences in fiscal capacities between the union on the one hand and states on the other and the latter among the states themselves. The constitution and conventions provide for devices for reduction of such imbalances.

The various fiscal devices adopted in reducing the fiscal imbalances are tax sharing, tax rental arrangement, revenue sharing, grant and grants-in-aid of several types. The application of these tools however depends upon the objectives to be achieved like equity, equalisation, efficiency, stabilisation and growth.

In India, the constitution under Article 280, provides for a constitution of a statutory body namely the 'Finance Commission (FC)' once in five years to look into the fiscal imbalances and to suggest suitable methods in the distribution of finances between the centre and states and among the states. Contrary to this, financial transfers are also flowing from the Centre to the states through other agencies namely, 'Planning Commission (PC)' a non-statutory body and from various central ministries which is known as 'discretionary transfers'.

Since the above agencies operate independently with their own objective, criteria and as such the impact is felt differentially by the Centre and states and between the states. In this background, this part of the Chapter examines the impact of federal transfers on Karnataka finances. Specifically it analyses the transfers made by FCs, PCs and Central ministries at the aggregate and disaggregate levels from 1990s onwards.

Before analysing the trends and impact of transfers on Karnataka state, it is relevant here to sketch the broad trends of statutory and non-statutory transfers in India and in Karnataka. The transfers made through different channels are presented in Table 12.14.

Table 12.14 reveals that at the all India level, the FCs transfers constitute 44 to 51 per cent from the Annual Plan Period 1990-92 to Annual Plan Period 2002-04. The share of plan transfers in the above periods ranged between 27 and 36 per cent and the share of discretionary transfers constituted 16 to 29 per cent in the same period. A cursory look at the trends reveal that there has been an increasing trend with regard to statutory and plan transfers as against a decline in the discretionary transfers. Similar trends are observed in Karnataka also.

Details of Statutory Transfers to Karnataka

Statutory transfers mainly comprise of share in certain taxes and duties and grants-in-aid. It is obligatory that all the states should get a share in the divisible taxes based on certain criteria. On the other hand grants-in-aid is given to achieve the objective of equity. Normally in India the FCs have been recommending grants-in-aid for those states whose revenue account is in deficit even after the devolution of share in taxes and duties. Thus grants-in-aid play an important role in the state's finances. The proportion of tax share and grants-in-aid in Karnataka is presented in Table 12.15. It may be observed from the table that the share of taxes and duties has registered a substantial increase over the years. The share of grants in the total statutory transfers though very less, of late its

TABLE 12.14

Central Transfers to Karnataka and All States under Various Agencies

(Rs. in lakhs)

Year	Karnataka				All States			
	Statutory Transfers	Plan Transfers	Discretionary Transfers	Total Transfers	Statutory Transfers	Total Plan Transfers	Discretionary Transfers	Total Transfers
Annual Plans (1990-92)	154887	66728	106840	328455	3763830	2342934	2493396	8600160
	(47.16)	(20.32)	(32.53)	(100.00)	(43.76)	(27.24)	(28.99)	(100.00)
VIII Plan (1992-96)	658196	321845	432998	1413039	15227173	9706331	7584058	32517562
	(46.58)	(22.78)	(30.64)	(100.00)	(46.83)	(29.85)	(23.32)	(100.00)
IX Plan (1997-01)	1222295	792780	451470	2466545	26886830	16195260	9198546	52280636
	(49.55)	(32.14)	(18.30)	(100.00)	(51.43)	(30.98)	(17.59)	(100.00)
Annual Plans (2002-04)	649207	650771	186975	1486953	14663903	10768025	4893740	30325668
	(43.66)	(43.77)	(12.57)	(100.00)	(48.35)	(35.51)	(16.14)	(100.00)

Note: (1) Statutory transfers includes share in income tax, estate duty and union excise duty and non-Plan grants such as statutory grants, grants to natural calamities and others.

(2) Plan transfers include grants and loans for state Plans.

(3) Discretionary transfers include grants and loans to centrally sponsored and Central Plan schemes, small savings loans, ways and means advances, loans to natural calamities and others.

(4) Figures in parentheses represent their relative share to total.

Source: Reserve Bank of India, *RBI Bulletins* (various years).

percentage share has been increasing. It was 7 per cent during 1990-92 and in the Annual Plan period (2002-04) it was 11 per cent. The lower share of grants-in-aid implies that the overall financial situation in the state is quite good. However, the signs of deterioration in the financial aspect is noticeable from Ninth Plan period as the share of grants-in-aid has almost doubled compared to Eighth Five Year Plan period.

The impact of statutory transfers is measured through its share in revenue receipts and expenditure. The information provided in Table 12.16 reveals that the percentage share of statutory transfers in the state's total revenue receipts and expenditure is almost constant from the beginning of 1990s to latest Annual Plan period (2002-04). However a marginal decrease is seen in the case of percentage share of statutory transfers in revenue expenditure in the above periods. The overall result that is discernible from the above trend is that the statutory transfers remain constant over the years and the state is mobilising more and more resources on its own.

TABLE 12.15

Share of Grants in the Total Statutory Transfers in Karnataka

(Rs. in Lakhs)

Plan Period	Share in Central Taxes and Duties	Statutory Grants	Total Statutory Transfers	Percentage of the Statutory Transfers
Annual Plans (1990-92)	144243	10644	154887	6.87
VIII Plan (1992-96)	625978	32218	658196	4.89
IX Plan (1997-01)	1143024	79271	1222295	6.49
Annual Plans (2002-04)	575673	73534	649207	11.33

Source: Same as in Table 12.14.

TABLE 12.16

Share of Statutory Transfers in Karnataka's Revenue Receipts and Expenditure

(Rs. in Lakhs)

Year	Total Statutory Transfers	Total Revenue Receipts	Total Revenue Expenditure	Percentage Share of 2 to Column 3	Percentage Share of 3 to Column 4
1	2	3	4	5	6
Annual Plans (1992-96)	154887	866765	892521	17.87	17.35
VIII Plan (1992-96)	658196	3688033	3774672	17.85	17.44
IX Plan (1997-01)	1222295	6489428	7385822	18.84	16.55
Annual Plans (2002-04)	649207	3682451	4236530	17.63	15.32

Source: Same as in Table 12.14.

It can be observed from the above that the state is getting a share in the taxes and duties. The tax share comprises of income tax, union excise duty and estate duty. However, estate duty was abolished by the central government in the year 1989-90. Further, the individual tax sharing policy has been replaced with global tax sharing since 2002-03. When the states were sharing individual taxes, their relative share in Karnataka has wide variations over the years. This information is given in Table 12.17. It is evident from the table that the share of income tax is far lower than the share of excise duties till the Eighth Plan period. However, a drastic decline is noticed in the share of excise duties from the Ninth Plan onwards. One of the reasons for the rise in the share of excise duties was doubling of the state's share from 20 to 40 per cent and a decline in the base of income tax over the years. From the foregoing paragraphs it is clear that the statutory transfers to Karnataka remained constant in relation to state's revenue and expenditure. The question, therefore, is what factors led to this kind of impact? This may be due to a combination of approaches of the various finance commissions (FC), the criteria and weightages adopted, method of assessment of state's non-plan expenditure, etc.

The broad approach of the FCs was to leave out the consideration of the requirements for the plan and to consider only the budgetary needs on the revenue account of the state governments. Further, separate criteria was adopted for different taxes with varying weightages. The criteria adopted by the FCs failed to match their avowed objectives. The FCs have given higher weightage to population factor and this has neither reduced the interstate disparities nor allowed developed states to maintain their economic levels. No FC adopted any incentive method to encourage the prudent financial management, though at times they pointed out its importance. Again, some FCs set apart a portion of excise duties specifically to the deficit states after devolution of taxes and duties. For instance, the Eighth and Ninth FCs set apart 5 per cent and the Tenth FC 7.5 per cent in the divisible share of excise duties for the deficit states. This is highly arbitrary and through which they neglected the advantage of grants-in-aid. This is also against the principle of tax sharing. Due to this, Karnataka had to loose around Rs. 400 crores from each of the awards of the above FCs. Almost all the FCs recognised the importance of states' tax efforts, economy in expenditure, peculiar problems, etc. for distribution of tax share and grants but in reality they failed to apply them in any form. This has adversely affected Karnataka state as it has managed its finances quite prudently. There are inconsistencies between one FC to another on certain important issues. For instance, a few states including Karnataka have established *Panchayat Raj* Institutions in mid-80s based on Ashok Mehta Study Team Report. Karnataka government pleaded with the Ninth FC for special grants for the *Panchayats* but it turned down the state's request. On the other hand, the Tenth FC recognised the importance of *Panchayats* and it set apart a certain amount for distribution among different tiers of *Panchayats* in different states. Similarly, the Eleventh FC has provided grants to the *Panchayats* and it is almost double than what the previous FC provided. However, one disquieting feature in the distribution of resources between the states for *Panchayats* by the FC was adoption of unscientific criteria. More transfers have gone to those states, which have no interest in strengthening the decentralised bodies. Karnataka a leading state in decentralisation, got a raw deal from the FC allocation (Babu, 2002).

TABLE 12.17

Relative Share of Shared Taxes in Karnataka

(Rs. in Lakhs)

Year	*Income Tax*	*Estate Duty*	*Union Excise*	*Total Shared Tax Revenue*	*Percentage Share of Income Tax*	*Percentage Share of Estate Duty*	*Percentage Share of Union Excise Duties*
Annual Plans (1992-96)	46071	0	98772	144243	31.94	0.00	68.48
VIII Plan (1992-96)	242695	0	383283	625978	38.77	0.00	61.23
IX Plan (1997-01)	278502	0	344801	1143024	24.37	0.00	30.17
Annual Plans (2002-04)	0	0	0	575673	0.00	0.00	0.00

Source: Same as in Table 12.14.

Non-Statutory Transfers to Karnataka

Ever since the adoption of Five Year Plans, the Planning Commission (PC) makes grants and loans to states for plan purposes. The grants thus provided are block and unconditional. The ratio of grants and loans is 30 and 70 per cent respectively but for the special category states it is the reverse i.e., 70 per cent grant and 30 per cent loans. Before the commencement of Fourth Five Year Plan, there was no clear-cut criteria followed in Central Plan transfers. From Fourth Plan onwards, the PC adopted certain principles prepared by Prof. D. R. Gadgil and which is known as 'Gadgil Formula'. This formula was again modified in the year 1980. The various forms of Gadgil Formula and weightages given is presented in Table 12.18.

TABLE 12.18

Criteria for Interstate Allocation of Plan Assistance

(in per cent)

Criteria	*Original Gadgil Formula*	*Modified Gadgil Formula*	*Revised Gadgil Formula*	
	(1969)	*(1980)*	*(1990)*	*(1991)*
1. Population	60	60	55	60
2. Per Capita Income (below the national average income)	10	20	25*	25
3. Ongoing Irrigation and Power Projects	10	-	-	-
4. Tax Efforts (per capita tax level)	10	10	-	-
5. Fiscal Management	-	-	5	7.5
6. Special Problems	10	10	15	7.5

Note: * 5 per cent on the basis of distance of the per capita income from the higher per capita income.

Source: Government of India, Five Year Plans (various plan documents).

From Fourth Plan onwards, the Central Government has formulated certain schemes known as centrally sponsored schemes (CSSs) and central plan schemes (CPSs). These schemes are conditional in nature and the outlay are borne by both the centre and the States with varying proportions. The central transfers over the years have created strains in the centre-state relations in India. Mainly this is due to the dominance of non-statutory transfers in the total transfers and within this the CSSs and CPSs have grown enormously jeopardising the state's priorities. Not only this, the planning has put severe stress on the state's finances leading to pruning of their plan outlays, accumulation of debt due to high ratio of loans in the plan transfers. Besides these, there exists controversy in regard to criteria used for distribution of plan assistance and weightages given to the criteria. In this background, the following paragraphs bring out the impact of plan and discretionary transfers on Karnataka finances.

It may be observed from Table 12.16 that the share of statutory transfers in Karnataka during Ninth Plan period is more than the share of statutory transfers in all the reference periods. Non-statutory transfers as stated earlier are made to state plan schemes and for CSSs and CPSs. Discretionary transfers besides grants and loans for CSSs and CPSs include small savings loan and others. If we study only grants and loans to plan schemes i.e., between state plans and CSSs/ CPSs, in Karnataka, it is apparent that the share of the former category is more than that of the later in all the periods. However the share to the CSSs and CPSs was quite high till Eighth Plan period. As can be seen from Table 12.19 that the percentage share of CSSs/CPSs was 45 per cent during Annual Plan 1990-92 and it has gradually decreased to 22 per cent during later Annual Plan periods. This may be due to reduction in the number of CSSs/CPSs schemes as the states constantly put pressure on the Centre for the same in different forums particularly in the National Development Council (NDC) meetings. The other reason that is worth noting is that the Centre has asked the states to retain the small savings collections by themselves. On the whole the reduction in the share of CSSs and CPSs is a welcome trend, as the states will have free leverage in setting out their priorities.

A study of grants alone for state plans and CSSs/ CPSs reveal a distinct difference in different periods. This information is given in Table 12.20. It can be seen from the table that in Karnataka, the share of grants to state plans was lower than the share of CSSs and CPSs till Eighth Plan period and a reverse trend is observed from Ninth Plan onwards. Though, the share of CSSs/CPSs is decreasing from Ninth Plan onwards, still 46 per cent is very high.

TABLE 12.19

Relative Share of State Plan Schemes and CPS and CSS in the Total Plan Grants and Loans in Karnataka

(Rs. in Lakhs)

Year	*Grants and Loans to State Plan Schemes*	*Grants and Loans to CPSs & CSSs*	*Total Plan Grants*	*Percentage Share of State Plan Schemes*	*Percentage Share of CPSs and CSSs*
Annual Plans 1990-92	66728	54654	121382	54.97	45.03
VIII Plan 1992-96	321845	215781	537626	59.86	40.14
IX Plan 1997-01	792780	313690	1106470	71.65	28.35
Annual Plans 2002-04	650771	178875	829646	78.44	21.56

Source: Same as in Table 12.14.

TABLE 12.20

Share of Grants to State Plan Schemes, CPSs and CSSs in Karnataka and All States

(Rs. in Lakhs)

Year	*Karnataka*				
	State Plan Schemes	*CPS and CSSs*	*Total Plan Grants*	*Percentage Share of State Plan Schemes*	*Percentage Share of CPSs and CSSs*
Annual Plans (1990-92)	21536	53262	74798	28.79	71.21
VIII Plan (1992-96)	106228	203335	309563	34.32	65.68
IX Plan (1997-01)	253219	304489	557708	45.40	54.60
Annual Plans (2002-04)	210631	176945	387576	54.35	45.65

Source: Same as in Table 12.14.

The preceding analysis of central transfers to Karnataka brings out that the situation as regards statutory and non-statutory remains almost same over the years. Karnataka state comparatively managed its finances quite well over the years. For this the state should have been rewarded with fiscal incentives. But the transfer policies adopted by various FCs were not of much help for such states. Coming to the non-statutory transfers if we take both grants and loans, the share of state plan schemes has been increasing against a decline in the share of CSSs and CPSs. But the loan component is high with regard to state plan schemes and as such its share appears to be high. On the other hand if we consider only grants portion for both state plans and central sector schemes the situation has changed in the later years but still, the share to the latter one is quite high.

12.4 Government Expenditure

12.4.1 Trends and Issues

Trends in public expenditure as a proportion of GSDP reveal that the total expenditure (revenue and capital) has had a decline from 19.83 per cent in 1990-1991 to 18.35 per cent in 2003-04. While this appears to be in line with the fiscal consolidation ideology of the governments in general in reducing the size of fiscal and revenue deficits one has to examine the nature of expenditure cuts and its behaviour over a period to assess the impacts of such reduction on the economy. Data pertaining to government expenditure under revenue and capital accounts reveal that the decline in the percentage share of expenditure in GSDP during the period 1991-92 to 2001-02 has been largely an outcome of capital expenditure rather than the revenue expenditure (Table 12.21). In addition, the proportion of money spent on revenue account has been far higher than that of the capital expenditure all along. However, revenue and capital categorisation alone should not lead one to such judgments that growth in former is a bane and that of the latter is a boon to the economy in view of the fact that a large portion of the expenditure related to human development such as education, health care, etc. is accounted under revenue category. Nevertheless the rapid growth in the revenue expenditure in the present context is a cause for worry due to the fact that a large component of revenue expenditure is committed in nature such as salaries, pension payments, interest payments, etc. These three items in proportion to revenue expenditure increased

TABLE 12.21

Expenditure Indicators (Percentage of GSDP)

	1980-81	*1985-86*	*1990-91*	*1993-94*	*1995-96*	*2001-02*	*2003-04*	*2004-05 (RE)*
Revenue Expenditure	14.41	18.12	17.02	16.23	17.82	17.00	16.06	16.77
Development Expenditure	12.37	14.43	18.23	13.98	13.54	12.68	10.96	11.93
Social Services	5.56	7.04	6.67	6.36	6.53	6.07	5.58	5.59
Economic Services	6.81	7.39	7.65	7.62	7.01	6.61	5.38	6.34
General Services	4.11	5.59	5.03	4.98	5.23	5.68	6.92	7.08
Interest Payment	1.00	1.4	1.87	1.88	2.05	2.45	2.8	2.55
Wage Bill	4.24	4.88	5.66	5.14	4.86	4.59	4.17	3.73
Pension	0.69	0.82	1.12	1.07	1.09	1.50	1.43	1.39
Subsidies (of which)	NA	NA	0.17	0.26	1.18	2.73	1.73	1.84
Power	NA	NA	-	0.08	0.50	2.10	1.26	0.95
Transport	NA	NA	-	-	0.07	0.13	NA	NA
Irrigation	NA	NA	-	-	-	-	NA	NA
Food	NA	NA	-	0.12	0.37	0.19	NA	NA
Other Subsidy	NA	NA	0.13	0.07	0.23	0.31	NA	NA
Capital Expenditure	2.76	2.4	2.81	3.11	2.43	1.92	2.29	2.78
Total Expenditure	**17.17**	**20.52**	**19.83**	**19.34**	**20.25**	**18.92**	**18.35**	**19.55**

Source: Government of Karnataka, *Accounts at a Glance 1960-2005*.

from 41 per cent in 1980-81 to 45 per cent in 1991-92 and further more to 52 per cent in 2000-01. As a result a larger share of revenue receipts have been increasingly diverted to meet these committed expenditures. Proportion of resources utilised for these three items has increased from 38 per cent in 1980-81 to 47 per cent in 1991-92 and further to 63 per cent. The trend graph (Figure 12.3) clearly reveals that, a sharp increase, which had occurred in 1984-85, has resulted in a higher level of revenue expenditure thereafter. Hence, any reduction in such expenditure is possible only when the level of commitment itself is reduced. No amount of tinkering at the surface can improve the situation or in other words reduce the level of expenditure. The state government for long could not meet this expenditure from the revenue receipts, which should normally be the case. This inability, however is not of a recent origin, but dates back to mid 1980s. This growing expenditure is met out of the borrowed funds basically meant for capital investments. As a consequence of the diversion of borrowed funds, the state has been suffering inadequate capital investments and there has been shortage of economic infrastructure in the state. This also results in an additional burden in the form of growing interest payments in the revenue account. The Figure 12.3 clearly reflects that the capital investments have been abysmally low marked by sharp declines during the time periods 1987-88 to 1989-90, further 1991-92 to 1992-93 and the period after 1993-94. This clearly reveals that the state government is tiding over its fiscal crisis by increasingly cutting down the capital investments.

FIGURE 12.3

Revenue and Capital Expenditure in Proportion to GSDP Total

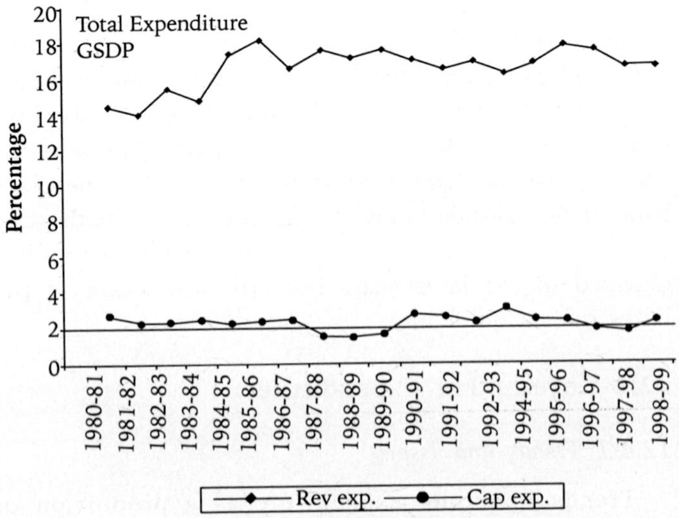

This serves as a big blow to the economy, which is already reeling under severe infrastructure inadequacy, Added to this is the problem faced by the state in the slow growth of private investment. It is observed that the severe infrastructure bottlenecks are largely responsible for the slow growth in the private investment. There is a need to urgently address these issues, as unless and otherwise industry in the state becomes globally competitive, the industry cannot survive the fierce global competition. The state has to step up capital investments in the direction of social and economic infrastructure.

Rapid growth in public expenditure cannot be treated as bad instead it may help in augmenting the overall development in the event moneys are well spent. Some idea about the nature of government expenditure is obtained when the items of expenditure are studied under certain meaningful categories such as functional categories and economic categories.

Functional categories such as general services, social and community services and economic services reveal that (Table. 12.21) over a period the state's expenditure under economic services in the initial period i.e. from 1980-81 to 1990-91, had increased from 6.81 per cent of GSDP to 7.65 per cent after which it has been by and large on the decline and reached its lowest level in 2001-02 i.e. 6.61 per cent (Figure 12.4).

FIGURE 12.4

Total Expenditure by Functional Categories

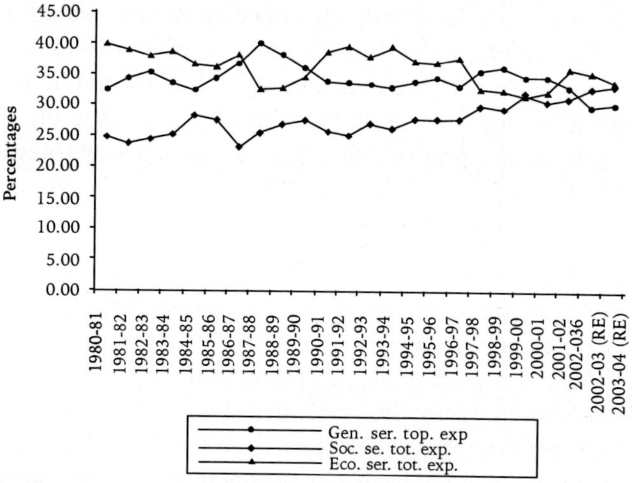

Public investment is very essential in certain crucial economic infrastructure such as power, irrigation, and

TABLE 12.22

Expenditure on Economic Services (Rev.+Cap. Accounts)

(Rs. in Crores)

Year	*Agriculture and Allied*	*Irrigation and Flood Control*	*Energy*	*Transport*	*Total*
1992-93	510.87	826.16	202.34	294.41	2413.92
*	1.55	2.5	0.61	0.89	7.31
**	21.16	34.22	8.38	12.2	
1993-94	597.68	1030.70	292.81	265.75	2913.73
*	1.4	2.41	0.69	0.62	6.82
**	20.51	35.37	10.04	9.12	
1994-95	636.71	1118.12	286.86	311.9	3108.96
*	1.26	2.21	0.57	0.62	6.15
**	20.48	35.96	9.23	10.03	
1995-96	891.01	1210.95	460.75	340.50	3578.94
*	1.51	2.06	0.78	0.58	6.08
**	24.89	33.84	12.87	9.51	
1996-97	856.55	1422.31	975.66	311.79	4267.61
*	1.22	2.02	1.39	0.44	6.07
**	20.07	33.33	22.86	7.31	
1997-98	854.16	1419.06	614.41	364.50	3933.36
*	1.11	1.85	0.80	0.47	5.12
**	21.72	36.08	15.62	9.27	
2003-04	1356.36	2060.52	234.08	821.63	7125.45
*	1.02	1.56	0.18	0.62	5.38
**	19.04	28.92	3.29	11.53	

Note: * indicates percentage to GSDP.

** indicates percentage to expenditure on economic services. There are other items of expenditure under economic services, hence these totals do not add up to 100 per cent.

Source: Government of Karnataka, compiled by the Finance Department.

roads. Government spending on each of these items has had a declined share in GSDP (Table 12.22). As said earlier the state is already experiencing severe inadequacy in the economic infrastructure and a further reduction in the expenditure will aggravate the infrastructure inadequacy and thus will have an adverse effect on the overall development of the state. Government's responsibility in these areas continues, as the desired private investment is yet to take place in adequate quantity.

Social services also reveal similar pattern wherein there is an increase in the percentage share in the first period and there is a decline in the second period, but of a lesser degree. Social sector in particular, essential sectors such as primary education, health care and rural development need to be given an increased attention in view of the fact that private sector plays a limited role in these sectors. On the contrary, the proportion of general services, which is termed as non-development expenditure, has increased from 4.11 per cent (1980-81) to 6.33 per cent (2003-04) within the general services the items that have had a sharp increase are interest payments, pension and retirement benefits and administration of justice.

From among the economic categories, the items that account for a large share are government wages and salaries (inclusive of pension) owing to the recent revision effected by the Fifth Pay Commission and current transfers. Interest payments, salaries and pensions together constitute a very large share in the total revenue expenditure and has also been on the increase. Subsidies have also been on the increase much against the reform agenda to reduce the subsidy bill.

Based on the broad trends of expenditure under the functional and economic categories, one can conclude that while the government expenditure as a proportion to GSDP has had a small decline, the sectors that have been adversely affected are the economic and social services.

12.4.2 Subsidies in the State

Issues pertaining to the low and uneconomic pricing of public services and the resultant increase in the implicit subsidies have been addressed in the recent literature (Rao *et al.*, 2003). There has been inadequate effort on the part of the state government to recover the cost of the public services even from those who can afford to pay towards these services. The quantum of implicit subsidy has grown substantially during the reform phase. The study observed that "despite large investments to irrigation, water supply and sanitation, higher and technical education and various other public enterprises, the state has not been able to recover the costs to make these activities viable and generate resources for additional reinvestments in these sectors." (Rao *et al.*, 2003:1).

The detailed sectoral studies for Karnataka reveal that subsidy level, both implicit and explicit, has been observed to have sharply increased in the state. A macro view of subsidy reveals that budgetary subsidy in absolute terms has increased from Rs. 1952 crores in 1990-91 to Rs. 4885 crores in 1998-99.There is yet another disappointing feature in the form of sharp decline that has occurred in the cost recovery rate. It has declined from 7 per cent to 2.5 per cent during the above reference period. (Rao *et al.* and Amarnath, 2003). Water supply and sanitation services account for a whopping Rs. 1303 crore subsidy during the 1990-99 period (Saleth and Sastry, 2003). Subsidy for food and agriculture comprising of irrigation and power was very high at Rs. 4058 crores (Deshpande, *et al.*, 2003). Irrigation sector also has a huge subsidy which has also substantially increased. It has increased from Rs. 711 crores in 1990-91 to Rs. 2335 crores in 1998-99, recovery rate has had a sharp fall from 2.41 per cent to 0.88 per cent during the above reference period. (Raju and Amarnath, 2003).

Power is yet another sector that has accounted for a large and increasing subsidy especially from the year 1994-1995. It has increased from Rs. 207 crores in 1994-95 to Rs. 1212 crores in 1999-2000. There is also an element of cross subsidy that is borne by a certain category of consumers which has also been on the increase (Vivekananda, 2003c). Housing sector accounts for a sharp increase in the direct or explicit subsidy. It has increased from Rs. 13 crores in 1990-91 to Rs. 127 crores in 1998-99 (Gayithri, 2003) State government is incurring not only a direct outflow of resources in the form of explicit and implicit subsidy but also is incurring heavy revenue loss to its exchequer on account of various concessions and exemptions. While the direct subsidy has increased from Rs. 29 crores in 1990-91 to Rs. 167 crores in 2001-02 that of implicit subsidy has grown from Rs. 147 crores to Rs. 232.54 crore in the above period. There has been a reduction in the recovery rate too (Gayithri, 2003). Subsidy in higher education is huge Rs. 160.55 crore in 1990-91 and has grown to Rs. 818.6 crore in 1998-99. (Narayana, 2003). All these studies reveal that subsidy growth during the reform phase is quite sharp. There are also problems of poor targeting of the benefits thus the benefits of subsidy have reached the undeserving.

12.4.3 Karnataka Reform Initiatives

Karnataka government commenced its introspection over the fiscal state of affairs with the release of White Paper on state finances in March 2000. The White Paper laid out the fiscal crisis in the state and suggested suitable fiscal reform measures over a medium term. In accordance with that the state government has since framed Medium Term Fiscal Plans (MTFP) commencing in the financial year 2000-01. MTFP has now been made a rolling Annual Document to reflect the previous reform measures, their implementation and the future targets. Currently the fourth MTFP is in place for the period 2004-05 to 2007-2008.

Karnataka is one of the first states to bring in to effect the Fiscal Responsibility Act (FRA) from April 2003, which provides the statutory backing to the MTFPs. The broad features of FRA are as given in Box 12.2.

Among the key strategies laid down in the MTFP 2003-04 to 2006-07 include (*Government of Karnataka*, 2003):

- improving revenue collection by improvising the rate structure, administration, and enforcement;
- mobilising greater non-tax revenue by revising rates and phasing out implicit subsidies;
- reducing budgetary support to public sector enterprises;
- introducing budgetary reforms to promote accountability, flexibility, and performance; and
- effecting reforms in governance to strengthen performance.

BOX 12.2

Fiscal Responsibility Rules, Government of Karnataka 2003

- MTFP to be laid before the Legislature every year.
- State government should take measures to reduce the level of revenue deficit to nil and that of fiscal deficit to three per cent of GSDP by 2006.
- Not give guarantee over and above the ceiling set under the Karnataka ceiling to Government Guarantees Act 1999.
- Ensure that total liabilities do not exceed 25 per cent of GSDP by the year 2015.
- Ensure greater fiscal transparency in governmental fiscal operations: disclose contingent liabilities, tax expenditures, subsidy payments, etc.
- Enforce compliance: Budget has to be consistent with MTFP targets and objectives—trends in expenditure and revenue to be reviewed every half year.
- Every rule made under this Act to be laid before each house of legislature as soon as it is made.

Thus the state finances have for long ailed on account of adversities on both revenue and expenditure fronts. Reform initiatives have shown some positive results by way of reduction in fiscal deficit and attainment of revenue surplus in the recent past. However, the state government has to address the issues of declining investments in the social and economic sectors especially in view of the fact that Karnataka's human development does not compare very well with other states. In addition, the revenue-expenditure gap has for long created debt burden on the states government that has considerably grown over a period. These issues are dealt with in the following section.

12.5 Public Debt of Karnataka

In India, the adoption of Five Year Plans has compelled the state governments to borrow from various sources including the centre to finance their plans. Besides, the centre provides loans to the centrally sponsored schemes and for other non-plan schemes. This has put heavy burden on the state's finances in the form of interest servicing and repayment of principal debt. The problem is so acute that the poor and the backward states and sometimes the advanced states borrow fresh loans from the Centre to repay their outstanding debt. Further, due to various restrictions by the Central Government upon the states' borrowings a shift towards high cost borrowings has emerged in recent years.

12.5.1 Growth of Public Debt

Public debt of state governments broadly comprises of internal debt and loans and advances from the Central Government. The important sources under internal debt are market loans, loans from the financial institutions. Loans and advances from the Centre include among others loans for state and central plan schemes, small savings loans (now totally transferred to state governments). Besides, state governments also utilise public savings under public account such as provident funds, small savings funds, pensions, etc.

In Karnataka, as in other states, the size of debt has been growing at a rapid rate particularly in recent years. As can be seen from Table 12.23 the total outstanding debt (excluding public account borrowings) during 1990-91 was Rs. 3,988 crores and the same has gone up to Rs. 34,910 crores in the year 2004-05 (budget estimate), a rise of 7 times in 15 years. The growth in current borrowings has also been witnessing a rising trend in the present decade (2000s). The total current borrowings during 1990-91 were Rs. 777 crores and it has risen to Rs. 8059 crores in the year 2004-05 (BE). The trend in the growth of debt will be clearer if we compare the position of 2000s to the previous decade. It can be observed from the Table 12.23 that the average annual growth rate of total outstanding debt was 15.68 per cent during 1990-1999 and in the 2000s it is 17.61 per cent. The growth rate of current borrowings was 14.92 per cent during the period 1990-1999 and in the 2000s (2000-2004) it is 27.13 per cent.

The state's growth rate of current borrowings has witnessed sharp increase during 2000s as compared with the position in the previous decade (1990s). Between the two types of debt, the internal debt has grown at a phenomenal rate from 19.02 per cent in the 1990s to 31.72 per cent in the 2000s. On the other hand the growth rate of loans and advances from the Centre rose from 11.11 per cent in 1990s to 16.34 per cent during 2000s. However, the outstanding debt has grown by 2 per cent in the same period.

Generally the growth or otherwise of public debt is measured in relation to state income i.e. gross state domestic product (GSDP). It is interesting to observe that the ratio of outstanding debt to GSDP was 17 per cent in the year 1990-91 and it has risen sharply to 24 per cent in the year 2004-05. If we include liabilities under public account while analysing public debt, the growth of total debt would be much higher. For instance, the total liabilities as per cent of GSDP during 1990-91 work out to 18 per cent and in the year 2003-04 stand at 24.26 per cent. However, in relation to other states, the ratio of debt to GSDP in Karnataka is slightly less. It may be noted from the Report of the Eleventh Finance Commission that the ratio of debt to GSDP for all states between 1993-94 and 1999-2000 hovers around 21 per cent to 24 per cent. In contrast to this, in Karnataka it ranges between 16 per cent and 19 per cent in the same period (Government of India, 2000). Even during 2002-03, Karnataka stands third

TABLE 12.23

Growth of Public Debt in Karnataka

(Rs. in Crores)

Year/Period	*Current Borrowings*			*Total Outstanding Debt*
	Total Internal Debt	*Loans and Advances from GoI*	*Total Public Debt*	
1990-91	317.68	459.70	777.38	3987.64
1991-92	185.91	528.00	713.91	4533.91
1992-93	560.27	669.71	1229.98	5193.65
1993-94	1782.25	688.90	2471.15	5906.02
1994-95	1695.76	1221.32	2917.08	7136.96
1995-96	539.50	807.61	1347.11	1347.11
1996-97	1364.34	1065.26	2429.60	9189.25
1997-98	827.75	1133.18	1960.93	10446.61
1998-99	871.96	1552.00	2423.96	12465.22
1999-00	2324.85	927.72	3252.57	15147.26
2000-01	2295.57	1075.65	3371.22	17997.94
2001-02	3705.36	2176.88	5882.24	22432.53
2002-03	7981.81	1544.22	9526.03	26169.32
2003-04 (RE)	9065.00	2284.27	11349.27	30188.38
2004-05 (BE)	5820.90	2238.05	8058.95	34910.28
CAGR				
1990-1999	19.02	11.11	14.92	15.68
2000-2004	31.72	16.34	27.13	17.61

Note: CAGR-Compound Annual Growth Rate; RE-Revised Estimate. BE-Budget Estimate.

Source: Website of Finance Department, *Accounts at a Glance for 1960-2003*, Government of Karnataka.

lowest state in the debt-GSDP ratio among the 17 general category states (Government of India, 2005).

12.5.2 Composition of Public Debt

Debt comprises of internal debt and loans and advances from the Centre. Again, each of these categories of debt has many items. A study of these would throw light on the relative position of each of these items in the total debt. The share of former in the total debt during 1990-91 was 40.87 per cent and that of the latter 59.13 per cent. However their shares have undergone changes in recent years. They were 72.23 and 27.77 per cent respectively of internal debt and loans and advances during 2004-05 (BE). Further, among many sources of debt, the average share of loans for state plans account for 27 per cent; ways and means advances 17 per cent, market loans 16 per cent and other miscellaneous items account for 60 per cent. Another observation is that there is no consistency in the yield from market borrowings over the years. The main reason for this is that the Centre fixes the quantum of market loans to be raised by each state and the states have no freedom on this source. The decline in the share of Central loans and advances may be attributed to two main reasons. First, the borrowings against the collection of small savings by the states from the Centre no longer exists as states themselves maintain this fund in their public account with effect from 1-4-1999. Second, the debt-swap allowed by the Central Government in recent years.

12.5.3 Burden of Debt

Public debt entails repayment of principal and interest charges on the part of the borrower. Repayment of principal debt is charged to capital account and interest servicing is met from the revenue account. Besides, the government has constituted a 'sinking fund' under revenue account for the purpose of discharging market loans. But the amount earmarked under this Fund in different years is very negligible. Not only this, the government decided to stop providing funds under this Fund from the year 1999-00 onwards. Interest servicing and repayment of debt in relation to revenue expenditure and capital disbursement respectively provides an indication of the extent of the debt problem in the state. The extent of the interest payment problem is also measured in relation to revenue receipts of the state. Further, the magnitude of the total debt problem i.e. interest and principal debt payments together can be observed from the ratio of debt discharged to the GSDP.

Appendix Table A-12.3 provides various indicators denoting the extent of debt problem in the state. The most important aspect of burden of debt is interest payment. The table shows that interest payments as per cent of total revenue receipts during 1990-91 was 11.19 per cent and in the year 2004-05 (BE) it stood at 15.36 per cent. In relation to revenue expenditure its share was 10.97 and 15.41 per cent respectively in the above years. The interest payments as a per cent of total revenues and expenditure are increasing continuously till the year 2002-03 and thereafter a decline is noticeable. The broad and the most important indicator of the magnitude of the debt burden in the state as said earlier is the ratio of debt servicing (interest and principal) to GSDP. Debt servicing as a per cent of GSDP increased very sharply from 2001-02 onwards. The ratio during 1990-91 was 3.25 per cent and it has gone up to 8.44 per cent in the year 2003-04. However, in the year 2004-05 (BE) the ratio declined to about 5 per cent.

12.5.4 Contingent Liabilities

Apart from the above, the state government has given approvals and guarantees for raising loans by various authorities like state government undertakings, cooperative societies, local bodies, etc. It is a known fact that most of the state owned boards and corporations and societies run under losses and some have become sick. The net worth of many companies has become negative. In such situations the state has to take responsibility of servicing their outstanding debt and interest falls on the government. Thus, outstanding guarantees indicate the risk exposure of the state government, and should therefore be compared with the ability of the government to pay from its revenue receipts. The ratio of total outstanding guarantees to total revenue receipts of the government would indicate the degree of vulnerability of the state government. Table 12.24 presents the position of total outstanding guarantees given by the state and its ratio to the revenue receipts. The table brings out that the total outstanding guarantees given by the Karnataka government during 1990-91 was Rs. 2258 crores and the same stood at Rs. 13314 crores in the year 2002-2003 a five-fold rise in 13 year period. The ratio of outstanding guarantees to total revenue receipts works out to 58 per cent and 82 per cent respectively during 1990-91 and 2002-03.

TABLE 12.24

Outstanding Guarantees Given by Karnataka Government

(Rs. in Crores)

Year	*Total Outstanding Guarantees*	*Total Revenues*	*Per Cent of Outstanding Guarantees to Total Revenue*
1990-91	2257.63	3892.18	58.00
1991-92	3057.39	4775.47	64.02
1992-93	2255.11	5421.66	41.59
1993-94	3640.04	6324.65	57.55
1994-95	3861.80	6968.39	55.42
1995-96	4669.00	8543.45	54.65
1996-97	4887.00	9622.18	50.79
1997-98	5594.00	10613.39	52.71
1998-99	8023.00	11230.44	71.44
1999-00	9829.00	12906.45	76.16
2000-01	13004.13	14822.72	87.73
2001-02	12279.17	15321.26	80.14
2002-03 RE	13313.68	16168.73	82.34

Note: RE–Revised Estimate.

Source: 1. Government of Karnataka, *Budget Documents* (various years).

2. Government of Karnataka, *Report of the Comptroller and Auditor General*, (various years).

12.5.5 Overview

Borrowings should finance the plan expenditure and should not be used for unproductive activities. In other words, borrowed funds on the one hand should be used efficiently and prudently for capital expenditure, which earns higher returns, and productivity of the economy resulting in increased government revenue and on the other it should not be used for financing revenue expenditure. If the mismatch between the revenue and expenditure is of a temporary nature then adjustment could be made from the borrowings. But if the mismatch persists for a long period and grows in volume, debt tends to become unsustainable.

The analysis of public debt of Karnataka unravels that its current as well as outstanding debt has been growing at a faster rate particularly in the current decade (2000s). Servicing of interest on the debt has also been increasing. Apart from normal sources, the state has gone for high cost debts in recent years. The interest rates on small savings loans, provident funds, and capital market bonds are high compared to other debt instruments. These have compounded for high interest servicing in recent years.

Since 1996-97 the state is witnessing revenue account deficit and the deficit from 1998-99 was huge. A deficit in the revenue account implies that no funds are available from current revenues for meeting plan expenditure and further implying that the entire plan expenditure is financed through borrowings. Thus, the huge revenue deficit create a kind of vicious circle of deficit-induced borrowings, interest payments and increased indebtedness.

Further, the state had established a few enterprises like Krishna Bhagya Jala Nigama Ltd. (KBJNL), Karnataka Neeravari Nigama Limited. (KNNL) for developing infrastructure and utilisation of irrigation potential. The state has mobilised off-budget resources through these agencies and the liabilities on these are to be met from the budget. The bonds floated in mid-1990s under KBJNL are now due for redemption. This would put more pressure on the state's finances in the coming years.

The size of debt is linked to the fiscal performance and the burden of debt could be reduced if corrective measures are taken in the fiscal arena. In this direction Karnataka state has initiated fiscal reforms in earnest way. It had passed a legislation namely 'Fiscal Responsibility Act, 2002'. Under this Act, Medium Term Fiscal Plans (MTFP) have been adopted from time to time. The latest one in this series is MTFP for 2004-2005 to 2007-08. It has specified time bound targets for eliminating/reducing revenue and fiscal deficits. With regard to controlling the growing debt the direct measures adopted include prescribing ceiling limit on borrowings, capping on guarantees, elimination of off-budget borrowings, debt-swap, etc.

The Planning Commission has identified six criteria to measure whether a state is debt stressed or not. These criteria are:

1. 30 per cent for debt to GSDP ratio;
2. 300 per cent for debt to total revenue receipts ratio;
3. 18 per cent for interest as a ratio of total revenue receipts;
4. 1.25 for the ratio of debt growth to revenue growth;
5. 50 per cent for the ratio of revenue deficit to fiscal deficit; and
6. 25 per cent for the ratio of fiscal deficit to total revenue receipts.

The fiscal reform measures initiated by Karnataka seem to bear fruits from the year 2003-04. The position of state with regard to the above criteria brings out that except in one indicator i.e. the ratio of debt to GSDP in all other criteria it is below the norms set.

However, this does not mean that the state is free from debt problem. It all depends on the outcome of the fiscal targets outlined in the policy measures in the coming years. It has to pursue vigorously in meeting the fiscal targets enunciated to keep debt burden under check.

12.6 Fiscal Decentralisation in Karnataka

In Karnataka, decentralisation effort commenced in 1980s and in that direction it passed a Legislative Act in the year 1985. Based on this Act elections were held for rural local bodies in the year 1987. The success of reforms towards decentralisation in Karnataka, in a sense paved the way for the 73rd and 74th Amendment Acts to the Constitution in the year 1992. The 73rd Amendment Act relates to rural bodies and the 74th Act to that of urban bodies.

Among many prerequisites for the success of decentralised governments, resources occupy an important place. Within resources, questions such as fiscal powers entrusted, extent of resources/grants devolved, nature of grants transferred, and the role of State Finance Commission, etc. need to be understood while analysing financial relation in a multi-governmental system.

12.6.1 Local Body System

Karnataka as per 73rd Constitutional Amendment dictate established three-tier *Panchayat Raj* Institutions (PRIs) during 1994 and 1995. Elections were held for PRIs again in the year 2000. At present there are 27 *Zilla Panchayats,* 176 *Taluka Panchayats* and 5650 *Grama Panchayats* in the state. The state government has transferred a large number of functions to PRIs. The State Panchayat Raj Act, 1993 has three separate Schedules containing the functions to be performed by the three tier *Panchayats*. Schedule-I has roughly about 29 sectors/programmes entrusted to GPs; Schedule-II with 28 functions meant for TPs, and Schedule-III with 31 sectors/ programmes for *Zilla Panchayats*. Though the state has entrusted the functions to different tiers under the above three schedules, the functions enumerated under Schedule-I are yet to be transferred to GPs. The total number of schemes (Plan and non-Plan) transferred to PRIs from all the three Schedules account for 665. No other state in India has transferred this large functionaries/schemes to PRIs. Article 243(G) of 11th Schedule of the 73rd Constitution Amendment Act lists 29 subjects for consideration of states to be delegated to PRIs. Karnataka has transferred almost all the subjects listed under the above Article to PRIs.

The structure of urban local bodies (ULBs) is different from that of rural ones. The state government has reconstituted the ULBs according to the 74th Constitution Amendment Act. At present there are 6 corporations, 41 city municipal councils, 82 town municipal councils, and 93 town *panchayats,* thus totaling 222 ULBs. The ULBs have been performing some vital functions such as providing roads and bridges, water supply, streetlights, public health and sanitation, solid waste management and many other amenities required by the community. The 12th Schedule of the 74th Constitutional Amendment Act has listed 18 functions for delegation to ULBs. Out of this, the state has already delegated 11 functions to ULBs and the remaining are under consideration.

12.6.2 Fiscal Powers of Local Bodies

In Karnataka, among the three-tier *panchayats* only *Grama Panchayats* have been entrusted with some tax powers. No other tier is bestowed with this power. On the other hand all the ULBs are empowered with taxing powers. Further both rural and urban bodies are empowered to collect non-tax revenues from various sources. The state government provides grants to both PRIs and ULBs in the form of share from its own revenues. The Centre also provides grants for its sponsored schemes and on the recommendations of Union Finance Commission. Again both rural and urban bodies are empowered to raise loans for developmental purposes. Thus various income avenues have been provided to local bodies (rural and urban) in the state.

12.6.3 Resource Position of Local Bodies

In the light of the above fiscal powers, it is important here to analyse the income levels of local bodies (LBs) in the state. In this direction the issues such as the extent of resources available, revenue sharing between the state and local bodies, share of rural and urban local bodies, and the recommendations of State Finance Commission, etc. merit high. The major problem in studying some of the above issues is non-availability of disaggregated data at the state level for both rural and urban bodies and for long years. Though the Eleventh Finance Commission Report provides information on own and devolved funds they do not tally with the information furnished in the annual municipal statistics and other state government reports. Notwithstanding this lacuna the available information broadly highlights the direction and trends in the LBs resources in the state.

As mentioned earlier the GPs in rural areas and all urban bodies have been given some taxation powers. The major tax source for both rural and urban bodies is property taxation. All the major and elastic tax sources rests with the state. The resources of local bodies (rural and urban) consist of own tax and non-taxes, loans, grants-in-aid from state and centre. The extent of resources available for LBs *vis-à-vis* the state is presented in Table 12.25 It can be seen from the table that the total resources available for LBs in the state during 1991-92 was Rs. 1,787 crores and in the year 1999-00 it was Rs. 5,307 crores, a three-fold increase in the nine-year period. Other indicators also throw light on the resource position of LBs in the state. The same table reveals that in the combined revenues of state and LBs, the share of the latter during 1991-92 was 27.23 per cent and in the year 1999-00 it was 29.14 per cent recording a two per cent increase in nine-year period. In relation to state income i.e. gross state domestic product (GSDP) there is not much difference over the years. In fact, there was a decline from 1994-95 to 1997-98. On an average it accounts for 5 per cent per annum. In terms of per capita availability, there is an increasing trend over the years. It was Rs. 397 in 1991-1992 and during 1999-00 it stood at Rs. 998.

While studying the resources of LBs it is also important to understand the financial relationship between the state and LBs, ratio of own revenue and grants-in-aid and share of rural and urban bodies in the grants-in-aid, etc. It can be seen from Table 12.26 that the transfers effected from the state to LBs in the year 1991-92 was Rs. 1206.73 crores and the same has increased to Rs. 4640.43 crores in the year 2001-02. The transferred grants in the total revenue of LBs which accounted for 67.53 per cent in 1991-92 increased to 73.78 per cent in 1999-2000. There is not much variation in the share of grants in the total revenues of LBs over the years except during 1991-92 and 1997-98. On an average the transfers account for 76 per cent per annum. Further, the revenues transferred to LBs from the state's own revenue during 1991-92 was 34 per cent and in the year 2001-02 it stands at 42 per cent. Thus, the share of LBs in the state's own revenues has been increasing over the years. Between rural and urban, the table reveals that the grants transferred to PRIs from the state's own revenues are far greater than the devolution made to ULBs. The share of PRIs during 1991-92 was 34 per cent and in the year 2001-02 it was 37 per cent. On the other hand the share of ULBs stood at 0.33 per cent

TABLE 12.25

Total Revenues (Own and Transferred) of All Local Bodies (PRIs & ULBs) in Karnataka

(Rs. in Crores)

Year	*Revenue of PRIs*	*Revenue of ULBs*	*Total Revenue of All LBs*	*State's Total Revenue*	*Total Revenue of State & LBs*	*GSDP*	*Percentage share of LBs Revenue in the Combined Revenue*	*Percentage of LBs Revenue in the GSDP*	*Per Capita Revenue of all LBs*
1991-92	1512.99	273.85	1786.84	4775.47	6562.31	30008	27.23	5.95	397
1992-93	1643.59	281.82	1925.41	5421.66	7347.07	33026	26.21	5.83	419
1993-94	1837.54	321.09	2158.63	6324.65	8483.28	42739	25.45	5.05	460
1994-95	2185.66	326.09	2511.75	6968.39	9480.14	50535	26.49	4.97	524
1995-96	2454.41	430.73	2885.14	8543.45	11428.59	58861	25.24	4.90	589
1996-97	2901.39	475.97	3377.36	9622.18	12999.54	70360	25.98	4.80	675
1997-98	3440.72	568.35	3440.72	10613.39	14054.11	76790	24.48	4.48	675
1998-99	3804.04	751.45	4555.49	11230.44	15785.93	90623	28.86	5.03	874
1999-00	4235.77	1071.09	5306.86	12906.45	18213.31	96179	29.14	5.52	998

Note: Per capita is calculated by using projected population.

Source: 1) Government of Karnataka, *Budget Allotment for Zilla Panchayat Plan and Non-Plan* (various years).

2) Directorate of Economics and Statistics, *Statistical Abstract of Karnataka* 1998-99, Government of Karnataka.

3) Directorate of Economics and Statistics, *Municipal Statistics* (various years).

and 5.12 per cent respectively in the above years. In per capita terms also it was more in the case of PRIs than that of ULBs.

12.6.4 Dependency Level

As brought out above, the LBs receive grants/ transfers from the higher-level governments. The share of transfers in the LBs' total revenues broadly indicates the extent of dependency on the higher-level government for their resources. The dependency level of all local bodies as revealed from Table 12.25 and 12.26 was to the extent of 76 per cent. However, it is useful to look at this issue from the rural and urban points of view. This information is presented in Table 12.26. It may be observed from the table that the dependency level of rural local bodies on the state transfers was larger than that of urban bodies. On an average, the transfers to PRIs in their total revenues account for about 80 per cent. On the other hand the share for ULBs on an average account for 37 per cent. The high dependence of PRIs is understood, as the two higher tiers of *Panchayats* entirely depend upon the grants from higher-level governments.

TABLE 12.26

Resources Transferred from State's Own Revenue to Local Bodies

(Rs. in Crores)

Year	*Transfers to PRIs*	*Transfers to ULBs*	*Total Transfers to All Local Bodies*	*State's Own Revenue*	*State's Total Revenue*	*Percentage Share of LBs in the State's Own Revenue*	*Percentage Share of ULBs in the State's Total Revenue*	*Percentage Share of ULBs in the State's Own Revenue*	*Percentage Share of PRIs in the State's Own Revenue*
1991-92	1194.95	11.78	1206.73	3521.48	4775.47	34.27	25.27	0.33	33.93
1992-93	1347.51	124.67	1472.18	3900.35	5421.66	37.74	27.15	3.20	34.55
1993-94	1568.93	123.93	1692.86	4545.91	6324.65	37.24	26.77	2.73	34.51
1994-95	1751.05	146.93	1897.98	5136.98	6968.39	36.95	27.24	2.86	34.09
1995-96	1974.1	115.13	2089.23	6509.35	8543.45	32.10	24.45	1.77	30.33
1996-97	2360.55	193.75	2554.3	7110.15	9622.18	35.92	26.55	2.72	33.20
1997-98	2752.98	274.81	3027.79	7676.27	10613.39	39.44	28.53	3.58	35.86
1998-99	3089.01	332.37	3421.38	8412.96	11230.44	40.67	30.47	3.95	36.72
1999-00	3499.95	415.66	3915.61	9514.32	12906.45	41.15	30.34	4.37	36.79
2000-01	3854.83	531.43	4386.26	10760.51	14822.72	40.76	29.59	4.94	35.82
2001-02	4076.63	563.8	4640.43	11018.52	15321.26	42.11	30.29	5.12	37.00

Source: 1) Government of Karnataka, *Budget Allotment for Zilla Panchayat Plan and Non-Plan* (various years).
2) Directorate of Economics and Statistics (2002), *Statistical Abstract of Karnataka–1998-99*, Government of Karnataka.
3) Directorate of Economics and Statistics, *Municipal Statistics* (various years), 4) Reserve Bank of India, *RBI Bulletins* (various years).

TABLE 12.27

Share of Own Revenues in the Total Revenues of Local Bodies

(Rs. in Crores)

Year	*Total Revenues of PRIs*	*Total Revenues of ULBs*	*Transfers from State to PRIs*	*Transfers from State to ULBs*	*Percentage Share of Transfers in the Total PRIs Revenues*	*Percentage Share of Transfers in the Total ULBs Revenues*	*Per Capita Revenue of PRIs*	*Per Capita Revenue of ULBs*
1991-92	1512.99	273.85	1194.95	11.78	78.98	4.30	479	192
1992-93	1643.59	281.82	1347.51	124.67	81.99	44.24	510	192
1993-94	1837.54	321.09	1568.93	123.93	85.38	38.60	562	211
1994-95	2185.66	326.09	1751.05	146.93	80.12	45.06	656	209
1995-96	2454.41	430.73	1974.1	115.13	80.43	26.73	724	268
1996-97	2901.39	475.97	2360.55	193.75	81.36	40.71	641	287
1997-98	3440.72	568.35	2752.98	274.81	80.01	48.35	980	332
1998-99	3804.04	751.45	3089.01	332.37	81.20	44.23	1066	427
1999-00	4235.77	1071.09	3499.95	415.66	82.63	38.81	1164	592

Source: Same as in Table 12.25.

12.6.5 Finances of Panchayati Raj Institutions

Within PRIs, the transfers consist of Plan grants and non-Plan grants. Further, the plan grants comprise of both state and centre. The share of these two and the trends over the years is presented in Table 12.28. On an average the share of Plan grants accounts for 37 per cent and that of non-Plan grants 63 per cent. The Central share in the PRIs plan grants on an average account for 46 per cent. Further, the Plan grants transferred to PRIs from out of state Plan outlay has been increasing in absolute terms but in percentage term it had been declining. Even the decline is seen in absolute terms from the year 2002-03 onwards.

b) provision of tax powers to the LBs, and

c) to make grants-in-aid to LBs from the state.

As per the constitutional obligation, Karnataka government constituted a three-member SFC in the year 1994. The Commission in turn submitted two separate reports—one for PRIs and the other for ULBs to the government in the year 1996. Again, a second SFC was constituted and it had submitted its report in 2003. The state government had accepted the first SFC report and action was initiated on the recommendations. On the other hand, the state is yet to act on the second SFC report. One of the important recommendations made by the First SFC Report was sharing of 36 per cent of the state's non-loan gross own tax and non-tax revenues with the LBs. Of this, the share fixed for PRIs was 30.6 per cent and for ULBs 5.4 per cent. It had also made recommedations on the shares of different tiers of PRIs and the criteria for distribution of resources horizontally. But the government has not accepted these recommendations. With regard to the criteria for horizontal distribution particularly for PRIs, the state has been following 12 criteria since 1987-88 for

TABLE 12.28

Trends in the Grants Devolved to PRIs (Three-tiers) in Karnataka

(Rs. in Crore)

Year	*Plan Grants*	*Percentage Share of Plan Grants in the Total Grants*	*Non-Plan Grants*	*Percentage Share of Non-Plan Grants in the Total Grants*	*Total Grants*	*State's Total Plan Outlay*	*PRI's Share of Plan Grants in the State Plan Outlay*	*Percentage Share of PRIs Plan Grants in the State Total Plan Outlay*
1990-91	545.28	43.99	694.22	56.01	1239.5	1306	545	41.73
1991-92	675.04	44.62	837.95	55.38	1512.99	1937	675	34.85
1992-93	670.08	40.77	973.51	59.23	1643.59	2625	670	25.52
1993-94	739.61	40.25	1097.93	59.75	1837.54	3621	793	21.90
1994-95	972.61	44.50	1213.05	55.50	2185.66	4175	973	23.31
1995-96	1100.31	44.83	1354.10	55.17	2454.41	4648	1100	23.67
1996-97	1272.84	43.87	1628.55	56.13	2901.39	5311	1213	22.84
1997-98	1419.74	41.26	2020.98	58.74	3440.72	5605	1420	25.33
1998-99	1447.03	38.04	2357.01	61.96	3804.04	6513	1447	22.22
1999-00	1527.82	36.07	2707.95	63.93	4235.77	7087	1528	21.56
2000-01	1696.96	36.98	2892.47	63.02	4589.43	8506	1697	19.95
2001-02	1834.30	37.99	2993.63	62.01	4827.93	9605	1834	19.09
2002-03	1241.20	27.41	3286.47	72.59	4527.67	9522	1241	13.03
2003-04	1302.27	27.51	3431.45	72.49	4733.72	10670	1302	12.20
Total of 14 Years	16445.09	37.43	27489.27	62.57	43934.36	81131	16438	20.26

Source: 1. *Economic Survey* 1997-98 and 2004-05, Government of Karnataka.
2. Reserve Bank of India, *RBI Bulletins* (various issues).

12.6.6 State Finance Commission and Local Bodies

Article 243(I) of 73rd Amendment provides for constitution of a State Finance Commission (SFC) by every state once in five years. The main objective of this SFC is to review the financial position of the LBs and to make recommendation to the Governor of the state on:

a) to distribute the resources between the state and LBs according to their responsibilities;

distribution across the *Zilla Panchayats*, 6 criteria in case of *Taluk Panchayats* since 1998-99 and a uniform fixed share for each of the *Grama Panchayats* since 1994-95.

The state government accepted the first recommendation i.e. to share 36 per cent of its own revenues with the LBs. With regard to other recommendations it agreed partially. If we observe the transfers being effected from the state to LBs over the years (Table 12.26) one thing becomes clear that it has been transferring more than what the SFC has recommended. With regard to shares between the rural and urban bodies, the state has committed to reach that level over the years. But the information shows that the share of ULBs in the total transfers from the state is still lower than the share fixed by the SFC. Thus, there exists discrepancy in the grants transferred between the PRIs and ULBs. The other important recommendation of SFC was discontinuation of sharing of individual taxes with the LBs. This has been accepted and implemented. Further, it has not recommended tax powers to higher two tiers of *Panchayats*. The state has complied with this recommendation also. Thus the local bodies in Karnataka get a share from the whole revenue of the state rather than sharing of individual taxes and thereby enabling the LBs to enjoy some stability in the flow of resources from the higher level governments to LBs.

The above analysis brings out that the resources available to LBs in Karnataka are far greater when compared to other states in India. However, the fiscal autonomy of LBs especially the rural ones is very limited. The dependency level of LBs on the state transfers is very high. The total revenues of LBs are not keeping pace with the growing state income (GSDP). The own resources of PRIs is far less than that of ULBs. Though the LBs are empowered to borrow, in reality they have not attempted except a few city corporations. There is no evidence of any *Panchayat* resorting to borrowings for development purposes. The reason for non-tapping of this source is stiff conditions laid down by the state on the LBs' borrowings. The ULBs are still getting lesser share from the state than what the first SFC had recommended

Of the total transfers from the state to PRIs, the share of non-Plan grants is more than that of Plan grants. Of late, the percentage share of plan grants of PRIs in the state's total plan outlays is declining. The decline has occurred even in absolute terms since 2002-2003. The transferred resources from higher-level governments especially to PRIs are by and large tied to programmes and schemes.

12.7 Conclusions and Policy Implications

The foregoing analysis of the fiscal situation in the state reveals that for long the state finances suffered fiscal adversities with some respite achieved in the recent past. Karnataka state however has been observed to be better placed than many other states as indicated by various fiscal indicators. This should not result in complacency, as the state needs to address many fiscal issues in the process of achieving higher social and economic development. Marked decline in the quality of public expenditure in terms of low and falling social and economic sector investments and small productive capital investments of the state, will pose problems in the attainment of higher growth and its sustenance.

The state's resources in terms of tax GSDP ratio have been marginally strengthened as revealed by the Budget and revised estimates for the years 2003-04 and 2004-05 respectively. However, the ratio is lower than the level prevailed in 1990-91. Also, there has been a track record of not being able to adhere to the budgeted levels in earlier years, and there is a need to set right this.

There is a need to tap adequate returns from the huge investments made by the government in the irrigation, power, water supply, etc. Wherever there is a need for subsidy for the deserving sections of the society there is a need to properly target them and set time deadlines. This will help avoid perennial growth of expenditure on account of these schemes. Apart from the measures to restructure the public expenditure there is an urgent need to address the issues pertaining to the quality of public expenditure. This is an important issue that has not received the attention of the policy makers. In order to address this there is a need to review all the government programmes and eliminate the ones that have outlived their utility or are duplicative in nature. The government in its eagerness to announce more and more programmes has been thinly spreading the funds over many programmes. It is disappointing to note that budgets continue with the practice of announcing many popular programmes. The time is ripe to reduce the size of committed expenditures, which constitutes a sizeable proportion of revenue expenditure. As mentioned elsewhere in the Chapter, expenditure cannot be reduced unless the commitment itself is reduced. These commitments are in the nature of huge public debt stock that the state has accumulated, the large base of employment created, etc. There is a need to improve the expenditure planning and management and also effectively introduce outcome budgeting that will aid in tracking the performance of government programmes.

The analysis pertaining to fiscal decentralisation brings out that the resources available to LBs in Karnataka are far greater when compared to other states in India. However, the fiscal autonomy of LBs especially the rural ones is very limited. The dependency level of LBs on the state transfers is very high. The total revenues of LBs are not keeping pace with the growing state income (GSDP). The own resources of PRIs are far less than that of ULBs. Though the LBs are empowered to borrow, in reality they have not attempted except a few city corporations. There is no evidence of any *Panchayat* resorting to borrowings for their needs. The reason for non-tapping of this source is stiff conditions laid down by the state on the LBs borrowings. The ULBs are still getting lesser share from the state grants than what the first SFC had recommended.

Of the total transfers from state to PRIs, the share of non-Plan grants is more than that of Plan grants. Of late, the percentage share of plan grants of PRIs in the state's Plan outlays is declining. In summary, fiscal decentralisation has not taken place in real spirit in the state despite the 73rd and 74th Amendments to the Constitution. There is a need to strengthen the local bodies in terms of their resources and clearly define their roles and responsibilities in providing the services to the public.

References

Babu, M. Devendra (2002). "Eleventh Finance Commission's Recommendations and the Local Bodies: Impact Across the States", *Management in Government*, Vol. XXXIV, No. 2.

Deshpande, R.S. Bhende, and Raveendra Naik (2003). "Volume and Composition of Subsidies in Food and Agriculture Sector", in Govinda Rao (ed.), *Volume and Composition of Budgetary Subsidies in Karnataka*, Monograph, ISEC, Bangalore.

Gayithri, K. (1997). "Role of Infrastructure in Industrial Development in Karnataka: A District level Analysis", *Arthavijnana*, pp. 185-205.

———. (2003a). "Industrial Incentives in Karnataka", in Govinda Rao (ed.), *Volume and Composition of Budgetary Subsidies in Karnataka*, Monograph, ISEC, Bangalore.

———. (2003b). "Industrial Incentives in Karnataka—A Study of Capital Investment Subsidy", *Mimeograph*, ISEC, Bangalore.

———. (2003c). "Housing Subsidies in Karnataka", in Govinda Rao (ed.), *Volume and Composition of Budgetary Subsidies in Karnataka*, Monograph, ISEC, Bangalore.

Goswami, Omkar *et al.* (2002). *Competitiveness of Indian Manufacturing Results from a Firm-Level Survey*, CII.

Government of India (2000). *Report of the Eleventh Finance Commission* (for 2000-2005), New Delhi.

———. 2005, *Report of the Twelfth Finance Commission*, New Delhi.

Government of Karnataka (1982). *Package of Incentives and Concessions for New Industrial Investments in Karnataka*, Bangalore.

———. (1996). *Industrial Policy Resolution*, Bangalore.

———. (2001a). *Medium Term Fiscal Plan for Karnataka 2000-01-2004-05*, Finance Department, Bangalore.

———. (2001b). *First Report of the Tax Reforms Commission*, Bangalore.

———. (2003). *Medium Term Fiscal plan for Karnataka*, 2003-04 – 2006-07.

Institute for Social and Economic Change (1994). "Industrial Potential in Karnataka", *mimeograph*, Bangalore.

Raju, K.V. and Amarnath (2003). "Irrigation Subsidies in Karnataka: A Growing Constraint for Reform", in Govinda Rao (ed.), *Volume and Composition of Budgetary Subsidies in Karnataka*, Monograph, ISEC, Bangalore.

Rao, Hemlata and Amarnath (2003). "A Macro view of Government Subsidies in Karnataka", in Govinda Rao (ed.), *Volume and Composition of Budgetary Subsidies in Karnataka*, Monograph, ISEC, Bangalore.

Rao, M. Govinda and V. B. Tulasidhar (1986). "Economic Analysis of Sales Taxation in India", International Bureau of Fiscal Documentation, July, pp. 288-299.

Rao, M. Govinda (2003). "Volume and Composition of Budgetary Subsidies in Karnataka", *Monograph*, ISEC, Bangalore.

Narayana, M.R. (2003). "Volume and Composition of Budgetary Subsidies to Higher Education in Karnataka State", in Govinda Rao (ed.) *Volume and Composition of Budgetary Subsidies in Karnataka*, Monograph, ISEC, Bangalore.

Saleth, Maria and G.S. Sastry (2003). "Subsidy in Water Supply and Sanitation Sector in Karnataka: Magnitude, Effects and Policy Issues", in Govinda Rao (ed.), *Volume and Composition of Budgetary Subsidies in Karnataka*, Monograph, ISEC, Bangalore.

The New Indian Express (2002). A report on "Stamp Duty Exemption, Latest Sop to Woo Investors", 20 March, Bangalore.

Tulasidhar, V.B. and M. Govinda Rao (1986). "Cost and Efficacy of Fiscal Incentives: Case of Sales Tax Subsidy", *Economic and Political Weekly* XX1 (41): 1799-1806.

UNCTAD (1998). *World Investment Report*, UNCTAD, New York.

Vivekananada (2003). "Subsidies in Power Sector" in Govinda Rao edited volume and *Composition of Budgetary Subsidies in Karnataka*, Monograph, ISEC, Bangalore.

APPENDIX A-12.1

Commercial Taxes in Karnataka

(Rs. in Crores)

Year	*Agricultural Income Tax*	*Professional Tax*	*Sales Tax*	*Entry Tax*	*Entertainment Tax*	*Betting Tax*	*Luxury Tax*	*Commercial Taxes*
1990-91	7.23	40.23	1316.92	65.49	42.01	11.6	6.46	1489.94
1991-92	9.07	47.89	1653.23	82.06	48.33	8.61	7.81	1857.00
1992-93	10.86	61.07	1775.79	109.84	49.64	9.95	10.48	2027.63
1993-94	9.01	77.99	2277.9	132.68	59.29	8.98	11.65	2577.50
1994-95	16.82	92.4	2505.76	117	47.05	14.05	16.43	2809.51
1995-96	49.73	105.76	2954.45	168.34	45.05	13.47	20.8	3357.60
1996-97	39.53	119.42	3510.19	199.44	34.20	11.81	31.21	3945.80
1997-98	30.05	102.96	3828.78	234.38	55.28	9.13	32.65	4293.23
1998-99	48.5	114.27	4265.17	273.13	56.27	11.78	42.16	4811.28
1999-00	34.8	132.78	4683.23	337.6	60.11	11.89	45.06	5305.47
2000-01	23.48	151.56	5386.33	473.02	50.73	14.29	66.60	6166.01
2001-02	2.63	0	5269.43	498.11	48.93	13.71	79.27	5912.08
2002-03 (RE)	1.55	0	5781.47	509.78	42.15	13.10	82.38	6430.43
2003-04 (BE)	28.31	0	6700.81	540.76	45.04	14.41	101.70	7431.03
Growth Rate	-0.98	12.96	12.86	18.43	0.12	2.69	24.41	12.76

Note: RE: Revised Estimates.
BE: Budget Estimates.

Source: Website of Finance Department, *Accounts at a Glance for 1960-2003*, Government of Karnataka.

APPENDIX A-12.2

Non-Commercial Taxes in Karnataka

(Rs. in Crores)

Year	*State Excise*	*Taxes on Motor Vehicles*	*Stamps and Regtn. Fees*	*Land Revenue*	*Electricity Duty*	*Forest Development Tax*	*Health Cess*	*Education Cess Tax*	*Own Tax Revenue*
1990-91	429.69	192.43	144.28	15.36	52.71	5.13	2.12	0.46	2332.12
1991-92	510.32	227.47	206.01	17.17	76.15	4.96	0.8	0.32	2900.2
1992-93	515.33	220.51	224.38	16.78	85.85	6	0.89	0.44	3097.81
1993-94	639.07	259.78	240.85	16.07	70.69	7.68	0.48	0.22	3812.34
1994-95	713.47	290.99	372.49	19.78	69.69	11.18	1.69	0.51	4289.31
1995-96	820.2	456.03	536.53	28.56	62.51	10.34	1.29	0.87	5273.93
1996-97	843.87	325.75	487.63	46.03	106.5	11.38	0.32	0.56	5767.84
1997-98	863.69	444.31	609.39	44.58	140.19	8.65	0.98	6.85	6411.87
1998-99	1005.19	386.79	548.11	38	140.25	8.36	2.29	2.77	6943.04
1999-00	1215.2	448.82	565.79	38.73	155.58	7.58	3.74	3.45	7744.36
2000-01	1523.13	501.82	638.12	43.16	162.1	6.82	1.54	1	9043.68
2001-02	1976.94	712.37	855.04	49.54	53.04	6.75	2.01	1	9568.777
2002-03 (RE)	2050.00	785.37	119.60	62.50	34.17	13.47	0.99	6.80	9503.286
2003-04 (BE)	2303.84	880.39	135.40	69.89	117.86	14.82	1.36	9.35	10963.88
Growth Rate	13.75	11.75	3.22	12.79	2.19	4.99	4.23	26.32	12.42

Source: As in Appendix A-12.1.

APPENDIX A-12.3

Burden of Debt in Karnataka

(Rs. in Crores)

Year	Interest Payments*	Debt Repaid	Total Interest and Debt	Outstanding Debt	Total Revenues	Total Revenue Expenditure	GSDP	Interest Payment as Per Cent of Total Revenue	Interest Payment as Per Cent of Revenue	Interest and Debt Repayment as Per Cent of GSDP
1990-91	435.61	323.57	759.17	3987.64	3892.18	3971.09	23332	11.19	10.97	3.25
1991-92	514.53	167.64	682.17	4533.94	4775.47	4954.12	30008	10.77	10.39	2.27
1992-93	593.71	570.22	1163.93	5193.65	5421.66	5591.69	33026	10.95	10.62	3.52
1993-94	717.97	1758.79	2476.76	5906.02	6324.65	6208.25	42739	11.35	11.56	5.80
1994-95	871.43	1686.14	2557.57	7136.96	6968.39	7264.52	50535	12.51	12.00	5.06
1995-96	1047.55	460.91	1508.46	8023.17	8543.45	8481.18	58861	12.26	12.35	2.56
1996-97	1208.06	1263.78	2471.84	9189.25	9622.18	10201.08	70360	12.55	11.84	3.51
1997-98	1393.81	703.58	2097.39	10446.61	10613.39	10890.21	76790	13.13	12.80	2.73
1998-99	1616.61	405.34	2021.95	12465.22	11230.44	12445.61	90623	14.39	12.99	2.23
1999-00	2012.30	570.52	2582.83	15147.26	12906.45	14677.2	96179	15.59	13.71	2.69
2000-01	2387.55	520.55	2908.10	17997.94	14822.72	16684.95	105396	16.11	14.31	2.76
2001-02	2682.89	1447.65	4130.54	22432.53	15321.26	18605.70	109461	17.51	14.42	3.77
2002-03	3291.89	5789.2	9081.09	26169.32	16168.73	18814.50	118540	20.36	17.50	7.66
2003-04 (RE)	3694.25	7330.21	11024.46	30188.38	21731.84	23050.28	130678	17.00	16.03	8.44
2004-05 (BE)	3919.64	3337.05	7256.69	34910.28	25510.31	25437.48	147956	15.36	15.41	4.90

Note: * includes interest on provident fund, etc.

Source: As in Appendix A-12.1.

Chapter 13

Environment, Biodiversity, Climate Change and Urbanisation

13.1 Introduction

The economy and environment have close inter linkages. Development has an impact on the environment and in turn the environment also impacts on development. This chapter examines some of the issues related to environment and its implications for growth and development. Specifically we discuss the environment in general (issues like air quality, water quality, etc.), biodiversity, wetland and coastal zone management, climatic change, urbanisation and urban solid waste management.

13.2 Environment

13.2.1 Introduction

This section discusses the issues relating to urban environment and its causes and consequences. The main variables used in the discussion are population growth, population density, land use, transportation, air and water quality, and solid waste. Here an attempt is made to provide answers to the questions: a) is Karnataka a high population growth state and which are the highest and least growth regions and their possible consequences, b) is Karnataka a high density state and which are the highest and least population density regions and their possible consequences, c) land use pattern of selected cities of Karnataka and their problems, d) existing urban transportation system and their problems, e) current air quality in selected urban areas and their associated problems, f) current water quality and their associated problems, g) existing solid waste situation and their associated problems, and finally h) policy direction for efficient environmental management.

13.2.2 Population Growth Dimension

Rapid population growth has been identified as the most common denominator for all environment and development related issues. By looking at the urban population growth trend one can find that Karnataka is not an exception to this conclusion. It may be recalled that towns of Karnataka have been growing fast due to the process of infilling of additional population added during 1901-91. As a result, almost, 24.5 per cent of the towns have recorded very high growth of more than 3 per cent per annum followed by a very significant proportion of towns (56.2 per cent) in the range 1-3 per cent growth. In terms of the regional pattern of growth, southern Maidan has emerged as the most prominent region with highest concentration of towns with high growth followed by northern Maidan (Table 13.1). Obviously, these regions have been experiencing high population pressure and hence, innumerable environment and resource associated problems.

TABLE 13.1

Population Growth of Cities and Towns of Karnataka by Region: 1991

Per Cent Annual Growth	*Coast*	*Malnad*	*Southern Maidan*	*Northern Maidan*	*Karnataka*
Negative	13.0	10.4	0	4.9	5.8
Less than or Equal to 1	26.1	18.2	3.1	14.7	13.4
1–3	47.8	55.8	62.5	52.4	56.2
More than 3	13.0	15.6	34.4	27.9	24.5
Total	**100.0**	**100.0**	**100.0**	**100.0**	**224***

Note: * Growth data is available for 30 new towns.

Source: Census, 1991.

13.2.3 Population Density Dimension

The main indicator of population pressure is population density. In Karnataka almost 40 per cent of the towns have population density more that 5000 persons per sq.km and in particular, 13 per cent of them have as high as more than 10,000 population density. Higher concentration of towns with high growth rates in southern Maidan has obviously, emerged as the region with higher concentration of towns with high population density followed by northern Maidan (Table 13.2). Hence, for obvious reasons of high population pressure southern Maidan has been facing acute environment and resource related problems as compared to other region. This is in addition to more specific environmental problems being experienced by individual regions. The most prominent environment problems that one can identify are related to land use, air and water quality and pollution. In particular, more specific environment related problems being experienced by the state are degradation of coastal region, rapid development of illegal residential layouts in urban areas, proliferation of slums, degradation and conversion of lakes in urban area, insufficient open space, overexploitation of groundwater, deteriorating water quality, lack of sewerage system and disposal facility, lack of household toilet facility, improper waste and hazardous waste management, poor air quality due to high SPM and RSPM levels, air pollution and high noise level in industries, (Government of Karnataka, 2004).

TABLE 13.2

Percentage Distribution of Towns by Population Density, Karnataka: 1991

Population Density	*Coast*	*Malnad*	*Southern Maidan*	*Northern Maidan*	*Karnataka*
Less than or equal to 1000	20	12.3	11.4	15.1	13.8
1000-3000	50	25.9	17.1	30.2	27.5
3000-5000	13.3	27.2	18.6	13.7	19.3
5000-10000	13.3	23.5	35.7	27.4	26.8
More than 10000	3.3	11.1	17.1	13.7	12.6
Total	**30**	**81**	**70**	**73**	**254**

Source: Census, 1991.

13.2.4 Land Use Dimension

Land use is the economic pulse for orderly function of activities in urban area. Hence, land use planning acquires greater significance in urban planning. In Karnataka, urban planning process is being implemented and updated as per the well defined town planning legislations. Accordingly, the total urban land is marshalled into broad land use types residential, commercial, industrial, parks and open spaces, transport and others as per the prescribed population norm to meet the requirements. For instance, as residential area requirement is more, almost 50 per cent of the area is earmarked for residential use. By and large, population density criterion (125 persons per hectare) is being used to derive the extent of residential land requirement in urban areas. Similarly, 15 per cent of the area is the prescribed norm for parks and open spaces (Government of Karnataka, 2004). However, the pace with which the towns and cities of Karnataka are growing, let alone land use norm, even the total urban land area requirement is not being met in almost all the towns of Karnataka. The per cent area norm under residential land is met only in Gulbarga and to some extent it is very close in the proposed 2011 land use for Bangalore and Hubli-Dharward. While, land use norm under open space is met only in Mysore and its share is very close to the norm in the proposed land use for Bangalore (Table 3.3). In terms of per capita availability of various land use types, Bangalore has the least per capita availability under all the land use types as compared to other cities of Karnataka. Hubli-Dharward stands next to Bangalore in per capita land use type availability (Table 13.4). The desired norm for various types of land use in an urban area is indicated in Table 13.5. The rapid population growth being experienced by Bangalore, the least availability of various land use types is a matter of very great concern as they impose serious impact on the quality of life of Bangalorians. In the absence of planned growth of the city and non-availability of the extent of the required land use types, particularly the residential land, the city has been experiencing greater extent of unplanned growth with illegal layout and unauthorised constructions to accommodate the growing population. In the absence of planned development these areas obviously lack basic

TABLE 13.3

Percentage Distribution of Land Use Types by Selected Cities of Karnataka

Land Use	*Bangalore*		*Gulbarga*	*Mangalore*	*Mysore*	*Hubli-Darward*		
	2011	*1995*	*1997*	*1992*	*1998*	*2011*	*2000*	*1986*
Residential	43.2	34.8	59.4	17.6	38.9	42.8	30.8	24.9
Commercial	2.9	2.4	5.0	1.4	2.2	6.1	3.2	3.6
Industrial	6.8	7.2	8.9	4.9	11.8	4.7	5.1	5.4
Open Spaces	13.8	7.5	6.5	2.8	17.2	10.1	6.4	13.2
Public Utilities	8.7	9.2	10.3	2.4	7.8	14.7	16.9	7.5
Transport	20.7	31.5	9.0	6.8	15.2	21.6	21.9	28.1
Others	3.9	7.4	0.9	64.1	6.9	0.0	15.7	17.2
Total	100	100	100	100	100	100	100	100

Source: Town Planning Department, Government. of Karnataka.

TABLE 13.4

Per Capita Availability of Land Use Types by Selected Cities of Karnataka

Land Use	Bangalore	Gulbarga	Mangalore	Mysore	Hubli-Darward		
	2011*	1995	1997	1992	1998	2011	2000	1986
Residential	4.3	2.4	9.4	15.4	6.8	6.2	4.0	2.7
Commercial	0.3	0.2	0.8	1.2	0.4	0.9	0.4	0.4
Industrial	0.7	0.5	1.4	4.3	2.1	0.7	0.7	0.6
Open Spaces	1.4	0.5	1.0	2.5	3.0	1.5	0.8	1.4
Public Utilities	0.9	0.6	1.6	2.1	1.4	2.1	2.2	0.8
Transport	2.1	2.2	1.4	5.9	2.7	3.1	2.8	3.1
Others	0.4	0.5	0.1	55.9	1.2	0.0	2.0	1.9
Total	9.9	6.9	15.7	87.2	17.6	14.5	13.0	10.9

Note: * Estimates.

Source: Town Planning Department, Government. of Karnataka.

TABLE 13.5

Desirable Land Use Pattern for Cities and Towns
(in Percentages)

Land Use Category	Population Size		
	More than 150000	150000–50000	Less than 50000
Residential	40.0	45.0	50.0
Industrial	8.0	7.0	6.0
Commercial	3.5	3.0	3.0
Parks, Playgrounds and Open Spaces	10.0	10.0	8.0
Transport and Communication	24.0	22.0	22.0
Public and Semi-public	10.0	9.0	8.0
Others	4.5	4.0	3.0
Total	**100.0**	**100.0**	**100.0**

Source: Gowda (1972), *Urban and Regional Planning*, Prasaranga University of Mysore, Mysore, p. 88.

infrastructure and facilities like piped water and sanitation, proper roads, solid waste disposal, permanent house structure thus reducing these areas into larger slums. On the other hand, with rapid realisation about the health care and physical fitness of the body, early morning walk has become almost an integral part of the daily routine among all the age groups of most of the Bangalorians. This has resulted in crowded parks as an indicator of lack of open space in Bangalore which is already limited as per the norm. Further, in the absence of planned cultural and religious land use, residents demand for such facility has resulted in conversion of several parks and playgrounds whose availability itself is limited into cultural and religious centres, thus destroying the functional and environmental identity of the open spaces. With rapid increase in number of multi-storied residential buildings indiscriminately without land use and land capability considerations has already imposed serious environmental problems like formation of heat islands and thermal inversion thus causing significant change in Bangalore's temperature. Poor infrastructure and service facilities, development of slums, air and water quality and noise are the other problems being faced by the city. Bangalore being the IT capital of India, unfortunately lacks vision for its long term perspective plan for its environmentally sustainable growth and development. Hence, it is high time to develop such a vision document by including environment and ecological components. Unless proper care is initiated well in advance through efficient urban and environmental planning process other major cities of Karnataka would follow the development path of Bangalore in the immediate future. With all possibilities the immediate next victim would be Hubli-Dharward.

Lack of a development vision for Bangalore has resulted in another serious problem of peri-urban region. Improper development of peri-urban region has led to coexistence of both affluence and poverty in the region. In the peri-urban region, while, multinational companies have developed IT industries with ultra-modern infrastructure, several land developers have developed innumerable American dreamland residential colonies to serve IT professionals with self-contained ultra-modern facilities. On the other hand, other areas have remained as 'urban' region with acute resource and environmental problems. More prominent among them are higher concentration of households with large size, higher illiteracy rate, higher share of unskilled and primary sector workers, higher share of medical expenses as compared to city, larger share of *kutcha* or semi-*pucca* house structure, least water and sanitation facility, poor solid waste disposal provision and high concentration of slums and uneven city-peripheral transport facility (Sastry, 2004; BMTC, 2003; Ramachandran and Sastry, 2001). Similar peri-urban regional problems may be found in other large cities of Karnataka.

13.2.5 Transportation Dimension

Another essential urban function is residents' travel for various activities. This contributes significantly to both economy and environment. While travel by residents contribute to the economy, the means or mode of travel impose serious environmental problems through emission of pollutants to the city environment. With rapidly growing cities improper planning processes have led to inadequate infrastructure and services. One such inadequacy is the lack of efficient urban public transport system and transportation planning. This has obviously resulted in rapid increase in private modes of transport. As a result, the number of vehicles registered in urban areas have increased enormously (Table 13.6). Interestingly, two wheelers, the most affordable means of transport for the urban middle income group forms almost 75 per cent of the total registered vehicle. In the absence of efficient urban public transport system, middle income households are forced to develop their private transport system to meet the situation. This has not only imposed financial burden on the middle income class, but more significantly has contributed almost 60 per cent of the total pollution load to the city environment, the impacts of which are manifold.

Here an attempt has been made to estimate the pollution load contributed to the city environs by the urban transport system through emission of various pollutants. The main pollutants emitted by the urban transport sector are suspended particulate matter (SPM), sulpher dioxide SO_2, oxides of nitrogen NO_x, hydrocarbon (HC) and carbon monoxide (CO). The pollution load emitted by each vehicle type, has been estimated by using the constant factor of emission per 1000 kms under each pollutant and average distance travelled by each vehicle per day (KSCST, 1995). Accordingly, in Bangalore the total pollution load emitted by the transport sector per day is almost 2856.7 tonnes which is the highest among the selected cities of Karnataka (Table 13.7). As per the previous estimate, per day pollution load emission by the transport sector has increased by 149.5 per cent during 1992-2004.

TABLE 13.7

Estimated Pollution Load Emitted by Vehicles to the Environment by Pollutant Type and Cities: 2004

City	*SPM*	*SO_2*	*NOx*	*HC*	*CO*	*Total*
Bangalore	37.3	30.7	318.8	791.1	1678.7	2856.7
Mysore	1.8	0.2	0.6	89.0	151.4	243.0
Dharward	1.2	0.1	0.4	58.6	99.6	159.9
Mangalore	1.1	0.1	0.4	56.2	95.6	153.4
Belgaum	1.7	1.7	20.5	36.5	77.6	137.9
Gulbarga	0.7	0.1	0.2	35.4	60.2	96.7
Bijapur	0.6	0.1	0.2	27.7	47.1	75.7
Bellary	0.5	0.0	0.2	24.0	40.8	65.5
Bidar	0.2	0.0	.0.1	10.5	17.8	28.5

Source: Derived from number of registered vehicles data, Transport Department, Government.of Karnataka, 2004.

For details see Appendices A-13.1 and A-13.2. This is a matter of great concern, as they impose serious health and environmental problems. The maximum contribution is from carbon monoxide while, minimum load varies among SPM, SO_2 and NOx. The main source of carbon monoxide emission is from incomplete fuel combustion in motor vehicles. The effects of this pollutant are deprivation of tissues of oxygen, aggravation of cardio-respiratory diseases. Bangalore has been known for asthma problem since beginning mainly due to pollen grains emanating from high concentration of trees on account of its popularity as a garden city. Of late this problem is being aggravated on account of most inefficient transportation planning and emission of very high quantity of carbon monoxide into the city environment. Similarly, the emission of said pollutants into the environs of other cities though small but, are

TABLE 13.6

Number of Registered Vehicles by Type and Cities in Karnataka: 2004

City	*Two Wheeler*	*Three Wheeler*	*Small Passenger*	*Big Passenger Vehicle*	*Goods Vehicle*	*Others Vehicle*	*Total*
Bangalore	1433539	75328	309648	19683	83722	12841	1934761
Mysore	246721	13087	31216	1949	7632	5813	306418
Dharward	128152	9233	20117	2284	17843	7267	184896
Mangalore	107809	12210	37624	3415	10345	537	171940
Belgaum	131961	5213	14450	1993	11561	3214	168392
Gulbarga	84525	5189	7566	1243	5003	8951	112477
Bijapur	55624	2447	5062	2083	9676	7026	81918
Bellary	61082	1891	4993	467	2790	6978	78201
Bidar	25198	1365	3091	414	1693	1849	33610

Source: Transport Department, Government of Karnataka.

significant as compared to their population size. Hence, unless early precautionary measures are taken with efficient urban transportation planning process in particular and urban planning and environmental management in general, the existing popularity of Bangalore as an 'air-conditioned' city would gradually turn into a 'health hazardous city'. In Bangalore, the city transport service called BMTC as on date is operating 3125 schedules with a fleet of 3207 buses with 45000 trips per day by serving the city and its region by transporting 28 lakh passengers. Towards realising its commitment to clean air, BMTC has introduced buses with Euro I and II emission standards in order to maintain clean air in the city environs. In addition, BMTC has planned to introduce *Jalashakti Vahinis*—buses operated with fuel which is a combination of diesel and vapourised oxygen. Towards clean fuel, unleaded petrol has already been introduced in the city to reduce 'lead content' another most dangerous pollutant in the atmosphere.

13.2.6 Air Quality Dimension

The main factors responsible for air quality deterioration in urban areas are urban transportation, industrial activity, biomass burning and incineration of solid, biomedical and hazardous waste substances. Structurally, causes and consequences of air quality deterioration are industrial activity, vehicular usage, population growth, population density, and high mortality (Sastry, 1985). As a part of national air quality monitoring network, air quality monitoring is being done under residential, commercial and industrial land use in selected cities of India and more so in Karnataka. The air quality data on the pollutants SPM, SO_2, NOx for Bangalore and Mysore have revealed a great concern about higher values of SPM in commercial and residential areas of Bangalore, while in Mysore it is well within the limit (Table 13.8). Similar air quality data for 25 sample locations (10 industrial, 9 commercial, 5 residential and 1 sensitive) in 14 cities of Karnataka is being monitored and recorded by the Karnataka State Pollution Control Board. It is interesting to note that out of the three pollutants regularly being monitored, sulpher dioxide and oxides of nitrogen are well within the stipulated standards in all the 25 sample locations. However, SPM has crossed the upper limit in all the land use type and more prominently in commercial areas. In industrial areas one out of 10 sample locations in HSSK Ltd, Hassan has recorded 477 (360 limit), while, two sample stations

TABLE 13.8

Pollutants Load in the Atmosphere by Land Use Type and Cities: 1999-2003

Pollutant	*Land Use*	*Standard*	*1999*	*2000*	*2001*	*2002*	*2003*	*2004*	*2005*
					Bangalore				
SO_2	Industrial	80	33.0	28.0	26.0	11.0	16.0	16	9.1
	Commercial	60	44.0	37.0	31.0	12.0	11.0	7.8	-
	Residential	60	38.0	32.0	26.0	12.0	12.0	6.7	8.0
Nox	Industrial	80	22.0	26.0	27.0	17.0	16.0	37.5	51
	Commercial	60	31.0	46.0	50.0	21.0	31.0	46	-
	Residential	60	26.0	31.0	34.0	24.0	26.0	28.4	54
SPM	Industrial	360	75.0	114.0	114.0	113.0	111.0	139.3	155
	Commercial	140	233.0	181.0	274.0	207.0	160.0	195.7	-
	Residential	140	173.0	160.0	162.0	122.0	119.0	181.4	150
					Mysore				
SO_2	Industrial	80	30.4	30.83	21.1	20.00	20	11	10
	Commercial	60	31.3	30	20	20	20	11	11
NOx	Industrial	80	-	-	30	29	27	17	22
	Commercial	60	-	-	28.5	30	27	18	22
SPM	Industrial	360	-	-	30	106	103	92	87
	Commercial	140	-	-	73	112	107	96	99

Note: All figures indicated in the above tables are in mg/m^3.
Source: CPCB, Dept. of E&E, Government. Karnataka.

out of 5 residential stations located in Bellary (regional office sample) and Chickmagalur (shariff colony sample) have crossed the upper limit and in particular Chikmagalur has recorded very high value of 539 (almost five times the limit—140 limit). In the case of commercial land use sample, it is a matter of very great concern as seven [Gulbarga (2:156,541), Davangere (1:280), Hassan (1:432), Hubli (1:490), Gadag (1:276) and Karwar (1:293)] out of 9 sample locations have crossed upper limit (140) thus calling immediate measures to reduce the level (KSPCB, 2004). This analysis is consistent with the air quality results for Bangalore. To corroborate this problem, as per the industrial air pollution control status for the year 2002-2003, only 89.7 per cent of the industrial units which come under the purview of Pollution Control Act have the air pollution control system under operation, and small scale sector has the lower compliance rate with only (88.3 per cent) of units with air pollution control system under operation. It is a well known fact that small scale sector with limited investment and land resources are unable to install pollution control measures effectively and hence, have been contributing significantly to both air and water pollution. This is in spite of highest number of units having undergone inspection towards pollution control and innumerable pollution control incentives being given to them (KSPCB, 2004). Major concentration of polluting units are found in Mysore, Belgaum, Bellary, Dakshina Kannada, Dharwad, Gulbarga, Shimoga, and Uttara Kannada districts. Bangalore rural and urban districts, for obvious reasons, has the highest concentration of pollution prone industrial units (Appendix A-13.3). Obviously, pollution load in these regions are high and require constant monitoring. (As per the KSPCB Regional Laboratory at Rajajinagar, Bangalore air monitoring in other cities of Karnataka are also followed as per the national air quality monitoring procedure.)

Seasonal analysis of the pollution levels of SO_2, NOx and SPM by land use types in Bangalore for the years 2001 and 2000 has revealed significant seasonal variations in all the said pollutants in the city. The pollution level of SO_2 is consistently the highest during winter and more so in commercial areas, and least during summer. By and large, NOx has revealed high values in spring and again in commercial area and lower values in the summer. By and large, the levels of SPM is highest in winter and more so in commercial area and least in the autumn (Table13.9). Hence, commercial areas of Bangalore have emerged as the highest polluted areas by all the three pollutants level and mostly during the winter. This is the season when the wind speed is comparatively low and hence, the chances of dilution of

TABLE 13.9

Pollution Levels of SO_2, NOx and SPM by Seasons in Bangalore: 2000 and 2001

Seasons	*2000*			*2001*		
	Industries	*Commercial*	*Residential*	*Industries*	*Commercial*	*Residential*
			Sulphur Dioxide			
Winter	19.23	26.07	21.90	34.03	34.38	34.54
Spring	11.04	15.23	10.54	27.49	31.35	26.33
Summer	18.52	19.25	NA	9.00	9.28	8.58
Autumn	26.83	33.55	26.70	9.43	8.87	8.34
			Nitrogen Dioxide			
Winter	34.29	46.59	44.19	26.11	37.55	32.87
Spring	35.67	67.19	46.30	28.45	24.46	32.16
Summer	38.56	39.70	NA	9.14	16.95	29.48
Autumn	22.64	54.76	31.33	16.13	21.10	18.24
			Suspended Particulate Matter			
Winter	126.93	156.26	142.68	93.95	202.54	170.00
Spring	147.29	193.26	129.32	88.24	155.26	143.77
Summer	43.17	176.97	NA	112.41	171.79	82.71
Autumn	28.95	148.50	64.62	90.44	213.94	125.31

Note: All figures indicated in the above tables are in mg/m^3

Source: CPCB, South Zone.

the said pollutants level is remote. As a result, commercial areas of the city are highly polluted during winter thus, calling for appropriate policy measures for their dilution. Of course, the main contributor to this problem is the intra-city transport which requires adequate planning measures in terms of redesigning the transportation routes, use of less polluting auto fuels and promotion of environment- friendly domestic and commercial vehicles in the city.

13.2.7 Water Quality Dimension

The status of water pollution control has revealed a more shocking situation in Karnataka as only 61.95 per cent of the water polluting units have water pollution control system under operation and again like air pollution situation, the small scale sector has the least share of units (58.66 per cent) with water pollution control system under operation (Appendix 13.4). Hence, unless proper care is taken well in advance, pollution problems of small scale units may go out of control by posing serious threat to both resources and environment. It has been well recorded that availability of both ground and surface water are decreasing rapidly on account of pollution problems. Due to least compliance of water pollution control standards by the polluting units and letting of untreated sewage from cities and towns into rivers, lakes, tanks and other water bodies, major river systems in the state are heavily polluted. In Karnataka, out of 218 urban local bodies, only 36 local bodies excluding Bangalore city and its surrounding municipal councils have underground drainage facility. However, household connections to UGD in these towns is not 100 per cent. The remaining 182 urban local bodies are yet to get underground drainage facility. Further, even among 36 urban local bodies where UGD facility exists, treatment facility is not complete, as in 16 local bodies only oxidation facility exists, while 6 local bodies have just primary treatment facility. Other 9 urban local bodies do not have treatment plant. In this background, to protect the river water quality, two river monitoring programmes are being simultaneously implemented by the KSPCB by covering all the major river stretches in the state (30 monitoring stations under Monitoring of Indian National Aquatic Resources (MINARS) programme; 19 monitoring stations under Board's programme) (Appendix A-13.4). An analysis of river monitoring data for all major river stretches for almost five years have revealed that most of the river stretches have constantly revealed the water quality rating as C—drinking water source after conventional treatment, and D—propagation of wildlife and fisheries and shifting between the rating C and D. In particular, more problematic river stretches which are located close to industrial units are detailed in the Table 13.10.

TABLE 13.10

Highly Polluted River Stretches in Karnataka

River Stretch
Bhadra River Shimoga:
Upstream of MPM and VISL, Bhadravati.
Downstream of MPM, Bhadravathi.
Tungabhadra River, Davangere:
Upstream of Harihar Polifiber.
Downstream of Harihar Polifiber.
Kali River, Uttara Kannada:
Upstream of West Coast Paper Mills
Downstream of West Coast Paper Mills.
Hebbala River, Mandya;
Hebbala village, near Mandya.
Kabini River, Mysore District:
Intake of KIADB, Nanjanagud.
Bathing Ghat, Nanjanagud.
Tungabhadra River
Haralahalli bridge.
Arkavathi River
Downstream of Kanakapura.
Krishna River
Downstream of Devasagara bridge.
Bhima River
Downstream of road bridge Ghanagapura Village.

Source: Karnataka State Pollution Control Board, *Annual Reports 1996-97 to 2002-03.*

However, the main efforts of the monitoring is to bring the river water quality to the B grade—bathing quality standard. Similarly, the polluted stretches of the river Cauvery is being also monitored under national river monitoring network in the towns of K. R. Nagar, Kollegal, Nanjanagud, and Srirangapattanam located along the river Cauvery. As a part of lake monitoring system, several lakes in and around Bangalore like Ulsoor, Bellandur, Labagh, Nagavara, Jogupalya, Kamakshipalya are being monitored regularly for water pollution by the pollution control board.

13.2.8 Solid Waste Dimension

One of the consequences of rapid urbanisation is the generation of huge quantity of urban solid waste. Inefficient management and disposal of urban solid waste has been posing serious environment and health related problems. It is a well-known fact that the quantity of solid waste generation is positively associated with the level of development and their composition is also highly complex as higher level of development would generate larger quantity of hazardous waste. This problem is becoming more acute with rapid urbanisation and level of development. The main sources of solid waste generation are urban residential and commercial sector, industrial activities and hospitals. Accordingly, they have been named as municipal solid waste, hazardous waste, and biomedical waste. In Karnataka 21, 43,280 metric tonnes of municipal solid waste, 92,975 metric tonnes of hazardous waste, and 15,786 metric tonnes of biomedical waste was generated in 2003 (*State of the Environment Report and Action Plan 2005*, Department of Ecology and Environment, Government of Karnataka).

Municipal solid waste is mainly composed of organic, plastic, paper, and other wastes, putrescrible (72 per cent), paper (11.6 per cent), dust and ash (6.7 per cent), plastic (6.2 per cent), glass (1.4 per cent), clothes (1 per cent), hazardous waste (0.9 per cent), and metals (0.2 per cent). Almost 40 to 50 per cent of the total municipal waste produced in Karnataka is generated by the 6 city corporations. Though, adequate legislations exist for collection, transportation and disposal of municipal solid waste, and to levy cess to meet the financial burden in its management, by and large both collection and disposal is not efficiently managed for the institutional constraint and lack of scientific knowledge about its problems. As a result, even whatever quantity of solid waste is collected is not being properly disposed. Even Bangalore, the capital city of the state is not free from this problem, as only 50 per cent of the total solid waste generated per day (2,500 tonnes per day) is being collected and dumped in a most unscientific way. Recently, the municipal corporation of Bangalore has entered into an agreement with a private firm for generation of power using the municipal solid waste. The problem is more serious in other urban areas. It is interesting to note that out of 226 urban local bodies in the state, 226 have identified proper solid waste disposal landfill sites as recently as 2005 and Puttur and Karwar acquire special significance for undertaking the process of scientifically designed landfill sites in their towns. Rapidly growing towns and cities, and increase in the magnitude of generation of municipal solid waste and their improper management would impose serious health and environment related problems.

Hazardous waste is the most harmful residue generated out of the industrial process, effluent treatment plants and expiry date crossed manufactured products. Karnataka has 1662 hazardous waste generating units that generate 92975 metric tonnes of hazardous waste per year. Spatially, Bangalore has the highest concentration (592) of units followed by Mysore, Belgaum, Dharwad, Dakshina Kannada, Gulbarga, Bellary, Tumkur, Bidar and Raichur. However, by quantum of generation of hazardous waste, Bellary stands first followed by Koppal, Bangalore, Uttara Kannada, Dakshina Kannada, Mysore, Belgaum, Dharwad, Bidar and Shimoga (Appendix A 13.8). Out of 92,975 metric tonnes of hazardous waste per year 31.24 per cent is recyclable, 4.35 per cent incinerable, while, the remaining 64.4 per cent need to be disposed safely into landfill. The Karnataka State Pollution Control Board has recently identified two disposal sites one in Siddlaghatta in Kolar district and another near Dobbaspet in Bangalore rural district. Hence, whatever waste generated so far was stored by the units themselves with greater amount of risk involvement.

Biomedical waste or hospital waste is another type of waste generated during diagnosis, treatment, immunisation and research processes involving human beings and animals. Only 20 per cent of biomedical waste is infectious and almost 77 per cent is noninfectious with a minute 3 per cent involving hazardous waste. In Karnataka by and large 43,257 metric tonnes of biomedical waste is generated per annum from approximately 9748 units. The main sources of generation are government. and private health care establishments, blood banks, diagnostic laboratories, small clinics and veterinary clinics. Though the major share of biomedical waste is non-infectious, improper handling and disposal would impose serious health and environmental problems. In Karnataka, the management of biomedical waste is purely a private affair. In medium size cities disposal of biomedical waste is done through burial within the hospital premises. However, due to huge costs, many of the health care establishments, particularly small establishments resort to illegal methods of disposal through community bins. Recently, the Karnataka State Pollution Board has encouraged setting up of bio-medical waste treatment facilities at all districts. As on date, 10 biomedical waste treatment facilities are operating in the state (two in Bangalore, one each at Mysore, Belgaum, Gulbarga, Bijapur, Shimoga, Davangere, Mangalore and Dharwad (Department of Ecology and Environment, Government of Karnataka). With rapid urbanisation, increasing number of health conscious urbanites and prevailing inefficient disposal methods would pose very serious health and environmental problems in urban areas.

13.2.9 Policy Dimension

Environmental protection is a constitutional obligation both from the government and from the citizens' point of view. Accordingly, several legislations have been enacted to protect the environment. The main legislations are Water Pollution Control Act, 1974; Air Pollution Control Act, 1981; Environmental Protection Act, 1986; Hazardous Waste Management Act, 1989. Well-defined institutional structures have been established both at the centre and the state for efficient environmental protection and management. However, due to complexity of the environmental issues, environmental protection is posing serious challenge.

Rapid urbanisation and higher growth rate of cities in Karnataka have led to cities with high population densities. Obviously, high growth and high density cities have not only imposed high pressure on land but, demand more resources and services, and hence, environmental degradation. Karnataka's urbanisation has been a lopsided one as higher level of urbanisation is taking place in southern Maidan and particularly in Bangalore and its region. Hence, there is a need for policy direction to encourage balanced urban development.

Urban land use pattern have shown inadequate land under various types thus posing serious problems specially on residential use and open spaces. Hence, suitable urban planning process need to be initiated with adequate environmental management controls to encourage sustainable urban development of various urban centres.

Urban transportation system is very poor resulting in poor air quality in urban areas. Hence, in order to maintain urban air quality rapid mass transport system need to be developed more efficiently with adequate fleet strength, with suitable pollution control measures. The pollution load emitted by the transport sector has been an alarming one which need to be reduced to a minimum level to achieve both health and environmental protection.

Air pollution levels in cities are becoming more problematic especially in commercial and residential areas. While, transportation is one of the causes, industrial activities have also contributed to the problem. Seasonally, the pollution levels of various pollutants are high in winter and least in autumn. Hence, in addition to streamlining the transport sector, efficient monitoring of industrial units is of utmost importance.

Water pollution has also become a serious issue due to poor implementation and monitoring of water polluting industrial units. In addition, letting of untreated urban sewage has polluted almost all the river stretches of Karnataka. Efficient implementation of water pollution control laws and establishment of treatment facilities for urban sewage are the priorities to safeguard the water resources of the state.

Solid waste generation has been posing serious environmental issue mainly due to inefficient management and associated poor institutional structure. It is high time to develop appropriate institutional arrangement for efficient and timely disposal of all types of solid waste in an environment friendly way.

13.3 Biodiversity Conservation: Status and Management

13.3.1 Introduction

Biodiversity conservation is part of the larger objective of promoting sustainable development. Biodiversity loss not only affects current economic growth but also the capacity of the economy to sustain future economic growth. Biological diversity or biodiversity in short is an umbrella term used to describe the number, variety and variability of living organisms in an assemblage. Biodiversity may be described in terms of genes, species and ecosystems. Genetic diversity is the sum of genetic information contained in the genes of individuals, plants, animals and micro-organisms. Species diversity refers to the variety and variability of species in a given region or area. Ecosystem diversity can be defined as the variety of habitats, biotic communities and ecological process in the biosphere as well as the diversity within the ecosystem.

13.3.2 Biodiversity Loss: Causes and Impact

Biodiversity loss is caused by both proximate and fundamental causes. Proximate causes include logging activities, agricultural clearance of forest land, pollution, etc. Fundamental causes include economic, institutional and social factors. Population growth, poverty and ill defined property rights are important factors driving biotic impoverishment, habitat loss, species and genetic decline. Moreover, environmental goods such as biodiversity, the costs and benefits of which are both uncertain and concentrated in the future are heavily discounted which accelerates biodiversity loss. Distortions due to missing markets or the inability of existing markets to capture the true value of natural resources are also factors behind biodiversity loss. Intervention failures or policy failures due to government actions in intervening in the working of the market such as giving financial incentives for deforestation or concessions for selling timber and other forest products at less than socially optimum levels are other factors behind biodiversity loss. Biodiversity loss has both human and non-human impacts as well as inter-generation and intra-generational impacts. For instance, the benefits of biodiversity conservation will accrue to the present generation but the costs of biodiversity loss will be borne by the future generations. The benefits of biodiversity conservation may accrue to the global community, whereas the costs may often be borne by the local community. Poor people and less developed countries who depend on natural resources for their livelihoods are affected the most by biodiversity loss. The developing countries are rich in biodiversity such as forests, wetlands, aquatic environments, etc. However, the biodiversity of the developing countries are under threat due to demographic and economic pressures, faulty incentive mechanisms and policies, etc. as noted above.

13.3.3 Biodiversity Conservation and Development

Although biodiversity conservation is part of the objective of realising sustainable development, there are trade-offs between development and conservation. Even if development becomes more sustainable, biodiversity loss will take place. The challenge facing developed and developing countries alike is to minimise the trade-offs between development and conservation.

Policies for conserving biodiversity depend upon the perceived costs and benefits of biodiversity conservation. This necessitates a comparative assessment of the benefits of biodiversity conservation vis-á-vis the benefits foregone or realisable from alternative land use options of forests such as for utilising and sustaining agriculture, animal husbandry, tourism and recreation and other activities (Ninan, 2001). However, an assessment of the benefits of biodiversity conservation as against alternate land use options poses problems and challenges since many environmental goods and services are not traded or difficult to measure. A number of valuation techniques have been developed to value biodiversity, etc. Similarly recent policy initiatives to declare protected areas or sanctuaries to protect habitats, biodiversity, wild life, etc., have focussed attention on their social costs since most often they tend to exclude local or indigenous communities from their planning and implementation, without giving them a stake in conservation or providing sustainable livelihood options. These adverse social impacts can affect the quality of success of these policy initiatives. These initiatives also tend to ignore or underrate the importance of traditions and customs as well as of local communities and institutions in conserving natural resources. The economic case for valuing biodiversity rests on the premise that if natural resources are properly valued rational decisions are possible, especially in the case of resources like forests which have alternate uses and economic valuation will help in prioritising investment decisions. Also policy makers and planners respond to price signals and economic valuation of biodiversity will help in facilitating this. Biodiversity does have positive economic values which needs to be taken into account. The reality nevertheless is that choices and trade-offs have to be made in the context of scarce resources and the need for measures to conserve biodiversity. Powerful social and ethical grounds can also be mustered for programmes which are designed to improve the welfare of poor people in developing countries but which involve some reduction in biodiversity. Unless and until the social and economic implications are clearer, governments are likely to continue to give insufficient weight to biological degradation. Improving the economic case for biodiversity conservation is, therefore, an important goal (ODA, 1991). Ultimately how much of biodiversity to conserve *vis-à-vis* promote development is a social issue.

13.3.4 Bio-rich Areas of Karnataka

The Western Ghats

The Western Ghats, spread over six states *viz.*, Kerala, Karnataka, Tamil Nadu, Maharashtra, Goa and Gujarat is one of the 25 biodiversity hot spots listed in the world (Myers *et al.*, 2000). The Nilgiri biosphere is located in this region. The Western Ghats runs to a length of about 1600 kms more or less parallel to the west coast of India starting from the mouth of river Tapti in Dhule district of Maharashtra and ending at Kanyakumari the southern most tip of India in Tamil Nadu (Tewari, 1993). The Western Ghats cover an area of 0.16 million sq. kms with elevations of 6000 m above MSL. The population of this region was about 38.55 million as per the 1981 Population Census. The region generally receives 2000 mm to 7000 mm of rainfall and is rich in natural resources. Almost a third of the geographical area of the Western Ghats is under forests of diverse types—evergreen to semi-evergreen forests, moist to deciduous forests, etc. The region is rich in forest and hydel resources, and biodiversity. Most of the rivers in peninsular India such as the Godavari, Krishna, Cauvery, Kali Nadi and Periyar have their origin in the Western Ghats. The health of these water courses is intimately bound up with the health of the forest catchments in the Western Ghats. The water harvested from the Western Ghats provides irrigation and hydro-electric power to the eastern plains (Western Ghats Forestry Project, KFD and DFID, 1999).

The Western Ghats region, as stated earlier, is rich in biodiversity. It is a treasure house of several known and unknown flora and fauna, including several mammallian species in the endangered list such as the Lion-Tailed Macaque (*Macaca silenus*), Four-Horned Antelope (*Tetracerus quadricernis*), Fishing Cat (*Felis viverrina*), Loris (*Loris targligradus*), Nilgri Langur (*Presbytis johni*), Nilgri Tahr (*Hemitragus hylocrius*), Mouse Deer (*Tragulus memmina*), Indian Gaur (*Bos gaurus*), Brant Malabar Squirrel (*Ratufa indica*) and the Malabar Civert (*Viverricula megaspita*), etc. The forests of the Western Ghats harbour some of the best wildlife areas of the Indian subcontinent with the last remnant populations of such major animals as the tiger, panther, elephant, gaur or Indian bison, etc. Other groups like birds and amphibians, etc. are equally rich in species. The specialised climatic conditions of the Western Ghats may also explain the restricted distribution or 'endemism' of many species. The Karnataka Western Ghats accounts for over 47 per cent of the endemic species in the entire Western Ghat region (Table 13.11). Over 57 per cent of endemic mammals, over 89 per cent of endemic birds and over 53 per cent of endemic amphibians in the Western Ghat region are found in the Karnataka Western Ghats.

TABLE 13.11

Distribution of Endemic Vertebrates in the Western Ghats

Class/States	*Western Ghats*	*Karnataka*	*Karnataka as per cent to Western Ghats*
Mammals	14	8	57.1
Birds	19	17	89.5
Reptiles	97	36	37.1
Amphibian	94	50	53.2
Fishes	116	50	43.1
Total	**340**	**161**	**47.4**

Source: National Biodiversity Strategy and Action Plan (NBSAP), Ministry of Environment and Forests, Government of India, December 2002, p.40.

Commercial forestry and various other human interventions in the forests have unintended effects on the wildlife. Fragmentation of the forest impedes the migratory movements, especially of large herbivores like the elephant resulting in lower carrying capacity and increase in man-animal conflicts (KFD and DFID, 1999). A study of the Western Ghats which estimated changes in the forest cover over a 25 year period between 1973 to 1995 in the southern parts of the Western Ghats using satellite data revealed a loss of 25.6 per cent of the forest cover. While dense forest was reduced by 19.5 per cent, open forests were reduced by 32.2 per cent. The study observed a five-fold increase in forest loss between the periods from 1920-60 to 1960-90. The southern stretch of the Western Ghats extending to about 40,000 sq.kms. has experienced the most significant loss during 1973-1995 with an estimated loss of 2729 sq. kms. of forest with an annual deforestation rate of 1.16 per cent. Increase in plantation and agricultural areas due to population pressure were the major factors behind this rapid loss of the forest cover in these parts of the Western Ghats (Jha, Dutt and Bava, 2000). The above discussion shows the significance and richness of the biodiversity of the Western Ghats. Due to demographic and economic pressures, market failures and inappropriate policies, the biodiversity of the region is under various stages of degradation and, therefore, need to be conserved through appropriate policies, etc. (Ninan, 2001).

The West Coast Region

The West Coast of India has a coastal length of 3,446 km and is characterised by a various types of ecosystems and habitats (NBSAP, 2002). Further, a large number of wetlands, backwaters, estuaries and creeks, mangroves, salt marshes, lagoons which support a plethora of flora and fauna including turtles, aquatic birds and fish species dot the coastal belt. This region also supports considerable economic activities and is the location of major industrial concerns, ports and fishing harbours. The development activities along the coast pose severe threat to the ecology of the region. Among the major activities which influence the biodiversity and ecosystem health, the most important is fisheries along the coastal belt leading to over exploitation of fishery resources. Unplanned industrialisation along the coast has also ruined or affected pristine coastal habitats (NBSAP, 2002). The coastal ecosystem of Karnataka which extends to about 300 km is strewn with wetlands, beaches and mountains. The region is significant both from an economic and ecological viewpoint and biodiversity in particular. Issues related to the coastal ecosystem of Karnataka and its management are dealt with in detail in a latter section.

Wetlands in Karnataka

Wetlands are an important ecosystem and provide a wide variety of goods and services including water recycling and purification, groundwater recharge, nutrient cycling, flood control, etc. They also support a wide range of economic activities including agriculture, aquaculture, tourism and recreation, transport, etc. The wetlands like other ecosystems are degrading fast due to anthropogenic and other factors. Karnataka is well endowed with natural and man-made wetlands. Wetlands cover about 2.72 million hectares of the total geographic area of Karnataka. This includes 2.54 million hectares of inland wetlands and 0.18 million ha of coastal wetlands. As in the rest of India and elsewhere Karnataka's wetlands too are degrading fast due to demographic, economic and other pressures. These wetlands are also noteworthy for their biodiversity especially avian and fish species. Issues related to Karnataka's wetlands and their management and avian and fish biodiversity are discussed in more detail in a latter section.

13.3.5 Status of Biodiversity in Karnataka

Status and Changes in Vegetative Cover of Forests

One way of assessing the status of biodiversity in Karnataka is to analyse the status of our forests, particularly the extent of forest cover and changes over time as well as the quality of our forests. Forest Survey of India based on satellite imagery data publishes biannually the *State of India's Forests*. These provide information regarding the forest cover across the states and up to district level and also in terms of forest types *viz.*, dense forests (those forests with crown density of over 40 per cent), open forests (forests with crown density of 10 to less than 40 per cent), scrubs (those with crown density of less than 10 per cent) and mangroves. Information regarding the forest cover and forest types and changes between 1995 and 2001 for India, Karnataka and selected districts in Karnataka are presented in Table 13.12. Interestingly while for India as a whole the forest cover has increased between 1995 and 2001, for Karnataka the forest cover has reduced for the same period. As a result Karnataka's share in total forest area of the country declined in the five year period ending 2001 from 5.8 per cent to 5.5 per cent. More significant is that while for India as a whole the dense forest cover has increased (from 55.1 per cent to 57.7 per cent) between 1995 to 2001, Karnataka has reported a decline in the dense forest cover (from 70.1

TABLE 13.12

Changes in Forest Cover and Forest Types between 1995 and 2001: India, Karnataka and Selected Districts

Country/State or District	*Forest Assessment Year*	*Total Forest Area (including Scrub Area under) (in Sq. Kms)*	*Forest Types*			
			Dense	*Open*	*Scrub*	*Mangrove*
			(Per Cent Distribution)			
India	1995	699407	55.1	35.6	8.7	0.6
	2001	722856	57.7	35.8	6.5	—
Karnataka	1995	37011	70.1	18.5	11.4	0.0
	2001	40236	65.0	26.9	8.1	—
Uttara Kannada	1995	7865	94.0	5.4	0.6	Negligible
	2001	7808	83.3	16.7	0.01	—
Shimoga	1995	5092	78.8	17.9	3.3	—
	2001	4509	69.1	30.1	0.8	—
Dakshina Kannada	1995	3647	75.9	24.0	0.1	—
	2001	4049	73.3	26.6	0.1	—
Kodagu	1995	3392	96.7	1.9	1.5	—
	2001	3010	86.6	13.3	0.1	—
Chickmagalur	1995	3469	85.1	10.9	4.0	—
	2001	3605	85.1	13.5	1.4	—

Note: Dense Forests—Those with crown canopy cover of 40 per cent and above; Open Forests—those with crown canopy cover of above 10 per cent to below 40 per cent; and Scrubs with crown canopy cover of below 10 per cent

Source: The State of Forest Report 1995, Forest Survey of India, Ministry of Environment and Forests, Dehradun; *www.indiastat.com*.

per cent to 65 per cent) and a substantial increase in the area under open forests (from 18.5 per cent to 26.9 per cent). Not only has the forest cover declined in districts such as Uttar Kannada, Shimoga and Kodagu but also the dense forest cover in these districts has reduced substantially over the period 1995 to 2001. This has serious implications for the biodiversity in the region and sheds light on the degradation of biological resources in the state.

Status and Changes Over Time of Endangered Species

Another indicator of the status of biodiversity is to examine the status and changes over time of endangered or threatened wildlife species. State forest departments in India collect wildlife census estimates (wildlife population estimates to be more precise) for selected wildlife species in India across states every four or five years. Such wildlife populations estimates are available for some endangered wildlife species such as tigers, elephants, and leopards. Although state forest departments call these as wildlife census they are in fact only estimates of wildlife population since it is impossible to enumerate or count all animals as done in population census. Wildlife population estimates are usually estimated on the basis of pug marks, block count and waterhole count methods, line transect methods, etc. In very sophisticated cases camera trappings are also done. These estimates will give a rough idea of the status of biodiversity especially of selected wildlife species and changes in their numbers over time. Table 13.13 presents the wildlife population estimates for tigers, elephants, and leopards for India and Karnataka between 1972 and 2001-02 for selected years. As evident, in the case of tigers there is an improvement in their numbers in Karnataka during the period from 102 to 401 tigers whereas for all India although the tiger population has increased from about 1827 in 1972 to 4334 in 1989, thereafter their numbers have fluctuated and declined to 3642 in 2001-02. In the case of elephants and leopards the data show that overall there is an improvement in their numbers both at all-India level and also in Karnataka though the increase in elephant and leopard population is slower in recent years. Though the data suggest that the population of these endangered species has improved partly due to conservation efforts, the threats faced by these wild animals is far from removed as evident from continued poaching of these animals, habitat loss, flourishing trade in wildlife products, etc. Moreover, wildlife experts such as Bittu Sahgal opines that the actual number of tigers in India is just half of that indicated by the wildlife census.

TABLE 13.13

Wildlife Population Estimates of Tiger, Elephant and Leopard in India and Karnataka and Changes Over Time: 1972 to 2001-02

Year	*Tiger*		*Elephant*		*Leopard*	
	Karnataka	*India*	*Karnataka*	*India*	*Karnataka*	*India*
1972	102	1827	-	-	-	-
1977	-	-	1187	-	-	-
1979	156	3015	1195	-	-	-
1984	202	4005	-	-	238	4747
1989	257	4334	4420	-	283	6767
1993	305	3750	5500	25541	455	6828
1997	350	3836	6088	29010	620	7787
2001-02	401	3642*	6088	28274	-	-

Notr: * indicates preliminary estimate.
Source: www.indiastat.com.

13.3.6 Strategies for Biodiversity Conservation

Both *ex situ* (eg. establishment of germ plasm banks, zoos, biodiversity parks, etc.) and *in situ* measures (e.g. establishment of national parks and sanctuaries, etc.) have been adopted to conserve biodiversity. Area based and species based conservation programmes have been implemented to promote biodiversity conservation. The area based programmes primarily seek to improve the forest cover and ecology of degraded forest lands which will also impact on biodiversity. The species based conservation programmes seek to improve the numbers and habitats of selected endangered species such as tiger and Asiatic elephant. These are considered as keystone or umbrella species and given the large habitat requirements of tigers and elephants, when you protect the tiger or elephant you protect the entire ecosystem. In the following section, some important area based and species based conservation programmes implemented in Karnataka are discussed.

Area-based Programmes

a) The Western Ghats Forestry Project 1992-2000

The Western Ghats Forestry Project funded by the Department of International Development (DFID), United Kingdom (UK) government was implemented by the Karnataka Forest Department (KFD) to consolidate and improve the existing forests, raise fuelwood, and small timber resources on the degraded hillocks and to strengthen institutional capabilities through research and training, etc. The primary objectives of the project were: i) to maintain the ecological balance and environmental stability; ii) to ensure the sustainability of living standards of those whose livelihoods derive in whole or in part from the forest; and iii) to ensure sustainable yield of all categories of produce proper to the natural forest. The strategy to achieve these objectives consisted of the following: a) assist institutional development in KFD, b) ensure that poor people, women, tribals and other disadvantaged groups who are substantially dependent on the forests are not worse-off and are preferably better-off; c) minimise further loss of forest cover and resources and their services; and d) achieve increasing understanding of the Western Ghats ecosystem. The target was to involve the communities living close to the forests to have a stake in the conservation and sustainable management of forests by making them partners in management and as well as in planning. The Joint Forest Planning and Management (JFPM) were to be attempted through the institution of village forest committees. The total estimated outlay of the project was Rs. 69.05 crores (at 1990-91 prices) or 18.079 million pound sterling for local costs. The money was an outright grant by UK to the Government of India. It was transferred to the Karnataka government as a 30 per cent grant and 70 per cent loan repayable over 15 years at 9.8 per cent interest. A further 5.22 million pound sterling was also earmarked to be spent directly by the donor on training consultancy and equipment, which were not part of the loan cum grant from government of India to government of Karnataka. The project started from October 1992 and ended in March 2000. The total local cost expenditure came to around Rs. 111.54 crores.

The Western Ghats Forest Project (WGFP) focused on different core issues. The major part of the project expenditure was spent on raising new plantations and their maintenance. The total plantation area rose to around 56598 hectares with majority of the plantation going to JFPM areas as the project progressed. The total expenditure on planting was estimated to be Rs. 69.57 crores or around 62.4 per cent of the estimated total expenditure of Rs. 111.54 crores. The average cost worked out to be around Rs. 12, 292 per hectare. The economic and social benefits of acacia plantations raised under the project were also looked into and these revealed that such plantations had made significant contribution to the rural livelihoods and environmental protection among the local community in the coastal areas. The planning and management systems mainly included the micro plans and participatory rural appraisal, management information systems, and geographic information systems. By March 1999 there were around 479 village forest committees (VFC) which were formally registered, 308 in Kanara and 171 in Shimoga circle. Between 1993 and 2000, 539 VFCs with a membership of 49761 persons was formed. There were a significant number of VFCs managed only by women. A social impact assessment by Outreach, an NGO in 1998 showed that there was a genuine effort on the part of the KFD to enter into participatory mode with the people and relations had improved in all villages studied. Although NGOs were committed to the participation of local communities its link with the KFD was weak. To make the VFC's sustainable, self-help groups and users groups were introduced.

Non-timber forest products (NTFPs) play a significant role in rural livelihoods and the Western Ghats project experience threw up many interesting findings. A study in 1997 revealed that around 45 per cent of the household income came from NTFP collection with clearly discernible gender preferences for different products. The participatory management regime for the NTFP was developed in the Kanara Circle through different case studies and experiments. A NTFP society was formed and the collectors would give the materials to this society. The society would in turn sell the products at the highest price. However, the efficiency of these endeavours are yet to be fully studied.

There was also quite a bit of emphasis on training and human resource development and research. The core areas of research were tree improvement, biodiversity and socio-economic research. The key findings of the Forest Research Institute's socio-economic studies found that women preferred different types of NTFPs and that out of 65 species planted under the Western Ghats project the survival rates of 30 species was very low (between 0 to 10 per cent). The Western Ghats Forestry Project (WGFP) was mainly intended to improve the conservation status of the forests but went beyond these objectives and contributed to development of institutional capabilities, improving planning and management system and institutionalising the participatory approach.

Table 13.14 presents an overview of the WGFP for the period October 1992 to March 2000. The final project document (FPDP) provisions are given in constant 1990-91 prices.

b) Forestry and Environment Project for the Eastern Plains of Karnataka

The Forestry and Environment Project for the

TABLE 13.14

Overview of the Western Ghats Forestry Projects for the Period October 1992 to March 2000

Component	*Provision as per FPD*		*Cumulative Totals October 1992 to March 2000*		
	Physical	*Rs. Lakhs*	*Physical*	*Rs. Lakhs*	*Percentage of Total*
1) Afforestation (ha)	-	-	-	-	-
Kanara Circle	42000	-	49943	-	-
Shimoga Circle	19200		6654.5		
Total	61200	3856.6	56597.5	6957.425	62.38
2) Buildings Completed	212	373.4	465	800.445	7.18
3) Vehicles (No)	114	181.4	75	218.384	1.96
4) Training Nos. Trained	9556	111.2	29064	169.234	1.52
5) Equipment (Lump Sum)	-	403.4	-	197.234	1.77
6) Staff (Lump Sum)	-	774.5	-	954.418	8.56
7) Operating Costs	-	989.5	-	1692.555	15.18
8) Repairs and Maintenance (Lump Sum)	-	174.6	-	163.085	1.46
Grand Total		**6864.6**		**11153.480**	**100.00**

Source: Western Ghats Forestry Project, *Project Experience and Achievements 1992-2000*, Karnataka Forest Department and DFID, Bangalore, December 1999.

eastern plains of Karnataka funded by the Japanese Overseas Economic Cooperation Fund envisages to treat 5.45 lakhs hectare area with tree planting and soil and water conservation works in 141 *talukas* spread across 23 districts of Karnataka. Out of the 5.45 lakhs hectare of land for treatment, 2 lakhs hectare is in reserved forests and in non-forest lands which is envisaged to be treated with tree planting and soil and conservation works through 12 specific technical models of treatment. The remaining is on private farm lands envisaged to be treated through the sale/distribution of 23700 crores seedlings of a wide variety of species required by the farmers and by extending them advisory services in tree cropping and tree husbandry. The salient features of the project are as follows:

- Afforestation, soil and water conservation in areas of Eastern plains.
- Conservation and maintenance of ecologically sensitive areas of Eastern plains.
- Supply of fuel, fodder, green manure, small timber, minor forest produce, fruits, and medicinal plants from the community forestry and farm forestry plantations.
- Distribution of seedlings of above species for farm forestry.
- Carrying out publicity and extension programmes.
- Conservation and development of lakes and tanks.
- Employment generation in wasteland and degraded forests.
- Implementation of JFPM.
- Construction of residential and non-residential buildings and civil structures for staff and office purpose.

The project is implemented at a cost of Rs. 722.489 crores, out of which Rs. 568.869 crores is reimbursable by the JBIC and the balance of Rs. 121.895 crores is to be borne by the state government. The cumulative financial achievement since inception of the project upto the end of March 2004 is Rs. 620.629 crores.

Appendix A-13.9 gives the details of the financial progress of the Eastern Plains Project.

India Eco-Development Project

The India Eco-Development Project funded by the World Bank was implemented as part of the efforts of the government of India to address urgent global biodiversity needs. The project aimed to conserve biodiversity in seven critical protected areas (PAs) of India, which also included the Rajiv Gandhi National Park at Nagarahole in Karnataka. The project was for a period of 5 years with a total outlay of Rs. 39 crores. It started in the year 1997-98 and was a centrally sponsored scheme.

The main objectives of the India Eco-Development Project were:

- To improve capacity of PA management to conserve biodiversity and increase opportunities for local participation in PA management activities and decisions.
- To reduce negative impacts of local people on biodiversity, reduce negative impacts of PA's on local people, and increase collaboration of local people in conservation efforts.
- To develop more effective and extensive support for eco-development.
- To ensure effective management of the project.
- To prepare future biodiversity projects.

The following Table 13.15 gives the financial target and achievements of the project in Karnataka over the five year period from 1998-99 to 2002-03.

TABLE 13.15

Targets and Achievements of the India Eco-Development Project in Karnataka from 1998-99 to 2002-03

(Rs. in lakhs)

Year	*Target*	*Achievement*
1998-99	1170	160.70
1999-00	1000	221.67
2000-01	1100	299.05
2001-02	1100	475.00
2002-03	570	352.90
Total	**4940**	**1509.32**

Source: Annual Reports of the Karnataka Forest Department, Government of Karnataka.

Other Central and State Sponsored Schemes of Karnataka Forest Department

There are several other centrally and state sponsored schemes implemented by the Karnataka Forest Department which have implication for forest development and biodiversity conservation. These are discussed below in brief.

a) Indo-Norwegian Project for Lake Development in Bangalore City

Indo-Norwegian Project for Lake Development in Bangalore city started a project for three years for three lakes *viz.*, Madivala, Hebbal and Agaram lakes. It had an assistance of about Rs. 4 crores. It started in the year 1997-98. The important objectives of the project are:

- To restore and develop lakes for posterity, which helps in the restoration of depleting groundwater table.
- To have treatment of sewage to generate alternative sources of raw water by achieving a desirable chemical physical and biological standard for the lake water, to also prevent contamination of underground aquifers from wastewater.
- To improve and recreate a habitat for water birds and other animals and wild plants.
- To treat waste water and impact through forestry and vegetation approaches and for a better utilisation of space for greening the area.
- Improve urban sanitation and health conditions especially for the weaker section of society living nearby.
- Better utilisation of the lakes for the purpose of education and research.

b) Integrated Ecological and Environmental Development for Mysore Urban Region (Norwegian Assistance)

This project was also for a period of three years and it started in the year 1997-98. The main objective of the project was to maintain the ecological and environmental stability of the Chamundi Hills and surrounding urban and rural areas and to promote tourism by enhancing the aesthetic beauty of the hills. The project went on until 2001-02.

The following Table 13.16 gives the details of the total physical target and achievements of both the above mentioned projects for four years from 1997-98 to 2000-2001.

TABLE 13.16

Targets and Achievement of Bangalore Tanks Project and Integrated Ecological and Environment Development Project

(Rs. in Lakhs)

Project	*Total Physical Target from 1997-98 to 2000-01*	*Financial Achievement from 1997-98 to 2000-01*
Integrated Development of Bangalore Tanks Project	400	417.79
Integrated Ecological and Environmental Development of Mysore Urban Region	380	304.46

Source: Annual Reports of Karnataka Forest Department, Government of Karnataka.

c) Area Oriented Fuel and Fodder Scheme

This scheme is being implemented in the state with the Central assistance on 50:50 basis since 1990-91.

The scheme is being implemented on watershed basis in fuelwood deficit districts. Fuel and fodder species are raised to meet the requirements of the people. Fuel fodder plantations are raised in forest areas in forest deficit districts like Bangalore, Dharwad, Gulbarga, Kolar, Chitradurga, Belgaum, Hassan, Mysore and Bijapur. Only planting works are undertaken in Bellary and Mandya districts. The following Table 13.17 gives the physical targets and financial outlays and the achievements from 1997-98 to 2002-03.

TABLE 13.17

Targets and Achievements of the Fuel and Fodder Scheme

Year	*Physical Target (in Hectares)*		*Financial Outlay (Lakhs)*	*Financial Achievement (Lakhs)*
	Maintenance	*Planting*		
1997-98	9469	5286	298	196.75
1998-99	5421	855	460	NA
1999-00	6304	2953	356	151.38
2000-01	9199	1388	427	171.62
2001-02	5139	2701	387.10	145.82
2002-03	7024	1850	81.42	30

Source: Annual Reports of Karnataka Forest Department.

Other Schemes

CSS of Conservation and Development of Non-Timber Forest Produce including Medicinal Plants

This scheme with 100 per cent Central assitance was being implemented in the state. Under the scheme plantations of medicinal value are being raised.

Ecotourism

This scheme is to facilitate visitors to the forests enough basic amenities with an intention of encouraging non-consumptive use of forest and wildlife. These schemes are meant to provide lot of eco consciousness for the people who visit the forests and get support for successful and sustainable forest conservation. This was implemented in 1993-94.

Van Vigyan Kendra

This scheme under state sector was started in 1996-1997. Initially it was established in 10 districts and the other districts of the state would be covered subsequently under the scheme. Farmers will be imparted training in raising nursery and plantations in the *kendras*. They will be exposed to recent developments and other advances in the field of forestry and development.

Development of Degraded Forests

Degraded forests are brought under Forest cover through afforestation. Development of Degraded forests Scheme is being implemented since 1992-93. Keeping in view the site quality and the local demands of the public, species of timber fuel and fodder are planted.

Greening of Urban Areas

This scheme is undertaken in the cities and towns of the state to give fillip to tree planting and also meet the aspirations of the people for tree planting with the objective of improving and maintaining better environment through creation of avenue plantations, tree parks and woodlots.

Social Forestry Project

This scheme continues as a state scheme to maintain the permanent assets and personnel created under the World Bank and ODA aided social forestry projects, which ended on March 31, 1992. Under this scheme provision has been made to incur the salary expenditure of 2585 staff and for maintenance of vehicles and office expenses.

Soil Conservation and Afforestation

This scheme envisages measures to prevent soil erosion in the degraded and eroded areas through afforestation activities and soil conservation activities. This scheme also contributes towards the production of fuelwood, fodder, green manure, small timber and agave fibres, etc.

Integrated Afforestation and Eco-development Project

This is a 100 per cent central assisted scheme being implemented in Mandya district. The salient features of this scheme are integrated development of wastelands, soil conservation in degraded forest and maintaining the environment ecological balance.

Soil Conservation in the River Valley Project

This scheme is being implemented in the catchment areas of Tunghabhadra river in Dharwad and Raichur districts, Nizamsagar and Nagarjunsagar in Gulbarga district by taking up afforestation work.

Minor Forest Produce

This is a scheme implemented in Uttara Kannada distict during 1997-98. The scheme tries to raise minor forest produce.

Integrated Development of Western Ghats

The scheme is being implemented in Belgaum, Chickmagalur, Dakshina Kannada, Dharwad, Hassan, Kodagu, Mysore and Uttara Kannada districts of the state which are covered by Western Ghats forest belt. The main objectives of the scheme are fulfilment of minimum needs of the rural folk by providing small timber, fuel, food, fodder, grass development of forests and maintenance of the ecological balance.

Roadside Plantations Scheme

This scheme is to do avenue planting with an objective of providing shade to travellers and usufructs to the local community. The scheme improves the aesthetic sense and utilisation of roadside wasteland strips.

Raising of Seedlings for Public Distribution

This scheme is to encourage planting in private lands with seedlings of the choice of the local people being raised and distributed to them. The scheme is being implemented since 1993-94 and will help in increasing area under tree cover and save the forests indirectly and meet their demand directly.

Tribal Sub-plan (State)

This is a scheme for the development of tribals. Social security plantations are raised on the lands of beneficiaries. This programme has helped in development and improvement of the conditions of the tribal people.

A summary of the financial outlays and achievement under various schemes from 1997-98 to 2002-03 is presented in Appendix A-13.10.

Species-based Conservation Programmes

Project Tiger

Project Tiger has been under implementation since 1973 as a Centrally sponsored scheme of the government of India. The main objective of Project Tiger is to ensure a viable population of tigers in India for scientific, economic, aesthetic, cultural and ecological values and to preserve for all time areas of biological importance as a natural heritage for the benefit, education and enjoyment of the people. The scheme envisages wildlife management, protection measures and site specific eco-development to reduce the dependency of local communities on tiger reserve resources. Initially, the Project started with 9 tiger reserves covering an area of 16,339 sq.km., with a population of 268 tigers. At present there are 27 tiger reserves covering an area of 37,761 sq.km. with a population of 1498 tigers. This amounts to almost 1.14 per cent of the total geographical area of the country. The selection of reserves was guided by the need to give representation to different ecotypes of wilderness areas across the biogeographic range of tiger distribution in the country. Project Tiger is undisputedly a custodian of major gene pool. It is also a repository of some of the most valuable ecosystem and habitats for wildlife. Project Tiger has put the tiger on course of recovery from the brink of extinction, and has resurrected the floral and faunal genetic diversity in some of our unique and endangered wilderness ecosystem. The population of tigers in the country has increased significantly to about 4000 from less than 2000 at the time of launch of the project.

The Bandipur Tiger Reserve in Karnataka is one of the tiger reserves set up during 1973 under the Project Tiger. Bhadra Wildlife Sanctuary was also declared as a tiger reserve under the scheme during 1998. In 2000 the government of India approved the inclusion of Rajiv Gandhi National Park, Nagarahole in addition to Bandipur and Bhadra Tiger Reserve in Karnataka under the centrally sponsored Project Tiger. The government of India gave 100 per cent financial assistance in respect of non-recurring expenditure and 50 per cent of financial assistance in respect of recurring expenditure.

Table 13.18 gives the target and achievements of the Project Tiger (for Bandipur and Bhadra Tiger Reserves) over the 11 years from 1992-93 to 2002-03.

Karnataka Tiger Conservation Project

Karnataka Tiger Conservation Project (KTCP) supported by the Save the Tiger Fund and several donors of the Wildlife Conservation Society, New York in association with the state government and local conservation partners has been implemented in Nagarhole, Bhadra, Bandipur, and Kudremukh National Parks/Sanctuaries in Karnataka from January 1998 to June 2001. The KTCP was implemented in four sites covering an area of 2600 sq. km in the above national parks and sanctuaries. The total investment in the project was Rs. 17 million (USD 375000). Of this Rs. 9.05 million (USD 210000) was provided by the project in the form of equipment and other support services directly to the Karnataka Forest Department; the remaining amount was invested in research, training conservation, etc. The densities of tiger recorded in three sites ranged from 3.4 tigers/100 sq.

TABLE 13.18

Target and Achievements of the Project Tiger in Karnataka for the Period from 1992-93 to 2002-03

(Rs. in Lakhs)

Year	*Target*	*Achievement*
1992-1993	53.15	49.87
1993-1994	67.00	43.56
1994-1995	55.00	72.75
1995-1996	57.00	38.83
1996-1997	60.00	40.21
1997-1998	72.00	23.33
1998-1999	80.00	36.26
1999-2000	150.00	64.33
2000-2001	200.00	160.41
2001-2002	285.00	124.44
2002-2003	260.00	116.71
Total	**1339.15**	**770.70**

Source: Annual Reports of the Karnataka Forest Department.

km in Bhadra to 12 tigers/100 sq. km in Bandipur to 11.5 to 15.2 tigers/100 sq km in Nagarhole. The project enhanced the enforcement capacity of the Karnataka Forest Department through purchase of patrol jeeps, wireless equipment, etc. A noteworthy feature is the voluntary resettlement of tribal and local communities from within the national parks/ sanctuaries to resettled areas outside the park limits. As a result, over 200 families from Nagarhole and 435 families from Bhadra accepted the rehabilitation package offered by the government and relocated to areas outside the park/sanctuary limits (Karnataka Tiger Conservation Project, Final Report, 1998-2001, Wildlife First, Wildlife Conservation Society, New York and Centre for Wildlife Studies, Bangalore).

Project Elephant

Project Elephant was launched in February, 1992 to assist states having free ranging populations of wild elephants to ensure long-term survival of identified viable populations of elephants in their natural habitats. The project is being implemented in 12 states including Karnataka. States are being given financial as well as technical assistance in achieving the objectives of the Project. Help is also provided to other states with small populations of elephants for the purpose of census, training of field staff and mitigation of human-elephant conflict. The project was predicated on the need to focus conservation action on the Asian Elephant and its habitat, which currently face a number of threats. The main threats include:

a) Reduction and fragmentation of habitat and consequent isolation of populations into small and genetically unviable units.

b) Conflicts between wild elephants and human populations, leading to loss of human life and property and retaliatory killing of wild elephants.

c) Poaching of elephants for ivory and, in some parts of the country for meat.

d) Elephant mortality due to other causes, such as from transmission lines, rail lines, highways, etc., passing through the elephant habitats and other natural causes such as floods.

e) Inadequate finance, infrastructure and human resources for proper implementation of management priorities at the field level.

Achievements

- An amount of Rs. 7.66 crores (Rs. 2.28 crores for Northeastern states) was released (till 31st December, 2002) to the elephant range states for the purpose of habitat management, mitigation of man-elephant conflict, payment of *ex-gratia* relief for loss of life, human and crop caused by wild elephants, strengthening of anti-poaching measures, capacity building of the field staff, registration of domesticated elephants using microchips, etc.

- Fourteen elephant reserves have been set up (during the year) (till December, 2002) which include Singhbhum (Jharkhand); Garo Hills (Meghalaya); Mayurbhanj, Mahanadi and Sambalpur (Orissa); Eastern Dooars and Mayurjharna (West Bengal); Wayanad, Nilambur, Anamudy and Periyar (Kerala); Kameng (Arunachal Pradesh); Mysore (Karnataka) and Shiwalik (Uttaranchal).

- Training programmes for officers and field staff of elephant reserves was organised at Bandipur (Karnataka), Rajabhatkhawa (West Bengal), Kaziranga (Assam) and Dehradun (Uttaranchal).

- Arrangements for refresher courses for elephant veterinarians were made with the help of the Assam Agricultural University (Guwahati) and Kerala Agricultural University (Trichur).

- Elephant census was carried out in the states of Orissa, Jharkhand, Uttaranchal, Karnataka, Kerala, Tamil Nadu and Andhra Pradesh.

During the year 2003-04 an amount of approximately Rs. 3.05 crores was allocated to the elephant range states to enable them to provide financial assistance for habitat management of man-elephant conflicts, payment of *ex gratia* relief for loss of life, strengthening of anti-poaching measures, capture and translocation of problem elephants, etc. Permission to capture 33 problem elephants in West Bengal and Assam was given in order to reduce man-elephant conflicts. An amount of Rs. 142.30 lakhs was released to the elephant range states to strengthen their anti-poaching and anti-depredation activities.

Project Elephant in Karnataka is basically concentrated on the Karnataka portion of the Nilgiris and Eastern Ghats elephant reserve. This part of the elephant reserve falls in the districts of Mysore, Kodagu, Mandya, Bangalore, Chickmagalur, and Shimoga forming two blocks. Most of the reserve area comes under the Western Ghats and its foothills contiguous to the Nilgiris including isolated hill ranges. This portion of the reserve has 6670 sq. kms of forest area.

Table 13.19 gives the details of the targets and achievements of Project Elephant in Karnataka over the period 1992-93 to 2002-03. Financial achievements are well below the target, although there has been improvement in performance in recent years. Wildlife census data presented earlier suggest an improvement in elephant population in the state, although poaching of elephants continue.

TABLE 13.19

Details of the Financial Targets and Achievements of the Project Elephant in Karnataka

(Rs. in Lakhs)

Year	*Target*	*Achievement*
1992-93	40.66	19.87
1993-94	50.00	15.82
1994-95	75.00	0.00
1995-96	560.00	0.00
1996-97	452.00	0.00
1997-98	100.00	0.00
1998-99	135.00	22.77
1999-00	100.00	34.98
2000-01	100.00	25.00
2001-02	100.00	62.98
2002-03	100.00	55.53
Total	**1762.66**	**236.95**

Source: Annual Reports of the Karnataka Forest Department.

Medicinal Plants

Recognising the importance of conserving medicinal plants, the government of Karnataka has initiated a number of measures to encourage cultivation of medicinal plants, including on private farm lands.

The Karnataka State Forest Medicinal Plants Authority was set up in 2002 to focus on the development of medicinal plants in Karnataka. The office is set up near Bannerghatta. The major objective of this authority is to provide guidelines and arrange financial assistance to the local community to grow medicinal plants. The most suitable medicinal plants according to the soil nature and weather condition are advised to the local community. The authority plans to improve growth of the medicinal plants all over Karnataka in the coming years.

People's Biodiversity Registers

The Biological Diversity Act, 2002 marks a milestone in the country in the efforts to conserve our biological resources. One of the important provisions of the Act is for documenting and safeguarding local knowledge through the establishment of people's biodiversity registers (PBRs).

People's biodiversity registers will be local level documentation of biodiversity and associated knowledge along with related management issues. It is generated through a broad-based process designed and led by local community and also involving technical and administrative inputs wherever appropriate. It's mostly in all Indian languages and also in English and databases are updated continually. They are organised so as to generate a variety of products desired by the people including reports on response to specific queries or videotapes. The computerised components of PBRs may be based in computers at all *panchayats* and municipalities with servers located at district level. The PBRs help the local community arrive at management decisions on their own and help local bodies propose development schemes. It helps people share their specific knowledge of uses and management of biodiversity resources, like for instance the use of catch crops in pest management, access information on prices and on marketing opportunities for their biodiversity resources, and also help in continuation of traditional practices of conservation and sustainable use of biodiversity by facilitating their recognition and incorporation in the biodiversity management plans. It also help preserve the biodiversity related knowledge of the people for the posterity through its coding and recording. It also has a role in solving disputes which pertain to rights of local communities over natural resources *vis-a-vis* neighbours, nomadic communities and government. PBRs are organised so as to generate a variety of products desired by the people.

The PBR component of the overall BIS will be ultimately built out of data collected by the local people who are the owners of the data. The data thus collected will be stored as close to the study area as possible with complete control by and full access to the owners and restricted access to the outside users. The use of network informatic system and the web are suggested to be used for the purpose. A computerised PBR database with uniform structure all over the country should be designed so that all the issues of corroboration data exchange, scientific scrutiny and analysis could be addressed. The PBR will essentially be in the local language of the people as its a people's document. This implies the use of 15 official languages of the states and 10 scripts, and more realistically many more languages such as Gondi, Santhali, Kuki Kinauri and so on. Moreover the data from any one locality should be accessible to a user in another locality with a different language and script. This is done by giving numeric ID's to data, which is common to all locations. Location specific data e.g. local name of the species when accessed at different location will be transmitted in the local script.

State Biodiversity Board

Another important provision of the Biological Diversity Act, 2002 is the setting up of National and State Biodiversity Boards. The Karnataka Biodiversity Board started functioning from August 1, 2003 as per provisions of the Biological Diversity Act 2002. The prime objective of the Board is to foster the institutional setup for documentation, sustainable use and development of the rich biodiversity for the state. The Karnataka Biodiversity Board has initiated several measures to conserve and protect the rich biodiversity of the state. The functions of the board are as follows:

- Advising the state government on matters concerning conservation, sustainable use, fair and equitable sharing of benefits arising out of the use of biological resources and knowledge.
- Regulation and rating of approvals for commercial utilisation of biological resources in consultation with biodiversity management committees.
- Coordination and technical assistance to biodiversity management committees.
- Commissioning and sponsoring of studies, investigations and research related to biological resources.
- Identification and promotion of heritage sites of biodiversity importance.
- Devising methods for validation and certification of the information collected through bio surveys.

In order to promote participatory and community based biodiversity conservation the Karnataka Biodiversity Board has initiated measures to set up biodiversity management committees by every local body within its area of jurisdiction. So far, 275 biodiversity management committees have been constituted covering 8 priority districts. These committees have been constituted for the purpose of promoting conservation, sustainable use and documentation of biological diversity including preservation of habitats, conservation and land races, folk varieties and cultivates and domesticated stocks and breeds of animals and micro-organisms and chronicling of knowledge relating to biological diversity.

13.3.7 People's Struggles and Biodiversity Conservation

Movements by environmentalists and the civil society for protecting the environment and biodiversity have been an important factor in arresting if not reversing biodiversity loss in Karnataka, as in other state. The biorich regions also happen to be those areas with best development potential and hence balancing the needs of development while conserving biodiversity is a major challenge for planners and policy makers. Karnataka has witnessed several struggles against diversion of forest areas for non-forest uses, especially location of hydro-electric and industrial project, mining, as well as policy requiring tribals to relocate out of protect areas. The Appiko movement pioneered by Pandurang Hegde (similar to Chipko movement of Sundarlal Bahuguna) was one of the earliest movements in Karnataka that sought to protect the environment and pristine forests of Uttara Kannada. While a detailed account of various such movements and struggles in Karnataka is not made due to constraints of space, mention may be made of the movement to protect the Kudremukh National Park, which has been in the news in the recent past.

The first movement is against the iron ore mining that is on for the past 33 years in the Kudremukh—already 3 years beyond its original tenure of 30 years—and efforts are made to extend for another 20 years at the behest of TNC's—in this case the Japanese giant

Nippon company. The other is against the establishment of the Kudremukh National Park for which the government has already issued the third and final notification required as per law. This programme uproots about 15 thousand Adivasis—the Goudlu and the Malekudias, two sister tribes inhabiting these jungles from time immemorial—and about 10 thousand non-Adivasi peasantry living here since centuries. Indirectly it also affects the livelihood of another 10 to 15 thousand rural population living on the periphery of the national park. This programme is undertaken in the name of preserving the ecology and environment of the thickly wooded stretch of 603 sq.km. comprising 5 erstwhile state forests in Sringeri, Koppa and Mudigere *talukas* of Chikmagalur district and Belthangady and Karkala *talukas* of Dakshina Kannada and Udupi districts respectively. Mining has destroyed vast tracts of shoal forests and meadows, which are the chief source of the rivers and streams originating in these hills. Over 2,000 hectares of forest area has been denuded in the past 33 years. And in the name of afforestation to compensate for the forests destroyed due to mining, the KIOCL has bulldozed extensive grasslands over the hill slopes and planted acacia and eucalyptus, which in turn only profit the company as well as the polyfibre industry, while harming the natural forests and ecosystem. In June 2000, the huge pipes carrying the ore concentrate from the hilltop to Mangalore burst spilling lakhs of tonnes of the ore slurry into the evergreen forests and the seasonal streams. In fact the pipes had been designed to last only for 30 years—i.e. the original lease of the company—five such breakages have already occurred in the past 3 years, spilling over 4,000 tonnes of slurry every time, but they have gone unreported. This time the slurry flowed into 'Yennehole' rivulet causing it to rise in 4 to 5 feet of flood full of iron ore slurry. This flood, apart from killing all the marine life in the rivulet, flowed into the farms and fields on its banks. This caused heavy loss to the standing crops and almost irreparable damage to the fields. The sufferers were mainly poor farmers, majority of whom are *adivasis*. The government has not properly assessed the loss to the farmers and have them adequately compensated by the company. The company has also not cared to compensate the poor farmers. The opposition to mining here has a history of over 15 years. As environmental awareness gradually spread in the country during the seventies and the eighties the concerned people started having a fresh look at some of the 'prestigious' projects of the country. And Kudremukh was no exception. First, some journalists, and then activists of the Parisara Jagruthi Vedike (Forum for Environmental Awareness), an independent environmental group at that time, probed into the 'protected' and 'prohibited' areas of the project and brought photographs of the devastating assault on the very sensitive region. The myth of development began to melt. The company had shown utmost disregard for all Environment Protection Laws. River Bhadra was polluted, thick forest areas were denuded, high ranges were brought down or badly bruised there was all-round degradation and destruction of the ecosystem. But at that time the reaction was quite limited and the demand was only for adhering to all standards and guidelines of mining and environmental protection, and for taking utmost care as regards the sensitive ecology of the region. But the government and company went ahead despite all the opposition. The environmentalists kept up the pressure and the outcome was some cosmetic 'redressal' of the damage, the exercise to 'make up for the lost forests' and all the company's attempts to browbeat the critics and 'win' environmental laurels! People living around both these areas and downstream Tunga and Bhadra sensed the intentions of the government and started protesting. They opposed the extension of mining activity and wanted the mining to stop immediately after the expiry of the original lease of KIOCL; they in fact would rather have it closed forthwith. Karnataka Vimochana Ranga (KVR) took up the struggle against extension of mining to Tungamoola (source of Tunga i.e. Gangadikallu) while the Bhadramoola (Nellibeedu) struggle was led by Karnataka Rajya Rytha Sangha (KRRS). The Okkootta organised a series of protest marches, demonstrations, mass awareness campaigns, *gherao* of 'peoples representatives' prevailing upon them to sign bond papers stating that they opposed extension of mining to *Tungamoola*, etc. All this culminated in a huge rally of the people of Tunga riverbanks in Shimoga City in 1994. None other than Sunderlal Bahuguna, the well-known environmentalist addressed this rally. At the other end the people of Bhadra also kept up the pressure on the government and the two streams began supporting each other's struggles. The then central government, at the behest of Nippon company mounted pressure on the Karnataka government to accede to the extension of mining to Nellibeedu and Gangadikallu for a period of 20 years and issue licence to that effect. The company silenced the opposition of the Karnataka Forest Department for the extension proposal by offering

Rs. 1.5 crores per year to it for afforestation programmes (the earlier offer of one crore rupees had failed to satisfy the 'environmental concern' of the KFD!). The two streams of Tungamoola and Bhadramoola struggles joined together with several other organisations and individuals and an umbrella organisation 'Save Tunga-Bhadra Struggle Forum' (*Tunga-Bhadra Ulisi Horata Okkoota*) was formed in September 1999 to continue the movement. The movement to protect the Kudremukh National Park and the surroundings continues. It may be noted that mining activity will cease by 31st December 2005 due to an order passed by the honourable Supreme Court of India on a petition filed by wildlife NGOs. Also the government has assured that there will be no forcible eviction of tribals and non-tribals from the Kudremukh National Park areas.

13.3.8 Challenges Ahead and Policy Suggestions

Balancing the needs of development and protecting the environment and biodiversity poses a major challenge to planners and policy makers. There is no easy magic formula to attain this and will need to be framed keeping in view local condition, planning, goals, etc. Although there have been demands to increase the extent of protected areas and also focus on less important biorich areas, the immediate concern should be to improve the status of the protected areas which are facing several threat factors. The need for improving the infrastructure and also enlisting the local communities, especially tribals for this end needs to be emphasised. Secondly, the traditional approach to conservation requiring tribals to vacate from national park areas has led to social and political upheavels. Although participatory and community based biodiversity conservation has been emphasised no serious attempt has been made to implement this and effectively continues to be a top-down approach. It may be mentioned that 3800 VFCs have been constituted involving local people. Each VFC, will have a micro plan in accordance with the prescription of micro plan, forest area and plantations allotted to them will be managed. Co-management involving the state, the tribals and other local communities, representatives of the civil society, may be a better option to conserve our biodiversity. There is a need to enhance the penalties for forest offences, especially poachers and timber smugglers. Lastly, in the context of biopiracy necessary changes in our institutional and legal framework need to be put in place to protect our biodiversity.

13.4 Wetlands in Karnataka

Wetlands are one of the most productive ecosystems, comparable to tropical evergreen forests in the biosphere and play a significant role in the ecological sustainability of a region. They meet many crucial needs such as drinking water, protein production, water purification, energy, fodder, biodiversity, flood storage, transport, recreation and climate stabilisers. Wetlands play an important role in improving the water quality by filtering sediments and nutrients from surface water. Wetlands also help in nutrient cycling. However overloading with nutrients beyond its threshold impairs its ability to perform basic functions.

Wetlands of Karnataka are classified into inland and coastal wetlands, both natural and man-made. Inland natural wetlands include lakes and marshes; inland man-made wetlands include reservoirs, tanks and waterlogged plains. Coastal natural wetlands include estuary creek, kayal, mud flat, mangroves and marsh vegetation; coastal man-made wetlands include salt pans. Wetlands cover about 2.72 Mha of the total geographical area of Karnataka, of which inland wetlands cover 2.54 Mha and coastal wetlands 0.18 Mha. Totally there are about 682 wetlands scattered throughout Karnataka covering about 271840 hectares. Out of these, 7 are inland natural (521.25 ha), 615 inland man-made (2,53,433.75 ha) 56 coastal natural (16,643.75 ha), 4 coastal man-made (1181.75 ha). Inland wetlands cover 93.43 per cent (254015 ha) of the total wetlands area, while the coastal wetlands cover only 6.7 per cent (17,825.5 ha). Tanks (561) rank first in the number of wetlands and account for 79,087.5 ha. Reservoirs come next in number (53) with an area of about 1,74,290 ha. Lakes are fewer in number (5) covering 437.5 ha. (Rege *et al.*, 1996; *vide* Ramachandra, *et.al.*, 2002: 17).

13.4.1 Major Threat Factors Contributing to Wetland Loss

1) **Hydrologic Alteration:** Wetlands consists of multiple linked paths (waterways, habitat types, biodiversity on the site) that interact through energy flows, chemicals and physical transfers, moving biota and water flows. Watershed conditions of downstream wetlands are linked as they influence the soil and hydrologic regime of the downstream areas. Land surfaces are subject to alteration through-human use and manipulations, e.g.: intensive cropping, deforestation, intensive grazing and alteration of water flows.

2) **Agricultural Activities:** The conversion of wetlands to paddy fields has increased the gross spatial extent of wetlands. This helps in profound changes in irrigation pattern. The demand for water to irrigate crops results in construction of large number of reservoirs, canals and dams significantly altering the hydrology of associated wetlands.

3) **Pollution:** The degradation of water quality is a direct consequence of population growth, urbanisation and industrialisation. Unrestricted dumping of sewage with toxic chemicals has polluted many fresh water wetlands making them unfit for drinking, fishing and bathing.

4) **Legal Policy Failures:** Wetlands jurisdiction is diffused and falls under various departments like agriculture, fisheries, irrigation, revenue, tourism, water resources and local bodies. The lack of a comprehensive wetland policy with each government having its own development priorities, works against the interests of the conservation of wetlands resulting in intended or unintended 'spillover' effects further aggravating the problem. At the policy level wetlands are too often taken for granted and are considered as wastelands and targeted for development and diversion to other uses.

5) **Direct Deforestation in Wetlands:** Mangrove forests are valued for production of fish, livestock, fodder, fuel and building materials, local medicines, honey and bee wax and for extracting chemicals used in tanning leather. All land uses of farming and fisheries production have replaced many mangrove areas and continue to pose threats to the forests. The loss of wetland forests, coastal or riverine reduces the ability of wetlands to slow water and trap suspended sediments.

6) **Global Climate Change Effects:** Wetlands are the single largest sources of CH_4, a gas that is a major contributor to the atmospheric trapping of heat which leads to global warming.

7) **Introduced Species and Extinction of Native Biota:** Wetlands are threatened by exotic species such as water hyacinth and salvinia. These exotic species pose problems by clogging waterways and competing with native vegetation. As habitats are changed exotic plants may be favoured over native vegetation. When wetlands lose native species of animals and plants, they are thought to be of lower value making it harder to justify their defence.

13.4.2 Status of Wetlands in Karnataka

A review of the status of wetlands in Karnataka observes that large wetlands areas in Karnataka have been diverted for non-wetlands purposes. A total of 642 tanks in 15 districts were surveyed and the following observations were made (Ramachandra *et al.*, 2002):

1) The waterfowl census has served as biological indicators for gauging the health and productivity of the wetlands in the absence of wider ecological information. However efforts still appear seriously inadequate when all the wetlands of the state are considered. There is an urgent need to create awareness on the need for protection, conservation and restoration of wetlands for posterity.

2) Three wetlands, Badranakere in Kolar District and Bellandur tank and Byramangala reservoir (in Bangalore) are of global importance as they supported more than 20000 birds. However, due to inflow of urban sewage Bellandur tank is highly polluted. It is unfortunate that none of the 3 wetlands have legal protection.

3) The rapid loss of wetlands habitat and biodiversity is mainly due to the growing population and resultant urbanism and its many negative impacts like encroachment in catchment area, sedimentation, pollution, etc.

4) Wetlands around cities and towns are being used for easy and inexpensive disposal of urban sewage.

5) Visits to selected wetlands revealed that pristine waterfowl habitats like the herons in Ranganthittu Bird sanctuary in Mysore, Gudavi and Mandagadde in Shimoga are often prone to floods. The habitat quality of these wetlands is also changing so that they are no longer able to support the waterfowls throughout the year.

6) Lakes and ponds near cities and towns are becoming eutropic with excessive growth of vegetation and algal blooms. Most of these water bodies are losing seasonality and their ecological values are not being sustained. The introduction of exotic fish species has greatly upset the endemic fish diversity.

7) Over the years the number of tanks have decreased from 267 to 117 and some birds have shrunken in size.

8) Water from wetlands is increasingly drawn for agricultural purposes, as in Mandya, Hassan, Tumkur and Chickmagalur. Wetland birds are frequently found in cultivated tracts surrounding the wetlands. The agricultural run-off with high pesticide content affects the wetlands and the birds dependent on them.

9) In hilly regions water from coffee pulpers is being drained into natural streams, rivulets and ponds. As a result the wetlands are seriously affected and ecologically destroyed.

10) Mega projects like Cogentrix, etc. have threatened major wetlands in the coastal and hill regions of Karnataka, especially the Western Ghats. The Kaiga Nuclear Power Project has further dampened the prospects of reviving vulnerable and fragile ecosystems like mangroves, estuaries, rivers, and ocean basins and the associated shore regions.

11) Wetlands in urban and suburban areas face imminent threat. Leaving good shore space (up to 2 km) can protect wetlands in rural areas. Effluents from industries, urban sewage, and solid waste especially plastics should not be diverted or dumped into wetlands.

12) Management plans for each of the 25 national parks/sanctuaries in Karnataka supporting a vast stretch of diversified wetlands need immediate attention.

13.4.3 Bangalore—Case Studies

Hebbal Lake situated on NH 7 has been severely affected by sewage and industrial affluents from the BEL factory and Vidyaranyapura. The lake was eutrophic due to excessive sewage inflow. The preliminary socio-economic survey carried out in the region sorrounding the Hebbal Lake through contingent valuation method showed high level of dependency on wetlands for groundwater, food, fodder, fuel, etc. The lake has since been restored now. The lake even in its present state supports irrigation and acts as a source of fodder to livestock in the neighbouring areas (Kiran and Ramachandra, 1999).

Madivala Lake, a perennial lake located in the south eastern part of Bangalore city has been reduced from 114 ha to around 100 ha due to encroachments by the BDA for laying road and also illegal development of private layouts. Direct discharge of sewage has increased the pollution of the lake. Low DO, high alkalinity, hardness, coliform bacteria, and predominance of microcystis pollution indicating algae are deteriorating the water quality (Ramachandra *et al.*, 2002)

Ulsoor Lake, one of the important lakes of Bangalore, has very broad and deep feeder channels through which sewage flow. The run-off and discharges from automobile workshops, aeronautical industry, etc. affects the lake. The same is the case with Amruthalli Lake and Rachenahalli Lake.

The results obtained from 12 month sampling for 7 tanks in and around Bangalore city revealed that most of them were polluted due to inflow of domestic sewage and industrial effluents (Table 13.20). Bannerghatta tank was relatively clean due to its location and Sankey was unpolluted as water was mainly used for boating and watering the forest nursery. In contrast Madivala, Ulsoor, Yediyur, Kamakshipalaya, and Hebbal were polluted so as to render the water unusable for any purpose.

13.4.4 Wetland Management and Restoration: Challenges Ahead

With a view to improve wetland management and arrest wetland loss the following merit attention:

1) Improved quality of reporting tends to reduce the threat between protected and unprotected sites. Detailed information is usually available on the threats occurring at protected sites; whereas for many of the unprotected sites little information is available and some of the less obvious but nevertheless serious threats such as water pollution, siltation, eutrophication may have been overlooked.

2) Effective legal policies need to be formulated to prevent illegal hunting, fishing, etc. and for the following:

   - drainage or conversion of land for agricultural purposes and human settlements;
   - cutting of wood for domestic purposes;
   - pollution from domestic sewage, industrial waste, pesticides and fertilisers;
   - siltation;
   - overgrazing by domestic livestock;
   - commercial logging;

TABLE 13.20

Tanks in Bangalore—Area, Location, Existing Condition and SCM of Wetlands

Tank	*PH.*	*EC*	*DO*	*BOD*	*COD*	*TS*	*TDS*	*TSS*	*Remarks*
Banner-ghatta	8.1-9.7	0.20± 0.06	6-7.8	2±0.79	19.4± 7.2	78-242	93.8± 27.7	20-132	Alkaline water body due to dissolved alkaline substances, less dissolved solids with no major sources of pollution.
Sankey	1.2-8.4	Centre 0.49ms/cm Outlet 0.55	Inlet 6.6± o.9 Centre 6.7±0.9 Outlet 6.6± 1.0	1.7±7	Inlet 15-105 Centre 14-94 Outlet 12-112	Inlet 260-446 Centre 264-398 Outlet 276-408	Inlet 238 Centre 234.18 Outlet 247.2		Slightly alkaline. Water with low EC and solids value indicating no major source of pollution and less plankton density. DO,BOD and COD values indicate less pollution.
Kamakshi-palaya	6.5-7.5	1.27-2.09	0.5-3.9	27-192	170-621		Behind slum 710 Towrds Outlet 843.3	108-410	Acidic water, highly polluted indicated by EC, TDS. Lower DO values indicate septic condition of tank.
Madivala	7.2-9.1	Inlet 0.7-1.3 Centre 0.63-0.79 Outlet 0.63-0.79	Inlet 1.8-8.0 centre 2.3-8.2 outlet 2.6-8.3	4-42	46.2-282	464.3	-	-	The PH is acidic the EC value indicates high amount of dissolved salts.BOD and COD values indicate sewage run-off.
Yediyur	7.5-10.1		Inlet 3.9-8.9 Centre 4-10	Inlet 14.32 Centre 17-31	Centre 84-378	Inlet 167.5 Centre 151.8	Inlet 208-428	-	Indicates pollution by domestic and industrial waste.
Hebbal Tank	7.5-8.9	1.2-1.5	Inlet 2.6-7.1	Inlet 22.5± 5.8 Centre 20±4.8 Outlet 20.6±5.2	56-386	Inlet 600-968 centre 702-766 outlet 556-702	-	-	Sewage and agricultural run-off contamination.
Ulsoor	7.5-11	0.6-1.2	6.9	10-31	Inlet 231.4 Centre 216 Outlet 221.3	460-884	-	-	High PH due to sewage and high plankton activity; high dissolved solids.

Note: EC-Electrical Conductivity; DO-Dissolved Oxygen; BOD-Biological Oxygen Demand; COD-Chemical Oxygen Demand; TS-Total Solids; TDS-Total Dissolved Solids; TSS-Total Suspended Solids.

Source: Ramachandra, Kirsan, and Ahalya (2002). *Status, Conservation and Management of Wetlands*, Centre for Ecological Sciences, Indian Institute of Science, Bangalore, Allied Publishers, August, pp.155-158.

- cutting aquatic vegetation for fodder, fuel etc;
- harvesting of eggs of water birds and/or reptiles; and
- eutrophication.

Problems such as the encroachment of agricultural land, illegal settlements and hunting, overgrazing, overfishing, logging and the cutting of aquatic vegetation could at least in theory be resolved by an improvement in law enforcement and best management practices. However, problems such as siltation caused by erosion in the watershed, pollution from urban and industrial development, contamination with pesticides and fertilisers in the run-off, diversion of water supplies for irrigation and disruption of river flow by damming projects and food control of the authorities responsible for the protection areas. The mitigation of these threats can only be achieved through a general improvement in the management of the water resources at regional level. This would require an improvement in the protection and management of watersheds. Strict controls on all forms of water pollution and better land use planning are needed (Ramachandra, *et al.*, 2002).

With a view to improve wetland management and arrest wetland loss, the government initiated measures for conservation and development of identified wetlands in the state under the National Wetland Conservation Programme. As part of this programme Government of India in the Ministry of Environment and Forests have sanctioned:

1. Bonal Tank in Gulbarga Forest Division–sanctioned amount is Rs. 36.55 lakhs for the year 2004-05.
2. Gudavi Bird Sanctuary in Shimoga Wet Land Division–Sanctioned amount is Rs. 31.30 lakhs for the year 2005-06.

Three proposals pertaining to Hidkal backwaters (Belgaum district), Ghataprabha, Bird sanctuary and Magadi wetland (Gadag forest division) are under consideration of Government of India.

13.5 Coastal Ecosystem and Development in Karnataka

13.5.1 Introduction

The coastal ecosystem of Karnataka is a 300 km mosaic of monsoon wetlands, beaches and mountains with up to 2000 metres. The coastal ecoregion of the state is separated by Western Ghats connected by a number of rivers forming estuaries. Coastal wetlands provide enormous economic benefits; direct and indirect. This coastal region provides fishery and plant products, water supply to urban and rural population, flood control, erosion buffering, wildlife habitat, recreation and tourism. The combined vast natural resources of both sea and estuaries generate millions of rupees worth sustainable output, which is significantly being eroded by overexploitation and ill concerned projects. This has led to serious loss of natural resources particularly affecting rural people.

West coast of India has a coast length of 3,446 kms along 5 states and one union territory, Lakshadweep. The Karnataka state has a coastline of 300 km. The coastal region includes the inter-tidal (shore and beach), subtidal and offshore region. Mangroves of Karnataka cover over an area of about 6000 ha of which 1000 ha is in Uttara Kannada district (Rao, 2001). The mangroves are found along Kalinadi, Gangavali, Aghanashini estuaries and at the confluence of Chakranadi, Kollur and Haladi rivers. The mangrove forest of 100 hectares in Kundapura has been declared as a sanctuary.

The coastal population in Karnataka is likely to increase from 0.81 million (1991) to 1.60 million (2021) (Centre for Policy Research, 2001). With high density of population (400 per sq. km to 1500 per sq. km in Mangalore) the coastal ecosystem tend to impact closely the livelihoods of local communities living around the area. During the last 15 years more than 17000 hectares of area and 50000 people were displaced in coastal region of Karnataka due to industrial projects such as harbour, refinery, naval base (sea bird) and hydro-electricity projects (Central Water Commission, 1996). The local population both rural and urban is therefore an important stakeholder in the environmental conservation. The narrow stretch of 30-80 km land between the Western Ghats and Arabian Sea, which extends to 300 km of coastline, is the coastal ecosystem of the state. This area consists of 21 small and major rivers, 550 tanks, wetlands estuaries and mangrove forests, fallows, etc. The mangrove forest of Gangolli is one of the 17 major mangrove forests. It has been documented that more than 310 different species of marine fish, 55 types of reptiles, 225 types of birds, etc. are found in Dakshina Kannada district. In the coastal waters, estuaries more than 1.5 million tonnes of shells are collected annually which is used for producing lime. Annually, 151000 tonnes of marine fish is landed in Karnataka.

The Table 13.21 lists out some of the species occurring in and around coastal Karnataka.

The Western Ghats of India is considered as one of the 25 global biodiversity hot spots owing to its concentration of endemism (Myers *et al.*, 2000). The Western Ghats are biologically more diverse and have been more extensively studied compared to Eastern Ghats. The biodiversity of the Western Ghats is under threat owing to deforestation, which not only contributes to loss of timber but also has a severe impact on soil and water quality and even climate (Repetto, 1990). From the Western Ghats originate 38 east-flowing rivers such as Cauvery, Tunga, Krishna, and Godavari and 27 west-flowing rivers such as Kali, Sharavathi, Seetha, and Nethravathi. Data on fish fauna of the Western Ghats are limited. Dahanukar *et al.* (2001) predicted 345 species and a major contribution of it comes from the districts of Karnataka. The threat status of the fishes in the Western Ghats suggests that nearly 41 per cent of the fish fauna is threatened and hence conservation measures are essential. The northern region of the Western Ghats contains various food fishes, aquarium fishes and larvivorous fishes. Sarkar and Yadav (1996) have suggested that many of these fishes are highly valuable for bio-control of malaria. However, various human impacts including pollution, heavy harvest, construction of dams, and introduction of exotic fishes have threatened these fishes.

The coastal ecoregion of Karnataka has been the subject of considerable studies. Most of the studies have concentrated on the diversity of flora and fauna. However, one of the major studies initiated by Centre

TABLE 13.21

Species of Fauna and Flora Occurring in and around Coastal Karnataka

Species	*Types*	*Zones*
Estuarine vegetation		
Mangroves	9	Coastal saline
Shrubs	7	Coastal sand dune
Alga	3	Back waters
Trees	4	Back shore
Birds	8	Mainly pelagic visiting coast
Birds	12	Breeding in estuaries, lagoons and coastal mudflats
Reptiles, Turtles and Sea snakes	8	Marine and estuarine
Marine Mammals	7	Marine and estuarine
Land Mammals	2	Mangroves, tidal marshes, creeks are becoming rare and uncommon
Marine Vertebrates		
Sharks	60+	Deep sea and estuary
Skates	10	Muddy sea floor
Rays	18	Muddy sea floor
Marine Fish and Crustaceans of Commercial Value		
Fin fish	200+	Deep sea, lagoon
Prawns	80	
Lobsters	6	
Crabs	8	
Marine and estuarine invertebrates		
Gastropods (Chunks and Turboes)	15	Estuaries/mudflats/offshore
Bivalves (Oysters and Mussels)	20	Estuaries/mudflats/offshore
Holothurians (Sea Cucumbers)	12	Estuaries/mudflats/offshore
Cephalopods	8	Estuaries

Source: Madhyastha, N.A. (2002). "Importance of Coastal Biodiversity", Paper presented at the Workshop Coastal Zone Management in Karnataka, Mangalore.

for Ecological Sciences of the Indian Institute of Sciences, Bangalore is a breakthrough in the research studies. A novel experiment to study the biodiversity was initiated in 1994 when 18 colleges and NGOs joined to form the Western Ghats Biodiversity Network (Gadgil, 1996). During the 3-year period of 1996-1999 vast information on the biodiversity was collected. The studies have recorded ongoing changes in the landscape, its impact on the biodiversity and the socio-economic forces behind these. It was observed that there has been an erosion of concern for the conservation of natural resources (Achar, 1997; Bhat, 1997) among younger generations. The preservation of natural resources as such does not generate returns and ensures little security. Further, several alternative economic options have opened up. The importance of fish in this particular ecosystem led to studies on their composition, population dynamics and community studies. It has been well documented that the composition of fish species has been changing over the years. Some of the species such as fishing cat, otter, and estuarine-crocodiles are now rarely found and are included in Schedule I (Endangered and highly protected species) of the Wild Life Protection Act (1972). Some of the grasses grown in tidal rivers of the district are recorded as extinct and induced in IUCN Red Data Book of Rare and Endangered Plants (Hussain and Achar, 1999).

Some of the important reasons for the degradation of the coastal biodiversity are: increase in fishing operations, increase in pollution, foreign fishing, destructive fish harvesting practices, absence of alternative livelihood opportunities, increased exports and developmental projects.

13.5.2 Marine Fish Production, Effort and Utilisation

The share of Karnataka to the India's fish production declined from 10 per cent in 1970 to 5 per cent in 1998. The share of pelagic fishes declined from 75 per cent in 1970 to 54 per cent. The mackerel production declined from 46,000 to 27,000 tonnes and oil sardine from 33,000 tonnes to 8600 tonnes during 1970 to 1998. The marine fish production is stagnating around 165,000 tonnes which is much below the potential level of 425,000 tonnes. During the last one decade (1990-98) the standardised fishing effort on demersal fishes has increased from 93,000 actual fishing hours to 600,000 actual fishing hours. Similarly, the standardised actual fishing hours on pelagic fishes has increased from 138000 to 146000 showing the sign of biological and socio-economic unsustainability. Realising the possibility of overexploitation the state enacted the Marine Fisheries Regulation Act of 1986. The overall package seems to prescribe limited entry, protecting breeding grounds and period through compulsory registration and imposing restrictions on fishing in specified areas by specified gears. The Act is not vigorously implemented due to lack of exact quantitative information on biological and socio-economic impact.

Changes in the fish utilisation have adversely affected the coastal poor. Due to the concentration of fish landings in fishing harbours the fisherwomen and small processors are facing problems of non-accessibility of fish for local village households and small scale women processors. Competition from the fish meal producers and exporters has increased as the fish-meal and oil is one of the major ingredients of aqua and shrimp feed. The percentage of production exported has increased from 6 per cent in 1990 to 13 per cent in 2000 in India. The share of fishes in the total marine export has increased from 26 per cent in 1990 to 48 per cent 2001 in India indicating less availability of such fishes for domestic consumption.

The destructive fishing practices by the deep sea fishing vessels of Indian and foreign companies are other causes of decline in the marine fish production. However, the Agreement on Technical Barriers to Trade (TBT) of WTO ensures that member countries do not use technical regulations (the process and production methods) as disguised measures to protect domestic industries and operate as a barrier to market access. It prohibits the adoption of any discrimination between domestic and foreign production methods for the production of like products (same physical characteristics). The GATT clearly states that the trade restrictions in the interest of environmental conservation are permissible if such measures are made effective in conjunction with restrictions on domestic production. Hence a blanket ban on foreign trawling is not possible unless the Government of India takes steps to ban trawling by the domestic fishing companies.

13.5.3 Industrial Pollution in Coastal Karnataka

It was reported by the Karnataka Pollution Control Board that the total industrial discharges per day from 4 mega industries in Mangalore is 28,730 cubic metres. The discharges from other small-scale industries are not known since the Pollution Control Board does not monitor them. The development of the Mangalore Port has led to an increase in the coastal shipping traffic from 7,284 thousand tonnes to 13,888 thousand tonnes in 1998. The transport of petroleum, oil, and lubricants has increased from 612 thousand tonnes in 1991 to 8,318 tonnes in 1998. The oil spill of the grounding of MV River Princess 26 metre long carrier at Goa last September has affected the marine life according to NIO and also tourism industry. The coastguard has expressed its helplessness with some 40 tonnes of oil left over with the said grounded ship (Table 13.22).

13.5.4 Urban Waste and Infrastructure Development

Most coastal pollution in India arises from land-based sources—industrial, domestic wastes, and agricultural run-off. It is reported that in Gujarat, industries are discharging over 200 mld of effluents, which are acidic, oxygen depleted, and sediment laden. The total untreated sewage discharge into the sea is estimated to be 410,000 million litres (Elrich de sa, 1999). Though the rivers and estuaries are relatively clean with the pressure of the urban and industrial growth taking place the stress is increasing. The scientific underground drainage system was introduced

TABLE 13.22

Mega Industries and their Effluents in Mangalore

Name of the Industry	*Year of Establishment*	*Raw Materials Used*	*End Products*	*Source and Quantity of Water (m^3/day)*	*Amount of Effluent Discharged (m^3/day)*	*Effluent Contents*
MCF	1976	Naptha, Ammonia, Phosphoric Acid	Urea, Ammonimum Bicarbonate, Diammonium Phosphate	Nethravathi River 15400	7200*	Ammonia, smaller quantities of chromium and venedium.
KIOCL	1980	Iron Ore	Iron Ore Concentrate, Iron Oxide Pellets	Bhadra River 40000	15000	Non recovered particulate metals with high PH.
MRPL	1996	Crude Oil	Petrol Diesel Kerosene	Nethravathi River 20016	2880	Non-recovered hydrocarbons with heavy metals and oil and grease.
BASF India Ltd.	1996	Sodium Sulphate Anhydrous Acticide, Acrylic Acid, Caustic Iye, etc.	Dyes and Dispersions	Nethravathi River 273	3650	Increase BOD, suspended solids, heavy metals such as chromium and cadmium.

Note: MCF-Mangalore Chemicals and Fertilisers; KIOCL-Kudremukh Iron Ore Company Limited; MRPL-Mangalore Refinery and Petrochemicals Limited.

Source: Karnataka Pollution Control Board, Regional Office, Mangalore.

to the Mangalore city in 1965, to cater to the needs of a 1.5 lakh population. The total drinking water supply has increased from 43.5 mld, catering to the needs of 1.80 lakh population in 1971 to 20 mgd in 1998 catering to the needs of 5 lakh population with an almost equal floating population. With a conservative estimate that 85 per cent of the drinking water goes as sewage, there is a need to have sewerage system for 15 mgd. The existing drainage scheme was designed for a prospective population of 2 lakhs at 30 gallons per capita per day. The underground drainage scheme was introduced to collect and treat the sewage before the effluents flow into the Nethravathi and Gurupur river. Basically it was designed to treat domestic sewage, which was organic in nature. The domestic sewage comprising of water carried waste generated from lavatory, urinals, bathroom, washing and kitchen. Under this system there were 8 wet wells networked through pipes and more than 1000 manholes. All sewage of one zone, generated from households and commercial establishments would reach 5 wet wells and be pumped to the treatment plant at Kavoor with 5 mgd capacity. The sewage collected by 3 wet wells of the other zone reach the treatment plant at Jeppinamogaru with 1 mgd capacity. The treatment of sewage water was meant only to segregate the semi-solid wastes from the liquid wastes through the rotation process. The effluent was released to the river without further treatment. The solid part of the sewage was dumped into the drying yard, where the remaining part of the sewage water drains to the nearby fields and small creeks which ultimately join the Gurupur estuary. Sewage treatment produces a toxic sludge that must be disposed of or recycled to the land as fertiliser, which improves soil structure. However this system was not functioning effectively for the last one decade. Further, the MCC, Mangalore is in the process of establishing 2 more STPs at Surathkal and Pachanady. The treated effluents are being proposed for the utilisation in major industrial units located at Mangalore. The capacity of Surathkal and Pachanady STP is 15 mld and 8.75 mld respectively. These are in addition to existing STP.

Realising the importance of urban infrastructure development, the state government started Karnataka Infrastructure Development Corporation and with financial support from the Asian Development Bank and implementing Karnataka Urban Development and Coastal Environmental Management Project with an investment of Rs. 1056 crores. The project is being implemented in 10 coastal cities for the purposes such as capacity building, water supply, urban environment, roads bridges and coastal environmental management. Though the project has some positive impact on improving the quality of sewage water and urban water supply, this would cover only a part of the cities and most of the suburban areas and nearby villages are left untouched. Normally, it is the coastal poor who will not get access to such improved infrastructure and the open access sources of water and land also get reduced. Further, a majority of the poor will not be able to pay higher tax and price for such services. It is estimated that the interest burden of the amount at 13.5 per cent would be huge which will be a burden on the poor and lower middle-income groups.

13.5.5 New Strategies for Coastal Industrial Development

The state announced the policy for coastal regional development during the Second Coastal Investors' Meet 2003 to encourage capital investment for utilising coastal resources to generate economic growth and development. The Coastal Investors Meet was attended by a large number (800) of potential entrepreneurs including 53 foreign delegates representing areas such as tourism, biotechnology, infrastructure, information technology, ports, housing and urban development, etc. another class of stakeholders. The state government came out with many schemes to grant support and attract entrepreneurs to invest in three coastal districts. The policy makers highlighted the availability of vast resources available. The outcome of the Meet was the assurance of capital investment to the extent of Rs. 60,000 crores within a span of next 3 years, which could generate employment for 5,000 persons. The state authorities issued final approval and letters of intent for a couple of tourism and entertainment industry. However, The public-private partnership model by the government of Karnataka, for example Coastal Agenda Task Force makes recommendations on the coastal development without placing them for public debate. As the development of the urban areas and the region is necessary, the way in which these development projects are implemented is the concern. There is an immediate need to improve the efficiency and transparency in governance. The non-coordinated approach in the planning for environmental, industrial and urban segments by state government departments is the prime reason for the degradation of urban wetlands and trees. The pressures on the fragile coastal ecosystem were well predicted by Department of Forests and Ecology–Danida study as early as in 1993.

The Government of India has notified the policy for special economic zones (SEZs) under a government resolution, which will apply to all SEZs in the country. This includes the SEZ in Hassan and approved SEZ in coastal Karnataka at Baikampady, Mangalore subject to the framework for SEZ determined by the government of India (GoI) from time to time. As per the state policy, all SEZs in the state will be declared as 'Industrial Township' (notified area). The management of the SEZs will be under the designated development commissioner who will grant all the permissions as single-point clearance from his office. These will include registration of the unit, allocation of land, permission for construction of building and approval of building plan, power connection, environmental clearance, water requirement, etc. The SEZ authority will ensure continuous and quality power supply to SEZ units. SEZ units will be granted automatic approval to set up captive power plant. All types of environmental clearances will be granted by the Development Commissioner, except for those falling under the purview of Government of India. The SEZ developer will be granted approval for development of water supply and distribution system to ensure the provision of adequate water supply for SEZ units. Implementation of labour laws within SEZ will be simplified. A consolidated annual report (CAR) has been designed which will be filed by industrial units once in a year. The industrial units in SEZ will be declared as 'public utility service' under the provisions of Industrial Dispute Act. There will be exemption on payment of stamp duty and registration fees on transaction of land as well as financial agreement, deeds, etc. Sales tax and other state taxes will be exempted on transactions within SEZ. Inputs made to SEZ units from DTA units will also be exempted from sales tax. Exclusive arrangements will be made within SEZ for law and order. A Committee headed by the Chief Secretary has been constituted to review promotion, development and function of SEZs in the state.

13.5.6 Coastal Tourism

Beach and sea as a centre for tourism and recreation is a recent phenomenon in our country. It began with the Hippies during sixties with hand picked centres like Goa, Gokarna (Karnataka) and Kovalam in Kerala. In Karnataka, the government has identified Mangalore, Someshwar, Ullal, Panambur, Suratkal, Malpe, Bhatkal, Karwar, Murdeshwara, Kundapur, Honnavar, Gokarna, Kumta and Mulki as coastal tourism centres. The adverse effects of mass tourism on coastal ecology have many facets: construction of resorts, highways, destruction of coastal habitats like sand dunes, coastal vegetation, mangroves for landscaping and recreation, contamination of water bodies from fertilisers and pesticides, disturbing coastal and marine life by mass human pressure could affect the livelihood of traditional communities.

13.5.7 Coastal Aquaculture

The state policy for encouraging the coastal shrimp farming was guided by the export promotion and foreign exchange earnings. According to Marine Products Export Development Authority (MPEDA, 2002) the quantum of export earnings from captured shrimp has been more or less around 50-55 thousand tonnes, in spite of several fold increase in the fishing effort. Thus it is logically concluded that the only alternative for augmenting export earnings is to culture shrimp. However, while promoting the coastal shrimp culture it was assumed that no significant diversion of cropping pattern suitable for rice crop would take place; farmers would be able to realise the benefits of the new technology without any constraints; and income from other sources would be generated with the adoption of shrimp culture (Sampath, 1993). The State Land Leasing Policy was amended to suit the capitalistic shrimp farming. The 1995 Amendments to Land Reforms Legislation accorded aquaculture the same status as other agricultural activities. Thus the croplands could now be leased for aquaculture for a period of not exceeding 20 years and also the purchase of land for aquaculture was made easier by raising the land ceiling to 40 units per person or 200 units per family equivalent to 427.53 hectares per family. The 1995 Amendments also relaxed the category of those who were allowed to acquire agricultural land. The income limit of Rs. 50,000 annually was raised to Rs. 200,000 per year (Government of Karnataka, 1995). The subsidies provided by MPEDA included 25 per cent capital subsidy for new farm development, and a subsidy of Rs. 450 for feed and Rs. 300 for seeds per hectare and Rs. 500,000 for hatcheries. During 1991-94 NABARD extended a total outlay of Rs. 1.20 crores in Karnataka out of the total of Rs. 240.50 crores in 8 coastal states (Kurien, 1999). The share of cultured shrimp from the total export of shrimps from India increased from 33 per cent (8,300 metric tonnes) in 1988-89 to 52 per cent (53,300 metric tonnes) in 1998-99 and in value terms it increased from 48.78 per cent to 74.50 per cent during the corresponding period (per communication from MPEDA).

According to the ruling of Supreme Court in 1996 (Judgement on writ petition No.561) the modern shrimp farms should have been closed down by the end of March 1997. The Court also ordered that an authority be constituted to oversee the closure of shrimp farms, and that compensation was required from shrimp farms for the damage which they had caused in terms of soil erosion and depletion. Shrimp farms were required to pay compensation to people and workers who would lose income and jobs once farms were closed. However, in March 1997 based on the fresh batch of review petitions from the Central Government, MPEDA and four state governments, the Supreme Court gave an interim order on its own order of December 11, 1996. The Supreme Court extended the deadline for closing all farms to April 1997 and further extension was given. The review petitions were still being heard and the demolition order stayed indefinitely. The government of India constituted the Aquaculture Authority of India (AAI) in February 1997 with its headquarters in Chennai. The AAI has developed packages of practices and guidelines for undertaking traditional improved shrimp farms. The licences to start traditional improved shrimp farms were given by the AAI based on the recommendations of the district administration. However, the issues of monitoring the compliance of stocking density limits and determination of the number and hectarage of farms in an area are some of the problems. Further, imposing the limits on stocking density would counter the efficiency criteria, since the full production potentials are restricted. Hence it is suggested that instead of limiting the stocking density the government should have the right to impose standards on the waste discharges in the name of public health and safety (Yap, 1999).

In Karnataka most of the shrimp farms are located in Uttara Kannada and Udupi districts. It was reported that nearly 30 per cent of the total potential area of 8,000 hectares has been under shrimp farming against the Indian average of 14 per cent utilisation. Table 13.23 presents the details of the land available for shrimp culture in Uttara Kannada.

Most of the *gazani* land suitable for shrimp culture is under private ownership. Aghanashini estuary has the maximum potential area suitable for shrimp farming. Table 13.24 presents the details of the size of shrimp farms. The Table 13.24 shows that 50 per cent of the farmers cultivate only 7-8 per cent of the total water spread area indicating the dominance of big farmers.

TABLE 13.23

Total Land Available for Shrimp Culture in Uttara Kannada

(in ha)

Taluka	*Estuary*	*Government Land*	*Private Land*	*Total Land*
Karwar	Kali	60.00	1006.90	1066.98
Ankola	Gangavali	4.25	100.91	105.16
Kumta	Aghanashini	2.00	2529.43	2531.43
Honnavar	Sharavati	1.34	127.08	128.42
Bhatkal	Venkatapur	-	36.46	36.46
Total		**67.59**	**3800.86**	**3868.45**

Source: Marine Products Development Authority, Karwar and Brackish Water Farmers' Development Agency, Udupi.

TABLE 13.24

Breakup Details of Area under Shrimp Production in Uttara Kannada

Size of Shrimp	*Total Area (Ha) Farm (Ha)*	*Water Spread Area (Ha)*	*No. of Farmers in Shrimp Farming*
0 - 2	193.00	113.00	178
2 - 5	310.00	173.00	94
5 - 10	255.00	131.00	48
Above 10	1342.00	1050.00	52
Total	**2100.00**	**1467.00**	**372**

Source: Marine Products Development Authority, Karwar and Brackish Water Farmers' Development Agency, Udupi.

Table 13.25 presents details of scientific shrimp farming during 2001-2004 and reveal how the utilisation of the coastal *gazani* land for shrimp farming has remained stagnant after the introduction of regulations for controlling the shrimp farms within the CRZ. The Table 13.25 shows that the area utilised has stagnated around 1,100 hectares and the total production has declined from 1,135 metric tonnes to 473 metric tonnes.

One issue where there ought to be no conflict between shrimp growers and non-shrimp growers is that of organic loading, pollution and enrichment.

TABLE 13.25

Scientific Shrimp Farming in Uttara Kannada during 2001–2004

Year	*Potential Area Available for Shrimp Farming (ha)*	*Area Developed for Shrimp Farming (ha)*	*Area Utilised*	*Total Production (MT)*		
				Ist Crop	*IInd Crop*	*Total*
2001 - 02	5500	1550	1100	835	300	1135
2002 - 03	5500	1650	1060	450	350	800
2003 - 04	5500	1560	1100	296	180	473

Source: Marine Products Development Authority, Karwar and Brackish Water Farmers' Development Agency, Udupi.

Aquaculture is unique in that unlike other industries it is also adversely and directly affected by the waste it generates. Effective waste treatment and pollution abatement can be considered the core of sustainability. It is as much to the interest of the shrimp culture industry to clean up its own wastes as it is to the community at large. This should now be increasingly clear to most growers. Some aquaculture systems also reduce wild supplies through excessive seed stock collection. The salinisation of coastal cropland owing to unregulated shrimp cultivation has generated its own crisis. There are ample evidences to believe that the common water bodies have been shrinking through degradation and encroachment and siltation, etc., which is not properly reflected in the official data. Another threat to fisheries and aquaculture is found to be from industrial pollution. Both biological oxygen demand (BOD) and total coliform are found to be on upward trend in many rivers of Karnataka (Nadakarni, 1999). As reported by the Central Pollution Control Board (1997) in Andhra Pradesh out of 2466 million litres per day discharged as wastewater 2116 million litres are from aquaculture where the growth of aquaculture has been maximum (CSO, 1997).

13.5.8 Environmental Concerns in Coastal Karnataka

During 1990s the threat to coastal environment came from outside the industry. Many mega industries such as ship breaking industry at Thaneerbhavi was opposed by the Fishermen's Action Committee by bringing pressure on legislators and later by filing a writ petition. Finally the government had withdrawn the permission given even before the court heard the case due to strong public pressure. In 1995 the Dakshina Kannada District Fishermen's Environmental Protection Committee was constituted to oppose the release of pollutants into the sea by the MRPL a joint venture of the government of India and Birla Group. In 1995 a compulsory fishing holiday was declared throughout the state and a big *jatha* was organised at Mangalore. When the government did not respond to it the Environmental Protection Committee gave a notice to the Deputy Commissioner that the fishermen themselves would remove the pipeline carrying the pollutants to the sea. The matter ended with violence during the 'rasta roko' programme and police firing. The government conceded to the demand and directed the company to install pollution abatement equipment at a cost of Rs. 15 crores within two years. But before the end of two years the company filed a writ in the High Court explaining its inability to install, as it is the responsibility of the government, which collects tax. The government has issued an order during 1995 that it will not establish any mega industry in Dakshina Kannada District without conducting carrying capacity study. The government of Karnataka with support from the Danish Government undertook an Environmental Master Plan Study (EMPS) between 1993-95. Dakshina Kannada was targeted because it was projected that industrial and urban growth in the region will increase substantially over the next decade. While these developments will lead to more employment opportunities and some welfare gains to citizens, there was some concern about the long-term impact on the natural resources and ecological system. The EMPS team prepared the environment management plan, which consists of a framework and actions ensuring that the activities will take place with the bearing on environment. The Environmental Master Plan spells out specific interventions to be taken by local and state level organisations to ensure that the region will develop on a sustainable basis. The government of Karnataka accepted the recommendations made by the EMPS team but they were not implemented. The local self government and affected people must have the final say in case of all establishments both developmental/industrial and tourism projects.

13.5.9 Coastal Zone Management in Karnataka

The coastal zone is considered as a unique ecosystem consisting of sea, estuaries, wetlands, mangrove forests, agriculture and fisheries, rivers and other resources. The Coastal Regulation Zone Notification of 1991 enacted under the provision of Environment (Protection) Act 1986 provides for the conservation of this ecosystem by prohibiting certain types of industrial and developmental activities. Under the provisions of CRZ notification the state governments were asked to prepare Coastal Zone Management Plan (CZMP) to clearly demarcate the coastal zones into CRZ I, CRZ II, CRZ III and CRZ IV and specifically provide survey numbers and map. However, due to inordinate delay in the preparation of the CZMP and its implementation by the state and district administration, many violations took place taking advantage of the loopholes in the implementation process and also in the absence of awareness about the various provisions of the notification among the public. The Committee on CRZ violations constituted by the High Court of Karnataka in 2001 in response to public interest litigation has reported that Tannirbhavi power company in Dakshina

Kannada and Murdeshwar complex in Uttara Kannada were among the 45 violations along the Karnataka coast. Though, the committee has categorically mentioned that such industrial projects such as thermal power plants should not have been allowed, in the absence of a clear information on the ecological impacts and the pressure of industrialisation in the coastal regions, it is likely that there will be more demand for the utilisation of coastal resources for developmental/industrial projects. Though, CZMP has been implemented by the state and district administration, many difficulties were experienced by the coastal communities particularly for the construction of dwelling houses by the local poor and middle income groups due to wrong classification of the CRZ areas particularly in the Udupi and Uttara Kannada districts. The district administration/*Zilla Panchayats* are not willing to give licensc for the construction/repair of houses by the local people under hesitation of CRZ violations. Though the state government has acted upon the directive of the High Court to constitute district committees for issue of licences for construction activities, the local communities are not able to get the required licence in the absence of information.

To facilitate and ensure effective implementation of CRZ notification, the Department has established regional offices in the coastal districts as an internal mechanism to the authority constituted by GoI. Required infrastructure facilities have been provided to all the three offices in the coastal districts. In order to facilitate quick disposal of cases pertaining to grant of building licences, the Department has issued Government Order appointing the regional directors (environment) of the three coastal Districts as designated officers for the purpose of examining requests for grant of building licences in the CRZ area. The designated officers shall have jurisdiction over the entire areas falling in coastal regulation zone within their respective divisions. They shall examine and verify applications for issue of building licences by refrence to CRZ regulation and guidelines. The designated officers shall certifiy whether the proposed building is likely to offend the CRZ regulations. While doing so the designated officers shall be entitled to call for any expert opinion from any body or individual, if any such opinion is considered necessary. After examining the proposal for issue of building licence the designated officers shall forward the applications with his 'no objection certificate' to the concerned licensing authority for issue of licence. If, however, the proposed building violates the provisions of the CRZ notification, the designated officer shall issue an endorsement to the applicant and ensure that the concerned licensing authority is informed of the fact that the proposed building will constitute a violation of the CRZ notification. In case of building located in somewhat uncertain areas, where there may be suspicion of a possible CRZ violation, the designated officer shall recommend that the licensing authority obtains an undertaking from the applicant that he/she is agreeable to removing at his/her own expense the structure or any part thereof found to be in the violations of CRZ Regulation once the demarcating is done. Therefore, it is not correct to observe that the local communities are not able to get the required licences in the absence of information.

13.5.10 Important Issues in the Implementation of Coastal Zone Management

One problem that has been identified in the state of Karnataka is that private lands have come under the classification of CRZ I. While prohibitions exist on construction of residential areas, there is no compensation to the owners to offset the losses that accrue from what in effect becomes a dead investment. This leads to considerable conflict and resentment towards conservation measures. The same goes for private lands within the 'No Development Zone'. Fishing communities have petitioned state governments to either compensate them for their losses or to permit only bonafide fishing communities to build residential homes in the No Development Zones of the CRZ. For marine conservation as well, a system that ensures ground level monitoring and feedback would be beneficial.

The permission to establish non-polluting industries within the special economic zone should be clearly defined. The definition and scope of non-polluting industries and the need for which has to be established within CRZ, etc. needs explanation. In the absence of such detailed explanations it should not be allowed. Further, all new special economic zones should be established outside the CRZ area only. Declaring the coastal region, as a special economic zone is contrary to the very spirit of the notification—which is the special protection of the coastal environment ensured by a system of specific prohibitions and detailed norms for development. Special economic zones seek to do away with all 'restrictions' to uncanalised development and exploitation of coastal resources. A large section of the population depends on coastal resources for their livelihoods.

The CRZ notification was introduced with the objective of protecting the traditional coastal fishing and agricultural communities and their surrounding natural resources. The right over coastal resources and coastal spaces is the customary right of the fishing community and poor coastal communities. The notification does not mention how the setting up of special economic zones in coastal areas will protect or enhance the lives of the coastal communities.

The rationale for permitting SEZ within CRZ areas, and certainly activities such as hotels, golf courses, and 'non-polluting' industries do not have to be located within 200 metres of the HTL. The reasons for the same have been outlined above. The permission for the construction of schools and dispensaries within CRZ of the special economic zone should be allowed only if no such facilities are available within the radius of 5 kilometres. The removal of the public hearing clauses in the EIA notification especially for the oil exploration and the rare earths mining in coastal areas can have negative impacts for marine conservation. The objective of laying down environmental clearance procedures must be viewed as completely independent of other commercial and trade related procedures and restrictions.

13.5.11 Regulations for Sustainable Development of Coastal Areas

Ecologically Sensitive Areas under the Environment (Protection) Act, 1986

There are several options for marine resource conservation within the Environment (Protection) Act. Section 3(2)(v) allows the Centre to restrict areas where any industries, operations or processes or class of industries, operations or processes shall not be carried out or shall be carried out subject to certain safeguards. An example of this is the declaration of Ecologically Sensitive Areas (ESAs). Rule 5 (1) states that the Centre can impose prohibitions and restrictions on the location of industries and the carrying on of 'processes and operations' in different areas. It also states that the Central Government can follow certain factors while imposing such prohibitions. This includes Rule 5(1)(v) the biological diversity of the area which, in the opinion of the Central Government needs to be preserved. Some of the advantages of using the concept of an ESA for conservation are, flexibility, no displacement and inclusive (ESA/EFA extends to any kind of ecosystem like coasts, forest, plains, etc.)

Wildlife (Protection) Act, 1972 (WLPA)

The WLPA accords protection to species on its different Schedules I–IV. However the harvesting or hunting or trade in these species is prohibited and becomes a punishable offence except in particular cases, therefore a great deal of care needs to be taken before commercially important yet endangered species can be put on the WLPA Schedules. The Act also empowers the central and state governments to create national parks and wildlife sanctuaries. But since the creation of these 'protected areas' (PA) place curbs on the continuation of rights of local communities, they have been unpopular among local communities. However there still exist certain provisions which need to be examined closely by government, officials and PA managers in order to overcome problems created for local communities, which would contribute to successful management of the coastal ecosystem.

The Territorial Waters, Continental Shelf, Exclusive Economic Zone And Other Maritime Zones Act, 1976

This Act defines the following terms: territorial waters = 12 nautical miles, contiguous zone = 24 nautical miles, continental shelf = 200 nautical miles or the continental margin, the exclusive economic zone = 200 nautical miles from the baseline. The Act gives the union government exclusive jurisdiction to preserve and protect the marine environment and to prevent and control marine pollution as regards the EEZ. The central government can declare an area as a designated area for the purpose of conservation and make provisions as are necessary for the protection of the marine environment.

The Maritime Zones of India (Regulation of Fishing by Foreign Vessels) Act, 1981

The maritime zones refer to the territorial waters or the EEZ of India. The permits and licences that are issued under the Act can stipulate certain conditions which can also be in accordance with the provisions of the State's Marine Fisheries Regulation Act's conditions and regulations, and also based on scientific knowledge of the implications of particular kinds of fishing.

Karnataka Marine Fisheries Regulation Act

There are several options that exist for the control of fishing and its impacts on the marine ecosystems and endangered marine species. The State Marine Fisheries Regulation Acts have the power to decide on the regulation or prohibition of fishing and/or of using particular types of vessels or fishing gear and also on the prohibition of fishing for particular vessels in specified areas. There are options within this Act to favour traditional fishing practices, thereby being more equitable in nature.

13.5.12 Vision for the Sustainable Development of Coastal Areas

- There is a need to enrich knowledge on ecological enrichment capacity of the coastal biodiversity. In all developmental and conservation programmes consent of actual stakeholders should be taken.
- Formation of a coastal biodiversity board to work as a nodal agency for the approval of all the developmental projects under the ministry of environment and forests. It should also provide common forum for all the line departments.
- Pollution monitoring and control centre should be established and its service should be accessible to non-governmental organisations. Further entire responsibility of giving consent to industries may be transformed from the pollution control board to the local self-governments.
- The small-scale ecofriendly fishing should be encouraged through linking of their products with separate marketing network of eco-labelling programme.
- The livelihood securities of village communities should be the top priority in undertaking any developmental projects.
- Information needs to be shared among and with all the stakeholders before informed decisions and actions can be taken.
- Development decisions within the mainland areas should take into consideration its impacts on the marine and coastal ecosystems as well. For example dam construction is known to decrease nutrition supply to estuarine rivers and seas, etc. Such issues therefore become part of marine conservation as well.
- Integration of agro-climatic regional planning with infrastructure development.
- Planning to be linked with the ecological friendly poverty eradication process.
- Social development programmes of state, Centre and local self-governments should provide basis for development.
- Develop political capability of NGOs under liberalisation and involve them in the process of policymaking.

13.6 Climate Change and Its Impact in Karnataka

13.6.1 Introduction

Climate change refers to a long-term shift or alteration in the climate of a specific location, a region or the entire planet (Shukla, 2003). Climate change primarily manifests itself in terms of temperature increase, sea level rise and variability of precipitation pattern, change in the frequency and intensity of extreme events like cyclones, etc. Effects of such primary changes are observed on humidity, water availability, flooding and water logging, vegetation growth, structural instability, landslides and land erosion. These changes act as the main force causing various impacts on sectors like water, land, forest, coastal zone and quality of life through visible changes in health and hardships.

Water is fundamental to human life, and to many activities such as agriculture, industry, power generation, transportation, and waste management. Hence, apart from the availability of clean drinking water, the potential effects of climate change on hydrology and water resources resulting in possible changes in the water balance and instream flow are important. Land is affected by climate change through soil changes. This includes the accelerated decomposition of organic matter that releases nutrients in the short-run but may reduce fertility in the long-run. Soil temperature influences rates of organic matter decomposition, nutrient release and intake, and plant metabolic processes. Forests meet nearly 40 per cent of the India's energy needs and 30 per cent of its fodder needs. The climate is further, one of the most important determinants of vegetation pattern, which in turn has shaped societal development over centuries. Further, the spread of diseases due to changes in global temperature are expected to change the incidences and spread of major diseases in the country.

Furthermore, processes like volcanic eruptions, changes in the sun's intensity, very slow changes in ocean circulation or land surfaces (which occur on time scales of decades, centuries or longer), anthropogenic activities like fossil fuel combustion, industrial activities, agriculture systems, changing land use patterns, and waste decomposition that releases greenhouse gases into the atmosphere, also contribute to climate change over a period of time.

13.6.2 Present Scenario of Climate in Karnataka

Temperature Changes

Karnataka has seen a visibly increasing trend in mean and maximum temperatures over the past 30 years and more (Figures 13.1 and 13.2). Effects are felt in terms of continuous droughts in northern Karnataka during the recent years in districts such as Raichur, Bellary, Bidar, Dharwad, Bijapur and Gulbarga (Reid, 2000).

FIGURE 13.1

Average Yearly Mean Temperature by District in Karnataka

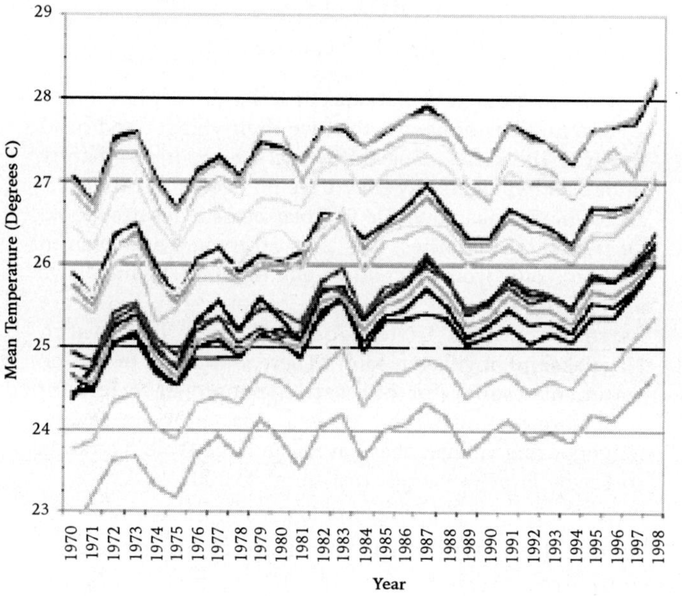

Note: The figure shows the trend of total yearly precipitation for 18 districts.

Forests and Temperature Changes

The impact of climate change specifically as an increase in temperature has been observed to be highly significant in the forested regions of the state. The dense forests of Malnad constitute one of the six major biosphere reserves in India. Based on a method developed by Hulme (1994), scenarios of climate change in this region of the Western Ghats were modelled for greenhouse gas forcing (Ravindranath *et al.*, 2003). For any given scenario of temperature and precipitation change for a given year it was observed that lower latitudes will experience the least change from baseline climatology of the region, while higher latitudes show greatest change (Table 13.26). Even moderate climate sensitivity projections are predicted to cause temperature changes any where from 1.05°C to 1.40°C in the region.

FIGURE 13.2

Highest Temperatures at Select Places of Karnataka

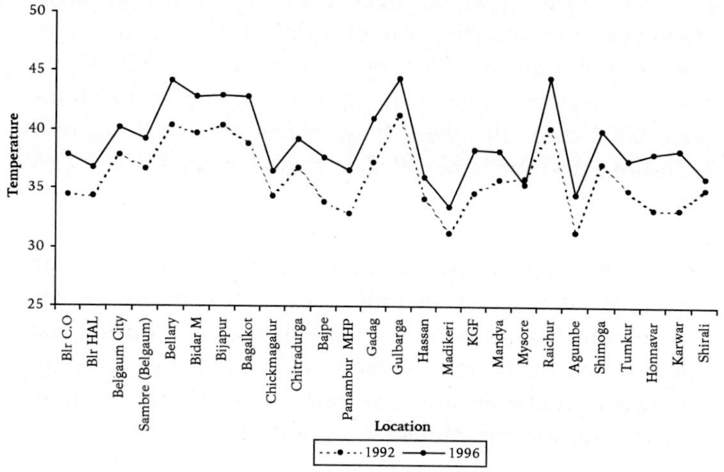

TABLE 13.26

Projected Scenarios of Climate Changes in Western Ghats Region

Scenario	*Year*	*Temperature*			*Precipitation*		
		10°N	*15°N*	*20°N*	*10°N*	*15°N*	*20°N*
Case 1	2020	0.26	0.30	0.35	<2	3	5
	2050	0.60	0.68	0.80	3	6.5	12
	2080	1.05	1.19	1.40	5	12	20
Case 2	2020	<0.15	0.20	0.20	-4	-3.5	-3.5
	2050	0.43	0.45	0.46	-8.5	-7.5	-8.0
	2080	0.75	0.79	0.80	-15	-13	-14
Case 3	2020	0.35	0.40	0.50	6.5	9	14
	2050	0.80	0.90	1.15	15	21	30
	2080	1.35	1.60	2.00	25	36	55

Notes:

Case 1: The central scaling factor and the moderate climate sensitivity global-mean temperature projection.

Case 2: The lower scaling factor and the low climate sensitivity global-mean temperature projection in the case of temperature projections or the high climate sensitivity global-mean temperature projections in the case of precipitation projections.

Case 3: The upper scaling factor and the high climate sensitivity global-mean temperature projections.

Changes in temperature are in degree C change from the present (1961-1990): changes in precipitation are in per cent change from present (1961-1990).

Source: Ravindranath *et al.* (1998).

Precipitation Changes

Karnataka is a tropical state. Annual normal rainfall is 1,139 mm received over 55 normal rainy days. However, the distribution of rainfall over space and time is not uniform. The Western Ghats, including the Malnad region, receive an annual normal rainfall of 4000-8000 mm; the west coast plains receive 3000 mm or more, the northern Maidan region receives 1500 to 500 mm, decreasing west to east while the southern Maidan receives 2000 to 460 mm, decreasing west to east. Seasonal rainfall distribution patterns for Karnataka as a whole indicate that approximately 71 per cent of the annual normal rainfall is received during the southwest monsoon season, 17 per cent during northeast monsoon and the remaining 12 per cent is received during pre-monsoon period (Figure 13.3).

For the 20 year period between 1961-1981, a comparison of normal rainfall with the percentage deviation of actual year-wise rainfall reveals that though annual rainfall was normal in 9 years, it fell below normal in 6 years and was above normal in 5 years (CMDR, 2004).

FIGURE 13.3

Total Yearly Precipitation by District in Karnataka

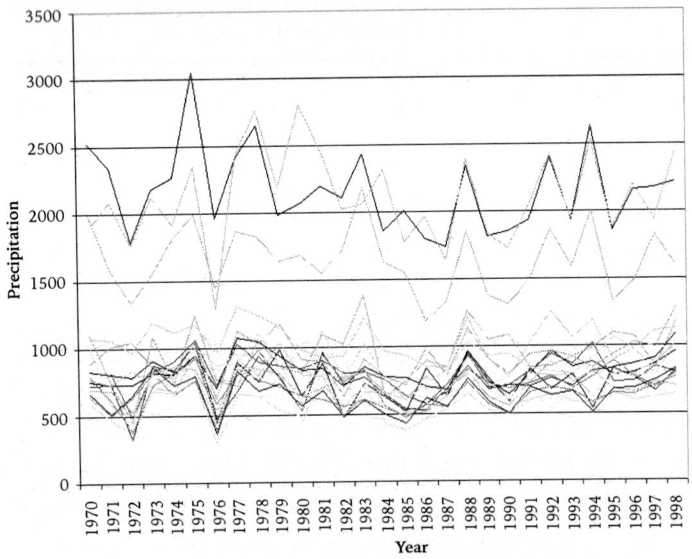

Note: The figure shows the trends of total yearly precipitation for 18 districts.

For the past four years (1999-2003), Karnataka has suffered from the adverse fallout of monsoonal failure as well as deficient post monsoonal precipitation. Rainfall deficiency during the 2001 monsoon was nearly 20 per cent, as compared to the normal. According to the Drought Monitoring Cell, Karnataka is next only to Rajasthan in terms of total area affected by drought (CMDR, 2004) (Boxes 13.1 and 13.2).

BOX 13.1

Precipitation of Drought in Karnataka

While monsoon has been good in most parts of the country, large parts of Karnataka have received below average rainfall–in as many 125 *talukas* sowing of the *Kharif* crop has been delayed. A total of 159 *talukas* in Karnataka have been declared drought-affected while another 20 are facing an acute water shortage. Worried about the farmers who face the impact of drought for a third consecutive year, the state government has decided to resort to cloud seeding to bring rain to the affected areas, at a cost of Rs. 5.65 crores. This is the first time in the country such an exercise is being planned on such a large scale—an aircraft armed with chemicals will 'seed' rain from clouds, an artificial way of making rain-bearing clouds precipitate in designated regions, *http://www.ndtv.com,* June 2, 2003.

BOX 13.2

Drought in Kolar District

The severe drought in Karnataka's Kolar district has forced a large number of people to leave their villages and head towards the cities. For three years now, it has barely rained and villagers say they have no choice but to leave. Eguva Maddalakana village in Kolar bears a deserted look. Of the 60 odd families, less than 30 remain and even in those it's only women, children and the old. The men have all left for the cities in search of jobs. The fields are barren, there is little food and even less water. Nagalakshmi, a villager, said, "There is no food to eat, no water, no fodder for our cattle, people have left for Bangalore to find work." It's the same story in several neighbouring villages that have seen large-scale migration to towns *http://www.ndtv.com,* June 9, 2003.

A detailed study of the impact of drought on agriculture carried out in 18 sample *talukas* of Karnataka, taken together as well as for two broad *taluka* categories, Category A and Category B, reveals several interesting findings (CMDR, 2004). Briefly stated, both Category A and Category B *talukas* show negative deviations in annual rainfall from the normal, except the slight positive deviations for Channapatna, Bangarpet, Hospet, Yadgir and Raichur in 2001, all of which belong to Category B *talukas* (Figure 13.4).

13.6.3 Impacts of Climate Change in Karnataka

Water Balance

The impact of local, regional and global changes in climatic patterns are predicted to be highly significant, particularly upon the water resources and water balance, for example, increased evaporation, a result of higher temperatures, combined with regional changes in precipitation characteristics (such as total amount,

FIGURE 13.4

Percentage Deviation in Annual Rainfall from Normal

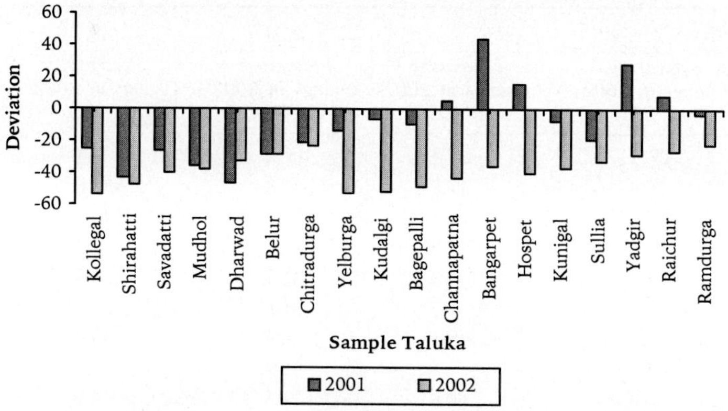

Note: Category A contains 7 sample *talukas* that recorded deficits in their respective *taluka* level average rainfall during both 2001 and 2002.

Category B includes the remaining 11 sample *talukas* with a recorded rainfall deficit in 2002 only.

Source: *Incidence and Effects of Drought*- report by CMDR, January 2004.

variability, frequency and intensity of floods and droughts, soil moisture and water supplies for the irrigation and hydroelectric power generation. Increased monsoonal precipitation does not necessarily lead to higher agricultural production. Increase in run-off may have positive results for hydropower or drinking water supply, but in numerous drainage systems, particularly altered systems, it may lead to waterlogging, salinity and sedimentation.

Although most of the rates of sedimentation observed in catchments in Karnataka are predominantly due to deforestation and land degradation, it is possible that increased precipitation will increase sedimentation rates, particularly if land degradation continues. The observed average rate of sedimentation ranges between 2.19 to 23.59 ha-m/100 km^2, where as the threshold level is between 0.29 and 4.29 ha. Most of the tanks have been silted up to more than 30 per cent of their capacities reducing their command area by 35 per cent. The rate of silt deposition in irrigated tanks is estimated at 8.51 ha-m/100 km^2/yr against the assumed siltation of 3.02 ha-m/100km^2/yr (AFC, 2000).

In a study that attempted to quantify the impacts of climate change on water resources in India, impacts are projected to be different for different catchments (Gosain and Rao, 2003). The study modelled water balance components expressed as a percentage of rainfall. The model predicts that in the case of the Cauvery basin an increase of 2.7 per cent rainfall will occur. Run-off will fall by 2 per cent, while actual evapotranspiration increases by about 2 per cent. In the Krishna river basin however, change in rainfall with respect to the control has been predicted as a negative, -5.8 per cent, while run-off will fall by 2 per cent and the actual evapotranspiration will increase by 2.6 per cent. This may be either due to an increase in temperature and/or changes in rainfall distribution patterns in time.

Land Use and Cropping Pattern

Rainfall and temperature changes, both have immediate impacts upon land use patterns. Changes in cropping patterns, decline in productivity and movement in pre and post prices in Karnataka is predicted with the changing climate scenario (CMDR, 2004). In tropical Asia it is estimated that although wheat crops are likely to be sensitive to an increase in maximum temperature, rice crops would be vulnerable to an increase in minimum temperature. The adverse impacts of likely water shortage on wheat productivity could be minimised to a certain extent under elevated CO_2 levels; these impacts, however, would be largely maintained for rice crops, resulting in a net decline in rice yields. Acute water shortage conditions combined with thermal stress could adversely affect wheat and, more severely, rice productivity even under the positive effects of elevated CO_2 in the future. One study assesses that the loss in farm-level net revenue will range between 9 and 25 per cent for a temperature rise of 2-3.5°C (Kumar and Parikh, 1998). A rise in mean temperature of 2°C and a 7 per cent increase in mean precipitation will reduce net revenues by 12.3 per cent for the country as a whole, while agriculture in the coastal regions of Gujarat, Maharashtra and Karnataka is likely to be affected negatively.

According to a study by CMDR (2004), drought impacts were observed in the *kharif* seasons of both 2001 and 2002, as compared to normal years for all *talukas* of the two categories of A and B (mentioned above). While in Category A *talukas* with two consequent years of deficit rainfall, the situation further deteriorated in 2002, there appears to have occurred a recovery to the extent of nearly 20 per cent on an average in Category B *talukas*, with deficit rainfall only in one year. Their studies can be taken as evidences of emerging climate change impacts on crop seasons.

More generally, the continuance of drought conditions in a particular region over a prolonged period of time is logically expected to make farmers to shift away from the cultivation of high water intensive crops (such as paddy and sugarcane) to less water intensive crops (e.g. *jowar* and maize) (Table 13.27).

Consider the B category *talukas*. In *kharif* 2001, the decline in net sown area as compared to normal is greatest for the low water intensive (LWI) crops (-37

TABLE 13.27

Changes in Cropping Pattern in Percentage Net Sown Area (NSA)

Taluka Category	*Crop Type*	*Kharif*			*Rabi*		
		Percentage Change in 2001 over 1990s	*Percentage Change in 2002 over 1990s*	*Percentage Change in 2002 over 2001*	*Percentage Change in 2001 over 1990s*	*Percentage Change in 2002 over 1990s*	*Percentage Change in 2002 over 2001*
A	Low	9	-96	-17.1	-10.1	-5.2	5.4
	Medium	-25.6	-17.5	10.9	17.6	-20.8	-32.6
	High	105.6	96.9	-4.2	-73.1	-33.7	146.3
B	Low	-53.7	-17.7	77.5	-19	-33	-17.3
	Medium	-17.2	-15.9	1.6	-4.3	-31.9	-28.9
	High	-16.3	1.6	21.4	-40	-91.8	-86.3
C	Low	-37.4	-15.6	34.8	-16.1	-24	-9.4
	Medium	-21	-16.6	5.5	8	-25.7	-31.2
	High	-0.7	13.8	14.6	-50.5	-73.3	-46.1

Notes: The classification of crops according to the intensity of water requirement are as follows:
Low: Jowar, Bajra, Ragi, Horsegram, Sajji, Save, Castor seed, Navane, Cow gram, Linseed, Alasande, Sesame, Black gram, Tur dal, Bengal gram, Green gram, Onion;
Medium: Sunflower, Wheat, Maize, Cotton, Groundnut, Chilli, Potato, Mango, Turmeric;
High: Paddy, Sugarcane, Banana, Betel nut, Coconut, Silk, Rubber, Geru

Source: Incidence and Effects of Drought-CMDR, 2004 Report.

per cent), followed by the medium water intensive (MWI) and high water intensive (HWI) categories. During the second year of drought, while the NSA increased by nearly 35 per cent for the LWI category over the previous year (2001), for the HWI crop category there was an improvement to the lesser extent of 21 per cent. The switching to LWI crops comes out more marked in the *rabi* seasons of the drought years. In *rabi* 2001, the percentage decline in the NSA of LWI crops is 16 per cent as compared to the 40 per cent decline for HWI crops. In case of HWI crops, in *rabi* 2002 the difference between these two crop categories is higher (86 per cent) with the LWI category recording a percentage decline of 9 per cent.

Moreover, for all *talukas* taken together, the shortfall in average yield rates in the *rabi* season is much in excess of 50 per cent from the normal figures in both the drought years, irrespective of the agricultural season.

Coastal Areas

Karnataka is endowed with a coastline of over 300 km, a strip between Kasargod and Karwar. The average population density of the coastal districts is 275 persons per square kilometres. The region is overshadowed by the Western Ghats mountain range to the east and has the Arabian Sea to the west. Characterised by heavy rainfall, hot climate and a short and mild winter, the tropical climate results in rich agricultural production in the region. While the majority of the crop is dominated by paddy, arecanut, coconut farming, besides rubber, cashew, sugarcane, grain and grams crops; localised specialties like the jasmine flower, Udupi brinjal (*gulla*) are also important. Fishing is also an important occupation. In effect, the coastal region is an important and critical region for Karnataka.

The coastal zone is also one of the most sensitive regions of Karnataka. This is because coastal ecosystems are influenced by a wide range of climate related factors including ocean currents, sea level changes, local precipitation, temperature changes, fresh water hydrologic changes, as well as changes in surrounding ecosystems. Some of the major problems in the context of Karnataka's coastal zones are erosion, flooding, subsidence, salinisation and the deterioration of coastal ecosystems. The washing of soil and sediment, which occurs to a marked degree in the Western Ghats, causes a large amount of sediments to pass into the sea along the states coasts, and contributes to the building of beaches and other shore features. At the same time, erosion due to cyclonic storms takes place all along the coast. River flooding (the temporary inundation of coastal areas by river water) also occurs in coastal areas, estuaries, and deltaic areas.

Sea level rise has been identified globally as the major threat to coastal regions, its impacts due to a combination of global sea level rise and local trends. In Karnataka probable impacts as a result of increase in sea level include–land loss and population displacement, increased flooding of low lying coastal areas, agricultural impacts like loss of yield and employment resulting from inundation, salinisation, and land loss, impacts on coastal aquaculture and impacts on coastal tourism, particularly through the erosion of sandy beaches. A study using available shoreline changes over a short span of 10-15 years along the Indian coastline, predicts a global sea level rise of 10-25 cm every 100 years. Along the Karnataka coast, however, a relative decrease in the sea level has been predicted (MoEF, 2004).

A different study, carried out by the School of Environmental Sciences, Jawaharlal Nehru University (1993), predicts that 0.15 per cent of the total 19.179 Mha of coastal Karnataka will be inundated by rising seas. Of the 44.81 million people in coastal Karnataka, 0.25 million (0.56 per cent) would be affected for each one metre increase in sea level.

Forests

Forests are subject to a range of anthropogenic pressures including grazing by livestock, unsustainable extraction of forest produce and conversion to other land uses. Climate change is an additional stress factor, contributing to the degradation of the state's forest ecosystems. Karnataka's tropical forests are rich in floral and faunal species, and include regions in the Western Ghats, internationally known as a biodiversity hotspot. Climate change, can affect this diversity, particularly through changes in productivity and forest regeneration.

Karnataka hosts several forest types. These include fragile coastal mangroves systems, tropical wet evergreen forests of the Western Ghats, pockets of *shola* forests interspersed with high altitude grass-lands, and the tropical thorn scrub forests of the northeastern plains, which have evolved specifically in response to scanty rainfall and high temperatures. These forests are a source of livelihood to many people, in addition to their role as carbon sinks. They are further rich in both floral and faunal diversity. Karnataka has 20.5 per cent of its geographical area as forests, which fall under the jurisdiction of the state forest department. Nearly 16 per cent of the total geographical area (TGA) of the state is under good canopy cover (canopy density > 25 per cent) while the remaining is either degraded or devoid of tree cover. The lack of sustainable land use practices combined with forest degradation have further contributed to severe soil erosion in the plains. As per the estimates of the state government about half of arable land in the state needs protection. Out of 125.85 lakh ha, 68 lakh ha (57 per cent) needs soil conservation measures (Kushalappa, 2003).

A study by Ravindranath and Sukumar (1998) was carried out under two scenarios—increase in greenhouse gases (GHG) and an increase in GHG and aerosol concentration. Under Scenario One, a shift in vegetation type along the altitudinal as well as west-east gradient is predicted for the Western Ghats. In the absence of proper management, the present day plantations of exotics such as wattles (*Acacia* species) could invade the grasslands. Longer dry spells may cause increase in dry season fires, threatening the moist and dry deciduous forests. Under Scenario Two, a change in precipitation pattern is projected that will weaken the Indian summer monsoon (Ravindranath *et al.*, 2003).

Health and Climate Change

Climate change is expected to affect human health, both directly through increased mortality due to extreme temperatures and weather events, and also indirectly through effects on morbidity, changes in food production, exacerbated air pollution, demographic displacement and the redistribution of biological organisms that transmit vector-borne diseases (Mc Michael *et al.*, 1996). If climate change occurs at the level projected by current global circulation models, it may have important and far-reaching effects on infectious diseases, especially those transmitted by poikilothermic arthropods such as mosquitoes and ticks. Although most scientists agree that global climate change will influence infectious disease transmission dynamics, the extent of the influence remains uncertain.

A study on the occurrence of malaria in Karnataka reveals that the annual parasite index (API) and slide positivity rates (SPR) show similar trends from 1975-1995: high malaria levels in the 1970s decreasing to low levels in 1985 and then increasing in some districts again in the 1990s. Average yearly mean temperature increased in all districts of Karnataka from 1970 to 1998, whereas the precipitation trend fluctuated. January, April, May and December mean temperatures with lags impacted on the incidence of malaria of the next calendar year. April and November precipitation all significantly correlated with API and SPR in a number of districts. The high correlations for these months is logical in terms of the climate of Karnataka. December and January are the two coldest, while April and May are the two hottest months. In general, the study shows that malaria rates and climatic variables were significantly correlated in the districts of Karnataka. There has been regional clumping with greater percentage of the variability in malaria rates predicted by climatic factors in the centre interior of the state, and lesser in the north, south and west. Also, the southern interior districts' malaria rates were more significantly correlated with precipitation than mean temperature, whereas the northern districts' malaria rates were more significantly correlated with mean temperature than precipitation (Reid, 2000).

It is suggested that most affected will be children, senior citizens, chronically ill people, disabled people, people living off the land and pockets of overcrowded and poorly serviced settlements in urban and rural areas.

Transport

The effect of climate change on transport is not very clear. However, transportation by air is known to be sensitive to adverse weather conditions; major system-wide effects sometimes follow from flight cancellations, rerouting, or rescheduling. There is a high level of confidence that sea-level rise will increase the cost of protecting infrastructure located in the coastal regions. A future climate with an increased number of rainy days, rainstorms and higher rainfall intensity may increase vehicular accidents and injuries in accidents, and result in longer travel time and increased delays. In addition, maintenance costs and durability of infrastructure are also dependent on weather events.

The Western Ghats, through which the Konkan Railway passes, normally experience moderate to heavy rainfall. An increase in temperature is expected to possibly effect stability and strength of building materials due to high evaporation rates and the efficiency, carrying capacity and composition of passengers who may be affected due to the need for air conditioning. Passenger traffic may shift to higher classes with air conditioning. An increase in rainfall could further cause ground and surface water level changes resulting in flooding and waterlogging. Extreme events like high velocity winds and storms could damage railway tracks, roads and communication lines.

13.6.4 Climate Change and the Future of Karnataka

Climate change effects are visible only slowly, but very remarkably and irreversibly over long periods of time. The net effects are permanent losses of soil, soil fertility, forest cover, changes in water resources and surface hydrology and increasing human health problems. These invariably lead to a cycle of human misery and migration due to threats to food and livelihood security and increased risks. Therefore, several major steps are required to arrest this trend of ecological disaster. Policy interventions need to be woven into other sectoral, social and economic measures.

Policies requiring immediate recognition include:

- Forest protection and conservation policy (on JFM, compensatory plantation, stoppage of forest lands for non-forest uses).
- Strict imposition of Coastal Zone Regulation.
- Watershed and rain water harvesting programmes to increase available water resources.
- Soil conservation policies.
- Wetlands conservation and development.

Karnataka is one of the leading states in taking initiatves in changing its fuel mix from coal to renewable sources such as wind, etc. and from naptha and biomass. Also from city wastes for Karnataka, there are several CDM projects and there are a lot of potential areas for CDM. An inventory of biodiversity and ecological hot spots is necessary for constructive follow-up action. A timely integrated approach towards research and policy development and implementation, would help abate potential ecological disaster that may ultimately affect the rich culture of Karnataka.

13.7 Urbanisation In Karnataka

Karnataka's urbanisation has been discussed in comparison with the national pattern, and the state and its regional patterns. The main variables used for the analysis are the number of towns by size-class, population concentration by size-class, population size and growth of towns and functional specialization of towns. The functional specialisation of towns has been identified using mean and two standard deviation of the share of workers in various occupation categories in each town. The present analysis attempts to answer a) the pattern of share and growth of urban population, b) pattern of concentration of towns and their population by size-class, c) growth pattern of towns by size and region, d) functional specialisation of towns by region, e) interrelationships among size, growth, and functional specialisation of towns, f) potential growth centres for future urban development, and g) existing and proposed hierarchy of urban centres in the state.

13.7.1 National and State Patterns of Urbanisation

Karnataka accounts for almost 6.3 per cent of national urban population and 5.5 per cent of total number of towns in the country. In the share of urban population, Karnataka (33.98 per cent) stands much above the national average (27.78 per cent). With conducive location characteristics for industrial and commercial development, the two main engines of urbanisation, Karnataka's urbanisation has been consistently progressive with gradual increase in urban population from 12.59 per cent to 33.98 per cent during 1901 and 2001. In particular, during 1901-2001, the state's urban population has increased by almost 11 times with annual growth of 9.91 per cent. As a result, the share of Karnataka's urban population has been on the much higher side as compared to the national pattern during 1901-2001 (Figure 13.5). By descending order of share of urban population, Karnataka (33.98 per cent) ranks sixth with Gujarat (37.35 per cent) and Punjab (33.95 per cent) as immediate neighbours on its either side by ranking fifth and seventh places respectively. The highest and least urbanised states in the country are Tamil Nadu (43.86 per cent) and Bihar (10.47 per cent) respectively (GoI, 2001).

FIGURE 13.5

Urbanisation: 1901-2001

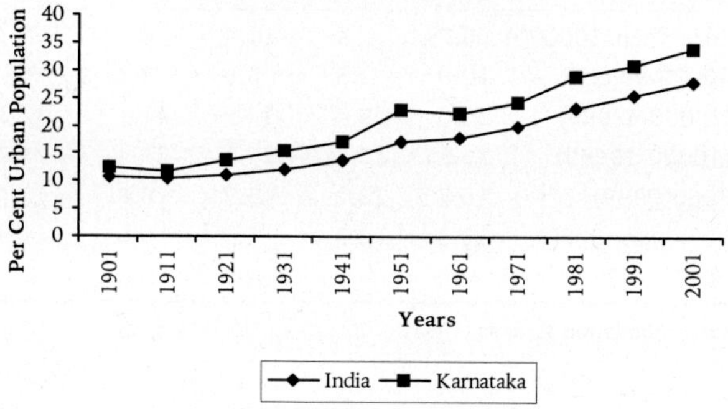

Source: *Census of India*, Various Years, Government of India.

However, decennial growth trend of urban population of Karnataka has shown a criss-cross pattern by hovering around the national pattern. In particular, urban population growth trend of Karnataka has exhibited two peaks one in 1951 and another in 1981 (Figure 13.6). The main reason for such high urban population growth during 1941-51 in the state is the strong initiation towards industrialisation. This is the period in which both Government of India and Government of Karnataka have encouraged massive industrial development through establishment of several large and medium scale public sector industrial units like Hindustan Machine Tools (HMT), Indian Telephone Industry (ITI), Bharath Electronics Ltd. (BEL), Hindustan Aeronautics Ltd. (HAL), Government Electric Factory (GEF), Radio Manufacturing Company, etc. in the state. The second boom in urban population growth during 1971-81 is also attributed to industrialisation and commercialisation, but with more dent on development of information technology (IT) sector in the formative stage. A similar spurt in the growth of population and manufacturing workers during 1941-51 and 1971-81 was evident in Bangalore, the capital city of Karnataka (Rao and Tewari, 1979).

FIGURE 13.6

Urban Population Growth: 1901-2001

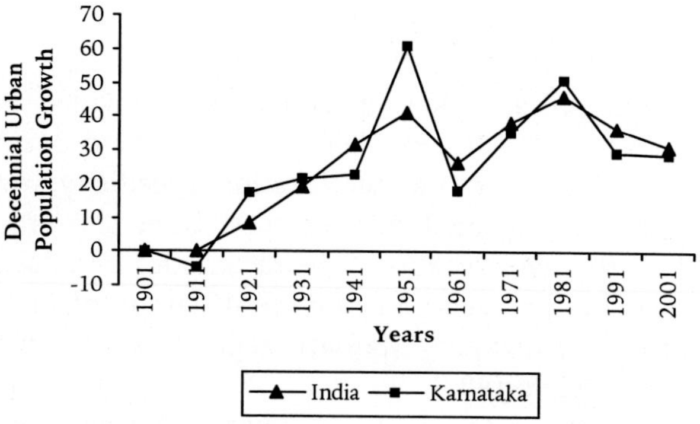

Source: *Census of India*, Various Years, Government of India.

In Karnataka, a number of towns have increased marginally by 8.2 per cent while, population has increased by 990.2 per cent. This clearly implies that instead of diffusion of additional urban population to more number of towns, the process has been in the form of infilling into the existing urban areas during 1901-2001 through the process of migration and natural growth. This process would obviously lead to rapid growth of towns in the state. While, country has experienced both diffusion of urban population which has experienced 1003.7 per cent growth into new towns which has recorded 172.3 per cent growth as well as infilling into the existing towns during the said period.

In the beginning of the century, distribution of towns in Karnataka by size class has revealed a typical pyramidal shape with highest and least concentration in class VI (less than 5,000 population) and class I towns (more than 100,000 population) respectively. However, subsequent urban development policies which encouraged higher size towns has led to redistribution in concentration of towns by eroding the pyramidal base. As a result, the concentration has been shifted towards middle order towns [III (20,000-49,999) and IV (10,000-19,999) classes]. The same growth pattern is evident at the national scenario as well.

In the case of concentration of urban population by size-class, it began with almost a similar pattern that of town concentration, but with a slightly disturbed pyramid. However, gradually, it assumed a perfect inverted pyramid with highest and least concentration of population in class I and VI towns of Karnataka during 1901-91. While, at the national level, the process has been that of the most distorted inverted pyramid turned into a perfect inverted pyramid during the same period. This reflects that both state and national urban development policies have consistently encouraged high concentration of population in class I cities thus stressing the' top heavy' character of Indian urbanisation.

13.7.2 Regional Pattern of Urbanisation

Physiographically, Karnataka has been divided into coastal, malnad, southern Maidan and northern Maidan regions according to the set location specificity. As a result, the development policies have been encouraged according to these locational characteristics and hence, urbanisation pattern. By per cent share of urban population, southern Maidan region is the most urbanised region (48.8 per cent) while, coastal region (7.6 per cent) is the least urbanised. However, both Malnad and norther Maidan for obvious constraints have revealed almost medium level of urbanisation. By overall growth of urban population, coastal region has experienced rapid urbanisation followed by southern Maidan. The main reason for higher level of urbanisation in coastal region is that in spite of restricted geographical space, coastal region has comparatively accounted for more towns and intensive industrial activities due to its location advantage and abundant natural resource base. For obvious location advantages and infrastructure facility southern Maidan has recorded the second highest urban population growth in the state. While, Malnad with its physiographic constraints has recorded the least growth of urban population.

By regional concentration of towns, surprisingly, Malnad, the ecologically fragile region has the highest concentration of towns and least being the coastal region (Tables 13.28 and 13.29). In particular, by size-class, Malnad has the highest concentration of town sizes IV, V and VI and second highest concentration of the most significant town size I and town size III. Malnad is a resource rich region. Hence, innumerable small towns have emerged as growth centres to provide minimum urban functions and services to these large rural hinterlands to maintain rural—urban symbiosis. Malnad region has been identified as urban and industrial dominant and highly developed region (Sastry and Rao, 2002). While, southern Maidan has the highest concentration of the most significant size class, the class I town, northern Maidan has the highest concentration of class III town (Tables 13.28 and 13.29).

TABLE 13.28

Percentage Distribution of Towns by Size and Region

Town Size	*Coast*	*Malnad*	*Southern Maidan*	*Northern Maidan*	*Total*
I (More than100000)	9.5	28.6	38.1	23.8	100.0
II (50000-99999)	17.6	11.8	35.3	35.3	100.0
III (20000-49999)	7.3	28.0	28.0	36.6	100.0
IV (10000-19999)	14.1	31.0	26.8	28.2	100.0
V (5000-9999)	12.8	46.2	28.2	12.8	100.0
VI (less than 5000)	16.7	41.7	12.5	29.2	100.0
Total	**11.8**	**31.9**	**27.6**	**28.7**	**100.0**

Source: Population Census, 1991.

TABLE 13.29

Percentage Distribution of Towns by Size and Region: Karnataka

Town Size	*Coast*	*Malnad*	*Southern Maidan*	*Northern Maidan*	*Karnataka*
I (More than 100000)	6.7	7.4	11.4	6.8	8.3
II (50000-99999)	10.0	2.5	8.6	8.2	6.7
III (20000-49999)	20.0	28.4	32.9	41.1	32.3
IV (10000-19999)	33.3	27.2	27.1	27.4	28.0
V (5000-9999)	16.7	22.2	15.7	6.8	15.4
VI (less than 5000)	13.3	12.3	4.3	9.6	9.4
Total	**100**	**100**	**100**	**100**	**100**

Source: Population Census, 1991.

By population growth performance of towns, almost 56.2 per cent of towns have experienced 1-3 per cent annual growth followed by 24.5 per cent of the towns with more than 3 per cent growth thus, contributing significantly to rapid urbanisation process in Karnataka. It can be recalled that the main reason for rapid growth of towns in Karnataka has been due to infilling of additional urban population added during 1901-1991 to the existing urban population into the existing towns. By regional concentration of growth performance of towns, southern Maidan has the highest concentration of towns with annual growth of 1-3 per cent and more than 3 per cent followed by northern Maidan (Table 13.30). Southern Maidan with its conducive location advantages is comparatively known for its industrial and commercial concentration and development. Hence, by and large, individual growth performance of towns is much faster and prominent in southern Maidan. Interestingly, Malnad region even with its location constraints has also exhibited a comparatively higher growth performance of towns (Table 13.30). Malnad is a resource rich region. Hence, innumerable small towns have emerged as growth centres to provide small urban functions and services to these large rural hinterlands to maintain the rural-urban symbiosis. Malnad region has been identified as urban and industrial dominant region (Sastry and Rao, 2002).

TABLE 13.30

Population Growth of Cities and Towns of Karnataka by Region: 1991

Per Cent Annual Growth	*Coast*	*Malnad*	*Southern Maidan*	*Northern Maidan*	*Karnataka*
Negative	13.0	10.4	0	4.9	5.8
Less than or equal to 1	26.1	18.2	3.1	14.7	13.4
1-3	47.8	55.8	62.5	52.4	56.2
More than 3	13.0	15.6	34.4	27.9	24.5
Total	**100.0**	**100.0**	**100.0**	**100.0**	**224***

Note: * indicates growth data is available for 30 new towns.
Source: GoI, Census, 1991.

By functional classification of towns, the quality of urbanisation in Karnataka is still in the primitive stage as highest number of towns (31.1 per cent) are specialised in primary activities followed by tertiary sector (27.2 per cent). Only 14.2 per cent of the towns are specialised in manufacturing sector. Interestingly, due to dominance of more functions in a single town, quite a significant share of towns (26.4 per cent) have been identified as multi-functional towns (Table 13.31).

By physiographic regions, coastal zone has the highest concentration of towns, which are specialised in tertiary sector (40 per cent) followed by secondary sector (26.7 per cent). The coastal region for its rich resource base and location specificity has attracted large number of industries and associated service sector. Malnad region for its obvious locational specificity and rich natural resource base has encouraged larger share of towns (40.7 per cent), which are specialised in tertiary activities followed by primary activities (32.1 per cent). Surprisingly, Malnad, the well-known forest region has encouraged large-scale agriculture (Sastry and Rao, 2002), which in turn has contributed significantly to functional specialisation of towns in primary sector. Southern Maidan with its locational advantages for industrial and commercial activities has encouraged significantly the towns, which are specialised in secondary (24.3 per cent) and primary sectors (24.3 per cent). In addition, southern Maidan

TABLE 13.31

Percentage Distribution of Towns by Functions and Region

Functional Category Growth	*Coast*	*Malnad*	*Southern Maidan*	*Northern Maidan*	*Karnataka*
Primary	13.3	32.1	24.3	43.8	31.1
Secondary	26.7	4.9	24.3	9.6	14.2
Tertiary	40.0	40.7	18.6	19.2	28.3
Others	20.0	22.2	32.9	27.4	26.4
All Towns	11.8	31.9	27.5	28.7	100.0

Source: Census, 1991.

which has efficient infrastructure facilities to encourage simultaneously trade, transport, communication and other services has the highest concentration of towns specialised in more than one function (32.9 per cent). While, northern Maidan for its obvious high agriculture and irrigation potentials and associated infrastructure has led to the highest concentration of towns with specialisation in primary sector (43.8 per cent) followed by tertiary sector (19.2 per cent). Like southern Maidan, northern Maidan has the second highest concentration of towns, which are specialised in multifunction (27.4 per cent) (Table 13.31).

An integrated analysis of towns by size, growth and functional specialisation by region has enabled to identify a few typologies of towns and their potential growth centre performances. In coastal region, cities and large towns like Mangalore, Udupi, Sirsi, and Puttur, which are multifunctional, are growing rapidly as compared to other functional towns. While Mangalore and Udupi are coastal towns, Puttur and Sirsi are in the midst of forest resource base and all of them are located in an ecologically sensitive zone. Hence, their growth process and pattern need to be regulated to maintain both forest and coastal ecology. In particular, Udupi has recorded very high growth (97.1 per cent) during 1981-91, thus attracting administrators and policy makers to take special care in the growth process of Udupi town. Incidentally, to recognise the importance of Udupi, which was a part of Dakshina Kannada district till 1995 has been recently carved out as a separate district along with a set of villages and towns. In fact, both Mangalore and Udupi with their rapid growth and associated urban environmental problems of industrial pollution, solid waste and sewerage disposal have been posing serious threat to the coastal ecology. In addition, the other coastal and coastal zone towns Karwar, Bantval, Dandeli, Puttur, Bhatkal, Yellapur, Honnavar, and Karkala with multifunctional specialisation and higher population growth have emerged as potential growth centres for future investments and development. Hence, these potential growth centres need adequate growth regulations for their sustainable development. Similarly, several newly emerged project towns have recorded significant population decline mostly due to decline in the project activities.

In Malnad region, which has higher concentration of towns specialised in primary and tertiary sector activities due to difficult terrain needs adequate care in promotion of urbanisation in the region. As a result, towns like Arkalagud, Heggaddadevanakote, Mundargi, Hangal and Navalgund which are specialised in primary sector, and Chennarayapatna, Haveri, Kushalnagar and Hubli-Dharwad, which have multifunctional specialisation, have recorded high population growth, thus emerging as potential growth centres. Hence, these towns need to be encouraged by making use of their available regional or local resource base. Like coastal region, Malnad is also an ecologically sensitive region. Hence, adequate care is required while development of these towns.

In terms of concentration of towns with functional specialisation, southern Maidan with almost equal share in primary, secondary of course with a slight lower share in tertiary sector has emerged as functionally balanced region. Especially, southern Maidan has accommodated Bangalore, the capital city of Karnataka that has accounted for almost 31 per cent of state's urban population and the entire state depends on it for various functions and services. The main concern of the southern Maidan is increasing concentration of population in Bangalore, which needs to be discouraged, in order to encourage balanced regional development. In this context, several towns of this region like Krishnarajpet, Holalkere, Siriguppa, Hadagali specialised in primary sector; Maddur, Mulabagal, Anekal, Harihar, Kanakapura and Vijayapura specialised in secondary sector; Hosadurga, Tumkur, Kolar, Bagepalli, Bangarpet, Challekere, Chintamani, Chitradurga, Davanagere, Hiriyur, Koratagere, Kunigal, Malur, Pavagada and Srinivaspura. have emerged as potential growth centres with higher population growth performance. Hence, these potential centres need adequate encouragement based on the available local resource base.

Similarly, northern Maidan due to high irrigation potentials, has accounted for major share of towns with specialisation in primary sector and in particular agriculture based activities followed by multifunctions. The region has concentration of cities like Belgaum, Gulbarga, Bidar, and Bijapur and Raichur which are specialised in bi-and multifunction. In addition several towns like Indi, Mudhol, Gangavathi, Manvi, Sindhanur, Hatti, Mudebihal, Badami, Bhalki, Mahalingapur, Sadem, with higher population growth have emerged as potential growth centres which need to be encouraged with appropriate regional perspective of course based on the available regional resource base. Hence, with proper choice in identification of potential growth centres across the state by keeping regional, state, and national perspective the state would induce balanced urbanisation process.

FIGURE 13.7

Population Trends in Million of Capital Cities

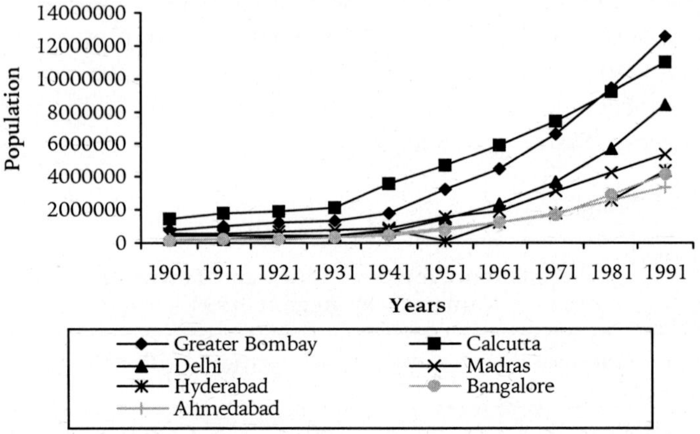

FIGURE 13.8

Percentage of Population Growth in Capital Cities: 1981-91

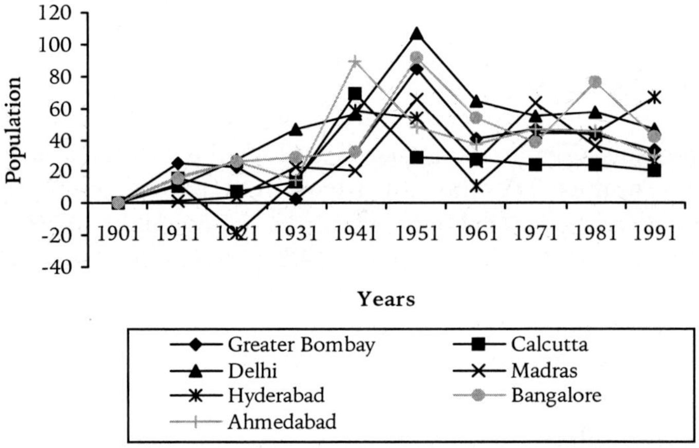

13.7.3 Growth Pattern of Bangalore

Bangalore, the globally known software city and capital of Karnataka is known for its trade and commerce and industrial development since its inception. As a result, it has become one among the million cities of India as early as 1961 and whose growth and development is comparable with the seven 'million' and capital cities of India. As per 1991 Population Census, Bangalore ranks sixth next to Hyderabad. Population size trend of Bangalore has been smooth all along and very close to the baseline unlike Greater Bombay, Calcutta and Delhi (Figure 13.7). While, growth trend has shown a bi-model pattern with growth peaks at 1951 and 1981 (Figure 13.8). The main reason for such high population growth during 1941-1951 was, as said earlier, large scale industrial development encouraged by both governments of India and Karnataka. While, 1971-1981 growth is also attributed to industrial development and area expansion (Sastry, 1988), it is mainly due to the formation stage of IT sector in Bangalore.

Functional Specialisation, Causes and Consequences of Growth

By functional specialisation, Bangalore has consistently emerged as a bifunctional city with specialisation in manufacturing and service sectors. In addition, trade and commerce for obvious location specificity has acquired greater significance. However, since 1984 the main instrument for Bangalore's rapid growth is IT sector with the establishment of a multinational company, the Texas Instruments followed by STPI first earth station and a group of 13 companies. Especially, during 1991-99 the number of IT units has increased by 361.5 per cent while, sales in terms of export has recorded an unparallel increase by 22566.7 per cent. More significantly, growth in export of software in a single year (2000-01) was as high as 73 per cent. For smooth functioning of the IT sector, it has attracted highly skilled IT professionals from all over the country whose number is estimated as 1.5 lakhs. This has obviously developed the multiplier effect to attract resources and population to the city. As a result, the city had started expanding its boundaries on all sides to accommodate IT units and its professionals. Such expansion has been more prominent in the southeast sector of the city (Hosur Road, Koramangala, HAL, Whitefield) which has been proposed as IT corridor running from Old Madras Road to New Madras Road (DIT, undated).

The area of the city has recorded significant increase by 92.1 per cent and the population by 37.8 per cent during 1991-2001. While, IT development has been in progress, the corresponding infrastructure and services required for smooth functioning of IT sector has not geared up. The main victim of such expansion is the peripheral areas of the city as it has experienced uneven development and severe environmental problems with unique 'urban' characteristics which is quite different from the city. Some of the characteristics are higher concentration of households with large size, higher illiteracy rate, higher share of unskilled and primary sector workers, higher share of medical expenses as compare to city, larger share of *kutcha* or semi-*pucca* house structure, least water and sanitation facility, no solid waste disposal provision and high concentration of slums and uneven city peripheral transport facility (Sastry, 2004; BMTC, 2003; Ramachandran and Sastry, 2001).

State Urban Development Policy

Spatially, Karnataka's urbanisation has been a lopsided one mainly due to higher level of urbanisation in the regions adjoining the state capital, Bangalore that is located almost in the southern tip of the state boundary. Of late, rapid infrastructure development along the major corridors of the state have encouraged rapid urbanisation, along those developing corridors and in particular along the Bangalore-Belgaum corridor which is a part of the golden quadrilateral national road network, Bangalore-Mysore corridor, a miniature of the golden quadrilateral being exclusively developed by the state, and Mangalore-Karwar corridor as a part of the west coast corridor. It has been identified that almost 84 per cent of the state urban population is concentrated in these rapidly urbanising corridors. As a result, almost 74 per cent of the total urban investment is concentrated in these corridors.

By population size of towns, the following more conspicuous six hierarchic order of urban centres have emerged in the state (Table 13.32). Spatially, one can find both gaps and overlaps in the existing hierarchic structure of towns. Hence, for balanced urban development in the state, reordering in the existing hierarchic levels is very much essential. In order to achieve this objective the proposed hierarchy of urban centres has been discussed as below. The importance of Bangalore as the capital city and globally known software centre needs to be maintained by encouraging its sustained growth in the state as the first order

TABLE 13.32

Hierarchy of Urban Centres in Karnataka

Order	*Town*	*Population*
I	1. Bangalore	4130288
II	1. Mysore	653345
	2. Hubli-Dharwad	648298
III	1. Mangalore	426341
	2. Belgaum	402412
IV	1. Gulbarga	310920
	2. Davanagere	287233
	3. Bellary	245391
V	1. Bijapur	193131
	2. Shimoga	193028
	3. Tumkur	179877
	4. Raichur	170577
	5. Kolar Gold Fields	156746
	6. Bhadravati	149257
	7. Hospet	134799
	8. Gadag-Betigeri	134051
	9. Bidar	132408
	10. Mandya	120265
	11. Hassan	108706
	12. Chitradurga	103435
VI	1. Gangawati	81156
	2. Bagalkot	76903
	3. Ranebennur	67442
	4. Harihar	66647
	5. Chickmagalur	60816
	6. Others	-

Source: *Population Census of India*, Town Directory of Karnataka, 1991.

TABLE 13.33

Proposed Hierarchy of Urban Centres in Karnataka

Order	*Town*
I (1)	1. Bangalore
II (5)	1. Mysore
	2. Hubli-Dharwad
	3. Mangalore
	4. Belgaum
	5. Gulbarga
III (16)	1. Harihar-Davanagere
	2. Bellary
	3. Bijapur
	4. Shimoga-Bhadravathi
	5. Tumkur
	6. Raichur
	7. Kolar Gold Fields
	8. Hospet
	9. Gadag-Betigeri
	10. Bidar
	11. Mandya
	12. Hassan
	13. Chitradurga
	14. Gangawati
	15. Bagalkot
	16. Madikeri
IV	Other Towns

Source: Derived from Census of India Town Directory of Karnataka, 1991.

urban centre and also encouraging it as an important national metro in the south along with four other metros of the country. This can be achieved mainly by reducing the existing functional gaps between Bangalore and other four national metros. At the second hierarchic order, it is preferable to have five cities: Mysore, Hubli-Dharwad, Mangalore, Belgaum and Gulbarga. These five second order centres, which have well spatially ordered locations would reduce the existing spatial gaps. In this context Mangalore, Belgaum and Gulbarga have to be brought to the levels of Mysore and Hubli-Dharward through appropriate policies. Similarly, it is preferable to have spatially well interspersed 16 third order urban centres, which would further reduce both functional and spatial gaps. These towns and cities are Bagalkot, Bellary, Bijapur, Bhadravati-Shimoga, Bidar, Chitradurga, Chickmagalur, Davanagere-Harihar, Gadag-Betigeri, Hassan, Hospet, Kolar Gold Fields, Madikeri, Mandya, Raichur, and Tumkur.

By size, growth and functional typology, both large and medium towns that are specialised in tertiary, secondary and multifunctions with their rapid growth process have emerged as potential growth centres in the coastal region. Incidentally, many of these towns are located in the well-known west coast corridor between Mangalore-Karwar. Similarly, In Malnad region, several large, medium and small towns with specialisation in primary and tertiary sector and multifunctions (cultural and religious) have emerged as growth centres with their rapid population growth. In both southern and northern Maidan regions several large, medium and small towns specialised in primary, secondary, tertiary and multifunctions have emerged as potential growth centres with their rapid growth. Incidentally, many of these towns are located all along the Bangalore-Mysore infrastructure corridor and Bangalore- Belgaum golden quadrilateral corridor. In addition, many of these potential towns are the part of the proposed hierarchic model to be encouraged for balanced urban development in the state. All these reoriented urbanisation process if encouraged with appropriate development perspective would promote balanced regional growth for which the state sevelopment policies have been striving since the formation of the state (Table 13.33).

13.8 Urban Solid Waste Management

Urban solid waste management (SWM) is a major challenge facing governments in developing countries. However, viewed from the global context, it appears that only a limited attention has been bestowed on waste management in these countries, especially on the need to develop an integrated approach such that it is both cost effective and efficient. In India, too, the situation is no different. Today, one of the most important issues facing the country pertaining to the development of the urban[1] (Appendix A-13.7) areas is the problem of SWM. With about 17 per cent of the global population and a staggering urban population of about 27 per cent of the country's total population[2] (World Bank, 1998), urban SWM in India represents a formidable challenge. The situation assumes more serious proportions if we consider the fact that while the country's overall annual population growth rate is about 2 per cent, the estimated urban population growth rate is much higher—around 3.5 per cent per annum (World Bank, 1998).

Although there is a dearth of precise and reliable data on waste generated in the country because of non-availability of such information at the municipal level, it is officially estimated that the country generates about 30 million tonnes of urban solid waste annually[3] (Government of India, 1998). The per capita waste generation in India varies between 0.1 kilogrammes and 0.6 kilogrammes per day, with an average of 0.33 kilogrammes (Bhide, 1990). It is also estimated that the per capita waste generation in a typical Indian metropolitan city is expected to increase by 1.33 per cent per year (Shekdar, *et. al.*, 1991). According to a survey conducted by the Central Pollution Control Board (CPCB), the present annual solid waste generation in Indian cities has increased from 6 million tonnes in 1947 to 48 million tonnes in 1997 and is expected to increase to 300 million tonnes per annum by 2047 (CPCB, 2000). This can be mainly ascribed to excessive urbanisation and the resultant slumming of the cities. Interestingly, studies show that there is a large difference between urban and rural levels of waste generation, which reflect the economic extremes existing within Indian society (WHO, 1991). The larger cities are centres of major economic activity, which is manifested in the prosperity and the culture of consumerism among the residents, together with increased waste.

Solid waste may be categorised according to its source as: (a) domestic solid waste; (b) commercial and industrial solid waste, which is bulky but not hazardous; and (c) hazardous waste from industries and hospitals that require special handling. The waste composition varies significantly across different areas within urban centres, such as between residential, commercial/market and industrial areas. Furthermore, as in most low-income developing countries, an important fact about urban solid waste in India is its high content of organic matter that amounts to anywhere between 30 and 75 per cent of total generation (Venkateswaran, 1994). The percentage of luxury waste-material such as paper, plastic, metals and glass is comparatively low (Bhide and Sundaresan, 1984). Although economic prosperity is one reason for the generation of more luxury waste materials, as observed in developed countries, the low content in India may be explained by the fact that traditionally such waste materials are segregated at source for reuse. As such compared to their total generation, the percentage of these materials which get incorporated into the city waste stream is smaller. According to one estimate, urban solid waste in India generally contains up to 20 per cent recyclable matter (Government of India, 1998). Efforts to further encourage recycling activities should therefore be made to reduce the quantity of waste that eventually gets dumped in the cities and require disposal.

Given its high organic content and moisture, waste disposal and processing are important in waste management practices in India. It is argued that the

1. Though the Census of India classifies urban areas according to population size, the official definition of 'urban' in India is any place so designated or any place with: (i) a minimum population of 5000; (ii) at least 75 per cent of the male working population involved in non-agricultural activities; and (iii) a population density of at least 400 per square kilometre. However, one peculiar characteristic of urbanisation in India is that it, to a great degree, suffers from 'official under-urbanisation' because the estimations do not include numerous large urbanised villages with populations up to 20,000 inhabitants, which are urban in every sense except in name. One explanation for the phenomenon is that staying 'rural' has many financial benefits for the community: electricity and water are highly subsidised, land and property are taxed more lightly and these areas qualify for various rural development funds and development programme initiated by the central and state governments.
2. Out of 1027 million (or 102.7 crore) population of India, as per Census 2001, 742 million live in rural areas and 285 million in urban areas comprising 72.2 per cent and 27.8 per cent of the population respectively.
3. Unofficially, the estimate is put around 60 million tonnes of waste generation annually.

best method for disposing of garbage is by composting it in sanitary landfills (Appaswamy, 1994). However, the most common practice in the country is dumping at landfill sites located around the city that are generally uncontrolled dumps. Dumping is also carried out illegally on private farmlands located in the city vicinity. One reason for this is the lack of landfill space in the cities. Often, sitting plans for potential landfills are strongly opposed by residents in the surrounding locality, which causes complications.

The municipal body is the main group involved in most urban SWM systems in India. Although other sub-systems, such as private organisations engaged in waste processing and informal recycling system, are actively involved in the waste management process in India, their activity is dependent on the operation of the municipal body (Sudhir, *et.al.*, 1996). It is broadly estimated that 10 to 40 per cent of the municipal budget is utilised for SWM (Bhide, 1990). Yet, it is generally argued that the Indian waste management system is starved of a resources when the demands of increasing urbanisation are taken into account (Shekdar, *et.al.*, 1992). Hence the services provided by the municipal authority are, for the most part, inefficient. It is estimated that, on average, 30 per cent of disposed solid waste are left uncollected (NIUA, 1989).

To address the problem of SWM in the country, the Ministry of Environment and Forest (MoEF), Government of India, has brought into force the Municipal Waste (Handling and Management) Rules, 2000. This specifies that the primary responsibility to manage SWM in the cities will now rest on the urban local bodies (ULBs). Although others such as private organisations engaged in waste processing and recycling system are involved in the country's waste management process, their activity is dependent on the operation of the municipal body. Further, as in most developing countries, there is an active informal network in the SWM process in Indian cities comprising of waste pickers, itinerant waste buyers and junk dealers. Existing as a parallel system with the formal process, it makes a significant contribution to the overall waste management process in Indian cities. There are varying estimates of the quantum of waste recovery taking place by the informal sector ranging from 6 to 7 per cent to around 15 per cent of waste generated (Bhide, 1990).

13.8.1 Solid Waste Management Status in Karnataka

Waste Flow in the Cities

The status of urban SWM in Karnataka is no different from the national scenario. Being one of the more urbanised states in the country with about 237 towns and urban agglomerations (Appendix A-13.6) and an urban population of about 34 per cent as compared to the national figures of about 27 per cent, the problem SWM is equally grave in Karnataka. According to the state of the Environment Report and Action Plan 2003 (Government of Karnataka, 2004), on an average 40 to 50 per cent of the total municipal waste in the state is generated in the six municipal corporations of Karnataka (Table 13.34).

TABLE 13.34

Municipal Sold Waste Generation per Day in Six City Corporations of Karnataka for 2002

City	*Population (2002)*	*Waste Generated (tonnes/day)*	*Waste Collected (tonnes/day)*	*Per Capita Waste* Generated (Grams/Day**)*
Bangalore	5882162	2500	1400	425.0
Mangalore	551701	250	200	453.1
Hubli/Dharwad	801442	250	200	311.9
Mysore	794677	230	183	289.4
Belgaum	516155	120	100	232.5
Gulbarga	452944	120	100	264.9
Total	**8999081**	**3470**	**2183**	**386**

Note: * indicate per capita waste generated=Waste generated/population.
** Figures rounded to the nearest decimals.

Source: Government of Karnataka, 2004.

Waste generation levels in a few other urban centres as estimated by studies carried out by Infrastructure Development Corporation (Karnataka) Limited (IDeCK) in 2003, is presented in (Table 13.35).

A case analysis of waste management practices in Bangalore city, studied as a proxy for similar urban centres (Beukering *et al.*, 1999), throws specific insights about waste generation and composition in cities. According to this study, commercial establishments are the major contributors of municipal waste in the city, accounting for about 39 per cent of the total while households (domestic waste) contribute about 18 per cent (Table 13.36). The waste generated by various other institutions accounted for 4 per cent. Although industries also generate a significant among the solid waste, this is generally high quality recyclables and is recovered by recycling and reuse.[4]

TABLE 13.35

MSW Generation in Select Cities/Towns

Size-class	*ULB Name*	*Population (2001)*	*Total Amount of Municipal Solid Waste (MSW) Generated per Day*	*Total* Amount of MSW Collected per Day Generation (Grams)*	*Per Capita*
Class I	Hospet	163284	60.75	35.3	372.05
	Hassan	116628	50.70	36.0	434.72
	Gadag	154849	65.70	35.4	424.28
	Bidar	172298	51.06	45.0	296.35
	Chitradurga	122549	50.00	20.3	408.00
	Bhadravathi	160392	52.00	45.0	324.21
	Bellary	317000	90.00	62.0	283.91
	Davangere	363780	180.00	130.0	494.80
	Mandya	131211	35.00	25.0	266.75
Class II	Gangavathi	93249	35.00	18.0	375.34
	Channapattana	63561	25.00	20.0	393.32
	Ramanagara	79365	30.00	20.0	378.00
Class III	Maddur	26456	7.00	6.0	264.59
	Arasikere	45160	14.00	13.5	310.01
	Belur	20225	8.00	6.0	395.55
	Holenarasipura	27018	12.00	10.0	444.15
	Ullala	49862	16.00	16.0	320.89
Class IV	-	-	-	-	-
Class V	Alur	6133	1.00	1.0	163.05
	N.R. Pura	7441	5.00	1.0	671.95
Class VI	Shringeri	4253	1.50	1.5	352.69

Note: Figures rounded to the nearest decimals.

Source: Table prepared from SWM data provided by Infrastructure Development Corporation (Karnataka) Limited, Bangalore.

This case study of Bangalore city also showed that the waste generated largely consists of organic and other biodegradable matter (43 per cent of the total generation). Comparatively the percentage of recyclables like paper, glass, plastic, metals, card board/packaging materials, and rubber was lower at about 36 per cent (Table 13.37). Plastic and glass are largely segregated at the household level or by rag pickers. However, the waste that flows into the public dustbins is mixed waste, often containing household hazards like glass pieces, batteries, polythene bags, etc. Though the study showed that the amount of environmentally unfriendly wastes like polythene carry bags is rather low, its impact is still serious given its potential harmful characteristics. Moreover, of the total waste generated, 1451 tonnes of waste per day was collected in public dustbins located at different points in the city (Table 13.38). The analysis showed that about 245 tonnes of waste per day was gone or unaccounted waste. This included debris and unorganised waste that remained uncollected. More worrying is the fact that about one

TABLE 13.36

Source-wise Generation of Solid Waste in Bangalore

(Tonnes per Day)

Stakeholders	*Volume*	*Percentage*
Households	650	18.00
Commercial Establishments	1456	39.00
- Markets	369	
- Hotels	1066	
Institutes	128	4.00
- Hospitals	20	
- Offices	15	
- Educational Institutions	92	
Industries	1399	39.00
Total	**3613***	**100**

Note: *Although various estimates put the total waste generated in Bangalore at around 2000 to 2500 tonnes per day, in this study the estimate of 3613 tonnes per day is mainly because industrial waste (approximately 1400 tonnes per day) was also considered as a component of the total urban solid waste generated in the city.

Source: Beukering *et al.*, 1999.

TABLE 13.37

Physical Composition of the Waste Generated in Bangalore

(Tonnes per Day)

Composition	*Percentage*	*Share of the Waste that Goes to Public Dustbins (Percentage)*
Glass	2.9	0.24
Plastic	6.7	0.48
Paper/Card Board	16.5	3.12
Metal	1.5	0.05
Rubber	9.9	0.0
Organic Waste	33.4	55.12
Other Biodegradable	9.2	1.92
Hazardous Hospital Waste	2.0	1.06
Miscellaneous*	17.9	

Note: *This includes old clothes, gunny bags, coconut shells, debris, etc.

Source: Beukering *et al.*, 1999.

4. In this study, other types of industrial wastes such as sludge, effluents, etc. were not taken into consideration as the focus was on urban solid waste. Only the solid waste generated by industries was considered.

per cent of the hospital waste got mixed with municipal waste in the public dustbins. This problem is also pointed out in the State of the Environment Report and Action Plan–2003, which says, "... about 1 to 2 per cent of biomedical waste gets mixed with municipal solid waste in the community bins" (Government of Karnataka, 2004: 135). Given the extent of scavenging at the dumpsites, this is a dangerous trend.

TABLE 13.38

Municipal Solid Waste Disposal by Source in Bangalore

(Tonnes per Day)

Waste Producers	*Waste Generated*	*Waste Disposed*			
		Public Dustbin	*Composted Privately*	*Incinerated Waste*	*Dumped/ Gone Waste*
Households	650.5	346.7	56.0	0.0	27.4
Commercial Establishments	1435.9	1055.9	0.0	0.0	4.9
Markets	369.5	246.1	0.0	0.0	1.9
Hotels	1066.4	809.7	0.0	0.0	3.2
Institutes	127.5	44.7	0.0	0.3	21.2
Hospitals	20.4	16.0	0.0	0.3	4.1
Offices	14.8	14.8	0.0	0.0	0.0
Educational Institutions	92.4	13.9	0.0	0.0	17.2
Industries	1399.2	3.8	0.0	0.0	191.6
Total	**3613.0**	**1451.0**	**56.0**	**0.3**	**245.4**

Source: Beukering *et al.*, 1999.

Stakeholders in the Refuse Collection and Disposal Services

The main stakeholders in the urban SWM process are the waste processors (all agents directly active in waste processing–that is, service producers) and waste generators (all agents generating and consuming services provided by the waste processors)–

- The waste processors consist of waste pickers, itinerant waste buyers, middlemen like junk dealers and wholesalers, the urban local body, and various recycling units, both private and government. While the first three agents constitute the informal network, the others are formal agents.[5]
- The waste generating categories comprise mainly of four types of agents, *viz.*, households, commercial establishments (markets and hotels), institutions (offices, educational institutions and hospitals), and industries (large, medium and small).

As laid down in the Karnataka Municipal Corporation Act, 1976, keeping the city clean is a responsibility of the civic administration. But the municipal bodies alone cannot perform this activity. The SWM process has various dimensions that require the involvement of the private, the non-government and the informal sector. This necessitates cooperation and coordination among the various agents, rather than an insular approach, for better management of urban waste. While the three agents in the informal sector and the municipality are directly involved in the waste collection activities, waste processing is done by the recycling units that receive the recyclables from the middlemen and the municipality.

However, one problem often observed is the multiplicity of agencies dealing with SWM services. In Bangalore, for instance besides the Municipal Corporation, the other agencies involved are Bangalore Water Supply and Sewage Board (BWSSB), The Metropolitan Region Development Agency (BMRDA) and the Karnataka Urban Infrastructure Development and Finance Corporation (KUIDFC). Because of this gaps and duplications can be observed in the provision of service and planning (Aziz, *et al.*, 2002). For example, both BMRDA and Bangalore Development Authority (BDA) have jurisdiction over the BDA area although BMRDA was constituted with a mandate to look after larger areas. Further, sewerage is with BWSSB, but this is not coordinated with the BMC which also has responsibility relating to drainage and SWM. With regard to slum upgradation, this responsibility is split among different agencies with no common line of direction for the development of slums as a result of which these areas are very badly serviced.

However, often, external actors—particularly the struggle between local and state level politics—influence the process for delivery of SWM services in both positive and negative ways. When the Bangalore Agenda Task Force (BATF) was constituted in November 1999 to provide an opportunity to public-private partnership, the Bangalore Mahanagara Palike (BMP) with the support of BATF launched the 'Swachha Bangalore' programme. Through door-to-door solid waste collection system, this programme targeted

5. This division is arbitrary. Informal stakeholders are generally those who are not registered with the municipality and do not pay tax. For a number of recycling plants located in Bangalore, this characteristic also holds. Moreover, they often employed informal labour. However, since the majority of recycling plants are registered, they are grouped as part of the formal sector.

to bring cleanliness in the 128 health wards[6] in the city that are managed through Pourakarmikas of the corporation. The BATF managed to get pushcarts to collect door-to-door garbage costing Rs. 5500 a piece. But now with the new government in the state going slow on the fate of BATF, the continuation of such a partnership is dependent on the political will and the power of the civic leaders. The Bangalore Mahanagar Palike, today, does not have an annual maintenance contract in place and the net result is that many of the pushcarts are lying around with broken wheels and parts missing (*Times of India*, Bangalore Edition, 27 July 2004).

Solid Waste Management (SWM) Practices

SWM encompasses the range of activities, such as: (i) prevention, either by reducing the content of waste or by reusing it; (ii) recycling the waste into secondary raw material or as a source of energy; and (iii) disposal through land-filling. But, the reality is quite different from these environmentally sound options. A major problem regarding urban SWM pertains to the collection of waste generated. Though, door-to-door collection has been introduced in some wards of Bangalore and Mysore, a major portion of the waste generated gets collected in public dustbins and the waste that reaches disposal sites is usually mixed, containing plastic, glass, metals, etc. as waste segregation is not practised in most of the urban areas (Government of Karnataka, 2004). Moreover, a large quantity of waste that gets collected in the public dustbins remains uncollected (Tables 13.34 and 13.35). The waste collected is dumped in an uncontrolled manner or burnt in the open air, causing high levels of environmental damage.

Most of the urban localities in the state do not have appropriate dumpsites to dump the garbage and to compost it. In some cases, the municipal land is used for the purpose and in some other cases government land in the city outskirts are used (Table 13.39). Since the capacity of such dumpsites is inadequate in relation to the requirement (Appendix A-13.7) in cities like Bangalore it is common for the municipality to dump garbage in open spaces and on roadsides in the city outskirts. As on March 2005, all the local bodies have filed applications for authorisation under Municipal Solid Waste (MSW) Rules and the Karnataka State Polution Control Board has granted authorisation to all of them under Municipal Solid Waste (Management and Handling) Rules 2000. At Puttur and Karwar scientifically designed landfill site is ready and being used.

TABLE 13.39

Number of Dumpsites-City-wise (Notified and Unnotified)

Centre name	*No. of Legal Dumpsite*	*Area of Legal Dumpsite*	*Distance from City*	*No. of Illegal Dumpsite*	*Quantity of Waste to Dumpsite*
Bangalore	Nil *	0	0	N.A**	370 tonnes/day
Belgaum	1	8 acres	2 kms	1	N.A.
Gulbarga	1	15 acres		2	N.A.
Hubli	2	28 acres	3 kms	1	N.A.
Dharwad		10 acres	3 kms		
Mangalore	1	70 acres	15 kms	Nil	200 tonnes/day
Mysore	1	4 acres	5 kms	Nil	183 tonnes/day

Note: 1) N.A.= Not available.

2) * According to a Government Order No. RD 126 LGB 94, dated 11.11.1994, 9 landfill sites have been leased to the BCC from the government but these are still not been used due to local opposition and litigations.

3) ** dumped in the city outskirts (16-27 kms).

Source: City Corporations, Respective Cities.

For the efficient management of the solid waste, infrastructure facilities for storing, transporting, and dumping the garbage is needed. The general impression is that the number of dustbins provided is inadequate considering the quantity of waste generated and, these are typically of R.C.C. with capacities varying between 540 to 1100 litres which are difficult to maintain (KUIDFC, 2003). In a study carried out by the Institute for Social and Economic Change, Bangalore (Aziz, *et al.*, 2002), discussions with citizens also brought out the point that the dustbins are often not located at the right places because of which, in many cases, the garbage gets thrown in the vicinity and around the dustbins and not into them.

As for transport vehicles, municipalities either own or hire lorries/trucks, tractors, tippers and tricycles of different capacity. The general complaint among municipal authorities is that the number of vehicles available with them is woefully inadequate to the task of transporting garbage to the dumpsite. If one did an exercise relating the quantity of garbage generated in the urban area with the number of vehicles in functioning condition that are with the urban local body, and multiply by the capacities and trips that can be made in a day, this complaint appears to be genuine

6. Bangalore city has 100 administrative wards. These have been divided into 277 health wards for functional convenience. Of these, 147 health wards including two markets are under private contract system of cleanliness. The remaining 128 health wards are managed through *pourakarmikas*.

(Aziz, *et al.*, 2002). Some data about the number of public dustbins and transport vehicles with the urban local bodies is given in the following table (Table 13.40).

Regarding the work force employed for SWM, also, the situation is different in different city corporations. Generally speaking the number of *pourakarmikas*/health workers on the role of the municipality is determined by their load of work in the municipality in terms of not only managing waste but also cleaning the open and underground drains and municipal urinals. But traditionally, the practice is to deploy the work force according to the city population. It is now accepted in Karnataka, *vide* Government of Karnataka Circular No. HMA/118/MNM/17, dated June 30, 1997[7], that for a population of 500 in the city there should be one

TABLE 13.40

Infrastructure and Manpower of Select ULBs

Name of ULB	*PDBs*	*Number of Vehicles*
Ullal	40	1
Tumkur	450	6
Ramanagaram	150	2
Channapatna	65	2
Mandya	560	6
Maddur	74	1
Kundapur	100	2
Hassan	1560	7
Kolar	350	6
Chickmagalur	150	5
K.G.F.	129	8

Source: KUIDFC (2003).

BOX 13.3

Strategies Identified Here to Address the Problem of Urban Solid Waste Management

Strategies 1	*Measures* 2	*Interventions* 3
1. Increasing waste segregation through source separation.	• Create public awareness.	• Use of media and newspaper. • Role of NGOs/CBOs. • Facilitating collection from source.
2. Strengthening institutional Interventions	• Increasing NGOs' involvement and encouraging community participation. • Privatisation of municipal solid waste systems. • Integrating the contributions of informal sector, particularly waste pickers' contribution, in the process of waste removal and recovery. • Developing and strengthening regulatory mechanisms, especially relating to hazardous waste.	• Strengthening the municipality SWM system by increasing its resources (levying taxes on related services) and its authority by giving it policing powers to prevent public littering and ensure public conformity to civic regulations. • Policy changes in the urban local government allowing for interface with the non-government and private organisations. • Recognised community representation in the municipal solid waste system (formation of resident welfare associations or area committees with people's representation) • Official policy for door-to-door collection either under the municipality, or a community organisation, or through private initiatives. interventions.
3. Increasing waste recovery	• Enhancing capacities of waste processing and recycling units.	• Government policies for providing facilities and exemptions to the recycling units to enable them to increase their production and to sell their products at a competitive price.
4. Popularising reuse practices	• Government itself setting an example. • Educating public.	• Writing down this in the government's purchase rules. • Advertisements in TV & assistance to NGOs to demonstrate in the community.

7. Quoted by the Karnataka State Finance Commission, Report of the State Finance Commission, Government of Karnataka, Bangalore, 1996, pp. 136.

Pourakarmika. However, the ratio between the health workers and the population varies between cities (Government of Karnataka, 2004). For instance, in Bangalore for every 301 persons there is one health worker, whereas in Gulbarga for a population of 631 persons one worker is available (Government of Karnataka, 2004). The following table (Table 13.41) presents the number of *pourakarmikas* working *vis-à-vis* the required number. It is evident that the number of these workers falls short of the desired number in the cities under reference. The overall gap in respect of the 5 cities is 46 per cent, thus pointing to the fact that the municipal administration functioning under severe constraints with regard to their workforce (Aziz *et al.*, 2002).

TABLE 13.41

Actual Number of *Pourakarmikas* and their Desired Number

Name of the City	*Estimated Population (in Lakhs in 1998)*	*Desired Number of Pourakarmikas*	*Actual Number of Pourakarmikas*	*Percentage of Gap*
Bangalore	50.00	10000	5504	44.96
Mysore	7.58	1516	863	43.07
K.G.F.	2.65	530	306	42.27
Robertsonpet	1.75	350	125	64.29
Shimoga	2.59	518	388	25.10
Bijapur	2.30	460	176	60.74

Source: Aziz *et.al.*, 2002, p. 7.

13.8.2 Agenda for the Future

Considering the present rate of waste generation in the state, it is estimated that by 2011 the projected municipal waste generation will be about 7424.8 metric tonnes per day (Government of Karnataka, 2004). While only about 9 per cent of the recyclable material (plastic and paper) is recovered due to non-segregation of wastes, it is hoped that this can be increased to 15 per cent by 2010 by practicing segregation (Government of Karnataka, 2004).

It is thus obvious that urban refuse collection and disposal service need to receive priority in future efforts. The priority areas that need to be addressed are:

- inadequate municipal service;
- unscientific disposal system;
- lack of civic awareness/waste management leading to unsegregated waste generation and disposal;
- existence of an extensive informal network driven mainly by market forces and functioning at subsistence level;
- insufficient capacity for waste processing, particularly organic wastes which is abundant; and
- a small market for recycled waste products and poor marketing of these products.

As of now, very little concerted effort has been made in this direction. Considering that a number of marginal and poor sections are active in the process as informal labour, any strategy to strengthen the waste management service needs to benefit the society as well as allow for income generating opportunities to the poor along its route. No amount of urban planning will translate into reality unless the government takes the required initiative and makes the necessary inputs, which do not have to be only financial. The BATF initiative on the part of the state government was a positive step in this direction. However, as matters stand today, its future is in doubt.

References

Achar K.P. (1997). "Documenting People's Knowledge & Priority for Biodiversity and Conservation through Peoples Register: A Case Study of Mala Village Panchayat, Karkala taluk, Karnataka", WWF, India, New Delhi, KSCST, Bangalore and Bhuvanendra College, Karkala.

AFC (2000). *Karnataka Tank Improvement Project AFC Report*.

Appaswamy, P. (1994). "Institutional Options in the Provision of Urban Services: The Case of Solid Waste Management in Indian Cities", Paper presented at the Workshop on *Linkages in Urban Solid Waste Management*, 18-20 April, Indian Institute of Science, Bangalore (unpublished).

Australian Agency for International Development (2001). *AusAid Strategic Plan: Improving Effectiveness in a Changing Environment*, Australia.

Aziz, Abdul, N. Sivanna, M. Nageswara Rao, Madhushree Sekher, C. Charles Nelson, B. Vijaya Kumar (2002). *Sustainability in Practice: Exploring Innovations in Domestic Solid Waste Management in India*, Institute for Social and Economic Change, Bangalore (unpublished).

Bangalore Metropolitan Transport Corporation (2003). *Annual Report*, 2003.

Beukering, van Pieter, Madhushree Sekher, Reyer Gerlagh and Vijay Kumar (1999). "Analysing Urban Solid Waste in Developing Countries: A Perspective on Bangalore, India", *CREED Working Paper Series No.24*, International Institute for Environment and Development, London.

Bhat, D. (1997). "Documenting Peoples Knowledge & Priority for Biodiversity Conservation: A Case Study of Kalasa Village, Sirsi Taluk, Karnataka, Sahyadri Parisara Vardhini, Yedahali", Karnataka State Council for Scicne and Technology, Bangalore & BCPP, WWF, India, New Delhi.

Bhide, A.D. and B.B. Sundaresan (1984). *Solid Waste Management in Developing Countries*, Indian National Scientific Documentation Centre, New Delhi.

Bhide, A.D. (1990). *Regional Overview on Solid Waste Management in South East Asia Region*, World Health Organization, New Delhi.

BWSSB (2002). *Bangalore Water Supply and Environmental Sanitation Master Plan*, Bangalore.

Central Water Commission (1996). Status of Projects monitored by Central Water Commission, 1993 – 1994, Central Water Commission, New Delhi.

Centre for Policy Research (2001). *The Future of Urbanisation, Spread and Shape in Selected States*, New Delhi.

CPCB (2000). *Management of Municipal Solid Waste*, Central Pollution Control Board, New Delhi.

CMDR (2004). *Incidence and Effects of Drought: A Case Study for Karnataka*.

CSO (Central Statistical Organisation) (1997). *Compendium on Environmental Statistics*, Government of India, New Delhi.

Dahanukar, N., R., Rant, M. Mahabaleshwarkar and S. Kharat (2001). "Changes in Fresh Water Fish Fauna in Northern Western Ghats", Pune, India in *Tropical Ecosysytems: Structure, Diversity and Human Welfare*. Proceedings of the International Conference on *Tropical Ecosystems* , edited by K.N. Ganeshayer, R. Umashankar and K.S. Bawa, pp. 724-726, Oxford-IBH, India.

Elrich, de sa, (1999). "Present Status of The Coastal Environment in India", *Coastin*, September p5.

Gadgil, M. (1996). "Documenting Diversity: An Experiment", *Current Science*, 270 (1996), pp. 36-44.

Gosain, A. K. and Sandhya Rao (2003). "Impacts of Climate Change on Water Sector", pp.171-192 in *Climate Change and India- Vulnerability Assessment and Adaptation*, P.R Shukla , Subodh K. Sharma, N.H. Ravindranath., Amit Garg, Sumana Bhattacharya (eds.), Pub. Universities Press (India) Private Limited.

Government of India (1991). *Census of India*, Town Directory of Karnataka, New Delhi.

———. (1998). *Launching a Clean City Campaign in the States in the 50th Year of Independence*, Brochure Published by the Ministry of Urban Affairs and Employment (Department of Urban Development) in Quarterly Journal of the All India Institute of Local Self-Governance, Vol. LXIX, (2), April-June: 96-105.

———. (2001). *Census of India*, Provisional Population Totals, New Delhi.

Government of Karnataka (1995). *Karnataka Land Reforms (Amendment) Act, 1995*, Bangalore.

———. (2003). *Annual Report 2002-03*, Urban Development Department, Bangalore.

———. (2004). *State of the Environment Report and Action Plan–2003*, Department of Forest, Ecology and Environment, Bangalore.

Hulme, M. (1994). "Validation of Large-scale Precipitation Fields in General Circulation Models", in *Global Precipitations and Climate Change*, M. Desbois and F. Desalmand, (eds.), pp. 387-406 Springer-Verlag, Berlin.

Hussain, S.A. and Achar K.P. (eds.) (1999). *Biodiversity of the Western Ghats Complex of Karnataka: Resource Potentials and Sustainable Utilization*, pp. 253, Biodiversity Initiative Trust, Mangalore.

Karnataka Forest Department and Department for International Development (1999). *Western Ghats Forestry Project–Project Experience and Achievements 1992-2000*, Project Directorate, Western Ghats Forestry Project, Bangalore, December.

Karnataka State Pollution Control Board (2004). *Annual Report*, 2004.

Kiran R., & Ramachandra T.V. (1999 March). "Status of Wetlands in Bangalore and Its Conservation Aspects", *ENVIS Journal of Human Settlements*, pp. 16-24.

KSCST (1995). *Air Quality in Bangalore: A Status Report on Atmospheric Pollution in Bangalore City*, Karnataka State Council for Science and Technology, Indian Institute of Science, Bangalore

KUIDFC (2003). *State of Urban Infrastructure in Karnataka*, Karnataka Urban Infrastructure Development and Finance Corporation, Bangalore. (Draft report).

Kumar, K. and J. Parikh (1998). "Climate Change Impacts on Indian Agriculture: The Ricardian Approach" in A. Dinar, R. Mendelsohn, J. Everson, J. Parika, A. Sanghi, K. Kumar, J. McKinsey, and S. Lonergan (eds.), *Measuring the Impact of Climate Change on Indian Agriculture*, World Bank, Washington DC.

Kurien, J. (1999). "State and Shrimp: A Preliminary Analysis of The Economic and Ecological Consequences of India's Fishery Policies", *FAO Fisheries Report* No. 572, Supplement, FAO, Rome.

Kushalappa, A.K. (2003). *State of Environmental Report and Action Plan 2002-2003*, Draft Final Report:- Land and Forest Degradation Sector.

Mc Michael, AJM Ando, R. Carcavallo, P F Pstein, A. Haines G., Jendritzky, L. Kalkstein, R. Odongo, J. Patz, and W. Pivr (1996). *Human Population Health In Climage Change 1995: Impacts, Adaptations and Mitigation of Climate Change*. Contribution of Working Group 11 to the Second Assessment Report of the Intergovernmental Panel on Climate Change [Watson, R.T., Mc Zinyowera and R.H. Mois (eds.)], NY, USA, pp. 561-584.

Ministry of Environment and Forests (2004). *India's Initial National Communication to the United Nations Framework on Climate Change*, p.268.

MPEDA (2002). *Marine Products Export Review*, various issues, Marine Products Export Development Authority, Cochin.

Myers, N., R.A Mittermeier, C.G Mittermeier, G.A.B da Fonesca, and J.Kent, (2000). "Biodiversity hotspots for conservation priorities", *Nature*, 403, pp. 853-858.

Nadkarni, M.V. (1999). "Environment in Karnataka: A Status Report", *Economic and Political Weekly*, 34(38): 2735-2744.

NBSAP (2002). *National Biodiversity Strategy and Action Plan*, Ministry of Environment and Forests, Government of India, December.

Ninan, K.N. (2001). "The Economics of Biodiversity Conservation–The Case of Tropical Forests in the Western Ghats", ISEC, Bangalore, *Mimeo*.

NIUA (1989). *Upgrading Municipal Services: Norms and Financial Implications* (Vol. I), National Institute of Urban Affairs, New Delhi.

Overseas Development Agency (1991). *Biological Diversity and Developing Countries: Issues and Options*, Natural Resources and Environment Department, London.

Ramachandran, H. and G. S. Sastry (2001). "An Inventory and Typology of Slums in Bangalore", in Hans Schenk (ed.) *Living in India's Slums*, Manohar, New Delhi.

Ramachandra, T.V., R. Kirsan, N. Ahalya, (2002). *Status, Conservation and Management of Wetlands*, Centre for Ecological Sciences, Indian Institute of Science, Allied Publishers, August.

Ravindranath N.H., R. Sukumarand P. Deshingkar (1998). "Climate Change and Forests: Impacts and Adaptation-A Regional Assessment for the Western Ghats, India", *Report on Atmospheric Environment Issues in Developing Countries Series*– No.4. Stockholm Environment Institute.

Ravindranath N.H, N.V. Joshi, R. Sukumar, K. Indu, Murthy, and H.S. Suresh (2003). "Vulnerability and Adaptation to Climate Change in the Forest Sector", in *Climate Change and India- Vulnerability Assessment and Adaptation*, P.R Shukla, Subodh K. Sharma, N.H. Ravindranath. Amit Garg, Sumana, Bhattacharya (ed.)., pp. 227-265, Universities Press (India) Private Limited.

Rao V. L., S. Prakasa and V. K. Tewari (1979). *A Structure of an Indian Metropolis*, Bangalore.

Rao, A.M. (2001). "An Overview of Indian Mangroves", M.S. Thesis. University of Strathelyde, UK.

Rege, S.N., Shreedhara, V., Jagadish, D.S., Singh, T.S., Murthy, T.V.R., and Garg, J.K. (1996). *Wetlands of Karnataka* (project report). Ahmedabad, India: Karnataka State Remote Sensing Application Centre, Bangalore and Space Applications Centre (ISRO).

Reid S.J. (2000). *Ozone & Climate Change: A Beginners Guide*, Gordon & Breach Sci Publishers, p. 210.

Repetto, R. (1990). "Deforestation in the Tropics", *Scientific American*, 262:18-24.

Sampath, V. (1993). "Development of Aquaculture and Coastal Fisheries in India: Ecological And Economic Aspects", Proceedings of the workshop on *Coastal Fisheries and Aquaculture in India*, Zentrum fur Marine Tropenkologie (ZMT), Bremen, Germany.

Sarkar, L. and B.E., Yadav (1996). "Larvivorus Fishes of Western Ghats, Maharashtra: Biocontrol of Malaria", *Geobios new reports*, 15:137-138.

Sastry, G. S. and Janarthan Rao (2002). "Emerging Development Issues in a Hill-Forest Region", *Social Science Review*, 4(2): 58-78.

Sastry G. S. (1985). *Metropolitan Cities Environment: India*, Nagaralok, 17(3): 1-11.

———. (1988). "Bangalore Metropolitan Transportation Planning: Some Observations and Suggestions", *The Indian Geographical Journal*, 63 (1), pp.10-21.

———. (2004). "Socio-Economic and Ecological Characteristics of Peri- Urban Region", International Workshop on *Energy and Transport in Peri-Urban Interface*, 12-14 July, TERI, Southern Center, Bangalore.

Shekdar, A.V., K.N. Krishnaswamy, V.G. Tikadar and A.D. Bhide (1991). "Long Term Planning for Solid Waste Management in India", *Waste Management Research*, Vol. 9:511-523.

Shekdar, A.V., K.N. Krishnaswamy, V.G. Tikadar and A.D. Bhide (1992). "Indian Solid Waste Management Systems: Jaded Systems in Need of Resource Augmentation", *Waste Management Research*, 12:379-387.

Shivaramakrishan, K. C. (2002). Seminar Presentation on Future of Urbanisation.

Shukla, P. R. (2003). "Climate Change Vulnerability Assessment and Adaptation: The Context", in Shukla. P.R, Subodh, K. Sharma, N.H. Ravindranath, Amit Garg, Sumana Bhattacharya (eds.), *Climate Change and India: Vulnerability Assessment and Adaptation*, pp. 1-28, Universities Press (India) Private Limited.

Sudhir, V., V.R. Muraleedharan and G. Srinivasan (1996). "Integrated Solid Waste Management in Urban India: A Critical Operational Research Framework", *Socio-economic Planning Science*, 30, (3): 163-181.

Tewari D.N. (1993). "Conservation of Biodiversity", Paper presented at the Indo-British Workshop on *Biodiversity and Forest Ecosystems*, organised by Karnataka Forest Department and DFD, held on 4-6 February at Bangalore.

Venkateswaran, Sandhya (1994). "Managing Waste: Ecological, Economic and Social Dimensions", *Economic and Political Weekly*, Vol. XX, (19), November 5-12:2907-2911.

WHO (1991). *Regional Overview of Solid Waste Management in South East Asian Region*, World Health Organization, New Delhi.

World Bank (1998). *World Development Indicators, 1998*. The World Bank, Washington DC.

Yap, W. G. (1999). "Viewpoint On Formulating Policies For Sustainable Shrimp Culture", FAO *Fisheries Report No.572*, Supplement. Rome.

APPENDIX A-13.1

Emission Factors for Vehicles

Type of Vehicle	*Pollutant (kg/1000 kms)*				
	SPM	*SO_2*	*No_x*	*HC*	*CO*
Light Duty Petrol Powered	0.33	0.08	3.20	6.00	40.00
Light Duty Diesel Powered	0.45	0.39	0.99	0.28	1.10
Heavy Duty Diesel Powered	0.75	1.50	21.00	2.10	12.70
Motorcycles	0.20	0.02	0.07	10.00	17.00*

Note: * It was taken as 21.25 in place of 17 to accommodate high quantity of CO emission from three wheelers. The emission from three wheelers is estimated to be one and a half times that of two wheelers.

Source: WHO Offset Publication No. 61.

APPENDIX A-13.2

Average Distance Covered by Various Categories of Vehicles in Bangalore City (Year of Information 1992-93)

Vehicle Description	*Average Distance Covered Km/Day*
Petrol Driven Vehicles	
2 wheelers	40
3 wheelers	75
4 wheelers	70
Diesel driven vehicles	
Heavy motor vehicles (buses	207
Heavy motor vehicles (goods)	40*
Light motor vehicles)	75
Heavy motor vehicles (tractors, trailers, etc.)	100

Note: * within city limits.

Source: South Zonal Office, Central Pollution Control Board.

APPENDIX A-13.3

Distribution of Polluting Industries by Hazardous Waste Generated in Karnataka State (District-wise)

District	*Units Identified under HWM Rules*	*Hazardous Waste Generated in MT/A*
Bangalore (Rural and Urban)	859	13190
Dakshina Kannada and Udupi	37	4594
Mysore	111	5955
Chamrajnagar	2	1
Kodagu	1	0
Gulbarga	37	683
Bijapur	11	81
Belgaum	103	575
Bagalkot	30	60
Bellary	36	29993
Dharwad	51	2418
Uttara Kannada	19	4403
Haveri	12	4
Gadag	6	41
Mandya	11	51
Tumkur	62	255
Hassan	17	247
Chickmagalur	9	345
Bidar	24	5987
Raichur	19	635
Koppal	16	17064
Davangere	37	2065
Chitradurga	32	32
Shimoga	59	4056
Kolar	61	240
Total	**1662**	**92975**

Source: E&E, Government, Karnataka.

APPENDIX A-13.4

Status of Water Pollution Monitoring in Karnataka:2005

Type of Industry	*Total No. of Industries*	*ETP under Operation*	*ETP under Construction*	*ETP under Planning*	*Connected to UGD*	*Defaulters*	*Closed Industry*
Large	1194	761	16	27	256	4	130
Medium	1792	732	17	26	692	5	320
Small	11027	3849	88	225	3922	108	2835
Total	14013	5342	121	278	4870	117	3285

Source: Department of E&E, Government, Karnataka.

APPENDIX A-13.5

The Indian Census Classification of Towns/Urban Agglomerations

It is the tradition in the Indian censuses to classify the towns/urban agglomerations into six size classes according to their population size *viz.*, Class I, II, III, IV, V and VI. The population range of these six size classes is as below. Class-I is sub-classified into seven sub-classes M7 to M1 according to the population size of the urban agglomeration/city.

Size-class	*Sub-classes*	*Population*
Class I	a) M7	5000000 and above
	b) M6	2000000 - 4999999
	c) M5	1000000 - 1999999
	d) M4	500000 - 999999
	e) M3	300000 - 499999
	f) M2	200000 - 299999
	g) M1	100000 - 199999
Class II	-	50000 - 99999
Class III	-	20000 - 49999
Class IV	-	10000 - 19999
Class V	-	5000 - 9999
Class VI	-	Less than 5000

APPENDIX A-13.6

Class-wise Population of UA/Towns in Karnataka, 2001

The following table presents the total number of towns and urban agglomerations and total population for the different size classes of towns in Karnataka as per 2001 Population Census.

Size-class of Towns	*No. of UAs/Towns*	*Population*
All Classes	237	17919858
Class I	24	12043036
Class II	27	1726134
Class III	101	3096525
Class IV	53	839021
Class V	27	192477
Class VI	5	22665

APPENDIX A-13.7

Projected Requirement of Land for Dumpsite (Composting) and Landfill Site for Next 10 Years

As per the guidelines given in the national manual on Municipal Solid Waste Management published by the government of India, Ministry of Urban Development in May 2000, the requirement of land for dumpsites in selected cities of Karnataka are as follows:

City Corporation	*Area Required for Dump-site (Composting)*	*Area Required for Landfill Site*
Bangalore	112.5 acres	129.6 acres
Mysore	13 acres	11.91 acres
Belgaum	8 acres	7.04 acres
Mangalore	13 acres	12.95 acres
Gulbarga	8 acres	6.216 acres
Hubli/Dharwad	13 acres	12.95 acres

Landfill area required for Bangalore is 129.6 acres, according to AusAid-2001 (AusAid, 2001). In the same manner the landfill area requirement for other cities has been calculated.

APPENDIX A-13.8

Distribution of Polluting Industries by Level of Pollution and Hazardous Waste Generated by District

District	*Red*	*Orange*	*Green*	*Total*	*Hazardous Waste Generating Unit*	*Hazardous Waste Generated per annum (in MT)*
Bagalkot	86	62	14	162	15	676.74
Bangalore(Rural)	200	99	145	444		-
Bangalore (Urban)	1349	469	2218	4036	592	11928.13*
Belgaum	381	71	102	554	70	3578.58
Bellary	318	59	310	687	25	28449.60
Bidar	163	28	77	268	25	5076.75
Bijapur	88	22	21	131	8	38.29
Chamrajnagar	3	2	5	10	1	45.60
Chickmagalur	4	19	106	129	3	783.0
Chitradurga	73	4	118	195	6	55.0
Kodagu	1	0	0	1	0	-
Davanagere	114	46	143	303	9	24.0
Dakshina Kannada	197	116	353	666	38	2773.13
Dharwad	159	143	124	426	51	1517.81
Gadag	6	10	14	30	10	75.72
Gulbarga	179	398	54	631	26	374.70
Hassan	63	33	121	217	15	651.94
Haveri	12	9	11	32	11	36.0
Koppal	36	72	30	138	20	16852.33
Kolar	113	43	140	296	9	316.06
Mandya	97	59	57	213	8	23.52
Mysore	273	108	290	671	80	4348.72
Raichur	66	40	175	281	24	396.58
Shimoga	140	32	170	342	16	3559.33
Tumkur	108	47	37	192	25	140.39
Udupi	119	0	48	167	-	-
Uttara Kannada	171	63	90	324	20	4390.60
Karnataka	4519	2054	4973	11546	1096	86136.56

Source: * Bangalore Rural and Urban Districts.

Note: KSPCB as on 31-3-2002 and 2002-03 *Annual Report.*

APPENDIX A-13.9

Details of the Financial Progress of the Forestry and Environment Project of Eastern Plains of Karnataka: 1996-97 to 2003-04

Category	*1996-97*	*1997-98*	*1998-99*	*1999-00*	*2000-01*	*2000-02*	*2002-03*	*2003-04**	*Cumulative***	
	Achieved Progress in Rupees (Crores)								*Target*	*Achieved*
Afforestation	2.051	38.892	70.379	77.568	68.498	86.105	40.753	34.541	454.605	418.77
Civil Works		1.427	8.894	13.828	17.722	7.941	1.958	1.096	74.072	52.865
Salaries		6.169	11.926	15.249	16.141	17.438	16.787		76.933	83.710
Equipment	0.016	0.265	1.153	0.760	2.448	5.703	6.902	13.050	63.185	30.298
Repair	0.013	1.375	1.003	1.973	1.799	1.704	1.747	2.298	19.262	11.912
Overseas Training		0.807	1.128	0.662	0.841	0.554	0.889		14.401	4.880
Local Training		0.063	0.849	0.479		0.674	1.088	1.250	11.205	4.403

contd. ...

...contd. ...

Category	*1996-97*	*1997-98*	*1998-99*	*1999-00*	*2000-01*	*2000-02*	*2002-03*	*2003-04**	*Cumulative***	
	Achieved Progress in Rupees (Crores)								*Target*	*Achieved*
Vehicles		0.614	1.185	0.828	0.399	0.678	0.640		5.855	4.344
Research	0.020	1.635	2.549	4.549		0.187	0.296	0.194	2.971	9.430
Total	**2.100**	**51.247**	**99.066**	**115.846**	**107.848**	**120.983**	**71.060**	**52.429**	**722.489**	**620.629**

Note: * March 2004 provisional.

** Revised target.

Source: Status report of the Eastern plains (2004), Karnataka Forest Department, April 2004.

APPENDIX A-13.10

Financial Outlays and Achievements of Different Schemes from 1997-98 to 2002-03 (in Lakhs)

Schemes	*1997-98*		*1998-99*		*1999-00*		*2000-01*		*2001-02*		*2002-03*	
	Phy.	*Ach.*	*Phy.*	*Ach.*	*Phy.*	*Ach.*	*Phy.*	*Ach.*	*Phy.*	*Ach.*	*Phy.*	*Ach.*
CSS of Conservation and Development of NTFP Including Medicinal Plants	—	—	50	—	55	—	55.3	27.9	36.12	—	—	—
Ecotourism	20	12.3	30	11	10	6.96	0.1	—	5	—	1	—
Van Vigyan Kendra	15	3.15	10	2.46	5	2.45	0.1	—	2	2	1	1
Social Forestry Project	867.9	628.8	947.7	690	195.7	148	233.9	144.7	243	150.4	169.4	110.4
Soil Conservation and Afforestation	109.9	51.2	84	30.9	76.8	33	75.8	33.8	93.65	46.8	98.75	46.16
Integrated Afforestation and Eco-development Project	43.6	15.1	200	—	172	54.7	210	—	176.5	10.38	61.5	—
Soil Conservation in the River Valley Project	90.2	8.4	91.6	10.7	113.3	18.4	111.7	19.6	105.3	10.4	167.2	0.68
Minor Forest produce	50	6.9	5.9	3.0	9	2.05	11.7	6.05	11.7	4.95	34.5	25.3
Integrated Development of Western Ghats	305.4	155	131	—	400.4	153	569.4	183.4	330.4	113.4	168.6	66.7
Development of Degraded Forests	100	58	130	51.7	20	17.1	5	3	60	26.28	70	53
Greening of Urban Areas	185	130	180	52	45	7.2	40	6.4	60	42.1	5.0	2.94
Roadside Plantations Scheme	75	46.8	50	27.2	5	3.5	0.1	—	5	1.98	3	2.54
Raising of Seedlings for Public Distribution	67	32.4	25	18.2	3	2.5	0.1	0.98	6.5	0.5	3	1.85
Tribal Sub Plan (State)	20	13.6	66	17.7	100	22	86	9.99	108	15.8	14	13.3

Note: Phy—Financial Outlay/target.

Ach—Financial Achievement.

Source: Annual Reports of the Karnataka State Forest Department, Government of Karnataka.

Chapter 14

Agricultural and Allied Sectors: Need for Re-Engineering

14.1 Introduction

14.1.1 Introduction

Agricultural sector of Karnataka is characterised by vast steppe of drought-prone region and sporadic patches of irrigated area. Thus a large share of agricultural land of the state is exposed to rainfed conditions with severe agro-climatic and resource constraints. Given this, farmers have no other option but to grow low value- high risk crops at the cost of an erratic performance. Coexisting with this are a few patches of high-value and high-tech agriculture emerging recently in the state. In an overall analysis agricultural sector of the state is known for its achievements on the growth front despite severe climatic and strong resource constraints. As a consequence Karnataka's agriculture is both diversified and segmented in many ways. It is a matter of deep concern that even though this sector directly impacts the overall growth as well as distribution performance of the state economy, it has not been on the forefront in investment portfolio during recent past. It is feared that the sector may confront another strong phase of stagnation.

Despite the presence of severe climatic and resource constraints agricultural sector of Karnataka could record satisfactory growth performance to remain at the median level in any cross-section comparison.

As history tells us, Karnataka has always taken pragmatic initiatives on policy front be it land reforms, democratic decentralisation, understanding regional diversity or human development (through HDI) at desegregated level and understanding WTO for rigorous participation in international trade. Despite all these in most of the across states comparisons, Karnataka occupies the unenviable position being placed at the average or the median level. (Bhalla and Singh 2001, Deshpande *et al.* 2004) From one point of view, this can be interpreted as an average response to the developmental initiatives and not buckling down under the pressure of acute production constraints. But from another viewpoint, this also indicates inability to climb up in the developmental hierarchy despite remaining at an average level for a long time. Probably, the developmental efforts are so critically managed that the state continues in the position without sliding down in the hierarchy and at the same time unable to climb up in comparison with other states of the country. This directs us towards search of new drivers of growth and enhance the developmental efforts with strong initiatives to cross the barrier of being at an average level for a long spell. In the present liberalised economic scenario, it is expected that such impetus will come mainly from the private investment supported by market participation and vigorous public policy drives. That will require placement of growth in the most crucial growth drivers to hold ahead a promise and attract fresh investment from private sector. (Deshpande and Raju 2001).

In view of the slowdown in yield growth (some times negative), during nineties across the country, total factor productivity growth in Karnataka has also decelerated. The exclusive dependence on seed-fertiliser approach to productivity growth with inadequate emphasis on organic treatments, has led to depletion of soil fertility and inadequate environmental support for a sound farming system. The emphasis has been more on backward and forward linkages for agricultural development and less on the environmental support for establishing a sustainable farming system. Related to this is the depletion of vegetative forest cover leading to lower atmospheric humidity, heavy surface run-off, reduction in moisture holding capacity and microbiological activity in the soil resulting in disturbance of very biological equilibrium (KAC, May 2001, Bisaliah, 2004a). Under this shadow and the afore said promises we are setting forth this analytical review of the agricultural development experience of the state.

14.1.2 Macro Performance

Agricultural sector engages more than 60 per cent of Karnataka's work force. There is some evidence of shift of the workers out of agricultural sector (Lewisian shift), but this movement is not very sharp. It is also accompanied by the declining share of SDP generated from agricultural sector, and at a faster pace than the change in the workforce. Consequently, the SDP per worker in the sector is declining in real terms. During the last decade this trend has become sharper than earlier. The share of agriculture in GSDP has decreased from 33 per cent in 1993-94 to 25.3 per cent in 2000-2001. (Appendix A-14.1)

> The share of GSDP generated from agricultural sector is sliding down at a faster pace than the workforce engaged in the sector. As a consequence the per capita real GSDP from agriculture is declining.

Although per capita income has shown considerable increase owing to the growth of secondary and tertiary sectors, the per capita GSDP in rural areas from agricultural activities remains at around Rs. 5372. Therefore, the low-income generations in agricultural sector and increased inter-sectoral inequalities are bare truths and need to be kept in view.

14.1.3 Basic Structure and Sectoral Interdependence

The growth rates of GSDP and NSDP across various sectors as can be seen from the Table 14.1 that makes the issue clearer. It can be seen that the growth rate of both NSDP and GSDP originating from agriculture have been much lower than the secondary and the tertiary sectors. In the case of NSDP the growth rate of all the sectors is around eight per cent per annum whereas, that of the primary sector is just about five per cent, which is much below the aggregate growth rate. In one way, it is a good indication as the non-farm income is growing at faster rate and therefore may be conducive to absorb the incremental work force from agriculture, but one must also recognise that agricultural sector also has the potential to grow equally well, to maintain the balance in the quality of life of people living in rural areas and urban areas.

Even though agricultural sector (and primary sector at broader level) recorded relatively lower rates of growth, the aggregate growth of the state economy seems to be quite sensitive to the performance of agricultural sector due to the strong interlinkages. It can be seen from the Figure 14.1 that all the troughs experienced by the agricultural sector during 1993-1994, 1996-97, 1998-99 and 2000-01 are clearly echoed in the aggregate growth performance of GSDP. In other words, this strikes a warning that the growth performance of agricultural sector cannot be taken for granted. It is clear that if agriculture does not perform the other sectors may not fill the void, and we are still far from the phase of an economy that can thrive on secondary sector growth despite poor performance of agricultural sector. The concern is emboldened when one notes that the majority of workers and highest density of poor are located in agricultural sector (Figures 14.1 and 14.2).

> It is a fact that the growth performance of agricultural sector eventually dictates the overall growth of the state economy.

TABLE 14.1

Growth Rates of GSDP and NSDP across Various Sectors 1993-94 to 2002-03 (at 1993-94 Prices)

Sectors	*GSDP*	*NSDP*
Primary Sector	3.201	3.204
Secondary Sector	6.953	5.560
Tertiary Sector	9.959	10.408
All the Sectors	**7.099**	**6.896**

Source: Government of Karnataka (2003a).

FIGURE 14.1

Intersectoral Comparison of Growth in SDP: 1993-94 to 2000-01

(a) Agriculture

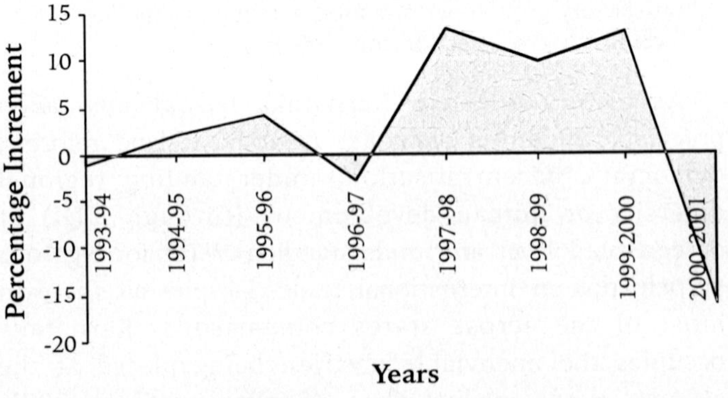

(b) Primary

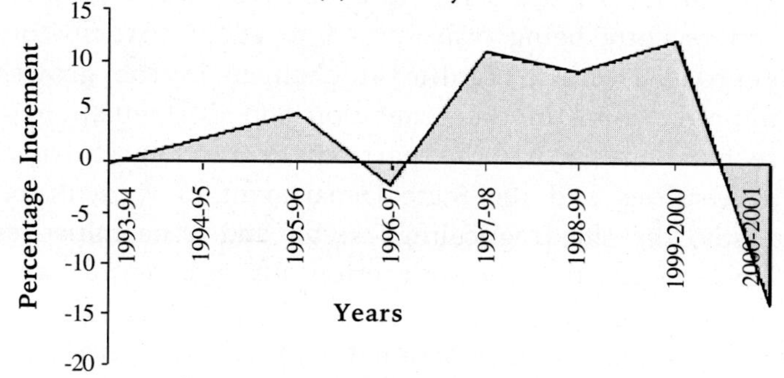

(c) Total GSDP

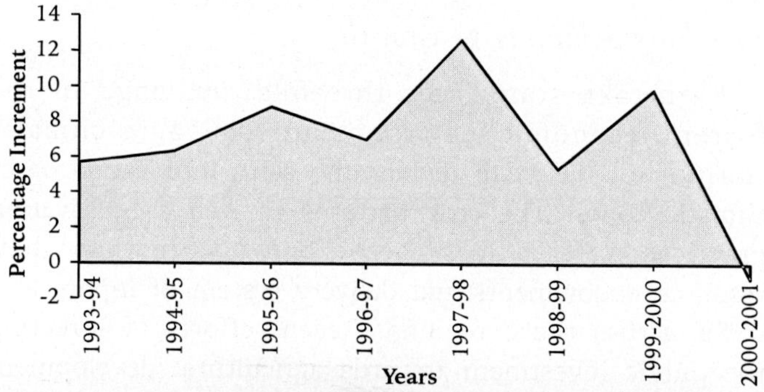

Source: Government of Karnataka, *Economy Survey of Karnataka*, Bangalore.

FIGURES 14.2

Intrasectoral Performance of the Primary Sector

(a) Sectoral Shares of GSDP at Factor Cost by Industry of Origin-At Constant (1993-94) Prices: Triennium Ending 1994-95

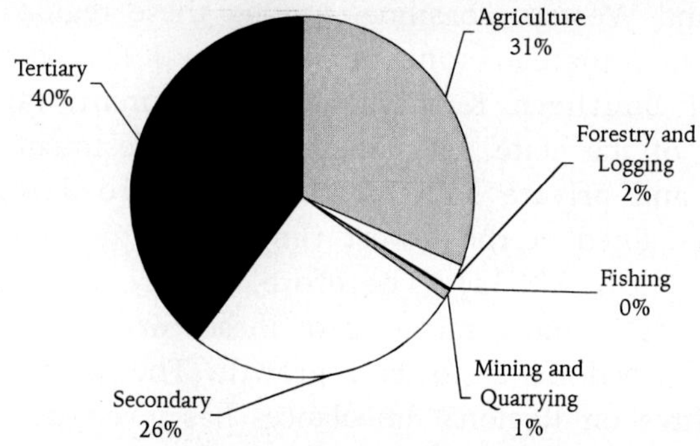

(b) Sectoral Shares of GSDP at Factor Cost by Industry of Origin-At Constant (1993-94) Prices: Triennium Ending 2000-01

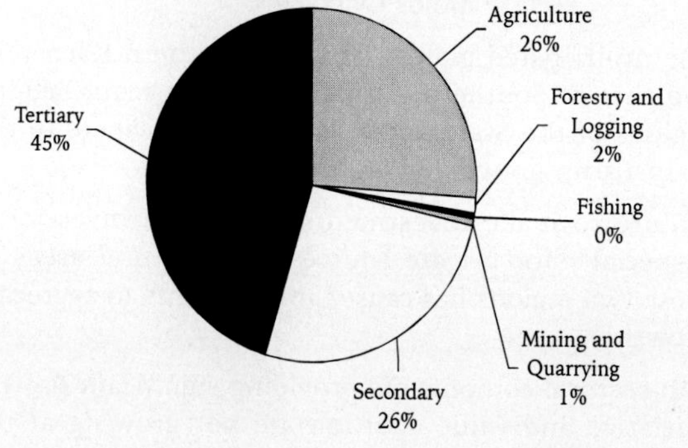

Source: Government of Karnataka, *Economy Survey of Karnataka*, Bangalore.

It is a fact that the share of agricultural sector in total GSDP is going down, but the GSDP originating from the sector is increasing albeit at a slower pace than expected. However, the internal composition of GSDP from agriculture is changing fast. The contribution of crop sector is in tune with the past trends but there are sharp changes in the horticultural and allied agricultural activities. This is a welcome change and similarly the agro-processing sector is also emerging strongly on the scene. Overall, the internal structure of the SDP originating from agricultural sector is undergoing fast changes.

Trade sector is one among the many subsectors that gave boost to the process of such changes. It is true that Karnataka is not the frontline state in international trade in the country, even though during the last decade it has recorded significant gains in the exports of some of the agricultural commodities (Appendix A-14.2). A quick view of the performance of agricultural trade during last five years indicates strong as well as weak spots. Among the weak spots coffee trade is a matter of deep concern showing a continuous decline so also the tobacco based products. These two commodities were the forerunners in the international trade sector of the state and therefore need immediate attention. But at the same time silk products, Bangalore rose, onions, gherkins are picking up as new favourites.

Exports of agricultural commodities like rose onion, silk products, gherkins are quite promising and indicative of a trend in future.

The trends in the other products like spices, cashew and flowers have to be closely monitored. The export earnings have improved significantly during the last decade, but the share of agricultural exports to total exports is declining mainly due to the growth in the exports of non-agricultural commodities.

14.1.4 Capital Formation and Investment

Capital formation both from public and private sector had been growing at a steady pace till 1998-99 but picked up only after that (Figure 14.3). The investment from private sector in agriculture is keeping pace with public investment but not with aggregate growth during the last four years of this decade. A part of this is the reflection of the general trend in capital formation in the state economy, but slackening of the investment in agri sector is an issue that cannot be overlooked. There is no necessity to re-emphasise the fact that the growth performance is a reflection of the trends in capital formation and therefore, the lower rates of growth in the sector are probably due to the pace of capital formation.

FIGURE 14.3

Estimates of Gross Fixed Capital Formation Sources in Karnataka-Agriculture

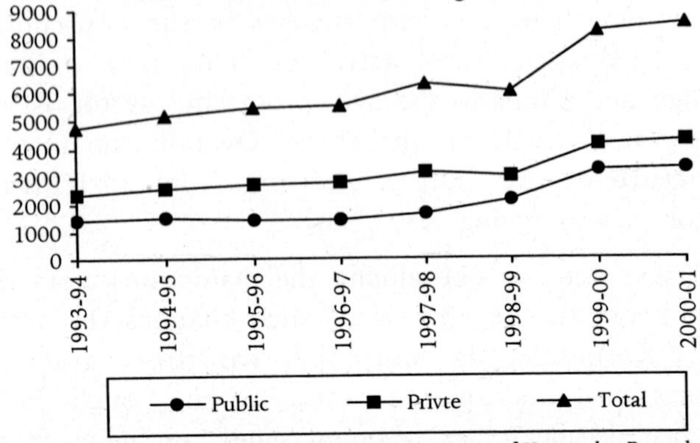

Source: Government of Karnataka, *Economy Survey of Karnataka*, Bangalore.

14.1.5 Sectors of Growth and Promise

At macro level the contribution of horticultural and food processing sector has been increasing during the later part of nineties. Similarly, cash crops like oilseeds, vegetable crops, sericulture and sugarcane are depicting good promises. Among the major sectors of growth, horticulture, floriculture, sericulture and post harvest processes also feature prominently. Trade in agricultural commodities is another promising contributor but it is largely located among a few commodities. Trade in horticultural and commercial crops is certainly a new recognised avenue of growth in the state. We shall get into a detailed analysis of some of these.

14.1.6 Interventions of the Donor Agencies

Karnataka state is one of the states that have benefited from the international donor agencies. First, major intervention came through the World Bank aided projects in irrigation sector as well as the USAID projects in agricultural extensions. These programmes steered the direction of the ongoing developmental efforts towards irrigated agriculture and made possible the availability and dissemination of technology. This was followed by interventions in tank irrigation sector and watershed development programmes by a few donor agencies. World bank and DFID recorded a significant presence in these sectors through their programmes. Four distinct directions of growth emerged due to the donor agencies interventions along with the state partnership during the last five decades. First, surface irrigation was established as the major growth initiator and that stepped up the growth in irrigated agriculture. Second, rainfed agriculture and watershed development programme in the state were taken up on large scale and recently being transformed to adopt participatory approach. Third, significant changes in the growth initiative came in the generation and dissemination of technologies with the participation of agricultural universities and the State Department of Agriculture. Lastly, the allied agricultural sector and trade initiatives have provided a new direction for enhancing value addition in the sector. In an overall analysis the interventions of international agencies have been the strong determinants of growth initiatives in the state.

14.1.7 Impediments to Growth

Karnataka state faces threefold challenge in the current economic environment. The agro-climatic situation of the state divides the state into varied agro-climatic zones. The crop patterns as well as cultivation practices differ across these zones. More than that, resource endowments and delivery system of inputs also differ across these regions. Recent efforts of directing the public investment towards agricultural development have not yielded the desired results to merge the differences in developmental initiatives across regions. Broadly, one can group these regions into five zones according to the agrarian and agro-ecological systems, namely: the Bombay Karnataka zone, the Hyderabad Karnataka zone, Southern dry zone; Southern irrigated zone, and Western coastline. Among these regions, the unirrigated plateau zone of Northern Karnataka and that of Southern Karnataka are the main lagging regions of the state. Even in terms of investment from public and private sources, these two broad regions have remained at the lowest rung in the development ladder (GoK 2003a). Therefore, failure to initiate investment in the rural areas of these two regions, has caused impediments to spur growth. The High Power Committee on Regional Imbalances has given its report and their recommendations significantly cover the agricultural infrastructure component (GoK, 2003a).

Major Obstacles

- The un-irrigated plateau zone of Northern Karnataka and that of Southern Karnataka are the main lagging regions of the State and these must participate in the mainstream growth.
- Failure to make investments or initiate investment (especially for private sources) in the rural areas of these two regions has caused impediments to aggregate growth.
- Sub-sectoral components providing significant growth initiative and value addition are not growing at the desired rate of growth.

An important challenge that the state faces presently is to facilitate private investment in the backward areas of the state. While initiating such schemes, it is essential to understand the resource endowments and competitive advantages of these regions to participate in the mainstream growth pattern. Hitherto, agriculture was considered as the only alternative to bring these regions into mainstream growth. Unfortunately, the climatic and weather patterns do not support such initives, and weather induced instability continues to inflict misery on agriculturists in these areas. Therefore, the growth culture has to be created in the allied agricultural sectors fuelled with private investment. These can include horticulture, floriculture, especially the dry land horticultural crops and food processing. In the recent past, it has been observed that horticultural crops have been picking up both in terms of area as well as productivity in these regions despite the climatic constraints but post-harvest and trade participation is still lacking. The state government is taking many initiatives to boost horticultural development in these regions. Contracting of horticultural crops to a consortium of small and marginal farmers with an assurance to provide them proper marketing facilities will go a long way in bringing this group of farmers into the mainstream development process.

Challenges

- Facilitating private investment in the backward areas of the state.
- The availability of funds to initiate agricultural and rural development schemes in the fragile regions with significant value addition.
- Participation of people in the process of liberalisation by enabling a proper conduit towards the most deserving regions and groups of farmers.

The third and important problem faced by the state is in terms of participation in the process of liberalisation by enabling a proper conduit towards the most deserving regions and groups of farmers. The state has been performing satisfactorily, as far as its participation in the international trade is concerned. In the past four years, the state has shown good progress on the front of exports of agricultural products but that is less than its potential. If this tempo has to be sustained and enhanced in future, it is necessary to support the agricultural and horticultural sectors in terms of crucial information as well as creating an enabling environment for the participation. The state has set up a Cell to advise on the WTO related issues. The WTO Cell submitted its first report and noted that the state has a strong potential to participate in the international trade (WTO Cell Report 2001). This can be harnessed for fuelling the growth process with the help of private-public partnership in the investment.

14.2 Performance Over Five Decades

14.2.1 Introduction

Performance of the agricultural sector is analysed from two prominent viewpoints. First, natural point of view is the growth in crop economy and its influence on the aggregate performance of the sector. That is taken as the main pointer to understand development trends. Second, the input/resources as the strong drivers of production growth are analysed to indicate the direction of growth. Given the predominant rainfed nature of Karnataka's agricultural sector, the staggering growth trends do not strike any surprise. But, probably the state has been able to internalise these constraints with a well-adjusted crop pattern on one hand and development of resources on the other.

Availability of resources and conversion of these inputs to outputs in the production process is certainly a major determinant of growth. The role of resources is therefore crucial especially in the context when the trends in resource depletion become evident. Similarly, the increasing cash component in the cost of cultivation has brought into focus the policy needs in the input sector.

14.2.2 Crop Production: Phases of Stagnation and Growth

One can broadly classify five phases of growth and stagnation in Karnataka's agricultural economy (Figures 14.4 and 14.5). The first phase that ended in 1955-56, recorded slight growth especially in foodgrains sector. This was followed by a strong phase of stagnation in the economy, which ended up in 1966-67, but with a severe drought. The state could pick up the advantages of the technological changes during the third phase, and this phase of growth came to a grinding stagnation in 1978-1979, and the decade of eighties saw a fluctuating behaviour in Karnataka's agricultural economy dominated by foodgrains that highlights the stagnation. Cotton and a few other commercial crops however, picked up slightly during this period. Followed by this during nineties the state witnessed some revival of growth in foodgrains sector but the two major commercial crops (cotton and oilseeds) are showing signs of deceleration specifically in the yield trends. The area under *jowar* and *ragi* has been declining but that under paddy is increasing. The area share of commercial crops has gone down but that of foodgrains has increased (Figure 14.6 and 14.7). It comes out very clearly from the analysis that there is a scope for realignment of cropping pattern based on efficient productivity of different crops across zones. Among these sorghum hybrids can be specially promoted in summer season in irrigated regions. In order to increase the productivity of pulses and oilseeds, these crops have to be raised in assured rainfall and in irrigated areas to the extent possible. Cotton as well as sugarcane crops have to be tailored to market needs of the crops in terms of quality and demand.

FIGURE 14.4

Production of Foodgrains, Oilseeds and Cotton ('000 Tonnes)

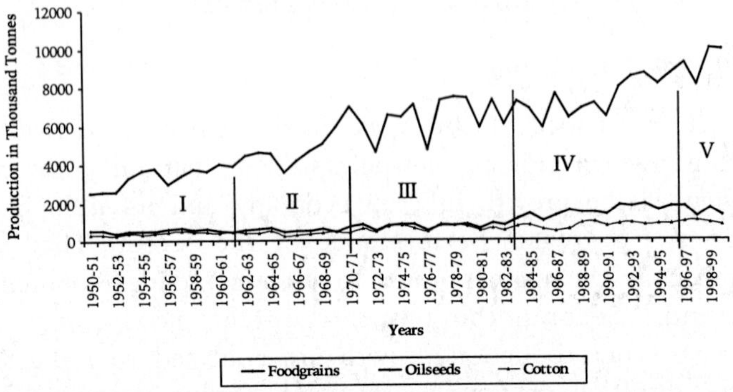

Source: Directorate of Economics and Statistics, Government of Karnataka, Bangalore.

FIGURE 14.5

Yields in Kgs of Foodgrains, Oilseeds and Cotton Per Hectare

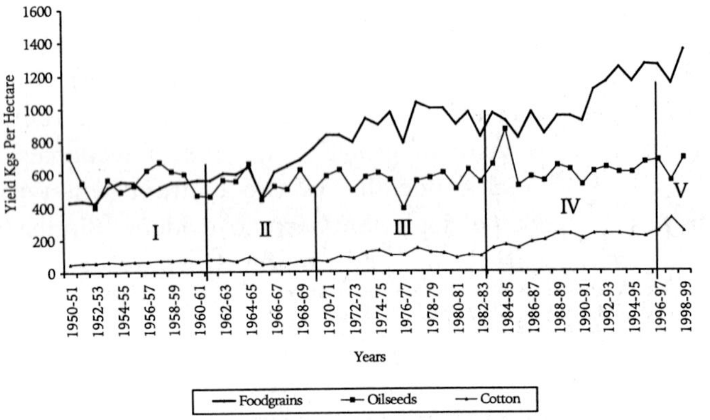

Source: Directorate of Economics and Statistics, Government of Karnataka, Bangalore.

FIGURE 14.6

Area Share of Different Crops at Triennium Ending 1988-89

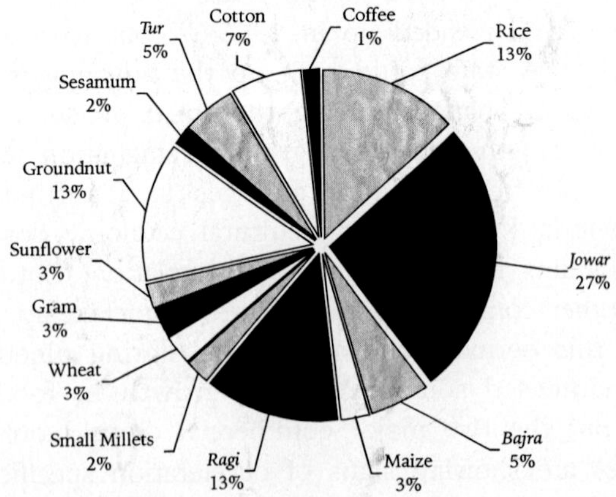

Source: Directorate of Economics and Statistics, Government of Karnataka, Bangalore.

FIGURE 14.7

Area Shares of Different Crops at Triennium Ending 1997-98

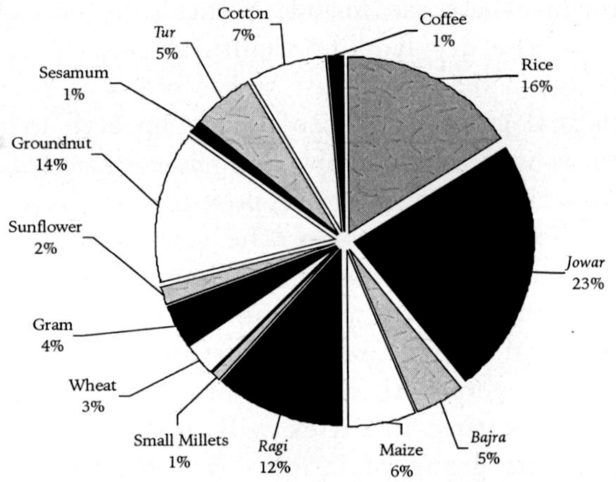

Source: Directorate of Economics and Statistics, Government of Karnataka, Bangalore.

The growth performances of various principal crops during the last decade indicate a mixed picture (Appendix A-14.3). It can be seen from the table that the last decade has not been very bad in the crop economy sector despite the droughts at the end period. In terms of yield, we note very good results for all the crops. Highlights are *jowar*, *ragi*, pulses and sesame (Figure 14.8). One cannot however, neglect the fact

FIGURE 14.8

Annual Compound Growth Rates in Crop Economy: 1990-91 to 1999-2000

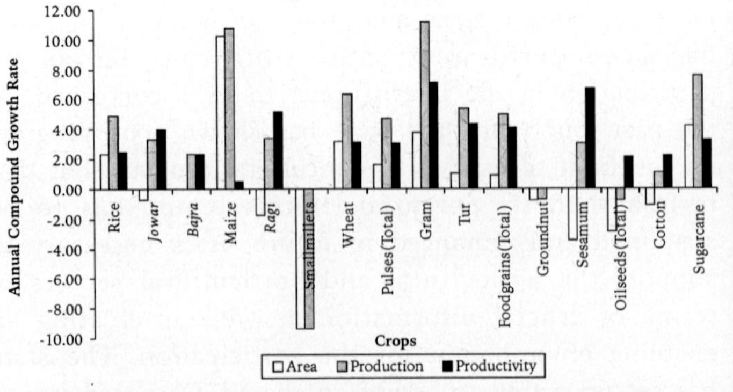

Source: Directorate of Economics and Statistics, Government of Karnataka, Bangalore.

that the allied agricultural sector has sustained the growth rates at the aggregate level despite the failure of the crop economy. This situation could have been averted by managing the crop failures at different stages but that is always a problem. It is needed that the remote sensing data could be used effectively to monitor crop conditions at regular intervals during the crop growth cycles.

14.2.3 Land Use

Land use and policy in Karnataka has been a matter of concern in the recent past. Government of Karnataka recently brought out a document on the Land Use Policy (Government of Karnataka, 2003a). The necessity of such document emerged from five different facets. First, land as a fixed resource, is fast approaching its optimum allocation and therefore there is an emergent need for reviewing the land use pattern. Second, there is a significant share of utilisable but wasted land resource that has to be brought under economic use. The current fallows reported as 12.9 lakh ha in 1991-92 increased to 16.7 lakh ha in 1997-98 and 17.28 lakh ha in 2001-02. Third, the pressure of commercialisation caused significant changes in the cropping pattern, and fears are being expressed in some quarters that this may threaten the food security. There is an increase of around 11.44 per cent in the use of land for non-agricultural purposes. Fourth, the demographic pressures and the land reforms together have caused the average size of holding to shrink over the last three decades. This has increased the number of marginal holdings. Lastly, the process of urbanisation is also exerting stress on the land use in the urban hinterlands.

Land Use Policy Issues

- Land being a fixed resource, it is fast reaching its optimum allocations across uses.
- There is a significant share of utilisable but wasted land resource.
- The pressure of commercialisation is increasingly forcing out the productive land resource for non-agricultural uses.
- The process of urbanisation of land use is quite fast.
- The demographic pressures and the land reforms together have caused the average size of holding to shrink bringing more cultivators below the economic viability threshold.

Over a period of time the fallow land is growing at the rate of 2.02 per cent per annum. However, in certain years like 1998-99, 1999-00 and 2001-02 the percentage of fallow land reached about 10 per cent of the total geographical area (GA) of the state. This was mainly because of the deficient rainfall and also the inability of the government to provide irrigation facilities in these years. The percentage of net sown area (NSA) to the total GA seems to have been grown negatively at the rate of 0.42 per cent (Appendix A-14.4). Though the figure is not statistically significant, but the point of concern is the proportion of NSA to the total GA has been decreasing over years, which is not a development symptom. Because, as it is mentioned already, the population in the state and the country is growing at the rate of about 1.75 per cent per annum, if the NSA declines there will be threat in terms of food security for the state.

14.2.4 Operational Landholdings in the State

It is interesting to observe that number of marginal and small holdings are increasing and also the total area of these marginal and small holdings, but the average area operated by these marginal and small farmers is shrinking at a faster rate (Appendix A-14.5). The average size of operated area of all the land size classes is declining. This clearly reveals the increasing fragmentation of landholdings in the state and marginalisation of the size of holding. Increasing marginalisation of the size of holding also indicates that the economic viability of large number of small and marginal holders is now more sensitive to the fluctuations associated with natural and market associated shocks. This increased economic fragility due to marginalisation of holding is clearly reflected in the current phase of farmers' distress. The shrinking sizes of holding and high density of unviable farmers are together causing marginalisation in the quality of life also, and that has serious implications (Figure 14.9). The new phase of land reforms therefore, needs to concentrate on efficient operations in land market, marginalisation of the size of holding, legalising tenancy market and reviewing the policies to encourage larger generation of marketable surplus.

Number and total area of marginal and small holdings are increasing but the average area operated in all classes of ownership holders is shrinking at faster density of economically non-viable holdings. Number of holdings under 1 hectare have trebled in the three decades (1970-2000).

14.2.5 Irrigation and Water Resources

Karnataka is the eighth largest state of India where six per cent of India's water resources are located (Table 14.2). Rainwater, the only source of both surface water and groundwater in Karnataka, ranges from 450 mm

FIGURE 14.9

Operational Holdings

(a) Number of Operational Holdings

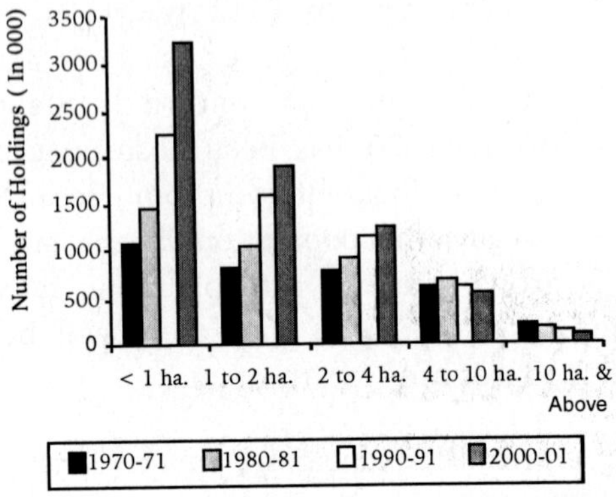

(b) Area Operated

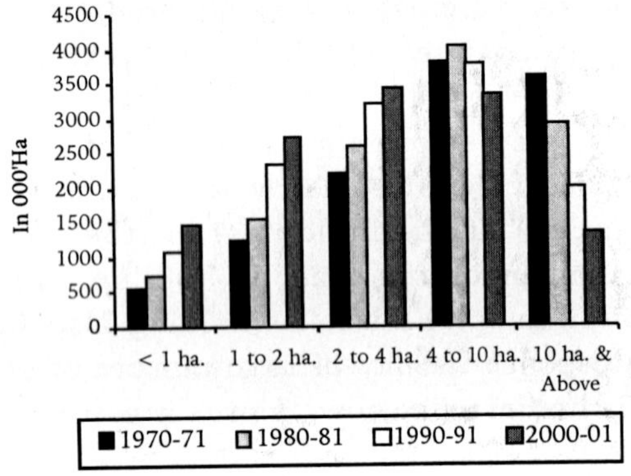

Source: Directorate of Economics and Statistics, various reports of the *Agricultural Censuses*, Government of Karnataka, Bangalore.

TABLE 14.2

Basic Irrigation Infrastructure in Karnataka: 1980-1999

Infrastructure	*1980*	*1990*	*1999*
Length of Canals (Kms)	5430	4634	5257
Number of lift Irrigation Schemes	437	24983	7900
Number of Electric Irrigation Pump Sets (Lakhs)	2.85	7.46	11.46
Number of Diesel Irrigation Pump Sets	36468	38517	38019
Gross area Irrigated by Iirrigation Open Wells (Lakh Acres)	10.4	16.61	14.14
Gross Area Irrigated by Tube Wells (Lakh Acres)	0.019	5.58	15.31
Gross Area Irrigated by Canals (Lakh Acres)	18.12	27.08	31.9
Gross Area Irrigated by Tanks (Lakh Acres)	8.72	6.65	6.79
Gross Area Irrigated by Lift Irrigation (Lakh Acres)	0.73	3.54	3.01
Gross Area Irrigated by Other Sources (Lakh Acres)	3.56	4.95	7.25
Gross Area Irrigated by All Sources (Lakh Acres)	41.56	64.44	78.42
Net Area Irrigated by All Sources (Lakh Acres)	33.74	52.25	62.68

Source: Data obtained from Brochure on Irrigation Statistics in Karnataka, Directorate of Economics and Statistics, Government of Karnataka, Bangalore

normal annual precipitation in Molkalmuru of Chitradurga district to 3500 mm in parts in the Western Ghats. The economically utilisable water from the river systems is 1695 TMC. With this availability only about 18 lakh hectares are under major and medium irrigation projects and the State has invested about Rs. 15000 crores in this since 1975. Annually, more than Rs. 2000 crores is spent on operation and maintenance in surface irrigation. With all these, only about 22 per cent of net sown area is irrigated and the potential estimated through surface irrigation is about 26.77 lakh ha. Between 1970 and 2000, the proportion of area irrigated by canals increased from 37 to 39.31 per cent; that by tanks reduced drastically from 32.14 per cent to 9.71 per cent, irrigated area under wells increased from 23 per cent to 37 per cent, and that by other sources increased from 8 per cent to 14 per cent. While the area under irrigation wells is rapidly increasing, that under tanks is drastically reducing creating an alarming lopsided extraction of groundwater with least regard to the recharge efforts. There exists a wide gap between potential and the actual area irrigated both under surface and groundwater irrigation. On the supply side this gap is indicative of the shortfall of both surface water and groundwater due to vagaries of monsoon, and on the demand side, this gap is indicative of lack of efforts towards efficient use of surface and groundwater for irrigation.

During 1980-2001 the growth in irrigated area by bore wells increased by 33 per cent and the number of bore wells by 34 per cent. However, the area irrigated per bore well increased only marginally from 2.67 acres in 1980 to 3.93 acres in 2001. Up to now, 43 *talukas* have come under the category of overexploitation of groundwater and in another 29 *talukas* the 50 per cent limit of exploitation has been exceeded. This precisely is a caution to both the farmers and the government regarding the limits to groundwater extraction per well, even though the bore well depths are increasing up to 1000 feet in different parts of Karnataka.

The area under irrigation by borewells is rapidly increasing; that under tanks is drastically reducing which indicates the alarming extraction of groundwater with least regard for the recharge efforts. Micro-irrigation (drip and sprinkler) in the groundwater irrigated zones will help to spread the available water on larger areas and at the same time increase the efficiency of irrigation.

Irrigation and water use sector in Karnataka poses quite a few problems. First, in the surface irrigation sector, the overuse of water wherever available and consequent environmental problems are quite visible. Moreover, surface irrigation has its limitations in the form of available potential. Measures to reduce the conveyance losses and overuse of water in the farmers' fields are on the top priority. In the case of paddy, instead of standing water, intermittent irrigation will save 40 per cent water. The legal step taken on 14th June 2000, providing state support to Water Users' Associations in the form of a concrete institutional frame will help to shift to distribution of water on volumetric basis. Second, as a support conjunctive use of water is being encouraged. In addition to these, steps have to be initiated to enhance irrigation literacy rational water and energy prices. Third, the water use efficiency in groundwater irrigation is a matter of serious concern. It varies from Rs. 74 per acre-inch in Southern Dry Zone to Rs. 2700 in Southern Transitional Zone (Chandrakanth, 1998). The variation is both due to agro-climatic conditions and crop pattern. Lastly, decline in tank irrigation (the recharge engines) on one hand and faster exploitation of groundwater on the other exert pressure on the sector, which needs attention.

14.2.6 Seeds and Nutrition Management

Seeds

Although precise estimates of volume of Karnataka's seed industry and size are not available it is valued roughly around Rs.400 crores. The industry is participated by both private and public sector companies/corporation involving production as well as marketing of seeds. The share of private seed companies in the high volume-low profit crops is minimal, whereas in *jowar*, maize, *bajra* and sunflower the private seed companies have major share.

The demand and supply scenario for seeds in 2004-2005 indicates a large mismatch between the actual requirement and production/availability in several crops like *ragi*, *jowar*, green gram, red gram, groundnut and sunflower. (Appendix A-14.6). Unfortunately the perspective seed plans (requirement and production) have not been drawn up resulting in frequent/sudden shortfalls and mismatches. The state agencies meet only 30 per cent of the total requirement and about two-thirds has to be met from private initiatives. Therefore, the role of private seed industry is quite strong in the seed market.

Keeping in view the strong presence of private seed industry in the sector, one cannot rule out the circulation of spurious material. A complete review of the existing legal framework therefore, is an essential prerequisite. The TRIPS requirement of WTO will also require the tightening of legal framework. It is a welcome feature that private sector is dominant in the seed supply but then the responsibility of proper and stringent quality of supply needs to be ensured by the state agencies. Present infrastructure of seed testing laboratories is not adequate and more than that these need to be the members of International Seed Testing Association to maintain those standards.

Integrated Nutrient Management

Integrated Nutrient Management (INM) approach aims at efficient and judicious use of all the major plant nutrients in an integrated manner, so as to optimise the economic yield without deleterious effect on physico-chemical and biological properties of the soil. Thus, the basic concept underlying the principles of INM is the maintenance and possible improvement in soil fertility for sustained crop productivity on a long-term basis. Enhance crop and soil productivity through a balanced use of mineral fertilisers combined with organic and biological sources of plant nutrients to ensure sustainability of the production systems. The major components of INM are fertilisers, organic manures (FYM/compost), legumes, crop residues/recyclable wastes, and biofertilisers.

Challenges for Sustainability

- Expanded food needs to be met primarily from increases in yields per hectare.
- Move the Green Revolution into the ecologies, systems and population segments that have not been benefited significantly.
- Food production efforts should take into account the declining environmental quality. These efforts should be coupled with those enhancing environmental quality.

Several studies have indicated that Karnataka state has a net negative balance in soil nutrients to the tune of about 43211 tonnes (1999-2000) that is not met through fertiliser applications. This in itself is not alarming but provides a caution for future policy. Nutrient balance in agriculture in Karnataka is relatively more satisfactory when compared with many other agriculturally leading states in the country except in case of potassium where there is sustainable mining of soil resources. The nutrient ratio ($N:P_2O_5:K_2O$) of fertiliser consumption in the state is 5.1 : 2.1:1 which is near optimal and much more balanced than many other States and the country (Figures 14.10 and 14.11.). Five out of 10 agro-climatic zones of the State had net negative balance of nutrients and that needs to be noted. The nitrogen and phosphorous usage was in excess of their crop removal in all agro-climatic zones except in coastal zone.

FIGURE 14.10

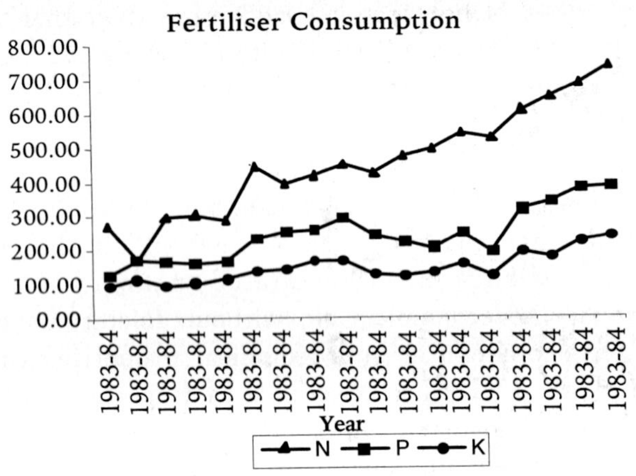

Source: Directorate of Agriculture, Government of Karnataka.

FIGURE 14.11

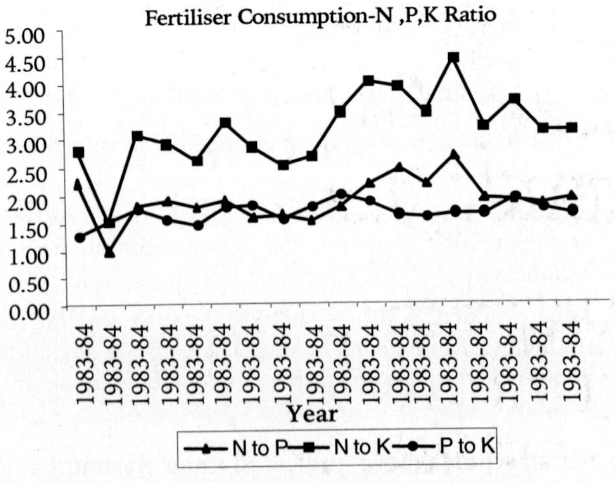

Source: Directorate of Agriculture, Government of Karnataka.

14.2.7 Integrated Pest Management

Agro-ecosystem analysis forms the basis for designing an efficient Integrated Pest Management (IPM), it encompasses various components like mechanical interventions, utilisation of biodiversity, pest resistant cultivars, cultural manipulations, use of semio chemicals (Pheromones, Kairomones), exploitation of biological resistance in the environment and botanical insecticides, besides target-specific selective insecticide usage. Though the value of pest management in sustainable agriculture is well recognised, very little is being adopted at the field level. While the reasons for increased pesticide consumption during the period from 1970 to 1990 are well known, the causes for declining pesticide consumption from 1990 onwards could be attributed to: (i) crop habitat diversification bringing in new crops and new plant types into cultivation, (ii) low pesticide usage crops occupying larger area across the country, like soyabean, sunflower, etc. (iii) slow increase in development and use of alternate pest control strategies, and (iv) climatic aberrations such as drought from 2000-01 onwards. Change in pest control strategies in pesticide-hungry crops like cotton, pulses and vegetables coupled with steady awareness on biological or organic farming paved way for promotion of IPM in these crops. There is very little awareness among the farmers about the use of natural enemies and the adverse effects of pesticides on these beneficial fauna. Though there are many instances of successful biocontrol-based pest management practices in different crops, there is still a wide gap between demand and production of bioagents both under public and private sector.

14.3 Infrastructure: A Shift Parameter

14.3.1 Introduction

Availability of infrastructure and its quality are among the major variables causing upward shift in the production surface. Infrastructure development in agriculture has not been quite satisfactory over the last two decades. Most of the studies analysing agricultural development of the state have highlighted the infrastructural bottlenecks (Deshpande and Raju, 2001; GoK, 2003). It is an indisputable fact that infrastructure with public investment provokes development and private capital formation. It helps to shift the production surface; at times even without explicitly participating in the production process. We are reviewing here agricultural education, research, marketing, mechanisation and credit sectors. Irrigation and other input sectors have been included in the earlier section on resources.

14.3.2 Agri-Education, Research and Extension

The triad system of education, research and extension is the key to catalyse and sustain development of agriculture and achieve farming prosperity. Impediments in the agricultural university system are spread around various issues that include: adoption of a rational personnel policy; manpower assessment; inbreeding in faculty development; growth *vis-à-vis* student admissions, inflow of research; projects, extension outputs, assignment on consultancy, availability of infrastructure; deteriorating financial health due to block grants from the Government of Karnataka including the externally funded projects, and the thinly spread resources. All these together have been the standing constraints but despite these the agricultural education and research system have contributed meritoriously to the growth of the sector in Karnataka.

The two agricultural universities in the state helped to create and nurture novel streams of training manpower to meet the demands of serving a rapidly developing agriculture sector and has acquitted itself in many fields within as well as outside the state. This is now appropriate to facilitate: (i) linking of the undergraduate and post graduate study programmes to the job market, (ii) skimming out a small but brighter segment of the students to pursue excellence in areas of agricultural research and teaching, (iii) exploring overseas student market on a pro-active mode and also (iv) achieve at least 50 per cent of student admission on high merit. Suresh Pal and Alka Singh (1997) have clearly established that Karnataka is one of the states where both research and extension intensities measured in terms of investment as a per cent of agriculture GDP, and growth of real investment in these areas are low. This should be a concern of public policy, while allocating resources for both agricultural research and extension.

Research and Extension

Research and extension being 'interactive' but, independent departments in the agricultural universities has probably outlived the original intent and purpose. At an operational level, research and extension should reflect convergence and synergy. In the post-Green Revolution technology environment, there have occurred significant paradigm shifts in the nature of demand for technology and extension services owing to the second-generation problems. Hence, research in the immediate future should focus on ecological and environmental interface of agriculture. A strategy of 'contract research and extension' consultancy can satisfy the market-driven demands through letting commercial considerations of technology inputs outside the public research extension system, while sparing the needs of small farmers, especially farming in dry land ecosystem, to be met by the 'public good' focus of the agricultural universities and the line departments. Prioritisation and reprioritisation of focus areas in research should be part of a continuous process.

The Department of Agriculture has the traditional responsibility to provide the extension services to the farmers, acting as a critical bridge between technology generation centres (mainly the agricultural universities) and the farmers. Of late the effectiveness of this public extension system has been a concern in some quarters. The fact that the extension intensity in Karnataka is the lowest heightens this concern. Private participation in agri research, extension and marketing is becoming increasingly important with the advent of biotechnology and protection being accorded to intellectual property. In the absence of public regulation of such services the resource-poor and gullible farmers are becoming victims of exploitation by the unscrupulous traders and moneylenders interested in selling spurious material. There is an immediate need for revamping and revitalising the existing agricultural extension system in the state so as to conform to the new priorities in agricultural research with adequate financial support. The existing public outlay on agricultural research and education is too meagre and needs to be stepped up substantially. There is a need for reordering the priorities in agricultural research and redefining the relative roles of public and private sectors in research and extension. It is imperative therefore to make a critical assessment of the present system and institute reforms to make the system responsive to address changing needs.

14.3.3 Farm Mechanisation

Mechanisation in agricultural sector of Karnataka could not record significant spread as it confronts several challenges. These include small and scattered land holdings, low investment capacity of majority of farmers, low farm power availability, non-availability of good quality improved equipment and machinery in the vicinity of farmers, large areas under rain fed farming, farm equipment reserved for small-scale industry, difficulties in mechanisation of commercial and horticultural crops and also dry land agriculture and hill agriculture, weak field extension machinery, etc. The present level of investment in agricultural machinery is of the order of about Rs.50 thousand crores annually consisting of about Rs.30 thousand crores for tractors, power tillers, combines, pump sets and other crop production machinery and Rs.20 thousand crores for post-harvest and processing machinery.

The changes in the use of agricultural implements in Karnataka indicates a decline in the use of indigenous implements during the period 1997 and 2003, which suggests a slow replacement of modern instruments (Appendix A-14.7). The usage of the seed-cum-fertiliser drill and other tractor and power-operated machinery is on the rise whereas a negative growth in the usage of a few implements like combines and power tillers can be attributed mainly to the difficulties in owning high-cost specialised machines and hence going for custom hiring. In the use of irrigation equipment, electric pumps as well as sprinklers have shown positive growth rate at the cost of the manual lifting devices that indicates a negative growth. While a considerable shift towards mechanisation is noticed there exists equal amount of gaps in the adoption that needs to be filled. Karnataka hardly owns 200 of the farm machinery industry, out of more than 16000 in India, and most of them are concentrated in Bangalore.

Agricultural Electronics

This is an emerging new field in the application of science and Technology in agricultural sector. Karnataka is one of the leading users and innovators in the field.

14.3.4 Marketing: Ready for Reforms

Currently there are 141 main markets and 342 sub-markets functioning in the state (Appendix A-14.8) and the Department of Agricultural Marketing controls these markets by enforcing the various Acts, like Karnataka Agricultural Produce Marketing (Regulation) Act, 1966 and Rules 1968 (Appendix A-14.9). The implementation of these however, has not been effective in reducing the market imperfections even though the components of Act promise a perfect marketing situation (Box 14.1).

Despite these, the marketing institutions and the infrastructure have effected quite a few changes in the agricultural marketing sector. These include: (i) increase in the market arrivals as a share of total output, (ii) reduction in the market inefficiencies in terms of unauthorised charges and irrational grading, (iii) dissemination of market information at the regulated market yard; (iv) better storage facilities and place to stay was created for the farmers, (v) marketing charges payable by farmers were either dropped, standardised or liability shifted to the buyers, and (vi) significant reduction in the sale in the village and in the proportion of distress sale.

BOX 14.1

Components of APMC Act

- Monitoring of marketing practices by Regulated Market Committees.
- Licensing of functionaries.
- Open auction or close-tender system.
- Issue of sale slips showing quantity and price to the farmers.
- Well-publicised time and days of sale.
- Correct weighment of the produce by licensed weigh man.
- Prescription of rational market charges.
- Provision of payment to farmers within stipulated period.
- Mechanism of dispute settlement.
- Dissemination of market related information.
- Provision of amenities to the farmers in market yards.
- Reduction of physical losses during buying and selling.

BOX 14.2

Lacunae in Agricultural Marketing

- Late payment to farmers.
- Underpricing of the produce.
- Arbitrary grading.
- Non-issue of sale slips by the traders.
- Congestion and delays due to lack of proper infrastructure.
- Traders organising themselves into informal cartels.
- Lack of understanding about the market regulations promoting sale of produce outside the market yards.
- Misutilisation of funds collected as cess and market fee.
- Emerging of APMCs as monopolistic centres of sale and purchase.

Among the main problems of marketing sector inadequacy of market infrastructure has been the main reason for market imperfection. A few studies have shown that, there has been significant increase in horizontal and vertical integration of agricultural markets and that larger share of the marketable surplus reaches the market. However, lot remains to be done in creating adequate marketing infrastructure in rural areas (Box 14.2). Incidentally, there was virtual absence of any private investment in this sector. It is high time now that the investment in this sector also comes from private sources. Conducive environment for attracting private investment would be required.

14.3.5 Institutional Credit

Institutional credit has played a significant role in enhancing the growth rates in agricultural sector during and after the phase of the Green Revolution. But the changes of pace and pattern of the contribution of agricultural credit emerge as a significant issue. In general the credit flow to the agricultural sector is declining and Karnataka is not an exception. This issue emerged boldly on the background of the farmers' distress in the state.

> Almost all the districts in Karnataka have experienced a shrinking flow of credit to agricultural sector during the decade of nineties. The supply of agricultural credit as a proportion to net bank credit has been declining in Karnataka. Possibly that explains the emergence of informal moneylenders during this decade.

Growth rates in total credit and agricultural credit for the entire period of 1981-2000 as well as two sub-periods, *viz.*, 1981-1991 and 1992-2000 in 19 districts of Karnataka (Appendix A-14.10) indicate that the total credit (including agriculture and other sectors) for the whole of the state grew at the rate of 15.6 per cent per annum during 1981-2000. There is no specific pattern, but still one clear observation emerges out of the table that almost all the districts have experienced a reduced flow of credit to agricultural sector during the decade of nineties. The total credit flow has increased marginally. The pattern is almost similar in developed as well as backward districts of the state. It was noted that ACBC in the state was 24.5 per cent during the period 1986-1990 and declined to 16.9 per cent by 1996-2000. This suggests that the supply of agricultural credit as a proportion to net bank credit has been declining in Karnataka. This was almost uniform across the districts. Nevertheless, the proportion of agricultural credit has been declining and still, the banks have achieved the fixed target in all districts except a few, that points out to the process of fixing lower targets. Above all, the share of Cooperative banks in the institutional credit for agriculture and allied activities has declined. This has to be looked into carefully. It is high time that a 'fresh rural credit survey' was undertaken in right earnest.

As regard the credit per hectare of gross cropped area across different categories of districts, it was observed that the district/group of districts where banks achieved the higher ACBC, the supply of credit per hectare of gross cropped area was less. For instance, although ACBC was only 10 per cent in developed category of districts, the credit per hectare of gross cropped area was Rs.7706 for the period 1996-2000. Similarly, the ACBC were 31.5 per cent and 44.2 per cent in backward and highly backward categories of districts, but the credit availability per hectare of gross cropped area were Rs.1665 and Rs.2408 respectively during the period 1996-2000. An increase in the amount of credit per loan account was associated with a decline in the number of farmers having access to the formal credit. This implies that the bankers have been adopting both price and non-price credit rationing strategies while selecting the agricultural borrowers and fixing the credit limit.

14.4 Allied Sectors: A Powerful Backup

14.4.1 Horticulture and Floriculture: Future Key Sectors

In Karnataka, horticultural crops occupy about 15.21 lakh hectares of area with an annual production of about 96.60 lakh tonnes. Although the area comprises only 14.25 per cent of the net cultivated area in the state, the total income generated from the horticultural sector accounts to over 40 per cent of the total income derived from the combined agriculture sector. This accounts for 17 per cent of the GDP of the state. Fruits, vegetables and flowers occupy an area of 3.15, 2.59 and 0.21 lakh ha, respectively. Of late, floriculture industry is picking up fast with great export potential. The annual income generated by the horticultural crops amounts to over Rs. 6000 crores.

> - Karnataka occupies the first position in area under sapota, onion and flower crops. It stands second in the case of lime, and grapes. It has the distinction of having large number of fruit crops and the area under horticulture/floriculture in the State is increasing fast.
> - Karnataka state is one among the major fruit exporting states.

Karnataka is highly progressive with regard to vegetable production, because of equitable climatic conditions, without extreme temperatures. Karnataka has second largest area under coconut, the total area of about 4 lakh hectares, over 2 lakh hectares are under rainfed cultivation. The productivity of coconut is three times more under irrigated conditions than under rainfed conditions in the state. In Karnataka there are over 300 horticulture nurseries in government sector and over 500 functional nurseries in private sector. These nurseries produce over 10 million fruit plants and 50 million ornamental plants in every year. The total value of the nursery turnover is more than Rs.500 crores every year. In 2004 the horticulture crops grown in an area of 1.20 lakh hectares are provided with drip irrigation and the adoption of drip is to the extent of near 100 per cent, which helped those areas where water availability is scarce. Another significant development that has taken place in Karnataka is related to the dry land horticulture, which has been formed purely under rainfed conditions, and various water conservation techniques.

Karnataka is on the forefront of area and production of many crops but there exists significant potential to increase the area under fruit crops in the North and Northeastern dry regions with crops like mango, grapes, sapota, lime/lemon, pomegranate, fig and papaya. In eastern dry zone, selection of crops should be aimed at low water requiring crops such as mango, grafted jack, anona, *amla*, wood apple and jamun. Crops selected for these areas should be hardy, such as tamarind, anona, jamun, rose apple, grafted cashew, *ber* and wood apple. The non-arable areas under Northeastern and Northern dry zones are suitable for *ber*, tamarind, wood apple and anona; while Central, Southern and Eastern dry zones are suitable for mango, jack and *amla*. In transition zones, cashew, sapota, jack, wood apple, *amla* and *jamun* are better suited. Hilly zone is suitable for garcinia, pineapple, cashew and jack. Bread fruit, rose apple, komarach, garcinia and cashew are specially suited to the non-arable areas of the coastal zone (zone 10) (Appendix A-14.11). There is considerable gap in productivity of mango (8.2 MT/ha), banana (25.6 MT/ha), sweet orange (7.2 MT/ha), lime/ lemon (4.5 MT/ha), mandarin (9.8 MT/ha) and guava (7.4 MT/ha) between Karnataka and other highest productivity States. There is ample scope to increase the productivity of the above fruit crops by following high-tech horticulture.

Karnataka's export of horticultural commodities is about Rs. 1250 to Rs. 1400 crores of which coffee alone contributes Rs. 830 crores followed by cashew worth Rs. 236 crores and horticultural and processed products about Rs. 132 crores. Horticultural exports of the state are covering large number of countries. (Appendix A-14.12) Horticultural crops contribute 95 per cent of the state's export of agricultural products. Given the growth rates in area under the horticultural crops in the state, one can easily foresee that the state would emerge as one of the major fruit-exporting region of the country, provided the institutional and investment support is conducive for small development.

Floriculture

Karnataka is well known for floricultural production accounting for 24.43 per cent of the country's total area under floriculture in 1999-2000. The area under floriculture has increased from 0.05 lakh hectare in triennium ending 1982-83 to 0.22 lakh hectare in triennium ending 1999-00.

> There has been consistent increase in flower exports from Karnataka. The value of exports increased from 37.73 crores in 1998-99 to 45 crores in 2000-01 accounting for 34 per cent of the total countries total floricultural exports in 2001-01.

The annual compound rates of growth in flowers is 9.53 per cent per annum during 1978-79 to 1999-00. The production growth mainly comes through area expansion and during this phase the productivity has not increased substantially. The district-wise growth rates of area and production of flowers are shown in Appendix A-14.13. The growth of traditional flowers is not uniform throughout the state. Among the four agro-climatic regions in Karnataka, the southern region experienced highest growth rate both in area (10.26 per cent) and production (10.61 per cent) between 1980-81 and 1999-2000. The improvement in productivity is not very significant; the increment is just 0.36 tonnes per hectare in 22 years. It is clear from the table that the flowers experienced a growth rate of 8.59 per cent in area and 10.24 per cent in production between 1980-81 and 1999-2000. If we consider the individual flowers, crossandra witnessed an annual growth rate of 12.93 per cent in area and 11.07 per cent in production. Marigold registered 9.63 per cent growth in area and 9.88 per cent in production. Whereas, tube rose witnessed 8.50 per cent growth rate in area and 9 per cent growth rate in production (Figure 14.12 and Appendix A-14.14).

Karnataka accounts for nearly 75 per cent of the flower exports from the country. The hi-tech floriculture made its beginning in Karnataka in early nineties, and soon it anchored itself firmly in the state. There are 20 big and 100 small hi-tech flower producers operating in the state at present (2004). The rose export alone accounted for the 90 per cent of the total exports. The rest constitute the Carnations, Gerbera,

Chrysanthemum, and Bird of Paradise, etc. A large proportion of these products are exported to Amsterdam, Germany, Italy, UK, Australia, Japan, and Middle East (GoK: 2001:11).

FIGURE 14.12

Area and Production Growth Rates of Flowers in Karnataka between 1980-81 and 1999-2000

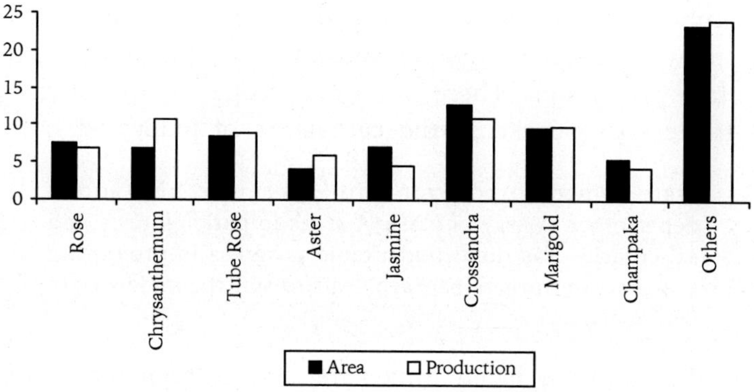

Source: Directorate of Horticulture, Government of Karnataka.

14.4.2 *Forestry and Agriculture: A Symbiotic Relationship*

Karnataka state has a total of 38,284.28 sq.kms of area under forest, which is 19.6 per cent of its geographical area. Only about 50 per cent of the forest area has good tree cover. About 6360 sq. kms of forest area has been notified for protection of wildlife and biodiversity. The state enjoys a wide variety of agro-climatic zones, with the forests ranging from the lofty tropical wet evergreen forests to the thorny scrub forests. The National Forest Policy has prescribed that one-third of geographical area is only about 20 per cent and enhancement requires greening of all community lands and wastelands. It is seen that nearly 51 per cent of recorded forest area is devoid of tree cover. Out of the total of 18850 sq.kms of tree covered forest area, over 6300 sq.kms are protected areas and preserves; an additional 2000 sq.kms consist of ecologically sensitive areas on the ridges and steep slopes of the Western Ghats. Approximately 10000 sq.kms can be called productive forests to sustain supplies to the needs of community, industries and the market. The forest survey of India has estimated that the total growing stock of Karnataka is approximately 272.4 million cubic metres as given in Table 14.3.

Forest Types and Extent in Sq. Kms

Evergreen and semi evergreen forests-5800, Moist deciduous forests-5780, Dry deciduous forests-7270, Scrub and thorny forests-8340, Unwooded areas-11090.

TABLE 14.3

Forest Resources of Karnataka

Forest Type	*Area in Sq.Kms*				*Volume in '000m³*			
	D1	*D2*	*D3*	*Total*	*D1*	*D2*	*D3*	*Total*
Teak	471	892	83	1401	10517	12117	176	22810
Bamboo	-	135	-	135	-	49		49
Deciduous	-	504	77	581	-	2187	85	2272
Miscellaneous	1043	21807	7376	30226	14763	210616	21901	247280
Total Growing Stcok	1514	23338	7536	32388	25280	224969	22162	272411

Note: D1-Crown density 70% above; D2-Crown density 40% -70%; D3-Crown density 10% - 40%

Source: Department of Forest, government of Karnataka.

Annual increment estimated by FSI is 5.5m³, which works out to an average of 1.45 cum/ ha p.a. However considering that this increment is derived from only 49 per cent of tree covered forest, the increment is about 2.9 m³ per ha p.a. Per capita forest area in Karnataka is 0.08 ha. The department of forest as resource has not received its due attention. It was noted that there is a small decrease in the area under forest in the state. A Forestry Action Plan was prepared in 1997 to achieve higher investments and growth in the forestry sector, including social forestry. The Forest Policy Proposals of the state indicate that about 10,000 sq. kms of productive forests are available for intensive management. Methods to manage these areas depending on the forest type, the present condition, increment and methods to improve productivity have been given.

An analysis of allocations for the forestry sector during the period from 1992-93 and the corresponding expenditure during the period have shown that total allocations under both, plan and non-plan have risen from Rs. 1176.818 million in 1992-93 to Rs. 2831.2 million during 2003-04.

The expenditure has risen from Rs. 1106.795 million in 1992-93 to Rs. 2475.434 million during 2002-03. The non-plan expenditure has risen from Rs. 671.36 million in 1992-93 to Rs. 1374.3 in 2002-03, which is more than double (Box 14.3). The allocation and expenditure under plans have also nearly doubled. But these are not keeping pace with the increasing prices and have little to do with actual needs. It is also true that most of plan expenditure during the decade has been made in social forestry sector, on less productive non-forest lands and partially on degraded forests. Very little attention or allocation has gone to productive forest areas to improve the growing stock and its increment potential. It can be said that investments in production forests will have to depend either on institutional finance or the forest development fund or private sector, if high productivity has to be achieved.

BOX 14.3

Proposals Indicating Investments

- Evergreen and semi-evergreen forests: Rs. 731.25 million.
- Moist deciduous forests: Rs. 2110.0 million.
- Dry deciduous forests: Rs. 1320.0 million.
- Unwooded and scrub forests: Rs. 980.0 million.
- Greening of non-forest public lands: Rs. 2012.0 million.
- Agro forestry, including bamboo expansion: Rs. 593.5 million.
- Commercial plantations: Rs. 960.0 million.
- Sandal and Rosewood planting: Rs. 200.0 and Rs. 100.0 million respectively.
- Peelable timber (soft-wood) and pulpwood: Rs. 100.0 million each.
- Cashew and other non-timber forest produce (NTFP): Rs. 175.0 million.
- Plantations in Forest Corporation lands: Rs. 300.0 million.
- Revamping all forest corporations: Rs. 30.0 million.
- Nature conservation and eco-tourism: Rs. 505.0 million.

Among the forest products we have broadly two components namely the timber and the non-timber forest products. The contributions from forest sector come from these sources. Major revenue share is generated from NTFP and it is available in all the administrative units. Its utilisation and environment is prescribed in the forest policy. The system of doling rights of NTFP to LAMP societies at nominal cost causes significant revenue loss. It is necessary that the user groups pay the value of NTFP at wholesale price excluding the cost of collection and supervision. A part of revenue thus collected could be used for regenerating and the resources.

The public investment in forestry sector has to be reviewed as the allocations hitherto were never need based and most often *ad hoc* in nature.

Sandalwood is the most important forest product of Karnataka. Karnataka state has average sandalwood yield of 1000 MT per annum and record plantation of 8500 ha. till 2002. But due to various problems annul yield actually realised has gone down to 250 MT per annum. Experts have suggested that extensive management of sandalwood has failed to yield the desired results and therefore the state has to concentrate on intensive sandal management.Under the intensive sandal cultivation it is suggested to grow sandal trees with a compatible host and under small protective states. It is also worthwhile to consider privatising sandalwood cultivation as well as some of the major forest trees. Rosewood (*Dalbergia Latifolia*) is another important and high-valued forest product, which attracts better prices in the national and international markets. Allowing privatisation of rosewood plantation will not only help to generate larger income through forestry and make forestry as a popular ancillary vocation, but it will also stop green felling of rosewood trees and illegal trade in timber. Pulpwoods including dry bamboos and other pulpwood have a large demand and it is met out of the state plantations. There is a good scope for the private growers to partake in the cultivation of pulpwood.

State owned corporation with assistance from forest department by way of lease of areas in parks, forests and sanctuaries has done remarkable progress in promoting eco-tourism through package deals to suit the middle class and above.

Eco-tourism is an important and emerging area of economic activity. High-tech national and multinational corporates are willing to invest and share the eco-tourism facilities. This concept is presently in its infancy and can grow fast with vigorous efforts made through aggressive salesmanship by contacting large corporates, especially in the growing IT industry in Karnataka.

14.4.3 Sericulture: Need for Continued Monitoring

Karnataka is a major silk producing state with nearly 46.2 per cent of share in Indian production out of 14617 MT during 2002-03. Sericulture in the state is spread over 27 districts with 88909 ha (2002-03) of mulberry including 17424 ha under rainfed cultivation. The silk production has steadily increased in the state.

The silk production has steadily increased from about 2,500 tonnes about two decades ago to the present level of over 8,700 tonnes. But there has been an influx of Chinese silk into Indian market in recent years

This expansion has been mainly attributed to the implementation of World Bank assisted Karnataka Sericulture Project (KSP-I) and KSP-II component of National Sericulture Project (NSP) during eighties and nineties. There has been substantial reduction in the area of mulberry during recent years, which however, is not commensurate with the cocoon and raw silk production indicating higher levels of productivity in recent years. The influx of imported silk is mainly catering to the needs of power loom sector. This has necessitated conceptualisation of a two-way approach towards streamlining the raw material requirements of the industry namely, (i) CB variety to meet the handloom sector; and (ii) Bivoltine variety to meet the power loom sector.

Sericulture sector in Karnataka has demonstrated significant strides during the last three decades. The domestic market demand for silk yarn as well as silk cloth has been increasing at a faster rate. Silk is a commodity consumed largely by the upper income strata of the society and therefore, the income-elasticity of demand is above unity. It is also supported by the trade sector, wherein sericulture has a significant role to play. These strengths of the sericulture industry can make silk as one of the important commodities in domestic as well as international trade of Karnataka. Unfortunately, the sector is facing declining capital formation and lack of modernisation. Consequently, the industry has remained labour-intensive and therefore, it is not cost-effective as required. Obsolete machines and technology still predominate the industry. These sectors have to be attended, if a significant presence is intended in the international market.

14.4.4 Livestock and Fodder Development

Livestock in the state is a wealth in terms of genetic diversity and its contribution to farming and livelihood systems. Strong complementarities exist between crop cultivation and animal husbandry. The contribution of livestock to the state's gross domestic product (GDP) is steadily increasing in the last two decades. The contribution of livestock sector in GSDP at current prices during 2000-01 was 20.2 per cent and that has increased from 18.4 per cent during 1993-94 to 22.55 per cent at constant (1993-94) prices during 2000-01. But the total cattle population at the state level has decreased by 6.3 per cent between 1990 and 2003, within the total cattle population, indigenous cattle have considerably declined by 16.1 per cent during the period 1990 to 2003, whereas crossbred cows have increased by 122 per cent during the same period. At the same time both sheep and goats' population has increased by 53.5 per cent and 14.9 per cent respectively during this period. The interesting trend in livestock population to be noted from Table 14.4 is that between 1997 and 2003 all species of livestock, except crossbred are showing declining trend in their growth.

While livestock population has increased, grazing lands such as cultivable and uncultivable wastelands and pastures (excluding forests) have declined by 6 per cent during 1991-92 to 1999-00. Even the area under forests does not support the increasing demand of fodder by the increasing number of ruminant livestock due to its own degradation. The quality of ruminants in terms of productivity, as also the carrying capacity of grazing lands is fast declining in many areas of the state. The unregulated and continued pressure of grazing on uncultivated lands has led to their further degradation and hence one of the major causes of ecological imbalance. The decrease of population is due to economic consciousness of rural people in maintaining the more animals especially low yielding local breed and reduced draught bullock power as ploughing machineries and transport facilities are largely available in almost all the villages like tractors, power tillers, etc. The farmers concentrating on maintaining the productive animals like crossbed cows for regular income with the network of dairy co-operatives giving fixed price and market for milk through District Milk Unions & Karnataka Milk Federation.

TABLE 14.4

Composition of Livestock Species in Karnataka (in lakhs)

Livestock Species	*Year*		
	1990	*1997*	*2003***
Indigenous	94.6 (40.7)	95.4 (33.3)	79.4 (31)
Cross-bred	7.2 (3.2)	13 (4.5)	16(6.2)
Total Cattle	101.8 (43.8)	108.4 (37.9)	95.4 (37.2)
Buffaloes	40.4 (17.4)	44 (15.4)	40 (15.6)
Sheep	47.3 (20.3)	80 (28)	72.6 (28.3)
Goats	39 (16.8)	48.7 (17)	44.8 (17.5)
Pigs	3 (1.3)	4 (1.4)	3.1 (1.2)
Others*	1 (0.4)	1 (0.3)	0.5 (0.2)
Total	**232.5 (100)**	**286.1 (100)**	**256.4 (100)**

Note: Figures in parentheses indicate percentages to total.

*Includes horses, ponies, mules, rabbits and donkeys (dogs not included).

** Provisional.

Sources: Quinquennial Livestock Census, 1990, 1997 and 2003, DA&VS, GoK, Bangalore.

The average estimated milk yield per day in milk and milch indigenous cow was 2.266 and 1.356 kgs respectively during 2000-01. In the case of cross-bred cows it was 5.994 kgs for in milk cows and 4.745 kgs for milch cows during the same year. Average estimated milk yield per day per in milk and per milch buffalo during 2000-01 was 2.987 and 2.101 kgs respectively. The total estimated milk production during 2000-01 from buffaloes was 18.80 lakh tonnes, 40.9 per cent of total milk production.

More than 58 per cent of the total milk production comes from cows (Table 14.5). This is quite interesting when compared with the country. Further, milk production from cows has increased from 16.31 lakh tonnes during 1994-95 to 25.39 lakh tonnes during 1998-99, an increase of around 56 per cent. Similarly buffaloes milk production has increased from 13.58 lakh tonnes to 16.61 lakh tonnes, an increase of around 22.3 per cent during the same period.

TABLE 14.5

Changing Pattern in Milk Production in Karnataka

('000 Tonne)

Year	*Goats*	*Buffaloes*	*Cows*	*Total*	*% Variation over Previous Year*
1994-95	14	1358	1631	3003	9.76
1998-99	31	1661	2539	4231	6.57
2000-01	43	1880	2675	4598	2.79

Source: *Report on Integrated Sample Survey for Estimation of Production of Milk, Egg, Wool and Meat* (2001-2002), Directorate of Animal Husbandry and Veterinary Services, Govt. of Karnataka.

KMF markets milk and milk products through a network of cooperative societies. It is a cooperative apex body. The federation has 17 dairy processing plants with a processing capacity of 24.15 lakh litres a day and 42 chilling centres with 13.74 lakh litres of chilling capacity and two product dairies equipped to produce 25 MTs of milk powder per day. The four cattle feed plants at Rajanukunte, Gubbi, Dharwad and Hassan produce on an average 400 MT of cattle feed per day. The average daily milk procurement was 25.3 lakh kgs in November 2002. The other details related to dairy development in the state can be seen from Table 14.6.

The population of sheep and goat has increased because they are drought resistant animals and service even on the dried blades of grass and leaves. This is the reason farmers depending on animal husbandry have survived and not went to the extreme step of committing suicides unlike farmers who depended exclusively on agriculture in case of drought vagaries of monsoon and failure of agricultural crops and low prices of agricultural produce.

FIGURE 14.13

Milk Production in Karnataka

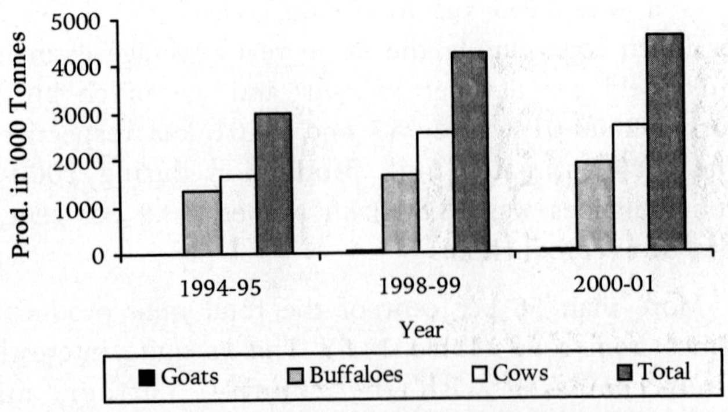

Source: Directorate of Horticulture, Government of Karnataka.

The target for dairy cooperative societies (DCSs) to be registered during 2002-03 is 473. And the KMF's Perspective Plan 2005 aims at enhancing and extending Karnataka dairy development infrastructure, and for this an agreement with NDDB for financial assistance of Rs. 250 crores has been signed. Under this, another 1500 dairy cooperative societies, covering 17.5 lakh members will be formed.

TABLE 14.6

Dairy Development

	2001	*2002-03**
Dairy Cooperative Societies Registered	364	322
Dairy Cooperative Societies Functional	450	473
Members Enrolled	47837	58908
Milk Procured (Lakh Tonnes)	7.51	8.10
Animals Treated (Lakhs)	4.77	5.07
Animals Inseminated (Lakhs)	10.15	11.17

Note: * Anticipated

Source: *Economic Survey 2002-2003*, Government of Karnataka.

Meat Animals

It is generally the sheep and goats, which are considered as meat animals in Karnataka. Other than these, pig and poultry are also being extensively used for meat purposes. The share of sheep and goats' meat in the state's total meat production (excluding poultry meat) was 66.4 per cent during 2001-02. The impact of KMF programme is spectacular in some districts of the state. For the dry region of the state, sheep and goats being drought resistant are important animals for small and marginal farmers. Even the landless labourer keeps sheep and goats unlike dairy animals where land should be available for fodder production. Adequate emphasis has to be given for the development of these. Strengthening of the Sheep and Wool Development Board (to launch the cooperative sheep production programme on two or three tier basis on lines with cooperative dairy development movement) requires immediate attention. Modern slaughter houses can help the poor farmers in drought affected districts. Poultry development has mostly benefited the capitalists. However small farmers have not reaped similar benefits even though these are suitable for them. Beef and buffalo meat constitutes 15.1 per cent and 10.7 per cent of total meat production respectively during the same period. The share of pork was 7.7 per cent of total meat production during the same year (Table 14.7).

Sheep farmers are selling sheep and goat to traders at shandys on the basis of approximate body weight by which farmers will not get their due price. Hence it is better to introduce weighing machines in all livestock shandys or markets where sheep and goat are sold. So that farmers can know the live body weight before selling to get fair price. Agriculture Producers' Marketing Committee or Sheep Farmers' Fodder Cooperative Societies or Sheep Breeders' Associations or SHG or unemployed youths can install weighing machines. Modern slaughterhouses and good meat selling centres are to be encouraged in the interest of public health. NABARD is encouraging to set up of chicken centres with loan facility under venture capital fund scheme.

TABLE 14.7

Production of Meat, Egg and Wool

	1990-91	*1997-98*	*2001-02*
Mutton ('00 tonnes)			
Sheep	232.82 (41.7)	285.44 (39.4)	329.94 (39.5)
Goat Meat	182.23 (32.7)	218.27 (30.1)	224.50 (26.9)
Beef ('00 tonnes)			
Cattle	72.03 (12.9)	108.21 (15.0)	126.31 (15.1)
Buffalo	46.14 (8.3)	66.57 (9.2)	89.11 (10.7)
Pork ('00 tonnes)	24.27 (4.4)	46.04 (6.4)	64.40 (7.7)
Total Meat ('00 tonnes)	557.49 (100)	724.53 (100)	834.26 (100)
Egg (Lakhs)	12848 (100)	18124 (141)	20273 (158)
Wool (Tonnes)	3808 (100)	4691 (123)	5757 (151)

Source: Government of Karnataka, *Report on Integrated Sample Survey for Estimation of Production of Milk, Egg, Wool and Meat for the Year* 2001-02, Directorate of Animal Husbandry and Veterinary Services, Bangalore.

Note: Figures in parentheses indicate percentages to total.

Pig and poultry are also being extensively used for meat purposes. The consumption of pork is less. Poultry development has mostly benefited the capitalists. Toning up the existing piggery activities with suitable personnel can also encourage piggery farming. Integrated poultry farming system with more capital investment is increasing. Backyard poultry with low inputs and low technology units needs to be popularised to supplement the income of the farmers and improve the nutritional status of rural farming population.

Feed and Fodder

Fodder development on livestock farms and on agricultural lands is becoming one of the major activities of the department of animal husbandry and veterinary services. At farms, root slips and fodder seeds are produced and supplied to farmers. Training is being given to farmers in fodder cultivation. Fodder development banks have also been set up at livestock farms. Fodder production target of the state for 2002-03 is 7562 tonnes.

Generally, livestock to a large extent have to fend themselves, except in the case of bullocks and lactating animals, which are supplemented and stall-fed with good quality feeds and fodder. It has been estimated that agricultural residues provide around 40 per cent, grazing 31 per cent, green fodder (cut and cultivated) 26 per cent and grain and concentrates around 3 per cent of total consumption by livestock. By and large the nutritional constraints in dairy production are real and the condition under which stall-feeding through concentrate feeding and cultivated fodder becomes viable options are still not clear.

Stall-feeding is to be encouraged with incentives like providing fodder, seeds, etc. As many of the small, marginal and landless agricultural labourers own dairy animals provision of green fodder at market rates can help by encouraging farmers with irrigation facilities to grow and sell fodder in the market. A community fodder production programme can be initiated with appropriate incentives from the government. Fodder growing farmers' associations for mere production of fodder can well suit the situation as farmers can afford to purchase because of regular income from dairy animals. Fodder productivity in forest lands and waste lands, grazing lands can be taken up with drought resistant varieties. Turfing on tank bunds can also be thought of for fodder production and extension programmes in fodder production have to be chalked out.

14.4.5 Fisheries: Marine and Inland

Fisheries is the one of the most important and emerging non-farm activities in Karnataka. The exports of fish and other aqua products have picked up significantly during the last five years. It is quite an encouraging trend and therefore, the sector needs a closer look as a development initiator. Karnataka have good proportion of marine as well as inland fisheries production.

Marine Fisheries

In Karnataka, fisheries contribute 0.7 per cent of the gross GDP and 3.18 per cent of the net GDP to the state's economy at current prices. The gross GDP from fisheries sector increased from Rs. 3702 lakhs in 1980-1981 to Rs. 6666 lakhs in 1996-97 at 1980-81 prices, and at current prices it increased from Rs. 3702 to

FIGURE 14.14

Fish Production of Karnataka: 1984-85 to 2002-2003

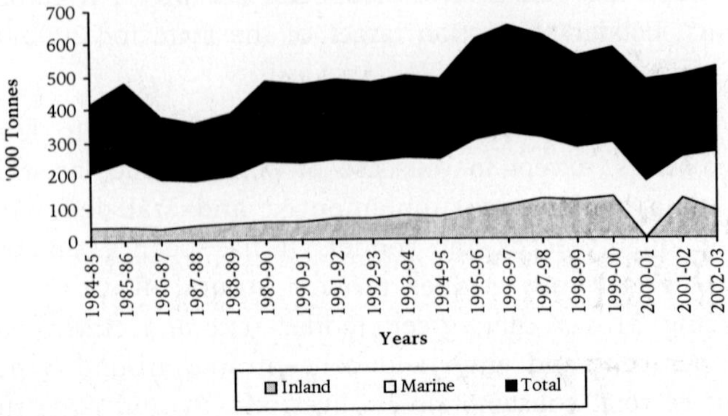

Source: Directorate of Fisheries, Government of Karnataka.

Rs. 39575 lakhs. Though the share of agriculture in the total GDP is decreasing, the share of fisheries within the agriculture and in the total is increasing—the share of agriculture in the state GDP has decreased from 40.68 per cent in 1980-81 to 30.31 per cent (at 1980-81 prices) in 1996-97 while, during the corresponding period, the share of fisheries in the total net state domestic product increased from 2 per cent to 3.18 per cent. The foreign exchange earnings of fish and fishery products of Karnataka doubled during the last decade and increased from Rs. 3812 lakhs in 1990-91 to Rs. 6270 lakhs in 2003. However, the share of Karnataka in the total Indian marine exports has declined from 5 per cent to 2.5 per cent indicating the lack of proper incentives to export from Karnataka ports on the one hand and decline in the production of exportable varieties. Over the years the share of Karnataka has declined due to decline in the capture shrimp fisheries on the one hand and also the decline in the cultured shrimp production (Appendix A-14.15). Further, under EU regulations many of the fish processing companies are not eligible for exporting to EU countries. This has made them to lift the fresh fish and transport shrimp directly to their counterparts in Kerala, which have upgraded their factories as per the EU standards.

The share of Karnataka in the total Indian marine exports has declined from 5 per cent to 2.5 per cent indicating the lack of proper incentives to export of marine fish from Karnataka.

Inland Fisheries

The state of Karnataka has a vast water spread area of 5.20 lakh ha comprising 74 reservoirs, 6015 major tanks, 19697 minor tanks, 3000 km irrigation cannels and 5813 km of river stretch. Karnataka accounts to about 13 per cent of the country's aquaculture resources and is in the 3rd place. However, these resources are not effectively put to aquaculture production and the state stands at 7th position in terms of freshwater fish production in the country. The low productivity of these water bodies is mainly because the aquaculture production of the state mainly comes from common property resource (tanks and ponds).

During the last one decade, while the marine fish production has almost remained unchanged excepting some variations in between specially, the inland fish production is showing a steady positive progress and the total production has increased from 55848 MT in 1989-90 to 121196 MT in 2001-02, registering an overall increase of 117 per cent. If the inland fisheries resources are properly conserved and put for scientific fish production practices, there is a good scope to double the aquaculture production in another decade and it can be even increased three times by 2025. Potential of different districts is presented in Appendix A-14.16. It is quite clear that the inland fishery has a good spread across regions.

Fish and fish products of Karnataka have been gaining a good export market (Figure 14.15). Even though the quantum of trade is growing very fast after 1995-96, the

FIGURE 14.15

Exports of Fish Production

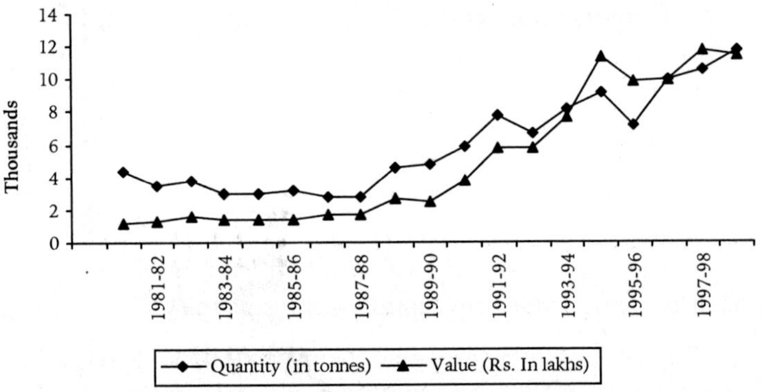

Source: Directorate of Fisheries, Government of Karnataka.

unit value of fish trade is sliding down. Among the export products, baby cattle fish earns highest forex followed by frozen ribbon fish and frozen whole fish. Karnataka's fisheries sector is yet to make its presence felt in the other marine and inland fish products.

Next Phase in Fisheries Development

Fisheries (both marine and inland) is emerging as a strong economic sector in Karnataka even though the coastline of the state is not very vast enabling a strong participation in international trade unlike some other states. However, the scope for marine and inland fisheries is quite encouraging and Karnataka has been able to make its presence felt consistently in the international market. However, the impediments are quite a few. It is very clear that Karnataka has not been able to keep with the international prices and the unit value of exports of fishery has been declining in the recent past (Figure 14.16).

It has declined both due to pressure of international market as well as the quality of fish and aqua products exported to different destinations. In addition to these, the institutional structure enhancing the international trade in fish is not very conducive and well settled. There are a large number of middlemen operating in the system and that cuts down the profits and causes disincentives in the product process. Market margins have been increasing and as a result the producers do not get the largest share of the market prices. Keeping in view the potential of inland as well as marine fisheries and other aqua products from Karnataka it will be quite prudent to support this sector with a new influx of capital in terms of cold storages, infrastructure, market facilities and processing of the products. Unfortunately, the institutional structures in these areas have also been quite weak and it is essential that the private-public

FIGURE 14.16

Unit Value Per Kg of Fisheries Export (in Rs.)

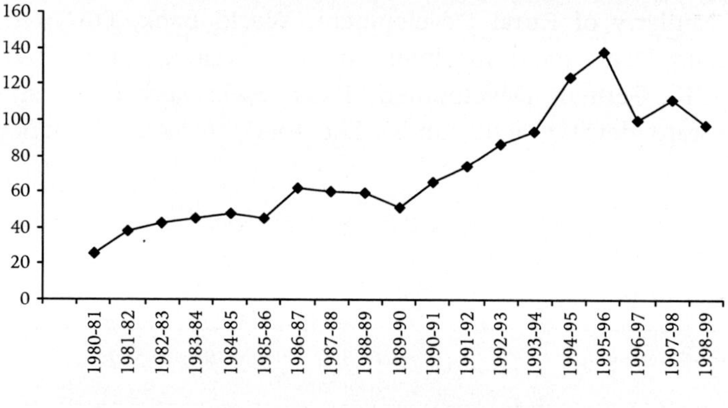

Source: Computed based on the data collected from FAO.org.

partnership can be strengthened for positive trade participation. As a result, trade in fish and fish products can pick-up. It is essential to bear in mind that such infrastructure has to be created separately for inland as well as the marine fish production.

14.5 Problems, Prospects and Promotion

14.5.1 Introduction

Agricultural sector in Karnataka is strongly categorised by the phases of growth and stagnation. Unfortunately, the stagnation phases are longer than the short spans of growth. Despite this the state has successfully maintaining aggregate growth in agricultural sector in a neighbourhood of 2 to 3 per cent per annum. However, the potential of growth in agricultural sector is much higher than what is demonstrated during the last three decades. This growth potential remains underexploited due to four major constraints. These include, high proportion of rain fed agriculture, domination of low-density low value crops forces into low productivity crops, meagre value addition in crop enterprises with little scope for diversification and restricted availability of resources. These problems have been on the scene right from early sixties and efforts have been made to overcome some of these impediments, however we have not fully succeeded in totally winning over these constraints. It is necessary, therefore, to view the habitual low productivity stagnation trap as the most important element to conform. This can be achieved by added attention to rainfed agriculture, watershed as the basis of directing the growth efforts, diversification and impetus of new technology. These factors, if attended to in proper direction, probably will provide better growth potential.

14.5.2 Productivity: Stagnation and Impediments

The aggregate crop production trends in the state have been slowing down during the last decade. There are some productivity gains in the foodgrain sector; however, the commercial crop sector requires an immediate productivity boost.

> Karnataka state has the second largest share of drought-prone region of the country that has the probability of drought in neighborhood of 20 per cent. This sets back the clock in productivity growth with at least two bad years in almost every decade.

It is very clear that the yield rates of commercial crops that include oilseeds, fibres, sugarcane, pulses and other commercial crops like sericulture, horticulture have been stagnating. There is a little addition on the new technology front to boost up the yield trends. It has been observed that these crops have also demonstrated large yield gaps and a few of them are also unreachable by the safety-net programmes. Another important impediment that causes this stagnation is the meagre increments in irrigated area in the state. Two years in almost every decade have been affected by drought. This sets back the clock in productivity growth. Unfortunately, the research and development (R&D) efforts in introducing new technology among the stagnated crops have not been directed towards locating drought tolerant varieties of the food crops as well as the commercial crops. It will be essential therefore, to step up the investment in agricultural research specifically concentrating on commercial crops and market-oriented food crops. This will also enhance the market access of the poor farmers and in turn provide them value addition with the positive developments in market forces.

14.5.3 Watershed Development: Experience and Prospects

Karnataka state has the highest proportion (79.87 per cent of geographical area) of drought prone area among all major states in the country and in absolute terms Karnataka has second largest area (152.16 lakh ha) under drought zone, which is next to Rajasthan (218.95 lakh ha). The rain fed area contributes around 62 per cent of the agricultural production in the state. Bulk of pulses and oilseeds are grown under rainfed conditions. Sizable proportion of drought-prone area in the state not only impinges on the growth performance of the state but also perpetuates regional inequality. The programmes like Drought Prone Area Programme, Arid Zone Development Programmes sponsored by the Central Government were being implemented in the state. However, the scope and coverage of these programmes are very limited. Following the initiatives proposed in the mid-term appraisal of Seventh Five Year Plan many state governments initiated watershed development programmes. National Watershed Development Programme for Rainfed Agriculture took shape in its three incarnations. Other such Pogrammes under the Ministry of Rural Development were also initiated during 1980s.

The concept of dry land development on watershed basis was initiated during 1983 with identification of 47 model watersheds by the ICAR. Out of these 47 model watersheds, 4 were in Karnataka managed jointly by SAUs and Dept. of Agri.; 2 in the red soil area (Mittemari in Bagepalli *taluka* and Bommanahalli in Mysore *taluka*) and two in black soils (Joladarasi in Bellary and Yernal in Bijapur). Two of these four projects *viz.*, Mittemari and Yernal received National Productivity Awards for best team work. This was followed by four World Bank assisted programmes, one each in Karnataka, Maharashtra, Andhra Pradesh and Madhya Pradesh. The major landmark in the efforts of resource conservation in Karnataka has been the establishment of Dryland Development Board (DLDB) during the year 1984. In the very first year, the Government of Karnataka started the programme in 19 districts through the four Divisional Dryland Development Boards. The convincing success in these watersheds led to the acceptance of the principle by the Government of India to implement the dryland development programmes on watershed basis. Karnataka has adopted various types of watershed development programmes financed by Ministry of Agriculture, Ministry of Rural Development, World Bank, DANIDA, and Department for International Development (DFID), UK, German Development Bank, Swiss assistance and State development funds. The total amount of money

BOX 14.4

Comparison of Watershed Development Programmes: Karnataka

State Run Programmes	*Projects Run Purely by Non-Governmental Organisation (NGO)*	*Projects with Co-ordination of State Agency and NGO*
• Implemented by technocrats therefore technically sound.	• Technically focused towards NGO's specialisation.	• Hybrid approach involves best of both state agencies and NGOs.
• Top-down approach in planning and implementation.	• Lack of sufficient and trained technical people that impinges on the span of technical aspects.	• Technically sound and conditioned by the dominance of the partners.
• Structures and activities do not have location specificities.	• Non-holistic approach as activities taken up are influenced by past experience or expertise of the NGO.	• Bottom up and top down mix up.
• Number of line departments are involved in the implementation and this process provokes low co-ordination among them.	• Participative approach in planning and implementation of the project.	• Low overhead cost
• High density of administrative staff.	• Less overhead charges and low pilferages.	• Approach is holistic in nature.
• High overhead charges and therefore chance for more pilferages.	• Participation of community is conditioned by the voluntarism of the NGO.	• Participation is ensured and people friendly.
• Forced participation of the community.		• Focused on livelihood.

Source: Deshpande and Nikumh (1993); Deshpande and Narayanamoorthy (1999) and Deshpande, Bhende and Erappa (2003).

invested through these programmes between 1984-85 and 1999-00 was Rs. 632.0 crores and the total area treated was 21.53 lakh ha (Appendix Table 14.17).

A number of studies compared the experience of these institutions with the one gathered from the state-run programmes and found that the programmes taken up voluntarily provided exemplary results compared with the state run programmes (Box 14.4). The NGO initiatives emboldened another important aspect of the programme, namely, incorporation of the perception of the people about the watershed development interventions. It was soon realised that without a proper approach, participation in the programme will be difficult, and such failure will not sustain the intervention in the field. Moreover, participation was quintessential for ensuring the effectiveness, equity and institutional sustainability of the programme. This was however, a good beginning of involving farmer but by design, it would not have spread the technology with the desired speed. In such experiments many times the farmers know only of the names of the terminology used but they are aware of neither its influence nor the necessity of its components in the overall design.

Since inception of the watershed development programmes till March 2003, about 29.11 lakh ha of the area has already been treated under watershed development programmes. The total amount spent on watershed development programmes in the state accounts for roughly Rs. 775.89 crores up to the end of March 2003. Even then out of the total geographical area around 190.5 lakh hectares, 116.9 lakh hectares and an additional 12.8 lakh hectares of forestland require watershed treatment and maintenance. Proportion of the available area covered under watershed programmes varied across districts in the state and it ranged from less than 2 per cent of area available for watershed development in Dakshin Kannada and Shimoga districts to more than 60 per cent in Bidar district. The average amount spent per hectare on watershed development amounts to Rs. 3342, Rs. 3024 and Rs. 2320 per hectare in the case of category I, II, III districts, respectively. Nearly 87.80 lakh hectares of land is yet to be treated under watershed development programme. The Department of Watershed Development, Government of Karnataka has already planned to develop about 21.92 lakh hectares of untreated land by spending an amount of Rs. 1250.47 crores under different ongoing schemes in the next 5-6 years.

TABLE 14.8

Area Covered and Amount Spent on Watershed Development: Cumulative up to March 2003

(Area in Lakh ha. and Rs. in Lakhs)

% of Available Area Treated	*Districts*	*Area Available for WSD*	*Area Developed*	*Amount Spent*
Category. I Less than 20	D. Kannada, Shimoga, Kodagu, Raichur, Chickamagalur, Davangere, and Mysore	30.00	3.04	10149.88
Category. II 20 to 30	Kolar, Chitradurga, Bellary, Tumkur, Dharwad, Bijapur, Bangalore (U & R), Mandya and Gadag	42.21	9.88	29877.97
Category. III More than 30	Hassan, Udupi, Haveri, U.Kannada, Gulbarga, Chamrajnagar, Bagalkot, Belgaum, Koppal and Bidar	44.69	16.19	37560.70
All	**State**	**116.90**	**29.11**	**77588.55**

Source: Government of Karnataka, Directorate of Economics and Statistics and *Agricultural Censuses* for various years.

The remaining area of 65.88 lakh ha not covered under any development programme would require Rs. 3952.38 crores for treatment. The details about the area available for watershed development, area treated, proposed and area remaining to be treated along with amount required for development is provided in (Appendix A-14.18). An additional amount of Rs. 592.90 crores would require meeting the expenditure on technical support and management cost at 15 per cent of the development cost during the project period.

Karnataka state is presently implementing 3681 micro-watersheds under different schemes. It is pertinent to note that the guidelines for implementation and priorities are not the same for all the watersheds even though most of them are implemented by Watershed Development Directorate.

14.5.4 Achievements in Watershed Development

Good examples of sustained productivity by developing dry lands and adopting improved crop production practices are available from Mittemari, Kabbalanala, and Kallambella Watershed Projects. Increase in the area under dryland horticulture and dense forest are reported almost from all the watersheds. Improvement in groundwater level and reduction in silt load due to catchment area treatment have been observed. Improvement in the availability of

TABLE 14.9

Measured Improvements due to Watershed Development

Name of the Watershed	*Measured Values*	
	Before the Project	*After the Project*
Crop Yields		
Mittemari Watershed, Kolar		
Ragi + Redgram (10:2 proportion)	6.5 + 0.0 q/ha	10.16 + 1.71 q/ha
Groundnut + Redgram (8:2 proportion)	3.0 + 0.0 q/ha	8.14 + 2.26 q/ha
Kallambella Watershed, Tumkur		
Ragi	16.32 q/ha	20.77 q/ha
Groundnut	12.12 q/ha	13.16 q/ha
Achulu Watershed, Kabbalanala		
Ragi	22.0 t /32.5 ha	61.0 t / 32.5 ha
Area Under Dense Forest		
Hirehalla Watershed, Belgaum	47 ha	345 ha
Area under Dryland Horticulture		
Chandakavate Watershed, Bijapur	380 ha	2437 ha
Reduction in Silt Load (RVP)		
Allapur Ah 5f 5b (1986)	4.06 ha m/100sq.km	1.11 ha m/100 sq.km
Kushnoor NK 2g (1999)	4.86	1.38
Average Yield in Bore wells		
Kallambella Watershed	850 gph(Outside watershed)	2321 gph(Inside Watershed)
Employment		
Mankanihalla, Bagalkot (NWDPRA)	43.6	48.9

Source: Unpublished reports of State Watershed Development Department.

employment due to watershed development and follow up activities have been reported in several studies (Table 14.9)

In recent years more refined remote sensing through satellites has become a handy tool for monitoring the changes. Repetitive nature of satellite images is of great advantage in assessing the post project changes in a given area. A study by ISRO through its regional remote sensing service centre at Bangalore in 1998, using 1988 and 1996 satellite images has brought out the changes in development indicators (Appendix A-14.19).

A comparison of the remotely sensed images spaced 5-7 years apart (pre-and post-project) revealed favourable influence of watershed treatments. Biomass and cropped areas increased at the expense of wastelands, plantations and forest areas increased and the number of water bodies and water spread areas also increased. Substantial increase in area under fruit crops was observed due to horticultural programmes.

Prioritisation for Watershed Development

The basic criteria for prioritisation of watersheds should be the status of its degradation. However, this is not strictly followed in the 6 ongoing programmes in the state. One of the major ongoing programmes on catchment area treatment is river valley project covering 106.88 lakh ha to consider the silt load in water for prioritisation. NWDPRA and RDPR programmes consider rainfall and area under irrigation (Appendix A-14.20). The externally assisted World Bank (Sujala), ISPWDK, DFID and KWDP have their own guidelines for selection. However, the best criterion would be to depend on satellite imagery and the matic maps prepared by KSRSAC, which is still under preparation. It may be reiterated that the remote sensing data can be used effectively in managing land and water resources.

The state watershed development department has suggested to prioritise the *talukas* based on the rainfall and agricultural backwardness (Table 14.10).

TABLE 14.10

Prioritisation of *Talukas* for Watershed Development

Category	*No. of Talukas*	*Total Geographical Area (Lakh ha)*	*Area Available for Watershed Development*	*Area Treated till 2003*	*Ongoing Programme (Next 5-6 years)*
I	37	47.15	31.85	9.04(252.93)**	7.62(436.76)
II	56	61.80	36.54	7.98(223.66)	6.60(383.22)
III	46	44.23	28.73	8.92(229.94)	5.28(297.63)
IV	36	37.32	19.78	3.16(69.36)	2.42(132.86)
Total	**175**	**190.50**	**116.90***	**29.10(775.89)**	**21.92(1250.47)**

Note: * Does not include 12.80 lakh ha of degraded reserve forest area.
** Figures in the parentheses indicate Rs. in lakh.

Source: Watershed Development Department, Government of Karnataka, Bangalore.

14.5.5 Biotechnology and Seeds

In a broader sense biotechnology can be defined as 'the application of all natural sciences and engineering in the direct or indirect use of living organisms or parts of organisms, in their natural or modified forms, in an innovative manner in the production of goods and services and/or to improve existing industrial process. The market application of outputs is typically in the general areas of human health, food production, industrial bioprocessing and other public goods and environmental settings'.

Current Status and Growth of Biotechnology in Karnataka

Realising the immense potentials the state government starting with the establishment of the Department of Biotechnology has taken significant initiatives. The infrastructure advantage available in the state has attracted large number of companies and increased the investment in biotechnology, as compared to other states. As a result the state has become the leader in the biotechnology sector in the country. Presently, Karnataka has more than 40 biotech companies have been established in Karnataka between 2000-2003. This rate of growth far exceeds any other state. Karnataka has attracted maximum venture capital funding in the biotech sector in the country (over Rs. 100 crores). Almost 90 per cent of biotech companies in Karnataka are in and around Bangalore. The Bangalore Helix–the Biotech Research Park when completed would be spread over 90 acres. The park shall provide world-class infrastructure with water, power and telecom connectivity. Sectoral development of BT covers agriculture, health, industry and others. From a sample of 92 companies, contract research and bioinformatics has more number of companies of about 30 per cent. Followed by agri-biotech and health biotech companies with around 25 and 20 per cent respectively. The infrastructure facilities in terms of high level research and academic institutions, industry, information technology, etc. in the state have been attracting large number of firms.

More than 40 biotech companies have been established in Karnataka between 2000–2003. This rate of growth far exceeds any other State. Karnataka has attracted maximum Venture Capital funding in the Biotech sector in the country (over Rs. 100 crores).

Investment in Biotechnology

The state has provided a very congenial weather for establishment and development of biotech companies. Such companies increased from 35 to 92 between 1999-2000 and 2003-04 at an average annual growth rate of 28 per cent (Figure 14.17). Biotechnology is a capital-intensive sector, where the state has seen significant rise in investment, at an annual average rate of 61 per cent. Similarly the total revenue has risen from Rs. 355 crores to Rs. 1700 crores (Figure 14.18). Greater

FIGURE 14.17

Distribution of Biotech Companies

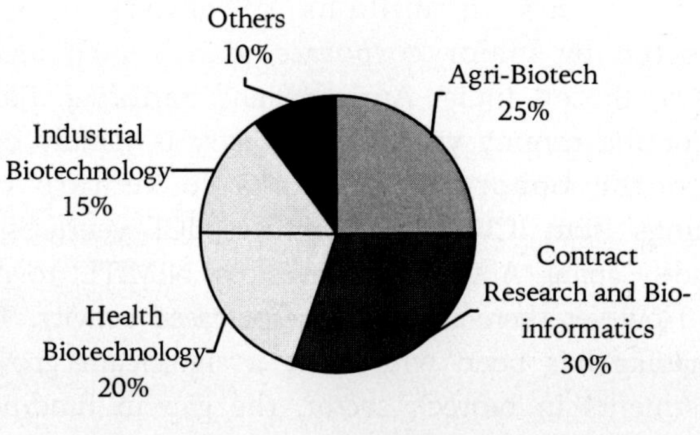

Source: Government of Karnataka, Department of Science and Technology, Bangalore.

potentialities of biotechnology are expected from its strength in augmenting the export sector. This can be seen from the rapid increase in export in the state. The exports from biotechnology sector have increased from Rs. 117 crores to Rs. 750 crores at an average annual growth rate of 61.5 per cent during 1999-00 to 2003-04 (14.19).

FIGURE 14.18

Growth of BT Sector in Karnataka (1993-94 to 2003-04)

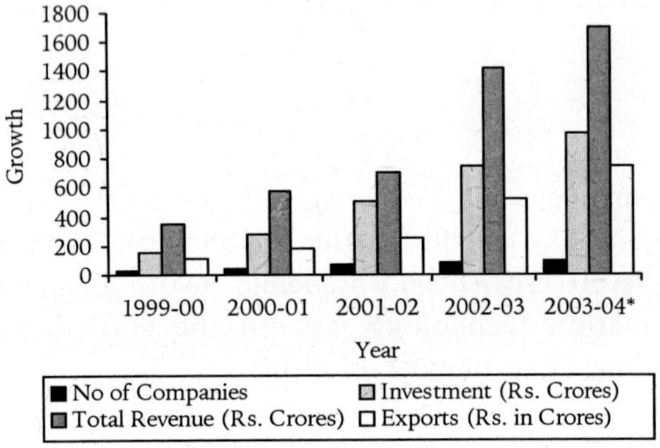

Note: * Projected growth.

Source: Government of Karnataka, Department of Science and Technology, Bangalore.

FIGURE 14.19

Average Annual Growth Rate (%)

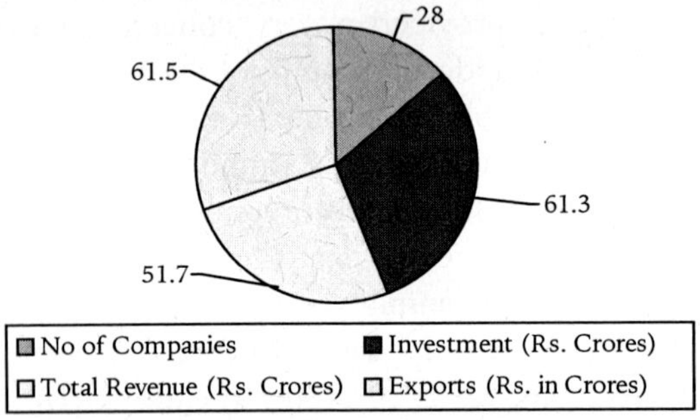

Source: Government of Karnataka, Department of Science and Technology, Bangalore.

Role of Financial Institutions

Investments in millions of dollars have been projected by major corporate giants such as Astra Zeneca, Biocon India, Aurigene and Sartorius, Biogenus Inc for the coming year. The industry is rapidly opening up to the opportunity, thanks to venture capital fundings from ICICI, UTI Ventures, ICF ventures, West Brigade Capital, Angel Fund Investors, NIMITLI to name a few. However there is room for increased activity. Though Karnataka has been witnessing a significant growth in investments in biotech sector, the gap in funding new biotech startups are still persistent partly due to longer gestation period. Considering the fact that biotechnology is a knowledge based industry and protection of IP rights of the findings is much important. The research institutions and companies involved in biotechnology research in the state have acquired 240 patents rights, out of which 177 are international patents. This indicates that biotechnology firms in the state are in the forefront of developing the sector.

14.6 Development Imperatives

14.6.1 Assessing the Challenges

The agriculture in Karnataka has to cope with the new challenges of achieving effective food security by raising the employment and purchasing power of the poor through the diversification of agriculture as well as facilitating shift of labour force from agriculture to the rural non-farm sector and making our agricultural products internationally competitive through the adoption of new cost reducing technologies. In order to track the policy imperatives, it will be essential first to bring together the challenges confronting the agricultural sector of Karnataka. Identification of such challenges can provide us material to locate the drivers of growth and the sub-sectors that need immediate attention. For policy these challenges emerge very clearly from the discussion that we had in the earlier section in this chapter. The first and foremost constraint that requires to be recognised is the large proportion of rain fed areas present in the agricultural sector in the state. Added to this, the variability in rainfall makes the situation worse in terms of droughts. Therefore, the development focus on rainfed agriculture becomes the primary concern to confront. In this context, watershed development approach can help to a large extent but it is necessary to supplement these efforts with a strong non-agricultural employment support. This also has to be supplemented with a fresh thinking on the natural resource conservation and interface between human and natural resource development.

Karnataka is not an exception among the other Indian states facing shrinking size of landholdings referred to as marginalisation of the size of holdings. The smaller size of landholdings not only restricts adoption of high-value addition crops in the state but also strongly constrain the growth of the crop economy. This also has brought down the viability threshold of the farmers as a group and made them economically fragile. In addition to this the support from Research and Development in the field of agriculture has decelerated in the recent past. We are expecting some new impetus to the technology and vying for the second revolution in the sector. This is feasible only if the Research and Development is stepped up and in the present can develop with public-private partnership. Biotechnology is one of the important ingredients in this development process.

Market is the driving force for the new growth thinking but it is severely restricted by the inadequate infrastructure and institutional setup. The Essential Commodities Act, Agricultural Produce Marketing Act, The Small Scale Industry Reservation and so on need to be thoroughly reviewed and revamped with a view to abolish all legal impediments under these Acts that restrict the entry of foreign direct investments in marketing storage and processing. Infrastructure is also a strong bottleneck in the other developmental fields in the agricultural sector. It will be essential to strengthen the infrastructural base so as to participate positively in domestic as well as international trade. Horticulture and floriculture are emerging sectors of the state, which can bring value addition and allow them to percolate up to the smallest grower, but this process needs to be supported by a proper infrastructural build-up. This process can also help to boost up the trade in marine and inland fisheries. In addition to these, we have listed out major challenges in the Box 14.5; their possible responses for enabling the development process are given there. In addition to these, it will be necessary to discuss some of the important sub sector-wise constraints presented above.

14.6.2 Focus on Rainfed Agriculture

We need to recognise the specific development support required for three major farming situations *viz.* rainfed agriculture, well (private) irrigated agriculture and canal (public) irrigated agriculture. Under well-irrigated farming situation, with water use efficiency as the central point, profitability of crops coupled with economic use of water, avoidance of water-intensive and mono-cropping systems should form the core aspects among others. In case of canal irrigated farming, water release discipline, management of drainage, proper crop planning and balanced use of fertiliser along with organic manures should be emphasised. In case of rain fed agriculture, adequate attention must be directed towards proper soil and water conservation measures, use of adequate amount of organic manure, adoption of improved agronomic practices, mixed cropping with tree crops as compulsory components and mixed farming could be major technological choices.

Added to these technological dimensions is a major study by Rao (2004) on drought prone areas (including Karnataka) so as to provide a social science perspective on the development of drought-prone areas. Rao (2004) in his major study on farmers in drought-prone areas has analysed farmers' response to technical and market opportunities and assessed the adequacy of institutional and policy required. The study concludes that, farmers in drought-prone areas are responsive to market signals and are willing and able to use modern inputs, ready to undertake risk and investment, and capable of

BOX 14.5

Major Challenges in the Agricultural Sector

Major Challenges	*Responses for Enabling the Acceptance*
Threatened stagnation in agri-growth. Possibility of decelerating growth.	Locating growth in the emerging growth inducing crops/sectors.
Low value addition in agricultural sector.	Removal of marketing bottlenecks and enabling remunerative price situation.
Fast approaching optima on technological front.	Investment boosting in R&D sector.
Large proportions of rainfed/dry land area.	Technological options and diversification of economic base.
Marginalisation of agricultural land base.	Group initiatives and arresting the process through institutional options.
Inadequate growth in public and private investment.	Attracting private investments in the sunrise sectors. Locating sub-sectors with new growth options.
Regional disparities in investment, technology adoption and growth	Prudent regional allocation of growth inducers.
Inadequate safety nets.	Revamping and redesigning the safety net programmes. Effective delivery.
Conflicting growth *versus* environmental options.	Resolving the issues amicably. Reducing the intensity of negative externalities.

squeezing positive net returns from crop production even in harsh environment and volatile markets. Government has pursued short-sighted policies of concentration of attention, investment and efforts on relatively small but dynamic and politically articulate pockets in agriculture, neglecting the main body. In spite of crop yield improvements in drought-prone areas, development gap between green revolution and drought-prone regions has widened. Lack of institutional and policy support could be the single most important factor impeding the progress of drought prone agriculture. Institutional and policy support is weak, undependable and indifferent towards backward areas and poorer sections.

The study by Rao (2002) has indicated the needed focus in three basic areas *viz.*-human development, resource development and institutional development for providing basic foundation for agricultural growth and development. With respect to resource development, land and water are two critical inputs (Algah, 1999). Lack of attention to conserving and augmenting the productivity of these two critical inputs would prove to be costly. One of the main strategies followed in improving agriculture in drought prone areas is watershed development, which takes a comprehensive and integrated view of land and water resources in watershed. The studies by Deshpande and his associates (1993, 1999 and 1999) have brought out the desirable impact of watershed on yield, employment and shifting towards high value crops, but have also brought out faulty implementation strategies adopted. Unless development administration addresses these issues, the pay-offs from watershed investment will be low.

14.6.3 Developing the Initiatives for the Small Farmers

Karnataka is a state of small and marginal farmers. In another decade, the percentage of small and marginal holdings to total holdings in the state would be around 80. Further, it is also reported that productivity, technical as well as allocative efficiencies were higher on medium and large farms than on small and marginal farms. Hence the challenge is to create an appropriate development environment for 80 per cent of holdings in the state (Bisaliah and Krishnegowda, 2001). A study by Chengappa, *et al.* (1996) has brought out source of the major problems faced by small farmers in the State.

Small and marginal farmers are caught up in a vicious circle of low investment, low productivity, and low income. The challenge is to empower them with appropriate changes in policy front, technology front and institutional front to enable them to get these constraints released unless some of these addressed through group action by small and marginal farmers with the support of appropriate policy-technology-institution matrix, their survival in the wake of liberalisation will be in danger. Land legislation to enable them to lease in and lease out land and legislation to prevent further subdivision beyond the threshold limit could form a part of policy change. Organisation of group action in rebuilding depleted and degraded natural resource base, in input and output marketing, in putting pressure on agricultural research institutions to develop low cost and risk-free technologies, in approaching the credit institutions for loans, in dealing with agri-business firms, and in availing the benefits public extension system could provide a stage for developing a strong development constituency of small and marginal farmers.

14.6.4 Rebuild Natural Resource Base: Organic Approach to Farming

It may be recalled from earlier analysis that seed-fertiliser-chemical approach to productivity augmentation has depleted and degraded the natural resource base for sustainable agricultural growth and development. With this strategy, the very biological equilibrium has been disturbed. Unless this equilibrium is restored by rebuilding natural resource base the sustainable agricultural growth with competitive edge will not be possible. Holistic development of natural resources seeking sustainable livelihood security for all life forms in the region is the focal point for future strategy. This would warrant search for technologies, policies and institutional approaches for rebuilding the natural resource base. Restoration of soil health and fertility through appropriate technology package including vegetative cover would be crucial. At the community level, vegetative cover around the village on main roads leading to farms, on tank/canal bund and on common land will have to be promoted to provide sound environment support to agriculture, in addition to building up vegetative cover at the farm level. Recently, Government of Karnataka (2004) has come out with State Policy on Organic Farming, and articulated very well the advantages of organic farming technology *vis-à-vis* green revolution technology. The policy document has also very well recognised the principal requirements for organic farming, policy objectives on organic farming and strategies for promotion and revival of this traditional system of farming.

One important dimension that needs to be made explicit is that organic farming in its pure form is a slow process and its sustainability in the short run is difficult in view of constraints on availability of organic matter considerable price premium expected for organically produced products, and lack of faith in the Indian system of certification for organic products in the international market (Bisaliah, 2004). Hence what is needed is to make a gradual transition by producing adequate organic matter by building appropriate institutional structure at the village level for organic farming and by using a judicious mix of both modern and organic farming technologies. Hence any ambition with organic farming fundamentalism to make a big leap forward in pure organic farming strategy is likely to meet with disappointment.

Forest Development

There has been a tendency to use the statutes and controls as bargaining power for gains and not as instruments of service to the cause of conservation, rational utilisation and help to the user community. This approach will change only if more rural institutions like *Panchayats*, village forest committees, self-help groups, etc. are empowered under the existing Acts and rules to become agencies of control, investments, conservation and returns, higher investments, productivity, harvests and utilisation should be the objectives of management. Statutes and empowerment coming in the way of these developmental attributes should be continuously reviewed and amended to cut the red-tape in administration. Another area of worry is the complicated judicial system, where delays, trials and punishments do not help the cause of conservation and development of biodiversity, which is so vital to the healthy existence of a man and the animals. Ceiling on landholding and provisions under Karnataka land Reforms Act come in the way of industrial plantations. Rising of trees and forest crops should be termed as 'plantation' under categories like tea, coffee, rubber, linolae, etc. which enjoy some exemptions under the Act. Credit policies need some relaxation for tree cultivation. Insurance for trees and forests should be available to cover calamities.

14.6.5 Infrastructure: Key for the Growth Momentum

Market and Prices

With liberalised international trade in agricultural and horticultural commodities under WTO, the farmers of Karnataka (like their counterparts in other parts of the country) are likely to encounter the situation of volatile prices (more towards downward). Unless safety net in the form of Minimum Support Price (MSP) Policy is properly defined (especially with respect to cost components) and implemented the farmers' economic interests will be adversely affected. With respect to cost of production, which is one of the factors considered in deciding (MSP), the contest on definition and cost components is still unresolved. Farmers argue for including managerial input/cost as an item in total cost of production, and for measuring and costing of risk. But the CACP, Government of India, is yet to consider managerial cost (even though it is computed) and risk cost (at least normal coverage insurance premium paid by the farmers). Unless these are considered among others, the MSP will not be a remunerative price. Hence any perspective on providing safety net to farmers should keep this in view.

The problem is not merely the definition of cost components and their consideration in deciding MSPs for various farm commodities, but also even the announced prices have less of relevance to farmers of Karnataka. The Agricultural Policy Resolution of Government of Karnataka (1995, Para 35) observes as follows:

"The problem of farmers is not merely one of price, but also of the market structure operating for agriculture products and also the conduct of this structure. Two studies (Report No. 8, July 2003 and Report No. 10, March 2004) conducted by KSAPC have brought the inadequacies and exploitative nature of marketing system and indicated the need for some structural changes in the system. With liberal trade regime, the role of private trading is not merely inevitable but also important. What is needed is to strengthen the marketing system in the public sector especially regulated markets, which are still dominant market outlets for farmers in case of pulses, oilseeds and maize. In addition to regulation of malpractices by traders and commission agents in regulated markets and addressing the problems of inadequacies, there are many directions in which improvements are acquired. For example, provision of information to farmers about the benefits of sale in regulated markets, streamlining of pledge loan scheme, and amalgamation of regulated markets are some of the suggestions made by KSAPC (Report No. 10, March 2004). Added to this is the need for the system of matching the demand with agricultural production plans. Further group marketing by farmers, farmers markets and strengthening of rural periodic markets, agricultural marketing extension

(KSAPC, Report No. 10, March 2004) and incentive for private sector to participate in market developments are some of the suggestions. Even though private marketing needs to be encouraged with minimum regulations, the need for strengthening public and cooperative marketing sector is to be recognised, since this sector provides some kind of reference point to farmers for making choice of market outlet for sale."

Some of the important issues that feature in the changed circumstances can be grouped into three groups. First group includes domestic market reforms and making the domestic market competitive and non-discriminatory. A proper conduit between the domestic and international market has to be established. Second comes the identification of commodities and the sectors that need to be encouraged in these circumstances. Third component involves preparedness for the likely market shocks and therefore putting in place a proper safety net programme. Specific issues that would require attention would be:

i. Creating a market access for domestic products *vis-à-vis* imported agricultural commodities.

ii. Elimination of all market imperfections. A comprehensive review of existing legal instruments be undertaken with a view to simplifying and synchronising them. The policy of levy on rice millers and sugar mills, monopsony purchase of cotton in Maharashtra, statutory rationing system in West Bengal and system of state advised prices of sugarcane need to be phased out.

iii. Creation of market incentives for the farm produce that require special treatment due to vulnerability to international price fluctuations.

iv. Establish an effective price monitoring system. Market information kiosks involving information on prices, quality, international trade centres and technology need to be setup. Statistical system and database should be strengthened to improve the coverage and quality of agricultural marketing related information and to reduce the time lag in its availability. Cooperatives and group marketing by farmers should be encouraged.

v. Market intervention system either to private agencies or by the State agencies. PRIs, NGOs and self-help groups be effectively involved in improving awareness about post-harvest handling methods and creation and maintenance of infrastructure at primary market level. A selective MIS needs to be put in place for commodities, which are not covered by the minimum price support programme.

Research, Extension and Development

Agri research and extension are the keys to provoke development and dissemination of the technologies. There are quite a few issues that emerge in this context. First, with regard to research focus, either in the public or private sector, the controversy on biotechnology needs to be sorted out. Biotechnology has emerged as one of the most innovative and powerful tools to increase agricultural productivity in a sustainable basis (Alagh, 1999). It holds promise for increasing the productivity; quality, efficient processing and utilisation of products and at the same time reduce reliance on agro-chemicals and other external inputs. But while accepting these arguments, the need for biosafety cannot be contested. The vision is that application of biotechnology to evolve new genetically engineered strains of plants, animals, fishes and plants of high nutritional quality, resistance to pests and diseases and healthy attuned to environment-friendly farm practices will have to be evolved. While doing so issues such as proper testing of transgenic and biosafety will have to be addressed. Intensified research efforts are needed in the application of biotechnology for increasing shelf life and converting foodstuffs into more palatable, nutrious and stable forms. Also public awareness relating to benefits of biotechnology and IPR related issues will be necessary to harness benefits of the frontier science. In fact advances in biotechnology genomics and information technology have created immense possibilities for their application in agriculture.

The need for restructuring public extension system is often argued and accepted platforms of reform. (Bisaliah, 2004). There are a large number of components that involve in any such reform. Agricultural development segmentation, shrinking land holding size, changing pattern of demand for farm products, changing behaviour of farmers who are not merely knowledge seekers but also knowledge providers, emergence of multi-agency system of extension, emergence of complex decision making process due to transition from protected to competitive agriculture, broader extension agenda (which goes much beyond production pursuit) encompassing extension services for natural resource management, marketing, poverty alleviation, mainstreaming women into extension process and environment concerns and trade are the triggers of change in extension system.

Added to these triggers for regearing agricultural extension system the need for public sector extension systems to operate in a partnership mode involving farmers associations, NGOs agri-business firms, etc. is well placed. Further some regulation of private sector, especially with respect to material inputs (seeds, fertilisers and pesticides) supply may be warranted. Given these, there are three major issues, which need to be addressed with respect to public extension system. First, whether the existing institutional structure is adequate to address the extension needs of agriculture sector under emerging technological and development environment? Second, what kind of changes are needed in the extension service package (addition of marketing and natural resource management, etc.) offered at present? Third, are the extension education methodologies followed at present for a segmented agriculture sector relevant? (Bisaliah, 2004)

Towards Improvement in the Delivery System

Time and again it has been said that the public expenditure incurred on the development schemes in rural areas do not reach the intended beneficiaries. The usual process of formulation of a development scheme begins either at the state headquarters or dished out by the Central Government. Most of the schemes have inbuilt mechanism of monitoring and strict adherence to the specified norms as visualised at the headquarters of the state in the process of designing such schemes. It is very rarely that any scheme is discussed with the end beneficiaries or administrators at grass root level before its formulation. Therefore, the evaluations of different schemes have pointed to three defects, *viz.* i) defects in formulation of the scheme, ii) defects in implementation of the scheme, and iii) non cooperation by the beneficiaries. Rarely evaluations have pointed to the lack of investment or misuse of funds.

It is noted by a number of analysts that the state agricultural sector and rural sector have major bottlenecks in terms of density and availability of infrastructure. Among the major rural services, we include density of roads, transportation system, communication system, agricultural extension system, agricultural markets, processing units and input delivery system. Looking into the available statistics it is not difficult to reach a conclusion that most of the rural services in Karnataka have been inadequate and are characterised by difficult access. Across the plan periods large sums have been spent on infrastructure and public investment in agricultural sector, however, even today, barring a few examples, the delivery systems of services in rural areas have been extremely unsatisfactory. It is, therefore, essential to boost the service network in the rural areas so that the production efficiency can be harnessed fully. Lack of efficiency and availability of services in the rural areas have a circular and self-perpetuating logic. Non-availability and difficult access to services make the production system inefficient and such production system finally causes inefficiency in distribution. In order to break the vicious circle it is essential that there is a substantial improvement in the rural infrastructure availability. Karnataka always comes at somewhere around the average level in an interstate comparison in the country in terms of many indicators. It has been observed that over the last 20 years the position of the state has not changed substantially. In other words, the state has retained more or less an average growth rate even in the infrastructural indicators. Therefore, lack of infrastructure becomes an important bottleneck and it is essential to attend to this on priority. It has been noted that a substantial amount of the state expenditure being incurred on inefficient subsidies, which unfortunately are the cause as well as the result of inefficient production system. A logical answer to this tangle is to reorient the expenditure on inefficient subsidies towards revamping and providing better quality of delivery system in the rural areas. The total subsidy amount in the latest year in the agricultural sector touched 601.64 crore rupees during 1995-96 (GoK, 2000c). It was 1.56 per cent of GSDP in 1995-96 and scaled down to 1.02 per cent of GSDP in 1999-00. Even if half of this expenditure is diverted towards better delivery systems probably, it will add to improve the efficiency production.

There are many challenges confronting Karnataka agriculture such as severe climatic and natural resource constraints, slow technology adoption, landholding based marginalisation, biological disequilibrium in farms, depletion of natural resources, both the opportunities and threats of GATT/WTO, declining trends in capital formation for agriculture and different development needs of diversified farming system. All these concerns and challenges would warrant a proper response to prevent further rural-urban development divide.

Breeding and Managing Crops to Conserve Water

It is crucial to breed crop varieties to adapt to high stress environments like drought. This requires researchers to involve farmers in the process of selection to enable scientific breeding. In addition, increase in water harvesting efforts, conservation tillage, integrated nutrient management, alternate wet-dry irrigation and aerobic rice cultivation are crucial to conserve water.

Research on the Effects of Climatic Change on Water Resources

The onus of the severest consequences of global climatic change will fall on developing countries due to their poor resilience capacities and are largely dependent on agriculture for their sustenance. Agriculture is the largest user of water resources and changes in quantity and reliability of water supplies due to climatic change threaten the welfare of poor farmers. The largest impacts will be on the developing countries—rural areas dependent on agriculture for income and employment.

Reforming Policies to Improve Water Quality

Problem of poor quality does not receive adequate attention in many developing countries. Hence polluted and unsafe water is increasing cost of health care and threatening ecosystems. Therefore investing in water quality monitoring, establishing feasible quantifiable water quality standards for different uses, incorporating water quality standards in water rights systems and educating policy makers about water quality and environmental water uses are the need of the hour. Challenging task is making polluters pay and changing people's habit of using and discharging low quality water. Further adequate investment is needed for water treatment and sewage disposal in semi urban and urban areas. Good quality water is vital for sustainability of ecosystems which regulate quantity and quality of water. It is necessary to devise policy to subsidise small farmers directly for environmental services for protecting upper watersheds.

Incentives for Efficient Use of Irrigation Water

Even though pricing water for irrigation is inherently difficult, complex and faces resistance from farmers, increasing water scarcity and falling financial resources for water development, necessitate such a reform. In water pricing system, incentives for efficient water use can be designed. The Water Users Association can be empowered to regulate water distribution within the group of water users, charge an initial fee for basic quantity of water to cover the operation, maintenance and depreciation costs. For any demand above the basic quantity, the users need to pay an efficiency price equal to the value of water in alternative uses.

14.7 Drivers of Growth

14.7.1 Crop Husbandry: Is Diversification a Key?

Karnataka has a traditional foodgrain dominant crop pattern. The cropping pattern has shown some changes in the last five decades which have not been significant enough to provide growth initiative and trade friendliness to the agricultural sector. However, the changes are in the right direction with a few commercial crops emerging slowly but strongly on the scene. The productivity has not still emerged as a driving force. It has been argued strongly that diversification of the crop economy will provide new growth initiatives in the state. This argument emerged out of the observations made in northeastern states of the country where the productivity plateaus in the food economy have been almost reached. Karnataka however, presents a totally different picture with a large number of marginal and smallholdings totally committed to growing foodgrains under the pressure of natural uncertainties. Therefore, it would be difficult to induce these farmers to diversify *en-mass* into a new area and new crops. Certainly, such inducement has to be price driven and therefore, emanates from the market-oriented commercial crops. Hitherto, Karnataka has been on the forefront of certain commercial crops/commodities that have proved their presence beyond doubt in the production sector (e.g. sericulture). In addition to this, the recent phenomenon of diversifying into horticulture and floriculture has provided a new driver to the economy. Despite all these, the most intriguing question remains un-answered viz., will the marginal and small farmers capably participate into the cultivation of these new vocations? The impediments are basically on four sides. First, do we have the technology for such crops to be adopted by the small and marginal farmers that is accessible and farmer-friendly? Unfortunately, the answer to this question is quite obviously NO. We certainly posses technologies that can support a large farm but will be unviable and are not feasible to be adopted by majority of the small farmers. The second question originates out of this and that is addressed to the economic strength of the small and marginal farmers of Karnataka to participate in this process of diversification. *Prima facie* it seems quite difficult for the farmers of Karnataka to participate in this changed environment of diversification process. But it can be made feasible by providing a price and market-led incentive structure. The third question originates from the food security domain and it has been time and again said that commercialisation of agriculture and diversification would push back cultivation of foodgrains. That will also impact the food availability thereby pushing the foodgrain growers and consumers to the wall. This argument has been put forth strongly in the recent past. It would be however, difficult to perceive a situation in which most of the foodgrain growers will participate in the transformation process towards commercial farming and therefore such threats is difficult to perceive. More than that, the reduced load on the foodgrain economy will help the price trends and that will benefit the weaker farmers' group who has stayed back in food economy sector. Lastly, the process of diversification always argues for the crops, which are market-friendly and have better price incentive in the market. Unfortunately, the marketing infrastructure itself is a challenge and we may have to deal with this challenge in the coming decade. Probably, there lies the key to provide the diversification to Karnataka's agriculture.

14.7.2 Rainfed Agriculture: Converting a Liability into an Asset

Karnataka is one of the states having meagre area under irrigation and vast drought prone tracts. It is well known that, about 80 per cent of the state is under rainfed conditions and major share of this falls in dry agro-climatic zones. Therefore, regular visits of droughts to the state are neither unexpected nor avoidable. Frequent droughts leave the state economy depleted with resources and that too with regular frequency. In such a situation, it will be necessary to work on a hypothesis that the rainfed agriculture itself becomes the vanguard of new growth initiative. It has been recorded that, despite the presence of vast rainfed areas in the state, Karnataka could record a growth rate in the neighbourhood of 3 per cent consistently over the years except a few patches of stagnation. In addition to that, Karnataka is not one of those hopelessly placed states in terms of its quantum of poverty and poverty reduction performance. In this context, it will be essential to review the potential contribution of rainfed agriculture to the growth of the state's agricultural sector.

Except a few spots of irrigated agriculture, most of the state depends on cereals and pulses as major commodities to support livelihood system. The productivity of these commodities has not been growing with the same pace as that in the other neighbouring states but the small commercial agricultural sector comprising oilseeds, cotton, sericulture, sugarcane, horticulture and floriculture under rainfed conditions have been keeping the state on the present growth path. It will not be imprudent to design and place the growth of agricultural sector in these emerging cash-intensive and high-density agriculture. Rainfed agricultural technology for all these crops is available across the shelf and has shown proven results but needs to be propelled and made farmer-friendly. In that perspective, the rain fed agriculture of Karnataka can still direct the path of growth and will not remain as an impediment on growth in the coming decades.

Watershed Development: Towards Sustained Development

The technology for conservation of natural resources is well documented and sustainable production systems have been identified through several years of experience of the community. The systems are further refined and modified in several agricultural universities and research institutions. The task before us is to formulate them in to implementable programmes and create an organisational set-up to translate these programmes in to actions. As the degradation of natural resources has already advanced to critical stage, the remedial measures will have to be on a 'mission mode'. The task of individual players (development departments and NGOs) should be well defined and focused, the activities of different departments will have to be suitably coordinated to achieve the desired goal in the stipulated time. Though the major responsibility of regeneration rests with the government, people's involvement is essential for sustainability. Watershed development is an infrastructure development programme in agriculture and envisioning such a marine programme with participation of people can make it one of the best anti-poverty programmes. Several departments are simultaneously working in a district without much concern for convergence of common goals. This results merely in wastage of scarce resources. *Zilla Panchayat* should be in a position to keep track of all the programmes at the district level and facilitate convergence of different departments that promote economic activities and generate increased employment opportunities. Involvement should be something more than mere 'participation' or 'work for wages'. The money collected as contributions can be made use of the watershed work itself. To get the landowners and the landless equally interested in the programme, a watershed plus approach is suggested by the Planning

Commission (Box 14.6). Conscious efforts to promote non-farm employment and increased land access to the landless as well as promotion of self-help groups (SHG) form a part of the new approach. However, all care is necessary to ensure that these 'plus' activities will not shadow the basic programmes of watershed development. Watershed development programmes to show the desired results will have to be on a 'ridge to valley' concept and implemented fully on the entire catchment. Traditional methods of water harvesting and conservation of water need to be encouraged. Quite often, this is not happening either due to shortage of funds or due to guidelines restrictions. This half-hearted effort will not serve the purpose and often wastes resources. The approach should reaffirm to implement the programme fully. It is necessary that WDD prepares GIS maps showing the area covered under different programmes and reconcile the statement of area treated and expenditure incurred.

Watersheds are to be prioritised on the basis of their erosion/degradation status rather than on their 'agricultural backwardness' and rainfall as done at present. Land use land cover maps based on the concept of Integrated Mission for Sustainable Development (IMSD) prepared by remote sensing agencies to be made use of for this purpose. The resource inventory of selected watersheds will have to be made by KSRSAC or ISRO; the same agencies can also be entrusted with the impact study of the completed watersheds. The major drawback in the watershed development programmes implemented so far has been the poor planning for withdrawal and post-project maintenance. It is almost universal that the pace of development reduces and the structures built under government cost are neglected once the active participation and funding by government is stopped. Therefore, the future programmes will be implemented on partnership principles between governmental, non-governmental organisations and the people. Planning Commission suggests an increase in the cost to be shared by the community from 25 per cent in Tenth Plan to 50 per cent in Thirteenth Plan. Same norm could be adopted by the state on all works carried on individual holdings and productive community lands. In case of government wastelands, however, the entire cost has to be met by the government itself.

Two major drawbacks in the watershed development programmes implemented so far have been the poor planning for withdrawal, post project maintenance and frequent shifts in the designs of implementation.

BOX 14.6

Watershed Plus Paradigm Shift to Involve Larger Section of the Community

- Programme specific and focused project approach.
- Greater flexibility in implementation.
- Well-defined role for state, district and village level institutions.
- An exit protocol for project implementing agencies (PIAs).
- A twin track approach that provides for short-term and long-term benefits in the implementation of projects.
- A combination of government organisations/NGOs as PIAs.
- A greater role for women.
- An effective role for *Panchayat Raj* Institutions (PRIs).
- Bringing self-help groups comprising rural poor, especially those belonging to SC/ST categories to the forefront.
- Establishing a credit facility from financial institutions.
- Transparency in implementation.
- Effective use of remote sensing data furnished by the National Remote Sensing Agency.

Source: Department of Land Resources, Ministry of Rural Development, GoI, 2001.

14.7.3 International Trade as Growth Booster

Karnataka state is emerging as a strong player in agricultural trade scenario. It is not only the IT products but horticultural produce, processed products and floriculture are the forerunners in the process. The state has also a very conducive climatic pattern and investment atmosphere to encourage trade. But there are two major bottlenecks that hinder the initiatives. First comes in the form of non-availability of infrastructure, and that causes the price spread. Consequently, the grower does not benefit and incentive is not created. Second, there is a lack of institutional set up to encourage and step up the process of integration of the chain from grower to the final destination. The value addition to this process will act as the best incentive. It is essential to facilitate the emergence of vertical integration between farmers, processors and retailers to facilitate high value addition in agriculture. In the coming years, Karnataka agriculture will have to put in place food safety laws and set up appropriate mechanism for enforcement on sanitary and phyto-sanitary standards and also promote large processing facilities with state of the art technology.

Strategies for Increasing the Export of Horticultural Produce

The last decade has been very important from the point of view of emergence of horticulture as the most important field for diversification. While our total production of horticultural commodities and our world standing is a matter of great pride, our productivity and quality leave much to be achieved. In the era of globalisation, produce has to be of international quality and globally competitive. The future expansion of horticulture has to be in arid and semi-arid areas and on underutilised crops. The demand for horticultural produce is on the rise due to increasing population, changing food habits, realisation of high nutritional value of horticultural crops and greater emphasis on post-harvest management and value addition. There is also considerable potential to exploit export opportunities. However, several challenges *viz.* fast eroding gene pool, rapid population build up, shrinking land and other natural resources, serious production constraints, both biotic and abiotic and huge post-harvest losses.

Horticultural sector of Karnataka calls for immediate policy attention and growth boosting investment. This sector can emerge as the main driver of future growth. First, the data on horticultural produce, incorporating the quality and quantum of products should be readily available to direct and place the growth efforts. Varieties covering long shelf life, fibre content, colour and proper timings of harvest of various fruits have to be popularised. Second, low cost greenhouses and other technologies suitable for different agro-climatic regions will help to step up the value addition. Focus has to be on dry-land horticulture and since the supports extended by National Horticultural Board as well as APEDA have proved growth boosting, it needs to be stepped up. Third, a need for quality planting material and its mass multiplication. This has to be supported by tapping proper segments of domestic and international markets. Lastly, even though the Directorate of Horticulture of the state should be credited with the achievements on growth front, but it will be better to have Horticultural Research and Development Council be established to develop functional linkages with agencies involved in promotion of agricultural crops.

Sericulture: Need to Extend Caution

Silk sector of Karnataka has to compete with international quality of silk and therefore, it is required that not only the quality of the yarn produced has to be monitored but also the cost of such production is maintained in a competitive regime. The silk marketing process has also to be revisited, as still there is no pro-active and aggressive marketing strategy to make the product available at international level and of the type. Some of the important measures that need to be taken in order to make silk sector vibrant could be described into four major components. In the production sector, it is necessary to minimise the dependence of important silk by producing bivoltine and multivoltine cultivars. Maintaining the quality of production of silk and modernisation of the production sector is quintessential. Mulberry cultivation as an essential ingredient of silk industry requires attention on the front of type of cultivars, crop management and integrated nutrition management. Large-scale commercialisation of the professional and farmers participation in an integrated framework will help to increase value addition. It is also necessary to keep in view the international standards of the products so as to place our products in a global competitive situation. Second, the market of silk, silk yarns has to be properly tapped at a price affordable to the producers. It is required to strengthen the symbiotic relationship between industry-state and market to create a policy framework, so as to put the silk industry on a newfound growth path. Third, it is required to rationalise and reconstruct the industry portfolio for specific requirement so as to deploy the scarce resources to the areas that need to be modernised. Lastly, it is felt necessary by the stakeholders and expressed that upgradation, physical and social infrastructures are essential to enhance the capabilities of the industry's portfolio. There needs to be a quantum jump in the infrastructure and mechanisation.

By 2005, the textile sector would have been fully integrated into the WTO General Agreement on Tariffs and Trade (GATT) and all quotas will have disappeared, while it is difficult to give a precise picture of the global textiles and clothing market after 2004, countries which are fully using their quotas in the years preceding 2005 will probably increase exports after that date and other countries may not benefit. Since the textiles and clothing sector is fully integrated into WTO/GATT, the countries and companies, which adapt first to the challenges of the new market will be better placed to secure their market position. In view of this, it is certain that the changes in the textiles and clothing sectors will bring more risks and challenges than new opportunities, particularly for smaller exporters in developing countries and economics in transition. Comprehensive preparation is a must to manage these risks and take action to secure existing or additional markets.

> The Agreement on Textiles and Clothing will end on 31st December 2004 and with the quota system for international trade in textiles and clothing. As a result, trade in these sectors will undergo a fundamental change. That necessitates a close monitoring to sustain growth of this vital sector.

Trade in Fisheries Sector

The inland fish production of the state is about 1.2 lakh tonnes, which does not reflect efficient resource utilisation through adoption of focused development plans. It would be possible to achieve about 1 lakh tonnes of fish production by using minor tank resources efficiently. In order to achieve this goal, it is essential to rejuvenate *taluka* level nurseries that were existing earlier, encourage establishment of private seed-rearing facility in the command area of large major tanks of more than 100 hectares with technical and financial assistance. It is also desired to optimise some of the new concepts like rearing of fish seed in pens and cages in major tanks and small reservoirs. It should be made mandatory to use these technologies instead of depending on rearing farms for seed stocking.

Aquatic weeds have become a major menace in some of the perennial and canal connected tanks. It is proved beyond doubt that repeated manual and or mechanical methods of weed control are effective in controlling weeds. It should be made mandatory to stock grass carp in all the weed infested tanks so that a biological control of weeds could be possible. If grass carp is not available in the state, it could be imported from areas of availability. Weed control and desilting of tanks could also be achieved through participatory approach involving all the tank water users for various purposes. Medium-sized carps such as *Fimbriatus Calbasu*, *Pulchellus*, *Dubius*, etc. and cat fishes such as *Clarius*, *Ompok*, *Mystus*, etc. and different species of murrels formed a lucrative fishery about three decades back. Rejuvenation of all these resources demands strategic planning and implementation in a phased manner. Some of the exotic fish species like *Clarias Garipennus* have gained entry into the state without any control/ check. It is essential to formulate suitable state policy for checking unauthorised entry of non-certified exotic fish species.

The fish produced at the farm site does not fetch competitive price to the farmer due to monopoly of small group of buyers. It is pertinent to establish ice plants in close proximity of each cluster of tanks to maintain fish quality and facilitate better marketing network. The culture of fresh water prawn under monoculture and polyculture system could be an important commercial proposition in tanks established in saline and alkaline soils and in other areas of reservoir commands. The cost effectiveness of the technology, easy seed availability, availability of formulated feed, management of culture systems, etc. demand a serious attempt in popularising the technology of freshwater prawn production. The government/some private agency should take up seed production so as to facilitate easy seed availability for the interested farmers. The knowledge transfer and capacity building of farmers through trainings and large-scale demonstration should be prioritised to produce export-oriented product of high market value. Most of the fish stocks being used for seed production are believed to be inbred leading to genetic depression. A continuous genetic improvement programme for important fish species and genetic improvement of indigenous fish species needs to be addressed by the scientific community in a phased manner.

Facilitate the institutions that can improve the governance of marine and coastal resources. Develop eco-friendly technologies for harvesting inshore resources. Develop proper low cost technologies for the introduction of artificial reefs, which could also act as a barrier to destructive fishing practices by bottom trawlers. A uniform fishing ban during the breeding period needs to be implemented. However, while doing so interest of small-scale fishers should be protected. The state should implement the provisions of the FAO Code of Conduct for Responsible Fisheries. FAO recommends 30 trawlers for every 10 km of coastline. However the existing number of trawlers is three times more than the required number and hence limited entry concept needs to be implemented. The Supreme Court of India has banned mechanised fishing within five km from the shore and the Karnataka state has also prohibited the operation of mechanised fishing in the inshore areas, which should be implemented strictly. The Department of Fisheries should undertake the task of identifying the fish breeding grounds with the help of local fishing communities and scientists. Till such time all wetlands and backwaters should be declared as fish breeding centres under the provision of the Karnataka Marine Fisheries (Regulation) Act. A notice to *Panchayats* could be issued indicating the reason for declaring such areas and seek their cooperation in protecting these areas from pollution and fishing. The

Department of Fisheries could spell out the permitted and prohibited activities in these areas.

14.7.4 Vision and Challenges

Agricultural sector of Karnataka has been going through the phases of stagnation and growth during the last five decades. It is characterised by large share of rainfed area, frequent bouts of droughts and has only about 20 per cent area under assured irrigation. Despite these constraints, the sector has contributed positively towards the aggregate economic growth of the state. In fact, it is the growth of agricultural sector that dictates the overall growth rate of the state's economy even though its share in GSDP is declining. Following Lewisian process, it was expected that in the process of growth, the workforce from agricultural sector would be transferred to the tertiary and secondary sectors, but probably this process is not strong enough in Karnataka. As a result, the share of GSDP originating from agriculture is declining at a faster rate than the workforce dependent on the agricultural sector. Consequently, the per capita share of GSDP is also declining in the sector. Added to this, agricultural sector has been facing more or less stagnating trends in capital formation during the past decade.

There are three major impediments to growth in the agricultural sector of Karnataka *viz.* the lagging northern Karnataka regions due to large share of drought-prone area coupled with low private capital investment. Regional disparities, therefore, became quite sharp in the face of failure of initial investments in these regions. Agricultural sector of Karnataka is also facing impediments in the form of growth initiatives in the post-harvest processing as well as value additions in the production process. These impediments are emboldened by regional imbalances, frequent drought conditions and inefficiency in managing irrigated agriculture. The future vision therefore, would require concerted efforts towards removing the regional imbalances in growth by promoting private as well as public initiatives in value addition focused on the post-harvest sector and picking up growth leads from the allied agricultural sector to participate pro-actively in domestic and world trade.

In the crop production sector, the phases of growth and stagnation indicate that we are likely to confront a technological bottleneck in the coming decade as the yield rates have been reaching close to the technological optima. That would require placement of growth in the non-food crop sector, without neglecting the food security issues. Oilseeds, pulses, sugarcane, maize and other millets are the crops that need to be attended to on technological as well as trade fronts.

There are quite a few issues concerning the land use policy and land reforms in the state. The significant share of utilisable but wasted land resources need to be brought under economic cultivation and the process of urbanisation has to be carefully monitored. Marginalisation of the size of holding and increasing number of the small and marginal farmers is an issue that has to be attended through a fresh process of reforms. It can either be done by consolidating the small patches of holdings but probably better achieved through informal cooperation among the small and marginal farmers in the production process. This has to be done for selected crops and crop groups by developing proper market chains or forward markets. Land augmentation by private irrigation could have been one of the strategies, however in the present situation of overexploitation of groundwater and limited availability of surface water resources, it will not be a prudent strategy to emphasise on irrigation alone. It will be more pragmatic to transfer the resources towards enhancing productivity in rainfed agriculture by undertaking selective watershed development programme.

Rainfed agriculture is the sector in which growth initiatives have to be located in the coming decade. This is justified on two counts *viz.* efficiency of the production process and equity across region. Returns to investment in watershed development specifically under rainfed conditions are quite encouraging and therefore, the future strategy has to be guided by investment towards selective watershed development projects specifically under rainfed conditions. This will also establish indirectly equity between the high growth irrigated patches across the state and lagging rainfed regions specifically in the northern Karnataka. Watershed development strategy however, is recommended to be selective in its approach and the areas to be focused during the next decade have been indicated. Naturally, forestry is the major component in the natural resources management sector along with the watershed development. Forestry resources have to be utilised economically in order to supplement and enhance the aggregate agricultural growth. The investment portfolio for the forestry sector is indicated.

Under the input sector, the gap between supply and demand for seeds and fertilisers has been strongly felt. The strong presence of private sector in the manufacturing and distribution of seeds is a welcome feature however, even with the the requirements are not met in terms of quality of seeds, typology of seeds and the quantum but probably the current initiatives on biotechnology will help in improving this situation in the coming decade. Integrated Pest Management (IPM) and Integrated Nutrition Management (INM) are the two major planks to deal with increased use of pesticides and managing the soil nutrition capabilities. These sectors have to be emphasised in terms of investment as well as extension network. The best way to achieve this is to strengthen the Krishi Vigyan Kendras and the Rayat Sampark Kendras.

Agricultural sector in Karnataka has also been severely constrained on the front of infrastructure specifically the markets, credit and investment in Research and Development. It has been noted that the density of markets is quite insufficient to deal with the requirements of increased production of various commodities. In addition to this, the process of globalisation has put forth a fresh challenge in the form of integrating domestic marketing system with the world markets. The marketing infrastructure in Karnataka needs to be readied for integrating with the global market and to participate effectively in the international trade. This is feasible only with the initiatives from private sector supported by state initiatives developing in the marketing infrastructure.

Another important bottleneck identified through our analysis is the availability of agricultural credit. Unfortunately, credit has not been supporting agricultural sector as it had during seventies and eighties. This has a telling effect on capital formation and lack of infrastructure in the sector. It needs to be underscored that credit institutions have not been meeting immediate requirements stipulated even by the Reserve Bank for providing the credit to the agricultural sector. Similarly, investment in Research and Development as well as availability of material for extension are also severely limited. These sectors are the deserving candidates for additional investment in the coming decade.

The availability of funds from public sources to initiate agricultural and rural development schemes in the fragile regions itself is a challenge. Therefore, it is required that private initiatives can be taken either in terms of corporate farming or bulk purchase and trade facilities. The requirement of investment in the backward regions can also be met by siphoning the excess savings from well-endowed regions to the deserving backward areas. This can be achieved by floating low interest investment bonds to be purchased by the private contributors from developed regions of the state. Development Boards specially set up to guide the process of development of these regions can take initiative in this respect.

Horticulture, floriculture, sericulture and fisheries are the allied agricultural activities which have been emerging very fast as new growth drivers are contributing to the aggregate economic growth. These four sectors have opened up the new avenues in proactive-active participation in international trade. Karnataka's participation in international trade under horticulture, floriculture, sericulture and fisheries is quite laudable, however constrained by investment, availability of infrastructure and proper exposure to the trends in the international market. Specific focus by specialised institutions (like KAPPEC) needs to be emphasised to promote the participation of these four vanguards of trade in the international sector.

Incidentally, our farmers will produce more if we can consume more. Opportunities for assured and remunerative marketing will determine the interest taken by small farmers in enhancing productivity. Our agriculture in the fifties, sixties, seventies and eighties was referred to as a gamble in the monsoon. It is now becoming increasingly a gamble in the market. Therefore, both monsoon and market management are essential for ensuring the economic well-being and livelihood security of farming families. Finally, there are a few action points which we note below:

- Capital formation in the agricultural sector must grow at least at the rate of more than five per cent per annum to supplement the aggregate growth of the sector. This is feasible by inducing private capital formation through public sector initiatives.
- Emerging regional disparities should be high on the agenda and all efforts should be made to seek participation of the lagging regions in the main stream growth. This would require additional investment in the lagging regions in terms of infrastructure, production and processing institutions. Future infrastructural investments therefore, have to be carefully directed towards these regions.
- Irrigation sector has been absorbing a large share of the funds from the state treasury. It is necessary that irrigation sector becomes self-sufficient and in terms of its returns to

investment there is necessity that the sector contributes to the aggregate revenue efforts. The additional revenue gained should be used for the development of rainfed agriculture.

- Rainfed agriculture both in terms of technology as well as Research and Development needs to be taken on priority. It would be worthwhile to chalk out a time bound programme to boost the growth in rainfed regions of the state. Any such attempt would require a separate study however, the present Watershed development schemes if implemented under one single umbrella and focused on a few weak regions would add to achieving this goal. Livestock activities provide a good support mechanism. Sheep and goat rearing on cooperative basis can be explored as one of the best drought proofing mechanism.
- Next phase of land reforms should provide flexibility as well as free operations in the land market without tampering with the Land Ceiling Act. This should make land economically productive in terms of its distribution and uses. The unabated conversion of agricultural land to non-agricultural uses has to be checked.
- In the input sector, availability of major inputs like seeds, fertiliser and extension of major programmes like IPM, INM, post-harvest processing needs to be located specifically in the regions, which are lagging behind. Investment required for this can be made available through public resources so that incentives are created for attracting private investment subsequently. Post-harvest processing should receive high priority in the investment portfolio.
- Reforms in agricultural marketing are long due and after the submission of Guru Committee and Patil Committee Reports, we are yet to take action on the points indicated by these two Committees. It is necessary that marketing infrastructure should be made conducive to face the challenges of globalisation and participation in the international trade.
- Credit to agricultural sector has been quite depressing and unless the credit flow to the sector increases substantially from the institutionalised credit suppliers it will be difficult for the sector to achieve a higher level capital formation and thereby influence the aggregate production structure.
- Investment in research and development and extension, both from public as well as private sources has to be undertaken to supplement the present efforts. Raitha Samparka Kendras and Krishi Vigyan Kendras can be better conduits for this purpose.
- Horticulture, floriculture, sericulture and fisheries are the emerging vanguards in the trade sectors. It will be essential that the state undertakes policies to provide incentives to the producers and traders in these growth drivers to participate proactively in international trade along with post-harvest processing.

The Karnataka government has established a Karnataka Biotech Vision group, in charge of carrying out studies and formulating policy recommendations. The group is composed of representatives from the Karnataka Ministry of IT and BT, as well as personalities from the academic and corporate world. The recommendations of the Vision Group constituted the core of the Millennium Biotech Policy–2001. This policy focuses on leveraging the biotech strengths of Karnataka for an overall development; sustenance and maintenance of the preeminent position of Karnataka in the field of biotechnology; to attract more investment into the state as well as create a conducive business environment by offering attractive incentives and concessions for the growth of biotech sector. An independent body, the Karnataka Biotechnology Development Council has then been appointed to implement this policy. In 2002, Bangalore Bio, a biotech congress was organised.

In order to bridge this gap and provide world class infrastructure to the biotech companies setting up their shops in the state a Biotech Park as envisaged in the Millenium Biotech Policy is being set up with world class infrastructure and incubation facility in Bangalore. It is happy to note that the Department of IT and Biotechnology, has also initiated the process of setting up a Marine Biotech Park in Uttara Kannada district. The centre would conduct high-end research in the area of Marine Biotechnology and would be first of its kind in India.

The sector being nascent, it is the responsibility of the government to provide adequate infrastructure for the quality output of international standard to generate. Biotechnology is knowledge-based capital-intensive and has long gestation period and has a high technological risk. It is the task of the government to play a critical role in aiding this sector by providing world class infrastructure to these startups so that the sector could take shape without much hassle.

References

Bhalla, G.S. and Gurmail Singh (2001). *Indian Agriculture for Decades of Development*, Sage, New Delhi.

Bhende, M. J. (2000). *Cropping Pattern and Resource Use Efficiency in Major Crops: A Case Study of Karnataka*, ADRT Unit, Institute for Social and Economic Change, Bangalore.

Bisaliah, S. and K. Krishnegowda (2001). "Creating Appropriate Development Environment for Small Farmers", U. A. S, Bangalore, *Mimeo.*

Bisaliah, S. (2004). "Sectoral Report on Economics, Extension and Management", Prepared for the Committee, constituted by parliamentary Standing Committer on Agriculture, Government of India, *Mimeo.*

Bisaliah, S. (1997-98). "Monitoring and Evaluation of Agricultural Research System", *Journal of IAUA*, (9-10) (1-2).

Bisalaiah, S. (2004). "Production and Marketing of Organic Farm Products: International Perspectives and Lessons for Karnataka", *Mimeo.*

Chandrakanth, M.G., B. Shivakumaraswamy, M.S. Shamsundar, S.N. Satisha, G. Basavaraj and Sushma Adya (1998). "Equity Issues in Ground Water Development—An Institution's Analysis of Failed Irrigation Wells in Karnataka", A Research Paper submitted to the Ford Foundation, University of Agricultural Sciences, Bangalore.

Chengappa, P.G. *et al.* (1996) *Economic Viability of Small Farmers in Karnataka: A Reconnaissance Study*, U.A.S, Bangalore.

Deshpande, R.S. and K.V. Raju (2001). *Rural Policy for Growth and Poverty Reduction*, Agriculture Development and Rural Transformation Unit, Institute for Social and Economic Change, Bangalore'

Deshpande, R.S., Bhende M.J., Thippaiah P. and M. Vivekananda (2004). "Crops and Cultivation", *State of the Indian Farmer: A Millennium Study* Vol. 9, Academic Foundation and Ministry of Agriculture, Government of India, New Delhi.

Deshpande, R.S. and J. Prachitha (2004). "Building up of an Efficient Marketing System to Obviate the Need for Large Scale State Intervention in Karnataka", Research Report, Agriculture Development and Rural Transformation Unit, Institute for Social and Economic Change, Bangalore

Deshpande, R. S. and D. V. Gopalappa, (2004). "Economic Poverty and Inequalities", in D. Johnand and V.V. Paulson KRCR-JPC Publications, Bangalore.

Deshpande, R.S. and Nikumbh, S.R. (1993). "Treatment of Uncultivated Land Under Watershed Development Approach", *Artha Vijnana*, Vol XXXV (1), March.

Deshpande, R.S. and A. Narayanamurthy, (1999). "An Appraisal of Watershed Development Programme Across Regions in India" *Artha Vijnana*, Vol. XLI, (4), December.

Deshpande, R. S. and Thimmaiah, G. (1999)."Watershed Development Approach and Experience of National Watershed Development Programme in the Country", *Journal of Rural Development*, 18 (3).

Deshpande, R.S. and T. Raveendra Naika (2002). *Impact of Minimum Support Prices on Agricultural Economy: A Study in Karnataka*, ISEC, Bangalore.

Deshpande, R.S., Bhende M. J. and S. Erappa (2003). "Output and Impact Monitoring Study of KAWAD Project", *Research Report*, Agriculture Development and Rural Transformation Unit, Institute for Social and Economic Change, Bangalore

Karl, Hans. E. and B.J. Nanjundappa (1999). "Agricultural Policy In The Ninth Plan," *Memorial Lecture*, IAT, Bangalore.

Karnataka State Agriculture Price Commission (KSAPC) (2003). "Marketing Behaviour of Farmers in Karnataka", *Report No. 8*, July.

Karnataka State Agriculture Price Commission (KSAPC) (2003). "Procurement, Storage and Disposal of Agricultural and Horticultural Commodities", *Report No. 7*.

Karnataka Agriculture Commission (KAC) (2001). *Yield Improvement Mission*, Bangalore.

Government of Karnataka (2000c). *Karnataka Economic Survey, 1999-2000*, Department of Planning, M.S. Buildings, Bangalore.

———. (2001). *Report by the Cell on WTO and Related Issues in Agriculture and Food*, Department of Agriculture and Horticulture, Bangalore.

———. (2003a). *Economic Survey 2002-2003*, Directorate of Economics and Statistics, Bangalore

———. (2003b). *Report of the Committee on Regional Imbalances* (Chairman: D.M. Nanjundappa)

———. (2003c). Karnataka Watershed Development Department for the year, Bangalore.

———. (2004a). *Karnataka State Policy on Organic Farming*, Bangalore.

———. (2004b). "A Study on the Performance of Regulated Markets in Karnataka", *Report No. 10*, Karnataka State Agriculture Price Commission (KSAPC) Bangalore.

Pal, Suresh and Alka, Singh (1997). "Agricultural Research and Extension in India: Institutional Structure and Investments", NCAP, New Delhi.

Ramaswamy C. (2004). "Constraints to Growth in Indian Agriculture: Needed Technology, Resource Management and Trade Strategies", *IJAE*, 59(1), January-March.

Rao, V. M. (2004). "Rainfed Agriculture", *State of Indian Farmer: A Millennium Study*, Vol. 10, Academic Foundation and Ministry of Agriculture, Government of India, New Delhi.

APPENDIX A-14.1

Sector-wise Distribution of Gross State Domestic Product at Factor Cost by Industry of Origin 1993-94 to 2000-01 Per Cent to GSDP

Industry	*1993-94*	*1994-95*	*1995-96*	*1996-97*	*1997-98*	*1998-99*	*1999-00*	*2000-01*
Agriculture	33	31	30.3	29.5	25.2	26.8	27.3	25.3
Fishing	0.4	0.6	0.7	0.9	0.8	0.6	0.6	0.6
Primary Sector	36.3	34.5	33.5	33.1	28.9	29.9	30.1	28.0
Secondary Sector	25.4	26.4	26.3	25.7	27.4	27.6	25.4	25.1
Tertiary Sector	38.3	39.1	40.2	41.2	43.7	42.5	44.5	46.9
Gross State Domestic Product (GSDP) at Constant Prices (in Lakhs)	4107906	4791516	5621456	6517572	7304576	8784091	9497193	10449173
Per Capita GSDP at Constant Prices (Rs.)	8706	9966	11478	13180	14205	16673	18332	13335

Source: Website on Agriculture Department of Agriculture, Government of Karnataka & Central Statistical Organisation.

APPENDIX A-14.2

Export Performance of Karnataka State

(Value in Rs. Crores)

Commodity	*1998-99*	*1999-2000*	*2000-2001*	*2001-2002*	*2002-2003*	*2003-2004#*
Coffee Products	1043.72	1183.93	957.53	881.42	730.65	532.48
Silk Products	357.90	521.24	772.39	672.24	746.09	675.39
Cashew & Cashew Kernals	238.00	251.55	187.98	163.55	279.83	260.50
Agricultural & Processed Food Products	165.31	195.33	237.91	349.51	366.99	172.40
Spices	60.00	61.00	73.74	69.12	91.65	125.14
Tobacco/*Beedi*	7.79	16.25	3.23	2.70	3.72	-
Bangalore Rose Onion	-	-	38.62	48.35	39.38	57.99
Gherkins	-	-	-	120.00	139.00	140.70
Flowers**	37.73	40.66	40.00	40.00	42.00	45.00
Total Agri-Exports	1910.45	2269.96	2311.40	2346.89	2439.31	2009.60
Total Exports	10039.48	12854.25	16027.46	20145.58	26279.43	26862.91
% of Agri-Exports in Total Exports	19.03	17.66	14.42	11.65	9.28	7.48

Note: ** Quantity in Million Stems # Up to December 2003

Source: Karnataka Agro Processing and Export Corporation, Bangalore.

APPENDIX A-14.3

Annual Growth Rates in Crop Economy: 1990-1991 to 1999-2000

Crops	*Area*	*Production*	*Productivity*
Rice	2.36	4.90	2.48
Jowar	-0.70	3.31	4.04
Bajra	-0.01	2.34	2.35
Maize	10.26	10.79	0.48
Ragi	-1.73	3.38	5.20
Small Millets	-9.34	-9.36	-0.02
Wheat	3.17	6.37	3.11
Pulses (Total)	1.64	4.75	3.06
Gram	3.73	11.13	7.14
Tur	1.00	5.40	4.35
Foodgrains (Total)	0.87	5.01	4.10
Groundnut	-0.76	-0.74	0.02
Sesamum	-3.47	3.06	6.77
Oilseeds (Total)	-2.85	-0.81	2.11
Cotton	-1.09	1.08	2.20
Sugarcane	4.23	7.59	3.22

Source: Computations based on the data collected from Directorate of Economics and Statistics, Government of Karnataka, Deshpande and Gopalappa (2004).

APPENDIX A-14.4

Land Particulars in Karnataka State

Year	*Fallow Lands to Total GA*	*NSA*	*Area Sown More than Once*	*Total GCA*	*Cropping Intensity (GCA/NSA)%*
1990-91	9.17	56.21	13.14	63.6	113.14
1991-92	9.17	54.49	13.27	61.73	113.27
1992-93	9.17	56.21	15.72	65.05	115.72
1993-94	7.88	56.63	15.06	65.15	115.06
1994-95	7.91	56.64	15.23	65.26	115.23
1995-96	8.95	54.7	15.3	63.06	115.3
1996-97	9.04	54.7	14.76	62.77	114.76
1997-98	8.06	55.69	16.44	64.85	116.44
1998-99	10.86	52.89	16.09	61.4	116.09
1999-2000	10.86	52.89	16.09	61.4	116.09
2000-01	8.76	55.06	17.37	64.63	117.37
2001-02	10.05	53.85	17.92	63.5	117.92
GR in %	2.02	-0.42	2.52	-0.11	—

Note: NSA–Net Sown Area; GCA–Gross Cropped Area; GA-Total Geographical Area.
Fallow Lands, NSA, ASMO and GCA are expressed as per cent of the GA.

Source: Various Issues of *Karnataka at a Glance*, Directorate of Economics and Statistics, Government of Karnataka, Bangalore.

APPENDIX A-14.5

Numbers of Operational Holdings and the Average Area Operated: Karnataka

Particulars	< 1 ha.	1 to 2 ha.	2 to 4 ha.	4 to 10 ha.	10 ha. & Above	Total
Number of holdings (in '000)						
1970-71	1081	840	788	623	219	3551
1980-81	1489	1057	918	662	183	4309
1990-91	2262	1586	1163	636	129	5776
2000-01	3252	1909	1259	569	90	7079
% Change per annum	6.69	4.24	1.99	-0.29	-1.96	3.31
Area operated in '000, ha.						
1970-71	549	1221	2205	3792	3601	11368
1980-81	733	1543	2572	4018	2880	11746
1990-91	1072	2308	3200	3770	1971	12321
2000-01	1492	2742	3429	3317	1327	12307
% Change per annum	5.73	4.15	1.85	-0.42	-2.1	0.28
Average Operated area in ha.						
1970-71	0.51	1.46	2.8	6.09	16.43	3.2
1980-81	0.49	1.46	2.8	6.07	15.69	2.73
1990-91	0.47	1.46	2.75	5.93	15.28	2.13
2000-01	0.46	1.44	2.72	5.83	14.74	1.74
% Change per annum	-0.33	-0.05	-0.1	-0.14	-0.34	-1.52

Source: GoK (2003); *Agricultural Censuses*, various years.

APPENDIX A-14.7

Agricultural Implements in Karnataka

(in Thousands)

Name of the Implement	1997	2003	Growth (%)
Seed-cum-Fertiliser Drill	160.32	288.94	80.29
Sprayer and Duster	428.00	469.36	9.67
Paddy Planter	62.69	29.50	-52.95
Thresher	252.65	401.41	58.89
Seed-cum-Fertiliser Drill	312.62	753.69	141.08
Animal Cart	800.86	760.82	-4.99
Tractor (Wheeled)	50.56	61.24	21.10
Paddy Thresher	1.46	2.68	83.30
Multi-crop Thresher	3.27	3.90	19.26
Planter	3.87	6.39	64.97
Tractor Operated Combine	4.50	2.31	-48.53
Self Propelled Combines	7.64	4.22	-44.70
Power Tillers	27.45	27.05	-1.47
Power Sprayer	65.48	85.19	30.10
Electric Pumps	588.72	696.08	18.24
Sprinklers	50.16	65.83	31.22

Source: Government of Karnataka, *Livestock Census* for respective years.

APPENDIX A-14.6

Seeds Demand Supply-Scenario (2004-05): Karnataka

(in Quintals)

Crop		Agency-wise Seed Supply							
	State Requirement	UAS (B)	UAS (D)	KSSC	NASC	KOF	Total Govt. Agency	Private	Grand Total
Paddy	142300	2500	-	83000	10000	-	95500	90860	186360
Ragi	22445	600	-	15500	400	-	16500	100	17500
Jowar	30500	-	-	4000	350	-	4350	9730	14080
Maize	79690	500	25	-	100	-	625	275650	276275
Bajra	13340	-	-	1000	200	-	1200	23355	24555
Red Gram	17930	30	49	4850	200	-	5129	3800	8929
Black Gram	4705	-	25	5000	400	-	5425	850	6275
Cow Pea	3900	20	-	500	500	-	1020	2400	3420
Green Gram	10320	-	50	2300	300	-	2650	1650	4300
Groundnut	156520	-	112	7000	750	30000	37862	2000	39862
Sunflower	13940	100	100	1150	270	1000	2620	2600	5220
Soyabean	6320	370	40	3700	400	5000	9510	10600	20110
Cotton	7350	-	40	2400	60	-	2500	3588	6088
Total	**510747**	**4370**	**779**	**130400**	**14030**	**36000**	**185429**	**428163**	**613592**

Note: 1. UAS (B) /(D)—University of Agricultural Sciences, Bangalore/Dharwad.

2. KSSC—Karnataka State Seeds Corporation.

3. NASC—National Agricultural Seed Corporation.

4. KOF—Karnataka Oilseed Federation.

Source: Commissionerate of Agriculture of Karnataka, Bangalore.

APPENDIX A-14.8

Agricultural Marketing Activities in Karnataka: Some Indicators

Year	*Main Markets (Nos.)*	*SubMarkets (Nos.)*	*Total Markets (Nos.)*	*Total Markets per Lakh Ha of GSA*	*As % of Main Markets in India*	*Annual Turnover Value for Total Markets (Rs. in Crores)*
1990-91	116	295	411	3.392	1.747	2448.05
1991-92	116	303	419	3.563	1.722	3194.33
1992-93	120	304	424	3.421	1.772	3162.72
1993-94	122	307	429	3.497	1.792	3636.89
1994-95	124	320	444	3.504	1.814	4167.48
1995-96	128	324	452	3.665	1.88	4974.5
1996-97	133	329	462	3.745	1.937	5595.09
1997-98	137	332	469	4.01	NA	5554.37
1998-99	140	333	473	3.84	NA	6500.21
1999-00	140	333	473	3.915	NA	6647.81
2000-01	141	342	483	NA	NA	7512.21
2001-02	141	342	483	NA	NA	7902.39

Note: NA–Gross Sown Area is not available for the respective years.

Source: 1. *Statistical Abstract of Karnataka* for various years, Directorate of Economics and Statistics, Bangalore: Government of Karnataka.

2. Agriculture Produce Marketing Board, Bangalore: Government of Karnataka.

3. Fertiliser Association of India, 1997.

APPENDIX A-14.9

Regulated Agricultural Markets in Karnataka and India

Year	*Number of Markets*			
	Total		*Per Lakh Ha of GSA*	
	Karnataka	*India*	*Karnataka*	*India*
1990-91	411 (6.19)	6640	3.392	3.572
1991-92	419 (6.22)	6738	3.563	3.697
1992-93	424 (6.26)	6772	3.421	3.648
1993-94	429 (6.30)	6809	3.497	3.653
1994-95	444 (6.50)	6836	3.504	3.647
1995-96	452 (6.49)	6968	3.665	3.718
1996-97	462 (6.63)	6968	3.745	3.718
1997-98	469	NA	4.010	NA
1998-99	473	NA	3.840	NA
1999-00	473	NA	3.915	NA
2000-01	483	NA	NA	NA
2001-02	483	NA	NA	NA

Note: 1) Figures in parentheses are per cent to all India.

Sources: 1) *Statistical Abstract of Karnataka* for various years, DES, Bangalore.

2) Fertiliser Association of India, New Delhi 1997.

APPENDIX A-14.10

District-wise Growth Rates of Outstanding Credit by SCBs (Per Cent Per Annum)

Districts	*1981-91*		*1992-2000*		*1981-2000*	
	Agriculture	*Total*	*Agriculture*	*Total*	*Agriculture*	*Total*
Highly Developed						
Dakshina Kannada	15.1	15.9	9.1	13.7	8.4	11.9
Mysore	14.2	16.0	11.3	15.4	9.8	13.4
Mandya	21.9	16.7	10.2	12.1	14.3	13.4
Shimoga	23.9	17.6	7.3	9.6	13.9	11.9
Belgaum	15.2	15.8	12.9	13.7	11.9	13.0
Group Total	16.8	16.2	10.7	13.6	11.2	12.5
Developed						
Bellary	17.2	17.3	11.3	14.0	10.9	13.8
Bangalore	20.9	17.1	12.6	19.7	15.6	17.7
Kolar	17.6	15.3	8.0	13.7	12.7	13.7
Chickmagalur	11.3	13.9	23.7	24.3	14.1	15.7
Kodagu	13.0	15.1	20.5	21.8	12.2	13.7
Group Total	16.9	16.8	15.5	19.7	13.8	17.2
Backward						
Tumkur	21.4	19.1	11.3	12.8	15.3	14.6
Hassan	15.8	14.8	16.5	18.2	13.8	14.4
Chitradurga	21.6	19.3	16.9	15.9	16.3	15.5
Uttara Kannada	14.9	14.3	12.4	15.3	9.4	12.7
Dharwad	19.0	16.7	11.1	14.3	11.6	13.9
Group Total	18.6	16.9	14.0	16.5	13.5	14.2
Highly Backward						
Raichur	14.3	15.5	13.4	13.7	13.5	13.6
Bijapur	20.2	17.3	16.2	15.4	16.7	16.8
Gulbarga	17.0	22.3	15.1	14.2	14.7	17.3
Bidar	18.5	21.2	11.3	13.9	14.6	17.4
Group Total	17.1	18.2	15.3	15.5	14.9	15.7
All	**17.2**	**16.7**	**12.2**	**16.9**	**13.2**	**15.6**

Source: Reserve Bank of India (various issues of *Banking Statistics* from 1981 to 2000).

APPENDIX A-14.11

Area, Production and Productivity of Major Fruit Crops in Karnataka (1998-99)

Fruit Crops	*Area in '000 ha*		*Production in '000 MT*		*Productivity in MT/ha*		*Ranking in Production*
	Karnataka	*India*	*Karnataka*	*India*	*Karnataka*	*India*	
Mango	123.8	1401.6	1176.5	9781.8	9.5	7.0	4 (AP, Bihar, UP)
Banana	60.9	464.3	2010.4	15072.7	33	32.5	3 (TN, Maharashtra, Gujarat)
Citrus	32.8	488.1	347.8	4579	10.6	9.4	4 (Maharashtra,Punjab, AP)
Sweet Orange	14.5	62.2	153.3	772.8	10.6	12.4	3 (AP, Maharashtra)
Lime/Lemon	13.1	139.5	138.8	1259.8	10.6	9.0	2 (AP)
Mandarin	4.4	165.1	67.7	1674	10.6	10.1	5 (Maharashtra, AP, Rajasthan, Assam)
Sapota	24	50.4	424.8	667.6	17.7	13.2	1
Guava	12.6	151.3	157.3	1800.5	12.5	11.9	5 (Bihar, AP, UP, Maharashtra)
Grapes	7.5	42.6	226.6	1082.7	30.2	25.4	2 (Maharashtra)
Papaya	5.7	67.6	496.8	1582.4	87.2	23.4	1
Total	314.6	3726.8	5446.3	44042.4	17.3	11.8	3 (Maharashtra,TN)

Source: Directorate of Horticulture, Government of Karnataka, Bangalore.

APPENDIX A-14.12

Export of Horticulture Produce (1998-99)

Hortil. Product	*Qty. in Mt.*	*Value in Rs. Lakhs*	*% Share of Value*	*Destinations*
Fresh Mangoes	45407.59	7913.67	5.63	UAE, UK, Saudi Arabia, Bangladesh, Kuwait
Fresh Grapes	11525.41	3788.6	2.7	UK, Netherlands, UAE, Bangladesh, Germany
Other Fresh Fruits	44820.43	7172.9	5.11	USA, Bangladesh, Malaysia, Sri Lanka, Singapore
Fresh Onion	215693.6	17604.72	12.53	UAE, Malaysia, Singapore, Sri Lanka, Bangladesh
Other Fresh Vegetables	64654.63	10233.37	7.29	USA, UAE, Saudi Arabia, Sri Lanka
Walnuts	5327.9	6892.22	4.91	Spain, Germany, USA, France
Mango Pulp	38133.73	13856.43	9.86	USA, Saudi Arabia, Netherlands, Japan, UAE
Dried and Preserved Vegetables	145049.6	38305.29	27.27	Sri Lanka, UAE, USA, UK, Singapore
Pickles and Chutneys	21138.05	7595.68	5.41	USA, Saudi Arabia, Netherlands, Japan, UAE
Other Processed Fruits and Vegetables	34322.16	10811.15	7.7	USA, UK, UAE, Netherlands, Saudi Arabia
Fruit and Vegetable Seeds	6062.38	6633.93	4.72	USA, France, Italy, Japan, Pakistan
Floriculture	18721.06	9660.97	6.88	USA, Netherlands, UK, Italy, France
Total	**650856.5**	**140468.9**	**100**	

Source: Indian Horticulture Database 2000.

APPENDIX A-14.13

District-wise Annual Compound Rate of Area and Production of Floriculture in Karnataka (Between 1980-81 and 1999-2000)

Districts	*Area*	*Production*
Belgaum	9.53	9.79
Bellary	4.48	5.60
Bidar	19.55	19.48
Bijapur	10.37	11.54
Dharwad	12.55	9.77
Gulbarga	9.05	5.68
Raichur	10.99	9.25
Northern Dry Region	9.82	10.00
Bangalore Urban	14.82	20.69
Bangalore Rural	11.83	16.33
Bangalore	11.36	13.96
Kolar	4.99	5.31
Chitradurga	5.18	6.69
Tumkur	3.37	5.55
Central Region	7.10	9.04
Mandya	14.44	16.41
Mysore	9.00	8.41
Hassan	9.30	7.47
Southern Region	10.26	10.61
Uttara Kannada	7.28	4.25
Dakishna Kannada	7.81	8.17
Chickamagalur	7.03	0.47
Kodagu	12.33	5.46
Shimoga	7.71	6.40
Hills and Coastal Region	8.43	4.95
Total	8.54	10.24

Source: Computed from the data collected from Directorate of Horticulture, Government of Karnataka, Bangalore.

APPENDIX A-14.14

Flower-wise Average Yield in Karnataka (Tonnes/Hectare)

Name of the Flower	*Ending 1982-83*	*Ending 1999-00*	*Increase/ Decrease*	*% Increase/ Decrease*
Rose	2.48	2.03	-0.45	-18.02
Chrysanthemum	5.45	7.44	1.99	36.62
Tube Rose	7.45	8.51	1.06	14.22
Aster	7.52	8.00	0.49	6.47
Jasmine	4.99	5.20	0.21	4.12
Crossandra	2.98	3.93	0.95	31.80
Marigold	7.49	7.22	-0.28	-3.72
Champaka	4.96	3.71	-1.25	-25.22
Others	4.97	6.19	1.22	24.43
Total	**5.60**	**5.96**	**0.36**	**7.66**

Source: Data collected from Directorate of Horticulture, Government of Karnataka, Bangalore.

APPENDIX A-14.15

Contribution of Karnataka's Marine Fish Landings in India (in Tonnes)

Year	*India*	*Karnataka*	*% Share of Karnataka*
1970	1085607	116936	10.77
1980	1249837	115322	9.23
1985	1522517	118654	7.79
1990	2142713	178334	8.32
1996	2414649	139544	5.78
1997	2680713	154453	5.76
1998	2668484	139678	5.23

Source: Marine Fisheries Information Service T& E Ser. No. 41, 52, 67, 136. Annual Reports of Central Marine Fisheries Research Institute, Cochin.

APPENDIX A-14.16

Inland Fish Production from 1999-2000 to 2002-2003

(Metric Tonnes)

District	*1999-2000*	*2000-2001*	*2001-2002*	*2002-2003*	*Average*
Bangalore (U)	4630.15	3990.35	4268.35	3828.09	4179.21
Bangalore (R)	6003.98	6382.38	6920.38	4263.97	5892.68
Bagalkote	363.09	181.49	426.49	449.49	355.14
Belgaum	4184.98	3003.38	2160.38	1637.38	2746.53
Bellary	11489.07	10394.99	7660.57	6339.79	8971.11
Bidar	1284.65	1355.75	1130.75	720.75	1122.98
Bijapur	1902.17	1660.37	1673.37	1762.37	1749.57
Chamrajnagar	1522.6	1507.8	1984.8	1925.8	1735.25
Chickmagalur	4588.19	4302.99	4155.99	2796.99	3961.04
Chitradurga	5263.02	5896.51	4654.51	2798.93	4653.24
D. Kannada	1155.18	1112.28	1145.28	1086.27	1124.75
Davangere	3300.09	4079.65	3801.49	2906.49	3521.93
Dharwad	1977.84	2010.84	1358.84	1049.06	1599.14
Gadag	486.64	198.64	258.64	40.69	246.15
Gulbarga	3329.13	3531.63	4289.63	3925.63	3769.05
Hassan	5324.21	4448.51	7863.51	5126.51	5690.68
Haveri	2203.91	3102.91	2444.91	739.91	2122.91
Kodagu	914.48	1161.48	1065.48	540.56	920.05
Kolar	4768.54	4292.44	6282.44	4979.47	5080.72
Koppal	3578.52	3324.22	2382.22	1559.74	2711.17
Mandya	8754.82	8591.22	8750.22	7502.22	8339.62
Mysore	12356.37	16188.87	11901.87	5372.87	11454.99
Raichur	3463.92	3409.92	3433.92	2597.92	3226.42
Shimoga	11711.21	12753.71	9297.71	5006.71	9692.33
Tumkur	15358.69	13555.11	15318.99	11522.16	13938.74
Udupi	1659.89	1713.29	1731.29	1637.58	1685.51
U. Kannada	5070.99	5317.84	4833.84	4145.26	4841.98
Total	**126646.33**	**127468.57**	**121195.9**	**86262.61**	**115343.3**

Source: Government of Karnataka, *Statistical Bulletin of Fishers* (various issues), Directorate of Fisheries, Bangalore.

APPENDIX A-14.17

Completed Watershed Development Programmes in Karnataka (1984-85 to 1999-2000)

Name of the Programme	*Implementing Agency and Year*	*No. of Districts*	*No. of Watersheds*	*Total Geographical Area (ha)*	*Area Area Treated since Inception (ha)*	*Amount Spent since Inception (Rs. Crores)*
World Bank Assisted Watershed Projects	DLDB/Department of Watershed Development (1984-1993)	6	7	136337	136337	37.564
District Watershed Development Programmes	DLDB/Department of Watershed Development (1984-1993)	18	18	578420	515200	121.978
Participative and Integrated Development of Watersheds (PLDOW)	DLDB/MYRADA (1985-86-1993-94)	1	1	20300	9680	4.14
Swiss Assisted ISPWD-K Project	DLDB/WDD (1995-96 to 1999-2000)	5	5	74968	30000	12.595
KFW Assisted Integrated Watershed Management	DLDB/WDD (1995-96 to 1999-2000)	3	5	53627	24600	16.221
River Valley Projects (Tungabhadra, Nizamsagar and Nagarjuna Sagar)	A&H Department through Dept. of Agri. (Centrally Sponsored, 1963-64 Onwards)	15	723 (225 W/s Saturated)	106.88 lakh (Area to be Treated 26.15 Lakhs)	541800	91.119

Contd. ...

...Contd. ...

Name of the Programme	*Implementing Agency and Year*	*No. of Districts*	*No. of Watersheds*	*Total Geographical Area (ha)*	*Area Treated since Inception (ha)*	*Amount Spent since Inception (Rs. Crores)*
National Watershed Development Programme for Rainfed Areas (NWDPRA) 1990-91 Onwards as NWDPRA	A&H Dept. Through Dept. of Agri. in the State Sector coordinated by ZP 1986-87. As NWD,	26	141	872872	872872	182.995
i) Drought Prone Areas Programme ii) Desert Development Programme iii) Western Ghat Development	RD&PR *Zilla Panchayat* and Watershed Development Associations talukas	i) 15 ii) 6 iii) 11	423 in 81 blocks 130 in 22 blocks 40 talukas	-	-	75.600 (1995-99) 20.220 (1995-99) 53.54 (1995-99)
Karnataka Watershed Development Project (DANIDA Assistance)	A&H Department through Directorate of Agriculture I Phase 1990-91 to 1996-97	3	14	53000	23000	16.036
	II phase 1997-98 to 2004	4	12	-	-	-
Total					**2153489**	**632.008**

Source: Karnataka Watershed Development Department and annual reports of the RD&PR Department.

APPENDIX A-14.18

District-wise Watershed Area Developed/Available for Comprehensive Watershed Development: 2003

(Rs. in Lakhs, Area in ha)

District	*Area Available for WSD*	*Area Developed since inception*	*Amount Spent*	*Proposed Area*	*Amount Required*	*Area Yet to be Treated*	*Amount Required*
Dakishna Kannada	313935	5036	259.38	12559	698.05	296340	17780.4
Shimoga	580478	9570	481.91	69196	3522.38	501712	30102.72
Kodagu	315450	26069	570.18	21320	1257.5	268061	16083.66
Raichur	507555	50569	1706.08	38314	2021.93	418672	25120.32
Chickmagalur	458253	69768	2859.35	49989	3614.11	338496	20309.76
Davangere	484664	80464	2809.66	19659	1316.68	384541	23072.46
Mysore	339814	62236	1463.32	13621	853.28	263957	15837.42
Kolar	633066	129533	4781.1	227749	13000.4	275784	16547.04
Chitradurga	467692	97111	3314.77	139701	8096.05	230881	13852.86
Bellary	453031	99241	3345.22	64270	3664.92	289520	17371.2
Tumkur	742485	165159	5595.21	219428	12815.94	357898	21473.88
Dharwad	319555	76010	1687.56	156192	9276.26	87353	5241.18
Bijapur	533057	133336	3297.26	149427	8044.24	250294	15017.64
Bangalore (Urban)	89149	22500	649.91	6618	383.52	60031	3601.86
Mandya	270453	69307	2603.75	19760	1183.4	181386	10883.16
Gadag	343973	89759	1976.76	95468	5745.45	158746	9524.76
Bangalore (Rural)	368241	105975	2626.43	71087	4278.24	191179	11470.74
Hassan	448456	136310	4525.7	101246	6267.2	210900	12654
Udupi	197694	60491	990.43	9325	464.36	127878	7672.68
Haveri	347388	113418	3962.96	157902	9542.24	76068	4564.02
Uttara Kannada	265524	87009	1187.18	43283	2664.2	135232	8113.92
Gulbarga	1191880	390991	8642.89	60904	3024.87	739985	44399.1
Chamrajnagar	337619	113508	2219.62	127333	6590.13	96778	5806.68
Bagalkot	389991	134619	3121.83	134143	8090.74	121229	7273.74
Belgaum	660467	243133	5006.9	96266	4707.28	321068	19264.08
Koppal	296151	125801	3699.21	41193	1988.42	129157	7749.42
Bidar	334184	213910	4203.98	46111	1935.61	74163	4449.78
State	**11690205**	**2910833**	**77588.6**	**2192064**	**125047.4**	**6587308**	**395238**

Source: Government of Karnataka (2003c), Karnataka Watershed Development Department, Government of Karnataka, Bangalore.

APPENDIX A-14.19

Impact of Watershed Development Activities in District Watersheds as Monitored by Satellite Remote Sensing

Name of the Watershed and Zone where Located	*Total Geographical Area (ha)*	*% Increase in 5-7 Years in Respect of*				
		Irrigated Crops Area	*Fallow Lands*	*Waste Lands*	*Forest Vegetation*	*Water Body*
Kalyanakere, Bangalore (EDZ)	22356	4.3	0.4	-16.7	N.A	0.7
Kallambella, Tumkur (EDZ)	24360	19.4	N.A.	-9.7	5.2	0.3
Chitravathi, Kolar (EDZ)	46340	6.1	-20.5	-1.2	7.6	-1.2
Arasinakunte, Mysore (SDZ)	40290	11.8	-6.8	-6.3	1.3	N.A.
Lokapavani, Mandya (SDZ)	32646	7.3	-12.2	-14.8	8.6	-0.5
Devihalla, Hassan (SDZ)	34988	8.5	-10.2	-4.4	5.1	0.01
Hirehalla, Shimoga (SDZ)	28471	2.5	-15.4	-0.1	0.8	N.A.
Mugalikatte, Chickmagalur (CDZ	20104	6.8	N.A.	-8.2	N.A.	1
Ganjigunte, Chitradurga (CDZ)	39281	2.7	N.A.	-3.5	N.A.	0.3
Asundinala, Dahrwad (NTZ)	28850	2.5	-8	-0.2	3.8	N.A.
Hirehalla, Raicur (NEDZ)	31655	5	N.A.	-5.5	3.2	0.02
Muchkullanala, Gulbarga (NEDZ)	34774	6.9	-5.4	-11.1	N.A.	0.8
Doddahallanala, Bidar (NEDZ)	28785	4.1	-9.6	-9.3	1.4	0.1
Margutti (PIDOW) Gulbarga (NEDZ)	20300	10.9	-4.8	-12.5	3.6	0.8
Chandakavate, Bijapur (NDZ)	28016	6.4	-8	-11.1	7.4	N.A.
Hirehalla, Belgaum (NDZ)	31840	13.4	-2.8	-13.5	0.9	0.2
Sannabombrahalla Bellary (NDZ)	40812	11.5	-1.5	-1.4	2.3	N.A.
Tattihalla,U.K.(HZ)	17343	1.8	N.A.	-7	0.3	1.4
Sitanadi,D.K.(HZ)	38047	1.6	1.4	N.A.	1.2	0.1
Shanivarasanthe, Kodagu (HZ)	9462	4.3	N.A.	-12.8	9.2	N.A.

Source: Government of Karnataka (1998). *Monitoring and Evaluation of Watersheds in Karnataka Using Satellite Remote Sensing,* Watershed Development Department.

APPENDIX A-14.20

Ongoing Watershed Development Programmes in Karnataka (2000-2004)

Name of the Programme	*Area Treated (Ha)*	*Amount Spent (Rs. in Lakhs)*
District Sector Schemes		
Special Component Plan (SCP)	2755.3	142.36
Tribal Sub-plan (TSP)	490.68	53.60
Employment Assurance Scheme (EAS)	79878.19	5338.97
Drought Prone Area Programme (DPAP)	143391	9880.48
Integrated Wasteland Development Programme (IWDP)	81815	4421.89
Western Ghat Development Programme (WGDP)	25394	3814.85
Desert Area Development Programme (DDP)	59125.5	5013.88
Sampoorna Gramina Rojgara Yojana (SGRY)	27212	3334.88
Sub-Total	**420061.67**	**32000.91**
State Sector Schemes		
River Valley Project (RVP)	134305	4489.71
National Watershed Project for Rainfed Areas (NWDPRA)	102514	6353.17
Reclamation of Saline, Alkaline, Waterlogged Areas	1701	249.00
WD Training Centre	-	196.81
Sub-Total	**238520**	**11288.69**
Externally Aided Projects		
Sujala-World Bank Assisted (2002-04)	26115	3442.01

Contd. ...

...Contd. ...

Name of the Programme	*Area Treated (Ha)*	*Amount Spent (Rs. in Lakhs)*
NABARD	1405	75.90
DANIDA	20143	1387.51
KAWAD (2003-04)	34749	1818.13
Sub-Total	82412	6723.55
Grand Total	**740993.67**	**50013.15 (Rs. 500.13 Crores)**

Source: Karnataka Watershed Development and Annual Reports of the RD&PR Department.

Chapter 15

Industrial Development in Karnataka

15.0 Introduction

In contemporary discussions of the problems of developing countries, industrialisation is widely regarded as a key to economic development and improved standards of living. The advocacy of accelerated industrialisation is generally based on one or more of arguments like the income per head generated in manufacturing production is generally higher than in agriculture; growth of manufacturing industry is necessary in largely populated countries to absorb the surplus population on the land and put it to productive work; and people with higher income levels spend an increasing proportion of their income on non-agricultural products.

All these arguments make a strong case for industrialisation. Karnataka state all along the last century took a lead in this respect. In this Chapter, industrialisation is examined in all its aspects as it has taken place in Karnataka. One of the objectives of the study is to identify the factors responsible for the growth of industrialisation in Karnataka. This Chapter discusses the industrial sector at large i.e., large and mega industries, small-scale industries, the unorganised sector and public sector enterprises. Some analysis is also provided wherever Karnataka is having a unique position like sericulture and *agarbatti* industries. The changes in the industrial policy and its impact on industrial growth in the country as a whole and Karnataka in particular are analysed here. It covers industrial policies of the state, impact of these policies, special economic zones and industrial parks, foreign direct investment (FDI) as an instrument towards promoting large industries. Finally it sets a target for the next five years based on the picture as it emerges. A detailed analysis of the small-scale industrial sector, unorganised sector, tiny, and rural industries focusing on sericulture and *agarbatti* industry are also provided. Some analysis is also provided on the mega sectors Section-2 deals with SSI, tiny and village and cottage industries, Karnataka state public undertakings. Industrial policy of the state—fiscal and other incentives offered by the state, level and ratio of investment by both the public and private sectors in addition to the scale of sickness and trade unionism.

Since 1991-92 major reforms were introduced in Karnataka in the industrial policy sphere, apart from power sector reforms. An integrated and focused approach was employed simultaneously for boosting industrial sector, mobilising private funds including FDIs. The reforms were crisis-driven and leadership-driven.

One of the outcomes of the policy initiatives was that the onus for regional industrial development shifted to states and this is another area that has attracted the attention of academia and policy makers. With the disbanding of the 'licence raj', getting licences ceased to be the differentiating factor. The focus shifted to 'availability of quality power', infrastructure, incentives, procedures and clearances, and governance. These initiatives largely rest with state governments and it is here that many projects succeeded or withered. The focus shifted to policy management and development at state level and their impact in terms of regional development and dispersal. The development trend in Karnataka indicates that sufficient scope existed for a proactive approach to exploit the newly liberalised regime, which we will discuss when we analyse the comparative picture of states like Maharashtra, Tamil Nadu, and Andhra Pradesh. In this overall context and in the light of policy and institutional initiatives taken by Karnataka, we will study the progress made by the state so far and the prospects.

15.1 The Process of Industrialisation

15.1.1 History of Industrialisation in Karnataka

Karnataka has several factors favourable for a programme of rapid industrialisation. The state has a fabulous wealth of forests and minerals, the existence of which is the basis for several industries. Karnataka state is favourably placed in natural and raw material resources and was the first state in India to generate hydroelectric power. Since power was available in the state on a comparatively cheaper rate, the state could make a headway in industrialisation.

Karnataka's industrialisation got off to a start as early as in 1884 when the first textile mill was set up in the state. However, the sugar industry came into existence prior to this—in 1800 itself. The commencement of the flow of electricity from Shivasamudram in 1902 marked the beginning of a new era in the state's industrial development. Within a decade after the commissioning of the electricity generating station, the number of industrial establishments using electric power had risen to 80 which was a significant achievement in those days.

The decade 1931-1941 touched the highest watermark of industrial activity in the state. Gold mining was the most important organised industry. Cotton, silk, and woollen textiles were next in importance. Further, heavy industries like the Visveswarayya Iron and Steel Works, the Aircraft Factory, the Mysore Chemicals and Fertilisers, the Mysore Sugar Company and the Mysore Paper Mills were directly owned or aided by the government. Karnataka evolved an industrial policy of its own in order to help private effort and direct government enterprise in fields beyond the capacity of private effort. In 1944 the large industrial establishments were 605, employing about 77,518 persons. The concerns in which private capital was readily invested were rice and flour mills, brick and tile factories and the manufacture of *beedies*. The important cottage industries were weaving, pottery and tile-making, oil-pressing, basket-making, goldsmithy, blacksmithy, carpentry, mat-making, leather, *beedi* and *agarbatti* industries. The notable landmark in the history of industrial development in the state was the launching of Sir M. Viswesvaraya's scheme for rural industrialisation. In 1948, the Industrial Policy Resolution of Government of India had its impact on the policies of the state government and consequently the whole process had to be reoriented.

Rapid industrialisation was one of the central objectives of the five-year plans of the state. During the First Five Year Plan, the state had earmarked 4.3 per cent of the total outlay for industries. Some of the key projects include the expansion of the Mysore Iron and Steel works at Bhadravati, development of the existing government industries, namely, the Soap Factory, the Government Electric Factory, and the Government Porcelain Factory. During the Second Five Year Plan the outlay was stepped up to 7.2 per cent. Important schemes that were taken up during this plan period were the development of Government Sandalwood factory at Shimoga, completion of the second stage expansion of Government Soap Factory, finalisation of the setting up of New Government Electric Factory, completion of the first expansion of Government Porcelain Factory and the expansion of Mysore Implements Factory at Hassan. The sate government took over the erstwhile Mysore Spun Silk Mills at Channapatna in 1960. Sericulture, which is an important industry in the state, received further fillip. The state however faced acute shortage of power, which hindered the speedy development of industries. A number of development schemes were undertaken for resuscitation and development of rural and small-scale industries such as constitution of Mysore Small-scale Industries and Handicrafts Board, setting up of Mysore Small Industries Corporation Limited, formation of Mysore State Silk Handloom Weavers' Central Cooperative Society, etc. The Third Five Year Plan saw the setting up of the New Government Electric Factory, a large industry, over which Rs. 650 lakhs was spent during the plan period. The factory is engaged in the manufacture of transformers, motors besides switchgear and other electrical accessories. Many existing industries were either modernised or expanded. The Mysore (Karnataka) State Industrial Investment Corporation with an authorised capital of Rs. 5 crore was set up in 1960 with the state government subscribing Rs. 50 lakhs. The Corporation was set up with the primary objective of helping the existing and new industries by way of direct subscription to their share capital and/or by underwriting, issuing guarantees, and extending loans. During the Annual Plans, the government constituted a statutory board *viz.* the Mysore (Karnataka) Industrial Area Developmental Board with the main object of overcoming procedural difficulties in acquisition of lands in 1966-67. During 1967-68 the state government also announced a number of incentives for new industries. During the Fourth Five Year Plan, the policy of the state had been to expand and/or modernise the existing industrial projects and not to venture into new units. The main emphasis was promotion of new industries through Mysore (Karnataka) Industrial Investment Development Corporation and the Mysore (Karnataka) Industrial Area Development Board and offering a number of facilities and concessions. A survey of industrial establishments conducted by the Department of Industries and Commerce in 1969 indicated that there were 9,657 units in the state excluding Hindustan Aeronautics Limited and other defence industries with a total capital investment of about Rs. 318 crores and employing about 2.8 lakh persons. Bangalore city had almost 40 per cent of the industries with a third of the total capital investment. Only 167 of these units were in the large and medium sector, the vast majority remaining in the small-scale sector. The number of registered small-scale units rose from 2,377 in 1963 to 6,646 in 1970. However, Karnataka experienced acute shortage of power in 1972-73, which affected the industrial prospects of the state adversely. In the year, growth turned out to be negative in respect of some industries.

It was during the Fifth Five Year Plan in 1978 that small-scale and rural industrialisation were given a major thrust. With a view to encouraging small-scale and rural industries to solve the growing unemployment problem in the rural areas as also to exploit rural resources, Government of India had launched the programme of District Industries Centres (DICs) in various parts of the country. These centres were expected to act as a focal point for promotion of small-scale village and cottage industries and provide all-round services and support to the decentralised industries sector under a single roof at pre-investment, investment and post-investment stages. This programme was launched in Karnataka in May 1978 and the 7 rural industries projects existing then were converted into district industries centres. Besides, dispersal of industries to backward areas was given emphasis for increasing the incomes of the rural poor. In the state, 11 districts were notified by the government of India, as backward and these districts cover 66 per cent of the total area of the state. Any new industry to be set up in these districts of Belgaum, Gulbarga, Bidar, Bijapur, Dharwad, Hassan, Tumkur, Dakshina Kannada, Raichur, Uttara Kannada, and Mysore were eligible for concessional finance from institutions like the Industrial Finance Corporation, the Industrial Development Bank of India, etc. The concessional finance included lower rate of interest, exemption from payment of interest for the first few years, etc. Besides, out of these 11 districts, 3 districts *viz.*, Raichur, Mysore, and Dharwad were selected to qualify for a subsidy by the Central Government. Industries that were newly set up enjoyed also the exemption on sales tax and deferment for a specific period depending upon their location.

Karnataka's Draft Sixth Five Year Plan 1980-1985 had noted that the state's performance in the industrial field did not compare well with industrial states like Maharashtra, West Bengal, Gujarat, Tamil Nadu, etc. There was a tendency to adopt highly capital-intensive and high power-intensive units. The Draft Plan further observed that, by and large, the industrial sector had not developed commensurate with endowments and needs in the different parts of the state. Even though several incentives were given, decentralisation of industries into rural areas had not taken place. Industrial development in the large and medium sector had been retarded mostly due to very limited outlays provided in the previous plans. Further, the industrial progress in the state had been adversely affected by the power and energy cuts as well as by problems connected with raw materials and labour. The units, which suffered on account of these problems were the sandalwood oil factories at Mysore and Shimoga. The Seventh Five Year Plan document stated that most of the industries had been established since the late 1960s on account of availability of cheap power from the Sharavathi Hydel project and consequently many industries have become power intensive with proportionately low contributions to employment generation or value added. The state had to its credit 20 electro-metallurgical and electro-chemical industries, which consumed more than 60 per cent of the aggregate energy used in industry. In addition, half of the large and medium-scale industries were concentrated in Bangalore district leading to the accelerated growth of the metropolitan city. It was, therefore, necessary that a reorientation of industrial policy was considered necessary and it envisaged a correction of the imbalances in industrial development which have hitherto occurred and more a positive role by the state government and its agencies and organisations towards the dispersal of industries. It also laid emphasis on discouraging power-intensive industries and proposed that government should refrain from large-scale direct investment. It instead recommended the fostering of entrepreneurship among the people of the state. The thrust of maximising employment opportunities by encouraging labour-intensive industries, of emphasising those industries which would help forge sustained backward and forward linkages with other economic activities and of providing incentives to encourage the development of desirable large and medium industries. The central thrust of the policy was the reinforcement and expansion of village and small industries. The Seventh Plan envisaged a more positive role for the government in promoting and protecting village and small-scale industries through a strengthening of programmes.

15.1.2 Industrial Scenario in Karnataka

The growth rates of states varied widely and the range was quite significant. Growth rates of gross state domestic product (SDP) for different states are given below (Table 15.1).

TABLE 15.1

Annual Growth Rate Comparisons

(in Per Cent)

States	*1980-81 to 1990–91*	*1991-92 to 1997-98*
Andhra Pradesh	5.65	5.03
Tamil Nadu	5.38	6.22
Kerala	3.57	5.81
Karnataka	**5.29**	**5.29**
Gujarat	5.08	9.57
Maharastra	6.02	8.01
GDP (Nat. Accounts)	5.55	6.89

Source: Ahluwalia, 2000: 1638.

As can be seen from the above data, the growth rate of SDP of Karnataka remained stagnant during the period 1980–1991 and 1991–1998 at 5.29 per cent (Ahluwalia, 2000: 1638). In the industrial sector also the picture was similar. During the period 1997 to 2002, the industrial sector grew by 2.94 per cent and manufacturing sector grew by 5.39 per cent. So, while other states seemed to have exploited the liberalised regime and caught up with the growth path, somehow Karnataka does not seem to have exploited it. In fact, during this period the state net domestic income still maintained its growth rate, which was helped by other sectors like software (Figure 15.1 and Appendix A-15.13).

15.1.3 Policy Initiatives So Far

Karnataka has not been able to parallel the success that it had in software industry to manufacturing sector on the whole. While we see an active pursuit of policies in the case of software sector, we see only half-hearted attempts in the case of industrial sector. In response to changes in the Industrial Policy of Central Government it made only tentative changes through the

FIGURE 15.1

NSDP at Factor Cost (Percentage Change Over Previous Year)

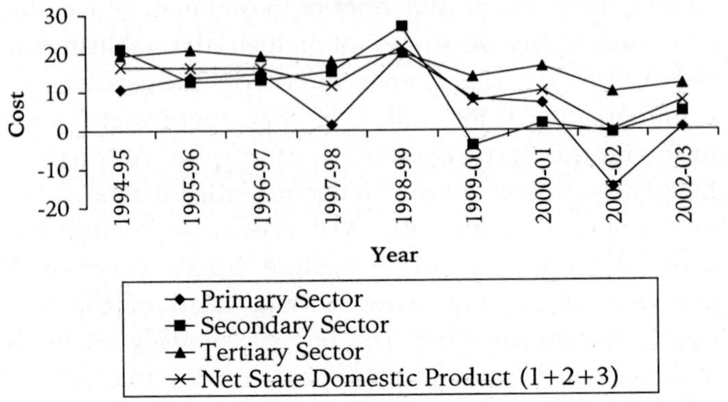

Source: Directorate of Economics and Statistics, Government of Karnataka, Bangalore.

New Industrial Policy Resolution, 1993–1998. It reclassified developed areas, which are eligible for incentives, introduced a scale of subsidy for tiny and small-scale industrial units, enhanced subsidy for thrust sector, introduced special incentive package for mega industries, etc. Single window agencies were empowered and given more discretion. Another New Industrial Policy, 1996 was introduced with a package of incentives and concessions for the years 1996–2001. It was introduced with many laudable objectives like:

- Active participation of industry in development of infrastructure.
- Development of potential growth centres.
- Growth thrust in export of value added groups.
- Proposals for improvement in performance of public sector undertakings.
- Simplification of rules and regulations and transparent administration.

The Policy settled for redefining small-scale sectors, announcing some sector-specific subsidies, empowering single window agency (SWA) to release subsidy, etc. It is clear from the provisions of Industrial Policy Statements that changes have not been perceived at state level about their changed role in promoting industrial growth, especially large and mega industries, and industrial parks. The emphasis was primarily on changing limits, reclassifying zones, changing procedures for releasing subsidies, empowering SWA for releasing subsidy, etc. The state had not still perceived the critical role it has to play in attracting investments. There was no clearcut strategy to attract FDIs. There is a mention of growth centres but these don't happen on their own and need concrete proposals for getting them started. Crucial time was probably lost in the initial phase of liberalisation and the state lost some momentum.

We see a series of initiatives in the form of Policies and Acts taken around 2000. New Industrial Policy, 2001–2006 was announced. There were also other policies announced to promote industries and economic growth. The relevant policies are (Gore, 2003):

- Industrial Policy, 2001;
- Millennium IT Policy, 2000;
- Millennium Biotech Policy, 2001;
- Millennium BPO Policy, 2002;
- Karnataka Infrastructure Policy, 1997;
- Karnataka Tourism Policy, 2002;
- Karnataka Export Promotion Policy, 2002; and
- Agro Food Processing Policy, 2003.

There were also Acts passed to improve the governance and institutional factors. The various Acts are (Gore, 2003):

- Land Reforms Act;
- Karnataka Industries (Facilitation) Act, 2002;
- Right to Information Act, 2000;
- Karnataka Transparency in Public Procurement Act, 1999;
- Zero Piracy Act, 2002;
- Reformed Labour Laws; and
- Karnataka Electricity Regulatory Commission for Power Reforms.

Karnataka's New Industrial Policy,[1] 2001 seeks ambitious targets in line with the thinking of the national policy makers and set about defining various initiatives that will be taken to fulfil that. It mentions that:

- Karnataka's mission is to achieve an economic growth rate of 8 per cent to 9 per cent over the next decade by promoting the rapid growth of a market-driven, knowledge-based, efficient, and competitive industrial sector.
- The proposed Industrial Policy will therefore aim to achieve an average industrial growth rate of 10 per cent to 12 per cent per year.
- Attract investments of at least Rs. 20,000 crore per year.
- Create on an average, employment potential of at least 1.5 lakhs per year.

It sought to achieve these objectives by providing 'high quality infrastructure, extending institutional support for technology upgradation, deregulating the business environment for an efficient, proactive and transparent administrative framework and catalysing the entrepreneurial as well as creative capabilities of the human resources'. The objectives and strategies through which these are sought to be achieved as mentioned in the Policy Statement can be seen in Appendix A-15.1. The Policy is a mirror of the industrial policy of the Government of India with focus on Karnataka's advantages, technology, knowledge sector, global reach and competitiveness, and broad based development through promotion of various sectors and regions.

The New Industrial Policy, 2001–2006 Statement sought to address issues relating to various contributory factors to industrial development like:

- technology upgradation,
- infrastructure,
- human resource development,
- deregulation of business environment,
- marketing assistance for the SSI sector, and
- streamlining the single window mechanism.

These are comprehensive enough and provide for a wide range of reforms and support. It also reconfigured the regional classification scheme for giving incentives into four Zonal Systems as developed areas, developing areas, backward areas, and growth centres and mini growth centres, specialised industrial parks and list of *talukas*. Besides encouraging investments in thrust industrial product lines, the policy has also announced series of incentives for exports and mega industries.

In keeping with the Central Government Policy for special economic zones (SEZ), Government of Karnataka also proposed to set up a SEZ at Hassan, which lies midway between Bangalore and Mangalore. It also has proposed to establish a SEZ exclusively for electronic hardware at Devanahalli and provided for converting existing Export Promotion Industrial Park at White Field, Bangalore and the proposed Export Promotion Industrial Park at Mangalore into SEZ (State Policy for SEZ). Sector specific SEZ for textiles at Hassan and for

1. New Industrial Policy 2001–2006, Department of Industries and Commerce, Government of Karnataka.

IT at Mangalore have been identified for development and have been approved by the government of India (Appendix A-15.2).

The government has set up an implementing agency named Karnataka Industrial Area Development Board (KIADB) which will promote SEZs either on its own or in association with private sector partners. KIADB has the mandate to promote various growth centres and specialised industrial parks[2] (Appendices 15.3 to 15.5):

i. Six Agro-Food Processing Parks at Malur, Bagalkot, Belgaum, Chitradurga, Maddur, and Jeevargi. The Government of India has released funds for these projects.

ii. Two Apparel Export Parks, one each at Bangalore and Bellary.

iii. A Special Economic Zone in Hassan.

iv. An Export Promotion Industrial Park in Mangalore.

v. Three Auto Parks, one each at Bidadi, Shimoga and Dharwad.

vi. A Knowledge Park dedicated to Biotechnology and related industries near Bangalore.

vii. A full–fledged Financial District near Bangalore.

Cluster Development Programme

The government of India has introduced Integrated Infrastructure Upgradation Scheme (IIUS) during 2003-2004 and the objective of the scheme is to enhance international competitiveness of the domestic industry by providing quality infrastructure through public-private partnership approach in selected functional clusters/locations which have greater potential to become globally competitive. The proposed scheme aims to select industrial clusters/locations with high growth potential which requires strategic interventions in providing: (a) physical infrastructure, (b) information and communication technology (ICT) infrastructure, (c) R&D infrastructure, (d) information dispersal and international marketing infrastructure, (e) ICT-induction and process engineering and process re-engineering and management consultancy service centre, and (f) any other physical infrastructure identified by cluster and approved by the Apex Committee. The proposed scheme is a central sector scheme with a provision of Rs. 675 crore in the Tenth Plan and initially 20-25 clusters/locations would be taken up for development. The government of India shall sanction up to 75 per cent of the expenditure and the rest to be brought in by the cluster SPV along with state contribution. Out of 7 applications sent to the government of India, 2 cluster projects have already been sanctioned.

The Karnataka Government has set up the Karnataka Udyog Mitra (KUM) as the nodal agency to guide and provide assistance to the entrepreneurs as well as to obtain the required clearances/consents/approvals/registrations/licence from the various departments at the implementation stage of a project (Department of Industries and Commerce). Nodal agencies are increasingly being used to deal with multiple agencies and approvals on behalf of investors and it is important to see to it that these themselves do not become bureaucratic over time and develop multiple windows. Different states have developed different mechanisms to manage SWA, and it has to be set up within the overall organisational context of the Industry Ministry but should have adequate powers to decide. Karnataka government also set up subsequently two high level committees to deal with large and mega industries, and SME segments. These were State High Level Clearance Committee (SHLCC) chaired by the chief minister to deal with large and mega projects and another state level single window agency headed by principal secretary industry to deal with small and medium enterprises.

The government also sought to give thrust to development of Bangalore city. It has also set up Bangalore Task Force Agenda, which was a joint initiative of leading individuals and government. The government took various steps to improve the road infrastructure, communication, and power in Bangalore and the city grew at impressive growth rates propelled by software industry.

These are bold initiatives and give wide ranging incentives and support and are matching with what other states can offer. It seeks to provide for ambitious growth through SEZ and growth centres, sectoral growth through specific parks, regional development through zoning system, more streamlines clearance procedures through empowered high-level single window agencies, etc. One can hardly find any fault with these or any gaps in the proposals, but it is yet to make an impact on the ground. It shows that in implementation the issues are still impeding the progress.

2. State Policy for SEZ, Government of Karnataka.

15.2 Industrial Performance: Karnataka

As per the index numbers of industrial production (IIP)[3] for Karnataka 1993-94=100, industry grows on an average by 6.17 per cent per annum in the nine year period ending 2002-03. The intra-year variations were wide apart ranging from a low of 2.37 per cent in 2002-2003 to a higher of 12.26 per cent in 1997-98. This essentially reflects the growth pattern of manufacturing sector, which ranged from 2.74 per cent in 2002-03 to 10.2 per cent in 1997-98. The average annual growth rate of manufacturing sector during this period was 6.14 per cent and that of electricity was 7.54 and mining was 7.22 per cent. Prior to economic reforms, the industrial performance (general) of Karnataka in eighties started off quite well with an impressive growth of 17.3 per cent in 1981-82, which progressively decelerated (Figure 15.2). In the major part of the eighties (1980-81=100) industrial growth on an average was around 7 per cent per year. With the change in base year to 1993-94 there is a break in the IIP series from 1993-94 onwards.

FIGURE 15.2

Trends in Industrial Production (Index)

(a) 1991-91 to 1993-94: Base 1980-81=100

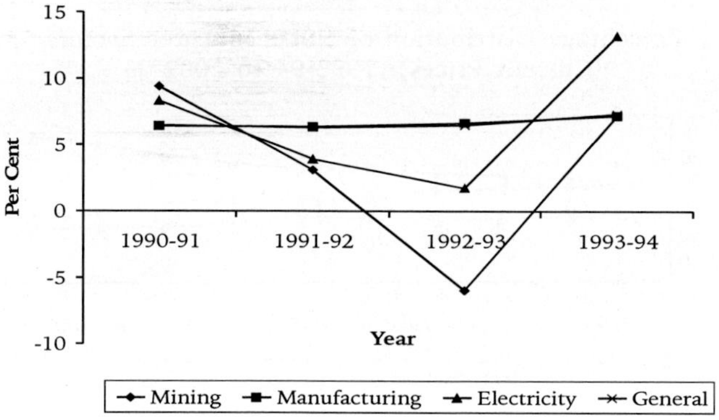

(b) 1994-95 to 2002-03: Base 1993-94=100

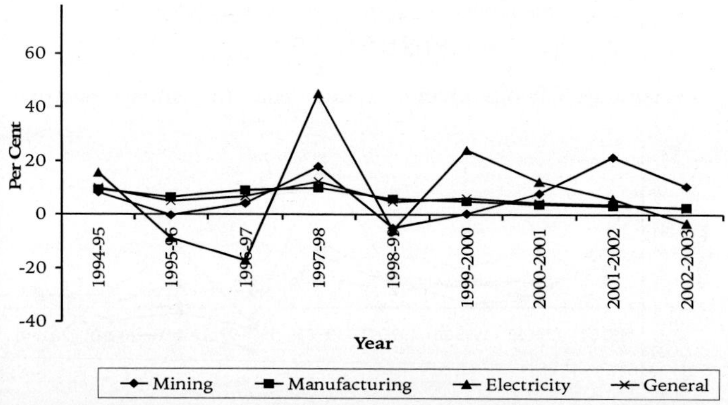

Source: Directorate of Economics and Statistics, *Index Numbers of Industrial Production*, Government of Karnataka.

In the interim period of three years 1990-91 to 1993-1994, the average annual growth was little less than 7 per cent. This, however, was maintained in the subsequent period with the annual average growth slowing down to 6.17 per cent from 1993-94 to 2002-03. With the change in the base year the role of manufacturing sector which was assigned a weight of 95.85 in the overall IIP in 1980-81 reduced to 89.30 in 1993-94. The electricity sector has taken a slightly bigger role with the change in the weight from 2.74 to 8.34. (Appendix A-15.14). If we look at the growth rate of various subsectors like capital goods, intermediate and consumer we observe no perceptible change years, during the years 2001–02 to 2002-03, taking it as a case if we want to study the impact of recent policy changes. The past trend shows that while consumer industry has been showing positive trend, capital goods and consumer durables show steady trend but lower growth rate around 3 per cent (Appendix A-15.15 and Figure 15.3). Basic goods registered an absolute fall (-) 0.19 per cent in 2002–03 while capital goods decelerated to 2.12 per cent during 2002-03 from 2.84 per cent in 2001-02 which itself was sharply lower i.e., just half of 5.76 per cent growth recorded in the earlier year 2000-01.

FIGURE 15.3

Average Annual Growth of Manufacturing Sector by Use Based Group

(a) 1990-91 to 1993-94: Base 1980-81=100

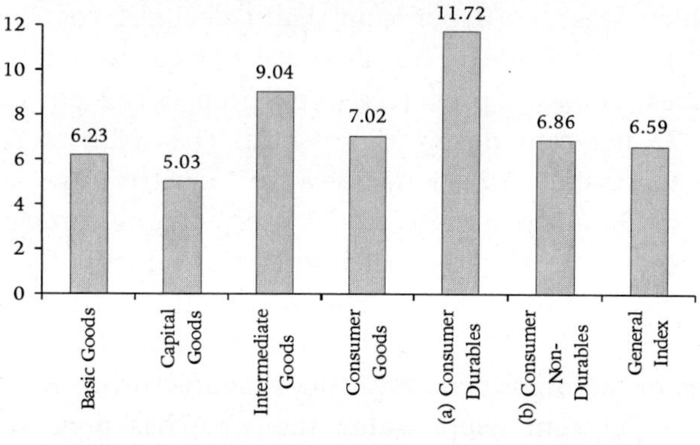

(b) 1994-95 to 2002-03: Base 1993-94=100

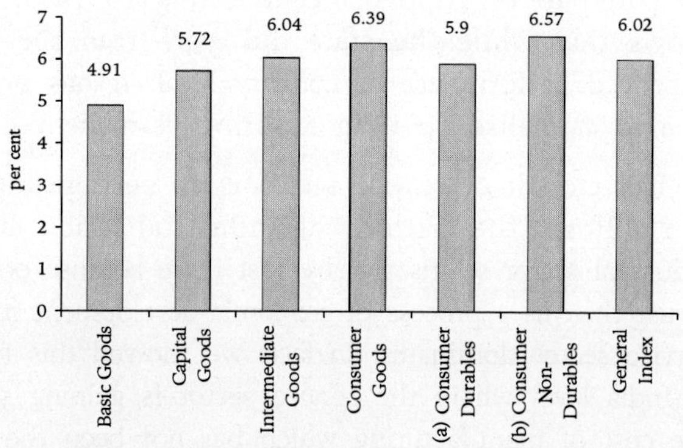

Source: Directorate of Economics and Statistics, *Index Numbers of Industrial Production*, Government of Karnataka.

3. Government of India have selected 1,307 units in the new IIP basket with base 2001-02. The terms and conditions of the data collection are the same as that of IIP with the base year 1987-88.

A comparative picture of net state domestic product at current prices of fast growing states is given in Appendix A-15.16 and its growth rates in Appendix A-15.17. It emerges from this that all these states exhibit excellent growth rates during the period 1993-2002, which is around 12 per cent. Surprisingly, it turns out that the growth rate during 1993-1997 has been much higher than 1997–2002. It emerges that the initial policy impetus given were not sustained and that we can say that even in these states the growth phase has not entered auto mode from where it can expand on its own base or momentum. These still need continuous impetus, which has to be given by the states.

Karnataka ranks among the top five industrialised states in India, and according to the state, it has made appreciable 'achievements in promoting hi-tech industries in key sectors like electronics, telecommunication, information technology, precision engineering, automobiles, readymade garments, bio-technology and food processing' (Karnataka Economic Survey 2002–03: 1, *des.nic.in*). Share of the secondary sector in the state's income fell from 25.40 per cent in 1993–94 to 23.83 per cent in 2002–03 and the share of manufacturing fell from 17.86 per cent to 14.68 per cent in the same period (Appendix A-15.18). The contribution of manufacturing to secondary sector which was at 70 per cent again declined to 61.6 per cent in 1993-94. The share of agriculture sector in states' domestic product also fell from 36.32 per cent to 23.23 per cent during this period. The share of tertiary sector mainly driven by software industry, rose sharply from 38.27 per cent to 52.94 per cent during this period. In real terms also software industry has done better and service industry grew at 10.10 per cent during 1993–94 to 2002-03 compared to secondary sector at 5.24 per cent and manufacturing sector at 2.91 per cent. Here again, the state has done well in the first half that is, during 1993-97 at 4.39 per cent compared to (–) 1.30 per cent during 1997-2002. This shows that while the state did gain from the overall improved performance at country level, it has not been able to capitalise on it in ensuring permanent gain.

The growth of service sector is an encouraging trend and follows the pattern of industrialisation but the industrial sector seems to have lost more because of lack of thrust than as a process of economic development in which service sector dominates. In fact, we showed this trend at all-India level where the service sector is gaining share at the cost of manufacturing which has not been the case if we take countries like China, Thailand, Korea, etc.

The trend of growth rates of secondary sector in recent years 2000–01 to 2002–03 is quite revealing. The general index of secondary sector fell from 4.54 per cent in 2000–01 to 2.39 per cent in 2002–03 and manufacturing sector fell from 3.77 per cent to 2.74 per cent. Power in fact fell drastically from 12.38 per cent to (–)3.22 and only mining rose from 8.03 per cent to 10.50 per cent. These are disturbing trends as these are not steady even at lower rate. On the other hand one can see that services has shown a positive and upward trend (Figures 15.4, 15.5 and 15.6). We can say that the policy changes are yet to get reflected in the industrial growth. In the reform-period the industrial slowdown in Karnataka is in line with the all-India trend. Only in the recent one or two years this is visible for the state. The industrial restructuring process whereby the state industries are adjusting to the competition whereby they slowed down production. With services sector gaining predominance, the role of manufacturing sector which decides the overall industrial performance is diminishing slowly (Table 15.2).

FIGURE 15.4

Percentage Distribution of NSDP in Three Sectors (Current Prices): 1993-94 to 2002-03

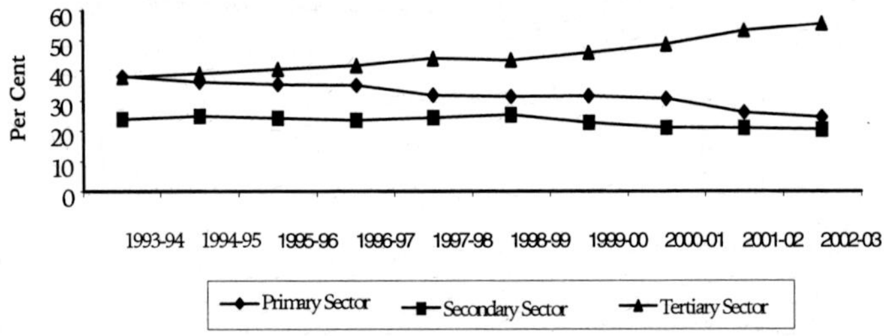

Source: Directorate of Economics and Statistics, Government of Karnataka, Bangalore.

FIGURE 15.5

Percentage Change Over Previous Year (Secondary Sector)

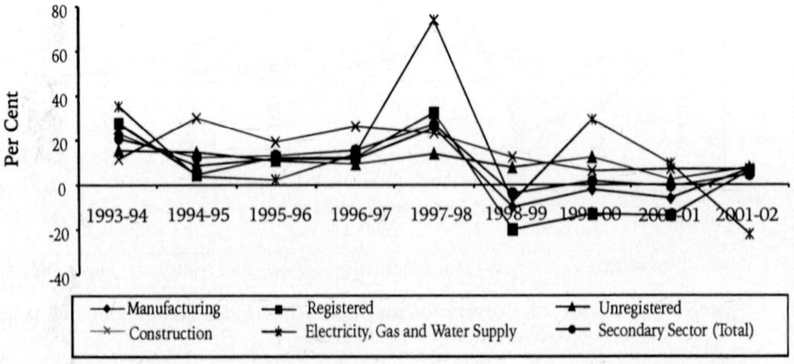

Source: Directorate of Economics and Statistics, Government of Karnataka, Bangalore.

FIGURE 15.6

NSDP (Secondary Sector) 1993 to 2002-03 at Factor Cost (Rs. Lakh)

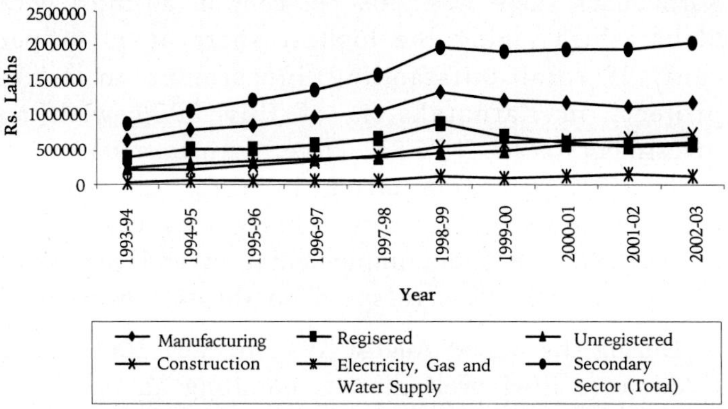

Source: Directorate of Economics and Statistics, Government of Karnataka, Bangalore.

TABLE 15.2

Trend in Index of Industrial Production of Karnataka: Base 1993-94=100

(in Percentage)

Periods	*Mining*	*Manufacturing*	*Electricity*	*Gen. Index*
1993–1997	2.92	12.14	-3.37	10.75
1997–2002	4.54	2.94	6.82	6.49
1993–2003	6.48	9.59	7.32	10.29

Source: Directorate of Economics and Statistics, Government of Karnataka.

The status of Karnataka's industrial development in terms of employment, output, value added in relation to other states is as follows (Table 15.3). Complete statistics can be seen in Appendix A-15.19.

TABLE 15.3

Important Parameters of Industrial Performances as per Annual Survey of Industries: 2000-01

States	*Total Factories (Nos.)*	*Total Employees (Nos.)*	*Value of Output (Rs. Crore)*	*Net Value Added (Rs. Crore)*
Karnataka	7010	474150	46258.83	8301.63
Maharashtra	18528	1172799	1849771.46	31260.98
Andhra Pradesh	14029	907055	61347.02	8878.67
Tamil Nadu	20601	1136265	103539.89	16536.32
Gujarat	14090	752013	127977.28	16855.87
All India	**131268**	**7987780**	**926901.86**	**143621.41**

Source: CMIE, *Monthly Review of Karnataka Economy*, August 2004.

The Table 15.3 shows that on the whole, the industrial base of Karnataka is quite low on all indicators when compared to other fast growing states. It needs to go for concerted efforts to boost industrial sector at all levels, that is whether it is SME segment or mega industries. Karnataka showed a positive trend in value of output. It can be seen that it is showing negative trend also but a negative trend in value added at (0.55 per cent).

Another comparative analysis that we can make is regarding value added per worker (Appendix A-15.20). The net value added per worker has been growing steadily but in a small measure from Rs. 1.82 lakhs in 1995–96 to Rs. 2.31 lakhs in 2000-01. This table shows the share of Karnataka at national level, and we can observe them that the share of Karnataka is small around 5 per cent and has not shown any perceptible increase during this period.

In Appendix A-15.21, we have given statistics relating to output and capital formation. We observe that there is hardly any trend in relationship between value of output, net value added and gross and net capital formation. In fact over the years we find that net value added per investment made varies from 3.19 times in 1990–91 to 4.56 in 1991-92 to 2.11 times in 1996–1997. This is a very poor trend especially in the face of spectacular gains made in productivity by China in their SEZs and overall economy. We found that attempts to relate output to capital formation and compute ICOR are quite futile.

TABLE 15.4

Plan Outlay for Industrial Sector

Industry and Minerals	*Rs. in Lakhs*
Village (V) & Small Industries (SI)	114021
Industries (Other than V & SI)	29039
Mining	2227
Total	**145287**

Source: Karnataka Tenth Plan–2002-07.

At the next level we can look at fresh investment made in the state in the last decade and plan period. The gross and net capital formation grew at best at modest rates. The Plan outlays earmarked for industries in the Tenth Plan is given in Table 15.4. This level of investment is grossly insufficient to achieve targeted growth rate of 10 to 12 per cent. It is to be noted that the present policies provide for industrial growth mainly through private sector but this level of investments fall short of requirements even for promoting industrial parks and to provide for subsidies and various incentives.

We can also look at fresh approvals given for new industries. The number of factories in Karnataka show a fluctuating trend as shown earlier which reflects sickness which is hardly encouraging. On the other hand if we look at the corporate sector performance, it has faired well when compared to all-India level on all parameters. Sales and gross fixed assets show fluctuating trend but at higher levels with sales at 16.10 per cent in 1995–96 to 18 per cent in 2002-03 gross fixed assets at 35.80 per cent and 12.70 changes during these years (Appendix A-15.22). The profit percentages are again unsteady but higher than all-India figures. This shows that corporate sectors located in Karnataka are doing better and seem to move in line with rest of country. What is of concern is the ratio of value of products to gross fixed assets which came down from 2.06 times in 1995-96 to 1.29 times in 2002-03 which also seems to be the all-India trend. So, productivity is an issue, which needs to be addressed at all-India level as well as Karnataka level.

However, the large industries in manufacturing are few and far between. This is evident from Appendix A-15.23, which gives approvals of letter of Intent (LI) and Industrial Licences (IL). The trend again shows initial good response to national industrial policy post-1991 but came down drastically from 1997-98, often figuring in single digits. KSIIDC Ltd, the State Financial Institution which deals with large industries had disbursed Rs. 66.6 crore to 85 units in 1990–91 and Rs. 182.13 crore to 79 units in 2001-02. In investments, it started at Rs. 5.30 crore to 5 units in 1990-91 and came down to Rs. 4.58 crore in 2001-02 after peaking in 1995-96 at Rs. 60.80 crore for 38 units. These trends are indicative of very low demand for loans and disbursal of funds, especially when compared to ambitious targets the state has set for itself.

TABLE 15.5

Trends in Investments

(Rs. in Crore)

	Under Implementation	*Total*
July 1999	2080.98	13504.38
July 2000	2630.35	17272.29
July 2001	3634.79	37192.98
July 2002	4762.56	39807.27
July 2003	7081.10	42704.68
July 2004	7598.91	43487.35
July 2005	58431.00	176532.00

Source: Monthly Review of Karnataka Economy, CMIE, September 2005.

One indication of future growth path of industrial sector of Karnataka can be the quantum of projects under implementation (Table 15.5). In July 2005, Karnataka's share was 7.03 per cent in all-India with Maharashtra taking the highest share at 11.46 per cent. If total outstanding investment in 1,234 projects in Karnataka as of July 2005 with an investment of Rs. 1,76,532 crore, Karnataka ranks 5th with 7.94 per cent share in total outstanding investment in the country. This shows that major investments are under implementation and that state has to take initiatives to speed up these investments.

During the period August 1991 to May 2005, 2,327 IEMs were filed in Karnataka entailing an aggregate investment of Rs. 78.077 crore. In this respect also while Maharashtra occupies the 1st place Karnataka is ranked 7th among the major states. Its share in all-India is over 5 per cent.

15.2.1 Implementation Record

Paul, as quoted earlier, citing a report in *Economic Times*, mentions that Maharashtra and Tamil Nadu have been successful in attracting investment proposals but the conversion of these proposals into actual projects was a disappointing picture (Appendix A-15.24). According to the Report while Maharashtra had done the best with 55 per cent success rate in conversion, other states like Gujarat at 43 per cent, Karnataka at 38 per cent and Tamil Nadu at 26 per cent performed not so well (Paul, 2000: 3861).

Of the 104 projects approved in Karnataka only 16 projects which were worth Rs. 3,400 crore, were completed over a period of 1991–92 to 1998–99 and in value term it was only 5 per cent of the value of the proposals. Nearly 23 projects worth Rs. 14,400 crore were waiting for clearance. Of the 104 projects worth Rs. 68,787 crore, 17 were large projects in the range of 1,000 crore and above with value of investment totalling Rs. 43,857 crore, 12 projects were in the range of 500–1,000 crore, with the total value of investment Rs. 8,095 crore, and 62 units in the range of 100–200 crore valued at Rs.15,950 crore (Paul, 2000: 3863). Projects proposed in Bangalore, seems to have had better success rate than those in other districts of Karnataka. Several reasons were advanced for lack of progress of projects including demand of bribes, amount of paper work, process time, and staff behaviour (Paul, 2000: 3868). The study also points out, "Foreign investment appears to be a minor element in the totality of projects" (Paul, 2000: 3863). Share of public sector was also minimal. One thing encouraging from the study is the size of the proposals, which were approved. Also, the projects approved belonged to various industries like steel, cement, consumer goods, information technology and services.

A list of large projects above Rs. 200 crore is given in Appendix A-15.25. The cumulative of all industries is Rs. 39,873.91 crore which however includes non-manufacturing industries also.

15.2.2 FDI Approvals

One more indicator, which we can consider is FDI approvals and investments in the state. A statement of approval of foreign collaboration and FDI proposals for select states is given below. During the period 1991 to 2002, the FDI approval given for units to be located in Karnataka was Rs. 21,586.53 crore and its share in all-India approval in value terms is 7.70 per cent (Table 15.6). In this we can observe that Maharashtra and Delhi have done quite well.

TABLE 15.6

FDI Approvals: 1991-2002

State	*No. of Approvals*			*Amt. of FDI*	*Share*
	Total	*Tech.*	*Fin.*	*Approved (in Crore)*	*In Value (%)*
Karnataka	1950	448	1502	21586	7.70
Maharashtra	3959	1146	2813	48660	17.35
Delhi	1951	214	1737	33688	12.10
Tamil Nadu	2152	542	1610	23236	8.20
Andhra Pradesh	1010	239	771	13068	4.66
All India	21926	7039	14887	280442	-

Source: India Investment Centre, Report, 2003.

If we see this along with the success rates of actual implementation in Karnataka, it is picture considering the fact that the state plans to attract Rs. 20,000 crore every year during the policy period. We do see good growth rates in state net domestic products but not so much in manufacturing sector. The growth rates of manufacturing are not consistent and sometimes declining also. The state is not successful in retaining the projects and investments. Inconsistent growth in the state also shows that the impact of the industrial policies made at both central and state level is yet to be felt in reality. It is not getting translated into projects and investments. It would require much more drastic and wholehearted approach if it has to achieve its objectives. Of these, one of the major hurdles will be governance and institutional mechanisms, as it is increasingly becoming evident globally among all developed countries and equally applicable in India and its states.

15.3 Plan and Strategies for Karnataka

Industries Sector: 2005-06 to 2009-10

We can now piece together the trends in manufacturing growth and investment and make prognosis regarding the plan for the period 2005-06 to 2009–10 (plan is made for this period as it is expected to take effect from next budget year). This section will portray the industrial growth rate targets, and investments potential and targets, and strategies for mobilising the investments. Side by side existing position is also given to appreciate the size and complexity of the action involved. The strategies are suggested in terms of projects to be followed up, tapping FDI market, milestones, and tackling governance issues.

We observed that the industrial growth rate has not been showing significant increase besides exhibiting high volatility indicating that the growth rates have not still stabilised. The state net domestic product again has been growing at the rate of 8.92 per cent in the recent period but the Tenth Five Year Plan targets 8 per cent growth rate NSDP and 10 to 12 per cent growth rate in industrial sector. The Plan also assumes that the state will be able to attract Rs. 20,000 crore during the Tenth Five Year Plan period.

It is suggested that the Plan targets for industrial sector be kept the same for this period—2006-2010 also. The optimism can be misplaced, if we go by past trends or present rates, but we are proposing this for many reasons. Firstly, it is important that the effect of plan should be such that it targets a rate higher than the current rate. Secondly, as we saw earlier Karnataka has taken many initiatives in the last few years, which should start yielding result now. Thirdly, it has earned global image in software industry, which it should try to leverage for promoting Karnataka as a destination for manufacturing and FDI. Fourthly, many mega projects like international airport, petrochemical and aromatics, gas-based power plant, gas pipeline project, etc. are in various stages of finalisation and are in the process of getting launched.

TABLE 15.7

Industries Plan Targets

State Net Domestic Plan	
Recent Ave. Growth Rate: Karnataka	: 5.29 per cent
Present Growth Rate: All India (2000–03)	: 8.2 per cent
Projected Growth Rate: (2005-06 to 2009–10)	: 8 per cent per annum
Industrial Growth Rate	
Recent Growth Rate: Karnataka	: 8.92 per cent per annum
Present Growth Rate: All India 2003–04	: 7.3 per cent
Projected Growth Rate	: 12 per cent per annum
Investment Flow	
Tenth Plan Outlay for Industries	: Rs. 290.39 crore for five years
Gross Capital Formation (as of 1998)	: Rs. 5341.88 crore
Projected Level of Investment	: Rs. 20,000 crore per annum
FDI Flow	
Inflow so far for the Period for Karnataka (1991–2000)	: Rs. 21,586.52 crore (Approvals)
Jan. 1997 to Dec. 2004	: Rs. 22,685.24 crore (Approvals)
Suggested FDI Target for Karnataka for five years	: US $ 1 to 2 billion
FDI Approval at All-India Level (1991–2004)	: US$ 36.62 billion
Jan.–Dec. 2003	: US$ 3.1 billion
Jan. 1997 to Dec. 2004	: Rs. 2,05,468.57 crore (Approvals)
All India Level	
Projected FDI for next five years	: US$ 100 billion.
Large and Mega Projects (CMIE)	
Various Projects under Implementation in Karnataka: Cumulative (July 2005)	: Rs. 1,76,532 crore
Projects under Implementation: 2004-2005	: Rs. 58,431 crore
Mega Projects Approved 1991-92 to 2004-05	: 296
Investment	: Rs. 1,66,343.5 crore
Employment	: 572552
Medium and Large Industries Approved 1998-99 to 2004-05	: 2107
Investment	: Rs. 29,30,165 lakh
Employment	: 658439

Source: Based on data obtained from various sources such as, Department of Industries and Commerce, Govt. of Karnataka, CMIE, Plan Documents of Govt. of Karnataka.

If we look at the targeted growth rates (Table 15.7) it does not look beyond reach as such rates have been achieved in the past. The pipeline projects itself are quite huge and significant and if these are converted into actual investments and projects, the target will be easily reached. For this, as pointed out in the discussion above, it is important to improve administration, make suitable policy changes in areas mentioned earlier and improve overall governance.

If we look at national level inflow of FDI, it is discouraging. FDI inflows in 2001 at all-India level was US$ 4.3 billion, of which manufacturing sector accounted for less than 30 per cent, unlike China where FDI inflows into manufacturing account for 60 per cent. This shows again the poor performance of the nation in attracting FDI and the scope that exists if we go for it aggressively (DIPP, 2004: 84).

However even at national level, FDI targets are only US$ 7–8 billion in the Tenth Plan. But according to the DIPP potential exists for US$ 100 billion over next five years and privatisation itself has the potential to absorb US$ 49 billion. It stresses sectoral targets and commitment from respective ministries to implement reforms, "Active participation of State governments is required in attracting FDI" (DIPP, 2004: 84).

The share of states of cumulative FDIs made from 1991 to 2002 which are given in Box 15.3 places Karnataka's share to 7.70 per cent only. In its efforts to increase its share above 10 per cent which is very important as it could fetch the state FDI of US$ 10 billion to US$ 15 billion in the next five years. This is very vital to the state as on its own it will not be in a position to mobilise the investments that it needs, if it has to ensure a growth rate of 12 per cent. But there appears to be some visible improvement in the latter period. If we take the period January 1997 to December 2004, the state's position appears far better (Table 15.8). The foreign collaboration proposals approved by the government of India for Karnataka for the 15 year period ending 2004-05 were 2,620 projects with an amount of Rs. 24,912 crore. Though the number of proposals approved were largest at 320 in 2001-02, amount-wise it was highest at Rs. 5,374 crore in 1998-99.

TABLE 15.8

Share in FDI

Share (per cent)

	1991-2002	*Jan. 1997-Dec. 2004*
Karnataka	7.70	11.04
Maharashtra	17.35	17.31
Delhi	12.00	5.91
Tamil Nadu	8.30	7.42

Source: Centre for Monitoring Indian Economy (CMIE).

Internal mobilisation also has to improve a lot. It has to strengthen its profit making PSUs and decide on loss making units. It should also coordinate with the Central Government to improve the performance of central PSUs as these invariably lead to further sickness through its ancillary units.

Thirdly, relationship should be developed with Indian corporates. It should be understood that some of these corporates themselves have become MNCs over the years and they are also investing aggressively in other countries. It should sell aggressively to the India Inc. also, as they have more credibility in approaching foreign companies for forming JVs.

It is important to develop a project orientation and move from policy orientation. In policy orientation the emphasis is more towards making pronouncements, issuing guidelines, streamlining procedures, and prescribing the incentives and subsidy scheme and structure. In the end, the tendency of the government is towards wait and watch, and react to proposals. In project orientation, the emphasis is on being proactive in identifying projects, targeting investors in promoting SEZs, in customising incentives. The emphasis should be more towards identifying shelf of large and mega projects and make targeted search. The players in areas like industrial park and township development, port development, airport development, gas pipeline laying are small in numbers and it is important to sell the projects on individual basis. In mega project it is important to proceed with customised policy framework. Generalised policy framework can work only with large and medium-scale industries.

Promotion of SEZ should be taken on highest priority basis and blueprints should be developed immediately. A study of SEZs in China and other countries showed that hardly any time is lost in reaching the completion stage once the policy decision has been taken. A cross-country comparison of countries like China, Malaysia, Bangladesh, and Sri Lanka can be seen in Appendix A-15.7. It shows that in benefits we are comparable but we lack mainly in implementation. If the SEZs are to be made popular, Mc Kinsey has suggested that it should focus on: (a) closer proximity to ports and industrial hubs, (b) areas extending to 50 to 100 square kms to attract sizeable number of industries, (c) relaxed labour laws, (d) independent power producers, and (e) investment by government in roads, ports, telecom (*ibid*: 77). A brief write up on Shenzhen SEZ in China can be seen in Appendix 15.6, based on the work of Ge (1999). The story of this SEZ should be very inspiring and it requires deeper study to understand how it reached such heights.

One important lesson of general development and SEZ development in China is that most of these areas are coastal areas. Karnataka needs to develop Mangalore into a major port or need to identify one, which can be developed as major port. The recent crisis in JLN Port in Navi Mumbai, shows acute necessity for port in this region. Coastal Area Development should be one of the priority areas for Karnataka.

It is suggested that it should immediately prepare blueprint for SEZs in Hassan and other industrial parks as proposed in the industrial policy. It should identify international consultants, who can also help identify investors. It can also focus on specific industrial parks like biotechnology for which it has already plans, pharma, auto parts, etc. Without loss of time and proceeding on its own it can undertake preliminary work in the identification and acquiring of land, creating necessary regulatory frameworks, and developing interconnected infrastructure like roads, power, etc.

It should also identify 20 mega industries, which can be promoted in Karnataka in which the state has advantage. It should then target Indian and global corporates who would be interested in these projects. Each should have its own customised policies relating to incentives, location, and subsidies.

Finally the regulatory framework has to be made conducive for investors. According to the report (World Bank, 2004: 92) on doing business, principles of good regulation are:

- Simplify and deregulate in competitive markets.
- Focus on enhancing property rights.
- Expand the use of technology.
- Reduce court involvement in business matters.
- Make reform a continuous process.

It needs to commission series of studies on:

- Identification of thrust industries for Karnataka.
- Role of incentives and subsidies.
- Reason for investors dropouts after approvals, identification of irritants, and strategies for tackling these.
- Labour reforms at state level. In any case it has to think afresh on labour reforms for SEZs.
- Blueprint for improving governance. Even though there are SWAs and improvements in procedures it is still not clear why no

downsizing has taken place like in the case of DGTD in Central Government. Unless the industries department and SWAs are made more efficient, these may become one more stage in the process. The study should provide for pruning the industries department and approval agencies like it happened in Central Government.

- To fix specific targets and milestones for setting up SEZ at Hassan, port development, EPZ/ growth centre, mega industries, large industries.
- Strategy for leveraging on IT and exploit the presence of MNCs located in Karnataka as resource persons for attracting other corporates.

15.4 Small-Scale, Village and Cottage Industries

In the early stages of industrialisation, there was more emphasis on setting up giant undertakings in the public sector and in the process, the essential role that small-scale industries could play in complementary capacity in the larger projects was not given due recognition. This has resulted in the projects being over capitalised. With a view to becoming self-contained, the need to develop small-scale industries was embodied in the fundamental policy of the state for the equal distribution of the ownership of material resources among the communities at large and to ensure that the implementation of any scheme does not result in concentration of wealth. Karnataka, as mentioned earlier, possesses all resources and in-built infrastructure to march ahead in setting up industrial estates throughout the state to encourage entrepreneurs to start small-scale industries. The variety and range of products manufactured by the small-scale units in the state also reflect the progress made in the sector. They include sophisticated telecommunication equipment, machine tools, intricate castings, diesel engines, agricultural machinery, flow meters, hearing aids, electrical appliances and accessories, rubberised coir, foam rubber, moulded rubber goods, industrial plastic components, monofilament acrylic sheets, reinforced plastic products, insulators, scientific glass instruments, tanned leather, travel accessories, etc. The small-scale industries in Karnataka state today are recognised as the most dynamic and progressive sector of our economy. The progress achieved in this sector, particularly during the last decade and a half, in terms of the increase in the number of units and the volume of production, the variety of new products taken up, the employment opportunities created, the entrepreneurial skill developed, the increases attained in productivity, the extent of industrial dispersal achieved both spatial and ownership, the amount of capital mobilised for industrial progress testifies to its contribution to the economic growth of the state and the promise that it holds for the future.

It was during the Second Plan period that the small-scale industries were given a helping hand in their growth by provision of ready-built accommodation in different places. A network of industrial estates was formed for this purpose. The scheme for industrial estates envisaged the construction of worksheds for small-scale industrialists along with the provision of facilities and services like power, water, drainage and sewerage, roads, godown, post offices, banks, etc., all at one place. The first working group on industrial cooperatives set up in 1957 made useful recommendations for the development of these societies. The Mysore Small-Scale Industries and Handicrafts Board was constituted in the year 1959 with the object of advising the government generally on the production and growth of small-scale industries. In 1960, the state government set up a corporation called the Mysore Small Industries Corporation Limited with a capital of Rs. 10 lakhs for rendering various types of assistance to small-scale industrialists such as construction of industrial estates and their management, opening of raw material depots at important industrial centres such steel, coal, coke and non-ferrous metals and developing marketing facilities for the products of small-scale industries, etc. During 1968-69 the state government set up a testing laboratory and a tool room for small-scale industries through the Mysore Small Industries Corporation. Presently, there are a number of institutions like Karnataka State Small Industries Association, Karnataka Productivity Council, Consortium of Electronic Industries in Karnataka, Association of Women Entrepreneurs of Karnataka, CSIR Polytechnology Transfer Centre, Visweswaraya Industrial Trade Centre, etc. which have been servicing the small-scale industries in various ways. The state government is extending financial assistance to these institutions, giving the due recognition to their promotional activities and also their limited resources.

15.4.1 Income from Unregistered Sector

The entire village and cottage industries are in the organised sector and further, the structure of this sector is such that it differs from state to state and also within the state from district to district depending upon the availability of specific raw materials in that particular region. In Karnataka, as already mentioned, some of the populous and important cottage and household industries are sericulture, handicrafts, *agarbatti*, and handlooms. Most of these products are good value added items and have good prospects of earning good income and also foreign exchange for the country. As all these units fell under the unregistered category, it will be more appropriate to analyse the contribution of this sector to the state domestic product.

The unregistered sector, which is mostly the unorganised sector accounts for a relatively larger share in the domestic product and more so in the manufacturing sector. In 2002-03 its share in the NSDP was 55.73 per cent and in GSDP it was 44.37 per cent. In the nine year period 1993-94 and 2002-03 the income from this sector registered a maximum growth of 10.3 per cent (NSDP) in 2000-01 and lowest of 2.4 per cent (NSDP) in 1995-96. Its share to NSDP in this period hovered fractionally below 7 per cent (6.8 per cent) on an average (Table 15.9).

TABLE 15.9

Contribution of Unregistered Sector to Karnataka State Domestic Product: Base 1993-94=100 at Constant Prices

(in Percentages)

Period	*Annual Growth Rate of Income from Unregistered Sector*		*Share of Unregistered Sector to Income from Manufacturing*		*Share of Unregistered Sector to Total State Income*	
	Net	*Gross*	*Gross*	*Net*	*Net*	*Gross*
1993-94	-	-	38.44	39.15	6.9	11.0
1994-95	5.7	6.5	36.58	37.27	6.9	12.0
1995-96	2.4	4.2	36.66	38.93	6.7	11.7
1996-97	8.4	8.2	36.55	38.69	6.7	11.8
1997-98	6.4	6.5	34.33	37.87	6.7	12.8
1998-99	8.2	7.8	31.38	34.17	6.4	14.0
1999-00	6.4	5.8	36.97	43.75	6.5	11.0
2000-01	10.3	9.9	41.13	50.21	6.5	9.2
2001-02	7.2	6.7	48.27	55.06	7.0	8.9
2002-03	8.4	7.7	44.37	55.73	7.3	9.0

Source: Directorate of Economics & Statistics, Government of Karnataka.

There are wide fluctuations in the growth rate of income from unregistered sector in this period. From 5.7 per cent in 1993-94 it slid to 2.4 per cent in the following year but rose more sharply to 8.4 per cent in 1996-97 and after some slowdown it reached the peak of 10.3 per cent in 2000-01. As per the latest data for 2002-03 the growth rate was 8.4 per cent.

15.4.2 Unorganised Sector as Revealed by Economic Census 1998

The unorganised sector plays an important role in capital formation and generation of employment in the economy of the state and the country. The economic census provides information in respect of distribution of enterprises employing at least one hired worker on a fairly regular basis by location and activity and also estimates of employment. The Census is conducted at regular intervals of 10 years since 1980.

The latest Economic Census 1998 revealed that the number of enterprises as well as employed increased by 12.9 per cent and 3.4 per cent respectively between 1990 and 1998. Out of 19.12 lakh enterprises, agricultural enterprises formed 13.6 per cent in 1998, which was slightly more than 12.3 per cent recorded in the 1990 census. Over 60 per cent of the total enterprises were in rural areas in 1998 as compared with 61.0 per cent in 1990. Own Account Enterprises dominated 62.40 per cent of the total enterprises, (Table 15.10).

TABLE 15.10

Important Parameters of Unorganised Sector

All Enterprises	*1990 Census*	*1998 Census*	*Percentage Increase*
All Enterprises	1693700	1911631	12.87
OAEs	1074400	1192500	10.99
Establishments	619300	719131	16.12
Persons Usually Working	5083200	5253439	3.35
Hired Persons	2872400	2728372	-5.01
Concentration of Units			
Per Square Km	9	10	11.11
Per '000 Population	38	43	13.16
Average No. of Persons/ Enterprise.	3	3	0

Source: Third Economic Census 1998.

15.4.3 Structure of Small-scale Industries in Karnataka

Data on small-scale industries in Karnataka are available only in respect of those, which are registered and there are a number of unregistered units, which are operating in the state for which no data is available. The document on Seventh Five Year Plan for Karnataka reported that at the beginning of the Plan, there were about 2.6 lakh unregistered small-scale units providing employment to 11.7 lakh people. However, the Third All-India Census on SSI conducted for the reference period 2001-02 had covered the hitherto unknown area i.e. the unregistered SSI sector and the data are discussed separately. According to the data available from the Industries and Commerce Department, Government of Karnataka, the number of registered small-scale industrial units increased from a mere 3,890 in 1969-70 to 24,893 a decade later and to 1,05,567 industrial units in 1989-90. At the end of 2004-05 this number stood at 3,21,38. As may be seen from Appendix A-15.26 and Figure 15.7, the number of units registered in any single year was highest at 34,402 during 1997-98. There is no definitive trend in the pattern, which may be attributed to the various policies relating to small-scale units such as reservation, concessions, subsidies and the availability of credit. Many units were closed in the course of the period due to various reasons like sickness, competition, etc.

FIGURE 15.7

Registered SSI Units and Persons Employed

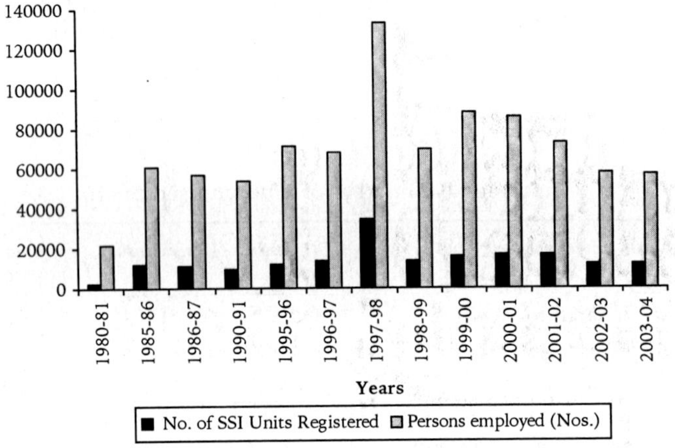

Source: Department of Industries & Commerce, Government of Karnataka.

15.4.4 *Employment*

SSI is a sector, which provides large-scale employment with lower investment. There is a significant progress in the employment provided by the small-scale industrial units. In 1969-70 the number of persons employed were 47,960 which increased manifold, to 18,28,978 in 2004-2005. The employment provided by these units during a year was as high as 1,32,978 persons in 1997-98, which was the year, when SSIs registered were also highest. However, the average employment provided per unit has come down sharply despite the increase in the number of registered SSI units. Although there is a significant growth in the number of registered units growth in employment provided by them is not concomitant with this. The per unit employment provided by these units on cumulative basis has been coming down consistently. At 16.0 persons it was highest in 1970-71 and during the eighties it hovered between 7.1 persons and 11.9 persons. In the nineties it touched a low of 6 persons and continue to remain at that level in 2004-05 also (Figure 15.8).

FIGURE 15.8

SSI Units Growth and Employment (Per Unit)

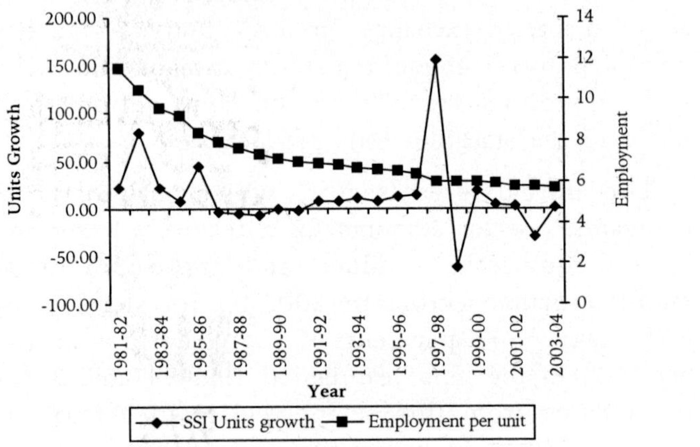

Source: Department of Industries & Commerce, Government of Karnataka.

15.4.5 *Investment in Registered SSI*

The investment made by the 3,21,676 registered SSIs in Karnataka in 2004-05 was Rs. 6,91,969.30 lakhs on cumulative basis. The investment made both in the eighties and nineties showed a mixed trend. During the eighties it ranged from Rs. 2,776 lakh in 1980-81 to Rs. 11,634 lakh in 1985-86 and in nineties there was a step up in investment and the highest investment was during 1999-2000 at Rs. 73,706 lakh and the lowest was Rs. 11,843 lakh in 1990-91. In the first four years from 2000 onwards there was a slowdown in each year. The investment per SSI unit significantly improved during the second half of nineties as compared with eighties. Here again, it was highest at Rs. 462.45 lakh in 1999-00 and the lowest was Rs. 83.44 lakh in 1990-1991. Beyond the year 2000, there was slowdown in per unit investment also (Figure 15.9).

FIGURE 15.9

SSI Units Growth and Investment (Per Unit)

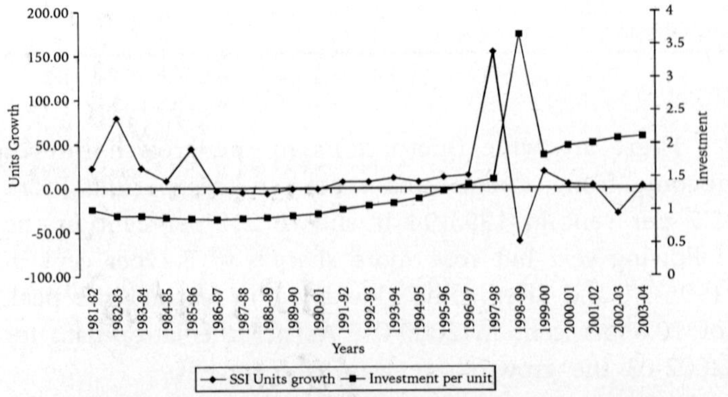

Source: Department of Industries & Commerce, Government of Karnataka.

15.4.6 District-wise Distribution of SSI Units

The distribution pattern of the registered small-scale industries (SSIs) among the districts in Karnataka reveals that majority of small-scale industries are concentrated in Bangalore urban district followed by Bangalore (Rural), Dakshina Kannada, Dharwad, Tumkur and Hassan districts. The state had set a target of 12,000 SSI units for the year 2003-04. This target has been overachieved by 220 units for the state as a whole. However, districts such as Bidar, Raichur, Kolar, Davangere, Gulbarga, Mandya, Mysore, Bangalore (R), Gadag, and Udupi were lagging behind the targets (Appendix A-15.27).

15.4.7 Policies Relating to SSI

As mentioned earlier Karnataka government has been extending financial assistance to SSIs. The Central Government has been giving the capital investment subsidy (CIS) to SSI introduced since 1971 and for Karnataka it has restricted this subsidy to 37 only backward *talukas* in three districts, namely, Mysore, Dharwad, and Raichur. But the state government took initiative to extend the CIS to other areas also simultaneously excluding Zone-1. Subsequent to the withdrawal of the scheme by the government of India in 1989 the state government took the entire onus of CIS. Basically the introduction of capital investment subsidy was essentially with the objective of dispersing industry to the backward regions, to compensate for the regional infrastructure inadequacy. The details of different packages right from 1983-88 announced by the state government are given in the Appendix A-15.8. Salient features of the incentives and concessions contained in recent package 2001-2006 *inter alia* include: i) the government would provide subsidy to all new tiny/small-scale industries; ii) there will be an additional subsidy to special category of entrepreneurs; iii) entry tax exemption, stamp duty exemption, concessional registration charges and waiver of conversion fee are the other incentives (Appendix A-15.9).

15.4.8 Marketing Assistance for the SSI Sector

The state has established the Karnataka Small Industries Marketing Corporation to provide marketing assistance to the small scale industries sector. These measures have helped the SSI sector to a great extent. However, with the coming into force of the Karnataka (Transparency in Public Procurement) Act, 2000, the special preference available to the small scale industries sector has been negated. In view of the serious sickness faced by the small-scale industries sector as a whole and the problems are getting much more serious with full implementation of the provisions of various agreements signed with the WTO, the New Industrial Policy 2001-2006 has therefore proposed to amend the Karnataka (Transparency in Public Procurement) Act, 2000 to provide purchase-price preference to SSI units of the state, which manufacture items reserved for SSI sector by government of India from time to time, in the following manner:

a) Seventy-five per cent of the items reserved by the SSI sector shall be procured from the units located within the state, through an open tender system;

b) SSI units of the state shall be offered a price preference of 15 per cent over the lowest price quoted;

c) This benefit will be available for a period of five years from 1st April 2001. The role of KSIMC will also be reoriented to help the SSI Sector to: i) improve quality of the products; ii) improve the production-manufacturing processes; iii) reduce prices; and iv) augment exports.

> **BOX 15.1**
>
> **Definition of SSI and Tiny and Medium and Large-Scale Industry**
>
> a) Tiny Industry: Tiny-scale industry is one in which the investment in plant and machinery is less than Rs. 25 lakhs irrespective of the location of the unit.
>
> b) Small-Scale Industry: An industrial undertaking in which the investment in fixed assets in plant and machinery whether held on ownership terms or on lease or by hire purchase does not exceed Rs. 100 lakhs.
>
> c) Medium and Large-Scale Industry: An Industrial unit, which is not classified as Tiny/Small Scale/Ancillary Industry shall be classified as medium/large-scale industry.

15.4.9 All-India Census of Small-Scale Industries

Taking cognizance of the need for strong data-bank on SSI sector, the government of India has launched a comprehensive census on SSI. So far three such censuses have been conducted in 1973-74, 1990-91 and the Third all-India census of small scale industries which is the latest was conducted during November 2002 to April 2003 and relates to the reference year 2001-02. Each census is an improvement over the others and in that sense, the Third Census is a unique one. Because registration of SSI sector is voluntary there exists a much larger size of the unregistered segment of SSI. For the first time, this census has thrown light on the hitherto unknown field i.e. unregistered sector by conducting a sample survey simultaneously with the complete enumeration of registered SSI units in such a way that the two sets of data become additive and give an overall picture of the SSI Sector.

Salient Features of the SSI Units as Revealed by the Census

The total size of the SSI Units in 2001-02 was 6,58,821 of which 1,10,487 units (16.77 per cent) were registered and 6,57,802 (99.8 per cent) were working units. The size of registered SSI units as per the Department of Industries and Commerce in 2001-02 was 2,86,189. There is a large divergence in these two sets of data. The SSI units as revealed by Third Census are much larger than those revealed in the earlier Second Census (1987-88). But the other parameters such as investment per unit, employment per unit, etc., have all decelerated (Table 15.11). But there is a difference in the coverage of units in the Third Census which covered all the units under the purview of the Small Industries Development Organisation (SIDO) like the earlier one upto March 31, 2001, on complete enumeration basis, whereas the unregistered units were covered through a sample survey in selected villages. So the Third Census data refers to the consolidation of all the units, registered and unregistered segments and each of those segments consist of small scale industrial undertakings and small scale service and business (industry related) enterprises (SSBEs). Karnataka has 7.2 per cent of the permanently registered SSI units in India. The number of working units in the state was 9.13 per cent while the closed units account for (3.93 per cent).

BOX 15.2

Definition of SSI and SSBE

The SSIs are industrial undertakings in which the investment in fixed assets in plant and machinery, whether held on ownership terms or on lease or by hire-purchase, does not exceed rupees one crore.

The SSBEs are industry related service and business enterprises with investment in fixed assets, excluding land and building, up to Rs. 10 lakhs, irrespective of the location of the units.

As compared to the earlier censuses, a noticeable change was in their structure, while the proportion of SSSBFs increased to 27.5 while per cent that of SSI was 73 per cent.

Structure of SSI Units as per Census

The SSI uits are dominated by a large unregistered segment (83.25 per cent) and rural units (58.52 per cent). Majority of ancillary units among SSI was smaller at 8,635 (1.32 per cent).

The number of women enterprises were 1,03,169 (15.66 per cent). More than 96 per cent of the units

TABLE 15.11

Comparison of Main Findings as per the All India Census of Registered SSI (SIDO) Units–Karnataka

Item	*All-India Census of SSI Units*					
	1st (1972)		**2nd (1987-88)**		**3rd (2001-02)**	
A. 1) Total Units as per Frame List	11020 (as on 30.11.1973)		59469 (as on 31.3.1988)		658821	
2) Working Units	7062		40525		657802	
	Total	**Per Unit**	**Total**	**Per Unit**	**Total**	**Per Unit**
B. Investment in Fixed Assets (Rs. in Lakhs) (Original Value)	4379	0.78	66085	1.63	842743	1.28
Investment in Plant and Machinery (Rs. in Lakhs) (Original Value)	2394	0.43	41597	1.03	348574	0.52
C. Employment (Nos.)	64385	11.0	244039	6.0	1638703	2.49
D. Value of Production (Rs. in Lakhs)	1970-4546		1985-86–215281			
	1971–5884		1986-87–289445			
	1972–7977		1987-88–252686		2001-02–1272687	
E. Net Value Added (Rs. in Lakhs)	**Total**	**Per Unit**	**Total**	**Per Unit**		
	2876	0.51	95245	2.35	-	-

Source: All India Census of SSI Units.

were propriety concerns. As for the management of these units 56.89 per cent were managed by the OBC category whereas only 10 per cent were managed by the SC and ST category together. Those managed by women accounted for about 15 per cent. Total employment was 16,38,703 persons and the per unit employment was 2.49 persons. The main source of power for these units was electricity (49.07 per cent) while another large section of the units (42.72 per cent) did not need power. About 3.46 per cent of units used traditional energy. The number of units engaged in exports was however small at 3622 and the value of exports stood at Rs. 51,361 lakhs. Exports mainly comprised of manufacture of all types of textile garments and clothing accessories and processing of edible nuts. As for the nature of activity, 49.53 per cent was engaged in services while 39.12 per cent was in the manufacturing, assembling and, processing. But in case of registered SSI units a higher number of units i.e. 70.95 per cent was in the manufacturing, assembling, and processing. Only 27.50 per cent was engaged in providing services. Among the top industries in terms of the number of units, flour milling had the maximum share followed by tailoring services. But in terms of fixed assets and value of plant and machinery it was the rice mills which had the lion share followed by manufacture of all types of textile garments, etc.

Gross Output

Manufacture of all types of textile garments, rice milling, manufacture of *beedies*, gold jewellery and cutting, shaping and finished stone were the major contributors to total gross output of SSIs. Total output in 2001-02 was estimated to be Rs. 8,730.28 crore. Distribution pattern according to different slabs of value revealed that 93.35 per cent of units had gross output less than Rs. 10 lakhs. Large output units (with output more than Rs. 1 crore) had a share of about 64.46 per cent of output with a share of only 1.10 per cent in the number of units (Table 15.12).

Loan Outstanding

Nearly 17 per cent of total SSI units have outstanding loans to institutions—a reason why banks are hesitant to meet their lending requirement. This percentage was quite high among the unregistered units i.e., 60 per cent. Of the total outstanding loan of SSI sector, 85 per cent belonged to unregistered sector.

TABLE 15.12

Percentage Distribution of Principal Characteristics by Gross Output Slabs

Gross Output Slabs Rs. in Lakhs	*No. of Units*	*Employment*	*Fixed Capital*	*Original Value of P & M**	*Gross Output*	*Export*
Up to 1 lakh	67.06	36.20	13.94	14.82	3.52	0.06
1 to 2	11.95	10.90	7.59	8.42	2.17	0.06
2–5	9.86	12.86	13.11	12.48	3.97	0.11
5–10	4.48	8.04	9.59	9.50	3.99	0.17
10–15	1.61	3.74	4.83	5.28	2.52	0.15
15–20	0.86	2.18	3.21	3.41	1.89	0.19
20–25	0.58	1.64	2.79	2.43	1.66	0.12
25–30	0.45	1.36	2.54	2.31	1.56	0.23
30–50	1.00	3.66	6.20	6.78	4.88	0.98
50–70	0.57	2.64	5.14	4.81	4.25	1.01
70–100	0.48	2.58	4.41	5.23	5.12	1.67
100–200	0.52	4.22	7.46	7.70	9.19	4.75
200–500	0.38	4.07	7.44	7.70	14.60	9.38
Above 500	0.20	5.91	11.76	9.13	40.67	81.12
Total	**100.00**	**100.00**	**100.00**	**100.00**	**100.00**	**100.00**

Note: * Plant and Machinery.

Source: Third All-India Census on SSIs 2001, 2002.

15.4.10 Industrial Sickness and Closure of SSI Units

Industrial sickness is a chronic problem and it is more rampant among the SSI Units. The Reserve Bank of India has been addressing this problem almost on an ongoing basis through various committees and working groups. The Karnataka government has also been looking into the problem and has evolved appropriate

BOX 15.3

Definition of Sick SSI

"A small-scale industrial unit is considered sick when:

(a) if any of the borrowal accounts of the unit remains substandard for more than six months, i.e., principal or interest, in respect of any of its borrowal accounts has remained overdue for a period exceeding one year will remain unchanged even if the present period for classification of an account as substandard is reduced in due course;

or

(b) there is erosion in the net worth due to accumulated losses to the extent of 50 per cent of its net worth during the previous accounting year, and

(c) the unit has been in commercial production for at least two years."

Source: RBI Working Group on Rehabilitation of Sick Units, Chairman: Shri Kohli.

measures to take care of the sick SSI units. These have been presented earlier in the policy latest Industrial Policy 2001-2006 relating to SSI. The Third all-India Census on SSIs 2001-02 has thrown light on the magnitude of sickness and incipient sickness. In the case of registered SSI sector, sick units in Karnataka accounted for 15.08 per cent of such units in the country. Incipient sickness formed 9.74 per cent while both sick and incipient sick SSI units accounted for 10.53 per cent. This order of sickness is relatively high for the state (Figure 15.10).

FIGURE 15.10

Number of Sick SSI Units A: Comparative Picture

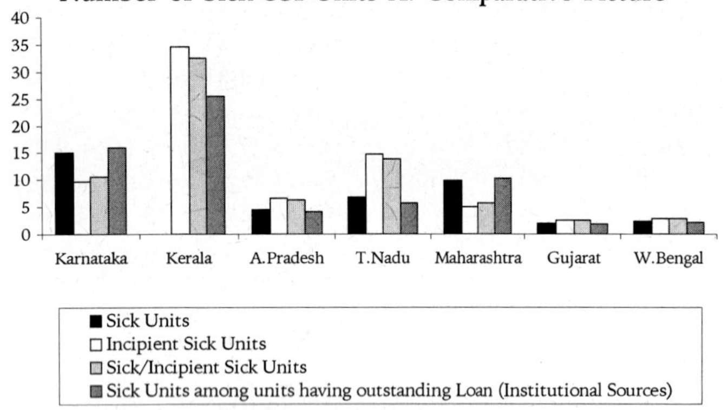

Source: Third All-India Census on SSIs 2001, 2002.

The number of sick units in Karnataka (with erosion of net worth by more than 50 per cent or delay in repayment of instalment loan by more than 12 months) was 11,593 in 2001-02 of which 5,538 were in the registered SSI units. The number of incipient sick SSI Units (decline in gross output over three consecutive years) was 66,400 of which 13,949 were the registered ones. The criteria adopted to identify the sick SSI units was different from those of RBI (Box 15.4). The number of sick units as per RBI criteria were smaller at 10,061 of which 5,007 were in the registered category. In the broader sense using both criteria, the number of units were 77,993 and out of this 19,486 were in the registered sector.

BOX 15.4

RBI Definition of Sick SSI

As per the RBI criteria, sick SSI units are those that are having outstanding loan with institutional sources whereas the census has used three strategies to identify the sick units such as, i) continuous decline in gross output compared to the previous two financial years; ii) delay by more than 12 months in repayment of loan taken from institutional sources; and iii) erosion in the net worth to the extent of 50 per cent of the net worth during the previous accounting year.

Causes of Sickness

There were many causes, namely, lack of demand, shortage of working capital, power shortage, marketing and labour problems, etc.

TABLE 15.13

Causes of Sickness of SSI Units

(Percentages)

Cause of Sickness	*Registered*	*Unregistered*	*Total*
Lack of Demand	56.12	74.65	31.67
Shortage of Working Capital	56.30	45.31	21.72
Non-availability of Raw Materials	13.32	13.13	5.96
Power Shortage	27.53	24.27	11.34
Labour Problems	7.86	7.14	3.31
Marketing Problems	41.31	42.55	19.11
Equipment Problems	11.84	12.21	5.48
Management Problems	4.43	2.69	1.41

Source: Third All-India Census of SSI Units.

Closure of Units

Closure of SSI units is a continuous feature, SSI units which did not operate even for a single day were treated as closed. As per the First Census (1973-74), 38.20 per cent of the registered SSI units was closed, in the Second Census (1990-91) almost an equal proportion 37.25 per cent was closed. The Third Census reveal an improvement in the situation. The percentage of closed units was smaller at 29.5 per cent. While sickness was the major problem, the other major reasons were: i) marketing problem, ii) lack of finance, and iii) could not survive competition. Across the districts, six districts, namely, Bangalore (Urban) (28.3 per cent), Belgaum (6.97 per cent), Dakshina Kannada (5.86 per cent), Bellary (5.52 per cent), Davangere (4.56 per cent), and Gulbarga (4.30 per cent) altogether account for over 55 per cent of the closed SSI units in the state.

15.4.11 Unregistered SSI Units

Structure of the Unregistered SSI Units

According to the summary results of the Third Census on SSI, out of the total size of SSI sector of 6,58,821 units in Karnataka, the unregistered units account for 83.25 per cent at 5,48,334 units whereas the registered sector 16.77 per cent. While all the unregistered units were working. Thus unregistered sector dominates the SSI sector in other areas also like the number of ancillary units among the SSI, etc. Further, the unregistered sector was dominated by the presence of small-scale service and business (industry related) enterprises (SSBES) i.e. 64 per cent which is the same as that of all-India.

BOX 15.5

Registration of SSI Units

Registration in the SSI units is voluntary. The registration is done with DICs firstly on a temporary basis and subsequently on the basis of the request of the concerned entrepreneurs on a permanent basis. The DICs registers the units as SSIs, ancillaries or SSSBEs as per the eligibility of units.

Registration under Factories Act: Registration of manufacturing units is mandatory under Factories Act.

Nearly 88 per cent of the SSIs in Karnataka are in the nature of perennial operation, 9 per cent seasonal and the rest are casual.

The reasons for not registering were mostly lack of interest and no knowledge of such provisions.

Source: Third All-India Census on SSI.

Out of 6,57,802 working SSI units in the state 3,84,920 or 58.52 per cent were in the rural areas. Once again, the unregistered category dominates the rural i.e. 86.34 per cent. However, in the registered category, urban units were more than the rural units i.e., 56,878 and 52,590 respectively.

As regards the nature of activity of the unregistered sector, majority of them were service oriented (53.93 per cent) as is reflected in the predominance of SSBEs followed by manufacturing, assembling and processing and the rest were for repairs and maintenance. More than 97 per cent of the unregistered SSIs are propriety units and partnership units account for 1.54 per cent. It is interesting to note that while SSI units managed by women were more in the registered category, within the unregistered sector only 15.9 per cent were managed by women.

Employment

Although the unregistered units had a higher employment of 11,67,204 persons, average number of persons, employed per unit was 2.13 (2.11 all-India) only as compared with 4.31 in the registered sector. However, in respect of employment per lakh of investment it was higher at 3.11, *vis-à-vis* 1.01 in the registered sector.

About 47.06 per cent of the unregistered SSI units used electricity as the main source of power, while an almost nearer this per cent 44.57 per cent did not need any type of power and another 3.45 per cent used traditional energy like firewood, etc.

In value terms, the fixed investment per unit, the gross output per unit and the plant and machinery per unit were all much lower i.e. less than one lakh for the unregistered sector.

Efficiency of Small-scale Industrial Units

SSI has shown resilience despite heavy competition and recession over the years. It still has the capacity and potential to generate high employment (Box 15.6).

BOX 15.6

Resilience of SSI

1) SSI despite lack of demand and shortage of working capital has generated more employment per rupee of investment than the organised sector. A good proportion of SSI units was sick, however their average investment–output ratio is almost at par with that of the organised sector.
2) The organised sector requires an investment of Rs. 5 lakh to generate employment for 1 person while SSI employs 7 persons with the same investment.
3) An investment of Rs.1 lakh in SSI generated 1,39,000 jobs as against 20,000 in large-scale companies.
4) SSI faired almost at par with the organised sector in terms of investment-output ratio.
5) While the organised sector needed an investment of Rs. 43,000 to generate an output of 1 lakh, the SSI needed 48,000 for the same.
6) Over 50,000 exporting units in the organised sector accounted for exports amounting to Rs. 14.2 lakh and the value of exports was only 5 per cent of gross output.
7) The registered SSI units accounted for 87 per cent of the total exports with only 14.5 per cent of exporting units.

Source: Third All-India Census of SSI.

15.5 Village and Cottage Industries

In the field of village and cottage industries Karnataka has made much headway. The important cottage industries are weaving, pottery, tile-making, oil-pressing, basket making, goldsmithy, blacksmithy, carpentry, mat-making, leather, and *beedi* manufacturing. In order to develop the cottage industries it was suggested that they should be encouraged in particular areas of the state, taking into account the availability of raw materials, the ready sale of finished goods, etc. in line with the organised industries already existing or proposed. On account of the advent of power to all parts of the state, even cottage industries were made to develop into small-scale and minor industries. The notable landmark in the history of industrial development of the state was the launching of Sir M. Visveswaraya's scheme for rural industrialisation. Designed to provide gainful employment to the unemployed and underemployed in rural areas, the rural industrialisation scheme was introduced on an experimental basis in 1950 in two districts of Bangalore and Kolar. Under this scheme, village group development committees were formed for groups of villages for expanding the existing ones. The rural industrial cooperative societies formed proved immensely beneficial to artisans and entrepreneurs in rural areas. This scheme was subsequently merged in the successive five year plans. A number of development schemes were undertaken for resusciation and development of rural and small-scale industries. A number of handicrafts cooperative societies were organised and some of them were financially assisted. Production items in the societies comprised net-weaving, sandalwood-carving, ivory-carving, *bidriware*, metalware, wooden toys and dolls, etc. A raw material depot at Mysore was set up to stock ivory, rosewood, etc., and to supply improved tools and equipment to artisans at subsidised rates. A central depot for coir products was also set up. The state government policy towards this sector had always been one of encouragement and special attention has been paid to their needs with a view to preserving the rich tradition of craftsmanship and hereditary skills of Karnataka craftsmen in producing unique products which bear testimony to the rich cultural heritage of the state.

15.5.1 Textiles

Handloom Industry

The Handloom industry in Karnataka is the largest cottage industry and about eight lakh people depend on this industry for livelihood and in magnitude of employment it is next only to agriculture. Therefore, it occupies an important place in the development of the state particularly of the economically weaker sections. At the national level this industry has been given due importance and recognition only during the Fifth Five Year Plan when it was felt that this industry needed assistance. But in Karnataka, the state government undertook several measures very much earlier, i.e. from 1956 onwards to improve this industry such as setting up of Mysore State Cotton and Woollen Handloom Weavers' Society and the Mysore State Silk Handloom Weavers' Central Cooperative Society. The handloom weavers at that time were given assistance by way of arrangements for a supply of raw materials and capital and for conducting demonstrations in the use of improved equipments and weaving new designs and also marketing of their finished products. The government continued to provide financial assistance in the form of loans, grants and investment to the various handloom weavers' societies.

Structure of the Handloom Industry

As per the Handloom Census data 1995-96, the number of looms were 63,088 from the household sector and 13,5117 from the non-household sector. Out of a total of 63,088 looms from the household sector 3,460 looms were stated to be idle and the number of working looms were 59,628. In the non-household sector the percentage of idle looms was higher at 14.11 *vis-à-vis* 5.5 in the household sector (Table 15.14).

The number of weavers and looms as per the Handloom Census 1995-96 indicate that the number of looms in power loom sector was higher than the handlooms. Yet, the number of workers and the families supported was higher in handloom than the powerloom (Table 15.15).

TABLE 15.14

Workforce in Handloom Industry

Details	*1995-96*
Household	
Total Looms Working	59,628
Total Workers	1,86,352
Average Workers Per Loom	3.13
Men	85,271 (45.76 per cent)
Women	74,981 (40.24 per cent)
Children	26,100 (14.00 per cent)
Non-Household	
Total Looms Working	11,610
Total Number of Workers	3,582
Average Workers Per Loom	3.24

Source: *Census of Handlooms*. 1995-96.

TABLE 15.15

Production of Handloom and Power Loom

Details	*Handloom*				*Power Loom*
	Silk	*Cotton*	*Wool*	*Total*	*Silk, Polyester Blends*
No. of Looms	13641	49384	13580	76605	88599
No. of Workers	23310	120166	47458	189934	127535
No. of Families	6573	34011	13101	53685	30998

Source: Department of Handlooms and Textiles, Government of Karnataka.

There are a sizeable number of societies (about 30 per cent), which have either stopped functioning or were on liquidation. This was higher in respect of cotton handlooms. Out of 643 registered societies, only 453 were working (70.45 per cent) (Table 15.16).

TABLE 15.16

Registered Weavers Societies as on March 31, 2003

Sector	*Total*	*Working*	*Stopped*	*Liquidation*
Cotton Handlooms	273	184	53	36
Silk Handlooms	81	53	25	3
Woolen Handlooms	207	149	54	4
Power Looms	82	67	13	2
Total	**643**	**453**	**145**	**45**

Source: Department of Handlooms and Textiles, Govt. of Karnataka.

The child workforce in the household category of looms was quite high at 14 per cent. The handloom industry is another sector, which provides employment to large size of women. Women and child workers constituted more than 50 per cent of the workforce.

Across the districts, Bijapur comes first with 34.6 per cent of the working looms, followed by Dharwad, Tumkur, and Chitradurga. These four districts accounted for over 65 per cent of the total working looms in the state in the household category. The non-household category also followed a similar pattern.

Textile Policy

The New Karnataka State Textile Policy 2004-2009 announced on February 21, 2004 aims at an overall development of ginning, pressing and spinning units, textile mills, handlooms, power looms, knitting and garment units. It also contemplates imparting training to handloom weavers, adoption of handloom technology upgradation, powerloom technology upgradation, welfare schemes for handloom weavers and the development of markets for handloom products with an objective to create edifice of textiles and apparel nature in state. It also aims at attracting private investment for high quality standard rationalisation of regulatory framework in addition to proactive and conducive environment (Box 15.7).

For the Tenth Five Year Plan, the state has set the target of handloom production of 377 million metres which could provide employment to 2 lakh persons. For the power loom production, similar targets are 1980 million metres and 1.32 lakh persons respectively. During 2004-05 as against the target of 75 million metres of handloom production, the anticipated production was lower at 70 million metres. For powerloom also it was lower at 425 million metres against the target of 450 million metres.

BOX 15.7

Textile Policy 2004-2009

The Textile Policy aims to boost textile industry in the state, which includes handloom, power loom, silk, woollen, mill sector and garment sectors. Further, it aims to provide additional employment of over 40 lakhs people by the end of 2010.

- The Policy proposes to revive and restructure the following handloom agencies:
  1. Karnataka Handloom Development Corporation.
  2. Karnataka Coop. Handloom Weavers Federation (Cauvery Handlooms).
  3. Karnataka State Coop. Woollen Federation.
- The Policy proposes development of six clusters in the state under TCID Scheme—Bangalore – Bommanahalli (readymade garments), Doddaballapur (power looms), Mandya, Chamarajnagar (silk), Bagalkote, Ilkal (handlooms), Rabakavi – Banahatti (power looms).
- Design development and textile design centre activation and revival of 1,000 idle handlooms and 15,000 power looms.
- Establishment of power loom parks in four places in the State—Bangalore, Davangere, Belgaum, and Gadag.
- Establishment of power loom complexes at 10 places in the state.
- Modernisation of power looms.
- Revival of financially weak mills on selected basis.
- Establishment of apparel park at Bangalore and Bellary.
- Establishment of Garment Training Institute for the development of human resources for requirement of apparel industry.

Garments

In 2004 (January–December 2004) 58 readymade garment exporters were registered with the Apparel Export Promotion Council in Karnataka. Bangalore is the major exporting centre with much export potential. The value of export of readymade garments from Karnataka is also increasing steadily from Rs. 2,553 crore in 2002 to Rs. 3,146 crore in 2003 and to Rs. 3,410 crore in 2004.

Setting up of Apparel Park at Doddaballapur in Bangalore Rural District

The government of India, with an objective to facilitate the textile industry, for a sustained a pre-eminent global standing in the manufacturing and export of clothing, have announced creation of a cluster of apparel industries in the National Textile Policy 2000. Karnataka with its own garment export worth Rs. 3500 crores enjoys top ranking among the Indian states. Bangalore has the potential to become the garment hub of the country. In accordance with this the financial sharing ratio between the government of India and government of Karnataka funding pattern has been kept in mind. Accordingly, a project report has been prepared for Doddaballapur Apparel Park for Rs. 32.97 crores Rs. 17 crores being the government of India share, Rs.10.18 crores being the state government grant and Rs. 5.79 crores loan to be raised by the nodal agencies.

15.5.2 Sericulture

Sericulture in Karnataka

India is the second largest producer of silk with 17,550 metres in 2000-01. Eighteen per cent of the global raw silk is produced in India. As against a low value of exports of Rs. 76 crore in 1971-72, the value increased manifolds to Rs. 2,747 core in 2004-05. About 60 lakh persons are engaged in plant cultivation, silk worm, egg production and rearing or in the predominantly small-scale reeling and weaving industry. About 57 per cent of the gross value of silk fabrics flow back to the cocoon growers with share of income to different groups (Box 15.8). Since silk is rooted in Indian social tradition, the domestic market is strong and most of the production is used locally. However, exports mostly fabrics, have expanded, particularly over the decade. Of the four varieties of silk—mulberry, tasar, eri, and muga—mulberry silk represents bulk of internationally traded silk (95 per cent). Karnataka accounts for the lion share of total Indian mulberry silk. Out of the total of 14,620 metres of mulberry silk produced in India in 2004-05 Karnataka alone has contributed 7,302 metres (50 per cent). Therefore, large-scale programmes/projects for expansion in Karnataka have had a major impact on Indian production.

Employment

Sericulture is highly labour intensive—one hectare of mulberry plantation creates 12 to 13 man-years of employment annually in mulberry cultivation, silk weaving, reeling, twisting, weaving and implements fabrication. Every 3.07 kgs of silk produced and used in handlooms generates gainful employment of one-man year. The potential is par-excellence and no other industry generates this kind of employment. An estimated investment of Rs. 15,000 to 20,000 (excluding cost of land and rearing space) is sufficient for undertaking mulberry cultivation and silk rearing in one acre of irrigated land. By adopting stipulated package of practices a farmer can attain net income levels of Rs. 35,000 per acre per annum. Women constitute over 60 per cent of those employed in downstream activities. Benefits of sectoral value addition primarily accrue to rural households. As the end product users are mostly from higher groups, the money flows from high-end groups to low-end groups.

BOX 15.8

Why Sericulture?

- High employment and export potential.
- Provides vibrancy to village economics.
- Low gestation, high returns.
- Women friendly occupation.
- Ideal programme for weaker sections of the society.
- Eco-friendly.
- Satisfy equity concerns.

Department of Sericulture, government of Karnataka therefore, accords well with government of India priorities for alleviating unemployment and rural poverty. Furthermore, the time is propitious for expanding Indian sericulture since production is dropping among the leading producers, notably Japan and Korea, due to high labour requirements and costs.

Area under Mulberry and Families Engaged in Sericulture

The mulberry cultivation in the state remains largely confined to 5 districts comprising the former kingdom of Mysore. However, over the period, large-scale cooperative trials with farmers have proved the feasibility of profitable sericulture in many other parts of the state. Mulberry area, cocoon and silk production have been expanding steadily. From 43,000 hectares in 1951-52, the area under mulberry had increased to 1.22 lakh hectares in 2001-02 but due to continuous spells of drought the area decline sharply to 77,998 hectares in 2004-05 (Table 15.17). Depending upon the monsoon conditions this area varies year to year but lately increased area under irrigated conditions is a notable factor. Over 86 per cent of the area is irrigated and over 1.89 lakh families are engaged in sericulture activities in 13,661 villages. Nearly 20,000 villages are sericulture villages which of late is declining. District-wise sericultural activities are concentrated in Kolar,

Bangalore (R), Tumkur, Mandya, and Mysore. The details of sericultural activities are given in Table 15.18.

TABLE 15.17

Area under Mulberry and Families Engaged in Sericulture

Year	Number of Sericulture Villages	Area under Mulberry ('00 hectares)		Total	Families Directly Engaged in Sericulture
		Irrigated	Rainfed		
1995-96	19578	113602	53758	167558	333339
1996-97	18533	113606	53758	167362	333339
1997-98	25933	100371	39655	140226	333339
1998-99	20477	104068	35974	140042	288420
1999-00	16132	93700	25000	118700	253752
2000-01	15448	93663	18894	122557	255941
2001-02	14867	99122	17036	116158	254155
2002-03	14820	73736	15167	88903	210113
2003-04	13891	68594	11184	79778	188614
2004-05	13661	67077	10921	77998	176924

Source: Department of Economics and Statistics and Department of Sericulture, Government of Karnataka.

TABLE 15.18

Sericultural Activities

Particulars	Unit	1995-96	1996-97	1997-98	1998-99	1999-00
Grainages						
Government	No.	98	96	94	94	94
Licenced Seed Preparers	No.	918	916	918	824	774
Layings Prepared						
Cross Breed	Lakh Nos.	1816	1780	1817	1777	1592
Bivoltine	-do -	99	67	71	83	55
Cocoons Produced						
Mysore Race	Lakh Nos.	16693	14683	15979	12650	7175
Reeling Cocoons	Tonnes	71209	70678	80658	76198	60810
Cocoon Markets	No.	63	64	64	59	59
Developmental Programme						
Chawki Rearing Centres	No.	657	657	657	410	429
Govt. Silk Farms	No.	95	96	98	98	99

Source: Department of Economics and Statistics, Government of Karnataka.

Silk Production

As said earlier Karnataka accounts for more than half of mulberry silk produced in India. The production of silk, which was barely 727 tonnes in 1951-52 increased manifold thereafter. In 2004-05 the output of silk was 7,302 tonnes (Table 15.20).

TABLE 15.19

Salient Aspects of Silk Industry

Particulars	Unit	1995-96	1996-97	1997-98	1998-99	1999-00
Silk Industry						
Govt. Silk Filatures	No.	5	5	5	5	5
Filature Basins	No	16391	19961	19138	20755	20389
Cottage Basins	No	3515	1784	1816	1921	1595
Charkhas	No	26749	22322	23176	23934	25060
Govt. Silk Weaving Factory	No	1	1	1	1	1
Govt. Silk Twisting Factory	No.	1	1	1	1	1
Spun Silk Mills	No.	1	1	1	1	1
Production of Reeling Cocoons	Tonnes	71209	70678	80656	76198	68920
Silk Production	Tonnes	8264	8328	9236	8939	8121
Marketing						
Silk Marketing Board	No.	9	10	10	10	10
Sericultural cum Farmers Cooperative Society	No.	109	109	111	60	110

Source: Department of Sericulture, Government of Karnataka.

Culminating with the declining acreage under mulberry, cocoon/silk produce also decline. But per hectare yield of cocoon/silk has increased as seen in Table 15.20.

TABLE 15.20

Production and per Hectare Yield of Cocoon/Silk

	2000-01	2001-02	2002-03	2003-04	2004-05
Cocoon Production	66518	73860	55851	44652	54210
Silk Production	8200	8728	6760	5949	7302
Per Hectare Yield (Kgs)					
Cocoon	590	635	628	560	695
Silk	72.8	75.1	76.0	74.6	93.6

Source: Department of Sericulture, Government of Karnataka.

Marketing of cocoons and silk has been regulated in Karnataka. There were 59 cocoon markets and 10 silk marketing boards functioning in the state. The quantity of silk yarn transacted in silk exchanges ranged between 1,484 tonnes in 1998-99 to 1,788 tonnes in 1995-96 and valued between Rs. 16,723 lakhs and Rs. 19,619 lakhs in this period respectively (Table 15.21).

TABLE 15.21

Transaction of Silk Yarn in Silk Exchanges

Variety	*Unit*	*1995-96*	*1996-97*	*1997-98*	*1998-99*	*1999-00*
No. of Lots Transacted						
Quantity	Tonnes	1788	1779	1736	1484	1685
Value	Rs. Lakhs	18289	19619	18010	16723	17099
Market Fee	Rs. Lakhs	366	392	360	334	342
Purchased by KSMB						
Quantity	Tonnes	343	422	260	270	275
Value	Rs. Lakhs	3838	4956	2935	3310	3009
Market Fee	Rs. Lakhs	77	99	58	66	60

Source: Department of Sericulture (Silk Exchange).
KSMB–Karnataka Silk Marketing Board.

Karnataka Silk Marketing Board

The Karnataka Silk Marketing Board markets silk yarn and fabric. It tries to stabilise the prices of silk yarn and ensures that the reeler gets a satisfactory return for his produce through direct purchases when there is a slump in the market. During the financial year 2002-03, prices showed downward trend due to unrestricted availability of foreign silk both from legal and illegal channels, which affected the sales. This is one such aspect, which hinders Karnataka silk production. In the year 2003-04 the turn over was Rs. 2152.54 lakh showed an improvement over 2002-03 (Table 15.22).

TABLE 15.22

Performance of the Karnataka Silk Marketing Board

(Rs. Lakhs)

Particulars	*2001-2002*	*2002-2003*	*2003-04*	*2004-05(up to Nov.)*
Turnover	3262.14	1729.80	2152.54	620.92
Profit After Tax	-26.85	-823.50	11.65	-144.96

Note: In view of the adoption of Accounting Standards (AS)2 by the company during the year 2002-03 method of valuation is changed from 'at cost' to 'at the lower of cost or net realisable value'. Normally prices during March would be the lowest. The market value as on 31-3-03 has been taken for valuation of stock, since it is lower when compared to the cost. Due to this change in method of valuation the loss has increased by Rs. 483.12 lakhs.

Source: Karnataka Silk Marketing Board, Bangalore.

The silk industry in Karnataka earned a foreign exchange worth Rs. 746.13 lakhs in 2002-03 which increased to Rs. 968.02 lakhs in 2003-04. The share of the Karnataka silk industry in all-India exports in terms of value has been increasing from 30.08 per cent in 2001-02 to 32.05 per cent in 2002-03 and furthermore to 34.80 per cent in 2003-04. Globalisation has impacted adversely the silk industry in Karnataka with imports of silk yarn from China to meet the domestic demand from states like Tamil Nadu, etc. The value of exports from Karnataka for 2003-04 suggest a higher share of 34.80 per cent (Table 15.23).

TABLE 15.23

Value of Exports of Silk Goods from Karnataka and India

(Rs. in Crores)

Particulars	*2002-2003*	*2003-2004*	*2004-2005(up to August 2004)*
Karnataka	746.13	968.02	352.35
India	2294.05	2779.19	1016.40
Share of Karnataka (percentage)	32.50	34.80	34.80

Note: 1. Figure includes silk yarn and silk waste.
2. Value of export of silk goods figures from Karnataka reflect the export consignments dispatched from ports *viz.*, Bangalore Airport and Bangalore ICD only.

Source: Central Silk Board, Bangalore.

15.5.3 Khadi and Village Industries

Karnataka is known the world over for the rich heritage blessed with a multitude of arts and crafts and is one of the leading states in the field of handicrafts in the country. Handicrafts from the State are now reaching practically all leading world markets. Karnataka state Handicrafts Development Corporation (KSHDC) set up by the government of Karnataka plays a leading role in the development of the artisans and craftsmen. Considering the potentiality of handicrafts of the state and also with a view to encourage crafts, the KSHDC has set up emporia within and outside the state, for exhibition and sale of handicrafts and also craft complexes/rural marketing and service centres/ production centres to provide multifarious facilities and services to the artisans. Besides, the corporation has been running raw material depots for supply of various raw materials to the artisans at reasonable rates.

The Karnataka state Khadi and Village Industries Board organises, develops and regulates *khadi* and village industries in the state. It renders financial, technical, and other assistance as may be necessary for developing *khadi* and village industries in the rural areas and help solve the problems of unemployment and raise the standard of living of the rural artisans. The performance of this sector can be viewed from the following Table 15.24.

TABLE 15.24

Production of *Khadi* Industries

Year/ District	Cotton Khadi		Woollen Khadi		Silk Khadi		
	Production ('000Sq.Mts)	Value (Rs. in Lakhs)	Production ('000 No. of Kambals)	Value (Rs. in Lakhs)	Production ('000 No. of Metres)	Value (Rs. Lakhs)	Value of Hand-made Paper (Rs. in lakhs)
1995-1996	14.56	431.57	2.85	538.25	1.49	300.60	88.57
1996-1997	16.25	549.92	3.60	886.57	1.98	386.12	71.62
1997-1998	18.02	760.90	2.30	892.30	1.19	520.19	71.72
1998-1999	17.54	609.70	2.70	864.30	2.60	496.12	123.38
1999-2000	18.16	766.02	1.80	756.42	1.996	440.46	162.95

Source: Khadi and Village Industries, Bangalore.

Production of *Khadi* Industries

In terms of cotton *khadi*, Davangere district has the highest production more than one-third of the state's output followed by Chitradurga district, Bellary district, Gadag, and Dharwad districts. These five districts account for 78 per cent of the state's output of cotton *khadi*. Belgaum district is the leading producer of woollen *khadi* (38.4 per cent). Chitradurga, Dharwad, and Bagalkot are the other important districts. For silk *khadi*, it is the Kolar District, which produces 63.53 per cent of the state's total output of silk *khadi*. Hand-made paper was mostly produced in Bangalore (Urban), Udupi, Shimoga, and Davangere districts. The value of production of all *khadi* industries stood at Rs. 2243.70 lakh during 2004-05 of which cotton segment was Rs. 805.25 lakh, silk and wool were Rs. 617.95 lakh and Rs. 650.00 lakh respectively. Polyvastra production is not very significant.

15.5.4 Agarbatti Industry

The *agarbatti* Industry in Karnataka is another traditional industry developed over generations by means of family activity. The growth of some of such family activities has been tremendous over the years and today the industry enjoys the position of having a premier position in the country. Karnataka is the main supplier of raw as well as finished *agarbatti* to the world. The market share of *agarbattis* from Karnataka is over 70 per cent. Though the art of making *agarbatti* was developed in the temple towns of Tamil Nadu, it has acquired a permanent place in Karnataka, which possesses rich sandalwood trees. Further this sector also received patronage from the royal family in the princely state of Mysore. The basic forest-based raw materials which were abundantly available in the forests of Kodagu and Malnad regions were the favourable factors for this industry to take firm root in this state. *Agarbatti* industry is traditional in character and is basically a handicraft cottage industry. In one respect, this industry, unlike the traditional conception of a handicraft industry associated with carvings, etc. and providing employment to very limited persons, is a real employment generator and is capable of providing employment to the weaker sections of both the urban and rural populace. Most of the persons engaged in fashioning *agarbatti* are main servants and the like in urban areas and marginal farmers, landless labourers, rural artisans, etc. in rural areas. This industry does not qualify for being considered as an industry since no investment in plant and machinery is involved as all *agarbattis* are individually handrolled. Similarly, it does not use power at any stage of manufacture and even the drying operations of *agarbatti* is carried out by natural solar power. The labour engaged in this industry does not require any educational qualifications nor power or machinery but has a relatively high turnover. The industry generates subsidiary employment to nearly four lakh workers. *Agarbatti* manufacturing is purely a supplementary occupation i.e. an activity carried on along with other occupations which are considered to be the main, with *agarbatti*-making included whenever time and inclination permits or when there is a need for additional income. The major workforce is from the weaker sections of the society and mainly of women. Therefore, it is an important poverty alleviation programme.

The initial investment involved is very small in other words, a person who can save Rs. 5000 can start his own manufacturing facility in a small way. The basic raw materials that are used in this industry are *jigat*, bamboo, charcoal, aromatic roots, and herbs that are basically forest-based. This industry will get a big push if adopted by the *Khadi* and Village Industries Board. *Agarbatti* making can be adopted during drought years when the government institutes food for work programmes.

Agarbatti Production

As most of these units are very small and consisting of many households they are not registered and hence data on *agarbatti* are not available. However, some estimates are available according to which the production of raw *agarbattis* is about 9,823 tonnes and the industry generates employment of around 54.57 lakh man-days. The All-India Agarbatti Manufacturers' Association (AIAMA) has estimated the *agarbatti* production mainly from the households, which is 2330 crore *battis* or 23,300 tonnes. However, this does not include the consumption other than households like shops and establishments or commercial vehicles, etc. If one takes into account those, the actual consumption would be 3 lakh tonnes per annum. Once again these estimates will also be an underestimation as these do not take into account: a) *agarbattis* exported from the country, b) *agarbattis* burnt in temples, and c) *agarbattis* consumed by armed forces.

Karnataka, renowned for fragrant *agarbattis*, sandalwood, sandal oil, and sandal soaps, has captivated the world. It has become a highly profitable business even though other states have made some headway into the business in recent years. According to industry sources the total number of units in Karnataka is around 3,303. About 3,000 units are in the category of having a turnover of 90.82 per cent. These units are family units in urban areas confined mainly to slums and such pockets and therefore has a special significance in the social order.

The cost of wages forms one-third of the value in respect of raw *batti* and 10 per cent in respect of finished *batti*. Given the target of production in terms of value at one crore, the initial investment required will be say, Rs. 25 to 30 lakhs. The area of concentration of these manufacturing units in Karnataka are Bangalore, Mysore, and Chintamani *taluka* in Kolar district. This industry also earns valuable foreign exchange for the country as can be seen from the quantum of exports (Table 15.25).

They are being exported to Kuwait, Bahrain, Australia, Saudi Arabia, Malaysia, France, Japan, Singapore, UK, USA, Canada, Italy, Hong Kong, Holland, and Nepal. Karnataka's share has been declining very sharply from 90.2 per cent to 55.4 per cent in a period of 4 years. The diversification of activities in the manufacture of *agarbatti* in other states have contributed to this reduced share. Gaya in Bihar is emerging as a strong competitor for Karnataka, which has a large commercial complex and captured the markets in northern India. The value of exports has more or less remained unchanged around Rs. 7.3 crore to Rs. 8.5 crore in the past 4 years. However, Karnataka still enjoys an all-India market.

TABLE 15.25

Exports of *Agarbatti*

Rs. in Crore

Year	*All India*	*Karnataka*	*Karnataka's Share in per cent*
1986-87	811	732	90.2
1987-88	871	742	85.2
1988-89	1106	856	77.4
1989-90	1440	798	55.4

Source: CHEMIXIL, Bangalore.

Employment

Applying the same estimates i.e. estimation on the basis of consumption of *agarbatties* by households only, employment/man-days have also been estimated by the AIAMA. The estimated employment generated is 6.03 lakh man-days per annum. Another source places the employment generation at 11,797 lakh man-days (Techsok, 1995-96) as detailed in Table 15.26.

TABLE 15.26

Employment in *Agarbatti* Industries

	Mandays in lakhs
Perfuming and Packing	41.99
Raw *Batti* Rolling	58.57
Bamboo Splitting	11.96
Pulverising Activity	0.15
Collection of Forest Product	2.60
Paper Tube and Carton Manufacture	2.70
Total	**117.97**

Source: All-India Agarbatti Manufacturers' Association (AIAMA).

Once again these estimates do not include activities like transportation, part-time selling, felling of bamboo trees, etc.

Income Generation

Income generation is estimated to be Rs. 150.65 crore for the industry as a whole and Karnataka accounts to 70 per cent of this. An important feature of *Agarbatti* industry is that it contributes to the sales tax of Karnataka, about Rs. 265 lakh, which is however far less than the potential to collect.

Patenting of *Agarbatti*

In order to protect the traditional, age old *Agarbatti* industry from any incursions, the AIAMA has approached the office of the Assistant Registrar of Geographic Indication Registry and made a written and oral submission to establish that *agarbatti* is an age old, traditional handicraft of this country. The office of the Registrar has made a favourable recommendation for the issuance of the patent. This will enable *agarbatti* industry to say with confidence, backed by law, that *dashangas, dhoopas, agarbattis,* joss sticks, and sticks are of Indian origin and that they have originated from the state of Karnataka. Mysore silk was the first commodity to secure such a patent from this state.

Problems Faced by *Agarbatti* Industry in Karnataka

This labour-intensive, foreign exchange earning industry is beset with persistent problems such as labour legislation, raw material shortage, stiff competition from foreign countries and heavy levies when many states including Kerala and Rajasthan have abolished taxes, Karnataka continues to levy taxes. *Agarbatti* manufacturing has been declared as a handicraft industry in 1983 by government of India and Karnataka government has declared it as an industry. Even if a unit employs more than one person in the *agarbatti* industry, it attracts the provisions of the Factories Act and the Minimum Wages Act. Secondly, due to certain problems relating to availability of raw materials, the production has been affected in Karnataka. Since all the raw materials are forest-based and because of some large-scale deforestation, most of these raw materials have become extinct in Karnataka. The present requirements are met by imports from various countries including Australia and other states, e.g. bamboo from Assam, *Jigat* from Tamil Nadu and Jammu and Kashmir, etc. According to AIAMS, the *agarbatti* labourers who are from the weaker sections, especially women need to be provided with education skills so that they can graduate to more skillful jobs. The *agarbatti* industry can definitely prosper better with mechanisation, which is available. Despite this, it is for the noble cause of helping the weaker sections that the industry has not mechanised.

15.5.5 Coir Development

Karnataka is one of the major coconut producing states in India. As per cultivation it takes the third place which is estimated to be more than 3.3 lakh hectares. And coconut produced is estimated to be 15–20 million nuts. With this potential, coir development is assuming importance in the state. In order to enhance the utilisation of available natural resources, a programme has been drawn for creating more number of defibering centres. In potential districts to take up manufacturing of value added products. It has been planned to increase the present husk utilisation for defibering from the existing 19 per cent to 50 per cent in a span of five years. The Central Coir Board has prepared a vision document for five years to promote coir activities in Karnataka and an action plan has been drawn. Karnataka is known for production of brown fibre and has vast potential for fibre extraction and value added products. The Karnataka Coir Development Corporation, Coir Cooperative Federation along with its primary societies are supported adequately through Coir Board and financial institutions to upgrade their technologies for quality fibre production and to generate rural employment particularly for women. Coir production in the three-year period ending 2004-05 shows an increasing trend (Table 15.27).

TABLE 15.27

Coir Production

Year	*Production in MTs*	*Value of Production (Rs. in Lakhs)*
2002-03	13500	313
2003-04	15000	353
2004-05	18000	480

Source: Economic Survey of Various Periods, Government of Karnataka.

15.6 Karnataka State Public Sector Enterprises

The earliest enterprises in the public sector were set up when there was hardly any industry in the private sector, especially in the then Mysore state. Barring a few industrial enterprises run by certain big houses like Tatas, Birlas, and Godrej, the rest of the industrial entrepreneurial scene in the private sector in the country as a whole was sparse. In 1950, there were in all 10 state enterprises, it increased to 14 in 1960, 19 in 1965 and to 59 in 1981. At the end of March 2000, there were 80 enterprises (*Public Enterprises Survey,* 1990-2000) Majority of them were manufacturing enterprises. It should be noted that PSEs in the state cover a wide spectrum and include many, which were started by the government in the pre-independence days, when Mysore state was a pioneer in industrialisation in the country. The Karnataka State Bureau of Public Enterprises set up by the state government in 1980 monitors the performance of these enterprises and prepares and publishes annual reports on the working of these enterprises. The 80 state public sectors have been classified in 7 groups on the basis of the commodities and services they deal with. Their performance for the year 2001-2002 is presented in Table 15.28.

TABLE 15.28

Sector-wise Performance of the PSEs 2001-2002 (Rs. Lakhs)

Sectors	*Nos.*	*Net Worth*	*Capital Employed*	*Profit**
Public Utilities	5	383126.44	1014627.89	37844.79
Financial Institutions	2	-39358.80	265555.05	-25747.58
Development Enterprises (Non-commercial)	5	22369.54	46651.58	-119.20
Development Enterprises (Commercial)	12	-2085.73	17242.76	-2799.78
Service Enterprises	18	355885.53	1322843.79	7317.12
Manufacturing Enterprises	30	-4748.84	73811.97	-12831.93
Marketing and Advertising Enterprises	8	16274.08	36850.12	1404.3

Notes: * Profit after income tax and prior period adjustments.
Source: *Public Enterprises Survey*, Government of Karnataka 2001-02.

Thus it is observed that both development (commercial) enterprises and manufacturing enterprises are loss-making sectors in the aggregate sense. Therefore, pressure is mounting on the ground that from revenue point of view also, government should try to reduce its share from these sectors. Furthermore, financial institution sector and the development (non-commercial) sector are also incurring net losses.

Further the total borrowings show an increasing trend (Figure 15.11). This is a matter of concern because usually the borrowings of the PSEs are from the state government and when they are unable to repay the loan, government has no other way but to convert the loan to an 'investment'. Thus, the total loss shown by an enterprise may be much more than what it actually amounts to.

FIGURE 15.11

Total Borrowings of State Public Enterprises in Crores of Rupees

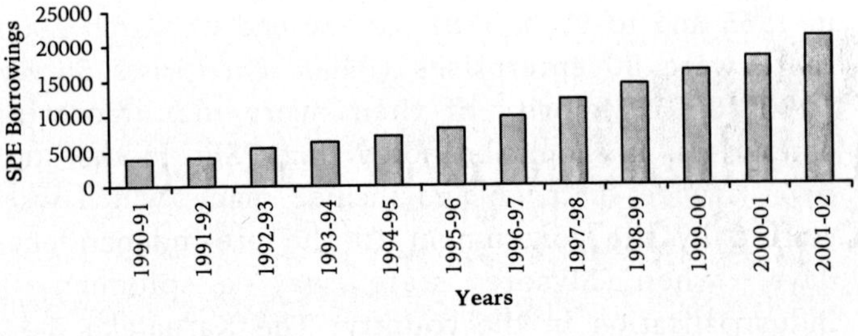

Source: *Public Enterprise Survey*, 2001-2002.

This compels one to rethink about government's commitment to reform measures with respect to the PSEs.

15.6.1 Public Sector Enterprises' Reform Programme of Karnataka

During the initial period of macroeconomic reforms in the 1990s, employment in the Karnataka PSEs recorded a sharp growth in 1992-93, which however slowed down in 1993-94 and thereafter till 1998-99, there was absolute fall in employment. Once again this trend was reversed in 1999-00 only to fall again in 2000-01. But in 2001-02 it turned around and registered another peak in the growth on par with 1992-93. So there was no definitive trend in employment in the PSEs (Figure 15.12).

FIGURE 15.12

Growth Rate of Employment in State PSEs

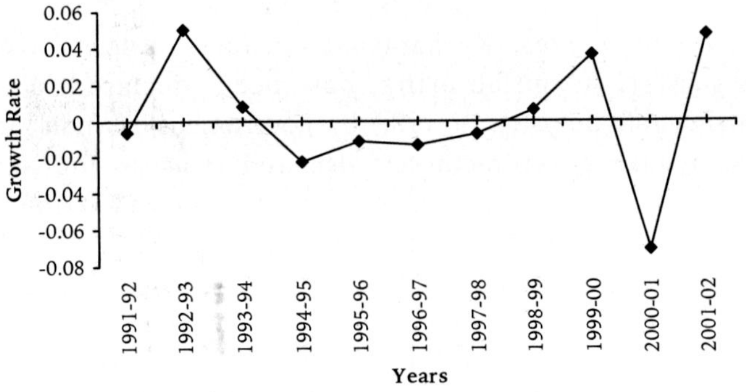

Source: *Public Enterprise Survey*, Government of Karnataka, 2001-02.

15.6.2 New Policy Initiatives

As the financial situation of the state government deteriorated, it became clearer that it is no longer viable for the government to inject more and more resources into the loss making PSEs. Government of Karnataka has brought out a policy prescription on public sector reforms and privatisation in Karnataka in consultation with the Public Sector Restructuring Commission in 2001 and the process of reform gained momentum from early 2002. The policies includes (*Public Enterprise Survey*, 1999-00):

"PSEs, whose activities are commercial in nature or which produce consumer goods, and where there exists a strong private sector presence, would be restructured through privatisation or closure."

1) To evaluate the state PSEs and suggest measures which would promote greater productivity and profitability within the next five years.

2) Suggest measures, which could promote autonomy and reduce or preferably remove budgetary support.

3) Evolve a long-term reform programme, which would enable government to identify PSEs that need alternative forms of management such as complete privatisation or disinvestment or merger etc. If any PSE needs government support to enhance its long-term profitability, strategies should be evolved to identify them.

Accordingly, during the first phase of reform drive, 20 commercial enterprises were selected and the second phase consists of another 20 enterprises.

The first phase of the reform drive is going to effect over 10,000 employees working in PSEs and 30 per cent of these enterprises, are currently profit making. Our discussion with several government officials dealing in this area reveal that the current idea of the department is to sell an enterprise while it is functioning satisfactorily (as it is then easier to privatise) rather than waiting for it to become sick over time and then opt for closure. This is indeed a welcome decision. Thus, after identifying an enterprise for privatisation, the strategy is to ask the management to identify and shed the extra manpower as it has been generally observed that it is difficult to sell even a profit-making enterprise which has excess labour. The government in turn would finance the VRS for the retrenched workers. Recognising the psychological trauma that an employee may go through at the sudden loss of a job, especially if he is young, government of Karnataka also attempted counselling services through experts.

15.7 Industrial Finance

There exists in the financial market a variety of non-banking financial institutions, all-India and state level institutions and a good network of commercial banks, which provide long and medium-term capital for industrial development. The Karnataka State Financial Corporation (KSFC), The Karnataka State Industrial Investment Development Corporation Limited (KSIIDC) and other institutions like the KVIC, NSIC, etc. have been providing the necessary financial infrastructure at the state level. These are dealt in detail in Chapter 7 and hence are not analysed in this chapter.

15.8 Infrastructure

Infrastructure includes transport, communications, electricity and other services like water supply, etc. Sustainable growth hinges around the existence of a critical minimum in terms of the availability of physical infrastructure, power, roads and highways, ports and telecommunication in particular. There has been a persisting demand–supply gap and infrastructural bottlenecks remain the major impediment to stability in growth let alone acceleration in growth. This is true not only in Karnataka but also elsewhere in the country at large. A critical issue in the development of the infrastructure development is financing. Chapter 5, has dealt in detail both the physical and financial issues of all segments of the infrastructure in Karnataka.

Across the districts in Karnataka, industrial development has still remained quite uneven and imbalanced. The major factor attributable for regional disparity in industrial development is lack of infrastructure. There are 12 districts of Karnataka, which are industrially lagging behind, namely, Bijapur, Uttara Kannada, Raichur, Gulobarga, Haveri, Gadag, Kolar, Shimoga, Hassan, Chickmagalur, Kodagu, and Mandya. More than 55 per cent of the industrial investment has occurred is in Bangalore urban district alone.

15.9 Concluding Observations and Vision

There is one area where the state faces a serious constraint—lack of able entrepreneurship. It is mainly for this that the state government emerged as a major investor in the country to mop up the rich resource potential of the state. The 1983 Industrial Policy of Karnataka envisaged a reduction of investment in the state managed and state owned industrial sector and at the same time training programmes for potential entrepreneurs, technical personnel and technicians in rural areas. It is interesting to note in this context that although Karnataka had the largest number of technical and orientation training institutes, according to the report of the Directorate of Employment and Training, Government of Karnataka, the state has been facing an acute shortage of highly qualified and skilled personnel in the public and private sector establishments, especially chemical engineers, chemists, commercial artists and designers, decorators and manufacturing managers. Apart from these occupations requiring high qualifications, jobs for skilled workmen like boiler attenders, crane operators, hydro-extract operators, assemblers at workshop machines, offset printing machine operators were also available in plenty. Again, shortage of photographers, technical assistants for overseas communication, plumbers, refrigeration and automobile mechanics, textile jobbers and stone modellers was also felt. The one area, which has become a perennial problem for Karnataka is the power shortage. There is a chronic problem of a wide gap between demand and supply of power supply. The state was dependent totally on hydel resources, which has been hit by the repeated failure of monsoons. Further, central investment in the state power sector was almost non-existent—the NTPC and NHPC had not set up any projects. When compared to southern region, Karnataka was deprived of home state quota of power as the Central projects were located in Tamil Nadu and Andhra Pradesh. It is also to be mentioned that the sate has no coal yards. This again is mainly due to the inadequate train routes available in the state. The railway route length in the state had, for years, remained constant though improved in the recent period with Konkan Railway, etc. and conversion of metre guage to broad guage, still some backward districts remain unconnected. Road length, needs a massive improvement in terms of coverage, quality, etc.

The industrial relations of late are improving in the state with the sharp decline in strikes, lockouts and lay-offs. The Electronics Industry is a major breakthrough in industrialisation of Karnataka. The registration of new industrial units suggest that textiles and food products are assuming significance. As per the ASI data indicators such as output per worker and labour productivity are lower than all-India. Data on index of industrial production in Karnataka also show an overall sharp deceleration in industrial production. This may be attributed to global recession and also the all-India phenomenon of slowdown. Karnataka in the early seventies had occupied fourth place in terms of many important industrial performance parameters but it slipped to sixth place in late eighties and continues at that level.

In respect of SSI, the state has been protecting and encouraging them through subsidies, incentives, and concessions. But the government has a substantial backlong in release of subsidies to the SSIs. A recent study revealed that majority of SSI units expressed dissatisfaction over the delays. Further the same study concludes that the basic objective of promoting industry in the backward areas is not being met very effectively through the Capital Investment Subsidy Scheme. Further there exists a large-scale closure among the SSI units that could not be arrested by the incentive measures. Many studies highlighted the need for strengthening infrastructure rather than offer fiscal concessions (Institute for Social and Economic Change, 2003).

The third problematic area is availability of raw materials particularly for small-scale sectors. Much of the raw silk produced in the state (the state ranks first in raw silk production) goes out of the state for manufacture of finished goods. Import of silk is another bottleneck for Karnataka. Some of the forest-based industries e.g. agarbatti, sandalwood oil factory face acute shortage due to depletion of forests.

Lastly, a word about the state public sector undertakings. The products of these units are facing severe competition on account of attractive substitutes e.g. KSIC silk fabrics, soaps and detergents, leather products, etc. First of all they are outmoded and not catching up with the changing fashions, taste of the customers; secondly, they are high priced due to higher wage costs. Most of the products manufactured are not durable consumer goods and thus do not cater to the requirements of the common man. It is for these reasons that they are saddled with huge unsold stocks and the net result is underutilisation of capacity. There is also a feeling that the industrial units established early in the state are finding it extremely difficult to face the competition from industries outside Karnataka. Recently the state has come out with a reform programme of its public enterprises. The only profit-making enterprises are in the category of public utilities service enterprises and marketing and advertising enterprises. All of them are loss-making and it is very huge in case of financial institution. Here again the cooperative banks and the state level financial institutions are responsible. The manufacturing enterprises are also incurring huge losses.

15.10 Policy Suggestions

The state possesses vast potential to explore new areas of industrial activity. There are huge deposits of iron ore, manganese, mica, and limestone. Limestone deposits support several cement mills and the ,state possesses a good number of mini cement plants. Many more can be set up. The deposits of iron ore and manganese—particularly Kudremukh iron ore available in the state should be processed into products instead of just being exported in primary form to other countries. Secondly, many agricultural and horticultural crops can facilitate setting up of more food processing units and more so when an exclusive and separate ministry has been created at the Centre for this. Some of them are sugarcane, coffee, coconut, arecanut, citrus fruits, pineapple, mango, and a variety of vegetables alongside food crops like *jowar, bajra* and *ragi*. Cotton is cultivated widely in the northern parts of the state where good quality long staple and other varieties could be used by the textile industry. Here again, much of this goes to Maharashtra, Tamil Nadu and Gujarat. Another area, which has considerable potential, is marine products. This industry is still in its infancy. In view of the long coastline, the state can improve its fishing network especially deep sea fishing and processing down the line. Fifthly the present emphasis is on non-power-intensive industries as against electro-metallurgical and chemical units. In view of the availability of skilled manpower, institutional support and infrastructure and considering the excellent educational and technical training facilities, the state ought to look towards high-tech areas such as electronics, computers and biotechnology for future growth. Sixthly, there is immense scope for growth in manufacture of garments for export as well as domestic consumption which could contribute a great deal to employment and income generation. Leather processing is a growing industry and there is potential for developing it. There are initiatives in this area recently. Leather garments and products are in great demand abroad and Karnataka with its supply of skins and hides and a considerable section of dependent population should be able to utilise the opportunity to develop it further.

On the state government side, government should speed up decision making and ensure that policy decisions are implemented forthwith. There is immediate need for improving roads as well as rail network to enhance the mobility within the state. Communication facilities such as telephone and telex must be improved. Good schools, adequate medical facilities, proper housing and adequate water supply are absolutely essential for any region or centre to attract industries. Coming to the power front, Karnataka immediately needs a few more thermal plants, coal-based and located in the coastal regions. It is equally essential to set up coal yards by Coal India Limited at Bangalore, Mangalore, and other cities to meet the needs of industrial consumers. In order to redress the small-scale industries of their problems, government may set up corporations for procuring products manufactured by SSIs for distribution domestically and abroad. The latest policy on SSI addresses this problem.

Flow of institutional finance would need to be stepped up. Some of the measures to alleviate industrial sickness should be that Karnataka should provide a mechanism with a monitoring cell in the state government. Government could work towards a moratorium on strikes and lockouts in the case of sick units. There is a unanimous view that the flow of funds for working capital requirements of small-scale industrial units is totally inadequate. A careful examination of the financial problems of SSI units is necessary.

References

Ahluwalia, Montek Singh (2000). "Economic Performance of States in Post–Reforms Period", *Economic And Political Weekly*, May 6: 1637–1648.

All India Agarbathi Manufacturers' Associations' unpublished report, *A Report on Productive Employment Generated by the Agarbathi Industry: Quantum Requirements for such Production*, Bangalore.

———. (2004). 53rd and 54th Annual General Body Meeting of All-India Agarbathi Manufacturers' Association, Ravikiran N Vimalkar, President AIAMA–Welcome Address.

———. (2003). "Importance of Agarbathi in a Globalised World–Generating Productive Employment and Exports", *Monograph*, Bangalore, December.

Centre for Monitoring Indian Economy (2004). *Monthly Review of Indian Economy*, August.

———. (2004). *Monthly Review of Karnataka Economy*, August.

Dengbol, Martinussen John (2001). *Policies, Institutions and Industrial Development: Coping with Liberalization and International Competition in India*, Sage Publications, New Delhi.

EPW Research Foundation (2002). *Annual Survey of Industries 1973–74 to 1999–98 A Database of the Industrial Sector in India*, EPW Research Foundation, Mumbai.

Ge, Wei (1999). *Special Economic Zones and the Economic Transition in China*, World Scientific, Singapore.

Gore, Vijay (2003). *Overcoming Investment Climate Known Constraints: Karnataka's Experience*, in a Seminar conducted by World Bank, New Delhi: July 30, *http://lnweb18.worldbank.org/SAR/sa.nsf/attachments/vginv*

Government of India. *Statement of Industrial Policy 1991*, Department of Industrial Policy and Promotion, *http://dipp.nic.in/publicat*

———. *Economic Survey 2003–2004*, *http://.indiabudget.nic.in*

———. *Third All-India Census of Small Scale Industries 2001-2002: Quick Results*, Development Commissioner (Small Scale Industries), Ministry of Small Scale Industries.

Government of Karnataka, *Annual Plan* 2004-05 for Handloom and Textiles – Brief Note of the Schemes, Department of Handloom and Textiles.

———. *Annual Report 2003–04*, Department of Industrial Policy and Promotion (DIPP), *http://dipp.nic.in/anrepo_e/dipp-03-04-annual-report.htm*

———. *Economic Survey 2002–2003* and *Economic Survey 2002–2004*, Department of Industries and Commerce (DIC).

———. *New Industrial Policy 2001–2006*, Department of Industries and Commerce.

———. *Final Report on Fourth Economic Census 1998*, Vol.I and Vol.II, Directorate of Economics and Statistics, November 2000.

———. *Economic Development of Mysore*, 1970, Bureau of Economics and Statistics, Government of Mysore.

———. *Economic Survey of Karnataka 2003–04*, Planning and Statistics Department, Feb 2004, *www.des.kar.nic.in*

———. (2001). *Policy on Public Sector Reforms and Privatization in Karnataka:* Karnataka State Bureau of Public Enterprises.

———. Proceeding of the Government of Karnataka on Public Enterprise Reform.

———. *Third All-India Census of Small Scale Industries 2001-2002*, Department of Industries and Commerce.

———. *Report of the High Power Committee on Redressal of Regional Imbalances*.

———. *Guidelines on Voluntary Retirement Scheme (VRS) in Public Sector Enterprises in Karnataka*, Proceedings of the Government of Karnataka, 10th August, 2001.

Institute for Social and Economic Change (2003). *Industrial Incentives in Karnataka–A Study of Capital Investment Subsidy in Bangalore Division*, sponsored by Government of Karnataka, Department of Industries and Commerce.

Karnataka State Bureau of Public Enterprises, *Public Enterprises Survey*, different issues.

Mendon D. K. (ed.) (1964). *Industrial Mysore 1964*, Tainudi Publication, Bombay.

Ota, Tatsuyiki (2003). *Industrial Policy in Transitional Economy: The Role of China's Special Economic Zone in Economic Development (Part I)*. *www.mng.toyo.ac.jp/publication.*

Paul, Samuel (2000). "Do States Have an Enabling Environment for Industrial Growth? Some Evidence from Karnataka", *Economic and Political Weekly*, October 28; 3861–3869.

Planning Commission (2002). *Report of the Steering Group on Foreign Direct Investment–FDI India*, Government of India, Academic Foundation, New Delhi.

———. *Tenth Five-Year Plan 2002–2007*, Government of India, *http://planningcommission.nic.in*

Rajeev M. (2002). "Whither Public Enterprise Reform in Karnataka?", *The Journal of the Institute of Public Enterprise*, 25: 55-69.

Ramanadhan, V. V. (ed.) (1995). *Privatisation and Equity*, Routledge, London.

Rao G. Hayavadana. *Mysore Gazetteer*, Vol II, Part IV.

Singh, N.K. (2003). "Workshop on Improving India's Investment Climate: Key Note Address", conducted by World Bank, Delhi July 30, *http://Inweb18/worldbank.org/SAR/sa.nsf?countries/India*

Srinivasan, T. N. (1992). "Privatisation and Deregulation", *Economic and Political Weekly*, XXVII (15) and (16), 11-18 April. Also republished in *Economic Policy and State Intervention*, selected papers by T. N. Srinivasan, edited by N S S Narayana, Oxford University Press, 2001.

Techsok (1995-96). *Study on Agarbatti industry by Technical Consultancy Services Organisation of Karnataka.*

World Bank (2004). *Doing Business in 2004–Understanding Regulation*, Oxford University Press, Washington.

Websites extensively referred:

http://des.kar.nic.in

http://dipp.nic.in

http://planningcommission.nic.in

www.indiabudget.nic.in

www.kumbanglore.com

APPENDIX A-15.1

Karnataka: New Industrial Policy 2001–2006

Objectives

a) Encourage rapid growth of sectors and markets in which Karnataka has strategic advantages.

b) Enhance value addition in products and processes through rapid technology upgradation.

c) Enable optimal utilisation of capacity and resources in different sectors *viz.*, agriculture, horticulture, animal husbandry, minerals and human capital.

d) Enable industry to access new markets—domestic and export through new products that meet global standards of quality and competitiveness.

e) Give impetus to knowledge-based industries and the service sector.

f) Create a market-driven environment with the private sector being the primary engine for growth.

g) Provide industry access to high quality infrastructure

h) Fully tap the potential of the small-scale sector and encourage establishment of new tiny and small-scale industries, particularly in the rural areas to achieve the twin objectives of employment generation and utilisation of local resources.

Strategy

a) Forge a strong partnership with the private sector in all aspects of Industrial Policy and its implementation to provide for a demand-driven decision making process in an increasingly market oriented economy.

b) Create a policy framework to facilitate competitiveness of local industry and enabling ease of doing business.

c) Enhance public and private expenditure to build efficient and competitive industrial infrastructure.

d) Give impetus to technology upgradation by forging symbiotic and mutually beneficial institutional arrangements between government, academic, R&D institutions and industry.

e) Focus on catalysing comparative advantages that Karnataka has in the global market by increasing its exports in information technology, biotechnology, food processing, electronics and communication, garments, machine tools, and precision engineering goods.

f) Assist the tiny, small and medium-scale industries to upgrade their technologies and manufacturing processes to face the increasing competition.

g) Radical restructuring of the state public sector undertakings as well as government infrastructure agencies and financial institutions by promoting private sector initiative in these activities.

Source: Department of Industries and Commerce, *New Industrial Policy 2001–2006*, Government of Karnataka.

APPENDIX A-15.2

SEZ in Karnataka

The Karnataka Government is working on the possibility of having a special economic zone in Mangalore in addition to the one in Hassan. The state government has also chalked out a project involving areas not covered under the Karnataka Urban Infrastructure and Coastal Environment Management Plan (partly funded by the Asian Development Bank). An export promotion industrial park (EPIP) is also being planned in the Mangalore district. Government is also proposing to establish an exclusive SEZ for electronic hardware near the proposed international airport at Devenahalli. Government is also proposing to convert existing export promotion industrial park at White Field, Bangalore and the proposed export promotion industrial park at Mangalore (which is under implementation in SEZ). Government may also consider establishing of SEZs in other parts of the state.

Source: Department of Industries and Commerce, Govt. of Karnataka.

APPENDIX A-15.3

Growth Centres

Government of India has appointed KIADB as a nodal agency for establishing growth centres in Raichur, Dharwad, and Hassan districts. Government of Karnataka has extended several incentives, subsidies and benefits for units operating from the growth centres.

Growth Centres under Zone D

1. Raichur Growth Centre

- An extent of 2,000 acres of developed land, located on National Highway, 6 kms from Raichur city—the regional hub of trade and commerce.
- Dedicated power lines and water supply of 13 MGD, proposed to be set up by KUWS and DB, and government body.
- Fully loaded Infrastructure.
- Additional land of 68.31 acres is under acquisition.

2. Dharwad Growth Centre

- Located on National Highway-4, 10 kms distance from Dharwad city.
- Extent of Area:

- 1st phase: 500 acres.
- 2nd phase: 842 acres.
- 3rd phase: 650 acres (Allotted to M/s Telco.)
- 4th phase: 243 acres (Housing Area.)

- Dedicated receiving and sub-station of uninterrupted power supply of 220KV and 110KV capacity. Load up to 30MW could be availed.
- Dedicated water supply line from River Malaprabha with treatment plant of 5 MGD capacity.
- Headquarters of CEDOK located (Centre for Entrepreneurship Development of Karnataka).
- Infrastructures like housing, recreational facilities, telephone exchange, banks, post office are existing in the centre.

3. *Hassan Growth Centre*

- Extent of 400 acres of developed land, located on National Highway-48 and 4 kms. from Hassan city—regional hub of trade and commerce.
- Fully developed internal roads and link roads and completely loaded infrastructure.
- Dedicated power lines and 28 numbers of 250 KVA transformers. Load up to 10 MW could be availed.
- Dedicated water supply lines of 2.5 MGD capacity from Gorur reservoir.

Mini-Growth Centres

KIADB has formed five mini-growth centres and two are in offing. Features of this scheme are basically similar to that of scheme of regular growth centre plans detailed earlier. Of these, two of the mini-growth centres are formed with assistance of government of India and remaining three have been formed with assistance from government of Karnataka. Brief profiles of project and location are given below:

1. *Aliabad (Bijapur District)*

- Extent: 158 acres with infrastructure fully provided.
- Allotment of land commenced.
- Nearest airport at Belgaum—205 kms., Hyderabad—275 kms.
- Good railway links with many world heritage sites/centres near by.
- Rivers: Krishna, Bhima, Dona, and Soogli.

2. *Malur (Kolar District)*

- Extent: 250 acres with infrastructure fully provided.
- Extent allotted 12 acres to 7 units.
- Just 50 kms from Bangalore.
- Well-known place for agro products and clay products.

3. *Amble (Chickmagalur District)*

- Extent: 50 acres with Infrastructure fully provided.
- Extent allotted 8.10 acres to 3 units.
- Just 200 kms. from Bangalore, pollution free climate of Western Ghats, famous for coffee and spices.

4. *Mundargi (3rd Phase) (Bellary District)*

- Extent: 89.52 acres with Infrastructure fully provided.
- Extent allotted 21.40 acres to 15 units.
- District is known for the deposits of iron ore and manganese.
- River Tungabhadra.
- Hub of trade and commerce in the region.

5. *Narasapur (Gadag District)*

- Extent: 180 acres with infrastructure fully provided.
- Extent allotted 19 acres to 2 units.
- Rivers Malaprabha and Tungabhadra.
- Distance to Hubli-60 kms. Airport at Hubli.
- Hub of trade and commerce in the region.

Source: Karnataka Industrial Area Development Board, Govt. of Karnataka.

APPENDIX A-15.4

Agro-tech Park

Karnataka is blessed by nature with 10 different Agro-climatic zones and produces around 12.4 million tonnes of horticultural crops in the various varieties like vegetables, fruits, spices, herbs, and flowers. Sixty-six per cent of the area of the state is under agriculture and an area of 12.7 million hectares of land is available for cultivation. Crops that are most sought after from this state are coffee, cashew, spices, fruits, vegetables, processed foods and pulps and marine products. Demand continues to rise for maize, rice, millet, sorghum, tobacco, and spice. The most fancied products of late are gherkins and rose onions. Exports from this state in this sector were about Rs. 1,549.35 crores and is expected to grow by 20 per cent annually.

KIADB in its role of facilitator for growth of industries in Karnataka is appointed as nodal agency for establishing Agro-tech parks by the government of Karnataka in Bagalkot, Belguam, Chitradurga/Sira, Maddur, Malur, and Jewargi (Gulbarga). Government of India has accorded approval initially for three parks at Malur (Kolar Dist.), Jewargi (Gulbarga Dist.) and Bagalkot.

These parks will be provided with complete infrastructure as in our other industrial areas. Along with the regular infrastructure board has plans to provide facilities for establishing:

- cold storage,
- dry storage,
- testing laboratory,
- packing and forwarding activities, etc.

Source: Karnataka Industrial Area Development Board, Govt. of Karnataka.

APPENDIX A-15.5

Export Promotion Industrial Parks (EPIP)

EPIPs are the destination for industrial units who have plans to export at least 33 per cent of their output in value offshore. These parks come with well-planned infrastructure, which is hallmark of KIADB's service. These parks are established with the sanction of Union Government of India to give impetus to growth of exports in the state. Government of Karnataka offers host of incentives and concessions to export oriented units.

Source: *http://sezindia.nic.in*

APPENDIX A-15.6

China: Shenzhen SEZ

Initially, four SEZs were set up in China in Shenzhen (close to Hong Kong), Zhuhai (near Macao), Shantou all three located in Guangdong Province, and in Xiamen (across Taiwan) (Ota, 2003: 131). Shenzhen surrounded by agriculture land, was a sleepy county named, Baoan County which was upgraded to municipal status in 1979. Shenzhen which is across from Hong Kong New Territories, was the largest SEZ at the time in terms of area. Shenzhen SEZ totaling 327.5 kilometres is about one–third the size of Hong Kong and more than one–half the size of Singapore (Ge, 1999: 46). Shenzhen was a backward area and its share of the GDP and exports in the Guangdong Province was below 1 per cent. "The length of paved road was measured at 8 kilometres, and the sewer pipeline at barely 0.5 kilometres" (Ge, 1999: 48). In the beginning these were in fact referred to as Special Export Zones and started with modest objectives. The objectives were clearer by 1985 and were more clearly spelt out as: "to experiment with the development of an outward–looking, market oriented economic system, and to serve the country as a 'window' and a 'base' along these lines" (Ge, 1999: 49).

To fulfil these objectives several initiatives were taken for: "attracting and utilising foreign capital, acquiring advanced foreign production and managerial technologies, developing a comprehensive economic structure, promoting foreign trade in accordance with the comparative advantages of the region, and gaining experience in economic reforms according to the international norm of market economies" (Ge, 1999: 49). Apart from industrial projects, agricultural undertakings, financial and banking services, real estate development, tourist facilities, R&D establishments, educational institutions, and housing were also targeted (Ge, 1999: 49).

The salient features are:

- Between 1980 and 1993, of the total 9,314 contracts signed over the period, nearly 76 per cent were foreign–direct–investment projects, comprising joint ventures, co-production, and wholly foreign–owned enterprises (Ge, 1999: 57).
- The overall fixed capital assets rose from 50 million RMB yuan to 2.6 billion yuan in 1985 to 16 billion yuan in 1993, i.e. 320 times.
- The total public expenditure rose 120 times during the period from 40 million yuan to 5 billion yuan.
- Construction activities grew at the annual rate of 36 per cent during this period and industry at 47 per cent. Light industry production accounted for about 70 per cent of industrial output.
- Actual utilisation of foreign capital rose from $ 26.6 million to $ 1.1billion in 1993 with the cumulative total capital tending towards to $ 6 billion. The major source of capital was Hong Kong.
- Wages in the SEZ were 1.5 to 2.5 times more than national average.
- GDP per worker, a measure of productivity was approximately 5 times that of national average.
- The value of exports increased 2000 fold, from $ 9.3 million to $ 18 billion in 1994.
- The import content declined from 85 per cent to 78 per cent suggesting more linkages with domestic industries.
- Exports grew at 56.6 per cent annually between 1979 and 1995, and by 1995 contributed 14 per cent to the nation's total exports.
- Its share of GDP of China was 1.37 per cent.

Source: Ge, 1999.

The maginificent development witnessed by the provinces, which had SEZs over a long period of time consistently will be evident from the table below. The growth rate of these provices outperformed consistently the national growth rates.

Industrial Production: China and Provinces with SEZ (100 Million Yuan)

	1980	*1985*	*1990*	*1995*	*Annual Average Gross Rate*
National	5154	9716	23924	91894	14.9
Guangdong	234	505	1,907	7,458	21.7
Fujian	81	173	531	2,881	26.9
Hainan	7	21	44	177	24.1

Source: Ota, 2003.

APPENDIX 15.7

Cross Country Comparison of Selected EPZs

Country	*No. of Zones*	*Incentives*	*Employment*	*Investor Countries*	*Sectors*	*Labour Laws*	*Workers Organisations*
Bangladesh	2 public EPZs; 3 public & 1pvt. EPZ under construction	10 year tax holiday duty free imports & exports.	2.2 million				
China	6 SEZs, 34 ETDZs	Govt. infrastructure (roads, ports, power), corporate tax 15 per cent, full refund of taxes on profits reinvested, duty free imports & exports.	18 million in foreign invested firms	Hong Kong, Taiwan, Japan USA	-	Flexible labour laws	Single trade unions
Malaysia	15 free industrial zones	-	-	Japan, Singapore, USA	-	Labour laws apply except pioneer industries	Restrictions electronics and pioneer industries
Sri Lanka	6 EPZs	10-20 year holiday for new, large export projects or thrust industries.	Estimates range within 90000	South Korea, Hong Kong	Apparel services rubber	Labour laws apply	No trade unions present, zones have emp. councils

Source: Foreign Direct Investment, Planning Commission 2002.

APPENDIX A-15.8

Rates and Ceiling for Capital Investment Subsidy under Various Policy Packages–Karnataka

Zones	*Tiny Ind.*		*SSI*		*M & L Ind.*	
	Rate per cent	*Max. Clng. (Rs. in Lakhs)*	*Rate per cent*	*Max. Clng. (Rs. in Lakhs)*	*Rate per cent*	*Max. Clng. (Rs. in Lakhs)*
			1983-88 Package			
I	Nil	Nil	Nil	Nil	Nil	Nil
II	10	0.5	10	5	10	10
III	15	0.75	15	7.5	15	15
IV	15	1	15	15	15	15
			1993-94 Package			
I	Nil	Nil	Nil	Nil	Nil	Nil
II	10	0.5	10	5	10	10
III	15	0.75	15	7.5	15	15
IV	15	1	15	15	15	15
			1996-2001 Package			
I	Nil**	Nil**	Nil**	Nil**	Nil**	Nil**
II	25	25	25	25	Nil**	Nil**
III	30	30	30	30	Nil**	Nil**
			2001-2006 Package			
A	Nil	Nil	Nil	Nil	Nil	Nil
B	10	6	-	-	-	-
C	20	10	-	-	-	-
D	25	12.50	25	12.50	-	-

Note: **: Only the tiny and small-scale Industries set up in developed areas in specified non-polluting high technology industrial units shall be eligible for an investment subsidy of 25 per cent of value of fixed assets, subject to a ceiling of Rs. 25 lakhs.

(1) Tiny Ind. – Tiny Industrial Units

(2) SSI – Small-scale Industries Units

(3) M & L Ind. – Medium and Large-scale Industrial Units

(4) Max. Clng. – Maximum Ceiling.

Source: Karnataka Industrial Policy for various periods, Department of Industries & Commerce, Govt. of Karnataka.

APPENDIX A-15.9

Salient Features of the Incentives and Concessions of the Industrial Policy Package 2001-2006 Relating to SSI

1. Investment Subsidy

a) The Government will provide subsidy to all new tiny/small-scale Sector industries. The details of investment subsidy available to tiny/small-scale sector industries in different zones will be as follows (refer Appendix A-15.10 for detailed classification):

Zone	*Particulars*	*Industry Sector Eligible for Subsidy*	*Investment Subsidy**
A	Developed Areas	Nil	Nil
B	Developing Areas	Tiny Industries	10 per cent value of fixed assets subject to a maximum of Rs. 5 lakhs
C	Backward Areas	Tiny Industries	20 per cent value of fixed assets subject to a max. of Rs. 10 lakhs
D	As detailed in Appendix A-15.10		Tiny and small scale industries 25 per cent value of fixed assets subject to a max. of Rs. 12.50 lakhs

Notes: * This would be available for industrial units making new industrial investments under expansion, diversification and modernisation.

(b) Additional subsidy to special category of entrepreneurs: In addition to the subsidy at 1 (A) above, additional subsidy to an extent of five per cent of the value of fixed assets subject to a ceiling of Rs. one lakh shall be available for tiny/small-scale units, except in Zone-A, in respect of entrepreneurs belonging to SC and STs and women entrepreneurs. This additional subsidy will however, be within the overall monitory ceiling indicated in Sub Para [a] of Para-1. Entrepreneurs who are covered under more than one special category is defined above will be eligible for special subsidy only under one of the special categories.

2. Entry Tax Exemption

Entry tax exemption will be extended to all new industries including large and medium-scale industries as detailed below:

a) During the implementation of the project on production machinery and equipments directly involved in the production process, subject to the condition that the benefit will be available for a maximum period of three years from the date of commencement of project implementation.

b) On commencement of commercial production (during the operational phase), on raw materials, components, semi-finished goods, sub-assemblies, consumables (excluding petroleum products like petrol, diesel, furnace oil, naphtha and LSHS used as consumables or for captive power generation units). Entry Tax exemption will be available as indicated below:

Zone	*Particulars*	*Entry Tax Exemption Period*
A	Developed Areas	Nil
B	Developing Areas	3 Years
C	Backward Areas	5 Years
D	As detailed in Appendix A-4.3	8 Years

3. Stamp Duty Exemption and Concessional Registration Charges

A. For Loan Documents

All new industries and also such units taking up expansion, diversification and modernisation will be eligible for 100 per cent exemption of stamp duty and reduction of registration charges to Re. 1 per Rs. 1000 in respect of loan agreements, credit deeds, mortgage and hypothecation deeds executed for availing financial assistance from state government and/or State Financial Corporation, Industrial Investment Development Corporation, Nationalised Financial Institutions, Commercial Banks, LRRBs, Industrial Cooperative Banks, KVIB/KVIC, Karnataka State SC/ST Development Corporation, Karnataka State Minority Development Corporation and other institutions which may be notified by the government from time to time.

B. For Registration of Land/Shed

The concession of stamp duty exemption and reduction of Registration charges will be available for lease deeds, lease-cum-sale and absolute sale deeds executed by industrial units in respect of industrial plots, sheds, flats allotted by State Infrastructural Development Agencies *viz.* KIADB, KSSIDC, KEONICS, KSIIDC, etc. and industrial cooperatives.

The concessions will be as under:

Zone	*Extent of Exemption on Stamp Duty*		*Registration Charges*	
	Tiny and Small Scale Industry	*Medium and Large-Scale Industry*	*Tiny and Small-Scale*	*Medium and Large-Industry*
A	Nil	Nil	Normal	Normal
B	100 per cent	50 per cent	Re. 1 per Rs. 1000	50 per cent of normal charges
C&D	100 per cent	100 per cent	Re. 1 per Rs. 1,000	Re. 1.00 per Rs. 1,000

In order to give an impetus for growth of certain sectors of industries for which the State has significant resource/technology base, 100 per cent exemption from payment of stamp duty and registration charges will also be available to the industries (Appendices A-15.11 and A-15.12).

4. Waiver of Conversion Fee

The payment of conversion fee for converting the land from agriculture use to industrial use will be waived for tiny and SSI units set up in all areas other than Zone A. This concession will be limited to a maximum extent of two acres only. Conversion of agriculture land to industrial land in identified industrial zones of respective municipal/town planning authorities and other local bodies will henceforth be automatic and orders issued in 45 days by the respective DCs, failing which conversion will be deemed to have been given.

In addition, the government has also announced relief packages for revival/rehabilitation of sick industries such as margin money scheme, extended period for payment of energy bills in easy instalments, etc. There are separate concessions for BIFR and non-BIFR cases.

Source: New Industrial Policy 2001-06, Dept. of Industries & Commerce, Government of Karnataka.

APPENDIX A-15.10

Classification of Zones

Sl.No.	*District*	*Zone*
1	Bangalore (Urban) & Bangalore (Rural)Excluding Kanakapura and Magadi *talukas*)	A
2	Dakshina Kannada	
3	Shimoga	
4	Tumkur (Excluding Pavagada, Sira and Gubbi *talukas*)	
5	Belgaum (Excluding Ramadurga *taluka*)	
6	Mysore (Excluding Heggadadevanakote *talukas*)	B
7	Dharwad	
8	Bellary (Excluding Kudligi, Hadagali, Sandur and Hagaribommanahalli *talukas*)	
9	Davangere (Excluding Harapanahalli *talukas*)	
10	Mandya	
11	Kanakapura and Magadi of Bangalore Rural District	
12	Bijapur	
13	Bidar (Excluding Aurad, Basavakalyan, Bhalki and Humnabad *talukas*)	
14	Raichur (Excluding Devadurga, Manvi and Lingsugur *talukas*)	
15	Chickmagalur	
16	Kodagu	
17	Kolar (Excluding Bagepalli and Srinivasapur *talukas*)	
18	Chitradurga (Excluding Molakalmuru, Holalkere and Hosadurga *talukas*)	
19	Hassan	
20	Gulbarga (Excluding Jevargi, Chincholi, Aland, Yadgir, Afzalpur, Shorapur and Shahpur *talukas*)	C
21	Uttara Kannada (Excluding Mundagod and Joida (supa) *talukas*)	
22	Chamarajnagar	
23	Gadag (Excluding Ron, Shirahatti, Naragund and Mundargi *talukas*)	
24	Udupi	
25	Haveri (Excluding Shiggaon and Byadgi *taluka*)	
26	Bagalkot (Excluding Bilgi *taluka*)	
27	Koppal (Excluding Kushtagi and Yelbarga *talukas*)	
28	Kudligi, Hadagali, Sandur and Hagaribommanahalli of Bellary District	
29	Ramdurg of Belgaum District	
30	Harapanahalli of Davangere District	
31	Pavgada, Sira and Gubbi of Tumkur District	
32	Heggadadevankote of Mysore District	
33	Growth centres at Raichur, Dharwad and Hassan	D
34	Mini growth centres at Bijapur, Bellary, Malur, Nippani, Gadag, Chikkaballapur and Chitradurga	
35	Agro Parks, Apparel Parks, Special Economic Zone, Export Promotion Industrial Parks at Mangalore, Auto Parks, Chemical Industrial Parks and Jewellery Parks (excluding those set up in Zone A)	
36	Aurad, Basavakalyan, Bhalki and Humnabad of Bidar District	
37	Jevargi, Chincholi, Aland, Yadgir, Afzalpur, Shorapur and Shahpur of Gulbarga District	
38	Kundgol of Dharwad District	
39	Devadurga, Manvi and Lingsugur of Raichur District	
40	Kushtagi and Yelburga of Koppal District	
41	Bilgi of Bagalkot District	
42	Mundargi, Ron, Naragund and Shirahatti of Gadag District	
43	Shiggaon and Byadgi of Haveri District	
44	Molakalmuru, Holalkere and Hosdurga of Chitradurga District	
45	Bagepalli and Srinivaspur of Kolar District	
46	Mundagod and Joida (Supa) of Uttara Kannada District	

Source: New Industrial Policy 2001-06, Dept. of Industries & Commerce, Govt. of Karnataka.

APPENDIX A-15.11

List of Key Projects in Core Areas

1. Electronics
2. Telecommunication
3. Informatics
4. Precision tooling/Tool Room Industries including units manufacturing dies, jigs and fixtures
5. Ready-made garments including leather garments (excluding leather tanning units)
6. Units manufacturing equipment for pollution control, effluent treatment plant and water recycling
7. Biotechnology
8. BioInformatics
9. Agro-Food Processing Industries

10. Equipment for utilisation of renewable/non-conventional source of energy and energy conservation
11. Hundred per cent Export Oriented Industries
12. Spinning mills, weaving units, power loom, knitting and textile processing
13. Cutting, polishing and processing of semi-precious stones
14. Pharmaceuticals industry including bulk drug and formulations
15. Floriculture
16. Industries manufacturing equipment for water conservation i.e. drip irrigation, etc.
17. Automobile industries for manufacture of two wheelers/ passenger cars, LCVs/HCVs
18. Machine tools/Auto Components
19. Jewellery
20. Cold storages
21. Cement and steel/steel alloys
22. Sugar industry
23. Grey iron and other foundries

Source: New Industrial Policy 2001-06, Dept. of Industries & Commerce, Government of Karnataka.

APPENDIX A-15.12

List of Industries not Eligible for Incentives and Concessions

1. Popcorn and ice candy making units
2. Coffee roasting and grinding
3. *Khadsari* units
4. Breweries and distilleries of all types
5. Photo studios and colour processing centres
6. Photocopying machines
7. Power laundries
8. Clock and watch repair shops
9. Cassette recording (audio and video)
10. Fertiliser mixing
11. Units using molasses/rectified spirit/denatured spirit as main raw material for manufacturing of potable alcohol
12. Repacking of drugs/medicines/chemicals, etc., without any processing and value addition, excluding formulation units
13. All types of saw mills
14. *Beedies*
15. Cigarettes
16. Cigars
17. *Gutka*
18. Tobacco-based Industries
19. Azoic Dyes
20. Fire Crackers
21. Reactive Dyes
22. Cyanide
23. Industries manufacturing and/or utilising ozone depleting substances

Source: New Industrial Policy 2001-06, Dept. of Industries & Commerce, Government of Karnataka.

APPENDIX A-15.13

Net State Domestic Product at Factor Cost by Industry of Origin–at Current Prices, 1993-94 to 2002-03
(a) Value in Rs. Lakh

Industry	*1993-94*	*1994-95*	*1995-96*	*1996-97*	*1997-98*	*1998-99*	*1999-00*	*2000-2001*	*2001-02**	*2002-03***
1. Primary Sector	1408934	1558095	1770080	2029788	2059086	2468832	2670140	2857087	2431265	2447211
2. Secondary Sector	887568	1074092	1209430	1366054	1573542	1995165	1917201	1952559	1941376	2035166
3. Tertiary Sector	1401726	1674323	2023309	2411236	2843062	3411627	3882282	4523697	4965644	5558254
Net State Domestic Product (1+2+3)	3698228	4306510	5002819	5807078	6475689	7875624	8469623	9333343	9338285	10040631
Secondary Sector:										
Manufacturing	650282	800832	867509	966598	1074908	1350107	1212944	1182586	1113192	1189775
Registered	395685	506240	530415	593880	667308	884640	710295	618335	534761	567085
Unregistered	254597	294592	337094	372718	407600	465467	502649	564251	578431	622690
Construction	199081	221442	288115	344239	435565	535470	602914	638768	684426	733191
Electricity, Gas and Water Supply	38205	51819	53806	55217	63069	109588	101343	131205	143759	112200
Secondary Sector 1+2+3	887568	1074092	1209430	1366054	1573542	1995165	1917201	1952559	1941376	2035166

Source: State Domestic Product: Karnataka 1993-94 to 20-02-03.
Directorate of Economics and Statistics, GoK, 2004.

Note: * Partially Revised Estimates
** Quick Estimates

(b) Percentage Variation over Previous Year (Concluded)

Industry	*1994-95*	*1995-96*	*1996-97*	*1997-98*	*1998-99*	*1999-00*	*2000-2001*	*2001-02*	*2002-03*
1. Primary Sector	10.6	13.6	14.7	1.4	19.9	8.2	7.0	-14.9	0.7
2. Secondary Sector	21.0	12.6	13.0	15.2	26.8	-3.9	1.8	-0.6	4.8
3. Tertiary Sector	19.4	20.8	19.2	17.9	20.0	13.8	16.5	9.8	11.9
Net State Domestic Product (1+2+3)	16.4	16.2	16.1	11.5	21.6	7.5	10.2	0.1	7.5
Secondary Sector:									
1. Manufacturing	23.2	8.3	11.4	11.2	25.6	-10.2	-2.5	-5.9	6.9
Registered	27.9	4.8	12.0	12.4	32.6	-19.7	-12.9	-13.5	6.0
Unregistered	15.7	14.4	10.6	9.4	14.2	8.0	12.3	2.5	7.7
2. Construction	11.2	30.1	19.5	26.5	22.9	12.6	5.9	7.1	7.1
3. Electricity, Gas and Water Supply	35.6	3.8	2.6	14.2	73.8	-7.5	29.5	9.6	-22.0
Secondary Sector 1+2+3	21.0	12.6	13.0	15.2	26.8	-3.9	1.8	-0.6	4.8

Source: State Domestic Product: Karnataka 1993-94 to 20-02-03.
Directorate of Economics and Statistics, GoK, 2004.

APPENDIX A-15.14

Index of Industrial Production in Karnataka: 1990-91 to 1993-94
(a) Base Year 1980-81 = 100

Division/Sector	*Weight*	*1990-91*	*1991-92*	*1992-93*	*1993-94*	*Average Annual Growth*
Mining	1.41	149.03	153.61	144.44	154.84	3.42
Manufacturing	95.85	262.53	279.31	298.01	319.55	6.68
Electricity	2.74	188.46	195.87	199.22	225.52	6.80
General		-	-	-	-	-

(b) Base Year 1993-94 = 100

Division/Sector	*Weight*	*1994-95*	*1995-96*	*1996-97*	*1997-98*	*1998-99*	*1999-00*	*2000-2001*	*2001-2002*	*2002-2003*	*Average AnnualGrowth*
Mining	2.36	108.22	107.77	112.18	132.31	125.77	125.98	136.10	165.22	182.57	7.22
Manufacturing	89.30	109.37	116.31	126.75	139.46	147.50	154.82	160.65	165.95	170.50	6.14
Electricity	8.34	115.53	105.38	87.18	126.49	119.26	147.88	166.19	175.94	170.28	7.54
General	-	109.86	115.20	123.11	138.21	144.63	153.56	160.53	166.77	170.76	6.17

Source: Directorate of Economics and Statistics, Bangalore.

APPENDIX A-15.15

Growth in Index of Industrial Production in Manufacturing by Use-based Groups: 1990-91 to 1993-94
(a) Base Year 1980-81 = 100

(in per cent)

	Weight	*1990-91*	*1991-92*	*1992-93*	*1993-94*	*Average Annual Growth*
Basic Goods	14.91	2.35	8.34	2.42	11.82	6.23
Capital Goods	10.7	5.63	2.74	5.12	6.61	5.03
Intermediate Goods	4.56	10.45	1	9.42	12.27	9.04
Consumer Goods	69.83	7.17	7.65	7.76	5.48	7.02
Consumer Durables	2.1	42.83	2.53	-0.19	1.7	11.72
Consumer Non-durables	67.63	5.6	7.95	8.21	5.68	6.86
General Index	**100**	**6.15**	**6.63**	**6.42**	**7.16**	**6.59**

(b) Base Year 1993-94=100

(in per cent)

	Weight	1994-95	1995-96	1996-97	1997-98	1998-99	1999-20	200-01	2001-02	2002-03	Average Annual Growth
Basic Goods	14.58	8.93	5.62	8.15	6.86	4.33	5.76	2.69	2	-0.19	4.91
Capital Goods	10.52	9.44	5.46	9.78	0.47	11.29	4.28	5.76	2.84	2.12	5.72
Intermediate Goods	24.16	9.45	6.33	9.7	8.04	6.05	5.9	4.81	3.58	0.47	6.04
Consumer Goods	50.74	9.66	6.28	8.85	13.6	4.67	4.47	2.68	3.15	4.14	6.39
Consumer Durables	13.6	9.89	5.9	9.89	11.65	7.26	1.78	1.64	2.74	2.34	5.9
Consumer Non-durables	37.14	9.57	6.43	8.47	14.32	3.74	5.47	3.06	3.3	4.77	6.57
General Index	**100**	**9.48**	**6.11**	**9.06**	**9.9**	**5.6**	**4.97**	**3.51**	**3.07**	**2.44**	**6.02**

Source: Directorate of Economics and Statistics, Govt. of Karnataka, Bangalore.

APPENDIX A-15.16

Net State Domestic Product of Select States at Current Prices

(Rs. in crore)

	State/Union Territories			
	Karnataka	Maharashtra	Tamil Nadu	Andhra Pradesh
1980-81	5587	15163	7218	7324
1990-91	20551	58137	27674	29867
1993-94	36982	101767	51643	51655
1994-95	43065	116507	61276	61789
1995-96	50028	140730	69719	71796
1996-97	58071	158683	79121	81517
1997-98	64757	172530	92690	1224946
1998-99	78756	191222	105793	1415093
1999-00	84696	217065	112741	1564048
2000-01	93333	210075	126100	1687818
2001-02	93383	237112	132567	1861117
2002-03	100406	263225	na	1995229

Note: Estimates prior to 1993-94 are based on 1980-81 series and estimates from 1993-94 and onwards are based on 1993-94 series.
NA–Not available

Source: Directorate of Economics & Statistics of respective State Governments (as on March 26, 2004).

APPENDIX A-15.17

Growth Rates: Net State Domestic Product of Select States at Current Prices

(in per cent)

Year	Karnataka	Maharashtra	Tamil Nadu	Andhra Pradesh
1993-94	21.63	20.52	23.12	20.03
1994-95	16.45	14.48	18.65	19.62
1995-96	16.17	20.79	13.78	16.20
1996-97	16.08	12.76	13.49	13.54
1997-98	11.51	8.73	17.15	5.24
1998-99	21.62	10.83	14.14	21.13
1999-00	7.54	13.51	6.57	8.71
2000-01	10.20	-3.22	11.85	11.82
2001-02	0.05	12.87	5.13	7.80
2002-03	7.52	11.01	N.A.	5.73

NA – Not available.

Source: Directorate of Economics & Statistics of respective State Governments (as on March 26, 2004).

APPENDIX A-15.18

Composition of Secondary Sector, Manufacturing, etc., in Net State Domestic Product at Factor Cost by Industry at Current Prices, 1993-94 to 2002-03

(Percentage Distribution)

Sl.No.	Industry	1993-94	1994-95	1995-96	1996-97	1997-98	1998-99	1999-2000	2000-2001	2001-02	2002-03
1.	Primary Sector	38.1	36.2	35.4	35.0	31.8	31.3	31.5	30.6	26.0	24.4
2.	Secondary Sector	24.0	24.9	24.2	23.5	24.3	25.3	22.6	20.9	20.8	20.3
3.	Tertiary Sector	37.9	38.9	40.4	41.5	43.9	43.3	45.8	48.5	53.2	55.4
	Net State Domestic Product (1+2+3)	100.0	100.0	100.0	100.0	100.0	100.0	100.0	100.0	100.0	100.0
	Secondary Sector:										
1.	Manufacturing	17.6	18.6	17.3	16.6	16.6	17.1	14.3	12.7	11.9	11.9
	1.1 Registered	10.7	11.8	10.6	10.2	10.3	11.2	8.4	6.6	5.7	5.6
	1.2 Unregistered	6.9	6.8	6.7	6.4	6.3	5.9	5.9	6.0	6.2	6.2
2.	Construction	5.4	5.1	5.8	5.9	6.7	6.8	7.1	6.8	7.3	7.3
3.	Electricity, Gas and Water Supply	1.0	1.2	1.1	1.0	1.0	1.4	1.2	1.4	1.5	1.1
	Secondary Sector 1+2+3	24.0	24.9	24.2	23.5	24.3	25.3	22.6	20.9	20.8	20.3

Source: State Domestic Product: Karnataka 1993-94 to 20-02-03.
Directorate of Economics and Statistics, GoK, 2004.

APPENDIX A-15.19

Interstate Comparison of Important Parameters of Industrial Sector Performance ASI-2000–01

States	Total Factories Nos.	Total Employees Nos.	Value of Output Rs. Crores	Net Value Added Rs. Crores
Andhra Pradesh	14029	90755	61347.02	8878.67
Bihar	1535	62905	7254.87	729.26
Chhattisgarh	1275	96389	12743.07	2492.77
Delhi	3498	120498	14297.95	2008.90
Gujarat	14090	752013	127977.28	16855.87
Haryana	4448	300882	44675.04	5570.54
Jharkhand	1500	173481	19277.81	4044.47
Jammu & Kashmir	356	23216	1342.72	159.47
Karnataka	7010	474150	46258.83	8301.63
Kerala	4853	313355	26710.55	3553.81
Madhya Pradesh	3221	253444	36712.34	6208.34
Maharashtra	18528	1172799	184971.46	31260.98
Orissa	1665	128662	13242.67	2351.68
Punjab	7137	358558	35018.49	4300.80
Rajasthan	5112	232177	30784.18	5258.02
Tamil Nadu	20601	1136265	103539.89	16536.32
Uttaranchal	744	43132	4884.41	961.36
Uttar Pradesh	9635	539739	64584.18	9577.02
West Bengal	6091	569838	39182.67	5699.17
All India	131268	7987780	926901.85	143621.41

Source: Transpose Monthly Review of Karnataka Economy.
Centre for Monitoring of Indian Economy, August 2004.

APPENDIX A-15.20

Leading Manufacturing Indicators: Karnataka

	Units	*1995-96*	*1996-97*	*1997-98*	*1998-99*	*1999-00*	*2000-01*
Factories	Nos	6730	7277	6854	7442	6952	7010
% to all India	Per Cent	4.92	5.48	5.04	5.65	5.28	5.34
Value of Output	Rs. Crores	30845	37268	42868	46167	42505	46259
% to all India	Per Cent	4.60	5.02	5.12	5.89	4.73	4.99
Net Value Added	Rs. Crores	6748	8772	8802	9309	8347	8302
% to all India	Per Cent	4.84	5.56	5.29	6.40	5.39	5.78
No. of workers	'000s	371	431	451	415	369	359
% to all India	Per Cent	4.86	5.98	5.90	6.52	5.87	5.85
VOP per worker	Rs. Lakh	8.3	8.64	9.50	11.13	11.53	12.88
Net VA per worker	Rs. Lakhs	1.82	2.03	1.95	2.24	2.26	2.31

Source: Centre for Monitoring Indian Economy, *Monthly Review of Karnataka Economy*, August 2004.

APPENDIX A-15.21

Principal Characteristics of Industrial Performance in Karnataka

(Rs. Lakhs)

Year	*Vol. of Output*	*Net Income*	*Net Value Added*	*Gross Value Added*	*Net Fixed Cap. Formation*	*Gr. Fixed Cap. Formation*	*Gr. Cap. Formation*
1990-91	1242437	206999	276914	327954	35704	86744	135768
1991-92	1517364	249309	342143	397753	19293	74903	136015
1992-93	1754241	314446	412190	475882	84387	148080	190039
1993-94	1876181	308142	413656	482052	90649	159045	168717
1994-95	2449771	464741	590619	672596	174055	256033	360526
1995-96	3084514	493145	674966	783272	228990	337296	464620
1996-97	3726782	610226	877222	1026246	265158	414182	500157
1997-98	4269078	542840	864723	1038591	360320	534188	549750

Source: EPW Weekly Research Foundation, *Annual Survey of Industries*, 2002.

APPENDIX A-15.22

Financial Performance of the Corporate Sector: Manufacturing Sector, Karnataka and India

	Units	*1995-96*	*1996-97*	*1997-98*	*1998-99*	*1999-00*	*2000-01*	*2001-02*	*2002-03*
Corporate Sector (Manufacturing Cos.)									
Sales									
Karnataka	% change	16.10	16.40	10.40	9.50	13.00	8.20	12.40	18.00
India	% change	11.90	6.20	8.70	17.10	17.70	-0.70	10.70	
Gross Fixed Assets									
Karnataka	% change	35.80	30.30	10.10	9.50	13.70	30.50	18.20	12.70
India	% change	19.40	16.60	14.10	12.40	10.60	8.50	6.00	
PBDIT									
Karnataka	% change	20.20	35.80	8.10	2.50	13.70	17.20	1.60	22.40
India	% change	4.70	4.20	2.50	9.70	9.30	2.00	20.80	
Profit After Tax									
Karnataka	% change	33.50	1.90	-3.00	-11.70	21.30	69.20	-63.40	137.70

Contd. ...

...Contd. ...

	Units	1995-96	1996-97	1997-98	1998-99	1999-00	2000-01	2001-02	2002-03
India	% change	-38.30	-22.20	-49.80	12.00	18.50	-52.10	247.80	
PBDIT/Sales									
Karnataka	per cent	12.90	15.60	15.10	14.30	14.70	16.20	14.70	15.10
India	per cent	12.50	12.20	11.60	10.90	10.20	10.30	11.40	
PAT/Sales									
Karnataka	per cent	3.60	3.20	2.80	2.60	2.70	4.70	1.60	2.90
India	per cent	2.30	1.70	0.80	0.90	1.00	0.50	2.40	
Debt/Equity									
Karnataka	times	1.43	1.61	1.75	1.62	1.53	1.39	1.40	1.25
India	times	1.35	1.48	1.54	1.43	1.41	1.48	1.32	
VOP/GFA									
Karnataka	times	2.06	1.75	1.60	1.63	1.64	1.42	1.24	1.29
India	times	1.70	1.50	1.45	1.50	1.59	1.44	1.52	

Source: *Monthly Review of Karnataka Economy*, Interstate Comparison, CMIE, August 2004, p. 11.

APPENDIX A-15.23

Industrial Approvals in Karnataka: 1990-1991 to 2001-2002

Item	1990-91	1991-92	1992-93	1993-94	1994-95	1995-96	1996-97	1997-98	1998-99	1999-00	2000-01	2001-02
Letter of Intent Issued	61	64	21	39	22	10	51	14	8	7	21	5
Industrial Licences Issued	23	33		6	10	2	6	4	3	3	7	2

Source: Technical Consultancy Services Organisation of Karnataka, (TECSOK), Bangalore.

APPENDIX A-15.24

Industrial Investment Proposals (State-wise) (August 1991-March 2004)

State/UT	IEL + LOI + DIL		Indus. Entre. Memo.		LOI + DIL	
	Nos.	%age	Filed	Invest. (Rs.Cr)	Granted	Invest. (Rs.Cr)
Maharashtra	11007	19.97	10449	237559	558	14567
Gujarat	6986	12.42	6548	201053	438	21028
Tamil Nadu	5076	9.03	4340	62143	736	11273
Uttar Pradesh	4837	8.6	4484	70350	353	9752
Andhra Pradesh	3922	6.97	3488	131844	434	10715
Haryana	3303	5.87	3070	37786	233	4318
West Bengal	2944	5.24	2854	48309	90	4047
Rajasthan	2639	4.69	2542	40461	97	1626
Punjab	2434	4.33	2251	50904	183	4887
Karnataka	2297	4.08	2064	61135	233	9598
Madhya Pradesh	2180	3.88	2039	43753	141	3160
Delhi	501	0.89	480	6503	21	30
All India	**56236**	**100**	**52318**	**1204732**	**3918**	**111136**

Source: Department of Industrial Policy and Promotion, *Annual Report*, 2003-04.

APPENDIX A-15.25

Major Projects on Hand: Karnataka (As of August 2004)

Projects	*Location*	*Cost*	*Status*
Karnataka Power Corpn. Ltd. (Bidadi Power Project)	Bidadi	4055.81	Proposed
Bangalore Mass Rapid Transit Ltd. (ELRTS Phase-I Project)	Bangalore	4000.00	Proposed
Nandi Economic Corridor Enterprises Ltd. (Bangalore-Mysore Infrastr5ucture Corridor Project)	Bangalore	3000.00	Proposed
Data Access (India) Ltd. (Telecom & Knowledge SEZ Project)	Kondasapura	2060.00	Proposed
Shoba Inner City Technopolies Pvt. Ltd. (Software Technology Park Project)	Sarjapur	2000.00	Proposed
Karnataka Housing Board (Township Project)	Iglurbannahalli	1800.00	Proposed
Reliance Industries Ltd. (Technology Park Project)	Bangalore	1600.00	Proposed
KVN Software Technologies Pvt. Ltd. (NS Info City 2 Project)	Doddaballapur	1500.00	Proposed
Bangalore International Airports Authority Ltd. (Devanahalli Airpoort Project)	Devanhalli	1260.00	Proposed
Soft City International Ltd. (Software Township Project)	Bangalore	1200.00	Proposed
Bangalore Water Supply & Sewerage Board (Bangalore Water Supply Phase-I Project)	Bangalore	1072.00	Under Implementation
Ind-Euro Pharma Ltd. (Drug Formulations Project)	Jigani	1012.50	Under Implementation
Chaitanya Properties Pvt. Ltd. (Township Cum Park Project)	Whitefield	1000.00	Proposed
Manipal-Eta Infotech (Software Park and R&D Centre Project)	Agara Village	1000.00	Proposed
Newscorp Ltd. (Convergence Centre Project)	Bangalore	1000.00	Announcement
Tata Power Broadband Co. Ltd. (Broadband Network Project)	Bangalore	880.00	Under Implementation
Unisys India Pvt. Ltd. (Bangalore Software Dev. Centre Project)	Bangalore	864.00	Announcement
Bangalore Water Supply & Sewerage Board (Bangalore Water Supply Phase-I I Project)	Bangalore	760.00	Announcement
GAIL (India) Ltd. (Mangalore-Coimkbatore-Bangalore Gas Pipeline Project)	Bangalore	660.00	Proposed
Infosys Technologies Ltd. (Sarjapur Software Dev. Centre Project)	Sarjapur	618.00	Under Implementation
UB General Invst. Ltd. (UB City Project)	Bangalore	600.00	Under Implementation
Bicon Ltd. ('Statin' Drug Capacity Expansion Project)	Bangalore	500.00	Proposed
Narayana Institute of Medical Sciences (Health City Project)	Bangalore	500.00	Announcement
Southern Railways (Bangalore-Mysore Railway Project)	Hosur Road	500.00	Under Implementation
Huawei Technologies India Pvt. Ltd. (Bangalore Software Dev. Centre Project)	Bangalore	480.00	Under Implementation
Karnataka Road Devp. Corpn. Ltd. (Bangalore-Mysore Road (SH-17) Project)	Bangalore	471.00	Announcement
Applicomp (India) Ltd. (Electric Appliances Project)	Attibele	450.00	Proposed
Bangalore Development Authority (Rajarajeshwarinagar Township Project)	Rajarajeshnagar	450.00	Under Implementation
Government of Karnataka (Bangalore-Devanahalli Expressway Project)	Bangalore	400.00	Announcement
Peenya Power Co. Pvt. Ltd. (Peenya Power Project)	Peenya	390.60	Under Implementation
Gas Transportation & Infrastructure Co. Ltd. (Chennai-Bangalore Pipeline Project)	Bangalore	325.00	Announcement
Container Corpn. Of India Ltd. (Cold Storage Project)	Bangalore	300.00	Announcement
Enron India Pvt. Ltd. (Internet Data Centre Project)	Bangalore	300.00	Proposed
Primenet Global Ltd. (Internet Gateway Project)	Bangalore	300.00	Under Implementation
Norland Investment Pvt. Ltd. (IT Park Project)	Bangalore	295.00	Proposed
Pritech Park Ltd. (IT Park & Allied Infrastructure Project	Bangalore	280.00	Proposed
ITC Hotels Ltd. (Bangalore Hotel Project)	Bangalore	250.00	Proposed
Lakeview Tourism Corpn. (Commercial Complex Project)	Hebbal	250.00	Proposed
Sunlife Technologies Ltd. (Multiplex Project)	Nagawara	235.00	Proposed
Supreme Buildcap Ltd. (Integrated Complex Project)	Devarabisanahalli	230.00	Proposed
Southern Railways (Bangalore-Sathyamangalam Rail Project)	Bangalore	225.00	Proposed
Agri Gold Estates & Entertainments Ltd. (A musement Parks Project)	Bangalore	200.00	Proposed
Pizza Corner India Pvt. Ltd. (Restaurant Project)	Bangalore	200.00	Under Implementation
Trilogy E Business Software India Pvt. Ltd. (Bangalore Computer Software Project)	Bangalore	200.00	Under Implementation
Wockhardt Hospital Ltd. (Bangalore Hospital Project)	Bangalore	200.00	Proposed
Total		**39873.91**	

Source: *Monthly Review of Karnataka Economy*, CMIE, August 2004, pp.138-139.

APPENDIX A-15.26

Registered SSI Units in Karnataka (Cumulative)

Year	*No.*	*Investment* (Rs. Lakh)	*Employment* in '000s
1970-71	5798	5750	92
1980-81	27669	26414	330
1990-91	115411	108867	808
1991-92	125969	127490	870
1992-93	137337	147262	933
1993-94	149951	167153	1003
1994-95	163454	193616	1077
1995-96	175310	226776	1148
1996-97	188839	262587	1216
1997-98	223241	329038	1349
1998-99	236663	388790	1419
1999-00	252601	462496	1507
2000-01	269155	527654	1593
2001-02	286119	575538	1666
2002-03	298148	616374	1723
2003-04	310438	653428	1779
2004-05	321676	691969	1829

Source: Department of Industries and Commerce, Government of Karnataka.

APPENDIX A-15.27

District-wise SSI Units Target and Achievements 2003-04 and 2004-05 (Up to 31.7.2004)

Name of the District	*2003-04*			*2004-05*		
	Target	*Achievements*	*%*	*Target up to 7/04*	*Achievements as on 31.7.04*	*%*
Bangalore (Urban)	960	1497	155.94	332	462	139.16
Belgaum	528	529	100.19	168	185	110.12
Bellary	405	407	100.49	123	60	48.78
Bijapur	370	382	103.24	104	53	50.96
Bidar	315	252	80	90	26	28.89
Chickmagalur	320	323	100.94	96	82	85.42
Chitradurga	365	361	98.9	100	72	72
Kodagu	60	61	101.67	16	14	87.5
Dharwad	660	676	102.42	206	146	70.87
Gulbarga	560	508	90.71	144	73	50.69
Hassan	610	610	100	178	23	12.92
Uttara Kannada	380	381	100.26	138	26	18.84
Mangalore (DK)	728	728	100	180	216	120
Kolar	470	421	89.57	132	31	23.48
Mandya	360	341	94.72	100	84	84
Mysore	680	595	87.5	196	60	30.61
Raichur	480	377	78.57	84	21	25
Shimoga	430	437	101.63	128	106	82.81
Tumkur	660	660	100	192	107	55.73
Bangalore (Rural)	774	736	95.09	148	72	48.65

Contd. ...

...Contd. ...

Name of the District	*2003-04*			*2004-05*		
	Target	*Achievements*	*%*	*Target up to 7/04*	*Achievements as on 31.7.04*	*%*
Bagalkote	305	330	108.2	68	21	30.88
Chamrajnagar	160	176	110	56	48	85.71
Davangere	420	386	91.9	124	73	58.87
Gadag	260	249	95.77	80	32	40
Haveri	210	262	124.76	64	45	70.31
Koppal	210	233	110.95	64	6	9.38
Udupi	320	299	93.44	100	19	19
Total	**12000**	**12220**	**101.83**	**3411**	**2163**	**63.41**

Source: Department of Industries and Commerce, Government of Karnataka.

Chapter 16

Tourism, Entertainment and IT-enabled Services

16.1 Tourism

16.1.1 An Overview

Tourism is an important service and entertainment linked economic activity. The promotion of any place as a tourist destination leads to the economic development of that area and opens various kinds of employment avenues for the local people as well. These are in the nature of tour operations, travel agencies, restaurants and hotels, and working as guides.

Tourism by its very nature is omnipresent in all segments of life. Tourism is an important service industry which contributes to the national and state income substantially. Travel and tourism in India are expected to generate Rs. 1,564 billion making India the 22nd largest tourism market in the world. It is projected to grow at an annual rate of 9.1 per cent through 2011. It accounts for 5.3 per cent of the GDP and 6 per cent of all employment. By virtue of having strong linkages with many other sectors of the economy, tourism brings about an overall development of the economy through increase in employment, stimulation of business activities, increase in business diversity, tax collection, and sales of goods and services. It enhances the community pride and concern for community history, culture, attractions and artifacts; participating in protection, excavation, restoration and maintenance of archaeological, historic and heritage sites, monuments and places, and enabling friendly conservation of natural resources as tourist attractions.

India is the leading destination in the South Asia Region with a share of 41.2 per cent of tourist arrivals to South Asia in 2000. According to World Tourism Organization (WTO), international tourism receipts in India have been estimated at US$ 3.3 billion ($1,250 per person) in 2000, with a growth of 9.5 per cent over the year.

Domestic tourism has grown substantially during the last few years due to the increase in income levels and emergence of a tourism oriented dynamic middle class. Government of India announced the first ever major Tourism Policy in November 1982. In July 1991, coinciding with the onset of economic reforms, tourism was declared as a priority sector attracting foreign investment. In May 1992, a National Action Plan was drawn up with the important objectives of: i) preservation of national heritage and environment, ii) increase in India's share in world tourism, iii) socio-economic development of areas, and iv) increasing employment opportunities, etc. A New National Tourism Policy 2002-2007 has now been drafted to keep pace with the developments taking place around the world with major features like facilitating the development of a dynamic private sector in tourism, providing for people's participation in development as well as sharing the benefits of tourism, coordinating the efforts of different government departments, enhancing infrastructure, liberation of the visa regime, uniformity and rationalisation of taxation structure and ensuring tourism safety and security. Certainly, Karnataka has a major stake in tourism in the country.

16.1.2 Tourism in Karnataka

As per the survey conducted by the Ministry of Tourism, Government of India, Bangalore-Mysore stretch of Karnataka is one of the most visited destinations in India by foreign tourists. The state of Karnataka, formerly known as Mysore is a state of strong contrasts, with the modern industrialised city of Bangalore at one extreme and expanse of rural farming areas at the other. It has some of the most interesting historic architectures in India. For the world-weary traveller, Karnataka's dramatically different theme destinations will be a perennial source of inspiration. In fact, Karnataka is Little India—this state has everything that India has to offer like, world heritage sites, breathtaking hill stations, spectacular water falls, exotic wildlife, gripping adventure options, sensational beaches, renowned pilgrim centres, colourful festivals, throbbing nightlife, etc. India's most well kept secret so far as tourism goes; Karnataka is all set to draw the customer on a mind-boggling spread of experiences (GoK, 2002-07).

As per the latest data available in 2004, Karnataka's share in the total foreign tourists' visits in India was 6.4 per cent and in respect of domestic tourists it was 3.62 per cent and is the seventh preferred state in case of domestic tourists and eighth preferred state in case of foreign tourists. The most preferred states in order of share in domestic tourists are Uttar Pradesh, Andhra Pradesh, Tamil Nadu, Rajasthan, Delhi, West Bengal, Uttaranchal and Karnataka. This order of preference is slightly variant insofar as foreigners are concerned i.e., Maharashtra, Tamil Nadu, Uttar Pradesh, Rajasthan, Delhi, West Bengal, Uttaranchal and Karnataka followed by Andhra Pradesh.

Important Tourist Places in Karnataka

Karnataka has been ruled and shaped under the reigns of many dynasties including the Mauryas, Satavahanas, Gangas, Chalukyas and the Vijayanagar kings. The individual dynasties and the rulers have uniquely offered distinctive arts, architecture, history and culture to the state. There are a large number of tourist attractions, as can be seen from Box 16.1.

The state provides varied nature of tourist attractions, wildlife sanctuaries at Bandipur and Nagarhole, the turbulent leap of Sharavathi at Jogfalls, the myriad coloured fountains of the picturesque Brindavan Garden at Mysore, the beaches of Karwar, the sun setting scene at Agumbe, the famous architectural beauty at Badami, Aihole and Pattadakal, the tall monolithic Gometeshwar statue at Shravanabelagola and Karkal, the devastating ruins of Hampi, the world famous Hoysala temples at Belur and Halebidu, dome of Golgumbaz at Bijapur and bird sanctuary at Ranganatittu, etc. Further there are many more attractive tourist spots, which have not come to light. This again reinforces the vast potential of the tourism sector in Karnataka.

World Heritage Centres

It is a matter great privilege and pride for Karnataka to have two ancient, important monuments included in the list of World Heritage Centres:

1. Hampi - Located in Hospet *taluka*, Anegundi *Gram Panchayat* in Bellary district.
2. Pattadakal - Located in Badami *taluka*, Aihole *Gram Panchayat* in Bagalko district.

The group of monuments at Hampi was included in 1986, and the groups of monuments at Pattadakal was included in 1987 (Appendices A-16.1 and A-16.2).

16.1.3 Tourist Arrivals

It is rather a complex exercise to assess the exact number of tourist arrivals at any given point of time. Nevertheless, the data provided by the Karnataka Department of Tourism are provided in Table 16.1.

TABLE 16.1

Tourist Visits in Karnataka

Years	*Domestic*	*Foreign*
1996-97	11760836 (7.36)	246862 (4.49)
1997-98	11996053(7.13)	249836 (4.51)
1998-99	15902666 (8.34)	229720 (3.93)
1999-00	18000000 (8.18)	208000 (3.53)
2000-01	14117464 (5.97)	140703 (2.59)
2001-02	8678670 (3.22)	59545 (1.15)
2002-03	11175292 (3.62)	249903 (3.72)
2003-04 (till Oct., 05)	4430814	530225 (6.39)

Note: Figures in parentheses represent Karnataka's share in all-India.
Source: Commissioner of Tourism, Government of Karnataka.

The data suggest a steady trend in the tourist visits. While the domestic tourist visits almost stagnated, that of foreigners increased manyfolds particularly in 2001-2002 and 2002-03. But it is a matter of concern that Karnataka is losing out on the domestic sector as its share in all-india which was high at 8.34 per cent in 1998-99 declined thereafter and stood at a low of 3.62 per cent in 2002-03. Places like Mysore, Belur, Halebeedu, Mangalore, Jog Falls, Bijapur, Hampi/Hospet, Gadag, Aihole, Chitradurga together account for over 85 per cent of the total tourist arrivals in the state.

The destination preference of tourists in Karnataka can be seen from Table 16.2.

It is interesting to note a discernable shift in domestic tourists' preferences. Traditionally preferred places like Mysore, Shravanabelagola, Belur and Halebeedu showed a decline in tourist visits. On the other hand, places like Hampi/Hospet, Aihole, Pattadakal, Chitradurga and Badami have come into

BOX 16.1

Tourist Places in Karnataka

Tourism type	*Places*	*Comments*
Hill Stations	Agumbe, Kudremukh Nandi Hills, Kemmanagundi, Madikeri, BR Hills	Mostly in Western Ghats
Wildlife Sanctuaries	Dandeli, Bhadra, and Cauvery Wildlife Sanctuaries, BR Hills Sanctuary	Mostly in Western Ghats
Bird Sanctuaries	Gudavi, Kaggaladu, Kokrebelur, Ranganthittu	
National Parks	Anshi, Kudremukh, Bannerghatta, Rajiv Gandhi (Nagarhole), Bandipur	Mostly in Western Ghats
Water Falls	Unchalli, Magod, Jog, Abbey, Kalhatti, Lalguli, Hebbe, Sivasamundram, Sathodi, Iruppu.	Along Cauvery and west flowing rivers
Beaches	Karwar, Gokarna, Marawanthe, Malpe, Kaupo, Murdeshwar, Mangalore	Coastline of Karnataka
Monuments/Heritage	Bidar fort, Gulbarga fort, Bijapur, Kittur, Badmi, Pattadakal, Aihole, Lakkundi, Hampi, Chitradurga, Tipu's fort, Bangalore palace, Hoysaleswara temple, Srirangapatnam, Chennakeswara temple, Mysore palace, Belur, Halebid	Spread all over the state
Pilgrim Centres	Basavakalyan, Gurudwara Nanak Saheb, Khwaja Bando Nawaz Durgah, Sharanabasaveswara, Banashankari, Yellamma temple, Gokarna, Banavasi, Karkala, Udupi, Mookambika temple, Murdeshwar temple, Mudabidri, Dharmasthala, Talacauvery, Nanjangud, Shivaganga, Sringerim Siddhaganga, Devarayanadurga, Iskon temple in Bangalore, Inam Dattatraya Peetha, Shravanabelagola, Melkote, Talakad, Lakkundi	All over the state
Cuisines	North Karnataka, Udupi, Malnad, Coorg	Specialised in regional goods
Fairs and Festivals	Kundadri, Agumbe, Kodachadri, Kudremukh, Nandi Hills, Kemmangaundi, Madikeri, BR Hills	Depicting cultural heritage
Romantic	Kundargi, Agumbe, Kodachadri, Kudremukh, Nandi hills, Kemmanagundi, Madikeri, BR Hills	Mostly in Western Ghats
Adventure	Western Ghats, Badami, Hampi	Rock climbing, trekking
Water Rafting/Sports	Kali river in Dandeli, Honnemaradu, Kemphole, Agumbe, Backwaters of Karwar and Gokarna beaches	Coastal and Western Ghat regions

Note: This list of names of places is not exhaustive, but only suggestive.

prominence. In the recent period the number of tourists' visits to these places has exceeded one lakh and this indicates that tourists prefer Karnataka as an important heritage destination.

16.1.4 Employment and Income from Tourism in Karnataka.

Tourism sector has a large potential for employment opportunities, both direct and indirect. Tourism industry in Karnataka is providing employment to about 1.56 lakh persons directly and to another 3.59 lakh persons indirectly. Estimated revenue generation from this sector is of the order of Rs. 734.71 crore in the year 2002-03. Further, this sector has another unique feature of having highest multiplier effect due to its strong linkages with the other sectors. Being a labour-intensive industry, tourism and its related activities generate income and provide employment to women, rural artisans, educated unemployed and youth. It also facilitates developments in the periphery of tourist destination in terms of power, water, transport, agriculture and allied sectors, *khadi* and village and small-scale industries such as handlooms, handicrafts and hotels, etc. This sector also has a high employment output ratio, i.e., for every additional investment of Rs. 1 million, employment generated is estimated to be of the order of 47.5 direct jobs and 89 indirect jobs that is in sub-sector of hotels, restaurants, shop establishments, etc. A private study has estimated the employment generation arising out of tourism in Karnataka both direct as well as indirect

TABLE 16.2

Domestic Tourist Visits to Popular Destinations in Karnataka

(No. in Lakhs)

Places	*1993-94*	*1994-95*	*1995-96*	*1998-99*	*2001-02*
Mysore	21.70	21.62	22.67	24.15	10.40
Mangalore	2.70	2.74	2.91	3.24	3.20
Belur	12.65	15.08	15.97	19.87	8.63
Halebidu	6.07	6.87	6.92	6.22	8.31
S'belagola	2.91	2.03	2.03	2.24	o.59
Bijapur	3.80	3.48	3.56	2.58	2.27
Badami	0.12	0.15	0.17	0.15	0.34
Aihole	1.35	1.05	0.97	0.96	1.83
Pattadakal	0.22	0.29	0.31	0.32	0.61
Jog Falls	0.53	4.14	6.02	6.22	0.32
Nandi Hills	2.70	2.78	2.83	2.50	-
Chitradurga	0.82	0.84	0.95	0.88	1.34
Raichur	0.67	0.71	0.76	0.79	0.39
Hampi	1.43	1.54	1.84	1.78	2.70
Hospet	0.67	0.79	0.93	0.77	
Udupi	-	-	-	-	0.61
Shimoga	-	-	-	-	0.80
Gadag	-	-	-	-	1.66

Source: Department of Tourism, Government of Karnataka.

placed at 369,335 persons of which direct would be 156,498 and the rest are indirect.

Karnataka attracted about 6.4 per cent of the foreign tourists who visited India in 2004 and takes the seventh position among all the states. As per the Ministry of Tourism, Government of India, the foreign exchange earned by tourism for the country has been increasing steadily from Rs. 9,920 crore in 1995-96 to Rs. 14,006 in 2000-01. Over the years the earnings have been recording a growth rate ranging between 8.12 per cent and 11.42 per cent per annum. Based on Karnataka's share as also the spending by foreign tourists, total foreign exchange earnings in Karnataka have been estimated at Rs. 32,212 lakh in 2000-01.

16.1.5 Tourist Infrastructure

As far as the integrated tourist infrastructure and facilities are concerned Karnataka is having fairly good infrastructure facilities in terms of internal transport, power, communication network, banking, good education and medical facilities, accommodation, tourist information, basic amenities, entertainment and recreational avenues, etc. A Study Report on Preparation of 20 years 'Perspective Plan for Development of Sustainable Tourism in Karnataka' reveals measures of satisfaction, some of which are shown in Figure 16.1. The study also highlights some of the specific aspects of dissatisfaction. For instance, foreign tourists were unhappy with the railway connection, banking facilities, emergency health care, domestic air connectivity within Karnataka, etc. Some of the other problems faced by the foreign tourists relate to cuisine food, local transport in small towns, accessibility to all the places of interest, insufficient ATM facilities and money changers at tourist places, safety and security in lonely destinations, harassment and cheating by the local miscreants, pollution and cleanliness, etc. The difficulties faced by domestic tourists are not different either. The report has strongly suggested a large number of improvements in infrastructure to make tourism a pleasure with safety.

Recently, the state government, however, has accorded special importance to tourism infrastructure projects like hotels and accommodation, information centers, landscaping, signage and transportation. But with the fast growing economy and considering the vast tourism potential in the state, the existing infrastructure facilities need to be strengthened and modernised on a fast track basis. Moreover, as infrastructure development require massive investments and it is not possible for the state government to provide all the infrastructure, attracting private sector to play a dominant role in tourism infrastructure is very important. This is the reason that Karnataka Government formulated the State's

FIGURE 16.1

Satisfaction Levels–Foreigners and Domestic Tourists

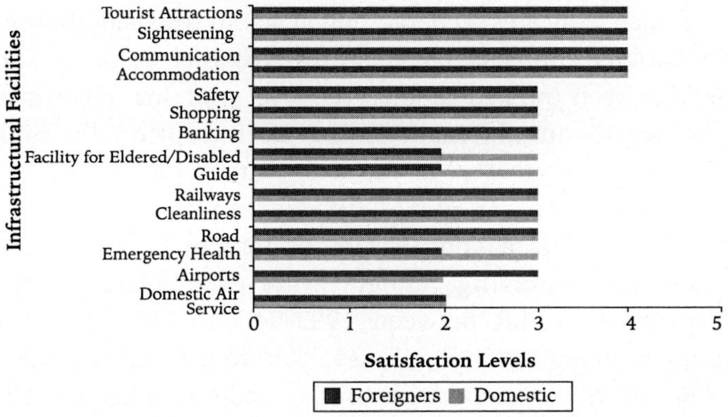

Tourism Policy in 1992. As for the institutional arrangements, the Karnataka Government, Department of Tourism has created two of its subsidiaries, namely Karnataka State Tourist Development Corporation (KSTDC) and Jungle Lodges and Resorts (JLR) to take care of the overall tour arrangements of the tourists.

In all, there are more than 100 travel and tour agents who are operating throughout the state. There are a good number of agents approved by the Indian Tourism Development Corporation. The state government has stipulated specific and stringent criteria and parameters for selection of tours and travel agents like location, furnished office, information collection, handling capacity and basic facilities, etc. Most of the approved travel and tour operators provide the services like hotel booking, ticket booking and package tours. The focus is to provide all possible tourist-friendly arrangements.

16.1.6 Investments on Tourism and Financing

During the period of the first Tourism Policy 1992-1997 the state government could mop up investments of over Rs.900 crore in 280 approved projects. In the second revised policy 1997-2002, master plan was drawn to attract a massive investment of Rs. 4,500 crore in tourism sector of which three-fourth was expected from the private sector and the rest from the state government. In the 11-year period 1992-93 to 2002-03 the state had approved 765 tourism projects in the private sector amounting to Rs. 1,364 crore.

The Department of Tourism, Government of Karnataka is the catalyst agent to promote tourism in the state. Further the department has the overall responsibility of implementing the state sponsored schemes through the state government budget and the centrally sponsored schemes with the assistance of Government of India and the projects taken up by private entrepreneurs in accordance with the Tourism Policy. The state plan schemes include (a) development of beach resorts, (b) tourist bureaus for disseminating information, (c) tourist publicity for aggressive marketing, (d) tourist promotion to create awareness about the places of tourist centres, through road signs, touch screen kiosks, documentary films, etc, (e) develop tourism as industry, (f) tourism festivals to promote and showcase art, culture and tradition of Karnataka e.g., Mysore Dasara, Hampi Utsav, Bijapur Utsav, etc, and (g) tourist lodges and buildings. The sports tourism which was hitherto looked after by the Tourism Department has since been discontinued from the Tenth Five Year Plan. There are 14 *yatrinivas\yatrikas*, 3 tourist complexes, 22 wayside facilities, 26 public amenities and 8 tourist reception centres which are maintained by the State Tourism Department. To promote private sector investment, the state has approved several projects in the private sector in the hotel industry (Appendix A-16.6).

The centrally sponsored schemes include tourism infrastructure facilities at tourist destinations whereby Government of India provides financial assistance to the state in the ratios of 80:20, 50:50 and 25:75 depending upon the nature of the project. These are *yatrinivas*, *yatrikas*, wayside ameneties, tourist reception centres, public convenience, drinking water facilities, and flood lighting of monuments, etc. and the available infrastructure is given below:

BOX 16.2

Tourism Infrastructure Facilities at Tourist Destinations

1.	*Yatrinivas*	:	24 (includes 7 under construction).
2.	Way Side Facilities	:	27 (includes 5 under construction)
3.	Public Convenience and Drinking Water Facilities		36 (includes 10 in the pipeline)
4.	Eco-tourism Facilities	:	8
5.	Tourist Village	:	1

The outlay for the state schemes during the Ninth Five Year Plan was Rs. 8,000 lakh and the expenditure amounted to Rs. 5,664 lakh. For the Tenth Plan period the outlay set is Rs. 7,500 lakh which is lower than the

Ninth Plan, but provides increased role of private sector in tourism industry. For 2003-04, the outlay proposed is Rs. 2,200 lakh which includes Rs. 500 lakh towards Central schemes. The revenue earned from tourism in the 15-year period ending 2004-05 showed a mixed trend. Nevertheless the revenue shot up from Rs. 5,179 lakh in 1990-91 to Rs. 734.71 lakh in 2002-03. But a slowdown is expected in 2004-05 to Rs. 606.06 lakh. The plan expenditure on tourism in Karnataka rose from Rs. 2.04 crore in 1990-91 to Rs. 17.00 crore in 2003-04. But it does not show any secular trend in between, rather it is a mixed trend (Appendix A-16.7).

The tourism related projects are financed by the: (i) Tourism Finance Corporation of India (TCFI), (ii) Karnataka State Financial Corporation (KSFC), (iii) Infrastructure Development Corporation (Karnataka) Ltd. (IDECK), Infrastructure Development and Finance Company (IDFC) and other state and all-India institutions such as IDBI, ICICI, and HDFC. So far, most of the assistance has been for setting up hotels and now with diversified tourism projects, adequate finances need to flow into the other segments also.

16.1.7 Tourism Promotion and Tourism Products

Apart from the Karnataka Department of Tourism, there are two subsidiary organisations functioning, which also provide direct facilities to tourists namely Karnataka State Tourism Development Corporation (KSTDC) and the Jungle Lodges and Resorts (JL&R). While KSTDC established in 1971 arranges package tours and provides hospitality facilities for tourists targeting the budget class, the JL&R provides eco-friendly tourism for upper class tourists both domestic and international. The Karnataka Government is also considering a computerised reservation system, which would act as a hub for the entire state and the southern states as well. Concerted efforts have been made to explore those interesting places, which have not come into limelight yet. Such efforts have revealed that there are around 280 unexplored places so far. KSTDC has about 29 NGOs listed for adventure tourism. The income generated by KSTDC rose sharply from Rs. 179 lakh in 1993-94 to Rs. 515 lakh in 2002-03.

The Jungle Lodges and Resorts (JLR) was established in 1981 as a joint sector organisation between M/s Tiger Tops Nepal and the Government of Karnataka. From 1989 onwards, it is fully owned by the Government of Karnataka. JLR has been set up with the primary objective to promote eco-tourism in a sustainable manner. The stakeholders of the JLR are the forests, the local communities and the customers who derive substantial benefits. It offers wildlife safari, trekking, sport fishing, river rafting, outdoor camping and also educates general public about the significance of various animals and creatures. Another pride of JLR is that it is ranked among the five wild life resorts in the world and is maintaining an exceptionally high standard. About 16,047 tourists visited JLR in 1998-99 out of which 75 per cent were foreigners. This organisation is a good earner of foreign exchange and has been reporting higher profit each year. Income generated by JLR between 1993-94 and 2002-03 more than doubled from Rs. 5,424 lakh to Rs. 12,607 lakh. JLR covers six important tourist projects like: (i) The Bannerghatta Nature Camp, Bannerghatta, (ii) Cauvery Fishing Camp, Bhuvaneswari, (ii) BR Hills Wildlife Adventure Resort, BR Hills, (iv) Kabini River Lodge, Kabini, (v) Devbag Beach Resort, Karwar and (vi) Kali Wilderness and Adventure Camp, Dandeli. JLR is now much sought after by other states wanting to develop eco-tourism (Gujarat, Chhattisgarh, Nagaland and Andamans). JLR is diversifying its activities to include consultancy and training also.

Tourism Products

Karnataka is offering a variety of tourism products: (i) adventure tourism targeting age group of 35-40, (ii) Ecotourism, (iii) heritage tourism (iv) religious tourism (v) spiritual tourism (vi) hill tourism, (vii) coastal and beach tourism, (viii) leisure tourism, (ix) business tourism, (x) entertainment tourism, (xi) education tourism, and (xii) wildlife tourism, etc.

To attract tourists the state organises various festivals such as Hampi Festival and Karnataka Rajyotsava Day on 1st November, Mysore Dasara festival in October, Pattadakal and Kittur festivals in January, Kite festival in July, Karavalli festival of Dakshina Kannada, Navarasapura festival, Hoysala festival all in February and so on. Apart from these festivals there are also few other religious and music festivals like Mahamastabhishek of Shravanabelogola, Badami festival, annual music festival of Dharwad, Chitradurga, etc. The Mahamastabhishek of Shravanabelogala is celebrated once in 12 years and the last such celebration was in 1993.

Another important product of tourism in Karnataka has been the implementation of a noval scheme called 'Athithi'—open your doors to opportunity. Karnataka, the India's theatre inspiration with its diverse tourism products is capturing the imagination of the traveller. The state invites each and everybody to be a part of Karnataka's tourism revolution by setting up a homestay.

This is an accommodation option wherein tourists are offered quality boarding and lodging in such off the volunteers' own home at an affordable cost. Running a homestay will be a rich and rewarding experience. A vastly popular concept worldwide, homestays are the perfect solution to cater to today's discerning tourist who prefers to experience a slice-of-life of the land that he is visiting, shorn of all the frills of star-rated hospitality. Homestays add a personal touch to the travel experience. Given our rich tradition of hospitality, a homestay is the best way to showcase the quintessence of Karnataka. There are some stipulations for volunteers to set up a homestay like being a native of Karnataka with a basic awareness of our culture, tradition and cuisines, etc. Above all, a personal touch and genuine warmth are what make homestays a resounding success.

Karnataka government launched recently a programme called, 'Connect' a private-public partnership from strength to supremacy. Connect is an initiative that will propel the comprehensive development of tourism in Karnataka by synergising the individual strengths of the tourism trade and the government to transform Karnataka into South-Asia premiere tourists destination. It is an institution that will ensure a level playing ground for all tourism service providers and aims to build a close and result oriented relationship between the two segments, foster collaborative initiatives and provide structure to the joint efforts of the private and public segments, facilitate exchange of ideas between the government and the private enterprises. The seven ways to Connect are: i) get noticed globally, ii) hit the road, iii) play host, iv) strike a deal, v) stay in touch, vi) get online and vii) invest.

Publicity

It was mentioned earlier that Karnataka Government has been organising various festivals for projecting the state as a paradise waiting to be explored. The Department of Tourism started the publicity drive from 1975-76 onwards and adopting an aggressive marketing plan for the tourism destinations. For this during 2002 a private agency namely M/s Stark Communications Private Ltd. was hired to promote and brand Karnataka tourism. The strategies adopted for this are:

(i) Participation in national and international tourism events.

(ii) Presenting of promotional literatures, electronic media like website.

(iii) Issuing advertisements in national and international magazines and newspapers.

(iv) An exclusive toll-free telephone line for tourist enquiries.

(v) A comprehensive Directory namely, *Karnataka Traveller* has already been brought out.

(vi) The department provides hospitality to the freelance journalists, photographers, travel writers, and farm tours. Delegates from Singapore and Japan also have availed this facility.

Karnataka has generated interest at key international trade fairs in Berlin, London and Dubai and has acquired a comprehensive website. The Karnataka Department of Tourism has been participating regularly in various tourists festivals such as India Festival of USSR in Karnataka, Karnataka Festival at New Delhi, India International Trade Fair, New Delhi, the India Tourism and Industrial Fair at Chennai, World Tourism Day, Asia Travel Market, ITB, Berlin, Expos, WTM, etc.

Further it had the privilege of organising the World Tourism Meet at Bangalore in April 1992 at the instance of Commissioner of South Asian Division of World Tourism Organization an affiliated body of the United Nations under the aegis of the Union minister of tourism. About 30 delegates from South Asia and also the member countries of WTO participated.

16.1.8 Karnataka Tourism Policy

A new dimension was given to the tourism sector by the state declaring it as an industry in November 1988. In 1992, State Tourism Policy was brought into focus for the first time in the country and private entrepreneurs were encouraged to invest capital in the tourism sector. Further refinements in policies formulated in 1992,1997 and 2002 aimed at more room for the private sector to play by deregulation, enhancing incentives of all kinds and provide improvement in tourist infrastructure in a balanced way so as to reduce regional disparities. The New Tourism Policy 2002-2007 envisages that 10 years from now, tourism will be Karnataka's most important economic activity, and would be accorded top priority. It will work very closely with private enterprises, international resources, local bodies and all segments of the tourism sector to make tourism as number one industry in the state. The Tourism Policy also emphasises the need for coordination among all connected departments such as Revenue, Finance, Energy, Public Works, Forest, Rural Development and Panchayat Raj, Karnataka Electricity Board, Ecology and Environment, Transport and Home.

According to the Department of Tourism, the state has accomplished all the provisions and measures contained in the first two policies. Encouraged by the considerable flow of investment from the private sector, the state government intends to give tourism a new thrust. Thus the latest policy 2002-2007 has made drastic changes by deregulating further making the tourism sector the most investor friendly and also highly remunerative. The most striking feature of the policy 2002-2007 is to make available all concessions offered under the Industrial Policy of Karnataka 2002-2007 for private investments in the tourism sector. The state government will function as a catalyst and confine itself to infrastructure development, dissemination of information and coordination of sectoral activities to create conditions for attracting substantial private sector investment in tourism sector. The Tourism Policy by and large aims at promotion of tourism related activities and enhancing employment and income generation across all sections of the society. Now private sector is encouraged to invest in hotels, beach resorts, eco-friendly resorts, wayside facilities, adventure/recreation centres like golf courses, aero sports, amusement parks and other tourism related activities. "The Vision and Mission Statement" of the Karnataka Tourism Policy 2002-2007 is summarised below:

- To be among the pre-eminent tourist destinations in Asia, with market leadership and dominance in the following segments:
  - Upscale tourism (both national and international),
  - Heritage tourism,
  - Ecotourism,
  - Conventions and conferences,
  - Exhibitions,
  - Cruises, and
  - Theme parks
- to be on par with the best in the world,
- to excel in every facet of the tourism industry, and
- to emerge as a benchmark for other destinations.

Awards

1. The Department of Tourism, Government of Karnataka has been conferred with the 'Best Tourism Performance State' award in 1998 by GoI which is the most highly acclaimed award in the industry.
2. Jungle Lodges and Resorts Ltd., Bangalore was awarded the 'Best Eco-Tourism Organisation of India' during 1999.
3. A special award was conferred in 1999 to Kabini River Lodges as 'one among the Top 5 wildlife resorts in the world'.
4. During 2003-04, the Government of India conferred yet another award to Karnataka Tourism for production of best publicity materials during 2003-04.

16.1.9 Assessment, Prospects and Concerns

There is a move by the Government of India for the first time to unlock forests for controlled tourism. So far, wildlife tourism is allowed under strict control in national parks and sanctuaries. But lot of scope exists to promote ecotourism with incentives built for NGOs and local communities. In order to promote foreign tourist arrivals, simplification of visa procedure and ensuring speedier visas for visitors, improvement and expansions of infrastructure are some of the features to be completed on a fast track basis.

According to the Union Ministry of Tourism, there has been an impressive growth in foreign tourist arrivals in the current year. Simplification of visa procedure and ensuring speedier visas for visitors, improvement and expansions of infrastructure are some of the features completed to attract more foreign tourists.

Tourism industry in India provides employment to about 50 million people (direct and indirect). Therefore, even a modest 10 per cent growth in tourism sector would generate 5 million new jobs every year and the major beneficiaries are the weaker sections of the society women and rural artisans. According to the World Travel and Tourism Council, India is the second fastest growing travel and tourism economy in the world. Following SARS in Southeast Asia, conflict in Iraq and weak global economy, tourism industry suffered a major setback in the past 3 years and now is staging to come back after a robust recovery. The set back led to a drop of 1.2 per cent in tourist inflows. Now there is a visible change in the trend, which is that US and Europe have become expensive destinations and hence opportunity has befallen on India as an alternative destination. It will be a great opportunity to attract more foreign tourists. Countries like Malaysia are attracting 15 million tourists whereas India could get only one-third of this. India can offer a variety of tourist's products with its comparative advantage.

India is now in the limelight in medical treatment at affordable cost and hospitals and therefore medical tourism is considered as a major area with a potential of Rs. 5,000-10,000 crore by 2012. Since southern states of Tamil Nadu and Karnataka are emerging as Asia's gateway to medical treatment, both the states should capitalise the opportunity to derive maximum benefit. In the Railway Budget 2004-05 there is a proposal by Railways to run tourist special, 'village-on-wheels' trains of ordinary sleeper class to places of religious and historical importance. Karnataka is bound to derive maximum benefit out of this.

Foreign tourists arrivals in 2003 were 2.8 million, a 14 per cent increase over 2002. Karnataka was one of the three preferred destinations besides Goa and Kerala and these three states have done a good job of marketing themselves. Foreign exchange earnings rose significantly to Rs. 17,049 crore in 2003.Tourism is a highly employment-intensive sector though it accounts for 1 per cent of GDP. It provides indirect and direct employment to 8-10 persons (all categories) per foreign tourist arriving in India. Karnataka gets 4 per cent of foreign tourists of the country; it may be little more now following its vigorous marketing lately.

Taking all these into account with a 5 per cent share of foreign tourists, the additional jobs that can be created will be around 1.4 million over the years.

There are some initiatives already taken by Karnataka. The state government is making all efforts to include Shravanabelagola, Belur and Halebeedu in the list of world heritage centres. As an improvement in infrastructure development with Rs. 330 crore investment on a 141 km highway, the Bangalore-Mysore Infrastructure Corridor (BMIC) is expected to be completed by March 2005. The four-lane road is designed for speeds of 100 kmph which should reduce travel time to Mysore making it possible to reach in 120 minutes. All these will open a gateway to attract more tourists to Karnataka.

Finally, tourism offers good career prospects. In view of the promising future of tourism in India, travel and tourism industry is capable of providing ample career and employment opportunities for students to take up short-term certificate courses as well as bachelor's and master's degree programmes in addition to specialisation in this sector like spiritual tourism, wildlife tourism, golf and rural tourism, etc. There is already an emerging trend in the career prospects which is to become a consultant who can operate from home. Again, the travel BPO industry is the latest addition, having ample scope for expansion.

The Tourism Policy 2002-2007 had announced several very attractive projects and proposals to promote tourism in the state. But there appears to be some delay in implementing these projects such as sound and light show in Mysore Palace, handing over of Brindavan Gardens to private entrepreneurs at an estimated cost of $40 million, development of Nandi Hills including ropeway and development of coastal circuit. Further the concessions and incentives announced in the Policy have not brought in any investment in tourism projects except hotels. This may be attributed to the reduced budget for tourism in the current year 2004-05. As against the department's initial demand of Rs. 55 crore or even that recommended by the Medium–term Fiscal Plan of Rs. 24 crore, the allocation is scaled down to Rs. 16.46 crore of which Rs. 6 crore is towards improving infrastructure, campaigns, promotion and advertising which is far inadequate. It may be noted that the neighbouring states have budget allocation 3 to 5 times that of Karnataka.

A 20 year perspective plan for 'Development of Sustainable Tourism', for all the states including the state of Karnataka has already been prepared by M/s Dalal Consultants and another similar document by TECSOK. The studies include a perspective plan for tourism development based on the Karnataka Tourism Policy 1997-2002, from 2000 to 2020. Some of the major estimates made by them are shown in Table 16.3.

As seen from Table 16.3, the likely investment is required in Karnataka to usher in a new area of tourism at Rs. 3,302 crore in 2020. This means the annual investment required on an average would be Rs. 165.10 crore. This is based on projected traffic flow of 5.26 lakh foreign tourists arrivals and 776.83 lakh domestic tourist arrivals by 2020.

As a vision, it can be stated that with special attention given to the concerns of tourists, encouraging private and NGO sectors and state government getting on infrastructural development on tourism, the state has a good opportunity to make tourism as a sustainable economic activity in the state.

16.2 Entertainment

Entertainment industry world over is changing much faster than many other industries. By and large,

TABLE 16.3

Projections of Certain Tourism Parameters for Karnataka

Measures/Indicators	*2000-2001*		*2004-2005*		*2009-2010*		*2019-2020*	
	TECSOK	*DALAL*	*TECSOK*	*DALAL*	*TECSOK*	*DALAL*	*TECSOK*	*DALAL*
Arrival of Foreign Tourists (in Lakh)	2.55	2.08	2.76	2.53	-	3.23	-	5.26
Employment Generation (in Lakh)	3.76	3.69	4.07	4.49	-	5.72	-	9.32
Arrival of Domestic Tourists (in Lakh)	107.82	180	116.71	244.9	-	359.8	-	776.8
Revenue Due to Tourism (in Lakh)	21478	19525	31445	28587	-	46039	-	1E+05
Foreign Exch. Earnings (Rs. Lakh)	34788	32211	47329	39153	-	49970	-	81396
Tourism Contribution to State GDP (in Lakh)	-	12	-	13	-	15	-	25
Total Tourists (in Lakh)	**11.037**	**182.1**	**119.47**	**247.4**	-	**362.1**	-	**782.1**
Investment Required (in Lakh)*	-	-	-	-	-	-	**33037**	

Note: *As per TECSOK average investment per year is estimated at Rs.370 crore for the next 10 years.

entertainment and tourism are everlasting services. Entertainment industry like tourism also provides large scale employment, but generates small proportion of income and revenues. The invisible benefits arising from entertainment are enormous. Karnataka is a major centre of entertainment activities of various types.

Entertainment broadly includes radio, TV broadcasting, art, music, dance, plays, theatres, cultural programmes, literature folk and rural, academies of all types, religious activities/festivals, etc.

16.2.1 Income from Entertainment

Identification of incomes, resource allocation, employment, etc. are extremely difficult for this activity (Appendix A-16.3). As part of state domestic product, recreation and entertainment are included in the category of 'other services' in the tertiary sector (Table 16.4). Recreation and entertainment contributed a very small proportion of about 0.24 per cent to Karnataka's GSDP in 1993-94, which rose to 0.32 per cent by 2002-2003. The income generated from recreation and entertainment, which was Rs. 9,555 lakh in 1993-94, increased to Rs. 3,6115 lakh in 2002-03 at current prices.

16.2.2 Revenue from Entertainment

The revenue from entertainment industry to the state is not significant. Its contribution is less than

TABLE 16.4

Contribution of Entertainment to Karnataka's GSDP

Year	*Value Added from Recreation and Entertainment (Rs. Lakh)*		*Contribution (in per cent) All at Current Price*		
	Constant Prices	*Current Prices*	*GSDP*	*Tertiary Sector*	*Other Services*
1993-94	9555	9555	0.24	0.61	3.49
1994-95	9828	10048	0.21	0.54	3.17
1995-96	10110	11159	0.20	0.49	2.97
1996-97	10399	14270	0.22	0.53	3.12
1997-98	10697	14378	0.20	0.46	2.55
1998-99	11003	16201	0.18	0.43	2.33
1999-00	11318	17134	0.18	0.40	2.08
2000-01	11642	33082	0.32	0.67	3.45
2001-02	11974	34651	0.32	0.64	3.62
2002-03	12317	36115	0.32	0.60	2.89

Source: Directorate of Economics and Statistics, *State Domestic Product*, Government of Karnataka, 2004.

half a per cent to the state's tax revenue. Further, as proportion to state's own tax revenue, its share is declining over the years from 2.65 per cent in 1987-88 to less than 0.39 per cent in 2002-03 (Table 16.5).

The main sources of revenue from entertainment is the entertainment tax (ET) levied on cinema theatres, video-shows centres and sports events. There were 1,070 cinema theatres in the state in 2002-03 of which 774 were permanent ones and 296 were temporary ones like tent theatres, moving theatres, etc. Table 16.6 gives the trend in the number of theatres in Karnataka.

In fact up to 1989-90 the number of temporary theatres were more than the permanent ones and from then on there was a continuous decline in the temporary theatres from 721 in 1987-88 to 296 in 2002-2003. On the contrary the number of permanent theatres which was increasing steadily from 599 in 1987-88 to 902 in 1998-99 started declining to 774 in 2001-02. Between 1990-91 (Accounts) and 2004-05 (BE) the revenue from ET was highest at Rs. 6,011.02 lakh during 1999-2000 and the lowest revenue was Rs. 3,420.05 lakh in 1996-97. The revenue estimates for 2004-05 is Rs. 3,830.00 lakh. Revenue from entertainment tax in some of the neighbouring states is much higher than in Karnataka. There are many reasons for low collection of ET in the state. The major ones are: i) leakage by evasion, ii) complex administrative process (e.g. licensing authority of entertainment units are being controlled by the Revenue Department of the state while enforcement of Entertainment Act is done by Office of the Commercial Taxes). There are a large number of concessions and exemptions to certain segments of films. Certain activities like live bands which are coming up in a big way in the city areas have elements of entertainment, but are not covered under the tax network. In Bangalore city alone there are about 60 live bands but many more are coming up in other places without licences. There are two major turf clubs in Karnataka one at Bangalore and the other at Mysore. Besides these, there are a good number of recreation and sports clubs operating in the state. There is a need for a regulating body to oversee the activities of these clubs and other recreation centres including live bands and video centres, cable operators, etc. Much of evasion is also because of the high rate of ET. At present it is as high as 70 per cent as compared to 25 per cent in Tamil Nadu. Secondly, it is also reported that the costs of tickets in cinema theatres are high in Karnataka.

16.2.3 Vision

The entertainment scenario is changing dramatically with a spectacular growth of the television sector, new formats of film production and distribution, privatisation of radio services, liberalising attitude of

TABLE 16.5

Revenue from Entertainment Tax

(Rs. Lakhs)

Year	*Cinematography Show Tax*	*Entertainment Tax*	*Other Items*	*Total*
1990-91	312.89	3767.07	120.55	4200.51
1991-92	374.40	4155.51	303.36	4833.27
1992-93	314.50	4462.09	186.98	4963.57
1993-94	574.18	5249.42	108.57	5932.17
1994-95	624.87	3934.10	145.81	4704.78
1995-96	348.83	4078.30	77.69	4504.82
1996-97	913.77	2428.86	77.42	3420.05
1997-98	1032.67	3850.99	644.06	5527.24
1998-99	1371.88	3970.32	285.04	5627.24
1999-00	1988.67	3613.87	408.48	6011.02
2000-01	722.29	4070.84	279.57	5072.70
2001-02	1020.02	3509.06	363.66	4892.74
2002-03	673.75	3563.64	344.14	4581.53
2003-04 (RE)	904.26	3409.00	48.74	4362.00
2004-05 (BE)	906.00	2733.70	190.30	3830.00

Source: Karnataka State Budgets, Government of Karnataka.

the government and easier access to and for international companies and many other factors. The entertainment sector in the country is expected to grow at a compounded annual growth rate of 27 per cent (KSFC News, Feb.-Mar. 2004). The government has opened up the entertainment sector and accorded it the industry status, and has allowed 100 per cent FDI in almost all areas of the sector, except print media and DTH broadcasting where FDI is restricted to 26 per cent and 20 per cent, respectively. As a result many large corporate houses have evinced keen interest to invest in this sector (Box 16.3). Further leading Chambers of Commerce such as FICCI and CII have identified entertainment as a fast growing industry. Revenues from this sector have been projected to increase to $10 billion in 2005 from $3 billion in 2002.

Future of entertainment sector lies in promoting production of animation films, development of studio infrastructure, reducing entertainment taxes and also reducing tax exemptions.

16.3 Software Services in Karnataka

16.3.1 Overview of the Development of Software Services in Karnataka

As reviewed in Chapters 2 and 11 on the development of IT sector in the state, Bangalore is recognised globally as the, Silicon Valley of the East. A temperate climate, friendly people, availability of a large pool of talented computer literate manpower, as well as the presence of a large number of research institutions of excellence and industrial outfits specialising in electronics, attracted a large number of firms to set up operations. This booming five centuries old city of more than seven million people has been described as a 'Software Mecca'. "When a foreign company wants to set up a software centre in India, it invariably comes to Bangalore," comments Anil Sharma, Head of US-based Hughes Software Systems (HSS) office in Bangalore.

TABLE 16.6

Number of Cinema Theatres in Karnataka

Year	*Permanent*	*Temporary*	*Total*
1987-88	599	721	1320
1988-89	606	680	1286
1989-90	607	667	1274
1990-91	628	619	1247
1991-92	670	571	1241
1992-93	696	517	1213
1993-94	714	524	1238
1994-95	731	484	1215
1995-96	731	496	1227
1996-97	735	486	1221
1997-98	761	481	1242
1998-99	902	537	1439
1999-00	778	434	1212
2000-01	775	383	1158
2001-02	774	347	1121
2002-03	774	296	1070

Source: Government of Karnataka, *State Domestic Product*, Directorate of Economics and Statistics.

16.3.2 Growth of Software Services

The software sector in the state has been growing hand in hand with the IT sector itself. While the IT companies (and also the investments) in the state grew from 782 in 1999-00 to 1285 in 2004, the BPO sector grew from 28 companies in 2001-02 to 52 by 2004. By 2002-03, the total investments in the IT sector in the state is of the order of Rs. 2029 crores, and in the BPO sector at Rs. 650 crores. In 2003-04, the total exports of the Indian software and services industry were US$ 12.5 billion (NASSCOM), with Karnataka contributing about 33 per cent of the total software exports. The ITES/BPO sector exports from Karnataka accounted for Rs. 2237 crores. Karnataka's share of software exports

BOX 16.3

Scheme for Financing Entertainment Industry

KSFC has adopted a new scheme for financing a part of the entertainment industry like production of feature films, construction of stand alone cinema halls and multiplexes, production of short TV serials and software for visual media publicity to be set up/produced/filmed within Karnataka.

Assistance under the scheme is available for meeting the expenditure on construction of buildings for multiplexes and cinema halls, purchase of capital equipments for multiplexes, cinema halls and software for visual media publicity and for production of TV serials, production and post production costs of feature films only.

Proprietary concerns, private limited companies promoted by reputed persons with good technical/financial background and with good net worth are eligible for assistance under the same.

The project cost should not exceed Rs.20.00 crores, with minimum promoters contribution of 40 per cent of the project cost and DER of not less than 1.50: 1.00.

TABLE 16.7

India and Karnataka's Software Exports

Year	*India*		*Karnataka*		*Share of IT in India's Export (%)*
	(Rs. in Crores)	*In USD*	*(Rs. in Crores)*	*In USD*	
1997-98	6,530	1,759	2,246	478	4.90
1998-99	10,940	2,600	3,915	833	7.60
1999-00	17,150	3,962	4,400	957	10.60
2000-01	28,150	6,217	7,475	1,600	13.80
2001-02	36,500	7,647	9,903	2,063	17.00
2002-03	47,500	9,693	12,350	2,572	20.40

TABLE 16.8

Software Exports Location-wise in Karnataka in 2003-04

Location	*Software Exports (Rs. Crore)*	*No. of Firms Registered with STPI*
Bangalore	17,474	1322
Mangalore	456	18
Mysore	180	31
Total (Karnataka)	**18,100**	**1371**

Source: *www.karnataka.com.* Information Technology in Karnataka and Software Technology Park of India.

TABLE 16.9

Karnataka's ITES/BPO Scenario in 2002-03

Total Number of BPO Companies	41
Total Investments	Rs. 512 crore
Total Exports	Rs. 988 crore
Total Employment Generated	18875

Source: "Information Technology in Karnataka" & STPI. *www.Karnataka.com.*

has grown consistently over the years as shown in Tables 16.7, 16.8 and 16.9.

It is not a surprise that the firms located in Bangalore do most of the exports. This skewed pattern is also apparent in the distribution of firms across the cities in Karnataka. Most of the firms are located in Bangalore. About 96 per cent of software exports from Bangalore are routed through the software technology park of india (STPI) in Bangalore. Mysore, Hubli and Mangalore are the other STPI centres in Karnataka. Over 1370 companies were registered with the STPI for the year ending 2003-2004. Box 16.4 and Table 16.10 indicate the top 10 software exporters for the year 2002-2003 and key players in each segment of the industry.

BOX 16.4

Top 10 Software Exporters for the Year: 2002-03

1. M/s. Infosys Technologies Ltd.
2. M/s. Wipro Ltd.
3. M/s. IBM Global Services India Pvt. Ltd.
4. M/s. Tata Consultancy Services
5. M/s. Digital Global Soft. Ltd.
6. M/s. I-flex Solutions Ltd.
7. M/s. Texas Instruments (India) Pvt. Ltd.
8. M/s. Cisco Systems (India) Pvt. Ltd.
9. M/s. Mphasis BFL Limited
10. M/s. Philips Software Centre Pvt. Ltd.

TABLE 16.10

Major Players in Different Segments of the Industry

Category	*Approximate Numbers*	*Illustrative Examples*
Major Indian Companies	100+	Infosys, Wipro, Sasken, TCS, Cognizant, Satyam, Mphasis, I-flex etc.
Foreign Equity Companies	400+	HP, Accenture, IBM, TI, Intel, Oracle, Huawei Technologies, GE, Delphi, SAP, Philips, Lucent, etc.
Medium Enterprises	700+	Mind Tree, Majoris, Tarang, Synergy, Mistral, Encore, Apex, Plantesia, vMoksha, Trigyn, etc..

Source: STPI, Bangalore.

As per NASSCOM-KPMG study, housing of R&D facilities of over 80 global firms including Intel, TI, HP, Philips, Motorola, Honeywell are ranked amongst the seven leading states in India for technical skills. In terms of their workforce, most of these are testimony to the attractiveness of Karnataka specially Bangalore for this technology sector.

Emergence of Bangalore as the Silicon Valley of India is not an overnight phenomenon. The foundation for the abundant technical manpower was laid over five decades back with the setting up of public sector units (PSUs) in electronics, electrical and machine tools. PSUs like Bharat Electronics Ltd. (BEL), Indian Telephone Industries (ITI), Hindustan Machine Tools (HMT), Hindustan Aeronautics Ltd. (HAL), Bharat Earth Movers Ltd., (BEML) and Bharat Heavy Electricals Ltd. (BHEL) helped create a private sector industrial infrastructure specialising in the development of high precision products and components. On another front, the high-tech labs and facilities created by research institutions like the Indian Space Research Organisation (ISRO) and the defence research establishments as well as the excellent research and development set up of the Indian Institute of Science (IISc) have been instrumental in sharpening the technological edge of the city. These PSUs and research institutions attracted talents from all over the country and gave Bangalore a distinctive cosmopolitan outlook. Box 16.5 highlights the initiatives taken by the government towards the infrastructure front for attracting investment in IT and ITES in Karnataka.

BOX 16.5

IT Infrastructure in Karnataka

- State of the art International Technology Park (ITPL) with 1.5 million sq.ft built up area.
- Six new Private Technology Parks with built up area of 6 million sq.ft.
- Over 100 Private IT Parks with more than 28.00 million sq ft of world class IT infrastructure in the pipeline.
- A specialised Electronic City at Bangalore and Mysore.
- Software Technology Parks at Mysore, Hubli and Mangalore with high speed data.
- Communications facilities.
- Best telecom infrastructure in the country.
- Total investment in IT Parks Rs. 4864 crores.

The encouragement to private investment in education ensured the setting up of several engineering colleges in Karnataka thus ensuring a steady supply of technical talents. Karnataka's educational institutions produce over 28 per cent of the country's IT professionals. Over 36,000 engineering students graduate every year from its 124 engineering colleges. There are 800 polytechnics and ITIs, and sufficient infrastructure to develop skilled manpower. The State's Education Policy initiated almost 50 years ago has actively encouraged the private sector in education—of 124 engineering colleges only 2 colleges are government run. Because of this early initiative the state has seen extraordinary investment in the field of education ensuring its comparative superiority.

The state government also played a significant role in encouraging the software industry by creating infrastructure including Electronics City and partnering with the private sector for setting up the International Technology Park. It was the first state ever to announce an IT Policy in the year 1997 to encourage and facilitate investments. This policy has been an important catalyst for the growth of the IT industry in the state. An updated policy came into force from March 2000 as the Millennium IT Policy of Karnataka Mahithi, (Appendix A-16.4). In order to attract new companies and support the expansion and modernisation of existing firms, the policy offered an attractive package of incentives and concessions including both financial and non-financial commitments from various departments in the government. Other initiatives from the government included the establishment of the first Indian Institute of Information Technology (IIIT) in Bangalore dedicated to post graduate and doctoral level programmes for the IT sector. Investor-friendly and transparent administration over the last decade, a progressive industrial, fiscal and infrastructure policy and single window clearances were other enabling factors which helped the software industry in Karnataka. The state offers several incentives like sales tax exemption for 10 years, entry tax exemption on computer hardware peripherals and other capital goods.

India and especially Karnataka have become a favourite destination for sourcing software and IT enabled services due to high levels of government support, quality of the labour pool, English language skills, cost advantages, project management skills and overall quality control. A favourable time zone difference with North America and Europe helps service providers achieve 24x7 internal operations and customer service. Leading organisations have established process and quality focus and many have received SEI-CMM Level 5 certifications. Out of the 63 companies from India, which have achieved this highest level of process maturity, 32 are located in Bangalore (*Economic Times,* November 1, 2004, pp.1.).

16.3.3 Economic Impact of the Software and Services Industry

Capital Investments

With 1,038 companies under STPI in 2001-02 (as of May 2002), and 1,154 companies under STPI in 2002-2003 (as of April 2003) the composition by categories, capital investments, and capital growth have been quite impressive (as can be seen from Table 16.11). The total capital investment grew from Rs. 1,383 crores in 2001-02 to 1,708 crores in 2002-03.

The boom in the software services have created immense employment and career advancement opportunities. Employee Stock Options (ESOPS), dollar earnings and performance linked bonuses—all created a special class of employment with high disposable income at a relatively young age. The Mercer Human Resources Cost of Living Survey ranked Bangalore as the fourth most expensive city in India. On an average, software professionals in Bangalore are paid 17 per cent more than their counterparts. Everything in the city is directly related to the boom in the technology sector—growth in the real estate for housing as well as commercial space, multi-cuisine restaurants, shopping malls, etc. Table 16.12 shows the estimates of economic impact of the software industry.

The ITES/BPO industry which currently employs over one lakh people has almost a similar number employed in ancillary services comprising recruitment, training, catering, transportation, construction and real estate, security and facility management. Ancillary services of business process outsourcing and ITES are expected to have a major impact on the local economy by creating large number of employment opportunities and high volume revenues. On an average ITES/BPO companies spend anything between Rs. 25,000 to 30,000 per seat towards ancillary charges. By 2008, the total demand created by ITES/BPO related ancillary industries are estimated and presented in Table 16.13.

16.3.4 Employment Opportunities

Karnataka has witnessed exceptional growth in the IT services and product companies. These companies are proving to be a large employment base for the state engineering graduates. At the same time, the growth in the BPO/ITES sector will create tremendous

TABLE 16.11

Capital Investment in Software Sector

Category of STP firms	*2001-02 Capital Investment in Rs. Crores*	*2002-03 Capital Investment in Rs. Crores*	*Growth in the Capital Investment in Per Cent*
Small and Medium Entrepreneurs	208	160	(-ve)
Major Indian Companies	283	523	84.80
Foreign Equity	892	1025	14.91
Total	**1383**	**1708**	**23.50**

Source: Software Technology Park of India, Bangalore.

TABLE 16.12

Economic Impact of the Software and Services Industry

(in Rs. Crores)

Year	*Jobs in IT/ITES (No.)*	*Software and BPO Exports*	*Cost of Support Services*	*Total Salaries Paid Out*	*Spends on Food and Rent*	*Spends on Clothing*	*Savings*
1999-2000	50000	5000	700	2100	504	151	630
2003-2004	250000	20300	2847	8541	2050	615	2562
BY 2008	810000	69000	9660	28980	6955	2087	11694

Source: Times of India, July 29, 2004. "How the Money is Earned and Spent", Development of Ancillary Services.

TABLE 16.13

Estimates of Ancillary Services of BPO

Ancillary Industry	*Amount in Rs. Crores*
Transportation	6000
Food items	1500
Training	1600
Facilities	1000
Technology	1000

Source: *Times of India*, July 26, 2004. "Ancillaries are growing as fast as BPO Industry".

employment opportunities for arts, science and commerce graduates. In IT services, around 35,000 new jobs are expected to be created every year. Infosys and Wipro are expected to create around 3,000 new jobs in IT services in the year 2004-05. In semi-conductor engineering space, Bangalore is emerging as the key global destination. LG, Nokia and Motorola, are conducting most of their handset work from here. In ITES/BPO, Bangalore will add around 30,000 jobs to its existing base of one lakh agents. The top recruiters in this space will be Accenture, Converges, IBM, 24/7 Customer, Infosys/Progeon, HP and Oracle. At the same time, IT vendors like Dell, HP, Oracle and Microsoft are creating thousands of technical support jobs in the city for their captive requirements.

16.3.5 Areas of Concern, New Opportunities and Vision

Bangalore has become a victim of its own success. By being the most attractive destination for the IT industry, it witnessed explosive growth in the last 12 years, which also created several problems. The exponential growth as an IT hot spot has not been matched by infrastructure facilities, forcing technology companies to look outside Karnataka for expansion. Most corporates fear that infrastructural bottlenecks, higher attrition levels and rising wage costs in the city will hurt their profitability. Many players are publicly stating their intentions to expand outside Bangalore where the economics of business looks more attractive. The growth has resulted in traffic jams, higher levels of environmental pollution, a heavier burden on the public transportation, power shortages and insufficient civic infrastructure. All these have led to higher cost of living. The perception of Karnataka as an IT-friendly state took a further beating with the latest State Budget increasing sales tax on computer hardware from 5.3 per cent to 13.8 per cent which is the highest on PCs in the country.

The road network, public transport systems, power and water supply have deteriorated over the years. To compensate for these shortcomings and deliver timely services to their clients, the players in the industry have substituted utilities by investing in alternatives. The ITES/BPO units are forced to invest in backup generator sets for uninterrupted operations. Lack of reliable public transport system forces them to depend on a fleet of vehicles to transport their employees to and from office. All these add to the cost and impact the industry's competitiveness. Another area of concern is the shortage of qualified manpower which has pushed up the wages and attrition rate to alarmingly high levels. This has led to investors shifting their attention to smaller cities where talent is available and operational costs, wages and attrition rates will be low. The limitations of operating in Bangalore will thus create an opportunity for other cities in Karnataka. The state can play an active role to encourage investments in the non-metro cities of Karnataka (Appendix A-16.5). Hubli, Mysore and Mangalore already have STPI centres and they can emerge as alternatives to Bangalore for many firms in the ITES/BPO business. However, these cities have to be made attractive to investors by mainly improving the connectivity to international gateways including Bangalore and Mumbai. Table 16.14 gives the status of the cities on different parameters on a scale of 10 as relevant for designing regional spread of this sector in future.

TABLE 16.14

Ranking of Cities in Karnataka on Different Parameters

	Hubli	*Mysore*	*Mangalore*
Physical Connectivity	4	3	6
Power Supply	6	4	4
Housing and Schooling	7	7	5
Communication Link	7	5	6
Talent Pool Availability	6	7	7
Cost of Living	2	7	9

Source: *Times of India* 7th August 2004. "Are Cities Geared up for IT?"

The vision for the future of software sector is therefore, one of continued growth, geographically and regionally spread over alternative STPI centres, catering to increasing opportunities of ITES/BPO services. The state policies to support with the necessary infrastructure has to be enhanced. The sector in turn can do the magic of increased flow of capital, profits, income and employment.

References

Government of India. Department of Tourism and *Report on the Preparation of 20 years Perspective Plan for Development of Sustainable Tourism 2002*, M/s Dalal Consultants and Engineers Ltd.

Government of Karnataka, *Theater of Inspiration-A Glimpse*, Department of Tourism.

———. *Karnataka At a Glance* of various years, Directorate of Economics and Statistics.

———. Commissioner of Commercial Taxes, Finance Department.

———. *Karnataka Tourism- Guidelines for Implementation of New Tourism Policy with effect from 1.6.1997*, Department of Tourism.

———. *Karnataka Tourism Policy 2002-07*, Department of Tourism.

———. Karnataka Tourism-website, Department of Tourism.

———. *Tourism Policy 1992-97*. Department of Tourism.

———. Directorate of Economics and Statistics.

———. *Economic Survey*, various years.

———. *Gazetteer*, various years.

———. *High Power Committee For Redressal of Regional Imbalances*, June 2002.

———. *Plan Documents*, various years.

———. *Socio-Economic Benefits of Tourism*, Nov.2000, TECSOK.

———. *State Domestic Product Karnataka 1993-94 to 2002-03*, Directorate of Economics and Statistics 2004.

APPENDIX A-16.1

Hampi

Hampi is the world's largest open-air museum. Hampi was the capital city of the powerful South Indian Vijayanagar Empire. Founded by Harihara and Bukka in 1336, it fell to the Muslim rulers of North India in 1565 after the disastrous Battle of Talikota and subsequently lapsed into decline and abandonment. The once proud city of victory is now a city of desolation. However, the ruins of these historical monuments have stood the ravages of man and time and still evoke memories of the grandeur of a bygone era. Hampi is set amidst an awesome boulder-strewn landscape along the banks of the Tungabhadra river 12 kms. away from the sleepy town of Hospet in Bellary district, Hampi was the magnificent capital of the mighty Vijayanagar kingdom. "The city is such that the pupil of the eye has never seen a place like it and the ear of intelligence has never been informed that there existed anything to equal it in the world," marvelled a 15th century Persian ambassador. There were opulent palaces, marvellous temples, massive fortifications, baths, markets, aquaducts, pavilions, stables for royal elephants and elegantly carved pillars. This was a city whose merchants offered diamonds, pearls, fine silks, brocades, horses and according to one Portuguese visitor, "every sort of thing on earth".

A visit to Hampi is a sojourn into the past. The best way to experience this world heritage site is to take a leisurely stroll through the eloquent ruins. Most of the important structures and ruins are located in two areas, which are generally referred to as the royal centre and the sacred centre. The Royal Centre in the southwest part of the site contains structures that seem to have been palaces, baths, pavilions, royal stables and temples for ceremonial use. The Sacred Centre is situated on the northern edge of the city along the banks of the holy Tungabhadra river.

The ruins of Hampi are extensive and fascinating enough to absorb your attention for several days. There is always something new to discover in Hampi. If you are in a hurry, a day or two will suffice to see all the important structures. Photography and archaeology buffs should plan on staying a little longer.

King's Palace

This is the largest enclosure, including two major platform structures, an underground chamber which must have served as a treasury or private audience hall, several other platforms, double fortification walls and several other interesting architectural elements.

Mahanavami Dibba

Equally impressive is the massive Mahanavami Dibba, where the kings once sat on gem-studded golden thrones and watched processions pass by. The platform sports densely carved bands of horses, soldiers and depictions of the various aspects of courtly life.

Queen's Bath

This structure has a very plain exterior but the interior is stunningly ornate, with graceful arched corridors, projecting balconies and lotus-shaped fountains that used to spout perfumed water for the ladies of the court.

Lotus Mahal

This visually appealing structure has two levels, with open pavilions at the bottom and balconies above. An elegant example of the fusion of the Hindu and Muslim styles of architecture, the Mahal derives its name from its beautiful, geometrically-arranged cusped arches that resemble the petals of a flower opening to the sun.

Elephant Stables

An imposing edifice with arched entrances and many domes that once housed the magnificent state elephants.

Pushkarni

This stepped water tank, excavated in the mid-1980s, was originally a part of the palace complex. Almost lyrical in its beauty, the tank is a tiered structure crafted from rectangular pieces of granite.

Hazara Rama Temple

This was a royal temple reserved for ceremonial use. The entire temple is embellished with reliefs depicting scenes from the epic 'Ramayana'. The walls of the enclosure are richly carved with friezes depicting processions of horses, elephants, dancing girls and soldiers attired in splendid weaponry. Inside, four exquisitely sculpted granite pillars add to the beauty of the *ardha mantapa.*

Vithala Temple

The Vithala Temple is Hampi's crowning glory, with a magnificent stone chariot standing in the temple courtyard. Equally impressive is the large *ranga mantapa* with 56 musical pillars that resound with musical chimes when struck.

Virupaksha Temple

Dedicated to Lord Shiva and his consort Pampadevi, this is the only temple that is still used for worship. Parts of the temple predate the Vijayanagar empire. The temple, with its nine-storied *gopuram,* towers above the other structures at Hampi. The ceiling of the *ranga mantapa* is beautifully painted with scenes from the epics and Puranas.

Lakshminarasimha

The awesome 6.7 mts. high monolith depicting the man-lion form of Vishnu is seated on a seven-hooded serpent.

Badavilinga

Located next to the Lakshminarasimha statue, it is 3 mts. high and stands permanently in water that flows through an ancient channel.

Ganesha Images

Two Ganesha images (Sasuvekalu and Kadalekalu) can be seen on the slopes of the Hemakuta Hill. One of them is enclosed in a temple with unusually tall pillars, while the other is in an open hall.

Source: Government of Karnataka (1983). *Karnataka State Gazetteer*, Part II.

APPENDIX A-16.2

Pattadakal

With its beautifully chiselled temples, this world heritage site on the banks of the Malaprabha river bears testimony to the richness of Chalukyan architecture. Pattadakal reached its pinnacle of glory under the Chalukya kings and was once used as a ceremonial centre where kings were crowned and commemorated. It has a cluster of 10 major temples, each displaying interesting architectural features. At the entrance of the site, you can see the 8th century temples of Jambulinga, Kadasiddeshvara and Galaganatha with their curvilinear *shikaras* or spires. The biggest temple, dedicated to Virupaksha, has a huge gateway, several inscriptions and a profusion of friezes from the epics. Facing the temple is a pavilion containing a majestic 206 metre high Nandi. The Mallikarjuna Temple is similar in design to Virupaksha Temple, but smaller in size. The ornate Papanatha Temple is yet another impressive piece of architecture, with delicately chiselled ceilings and a 16-pillared main hall. The Sangameshwara Temple dating from the reign of King Vijayaditya (696–733 AD) is the earliest temple in this complex.

Large number of stone weapons found along the river bank and the existence of giant stone graves nearby, are clear proofs of earlier inhabitation here in the pre-historic period. Several burnt brick structures which came to light during the excavations carried out near the Sangameshvara and Jaina temples, date back even earlier to the pre-Chalukyan era. In ancient days, according to inscriptions, the place was known by the names Kisuvolal (Red Town) or Pattada Kisuvolal. The literary work, *Hammira Kavya* of 1540 AD, quotes the place as Pattashilapura and Hammirapura. It reached its zenith during the reign of Badami Chalukyas and it was their sub-capital. It has been mentioned in the 11th and 12th century inscriptions, as well as in the literary work *Singirajapurana* of 1500 and *Hammira Kavya* as the place where Chalukya kings were crowned. The place continued to be an important centre under the Rashtrakutas and the Kalyana Chalukyas. Later it became a chief city for small region called Kisukadu-70. The Sindhas of Yarmabarige (Yelburgi) also ruled it for some time. From the temple architectural point of view, a significant feature of the place is the existence of the best temples of the early Chalukyan days in Dravidian and Nagara styles side by side. Out of 10 major temples 9 are Shiva and 1 Jaina and situated along the northern course of the river is considered as auspicious according to holy scriptures. The biggest temple in Pattadakal is Virupaksha, enclosed by a large *prakara*. According to an inscription, the temple was built by Lokamahadevi, the consort of Vikramaditya to commemorate his three victories over the Pallavas and occupation of Kanchi. Its original name was Lokeshvara or Lokapaleshvara. This was perhaps built in about first half of the 8th century. This temple has a sanctum, an inner passage, pillared by *navaranga* and triple entrances from the north, east and the south porches. It has a massive gateway in front from the east and a small gate behind. There are inscriptions and imposing stone carved figures inside the stone *mantapa*. A little inside is the four- pillared *Nandimantapa*, which has a fine large stone bull. On the pillars and walls are several figures of males, females, dwarfs and amorous couple. Just in front is the main shrine. The sanctum has a circuit path and installed on the square pedestal, a black Shivalinga. The famous Kailasa temple at Ellora was built on the model of the Virupaksha temple here. Another temple, that of Sangameshvara is in Dravidian style, and perhaps the oldest among the temples at this place, and consists of a sanctum, inner passage and *navaranga*. The sanctum and inner passage are enclosed by a pathway for *pradakshina*, which has several lattices of different design, sculptured on the outer walls various figures like Ugranarasimha and Nataraja. The navaranga has 20 pillars in 4 rows. Its exterior walls have stone-carved figures. The sanctum has a Dravidian tower. According to an inscription in Kannada dated 1162 AD, it was built by the early Chalukyan King Vijayaditya and was named Vijayeshvara. To the north of Virupaksha temple lies the Mallikarjuna, which was formerly known as *Trilokeshvara*. It is in close proximity with the former in design, construction and sculpture, but smaller in size. The porch has a beautiful image of Narasimha killing Hiranyakashipu and two female idols. Here are two grand images on both the sides of the entrance to the *navaranga*. The 18 pillars of the *navaranga* have figures pertaining to *Ramayana*, *Mahabharata* and those representing social conditions of those days. There is a Jain temple on the Pattadakal-Badami road. It consists of a *mukhamantapa*, a *navaranga*, *sukanasa* and *garbagriha*. Its construction may be of the 9th century AD. The Galaganatha temple lies to the north of the Virupaksha and faces the west. It has a *navaranga*, sukanasa and a *sanctum* with a *linga*. Around the sanctum is a circuit pathway. In several niches are small figures of Kubera, Gajalakshmi and others. On the external wall niche of the circuit pathway is a fine figure of Shiva. The *rekhanagara* style tower over the temple is very fine. It seems to have been constructed during the first half of the 18th century AD. The Papanatha temple, located to the south of the Virupaksha has a portico, a main hall, big antechamber and the sanctum with encircled pathway. At the doorway of inner eye are idols of door keepers, Nandi and Veerbhadra. Amorous couples and decorative carvings are found in the several parts of the temples.

To the north of the Mallikarjuna temple is the temple of Kashi-Vishveshvara of which only the sanctum and a passage is left. On the ceiling, Somaskanda is represented. Its sanctum has a *rekhanagara* tower. The structure is presumably of the 8th century. Apart from these major temples, several small Shiva shrines are seen here. According to the inscription on a Shiva stone pillar found near the Virupaksha, Sangameshvara and Mallikarjuna temples, this pillar with a trident emblem was put up by Jnana Shivacharya, who hailed from Mrigathanikahara, on the north bank of the Ganga. It also states about the gift of land by him to the Vijayeshvara. The abundance of Shiva temples here clearly indicates that the place was a great Shiva centre in ancient times. The place is the headquarters of the village *Panchayat*.

Source: *Karnataka State Gazetteer*, Part II, Government of Karnataka 1983.

APPENDIX A-16.3

NIC 98 Classification Used for Computing State Domestic Product (as Relevant for the Entertainment Sector)

1. Motion picture, radio, television and other entertainment activities, motion picture and video production and distribution [including documentaries and animated films or cartoons (also includes distribution of pictures and video tapes to other industries)].

   i) Motion picture production,

   ii) motion picture distribution and activities allied to film distribution,

   iii) video production and distribution, and

   iv) auxiliary activities of motion picture and video production, on a fee or contract basis, such as film editing, cutting and dubbing, etc.

2. Motion picture projection

   Radio and television activities (includes production of radio and television programmes, whether live or on tape and whether or not combined with broadcasting).

   i) radio activities, and

   ii) television activities.

3. Dramatic arts, music and other arts activities (includes the production, for the general public, of live theatrical presentations, concerts or dance programmes; light and sound shows; magician's shows and art and craft exhibitions, etc. Also included are the related activities such as operation of light and sound equipments, ticket agencies, concert and theatre halls and the design for scenery and lighting).

   i) Stage production and related activities, and

   ii) activities of the independent artists.

4. Other entertainment activities n.e.c (includes activities of ball rooms, video parlours, discotheques, amusement parks and similar attractions; circus; puppet shows and production of other kinds of entertainment not elsewhere classified).

   i) operation of circuses and race tracks, and

   ii) video parlours, amusement centres, and other entertainment activities n.e.c. This classification is used to compute the income generated by recreation and entertainment.

APPENDIX A-16.4

The Millennium IT Policy 'Mahithi'

The Government of Karnataka has announced a policy on information technology (IT) called Mahithi aimed at bringing the benefits of IT to the common man. Karnataka was the first state to announce IT Policy in the year 1997. This Policy has acted as a catalyst for the growth of IT industry in the state. The state government came out with this policy to refocus on the IT Policy and define it in a way that is most suited for the present.

The main objectives of the Millennium IT Policy are to:

- Utilise the power of information technology in the overall goal of the Government of Karnataka in eradicating poverty and empowering women.
- Effectively reduce unemployment by absorbing the major share of educated youth into the IT industry.
- Promote the usage of Kannada in information technology.
- Use e-governance as a tool and deliver a government that is more proactive and responsive to its citizens.
- Unleash the Karnataka incubation engine.
- Encourage business with non-English speaking countries.
- Maintain the pre-eminent position of both Bangalore and Karnataka in the field of information technology.

Education-Computers to be part of school and college curriculum, curriculum to be developed with inputs from industry, a premier institute called IIIT to be set up, 225 training centres all over the state, primarily for the purpose of training the unemployed educated youth in various IT skills to be set up, and set up more colleges.

Local language-The Government of Karnataka with the active cooperation of the Kannada *Abhivruddhi Pradhikara*, Kannada *Ganaka Parishad*, Kannada and Culture Department as well as several Kannada researchers has already evolved a common keyboard. The government is committed to complete the process of standardisation and prescribe standard formats and codes for all the software companies. The government will provide incentives for the development of Kannada software.

Welfare of Socially Disadvantaged-The Government of Karnataka proposes to use information technology to track beneficiaries of social welfare schemes.

E-governance-Computers to be used by different departments; departments to be supported by Karnataka Government Computer Centre as well as the National Informatics Centre.

Source: *http://www.bangaloreit.com/html/govtinformation/policies.htm*

APPENDIX A-16.5

Attractiveness of the Non-metro Cities in Karnataka

Hubli: Hubli is a STPI centre so it has the physical infrastructure and data connectivity for IT companies to set up operations. Population is around 8.5 lakhs. Power supply, housing and schooling, communication link and talent pool availability is more than 5 on a scale of 10.

Mysore: Mysore is only 150 kilometres from Bangalore and already has a large number of well-established IT companies with road and rail connectivity to Bangalore. Infosys has set up a Leadership Training Institute in Mysore. Mysore boasts of 5 engineering collages and 20 first-grade colleges. Talent pool is extremely good. It has a population of over 1 million. More than 30 software firms are already operating in Mysore.

Mangalore: Mangalore has excellent resources for quality manpower development. This city has a number of well-known engineering, medical and other colleges. Infosys has a large operation in Mangalore which employs 1,000 people.

Barring Mangalore the cost of living of other two cities are pretty low. All the three cities have poor connectivity with Bangalore. Only Mangalore touts a fully operational airport. However, on the housing and schooling front the three cities compare favourably with Bangalore. For start-up operation, IT firms should find the availability of talent pool in the three cities comfortably.

Source: Department of Industries and Commerce, Government of Karnataka.

APPENDIX A-16.6

Year-wise Statement Showing the Total Number of Tourism Hotels

Year	*No.of Tourism Projects Approved*	*Total Investment (Rs. in Lakhs)*
1992-93	47	2063.19
1993-94	48	3455.50
1994095	74	24681.32
1995-96	58	10298.26
1996-97	79	46302.27
1997-98	74	8191.56
1998-99	77	15116.97
1999-00	66	5202.52
2000-01	86	7454.95
2001-02	85	6556.95
2002-03	71	7106.34
Total	**765**	**136429.83**

Source: Commissioner of Tourism, Government of Karnataka.

APPENDIX A-16.7

Revenue and Expenditure including Plan Expenditure on Tourism

(Rs. Lakhs)

Year	*Revenue*	*Expenditure*	*Plan Expenditure*
1990-91	51.79	139.02	2.04
1991-92	51.96	373.32	4.04
1992-93	135.63	317.94	11.20
1993-94	81.85	495.86	5.10
1994-95	107.10	665.73	3.86
1995-96	139.87	782.45	4.66
1996-97	224.75	1253.60	9.24
1997-98	91.95	1422.40	9.41
1998-99	253.13	1165.46	7.84
1999-00	-	-	6.52
2000-01	290.71	951.63	10.04
2001-02	292.44	1370.13	8.90
2002-03	734.71	1757.73	13.15
2003-04 (RE)	572.44	1732.61	17.00
2004-05 (BE)	601.06	1500.74	13.60

Source: Budget Documents, Government of Karnataka.

Chapter 17

Vision of Development in Karnataka

17.1 Introduction

Karnataka has a long history of developmental visions. One can begin with what Bharat Ratna Sir M. Visveswaraya said to make Mysore (the erstwhile state of Kannada speaking people) a modern state with prosperity. As back as 1903 when he initiated the construction of the first ever hydel dam and power generation plant at Shivasamundram near Mysore, he had well thought out schemes of modernising the country by taking big leaps. He had realised the weakness and strength of the society simultaneously. In his own words:

> The people themselves are, as a rule, passive and unaggressive. They are guided rather by the opinion of the caste or community than by a common national standard of life, thought and work, by century-old traditions and superstitions rather than by the collective experience of the modern world. .... Through leaning on others, large number of people have become reduced to social parasites (1920: 8).

He went on to say:

> If, as suggested in this book, the utilisation of India's man power and material resources is placed in the forefront of national aims, if the people's general and technical knowledge is developed, if private initiative is stimulated, if all the latest inventions and discoveries are applied to increase production, if foreign experience is adapted to Indian conditions and fully utilised and useful foreign institutions readily adopted, if in short, all the improvements necessary and possible are introduced, the development of India, politically, economically and socially, will proceed at a pace which may be one of the outstanding futures of the coming generation (1920: 14).

The process of development in Karnataka had always kept this foresight at the backdrop and attempted to overcome the weakness at the same time with appropriate policy measures. The vision on development in the state today takes note of the history of Karnataka as well. Ever since the state's reorganisation, attempts were set in, to reduce regional imbalances and to bring social harmony in the state. In the beginning of the 1990s, with the new economic policies of the nation in which Karnataka also participated, further steps were taken to modernise the state and to bring about social and economic upliftment and harmony. It also called for the introduction of several new strategies and policies. Very recently, the then chief minister of Karnataka in 2000 wrote the following:

> Our vision is for our state to be the power house that drives our nation to emerge as a clear leader in this New Economic Order. As new technology emphasises the difference between the rich and the poor, we want to ensure the new economy makes a difference in the life of the common man. In the New Economic Order, we perceive knowledge to be the driver and the most obvious segments of the knowledge economy today are the information technology, and the bio-tech segments with infrastructure and education being the key facilitators (Krishna, 2000: 2).

A document prepared in the year 2000, entitled *Karnataka: Future Vision and Current Action*, aimed at an overall growth rate of 8 per cent to 9 per cent with enhanced agricultural growth rate at 1.19-2.5 per cent, an average annual industrial growth at 12 per cent; fully tap the world markets in information technology, attaining information technology (IT) related exports of US$ 10 billion per year; and an average annual growth of employment at 3.15 per cent during 2000-2010. In addition, by 2005, the state aimed at total literacy and primary health care for the entire population, reduction in population growth rate to 1.4 per cent, and attracting private investment in industrial sector to the tune of Rs. 20000 crores per annum, planting e-governance and total transparency at all levels. Many of these foresights are relevant even today with some differences, some requiring major shifts in emphasis and some with new directions on governance, fiscal discipline, devolution of power, and empowerment of the people as additional riders.

As elaborately discussed in various chapters of this volume, the experience and attainments during the last two-three decades need to be seriously reviewed for bridging the gaps and to set up new visions, steps and corrective measures. This chapter is addressed at that with two specific purposes. First, providing a set of revised vision statements for the state. The context being the period of economic reforms, and such a restatement is necessary at this stage. Any restatement of the outlook for the state requires drawing upon the lessons from the development experience in the past, laying down a revised road map for the next two decades, and setting out targets for the medium term. This is by no means an easy task. The analysis of development in the state dealt in the earlier chapters covered a variety of themes such as strengths and weaknesses on resources (human, natural and economic), performance and perspectives on sectors (e.g., agriculture, industry or service and so on), and large number of cross-cutting social dimensions (e.g., historical, cultural, social, political, and regional). With a long history of development in Karnataka, an analysis of only the most recent past period are taken to knit concrete vision statements. Second, with a detailed policy chapter devoted to a series of policies (priorities, investments and resource flows) and drivers (institutional, legal and administrative) coming at the end of this volume, this chapter acts as a link between the subject based analysis carried out in the earlier chapters and the Policy chapter.

The Planning Commission (2003) has brought out a national level Vision Document for the coming two decades. Whenever it is liberalisation strategy or structural adjustment programmes, while much of the reforms process has to do with the national level foresights and policy developments, the options at the state level are only marginal. But, there are very distinct region-specific issues to be dealt with. They have to do with regional imbalances, devolution of powers at the *Panchayat* level institutions, involvement of local communities and non-governmental organisations (NGOs), public-private partnerships, and creation of climate of competitiveness and efficiency, all of which at some degree of micro-level. Many of these are derived from openness of the economy with efficiency, accountability, transparency, and essential principles of governance. Unless the national and state level visions are complementary to each other, the process of development can become hampered. Hence, this chapter has a special space in this volume.

17.2 Macro-Perspectives and Sectoral Growths

Where does the state stand now in the dynamic process of development? Karnataka has all the potential for rapid growth, much higher than the national average rate of 8.1 per cent gross domestic product (GDP) growth, as targeted by the Tenth Five Year Plan document of the Planning Commission. The per capita income of Rs. 11,800 (at 1993-94 prices) in 2002-03 is far above the national average. The current rate of gross fixed capital formation (GFCF) has been about 47 per cent of the gross state domestic product (GSDP). GFCF has been increasing at an average annual rate of 22 per cent from 1993-94 to 2001-02. The infrastructural GFCF requirements for a stipulated 4 per cent growth rate in agriculture and around 10 per cent in all other sectors (same as stipulated at the all-India level by the Planning Commission for the Tenth Plan period), are estimated to be around Rs. 13,250 crores on an average (at 1993-94 prices) per year for the coming years (as against the current rate of Rs. 11,000 crores).

Sources of investment in the state have been domestic savings (at around 20 per cent of SDP), inflow of private and foreign direct investments (FDIs) and borrowings. The capital formation in the infrastructure sector has recently registered a high average growth rate of about 12 per cent. In the recent past, more that 75 per cent of the overall investments have been coming from the private sector, an indication of confidence in private governance and management. Since the private initiatives and investments have been rising in the state, it is indeed possible to peg the overall growth rate at 8 per cent of GSDP in the medium-term. This should be the overriding target for the state.

No vision is free from concerns of some sort or other. In the dynamics of growth, the major one is on annual fluctuations on the investment front. Total investment (excluding investment of less than Rs. 3 crores) has been fluctuating over the years. The annual growth of total investment has varied from (-) 25.98 per cent in 1993-94, 260.48 per cent in 1995-96, (-) 22.02 per cent in 1997-98 and to 209.43 per cent in 2000-01. However, the average annual growth of total investment over the same period is equal to 39.22 per cent, which is quite high. Part of the fluctuation is due to an influx of FDIs in the recent past. The state should encourage private-public hub investment, with a view to stabilising the investment rates, thereby the GSDP growth rates.

Karnataka's average per capita net state domestic product (NSDP) growth rate was 5.71 per cent in 2002-2003 (average over the last eight years), but not without annual fluctuations. The GSDP rose at a compound rate of 7.1 per cent during the same period. Stabilising these growth rates forms the first charge of the foresight for the future. Though high incremental capital output ratios (ICORs) have been observed in various sectors of the state, the very high correlations (0.8) between SDP and growth rates of GFCF (and also high share of 47 per cent) suggest that the state can target still higher growth rates around 8 per cent. Once such a high growth path is set in, subsequently it is no more necessary to maintain the high (ICORs). Then, the fluctuations in the GFCF rates will also be less and become tolerable. Feasibility of this can only be visible through properly setting targets on the sectoral composition of the SDPs.

The distribution of state income across primary, secondary and tertiary sectors shows a major shift towards the tertiary sector, and especially away from the primary sector. For instance, the share of tertiary sector in the state income increased from 38.3 per cent in 1993-94 to 50.0 per cent in 2002-03. This shift from primary to tertiary sectors is also evident at the national level. With new developments in the biotechnology sector enabling diversification in agriculture, completion of Upper Krishna River based irrigation and other schemes, and creating marketing facilities for horticulture and other agri-based industrial products, the share of agricultural contribution to the GSDP can be targeted higher. Based on the analysis of agricultural sector, the corresponding sectoral growth rate can be pegged at 4 per cent, higher than the observed average of 3.2 per cent since 1993-94, thereby also raising its share in GSDP.

There is another matter of concern, however, on the fluctuation in the sectoral incomes. Partly because of severe droughts in the state during the last four years and the fluctuations in the international orders on exports (also clubbed with threats from other competing countries such as China on Indian exports from the IT and biotechnology (BT) sectors), the income from both agriculture and service sectors has been highly fluctuating. As a demand management strategy it is possible to bring about a balance between domestic (i.e., internal) and foreign (i.e., external) demands, so as to reduce the impacts of variations in sectoral incomes. This calls for constant monitoring of the agricultural input and output flows, price mechanisms and supports, and distribution systems.

17.3 Resource Development

The state has a strong base in human, natural and economic infrastructure resources. The fundamental question now is about properly deploying them to attain enhanced human development. Invariably, one notices a mismatch between such resources and development targets. The reasons are many. Resources are site-specific, and not demand-specific. They may require refinements to meet the needs during this reform period. Therefore, instead of simply trying to match them with development targets mechanically, it is necessary to make them closer to actual needs, in time, by region and by scale. This calls for a vision to develop proper institutions, information system, and timely linkages to deal with the resources.

With more than 13 universities, 712 general education colleges, 97 medical colleges, 96 engineering colleges, 181 polytechnics, 300 industrial training centres, and several premier institutes/centres of research in pure and applied sciences, social sciences and humanities, management, information technology, biotechnology, fashion technology, legal education, and manufacturing and foundry technology, the state can be aptly called the "Brain Bank of India". To get the best of this Brain Bank, it is also necessary to build a strong base at the literacy and primary educational levels. The overall literacy rate being about 67 per cent in 2001 with its rapidly increasing rate over the last decade, the human resource growth should be carried upwards. Several steps are required for this. The state will have to introduce certain innovative methods to bridge the male-female literacy gaps (which is currently about 22 per cent). Clearly, this requires a well-conceived design and strategy to implement within the next 10 years. Likewise, it is visioned that the rural urban gap (currently at 10 per cent) in literacy be reduced to nil in 10 years. It is possible to attain all these dimensions of balanced literacy provided the income ability to spend and 'parent participation' are also increased in the literacy mission. While targeting universal literacy missions for the vulnerable sections such as Scheduled Caste (SC) and Scheduled Tribes (ST) categories, and girl child education through various schemes, corporate involvement may be invited. It is time now that the design of technical knowledge and skill formation in the state is pegged at the high school and diploma level education than at the levels of higher education. This message comes clearly from the demand side of the service sector, be it software engineering or business process outsourcing (BPO) call centres, transport and mobile phone and other communication sectors.

There is lot more to be done at the state and regional levels on enhancing the level of human resources in the state. While a large number of programmes have been launched to bring about increased literacy and basic education, it is time to seek partnerships between corporate sectors, NGOs and governmental organs to make this change an enduring one. Therefore, while a vision of complete literacy within the next 10 years may be set, it also requires a design of creating action hubs. The recently emerging corporate sectoral involvement in primary education and literacy drives seems to be a possibility in this direction.

The state has a strong base in natural resources with about 20 per cent under forest cover and another 10 per cent of geographical area as pasture and uncultivated lands, about 117 lakh hectares (62 per cent of geographical area) under agriculture and cultivation, about 7,663 trillion metric cube (TMC) of water resources per year (of which about 50 per cent is dependable for use), and about a maximum of 1,695 TMC (covering about 30 lakh ha of land under one form or other) under irrigation. The state is rich in mineral resources like iron ore (about 4,000 million tonnes of reserves) and limestone and dolomite (about 20,000 million tonnes), extraction of marine and inland fisheries of about 1.9 lakh tonnes of fish landings on a sustainable yield basis. A comprehensive document on natural resource assessment and use, and carrying capacity is necessary now.

The Western Ghat Region has been identified as one of the 8 biospheres in the country. The biodiversity resources of this region should be fully protected and conserved. The current forest cover of 20 per cent of geographical area should be enhanced to possible 30 per cent, though at the national level 33 per cent coverage is recommended. These foresights for the state will have several gains in terms of abating climate change, stabilising rainfall cycles and enabling the poor with some access to forest and grass resource-based (non-timber forest product linked) livelihood.

Two major technological strides that the state has taken should also be noted. The state has launched a massive programme in the development of IT sector. A document released by the government in 1997: *Information Technology Policy-1997,* clearly sets out the enabling role of the state in promoting private sectors to come up with venture capital investments in this sector. Specially designed IT Parks and Electronic Cities have been set up at Bangalore, Hubli, Mangalore and Mysore. The state, as a major stakeholder and buyer, has been highly supportive and encouraging the use of IT in education, revenue, employment, police, environment, transports and industry, all of which are popularly called e-governance. For instance, under BHOOMI, 20 million rural land records of 6.7 million farmers through 177 government owned kiosks are being delivered online. This has reduced, among others, red tape in the issue of land title records. Likewise, land transaction registration under Kaveri and Khajane for treasury and revenue records (connecting as many as 4500 *Zilla Panchayats* (ZP), *Taluka Panchayats* (TP) and *Gram Panchayats* (GP), computerising transactions of about Rs. 20,000 crores per year, from about 225 treasury offices) is already functional. The recent growth of the IT sector in BPO and software exports only indicate the manner in which all the infrastructure development have brought dynamism in the growth process of the state. The current rate of investment in the IT sector cumulated at over Rs. 2000 crores but the current rate of increase of about 15 per cent should be maintained on a continual basis. This will require good demand and efficiency management. On the export front, newer avenues of BPO options should be tried. Potential sectors are financial institutions, insurance, health care and hospital systems. On the domestic front, all the government departments should take up e-governance on a priority basis. For instance, computerising combined entrance test (CET), status of primary health centres (PHCs), primary school status, water supply, property tax records, performance of *Panchayat Raj* Institutions (PRIs), etc. should be completed in the next phase of five years. Having taken a major lead in decentralisation and devolution of power and governance at the grassroot levels, the state has to accomplish computerisation of all aspects of governance, fiscal records and accounts, sector-wise activity and employment status, quality of life, etc. at the ZP, TP and GP levels.

Second, with the release of the document: *Biotech Policy 2001* and the setting up of BT Parks, the biotechnology sector has come out with packages of assistance to the farmers, drug manufacturers and exporters of processed foods, seeds, etc. Biotechnology development being a capital-intensive activity, its growth has to be matched by state support. While biotechnology companies have been growing at an annual rate of 28 per cent in the recent five years, the sector may soon find it difficult to grow at this high rate. Special cells and kiosks to provide information to farmers, small and medium drug manufacturers may be required, as a strategy to create awareness and demand push.

17.4 Infrastructural Development

17.4.1 Communication Sector

Lack of capacity utilisation and existence of unmet demand pose contradictions in the planning and development of telecom services in the state. Efficient and competitive delivery of communication services is important for attraction and sustainability of economic development in the state. Information-technology sector and communication sector are mutually complementary. Having taken a major lead in the IT sector as IT Capital of India, the first step for the communication sector should be to take this technology to every village in the state. Several steps beyond e-commerce, e-governance, e-education and IT-enabled services are required. They include, training the youth in IT even at the high school level as a vocational training, setting up of IT kiosks in every village, policy coordination between communication sector and information technology and so on. Several corporate initiatives on public-private partnership basis should be internalised within postal, telecommunication and IT-enabled service activities.

17.4.2 Vision for the Power Sector

Though Karnataka is in lead in many other sectors, power sector reforms in the nineties have achieved only a moderate success. Invitation to independent power producers (IPPs) received very poor response. The only success of the sector during the reforms period has come from unbundling of generation, transmission and four distribution companies (electricity supply companies: ESCOMs). Some strides have been made to reduce loss and improved accountability. This is not enough. The future for Karnataka's power sector must be defined in terms of the building blocks needed to implement effectively and sustain these reforms at all levels of generation, transmission and distribution. Major steps (as highlighted in Chapter 5) are to restructure Karnataka Electricity Regulation Commission (KERC) itself, and bring the consumers much closer to the distribution system. That requires a vision of good governance, public participation, transparency, disclosure mechanism and, demand side management. For instance, the concept of 'power *adalat*' should be universally used even at the *taluka* levels. Introduction of cost-based power tariff has received maximum resistance in the state. While the annual burden of subsidies are on the rise, it is also time to realise that quality of power would also suffer, in turn, unless some rationality on power pricing is introduced. When it comes to power subsidy to agriculture, the solution seems to be a mix of policies on the use of groundwater as well as gradually raising power tariffs on a progressive basis. Alternative sources of energy such as solar and wind energies have ample scope in the state, which should receive some priorities.

17.4.3 Vision for Irrigation Sector

When it comes to water resources, as of 2001, there still remains a harvestable balance potential of about 11.63 lakh hectares to be covered under major and medium irrigation. With this, the total potential of exploitable water resources in the state can reach the order of 36.22 lakh hectares (including groundwater to the tune of 9.08 lakh hectares). This full potential of water resources should be realised in the next five years. This is a major step to raise income and employment status from agricultural sector.

As a strategy, the starting point for such a vital sector is Participatory Irrigation Management. Otherwise, the gap between investments and actual delivery would continue to widen over time. Rather than stating that farmers are begging for free water, it is time to set the framework as one of 'pay and get assured water'. Recent institutional reforms have focused on setting up 'financially autonomous' irrigation agency, like the Krishna Bhagya Jal Nigam Limited, as means of bringing farmers-orientation in services. The second main thrust is to fulfil the basic assurance of completing irrigation projects on time. Nearly 50 per cent of the potential arable lands are still waiting for irrigation facility in the state. At the same time, groundwater regulation should be viewed as a conservation policy, to be developed on a regional agro-climatic basis.

17.4.4 Vision for Road Sector

The foremost task for the development of road infrastructure is to restructure the Public Works Department. Good governance and accountability and timely delivery are the first charge for this department. The department should be made fully responsible only for road construction and maintenance. There is a need for major transformation among departmental workers. Training the existing staff and bringing modern technologies in road construction, maintenance and vigilance are required as the first move.

At present, road coverage is not adequate in the state. It is just about 69 kms per 100 sq. kms of area. The situation is very bad in rural areas and in north Karnataka. The foresight on roads in the state should be to raise the road coverage to around one km per one sq. km area. Such a goal should be targeted in the next 10 years, ahead of other developments. After all 'it is not the wealth that builds the road but it is the roads that build the wealth'.

17.5. Sectoral Visions and Initiatives

17.5.1 Re-engineering Agriculture Sector

Among the many production sectors in the state, in terms of involvement of about 44 per cent of the workforce in the state in 2001 (out of 235 lakhs), agriculture had the maximum links with the people for rural development and livelihood sustainability. As already mentioned, the new challenge for the agriculture sector is to reverse the downward trend in its growth and development. A new vision is necessary on all fronts of productivity growth, agriculture diversification, technological break and R&D investments, institutional arrangements and links with the private sector and taking the stride in a market economy.

While designing a revised strategy, it is necessary to recognise the basic characteristics of this sector. They are: large share of rainfed area, frequent bouts of droughts (particularly in northern districts), only about 20 per cent area under assured irrigation, technological bottlenecks on non-food crops, and no major breakthrough in institutional mechanisms. In addition to these, the size of holdings has been shrinking at a fast rate.

The first vision is about setting a revised growth rate for this sector, much above the current rate of about 2.11 per cent during the last 8 years. The starting point for this is food security. This is possible first by concentrating on several policy drives internal to the sector itself. They are, attending to the special needs of marginal and small farmers (with about 80 per cent of total landholdings of the state), policies addressed specifically on stabilising land productivity at an efficient level with revised emphasis from crop intensification to diversification, from land productivity to overall gain from agricultural diversification (horticulture, floriculture, poultry and dairying, etc.), from state monopoly in procurement to creation of market information and forward market facilities, attaining potential irrigation levels and large-scale programme on watershed programmes for the benefit of rainfed agriculture, private involvement in extension services, matching demand and supply of seed and fertilisers on time and so on. With such major shifts, it may not be difficult to stabilise agricultural outputs growing at 4 per cent per year.

The second major vision is on linking sectors other than agriculture to this sector, particularly the service sector. Market creation, credit facility, information on domestic and international prices and quantity in production and demands, creating intermediary institutions to liaison between farmer communities and international markets, R&D programmes from 'lab to land', zeroing on the right kinds of biotechnology, and such other value added activities should be considered to link agriculture sector with many other sectors. This will enable higher returns to agriculture with improved efficiency. For instance, the application of biotechnology to evolve new genetically engineered strains of plants, animals, fishes and plants of high nutritional quality, resistance to pests and diseases, and environment-friendly farm practices can raise productivity as well as stabilise the growth.

The third major vision is on institutional changes by establishing better links between public and private sectors to come closer to the farmers. Apart from new institutional structures such as contract farming, community farming, market intervention system either through private agencies or by the state agencies, PRIs, NGOs and self-help groups, and water user associations be effectively involved in improving awareness about post-harvest handling methods, and creation and maintenance of infrastructure at the primary market level.

The final vision is on a fresh look at the subsidies in the agriculture sector. The current total subsidy (other than power subsidy) in the agricultural sector is of the order of Rs 600 crore (during 1995-96). This is of the order of 1.02 per cent of GSDP in 1999-00. While subsidy by itself is not necessarily bad, diversification of its use away from crop sector towards better delivery systems (seed, market access, storage, information providing, etc.) can lead to improved efficiency and productivity gains.

17.5.2 Vision on Service Sector and Development

When it comes to employment and development, the role of service sector cannot be ignored. Among the many options that the state has, tourism and the development of software and BPO services are the major ones with new openings and opportunities.

With a strong historical and archaeological background the state is enormously endowed in providing yet another major social service through tourism. Karnataka is also the first state to formulate Karnataka Tourism Policy way back in 1992, and also having declared it as an industry (way back in 1988). The New Tourism Policy 2002-2007 envisages that 10 years from now, tourism will be Karnataka's most important economic service activity, and would be accorded top priority. The background for this sector is vast educated human capital and the variety of tourist attractions. Attainment of this goal is possible with privatisation of several aspects of tourism such as ecotourism, sports tourism, heritage and religious tourism. It also requires coordination among all connected departments such as Revenue, Finance, Energy, Public Works, Forest, Rural Development and Panchayat Raj, Ecology and Environment, Transport and Home, and the Karnataka Electricity Board.

When it comes to software development and BPO services, this is one sector that has the full potential to grow in the hands of private sector, Already it has crossed employment of over 20 lakh skilled engineers, with over 1,500 software companies and an export share in the country of over 25 per cent. The goal for this sector for the coming 10 years can be to raise the annual employment off-take to about 5,000 skilled persons, with another 5,000 in ancillary sectors. It is also hoped that this is one sector that will add substantially to the savings and reinvestment in the state.

17.5.3 On Banking and Financial Sector

Savings and capital formation are critical for the development of an economy. Historically, having taken a lead in the development of the banking sector in the country, Karnataka has also encouraged a mix of rural and cooperative financial institutions to come up. With such a mix, the agricultural sector, the small-scale industries (SSIs) and medium industrial sectors will benefit from the credit flows and easy access. This mission, though is quite advanced in the state, be targeted better by expanding the regional rural banks (RRBs) and cooperative banking outlets at every village level. For this the PRIs should work together with the banking sector to bring the needy farmers and artisans closer to the banks and to enable to get easy access to credits.

Some new visions to enable the growth of IT sectors in the hands of SSI are necessary now. For this, the banks and non-banking financial institutions should expand their easy credit policies to the IT workers and other youths engaged in service activities including tourism. Such a move ahead of the development of the service sector may be necessary to attract both capital flows into the state and its availability for the younger generations of hope in the state.

17.5.4 Process of Industrialisation

Karnataka has by now crossed several stages of industrialisation. To begin with, an 'old economy', with industries such as precision engineering, automobiles, readymade garments and food processing industries, manufacture of silk, cement, steel, paper, textiles, auto ancillaries, machine tools and foundries dominated. This phase also saw the growth of private sector in the state. Then came the second phase of a very strong public sector, both central and state. The third phase of industrialisation included the high-tech industries in the state. The notable ones are electronics, telecommunication, information and biotechnology. It is now time to bring about a balance between all these phases of industrial development, so that while employment and efficiency of delivery system have to be maintained, added dimensions of export outlets, and regional balanced growth are to be reckoned.

In the past, Karnataka had also taken a lead in the development of small-scale units. While the axe of economic reforms can easily fall on them, it will be necessary to bring about modernisation in them, provide market opportunities and easy credit facilities. A revised vision on the status of small-scale industrial units is now necessary. The New Industrial Policy 2001 states its intention to promote entrepreneurship and human resources to help develop this sector. It is one sector that can reduce the hardships of regional imbalances and reduce pressures on urban systems. But the reality is far from attainment. Fresh capacity building on production system, material management, and service delivery are necessary to revive this sector.

17.6 Employment and Social Security

While Vision 2020 of the Planning Commission has set out very high targets of employment creation through the development process (10 million job creation per year), there are some serious concerns in the state. The workforce in the state has increased from 1.9 crores in 1991 to 2.4 crores by 2001, of which about 19 lakh workers were employed in organised sectors, whereas another 19 lakhs were on the live register of employment exchanges. But growth rate of employment in the organised sector of Karnataka, in fact, declined from 3.12 per cent in 1993-94 to 0.44 per cent in 1999-00. This decline was also evident at the national level. However, the annual growth of employment in Karnataka remained higher than at the national level. The average annual growth of organised employment in Karnataka was 2.74 per cent during 1993-94 to 2000, which is about 3.7 times higher than at the national level (0.74 percent). The daily status unemployment rate in the state during 1999-00 was 43 per thousand, as against 71 at the national level.

A major cause of concern is the declining rate of employment in agriculture sector. Labour absorption in this sector over the decade has declined from 30 per cent to 26 per cent. The only way to reverse this downward trend is to give a different package of agriculturally diversified productions with horticulture, agro-processing, fishery, poultry and such other activities taking a major lead over the traditional food and plantation crops. A second major issue in employment situation is reducing child labour. Properly designed social security system for the unorganised sectors can reduce this tendency. Opportunities such as transparency and involvement of civic societies be created to address this long standing human problem.

Karnataka still has a high potential of sustaining the employment rate in the organised sector. This is possible because of high rate of technical and professional education in the state and the fast track service sectoral growth. However, several traditional unorganised sectors such as *beedi* making, silk industry, tile, fishery, horticulture and forest-related activities share almost 75 per cent of total employment in the state. The future of employment rate in these sectors can still be higher provided a clearly laid out goal is set out for such employment. Currently, the state is considering a bill on social security and raising employment in this and self-employment sectors. Good training in processing, packaging, and delivery management in many of these export-oriented products can enhance the off-take as well as value added services.

It is time to set out a clear vision on matters of social security at the state level. Currently, some provisions on this are available mainly from organised sectors and government sector in the forms of pension, gratuity, medical support, support for higher education of children and so on. However, the development process should also take along a large section of the people categorised as farmers, unorganised workers, and disadvantaged (widows, underprivileged, challenged and disabled), also needing a decent living space. This goal can be visualised by good partnerships between corporate sector, NGOs, trade unions and other civil societies. The existing public institutions like Stree-Shakti, SHGs and farmer's associations should be strengthened to work on these lines.

17.7 Vision on External Sector

It is noted that as many as 7 traditional exports of relevance for Karnataka (*viz.* readymade garments, coffee products, iron ore and minerals, engineering, silk products, chemicals and allied products and leather products) have all decelerated from 81.03 per cent in 1993-94 to 47.10 per cent in 1997-98 and further to 35.15 per cent in 2002-03. On the other hand, the composition of electronics and computer software has accelerated from 7.77 per cent in 1993-94 to 37.12 per cent in 1997-98 and to 53.18 per cent in 2002-03. However, given the resource base and employment links, there is ample scope to raise exports of traditional commodities, while taking further strides in exports of IT-based services through the expansion of BPO sector.

What is increasingly disturbing is the fact of annual fluctuations in export performances. This trend is not good for any state, in terms of export earnings, employment and investment patterns. It is time that a foresight of stable export performance is necessary (though there are also theoretical arguments on the advantages of fluctuating export regimes). Under World Trade Organization (WTO) regimes, such a stability may be difficult at a state level (perhaps even at the national level). But with the advent of e-information, e-export and other options, farmers and manufacturers should be provided advance information on prices, market trends and direction of trade regimes. It is then possible to set export targets consistent with the overall growth rates of the state, nation and global economies. As reviewed already, exports as a share of state GSDP have increased from 7 to 10 per cent between 1997 and 2003. Therefore, a target of 10 per cent or even higher share of exports can be reasonably visioned. Commodities being impacted from fluctuations in the international markets need to be given additional storage, assurance of domestic lifting and buy-back arrangements. Industrial organisations like CII, FKCCI, GMCI should be involved in providing these facilities.

Another major vision required at the state level is on FDIs. Given its expanding service sector base, and globalisation on several fronts, there is ample scope for the state in attracting foreign direct investments. Based on the current trend, the number of such projects can certainly jump to 200-300 per year; likewise to target an inflow of enhanced foreign capital into state to a tune of US$ 10 billion by 2010.

17.8 Human Development

Human development is the ultimate goal of all development efforts, to which human beings are ends in themselves. They should not be looked upon as mere resources. They have resources. They are not resources. Their resources should be used to develop themselves and incidentally also promote the community and national goals. This should be the perspective of all development efforts.

Human development can be viewed in terms of population growth and its concomitant components. The overall index of human development in Karnataka (ranked 7th at the national level in 1991) has marginally improved to 0.630 in 1998 from an earlier index of 0.47 in 1992.

Karnataka shares 5.31 per cent of the nation's total population (846.30 million) in 1991, which has declined to 5.17 per cent (1,027.02 million) in 2001. The share of rural population in the state was 66.02 per cent in 2001, and the state's decadal growth rate of population also has been declining currently with 17.25 per cent in 2001, which is lower than at the national rate. In fact, the share of rural population in the state declined from about 69 per cent in 1991 to about 66 per cent in 2001. These trends of demographic transition show some healthy signs of population dynamics moving towards sustainability based on carrying capacity of the state. Viewed from fast declining crude birth rate, death rate and infant mortality rate, as compared to the national level, Karnataka has shown trends of sustainable population dynamics. In the long run, it is visioned that the population growth can be stabilised at 1.3 per cent per year (an average of southern zone states in 2001). It is also envisaged that Karnataka can attain the replacement level fertility by the year 2010. However, there is one issue of regional variation in the fertility rates and population growths that needs to be addressed in the coming 10 years. These region-specific demographic deviations can only be reduced by bridging regional imbalances in employment, education, health care and access to better quality of life (such as roads, drinking water, electricity, etc.).

Talking about human capital, literacy and education are two major milestones. Literacy in the state improved from 56 per cent in 1991 to 67 per cent in 2001 and was higher than the national level (65 per cent), likewise at the categories by male and female, and in rural and urban areas. The thrust of vision on the future should, however, be on raising rural and female literacy rates, bridging the gender and rural-urban gaps to nil by the year 2010. The 1992 revised National Policy on Education made the commitment of 'Education for All' as a mission. This mission will also remind that one third of the population is yet to be covered in the coming years. Other major challenges in this literacy mission are the quality of basic education, reduction of dropout rates (particularly of girl child), and reduction in the long-standing gap of male-female literacy (of around 22 per cent). The next challenge is to implement the goal of Universal Elementary Education (pending as a 2002 Bill before the Parliament).

Looking at the demand-side of human capital, there is a need to switch away from higher education (university degrees) to secondary and technical/ vocational education (to raise vocational skills useful in industrial, maintenance and service sectors). In the areas such as floriculture, horticulture, herbiculture, maintenance, sales and service of automobiles, electronics, and IT/BT sectors, vocational and field training should be designed based on location-specific demands.

The vision of Universalisation of Elementary Education and transition from higher education to vocational, technical and professional education will require building a strong institution of public-private partnership and education-industry linkage. Resource mobilisation (estimated to the tune of about Rs. 4,000 crores additionally and pegging a GSDP share of higher than the present 4 per cent) is feasible only under such partnerships in operationalising the process of linking education to job orientation.

Next to literacy and education, the most important human needs are health and quality of life. The vision on health care has to make a major turn-around now. It is not simply provisioning or public spending but making the system work. That requires several institutional changes in the health care delivery system. The new mission is to cover the poor on all aspects of their health care needs. The buzzword today is the 'cooperative health care' system, in which even the poor 'pays' but also 'gets' the necessary health care. Programmes such as Yashaswini Health Plan need to be re-examined to make it on private and cooperative partnership basis. The *Panchayats* should have their own choice of health care management system, be they with the involvement of corporate sector, or NGOs, other private provisioning, or cooperative and charity-based health care systems.

Karnataka has taken a lead in its mission of meeting drinking water needs on an universal basis. Through various existing programmes of Karnataka Urban Water Supply and Drainage Board (KUWSDB), Urban Local Bodies (ULBs) and Rural Development and *Panchayat Raj* (RDPR) (through the ZP, TP and GPs), about 85 per cent of households are being covered by safe drinking water in the state. But the twist required in this mission is on quality of water, assured and timely supply and easy accessibility. This vision is most urgently needed to be covered by the state machineries, though much of the decisions and implementation and monitoring are to be left to the *Panchayat Raj* Institutions. A new direction of 'willing to pay' should be used to bring about these changes.

17.9 Social Development

The mission on social and economic transformation is to bring in more and more inclusion rather than excluding marginalised and weaker sections of the society with one or the other constitutional provisions. Two special groups among them deserve redefining the visions for the future. They are Scheduled Caste and Scheduled Tribe populations, and women. All through the plan period, several schemes and special component programmes were introduced. However, the social status and transformation among them are still at a slow ebb. The major thrust should be providing land for the needy landless people, providing better training on land management with agricultural diversification, ensuring literacy and education, better credit and easy access facilities for legal defence and social security, and their recognition in social and political arena.

The declining sex ratio in the state is a serious matter of concern. It was 964 in 2001 (lowest among the southern states). Several districts within the state have shown much sharper declines. A clearly spelled out mission to raise this to a social status that of other states like Kerala (highest) and Tamil Nadu (second highest) should be the goal of the day now. Female labour force participation in work situations, in PRIs and community-based decision making should be enhanced.

Finally, there is a question of social transformation with good governance. It is hoped that the long pending 33 per cent representation for women in assemblies and much higher rates in all local bodies is realised soon. The state and the Centre need to carry forward the politics of positive discrimination. Given the fact that more than 35 per cent of our population lives below the poverty line and the discrimination of and atrocities against Dalits and women never seem to stop, the state's intervention in this matter both to protect and empower them through legal measures and constitutional provisions become a priority. But this can be realised only with a revised approach of 'inclusion' process. In this context, the role of Civil Society Groups and NGOs has become doubly important and even critical, especially to the cause of the oppressed and the marginalised sections of the society.

17.10 Regional Balance

Ever since the state reorganisation took place in 1956, with five major regional segments coming together, namely, whole of old Mysore state, parts of old Bombay state, parts of old Hyderabad and Madras presidency states and Kodagu, there was a vision of making the state united on all aspects of development on a principle of regional balance. Several committees have gone into this question of balancing regional development in Karnataka.

This objective of balancing is far from complete till now. All the 12 districts from north Karnataka and 7 out of 15 from south Karnataka are below the state average per capita income in 2001-02. Interestingly enough, the high imbalances in northern districts are not attributable to low rates of resource allocations, nor due to low rates of provisioning of health and school facilities. However, in terms of overall composite index of development in the year 2002-03, 8 districts from north out of 12 and 6 districts out of 15 from south are below state average. These recent facts on development in a regional context suggest the resilience power of the northern districts to maintain higher status of overall development. Therefore, the moot question on the future of Karnataka's growth and regional development is about internalising the strengths of all those backward districts.

Implanting a balanced regional development requires some fresh thinking. Focus should be on dispersal of economic and investment activities spread over the backward pockets of the state. With the development of IT, improved communication system and provisioning of various e-governance opportunities, it is certainly possible to encourage the medium and small-scale industrial units to move to remote parts of the state. This should be the first charge towards the objective on regional balance. Both the High Power Committee (HPC, 2002) Report and Administrative Reforms Commission's Report (2001) have already emphasised these strategies.

Regional development should be viewed in the framework of decentralised development. After the major shift in the development strategy, switching from centralised to decentralised framework under the 73rd and 74th Amendments to the Constitution, devolution of decision power and economic instruments in respect of as many as 29 functions and activities have been transferred to *Zilla, Taluka* and *Gram Panchayats*. They have also been empowered to raise their own resources. Several line departments such as Education, Health, Public Works Department (PWD), Women and Child Welfare, Water Resources, etc., have supported them. Significant amount of training and empowerment have already been parted to their members, communities and officials of the line departments and RDPR department. Recently, the Karnataka government has transferred as many as 180 state sector functions to the *Panchayat Raj* Institutions. Therefore, the second charge on bridging the regional disparity can begin from the GP, TP and ZP. They will be the first and best judges on identification of the gaps, deprivations and remedial solutions acceptable to the communities. An operational and implementable activity mapping be prepared on all the 29 functions identified for the *Panchayat Raj* Institutions in terms of their capabilities, capacities for their effective implementations and monitoring. These functions should be so regrouped as to internalise the policies listed earlier. For instance, the *Zilla Panchayats* can concentrate on both promoting public-private partnership and attracting industrial hubs. The *Taluka Panchayats* can take up implementing public-private partnerships with taluka level growth centres. The *Gram Panchayats* should concentrate on internalising the local talents in promoting employment and artisanships. They can easily involve the self-help groups (SHGs) and other NGOs in some of these functions.

A variant of this process of decentralisation is the vision of 'small village clusters'. Since many of the villages may not have all the complementary resources (land, water, forest, livestock, etc.), it may be possible to encourage groups of villages to come together to take up common activities such as watershed development, establishing small rural industrial processing units, etc. This framework of promoting economic activity is meant to reverse the trend of rural people to migrate to urban areas, and take advantages of scale economies with emphasis on rural employment and promotion of artisanships.

The third major objective is on building a strong base of civil societies all around the state. Though a large number of activities are identified for the *Panchayats*, to the extent they have to deal with the society, there is a need for involving other institutions as well. The concept behind the evolution of such institutions is the principle of 'participation'. Viewed on these lines, the role of NGOs and government supported organisations such as self-help groups, *stree-shakti, Swashakti* (under a promotive scheme of Department of Women and Child Welfare), Water User Associations, Village Protection Committees of joint forest management (JFM), etc. and cooperative banks and certain segments of corporate bodies and hubs are important as civil society agents, regulators, monitors and implementers. Already there are a large number of NGOs in Karnataka, directly working on water resources, health, education, sanitation, poverty and women development. These public-private partnerships should spread to all the districts. At present, there are no clear constitutional provisions, though Karnataka has enacted several legal Acts to implement such moves. Establishment of Water User Associations and Village Water Supply and Sanitation Committees (VWSSCs) can be cited as some examples. But, there are more opportunities to expand this scheme of thinking.

17.11 On Devolution of Power and Governance

On matters of governance, three major policy developments are in place in the state today. First, Karnataka enacted a Transparency Act in 2000. Transparency in administration and procurements, right to information, simplification of procedures and single windows for clearance have been introduced. Government departments have undertaken massive reforms to bring efficiency and transparency into play. Second, decentralisation in the development process at three-tier levels namely, *Zilla, Taluka* and *Gram Panchayats*, has been introduced since 1992. Third, the state introduced *Lokayukta* as an anti-corruption institution at the state and districts levels, and several citizen charters and people's forums such as water and electricity *adalats*.

Decentralisation is a process of translating development at political, administrative and fiscal management levels with local level elected bodies under the 73rd and 74th Constitutional Amendments. With regular elections to PRIs since 1992 and after having gained some confidence in both fiscal and administrative decentralisation, the major shift now aimed as a vision for the future is devolution rather simply decentralisation. As a process of political decentralisation, it is necessary to put into practice a strict process of 'inclusion' of all sections of the village and women representatives as per the reservations and requirements. This be done based on the principle of participation and not simply as constitutional compliance or obligation. It is necessary to bring some pressures from citizen groupings at the wards and village levels on building up of database by elected leaders to deepen the democratic process and improve the quality of people's participation. Political participation up to the level of district development committees and at all decision making levels in *Gram Panchayats* is to be ensured. Administratively, it is absolutely necessary to transfer all the responsibilities of planning and implementation of development activities to local bodies and it is also necessary to make line departments fully accountable to the elected members of the PRIs. The RDPR and other departments should act as enabling agencies only. On fiscal and fund management the concept of devolution would mean the local bodies to have full powers in designing all aspects of budget including salaries, expenditures on developmental programmes, etc. and also mobilising resources. For an effective devolution, the funds should be made as untied as feasible.

References

Bali, Arun P. (ed.) (2001). *Refashioning the New Economic Order: Karnataka in Transition*, Rawat Publication, Jaipur.

Government of Karnataka (2000). *Karnataka: Future Vision and Current Action*, Karnataka State Industrial and Development Corporation Ltd., Bangalore.

———. (2001). *Functional Review Reports*, Karnataka Administrative Reforms Commission.

———. (2002a). *Taxation Reforms Commission Report*, Finance Department.

———. (2002b). *Report of the High Power Committee on Redressal of Regional Imbalances*, Department of Planning.

———. (2003). *State of Environment Report*, Department of Ecology, Forests and Environment.

———. (2004a). *Revenue Reforms Commission Report*.

Kalam, A. P. J. Abdul and Y. S. Rajan (1998). *India 2020: A Vision for the New Millennium*, Viking Press, New Delhi.

Planning Commission (2001). *National Human Development Report*, Government of India.

———. (2003). *India Vision 2020: The Report plus Background Papers*, Academic Foundation, New Delhi.

Visveswaraya, M. (1920). *Reconstructing India*, P.S.King & Sons, Westminster, UK.

World Bank (2004). *Fiscal Decentralization to Rural Governments in India*, Oxford University Press, New Delhi.

Chapter 18

Policy Directions and Drivers for Future Development

18.1 Introduction

Design of development policy is always linked to vision of development. The period under reference is the forthcoming phase of economic reforms process initiated since 1991. Strategically, it is the demand-driven situation at all levels: macro and micro; regional, district and village. Therefore, as much as the vision has to be reforms-oriented, the policy will have to be people-oriented.

Several measures by way of targets and directions are suggested in the previous chapter for a medium term of 5-7 years. Based on the analysis of past performance and the resource potentials, and the vision on sectoral and social dimensions, the overall GSDP growth rate at 8 per cent is suggested. This will have to be backed up by about 4 per cent growth rate in agriculture (all primary sectors), 10 per cent in the manufacturing and secondary sectors, and 12 per cent in the service sector.

Implementation of such a macro perspective requires a sea change in policies. It may be recalled that till the beginning of the Ninth Plan period, public policy in Karnataka was generally conceived within the framework of planning at the state level, which was, by and large, supply-oriented. But, in the context of economic reforms now, it requires a different basket of policy package. The Vision Statements elaborated in the previous chapter (also in individual chapters in the earlier parts of the book) require policy directions, drivers and strategies to bring about public-private partnership, good governance, transparency and accountability, and fiscal discipline and management of the economy to balance between regional development and economic growth with justifiable social welfare.

All these are very tall orders of demands on policy. Moreover, since much of the reforms package covers the nation as a whole, at the state level there may be very little scope for any divergence from some of the central directives. Keeping these in mind, only such policy changes and strategies that are within the purview and framework of state policy have been presented and discussed here. The policies so propagated can be viewed as those that can be within a feasible action plan of the state government and those that require a dialogue and creation of an environment of public and private partnerships. The policy imperatives so developed are based on the analytical and critical discussion of the subject matters dealt in different chapters earlier.

18.2 The Directions

18.2.1 Policy Priorities—Continuity and Change

Taking the policy drive from the past, four major diversions and changes are worth considering in this phase of economic reforms.

They are about:

- revival of agricultural sector,
- new phase of thrust on industry and infrastructural development,
- dismantling command and control regime, and
- promoting regional balance.

During the early period of planning in Karnataka, the main focus of development strategy was clearly on agricultural sector. During the present economic reforms period, as analysed in other chapters, some symptoms of neglect of agriculture sector was witnessed. Agricultural production has remained constant; its contribution to SDP has been declining; employment in the sector also has been going down. Investment outlays, which was between 40-50 per cent in sectors related to agricultural development has declined to 31 per cent (by the Ninth Plan period). The areas such as irrigation, application of scientific knowledge, provision of agricultural credit, use of seeds and fertilisers, as well as land redistribution which were receiving attention there have all stagnated. Such downturns have affected agricultural output, productivity and employment in the rural economy of the state. Therefore, the first policy priority now should be to bring back agricultural sector on the rails of continuity in development. As discussed in the previous chapter, launching this sector on a stable path alone can sustain growth in the rest of the economy.

The second major driver for development in the earlier plan phases was capital formation and industrialisation. The main instruments were: (a) setting up of a supportive network of institutions, (b) creation of infrastructure, and (c) massive flow of funds from the banking sector. But all these were driven by government initiatives. For instance, in the past, nationalised financial institutions provided long-term loan finance and venture capital, and the state government provided land and infrastructural supports such as industrial sheds. Government subsidy was a major policy instrument. Several state level institutions (in addition to the national level institutions) were established to enable these. They included the State Financial Corporation, the State Investment and Development Corporation, the Small Industries Corporation and the Industrial Area Development Board, Regional Rural Banks and so on. Concomitantly, in the past, spending on infrastructure was also stepped up, and the state government allocated between 30 per cent to 40 per cent of total plan expenditure during the early plans to power, transport, communication and technical education. Apart from this, the government provided a number of promotional subsidies and tax exemptions on infrastructural development.

With all these, it was noticed during the economic reforms phase so far, that the industrial sector was stagnating with about 25 per cent contribution to the SDP. Labour absorption from this sector had come to a stand still. The new policy question at this juncture was about creating jobs and absorbing lakhs of engineering graduates and technicians from the state universities and colleges. Therefore, a fresh look at strengthening the manufacturing and industrial sector was necessary. Now, the new policy thrust will have to be to decentralise more of the industrial units, in and around centres of engineering job shops. Such a policy will also neutralise the regional imbalances.

This, in turn, calls for a fresh look at the adequacy of infrastructural development. Not that investments on infrastructural development were not there in the past. But they did not come up as per the requirements and did not meet the demands efficiently. The main switch in policy required now is not just mobilising investable funds on infrastructural development, but to involving the private sector and making them also to manage them on a 'build-operate-transfer', 'build-own-operate', 'build-own-operate-transfer' or 'build-operate-share-transfer' basis. This policy would not only reduce the pressure on the state for funds, but bring about more and more efficiency and accountability.

The third major shift needed now is on the extent of 'command and control' in the production and distribution systems. Political economy of competitive electoral politics has led to large and widespread subsidies in 'people-oriented' sectors like power, irrigation, food and agriculture, housing, education and even industry. Now that a sharp change in the policy environment has been introduced by the national level economic reforms itself, shifting more and more in favour of competitive, and transparent system, the same policy is yet to find its strong roots at the state level. The buzz word for this change is public-private partnership. A thrust on institutional change required now is regulation, in place of command. The sectors requiring some major shifts in this direction are power, irrigation, communication, road, tourism, urban water supply and so on.

The fourth drive on the policy front to be pursued and given a new shape is on matters of regional imbalances. As stated and anlysed by the Nanjundappa Committee in 2002, it is clear that a new set of policy drives are required to make regionally balanced growth a true reality. Significant policy changes are required here. The direct interventions alone with additional doses of resource mobilisation for the development of backward regions do not yield much needed results. The policy should be quickly switching to devolution of power to *Panchayat Raj* Institutions to raise the resources and use them for their own development. The current rate of allocations of about 32 per cent of state budget for these institutions need to be enhanced on yearly basis. Additionally, creation of private entry space for economic activities in the backward regions may be necessary. Some notably potential areas are infrastructural development and maintenance (roads, communication system, tourism, electricity distribution, drinking water supply, cooperative health care system and so on). A fresh thinking on modifying the Second Finance Commission's Award is necessary to take cognizance of regional disparity in resource allocations.

18.2.2 New Strategic Considerations

The new strategies to be either introduced or strengthened in Karnataka can be summarily stated as:

- proactive planning,
- consultative and participative approach,
- public-private-hubpartnership,
- small industrial and agricultural clusters approach,
- newly emerging sectors, and
- from domestic to export-orientation.

A number of new strategies are to be introduced in the reforms period now. Among them, giving means and support for the IT, BT and service sectors for their global integration are a priority. The policy calls for providing such services as a state-level mechanism for certification and accreditation of human resource training agencies so that good quality human resources can be accessed quickly. Setting up of regionally spread IT and BT parks is another major step in this direction. But creation of the necessary infrastructure and communication system is yet to be geared up. Priorities should be given for an effective policy package to stimulate growth in the backward districts and in the rural economy more generally.

The post-reform approach of the state has broadly followed a liberal model, with an increased role for the private sector. This measure should be intensified. The new word in this policy package is 'public-private-hub partnership'. In sectors, which hitherto were exclusively under government control, such as roads and power, transport, tourism and so on, private sector participation is to be actively encouraged. Privatisation, restructuring and disinvestments are the directions in which the government has to move further.

Another major shift in strategy to be intensified now is on the external front. With the direction of structural adjustment having already been set, substantial switch from a purely domestic market-orientation to export-orientation is necessary. The potential on this exists not only in the newly emerging IT and BT sectors but also in the traditional sectors like textiles and garments.

All these require a switch to a proactive approach towards the market, may be newly termed as 'proactive planning'. To be proactive also requires instituting good governance at all levels, be it industry, infrastructure, service deliveries or social security. The role of the government should be more as 'supportive' and vigilant rather than purely providing incentives for markets to emerge. For instance, various incentives offered for industrial dispersal have not worked. Vigilance and governance have to go together on the part of government and regulatory institutions. Today, the choice of an industrial location is based on the economic calculation by investors and entrepreneurs as well as that of buyers. It is time to take advantage of new information and communication technology and decongest urban agglomorates. The economic strategy should be based on regional comparative advantage while the social development strategy should be based on the logic of assuring equity.

There are some newly emerging problems under the current economic reforms period at present. In simple terms, they can be called 'problems of the commons'. Two major issues noteworthy are, high degree of urbanisation and environmental stress. Both these issues require a mix of legal, economic and civil society-driven instruments of good governance. The new phase of industrialisation should consider the possibilities of 'small industrial clusters' in different districts to reduce the pressures on urban land and other resources. Equally important is to introduce all such policy drives to reduce out-migration from the rural economy, mainly hoping to get employment in the urban sector. Rather, with innovative approaches the private sector should be enticed to move to the rural sector. This is indeed possible with the recent advancements in information technology and modern communication systems. Strict rationalisation of the pattern of utilisation of peripheral urban and semi-urban lands and introduction of 'willingness to pay' principle to abate and reverse environmental damages and for the maintenance of ecological balance between land, water, roads, parks and lifestyles are absolutely necessary at the moment.

A strategy of consultative and participative approach is the key in achieving such revisions on the direction of development. It is time to understand and appreciate the advantages and limitations of market mechanism in the design of state policies. In the context of a state, there are a number of sectors and activities that fall outside the orbit of market dynamism—such as the presence of backward and deprived regions and economically and socially marginalised groups. Rather, they become the ultimate victims of market forces. Even in sectors like agriculture, irrigation and power, there are difficulties in introducing market-based pricing systems at the state level. In many of these situations, a 'gradualist method of pricing' and 'incremental incentive-based strategies' are to be tried out. As a driving strategy, it is time to involve social groups at different levels in implementing such intermediary market-based instruments. Participatory irrigation management to resolve the water management problems in the irrigation sector can be an example to cite. Bringing Karnataka Electricity Regulation Commission closer to people's groups is yet another strategy. *Panchayats* undertaking public distribution system, cooperative health care system, regulated price shops, etc. are some of the other possibilities. In all such cases, the market signals of price efficiency clubbed with social needs can be met simultaneously.

Another important constituent of Karnataka's economy is the small-scale industrial sector. In a market system, this sector will remain relatively weak in terms of productivity and economic performance, particularly in comparison to the IT services sector. But its employment potential and meeting local demands must be appreciated. The New Industrial Policy 2001 states its intention to promote entrepreneurship and human resources to help develop this sector. Revised policy thrusts on training, fresh capacity building on material management, storage, handling and marketing are necessary. The task at hand is to facilitate the transformation of small-scale industrial sector or traditional artisan-based organisation to one that can compete effectively without a host of subsidies.

18.3 Basic Thrusts

18.3.1 Addressing the Question of Poverty

Whichever measure one uses, poverty estimates in the state show the concentration in the northern districts. As many as 48 *talukas* were found to be suffering from abject poverty (with more than 40 per cent families below poverty line) in the state, of which 30 were from north Karnataka. (GoK, 2002a: 75, 110). The estimate of people below poverty line is 33 per cent, higher than among the neighbouring states. On the basis of head-count rating, 6 districts of north Karnataka were worst in 1999-00. More important for policy purposes is the fact that 60 per cent of the poor of the state lived in north Karnataka.

But the policy drives, directly addressed to poverty alleviation *via* food for work, employment guarantee scheme, Rural Landless Employment Guarantee Programme and many such programmes did not yield any major reversal of the poverty syndrome. Instead of directly concentrating on attacking poverty reduction, incentive-based income approaches may be necessary. Incentives to opt for vocational training and job assurance from the newly emerging service sectors (IT, communication, storage, packaging and handling, machine tools and repair and so on) should be simultaneously introduced. Agricultural production cycles being the most direct factor for the incidence of poverty, policies of crop and livestock insurance must be made universal. In the dry land areas, diversification of agriculture should be propagated. Likewise, revival of small-scale industrial units, creation of additional infrastructural development, introduction of social security systems for unorganised sector are some of the new policy directions now.

18.3.2 Governance and Devolution Measures on PRIs

Under the principle of public-private partnership, promotion, production, and distribution systems of goods and services and social development in general require well established institutions of governance and accountability. Generally these are well stated than practised. It is time now to bring about specific policy interventions to institute them and create an atmosphere of effective functioning of those institutions. Having established institutions like Right to Information Act, *Lokayukta*, several *adalats* (on telecom, water and power), unbundling of several governmental institutions and organisations (in financial, banking, power, water distribution and so on), a space for good governance has already been created in the state. More desirable policy interventions now required are:

- making all public units and departments attuned to transparency and fiscal responsibility;
- effective utilisation of information technology in all aspects of governance;
- promotion of private Indian and foreign investment, and private-public partnership in owning, managing and financing of social and economic infrastructure sectors, and for promotion of tourism development; and
- special promotional policies (including attracting foreign investment and increasing exports) on key sectors such as information and communication (including electronics), biotechnology, automobiles, handicrafts, readymade garments, general engineering, and agro-food processing industries.

On improving governance and performance at the PRI levels several new initiatives are necessary. They are:

i. **Political decentralisation:** To improve the inclusion process for marginalised and minority sections of the population in PRIs. Although seats are reserved for SCs, STs and women as means of establishing this inclusion process they do not seem to participate in the most visible accountability mechanism, the *Gram Sabhas*. Training for these sections on more participation should be made part of this political process of decentralisation.

ii. **Administrative decentralisation in PRIs**: At all levels of decentalisation, the PRIs should be trained in the preparation of their plans and decision making, be they at district level planning, or *gram* planning, and implementation. Flexibility in such designs is necessary rather than uniformly designed at the ministry and department levels.

iii. **A fresh look at designing of Activity Mapping**: On the activities transferred to PRIs (under Article 243G) for effective implementation of planning, devolution and peoples' participation is necessary.

iv. **A separate cadre of officers for PRIs**: Is necessary for the fast implementation of decentralisation process.

v. **On fiscal decentralisation**: Notwithstanding the recent reforms (such as direct transfer of funds to GPs, discontinuing deductions towards electricity charges from the untied grant at the source, systematising the enumeration and collection of property tax, fixing water user rates, etc.), the fiscal decentralisation continues to be weak. The number of schemes meant for PRIs be reduced and moved in the direction of providing untied grants. As long as most fundings are scheme bound and there is no space for actual local initiative, people evince little interest in local level planning.

18.3.3 Employment Creation

Under the Vision Statements, the Planning Commission (Government of India, 2003) set out an objective of creating employment in the country at the rate of 10 million per year. The Common Minimum Programme of the United Progressive Alliance (2004) reiterates a similar statement to introduce Employment Guarantee Act for at least 100 days of employment per year. Nothing of this sort has happened till now, though way back in 1992 the National Development Council approved the strategy for the removal of unemployment and severe under-employment over the next 10 years.

The root causes of unemployment, apart from fast rising adult population, are illiteracy and lack of skills to take up jobs as demanded in this era of economic reforms. These call for the obvious policy interventions at promoting the right kinds of human resources and development. But, policies on employment cannot be isolated from other dimensions of development, be they sectoral or regional.

President Abdul Kalam and Y.S. Rajan (1998) highlight the need to strengthen three sectors simultaneously. They are agriculture (for reasons of food and nutritional security), manufacturing (for reasons of economic and national security) and infrastructure (for servicing the above two). They argue, that these in turn can generate sufficient employment. All the three sectors should be emphasised to target a sustained eight per cent growth rate in real gross state domestic product. Referring to Karnataka, additional potential exists because of newly emerging sectors such as horticulture, floriculture, herbiculture, agro-processing, IT and BT and BPO sector and so on. Specific policy guidelines on all these sectoral levels are presented in the corresponding sectoral frameworks, and hence, are not elaborated here.

There are three elements to the strategy to expand employment: (a) redistribution of income in favour of the low-income groups, (b) creation of public investment (specifically in infrastructure), and (c) provision of incentives to private investment. All these are to be designed so as to bridge regional imbalance in employment. Otherwise, apart from the obvious rural to urban migration, there are growing implications of regional migrations as well. The possibilities of resource allocations to be linked to the rate of unemployment at the district levels can also be explored; but information on these is difficult to quantify.

18.4 Sectoral Policies

18.4.1 Industrial Policies: Some New Twists

The previous chapter has already noted the stagnancy of the growth of industrial sector in the state. For this, a vision with a growth rate of 10 per cent is to be emphasised now. While major thrust is put on IT and software industry, pursuit of policies in the case of industrial sector is also a necessity. Attraction of new private and FDI investments (to raise investments to the tune of Rs. 20,000 crores per year), effectively introducing single window agency, creation of industrial parks, special supports to small-scale units are some of the new twists required now. With these, an employment target of at least 1.5 lakh per year has to be targeted.

The New Industrial Policy 2001–2006 of Karnataka has already sought to address issues relating to various contributory factors to industrial development. They are technology upgradation, infrastructure, human resource development, deregulation of business environment, marketing assistance for the SSI sector, and streamlining the single window mechanism. It also reconfigured the regional classification scheme for giving incentives into a System of Economic Zones (SEZ) as developed areas, developing areas, backward areas, with special focus on growth centres and mini growth centres, export promotional industrial parks, and specialised industrial parks. The role of Karnataka Udyog Mitra as the 'nodal agency' should be enhanced.

But the implementation of all these require new approaches. In the era of economic reforms process it is important to move from a 'policy orientation' to a project orientation. In policy orientation the emphasis is more towards making pronouncements, issuing guidelines, streamlining procedures, and prescribing incentives and subsidy schemes and structure. In project orientation, the emphasis is on being proactive in identifying projects, targeting investors, promoting SEZs, and customising incentives. The emphasis should be more towards identifying shelf of large and mega projects and make targeted search. The players in areas like industrial park and township development, port development, airport development, gas pipeline laying are small in numbers and it is important to sell the projects on individual basis. For mega projects it is important to proceed with customised policy framework. Generalised policy framework can work only with large and medium-scale industries.

The government of Karnataka already has a general industrial policy, along with complementary policies for the general industrial policy and sector-specific industrial policies for the promotion and development of industries in the state. These policies include:

General Policies

- New Industrial Policy 2001-06

Complementary Policies

- Export Promotion Policy, 2002
- Infrastructure Policy for Karnataka, 1997
- Power Sector policy, 1997
- New Tourism Policy, 1997
- Karnataka Industries (Facilitation) Bill, 2002

Sector-Specific Industrial Policies

- Information Technology Policy, 1997
- Agro-Food Processing Industrial Policy and Package of Incentives and Concessions, 1999
- Industrial Promotion Policy for the Automobile Industry, 2000
- The Millennium Biotech Policy, 2001
- The Millennium BPO Policy, 2002

It is time now to have a review of all these policy statements and directives, to have a revised set for the next 10 years.

18.4.2 New Directions for Agriculture

Karnataka is characterised by natural phenomena of large share of rainfed area, frequent bouts of droughts and has only about 20 per cent of the area under assured irrigation. High dependency of farm labour, declining share of GSDP from agriculture and stagnating trends in capital formation and declining employment are the economic derivatives.

Therefore, this sector requires some new policy thrust for three basic reasons:

- First, the weak performance of the agricultural sector during the reforms period is a matter of serious concern. In fact, the slow growth of the sector, on which two-thirds of the population rely for livelihood, has always been a longstanding source of concern for policy makers. Stagnancy in crop agriculture is visible all over the state, partly due to yield rates having reached close to the technological optima. It would now require placement of growth focused on the non-food crop sector, without neglecting the food security issues. Oilseeds, pulses, sugarcane, maize and other millets are the crops that need to be attended to on technological as well as trade fronts.

- Second, invariably the northern Karnataka regions are heavily drought-prone. Dealing with such regions requires a mix of human development, resource development and institutional development for providing basic foundation for agricultural growth and development.
- Third, attention should be given to reduce hardships due to fluctuations in crop productivity (or failure) to move away from crop agriculture to agricultural diversification. The notable avenues are poultry, fishing, horticulture, floriculture, storage, packaging, food processing and so on.

Keeping these main visions, several sectoral policies are suggested:

Land Use Policy

Consolidating the small patches of holdings be achieved through informal cooperation among the small and marginal farmers in the production processes. This has to be done for selected crops and crop groups by developing proper market chains or forward markets. At the same time, it may be possible to pool the resources towards enhancing productivity and improving efficiency in rainfed agriculture by undertaking selective watershed development and rain harvesting programmes. It also means that instead of targeting on large wartersheds, it is time to promote small or mini watershed programmes covering around 500 ha. of land.

Supply-Demand Management

If there is one area in which agricultural policy has failed, it is in bridging the gap between supply and demands for seeds, fertilisers, market access, storage facility and transportation. For instance, the density of markets is quite insufficient to deal with the requirements of increased production of various commodities. The presence of private sector in many of these areas is a welcome feature.

Integrated pest management and integrated nutrition management are the two major planks to deal with increased use of pesticides and managing the soil nutrition capabilities. These activities have to be emphasised in terms of private investment as well as extension network. The best way to achieve this is to strengthen the Krishi Vigyan Kendras and the Rayat Sampark Kendras. On the issue of rural and agricultural credits, the cooperative banks should have a wider network covering up to the level of agricultural marketing.

Restoration of Biological Equilibrium of Soils

Restoration of soil health and fertility through appropriate technology package including vegetative cover would be crucial. At the community level, vegetative cover around the village on main roads leading to farms, on tank/canal bund and on common land will have to be promoted to provide sound environmental support to agriculture, in addition to building up vegetative cover at the farm level. Recently, the government of Karnataka has come out with a state policy on organic farming, and articulated very well the advantages of organic farming technology *vis-à-vis* green revolution technology.

Forest Development

Karnataka has not been able to implement joint forest management (JKM) effectively so far. New policy and legislations are necessary to make JFM as part of PRI and SHG linked activities, so that it can be replicated all over the state. The rich Western Ghat and other major forests do require special attention within the plan allocations for conservation. Being a plantation rich state, tree categories like tea, coffee, rubber, linolae, etc. should also be encouraged under private forest plantation activities. The biodiversity richness of the state should be strictly brought under the State Biodiversity Authority for effective protection and preservation.

Agricultural Marketing

Against the odds of WTO and international prices, the farmers of Karnataka are to be provided sufficient advance market information, advantages of regulated markets and safety net in the form of a minimum support price (MSP) policy. It is time that MSP considers managerial input/costs as much as all other input costs. This has already been reiterated in the 1955 Agricultural Policy Resolution of the Government.

Public market channels for non-cereal crops such as pulses, oilseeds and maize should be added. Further, group marketing by farmers, farmers' markets and strengthening of rural periodic markets, agricultural marketing extension and incentive for private sector to participate in market developments are the thrust policy directions. Karnataka also has rich experience in cooperative market systems. This should be strengthened.

It may also be possible to involve agencies like PRIs, NGOs and self-help groups in improving awareness about post-harvest handling methods and creation and maintenance of infrastructure at the primary market level.

Research, Extension and Development

The recently announced Central Government Policy on enhancing R&D investments, extension services are nothing but a revisit to the forgotten policy drives in the country. Biotechnology has a high potential in evolving new genetically engineered strains of plants, animals, fish and plants of high nutritional quality, resistance to pests and diseases and healthy growth attuned to environment-friendly farm practices and in reducing pesticide usage. It holds promise for increasing the productivity, quality, efficient processing and utilisation of products and at the same time reduce reliance on agro-chemicals and other external inputs. A new phase of training in extension services to cover risk management, on public-private partnerships with agri-business, material management, storage, processing are to be the new policy initiatives. Some of the new directions to be emphasised are:

- Breeding and managing crops to conserve water.
- Research on the effects of climatic change on water resources.
- Training on improving water quality and efficient use of irrigation water.

In this respect, privatisation of extension services through suitable accreditation mechanism needs to be considered to make this process of technological access faster.

Watershed Development: Towards Sustained Development

It is by now well recognised that though the major responsibility on regeneration of soils and land resources rests with the government, people's involvement is essential for sustainability. The watershed programme has emerged as an important avenue on this. However, several departments are simultaneously working in the districts without much concern for convergence of common goals. As a policy now, it is time to declare *Zilla Panchayat* as the nodal agency to replicate the programmme in all the districts. The Watershed Department may provide the necessary technical assistance. It is also time now to use modern information systems and GIS maps to design the programmes more effectively. Land use and land cover maps based on the concept of Integrated Mission for Sustainable Development (IMSD) prepared by remote sensing agencies to be made use of for this purpose. Watersheds should be prioritised on the basis of their erosion/degradation status rather than on their 'agricultural backwardness' and rainfall as done at present.

Linking with Trade

Agricultural diversification in the areas of horticultural and floricultural produce, processed agri-products, silk products and fishery products are the forerunners for catching up with the external sector. Information generation, market creation, extension training as mentioned above should be linked to these export objectives. More than these, one does not see the need for any other incentives or subsidies. Some additional investments are required to boost horticultural sector, particularly on cold storage. Training on varieties covering long shelf life, fibre content, colour and proper timings of harvesting various fruits have to be organised. These land-based activities can also reduce regional disparities in the state to a large extent. Specific focus by specialised institutions (like KAPPEC) needs to be laid to promote the participation of the upfront trade products in the international sector.

Sericulture: Pride of the State

In today's world, though Karnataka is the largest producer of silk in the country, it has to compete with international quality of silk. India is still a raw silk importing country. As a first step, it is necessary to minimise the dependence on imported silk by producing bivoltine and multi-voltine cultivars. Improving the quality of silk and modernisation of the production sector to reach the international standards is also necessary. Like all other export-oriented sectors, by 2005, under the WTO regime this sector has to be prepared to face the open economy. Additional skills and training for silk entrepreneurs on the new regimes, providing international market information using IT techniques and biotechnology-based developments on improving the productivity of mulberry worms are the new policy thrusts required now.

Challenges in Fishery Sector

The full potential of this sector in the state is still not tapped. For this, the policy interventions in terms of rejuvenating *taluka* level nurseries, establishment of private seed rearing facility in the command area of large major tanks of more than 100 hectares with technical and financial assistance, promoting new concepts like rearing of fish seed in pens and cages in major tanks and small reservoirs, weed control and desilting of tanks, promoting storage and transport facilities in the private sector to maintain fish quality and facilitate better marketing network, introducing biotechnology-based genetic improvements of fish species, extension training in knowledge transfer and capacity building of farmers through large-scale demonstration are some of the crash programmes required now.

Major Policy Guidelines at the Agricultural Sectoral Level

In terms of decisive policies, some of the major guidelines can be listed now:

- Capital formation in the agricultural sector must be made to grow at least at the rate of five per cent per annum. Inducing private capital formation is also important, particularly in seed development, storage, processing and transportation activities.
- The full potential of irrigation should be attained by the year 2010.
- Rainfed agriculture and livestock development should take advantage of new technologies such as biotechnology.
- Next phase of land reforms should provide flexibility as well as free operations in the land market without tampering with the Land Ceiling Act. The unabated conversion of agricultural land to non-agricultural uses has to be checked.
- Decongestion of farmlands is essential to enable dry land farming economically viable. This can happen through a deliberate plan to wean away a minimum number annually to alternate livelihood opportunities, as being initiated in China.
- Reforms in agricultural marketing are long due and particularly after the submission of Guru Committee and Patil Committee reports.
- Enhancement of investments in research and development and extension, both from public as well as private sources, to be targeted at Rs. 100 crores per year.
- Horticulture, floriculture, sericulture and fisheries are the emerging vanguards in the trade sectors. It will be necessary that the state undertakes policies to make the producers and traders in these growth drivers to participate proactively in international trade along with post harvest processing. Specialised institutions like KAPPEC need to be strengthened to promote the participation and making the farming community reach international markets in these products.
- Establishment of biotechnology parks exclusively for marine resource development should be undertaken.

18.4.3 Policies on Communication, IT and BT

In terms of its share in the state income, undisputedly communication sector is a major contributory to economic development in Karnataka. The objectives of service access (both telecom and postal services) and affordability of overall communication services are being kept in mind. In this respect, lack of capacity utilisation and unmet demands pose contradictions in planning and development of the telecom services in the state. Furthermore, improving the expressed demand for telecom services (i.e. basic, value added and broadband services by fixed and mobile services) deserve special consideration for implementation.

As already emphasised in Section 18.2.2, information-technology (IT) and communication sectors are mutually complementary. Many of the recent postal services use information technology for speedy and efficient delivery of services. The objectives of the Millennium IT Policy in 2000 (called Mahithi) includes important social and cultural aspects, such as, use of IT technology in the overall goal of the government of Karnataka in eradicating poverty and empowering women and to promote the usage of Kannada in IT. Promotion of and setting up of targets on e-commerce, e-governance, e-education and IT-enabled services (e.g., call centres/customer interaction services, BPO, insurance claim processing, medical transcription, legal database, online education, payroll/HR services and web services) are necessary now.

18.4.4 The Future of Power Sector

The review of power sector reforms in the state in the nineties indicates only a moderate success at best. The thrust of reforms was to attract independent power producers (IPPs) to boost generation of investments, which has not materialised much. The state has been attempting privatisation of power distribution for a few years now, but without concrete results. At the same time, the transmission and distribution (T&D) losses have increased (around 36 per cent), and the annual power subsidy burden has also increased to Rs 1,800 crores.

Looking forward, the Electricity Act 2003 (E-Act) envisages several paradigm shifts. With generation delicensed, IPPs can exploit open access to sell power directly to consumers and across regions. The tariffs have to be revised toward cost of supply. But these steps require proactive intervention by the state government, both in policy and rule-making.

The first step in this direction is reforming Karnataka Electricity Regulation Commission itself. The E-Act relies heavily on KERC's decision making authority to implement reforms—including open access rules and tariff rationalisation—as well as to guide future utility operations, including regulation of power purchase, utility performance, service quality, guiding on power purchase procurement, and ensuring competitive bidding and public participation.

Secondly, the E-Act's objective of eliminating cross-subsidies requires understanding customers' cost of supply, which relies heavily on customer load profiles. Further, demand-side management, loss reduction and improved customer management (metering and billing) are necessary for reducing costs and future capacity needs. Distribution companies must be required to collect and disclose such information, and implement metering and IT system judiciously where most needed.

The third policy thrust is on subsidy reduction. With tariff rationalisation, the current level of Rs 1,800 crores should be reduced to below 1,000 crores. Subsidy if required should be based on the principle of performance, targeted to specific consumers. Financial incentives to support for physical system upgrade, including loss reduction, metering and IT deployment should be introduced.

Finally, only transparency and public scrutiny of utility operations through the avenues for public participation and consumer grievance provided by the regulatory process can improve SEB governance.

18.4.5 Policy for Irrigation Sector

Having taken a lead in major irrigation systems in the country in the last century, time has come now in Karnataka to examine the entire irrigation policy afresh. The major issues are on sources of water, the irrigation technology and their productivity, sustainability, investment focus and financial discipline, and sector management.

To begin with, the full potential of surface water irrigation is yet to be achieved. The remaining 50 per cent of water works need about Rs. 15,000 crores of investment, which is a priority. The GoK (2002a) has already made a recommendation on this, to be attained in eight years.

On the matter of implementing participatory irrigation management very little has been achieved. Even today, major and medium irrigation systems in Karnataka have been wholly state managed with very little user's participation. The National Water Policies (of both 1987 and 2002) have also stressed the involvement of farmers in various aspects of the management of the irrigation system, particularly in water distribution and collection of water charges. It is necessary now to explore more and more financially viable private investments on irrigation projects (as was done with Krishna Jal Nigam Ltd.). This also means, farmers are also to be partners in decision making on water distribution and pricing systems. Though the state has already introduced Water Use Association Act in 2000, the scheme is still to take its deep roots. In the area of groundwater development, particularly, in the management of artificial recharging, treatment of aquifers, etc. private agencies can be encouraged to come up, either on a cooperative basis or on a corporate sector basis.

It is also necessary to make corrections on wrong policies made in the past. A case in Karnataka is lift irrigation schemes in certain districts. They need to be abandoned without wasting any more resources and time. Almost 40 per cent of the lift irrigation schemes implemented in the districts of Raichur, Gubarga, Bidar, Bellary and Bijapur are just not working, and even those working are providing just about 36 per cent of potential water.

A fresh look at the development of irrigation technology is required now. The emphasis on provisioning only is not enough. Technology development has also to be kept in mind for possibilities of sub-optimal distribution of water (e.g., timing, reliability and spatial distribution), deficiencies in agricultural extension, limited research on irrigation technology, insufficient piloting of innovations, poor design and project preparation.

18.4.6 Policy for Road Sector and Opportunities with Tourism

Though Karnataka is one of the well developed states of India, the growth of road network has not kept pace with the requirements. It is important to recognise the fact that road connectivity to rural areas is very necessary for improving the socio-economic conditions of rural people. Several reform steps are required to improve the road infrastrctures. The government of Karnataka has created a special cell, known as Karnataka State Highway Improvement Project (KSHIP) as a project implementation unit. But it should be delinked from PWD, just as Karnataka Road Development Corporation was set up in 1999. Moreover, PWD should also be delinked with its building and construction activities, and made responsible exclusively for road and bridge maintenance only.

There is also a need to change the current practices of contracting on construction but maintenance to be dealt by PWD or other departments. The policy should be one of build-operate-maintain on a private venture basis. Additionally, there is an urgent need to upgrade capacity building and human resource development in all the organisations associated with road development.

There is a necessity to augment the resources for highway projects by allowing private sector participation. It is estimated that to maintain the existing road network in Karnataka, about Rs. 9,000 crores are required at 2001 price level. In the long run, therefore, creation of a Karnataka Road Fund may be considered.

When it comes to tourism, apart from the New Tourism Policy 2002-2007, no major policy changes have occurred on tourism in the state, but there is a marked decline in tourism activity. With the high potentials in eco-tourism, religious, archeological and cultural tourisms, the private sectors should be fully opened up to create a healthy and user-friendly atmosphere for the growth of tourism in the state. Hotels, beach resorts, eco-friendly resorts, wayside facilities, adventure/recreation centres like golf courses, aero sports, amusement parks and other tourism related activities be opened up for the private sector to invest and manage them completely on their own all over the state.

18.5 Regional Policies

18.5.1 Alternative Strategies for the Development of Backward Regions

It is by now well recognised that a large number of backward regions in Karnataka lack basic social and economic infrastructure in general, as much as amenities for human development. However, infrastructure backwardness is not uniform among all the backward regions either. It is also increasingly revealed that a uniform policy for different types of backward regions is not feasible. Instead, differential strategies or flexibilities are needed as the first policy change for the development of differentially endowed and differentially developed regions. As analysed in Chapter 10, some regions are very well endowed with social infrastructure and may be lacking in economic infrastructure or infrastructure essential for the development of productive sectors. In some other regions, capital inflow may not be very difficult but because of lack of social overheads, capital may be shying away. There may also be a situation of lack of social capital in certain parts of the state, where government may have to explicitly encourage civil society groups, SHGs, NGOs to come up and take on the tasks of creating awareness, communicating with the governments about gaps and deficiencies and malfunctioning of public services and so on.

Secondly, the sectoral approach to deal with regional disparity has its limitations. Instead, major district and state level economic activities should be transferred to the PRIs, at the three-tier levels based on a model of area approach. This will make local participation effective, and economic and social deliveries transparent and accountable. Recently, the government transferred most of the state and Central schemes to the PRIs—321 to *Zilla*, 108 to *Taluka* and 43 to *Gram Panchayats*)—with a net additional transfer of about Rs. 4,000 crores per year.

Thirdly, there is no need to maintain uniform programmes on poverty alleviation, redressal of gender disparity and social exploitation directed from the state headquarters. They should be made area-specific regional issues, to be dealt by PRIs and SHGs. But they should work together. This way, additional parallel institutions overlapping on the PRIs are not needed.

Fourthly, in order to bring out the hidden potential, investment in productive non-farm sectors like horticultural processing, rural marketing, and services (including IT and BT) and artisanships need to be enhanced. This, in turn, requires policies of attracting capital and investors from within the region and from outside. This is a matter of public-private partnership and creating forward linkages.

Fifthly, in a country like India and equally so in Karnataka, backwardness of a region is also due to predominance of rural sector. Most of the villages are scattered and economically unviable to promote any one activity. This has led to considerable out-migration of rural artisans to urban environments. To overcome this shortcoming, cluster of villages as 'rural growth centers' like small towns need to be identified and create an atmosphere for attracting both investments and consolidation of skill.

Finally, at present, allocation of resources does not seem to be in response to any major disparity linked issues among the regions or districts (except for population size and area). The State Finance Commission takes note of rural area (28 per cent weightage), population (28 per cent), road length (9 per cent), and illiteracy (19 per cent) for allocating resources to PRIs. Though disparities in access to roads and literacy are two major stumbling blocks in attaining regional development, several other major social and economic maladies are left out. The major ones are health care, education, and quality of life (access to sanitation, drinking water and so on). Keeping these in mind, a new strategy on resource allocation is needed. Allocations be made directly linking on the disparities in the development of health care and education facilities, rather than simply linking it to the levels of illiteracy. Likewise, it be inversely linked to the status of drinking water supply and sanitation facilities.

18.5.2 Policies on Uneven Urbanisation Pattern

The growth process so far has led to more than national rates of migration and levels of urbanisation in the state. This has growth rise to several emerging problems and constraints and pressures such as—power shortage, roads and public transportation bottlenecks, water, sewerage, sanitation and air pollution problems. A closely connected issue is that of land utilisation in urban environment.

At the policy level, it is now necessary to develop and strengthen the towns all along the 'corridors' of the national highways, rather than converging around mega cities like Bangalore. The major ones are Bangalore-Belgaum corridor, the Mysore-Bangalore-Kolar corridor, and the coastal Mangalore-Udupi-Karwar corridor. This will take away significant pressures on Bangalore as a mega city. It is possible now to act on this policy because of improved communication and IT services.

Having witnessed the deficiencies in public services and peoples' willingness to pay for them, it is time to introduce sanitary, water supply and power systems based on cost linked tariff structures.

Thirdly, citizen forums are to be encouraged to act upon on a participatory basis to take up household linked sanitary, neighbourhood environments and social issues such as collection and disposal of garbage, recycling of wastes, security against crime and so on. In addition, regular Citizen Report Cards should be produced and widely publicised.

18.5.3 Policies on Natural Resource and Environmental Management

Forest Resources

Karnataka has about 20.5 per cent of the geographical area as forests, coming under the jurisdiction of Forest Department, of which nearly 16 per cent is under good canopy cover where canopy density is more than 25 per cent and the remaining is either degraded or devoid of vegetation or tree cover. Since 1978, the state has lost about 1,34,000 hectares (approximately about 3.5 per cent of forest area) by way of encroachment and conversion to non-forest use.

The Karnataka forests support around 4,500 species of flowering plants, about 500 bird species, 120 species of mammals, 160 species of reptiles, 70 species of frogs and 800 species of fishes, out of which 350 species are endemic. The Western Ghats which cover about 60 per cent of the forest area of Karnataka is considered as one of the 25 biodiversity hot spots of the world and form an important ecosystem. As these forests are sources of livelihood to millions of people living in and around the forests, they are subjected to severe anthropogenic pressures.

Loss of forest cover and its degradation, extinction and endangered status of biological species are the major issues in the state today requiring immediate policy interventions. First and foremost is to put State Biodiversity Authority into functioning. Second is to stop all conversion of forest areas to non-forest uses.

As far as forest management is concerned, a balance between the Forest department's regeneration and conservation efforts and community-based protection activities are necessary. Under Joint Forest Management, though by the end of 2003 as many as 3,799 village forest committees (VFC) are formed, their effective functioning is still a question. The position of the VFCs should be made more specific, in terms of their responsibilities and shares in the forest produce. Then, there is an issue of parallel roles between VFC and *Gram Panchayats* (GP). Under Article 243G, several forest related functions are transferred to the *Gram*

Panchayats. But VFC has to deal with specific and technical issues related to forests (to take up nursery work, protection and soil and water conservation works and so on). Therefore, it should be constituted as a part and parcel of the GP, but with independent charge on all matters of community forestry.

Water Resources

As far as water resources are concerned, several refinements on the policy are required. First, even though 'river basin' has been recognised as a planning unit in Karnataka, a concrete system to account for dynamics of water resources and issues related to it have not yet been developed. Second, as far as the State Water Policy 2002 is concerned, the establishment of State Water Resources Board is overdue. But it is also important to establish these boards at the basin level rather than as a centralised one. It is in this direction that it is time now to develop a complete 'water accounting system' at the basin level. The modern method of remote-sensing should be used to map both hydrological and economic activities to arrive at the linkages. Third, increasing groundwater exploitation is going to lead to a major environmental crisis in the state. It is high time that rules and regulations on groundwater use be made agro-climatic zone specific. Power subsidies are no more required for water pumping, except in the regions where alternative source of water is not available. Fourth, there are as many as 1,776 water user associations established by September 2002. But their functioning is still doubtful in the state. Just as JFM has evolved a structure of village forest committees, the water user associations may have to development specific rules regarding user charges and protection from overuse and exploitation of groundwater. Finally, revisions of water prices are overdue. The Department of Mining revises these once in 10 years. The revisions should be made more regularly and linked to cost of water supply and also the land productivity due to water use. Water pricing can also be linked to recycling and reuse of water rates.

Issues on Land and Soils

The major land and soil related issues requiring research and policy interventions are limitations of soil texture, surface crust formation and drainage, salinity, sodicity and erosion, slope conditions, gravel content, shallow rooting depth, gravelness, and climate.

Among many others, excessive irrigation and faulty water regimes seem to be causing severe soil erosions and degradations (including salinity). The second most important issue is of fragmentation of landholdings, encroachments and habitat destructions. It is time that the state evolved stricter policy regimes for the use of *Panchayat* lands, forest buffer lands and several other open access lands. Third, it is high time that the state encouraged organic farming in plantation and newly emerging diversified agriculture such as floriculture, horticulture and herbiculture. Likewise, assessment of biodiversity damages from mining activities should be carried first before launching such activities.

Since most of these natural resources have long-term use values, their use in the medium or short-term should be properly viewed. It is, therefore, strongly suggested that regular Natural Resource Accounting be carried out in the state. Furthermore, keeping in view of growing pollution and natural resource degradation, the state should introduce strict 'polluter pay' principle and introduce 'user charges' on the use of such resources (GoK, 2004).

18.6 Policies on Human Development

18.6.1 On Attaining Complete Literacy

Though introduced as part of National Literacy Mission since 1988, Education for All (EFA) has remained merely as a slogan in the country and the state. The outcome of the programme in the state is half way (i.e. among the identified 77.16 lakh non-literates in the 9-35 age group, thus far about 43.08 lakh have been converted into the category of literate).

To achieve the goal of Universalitation of Elementary Education, both the governments in the state and Centre have formulated an integrated programme (consolidating a variety parallel programmes) under the umbrella of 'Sarva Shiksha Abhiyan' (SSA). SSA is a holistic programme which envisages community involvement in a big way and community ownership is central to the SSA programme. To see the success of this programme, strict monitoring on girl child attendance, distribution of free textbooks and uniforms for girls, mid-day meal programmes, free school bags, and free text and notebooks to SC and ST girls, etc. are absolutely necessary. The *Gram Panchayats* have to play a major role here as they are closest to the situation. Likewise, in urban areas, the urban local bodies's may have to introduce a large number youths on part-time basis as para-teachers to take up literacy for the slum dwelling out-of-school children.

There is a need to link the policies of liberating bonded labour and children in hazardous activities and arrange for their education. Karnataka has introduced several programmes on these lines, though the off-take seems to be quite low. Incentives on programmes such as Baa Baale Shalege (bringing the girl child to school) or Akshar Dasoha should be extended to NGOs and social work organisations as well. Some of these programmes can yield the desired results only when programmes on gender equity, gender and parent sensitisation, representation of women in school committees, provision of toilets, safe drinking water supply, appointment of women teachers, and incentives to girls to attend schools, etc. are also matched.

18.6.2 Policies on Education

Karnataka is one of the states where educational development has been quite impressive though there are still many challenges in this connection, on which certain major policy twists are required.

First, in spite of reasonably balanced provisioning in respect of educational infrastructure, regional disparities in educational development are quite high between the districts of the northern and the southern regions, and between rural and urban areas. For instance, the gender disparities in northern districts are much larger than in southern districts. The redressal of this educational disparity requires some change in the management strategies, by bringing the PRIs, civil society institutions, and NGOs to work together to address all these problems in a united way. The state government should ensure that the teachers are in place in all the schools. PRIs should act as monitoring agencies to check the school facilities, girl student attendance, and also oversee that all eligible children are made to go to school.

Second, in order to operationalise the emergence of good educational performance, it is all the more necessary to develop a flexible approach to educational infrastructure and promotional activities. Only then, it is possible to meet the requirements at each district and *taluka* level, on a need basis.

Third, some special attention is now required to improve the girl child schooling. Though the parity index of enrolment in school education has improved over time but across the districts south Karnataka districts perform better than the north Karnataka districts. This indicates the low rate of girl's enrolment in the backward districts of north Karnataka. Once again, the *Gram Panchayats* should act as watchdogs on this social problem.

Fourth, there is a newly emerging problem in the educational setup in the state. It seems that no new lower and higher primary schools have been established in the state since 2001-02. But the unaided schools of all types are coming up in the state in large numbers. This trend will increase the inaccessibility of primary education to socially and economically backward people. The state spends about four per cent of its GSDP on education; and elementary education gets the highest share. However, the real expenditure per student has not increased significantly during the 1990s. It is also important to note that allocation of resources is more or less stagnant for the last 15 years. It is time to raise such allocations to at least six per cent of a GSDP. The backward regions like northern part of Karnataka should be given priority.

Fifth, there can be growing pressures at least for another 10 years on financial requirements for elementary education. The state has to find out appropriate alternative sources to meet the gap. Such type of sources may come from the corporate and banking sectors under the public-private partnership basis.

Finally, education should be based on an integrated planning rather than a plan for education in isolation. The integration could be with primary health care and nutrition, and gender-based social welfare, all of which are significantly correlated to the educational achievements of the children in the state.

18.6.3 Health and Nutrition Policy Options

Karnataka has made considerable improvements in the health sector as can be viewed from the health related indicators like improved life expectancy at birth, declining IMR or morbidity status. But, the state is still lagging behind on some of these aspects among the southern states (Joseph, 2003). Moreover, in terms of provisioning and access across all the regions in the state, the performance of the health sector is quite at variance. TB and HIV cases across the districts reflect the challenge that the health care delivery mechanism needs to be addressed in the years to come. Across the districts in the state as far as health expenditures and health care facilities are concerned, it seems the districts of south Karnataka are doing better.

Policy interventions in this sector has to take both the people and the technological advancements together. Recent advancements in IT supported health care facilities should be spread to every district in the state. For instance, tele-medicine systems, and creating more and more medical supports with modernised ayurveda and indigenous medical systems should be promoted by the PRIs.

There is need for a fresh look at provisioning of public health care facilities in the state. Public health delivery requires coordination between different sectors such as water supply and drainage, agriculture (e.g. salinity), industry (e.g. pollution), transport, health (e.g. vector control), urban development (e.g. waste management) and so on. The existing system of Health and Family Welfare Department is unable to meet the social needs of public health deliveries. To begin with, there is need to consolidate the various components of public health and create a Directorate of Public Health to work out the delivery system in close association with the PRIs. Programme design, implementation, and monitoring of all aspects of public health at the PRI and ULB levels should be left to this Directorate. It should cover all aspects of public health, namely, safe drinking water, sanitation, nutrition, vector control, immunisation and so on.

One way to begin this is to develop 'facility maps' at the district, *taluka* and village levels. This should be overlaid on the population, and infrastructural maps, from which the critical areas of health care needs can be identified.

In the recent period, the share of allocation on health sector has declined to around 3.6 per cent (from 5.44 per cent in 1997-98). Further, the resource allocation for rural health has been stagnating around 30 per cent of the allocation to the sector. In view of the regional imbalances at the rural levels, this share has to be stepped up to at least 50 per cent. Keeping all these and also the emerging need for additional allocations on public health, the first charge in policy is to raise this to at least to 6 per cent of the state allocations.

Nutrition is one aspect of health care which gets least priority in the health sector. Studies after studies have revealed that malnutrition is chronic in the state, and regional variations across the districts are quite alarming, particularly during the drought periods. Though there are a large number of schemes such as Mid-day Meal Scheme and Akshara Dasoha, PMRY, ICDS, PDS system and so on, there is no policy of a universal nutritional support. The policy should include special drives on leakages in the nutrition delivery systems (be it PDS, ICDS or Mid-day Meal Scheme). *Gram Panchayats* should be made responsible to monitor the schemes. They should ensure that the PDS offtake is 100 per cent, but also reaching the eligible population. *Anganwadi* workers should be subjected to repeated training to discuss the emerging issues of inaccess and ineffective delivery systems.

It is necessary to involve the civil society institutions such as Stree Shakti or Bal Vikas Samitis to take up the organisation of awareness camps (on nutritional values, links with health and population growth, etc.), distribution of nutritional foods and medicines, care for pregnant mothers and so on. There is also a need for transparency in the system, as food distribution is very conflict-oriented.

18.6.4 Policies on Housing

It is not very clear if Karnataka has a clearly laid out housing policy for the needy population, though a large number of centrally sponsored programmes are on the anvil. It may not be an overstatement to say that the deprived sections such as SC and ST population in the state suffer from housing shortage, defects and deficiencies as the major starting problem in their poor livelihood status.

Experience shows that public provisioning of housing for the vulnerable sections does not necessarily make them livable. The new strategies on this should be one of partnerships between the needy sections, the banking or financial institutions and the government. This also requires the government motivating the financial institutions to take up this as a social necessity. A large number of housing financial institutions have already come up in the state. But they should consider with certain flexibilities to cover the vulnerable sections as well as the rural economy, and not just the urban sector.

It is also necessary to reorient public schemes such as Rajiv Gandhi Rural Housing Corporation (RGRHC) as a full-fledged institution to administer the housing commitment of the state and to implement all the social housing schemes in rural areas. It is all the more necessary for them to work with PRIs, in identifying the housing needs. PRIs should also play a major role in enabling the financial institutions to reach the poor and needy with timely loans. The state should empower RGRHC to mobilise resources from the market on a guarantee of the state to meet the total housing needs both in the new housing and redevelopment streams in rural areas.

While targeting housing for the needy, the whole scheme should be viewed as an integrated one with the necessary infrastructures such as drinking water supply, roads, electricity supply, drainage and market facilities.

18.6.5 Drinking Water Supply and Sanitation

As much as housing needs, an equally burning issue in social development is about providing adequate safe drinking water and sanitation services. There are a large number of schemes and ongoing programmes in the state to redress this problem, both regionally and by rural and urban divide. But, many of these programmes (Chapter 5) are promotional, funded by multilateral agencies such as the World Bank or bilateral agencies such as DANIDA, and some under central schemes. But, in the long run, the basic problem will have to be tackled under the Constitutional empowerment of the PRIs. Article 243G clearly transfers this function to the local bodies. Apart from this constitutional provision, the state has already created highly specialised institutions such as Karnataka Urban Water Supply and Drainage Board (KUWSDB) to cater to the needs of urban areas. For Bangalore city, there is a separate board for this function. All added, the government is spending about 2.5 per cent of the total resource allocations on water supply and sanitation programmes. The very first policy change required is on raising this to at least 5 per cent.

Though various schemes have already covered about 85 per cent of the households in the state with some water provision or other, the extent of hardship and regional variations and frequency are matters of deep concern. The policy required now is in making water supply a basic right and ensuring 100 per cent coverage without any hardship.

In terms of priority and phasing the programmes, drought-prone districts should be given high priority to resolve the problem of inadequate water supply. Drinking water quality affected habitations should be taken up on first priority basis to provide safe drinking water through alternative sources or by treating water.

PRIs do not assign high priorities to sanitation as much as water supply. It is increasingly becoming clear that bad sanitation and physical hygiene can lead to various health problems, reducing the productivity and efficiency of human capital. Immediate attention needs to be given towards providing sanitation facilities like drainage and sewerage system to avoid adverse impact on health in both rural and urban areas. In urban planning, provision should be made for sewerage system, public toilets/latrines, garbage disposal place, site for sewage/wastewater diversion, STPs, etc. Slum development programmes should be given priority to provide basic facilities like drinking water and sanitation to slum dwellers covering all ULBs.

Operation and maintenance is a major problem in both water supply and sanitation system. The remedy can be through civil society interventions and in partnerships between public and private sectors. In villages, Village Water Supply and Sanitation Committees (VWSSCs) can be established.

Finally, clearly laid out policies on groundwater exploitation is necessary in the state. ULBs particularly have to establish special cess for the use of such water for gardening and washing, etc. apart from regulations on their layouts. Above all, water user charges should be uniformly introduced, without which it may not be possible for the PRIs and ULBs to maintain water and sanitation programmes in the long run.

18.6.6 Policies on Social Development

Since Independence both the governments in the state and Centre have launched a series of development programmes for the upliftment of the Scheduled Caste and Scheduled Tribe population in the country. Broadly speaking, the programme structure comprises: (i) policy goals and objectives in the shape of Directive Principles in Article 46; (ii) the legislative and physical infrastructure in the Fifth and Sixth Schedule; (iii) Articles 335 and 338 on job reservation; and (iii) financial support under Article 275 for funding schemes that promote development and welfare.

Scheduled castes and tribes in Karnataka present a most complex and mixed story of development. No doubt the Government of Karnataka has been doing its best in improving their livelihood status in terms of resource allocations, concessions and special provisions such as housing, roads, drinking water, special provisioning for schooling and so on. In the next phase of reforms process, a balance has to be struck between providing direct support to such vulnerable sections of the society with policies of reservations and concessions, and making them grow as part and parcel of the reforms process with empowerment, transparency, opportunities and rights.

The employment situation of scheduled castes in Karnataka presents a grim picture. Their entry in secondary and tertiary sector is not more than 10-12 per cent. But a large percentage (54 per cent) of them is in the category of landless agricultural labour. Land reforms have not helped them at all. High illiteracy and school dropout rates are recorded among the scheduled caste population. Likewise, access to safe drinking water and sanitation was very meagre.

One major policy change already in place is the introduction of decentralised governance at the Gram Panchayat root levels, thereby ensuring their political empowerment with an average of 20 per cent representation in *Panchayat* bodies. In actuality, it can be much higher. But what is important as a policy is to ensure that they are active representatives and not passive in terms of numbers. The role of *Gram Panchayats* in the process of social upliftment of the people is very important. It is with this objective that training for the *Panchayat* members on governance, awareness, design of programmes is necessary. These should specifically be designed on awareness creation on education, health, infrastructure and government polices. Furthermore, under the functions identified for them, the *Gram Panchayats* should take up providing basic amenities such as safe drinking water, housing, electricity to all poor families at their doorsteps.

Second, a major policy shift is required now on prioritising various schemes. The schemes developed for the benefit of scheduled caste and tribes can be grouped into two categories, *viz.*, Employment and Income Generation Schemes (Poverty Alleviation Schemes) and Minimum Needs Programmes. As a strategy for the coming decade, more and more of employment generating schemes should be introduced. Such empowerments can automatically create the purchasing power to meet the minimum needs in turn.

Third, a special emphasis is needed to uplift the agriculture dependent landless labour. The state has significant land area under barren, shrub and as cultivable waste (10.89 per cent of geographical area of the state are wastelands). Some of these lands can be brought under cultivation if newer technologies such as rainwater harvesting, introduction of BT, diversification to non-crop based agricultural uses such as poultry, fishery, horticulture, floriculture, etc. are taken up. The regional rural banks can come forward to make them loanable and yet be profitable activities.

Fourth, the cultural heritage of the tribals of Karnataka needs to be protected and promoted. The state is very rich in several tribal and ecology linked economic activities. These should be further encouraged with marketing support. This is one way that such a rich cultural heritage can become globalised.

Fifth, gender-based development is yet another major step required in the process of social development. To facilitate the social and economic development of women, the government through the Department of Women and Child, and the Women Development Corporation, RDPR, NABARD and so on, has implemented various schemes and programmes. Some notable ones are: vocational training for women and financial assistance. Fresh thinking on the lines of the activities under Self Employed Women's Association (SEWA) of Gujarat is necessary to make employment of women a true reality. In Karnataka, the formation of SHGs (with programmes like Stree Shakti in all the 27 districts) under the Swarna Jayanthi, Gram Swarozgar Yojana Programme and Swashakthi (in seven districts of north Karnataka) have been very instrumental in providing both training and credit programmes for women's overall development. It is also time to think if too many parallel programmes are desirable in the long run.

The state has already initiated several special employment-oriented programmes for women. Notable among them is Women's Milk Producers' Association. Similar empowerment programmes are feasible in the areas of floriculture, spice and silk industries. The SHGs should enable women to get easy loans to start and take up more and more self-employment-oriented jobs and works. Since women may have properties in their names, some amendments in the rules need to be made in the banking sectors to waive conditions such as mortgaging. PRIs and organisations such as Stree Shakti should come forward to deal with exploitation of women in several sectors such as silk weaving, *beedi* rolling, fishery and so on.

18.6.7 Policy for Better Social Security

Social security to safeguard life and property needs to be redefined in the context of reforms period. While the reforms process itself is targeted to welfare and better quality of life there are matters of dignity, empowerment, social status and security that need to be guaranteed. These are such issues that receive a low priority in the process of development, except perhaps poverty (as if it is a catch-all malady).

Except for the organised sector there are hardly any breakthroughs in social security schemes in the state. It is time to bring some new schemes of social security in the state. Schemes such as farmer's health insurance scheme, crop and livestock insurance scheme are yet to take off from the ground. Health support plans such as Yashaswini are catering to only limited sections of rural population.

On a parallel, the unorganised workers in the state require several social security and welfare measures. The Unorganised Workers Bill introduced in the Assembly originally in 2000 never saw the light of the day. It is time that the state reintroduces the Social Security Bill for the benefit of unorganised workers. If and when introduced, it would enable creation of social welfare funds, regulation of their employment conditions like health, safety and job security, regulate the working hours, standardisation of wages, overtime benefits, maternity benefits, insurance, pension, insurance, etc.

Then, there are several schemes to empower different sections of people in the state in terms of income earning power and dignity. The recently introduced women's self-help groups are an instance of empowering them on an economic basis. But this is still at an experimental basis. The experience of nearly 20 years in this respect prompts some new policy measures to make this institution to reach all sections of women. Some of the new directions required in this respect are:

- Currently the emphasis is only on internal lending and savings. But this process should enable women to take up other investment tasks to enhance their income and family security. The experience of Self-Employed Women's Association (SEWA) of Gujarat is important to draw upon a detailed plan in this direction.
- Some further features such as training on women entrepreneurships and participatory democracy is also necessary. For instance, the women representatives should not be counted just in terms of their percentage numbers but are to be ensured in attending meetings, participating in decision making, knowing about the programmes for women's development, etc.

18.7 Fiscal and Financial Policies

18.7.1 Policies on Financial Flows

Finance and financial infrastructure facilitate growth, provided the economy creates opportunities. The state has a positive role to play on both in creating such opportunities and developing new types of financial infrastructure to leverage such growth opportunities. In the past, Karnataka has been the lead state in the country when it came to the development of financial sector.

Both mobilisation of savings and capital formation are critical for the development of any economy. The role of financial institutions is to bring the savings closer to the investment climate. In Karnataka, the network of financial institutions, particularly banking and cooperatives, is fairly good, resulting in near about equalisation of savings mobilisation and capital investments. While this being so, the net inflow of capital from within the country or international capital markets is very low (FDI investments being about 12 per cent of total approved investments in the state). In the long run, the state may face a situation of credit crunch. For this, it is necessary to create a climate of attracting capital flows into the state. The growth and congenial investment environment in the state in industrial, information technology and biotechnology spheres should be highly publicised and pronounced widely to attract investment flows.

It is necessary to play a major lead role in developing or facilitating development of private sector to cater this segment. Agencies like Karnataka Information Technology Venture Capital Fund should be strengthened to allow large scale establishment of such service ventures. Knowledge industry requires considerable risk capital. While venture capital funds can provide initial risk capital, once the unit overcomes the initial phase, further expansion requires additional risk capital. Also, venture capitalists need an exit route.

In the process of developing knowledge industries, which are normally located in urban areas, one should not loose track of the aspiration and needs of people in rural sector. Though Karnataka is not on the top in micro-finance activities, it has considerable experience in this sector. It is important to strengthen micro-financial institutions to cover a large number of rural poor. While penetration of financial infrastructure is critical in this context, it is equally important on the demand side to generate necessary business opportunities for the rural people.

The cooperative credit institutions have played a major role and made some dent in the state on financial leveraging. Their network should be encouraged to spread to all the backward regions of the state. This network is particularly needed for micro-financing.

18.7.2 Fiscal Policy Drives

Karnataka is one of the first states in the country to introduce the Fiscal Responsibility Act (FRA) from April 2003, which provides statutory backing to the Medium Term Fiscal Plan (MTFP) in the state. The state has already brought out the MTFP Document in 2001 on fiscal reforms and discipline for the state. The government has periodically undertaken reforms of the tax and expenditure structures. Recently, a report of Tax Reform Commission was released in late 2001. Subsequently, the Revenue Reform Commission also submitted its report to the government. The most recent MTFP of 2003 spells out to reduce the fiscal deficit (as a ratio of GSDP) to 3 per cent by the year 2006.

Several committees and commissions appointed so far in the state have uniformly expressed that the tax system should be made simple and transparent. A simple tax system should have only a few tax categories, rates (and tax slabs), and very few exemptions. To achieve the objective of simplicity, exemptions based on 'forms or uses of commodities or nature of purchasers' will have to be eliminated. Some major steps in this direction have been taken in the recent budget formulations.

Revenue collection (as a ratio of GSDP) in the state is falling over the recent years. This is a matter of serious concern. Revenue from the state excise duties (which constitute the second most important revenue source after sales tax and related commodity taxes) has not been very buoyant during the nineties, reducing the annual growth rate from 13.37 per cent in the eighties to 10.91 per cent in the nineties. While the tax rates are being reformed and rationalised (e.g., fewer slabs) it is also necessary to broaden the tax base. For instance, under sales and professional service taxes several new products and sectors are yet to be added. Secondly, changes in the tax structure should be well planned in advance rather than on an *ad hoc* basis. If tax structures are framed on economic rationality then there cannot be any further case for exemptions or changing the rates of tax or expanding incentives and concessions through notifications and orders throughout the year. Such mid-course interventions and changes should not be allowed. Thirdly, considerable amount of improvements and modernisation are necessary in tax collection and administration systems, making them consumer-friendly. Tax kiosks (including user fee or charge kiosks), electronically furnishing the tax returns, introduction of transparent system of announcing submission dates (using e-mail system), incentives for early submission of tax returns, etc. are some of the modern methods that can be tried out. Only with such changes and improvements the buoyancy of tax collection will improve.

The Tax Reforms Commission, however, made an assessment that the effective tax rates in Karnataka are higher than those prevailing in the neighbouring states. Therefore, the new avenues in tax policy available now are to broaden the tax base, reduce the exemption basket and to improve tax administration. This is a mater of good governance. For this, computerisation (e.g., Khajane) of the entire tax system is required. It is high time that special studies on the effectiveness of tax subsidies, concessions and exemptions are made and a comprehensive view is taken.

Karnataka is one of the first states in India that has already progressed in the preparation for implementing a VAT. In its preparation, tax rates are being rationalised by reducing the number of slabs from 14 to 7 in sales tax. The bulk of the 600 scheduled commodities would be brought under 4 basic rates, 4 per cent, 8 per cent, 12 per cent and 16 per cent. Two special rates of 17.5 per cent and 25 per cent are being abolished and only 3 special rates of 1 per cent, 20 per cent and 28 per cent will be retained for a small group of commodities including bullion and specie, diesel, tobacco products and petrol.

Several new measures are also called for in the arena of non-tax revenues. Till now their role in raising the state income is quite unexplored. With the introduction of user charges in a number of public services such as water supply, road or bridge use, etc. non-tax revenues have a major scope in the state. Collections of royalty (say on minerals), access fees (irrigation charges), forest revenue, licence fees, etc. seem to be on the increase. The Revenue Reforms Commission in its final report on non-tax revenues recommended several steps to make this an important resource raising mechanism for the future. Forest revenues have grown at an average of 8 per cent over the last 4 years. Mineral revenues have grown at 12 per cent, cooperation revenue at 16 per cent and irrigation charges at about 20 per cent.

Till date, the non-tariff revenue options are not fully based on any principles such as 'willingness to pay', 'polluter pay' or 'linked to demand elasticity'. With market linked production and distribution system, it is equally important now to introduce some of these measures. For instance, maintenance of environmental sustainability requires balancing the demand and supply of environmental services, hence, application of one or the other principles of public finance. For instance, given the productivity of irrigation water, it is perfectly logical to charge water, based on the cost recovery of the irrigation system. Likewise, overexploitation of water (say by the groundwater users) should be paid, for the cost as well, a penalty. Progressive water use charges may have to be considered, apart from a heavy fixed charge for initial approval as capital charges.

Currently, the third MTFP is in place for the period 2003-04 to 2006-07. The key strategies laid down in the

MTFP 2003-04 to 2006-07 include (Government of Karnataka, 2003):

- Improve revenue collection by improvising the rate structure, administration and enforcement.
- Mobilise greater non tax revenue by revising rates and phasing out implicit subsidies.
- Reduce budgetary support to public sector enterprises.
- Introduce budgetary reforms to promote accountability, flexibility and performance.
- Effective reforms in governance to strengthen performance.

Several of these recommendations from the MTFP also require effective regulatory institutions (such as KERC) and vigilance (such as Lokayukta). One only hopes that the state launches a bold programme of tax reforms with state VAT system, modernisation of tax collection system, broad banding the tax base, non-tariff structures on user charges, makes independent regulatory authorities and several Acts on governance (such as Right to Information, Transparency) functional. It is only then that it is possible to take the development phase of the economy on the targeted eight per cent growth rate in the medium term.

References

Bali, Arun P. (ed.). (2001). *Refashioning the New Economic Order: Karnataka in Transition Jaipur*, Rawat Publication.

Government of India, Planning Commission (2003). *India Vision 2020: The Report plus Background Papers*, Academic Foundation New Delhi.

Government of Karnataka (2000). *Karnataka: Future Vision and Current Action*, Karnataka State Industrial and Development Corporation Ltd., Bangalore.

———. (2001a). *Medium Term Fiscal Plan for Karnataka 2000-01 – 2004-05*, Bangalore: Finance Department

———. (2001b). *Administrative Reforms Commission's Report.*

———. (2002a). *Report of the High Power Committee on Redressal of Regional Imbalances*, Department of Planning, Bangalore.

———. (2002b). *Taxation Reforms Commission Report.*

———. (2004a). *Revenue Reforms Commission Report.*

———. (2004b). *State of the Environment Report and Action Plan-2003*. Department of Forest, Ecology and Environment, Bangalore.

Howes, Stephen and Rinku Murgai (2003). "Karnataka: Incidence of Agricultural Power Subsidies", *Economic and Political Weekly*, April 19: 1533-1535.

Howes, Stephen, Ashok Lahiri and Nicholas Stern (eds.) (2003). *State Level Reforms in India*, Macmillan India Ltd. New Delhi.

Joseph, Mathew (2003). "Performance of the Southern States: A Comparative Study", *Economic and Political Weekly*, September 13:3915-3930.

Kalam, A. P. J. Abdul and Y.S.Rajan (1998). *India 2020: A Vision for the New Millennium*, Viking Press, New Delhi.

Paul, Samuel (1995). *Strengthening Public Accountability: New Approaches and Mechanisms*, Public Affairs Centre Research Paper.

United Progressive Alliance (UPA) (2004). "Common Minimum Programme", *The Hindu*, May 28:12

World Bank (2004). *State Fiscal Reforms in India: Progress and Prospects*, Oxford University Press, New Delhi.